FIELD OF ORGANIZATIONAL BEHAVIOR

1954

Management by objectives (MBO)
Peter Drucker developed a technique for involving employees in the process of planning and implementing strategic change in organizations (see chapter 16).

Peter Drucker

1958

Contingency approach to leadership
Fred E. Fiedler's pioneering research established the idea that different leadership styles are appropriate for different situations (see chapter 12).

Fred E. Fiedler

1958

Administrative approach to decision making
James G. March and *Herbert A. Simon* advanced the idea that limitations in information-processing ability lead people to make less than optimal decisions (see chapter 14).

James G. March   Herbert A. Simon

(Continued on inside back cover)

1964

The managerial grid
Robert R. Blake and *Jane S. Mouton* developed the grid training technique of organizational development (see chapter 16).

Robert R. Blake   Jane S. Mouton

1964

Expectancy theory of motivation
Victor H. Vroom's ideas contributed to the advancement of the expectancy theory approach to organizational motivation (see chapter 4).

Victor H. Vroom

PRACTICAL APPLICATIONS
BALANCED WITH
SOLID RESEARCH:

It's the Greenberg and Baron touch.

BEHAVIOR IN ORGANIZATIONS:
Understanding and Managing the Human Side of Work,
Fourth Edition

- **Increased attention to applications** — including more examples from operating companies plus relevant cases from the Cable News Network (CNN) — help your students easily relate the concepts to everyday issues.

- **New material and expanded coverage of issues like diversity** let your students see the many ways today's organizations deal with cultural diversity and ethical issues.

F ew American citizens are more proud than Maria Sanchez. Having grown up in a poor, rural Mexican village, she is now a department manager at Desert Power and Light, one of the fastest-growing utility companies in the United States. And based on the performance evaluation interview she is having with her boss, Dan Haskins, she is obviously doing quite well.

"You're clearly a fast-tracker, Maria," says Dan, "exactly the kind of employee we like around here. You have great technical skills and you're highly motivated. No one works harder for the company than you do."

"Thank you very much, Dan," replies Maria. "That means a great deal coming from you."

"There's only one small matter," Dan adds. "You have a communication problem. It's nothing serious, mind you, but you do have to work on it."

Dan's intercom buzzes, interrupting them. It's the receptionist, informing Dan that he must leave right away for an important meeting with the Utilities Commission.

Hearing this, Maria immediately stands up and gathers her things to leave. Dan extends his hand and shakes Maria's hand firmly as they walk toward the door. "As you heard," he says, "I've got to go now. Again, you're doing a terrific job, just work on that communication problem and you'll be fine. We'll talk about it more at your next evaluation session, six months from now."

As she walks back to her desk, Maria thinks about Dan's remarks. She is truly pleased that her hard work has been appreciated. Optimistic about her future with the company, now she wants to please him more than ever. "I'll show him," she thinks aloud. "I'll work on that communication problem."

Although Maria is proud of her Mexican heritage, she knows that she speaks with an accent, which sometimes makes her feel a bit self-conscious. As a result, she frequently refrains from making presentations with all the poise and confidence that her superior skills and knowledge merit.

Determined to turn things around, she goes on an all-out campaign to improve herself. She hires a private English tutor and takes classes in English composition and public speaking at a local community college—all at considerable personal expense. As a result of these efforts, it soon becomes clear to everyone at Desert Power and Light that Maria has become a poised and polished communicator. Now, instead of shyly hiding in the corner at meetings, she always sits up front and confidently speaks her mind.

487

- **Four special sections** further help blend research and practical applications and heighten your students' interest: *An International/ Multicultural Perspective, Focus on Research, OB in Practice,* and *A Question of Ethics*

- **A new and expanded Annotated Instructor's Edition (AIE)** provides you with many helpful teaching tools. **An outstanding supplement package** helps you motivate students to learn.

PRACTICAL APPLICATIONS BALANCED WITH SOLID RESEARCH:

It brings the concepts to life.

With examples from companies like Chrysler, Disney, and Air Florida the principles of OB take on real meaning for students.

Case-in-Point features further heighten student interest in the issues.

In this new edition authors Greenberg and Baron continue their tradition of presenting solid, current research while enhancing their presentation of the practical, applications-oriented side of OB.

- **More examples from actual companies** such as United Parcel Service, Kinney Shoes, Citicorp, and Avis illustrate the principles being discussed and show students how those findings relate to practical problems and issues of functioning organizations.

- **OB in Practice sections** show how the findings and principles of organizational behavior can and are being applied in many different work settings.

- **Case-in-Point features at the end of chapters** focus on companies like XEROX, GM, and Levi Strauss to illustrate the practical applications of OB and relate the issues to topics and findings in the text.

- **International/Multicultural Perspective sections** students the many ways OB can work to modernize organizations as they strive to deal with these new concerns.

PRACTICAL APPLICATIONS BALANCED WITH SOLID RESEARCH:

It prepares your students today to meet tomorrow's business challenges.

CASE IN POINT

"Getting your self-esteem from money, power and control is diminishing," says a psychologist who counsels managers who are finding themselves out of work in the 1990s.[1] Mergers, acquisitions, and the continued pressure to downsize in an attempt to reduce costs and become more competitive are causing U.S. companies to drastically cut their management ranks.

For these unemployed managers, finding a similar management position at another company is not likely. Most U.S. companies are cutting management jobs. There are more managers looking for work than U.S. industry can possibly absorb.[2] James Swalow, a vice president for A. T. Kearney management consultants, agrees: "A lot of people will walk out of these management positions and never see these kinds of jobs again."[3]

William Morin of Drake Beam Morin—an outplacement company that helps laid-off managers find new jobs and launch new careers—describes losing your job this way: "When you lose your job, even if it's in mass or as an individual, it's a loss of self-esteem, you're upset, you're angry, it's a sense of being out-of-control."[4] These managers have spent years working their way up the organizational hierarchy, only to find the hierarchy is being dismantled and their traditional management skills (directing and controlling) are no longer needed.

Being one of an army of unemployed managers looking for work is hard on a person's sense of self-esteem. Says one displaced manager, a former division president and a victim of a corporate takeover, the job market is "full of people like me. And it's getting cold and rude out there. Right now it's rare that you even hear back from your inquiries. That's what is so discouraging and disappointing. They are not even courteous enough to reject you."[5] It doesn't take long before displaced managers realize that the day of the traditional boss is dying, and the need to shift career strategies is becoming ever more apparent.

What do displaced managers do? James Cabrera, president of Drake Beam Morin, argues that managers must stop relying on the corporation to take care of them and start taking responsibility for their own careers. Losing your job gives you the opportunity to take control of your career. William Morin describes the silver lining (the benefits) of losing a job: "You really get in touch with yourself. A lot of people say they get in touch with their families, they get in touch with reality again, they are not servicing that god called the corporation anymore and they can kind of look inward, reattach to values and feelings and emotions they haven't had in years."[6]

Edgar Schein, a prominent career development expert, developed the concept of *career anchors*, the set of self-perceptions about values, preferences, abilities, and motives that serve to guide people into certain careers.[7] People are attracted to careers that match their career anchor. For example, some people are attracted to careers that offer autonomy and independence. Others look for careers that provide opportunities to express creativity and entrepreneurship. The traditional U.S. corporate management position has typically attracted people who seek careers that allow them to fulfill their career anchor—to exercise power and influence over other people. With companies changing, people attracted to the traditional corporate manager career are finding fewer and fewer jobs available. These people need to identify their niche, and then modify their career to fit the niche.

John Huey, a writer for *Fortune* magazine, investigated the job pursuits of displaced managers.[8] His research revealed several career paths. The first path is the traditional one—compete for one of the shrinking number of remaining corporate management jobs. *But*, the managers who land such jobs are finding out that even the nature of the traditional corporate management job is changing. Says Huey, the corporate management job of the 1990s means "you will have to transform yourself from an overseer into a doer, from a boss into a team leader or maybe just a team player."[9] Will the new corporate manager find his or her career anchor fulfilled by this new type of corporate management role? There is clearly reason for doubt. If the job changes too much, these people may have to change their career anchor, or explore new careers that provide them with the career anchor fulfillment they once found as corporate managers.

Changing Management Careers in the 1990s?

CNN

349

Current, informative, intriguing CNN cases bring the experiences of both business giants and smaller organizations into your classroom.

Allyn & Bacon's exclusive agreement with Cable News Network puts current CNN business programming at your command ... and into the text! An 80-minute video that includes eight custom edited segments from CNN's "Pinnacle" program, with interviews of business leaders such as Herb Kelleher of Southwest Airlines, and programs on current topics such as sexual harassment, workforce motivation, and the changes in management careers in the mid-1990s. The videos are integrated with cases and boxes in the text and reinforce text concepts.

CNN case studies are available on videotape for classroom use and are free to adopters upon request.

Just flip through this text looking for the CNN logo. Wherever it appears you'll find that Allyn & Bacon provides you with a stimulating CNN business video.

IMPORTANT CHANGES HAVE BEEN ADDED THIS YEAR:

It's the best edition yet!

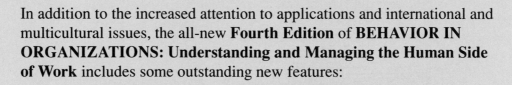

In addition to the increased attention to applications and international and multicultural issues, the all-new **Fourth Edition** of **BEHAVIOR IN ORGANIZATIONS: Understanding and Managing the Human Side of Work** includes some outstanding new features:

* **The latest research, findings, and applications in modern OB** help to keep the text the most current on the market — over 20 percent of the references are from 1990 or later!

* **Major content changes have been made within the chapters,** including coverage of literally scores of new topics — Impression Management, Positive and Negative Affectivity, Image Theory, The Five Robust Dimensions of Personality, Stress and Personal Health, New and Effective Techniques for Stress Management, Critical Issues in Careers in the 1990s, Transformational Leadership, and Champions of Technological Change to name just a few.

* **New special sections are included:** the all new *A Question of Ethics*, along with *OB in Practice* and *International/Multicultural Perspectives*. See pages 6 and 7 for descriptions.

* **Every chapter now begins with a new business vignette** to reinforce the practical, applications-oriented side of OB.

* **And some important changes have been made to the supplementary materials.** See pages 8 and 9 for descriptions.

investigating this topic, conceptual clarification and evidence regarding the value of various approaches to understanding individual power bases will probably be forthcoming.

Individual Power: How Is It Used?

As researchers take on the challenge of distinguishing among the various bases of individual power, one consideration facing them is the widespread overlap in the ways people use power. Only sometimes is a single source of power used; indeed, it is recognized that the various power bases are closely related to each other.[22] For example, consider that the more someone uses coercive power, the less that person will be liked, and hence, the lower his or her referent power will be. Similarly, managers who have expert power are also likely to have legitimate power because their directing others within the field of expertise is accepted. In addition, the higher someone's organizational position, the more legitimate power that person has, which is usually accompanied by greater opportunities to use reward and coercion.[23] Clearly, then, the various bases of power should not be thought of as completely separate and distinct from each other. They are often used together in varying combinations.

What bases of power do people prefer to use? Although the answer to this question is quite complex, research has shown that people prefer using expert power most and their coercive power least often.[24] These findings are limited to the power bases we've identified thus far. However, when we broaden the question and ask people to report exactly sources of power they have on their jobs, a fascinating picture emerges. Figure 11–6 depicts the results of a survey in which 216 CEOs of American corporations were asked to rank-order the importance of a series of specific sources of power.[25] The figures indicate the percentage of executives who included that source of power among their top three choices. These findings indicate not only that top executives rely on a broad range of powers, but also that they base these powers on

FIGURE 11–6

American CEOs: What Are Their Power Bases?

A survey of more [than] 200 American CE[Os] revealed that they obtained their po[wer] primarily through [the] support of others [at] different levels throughout the organization. (So[urce:] Based on data ap[pearing] in Stewart, 1989; Note 25.)

Source of power

- Support of the financial community (9)
- Management decision control (28)
- Expertise and knowledge (43)
- Support of senior colleagues (64)
- Support of the board of directors (70)
- Personality and leadership skills (83)

Percentage of CEOs who identified this factor as one of the top three sources of power in their jobs

---

Scores of new topics have been added to the text's comprehensive coverage.

The mix of illustrations in the text and in the chapter-opening stories has changed to include more flow-charts and diagrams — making this edition an even more effective tool for learning.

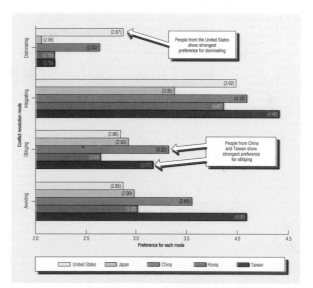

Conflict resolution mode / **Preference for each mode**

Dominating:
- (2.87) People from the United States show strongest preference for dominating
- (2.06)
- (2.65)
- (2.15)

Integrating:
- (3.92)
- (3.35)
- (4.10)
- (3.87)
- (4.40)

Obliging:
- (2.86)
- (2.93)
- (3.32) People from China and Taiwan show strongest preference for obliging
- (2.44)
- (3.17)

Avoiding:
- (2.85)
- (2.99)
- (3.55)
- (3.92)
- (4.06)

Legend: United States | Japan | China | Korea | Taiwan

FIGURE 10–8   Cultural Differences in Preferred Modes of Conflict Resolution

As shown here, people from *individualistic* cultures such as the United States showed stronger preferences than people from *collectivistic* cultures such as China and Taiwan for resolving conflicts through dominating. In contrast, people from collectivistic cultures showed stronger preferences for resolving conflicts through obliging and avoiding. (*Source:* Based on data from Ting-Toomey et al., 1991; see Note 37.)

to prefer strategies based more on obliging and avoiding. This is not to imply, of course, that cultural factors are all-powerful; on the contrary, all individuals, regardless of their cultural background, may adopt any approach to resolving specific conflicts, and may differ greatly, as individuals, in their concern for their own and others' face. But culture does appear to form an

important backdrop for conflict, so efforts to understand this important process—and how best to manage it—should certainly take cultural factors into account. To the extent that cultural influences are ignored or overlooked, the picture of conflict that emerges from ongoing research will remain incomplete.

FOUR SPECIAL SECTIONS MAKE THIS TEXT UNIQUE:

It stands out among the competition.

often do—affect performance at work. In the past, most individuals (especially men) tended to put their careers ahead of their family obligations. If their jobs called, they answered, even if it meant neglecting various aspects of home and family life. Now, however, the picture is changing. An increasing number of employees are putting the needs of their families on a par with—or even ahead of—those of their careers.[60] This trend is especially visible among employees in their twenties, who have watched older colleagues, older brothers and sisters, or even their own parents struggle with

 AN INTERNATIONAL/MULTICULTURAL PERSPECTIVE

Race and Career Outcomes in the United States: Different and Still Unequal

 First, the good news: the number of black people occupying managerial positions in the United States has risen substantially in recent years. In the 1970s, only about 3 percent of all managers were black; by the 1990s, this figure had doubled, to more than 6 percent.[61] In this sense, at least, black people have made visible, concrete progress. Now for the bad news: blacks occupying managerial positions continue to experience less favorable career outcomes than whites. They often receive lower performance evaluations than whites, and higher proportions of blacks than whites are stuck at career plateaus. What accounts for such outcomes? One answer involves what several authors have termed **treatment discrimination**.[62] In such discrimination, people belonging to minority groups receive fewer rewards, resources, or opportunities on the job than do others. Thus, they are not denied access to managerial jobs; but once in them, they are held back from attaining success by poorer treatment and reduced opportunities. We hasten to add that such treatment discrimination is not necessarily intentional; it may sometimes arise because other organization members, being unfamiliar with blacks, feel somewhat uncomfortable around them. Alternatively, treatment discrimination may occur because some people hold unfavorable implicit assumptions about blacks and other minority group members. In other words, they believe that such people are not capable of excellent work, even while supporting efforts to hire and promote them.

Is treatment discrimination a reality? Does it contribute to the poorer career outcomes experienced by blacks in the United States? A recent study by Greenhaus, Parasuraman, and Wormley examined these issues.[63] In this investigation, several hundred black managers and white managers provided information on their organizational experiences. Their supervisors also provided job evaluations for these managers and ratings of their promotability. Finally, the number of years the managers had occupied their present positions was used to assess the extent to which they had reached career plateaus.

Greenhaus and his colleagues proposed a model in which race exer... outcomes through its im... ganizational experiences... other words, they expec... race on career outcomes... erating through the me... organizational experiences... model was obtained. Rac... of promotability indirect... on job discretion and tw... mance evaluations. And a... blacks did perceive ther... discretion in their jobs a... ganizational acceptance t... in general, race seemed... than indirect effects on ca... words, blacks were more... plateaus, to report lower... to receive lower job pe... quite aside from the im... zational experiences.

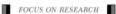 FOCUS ON RESEARCH

Physical Attractiveness and M.B.A.s' Salaries: Beauty Pays Off

 Beauty, it is often said, is in the eye of the beholder. But what are the effects of being perceived as physically attractive? Are those who are perceived as attractive any more or less successful on the job than those who are less attractive? Recent research has found that people are, in fact, biased against those who are generally perceived to be unattractive.[86] This is particularly important because unlike other forms of prejudice—such as those based on gender, race, and age—unattractiveness is not protected by any legislation.

One of the most dramatic effects of the bias in favor of attractive people has been shown in a recent study by Frieze, Olson, and Russell.[87] These investigators had four raters (two of each gender) judge the attractiveness of a large group of former M.B.A. students appearing in yearbook photos (the scale ranged from 1 = very unattractive, to 5 = very attractive). Then the people pictured were contacted and asked to complete a questionnaire revealing information about their salary history.

The connection between salaries and attractiveness rating was quite strong—and very interesting. Specifically, starting salaries for men, but not for women, were found to be related to their attractiveness. In fact, men who were rated as attractive (4 and above) had starting salaries

of $2,200 more than those believed to be unattractive (2 and under). As time went on, these differences became even greater! Both attractive men and women currently (in 1983) had higher salaries than their unattractive counterparts (see Figure 5–15). For men, each rating scale unit of attractiveness was found to be worth $2,600 per year (thus, those rated 2 received about $5,200 per year less than those rated 4). For women, the relationship was identical, although the figures were slightly lower—each unit was worth about $2,100 per year. Thus, women rated 2 received about $4,200 per year less than those rated 4. These findings are particularly dramatic when one takes into account that these are 1983 figures, and they represent a larger proportion of the overall salaries than they would given today's higher salaries.

These findings provide clear evidence of a bias against unattractive people (or in favor of attractive people) in the workplace. However, *why* these results occur is not clear. One possibility is that attractive people are believed to be more competent and, therefore, worth more. Attractive people also may have more self-confidence and project a more successful image of themselves. Of course, both factors may be operating, with each accounting for some degree of the observed effect.

We believe it is important to caution that al-

confidence before working on the tasks. More important, although positive feedback increased their self-confidence, it did not eliminate the difference in favor of men; women continued to report lower self-confidence throughout the study. Interestingly, men who received no feedback during the study reported self-confidence as high as that of women who had received positive feedback.

Together, these findings suggest that positive feedback about task performance may be especially important for women. Even in its absence, men express relatively high degrees of self-confidence. However, women report similar levels of confidence only when receiving encouraging feedback. This is a point managers who wish to foster advancement among women would do well to consider.

Regardless of the status of gender-based discrimination, the existence of other sources of prejudice is well established. For a closer look at another particularly

---

***International/Multicultural Perspective* sections reflect the many ways in which OB can help modern organizations deal with the growing internationalization of all business activities and the increasing cultural diversity of today's work force.**

***Focus on Research* sections describe important new research findings and show students the research process in OB.**

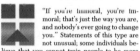

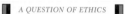

OB IN PRACTICE

Avis Employees *Do* Try Harder . . . Because They Own the Company

"We try harder" goes the old advertising slogan once used by Avis, the giant car-rental company. The phrase signified the willingness of Avis employees to surpass the service of its larger rival in the business, Hertz. That may have been decades ago, but since 1987, Avis employees have tried even harder than before. The reason is simple: the employees own the company (see Figure 4–14).

According to the job characteristics model, employees will be motivated to perform well when they believe that their work contributions are meaningful and important. You can expect people to recognize immediately the value of their work when they are part owners of the company. Avis employees participate in an *employee stock ownership plan (ESOP)*.[85] ESOPs work like this: The ESOP borrows money to buy the company, which is held by a trustee who represents the eventual shareholders. As the company pays off its debt, all employees receive shares of the company in proportion to their pay (up to a $30,000 per year federal limit). After fifteen to eighteen years, all 24 million shares ̶s̶ employees. An employee ̶ for his or her shares ̶eaving the company ̶eir shares back to the ̶new employees.

̶of ESOPs lies in their ̶e tax advantages. De-spite the benefits, ESOPs do not work unless they enhance workers' motivation. At Avis, the concept clearly works. Analysts have noted that since Avis's ESOP went into effect, the morale of its employees has improved dramatically, and its customers have noticed the improvement. Employees now make many more suggestions (and follow up on them!) and work harder than ever to improve performance standards. Avis employees are actively involved in all aspects of company functioning, and the company changes its operations as a result. In fact, changes ranging from billing procedures to baby seats have been credited to management's active attention to employees' suggestions.

Recent research by Katherine Klein suggests that Avis's success with its ESOP is not at all atypical.[86] Her survey of more than 3,800 employees participating in thirty-seven ESOPs revealed that responses to these programs were very positive. Specifically, employees in such plans tended to be highly satisfied with their jobs, highly committed to their companies, and unlikely to quit—especially when the plans were well run and profitable. The key is for management to be highly committed to employee ownership, and for the company to communicate clear and thorough information about how the plan is working. On the basis of such research, it is safe to conclude that ESOPs represent a form of organizational management that has great potential to effectively motivate employees.

FIGURE 4–14

Company Owners at Work at Avis

Whether they're auto mechanics, cleaners, or service assistants, Avis employees are highly motivated to perform at a high level because they collectively own the company.

A QUESTION OF ETHICS

Learning to Be Ethical: Citicorp Employees Play the Work Ethic Game

"If you're immoral, you're immoral; that's just the way you are, and nobody's ever going to change you." Statements of this type are not unusual; some individuals believe that you cannot train people to be more ethical than they already are. In recent years, however, this fatalistic outlook has been challenged by experts who counter that people *can* be trained in matters of business ethics.[35] Specifically, many businesses have trained employees to recognize the moral aspects of the decisions confronting them, to become more aware of their moral obligations, and to consider various ethical points of view.[36] The basic idea is very simple: as ethical scandals fill the pages of our daily newspapers, those charged with immoral conduct tend to falter, whereas those who maintain high moral practices tend to succeed. In short, if good ethics makes for good business, training employees to be ethical makes sense.[37]

This is the idea behind a novel training tool used by Citicorp to communicate ethical practices to its 90,000 worldwide employees.[38] It's called The Work Ethic, a board and card game that presents teams of players with ethical dilemmas (e.g., insider trading, conflicts of interest) and awards them points based on their selection of one of four predetermined solutions.

To paraphrase, one of the scenarios used goes something like this. You are to imagine that you are a corporate recruiter for your organization. A vice president asks you to find a new position for a manager who you know is a poor performer. This puts you in a difficult situation. The vice president wants this poor performer out of her department within a few months, but you cannot afford to anger the vice president because your own success depends on having good rapport with her. What would you do in this situation? You must discuss each of the following alternatives, and then select one:

1. Insist that the manager be counseled on his performance before he is transferred.
2. Say nothing about the manager's poor performance when presenting him for another job.
3. Refuse to get involved in transferring the manager.
4. Be frank about the manager's performance problems when presenting him for another job.

The idea of the game is to encourage dialogue. In this case, for example, there are many issues to discuss. It certainly is not easy to tell a superior that you will do what she wants only with a condition attached (in this case, arranging the transfer if the problem manager is counseled). Yet, that solution (1) merits the most points, twenty. Solution 2 receives minus-ten points, solution 3 rates zero points, and solution 4 is awarded ten points. If these point assignments don't happen to reflect what you might think would be the right thing to do, don't be alarmed. It doesn't mean you are unethical. The game is *supposed to* generate disagreement. In fact, players can disagree formally with preprinted answers by taking their cases to an appeals board made up of four of Citicorp's senior managers.

By engaging in dialogues created by the game, participants receive a clear message that senior management at Citicorp is *very* serious about ethics. Similarly, the company's policy to encourage employees to speak out on ethical matters without fear of censure is reaffirmed.

Specific ethical issues that reflect the varied activities of Citicorp's employees have been developed. For example, the game includes questions that address diverse matters such as credit card collections, recruiting, law, trading, international money management, and the like. The game has been played by 30,000 to 40,000 Citicorp employees in at least fifty-four nations, where it has been translated into the local languages. Obviously, Citicorp is very optimistic about the use of this training tool. To quote Kate Nelson, the head of communication for corporate human resources, "You can't overstate the importance of talking about ethics whether it's in a corporation or in our personal lives. Without training, even well-meaning employees can make bad decisions."[39]

HERE'S EVERYTHING YOU NEED TO TEACH — IN THIS ANNOTATED INSTRUCTOR'S EDITION:

It's your all-in-one-resource.

Here's your handy guide to in-text references and teaching aids. Complete with an extensive instructor's section containing a variety of useful features — chapter overviews and outlines, learning objectives, lecture and review questions, teaching suggestions, notes on the Case-In Point features, notes on the experiential exercises, and suggestions for supplementary videos and additional reading — this Annotated Instructor's Edition is designed to make your teaching simpler and more effective by giving you...

- Test Bank annotations

- Lecture Nuggets prepared by the authors to give you interesting background information and lecture ideas

- CNN Video annotations

PLUS AN OUTSTANDING SUPPLEMENTARY PACKAGE:

It's ideal for motivating students.

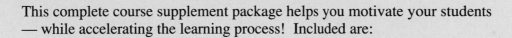

This complete course supplement package helps you motivate your students — while accelerating the learning process! Included are:

- **ANNOTATED INSTRUCTOR'S EDITION**

- **STUDENT STUDY GUIDE** with detailed learning objectives, definitions of key terms, review quizzes, and a fill-in-the-blank review guide.

- **INSTRUCTOR'S RESOURCE MANUAL** that contains...

  ✔ **A New Transparency Package.** 80 transparency masters, extensively revised, appear in the Instructor's Resource Manual (five for each chapter). There are new illustrations — ones not found in the text— and the artwork is now designed specifically for use in conjunction with *BEHAVIOR IN ORGANIZATIONS, Fourth Edition.*

  ✔ **A Test Bank** written by the author that includes over 1200 thoroughly revised test questions. These appear in a separate Instructor's Resource Manual. The questions are categorized as being either primarily factual, conceptual or applied in nature.

- **COMPUTERIZED TEST BANK.** In addition to the "hard copy" form, test questions are also available as part of Allyn & Bacon's *Test Manager,* an easy-to-use tool for preparing computer generated exams based on the text.

- **A CNN VIDEO LIBRARY** that truly brings OB to life! This 80-minute video includes eight specially edited segments from Cable News Network's "Pinnacle" and "Inside Business" programs, with interviews of business leaders like Herb Kelleher of Southwest Airlines, and programs on current topics like sexual harassment, workforce motivation, and the changes in management careers in the mid-1990s. The videos are integrated with cases or boxes in the text and reinforce text concepts.

Annotated Instructor's Edition

BEHAVIOR IN ORGANIZATIONS

UNDERSTANDING
AND MANAGING
THE HUMAN SIDE
OF WORK

Fourth Edition

Jerald Greenberg
The Ohio State University

Robert A. Baron
Rensselaer Polytechnic Institute

Instructor's Section Prepared by
Richard A. Grover
University of Southern Maine

Allyn and Bacon
Boston · London · Toronto · Sydney · Tokyo · Singapore

Editor-in-Chief, Behavioral and Social Sciences: Susan Badger
Senior Editorial Assistant: Dana Hayes
Production Coordinator: Deborah Brown
Editorial-Production Service: Sally Stickney
Cover Administrator: Linda Dickinson
Composition Buyer: Linda Cox
Manufacturing Buyer: Louise Richardson

Printed in the United States of America

10   9   8   7   6   5   4   3   2   1   98   97   96   95   94   93

ISBN 0-205-13831-4

BRIEF CONTENTS

A detailed contents begins on page iv following the instructor's section.

INSTRUCTOR'S SECTION CONTENTS

FOREWORD

Organizational behavior is a fascinating field that addresses some of the most important issues of our time. Still, in twenty years of teaching OB, I've found that students are often turned off by their textbooks. Some texts document research with little concern for practical applications. Others are dated or betray lack of knowledge of major developments in the field. Still others are, quite simply, dull.

Behavior in Organizations is refreshingly different. The authors are respected researchers who are able to draw on their important work on such topics as personality, conflict, stress, status, destructive criticism, attribution theory, bias in performance ratings, and organizational justice. However, *Behavior in Organizations* also has a strong and consistent applied focus; research examples are used to support key points without overwhelming substance. The book is full of interesting, recent, relevant examples and is engagingly written.

I've used the third edition of *Behavior in Organizations* with great success. Students report that they like the writing style. They appreciate the text's practical applications and action orientation. They find the chapter-opening vignettes and chapter-ending cases to be interesting and challenging and the experiential exercises at the end of each chapter to be illuminating. In short, this is an excellent, successful, well-received text; the authors could have been excused had they opted to make only cosmetic revisions.

But they did much more than a cursory revision. I am delighted with the fourth edition. Greenberg and Baron have maintained their engaging writing style and philosophy concerning the goals of the text while fully revising the content. Ethical issues in research, selection, training, conflict management, communication, and decision making are given expanded attention. International/multicultural perspectives are explored in segments such as motivation to manage in China, work goals around the world, the stress-deterrent effects of religiosity in Israeli Kibbutzim, and the management of diversity. OB in Practice sections deal with issues such as organizational commitment in the Magic Kingdom (Walt Disney World in Florida), managing wild ducks and mavericks, the role of habit in air-traffic disasters, creating an organizational culture, and approaches to empowerment. This edition contains more information on such current topics as impression management, the "big picture" of personality, positive and negative affectivity, coping styles, career issues in the 1990s, social influence, transformational leadership, and image theory. Some material has been appropriately reordered. Almost a quarter of the references are of 1990 or more recent vintage.

I'm looking forward to using the fourth edition of *Behavior in Organizations*. I recommend it highly.

Ramon J. Aldag
Professor of Management and
Co-Director of the Center for the
Study of Organizational Performance,
University of Wisconsin–Madison
Past President, Academy of Management

INSTRUCTOR'S SECTION PREFACE

Welcome to the fourth edition of *Behavior in Organizations* and its integrated *Instructor's Section,* collectively referred to as the *Annotated Instructor's Edition* (AIE). Guided by the generous comments and suggestions provided by users of the third edition, the authors have made an extremely informative and well-written introductory organizational behavior text even better. The text retains its strong foundation in research, and numerous actual organizational examples and illustrations have been added. The end-of-chapter Case in Point features are all new. They are also current and based on actual company situations. If you have not done so, take a few minutes to peruse the preface to the text to learn about the new and exciting changes that have been introduced.

Overview of the Annotated Instructor's Edition

Are there any changes to the instructor's edition? Yes—changes of an evolutionary, rather than revolutionary, nature. The previous edition's notes to the instructor, prepared by Angelo DeNisi and Robert Goddard, provided an excellent foundation on which to build. The basic format remains the same, but several sections have been added—specifically, in addition to the features found in the previous edition, this *Annotated Instructor's Edition* now includes the following: chapter outlines, learning objectives, Case in Point notes, Experiencing Organizational Behavior notes, and assorted new lecture and review questions reflecting changes in the text's content. Chapter overviews have also been expanded to include brief descriptions of the chapters' special sections (Focus on Research, An International/Multicultural Perspective, A Question of Ethics, and OB in Practice) and Case in Point and Experiencing Organizational Behavior features. Marginal annotations and cross-references to the test bank (at the bottom of relevant pages) are also included, printed in blue. (These last two new features are discussed in more detail below.)

Highlights of the Annotated Instructor's Edition

Each chapter begins with a Chapter Outline and Learning Objectives. Following these is a chapter overview that briefly describes the chapter's general content, special sections, and Case in Point and Experiencing Organizational Behavior features. This sec-tion is followed by Lecture and Review Questions. These questions address the major issues discussed in the text. You can use these questions in a variety of ways. For example, they can be used as the basis for lectures, review sessions, or as essay questions for examinations. Following this section are Other Teaching Suggestions, a potpourri of suggestions intended to allow you to pick and choose from these as you wish. Some suggestions directly address issues presented in the text, whereas others offer suggestions for working around the edges of the material covered in the text. The next section is the Case in Point Notes. This section provides an overview of each chapter's Case in Point, along with various tips and suggestions for using the case. Following this is an Additional Cases section consisting of supplementary cases and notes that can be used by teachers who prefer to use cases to teach OB or simply wish to include more cases in their course. Next is an Experiencing Organizational Behavior Notes section. These notes describe the Experiencing Organizational Behavior exercises found in the text and provide suggestions and comments for using the exercises. Additional Experiential Exercises are also provided for teachers who use an experiential approach to teaching OB or wish to add more experiential exercises to their classes from time to time. Each AIE chapter concludes with a section of Additional Readings. This section lists additional articles and books that can be used to supplement the material covered in the text.

In addition to the material provided in the instructor's section, the AIE text itself contains marginal annotations (called "lecture nuggets") and references to the test bank. These features are found *only* in the instructor's copy of the text and are printed in blue for easy reference. The lecture nuggets offer interesting "tidbits" of supplementary information about the topic being discussed in the section. Instructors may find these sidebars useful sources of additional information when preparing lectures. As you will see, these lecture nuggets come from a wide variety of sources. Also, at the bottom of relevant pages are references to specific test bank questions that are based on material appearing on that page. (In some cases, answers to questions appear over several pages; when this happens, the question numbers at the bottom of the page indicate the beginning of the range of pages on which the answer appears.)

Supplements

In addition to the instructor's section of this text, the AIE contains several improved resource materials that accompany *Behavior in Organizations*. The foremost among these are discussed here.

The Instructor's Resource Manual (IRM) Included in the IRM are eighty transparency masters, five for each chapter. As a special feature, illustrations not found in the student text have also been included. This collection of artwork is designed specifically for use in conjunction with this edition of *Behavior in Organizations*.

Thoroughly revised test bank questions also appear in the IRM. There is a total of 1,200 questions. As an aid to item selection, the questions are categorized as being either factual, conceptual, or applied.

Computerized Test Bank Test bank questions are also available in computerized versions for the Macintosh and the IBM-PC.

CNN Video This eighty-minute video includes eight custom-edited segments from CNN's *Pinnacle* program, with interviews of business leaders such as Herb Kelleher of Southwest Airlines, and programs on current topics such as sexual harassment, workforce motivation, and the changes in management careers in the mid-1990s. The videos are integrated with cases and special sections in the text and reinforce text concepts. A *Video User's Guide* is also available as a separate item for use with the CNN video.

Student Study Guide For your students, a *Student Study Guide* is available to supplement the text.

All the supplements are provided to instructors who adopt the fourth edition of *Behavior in Organizations*.

Note on Using Cases

The cases included in the text and the *Annotated Instructor's Edition* can be used in various ways. The two most common approaches are to ask students to read the case and then (1) to respond to the discussion questions following the case or (2) to use the classic case-analysis method involving problem diagnosis, generation of alternative solutions, evaluation of alternative solutions, and ultimately the selection, implementation, and follow-up of a preferred problem-solving strategy. For teachers who wish to use the classic case-analysis method, the guidelines for discussing cases using the case method are provided in the section that follows.

The Case Method of Discussion*

A case consists of conditions, attitudes, and practices that exist at a particular time in an organization's history. It usually describes a challenging problem or problems an organization is facing or has resolved. One of the assets of the case method is the extent to which it forces us to identify problems that may not be self-evident.

A second distinguishing feature of a case is the reality of the situation it describes. A problem might be posed as a question, for example, "Should a manufacturer adopt a program of national advertising?" A case suggests the same problem, but by including the condition under which it arises, it also acknowledges the complexity of the situation.

A case provides some, but usually not all, of the information available to managers at the time they need to resolve a problem. A case also frequently includes data on alternative courses of action. Because it attempts to reconstruct a real-life situation, a case is deliberately written in a way that requires the rearrangement of facts and an interpretation of these facts, including an evaluation of a company's opinions, behavior, and intentions. In addition, many but not all of the available facts are relevant to the solution of the problem. This simulates real life experience, since information used to solve an actual problem is rarely presented in a systematic and orderly fashion.

There is no right way to study cases. Each student will eventually discover an approach that best suits him or her. The following are simply some suggestions that may prove helpful.

- All case preparation has the same objective: to reach a decision about the issue or issues in the case in light of the facts given in the case and of the student's relevant knowledge. A full command of the facts in the case is a critical element in that process, and thus the case should be read carefully at least a couple of times. A first reading will give the general flavor of the situation and make possible preliminary identification of issues. Generally, there will be some guiding questions given at the end of the case; sometimes these will be omitted. The student should always be alert for issues or problems that have not been identified. At least a second reading is generally required to ensure full command of the facts. Part of a second reading should be a close analysis of quantitative data given in the case. As courses progress, the student will be learning many of the techniques of such analysis, so the

*Adapted from materials prepared by Professor Roy J. Lewicki, Ohio State University, College of Business, for instructional purposes.

fact that analyses may be rather superficial at the start should not be cause for dismay.

- At this point, it is useful to review all of the data to make sure that the issue or issues have been correctly stated. For example, the apparent issue in a case might be whether or not a supervisor is doing a good job, whereas the real problem is the basis being used for evaluation by the superior. Correct stating of the problem is often the most important part of decision making.

- When the issue is identified, it is usually helpful to list all possible courses of action. Remember that not all of these will necessarily be stated in the case itself. For example, an ever-present alternative, not always stated, is to do nothing.

- Once possible courses of action have been identified, a *pro* and *con* listing for each one is often helpful. Not infrequently, data in the case will be contradictory. For example, a person may say that she behaves in a certain way, whereas the record of her actions given in the case indicates quite different behavior. A student's judgment about the validity of data must be utilized here, and an objective of the whole educational process is the develop-

ment of the student's powers of judgment. Once again, students should not be unduly disturbed about the apparent quality of their judgment in the early stages of a course.

On other occasions, some very desirable information may not be available. In these instances, the student must make his or her judgments on the basis of information available, though from time to time an appropriate "solution" may be to ask for more data. A careful assessment of the probable cost of getting the data is required to support such a conclusion, however.

- After identifying possible courses of action and weighing the *pros* and *cons* of each, the final step in case analysis is to make a decision. In case analysis, as in real life, this is a first step that most people like to avoid; but in terms of the educational experience it is the most important part of the whole process. Bear in mind that making a decision and jumping to a conclusion are not the same thing. Some of the great decisions of human history have, no doubt, been based on intuition, and some successful administrators may well have uttered the legendary "Don't confuse me with facts. I've made up my mind." However, virtually all decisions are made

---

Ten Case Discussion Rules for Students°

1. Each remark must follow in some way from the last comment offered. Listen to what is said and build on it.
2. Attempt to relate the case to your readings and what you have learned in class. Don't just speak from experience, but connect your remarks to theory or the concepts of the course.
3. Only one person should speak at a time. Obviously it's more difficult to pay full attention to two or three people at once.
4. Control your personal evaluations of each other and use your intellect to try to understand *what* a person is saying as well as *why*.
5. Attempt to build a consensus on a conclusion or solution that reflects the *best* thinking of the group as a whole and not just an individual's view.
6. Practice active listening skills, and if you need more information to understand what someone is saying, ask for it. It's your responsibility to understand, so if you don't, then ask for help.
7. When speaking, put your ideas in a logical form and be sure you are understood. Help the listeners understand your message by making sense (logic) of it for them.
8. Avoid excessive rhetoric or preaching; the professor does enough of that. Try to stick to the facts of the case.
9. If you have to make assumptions about the case because there is not enough information, then state and support your assumptions clearly.
10. Test and evaluate what you have learned from the case. Share these learnings with others; it may help us all learn more.

°These rules were developed by Kenneth Murrell.

only after vigorous and logical analysis of all pertinent data, and this is the way the student should proceed.

Finally, it is important to remember that only infrequently is there a "right" decision. A decision may appear to you to be "right" in light of *your* assessment and weighing of the facts. Another person may evaluate the same facts in another way and thus have a different "right" answer. Virtually every business decision involves both judgment and straightforward assessment of facts. Techniques for analysis and weighing concrete data can be taught effectively by lectures, demonstrations, readings, and exercises. The important element of judgment apparently can be learned, if at all, only by making judgments about real situations. This is the purpose of the case method. As the late Professor Charles Gragg of Harvard put it in a well-known talk, the case method is used "Because wisdom can't be told."

A Balanced Conclusion

Looking back, we can honestly say that we have spared no effort in our attempt to place this new edition of our text on the fulcrum—to attain the ideal balance where research and practice are concerned. In this respect, we have heeded the words of Lord Chesterfield, who wrote

> Aim at perfection in everything, though in most things it is unattainable; however, those who aim at perfection and persevere, will come closer to it than those give it up as unattainable . . .

Whether, and to what extent, we have reached this goal can be judged only by you—our colleagues. So, as always, we sincerely invite your input. Please let us know what you like about the book and what features can stand improvement. Such feedback is always welcomed and does not fall on deaf ears. We promise faithfully to take your comments and suggestions to heart and to incorporate them into the next edition.

Jerald Greenberg

Jerald Greenberg
Abramowitz Professor of Business Ethics and
  Professor of Organizational Behavior
Department of Management and Human Resources
The Ohio State University
Columbus, Ohio 43210

Robert A. Baron

Robert A. Baron (seated)
Chair of the Department of Managerial Policy and Organization
Rensselaer Polytechnic Institute
Troy, New York 12180

ACKNOWLEDGMENTS:
SOME WORDS OF THANKS

Writing is a solitary task. Converting authors' words into a book, however, requires the efforts and cooperation of many individuals. In preparing this text, we have been assisted by many dedicated, talented people. We can't possibly thank all of them here, but we do wish to express our appreciation to those whose help has been most valuable.

First, our sincere thanks to our colleagues who read and commented on various portions of the manuscript. Their suggestions were invaluable and helped us in many ways. These reviewers include Mary Kernan (University of Delaware), James Mc-Elroy (Iowa State University), Paul Sweeney (Marquette University), Terry Scandura (University of Miami), Rodney Lim (Tulane University), Dan Levi (California Polytechnic University at San Luis Obispo), Taggart Smith (Purdue University), Rabi S. Bhagat (Memphis State University), Richard Grover (University of Southern Maine), Ralph Katerberg (University of Cincinnati), Richard McKinney (Southern Illinois University, Edwardsville), Paula Morrow (Iowa State University), and Shirley Rickert (Indiana University—Purdue University at Fort Wayne). Reviewers of the previous edition include Debra Arvanites (Villanova University), Jane M. Berger (Miami–Dade Community College), Angelo DeNisi (Rutgers University), Maureen Fleming (University of Montana), Hal W. Hendrick (University of Denver), Bruce Kemelgor (University of Louisville), Jack Kondrasuk (University of Portland), Mark Miller (De-Paul University), Suzyn Ornstein (Suffolk University), and Charles Regan (Manchester Community College).

Second, we wish to express our appreciation to Susan Badger, our editor at Allyn and Bacon. Her enthusiasm for this project was contagious, and her constant support and good humor certainly helped us bring it to completion in a timely and enjoyable manner.

Third, our sincere thanks go out to the production team at Allyn and Bacon. Although many people were involved in helping make this book so beautiful, we worked most closely with Dana Hayes, Deborah Brown, and Sally Stickney. Their diligence and skill with matters of design, permissions, and illustrations helped us immeasurably throughout the process of preparing this text. Nancy Bell Scott did a very professional job copyediting the text. It was a pleasure to work with such kind and understanding professionals, and we are greatly indebted to them for their contributions. With a team like this behind us—a group that can spot an undotted "i" or an uncrossed "t" from forty paces away—authors cannot help but look good.

Fourth, we wish to thank our colleagues who have provided expert assistance in preparing various features for this book. Rick Grover researched and wrote the very interesting Case in Point features that end each chapter, and he also did a fantastic job with the entire *Instructor's Section* of the *Annotated Instructor's Edition*. Linda Hoopes prepared a very useful *Student Study Guide* to accompany this text. We also wish to thank Jeff Miles for the research assistance he provided and for the truly fascinating "lecture nuggets" he wrote as marginal annotations for the *Annotated Instructor's Edition*.

Finally, Jerald Greenberg wishes to acknowledge the family of the late Irving Abramowitz for their generous endowment to the Ohio State University, which provided invaluable support during the writing of this book.

To all these truly outstanding people, and to many others too, our warm personal regards.

■ 1 ■

ORGANIZATIONAL BEHAVIOR: AN INTRODUCTION

CHAPTER OUTLINE

The Field of Organizational Behavior: A Working Definition
Organizational Behavior and the Scientific Method
Individuals, Groups, and Organizations: Three Levels of Analysis
Organizational Behavior: Further Characteristics of the Field

Organizational Behavior: A Historical Overview
Scientific Management: The Roots of Organizational Behavior
Human Relations: Social Factors in Work Settings
Classical Organizational Theory
Organizational Behavior in the Modern Era

Tools for Learning about Organizational Behavior: Theory and Research
Isn't It All Just Common Sense?

Theory: An Essential Guide to Organizational Research
Natural Observation
The Case Method: Generalizing from the Unique
Surveys and Correlational Research
The Experimental Method

Special Sections

An International/Multicultural Perspective   Are the Chinese Motivated to Manage?

OB in Practice   United Parcel Service: The Big Brown Bureaucracy That Really Delivers

A Question of Ethics   Ethical Obligations to Research Participants

LEARNING OBJECTIVES

After reading this chapter, you should be able to:
1. Describe the focus of the field of organizational behavior, including its three basic levels of analysis.
2. Characterize the features of the field of organizational behavior today.
3. Outline the historical developments and schools of thought leading up to the field of organizational behavior today.

4. Explain why the scientific study of the field of organizational behavior is necessary.
5. Describe the role of theory in the pursuit of knowledge about organizational behavior.
6. Characterize the major approaches to conducting research in the field of organizational behavior.

Chapter Overview

This chapter begins with a definition of the field of organizational behavior and its grounding in the behavioral sciences and the scientific method. The three levels of organizational behavior analysis (individual, group, and organization) are discussed, followed by an overview of the general characteristics of contemporary organizational behavior. In this section, the influence of the human resources, the contingency, the open systems, and the international perspectives on organizational behavior are described. The chapter then presents a brief history of the field, tracing its roots from scientific management, human relations, and classical organizational theory.

The end part of chapter 1 presents a discussion of the basic concepts of organizational behavior theory and research methodology. This section begins by addressing the question "Isn't it all common sense?" then moves on to a discussion of the importance of theory and research in understanding organizational behavior, and concludes by describing the major research methods used in doing organizational behavior research.

Starting in chapter 1 and continuing throughout the text, are special sections that present illustrations of the international/multicultural (e.g., comparing Chinese and Americans motivation to manage) and ethical (e.g., ethical obligations to research participants) dimensions of organizational behavior. Each chapter also includes an OB in Practice feature that describes how organizational behavior information is being used in real businesses (e.g., use of bureaucracy by United Parcel Service). Case in Point and Experiencing Organizational Behavior features are provided as supplements to the chapter. The case in this chapter illustrates how organizational behavior research is often done (research on the factors affecting quality circle success at Hughes Aircraft). As with the special features, all of the Case in Point sections throughout the text are based on real events that have taken place in existing organizations.

Lecture and Review Questions

What is organizational behavior?

Organizational behavior is the study of human behavior at work, considering three levels of analysis within organizations: the individual, the group, and the organization itself. This study's ultimate goal is the improvement of organizational effectiveness and individual well-being. The specific areas of interest that comprise organizational behavior are defined, in large part, by subsequent chapters of the text.

Why is the study of organizational behavior important?

Despite our confidence in common sense, little is actually understood about behavior in organizations. Issues concerning the most effective leadership style in a given situation, the nature of decisions made by individuals and groups, and the role of money as a motivational force in modern organizations continue to provide a multitude of opportunities for scientific research in organizational behavior. Also, as international competition becomes more heated, the competitive edge belongs to those organizations that are most effective. The field of organizational behavior provides a perspective and a methodology for determining how organizations can gain this edge.

How does the nature of organizations influence behavior within them?

The formal aspects of organizational design influence behavior by dictating tasks and responsibilities, determining patterns of communication, and identifying the locus of power. Informal aspects of organizational structure also influence behavior because informal networks and structures are often more important in day-to-day interactions than more formal ones. Finally, the culture of an organization influences the attitudes and expectations of most of its members.

Newcomers to organizations may feel like full members only when they adapt to the organizational culture in anything from the way they dress to their views on politics.

What are the major steps in the development of organizational behavior from scientific management, human relations, and classical organization theory to its current state?

Scientific management, human relations, and classical organizational theory contributed to the development of contemporary organizational behavior by highlighting the importance of work technology, \social relationships, and organizational structure, respectively. Interest in scientific management grew from attempts to improve productivity. This particular approach is based on the assumption that employees are motivated primarily by economic needs and that meeting these needs is the key to motivation. It emphasizes redesigning jobs so that workers are more efficient and outlines the actual movements workers perform to complete their jobs. Frederick Taylor, the most famous proponent of this approach, also believed that workers should be rewarded financially for increased productivity.

The beginning of the human relations movement can be traced to the Hawthorne studies conducted by Mayo and Roethlisberger. The emphasis of this approach is on ways of improving the social aspects of work and making jobs more satisfying to workers. Based on the assumption that a satisfied worker is a more productive worker, job satisfaction and work attitudes became major topics for study.

Classical organizational theory focused on the efficient structuring of organizations. From this perspective grew a number of principles of management that were intended to serve as rules for controlling organizational resources—chief among them employees. Certainly the most widely known set of management principles to emerge from classical organizational theory is the bureaucracy. As described by Max Weber, a bureaucracy is defined in large part by its rationality—the commitment to achieve organizational goals in the most efficient manner possible. Typical of the other principles of bureaucracy are emphasis on formal rules and regulations, impersonal treatment of all employees, division of labor, hierarchical structure, chain of command, and life-long career commitment. With its focus on organization structure, classical organizational theory called attention to the important role that formal organization structure has on organizational behavior.

What are the characteristics of contemporary organizational behavior?

Modern approaches to organizational behavior tend to have rather positive views of human nature believing that employees are capable of accepting responsibility and are valued assets of the organization. Efforts to motivate employees involve a contingency view that suggests the success of any program will always depend on factors in the situation. This view also accepts the premise that there are no simple answers to understanding behavior at work. Modern approaches to organizational behavior also view organizations as open systems. According to this view, organizations are dynamic, ever-changing, self-sustaining systems that operate to transform resources from the environment into various outputs.

Finally, contemporary organizational behavior also recognizes the importance of cultural differences as factors affecting how people behave in organizations. Doing business in a global marketplace demands that the field of organizational behavior take into consideration the sometimes dramatic differences in the way people from different countries and cultures go about doing work.

What distinguishes experimentation from other research methods in organizational behavior?

Natural observation and the case method make no attempt to change or control any aspect of a given situation. Although survey methods are somewhat more systematic in their approach, they also fail to exercise any control, and thus, it is virtually impossible to determine what causes a particular behavior by this method.

In an experiment, we attempt to control as many aspects of a situation as possible in order to make strong statements about causality. Thus, if we were interested in whether a new incentive plan would cause increased productivity, we would need to conduct an experiment. This would involve *randomly* choosing a group of employees and instituting the new incentive plan. The remainder of the employees would continue under the present system. This second group of employees (which we would call the control group) should be comparable to the incentive group (the experimental group) in every other way. If, over time, we observe the experimental group's performance to be higher than the control group's, we can conclude that it was the introduction of the incentive plan that caused productivity to increase since we equated the two groups on all other factors.

Other Teaching Suggestions

1. At this point, there still may be students who are convinced that much of organizational behavior is common sense. Challenge their common sense a bit. Cognitive dissonance research has always been a good area for such a challenge. If I paid $300 for a suit, and I learned that you paid $200 for the exact same suit, who will be more satisfied with the suit? Using common sense, not many students will come to the conclusion that I will. There's also a lot of recent work on escalation of commitment to a disasterous course of action that is counter-intuitive. Discuss this concept relative to the Vietnam war.

2. To really appreciate the impact of culture on behavior in organizations, you might discuss IBM. There are many books written about life with *Big Blue* that discuss the strengths of the norms for behavior (e.g., white shirts). Compare this to what has been written in the popular press about working for Apple Computers.

3. McGraw-Hill has available actual films of Frederick Taylor working with employees in an attempt to improve productivity. Some of these scenes involve immigrant workers and are quite revealing about prevalent views of workers, and people in general, at the time.

4. In the last five-to-ten years, much new material has been written about the Hawthorne studies that refutes some of the original conclusions on which the human relations movement is based. Ed Locke at Maryland argues that the results really support scientific management more than human relations. There is also the story of the immigrant girl working in the assembly room. Her father needed an operation; so she pushed the other workers to produce more, so they could earn more. Some have even called this immigrant girl the "Mother of the human relations movement." In any event, there may never have been a true Hawthorne Effect.

5. Daily life frequently provides examples of research results. Discussion of some of these studies might help students understand how empirical research works. For example, for years Bayer aspirin claimed that nearly 95 percent of all doctors surveyed recommended Bayer. However, the fine print said, "of those indicating a specific brand." Ask your students if they can think of another brand name of regular, unbuffered, non–extra-strength aspirin. Or how about an old Volvo claim that 90 percent of all Volvos bought in the United States in the last ten years are still on the road, when actually, 90 percent of all Volvos bought in the last ten years had actually been bought in the last two years. There are many other examples of companies using flawed research findings to help sell their products. Ask your students if they know any.

6. A Discussion about the ethics of experimental research might also be interesting. (Remind students that true experiments require random assignment to equivalent experimental and control conditions.) Then, ask about the nature of research needed to determine if cigarette smoking causes cancer, for example. What happens when the government decides to test a new drug to deal with AIDS? Some people, who act as the control group, must not be able to get

Chapter 1

the drug even though we believe it to be their only hope. Is this ethical? When is it ethical to withhold treatment or to induce a potentially dangerous condition, and when is it not? If you want to push this a bit further, ask your students how they feel about animal research.

7. Your students may well have served as subjects in someone's experiment. If not, they certainly are no different than the students who have served as subjects. How do they feel about acting as *guinea pigs*? Perhaps more importantly, how do they feel about the issues regarding whether their responses are the same as would be obtained from "real world" employees or managers?

Case in Point Notes

Using Research to Solve Organizational Problems: A Behind-the-Scenes Look

This case illustrates how organizational behavior research is often done in field settings. The research investigated the organizational factors that contribute to quality circle effectiveness and was conducted for the Hughes Aircraft Corporation. Participants in the study were quality circle members working in the company's Space and Communications Group. The researcher was Alan Honeycutt, a management consultant. The research process is fairly typical of applied research used to solve practical organizational behavior problems.

This case outlines the general sequence of decisions involved in doing applied survey research. The process starts with a request from Hughes Aircraft management to identify the organizational factors that contribute to the success of quality circles, proceeds to Honeycutt's review of the relevant OB literature on quality circles, the development of research questions and selection of research methodology, the review of proposed research with Hughes Aircraft management, the study design and development of the study questionnaire, the data collection process, and finally the analysis of the research data and formulation of study conclusions. By illustrating the general steps of the research process, students see what types of decisions and concerns the OB researcher has to deal with. Students will recognize that this research, like most research, is far from perfect and that sometimes the conclusions drawn from research are open to question.

The questions following the case are intended to make students think about each of the major stages of the research process. You may wish to expand on these questions by considering what other directions Honeycutt could have pursued at each decision point, and how different choices would have affected the nature of the research process. This procedure also allows students the opportunity to apply many concepts and terms and to design their own research projects. This procedure works particularly well when done in small discussion groups, and has also been effective when discussed with the class as a whole.

This case provides a good springboard for discussing research projects that you have done or are in the process of doing. Students seem to really like getting a behind-the-scenes peek at how OB research is actually conducted—with all of its difficulties, false starts, mistakes, messiness, but most important, the sense of excitement and discovery inherent in doing OB research.

The case concludes by discussing how Hughes Aircraft used the research to guide its effort to implement quality circles throughout other parts of the company and relates numerous additional questions raised by Honeycutt's research. This part of the case often stimulates discussion regarding other questions students might like to investigate and previews OB topics that appear in later chapters of the text.

Experiencing Organizational Behavior Notes

Organizational Behavior versus Common Sense: A Demonstration

This exercise introduces students to the complexity inherent in organizational behavior. Students are presented with a list of apparently simple statements regarding various organizational behavior phenomena. They are asked to indicate which statements are true, which are false, and also to indicate the degree of confidence they have in their answer.

The exercise is a real eye opener for students. By comparing their answers to the suggested answers provided, students quickly realize that much of what they thought was straightforward commonsense truth about organizational behavior is really quite complex. The exercise introduces students to the very important role of moderator variables in organizational behavior. What is true in one situation is not necessarily true in other situations.

Overall, this exercise provides students with the opportunity to realize for themselves that although they already know a little about organizational behavior, they—like all of the rest of us—have a lot more to learn.

Additional Reading

Campbell, D. T., and Stanley, J. C. (1963). *Experimental and quasi-experimental designs for research.* Chicago: Rand McNally. (This is the original source for most discussions of research designs.)

■ 2 ■

PERCEPTION: UNDERSTANDING AND EVALUATING OTHERS

CHAPTER OUTLINE

Perception: Some Basic Features
  Attention: Selectivity in Perception
  Attention and On-the-Job Safety: Reactions to Hazard
    Warnings
Social Perception: Understanding Others
  Attribution: Identifying the Causes of Others' Behavior
  Cognitive Factors in Social Perception
When Social Perception Fails: Errors in Our Efforts to Understand Others
  Errors in Attribution
  Halo Effects: When Overall Impressions Shape
    Specific Judgments
  Similar-to-Me Effects
  Stereotypes: Fitting Others into Cognitive Molds of
    Our Own Making
Impression Management: The Fine Art of Looking Good
  Impression Management: Specific Tactics
  Impression Management and Organizational Behavior

Social Perception and Organizational Behavior: Its Role in Job Interviews, Performance Appraisal, and Organizational Conflict
  Social Perception and Job Interviews
  Social Perception and Performance Appraisal
  Social Perception and Organizational Conflict

Special Sections

Focus on Research What's in a Name? The Origins of
  Company Reputations

An International/Multicultural Perspective In
  Search of Diversity: Matching Work Force to
  Customer Base at Kinney Shoes

OB in Practice Escaping the Echo Chamber: Or, How
  to Counter the MUM Effect

LEARNING OBJECTIVES

After reading this chapter, you should be able to:
1. Define *perception* and explain why it is an active process.
2. Define *social perception* and indicate its relevance to organizational behavior.
3. Explain how we employ *attribution* to understand the causes of others' behavior.
4. Explain various causes of error in social perception such as the *self-serving bias, contrast effects*, and *stereotyping*.

5. Describe the process of *impression management*, and indicate how it can influence important aspects of organizational behavior.
6. Indicate how social perception can affect *job interviews, performance appraisal*, and *organizational conflict*.

Chapter Overview

This chapter deals with perception, a topic that pervades most aspects of organizational behavior. The chapter begins by answering why perception is so important and then presents information on the role of attention as a determinant of what we perceive. The remainder of the chapter deals with various aspects of social perception—the process by which we come to understand others. Attribution theory and

the factors that lead us to make internal and external attributions are explained. Then the key aspects of social cognition—the way information is sorted, encoded, stored in memory, and recalled—are presented. Next, various errors in social perception are discussed: attribution errors, halo effects, similar-to-me effects, and stereotypes. This is followed by an extensive discussion of impression management, in which the tactics people use to create a favorable impression and the impact of impression management on various forms of organizational behavior are described. The chapter concludes by presenting three areas where social perception has been shown to have a major impact on organizational behavior: job interviews, performance appraisal, and organizational conflict.

Three special sections appear in this chapter. Focus on Research (What's in a Name? The Origins of Company Reputations) presents the findings of a study investigating the factors (signals) that contribute to the formation of a company's reputation. The International/Multicultural Perspective section (In Search of Diversity: Matching Work Force to Customer Base at Kinney Shoes) discusses how Kinney Shoes uses the similar-to-me effect to its advantage by staffing their stores with employees who are similar in ethnic and cultural background to the customers they serve. And an OB in Practice section (Escaping the Echo Chamber: Or, How to Counter the MUM Effect) reports on how Anheuser-Busch attempts to prevent the MUM effect—the tendency to avoid transmitting bad news to supervisors so as to prevent the formation of an unfavorable impression.

The Case in Point (Team-Based Performance Appraisal at Digital Equipment Corporation) describes how teams are used to conduct employee performance appraisals and the perceptual issues associated with this practice. And the Experiencing Organizational Behavior exercise (The All-Too-Powerful Impact of Stereotypes) demonstrates the subtle, but powerful, influence of stereotypes on our perceptions.

Lecture and Review Questions

What is the role of attention in perception, and what factors influence attention?

We are constantly being assaulted by information from our environment and it is impossible to process all of it. Thus, we selectively perceive some stimuli, while ignoring others. Specifically, we react only to those stimuli which get our attention, and only those stimuli are processed from the environment. What makes us notice some things and not others? Motivational state for one—we are more likely to notice restaurants when we are hungry. Another factor is our attitude. We tend to pay attention to stimuli toward which we are positively disposed, and we tend to ignore others toward which we are more negatively disposed. The other major factor here is the salience of the stimulus: the more salient a stimulus, the more likely it is to be noticed. Salience is said to increase as a stimulus becomes more intense, larger, novel, moves, and is in greater contrast to its surroundings.

What is attribution theory and how are attributions for behavior formed?

Attribution theory supplies a system of rules and relationships to help us answer questions about why people behave the way they do. Typically, we are trying to decide whether the behavior is due to something about the situation (an external attribution) or something about the person (an internal attribution). In trying to reach this decision, the theory says we consider whether other persons behave in the same way in the same situation (which would be called high consensus); whether the same person has behaved in the same way in this situation in the past (which would be called high consistency); and whether the person behaves in the same way in other situations (this would be called low distinctiveness). We are most likely to attribute behavior to the situation when consensus is high, consistency is low and distinctiveness is high; we are more likely to attribute behavior to the person when consensus is low, consistency is high, and distinctiveness is low.

What are schemas and how do they affect social perception?

A schema can be defined as a cognitive framework that helps us interpret the information we encounter in our environment. It includes definitions of the members of some cognitive category and also specifies relationships among behaviors. Person schemas help us to interpret interactions with others, while event schemas help us to deal with different situations. Schemas affect social perception in several ways. First, they influence attention in that we are more likely to notice events or actions that are *inconsistent* with an existing schema. Second, schemas influence how information is entered into memory (encoded), in that information relevant to a schema is more likely to be retained in memory (especially if it is inconsistent with the schema). Finally, information that is consistent with a schema is more likely to be recalled, so that the schema can remain intact. Also, it is worth noting that a stereotype can be considered simply as a schema that relates membership in some particular category to a set of inferred personal attributes.

What are some of the more important perceptual errors that occur?

Two of the more important perceptual errors involve the attribution process. One of these, known as the *fundamental attribution error*, refers to a general tendency to attribute the behavior of others to internal rather than external causes, discounting situational forces that might be present. The second of these is known as *self-serving bias* which refers to a tendency to attribute our successes to internal causes, but to attribute failures to external causes. In addition to these, there are several perceptual errors that do not relate to attributional processes. *Halo error* occurs when our overall impression of a person affects our judgment of the person's specific traits or behavior. *Similar-to-me effects* occur when we evaluate persons more favorably the more like us they are. There are actually several ways of viewing this similarity. Perceived similarity refers to the extent to which we feel others share our values and beliefs. Perceptual congruence refers to the extent to which supervisors and subordinates agree about what exactly constitutes good performance on the job. Demographic similarity refers to the extent to which two people share demographic backgrounds such as age, race, or sex. *Contrast effects* refer to a tendency to modify our reactions to a specific person on the basis of our recent reactions to other persons. Thus, reactions tend to be more positive when they follow poor interactions with others, and they tend to be more negative when they follow good interactions with others. Finally, *stereotypes* result from our beliefs that all members of some identifiable group share common traits or behaviors.

What factors contribute to forming a favorable impression?

People rely upon two major sets of tactics to create a favorable impression: self-enhancing and other-enhancing behaviors. Improving one's physical appearance (e.g., dress for success) is a common self-enhancing tactic. Another self-enhancing tactic is to solicit feedback regarding one's performance. Timing is critical when using this tactic. Always ask for feedback immediately following good performance and ask for feedback from powerful, high status people. Also, be sure to ask for feedback in a way that will put you in the most favorable light (e.g., entitlement, blame deflecting, or enhancement approaches to seeking feedback). Other self-enhancing tactics include claiming acquaintance with well-known, high status persons (name-dropping), referring to one's experience or competence, talking rapidly to convey the impression of intelligence and using self-deprecating comments to suggest modesty. Other-enhancing tactics for creating a favorable impression are based primarily on flattering and/or doing favors for the target person. As the research in the text shows, self-enhancing and other enhancing tactics, if done skillfully, do indeed create favorable impressions.

What is the role of social perception in job interview settings?

Since interviews involve first meetings between strangers, social perceptual processes play a major role in their conduct, primarily through their influence on first impressions. For example, interviewees who emit mostly positive non-verbal cues, such as smiling, tend to be evaluated more favorably than interviewees who emit mostly negative or neutral cues. Other research has found that perceptual errors such as similar-to-me effects and contrast effects also influence the outcome of an interview. In general, the brief interaction afforded by the interview, along with the face-to-face nature of that interaction and the absence of much history between the participants, all contribute to the extent to which the conduct and outcome of an interview is influenced by social perceptual processes and errors.

What role does social perception play in performance appraisals?

Research suggests that perceptual processes play a major role in determining appraisal decisions. One way in which this occurs is through the influence of expectations. Raters who observe an employee behaving in a manner not consistent with their expectations for that employee (even if the behavior exceeds the expectation in some cases), tend to rate that employee less favorably than they would an employee whose behavior was consistent with rater expectations. Attributions also play a role in this process. Raters observe ratee behavior, but must also consider the *cause* of that behavior. Raters have a tendency to give higher ratings to employees whose performance they believe is due to effort as opposed to other causes. Also, as noted earlier, schemas affect attention, encoding, and retrieval. Since appraisals are relatively infrequent events, most of the information used by raters must be retrieved from memory. Since schemas affect these memory processes, much of the information available to a rater is determined by the schema he or she has for a particular employee.

What role does social perception play in organizational conflict?

Attributions play a crucial role in organizational conflict. When a provocative action occurs, does it stem from an internal causes such as conscious desires (e.g., selfishness) or does it instead stem from external causes—beyond the control of the actor (e.g., an accident)? The attribution made regarding the cause of provocative action has a major effect on the degree of organizational conflict that results. As the research discussed in the text reveals, organizational conflict is the probable result when provocation is attributed to internal causes, but much less likely when an external attribution is made.

Other Teaching Suggestions

1. One of the most striking examples of differential attention is the kind of exercise one often encoun-

ters in law schools. The exercise involves problems with eyewitness testimony. In the course of a lecture, unannounced to the students, someone bursts into the classroom, begins screaming at another of the students, pulls a gun, and shoots at the student. The shooter flees and is pursued by the student he fired at. The professor then questions all the students about what they saw. The discussion that follows deals with details noticed or missed by various students. This model could be adapted for a business class, using videotapes (and less violence) to see how different people observe different details in an interview, a counseling session, negotiations, and so on.

2. People naturally form attributions about all behavior they observe, so it should be simple to generate some concrete examples of how the process works. One example that should be quite salient to students involves the reasons for poor performance on an exam. The instructor might conclude the student's performance was due to lack of effort (he or she didn't study) because the student did well on other tests in this class and did well in other classes. The student's perspective might be quite different. The discrepancy may not be due to different interpretation of the information available. Instead, we are likely to see *self-serving bias* in operation, as the student distorts some facts to reach the conclusion that the test or the instructor was unfair.

3. Advertisers are always trying to take advantage of halo effects by having celebrities tout their products. Thus, if we admire Michael Jordan as an athlete, we are supposed to trust his taste in breakfast cereals as well. This plan can backfire, of course, when controversy arises over a formerly respected athlete like Pete Rose. Now he can be more of a liability than an asset, as the halo works against the advertiser.

4. An interesting extension of the role of stereotypes and impression formation in the interview is evident in the suggestions for men and women interviewing for jobs when they graduate. Men are told to shave their beards, buy dark suits, and wear ties that are some shade of red. Women, on the other hand, are given more interesting suggestions. They are told to wear suits (not dresses), not to wear too much makeup or jewelry, and to wear their hair pulled back or neat. This is interesting because it's really tantamount to suggesting that women must be sure that their gender is never salient. The more women *look* like men, the more the interviewer is likely not to be biased against them.

5. The text discusses the role of social perception in performance appraisal, but some background might be relevant here. For over 60 years, researchers and practitioners assumed that the best ways to improve appraisal decisions were developing better rating scales or training raters. There are many types of

rating scales available, and many examples are provided in a book by Bernardin and Beatty. Despite these efforts, no one type of rating scale was found to consistently outperform others. The efforts devoted to training program design were also less than successful. Most of the early training was designed to get raters to reduce rating errors such as halo effects. The problem, however, is that when raters are instructed to reduce halo effects they will do so, even if there should be a relationship among ratings in different areas. It will be interesting to see if the newer emphasis on cognitive processes will be more successful. These approaches assume that the major problems facing a rater are reliance on memory (the behavior he or she has to evaluate occurred some time before the ratings are due) and a lack of standards which prevents really effective evaluations. Some dissenting voices, however, argue that the major problem for appraisals is simply that raters are not motivated to give accurate ratings. Instead, raters have other goals they are trying to accomplish through the rating process, and no interventions are likely to divert them from these goals.

Case in Point Notes

Team-Based Performance Appraisal at Digital Equipment Corporation

This case describes how Digital Equipment's Customer Support Center does performance appraisal within the context of self-managed work teams. When Digital's Customer Support Center in Colorado Springs, Colorado, implemented self-managed work teams as its primary work technology, it was faced with the challenge of devising a new way to appraise the performance of its employees. To meet this challenge, the company developed a team-based approach to performance appraisal that incorporates a combination of self-evaluation and peer-evaluation procedures. The details of the company's team-based performance appraisal system together with the a discussion of the advantages and disadvantages of the system are described in the case.

Following the case, students are asked to describe the general perceptual processes involved in performance appraisal. This is an excellent place to review the key aspects of social cognition. Students are then asked to consider the particular biases involved in self-evaluation (e.g., self-serving bias) and peer-evaluation (e.g., fundamental attribution error). The next question prompts students to consider why employees at Digital feel confident about the accuracy of the appraisals generated by their team-based approach. This question typically generates comments regarding the bias prevention effects of having multiple raters (peer-evaluations) and the bias-countering effects of mixing self with peer evaluations. Finally, students are asked to comment on the practice of screening peer-evaluation comments for harsh and/or inaccurate verbiage. This question will likely stimulate considerable discussion of individual differences in perception (e.g., what is cognitively categorized as harsh by one person may not be considered harsh by other people) as well as the type of information that should be included in performance appraisals.

Additional Case

The Case of Denise Morgan

Denise Morgan is a recent graduate of a major Ivy League school of business. She has recently successfully completed the Certified Public Accounting (CPA) exam, and has been interviewing with several accounting firms in the New York City area.

She has been particularly impressed with her interview experience at Van Dellen and Esterbrook, a medium-sized firm. There appears to be a high level of professionalism, and Denise has perceived that they regard her not as a rookie, but as a qualified, professional accountant. She has been led to believe, during the course of her third interview with Van Dellen and Esterbrook, that, if hired, she would be included as a member of a team of accountants handling would could be the largest single account for this firm. All in all, Denise is quite excited about the possibility of joining this progressive firm.

Upon receipt of an offer letter, which described her assignment to this special team as well as a *most* respectable salary offer, Denise accepted employment with Van Dellen and Esterbrook. She reported to work on Monday, and after completing what seemed like hours of paperwork, she met with the leader of the new team, Dan Gresham.

Denise had talked with Dan during the course of the interview process and had developed a positive impression of him as a supervisor. At no time during the interview process had Dan mentioned anything about Denise being a single female. He had discussed the possible new account, had introduced Denise to the other members of the proposed team (none of whom were female), and had described Denise's duties on the team should she accept the position. All in all, Dan seemed to be the ideal boss: knowledgeable, professional, and willing to assign challenging work to new people.

After welcoming Denise to Van Dellen and Esterbrook, Dan explained her responsibilities in some detail and took her down the hall to the "bull pen," the area where the associates who would be working together on the new account shared working space. Bill Jackson, an associate who was also assigned to the team, greeted Denise and helped her find an unused desk. He then said, "Denise, after Dan gets through showing you around, I'd like to take you to lunch. I've got a proposition for you."

At that remark, Dan rolled his eyes and groaned. "Denise, you've been here for three hours and you've already got your first proposition!"

Questions
1. What do you think led to Dan's last remark?
2. In terms of attribution theory (consensus, contingency, and distinctiveness), how might Denise interpret Dan's remark?

The Case of Denise Morgan: Teaching Note

Many students might conclude from his last remark that Dan is a male chauvinist. However, he has not given any indication of that up to this point. The fact that Denise is the first woman to be hired and assigned to his team may cause Dan to explore various behaviors to try to establish a sound working relationship with Denise. However, this remark is probably not an appropriate behavior.

Students should analyze Dan's last remark in terms of the attribution theory concepts of consensus and distinctiveness. Given the lack of information about Dan and Bill, reaching a *consensus* about the remark (Do other persons in the firm act in the same way?) may be difficult. *Consistency* in this situation seems to be low, as it was reported that at other meetings with Dan, he acted differently, with respect to chauvinistic remarks. *Distinctiveness* is high also, since Dan acted differently in other situations. Given what we know of this situation, we might attribute Dan's behavior to external causes.

Experiencing Organizational Behavior Notes

The All-Too-Powerful Impact of Stereotypes
This exercise provides students with the opportunity to see for themselves some of their own stereotypes. Students are asked to rate members of various occupations using a bipolar adjective scale (rating criteria include the characteristics: liberal, intelligent, greedy, dull, and their opposites). Upon completing the scale, most students will quickly recognize that their ratings of the various occupational group members differ. What does this mean? The obvious conclusion is that people who rate other people based on their occupational status are relying up their own stereotypes (schema).

Exercise instructions as well as follow-up questions and comments are provided in the text.

Source: Adapted from Jerri L. Frantzve, *Behaving in Organizations: Tales from the Trenches.* Copyright © 1983 by Allyn and Bacon. Used by permission.

The Reluctant Account Executive

This exercise involves role playing. Role playing involves interacting with others in various artificial situations as similar as possible to real life. It is not like acting in the usual sense, because there is no script; you make up your own words as you go along, providing the words support the basic facts of your given role.

It is a fairly painless way of giving and receiving feedback, because it is officially an experiment. Therefore, a critique of your performance need not make you feel as embarrassed as you would if it were real. Furthermore, constructive criticism from peers is far easier to accept and learn from than that from superiors and/or subordinates.

How to Role Play

In creating your part in role playing, accept the facts as given and assume the attitude and feelings supplied in your specific role. It is most important that you reflect these attitudes and feelings with overt behavior.

From this point on, modify your behavior or attitude as you feel a normal person would in the same situation; that is, relent from antagonistic behavior, especially if the other person's behavior makes you feel less angry.

At times, it may be best to react to the other person's behavior in an exaggerated manner in order for that person to get your message. (This technique is especially useful for helping the other person to learn.)

When facts or events arise that are not covered by your given role, make up things that are consistent with the way it might be in a real-life situation.

Why It's Often Difficult to Role Play

Individuals who have difficulty when asked to role play, often do so because they are either:

A. *Too used to following orders exactly.* If a role says think one way, these people are inclined to stay that way indefinitely instead of changing their behavior as their feelings are influenced by the other person's behavior;
B. *Not used to reflecting their feelings with behavior.* These people have learned that behaving unemotionally is less punishing than revealing their feelings; or
C. *Unused to giving feedback.* These people are unaware of the effects of giving immediate feedback to others.

Role Sheet for Charlie Shore, Supervisor

(Follow your instructor's directions in preparing for this role.)

You are the 38-year-old supervisor for an advertising account group of sixteen individuals in a large advertising agency. You have the typical problems any supervisor must

Source: Reprinted by permission from *Organization and People* by J. Ritchie and P. Thompson, copyright © 1988 by West Publishing Company. All rights reserved.

Role play instructions from an in-class exercise developed by Robert Goddard, Appalachian State University.

deal with—extended lunch hours, some absenteeism and tardiness—but basically a good team. The group has consistently been recognized for the high quality of its work. The client has now asked your agency to take on a brand extension of your current product. Because of the increased administrative demands—budgets, meetings, and so on—you and your management supervisor have decided that you need an assistant supervisor.

You are certain that your management supervisor is going to be promoted and that you are most likely to be his replacement. This means that the assistant you choose will probably make supervisor soon. In reviewing your team, you have observed that the majority of the members are young and too inexperienced to be considered good prospects for the assistant account supervisor position.

There is one individual, however, who stands out as an excellent prospect for the job if he would just change his attitude. Marc Stanton is a young man, about 26, who joined your account group as an assistant account executive right out of college. He is now the senior account executive on your staff and has had exposure in all areas—media, creative, and administrative—of your brand's marketing plan. He knows the brand's needs and has an excellent working relationship with the client.

The problem is that whenever you have asked him to work on the brand's long-term strategic issues, he doesn't seem interested. Although he has the best overall picture of the brand's needs, Marc is now content to limit his work to the day-to-day administrative duties of the brand. Many times you have told him that he has a good future with the agency and you would like to help him develop his leadership ability. Again and again, he shows little interest. You still think he is your best prospect, however, and so you have decided to talk to him once more about his attitude. He is on his way to your office now.

Role Sheet for Marc Stanton, Senior Account Executive

(Follow your instructor's directions in preparing for this role.)

You are the senior account executive on a sixteen-member advertising account group at a large advertising agency. Charlie Shore is your account supervisor. Most of the members of your group are much younger than you and are merely paying their dues in jobs that are simple and mundane. The advertising world is mostly administrative in nature, the pay is not good, and agency work is not at all glamorous. You feel that talent, especially yours, goes unrewarded and that anyone would be crazy to stay with an advertising agency.

But then, you really don't care. You are not going to be here much longer because you have already been accepted to graduate school. You want to get an MBA so that you can get a job in brand management. After all, the client side is where the real strategic brand decisions are made. You only took the agency job in the first place because it would make you a more attractive candidate for a top graduate business school.

There are some difficulties with your present position, however. You can't let Charlie know you are planning to return to school because you believe he will let you go. You need to work through the summer to save enough money for school. And lately he has been asking you to work on the long-term strategic plan for the brand, even though you know you won't be around to implement it. You just want to do what you're paid to do—the day-to-day administrative duties on the brand—and go home.

Now Charlie wants to see you again. He has asked you to come to his office. You wonder if it is about a problem yesterday when one of your assistants accidentally deleted a computer spreadsheet your group had been working on. You weren't able to retrieve it and it looked like you were at fault, but it wasn't a big deal. Oh, well, you can stall for time, it has always worked before. You only have a month before you give notice anyway. You will just complain about the poor pay, long hours, inexperienced staff, and low career potential. You are about to knock on Charlie's door.

The Reluctant Account Executive: Teaching Note

This role play gives your students the opportunity to experience perception in action. The two individuals in this scenario, Charlie Shore and Marc Stanton, have different perspectives on their futures with this advertising agency. Charlie sees the doord opening for promotion and advancement, while Marc sees his position as dead-end in nature.

Here are some suggestions for assigning and managing this exercise.

1. Have the class read the instructions of the first page of this exercise dealing with "How to Role Play."
2. Divide the class into three groups. The first will read only the role for the Supervisor, Charlie Shore. The second group will read only the role for the Senior Account Executive, Marc Stanton. The third group will read both roles.
3. Select one *Charlie* and one *Marc* to play their roles, in front of the class, acting out the confrontation. Instruct both participants to stay true to their roles according to the instructions at the beginning of this exercise.
4. Ask the *observers* who read the Charlie role if they believed the role actor accurately portrayed the role of the supervisor.
5. Ask the *observers* who read the Marc role if they believed the role actor accurately portrayed the role of the senior account executive.
6. Ask the *observers* who read both roles if their observations were any different from the other observers.
7. At this point, you could introduce some of the concepts of perception discussed in chapter 4.

Additional Readings

Bernardin, H. J., & Beatty, R. W. (1984). *Performance appraisal: Assessing human behavior at work*. Boston: Kent Publishing. (A comprehensive view of the appraisal process.)

Greenberg, J. (1988). Cultivating an image of justice: Looking fair on the job. *Academy of Management Executives, 2*(2), 155–158.

Walsh, J. P. (1988). Selectivity and selective perception: An investigation of managers' belief structures and information processing. *Academy of Management Journal, 31*, 873–896.

Chapter 2

∎ 3 ∎

LEARNING: ADAPTING TO THE WORLD OF WORK

CHAPTER OUTLINE

Theories of Learning: An Overview
Classical Conditioning: Learning by Association
Operant Conditioning: Learning through Rewards and Punishments
Observational Learning: Learning by Modeling Others

Reinforcing Desirable Organizational Behaviors
Schedules of Reinforcement: Patterns of Administering Rewards
Organizational Behavior Management: Positively Reinforcing Desirable Organizational Behaviors
Training: Learning and Developing Necessary Job Skills

Discipline: Eliminating Undesirable Organizational Behaviors
The Uses of Discipline

The Impact of Discipline: What Makes Punishment Effective?

Special Sections

OB in Practice Becoming Profitable by Teaching Customers Their Business

Focus on Research Testing an Operant Model among Sailboat Race Teams

A Question of Ethics Learning to Be Ethical: Citicorp Employees Play the Work Ethic Game

LEARNING OBJECTIVES

After reading this chapter, you should be able to:
1. Understand the concept of learning and how it applies to the study of behavior in organizations.
2. Identify and describe the three major approaches to learning and how they apply to understanding organizational behavior.
3. Name and distinguish between various schedules of reinforcement.
4. Appreciate how principles of reinforcement may be used in organizational behavior management programs to improve organizational functioning.
5. Understand the principles of learning that make organizational training effective.
6. Describe the conditions necessary for discipline to be effectively used in organizations.

Chapter Overview

In this chapter, students become aware of the major theories of learning and the many applications of learning theory to organizational behavior. The chapter differentiates among three basic types of learning: classical conditioning, operant conditioning, and observational learning. Each is defined, and specific examples of the role of each in the workplace are provided. The chapter then discusses the problems associated with reinforcing desired behaviors at work, presenting fixed and variable interval schedules and fixed and variable ratio schedules. Examples of different schedules of reinforcement (performance-contin-

gent as opposed to seniority-contingent pay systems) are drawn from several work settings.

A comprehensive plan for behavior management in organizations based on positive reinforcement is discussed, followed by analysis of the application of learning principles to training. The chapter concludes with ways to manage undesired behavior, focusing on punishment in the form of discipline. Guidelines for the effective use of discipline are provided and various issues involved with the use of discipline at work are discussed.

Three special sections appear in this chapter. The OB in Practice section (Becoming Profitable by

Teaching Customers Their Business) discusses how and why some companies are extending their learning programs to their customers as well as their employees. A Focus on Research section (Testing an Operant Model among Sailboat Race Teams) presents the findings of an ingenious study of the effects of operant contingencies used by skippers on the performance of sailboat racing crews. And a Question of Ethics section (Learning to Be Ethical: Citicorp Employees Play the Work Ethic Game) describes how the financial giant Citicorp uses principles of effective training to teach ethics to its 90,000 employees.

The Case in Point for this chapter (Getting Tough on Employees: Does It Pay Off?) describes how several CEOs (e.g., John Akers of IBM) use punishment and avoidance learning to increase the performance of their employees. The Experiencing Organizational Behavior exercise (The Reinforcing Value of Social Approval) demonstrates the effects of social reinforcers on organizational behavior.

Lecture and Review Questions

How does classical conditioning differ from operant conditioning, and how are they the same?

Both are models that explain how we come to learn new responses and both involve learning through some type of association. But classical conditioning deals only with reflexive or involuntary behavior. We cannot help but jump at the sound of an explosion or grimace when we taste something sour. These unconditioned responses are eventually paired with conditioned stimuli (the flash before the explosion), so that over time, we jump at the flash even if there is no explosion. Operant conditioning, on the other hand, deals with voluntary responses and learning through the use of rewards and punishments. This conditioning, based on the Law of Effect, is such that responses followed by positive outcomes (rewards) tend to be repeated, while behaviors followed by negative outcomes (punishments), or no outcomes (extinction), tend not to be repeated.

What is observational learning and how does it work?

Observational learning occurs by watching what happens to others. That is, someone observes another person engaged in a behavior, and then observes that person as he or she is rewarded, punished, or ignored. The observer then learns this relationship and comes to expect similar reactions if he or she were to engage in those same behaviors. In order for observational learning to work, the learner must pay attention to the model, remember what the model did, and then rehearse (at least mentally) that behavior. Then, assuming the learner is motivated, he or she copies the model's behavior. Typically, motivation to copy a model's behavior is highest when that behavior was seen as leading to a reward.

Describe the various schedules of partial reinforcement and discuss the effectiveness of each.

In most organizational settings, rewards are not administered every time a desired behavior occurs. This is known as partial reinforcement. There are four partial reinforcement schedules that vary along two dimensions: fixed versus variable and interval versus ratio. A fixed interval schedule means that, as long as the desired behavior occurs, it is rewarded after the passage of a fixed amount of time. The simplest example of this is a paycheck that is administered every week, as long as one works that week. Fixed schedules are easy to learn, but they do not result in consistent levels of performance. Over time, a person realizes that it will be another week before payday, and performance tends to drop, only to pick up again as payday approaches. Also, fixed interval schedules are not very resistant to extinction, so it will take little more than one week's work without pay for the person to stop coming to work.

Variable interval schedules operate in a similar fashion, but the amount of time that must pass with the behavior occuring changes. An example of this might be promotions based on performance. The level of performance tends to be more consistent because the person is never sure when the next reward will occur. Variable interval schedules are more difficult to learn than fixed interval schedules, but are also more resistant to extinction. Ratio schedules administer rewards based on the frequency with which desired behavior is exhibited. Thus, there are more frequent rewards if the behavior is exhibited more frequently. That is why performance tends to be higher under ratio schedules.

Fixed ratio schedules involve keeping the frequency required before reward a constant, such as paying a painter after every five rooms are painted. Since the person knows when a reward will be administered, performance is not consistent and this schedule is not particularly resistant to extinction even though it is easy to learn. Under a variable ratio schedule, the number of behaviors required before a reward changes, such as the way a slot machine works. The level of behavior is quite high (because of the ratio nature) and quite consistent (because of the variable nature) and, although these schedules are difficult to learn, they are quite resistant to extinction.

What is organizational behavior management and what are the major steps in developing such a plan?

Organizational behavior management is the systematic application of positive reinforcement principles to increase the frequency of desired behaviors at work. There are several steps that are critical for an effective plan. First, the desired behavior must be specified as exactly as possible; next, a base rate of occurrence for that behavior should be established; next, a criterion for change must be established; that is, we must specify what behavior and/or what frequency of behavior we want to obtain. At this point, the actual reinforcement process begins. Desired behavior is rewarded when observed but rather than wait until the target behavior is exhibited, we must reward behaviors that approach the goal. As employee behavior moves closer and closer to the target, behavior that is rewarded must more closely approximate the target behavior (this is known as shaping). Finally, after the goal is accomplished, the program should be periodically reviewed to determined if the learned behavior is still desired and still being exhibited.

What are the major learning principles involved in effective training programs?

Training programs are designed to get employees to perform at desired levels of behavior. Four major learning principles are relevant to this process. First, trainees should be allowed to actively participate in the process rather than being passive observers. Second, it is important to repeatedly practice the desired behavior. Third, the demands of the training program must closely match the demands of the job, thus enhancing the trainee's ability to transfer what is learned in training to the actual job setting. Finally, trainees should be given feedback concerning their progress in the training program.

What features of punishment tend to make discipline more effective?

Discipline involves changing behavior by attempting to eliminate undesired behavior. Therefore, it relies primarily on punishment. Punishment often evokes negative responses, especially from the person punished, but it tends to be more effective when:

1. the punishment is delivered immediately after the undesired behavior occurs—the longer the time lag, the weaker the association between the behavior and the punishment and the less effective the punishment will be;
2. levels of punishment should be moderate—punishment that is too weak can be ignored, and punishment that is too severe can cause perceptions of unfairness and serious negative consequences for the organization;
3. the punishment should focus on the undesired behavior, never the person—punishment should always be kept as impersonal as possible;
4. punishment should be consistent—every time any person exhibits an undesired behavior, it should be punished;

5. the reasons for the punishment should be clearly communicated—if employees don't understand why they are being punished, it will be difficult for them to change their behavior in the desired direction;
6. punishment should never be followed by non-contingent rewards—feeling guilty over having to punish someone, and then giving some reward just to make it up, actually results in the undesired behavior being rewarded, and makes it likely to be repeated.

Other Teaching Suggestions

1. One type of learning that will be discussed in more detail in chapter 9 concerns the ways in which we adapt to a new job. This process is known as socialization. Recall from chapter 1, the discussion of corporate culture as a determinant of norms at work. New employees learn these norms through the socialization process. In some cases, socialization could be quite explicit, as in an initiation period or an internship. In the army, socialization takes place during basic training, and in most police jobs, new officers are sent to some academy to be socialized before going on the job. You might relay to your students how you were socialized on your job and ask your students about all the norms they learned as they became socialized as college students.

2. Although extinction is discussed in the text, especially relative to how various schedules of reinforcement are resistant to extinction, further discussion of the topic might be useful. When young children begin eating solid food, an early reaction they have is to spit the food out. Unfortunately, some parents (myself included) laugh at this. The laughter is reinforcement, so the spitting continues, but getting the spitting to stop is easy since, presumably, the child only continues to spit out food to get a laugh—when the laughter stops so does the spitting. But not all undesired behaviors will respond to extinction. If an employee repeatedly comes in late to work, you cannot ignore it. If you do, the behavior will continue even though there is no apparent reward. The key is that coming in late is its own reward and needs no further reinforcement. Ask your students to think about other behaviors that provide their own reward. These behaviors can only be eliminated through punishment.

3. The basic principles of reinforcement can be illustrated by drawing two diagrams:

STIMULUS → DESIRED BEHAVIOR → REWARD

STIMULUS → UNDESIRED → PUNISHMENT
BEHAVIOR (OR NO CONSEQUENCES)

The rule, then, is never to let the lines cross such that undesired behavior leads to rewards, or that desired

behavior leads to punishment or is ignored. Ask students about situations that violate this rule. It is usually easier to think of situations where desired behavior is punished (e.g., the best typist is given the toughest manuscript to type), but your students can probably come up with several violations of each type. Steve Kerr discusses this problem in his article (cited in the chapter) about the "folly of expecting A while rewarding B."

4. Discipline is designed to change behavior, not simply to punish. Furthermore, vicarious learning has proven effective. Thus, it is reasonable to put someone in prison as a means of teaching that person, and showing others, the penalty for breaking a law. But in many states murder carries the death penalty. An emotional discussion will surely follow any question about the effectiveness of the death penalty. Review the principles for effectively administering punishment. How many of these apply to using the death penalty?

5. The final step in a progressive discipline program is termination. There are some who suggest that disciplinary programs can only be effective if there is the possibility of terminating employees whose behavior doesn't change. When an employee is terminated, however, there are some legal issues involved. You might want to investigate the doctrine of Employment at Will which, except for several specific exceptions, is the only real law concerning termination. It states, in essence, that any employer has the right to fire any employee at any time for any reason (be it good, bad, or no reason at all). The major exceptions occur when a law forbids termination for a specific reason (e.g., the Civil Rights Act makes it illegal to terminate someone because he is Black; the Taft-Hartley Act makes it illegal to terminate someone for advocating a union); when an employee is performing a statutory duty (e.g., jury duty, National Guard duty); when an employee has been denied due process (e.g., an employee is accused of stealing, but the theft is never proven); the employee has a contractual right to his or her job; or the termination is considered as contrary to public policy (this one is vague). Issues involved in termination and documenting a termination would be worth discussing.

Case in Point Notes

Getting Tough on Employees: Does It Pay Off?
This case describes the operant contingencies that CEOs (e.g., John Akers of IBM) have recently used to increase the performance levels of their employees. The primary operant contingencies used by these CEOs are punishment and avoidance learning (negative reinforcement). The case cites several behavioral consequences.

The questions following the case prompt students to first identify and describe the operant contingencies used by the various CEOs. Some students will identify the primary contingency as being punishment. Others will argue that avoidance learning is really the primary contingency being used. Ultimately, students come to recognize the both punishment and avoidance are being employed (i.e., a punishment contingency is established, followed by an avoidance contingency designed to avoid the punishment). Typically this first question has the effect of getting students to think through the meaning of each of the four operant contingencies.

Other discussion questions provide students with the opportunity to discuss the short- and long-term effects of punishment (question 2), extinction and positive reinforcement contingencies (question 3), and the reinforcement contingency histories of the executives themselves (question 4). Students should be encouraged to analyze the effectiveness of the CEOs' use of the various operant contingencies within the context of each of these questions. Particularly useful frameworks for analyzing the CEOs' behavior such as the principles for effectively using punishment and the steps for creating organizational behavior management are presented.

Additional Cases

The Case of the Assembly Line Bully

The Situation
Recently in a West Virginia auto plant operated by the XYZ Automobile Company, a welder hurled a tool at a fellow worker, setting off a furious fight. Before the fight was over,

Source: Case by Robert D. Goddard, Appalachian State University. The Hot Stove Rule of Discipline adapted from W. French, J. Dittrich, & R. Zawacki, *The personnel management process,* 2nd ed. Boston: Houghton-Mifflin, 1982.

the instigator had knocked the other out with a strong blow to the head.

The company fired the attacker and suspended the other employee for ten days. The local unit of the United Auto Workers protested that firing was too severe a punishment, but XYZ refused to back down.

After four months of arguing, the two sides took the matter to arbitration for a binding decision, as provided for in their labor agreement.

Arbitrator Dwight Perley first held a one-day hearing in the offices of XYZ to gather evidence from five witnesses to the incident.

Questioning those involved, Perley learned that the attacker was a Vietnamese immigrant, proud of his nationality and his family. His victim, it turned out, had been taunting this man for some time, heaping torrents of abuse on him about his native country and family, and making explicitly lewd remarks about the man's wife.

Lawyers for both sides studied the hearing transcripts and filed briefs. This took several months. Mr. Perley considered the facts for several weeks, and then gave his opinion.

Questions

1. Who was at fault? Carefully explain your decision.
2. What information would you need to decide this case if you were Mr. Perley, the arbitrator?

The Case of the Assembly Line Bully: Teaching Note

Overview and Issues

This incident is an excellent example of a highly volatile discharge case presented to an arbitrator. An employee attacked another employee and, following a furious fight, was discharged. The second employee was suspended for ten days. In arbitration, it was learned that the attacker had been repeatedly taunted by the victim, including explicitly lewd remarks about the attacker's wife. *At issue is the question of responsibility for the fight:* Is it that of the first person who physically attacked, or is it the person who initiated the verbal attack? Company responsibility is also at issue, since the maintenance of order in the workplace is a responsibility of management.

Analysis and Discussion

Company responsibility is not adequately addressed in the incident, and it is this issue that served as the crux of the arbitrator's decision, which is quoted below.

> "Such words would have provoked reasonable men into action," Mr. Perley wrote. "The company was aware of the continuing abusing language being meted out. Yet the company did nothing to alleviate the situation and stop the provocation."

> Unable to sustain the firing, the arbitrator then had to devise a fitting punishment. A 20-day suspension appeared most appropriate.

> So he ordered that the man be given back his job, and with it, back pay for all but twenty days of wages lost since the firing eight months earlier.

Transition

Discipline is rarely easy. A useful guide, however, is the *Hot Stove Rule*

The *Hot Stove* Rule of Discipline
Applying discipline is much like touching a hot stove. Effective discipline should be:
1. FOREWARNED: If the stove is red hot, people will know what will happen if they touch it.
2. IMMEDIATE: There is no question of cause and effect.
3. CONSISTENT: People are burned every time the stove is touched.
4. IMPERSONAL: People are burned not because of who they are, but because they touch the stove.

Emery Air Freight

The *power of positive reinforcement* is a topic that has been discussed by psychologists, organization behavior specialists, and managers for years. Much study has been done on the effects of positive reinforcement, but most of those studies have been with animals and humans in a laboratory setting. However, field studies, involving operating organizations, are now being reported in the literature, with some very interesting results. The case of Emery Air Freight is one of those.

The Program

Perhaps the most widely known example of the application of behavior modification in industry is that of Emery Air Freight. Under the direction of Edward J. Feeney, Emery selected behavior modification as a simple answer to the persistent problems of inefficiency and low productivity. In an air freight firm, rapid processing of parcels is important to corporate profitability.

Emery Air Freight began with a performance audit, which attempted to identify the kind of job behaviors which had the greatest impact on profit and the extent to which these behaviors were evidenced in the company. One area of special concern was the use of containers. Emery loses

Source: From *Introduction to Organizational Behavior* by Richard M. Steers. Copyright © by Scott, Foresman and Company. Reprinted by permission.

money if shipping containers are not fully loaded when shippd. Hence, one goal was to ensure that empty container space was minimized. Before the program was implemented, workers reported that they believed they were filling the containers about 90 percent of the time. However, the performance audit revealed that this was really true only about 45 percent of the time. In other words, less than half of the containers were shipped completely filled.

The Results

Through the use of feedback (in the form of self-report checklists provided to each worker) and positive reinforcement (praise), the percentage of full containers rose swiftly from 45 percent to 95 percent. Cost reductions for the first year alone exceeded $500,000, and rose to $2 million during the first three years. In other words, when workers were given consistent feedback and kept informed of their performance, subsequent output increased rapidly. As a result of this initial success, similar programs were initiated at Emery, including the setting of performance standards for handling customer problems on the telephone and for accurately estimating the container sizes needed for shipment of lightweight packages. Again, positive results were claimed.

Questions

1. To what do you attribute the increased percentage of full containers?

2. Do you think the increases in productivity noted will continue in the future? Why or why not?

Emery Air Freight: Teaching Note

The Emery Air Freight case is a quoted example of a successful positive reinforcement program in industry. Its successes have been documented, but there have been problems as well.

While the use of praise as a reinforcer proved initially to be a successful and inexpensive reinforcer, its effects diminished over time as it became repetitious. As a result, Emery had to seek other reinforcers. These included invitations to business luncheons; formal recognition, such as a public letter or a letter home; being given a more enjoyable task after completing a less desirable one; delegating responsibility and decision making; and allowing special time off from the job. Hence, the use of praise alone did not appear to have sustained effects and managers had to continually turn to new reinforcers to keep the program in operation.

You may wish to draw the discussion first to the effects of the initial program of positive reinforcement (praise) on productivity, then begin to draw out the students' opinions on the long-term effects of this program. Their responses to the questions provided at the end of the case should stimulate the class discussion. Perhaps their personal experiences with similar reinforcement programs could be worked into the discussion.

Experiencing Organizational Behavior Notes

The Reinforcing Value of Social Approval
This exercise allows students to witness first hand the reinforcing value of social approval. Detailed instructions for performing this exercise are provided in the text. Following the instructions are questions that ask students to analyze their data to determine the effect of social approval on social interactions.

A particularly valuable outcome of this exercise is the appreciation that students develop for the power of social reinforcers. Students often assume a very narrow definition of positive reinforcers (e.g., money and promotions). This exercise helps them to recognize that there are many non-financial reinforcers available to managers and coworkers that are often as powerful in their effects on organizational behaviors as are financial reinforcers.

This exercise involves out-of-class activity so you may wish students to start collecting data a week or so prior to your in-class discussion of operant conditioning.

Additional Experiential Exercise

Disciplinary Interview Role Play
General Instructions

Objectives
A. To practice giving feedback on disciplinary problems.
B. To explore how different attitudes and expectations affect the disciplinary process.

Task 1
A. In the classroom, participants should form three groups. One group will take the role of crew foreman, Nick D. Finger, one the role of shift foreman, Hermann Tripp, and a third group will be the observer. (Any extra participants can be observers.)
B. Carefully read the role you have been assigned, BEING CAREFUL NOT TO LOOK AT THE OTHER ROLE. You will be given ample time to discuss your role with the others who will be playing the same role.
C. Read over your role and think about how you would respond if you were actually in the situation described. Imagine how you would react to the situation, what your feelings and attitudes would be. Discuss how your role might work with the others playing that role.
D. Observers are to read both roles plus the observer's instructions, and discuss these with the other observers.

Source: By Robert D. Goddard, Appalachian State University.

Task 2
A. Form triads of Nick D. Finger, Hermann Tripp, and the observer.
B. The instructor will announce the start of the role play by announcing that Finger has just entered Tripp's office for the interview. Play your role naturally, based on how you would react, given what you know and how you feel. Portray your reactions as realistically as possible. If facts or events arise that are not covered by the roles, invent things that are consistent with the facts you do have and how you would anticipate your character would respond in a real-life situation.

Task 3
When the role play has finished, Hermann Tripp and Nick D. Finger should take a moment to note the following on paper for reference during the discussion while the observers organize their notes:

1. How did you feel about being in this situation?
2. How did you feel about the opposite person's role?
3. What matters did you agree on? What did you disagree about?
4. What was the source of your disagreement?

5. What problems did you have in getting your point across during the interview? What caused those problems?
6. What was the outcome, from your point of view, of the interview? Did it serve its intended purpose? What was that purpose?
7. What behaviors in the other person made him difficult to deal with? What behaviors made it easier?
8. Did you get a chance to discuss everything with the opposite person?

Task 4

Discussion by the instructor.

A. The participants' questions will be considered one at a time, with both Nick D. Finger and Hermann Tripp responding.
B. Observers will report.
C. The instructor will summarize salient points of the discussion and connect them to relevant concepts of interviewing and discipline.

Role Sheet: Nick D. Finger

You have just had a minor injury to the ring finger of your left hand because you did not deenergize a piece of equipment before you attempted to remove a rock stuck in a belt drive. While the injury is not serious, you have the misfortune of having your shift foreman, Hermann Tripp conducting a planned Safety Observation at that very moment. Tripp has called you into his office to discuss this violation of safety rules with you.

You have been this guy's target for a long time. You feel that Tripp is trying to get rid of you by using your poor safety record as an excuse. (You have been called into the office three times before for just such violations, but this is the first time you have been injured on the job. It looks like the finger will require a couple of stitches; nothing serious.)

You crew really likes you because you aren't afraid to help them get their jobs done. You have been with the company for 14 years, and have learned every facet of the operation of an underground mine. Your crew's production record is among the top of all of the units in your mine. Sure, you occasionally have a minor safety violation or two, but as far as you're concerned, the most important thing is to get the coal out of the ground. After all, *no one has ever been run off for running coal.* You know all of the shortcuts, and aren't afraid to use them to "get the rocks in the box."

Role Sheet: Hermann Tripp

You have finished a series of Planned Safety Observations of the unit foremen and crews operating during the shift under your leadership. You have observed a number of minor unsafe acts while out in the mine, and have decided to let those people who were not operating in a safe manner know that you won't tolerate that kind of activity on your shift.

You are proud that your shift has been recognized as the most productive shift at Camelback #3. The first shift of a mine is usually the most productive, but your second-shift crews have been out-producing the first shift consistently for the past 12 months. You are proud of that record and look forward to the performance appraisal interview you have in a couple of weeks with Larry Longwall, the superintendent.

The only thing that you have been having problems with is the lost-time incident rate, which has been on the rise over the past year. You are aware that The Company has recently begun to crack down on those superintendents and mine foremen who have had poor safety records. Your lost-time rate has climbed from 3.25 in January of 1986, to 10.66 in June 1987. You've heard from other foremen in other mines that their performance ratings have been hurt by excessive lost-time rates.

Nick D. Finger has been a source of constant irritation for you for the past six months or so. While his crew's production record has been good (his crew is the second most productive unit in Camelback #3), his safety record and that of his crew is appalling. He knows all of the shortcuts to get the coal out of the ground, but most of those shortcuts involve the violation of safety rules. Personally, you like the production results, but have let him know in no uncertain terms that his safety record is not acceptable. He has been in your office on three separate occasions for safety violations already this year.

According to The Company's progressive discipline system (The Basic Five-Step Correction Approach), you are at Step 4, the Corrective Interview step of the process. This is your chance to let Finger know that you will not stand for his poor safety performance. His (and his crew's) safety record are the main contributors to your 10.66 lost-time incident rate in June. *You may not get a raise because of Nick's safety record.*

When disciplining Nick, you remember the seminar you attended where the trainers discussed the *Hot Stove Rule* of discipline. As far as you can recall, they said that effective discipline is much like a hot stove, in that it should be:

FOREWARNED   If the stove is red hot, people will know what will happen when they touch it.

IMMEDIATE   There is no question of cause and effect. When the stove is touched, the person is burned NOW.

CONSISTENT   People are burned every time they touch the stove.

IMPERSONAL   People are burned not because of who they are, but because they touched the stove.

You know that Nick has been *forewarned,* you know that you will be administering the discipline within a half-hour of the occurrence of the safety violation (*immediate*), and you know that you have had Nick in your office on three other occasions for this type of problem (*consistent*).

What is hard for you to do now is to be *impersonal,* since this is going to hit you right in the wallet. Because of Nick, you may not get the raise you hoped for and you *need* the extra money to help support your aging parents. Even worse, if there is a cut-back, you could be laid off because of a poor lost-time rate. Right now, you are not very happy with Nick. In fact, you'd like to use him as kindling for your hot stove.

Disciplinary Interview Role Play: Instructions for Observers

On the basis of what you know about Hermann Tripp and Nick D. Finger and their situation, you have probably formed certain impressions of the situation. Most of what you have learned so far is factual in nature, but you also know that the facts may be less important than people's attitudes about and interpretations of them. In particular, people's perceptions and interpretations of the facts in a situation tend to be colored by their assumptions and expectations. People may form their interpretations by selecting certain facts to emphasize, while ignoring others. In the discussion between Finger and Tripp, you are to *observe silently, not entering into the discussion in any way.* Keep notes on your observations. The following questions are designed to provide clues as to what to watch and listen for:

1. Did Tripp get to the point quickly?
2. Was the problem defined in a non-threatening manner?
3. Did Tripp listen to Finger's side of the story?
4. Were the actions to be taken discussed with Finger?
5. Did Tripp work with Finger to decide how to correct the problem?
6. Were the results of the meeting documented?
7. In what ways was the *Hot Stove Rule of Discipline* violated?
8. Did you note any disagreements on the facts of this situation? Were the perceptions of each participant different? Why?
9. Did *personalities* become an important part of this meeting?
10. In what ways might Tripp have done a better job? In what ways might Finger have done a better job?

Disciplinary Interview Role Play: Teaching Note

Read over the Objectives, and divide the participants into Tripps, Fingers, and observers. (Any extra participants can be observers.) Assign each group to its own discussion area: different corners of the room, or the area next to the classroom. Have each participant/observer read his or her role, then discuss it with the other participants who are playing that role. For groups experienced in such exercises, discussion starts quite easily; for those requiring some guidance, a good question (which can be written on the chalkboard or flip chart) is, "What do we know about this situation?" A second helpful question is, "What do we expect in this interview?"

While the role groups are reading, meet with the observers to brief them on what they will do. Have them begin with the observer's instructions (tell them they will have time to read the other roles while the others talk). Emphasize that they'll be looking to see how the facts of the situation get selected and interpreted, and how different assumptions and expectations can impede communications. Mention that observers are to silently take notes and are not to intervene in the interview in any way.

Assemble triads (Tripps, Fingers, and observers), have them disperse around the room, and begin the role play by announcing that Finger has just entered Tripp's office.

Having participants briefly note their own reactions facilitates discussion later. Participants' desire for closure is also assisted by a few moments' reflection.

Discussion is typically rich and intense. The discussion begins with participants' questions—how they felt, the problems they experienced, and their assessment. The observers' reports should serve to highlight difficulties caused by assumptions and different factual bases for discussions. "What did you think and feel **then?**" is a good question. It is useful to ask about managerial implications during the discussion.

After a thorough discussion of these aspects of the experience, ask participants how the disciplinary interview could have been improved. What could Tripp have done? What could Finger have done?

The instructor's summary should note how frequently such difficulties arise. Using the *Hot Stove Rule of Discipline* should help individuals administer disciplinary problems. If proper procedures for preparing for disciplinary interviews are followed, and if proper procedures for conducting these types of interviews are adhered to, then they become means of developing employees. They become *coaching* sessions.

Additional Readings

Argyris, C. (1977, September–October). Double loop learning in organizations. *Harvard Business Review*, pp. 115–117.

Campbell, D. N., Fleming, R. L., & Grote, R. C. (1985, July–August). Discipline without punishment—at last. *Harvard Business Review*, pp. 162–166.

Copeland, L. (1985, July). Cross-cultural training: The competitve edge. *Training*, pp. 49–53.

McConnell, P. L. (1986, March). Is your discipline process the victim of RED tape? *Personnel Journal*, pp. 64–71.

Chapter 3

∎ 4 ∎

MOTIVATION IN ORGANIZATIONS

CHAPTER OUTLINE

The Nature of Motivation in Organizations
　　Motivation: A Definition
　　Motivation and the Work Ethic
Need Theories
　　Maslow's Need Hierarchy Theory
　　Alderfer's ERG Theory
　　Practical Applications of Need Theories
Goal-Setting Theory
　　Locke and Latham's Goal-Setting Theory
　　Practical Conclusions of Goal-Setting Research
Equity Theory
　　Adams's Equity Theory
　　Applying Equity Theory: Some Motivational Tips
Expectancy Theory
　　Basic Elements of Expectancy Theory
　　Practical Applications of Expectancy Theory

Creating Jobs That Motivate
　　Job Enlargement and Job Enrichment
　　The Job Characteristics Model
　　Practical Suggestions for Applying the Job
　　　Characteristics Model

Special Sections

An International/Multicultural Perspective　What
　Motivates Employees? Work Goals All Over the World

Focus on Research　Employee Theft as a Reaction to
　Underpayment Inequity

OB in Practice　Avis Employees *Do* Try Harder . . .
　Because They Own the Company

LEARNING OBJECTIVES

After reading this chapter, you should be able to:
1. Define *motivation* and explain its importance in the field of organizational behavior.
2. Describe *need hierarchy theory* and what it recommends about improving motivation in organizations.
3. Identify and explain the conditions through which *goal setting* can be used to improve job performance.
4. Explain *equity theory* and some of the research designed to test its basic tenets.

5. Describe the components of *expectancy theory* and their interrelationships.
6. Distinguish between *job enlargement* and *job enrichment* as techniques for motivating employees by redesigning jobs.
7. Describe the various components of the *job characteristics model.*

Chapter Overview

This chapter deals with motivation, one of the most important topics in organizational behavior. After defining motivation, the chapter briefly relates the notion of the work ethic to illustrate the potential relationship between working hard because you believe it is right, and working hard because of some external motivational force. The chapter then introduces the major theories of motivation, including their practical applications: need theories (Maslow and Alderfer), goal-setting theory, equity theory, ex-

pectancy theory, and job enrichment. As with previous chapters, research results related to each motivation theory are reviewed.

Three special sections appear in this chapter. An International/Multicultural Perspective section (What Motivates Employees? Work Goals All Over the World) discusses the findings of a survey comparing the work goals of respondents from seven different industrialized countries. The results show a remarkable degree of agreement about the relative importance of different work goals despite national differences. A Focus on Research section (Employee Theft as a Reaction to Underpayment Inequity) presents the findings of a field experiment investigating the propensity of employees to steal as a means of reducing feelings of underpayment inequity. Interestingly, the manner in which management explained the reasons for incurring underpayment inequity significantly affected the amount of theft that resulted. And an OB in Practice section (Avis Employees *Do* Try Harder . . . Because They Own the Company) describes how the Avis car rental company uses an employee stock ownership plan to motivate its employees.

The Case in Point (Motivation through Employee Involvement at United Electric Controls) describes the remarkable transformation of a dying company into a vibrant and competitive manufacturing business using employee involvement. This case is an excellent illustration of the motivation theories described in the chapter. The Experiencing Organizational Behavior exercise (Goal Setting and Personal Productivity) shows students how to apply goal-setting theory to help them get their own work done. A CNN video (*Intrapreneurship*) is available for use with this chapter. This video discusses how Bell Atlantic and Federal Express are nurturing intrapreneurship—developing entrepreneurship within an existing company—and it illustrates the motivational aspects of intrapreneurship—focusing on intrinsic and extrinsic rewards employees receive by participating on the intrapreneurship teams.

Lecture and Review Questions

What is motivation and how does it affect performance?

Motivation is defined as "the set of processes that arouse, direct, and maintain human behavior toward attaining a goal." Basic human needs, and deprivation relative to those needs, are seen as providing the drive that arouses the worker. Once aroused, the worker must choose among several alternative directions in which to point his or her energy. The motivational process includes identifying the direction most likely to satisfy the need that began the process. Once this energy is aroused and directed, motivation helps the worker persist until his or her goal is reached. Thus, assuming that a worker has the requisite ability and believes that improved performance will help satisfy his or her deprived needs, motivation will result in the worker exerting more effort toward performing well on the job. Notice, however, that motivation alone does not assure higher performance.

What is need theory and how does it contribute to the understanding of behavior at work?

There are actually two distinct need theories, but both deal with the identification of needs that, once de-prived, motivate behavior. Maslow's Hierarchy of Needs is the more famous of the two, and states that there are five basic sets of needs, which are (in ascending order): physiological needs, safety needs, social needs, esteem needs, and self-actualization needs. This theory suggests that we start at the lowest level of need (physiological). If these needs are not being met, they will be the only needs capable of motivating behavior (i.e., prepotent). Once these needs are satisfied, however, they are no longer capable of motivating behavior and the next highest level of need becomes prepotent. This process continues up the hierarchy although higher-level needs may never be fully satisfied, so may continue to motivate behavior. Alderfer's ERG Theory is closely related, except that he collapses Maslow's five need categories into three, which are (in ascending order): existence needs, relatedness needs, and growth needs. Alderfer's theory allows for more complex relationships among the needs in terms of which are prepotent, and, in fact, allows for more than one need to be capable of motivating behavior at once. The fact that people at work might be at different levels in the hierarchy helps explain why not everyone is motivated by the same rewards or outcomes, and suggests that programs such as a "Cafeteria of Benefits" where workers get to choose which benefits they want, make sense.

What are expectancy, instrumentality, and valence and how do they combine to determine force?

The major components of expectancy theory can be defined as follows: expectancy is the subjective probability that an increase in effort will result in improved performance; instrumentality is the perceived correlation between an improvement in performance and the likelihood of gaining various outcomes; valence is the attractiveness or desirability of those outcomes. Force is the product of these three processes, operating on an employee to increase his or her effort at work. This force, which is assumed to translate into effort (and performance if the conditions discussed earlier exist), will be positive and large to the extent that: (1) the employee believes that increasing effort will result in improved performance; and (2) improved performance is seen as leading to desired outcomes or the avoidance of negative outcomes. Thus, if the employee believes that he or she does not have the requisite ability to perform the job, there is no reason to increase effort since performance will not be affected (this is also true if the job is so simple as to require minimal effort). Further, even if effort will lead to improved performance, an employee is unlikely to increase effort if it is perceived that improved performance will not lead to any desired outcomes; worse yet if improved performance is seen as leading to undesired outcomes (e.g., higher expectations in the future). Note that the model is multiplicative, so if any term goes to zero, so does force. Note also that all terms are evaluated on the basis of an employee's perceptions.

How do goals motivate employees?

The underlying assumption of goal setting is that employees will exert more effort and channel that effort more effectively if they have clear, definable goals they are trying to reach. In fact, the research in this area generally supports the notion that the presence of goals results in higher effort and performance than the absence of goals. Those goals must be clearly defined in objective, measurable terms; they must be difficult but attainable; and employees must be committed to attaining the goals. This commitment is critical to the process and can be obtained by having the employee participate in setting the goals (although this is not essential—the commitment is essential). This approach is the basis for Management by Objectives and, as long as management is committed to the goal setting (or MBO) process and employees are given feedback about their performance relative to the goals set, it is one of the more effective means available to increase employee motivation.

What is equity and what role does it play in work motivation?

The concept of equity relates to perceptions of fairness. Equity theory is a social comparison theory where employees judge what is a fair return on their efforts by comparing their outcomes with the outcomes of someone else. If an employee's *rate of return* is less favorable than that of the comparison person, the employee perceives underpayment inequity and strives to restore equity, either by reducing inputs (i.e., not working as hard), or by trying to increase outcomes (i.e., increase in pay or some other reward). If an employee's rate of return is more favorable than that of the comparison person, the employee perceives overpayment inequity and may seek to restore equity by increasing inputs (working harder). It is also easy for the employee in this case to rationalize higher pay or differential reward, believing that he or she is worth the difference. Thus, overpayment inequity is not as much a problem as underpayment inequity. Organizations should always seek to maintain equity, so that each employee sees his or her rate of return as being equal to that of the comparison person. (Note that it is the rate of return that must be equal, not the absolute level of either inputs or outcomes.) When equity is perceived, employees are most likely to exert effort and be satisfied with their jobs since they believe they are being treated fairly.

How does job design affect employee motivation?

Designing jobs to make them more meaningful to employees is another method of enhancing motiva-

tion. Although scientific management (from chapter 1) was interested in designing jobs to make them more efficient, these newer approaches attempt to design jobs so that they are enjoyable for employees as well as more efficient. Job enlargement involves simply adding more tasks, while job enrichment involves more tasks that are at a higher level, allowing employees to have more control and assume more responsibility. The job characteristics approach, however, is more popular and somewhat more complex. Here, the emphasis is on redesigning the job to increase levels of skill variety, task identity, task significance, autonomy, and feedback to employees. Increasing the levels of these characteristics is seen as improving three critical psychological states: experienced meaningfulness, responsibility for outcomes, and knowledge of results. These states, in turn, have been found to increase feelings of motivation, the quality of work performed, and satisfaction with work, thereby decreasing absenteeism and turnover. Literature has provided generally good support for the job characteristics model.

Other Teaching Suggestions

1. The work ethic is one of the more fascinating topics being studied today. Basically, the Protestant Work Ethic can be understood as a belief that hard work is valuable for its own sake, regardless of whether it is instrumental in obtaining any rewards. There are some who claim that the work ethic is declining in the United States, and perhaps it is, but some of the controversy about the role of the work ethic stems from problems of definition. Some researchers ask workers about the outcomes they value on their jobs (actually, a concept that is close to valence from expectancy theory). These researchers tend to interpret responses indicating that workers desire extrinsic outcomes as evidence of a declining work ethic. But, if we look at the definition of the work ethic, we must recognize that the workplace is not the only place where this ethic finds expression. Some people devote great effort, for no monetary reward, to their gardening, to building furniture, or to cleaning and running a house. Surely these behaviors must be seen as possibly reflecting a strong work ethic.

Discussing students' views about declining work ethic might be interesting, especially if this were expanded to consider what students today want from work and what they believe their parents or grandparents wanted.

2. The notion of "Cafeteria of Benefits" was mentioned previously and this is worth expanding. The typical benefits package in most organizations is such that all employees receive the same basic benefits. (Managers and executives may have additional benefits, but the core of benefits is the same for everyone.)

So, for example, everyone in the organization may receive dental benefits, but these are most useful when you have children who need braces, and much less useful if you have dentures. A cafeteria approach allows employees to receive a budget for benefits, and to use that budget to purchase those benefits they really want. Thus, someone motivated by more basic needs might choose more life insurance or better medical benefits, while someone motivated by higher-order needs might select more vacation time. Some scholars argue that most employees are not consumers of benefits (that is, if left on their own, they would not adequately protect themselves against medical expenses and such), but the idea is interesting and it has been applied in a number of large organizations.

3. Equity theory is quite interesting because as a social comparison theory, it can be applied to a variety of non-work settings as well. For example, think about two people involved in a relationship. Both persons presumably feel they bring something to the relationship, but both also hope to get something out of the relationship. What happens when one person feels that his or her ratio of inputs/outcomes is less favorable than the other person's? How does this person try to restore equity in a situation where one's inputs **are** the other's outcomes? In order for the person to increase outcomes he or she must convince the other to increase inputs and any attempt to decrease inputs will presumably be met with resistance because this reduces the other person's outcomes. The alternatives in such a situation are to rationalize away the inequity or leave the relationship. You can probably think of a number of other examples.

4. Sometimes it is difficult for students to grasp expectancy theory because they tend to focus on the specifics of the model rather than on its logic. Expectancy theory is a rational decision-making model—people only take actions that they believe will benefit them in the long run. You may find it useful to refer to a nonwork example that is relevant to students. This example also helps students appreciate the fact that expectancy theory was really never meant to explain how person A reacted to a job versus person B. Instead, it was meant to explain where a given person chooses to exert his or her energies. Suppose, then, that I have three courses that have exams coming up on the same day. I have not kept up with the work and now I have a problem. I need an A in all three courses, but there is simply not enough time to really prepare for the three exams. How do I decide what to do? Suppose the three courses are Quantum Mechanics, Microeconomics, and Organizational Behavior. I begin with expectancy calculations, and I realize that if I haven't kept up with the Physics course, studying now won't help me. Thus, my expectancy is zero and the force operating on me to study Physics is zero. In both of the other courses, I realize that putting in the

effort to study will improve my chances of doing well on the exam. Now, assume that in both cases, an A on the exam will earn a B in the course, and I need at least one B for my grade point average (especially with that Physics course). The instrumentality for doing well on both exams, then, is about the same, but what about the valence of getting a B in each course? Well, Organizational Behavior is in my major, while the Microeconomics course isn't. Since I want to go on and get a Master's Degree, it's important to keep up my average in my major. Thus, the solution is clear. Expectancies and instrumentalities for the two courses are the same, but the valences differ in favor of the Organizational Behavior course and so that is the exam to study for.

5. Students are sometimes troubled by the fact that there are a variety of motivational theories. Are these theories contradictory or can they somehow be integrated into a larger view of motivation? It might be useful to try such an integration based on expectancy theory. We can take the basic components of expectancy theory and introduce need theory and equity theory as factors that help determine the valence of an outcome. That is, outcomes which help satisfy prepotent needs will always be more valent than outcomes which do not. Furthermore, regardless of whether an outcome satisfies a prepotent need, if the level of the outcome is not judged to be equitable (based on the comparison process outlined in equity theory), it will have little or no valence for the employee and will not lead to effort. There are surely other ways of putting the theories together, but this is a start.

6. As noted in the text, goal-setting and Management by Objectives are often effective ways of motivating employees. In fact, they are so effective that care should be taken in applying them. If goals are measurable, and accepted by employees, and management provides feedback and (especially) rewards goal attainment, then whatever is asked for in the goal is what the employee is going to give. It is critical, therefore, that managers be sure that the goals they set are the ones they truly want accomplished. If a goal is stated in terms of quality, an employee will focus on quality, even if quantity suffers. (This is also a variant on the "expecting A when rewarding B" theme.) Discuss situations where an organization might set what seems to be the right goals but, when we examine what behaviors would result, it becomes clear that there is a problem. For example, consider hospital administrators being asked to set goals concerning the number of beds occupied or police officers setting goals concerning the number of arrests made.

7. A number of years ago, Ed Locke and his associates conducted one of the more interesting studies on job redesign. After careful study of three clerical

jobs within a government agency, they introduced enriched jobs on an experimental basis, comparing enriched jobs with matched unenriched jobs. The results of the study indicated that productivity went up for the enriched jobs, but that there was no commensurate improvement in attitudes about the job (see chapter 5). In fact, the increased productivity seemed to be due more to effective manpower utilization on the enriched jobs, rather than to job enrichment itself. Furthermore, the introduction of job enrichment actually caused some problems relative to attitudes about the jobs. It seems that the workers, being good civil servants, felt that their enriched jobs should have been reclassified, resulting in more pay (**not** a part of the job enrichment). Since the jobs were not reclassified and the pay did not go up, some workers actually felt cheated because they were doing a job for which they were not being paid.

Case in Point Notes

Motivation through Employee Involvement at United Electric Controls

United Electric Controls of Watertown, Massachusetts, was transformed from a dying, outmoded company into a vibrant and competitive manufacturing business. The secret to United Electric's successful transformation, according to owners David and Robert Reis, is employee involvement. Prior to introducing employee involvement in 1988, the company's management was highly autocratic, its technology antiquated, and its balance sheet bleeding. The company was teetering on the brink of bankruptcy. The

Reises knew they had to radically change the way the company was run if they were to have any real chance of survival. Out of desperation, the Reises turned to their employees for help. Through a series of fits and starts they were able to empower their employees to take responsibility for the success of United Electric. It was not easy (they report on how scary it is for owners to truly loosen control). After only a couple of years, the company dramatically improved its performance, profit, and particularly, its level of employee motivation. The specifics of the employee involvement program at United Electric Controls are described in the case.

The discussion questions following the case focus on how United Electric's employee involvement program applies to the various motivation theories. Students are first asked to explain the success of United Electric's employee involvement program using need theories, expectancy theory, goal-setting theory, and job enrichment. The remaining questions prompt students to take a closer look at a number of the program's motivational features. Students typically are quick to recognize the job enrichment aspects of employee involvement. It is useful, however, to point out that extrinsic rewards are also important to United Electric's employee involvement program. This is an excellent place to integrate relevant aspects of reinforcement theory from chapter 3 with the other motivation theories presented in this chapter. Overall, this case points out how the various motivation theories presented in the text can be used together to enhance employee motivation and performance.

Additional Cases

Lincoln Electric Company

Holiday cheer arrived Friday for 2,045 employees of Lincoln Electric Co., who were rewarded for their year-long labors by bonuses averaging $17,380.78 per employee.

The bonuses were announced by the Lincoln Electric Co. Chairman William Irrgang at a Friday afternoon company meeting that was closed to the public. The company makes welding products and industrial motors.

The company announced allocation of $41.8 million in bonus money.

During the 52-year history of Lincoln Electric's incentive bonus, the bonuses have averaged 97.6 percent of an employee's annual earnings. Company management determines the size of the bonus for each worker based on merit evaluations.

Last year, as the company recovered from a recessionary slump, the year-end incentive cash bonus to employees

Source: From an Associated Press story printed in the Greensboro, NC, *News and Record*, December 7, 1985. Reprinted by permission.

amounted to nearly $37.1 million up from $26.6 million at the end of 1983.

The 1984 bonus to employees, most of whom live in northeast Ohio, was about 10 percent of the company's 1984 net sales of $363.6 million.

Richard S. Sabo, manager of public relations for the publicly held company, said this week that the company's net sales increased in 1984 and are expected to rise again next year.

"We do not maintain any reserve funds to make up for the bad years," Sabo said. "We pay out the maximum number of dollars available for the bonus with the intent of earning a new bonus fund next year."

Lincoln Electric earned 16.7 million, or $13.57 per share of common stock in 1984. About 40 percent of the company's stock is employee owned.

Located in the heart of a highly unionized industrial region, Lincoln Electric's workers have never belonged to a union. About 1,400 factory workers are paid piecework or a set amount per unit manufactured.

The company also guarantees at least 30 hours of work per week for employees even during recessionary times. The company has not laid off any worker since the early 1950s.

Lincoln Electric also requires workers to be flexible. During the company's slump in the early 1980s about 50 factory workers took on sales jobs.

Questions

1. How might you use Maslow's Hierarchy of Needs to describe the motivational aspects of Lincoln Electric's bonus plan and other policies?
2. Can the policies described in the above news story be related to expectancy theory? How?
3. In terms of equity theory, what problems might arise in the allocation of the bonuses described above?

Lincoln Electric Company: Teaching Note

Having the students read a handout of this case generally draws a lot of discussion. Lincoln Electric's bonus plan is legendary; in fact, many of your students may be familiar with it.

In terms of the three questions, students are likely to address the first question about the Hierarchy of Needs from the point that the bonus plans satisfy the physiological

and safety needs, but you may wish to draw them out about how money can satisfy the higher-level (growth) needs as well. Discuss the *symbolic* value of money with the students, showing them that money is a measure of social status, thereby satisfying esteem needs. Money may also be an internal measure of an individual's self-actualization needs.

The bonus plan has been in place for more than 50 years. What does this have to do with employees' perceptions of *instrumentality* in question 2? From the above employee comments, can you conclude anything about the *valence* of the bonus plan? How does the *no layoff* policy affect *expectancy, instrumentality,* and *valence?*

Question 3, dealing with equity theory, requires students to dig into the news story and look for how these bonuses are determined. The story states that, "Company management determines the size of the bonus for each worker based on merit evaluations." How might this method of determination affect worker perceptions about the fairness of the system?

In any event, I have found that the Lincoln Electric Co. story never fails to ignite student discussion. It is one of the best real-world illustrations about the importance of recognition of worker effort, and the worth of monetary incentives tied directly to productivity.

The U.S. Post Office at Newton, Massachusetts

My name is Ned Weinerman, and I would like to relate to you some of the experiences I encountered in 1986 when I was working on my summer job at a United States Post Office branch in Newton, Massachusetts. Before I describe these experiences, let me first describe to you how I came across this job and what I had to do in order to work.

Around January of 1986, the Post Office Department issued a bulletin stating that they were accepting applications for temporary help during the summer either working as a letter carrier during the day or as a mail sorter at the Post Office Annex in downtown Boston, Massachusetts, at night. This notice was posted at the school I attended then—the University of Massachusetts in Boston—and I assume at other colleges and universities throughout the nation. The only requirements for acceptance of the application were that the applicant had to have a high school diploma and that he or she had to be at least eighteen years of age on or before a certain date, and all applicants had to take a qualifying examination.

In February all of the applicants were contacted by mail telling them that on one of the Saturdays of that month a qualifying test would be given in order to select among the applicants. Naturally, I went for that test and found all it required was following directions by matching columns of numbers, seeing whether they were the same or whether they were different. The test required no great intellectual ability; however, strict attention to the test material was imperative and speed (the number of items that could be done in the allotted time limit) counted too. Thus, what the test was trying to do was find the quickest and most accurate

Source: By Joel Coreman, Suffolk University.

persons from among the applicants in order to fill the open positions.

I scored very high on the exam and was called in early May to come to the Post Office Building if I was still interested in the job. I appeared, and they gave me a list of post offices that had requested summer help. The closest to my house was the post office in Newton Center in Newton, Massachusetts.

Although Newton has just about any racial or ethnic group that can be found in the Boston area, the area which the Newton Center Post Office serves is largely populated with people who have a Jewish background (this is also a reason why I chose this post office instead of the others which were just as close to my house). Another point worth mentioning about Newton is that it is an upper-middle to upper-class suburban community. Also, another point which may or may not influence this report is that the residents of this town are considered by many to be snobs.

Now that I have described the community in which the post office is situated and serves, let me describe what my duties and actions as a mail carrier consisted of. The job can be broken down into two parts.

The first part, as I said, involved work within the post office building. What this consisted of was reporting to work from Monday through Friday (Saturdays we had off, while the permanent help had one weekday off) in the building anywhere from 6:30–7:00 A.M. During this period we set up our mail routes.

Setting up a mail route is not hard, but after doing it for about fifteen to twenty minutes, it becomes boring. The process consists of taking letters and putting them in the correct slots which represent addresses of families and homes that you will later deliver to. Each route (and there are twenty-four of them) has a different desk. After the letters and postcards had been sorted into their proper slots, the next step was to sort the magazines and other large matter into various piles and then set these piles in the order in which you would do the route.

This job, as I said, was not hard to learn; however, it did take practice to master the setup so that you did not have to take much time looking for the slots to match the addresses. The second part of the job was to pull the route down in the order it was to be delivered and then to tie it up and put it in bags which were delivered by trucks to the blue boxes you commonly see on the streets. Since we were temporary mailmen, it was our job to fill in for the regular mailmen who were on vacation. As a result, we usually would be on a route for a period of anywhere from two to three weeks. I cannot speak for the other temporary help at the Newton Center Post Office, but for me it took about a week to learn the scheme efficiently enough so that I could have my route pulled down in about the same time that the regulars had their routes pulled down and by the end of the second week on any route, I was able to have my route all pulled down and ready to go on the trucks while some of the regulars were still in the process of pulling down their routes.

Even though I finished getting my route down around 7:30, by post office regulations we were not allowed to leave the post office until 8:00 A.M. The reason for this, I was told, was that we might disturb some of the people we were delivering to if we arrived too early in the morning. Because I (and usually the other temporary helpers) finished early, the superintendent, Dan Weinbaum, would come over and ask us to do various jobs such as filing or filling out reports which, before the summer began and we arrived, he formerly designated to the permanent carriers who finished pulling down their routes early. To the permanent letter carriers, I learned, doing these jobs was considered an honor; however, they frequently made errors, and because of this Mr. Weinbaum preferred that we college students do this work.

Let me now describe the relationships that I and the other temporary help had with the permanent letter carriers. These men were all middle-aged to just around retirement age (35–60). None of the men seemed exceptionally bright to me, and also, as far as I could see, none of the men had any ambition whatsoever. My conclusion is that these men were there just to do a job and did not really show any interest or pride in the job. Another thing that I seemed to detect was a hostility to the people they were delivering to. The area of Newton that the post office served, as I said, was inhabited by upper-middle to upper-class Jewish residents living in beautiful (in my opinion) one-family houses. The letter carriers seemed to me to resent the Jews for all they had, and in the post office I sometimes overheard some of the familiar anti-Semitic stereotypes mentioned. Another point worth mentioning at this time is that most of the letter carriers were of Irish or Italian origin and rented apartments rather than owned their own homes, so I believe jealousy came very easily.

As far as my friendships with the regulars were concerned, they were just on a very casual, superficial basis. In the morning, we said the familiar "good morning, how are you?" and more or less left it at that. The only time we ever really talked to any great extent was when I was first learning a route and Mr. Weinbaum would delegate one of these men to help me or one of the other temps out in pulling down the route for us and telling us how to walk the route. This was learned in a matter of a few days, and then we could proceed on our own.

The other temps had basically the same relationship with the regulars as I did. As a matter of fact, it seemed that the letter carriers split into four close groups (there were twenty-four regular carriers) and then us three temporary carriers constituted another close group, and the only real friend that we had in the post office was the superintendent, Dan Weinbaum. Throughout the summer he constantly advised us on how to do things, and usually he sat with us and just talked to us while we were having coffee at about 7:00 in the morning when the coffee truck came around. During these breaks he would ask us how the job was going, about general things, and about how we should continue with our educations for the best jobs. He was the only one who told us this out of all the men who worked at the post office. I think the reason for this was that he was a college graduate himself, while the others in the post office just had high school educations, and they were not education-oriented. Here, I would like to add that when he did not sit with us, he would drink his coffee alone in his office while working.

The second part of the job involved delivering the mail to the houses. This job was easier than the job of sorting in the post office, if you consider the attention that had to be given to the two parts of the job. All this part required was for you to walk around from house to house and deliver the sorted mail. It goes without saying that the ease of this second job depended on how accurately you sorted in the first part, because if you made too many mistakes in either sorting or pulling down the route, you ended up in an area of Newton with the wrong mail. But as I said earlier, the job of sorting and pulling down was not very difficult, so this problem never arose except for a few missorted letters every so often.

One thing that made a noticeable difference between my performance and the performance of the regular carriers was the amount of time that it took me to do the route. Because of their ages (35–65) and my age (20) there was no question about who could do the route faster. On top of this (and I don't mean to brag), in high school I was one of the best distance runners in my league, so I was able to keep up a fast pace of delivering mail for the entire route. Another reason why I tried to cut the route time down was that we (all the mailmen) were allotted until 2:00 P.M. (from 8:00 A.M.) to do the route, so we would not have to return to the offices until 2:00 P.M. This meant that the less time it took us to do the route, the more time we could have to ourselves.

There was one experience I had that got a few mailmen mad. It came about because at the time, I was going out with a girl who lived on another carrier's route in our post office. After I finished doing my route, I always used to go over to her house and relax until 2:00. Usually I arrived after her mailman had delivered to her street, but this one time I finished my route early and arrived at her house before he had gotten there. When he came to her house, he noticed my car sitting in her driveway, and as he put the mail in her box, he saw me having lunch and yelled hello to me and just walked away. Later during the day back in the post office, I passed by him and he gave me a dirty look. I believe that most of the men went slowly because home was too far for them to go to, and the women would not let them relax in their homes at all so they were in no hurry to finish.

Another thing I did that got some of the mailmen mad was when they came back from vacation the first day, some of the women or girls would be waiting for me to come (I had made quite a few friends on the routes I delivered) so that they could give me a snack or a drink. What made it so strange was that the regular mailmen on these routes rarely, if ever, saw these people, and when they did see them on their first day back, all they asked was where I was and to say hello to me. This mailman did; however, rather reluctantly.

All in all, I can say that I had an enjoyable summer delivering mail. Although I did not make too many friends with my coworkers, I did meet a number of nice girls, some of whom I still go out with or at least keep in touch with.

Questions

1. How would you explain Ned Weinerman's motivation in terms of Maslow's Hierarchy of Needs?
2. How would you explain the regular carriers' motivation in terms of expectancy theory? Equity theory?

The U.S. Post Office at Newton, Massachusetts: Teaching Notes

This is a revision of a case written by an undergraduate student to describe the situation which existed during his former employment in the Newton Center Post Office during the summer of 1986. This case depicts some of the experiences common to undergraduates and shows the process of diagnosis and analysis in a management situation. It is not necessarily esoteric or unique in approach, but instead can be applied by all managers in everyday operations to aid their understanding of a situation. The bonus in this particular case is that the situation described is one that will provoke a good deal of empathy on the part of the undergraduate student, and once all the *war stories* have been heard, solicits a good deal of interest on the part of the class as the analysis pinpoints facts of a shared experience.

The most powerful use of the case seems to be in connection with an examination of individual needs in the daily work environment. Ned Weinerman, the temporary postal clerk, appears to be a normal undergraduate. The sheer normalcy of the situation offers a challenge to the students. By beginning to illustrate the process of motivation and response to inner needs, the case helps bring ideas expressed by the content (needs) theories of motivation to a point where they are translated by the student into his or her own real-world experience.

It might be good to start the discussion of this case by defining Ned Weinerman in motivational terms. Using Maslow, this most often centers around social or esteem needs, though there is often some disagreement about which need is preponderant. Weinerman does appear to demonstrate a high need for achievement, as demonstrated not only by his attitudes and accomplishments in the workplace, but in the style of his reporting of the situation in general.

Often it is helpful to point out how ordinary Weinerman appears and once his needs have been successfully defined in class, students have some confidence in their own analysis of the individual. It is fairly easy at that point to begin to see some realization on the part of the students about how to improve diagnostic skills using case analysis and apply them in their own situations with their own peers.

The interplay between the temporary and permanent carriers in the post office in Newton provides a rich demonstration of either equity of expectancy theories of motivation. It might be helpful to ask students to put themselves in the place of permanent help and to describe what they see when they view the expectancy or equity theory diagrams.

Experiencing Organizational Behavior Notes

Goal Setting and Personal Productivity

In this exercise students may put goal setting to work—for their personal benefit! Complete instructions are provided in the text. Students are asked to identify a work project that they want to get started on. They then use the principles for effective goal setting to set goals for performing their chosen task. Typically students have difficulty in putting some of these principles into practice. Students commonly set goals that are too general and often need coaching as to how to make them more specific. It is helpful to ask for a volunteer willing to share his/her goal with the class and then, as a class, apply the principles of effective goal setting to the volunteer's goal.

The exercise works best when students set goals during one class and then report the results of their goal setting (in small groups or to the class as a whole) during the next class. The Points to Consider provided with the exercise serve as a nice framework for discussing the students' goal setting experiences. Students really like this exercise because it not only gives them experience in goal setting, but it helps them complete work.

Source: By Robert D. Goddard, Appalachian State University.

Additional Experiential Exercise

Job Enrichment Exercise

This exercise is designed to help students understand how the process of job enrichment works and to nudge them into thinking how jobs might be enriched—even jobs which may seemingly not lend themselves to a job enrichment program.

Building on the job characteristics model of Hackman and Oldham (1976) described in the text, divide the class into smaller groups of 3–5 members. Using the core job dimensions of *skill variety, task identity, task significance, autonomy,* and *feedback,* ask each group to spend 15 minutes enriching one of the following jobs (the instructor may select the job or let the group select the job to be enriched):

1. Fast-food worker
2. College professor
3. Garbage collector
4. Linebacker coach
5. Daycare provider

Then have each group report back to the class on their plan for enriching the chosen job. Allow each group about 5–10 minutes for this phase of the exercise.

Follow up on the group reports with a general class discussion on topics such as:

1. Who might benefit from these enriched jobs?
2. What problems might certain workers complain about to management, given that they are now working on enriched jobs?
3. Do some jobs need enriching more than others? Which jobs, and why?

Job Enrichment Exercise: Teaching Note

Exercises such as this perform an important educational task—they get students to *think* about the topics presented in the text and in classroom lectures. They also involve students in the educational process itself—no small accomplishment!

You may wish to give students time to think about the assigned job to be enriched individually before assigning them to the task groups. In this way, each will have something to bring to the group discussion. You can vary the exercise by requiring individuals, rather than groups, to come up with an enrichment strategy for a particular job. You might have the students, either individually or in groups, choose a job to be enriched. This exercise can even be a homework assignment.

Additional Readings

Cissell, M. J. (1987, July). Designing effective reward systems. *Compensation and Benefits Review,* pp. 49–55.

Fitzgerald, T. H. (1971, July–August). Why motivation theory doesn't work. *Harvard Business Review,* pp.37–43.

Locke, E. A., Sirota, D., & Wolfson, A. D. (1976). An experimental case study of the success and failure of job enrichment in a government agency. *Journal of Applied Psychology, 61,* 701–711.

Nelton, S. (1988, March). Motivating for success. *Nation's Business,* pp. 18–19, 22–26.

▮ 5 ▮

WORK-RELATED ATTITUDES: THEIR NATURE AND IMPACT

CHAPTER OUTLINE

Special Sections

LEARNING OBJECTIVES

After reading this chapter, you should be able to:
1. Identify and describe the major components of attitudes.
2. Define what attitudes are, and describe their role in the study of organizational behavior.
3. Describe the major ways of changing someone else's attitudes.
4. Describe the process of *cognitive dissonance,* and how it leads people to change their own attitudes.
5. Identify and describe two major theories of job satisfaction, and techniques for measuring it.
6. Explain the major causes and consequences of job satisfaction.
7. Describe the major types of organizational commitment.
8. Describe the major causes and consequences of organizational commitment.
9. Define the prejudice of sexism, and discuss its underlying causes.

Chapter Overview

This chapter introduces the role of attitudes in organizational behavior and then discusses the factors related to attitude change or persuasion, including the nature of cognitive dissonance and dissonance reduction as a mechanism for changing attitudes. The chapter then presents the attitude of greatest concern in work settings—job satisfaction—and addresses the question: How prevalent is job satisfaction? How job satisfaction is measured is discussed, followed by a presentation of Herzberg's two-factor theory and Locke's value theory of job satisfaction. The chapter ends with a discussion of the causes of job satisfaction and the effects of satisfaction on organizational behavior. Organizational commitment, another key organizational attitude, is then defined and its causes and consequences discussed. Finally, the chapter turns to the topic of prejudice—negative attitudes about other organizational members. The prevalence of prejudiced based on gender and the existence of sexism in the workplace are the specific focus of this section.

Three special sections appear in this chapter. A Focus on Research section (Job Satisfaction: Can It Be in the Genes?) presents the findings of a recent study on monozygotic twins suggesting that job satisfaction is determined in part by genetic make-up. An OB in Practice section (Organizational Commitment in the Magic Kingdom) reports on how the Disney Corporation promotes organizational commitment among employees at Walt Disney World (The Magic Kingdom). A second Focus on Research (Physical Attractiveness and M.B.A.s' Salaries: Beauty Pays Off) describes a study finding in which people perceived as attractive are paid more than people who are considered unattractive, suggesting that attractiveness is another prejudice found in the workplace.

The Case in Point (Attitude Is Everything at Southwest Airlines) describes how important attitudes can be in the highly competitive airlines industry. In the context of relatively weak external forces, the attitudes of Southwest Airlines employees take on great importance. A CNN video about Southwest Airlines and its flamboyant CEO, Herb Kelleher, is available to text users. And the Experiencing Organizational Behavior exercise (Getting What You Expect: Anticipated Compensation of Women and Men) provides students with the opportunity to compare the compensation expectations of women with the expectations of men.

Lecture and Review Questions

What are attitudes and why are they of interest to management?

Attitudes can be defined as relatively stable clusters of feelings, beliefs, and behavior tendencies directed toward specific persons, ideas, objects, or groups. Attitudes have an affective component (feelings toward the object), a cognitive component (beliefs about the object), and a behavioral component. They are of interest to management within several contexts. Perhaps most important are workers' attitudes toward their jobs. Positive attitudes are usually referred to as job satisfaction. Negative job satisfaction can lead to poor performance, but is more likely to lead to absenteeism and turnover. Attitudes toward other members of the organization are also of interest to management, especially when these attitudes take the form of prejudice.

What are the major ways of changing others attitudes?

Persuasion is the major means of changing another person's attitudes. In the persuasion process, a target person is presented a message in which information is presented that is designed to change his or her attitude. As such, persuasion involves two general elements—the communicator and the communication (message). Persuasion is more effective when communicators are liked by those being persuaded, present themselves is a smooth eloquent style (speaking fast and convincingly), and probably most important when they are perceived as credible sources of information. Persuader credibility is determined by his or her apparent level of expertise and apparent motives (people who seem to have little to gain from changing our attitudes are usually considered more credible). Regarding the communication or message itself, persuasion is more effective when the message being communicated is clear and intelligible to the target audience and when it presents a view that is only moderately divergent from that held by the target audience.

What is cognitive dissonance and what role does it play in attitude change?

Cognitive dissonance is a state of tension that exists when a person becomes aware of inconsistency, either among various attitudes or between attitudes and behavior. When dissonance is perceived there is an immediate drive to reduce the dissonance by resolving the inconsistencies. Dissonance arousal and reduction also play a part in how attitudes are changed. Since dissonance can be the result of a discrepancy between an attitude and behavior, one way to eliminate the discrepancy is to change the attitude to make it consistent with the behavior. Thus, it is possible to influence someone to engage in a behavior that we know is inconsistent with the person's attitudes. In order to reduce the resulting dissonance, the person often changes his or her attitude. For example, when people are paid to buy a product they don't like, they often become more positively disposed toward the product, especially if they are paid a great deal of money, since the alternative to attitude change is admitting that they bought the product only because they were paid to do so. Faced with the dissonance arising from purchasing a product they don't like, they will start thinking of reasons to like the product, which would make the behavior more easily justifiable.

What is job satisfaction and how is it typically measured?

Job satisfaction is the set of attitudes people hold toward their jobs. Although we are interested in all aspects of those attitudes, most typically we focus on the affective reactions, and we talk about people who are relatively satisfied or dissatisfied with their jobs. Job satisfaction is most often measured using self-report questionnaires such as the Job Descriptive Index (although this instrument is more directly concerned with beliefs about the job than are most other job satisfaction measures), and the Minnesota Satisfaction Questionnaire. In addition, satisfaction can be measured by asking employees to describe incidents from their jobs that are particularly satisfying or dissatisfying and then searching for common themes in these descriptions (the critical incident approach). Meetings or interviews concerned with job satisfaction, especially those held as the employee leaves the organization, provide another means of measurement.

What factors have been identified as the major causes of job satisfaction and dissatisfaction?

Frederick Herzberg proposed a theoretical approach to determining the causes of job satisfaction. Based on critical incident data, he was able to identify a group of factors (labeled hygiene factors) which when not present on the job led to dissatisfaction. These hygiene factors were related to pay, working conditions, company policies, and relationships with coworkers. Although Herzberg maintained that the absence of acceptable levels of these factors led to dissatisfaction, their presence at these levels did *not* necessarily lead to satisfaction—all he could say was that employees would not be dissatisfied. Satisfaction was said to follow only from the presence of a different group of factors on the job. These factors (labeled motivators) were related to increased responsibility, recognition, and interesting work.

Herzberg's two-factor theory has received only limited empirical support and is best viewed as an intriguing, but unverified framework for understanding job satisfaction. However, it is important to note that Herzberg's two-factor called attention to the important role of such growth need related factors as the opportunity for personal growth and increased responsibility, thus stimulating much of the work that has been done on job enrichment.

According to Edwin Locke's value theory, job satisfaction is determined by the extent to which job outcomes (such as rewards) match those desired by the individual—the closer the match, the higher the level of job satisfaction. Thus the key to increasing job satisfaction is to minimize any discrepancy that might exist between the aspects of the job that one has and the aspects of the job that one wants. People differ as to the aspects of the job they desire, and therefore a major implication of value theory is that job satisfaction may be derived from many factors (in contrast to approaches specifying the importance of a few specific needs). In this respect, value theory is fully consistent with research on the causes of job satisfaction.

Research on job satisfaction reveals several other principle causes of job satisfaction. These causes can be broken down into two general categories: organizational and personal determinants of job satisfaction. Organizational policies and procedures concerning reward allocation, quality of supervision, decentralization of power, work and social stimulation, and pleasant working conditions are important determinants of job satisfaction. As for personal determinants, personality (e.g., self-esteem and locus of control), organizational status and seniority, and level of general life satisfaction are important determinants of job satisfaction.

What are the major consequences of job satisfaction and dissatisfaction?

Relationships between job satisfaction and a variety of behaviors have been observed. The strongest relationship, however, has been observed between job satisfaction and absenteeism—people who are dissatisfied with their jobs are more likely to be absent from work. A slightly weaker, though still meaningful, relationship has also been observed between job satisfaction and turnover—people who are dissatisfied with their jobs are less likely to remain on those jobs. It is worth noting that both of these behaviors are forms of withdrawal and the weaker relationship with turnover is due to the fact that the decision to leave an organization requires an employee to consider more than just his or her dissatisfaction with work. Actually, in the turnover process dissatisfaction causes an employee to think about quitting, triggering a search for alternative employment, the availability of which is an important factor in the ultimate turnover decision. The relationship between satisfaction and performance is less clear, although evidently increases in satisfaction do *not* cause increases in performance. The two may be related, however, in that higher levels of performance often result in rewards which may, in turn, lead to satisfaction. Finally, higher levels of job satisfaction are related to greater satisfaction with life in general and with improved health and well-being.

What is organizational commitment and what role does it play in organizational behavior?

Organizational commitment is the extent to which an individual identifies with and is involved with an organization and/or is unwilling to leave it. There are two major types of organizational commitment. The first type, continuance commitment, refers to the strength of a person's tendency to need to continue working for an organization because he or she cannot afford to do otherwise. The second type, affective commitment, refers to the strength of a person's desire to continue working for an organization because his or her personal goals are congruent with the goals of the organization.

Among the major types of organizational commitment are enriching jobs characteristics (e.g., responsibility, challenge, and autonomy), few alternative employment opportunities, personal characteristics (e.g., older and more experienced on the job), and the manner in which organizational newcomers are treated.

Organizational commitment affects several aspects of organizational behavior. High levels of commitment are related to lower levels of absenteeism and turnover, high levels of willingness to share and make sacrifices (organizational citizenship behaviors), and positive personal consequences (job satisfaction).

How does prejudice affect reactions to women in organizations?

Prejudice is simply a negative attitude toward members of a group based solely on their membership in that group. Although prejudice is widespread in our society, prejudice toward women at work is a particular problem in modern organizations. For example, women are not seen as leaders since they are not perceived as being as dominant or as self-assured as men. Women have a difficult time overcoming these prejudices because their success tends to be attributed to external causes such as luck or an easy task, even by other women. Also, there are some who believe that women have lower career aspirations than men, although this may be simply a reaction to what some see as career opportunities. All of these factors operate against women in the work-place and limit their access to managerial jobs. Yet, evidence suggests that these prejudicial views are largely incorrect. Female managers are at least as self-assured as male managers, and there is no evidence of performance differences between male and female managers. Nonetheless, many persist in thinking that women are not suitable for management. As long as this prejudice exists, it will be difficult for women to move to the top of the corporate ladder.

Other Teaching Suggestions

1. The chapter suggests that attitudes are an important consideration in our understanding of organizational behavior. But there has often been confusion over the differences among terms such as attitudes, values, and beliefs. For example, Yankelovich and his associates have received alot of press arguing that workers' values have declined, and that younger workers don't value hard work. These arguments are based on survey results often published in magazines such as *Time* or in the newspapers. But values are *basic* notions concerning right and wrong. Asking someone if he or she believes that hard work will be rewarded does not address the person's values. Bring in one of these surveys and read the items closely. Notice that many of the items tap beliefs or attitudes (which are much easier to change than values). Ask your students how they feel about the imminent demise of the work ethic.

2. Cognitive dissonance is discussed in the chapter as it relates to attitude change, but it's a fascinating variable in its own right. Barry Staw's dissonance study

of ROTC and the draft lottery (published in the *Journal of Personality and Social Psychology* in the early 1970s) has always been my favorite. At that time, we still had a draft, but had instituted a lottery system. Every year, there was a big drawing and each day of the year would be assigned a number. If you were born on that day in the year included in that lottery, that number would be your draft priority. Lower numbers were drafted first. But it soon became clear that, in any year, people with numbers above 150 would not be drafted. With this as background, Staw went to students enrolled in advance ROTC classes. These students were on scholarship and received a stipend as well. However, when they graduated, they owed the army four years service as an officer. If you believed you would be drafted anyway, and would have to serve two years as an enlisted person, it might make sense to put in the extra time, but do it as an officer. It might also be true that some students enrolled in this program to develop leadership skills or simply pay for college. One year, after the lottery, Staw surveyed advanced ROTC students, all of whom had already signed a commitment to the army. Since some of these students had high lottery numbers, they would not have been drafted and so lost the justification of preferring to serve as an officer rather than an enlisted person. Students with low numbers would have been drafted anyway, so they still had this justification. Staw asked these students why they thought the advanced ROTC program was worthwhile. The results were interesting. Students with low numbers (who would have been drafted) did not say many glowing things about ROTC, but tended to fall back on the argument that serving as an officer for four years was better than serving as an enlisted person for two. Those students with high numbers (who would not have been drafted), however, expressed much more positive views about ROTC, especially relative to developing leadership skills and helping to pay for college. I find this an ingenious study and an interesting demonstration of dissonance reduction.

3. The possibility of a causal relationship between job satisfaction and performance has always intrigued researchers and practitioners. It seems to make sense that happier workers are more productive workers, and such a relationship would mean that programs designed to increase satisfaction have a direct effect on the bottom line. Yet, when satisfaction is related to such phenomena as turnover and absenteeism (which also relate to the bottom line), increased satisfaction does not cause increased performance. It is interesting to discuss why we should not expect such a relationship to exist. For example, employees on machine paced jobs cannot increase their productivity regardless of their satisfaction, even if they want to. Also, if an employee is working as hard as he or she can, given current levels of ability, it would again be impossible

to improve performance even if the employee wanted to do so. Finally, it is probably true that many employees are satisfied simply because they do not have to work hard. Their jobs are not demanding, and that contributes to their satisfaction. Often, it is dissatisfaction with current levels of performance (for whatever reason) that motivates employees to work harder. Ask students to think of other reasons why the satisfaction-performance link is so weak, and have students recall situations where satisfaction lead to a decrease rather than an increase in performance.

4. Management is increasingly concerned with building commitment among employees as the benefits of committed employees become clearer. It has also been suggested that Japanese organizations do a better job of building commitment than American organizations. It is interesting to talk about some of the reasons for this. One major reason seems to be that Japanese firms are more committed to their employees than American firms are, and so Japanese companies receive higher levels of commitment in return. Some of the ways in which Japanese firms demonstrate their commitment include guaranteeing some employees life-time employment (although this usually applies only to male employees in large firms); by treating employees as members of an extended family (Japanese employees are often married and have receptions at company facilities); by narrowing the gap between management and employees (fewer status symbols for managers); and by soliciting employee suggestions and actually sharing information and decision making with employees (Quality Circles and more open communications both upward and downward). The results of these policies seem obvious as we continue to read about American firms' pleas for protection from the Japanese.

5. The role of attributions for success and failure as hindrances in the careers of women has been discussed. But there are far more subtle things that female managers must overcome. Authors such as Rosebeth Kanter have written about the perils facing women in management and what women can do to overcome the prejudice they face. It would be worth bringing in excerpts from some of these books. Students, especially male students, should be aware of the special rules society seems to have for women in management. Women must often deny family responsibilities, delay having families, avoid any relationships with male colleagues that might be considered questionable, and strive to act more like men. Recently, the popular press picked up the idea of a *Mommy Track* as another potential hindrance (although it may not have been proposed as one). All of these demands are, of course, added to the already considerable demands placed on any manager who wants to succeed.

Case in Point Notes

Attitude Is Everything at Southwest Airlines
This case describes the important role that attitudes play in achieving effectiveness and profitability at Southwest Airlines. Attitude is the number one selection criteria for employment at Southwest. Herb Kelleher, Southwest's CEO, relies heavily on his employees' positive attitudes for making the company a success. According to Kelleher, you can always teach skills through training so when it comes to hiring people, attitude is the primary concern. The case describes the various, often zany, ways in which Herb Kelleher promotes positive attitudes among his employees and the impressive results achieved as a consequence.

The discussion questions following the case direct students to discuss the relationship between attitudes and performance, and to explain the causes and consequences of job satisfaction on organizational behavior at Southwest Airlines. One important theme that typically emerges from discussion of this case is the relative influence of attitude as compared to external forces on organizational behavior. There are very few strong external forces operating at Southwest. For example, there is no mention of individual reward structure and clearly there are very few rigid work rules to direct individual performance. In this context, there is an opportunity for attitudes and their effects to be fully expressed.

For users of this text, a CNN video about Herb Kelleher and Southwest Airlines is available. This video provides considerable background information about Southwest Airlines that can be used to help students better understand and evaluate the case.

Additional Case

Ripping Off Mr. Gold's (A)

Instructions
Read the following case and answer the question below.

Source: By Jerry Saegert and George Eddy.

The Case
As the president and sole stockholder of Goldsmith's Lumber Company, Jake Goldsmith decided to seek the advice of his general manager, Daniel Rosenberg, about administering a polygraph test to all his employees. As he waited for Rosenberg to come to his office, Goldsmith wondered how

things could get into such a bind when his business was doing so well. When Rosenberg appeared, Goldsmith said:

"Well, Dan, what do you think we ought to do? I can't bring myself to believe that some of my long-time employees are robbing me! After all these years? How can it happen? And the kids! You know the security company is pushing me to give all our employees a polygraph test right away. But . . ."

"Jake, Jake, I agree with them wholeheartedly! I feel we should have done this a long time ago and gotten rid of these bums who are taking advantage of you. These three students I caught stealing materials should be fired immediately, and we should contact their parents to let them know what kind of kids they've got. We might also want to contact the police to see whether we should file charges. Also, if the polygraph tests show that any of the employees are stealing, I think we should fire them immediately, too. What are we waiting for?"

Goldsmith had become alarmed when he first was approached by several customers who told them that they had been offered merchandise by employees working in the yard section of the store where lumber, sheetrock, cement, steel products, roofing materials, and related items were kept and sold. The customers related that the salesman told them they didn't have to go inside and pay for the materials, but that they could just give a few dollars to the salesmen outside and no one else would be the wiser for such a transaction. Most of the employees in the yard section had been with Goldsmith's Lumber Company for many years prior to coming to Mr. Gold's Home Center, and he considered all of them to be quite loyal. Their jobs could be described as semiskilled; however, with pay above average for the Laredo area, with many benefits provided by the company, and a close association between employees and management, Goldsmith had delegated authority to these people so that they would consider themselves an important part of the company. Most of the employees were of Mexican background and regarded Goldsmith as the boss with total authority. Seldom were his decisions questioned.

After several years in the construction business in Laredo, Texas, Jake Goldsmith decided in 1963 to open his own lumberyard under the name of Goldsmith's Lumber Company. The purpose was to supply his own construction work and to have a place to store his equipment. For over 15 years, the lumberyard prospered and grew with its success coming not only as a supplier for Goldsmith's construction business, but also in sales to other customers. By 1980, as a result of the increasing demand for building supplies and home furnishings, he believed he should expand. Initially, he hesitated as to whether he should enlarge the present location or move to another one. He thought the problem in trying to decide whether to expand the present facilities of Goldsmith's Lumber Company was of a cultural nature. He wondered too, what to call the new facility. Laredo, Texas, a border city with its sister city lying in Mexico, has a predominantly Mexican population. In addition, Laredo's economy has been dependent significantly on its neighbors to the south for much of its business. The size of the store that Goldsmith wanted to open was unheard-of in this part of the state. Laredo still was considered a small town where people are suspicious of big-time operations. The possibility of alienating long-time customers who might

be ill at ease in a store of the size Goldsmith had in mind needed to be considered.

After extensive planning and replanning, checking with people in the field as well as traveling in various parts of the state to see if a trend could be detected, Goldsmith made the decision to go ahead. Accordingly, Mr. Gold's Home Center—his choice for a name—was started in March 1981 with a 30,000 square-foot building, housing a full line of building materials, home furnishings, and do-it-yourself tools and materials. In addition, there was an open lumber shed connected to the property from which standard lumber and building materials could be purchased.

Many of the employees from Goldsmith's Lumber Company were moved to Mr. Gold's Home Center to handle the business of the new store. The older employees had been with the firm for many years, and Goldsmith considered them traditionally hardworking and loyal. In addition, Goldsmith brought in his younger brother-in-law, Daniel Rosenberg, to be general manager of the store. Rosenberg had been a store manager with a large jewelry store chain in Houston, Texas for a number of years and had developed a style of leadership which was somewhat different from Goldsmith's. This style of leadership had been developed as a result of his experience in supervising a large operation in a highly competitive urban market.

As business increased at Mr. Gold's, it was obvious to Goldsmith that the skeleton work force would no longer be enough to handle the growing business. More qualified office personnel were hired, receiving became centralized under a separate department, and older employees were delegated more authority. Additionally, many high school students were hired for part-time work as the store was open seven days a week.

The store began to prosper as sales doubled through the first year and a half. With this tremendous growth, Goldsmith's problems began, foremost of which was internal shrinkage (commonly known as employee stealing). Goldsmith was well aware that in this type of retail business it is inevitable that some kind of internal shrinkage would occur. Accordingly, he made an even higher than usual allowance of four percent, which he built into his accounting criteria. Goldsmith realized that many small items would be shoplifted by professional shoplifters and others as a hobby, but he was unaware of the extent of internal shrinkage practiced by his employees. He did not expect this development due to the long-time employment of the majority of his employees. Mr. Gold's employed between 45–60 employees for sales depending on the peak period.

After contracting a security company in San Antonio, Goldsmith decided to use store walkers as a security team to try and stop the internal shrinkage. He considered some theft a normal consequence of doing business and in the past had made no reference to it, believing that it was not important. In fact, he thought that some of the items taken were left over and not saleable items, or scraps which could not really be sold for a profit. The security survey, however, suggested otherwise. After making its investigation, which included playing the part of customers in approaching salesmen in different areas of the store, the security team reported to Goldsmith in November 1982 that two people had been willing to sell goods in the yard without requiring the customer to pay the store, but paying the salesmen directly. In one case, the security investigator was not absolutely sure he could identify the salesman. In the other case, Goldsmith's legal counsel concluded that it was entrapment, and that he should not proceed against the employee. Moreover, this employee had eight years of service with the company, which Goldsmith considered had been outstanding.

Another factor that compounded the investigation was that business was progressing so rapidly and so well that all available personnel, including members of Goldsmith's family, were being used to keep the store going. Goldsmith doubted that it was sensible to terminate any employees who had experience due to the lack of time available to rehire and retrain people in the midst of the tremendous sales volume he was experiencing. Besides, Goldsmith still did not consider the theft problem to be of a sizable nature.

Nevertheless, he took several steps: (1) the one employee of eight years service who had been identified by the security investigator was transferred to another department; (2) Goldsmith moved an additional cash register closer to the lumberyard section of the store so that there would be little excuse for customers to have to go back into the store to pay for goods; (3) a voucher system was established whereby the customer was required to produce a paid receipt for any materials before they were taken from the yard; (4) the security people instructed several of the trusted employees to check on exits in departments other than those they were in charge of; (5) a system of two people was established in checking merchandise so that both would be responsible and no one person would have authority without the consent of the other; (6) a standardized security program was established which provided closer scrutiny and more control.

With these changes, Goldsmith considered operations to be moving along well. Business was still good and new people were hired for the lumberyard to keep up with the expanding customer demand. Most of these were high school students who worked afternoons and weekends. Due to the previous security problems, the entire hiring procedure was being revised. However, these changes were not totally implemented due to the lack of time, since all available people were fully utilized to make ends meet in just keeping the store going. After several months without further incidents, Goldsmith began to think that the problem of internal shrinkage was back under control. Unfortunately, his satisfaction was premature.

It was Rosenberg, enraged by the incident, who told him. Three high school students who worked in the lumberyard department were discovered to have taken several 50-pound boxes of wire fence staples and some public address system speakers which had been attached to the wall for calling employees but which were not used very often.

These items apparently had been thrown behind the building in tall weeds at the end of the late shift. For some reason, these part-time employees had failed to retrieve the items that evening, and Daniel Rosenberg saw them the next morning picking this material up when they were not supposed to be on the premises.

When accosted, two of the students denied any part in an illegal activity, while the other secretly approached Goldsmith and confessed that they were stealing. He also declared that other employees in the store were doing the same thing and had been for some time. Goldsmith was stunned. After his initial dismay, and before making any decisions, he contacted the security company in San Antonio that was still on retainer. Previously, the security company suggested that Goldsmith give a polygraph test to all his employees, but Goldsmith had rejected the idea because he concluded that internal shrinkage was not such a large problem. With this latest development, the security company again urged immediate polygraph testing of all employees.

Still Goldsmith hesitated. Countering Rosenberg's agreement with the security company as potentially troublesome, he demurred:

"I'm not so sure. As you know, we have been working up to twelve hours a day, almost seven days a week. We really can't afford to fire anybody! To make matters worse, I've talked with some of the department heads, who say that it's already known around the company that we've discussed the possibility of giving everyone a polygraph test. They tell me that many of the employees have said they would quit if they were forced to take it. Dan, I don't feel we can handle the store if all these people leave at once."

Rosenberg's response was emphatic: "Well, Jake, I just don't agree with you! There's no question that you've got to take action against these high school students we've caught . . . and as for the rest of them, well, if they're stealing from us, then I don't want them working here either. I'd rather work all day every day to keep those thieves out of this company. As fair as you've been with your employees and all the benefits you give them and the fact that they get wages as good as or better than other place in this town, I feel we're just making too many concessions. Jake, you just can't stall this any longer!"

Questions

1. What should Jake Goldsmith do with the three high school students who were caught stealing?
2. Do you think it is time to implement the suggestion of the security company and give polygraph tests to all of the employees of Mr. Gold's Home Center?

Ripping Off Mr. Gold's (B)

Instructions

Read the following case and answer the questions below.

The Case

Anxious to do the right thing, yet uncertain as to what was the best course of action to follow when he learned that his

Source: By Jerry Saegert and George Eddy.

supposedly faithful employees were stealing from him, Jake Goldsmith realized that he could not procrastinate indefinitely. He wished that he could be as positive as his store manager, Daniel Rosenberg, who faced the issue head on with a steadfast resolve that pressed on Jake powerfully. To Rosenberg, the remedy was so clear-cut that he began to be exasperated with Jake's indecision.

"What are you waiting for, Jake?" he persisted. "Fire them! Fire them all. That's exactly what they deserve. This is how they show their gratitude for all you've done for them! My God, boot them out the door! Right now!"

"Yes, Dan, I know you'd do just that if you were me. You wouldn't hesitate a minute . . . and maybe you are right. Yet, they've been with me for a long time and what have they really stolen? We don't know for sure. I'm not a vicious man; I'm not vindictive. You know that. Yes, you think I'm too easy and because of it, I'm being had. I know, I know."

The issue of internal shrinkage (employee theft) had been discussed many times between them without resolution, including the recommendation to use a polygraph on all store employees. The survey made by the security company Jake had engaged had demonstrated that stealing was taking place, and the investigator had urged the use of polygraph testing of all employees. Rosenberg agreed. It all commenced after the new store opened, after some 15 years in the lumber business, a 30,000 square-foot building with a full line of building materials, home furnishings, and do-it-yourself tools and supplies. Close to the main building was an open shed lumberyard from which standard lumber and related building materials could be purchased.

The security survey had confirmed the suspicions that salespeople in the lumberyard were selling merchandise and taking money directly from customers instead of sending them back to the cashier in the main building. The full extent of this practice had not been determined nor exactly how much money was going into the pockets of company salespeople as a result of bypassing the cashier. Jake thought, too, that some of his employees had been taking home nonsaleable items. Again, he did not know how much was being taken or how serious such practices were. Business was so brisk and everyone was so fully occupied it was difficult to find the time to check into the details.

While Jake was disturbed by the report of the security company, he still did not consider that stealing was a significant problem. He was dismayed, of course, that one of the employees implicated by the survey had been with him for eight years and had been regarded as an outstanding performer. Pressed by Rosenberg and the security investigator, Jake took several steps to tighten the security of the store. In particular, he installed a cash register out in the lumber yard and a voucher system so there would be no excuse for requesting the customer to return to the main building to pay for goods.

Business activity continued to increase and Jake's concern and attention to stealing incidents began to fade. Jake had to keep augmenting store personnel to satisfy the growing number of customers who appeared. Some temporary help was sought, including high school students who worked afternoons and weekends. Since the business volume was exceeding Jake's expectations when he decided to build this new facility, he was delighted that his judgment was proving astute.

Just when his euphoria was at its height, he was checked by Rosenberg who took him aside one morning and shattered his calm. Grimly, Rosenberg related that he had apprehended three high school students that morning trying to pick up and run off with materials they apparently had tossed over the fence the night before when they were working late in the lumberyard.

"Okay, Jake, what are you going to do?" he demanded.
"Well, I . . ."
"Oh, come on, Jake, damn it! Fire them! Immediately!"

"I want to think about it, Dan."
"Think about what, Jake? Surely you're not going to argue that I didn't catch these punks?"
"No, no, of course not, Dan. For God's sake! Just let me alone for awhile. I realize I've got to act, and I will, believe me. I just don't think it's as simple a matter as you do, that's all."
"Jake, Jake, don't worry yourself to death about it. It's not worth it. Get rid of them quick so we can go on about our business."
"Dan, you're a good manager and I rely on you. But, if I go ahead and fire these kids, and maybe somebody else, too—like Manuel—and hire replacements who are worse than what we've got now . . . what then, Dan?"
"Hell, Jake, that's just part of the hazards of doing business these days. You take all kinds of chances, but you keep trying. If the replacements are bad, try somebody else, and somebody else until you find what you want."
"All right, Dan, I hear you. Now go ahead with whatever you've got to do and let me think about this." He waved Dan out of the office. Mumbling that he did not know what there was to think about, Rosenberg left.

The next day Jake decided to terminate the three high school students. He did agree, however, not to contact their parents or take any legal action against them. "I want you to know," Jake lectured, "that this is a very serious matter indeed. I don't want you to forget it, just because I'm letting you off light like this. I could just as easily press charges against you, and you could end up with a record that would follow you the rest of your lives. So, remember that, and remember it well. If you think you can keep getting away with this sort of thing, you're going to be very, very sorry some day. Well, that's all I have to say. You can go now."

Two of the students departed immediately, while one lingered behind to talk to Jake in private. He told Jake that he was terribly ashamed of his part in the episode and that he was most grateful for Jake's leniency.

"Please keep my final paycheck, Mr. Goldsmith," he concluded. "for I'd like to have it reimburse the company for the trouble I've caused."

Feeling somewhat relieved that this unpleasant chore was behind him, Jake forced himself to think about the polygraph test for the store employees. He kept hearing Dan's insistent voice in his ear, saying over and over, "Get on with it, Jake, get on with it." To his expressed fear that many old-time employees would quit before submitting to this test, Dan's response was typically blunt.

"The hell they will, Jake. Oh, yeah, maybe one or two might go steaming off. But the rest of them? They're bluffing, that's all! You know damn well that they can't find jobs here in town that are as good as what they've got right now with you. So all this so-called talk about leaving is a bunch of baloney—nothing more."

After considerable agonizing over the possible adverse consequences, Jake reluctantly consented to have the polygraph tests administered to all his employees. He consoled himself with the though that Dan probably was right and, further, that the cost of the test was well worth the savings in getting rid of those cheating employees who otherwise would continue to steal from him.

Rosenberg was right. Only a handful quit the company, nowhere near the number who had indicated they would leave were they ever forced to be degraded and insulted by such a technique. Of those who took the test and remained, the polygraph told Jake that they did not feel they had done anything wrong when they took materials such as leftover paint and scrap pieces from the lumberyard, one employee admitted that what he was doing may have been wrong, helping himself to similar leftovers from time to time, but that this was peanuts to a company that was making such profits as Mr. Gold's Home Center.

"Look at the business you've got, Mr. Goldsmith! I didn't get much of anything and you know it. What I took would have been junked anyway. I never got anything that a customer would have bought. I don't steal! I've never put any money in my pocket from customers. But the way Mr. Rosenberg acts, you'd think I took the whole store home with me every night. You ask my customers about me. You'll see they like me and appreciate what I do for them. They always get the benefit of the doubt when I measure. I take care of them, Mr. Goldsmith."

"Well, I suppose so," Jake said.

"Are you going to fire me, Mr. Goldsmith?"

"Well, hmm. . . . ah . . . I . . . we'll see."

When he concluded mulling over this conversation, Jake decided not to fire anyone. Somewhat nettled by implied criticism by Rosenberg over this determination, Jake felt trapped by circumstances. The business flow seemed to engulf all his efforts to keep a staff on hand that was adequate to serve all the customers the store kept attracting. Each employee fired had to be replaced quickly, and there was no assurance that a new employee would prove to be better or even equal to the one displaced. Besides, Jake had yet to replace all the old employees who had quit over the issue of the polygraph testing. He did not think it made sense to aggravate the shortage of help by firing anyone whose transgressions perhaps were not so serious as they first appeared.

Now another disturbing personnel problem had surfaced. Morale had dropped appreciably, probably a reaction to the manner in which management had responded to the incidence of internal shrinkage. Listlessness had supplanted the prior enthusiasm employees had exhibited in performing their jobs. Moreover, the salespeople seemed to be avoiding him, and, even worse, they were no longer as respectful to Jake as they had been. Previously, it was customary for an employee to come to see him unhesitatingly when he or she had a problem—job-related or personal—with which the employee wanted help. Jake had welcomed these sessions and had encouraged them to become regular features of the working environment. Not only was Jake pleased to try to be of help, but these discussions were beneficial to him as he frequently learned of ways to improve store operations. With these informal communications networks drying up, Jake actually felt threatened by this isolation in his own store.

Wondering what he should do, he spoke again to Rosenberg. Several alternatives were reviewed such as giving the employees a bonus now instead of waiting the two months when it was normally due. Another option he mentioned to Rosenberg was to have a company-wide picnic.

"I don't like either of these ideas, Jake," he said in his usual positive manner. "You're just evading the central issue again."

"What do you mean, Dan? These are accepted practices in organizations."

"Oh come on, Jake, you know perfectly well what I'm talking about."

"Perhaps you would be good enough to explain."

"Now, don't get upset, Jake. I wouldn't get smart with you. But look at it squarely. What you are suggesting are merely diversions. Advancing the bonus smacks of some kind of payoff. And for what? They haven't done anything unusual. Aren't they supposed to sell our merchandise? And as for the picnic . . ."

"What's so bad about a picnic? Everyone likes a picnic."

"Well, for one thing, a picnic ought to be some kind of treat—a reward. Again, for what? A reward for those bums who are stealing from you that you wouldn't fire? As for the rest, you don't think you're going to buy loyalty with a few beers and hot dogs, do you, Jake?"

"Oh Dan, Dan, are you so hard? You can't possibly believe that all employees are bums or spoiled children, can you? . . . Ah, you see? Of course not, so give me an idea that's reasonable."

"Jake, I'm not unreasonable. I'm realistic, that's all. Of course, we've got some good employees who are putting out the way I think they should. The slackers are something else, and the thieves—no, I won't say any more about them right now. Just remember, Jake, if you let someone take advantage of you, he'll stomp on you. Now, Jake, I respect your experience and your success, but you're too soft. You've got to have discipline and that means you've got to be tough. Fair, of course, but tough, too."

"Dan, you've been right on many occasions, and you've made major improvements in receiving, merchandising, buying, and customer relations. But as for being tough, I just don't know. What do you mean by being tough now?"

"Call a meeting of all employees and tell them either to shape up or get out."

Questions

1. Did Jake handle the problem of the high school students' stealing correctly? What would you have done?
2. Would you have ordered the polygraph tests for all employees? Why or why not?
3. How can Jake regain the confidence and trust that his employees had previously shown? Will his proposed picnic and early bonus plans work? Why or why not?
4. In what way might Jake have contributed to the problem of internal shrinkage?

Ripping Off Mr. Gold's (A) and (B): Teaching Note

These cases raise issues of attitudes, values, leadership, motivation, and honesty.

The cases can stand by themselves. Case A can be taught alone as can Case B, or they can be taught as a series for prediction purposes. In sequence, they confront those students who prefer a hard-line approach with the difficulty of controlling outcomes through coercion, and thereby encourages the exploration of other choices.

Ripping Off Mr. Gold's (A) ends with Mr. Goldsmith, owner of Mr. Gold's Home Center, considering a recommendation from his general manager and younger brother-in-law, Mr. Rosenberg, to fire three high school students caught stealing and to administer a polygraph test to all employees as urged by a security company retained by Mr. Goldsmith to check on thievery in his enterprise. Students are asked questions about what Jake could do in this situation.

1. What should Jake Goldsmith do with the three high school students who were caught stealing?

   Your students' opinions will vary in this matter. Some may take the hard line and say that all employees who are caught stealing should be fired. Others might suggest that the employees be called in for counseling or some other remedial activity. Discussion might center on peer pressures to steal: "Everyone was doing it, and no one ever got warned about it" might be some students' perception of this situation.

2. Do you think it is time to implement the suggestion of the security company and give polygraph tests to all of the employees of Mr. Gold's Home Center?

   Again, students' opinions will vary. You may wish to introduce the idea of First Amendment rights concerning the use of polygraph tests in employment decisions. The perceived values and attitudes of Mr. Gold's employees should be a part of the discussion of this case. Also, the values of the owner, Mr. Goldsmith, and his general manager, Mr. Rosenberg, should be included.

   Ripping Off Mr. Gold's (B) carries on where Case A leaves off. Mr. Goldsmith has decided to fire the three high school students and to administer the polygraph tests to the employees. He does not feel good about these decisions. In fact, if Mr. Rosenberg had not pressed him about it, Mr. Goldsmith would probably have done nothing.

   The result of these decisions has been a change in the climate of Mr. Gold's Home Center. Employee's attitudes have changed for the worse, and the once-friendly atmosphere has turned to one of sullen resentment. Even given the employee reactions to these decisions, Mr. Rosenberg feels that Mr. Goldsmith has been too soft on his employees. Certainly, the two managers have different managerial styles and attitudes toward the employees of Mr. Gold's Home Center.

   Again, students are asked to respond to a number of questions about the case.

1. Did Jake handle the problem of the high school students' stealing correctly? What would you have done?

   Again, students' responses to this question will vary, according to their attitudes and values. Hard-liners (Theory X attitudes) will say that firing was the correct response, while other students might try to assess the climate of Mr. Gold's that might contribute to the attitude that "stealing is okay."

2. Would you have ordered the polygraph tests for all employees? Why or why not?

   The question of polygraph testing for employment is a hot one and involves legal issues which were not present when this case was originally written. Still, the attitudes of your students will color their responses.

3. How can Jake regain the confidence and trust that his employees had previously shown? Will his proposed picnic and early bonus plan work? Why or why not?

   Goldsmith has not demonstrated that he has analyzed carefully the full meaning of the losses incurred. The suspicion lingers that perhaps he has made too much of the internal shrinkage issue by concentrating more on the actions of his employees as opposed to evaluating what has been stolen, as well as whether any trend can be identified. Thorough study of these aspects might well cast a different light on the entire series of theft incidents. It still is not too late to take such action, and Goldsmith should be advised to do so. What is too late, however, is to *take back* the polygraph tests and the initial employee reactions to them. Now, Goldsmith must find some way to regain the confidence of his employees that he once enjoyed and which was important to him. While it is true that perhaps some of his employees might deserve the "shape up or get out" admonition Rosenberg has urged, it is inadvisable to broadcast such a declaration in a public meeting to all employees. Such actions should be accomplished strictly on an individual basis privately after an appraisal of the specific situation of each employee. Overall, Goldsmith needs to develop a greater appreciation for empathy as a basis for re-establishing the necessary communications linkages with his staff.

4. In what way might Jake have contributed to the problem of internal shrinkage?

   Students might be surprised at this question; they should not be. Jake apparently realized that employees steal from him from time to time, and even appeared to have tolerated stealing of spoiled or unsaleable items. Certainly, his attitude implicitly condoned stealing. His policy of overlooking stealing and merely transferring the long-time employee who was caught only added to the climate that stealing is an acceptable behavior.

Additional Comments

You may ask students to form groups and discuss the case. You might also expose them to the seriousness and costs of internal shrinkage in business today by assigning reading materials such as Chapter 19 in William F. Glueck's book, *Personnel: A Diagnostic Approach*, or the numerous current articles on the extent and cost of employee theft. It is estimated, for example, that $3.5 billion in merchandise is stolen from stores every year.

Experiencing Organizational Behavior Notes

Getting What You Expect: Anticipated Compensation of Women and Men

This exercise asks students to interview several classmates about their expectations regarding career choice, compensation, and opportunities for promotion following graduation. Specific instructions for doing the exercise, together with points to consider, are provided in the text.

As noted in the text, women continue to be compensated at a lower rate than their male counterparts. Generally, the results of this exercise are consistent with this inequity—females reporting lower compensation expectations than their male counterparts. Why? Sexism in the workplace seems not only to directly restrict the financial well-being of women workers, but also seems to influence their expectations. There are other plausible explanations as well. The exercise provides students with a springboard for discussing prejudice in work settings. As students will likely recognize, the most damaging kinds of prejudice are often those that are most subtle (e.g., what can be more damaging than prejudice that operates by lowering the aspirations of its targets?).

Additional Experiential Exercise

Whom to Leave Behind

Instructions

Read the following instructions and complete the information requested individually. Your instructor will then ask you to form groups and come up with a consensus opinion on *Whom to Leave Behind*.

The eight persons listed below have been selected for flight to another planet because tomorrow the planet Earth is doomed for destruction. Due to changes in space limitations, it has now been determined that only five persons may go. Any five persons qualify.

Your task is to select the five passengers. There are therefore three persons now on the list who will not go. Place the number *1* by the person you think should be removed *first* from the list of passengers; place the number *2* by the person you think should be removed *second* from the list; and, finally, place the number *3* by the person you think should be removed *third* from the list. Choose only three. These are the three persons who will not make the trip. They are to be left behind.

___ An accountant
___ An accountant's pregnant wife
___ A liberal arts coed
___ An intelligent female movie star
___ A black medical student
___ A professional basketball player
___ A biochemist
___ An armed policeman

Source: From Donald D. White and H. William Vroman, *Action in Organizations.* Copyright © 1977 by Allyn and Bacon. Reprinted with permission.

You are to select the three people to be left behind on your own. Then, together with your group, come up with another list of people to be left behind. After completing the group list, your instructor will ask each group to report whom the group decided to leave behind. If your list was in disagreement with the group's list, you may be called on to explain why your choice(s) were different.

Whom to Leave Behind: Teaching Note

In this exercise, those left behind are not nearly as important as the later discussion of how each group went about making that decision. Values about institutions and attitudes toward people and things will emerge from that discussion. In addition, interesting observations will be made about the group itself. You may wish to assign observers to make notes and comment on the values and attitudes of the group members.

This exercise can serve multiple purposes. It can illustrate individual values and attitudes, and it can also show how group values and attitudes can influence the individual's values and attitudes. This exercise is valuable in that the scenario presented is somewhat ridiculous and not one with which students would have experience. Therefore, their choices would be free from response bias—they would not put down what they think the instructor wants to hear. Their choices would likely reflect their values and attitudes toward what they perceive as the attributes and characteristics of the individuals listed.

By the way, there are no right or wrong choices of individuals to be left behind. A case can be made for each of the individuals listed to be included in the lucky seven. Students' choices should accurately reflect their attitudes and should provide a rich discussion!

Additional Readings

Organ, D. W. (1988). A restatement of the satisfaction-performance hypothesis. *Journal of Management, 14,* 547–558.

Schneider, B. (1991). Service quality and profits: Can you have your cake and eat, too? *Human Resource Planning, 14*(2), 151–157.

Schwartz, F. N. (1989, January–February). Management women and the new facts of life. *Harvard Business Review,* pp. 65–76. (The article that started all the discussion of a *Mommy Track.*)

▮ 6 ▮

PERSONALITY: INDIVIDUAL DIFFERENCES AND ORGANIZATIONAL BEHAVIOR

CHAPTER OUTLINE

Personality: Its Basic Nature
  Personality and Organizational Behavior
Work-Related Aspects of Personality
  The Five Robust Dimensions of Personality: A Look at
    the Big Picture
  The Type A Behavior Pattern: Its Effects on Task
    Performance and Interpersonal Relations
  Machiavellianism: Using Others on the Way to Success
  Locus of Control: Perceived Control over One's
    Outcomes and Fate
  Self-Monitoring: Public Image versus Private Reality
  Self-Efficacy: Beliefs in One's Ability to Perform
    Various Tasks
  Self-Esteem: The Importance of Self-Evaluations
  Positive and Negative Affectivity: Stable Tendencies to
    Feel Good or Bad at Work
Measuring Personality: Some Basic Methods
  Objective Tests: Assessing Personality through
    Self-Report

Projective Techniques: Ambiguous Stimuli and
  Personality Assessment

Special Sections

An International Multicultural Perspective Type A's
  and Type B's on the Job: Evidence from Two Different
  Cultures

OB in Practice Dealing with Problem Employees:
  Managing Wild Ducks, Mavericks, and Other Unruly
  Types

Focus on Research Champions of Technological
  Innovation: Profiling the Agents of a Crucial Form of
  Organizational Change

A Question of Ethics Information about Personality: Is
  It an Appropriate Basis for Organizational Decisions?

LEARNING OBJECTIVES

After reading this chapter, you should be able to:
1. Define *personality* and explain its importance to the
   field of organizational behavior.
2. Identify the *five robust dimensions* of personality, and
   indicate how they relate to various aspects of job
   performance.
3. Describe the following personality characteristics and
   indicate their relevance to important forms of
   organizational behavior: *self-monitoring,
   Machiavellianism, locus of control, positive affectivity,*
   and *negative affectivity.*

4. List the major traits of *innovation champions,* people
   who play a key role in their organization's adoption of
   technological innovations.
5. Describe the characteristics of *problem employees,*
   including *wild ducks,* or *mavericks,* and indicate how
   managers can best cope with such people.
6. Explain how personality is measured, and be able to
   comment on the ethical issues involved in the use of
   such information in organizations.

Chapter Overview

This chapter introduces the role of personality variables in organizational behavior. The chapter begins by defining the general nature of personality and then discusses several personality variables that have been found to influence behavior at work. This section opens with a discussion of the central dimensions that tend to underlie the vast array of personality traits.

These dimensions, referred to as the five robust dimensions of personality, are extroversion/introversion, agreeableness, conscientiousness, emotional stability, and openness to experience. Then several specific personality variables—Type A and Type B behavior patterns, Machiavellianism, locus of control, self-monitoring, self-efficacy, self-esteem, positive affectivity, and negative affectivity—are described in relation to their influences on organizational behavior. The chapter ends with a discussion of the two major methods available for measuring personality—objective tests and projective techniques, including a definition of measurement reliability and validity and a discussion of their use as criteria for assessing the accuracy of personality measures.

For special sections appear in this chapter. An International/Multicultural Perspective (Type A's and Type B's on the Job: Evidence from Two Different Cultures) describes the findings of a study of Type A and Type B personalities among bus drivers in the United States and India. The study found that these personality traits are not restricted to the United States and seem to exert similar effects on work behaviors regardless of culture. An OB in Practive section (Dealing with Problem Employees: Managing Wild Ducks, Mavericks, and Other Unruly Types) describes several types of problem behavior patterns representing characteristics that are opposite to the high self-monitoring personality. A Focus on Research section (Champions of Technological Innovation: Profiling the Agents of a Crucial Form of Organizational Change) describes a study investigating the personality traits of champions of change—individuals who emerge as active and enthusiastic promoters of technological change. Champions of change differed in several aspects of personality from other persons—higher levels of inclination to take risk, innovativeness, and achievement. A Question of Ethics section (Information about Personality: Is It an Appropriate Basis for Organizational Decisions?) provides several notes of caution about measuring personality and interpreting scores on personality measures.

The Case in Point (The Personality Behind Walmart) describes the personality of a fascinating man—the late Sam Walton, founder and former chairman of Wal-Mart Corporation. And the Experiencing Organizational Behavior exercise (Machiavellianism in Action: The $10 Game) provides students with a chance to observe High Machs (ruthless, self-centered people who manipulate others for their own gain) in action.

Lecture and Review Questions

What is generally meant by the term personality?
Personality can be generally defined as a unique but stable set of characteristics and behavior that sets each individual apart from others. That is, personality defines the lasting ways in which people differ from each other. Note that this definition implies that these lasting traits determine behavior, more so that situational factors. Note too, that this definition assumes people's behavior will be consistent across time and situations, although it is recognized that strong situational demands can often overwhelm personality and determine behavior.

What are the five robust dimensions of personality and how are they related to organizational behavior?

Over the years, numerous personality traits have been identified. However, analysis of these traits reveals five central dimensions underlying all of them. These dimensions, referred to as the five robust dimensions of personality, are: extraversion/introversion, agreeableness, conscientiousness, emotional stability, and openness to experience. Research has shown that several of these dimensions are closely linked to performance among persons holding a wide range of jobs. Other dimensions appear to only affect performance in certain types of jobs (e.g., extraversion predicts performance in managerial and sales jobs). Taken together, research on the five robust dimensions of personality supports the contention that personality plays an important role in organizational behavior.

What are the characteristics associated with Type A personalities and how do Type A persons fare at work?

Type A persons are generally hard driving, extremely competitive, impatient, often speak loudly and quickly, and tend to react quickly in many contexts. This pattern of behavior can be contrasted with that of Type B persons which is essentially the opposite in every way. Although these extremes are easily recognizable, most people fall somewhere in between, although they can be characterized as being closer to one type or the other. Type A persons are more prone to high blood pressure and heart disease, and they tend to die younger than Type B persons. On the job, Type A persons tend to work harder and faster at many tasks, and they tend to perform better at tasks where there are time pressures, or where they must work in the face of distractions. They tend to perform poorly, however, on tasks requiring patience or careful consideration or judgment. Also, Type A persons are more likely to be involved in interpersonal conflict on the job because they are more likely to lose their tempers and become irritable, and they tend to be less accurate than Type B persons. For all of these reasons, Type A persons usually do not rise beyond middle management. Instead, it is the Type B person who is more likely to rise to top management.

What is Machiavellianism, and what behaviors characterize persons high on this trait?

Machiavellians are persons who will use others and do anything in their power to succeed. Thus, they seem to base their lives on the strategies outlined by Machiavelli in his 16th century book, *The Prince*. *High Machs* are true pragmatists who believe that any means are justified in trying to accomplish their goals. They are confident, eloquent, and competent. They tend to seek situations where there is face-to-face interaction, few rules, and where others' emotions run high; they are also very good at political maneuvers. All of this allows them to manipulate those whose behavior is influenced by emotions, since High Machs' behavior is never influenced by emotion. When dealing with High Machs, it is possible to protect oneself by exposing them to others so that everyone sees them for what they are; by paying careful attention to what people do as well as to what they say; and by avoiding situations where emotions run high, since this is the type of situation High Machs prefer.

What is locus of control and how does it influence behavior in organizations?

Locus of control refers to the extent to which we believe that we control our own fate. Persons who believe they control their destiny are known as *Internals,* while persons who believe that their destinies are controlled by forces outside themselves are known as *Externals.* Again, most people fall somewhere between the extremes, but most can be characterized as relatively closer to one extreme or the other. Relative to Externals, Internals perceive stronger relationships between their efforts and performance and between performance and obtaining rewards. Internals tend to be promoted more quickly, earn more money, report higher levels of job satisfaction, and cope better with higher levels of stress. From the point of view of the organization, Internals tend to make better employees.

What is meant by self-monitoring, and how important is this in organizational behavior?

Self-monitoring is a personality trait that refers to our ability to adjust our behavior according to whatever situation we find ourselves in. High self-monitors are persons who can readily adjust their behavior in any situation so as to produce positive reactions from others—they almost seem to be different persons in different situations. Low self-monitors, on the other hand, tend to be the same in all situations and do not make any adjustments in their behavior as the situation demands. Thus self-monitoring involves a willingness to be the center of attention, a sensitivity to the reactions of others, and an ability to adjust one's behavior. High self-monitors are often more effective in boundary-spanning jobs that require interaction and communication with people from different backgrounds, as well as in any situation requiring clear communications. Finally, high self-monitors are more likely to resolve conflict through collaboration or compromise than through avoidance or competition, so they have greater concern for long-term solutions to conflict.

What is self-efficacy and what role does it play in organizational behavior?

Self-efficacy is a belief in one's ability to perform successfully at a given task. Since self-efficacy refers to beliefs about a specific task it is not, technically speaking, a personality trait. These beliefs tend to generalize, however, so we can treat self-efficacy much the same way we treat other personality traits. Feelings of self-efficacy develop through a person's own success at a task and through the observation of others performing the same task. Persons who are high in self-efficacy tend to set more difficult goals for themselves and tend to react to feedback that suggests they are not meeting these goals by increasing their efforts; persons who are low in self-efficacy react to similar feedback by giving up. Although self-efficacy is a relatively new variable in organizational behavior, there is reason to believe that it can play an important role in helping those individuals who have experienced failure or prejudice to overcome these problems and help themselves.

What is self-esteem and why is it important to behavior at work?

Self-esteem refers to a person's image about him or herself. The more positive that image, the higher level of self-esteem a person is said to possess. It has been shown that persons who have higher levels of self-esteem tend to be more satisfied on their jobs, are more highly motivated, and tend to have higher levels of productivity. In addition, high self-esteem individuals are more successful at identifying and then obtaining appropriate jobs. It should be noted, however, that although low self-esteem persons tend to be less desirable employees, self-esteem can be changed. Specifically, allowing persons to experience success on the job, and then training them to attribute their successes to internal causes (and to attribute failures more to external causes) can enhance self-esteem, making the individuals involved more valuable to the organization and better able to overcome feelings of helplessness that usually accompany low self-esteem.

What are positive affectivity and negative affectivity, and what are their effects on organizational behavior?

Positive affectivity and negative affectivity are lasting tendencies to experience positive or negative feelings, respectively. Persons high on positive affectivity tend to have an overall sense of well-being, see themselves as pleasurably and effectively engaged, and tend to experience positive emotional states. In contrast, persons high in the trait of negative affectivity tend to hold negative views of themselves and others, interpret ambiguous stimuli negatively, and tend to experience negative emotional states.

Recent research suggests that positive and negative affectivity exert important effects on organizational behavior. People who are high in negativity show less willingness to engage in helping behaviors and exhibit higher levels of absenteeism than do people who are high in positive affectivity. Furthermore, this research suggests that positive and negative affectivity may affect the nature and functioning of groups. This proposition, based on attraction-selection-attrition theory, posits that people with similar personalities are attracted to each other, tending to form groups. In most cases, only persons who share similar personalities will remain in the group. In this manner, individual personality traits can influence the nature and functioning of groups. Thus, a group comprised of people high in the trait of negative affectivity is expected to show the same negative affectivity-induced behaviors as seen in individuals.

What are some advantages and disadvantages of the major approaches available for measuring personality?

The most widely used method of measuring personality is some type of self-report inventory or questionnaire. These instruments consist of a series of statements, often self-descriptive, to which the person is asked to respond.

Inventories can be scored using objective scoring keys requiring little or no judgment and allowing for statements about relative standing on personality traits. In addition, research suggests that these questionnaires are the most valid means for assessing personality. Care must be taken, however, in the construction of such questionnaires. People will not always respond honestly when they are asked to describe themselves, especially if it is clear that some descriptions are more desirable than others. Projective techniques aim to overcome this problem by disguising the evaluation. Here, persons are presented some ambiguous stimulus (such as an inkblot) and are asked to tell what they see. Their responses can provide deep insights into their personalities, and it is difficult for people to present themselves in a desirable fashion since they do not know how their responses are being evaluated. Unfortunately, interpretation of data from these techniques requires a great deal of expert judgment, and those who administer these techniques must undergo extensive training.

Other Teaching Suggestions

1. Any class on personality tends to become more involving if the students are able to take and score some real personality measures to see where they fall. For example, measures of locus of control (Rotter) and self-esteem (Golding) are readily available. There are also scales available to measure various types of personal orientations such as assertiveness. It probably isn't necessary to bring in scales that measure every personality dimension discussed in the chapter, but a few examples would be useful.

2. On a somewhat similar note, one instrument that might be interesting to bring to class is the Minnesota Multiphasic Personality Inventory (MMPI). When most students begin to think about personality, they usually think about labels such as paranoia and schizophrenia. These are abnormal types, of course, and we are more interested here in normal types—one never hears of someone being institutionalized because of extremely low self-esteem. It would be interesting, however, to bring in the MMPI as an introduction to abnormal types. It probably takes too long to distribute the entire instrument and then have students complete it (it would also necessitate obtaining a scoring key), but you might read some of the items aloud. Respondents are asked to indicate whether they "Agree," "Disagree," or are "Not sure" if each statement applies to them. Statements deal with hearing voices, seeing plots, and floating outside of one's body, and usually elicit a reaction. It is important to point out that the assumption behind administering the MMPI is that a person has some problem in adjusting or functioning in the world, and the MMPI is designed to identify the nature of the problem. If you can get a scoring key, some of the more interesting scales do not deal with personality at all. There are items designed to determine if a person is just trying to make him or herself look good (such as agreeing with the statement "I have never taken anything that wasn't mine"), or if the person is just agreeing with all the bizarre statements. Although many would argue that the MMPI is not appropriate for work settings (unless you are trying to screen out psychotics) it is one of the more interesting personality measures available.

3. Self-monitoring is interesting psychological variable. It is usually argued that high self-monitoring is desirable, since it is equated with adaptability. Later on, however, we will be discussing leadership. Here, some people have speculated that adaptability may not be desirable. Indeed, presidential candidates are harshly criticized for behaving inconsistently across situations. But, isn't this what we would expect from high self-monitoring people?

4. Consideration of the negative side of high self-monitoring levels leads us to a consideration of how

some of these personality traits tend to cluster. The text points out that high self-esteem (which is clearly related to self-efficacy) is a prerequisite for Machiavellianism. Such persons would also tend to be high on a need for power and extremely low on need for affiliation. Furthermore, high self-monitoring would allow such persons to adopt to any situation in order to better manipulate others. Perhaps it is possible to have too much of a good thing.

5. A type of measure that is closely related to personality measures is an interest inventory. These measures attempt to assess the kinds of work in which people are interested so that they can seek jobs where they can do that kind of work. The assumption (and it has been proven in research as well) is that people perform best on jobs when they are interested in the kind of work they are doing. Copies should be available of the Strong-Campbell Interest Inventory (formerly the Strong Vocational Interest Blank) and some illustrative items and information on scoring (especially how the scoring keys were developed) should be interesting.

Case in Point Notes

The Personality Behind Wal-Mart

This is a case about the late Sam Walton, who died in April 1992. He was the richest man in America and he couldn't have cared less. He was the founder and chairman of the Wal-Mart Corporation—American's biggest retailer, with 1,650 Wal-Mart stores, 200 Sam's Clubs, and about 150 new stores opening each year—something he cared about a great deal. This case is derived from an interview with Sam Walton by John Huey of *Fortune* magazine. Huey flew with around the country with Sam Walton for several days, visiting numerous Wal-Mart stores. This case describes what Huey observed of this fascinating and driven man's personality.

The discussion questions that follow the case ask students to describe Sam Walton's personality using the personality types described in the text. Students are also prompted to consider how personality affects performance and interpersonal relationships.

Sam Walton was a folk hero to many people, as often becomes evident when discussing this case. Students really enjoy talking about him. Ask your students if any of them work for, or know someone who works for, Wal-Mart. Sam Walton tried very hard to visit as many of his Wal-Mart and Sam's Clubs stores as possible. Perhaps some students have met him. At the very least, if a student works for Wal-Mart, he or she is very likely to have interesting stories to share about Sam Walton. Such stories can provide wonderful illustrations of this legendary man's personality.

Additional Case

Different Strokes for Different Folks

George and Sam are two supervisors for a medium-size electronics firm in the Silicon Valley of California. They have both been with Jetronics for about four years and have worked with other electronics firms in the Valley. Both are around 35 years old, have similar educational backgrounds, and have been supervising teams of ten people for the last three years. They are similar, but oh, so different! Just ask Lillian Hill who has worked with them both.

Lillian worked in George's team for fourteen months before being transferred to Sam's group, where she has been for the last five months. She says that the difference is like night and day.

"George never trusted the members of the team to do the jobs he assigned them," said Lillian. "He was constantly checking up on you, making sure you followed his directions to the letter. He would assign me something, something I could easily handle, and then he would check on me at least four times a day to be sure things were going along OK. I never felt as though George could allow any of the team members to accept any credit for a job well done. He had to have all the credit.

"Since I was transferred (at my own request, I might add) to Sam's team, things are so much better. I really look forward to coming to work each day. When Sam gives me, or any other team member something to do, he treats us like responsible adults who know how to accomplish things. Sam is there if we need help, but he doesn't perch on our shoulder trying to catch us in a mistake.

"George was constantly checking on things. His favorite expression was, "I'm like General Motors. I sweat the details." Whenever any of us would come up with an idea, George would say "That's no good!" before he even gave it any thought. But somehow, if the idea was a good one, we'd see it introduced with his name on it eventually. George had to be the Golden Boy.

"When I first went into Cold Start (Sam's department)," Lillian continued, "Sam said that if I had any ideas about how to improve operations I should bounce them off him. He said that this was a *team*, and that all of the players (us workers) were important components of that team. He said that he was not planning on remaining supervisor of Cold Start forever, and that he wanted one of us to eventually have the chance to move up to his position when he was promoted.

"George was also a moody boss. When he was in a bad mood, he seemed to take it out on the rest of us. Nothing we did would be right. Everything we did would be wrong. And the worst of it was that you never knew from one day to the next what his mood would be.

Source: By Robert D. Goddard, Appalachian State University.

"Sam never gets personal—he is a true professional. His son may have thrown a baseball through the sliding glass door, and you'd never know it. He is always the same—and the contrast between him and George, well . . ."

Questions

1. How would you describe George as a supervisor? Sam?
2. How do the personalities of these supervisors influence the people who work for them?
3. Using some concepts discussed in the chapter, describe the personalities of George and Sam.
4. Do you think that George's style of supervision would suit the personalities of certain workers? What types of workers?

Different Strokes for Different Folks: Teaching Note

This case deals with the managerial styles of two supervisors, George and Sam, as seen by an individual who had worked with both. Managerial style is affected by personality, as evidenced by this case.

George trusted none of his workers, while Sam urged them to work on their own. Is this a contrast between Theory X and Theory Y?

George wanted all of the credit for ideas and was concerned with the tiniest of details. Sam actively worked to develop the decision-making capabilities of his team members and tried to prepare them for managerial responsibilities.

Questions

1. How would you describe George as a supervisor? Sam?

There are many responses possible for this question. As noted above, George had Theory X views of workers and did not trust them to work effectively without supervision. Sam, on the other hand, held Theory Y views of his team members. He delegated effectively, sought their ideas and opinions, and actively tried to develop their potential.

2. How do the personalities of these supervisors influence the people who work for them?

There is ample evidence in this case that George and Sam's personalities influenced Lillian's attitudes toward them. She said she looked forward to coming to work every day after transferring to Cold Start, while working for George was a task to be dreaded.

3. Using some of the concepts discussed in the chapter, describe George and Sam's personalities.

Students may wish to discuss locus of control. Type A/ Type B, Machiavellianism, social skills, self-efficacy, self-esteem, and the work-related motives of achievement, affiliation, and power.

4. Do you think that George's style of supervision would suit the personalities of certain workers? What types of workers?

An interesting concept, asking whether any workers would be happy working for George. Those workers who were Internals might be satisfied with a supervisor like George.

Experiencing Organizational Behavior Notes

Machiavellianism in Action: The $10 Game

This exercise offers students a way of observing High Machs (ruthless and self-centered people who are willing to manipulate others for their own gain) in action. Instructions for playing the "$10 Game," which involves dividing ten slips of paper, each representing $1, are given. The rule of the game is this: the money will belong to any two people who can agree on how to divide it. Following the exercise are questions that ask students to speculate on what happened in the game, what agreement was reached (and how it was reached), and if someone with a High Mach personality was discovered among the participants.

Additional Experiential Exercise

Change or Stability?

Would you ever consider skydiving for the thrills and danger it produces? Do you like to gamble? Would you like leading a life like Indiana Jones in the movies *Raiders of the Lost Ark, Indiana Jones and the Temple of Doom,* and *Indiana Jones and the Last Crusade?* If so, you may be a *high sensation seeker*—the kind of person who enjoys excitement, danger, and unpredictability. If, in contrast, the things just mentioned frighten you, and you prefer a life of calmness, order, and tranquility, you are probably a *low sensation seeker.*

Source: Adapted from an in-class exercise developed by Robert D. Goddard, Appalachian State University.

Are you a high sensation seeker, a low sensation seeker, or somewhere in between? To find out, please answer the questions below. For each, simply circle the letter of the choice (*A* or *B*) that best describes the way you feel.

1. A. I often wish I could become a mountain climber.
   B. I can't understand people who risk their necks climbing mountains.
2. A. A sensible person avoids activities that are dangerous.
   B. I sometimes like to do things that are a little frightening.
3. A. I would like to take up waterskiing.
   B. I would not like to take up waterskiing.

4. A. I would like to try surfboard riding.
   B. I would not like to try surfboard riding.
5. A. I would not like to learn to fly an airplane.
   B. I would like to learn to fly an airplane.
6. A. I would like to go scuba diving.
   B. I prefer the surface of the water to the depths.
7. A. I would like to try parachute jumping.
   B. I would never want to jump out of an airplane with a parachute.
8. A. I enjoy spending time in the familiar surroundings of home.
   B. I get very restless if I have to stay around home for long.
9. A. Sailing long distances in small sailing boats is foolhardy.
   B. I would like to sail long distances in a small, seaworthy boat.
10. A. Skiing fast down a high mountain slope is a good way to end up on crutches.
    B. I'd enjoy skiing fast down a mountain slope.

Change or Stability: Teaching Note

This is a self-assessment of one aspect of personality—sensation-seeking. Again, this is a dimension of personality that students find interesting. It also has an impact on such organizational topics as *reaction to change* and *risk propensity*.

Scoring Key

Have students score one point for each of the following responses; then have them add up their scores.

1. A	3. A	5. B	7. A	9. B
2. B	4. A	6. A	8. B	10. B

If their total sensation-seeking scores fall in the following ranges, interpret the scores according to the table below.

0–2 = Low
3–5 = Moderately Low
6–8 = Moderately High
9–10 = High

Additional Readings

Gist, M. E., & Mitchell, T. R. (1992). Self-efficacy; A theoretical analysis of its determinants and malleability. *Academy of Management Review, 17*(2), 183–211.

Pervin, L. A. (1989). Persons, situations, interactions: The history of a controversy and a discussion of theoretical models. *Academy of Management Review, 14*(3), 350–360.

∎ 7 ∎

STRESS: ITS NATURE, IMPACT, AND MANAGEMENT

CHAPTER OUTLINE

Stress: Its Basic Nature
Stress: Its Major Causes
    Work-Related Causes of Stress
    Personal (Life-Related) Causes of Stress
Stress: Some Major Effects
    Stress and Health: The Silent Killer
    Stress and Task Performance
    Burnout: Stress and Psychological Adjustment
Individual Differences in Resistance to Stress
    Optimism: A Buffer against Stress
    Hardiness: Viewing Stress as Challenge
    The Type A Behavior Pattern Revisited
    Tension Discharge Rate
    Coping Styles: Problem-Focused and
        Emotion-Focused

Managing Stress: Some Useful Tactics
    Personal Approaches to Stress Management: Tactics
        That Work
    Organization-Based Strategies for Managing Stress

Special Sections

A Question of Ethics Sexual Harassment: A Pervasive
Problem in Work Settings

OB in Practice A Tale of Lost Horizons: Or What Can
Happen When a Good Company Goes Bad

An International/Multicultural Perspective The
Stress-Deterrent Effects of Religiosity: Evidence
from Israeli Kibbutzim

LEARNING OBJECTIVES

After reading this chapter, you should be able to:
1. Define stress in terms of its physiological, behavioral, and cognitive components.
2. Describe several major work-related causes of stress and several personal factors that also contribute to stress in organizational settings.
3. Describe the impact of stress on personal health, task performance, and decision making.
4. Define burnout, describe its major components, and indicate why it occurs.

5. Explain how reactions to stress are affected by several personal characteristics, such as optimism, hardiness, and the Type A behavior pattern.
6. Describe physiological, behavioral, and cognitive techniques individuals can use to manage their own stress.
7. Describe several techniques that organizations can use to help manage stress among their employees.

Chapter Overview

This chapter introduces the topic of stress by defining what is meant by stress, including its physiological and cognitive aspects. The chapter then discusses the major sources of stress, including stress induced at work and stress induced by day-to-day living. Next, the chapter deals with the major effects of stress. Specifically considered are the importance of stress to our health and well-being, the effects of stress on task performance and decision making, and the role of stress in producing burnout. Ways that individual dif-

ferences in reactions to stress make some people more resistant to the effects of stress than others are also discussed. Attention is paid to the role of optimism, hardiness, the Type A behavior pattern, and tension discharge rates as key moderators of the effects of stress. Finally, the chapter presents several useful techniques for managing stress, both on and off the job.

Three special sections appear in this chapter. A Question of Ethics (Sexual Harassment: A Pervasive Problem in Work Settings) provides a discussion of a major organizational stressor—sexual harassment. Several illustrations of sexual harassment are provided. A CNN video about sexual harassment is available for use in conjunction with this section. An OB in Practice section (A Tale of Lost Horizons: Or What Can Happen When a Good Company Goes Bad) describes the stress and its consequences suffered by employees of Pan American Airlines during its financial decline and subsequent demise. And an International/Multicultural Perspective (The Stress-Deterrent Effects of Religiosity: Evidence from Israeli Kibbutzim) describes the findings of a study showing that being a member of a religious community seems to buffer the potentially harmful impacts of stress. Personal religiosity, however, was not found to protect individuals from the ill effects of stress.

The Case in Point (Stressed Out at Nordstrom Stores) presents a behind-the-scenes look at how Nordstrom Stores achieves a high level of customer service, and the stressors that its employees experience in the process. And the Experiencing Organizational Behavior exercise (Personal Worry List) provides students with a self-help activity targeted to get them to identify (and stop worrying about!) worries that are either not important or beyond their control.

Lecture and Review Questions

Describe the basic nature of stress.

In order to fully comprehend the nature of stress, we must consider three related issues: the physiological aspects of stress, the nature of various stressors in the environment, and a person's cognitive appraisal of a potentially stressful situation. The physiological aspects of stress refer to our bodies' reactions to stressful situations. Initially, there is an alarm reaction where the body prepares itself physiologically for the stress to come. This is followed by a resistance stage, where activation remains high, but subsides to levels that can be maintained over longer periods of time. Eventually, however, if the stress persists, the body's resources are depleted and exhaustion occurs. If stress persists past this point, serious biological damage can occur. Stressors are those aspects in the environment that can induce stress. These factors can vary dramatically, but tend to be so intense as to overload our systems, to evoke simultaneous incompatible responses, and to be uncontrollable. The cognitive component of stress refers to the individual's assessment of a potentially stressful situation. From this perspective stress occurs when a person perceives a situation is somehow threatening to a goal and feels that he or she will be unable to cope with the potentially threatening situation. Thus, stress can be defined as a pattern of emotional states and physiological reactions occurring in situations where individuals perceive

threats to their important goals that they may be unable to meet.

What are the major work-related causes of stress?

It seems that by their very nature some jobs are more stressful than others. Jobs that require making many decisions, constant monitoring of devices, working in unpleasant conditions, and performing unstructured tasks appear to produce more stress than other jobs. In addition, role conflict, competing demands, also results in stress, even though these effects may be diminished by warmth and support at work. Role ambiguity, uncertainty about what is required on the job, is also a source of stress, although most people endure modest levels of ambiguity without much problem. Work-related stress can also be the result of employees being overloaded (either by having too many tasks or by having tasks assigned them for which they lack necessary skills), or underloaded (having too few tasks or tasks that are not challenging enough) resulting in boredom and monotony, which are also stress inducing. Jobs which require an employee to be responsible for other people—their motivation, leadership, and discipline—are also more stressful than other jobs. Jobs that fail to provide employees with social support also tend to result in more stress. Social support seems capable of alleviating stress on the job by providing someone to turn to for help, by providing suggestions for ways of dealing with stress, and by simply providing someone to talk to about stressful events on the job. Lack of participation in decision making also induces stress on the job as employees feel they are out of control. Finally, stress on the job can be the result of specific events such as performance evaluations, poor working conditions, or any major change in the workplace (such as a merger).

What are some important life-related sources of stress?

Major stressful life events and daily hassles appear to be the major sources of stress in employees' personal lives. Stressful live events include such things as death of spouse or marriage—both these events require a major readjustment in a person's life. Most people who experience several such events in a single year often become seriously ill, although some persons seem to be more resistant to this type of stress than others. These traumatic events, however, do not occur frequently. Daily hassles refer to common day-to-day disruptions of our tranquility such as shopping, preparing meals, loneliness, noise, crime, and financial worries.

Some employees carry their own stress with them. What does this mean?

A growing body of research suggests that while stress is indeed generated by external conditions, it is influenced by personal factors too. Some people carry stress around with them, tending to experience rather high levels of stress no matter where they work. One study (details reported in the text) found that the level of stress experienced by people at the time they joined an organization was similar to the level of stress that they experienced nine months into their employment with the organization. The conclusion: Some stress at work seems to reflect personal dispositions and tendencies as much as conditions actually prevailing in an organization. Recall the effects of negative affectivity on organizational behavior discussed in chapter 6 (Personality). This personality characteristic may also be an important personal source of stress.

What are the major effects of stress?

The effects of stress are seen in all aspects of life. Stress has been found related to heart disease, high blood pressure, ulcers, and hardening of the arteries. Prolonged exposure to stress also appears capable of weakening the body's immune system. Stress is also related to task performance. Although it is widely assumed that stress initially arouses good performance, there are cases where even low levels of stress cause a decrease in performance. A large body of research indicates that as stress-induced arousal increases, task performance may at first rise, but at some point, begins to fall. The precise location of this *inflection point* (the point at which the direction of the function reverses) seems to depend, to an important extent, on the complexity of the task being performed. The greater the complexity, the lower the levels of arousal at which a downturn in performance occurs. Even with this in mind, however, there are some people for whom stress appears to be a motivational force, and their performance actually increases as they rise to the challenge.

What is the effect of stress on decision making?

The effects of stress on decision making are mostly negative. Individuals making decisions under high stress conditions make more errors than they do at other times. Under these conditions, individuals tend to make their decisions before considering all of the alternatives available to them (premature closure). And they tend to examine the alternatives that they do consider in a less systematic manner than they would under low stress conditions (non-systematic scanning).

Group decision making can also suffer when performed under high stress conditions. Groups tend to centralize authority and decision making when performing under stress. This creates a vicious cycle whereby group members become more stressed because they are deprived of opportunity to participate in decision making. Group members are also less likely to support the group's decisions because they have not had the opportunity to participate in the decision making process. Clearly, if the ultimate effectiveness of the group's decision depends upon group member acceptance, the centralization caused by stress is dysfunctional. However, the effects of stress on group decision making may not all be negative. Recent research shows that stress can exert a positive influence on a group's decision making process. Paradoxically, this research (described in text) shows that operating under stressful conditions tends to make group leaders more responsive to the inputs of group members. Clearly more research is needed in this area, but for now at least, it appears that the effects of stress on decision group decision making are more complicated than once assumed. Indeed, stress may have positive, as well as negative, effects on group decision making.

What are the causes of burnout and can it be reversed?

Burnout is a syndrome of emotional, physical, and mental exhaustion resulting from prolonged exposure to stress on the job. Burnout victims have low energy and always feel tired. In addition, burnout victims report headaches and feelings of nausea, tend to feel helpless and trapped, become cynical about others, and come to feel that they have not accomplished much in the past and are unlikely to do so in the future. Jobs where employees' efforts seem fruitless or unappreciated, offer poor opportunities for advancement, maintain inflexible rules, and promote leaders who have little concern for their subordinates, all contribute to burnout. Victims of burnout often seek new jobs or careers or withdraw from their jobs either by moving into administration or by just marking time on their jobs while no longer being involved. Burnout can be reversed if stress is reduced, if there is an increase in social support, and if the victims develop hobbies and outside interests.

What are some of the variables that have been identified as individual differences in reactions to stress?

Individuals clearly differ in their reactions to stress and several variables have been identified that seem related to these differences. One such variable is where the person falls on the optimism-pessimism dimension. Optimists are much more resistant to stress than pessimists. This seems to be because these persons react to stress by making and enacting plans to deal with the stress and because they are more likely to seek social support in times of stress. Another individual difference variable is hardiness. Hardy persons are those who show higher levels of commitment to their jobs and lives; they believe they can influence important events in their lives; and they perceive change as a challenge and an opportunity. Persons scoring higher on hardiness reported better health than those less hardy, even after encountering major stressful life changes. Also, Type A persons not only respond more strongly to stress, they actually seek out stressful situations. Finally, tension discharge rates refer to the rate at which individuals can dissipate their job-related stress at the end of the working day. Persons who cannot do this effectively (lower discharge rates) tend to bring stress home with them and to report poorer health.

What are some of the more effective techniques for managing stress?

In general, increasing physical fitness is a major factor in increasing a person's tolerance for stress. Losing weight, quitting smoking, and exercising regularly all help a person deal with stress. In addition, individuals can work on developing coping skills. Most of these techniques involve replacing strain with relaxation, such as relaxation training or meditation. Individuals can also manage stress by taking short vacations from work and developing outside interests.

Organizations can also help employees manage stress. Decentralization of authority reduces feelings of helplessness, allows employees more participation in decision making, helps insure fairer organizational policies, and enhances communications within the organization—all of which have been found to reduce work-related stress. In addition, organizations can help employees deal with and reduce stress by enriching jobs so that boredom is decreased and challenge increased. Organizations can also reduce stress found on particular jobs by eliminating hazardous or unpleasant working conditions. Finally, a growing number of organizations are implementing employee fitness programs to increase their employees' ability to resist stress.

An interesting way to extend discussion of stress-reducing techniques is to invite students to talk about what personal stress-reduction techniques they use, and/or what stress-management programs their employers offer.

Other Teaching Suggestions

1. There are several reactions to stress as noted in the text, but the most discernible ones are the physical reactions. It is often difficult to measure these reactions with much accuracy, although the symptoms range from chemicals in urine to perspiration and rapid heartbeat. If possible, it would be interesting to demonstrate some of these effects. Stress can usually be induced by having students perform a task with repeated interruptions, by showing a particularly frightening scene from a film (like the bathtub scene from *Fatal Attraction*), by asking personal and embar-

rassing questions (which do not really need to be answered), or by simply announcing a surprise exam worth half the course grade. It might be possible to then monitor (at least at a crude level) some of the physiological changes that follow. It should also be noted that this is the basic principle behind lie detectors which are increasingly being criticized as inaccurate.

2. One of the more interesting studies of stress was conducted some 30 years ago by Harry Harlow. Two monkeys were involved, one of whom received electric shocks if the other monkey made incorrect choices. The *executive monkey* as it became known, was supposed to guess which light was going to blink or behind which door a banana was hidden. When the executive monkey was correct, it was he who received the reward, but when he was wrong, it was the other monkey who received the shock. The monkey being shocked could do nothing to bring about or prevent the shock, so it was totally helpless. The monkeys watched each other with only a set of bars between them. After some time, one of the monkeys developed stress-related ulcers. Which one? Not the helpless monkey, but the executive monkey who was given the responsibility of keeping the other monkey from being shocked.

3. The entire Life Events Scale is available in the original article. Survey the class on their potential for health problems. You might also ask the class to think back to last year's events. You'll find that some class members have, in fact, collected a large number of stress points, yet have not had any health problems. This might be a good lead-in to a discussion of individual differences in reactions to stress.

4. Role conflict is indeed an important source of work-related stress. Is is also a way of life for *boundary spanners* such as foremen who, although they are still members of a work group, also represent the first line of management, thus spanning the boundary between labor and management. Lately, however, a new wrinkle in role conflict has been discussed. As women move out of traditional homemaker roles, and as the frequency of dual-career couples increases, more and more people must balance the demands of work with the demands of a family. Whether this translates to sharing responsibility for meals or truly sharing responsibility for parenting, it is clear that this represents a new source of stress. There has been a fair amount of research done recently on the problems of balancing work and nonwork aspects of one's life, and this might be worth discussing.

5. The text mentions several high-stress jobs, but let's focus on just one of those—air-traffic controllers. These people are doing a job that requires constant vigilance, and processing many separate bits of information in a generally monotonous work setting. All of

this is made even more stressful by the costs of a mistake. It should not be surprising that this was one of the first jobs for which psychological tests were used in making selection decisions. Also, given what was said about stress management, it seems reasonable that air-traffic controllers should be more concerned with shorter hours than with higher pay. What other kinds of jobs seem particularly stressful and why?

6. There are many examples around us of stress management techniques. If biofeedback equipment is available, the results of these techniques can be demonstrated quite graphically. Perhaps an even more dramatic demonstration, however, can be put together with the help of a local Lamaze class. Relaxation techniques are a major part of prepared childbirth, and it is amazing how relaxation and breathing exercises can help reduce perceptions of stress and even pain.

Case in Point Notes

Stressed Out at Nordstrom Stores

This case is about working as a salesperson at Nordstrom Stores, Inc., the nationwide chain of upscale department stores renowned for its outstanding customer service and profitability. Nordstrom employees have become known by counselors who treat them as "Nervous Nordies." Why are these employees nervous? Stress—lots of it! Where does all this stress come from? The case describes how Nordstrom man-

ages its sales force, providing numerous examples of organizational stressors. The case includes several illustrations of how Nordstrom's organizational stressors impacted various employees. Several moderators of stress are suggested in the case. For example, while Nordstrom's management system destroys some employees, other employees thrive within the system. Overall, this case is comprehensive in scope, touching many topics discussed in the chapter.

Following the case are a set of discussion questions asking students to identify the causes and effects of employee stress found at Nordstrom Stores, and to consider why it is that some people thrive under Nordstrom's system, but other people become so stressed that they become ill and/or leave the company. Discussion of this case is likely to be quite lively, particularly if any students have worked for, or are currently working for, Nordstrom as a salesperson. Stories about Nordstrom, similar to the one presented in this case, have appeared in several national newspapers and have appeared on *60 Minutes*. The publicity surrounding Nordstrom and its management practices excites students about this case.

A related discussion that has been very fruitful when discussing this case is to ask about jobs that students have had or are currently working in. What stressors do they experience? How much stress do they bring with them, as part of their personality? How much stress that they experience at work is a carryover from their college work? Count on this avenue of discussion to be very lively indeed.

Additional Cases

The Coach

Donald Bruce was in a dilemma. He was overcommitted and he knew it. Don had just taken on too much, but he didn't know how to deal with it all.

Background

Don is a faculty member in the College of Business at a medium-sized university. He has been on the faculty for about ten years and really loves his job. He is married and has three children, ages 16, 14, and 5. Up until four years ago, for him the world of intercollegiate athletics consisted of watching football and basketball on TV and reading about sports in the paper. Oh, he had been friendly with the university's soccer team coach and had supported the program since he had become a member of the faculty. And he had participated on his university's swimming team as an undergraduate, but that was 30 years ago. He had no ambitions of becoming a college coach in any sport.

All of that changed one day when he received a telephone call asking him to help start a women's club soccer

program at the university. It seems a group of female university students telephoned the men's soccer coach and asked him to recommend some faculty member who would serve as an advisor to the Women's Soccer Club. The men's coach mentioned Don's name, they called, and he agreed to serve.

Serving as advisor, however, was more than Don had counted on. The women had the goal of eventually having women's soccer designated as a varsity sport at the university. In order to do this, a strategy designed to meet that goal was formulated. The strategy was long-term in nature. During the first year, the club team would play other club teams in the state, gaining experience and learning. Then, the club team would try to schedule games with varsity teams, in order to show the athletic department that they were capable of competing on the varsity level.

In addition to his regular faculty duties, Don was expected to compile competition schedules, design and run practice sessions, try to raise funds to support the program, drive the bus to games, and attend to all of the many details associated with the operation of an athletic program. He found out that soccer is a year-round sport with a major fall season, indoor tournaments in the winter, and a short out-door schedule in the spring.

Donald Bruce was also an active consultant to various firms in the region. He conducted training seminars and held non-credit programs on a continuing basis. This work took him out of town at least three times a month. He also served on the National Council of a professional student organization. Additionally, Don was involved in research and publishing, and served the regional and national professional societies in his field.

He got little support from his boss, the department chairperson, for his work with the women's soccer team. When performance review time came along, his activities with the team counted for little compared with activities such as research and publication.

Needless to say, all of these activities placed demands on his time. He worked long hours and most weekends. After a period of time, Don's department chair noticed that there seemed to be a decline in his student evaluations. Requests for information and replies to memos appeared to take longer than in the past. Don was irritable at times and seemed to withdraw from the normal social activities of his department. His home life began to suffer, and he and his wife eventually separated and divorced. The financial difficulties created by the divorce settlement added to the tension Don was feeling.

Don began to have physical problems. He lost weight at a fairly rapid rate, even though he had not been involved in an exercise or diet program. He did not sleep well at night, often arising at 3:00 A.M. to read a book or magazine. Upon discovering some intestinal bleeding, Don went to his family doctor, who recommended a specialist. After extensive testing at an out-of-town hospital, Don underwent surgery to alleviate his symptoms.

As an activity in one of his classes, Don administered the Life Events Survey (see page IS-55) to his class. He decided to complete the scale while the rest of the class did. When his score totalled almost 400, Don knew that he would have to make some changes in his life.

Questions

1. What seems to be the problem with Donald Bruce?
2. If you were Don's friend or his family physician, what steps would you suggest Don take to overcome his problem?
3. In addition to individual strategies for coping with stress, what organizational strategies might apply in this case?

The Coach: Teaching Note

This is a classic case of how stress can affect an individual in the workplace. Don has taken on too many responsibilities and his performance has suffered as a result. He is doing a lot of things, but probably none of them well. Don is exhibiting many of the emotional and physical reactions to stress.

Don is suffering from both role overload and role conflict, topics that will be covered in more detail in chapter 8. Role overload and role conflict are complementary phenomena. When individuals experience conflict in competing roles (family member and faculty member) they often report difficulty in having enough time to get their work done.

Questions

1. What seems to be the problem with Donald Bruce?

   Don is suffering the physical and emotional effects of stress. As noted in the chapter, stress manifests itself in many ways. The irritability Don is experiencing, the decline in work performance, the physical symptoms of weight loss and intestinal bleeding, all could be manifestations of the stress he is experiencing.

2. If you were Don's friend or his family physician, what steps would you suggest Don take to overcome his problem?

   You might suggest some of the individual strategies for coping with stress suggested in the text, such as a program of physical activity, coping skills training, meditation, etc. A program of time management, for example, might help Don organize his life so that he would have the time to work on (and enjoy) all of these activities. A regular program of running or swimming might be the best way of managing stress for Don.

3. In addition to individual strategies for coping with stress, what organizational strategies might apply in this case?

   Delegation might be one method Don could employ for coping with the stress. Perhaps he could find someone who would be interested in managing the day-to-day details of the women's soccer program—a physical education graduate student who would like the experience of working with a program like this.

Stress is a problem in the work force today. This case is a true example of one such problem. Don did become involved in an exercise program and persuaded a graduate student to help with the soccer team. While Don does the scheduling and travels with the team, the graduate student handles all of the practices. He has remarried and his home life is very happy (he even has a gorgeous new baby boy). All in all, things are looking up for Don.

Bob Lyons

Part A

Those who knew Bob Lyons thought extremely well of him. He was a highly successful executive who held an important position in a large company. As his supervisors saw him, he was aggressive, with a knack for getting things done through other people. He worked hard and set a vigorous pace. He drove himself relentlessly. In less than ten years with his company, he had moved through several positions of responsibility.

Lyons had always been a good athlete. He was proud of his skill in swimming, hunting, golf, and tennis. In his college days he had lettered in football and baseball. On weekends, he preferred to undertake rebuilding and repairing projects around the house or hunt, interspersing other sports for a change of pace. He was usually engaged, it seemed, in hard, physical work.

Source: Reprinted by permission of *Harvard Business Review.* An excerpt from "What Killed Bob Lyons?" by Harry Levinson, January/February 1963. Copyright © 1963 by the President and Fellows of Harvard College; all rights reserved.

His life was not all work, however. He was active in his church and in the Boy Scouts. His wife delighted in entertaining and in being with other people, so their social life was a round of many parties and social activities. They shared much of their life with their three children.

Early in the spring of his ninth year with the company, Bob Lyons spoke with the vice president to whom he reported.

"Things are a little quiet around here," he said. "Most of the big projects are over. The new building is finished and we have a lot of things on the ball which four years ago were all fouled up. I don't like this idea of just riding a desk and looking out the window. I like action."

About a month later, Lyons was assigned additional responsibilities. He rushed into them with his usual vigor. Once again he seemed to be buoyant and cheerful. After six months on the assignment, Lyons had the project rolling smoothly. Again he spoke to the vice president, reporting that he was out of projects. The vice president, pleased with Lyons' performance, told him that he had earned the right to do a little dreaming and planning; and furthermore, dreaming and planning were a necessary part of the position he now held, toward which he had aspired for so long. Bob Lyons listened as his boss spoke, but it was plain to the vice president that the answer did not satisfy him.

About three months after this meeting, the vice president began to notice that replies to his memos and inquiries were not coming back from Lyons with their usual rapidity. He noticed also that Lyons was developing a tendency to put things off, a most unusual behavior pattern for him. He observed that Lyons became easily angered and disturbed over minor difficulties that previously had not irritated him at all.

Bob Lyons then became involved in a conflict with two other executives over a policy issue. Such conflicts were not unusual in the organization since, inevitably, there were varying points of view on many issues. The conflict was not a personal one, but it did require intervention from higher management before a solution could be reached. In the process of resolving the conflict, Lyons' point of view prevailed on some questions, but not on others.

A few weeks after this conflict had been resolved, Lyons went to the vice president's office. He wanted to have a long, private talk, he said. His first words were, "I'm losing my grip. The old steam is gone. I've had diarrhea for four weeks and several times in the past three weeks I've lost my breakfast. I'm worried, and yet I don't know what about. I feel that some people have lost confidence in me."

He talked with his boss for an hour and a half. The vice president recounted his achievements in the company to reassure him. He then asked if Lyons thought he should see a doctor. Lyons agreed that he should and, in the presence of the vice president, called his family doctor for an appointment. By this time the vice president was very much concerned. He called Mrs. Lyons and arranged to meet her for lunch the next day. She reported that, in addition to his other symptoms, her husband had difficulty sleeping. She was relieved that the vice president had called her, because she was beginning to become worried and had herself planned to call the vice president. Both were now alarmed.

Questions
1. How do you explain what is happening with Bob Lyons?

2. Evaluate the way in which his situation had been handled by the people around him.
3. As his boss, what actions would you take?

Part B

The vice president and Lyons' wife decided that they should get Lyons into a hospital rather than wait for the doctor's appointment which was still a week off.

The next day Lyons was taken to the hospital. Meanwhile, with Mrs. Lyons' permission, the vice president reported to the family doctor Lyons' recent job behavior and the nature of their conversations. When the vice president finished, the doctor concluded, "All he needs is a good rest. We don't want to tell him that it may be mental or nervous." The vice president replied that he didn't know what the cause was, but he knew that Lyons needed help quickly.

During the five days in the hospital, Lyons was subjected to extensive laboratory tests. The vice president visited him daily. Lyons seemed to welcome the rest and sedation at night. He said he was eating and sleeping much better. He talked about company problems, though he did not speak spontaneously without encouragement. While Lyons was out of the room, another patient who shared his hospital room confided to the vice president that he was worried about Lyons. "He seems to be so morose and depressed that I'm afraid he's losing his mind," the man said.

By this time the president of the company, who had been kept informed, was also becoming concerned. He had talked to a psychiatrist and planned to talk to Lyons about the psychiatric treatment if his doctor did not suggest it. Meanwhile, Lyons was discharged from the hospital as being without physical illness, and his doctor recommended a vacation. Lyons then remained at home for several days where he was again visited by the vice president. He and his wife took a trip to visit friends. He was then ready to come back to work, but the president suggested that he take another week off. The president also suggested that they visit together when Lyons returned.

Questions
1. Apparently, Bob Lyons had no physical reasons for his problems. What other explanation might there be?
2. Lyons' family doctor thought that rest would be the best treatment for Lyons. Do you agree or disagree? Why?
3. Did the president handle the situation correctly? Why or why not? What would you have done?

Part C

A few days later, the president telephoned Lyons' home. Mrs. Lyons could not find him to answer the telephone. After fifteen minutes she still had not found him and called the vice president about her concern. By the time the vice president arrived at the Lyons' home, the police were already there. Bob Lyons had committed suicide.

Bob Lyons: Teaching Note

The Bob Lyons case outlines the history of a dynamic, aggressive individual and his progress through the firm for which he has worked for more than nine years. Lyons is an active, athletic individual, quick to rise to the challenge. He becomes dissatisfied only when "things are a little quiet around here. I don't like this idea of just riding the desk, looking out the window—I like action." In the course of his career, Lyons had moved further and further away from the daily operations of the organization to a position which might be best described as near sedentary, one in which the daily organizational firefighting has given way to "a little dreaming and planning," a necessary part of the new position which he holds. The case traces Bob Lyons' gradual disintegration from a competent, indeed almost an ideal employee, to procrastination, irritability, minor psychosomatic illness, major psychological dysfunction, and ultimately to his suicide.

This case was originally written to illustrate the concepts of motivation and individual behavior. However, it ties in well with both the material on Type A/Type B behavior from chapter 6, and the material on stress and its resulting outcomes from this chapter.

The theme is dramatic. Hopefully, the students will not conclude that it is melodrama, pure and simple. Suicide is, unfortunately, something with which students on college and high school campuses have had to deal. Stress, role conflict, career development, and organizational responsibility for its members are central issues which could be addressed by the Bob Lyons case. The responses to the questions from *Part A* and *Part B* should lead to a lively class discussion of the issues mentioned above.

The evidence suggests that Lyons has moved from a job in which there was an excellent fit with his personality (outcomes of high satisfaction and excellent performance) to one which was a grave misfit (outcomes of extreme dissatisfaction and problem performance).

This case should be done as an in-class activity. Students should read *Part A* and respond to the questions. A discussion of the issues raised in *Part A* should be completed before the students proceed to *Part B*. Again, discuss the further developments and responses to the questions in this part before proceeding to *Part C*.

Responses to the questions from *Part A* are designed to find out something about Lyons and his personality. What makes Bob Lyons tick? What aspects of his personality lend themselves to the good individual-job fit evidenced in the first part of this case? A review of Type A personalities should help shape responses to the first question.

Good questions to help stimulate discussion might be: What makes Lyons run? What drives him? What role do you see work playing in Lyons' life? What might explain the symptoms we see developing here? How should the organization handle it? This is a classic case of the Peter Principle—promoting someone to their level of incompetency. Bob Lyons may be cognitively able to handle this new job and its different tasks, but is he emotionally able to handle this job? Did Bob's wife and the vice president do the right things to help Bob deal effectively with this problem?

After this discussion period on *Part A*, you should ask students to read *Part B*. The discussion of it is usually considerably shorter than that on the first part. You can get it started by reiterating your initial questions, then focus on the vice president's suggestion of a vacation, and the president's suggestion that he take a few more days off. Lyons' main need is to feel competent, active, constructive, and needed by his organization. The suggestion of a vacation and days off may be interpreted by him as a vote of no confidence and will provide little opportunity to satisfy that need.

Finally, with the discussion of *Part B* concluded, ask students to read *Part C*. Many students may laugh nervously. Many will feel a real personal impact. It is useful to explore the feelings of the class about the case at this point. Why the laughter? If the response is that the case is melodramatic, simply indicate that suicide is real, and that executive (and student) suicides are by no means unknown.

It is valuable to conclude the discussion by raising the issue of responsibility for career development and career management. We tend to focus on the organization, but the individual must also play a major role. Perhaps the greatest tragedy in the Bob Lyons case is his apparent inability to understand himself. In the absence of that understanding, the individual can hardly make a meaningful contribution to the individual-organization relationship with respect to career development and planning.

Experiencing Organizational Behavior Notes

Personal Worry List

This exercise is about worrying. Worrying is a cause of stress. Do we need to worry? The answer to this question is maybe, but only about some things. Some things are very important, and if we are in a position to do something about them, then it is certainly appropriate to be concerned. But some people seem to worry about everything. Is it necessary to worry so much, about so many things? Is this much worrying worth the price in terms of the stress generated? Not likely. This exercise leads students through the process of identifying the things that they are currently worrying about and then categorizing their worries according to those that are important or not impor-

tant, and those that they can do something about (can be controlled) and those that they cannot do anything about (cannot be controlled). Upon finishing the exercise, students come to recognize that worrying about things that aren't important and/or things that they can't control is an unnecessary source of stress, and in the interest of bettering their own health and performance, should be stopped!

Some students may recall a well-known prayer that makes a point similar to the point of this exercise. This prayer reads as follows:

> God grant me the serenity to accept the things I cannot change; courage to change the things I can; and wisdom to know the difference.

Additional Experiential Exercise

Life Events Survey

Instructions

The list below contains a number of events that can be stressful to the individual. Review and identify those events you have experienced during the past 12 months. Mark your score in the column headed *Your Score*. An event not experienced should be left blank. Add the individual event scores to obtain your *Total Score*.

EVENT	SCALE VALUE	YOUR SCORE
Death of spouse	100	_____
Divorce	73	_____
Marital separation	65	_____
Jail term	63	_____
Death of close family member	63	_____
Personal injury or illness	53	_____
Marriage	50	_____
Fired at work	47	_____
Marital reconciliation	45	_____
Retirement	45	_____
Change in health of family member	44	_____
Pregnancy	40	_____
Sex difficulties	39	_____
Gain of new family member	39	_____
Business readjustment	38	_____
Change in financial status	38	_____
Death of a close friend	37	_____
Change to a different line of work	36	_____
Change in number of arguments with spouse	35	_____
Mortgage over $10,000	31	_____
Foreclosure of mortgage or loan	30	_____
Change in responsibilities at work	29	_____
Son or daughter leaving home	29	_____
Trouble with in-laws	29	_____
Outstanding personal achievement	28	_____
Spouse begins or stops work	26	_____
Begin or end school	26	_____
Change in living conditions	25	_____
Revision of personal habits	24	_____
Trouble with boss	23	_____
Change in work hours or conditions	20	_____
Change in residence/schools	20	_____
Change in recreation/church activities/social	19	_____
Change in sleeping habits	16	_____
Vacation/Christmas	12	_____
Minor violations of the law	11	_____

Total score for previous 12 months _____

Life Events Survey: Teaching Note

The purpose of this exercise is to provide an opportunity for the student to measure the level of stress he or she has experienced over the past 12 months.

Scoring

The scoring process for the Life Events Survey is very simple. Students are to identify the Life Events they have experienced over the past 12 months and place the Scale Value for that event in the column headed *Your Score*. Note that if a student has experienced a particular Life Event more than once during the past 12 months, he or she should multiply the Scale Value for that event by the number of occurrences, and place the result in the *Your Score* column. Students are then to add up their scores and record the total score.

Note that some of the Life Events are considered pleasant events by most people. Christmas, personal achievement, marriage, and other events are probably not regarded as stressful, but research has indicated that these events can be as stressful as so-called problem Life Events.

Interpretation of this total score is also simple. If a student has a total score of more than 200 then he or she has experienced a high level of stress during the past year. Continued high levels of stress have been related to health problems in individuals. In fact, research has indicated that the accumulation of more than 200 total points in a year results in a better than 50 percent chance that the individual will sustain some type of major illness in the following year. If students have Life Events Survey scores greater than 200, they should be encouraged to become involved in some of the stress management techniques described in the chapter.

Additional Readings

Elsass, P. M., & Ralston, D. A. (1989). Individual responses to the stress of career plateauing. *Journal of Management, 15*, 35–48.

Hall, D. T., Richter, J. (1988, August). Balancing work life and home life: What can organizations do to help? *Academy of Management Executive, 2*(3), 213–224.

Leigh, J. H., Lucas, G. H., & Woodman, R. W. (1988). Effects of perceived organizational factors on role stress-job attitude relationship. *Journal of Management, 14*, 41–58.

Wolfe, R. A., Ulrich, D. O., & Parker, D. F. (1987). Employee health management programs: Review, critique, and research agenda. *Journal of Management, 13*, 603–616.

Source: Reprinted with permission from *Journal of Psychosomatic Research, 11*(2), T. Holmes and R. Rahe, "The Social Readjustment Rating Scale," copyright 1967, Pergamon Press plc.

▮ 8 ▮

GROUP DYNAMICS: UNDERSTANDING GROUPS AT WORK

CHAPTER OUTLINE

LEARNING OBJECTIVES

After reading this chapter, you should be able to:

1. Define what a group is and distinguish it from other collections of people.
2. Identify different types of groups operating within organizations and understand how they develop.
3. Describe the different roles played by individuals within organizations.
4. Understand what norms are and how they develop within work groups.
5. Distinguish between different types of status and explain how each influences organizational behavior.
6. Identify the causes and consequences of group cohesiveness within organizations.
7. Describe the phenomenon of social facilitation and explain various reasons for its occurrence.
8. Describe the social loafing effect and some ways of overcoming it.
9. Distinguish between additive, compensatory, disjunctive, and conjunctive groups, and summarize how well they perform relative to individuals working alone.

Chapter Overview

The topic of groups and their function in the workplace in this chapter is defined as formal and informal groups that exist in organizations. The chapter discusses various reasons why people join groups, the stages involved in the development of groups, and some suggestions as to how managers can facilitate the development of groups. The structure of work groups is discussed next, emphasizing the various roles individuals play in groups and the various types of role conflict that can arise. This section also dis-cusses the development of group norms and their impact on group member behavior, and the causes of group cohesiveness and its critical function in group dynamics. The chapter then turns to various aspects of group performance. Social facilitation, or perfor-mance in the presence of others, is discussed, as is social loafing, one of the potential problems facing groups at work. Finally, there is a discussion of various types of group tasks—compensatory tasks, disjunctive tasks, and conjunctive tasks—and how type of task affects group performance.

Three special sections appear in this chapter. A Focus on Research (Choosing to Work Alone or in Groups: Experimental Evidence) presents the findings of a study investigating conditions under which people choose to work in groups or alone. Results show that people prefer to perform work in groups when they are relatively unfamiliar with doing the work. When they are familiar with a particular task, they prefer to work alone. An International/Multicultural Perspective (The Norms of Working Relationships: A Cross-National Comparison) discusses research showing that work-related norms reflect the deep-rooted norms of the broader societal culture within which the work is performed. And an OB in Practice section (Habitual Routines as an Impediment to Group Performance: The Catastrophic Example of Air Florida Flight 90) illustrate how groups—like individuals—can develop habitual routines, the consequences of which can sometimes be disasterous.

The Case in Point (Making Teams Work at Monsanto) describes how self-regulated work groups are developed and implemented at Monsanto's Pensacola, Florida, chemical and nylon manufacturing plant. This case illustrates how difficult it is to introduce self-regulated work groups into the workplace. And the Experiencing Organizational Behavior exercise (The Social Loafing Effect: A Classroom Demonstration) creates a group activity in which social loafing is likely to occur.

Lecture and Review Questions

What is a group and what types of groups can be found at work?

A group is a collection of two or more interacting individuals with a stable pattern of relationships between them who share common goals and who perceive themselves as being a group. This broad definition of a group allows the consideration of a wide variety of work groups.

Formal groups are those created by the organization and intentionally designed to direct group members toward some important organizational goal. Such groups include command groups (top management teams), task groups, standing committees, ad hoc committees, and task forces. In addition, boards are formal groups in organizations, elected or appointed to manage some entity and similar to commissions, which are more common in the public sector. Finally, self-regulating groups are a special type of formal group in an organization where members schedule their own work, are responsible for the quality of their work, and are responsible for supplies and even hiring required personnel.

Informal groups develop naturally among employees with no direction from management. Informal groups within organizations include interest groups and friendship groups. Both formal and informal work groups can be important determinants of behavior in organizations.

Why do people join groups?

People join groups for a variety of reasons. For some, being a member of a group provides as sense of security—safety in numbers. Groups also provide a means of accomplishing something that is not achievable by a single individual (mutual benefit). Working as part of a group certainly helps to fulfill social needs and often provides individuals with the opportunity to enhance their self-esteem, through their affiliation with a successful and respected group. Being with other people who share your interests (mutual self-interest) is another good reason for joining groups. And finally, people often join groups simply because they often come into contact with each other and discover they have something in common (close physical proximity). As is the case with most organizational behaviors, a person's motivation for joining a group probably involves some combination of these reasons.

What are the major stages in group development?

It is generally believed that there are five stages in the development of a group. They are called: forming, storming, norming, performing, and adjourning. Forming is the stage where group members become acquainted with one another, try to establish roles, and determine what behaviors are acceptable within the group. This stage lasts until the members begin thinking of themselves as a group. The storming stage is characterized by conflict as members show hostility toward each other and the group's leadership. Norming is the stage where the group becomes most cohesive and group identification becomes strongest. The norming stage ends as shared responsibilities and close relationships develop and a commonly accepted way of doing things in the group emerges. Performing refers to the stage where all questions of relationships and leadership have been resolved and the group gets down to work. Finally, adjourning refers to the time when the group dissolves, either because goals have been met, or simply because the group can no longer survive intact.

What are the functions of roles in group behavior?

Roles can be defined as the set of typical behaviors exhibited by a person in a given social context. There are certain behaviors expected of any role incumbent, and these are referred to as role expectations. One aspect of roles and expectations in a group is the notion of role differentiation. That is, in order for a group to function effectively, certain group members are expected to play certain roles. For example, there is usually someone who plays a task-oriented role and is expected to work harder than others to help the group reach its goals, and someone who plays a socioemotional or relationship-oriented role, and is expected to be supportive and make others feel good. But these role expectations can be a source of role stress (see the previous chapter), since most persons occupy several roles and the expectations of the different roles may cause role conflict. The type of role conflict that results from the incompatible demands of two different roles occupied by one person is called *interrole conflict*. Intrarole conflict, on the other hand, develops when different members of the group have conflicting expectations about the behavior of a single person in a single role. Role conflict can have a negative effect on task performance as well as on personal well-being.

What are group norms and how do they operate?

Group norms are the informal rules that guide group members' behavior (as opposed to formal, written rules). Norms can refer either to behaviors that should be exhibited (prescriptive) or to behaviors that should be avoided (proscriptive). These norms develop over time due to precedents for group behavior established by group members themselves, or they can be carried over from other situations. In addition, they can develop as a result of explicit statements about what to do or not to do, or they can develop out of critical events in the group's history. Norms not only define the realm of acceptable group behavior, they also carry with them the penalties for failure to comply with the norms.

What role does status play in the structure and behavior of groups?

One of the potential rewards for group membership is the status associated with being a member of a prestigious group. Status, here, can be defined as the relative social position or rank given to a group or group members by others. Formal status refers to attempts to differentiate between degrees of formal authority given employees by an organization, and is usually accomplished through the use of status symbols. Informal status refers to the prestige accorded certain individuals (often with well-defined characteristics such as age) that are not formally dictated by the organization. Status differences affect expectations concerning influence patterns as well as the way people communicate with each other.

What is group cohesiveness and what is the impact of cohesiveness on group behavior?

Group cohesiveness can be defined as the pressures operating on members to remain a part of the group. Cohesiveness is the result of mutual attraction among group members, shared goals, and a shared commitment to reach those goals, and can be seen as a sense of solidarity or belonging. Cohesiveness tends to develop as initiation into the group becomes more severe and as the external threat of competition increases. In addition, cohesiveness tends to be higher when group members spend a lot of time with each other, when groups are smaller, and when they have experienced success. Group cohesiveness increases commitment to group goals, increases the participation of group members in group activities, and reduces absenteeism. Thus, cohesiveness often leads to increased productivity. However, if the group's goals are contrary to the organization's goals, cohesiveness can actually reduce productivity. Furthermore, members of cohesive groups may be so committed to fellow group members that they may be unwilling to challenge ideas from the group, leading to groupthink. In general, though, cohesiveness appears to enhance productivity, but only when the manager's style supports group efforts.

What is the phenomenon known as group facilitation?

Social facilitation refers to the fact that, in many situations, persons tend to perform tasks better in the presence of others than alone. Actually, there are situations where the presence of others results in a decrement of performance, but it is still referred to as social facilitation since the presence of others is exerting an influence. Zajonc noted that the presence of others hurts task performance when the task has not yet been learned, but helps in the performance of well-learned tasks. Zajonc suggested that this was because the presence of others is arousing and so strengthens our dominant response in any situation—when we are still learning a task, our dominant response is often incorrect, but when we have learned the task our dominant response is correct. Cottrell modified Zajonc's view and suggested that the presence of others is only arousing when we see those others as a source of positive or negative evaluations. Thus, he suggested that evaluative apprehension is really the driving force behind social facilitation. Markus modified this view further by suggesting a distraction-conflict explanation. She argues that an audience creates a conflict of attention among those performing a task—performers are directed toward the demands of the task, but are also distracted by the audience. Thus, others can distract us, cause concern over evaluation, or direct our attention to the task. In any case, the presence of others is arousing and strengthens dominant responses.

What is meant by "social loafing"?

When individuals work together as a group, the effort exerted by each person is usually less than the effort each person would exert if he or she were working on the task alone. In fact, the greater the number of people working together, the less effort each one puts forth. This phenomenon is known as *social loafing*. This phenomenon may be explained by the Social Impact Theory which suggests that the impact of any social force is divided equally among its members. Thus, the larger the group, the less force any task exerts on each individual group member and the less effort is put forth. This could be a serious problem, but several strategies have been identified that can reduce social loafing. One is to make each person performing the task identifiable. This means it would be possible to identify the performance of each individual, which reduces the loafing. Another strategy is to make work tasks more involving. Individuals are less likely to loaf when the task they are performing is highly involving and important. Finally, rather than rewarding employees for their individual performance, it has been suggested that they be rewarded for their contributions to the group effort, which focuses their attention more on group goals and group concerns.

What are the different types of group tasks?

Additive tasks are those where social loafing is most prevalent. These are tasks where the individual efforts of group members are simply added together. Compensatory tasks are those where the individual efforts of group members are averaged so that greater effort by one member can compensate for lesser efforts by another. A disjunctive task allows no compromise. The group must select a solution offered by one of the members of the group. In such tasks, in order for the correct solution to be accepted as the group solution, not only must the correct solution be obtained, but it then has to be supported by the group. A conjunctive task is one where group members must work in unison and so the group's performance is limited by the performance of the worst performing member.

Other Teaching Suggestions

1. The fact that every group needs members who will play key roles cannot be over-emphasized. Whether we think of the understudy who must go out on opening night after the star breaks her leg or the soldier who assumes command of the platoon after all the officers are killed, we are constantly reminded of how individuals will grow into roles when they are needed. Even if a group of rather lazy students are put together, eventually one of them will emerge as the task-oriented leader. It is also true that, as a society, we have a continuous need for heroes and villains. The specific persons cast in those roles may change, and it is even possible for one person to play several roles at different points in his or her life (the political career of Richard Nixon is a good example). It is also interesting to note the interdependence among he-roes and villains. Although there have been few examples like Sherlock Holmes who acknowledged his dependence on Professor Moriarty, it is clear that, without villains, we would have less need for heroes.

2. Status in organizations is a fascinating phenomenon to observe, as organizations are quite good at instilling many forms of status value. There may actually be some reasons for preferring a corner office, and larger offices are clearly more comfortable than smaller ones. Also, access to any exclusive privilege (such as the executive washroom) usually means less crowding. Nonetheless, all of these forms have taken on much more importance than they should simply because of the status organizations have given them. Status symbols actually help outsiders figure out the relative importance of people in an organization since we assume the person with the nicer office is in charge. It is interesting to note that the Japanese are much less concerned with office design as a status symbol and as a result many CEOs share offices. For some, this can be very disorienting. Closer to home, every executive at Milliken (except Mr. Milliken, Chairman of the Board) including the president occupy office carrels. They are all in a large room and, except for whatever decorations are chosen to personalize a space, the carrels are all identical.

3. The various studies conducted in the area of social faclitation and social loafing are quite fascinating and students would be interested in some of the details. The text refers to the original Triplett (1898) paper on "social facilitation." The paper is available and has been reprinted. I was always more impressed by the other explanations Triplett tested for why riders performed better when riding with others, and how he eliminated those explanations. One of Zajonc's earlier studies used roaches running a race with other roaches in the stands (cheering?). These are fun. Zajonc's paper in *Science,* on the other hand, is brilliant. In retrospect it seems clear that the presence of others facilitates the performance of learned responses and inhibits the performance of responses not yet learned, but it took Zajonc to figure that out. The papers on social loafing are also fun to read. Latane and his associates set fires in offices, had people drop their books in elevators, and even looked at tipping behavior (too many people in a party lowers the average tip left by each individual). These studies trace the development of these theories, but also provide some insight into the creativity of the researchers.

4. One of the issues relative to group processes that has been studied relates to the ways in which groups make decisions. Some of these, relating to the structure of groups, will be discussed later. Others deal with comparisons of different advocacy models. Is it better to have someone propose a solution and

then take a strong advocacy position against all comers, or is it better to have one person play "devil's advocate" once a solution has been proposed and look for all the shortcomings while others try to defend the proposal? There are a number of standard decision-making exercises available (several of them are included here), and it might be interesting to have students work on some of them using different decision criteria. Alternatively, they might work on the exercises with the condition that any solution is a consensus decision.

5. There are some other types of group phenomena that are not discussed in the text, chiefly because no one really understands them yet. One of these deals with the fact that the longer a group of people are held hostage, the more sympathetic they become toward their captors, and, generally, the more sympathetic their captors become toward them. It is interesting to note that the U.S. captives held in Iran for all that time did not seem to come out feeling very positively about their captors, but some of the captives released in Lebanon have had some positive statements to make about the goals of their captors. Why the differences? It would be worth discussing.

Case in Point Notes

Making Teams Work at Monsanto

This case describes the difficulties related to the introduction of self-regulated work groups in the workplace. The case focuses on the trials and tribulations experienced by employees of Monsanto Corporation's Pensacola, Florida, chemical and nylon plant in their ongoing effort to implement self-regulated work groups as their primary work technology. The reasons for introducing groups, the responsibilities, functions and dynamics of the groups, the group implementation processes and procedures, and the reactions of employees to the introduction of groups are described. The case concludes with a discussion of the impressive benefits that Monsanto has already realized as a consequence of its using self-regulated work groups.

The discussion questions that follow the case prompt students to discuss Monsanto's self-regulated work groups using the various aspects of group dynamics discussed in the chapter. This case is comprehensive in scope, providing students with considerable opportunity to apply what they have learned about the use and functioning of groups in the workplace.

Additional Cases

The Ohio Project Group

Fischer-USA, Inc., is a major engineering firm specializing in the design of installations that convert waste material into energy. The firm is a West German company having a branch in the southeastern United States. Fischer-USA employs a total of 42 engineers in this branch with a total employment of 65 people.

The 42 engineers are divided into project groups of 6–7 members. These project groups are responsible for the design of waste conversion plants to be constructed in various locations in the United States. The technology for this process is fairly recent, and Fischer-AG, the parent company, has been at the cutting edge of the development of this technology. Most of the leaders of the project teams have spent some time in Germany at the parent company learning this technology.

The Ohio Project group, consisting of six engineers, is developing a waste conversion plant for an Ohio municipality. The project has been ongoing for 18 months, and all six engineers have been with this project group since its inception. The Ohio group has worked together on all of these projects. These six engineers have developed a good working relationship among themselves. (See IE Table 8–1 for more detailed information about the "Ohio Six.")

However, the Ohio project has been quite troublesome. It is by far the largest waste conversion plant ever designed

Source: By Robert D. Goddard, Appalachian State University.

in the United States. The six project engineers have been working quite a bit of overtime, and it is obvious that they need additional engineering help. The branch manager, Bruce Charles, has been conducting interviews for an engineer and has finally found one he thinks will fit in well with the Ohio group.

Robert McCoy, P.E., is a recent graduate of the Master's in Civil Engineering program at a major California univer-

TABLE 8–1   The Ohio Six

Jim Jameson	(35 years old, married, two children, with Fischer-USA for six years)
Monte Miller	(38 years old, divorced, three children, with Fischer-USA for eight years)
Chris Kelly	(42 years old, married, two children, with Fischer-USA for fiften years)
George Oh	(29 years old, single, Chinese-American, with Fischer-USA for six years)
Steve Lilly	(34 years old, married, four children, with Fischer-USA for seven years)
Andy Joseph	(40 years old, married, two children, with Fischer-USA for five years)

sity. He has satisfied all of the requirements for the Professional Engineer designation and has given every indication in his interviews that he is knowledgeable and enthusiastic about the firm's ideas and projects. He was hired in June, and after two weeks on the job, his enthusiasm has been undiminished. The work is challenging and gives him the opportunity to showcase his engineering knowledge.

Robert plunged into the work assigned to him in the Ohio group. He worked hard and quickly became a contributing member of the group. Bruce Charles was impressed with the way Robert progressed. When a particularly difficult design problem presented itself, he was willing to work overtime on nights and weekends to research possible solutions. Robert was particularly adept with the computer system and used it to its fullest capability, since his university training had stressed computer-aided design. However, he was pretty much a loner both on and off the job, perhaps because he was black and the other group members were white.

After about three months with the Ohio group, Robert's learning curve had peaked, and he was a fully-contributing member. With his computer knowledge, as well as his more current education, Robert began to finish his assignments before their scheduled completion dates. He offered to help the other six members with their portions of the Ohio project, but each time Robert volunteered his assistance, he was rebuffed. He then would go to Bruce Charles and ask for another part of the project to work on.

One morning in December, Chris Kelly asked to see Bruce Charles about a problem. Bruce suggested that they meet for lunch and discuss the problem, and Chris readily agreed. During lunch, Chris elaborated on his concerns:

Chris: "I don't quite know how to say this, Bruce. I don't want you to get the wrong idea."
Bruce: "Just come right out with it, Chris. You know how we operate here, you've been here long enough."
Chris: "It is the new man, Robert. I've never worked with a more stuck-up, arrogant person in my life. And it's not just me; everyone in our group feels the same. He constantly flaunts his education and so-called 'superior knowledge.' No one can stand him."
Bruce: "He seems like he's working out well. His work is always done on time, and it is good work. So far, my impression has been very favorable—he's done all I've asked."
Chris: "Did you ask him to upset the morale of the Ohio group? He goes around trying to tell us how to do our jobs and generally sticking his nose into parts of the project he has no business messing with. We've been a good, productive group, and you've never had a complaint from us, even when we had to work all that overtime to complete the project proposal."
Bruce: "I'll tell you what, Chris. Robert has been a good worker, and I don't know if I can do anything about his arrogant attitude, as you call it. But I will talk with him and see what can be done."

After the lunch, Bruce went back to his office to think about what Chris had told him. He knew that Chris exerted a great deal of influence over the rest of the Ohio group, not only because of his seniority, but also because of his knowledge of the many facets of project operation. Chris was right, Bruce thought. No one in the Ohio group had com-

plained about anything before now. He did not want to lose any of the members of the Ohio Project Group.

On Monday of the following week, Bruce called Robert into his office. After reviewing Robert's work over the past six months, Bruce brought up the attitude problem described by Chris.

Bruce: "Robert, your work so far has been impressive. I don't believe that we've ever hired someone who has caught on so fast. But there is one problem that we need to discuss. Specifically, I want to talk about how well you and the other members of the Ohio group are working together. After all, this is a team effort; not a project that one person can complete."
Robert: "What do you mean?"
Bruce: "I've been approached by a member of the Ohio group who says that you are arrogant and that you constantly tell them how to do their jobs. This is a good team, and I don't want to lose any of you. I've been happy with the group's work up until this moment in time."
Robert: "I've never told them how to do their jobs. In fact, whenever I finish what I've been assigned, I have asked them if I could help them with their work. They never accepted my offer to help. I do have some knowledge of the computer and its capabilities that they don't, and I've offered to share that knowledge with them. Again, they have never accepted my offer. In fact, sometimes I feel that they shut me out of their activities because I'm black."
Bruce: "You were not hired by Fischer-USA because you are black. You were hired because you were the most qualified applicant, and I felt that you could do the job. You have proven that you can do the job, but you have a lot to learn about working with a team."
Robert: "These guys could be doing so much more than they do now. I know they can. They deliberately slack off on the job, talking about their bowling team and how well they are doing in their league. They talk about the Braves, the Falcons, the Hawks, any team that happens to be playing, when they could be working on the project or learning more about the computer."
Bruce: "Leave that part of the job to me, Robert. You do your job and try to get along with the rest of the group."

Robert and Bruce discussed a few more things and then the meeting was over. Robert left the meeting feeling disappointed. He knew that he had been doing his best, and he felt that the rest of the Ohio group was not.

Questions
1. What group norms were operating in the Ohio Project Group?
2. How does group cohesiveness impact on the behavior of members of the Ohio Project Group?
3. If you were Bruce Charles, how would you handle this situation?

The Ohio Project Group: Teaching Note

This case is a good illustration of how group norms affect individual member behavior, and how group cohesiveness affects group productivity. This case is ideally suited for introduction to small group materials.

Questions

1. What group norms were operating in the Ohio Project Group?

The Ohio Group had developed into a cohesive working group over a period of years. The members of the group had developed a set of unwritten rules—norms—as a result of their long-time close association. Among the norms students might identify are restriction of production and social activities (bowling, discussing sports, etc.). You may want to ask students if they identified any other norms.

2. How does group cohesiveness impact on the behavior of members of the Ohio Project Group?

As noted above, the group has been together for a number of years and has been successful. The fact that the firm has assigned the Ohio Project to this group means (to them) that Fischer-USA thinks it is competent. A cohesive group has shared goals and a shared commitment to achieving those goals. These goals may not be directed toward productivity; they may

be social in nature. This seems to be one aspect of the Ohio Project Group. The group members feel a sense of belonging to the group, and are committed to the well-being of its members—at least the long-term members. Robert is an outsider, younger, perhaps better-educated, and black. He is not interested in idle chit-chat about sports or the other activities of the group members. When he offered to help, he was rebuffed. It appears that the other members of the group have not accepted him, partially because of his actions, partially because of his demographics.

3. If you were Bruce Charles, how would you handle this situation?

This is the most difficult question for students to answer. You may have to help them through it. Charles could reassign Robert to another group, he could have an open discussion with the whole group to try to work things out, he could do nothing and hope that they can work things out by themselves.

The Case of the Changing Cage

Part I

The voucher-check filing unit was a work unit in the home office of the Atlantic Insurance Company. The assigned task of the unit was to file checks and vouchers written by the company as they were cashed and returned. This filing was the necessary foundation for the main function of the unit: locating any particular check for examination upon demand. There were usually eight to ten requests for specific checks from as many different departments during the day. One of the most frequent reasons checks were requested from the unit was to determine whether checks in payment of claims against the company had been cashed. Thus, efficiency in the unit directly affected customer satisfaction with the company. Complaints or inquiries about payments could not be answered with the accuracy and spped conducive to client satisfaction unless the unit could supply the necessary document immediately.

Toward the end of 1952, nine workers manned this unit. There was an assistant (a position equivalent to a foreman in a factory) named Miss Dunn, five other full-time employees, and three part-time workers.

The work area of the unit was well-defined. Walls bounded the unit on three sides. The one exterior wall was pierced by light-admitting north windows. The west interior partition was blank. A door opening into a corridor pierced the south interior partition. The east side of the work area was enclosed by a steel mesh reaching from wall to wall and floor to ceiling. This open metal barrier gave rise to the customary name of the unit—"The Voucher Cage." A sliding door through this mesh gave access from the unit's territory to the work area of the rest of the company's Agency Audit Division, of which it was a part, located on the same floor.

The unit's territory was kept inviolate by locks on both doors, fastened at all times. No one not working within the cage was permitted inside unless his name appeared on a

special list in the custody of Miss Dunn. The door through the steel mesh was used generally for departmental business. Messengers and runners from other departments usually came to the corridor door and pressed a buzzer for service.

The steel mesh front was reinforced by a bank of metal filing cases where checks were filed. Lined up just inside the barrier, they hid the unit's workers from the view of workers outside their territory, including the section head responsible for overall supervision of this unit, according to the company's formal plan of operation.

Part II

On top of the cabinets which were backed against the steel mesh, one of the male employees in the unit neatly stacked pasteboard boxes in which checks were transported to the cage. They were later reused to hold older checks sent into storage. His intention was less getting these boxes out of the way than increasing the effective height of the sight barrier so the section head could not see into the cage "even when he stood up."

The girls stood at the door of the cage that led into the corridor and talked to the messenger boys. The workers also slipped out this door unnoticed to bring in their customary afternoon snack. Inside the cage, the workers sometimes engaged in a good-natured game of rubber-band sniping.

Workers in the cage possessed a good capacity to work together consistently and workers outside the cage often expressed envy of those in it because of the nice people and friendly atmosphere there. The unit had no apparent difficulty keeping up with its work load.

Part III

For some time prior to 1952, the controller's department of the company had not been able to meet its own standards of efficient service to clients. Company officials felt the primary cause to be spatial. Various divisions of the controller's department were scattered over the entire twenty-two-story company building. Communication between the divisions required phone calls, messengers, or

Source: Adapted from "Topography and culture: The Case of the Changing Cage" by C. Richards and H. Douglas, 1957, *Human Organization, 16*(1), pp. 16–20.

personal visits, all costing time. The spatial separation had not seemed important when the company's business volume was smaller prior to World War II. But business had grown tremendously since then, and spatial separation appeared increasingly inefficient.

Finally, in November of 1952, company officials began to consolidate the controller's department by relocating two divisions together on one floor. One was the Agency Audit Division which included the voucher-check filing unit. As soon as the decision to move was made, lower-level supervisors were called in to help with the planning. Line workers were not consulted, but were kept informed of planning progress by the assistants. Company officials were concerned about the problem of transporting many tons of equipment and some 200 workers from two locations to another single location without disrupting work flow. So the move was planned to occur over a single weekend, using the most efficient resources available. Assistants were kept busy planning positions for files and desks in the new location.

Desks, files, chairs, and even wastebaskets were numbered prior to the move, and relocated according to a master chart checked on the spot by the assistant. Employees were briefed as to where the new location was and which elevators they should take to reach it. The company successfully transported the paraphenalia of the voucher-check unit from one floor to another over one weekend. Workers in the cage quit Friday afternoon at the one stand, reported back Monday at the new.

The exterior boundaries of the new cage were still three building walls and the steel mesh, but the new cage possessed only one door, the sliding door through the steel mesh into the work area of the rest of the agency audit division. The territory of the cage had also been reduced in size. An entire bank of filing cabinets had to be left behind in the old location to be taken over by the unit moving there. The new cage was arranged so that there was no longer a row of metal filing cabinets lined up inside the steel mesh obstructing the view into the cage.

Part IV

When the workers in the cage inquired about the removal of the filing cabinets from along the steel mesh fencing, they found that Mr. Burke, the section head, had insisted that these cabinets be rearranged so his view into the cage would not be obstructed by them. Miss Dunn had tried to retain the cabinets in their prior position, but her efforts had been overridden.

Supplemental Analysis

While the company has solved its problem, the workers in the cage did not regard their relocation as an unqualified success. The exterior boundaries of the new cage were still three building walls and the steel mesh. But the territory of the new cage had been reduced in size, a fact immediately perceived by workers who had felt cramped in the old cage. This territorial reduction was also obvious to higher-ups, who directed leaving an entire bank of filing cabinets behind in the old location to be taken over by the unit moving there.

Even worse, from the viewpoint of the voucher-check filing unit, was the fact that the new cage possessed only one door—the sliding door through the steel mesh into the work area of the rest of the agency audit division. The cage no longer had a private doorway directly into a corridor. This change made it impossible for workers in the new cage to stand at the door talking with messenger boys or to slip out unnoticed to bring in the customary afternoon snack. Some comments that were heard were: "We're going to be sitting on each others' shoulders!" "No more slipping out for water, girls!"

The old cage custom of afternoon snacking continued in new cage territory. Lacking a corridor, the food-bringers had to venture forth and pack their trade-goods through the work area of the rest of their section, bringing this hitherto unique custom to the attention of workers outside the cage. The latter promptly recognized the desirability of afternoon snacks and began agitation for the same privilege. This annoyed Mr. Burke, the section head, who initially forbade workers in the cage from continuing this old cage custom. But old cage culture proved stronger than this would-be inhibitor. Under continual pressure from Miss Dunn, he permitted one worker to leave the new cage at a set time every afternoon to bring food for the rest.

However, this rigidity irked cage personnel, accustomed to a snack when the mood struck, or none at all. Having made his concession to the cage force, Mr. Burke was unable to prevent workers in the society outside the cage from borrowing the snacking trait. Thus, the cage lost one of its highly valued overt symbols of separateness and superiority because the topographically structured rerouting of the snack-bringers' route through the main section work area made this privileged behavior visible to workers outside the cage. Workers in the new cage thus fell in status relative to others in their section, adding to their stress in the new section.

Because of Burke's insistence on rearranging the filing cabinets, the cage had lost its most highly valued overt symbol—the physical separateness of the unit from the rest of the section. With the new arrangement, he had no difficulty seeing into the cage from his desk just outside. This change resulted in increased supervision by Burke and corresponding decreased authority for Miss Dunn.

The section head did not approve of an untidy working area, and any boxes or papers which were in sight were a source of annoyance to him. He did not exert supervision directly, but would request Miss Dunn to "do something about those boxes." In the new cage, desks had to be completely cleared at the end of the day, in contrast to the work-in-progress piles left out in the old cage. Boxes could not accumulate on top of filing cases. Newly arrived checks were put out of sight as soon as possible, filed or not. Workers hid unfiled checks, generally stuffing them into desk drawers or unused file drawers. Since boxes were forbidden, there were fewer unused file drawers than there had been in the old cage. So the day's work was sometimes undone when several clerks hastily shoved vouchers and checks indiscriminately into the same file drawer at the end of the day.

The section head also disapproved of conversation on general principles. Since he could see workers conversing in the new cage, he requested Miss Dunn to put a stop to all unnecessary talk. Attempts by female clerks to talk to messenger boys brought the wrath of her superior down on Miss Dunn, who was then forced to reprimand and generally to restrict her workers in an activity they had previously enjoyed.

Not only was the freedom of movement of workers in the new cage restricted, but they found themselves being regarded with apparent dislike and rejection by Burke. All members of the cage social system reacted against Burke's increased domination occasioned by the altered topography. When he imposed his decision on the voucher-check filing unit, he became "Old Grandma" to its personnel. The cage workers sneered at him and ridiculed him behind his back. They clearly lost their faith in the leadership of their group by Burke as he superseded Miss Dunn. The loss of morale among members of the cage social system was obvious. Workers who formerly had obeyed company policy as a matter of course began to find reasons for loafing and obstructing work in the new cage. In many cases they were not fully aware of their actions, only knowing that they felt more tired and had to slip away for a few minutes oftener than before. One key worker developed a severe allergy and was off the job for nearly a month. She attributed her attack to nerves but never attributed the nerves to anything except the job.

Everyone in the cage experienced higher levels of anxiety and stress including Miss Dunn. The relocation, the changes in the work environment, the loss of status, and the increased level of direct supervision by Mr. Burke all contributed to the increased stress. One indication of the stress experienced by the workers in the cage was rubber-band snapping, or sniping. All knew that Mr. Burke would disapprove of this game. It became highly clandestine and fraught with danger. Yet sniping increased, indicating that the tolerance for stress threshold of the cage force had been exceeded. Members of the cage social system reacted with hostility toward Burke in this destructive and time-wasting interaction among themselves, further slowing work output in the cage.

Before a worker in the cage filed incoming checks, she measured with her ruler the thickness in inches of the bundle she filed. At the end of each day she totalled her output and reported it to Miss Dunn. All incoming checks were measured on arrival. Thus, Miss Dunn had a rough estimate of unit intake compared with file output. Theoretically she was able to tell at any time how much unfiled material she had on hand and how well the unit was keeping up with its task. Despite this running check, when the annual inventory of unfiled checks on hand in the cage was taken at the beginning of the calendar year 1953, a seriously large backlog of unfiled checks was found. To the surprise and dismay of Miss Dunn, the inventory showed the unit to be far behind schedule, filing much more slowly than before the relocation of the cage.

Questions

1. Describe some of the norms of the voucher-check filing unit prior to the move. How were these altered after the move?
2. Would some of the problems noted in the case have been avoided by involving the workers in this unit in the planning process prior to the move? How?
3. Describe the problems created by the change in interaction patterns caused by the move and by the different type of supervision exhibited by Mr. Burke.

The Case of the Changing Cage: Teaching Note

The *Case of the Changing Cage* is a case concerned with small work groups and change. It is one of the older classics and is still a favorite of many instructors who use it to drill students on the meaning of terms used in the basic social system conceptual scheme and to demonstrate the scheme's predictive power. The case is particularly effective for predictive purposes when it is presented in sequential parts. Normally, the case ends at Part IV, but we have included a section, *Supplemental Analysis*, to aid students in seeing the outcomes of the move. You might want to keep this section separate and bring it into the discussion after the students have made their predictions about the outcomes of the move.

The case is ideally suited for introduction to small group material and is a good complement to the first case in this chapter. The social system described is small with a limited number of variables and characteristics which are easily identified. This system is relatively closed and therefore easily analyzed in terms of internal dynamics, though it is the threat from the outside to which the workers in the case react. Because the case is presented in such clarity, it becomes a prototype for similar situations commonly found in organizations. In such situations, we have cultures relatively isolated from outside forces that will disturb their identity, change their practices, and interfere with the satisfaction which they enjoyed in the system before change.

Mr. Burke was, in effect, attempting to direct cultural change among members of the old cage society from his superordinate power position. But the old cage culture proved stronger than this would-be inhibitor, at least in regard to the afternoon snack policy.

All the unit's workers had, in the old cage, developed conventional understandings and values derived from a different tradition than those in the company hierarchy. The unofficial workers' charter envisioned their manipulating the unique topography of the cage for a maximum benefit to themselves while fulfilling the company-assigned function of locating requested checks at once. But in the new cage, old cage culture expressions were inhibited by Burke's company-oriented work-values. Members of the old cage social system were placed in a situation like that of a society recently conquered and undergoing forced acculturation by the conqueror. To remain in the good graces of Conqueror Burke, members of the old cage social system had to alter their behavior to conform to his expectations, ceasing behaviors learned by participation in old cage culture. Such forced changes met resistance and aroused conflicts and tensions such as have often been reported in acculturation situations. Cage workers, like adults in any society undergoing acculturation, had to unlearn former habits, end former customs, and acquire new ones. This again produced psychological stress, since individuals with previously acquired behavior patterns seem not to change them rapidly or cheerfully, especially when those patterns have been reinforced by positive sentiments and favorable emotions.

The discovery of a drop in efficiency of workers in the cage after relocation presented a new problem to the company. It had solved its problem of time-loss in the process of communication between units spatially distant within its building. But in doing so it had created an unforeseen new problem—a lowering of filing speed in the new cage which delayed filing just as effectively as several weeks of work stoppage would have. This drop in filing speed resulted directly from slight changes in the micro-environment of the cage, changes apparently not considered significant by the company hierarchy. Presumably, the planned rearrangement of desks and files within the cage dictated by Burke was aimed at increasing efficiency of unit operation. Yet his changes resulted in great inhibition of old cage cultural behavior, which upset the cage force. The direct imposition of his cultural standards, plus loss of overt symbols of dis-

tinctiveness and privileged status, plus the clear reduction in territory and enjoyed activities occasioned by the slightly altered topography of the cage were responsible for the drop in filing speed. For the distinct local customs, traditions and attitudes of old cage culture were vital components of the morale of cage workers. When they were inhibited, morale in the cage dissipated and filing achievement dropped. As a result, the company's ability to satisfy customers was impaired.

Experiencing Organizational Behavior Notes

The Social Loafing Effect: A Classroom Demonstration

The exercise creates a group activity in which social loafing is likely to occur. Detailed instructions for performing this exercise are provided in the text. Essentially, students are divided into groups of various sizes (the likelihood of social loafing increases with group size) and one student is randomly selected to perform alone. Students are then asked to perform a simple, additive task (several task suggestions are provided) within their assigned group. Ten minutes is allotted to perform the task. After ten minutes has

lapsed, each group counts the number of units produced and computes the average number of units produced per group member. At the board, the instructor then plots the averages at the board as a function of the size of the individual's work group. The class as a whole then analyzes the production results for evidence of social loafing. If social loafing occurred, the reasons for loafing are discussed. If social loafing did not occur then the discussion focuses on what factors may have prevented the phenomenon. Regardless of outcome, this exercise provides a rich basis for discussing social loafing.

Additional Experiential Exercise

3-D Tic-Tac-Toe Exercise

Instructions

I. Introduction

In making decisions and in planning and controlling operations, a company expects certain things from each manager. They are listed below, and they are the same for this exercise.

A. Recognize, define, and clarify the problem at hand.
B. Seek out all available information.
C. Describe the problem and analyze relevant facts.
D. Develop possible courses of action.
E. Evaluate possible plans and determine the final plan of action.

  1. Consider the framework in which the plan must operate as set by the situation, the organization, and the policies and procedures involved.
  2. Provide for alternate plans in the event future circumstances require changes.

F. Put the plan into action.
G. Observe closely the operation of the plan, checking results for the effects on future success.
H. Revise or adjust the plan as circumstances require.
I. Stay within the defined parameters.

Source: By Robert D. Goddard, Appalachian State University.

II. Definitions

A. *Referee:* The leader who directs the problem and who rules on points of procedure and scoring.
B. *Gatekeeper:* Person who calls each team when its turn to play comes.
C. *Small Groups:* One of the competing organizations or teams as assigned by the leader.
D. *Observer:* An individual assigned by the leader to study the performance of each group and report on how the game was played.
E. *Problem Board:* The three-dimensional tic-tac-toe apparatus located in a concealed area.
F. *Counter:* A small disc used to make moves on the board. Each group has a different color (red, blue, yellow).
G. *Group Representative:* Member designated to take the group's moves to the referee.

III. Responsibilities

Each member has the responsibility to contribute to the success of the group in competition with the other groups. You will learn only as much as you are willing to contribute.

IV. Regulations

A. A point is scored whenever the group succeeds in placing three (3) of its counters in a straight line on the board.

1. On one of the horizontal planes, this straight line may be across or diagonal.
2. On the vertical plane, the straight line may be vertical or diagonal.

(See 3-D Program sheet)

B. Before sending a representative to the board, each group will select the play desired and three additional alternate plays. In the event the first play has already been made by a competing group, the first alternate play will be used, etc. If none of the alternate plays can be used, the group will forfeit its turn.
C. The four alternate plays are to be written on a plain piece of paper, and taken by the group representative to the referee, who will place the counter in position according to the written instruction from the group.
D. The group representative may observe the board and report its status back to the group.
E. Members will alternate as group representatives. The order of selection is similar to a baseball batting order. Once the order has been determined, it must be followed exactly until the game is finished. No pinch-hitting is allowed.
F. The problem will continue until the allotted time has elapsed. In the event the *problem board* is filled before then, the referee will clear the board of all counters and start over without interruption and without notification to the groups.
G. *Time Limits:* Each group will be allowed 15 minutes before play begins, to read and study the instructions and to prepare a plan of action. After the group is notified that its turn has arrived, the group representative has only 30 seconds to deliver the group's instructions to the referee and observe the board. Each group then has approximately 1 minute and 30 seconds to determine the next move.
H. *Record of Progress:* Scores will be announced and tabulated on a blackboard for each group as the game progresses.

3-D Tic-Tac-Toe Exercise: Instructions for Observers

This exercise involves a number of the ideas about group process, performance, and communications found in the text. You are asked to evaluate how these ideas are demonstrated (or not demonstrated) in the group you will be observing. You will be asked to comment on your observations at the end of this exercise.

I. Stages of Group Development
Were all stages of group development observed in your group? If not, which were not observed?
What were the task and process behaviors observed for each stage? (see below for examples)

A. Forming
  1. *Task* Orientation to task.
  2. *Process* Testing and dependence.
B. Storming
  1. *Task* Emotional response to the demands of the task.
  2. *Process* Intragroup conflict.
C. Norming
  1. *Task* Open exchange of relevant interpretation and opinions.
  2. *Process* Development of group cohesion.
D. Performing
  1. *Task* Emergence of a solution.
  2. *Process* Functional roles emerge as a way of problem solving.

II. Norms
Did group members act to encourage certain behaviors? Did group members discourage certain behaviors by reacting and responding negatively to their occurrence? By what method did group members attempt to encourage compliance with the observed norms of the group?

III. Roles
A. Norm-Related Roles
  The extent to which group members comply with norms identifies one set of roles in a group. The *leader* adheres to group norms and generally makes a special contribution to thir identification and enforcement. The *regular* follows most, if not all, group norms; the regular contributes as a "good member." The *deviant* falls lower in the hierarchy; he or she deviates from the norms but is tolerated by others in the group. The *isolate* falls at the lowest level of the group hierarchy. The isolate does not meet group norms; therefore, the group rejects, and does not value, this member. Who were the leader, followers, deviates and isolates?
B. Functional Roles
  Task roles focus on goal accomplishment. *Maintenance roles* direct the group toward positive group interaction and interpersonal behavior. *Individual roles* focus on satisfying an individual's needs, which may distract from effective group functioning. Did you observe any of the functional roles described in IE Table 8–2?

IV. Decision Making
A. Groupthink
  Was there any evidence of the phenomenon of *groupthink* in this exercise? (See IE Table 8–3 for some of the symptoms of groupthink.)
B. Decision Making
  Did this exercise prove to be a good example of the group decision making process as opposed to individual decision making?
C. Effectiveness
  Was this an effective work team? Were their solutions and methods for solving the problem at hand creative?

V. Intergroup Relations
A. Perceptual Differences
  Did you perceive perceptual differences between the three groups participating in the exercise? What were they?
B. Interaction
  Was there much intergroup interaction? Describe the nature of this interaction.
C. Power Differences
  How well did the group cope with uncertainty? Did your group have more/less perceived power than the other groups?

TABLE 8–2   Functional Roles

Task-oriented roles	Initiator	Offers new ideas or suggests solutions to problems
	Information seeker	Seeks pertinent facts or clarification of information
	Information giver	Describes own experience or offers facts and information
	Coordinator	Coordinates activities, combines ideas or suggestions
	Evaluator	Assesses the quality of suggestions, solutions, or norms
Maintenance roles	Encourager	Encourages cohesiveness and warmth, praises and accepts others' ideas
	Harmonizer	Alleviates tension; resolves intragroup disagreements
	Gatekeeper	Encourages participation by others and sharing of ideas
	Standard Setter	Raises questions about group goals; helps set goals and standards
	Follower	Agrees and pursues others' activities
	Group observer	Monitors group operations; provides feedback to group
Individual roles	Blocker	Resists stubbornly, negative; returns to rejected issues
	Recognition seeker	Calls attention to self by boasting, bragging, acting superior
	Denominator	Manipulates group; interrupts others; gains attention
	Avoider	Remains apart from others; resists passively

Source: "Functional Roles of Group Members" by K. Benne and P. Sheats, 1948, *Journal of Social Issues, 2,* pp. 42–47.

3-D Tic-Tac-Toe Exercise: Teaching Note

This is one of the most interesting approaches to studying group processes that we have ever tried. It allows individuals to see the stages of group development in a concentrated setting. The competition aspect of the exercise highlights the "we/they" syndrome beautifully. Dealing with ambiguity and finding solutions to problems also are addressed in the exercise. Group norms, roles, tasks, power, interaction, and perception are integral elements of the exercise.

This exercise could just as easily be used to illustrate the processes of decision making, leadership, and communication. It is a powerful learning aid for many topics in organizational behavior.

Materials Required

You will need a copy of the QUBIC 3-D Tic-Tac-Toe game from Parker Brothers. Note that you will only use three levels of the board, and a 3" × 3" matrix for each board. You will probably want to put tape over the extra slots on each of the three boards used.

You will also need copies of the instructions form for each of the participants and observers (the first page of this exercise). Observers (at least one for each of the three groups) will need copies of the observer form. Each participant should also have copies of the 3-D Program Sheet and 3-D Problem Work Sheet, found at the end of this note. These forms will help groups in making decisions.

You will need a stopwatch or some method of measuring time in 30-second increments. Finally, you will need a cardboard box or some other suitable container to put the game board in to conceal it from the view of the groups.

Getting Started

You will want to assign members of the class to one of three groups (red, yellow, and blue, corresponding with the colors of the chips). Also, you will need at least one observer, gatekeeper, and referee per group.

Once the groups have been constituted, hand out the instructions form and give them 15 minutes to read it. You

will use this period to give instructions to the observers, gatekeeper and referee.

The referee is instructed to monitor the game board and to rule on points of procedure and scoring. Of particular importance to this referee is compliance with the written rules (Regulations, page 2 of instructions form) and the unwritten rules. These are especially important, as groups will probably not remember the unwritten rules; those in-

TABLE 8–3   Symptoms of Groupthink

Invulnerability	Members feel they are safe and protected from dangers, ostracism, or ineffective action.
Rationale	Members ignore warnings, by rationalizing their own or others' behavior.
Morality	Members believe their actions are inherently moral and ethical.
Sterotypes	Members view opponents as truly evil or stupid and thus unworthy of or incompetent in negotiations of differences in beliefs or positions.
Pressure	Members pressure all individuals in the group to conform to the group's decision; they allow no questioning or arguing of alternatives.
Self-censorship	Members do not voice any questions about the group's decision.
Unanimity	Members perceive that everyone in the group has the same view.
Mindguards	Members may keep any adverse information from other members that might ruin their perceptions of consensus.

Source: Based on "Groupthink" by I. Janis, June 1971, *Psychology Today.*

structions you will give immediately prior to the start of the game. There are two of these unwritten rules. They are:

1. Players are not allowed to talk while they are presenting their move to the referee.
2. Players are to place their team color at the top of the paper describing their move.

Any violation of either written or unwritten rules will result in the forfeiture of a move. The referee will simply state, "I cannot accept your move." The referee also checks the "batting order" provided by each group to ensure that they come up in the proper rotation. If not, the referee will state, "I cannot accept your move." The referee should also call out when a group has made a Tic-Tac-Toe. (Remember, more than one score can be made on one move.)

The gatekeeper is really a scorekeeper and timekeeper. This person will record on the blackboard or flipchart the score(s) called out by the referee. He or she will signal when each group will present its move to the referee by calling out the team color ("red," "yellow," or "blue") at the appropriate interval (usually 30 seconds). This person should have a stopwatch or other accurate timing device.

Observers will watch each group as it prepares and competes in the game. They will record their observations on the Observer form, along with any other observations they make concerning any of the other groups. Observers will discuss their findings at the end of the session.

Immediately before beginning play, you should announce the two "unwritten rules." You could do this by recapping the written rules and including these two. You don't want to draw too much attention to these two rules though, as they are crucial to the aspect of ambiguity that enriches this exercise.

The Competition

If all questions are answered, you are ready to begin play. Distribute chips to each of the groups and have them turn in their "batting orders" to the referee, who will check to make sure that each team follows it properly.

The gatekeeper will then call out the first team color, "Red." The first Red group member on the "batting order" will come up and present the sheet of paper listing the *team color* at the top (Red) and *four* moves. If either of these rules has been violated, the referee should say, "I cannot accept your move."

What usually happens is that the teams generally violate one or more rules the first few times. They either forget to put the team color at the top of the sheet, or they forget to put a total of four moves on the sheet. Perhaps they try to ask a question of the referee, or talk to someone (even themselves). If so, they have violated the rules, and the referee cannot accept the move. *No explanation should be given,* even though the temptation to do so is great. This creates real feelings of ambiguity and some hostility toward the referee. (You should choose someone for this job who is rather thick-skinned.)

Note: Even though the teams may have their moves rejected, they are not required to go back to the group. They can stay at the board and look at it. They can even bring up a 3-D Problem Work Sheet and record what they see for future strategy. Nowhere is this prohibited by the rules, although most people will just hang their head and go back to the group when their moves have been rejected.

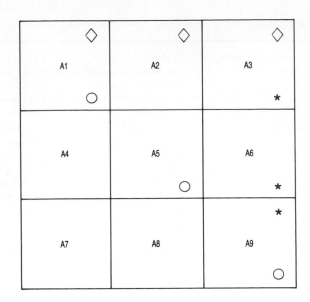

FIGURE 8–1

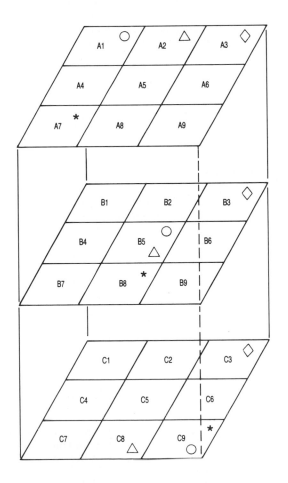

FIGURE 8–2

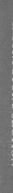

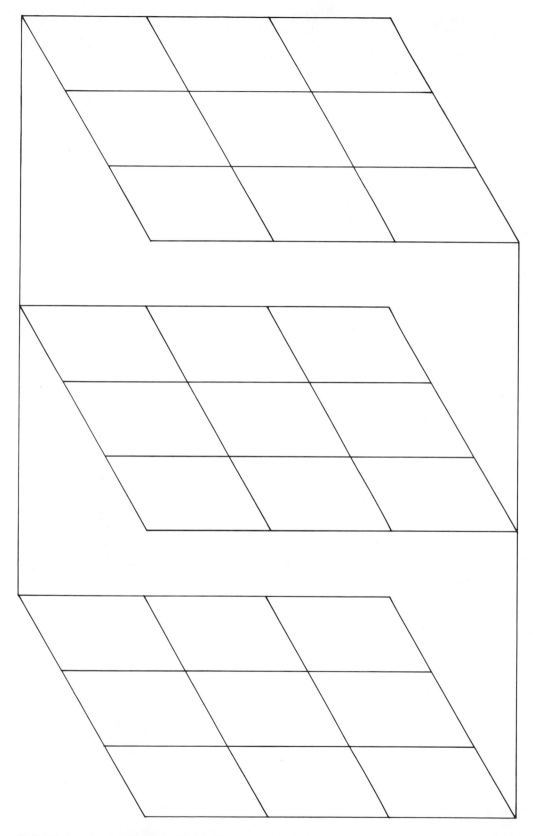

FIGURE 8–3   3-D Problem Work Sheet

The only time they *must go back* to the group is when the gatekeeper calls out another team's color.

The competition continues with the gatekeeper calling out team colors at 30-second intervals. Eventually, one or more of the groups will catch on and have a move accepted. The thrill of having a chip placed on the board is motivational for that group, and the others will try to emulate the successful group. Generally, there is not much inter-group communication during the course of the exercise, but when a group finally makes a Tic-Tac-Toe and the referee says, "Score for Red (Blue/Yellow)" the sense of accomplishment in the successful group is evident by cheers, etc. The other groups may work harder, or may even slack off in problem-solving activities.

It seems that there is always one group that never really catches on to the rules or strategy of the competition. It is interesting to note the behavior of the members of this group. Some of the elements of social learning theory can be evidenced in this exercise. Groups (and individuals) learn from successful behavior in other groups and try to emulate that behavior. If they are rewarded for that behavior (with a score), they will continue it.

When the game seems under control, and teams are scoring successfully, one strategy you may employ to alter the environment of the game is to decrease the interval between groups from 30 seconds to 15 seconds. If you do this surreptitiously, none of the groups will really notice it! When you debrief them at the end of the exercise, they may exclaim that you changed the rules in mid-game, or something to that effect. Of course, you may reply that the rules of the game of change constantly, and success-

ful groups and individuals are able to adjust to those changes.

The game ends when you decide, but we suggest that you run it for at least 30 minutes once you begin the actual competition.

3-D Program

Instructions

Points may be scored in the following manner:

1. On a single level.
   (a) Straight line across or vertically.
       Example: Figure 1–diamonds–A1–A2–A3, stars–A3–A6–A9.
   (b) Straight line diagonally.
       Example: Figure 1–ellipses–A1–A5–A9.

NOTE: POINTS MAY BE SCORED ON LEVEL B AND C IN A SIMILAR MANNER.

2. On a Tri-level.
   (a) Straight line vertically from level A to B to C.
       Example: Figure 2–diamonds–A3–B3–C3.
   (b) Straight line diagonally from edge-to-edge.
       Example: Figure 2–triangles–A2–B5–C8 or stars–A7–B8–C9.
   (c) Straight line diagonally from corner to corner.
       Example: ellipses–A1–B5–C9 or stars–A7–B8–C9.

NOTE: 2 OR MORE POINTS MAY BE SCORED IN A SINGLE MOVE.

Additional Readings

Gersick, C. G. (1988). Time and transition in work teams: Toward a new model of group development. *Academy of Management Journal, 31,* 9–41.

Goodman, P. S., Ravlin, E. C., & Argote, L. A. (1986). Current thinking about groups: Setting the stage for new ideas. In Paul Goodman and Associates, *Designing effective work groups.* San Francisco: Jossey-Bass. (Socio-technical effects on group dynamics.)

O'Connor, J. T. (1988). Architecture: Building corporate symbols. *Harvard Business Review, 66*(5), 131–133. (A view of a different type of status meant to differentiate between organizations.)

Schweiger, D. M., Sandberg, W. R., & Ragan, J. W. (1986). Group approaches for improving strategic decision making: A comparative analysis of dialectical inquiry, devil's advocacy, and consensus. *Academy of Management Journal, 29,* 51–71.

∎ 9 ∎

THE COURSE OF WORKING LIFE: ORGANIZATIONAL CULTURE, SOCIALIZATION, AND CAREERS

CHAPTER OUTLINE

LEARNING OBJECTIVES

After reading this chapter, you should be able to:

1. Define the term *organizational culture,* and indicate how such culture develops and how it can be changed.
2. Describe some of the ways in which organizational culture affects both individuals and the effectiveness of entire organizations.
3. Define the term *organizational socialization* and indicate how this process takes place in organizations.
4. Distinguish between individualized and institutionalized tactics of socialization, and indicate how these affect innovativeness and commitment among employees.

5. Summarize the potential advantages and disadvantages to both parties of *mentor-protégé* relationships, and describe the impact of early mentorship on protégés' later career development.
6. Describe important issues individuals confront in the early, middle, and later stages of their careers, and indicate how people today determine whether their careers are on track.
7. Describe the effects of work-family conflict, and indicate how these effects differ for females and males.
8. Indicate how unemployment affects the psychological and physical health of the people who experience it.

Chapter Overview

This chapter deals with the various issues facing employees as they proceed through their working lives. The chapter begins by discussing the factors that allow an organization to remain relatively stable despite employees coming and going. Specifically, the origin and nature of organizational culture are dis-

cussed, as well as the effects on organizational behavior of having a strong versus a weak culture. The importance of person-organization culture fit is explored, followed by a discussion of how organizational cultures change. Next, the chapter turns to the process by which new employees are socialized into an organization and its culture. Here, there is discussion of the major stages in the socialization process, and the programs that organizations use to socialize new employees. The effects of different types of socialization programs on organizational behavior are explained. In addition, the role of mentors in the socialization process, and the key aspects of mentor-protégé relationships are discussed. The next major section of the chapter deals with issues of careers and career management. The basic dimensions of career change are identified as are the various stages of life and career. The chapter concludes with a discussion of major career issues affecting workers in the 1990s and beyond—two-career families, gender differences in work-family conflict, and rising white-collar unemployment.

Three special sections appear in this chapter. An OB in Practice (Creating a New Organizational Culture: Some Practical Steps) describes how to change organizational culture, citing the experiences of several major companies—Dupont, Disney and Sharp—as examples. A second OB in Practice (Is Your Career on Track? Changing Perspectives on Personal Progress) describes how criteria for assessing career progress have changed over the past decades. Once judged primarily in terms of salary and promotions, today's definition of career success is much more likely to include criteria such as the opportunity for inner fulfillment and the amount of time available to spend with family. And an International/Multicultural Perspective (Race and Career Outcomes in the United States: Different and Still Unequal) discusses the ongoing discrimination against black and other minority employees in the U.S. workplace.

The Case in Point (Changing Management Careers in the 1990s?) describes how a growing number of displaced managers, laid off by corporate downsizing, are changing their careers to match today's realities. The Experiencing Organizational Behavior exercise (Personal Values Throughout Life) prompts students to identify their current values and compare them to past and future values. The point of this exercise is to demonstrate that values can change over the course of a lifetime. A CNN video (*Drake, Beam and Morin*) available for this chapter features a company that provides outplacement services to companies that are laying off employees. Many concerns expressed by the victims of white-collar and managerial employee layoffs are discussed, as are several career change and planning issues.

Lecture and Review Questions

What is organizational culture and how does it originate?

Organizational culture is the set of shared beliefs, expectations, and values held by members of an organization, to which newcomers must adjust. Once established, these beliefs tend to persist unless some dramatic events necessitate change. Although culture plays an important role in a variety of situations, perhaps the best way to observe a culture is by looking at the norms established for behavior in a given organization. Whether these are part of a formal corporate philosophy or simply informal rules for day-to-day dress, these norms are the clearest expression of an organization's culture. In many cases, these cultures can be traced to the founder of the company, a person who is often dynamic, with a clear vision of the future and a strong set of personal values. Through initial hirings and structuring, the views of this person often form the basis for the organization's culture.

Cultures can also develop as a result of the organization's trying to establish a niche in the marketplace and discovering that some ways of doing things are better than others. Finally, culture may develop from the need to maintain effective relationships among organizational members. The nature of these relationships is often dependent on the nature of the business and the nature of competition, but these needs are also strong forces in the development of a culture.

Do organizational cultures ever change?

Although cultures are generally resistant to radical change, some change is inevitable. External events may necessitate changes in how the organization does business and thus, in its culture. Also, over time, the persons entering the organization may change. Demographic shifts in population and the labor force may result in new employees who react differently to the organization's culture, often necessitating a change in the culture. Some change may actually be a function of the type of culture itself. That is, although many cultures are stability-oriented, it is the nature of some cultures to change with the times. Thus, the change may simply be a reflection of a larger culture. Finally, culture may change as the result of conscious efforts to alter the internal structure or basic operations of the company. Such alterations often involve changes in company policies about hiring and rewards which tend to lead to new forms for behavior, resulting in a new culture.

What are the major effects of corporate culture?

Organizational culture exerts a major effect on both individuals and organizational processes. Perhaps the most pervasive (if subtle) influence is that most people will simply adapt their behavior to go along with the organization's culture. Thus, if the culture stresses participation, most managers will simply become more participative simply because everyone else is. Also, although the evidence to date is sketchy, there is reason to believe that strong cultures (i.e., the basic aspects of the culture are accepted by most employees), and cultures that stress certain key traits (e.g., humanistic values, concern about quality, and innovativeness of products) result in higher levels of performance than other cultures.

What is organizational socialization and how does it occur?

Organizational socialization is the process by which individuals are transformed from outsiders to participating and effective members of organizations. This process can be described as encompassing three stages known as getting in, breaking in, and setting in. *Getting in* refers to anticipatory socialization that takes place as the potential new employee learns about the organization either from friends already working for the organization, from publications about the organization, or from organizational recruiters. During this stage in the socialization process, employees develop expectations about the organization. In an attempt to manage those expectations to keep them more in line with organizational realities, some organizations have taken to employing realistic job interviews as part of this process. *Breaking in* refers to the time when new members first assume their job duties. During this stage, the new member must master new skills and also be oriented to the practices and procedures in the new organization. *Setting in* refers to the period in which the new member moves to become a full, participating member of the organization. The socialization process can be either formal or informal, focused at individuals or groups. Socialization can also be sequential (where organizational membership follows from passing through a discrete set of stages) or non-sequential; it can be carried out by members of the organization itself (serial training), or by outsiders (disjunctive training); it can be designed to affirm the ability and self-confidence of recruits (investiture programs), or to strip away feelings of self-confidence so that recruits will be more receptive to new ways of doing things (divestiture programs); and newcomers can know in advance the duration of the socialization process (fixed programs), or not know exactly when they will gain full acceptance (variable programs).

What is the role of mentors in the socialization process?

Mentors are older, more experienced workers who teach, advise, and counsel younger workers, aiding in their development. Mentors help their protégés by providing emotional support and confidence, as well as providing key career opportunities and strategies for being successful when such opportunities arise. In return, mentors expect their protégés to work hard on assigned tasks and to be loyal support-

ers within the organization. They can bask in the reflected glory of their protégés. Mentors also get a lot of satisfaction out of feeling needed and being helpful. As such, mentors can be an important means for socializing new employees. Mentors are generally 8–15 years older than their protégés and are usually attracted to the protégé's initial performance or interpersonal style, although in some cases, the protégé formally appeals to the would-be mentor for help. The relationship usually goes through several stages beginning with the initiation stage, during which the relationship gets started and takes on importance for both parties. This is followed by the cultivation stage where the bonds strengthen, and the protégé makes rapid career progress, because of the assistance being received. The third stage, separation, occurs when the protégé feels the need to assert independence, there is some externally produced change in the relationship, or the mentor feels unable to provide guidance and support. Finally, there is the redefinition stage which follows only if separation was accomplished successfully, where the parties perceive their relationship primarily as one of friendship and they interact as equals. Although some of the early claims for the value of mentoring seem to have been exaggerated, having a mentor seems to ease the socialization process and provides the protégé with a real edge. This is unfortunate for women who usually have less access to mentors than men do for several reasons: the scarcity of female mentors, the more limited opportunity for interaction with top management, the perception that the failure of a female protégé will more adversely affect the mentor since women tend to be more visible in management ranks, and the reluctance of male managers to adopt female protégés because of the possible misinterpretation of the relationship.

What are the key dimensions to career changes and how does career development relate to life stages?

Careers can be defined as the sequence of attitudes and behaviors associated with work-related activities experienced by individuals over the span of their working lives. Although careers are all unique, they tend to develop along three key dimensions: vertical movement (promotions up the hierarchy in an organization), horizontal movement (changes in job functions), and radial movement (toward the inner circle of management). At the same time careers are developing along these dimensions, they are also undergoing other changes. Soon after a person takes a new position, there is a stage of career growth where the person acquires the skills needed to perform his or her current job competently. This is followed by stabilization which is the time the person is performing his or her job to the fullest capacity. The next stage is one of transition as the person prepares him or herself for the next career move upward. This cycle is repeated for as long as the career lasts. While these changes are taking place, however, the person is also aging and this process presents similar stages of change and stability. Around age thirty, decisions must be made about marriage and family; around age forty, decisions must be made about a last child, and people start thinking about how many years they have left. Finally, during their fifties, people begin thinking about how to spend their remaining years and retirement. These decisions and considerations must complement career decisions and moves.

What particular issues are related to the early, middle, and late stages in one's career?

The key issue related to the early stage of one's career is career planning. It is at this point that most people decide what course their future careers will follow, often on the basis of what have been called career anchors. These anchors are the set of self-perceptions we have of our abilities, talents, needs, motives, attitudes, and values. For some, these anchors are technical or functional in nature, and tend to guide careers according to the content of future work. For others, these anchors refer to managerial competence and tend to guide careers toward high level management positions. Another group of anchors is concerned with security and stability, and lead people to careers in large organizations, and employment with a single firm over their working lives. Another group refers to creativity or entrepreneurship and leads people to careers where they tend to start and run their own businesses. Finally, for some, career anchors emphasize autonomy and independence and lead people to careers where they work at their own pace and set their own goals, such as academia or writing. Also, at this stage in one's career is the issue of job changes. Decisions must be made about whether to move to different jobs and/or organizations and to resist attempts by organizations to seduce employees into making career decisions that are in the best interests of the organization, but not in their own best longterm interests. During the middle career stage (about age 40), people begin to realize that they will not accomplish all they planned, and so must decide what to do instead. Some employees simply burn out at this point, while others move into mentoring roles, and still others begin to develop outside interests and hobbies. All of this is related to the fact that the person has likely reached a career plateau from which further advancement is unlikely. These plateaus can be overcome, however, if the person retrains, takes another job, or develops an alternative role in the organization. Most late career issues revolve around the realization that goals which are still unmet will probably never be met, and that power and influence in the organization are on a decline. Issues here include planning for job succession (who will take over the job), and retirement.

What are the critical career issues of the 1990s?

Among the most critical career issues of this decade is the conflict between work and home life inherent in two-career families. When both parents pursue careers, child care becomes an important, and often heart-wrenching concern. Time for family activities gets squeezed and stress mounts. Work performance may also deteriorate due to the pressures of trying to balance the demands of family life and career. Of course all of these pressures are likely to be even more intense for single, working parents—a growing household pattern in the United States. What can organizations do to help employees balance work and family obligations? Flexibility seems to be the key. Examples of organizational flexibility include flexible work scheduling, job sharing, and work-at-home arrangements, practices that many companies are implementing to meet the needs of today's employees. For parents, on-site or subsidized child care services are also being provided.

The rising tide of unemployment among white-collar and management employees is another critical career issue for the 1990s. Considerable stress is experienced by people who lose their jobs and the survivors who remain. For those who are laid off there are feelings of being betrayed (anger) and fears emanating from uncertainty about what to do next. For many of these people, finding a new job in the same career is not realistic. Career change is necessary and help is needed. A growing number of organizations are assisting laid-off workers by providing outplacement services such as career development counseling for displaced workers. Employees who survive rounds of layoffs often suffer from survivor syndrome, characterized by feelings of guilt about not being laid off and feelings of anxiety—worry that they will lose their jobs during the next round of layoffs. Many survivors—fearing the worst—decide to quit their jobs rather than wait for the ax to fall. More often, employees who quit are the very employees the organization wants to retain (they were the ones who were not laid off). How can organizations manage the effects of the rising tide of unemployment among white-collar and managerial employees? Several actions seem to be particularly effective. Engage in open, accurate communication with employees. Run effective outplacement programs. And explain the criteria that will be used for choosing those who will remain and those who will go. By taking these actions, organizations may reduce the negative reactions on the part of survivors, and thereby increase the chances of attaining the goals they seek through reductions in work force: reduced costs and enhanced productivity.

Other Teaching Suggestions

1. When we think about corporate culture, we realize there are few large organizations with cultures as strong as IBM. The company works hard to maintain its culture and image, and any employee who comes in contact with the public must fit in. Men rarely wear beards or mustaches, suits are dark, and shirts are white, hair is short and neat. Executives are not allowed to drink at business lunches and the organization tolerates no improprieties. All of this strengthens IBM's culture and all employees have a clear idea of who they are and what the company stands for. But are there disadvantages to such a strong identity and such a strong set of norms? Although IBM may not have been the victim of any such problems, we can imagine other organizations with strong cultures (the army or police force), and it might be interesting to ask your students for examples where such strong norms might actually be a drawback, or might cause problems for society (e.g., Lt. Calley, Serpico).

2. Corporate cultures do not change easily, especially in large organizations, but, as the text notes, it is possible. Ten years ago, AT&T was by far the largest phone company in the United States. They operated almost with monopoly powers and, although the company generated profits, there was no real push to maximize income. Also, since there were no viable competitors, there was no push to worry about customer service needs. All that changed when AT&T was broken up, and the courts forced competition in the long-distance phone market. Now AT&T finds itself in a highly competitive market where they may not be leader on either price or quality, and they really have to hustle to get customers. I'm not sure how much has been written about the change in culture, but it would be worthwhile to speculate on what has happened as the company (the most publicly held company) was forced to move from complacency to tough competition.

3. The military is a unique arena for studying socialization. Many people have an image of boot camp (basic training) as a place where tough drill instructors literally beat recruits into shape. The image is quite false in several respects. The purpose of basic training is to provide recruits with necessary skills and to socialize them. Drill instructors are supposed to act tough and, especially at the beginning of basic training, to treat recruits as children. But, just as parents recognize when their children grow up and change their behavior, so do drill instructors. As one of the researchers involved in the Meglino, et al. study of realistic job previews, I was able to meet and get to know several drill instructors. They are generally quite articulate, knowledgeable, and dedicated to the people they lead. It's amazing to see how easily they can slip in and out of the role of task master. The point is, as socialization tasks go, it is hard to imagine one more daunting than taking a group of people just out of their teens, from all walks of life, and transforming them into cohesive units of soldiers prepared to die to defend their country.

4. Among Italians, the term godfather does *not* usually refer to people like Don Corleone. A godfather is someone who looks out for you and tries to ease the bumps along the road. In this sense, a godfather functions much the same as a mentor, and the stages in the relationship between mentor and protégé also work for the relationship one has with a godfather. Thus, although your students may not have been part of a true mentoring relationship in an organization, they may well have had a "godfather" at some point. Introducing this less formal relationship might be a good way to generate discussion about what issues really come up in mentoring relationships.

5. Perhaps one of the better ways to illustrate the issues involved in managing a career is to study the careers of some successful business people. Books about the lives of Lee Iacocca and Donald Trump provide the material needed. It might be interesting to contrast the careers of the son of immigrant parents (Iacocca) with that of someone like Howard Hughes who was born a millionaire and died a billionaire. It is also interesting to contrast leaders such as Iacocca and Trump with successful business leaders in Japan. The career paths of Japanese managers tend to reinforce feelings of organizational commitment and loyalty much more than the American system.

Case in Point Notes

Changing Management Careers in the 1990s?
This case describes how a growing number of displaced managers, those managers laid off by corporate downsizing, are changing their careers to match the realities of the 1990s. The case opens with a discussion of the effects of corporate downsizing on the availability of management jobs and the reactions of managers to being laid off. The case illustrates several new career directions that displaced managers are pursuing—general manager in a small organization, entrepreneur, consultant, and teacher. Also discussed in the case are several of the personal benefits that are experienced by displaced managers as a consequence of losing their jobs.

The discussion questions that follow the case prompt students to analyze the career shifts of displaced managers using the concepts and theories presented in the chapter (e.g., basic dimensions of career change). Students are also asked to consider the career anchors suggested by each of the careers described in the text and to compare them to their own career anchors. This exercise generally stimulates considerable discussion. It is also common for some members of the class to have either first-hand experience being a displaced manager or know (or be related to) someone ho has lost his or her management job. Ask these students what they, or their relatives or acquaintances, did in response to losing their jobs. This avenue of discussion is generally very productive as a means of illuminating the key concepts and issues presented in the chapter.

Additional Case

International Motors, Inc.

International Motors, Inc., is an imported automobile company, selling foreign cars in five southern cities. International Motors handles the "high roller" brands: Ferrari, Maserati, Lamborghini, and Rolls Royce. Each branch of IMI has direct responsibility for sales and service, and each branch manager reports directly to Jack Morrison, the president and owner of IMI.

Allen Lambert, the manager of the Atlanta branch, was meeting with Mr. Morrison, who was on one of his tours of all the dealership branches. Lambert has been with IMI for only four months, having been hired from Gordon Motors, a dealership that sold the Chevrolet line of cars and trucks. The emphasis at Gordon Motors was volume, volume, volume. Gordon Motors was very efficient, and sold the greatest number of new cars and trucks of any Atlanta dealership.

Prior to this conference, Mr. Morrison had met briefly with several of the Atlanta salespeople and service representatives. Morrison and Allen discussed several items of interest, and then the conversation continued:

Morrison: There's something I think we should talk about that's happening to your branch, Allen. Nothing serious, but it's something I want to alert you to.

Lambert: Nothing too gruesome, I hope. Our results have been pretty good this last quarter, haven't they?

Morrison: Nothing gruesome at all. It's just a question of your style of going about things. It seems that some of our people think they don't have a big enough say in terms of who is hired into the dealership.

Lambert: I thought they did have a big say. Before I hire anybody, a clerk, a sales rep, or a service person, that person is interviewed by the people who would be working most directly with him or her.

Morrison: Yes, but they think that you choose which candidates will even be interviewed. And then you make the final hiring decision.

Lambert: If that's the procedure they want to follow, I guess it could be arranged. I'm concerned, though, that total participation along those lines would be cumbersome and inefficient. We would spend too much time on recruiting and selection. Besides, I thought a branch manager was responsible for hiring employees.

Morrison: Yes, but I think the time invested would pay off. Your people would feel much more like they are part of a team effort.

Lambert: By the way, nobody ever told me about these problems. I would have been receptive to their ideas. Why don't they complain to me instead of running to you?

Source: By Robert D. Goddard, Appalachian State University.

Questions

1. Why is this case included in a chapter about organizational culture and socialization?
2. What kinds of attitudes does Allen Lambert have to change in order to be successful as the Atlanta branch manager of IMI?
3. Can you identify elements of the organizational structure at IMI?
4. What influence does Jack Morrison have on the culture of IMI?

International Motors, Inc.: Teaching Note

This case shows that exercises and cases do not have to be long and involved in order to illustrate a point. From what we have read in the introduction and the conversation between Morrison and Lambert, we can come to some suppositions about the culture of IMI.

First of all, IMI is *not* Gordon Motors. The culture at Gordon Motors was one of "Move 'em out the door." That is, as the largest volume dealer in a major city, the watchword at Gordon was probably efficiency. The whole organization was designed to move customers through the sales and service processes as quickly and efficiently as possible. In fact, in dealerships like this, there exists an "assembly-line" mentality. The more time you waste with a customer or an employee, the fewer sales you will make. The bottom line in high-volume dealerships like Gordon Motors is the daily/weekly/monthly/quarterly sales report.

Jack Morrison, the owner of IMI, takes a totally different approach. Selling "high-roller" automobiles is similar to selling jewelry. You do not have many transactions in a day or a week, but those you do have are large. Markups on the lines of cars sold by IMI, while not in the range of markups in the jewelry business, are still substantial. Developing a good relationship between the customer and the sales person or service representative is extremely important, because repeat and referral business is the lifeblood of firms like IMI.

Apparently, the culture at IMI had been one of participation in the selection of coworkers. Lambert was not used to this approach, and his idea of involving others was to let them interview selected applicants, still reserving the final hiring decision for himself. Lambert was violating the "natural order of things" at IMI.

Another aspect of the culture at IMI was employees going directly to the owner, Mr. Morrison, with any problem. The communications lines were open at all times. This probably was not the case at Gordon Motors; in fact, workers there probably never got a chance to see and talk with the boss.

Lambert is going to have to recognize the *norms* and *mores* of the culture at IMI. He is going to have to reassess his previously-learned attitudes and behaviors, and go through a change process if he is to be successful.

Experiencing Organization Behavior Notes

Personal Values Throughout Life
This exercise is intended to demonstrate how values can change over the course of a person's working life. Students are asked to write down the three values that are currently most important to them. They are then asked asked to list the three values that were most important to them five years ago. Finally, students are asked to write what three values might be important to them in ten years. Students then compare the three lists. Typically, the lists differ to some extent. What does this mean? Values can change as we change over the course of a lifetime. Changes in personal values clearly have important implications for career development. Various points to consider are provided with the exercise to facilitate discussion of the relationship between personal values and careers. This exercise is particularly useful as a means of introducing the topic of career anchors and the importance of matching career anchors with organizational culture when looking for a job.

Additional Experiential Exercise

Marriage/Career Expectation Survey

Female Form

This exercise is a useful one to help students clarify their expectations regarding careers and family life. Too often people enter into relationships without thinking about or discussing some of the items contained in this survey. The results can be disasterous.

You are to complete this survey as honestly as you can. There are no right or wrong responses to the statements on the survey. Choose your responses from the response key below:

1 = Strongly Agree
2 = Agree
3 = Neutral/No Opinion
4 = Disagree
5 = Strongly disagree

____ 1. It will be preferable for my husband to have at least as much or more education than I do.
____ 2. I expect to fully develop my career and for my husband to encourage me.
____ 3. If I am not employed, I will do all the housework; if I am employed, I will expect my husband to help me.
____ 4. I expect to stay home full-time with our children.
____ 5. It is preferable for my husband to make most of the financial decisions, regardless of whether (and how much) income I would bring to the household.
____ 6. Weekends will be time for my husband to relax, watch TV, etc., and I will strive to keep distractions (such as visitors and children) to a minimum for him.
____ 7. Substitute mothers can do an excellent job and will take care of our children while I work.
____ 8. I expect to have the major responsibility of raising our children regardless of whether I am employed or not.
____ 9. If there is a disagreement that we cannot resolve, I think the wife should most often give in to the husband.
____ 10. I expect to take some vacations either a) by myself, or b) with my husband, but no children.
____ 11. I may not want children, since I want to develop my career.
____ 12. I expect to be able to continue my education if I wish, even if we have children.
____ 13. I expect to be able to go out in the evening with my friends.
____ 14. Yard work and fix-it tasks will mainly be done by my husband.
____ 15. If my husband gets an excellent job offer elsewhere, I will expect to pick up and move to the new place. Therefore, his career will be more important than mine.
____ 16. I expect that my husband will sometimes have to put his career before our family, but I will not.

Male Form

This exercise is a useful one to help students clarify their expectations regarding careers and family life. Too often people enter into relationships without thinking about or discussing some of the items contained in this survey. The results can be disasterous.

You are to complete this survey as honestly as you can. There are no right or wrong responses to the statements on the survey. Choose your responses from the response key below:

1 = Strongly Agree
2 = Agree
3 = Neutral/No Opinion
4 = Disagree
5 = Strongly disagree

____ 1. It will be preferable for me to have at least as much or more education than my wife.
____ 2. I expect my wife to fully develop her career and I will encourage her.

Source: Copyright Dorothy Marcic, Metropolitan State University, St. Paul, Minnesota.

___ 3. If my wife is not employed, I will expect her to do all the housework; if she is employed, I will help her somewhat.

___ 4. I expect my wife to stay home full-time with our children.

___ 5. It is preferable for me to make most of the financial decisions, regardless of whether (and how much) income my wife brings to the household.

___ 6. Weekends will be time for me to relax, watch TV, etc., and I expect my wife to keep distractions (such as visitors and children) to a minimum for me.

___ 7. Substitute mothers can do an excellent job and will take care of our children while my wife works.

___ 8. I expect my wife to have the major responsibility of raising our children regardless of whether she is employed or not.

___ 9. If there is a disagreement that we cannot resolve, I think the wife should most often give in to the husband.

___ 10. I expect to take some vacations either a) by myself, or b) with my wife, but no children.

___ 11. We may not want children, since I expect my wife to develop her career.

___ 12. I expect my wife to be able to continue her education if she wishes, even if we have children.

___ 13. I expect my wife to be able to go out in the evening with her friends, as I do with mine.

___ 14. Yard work and fix-it tasks will mainly be done by me.

___ 15. If I get an excellent job offer elsewhere, I will expect my wife to pick up and move to the new place. Therefore, my career will be more important than hers.

___ 16. I expect to sometimes put my career before our family, but my wife will not.

Marriage/Career Expectation Survey: Teaching Note

This exercise is a useful one to help students clarify their expectations regarding careers and family life. Too often people enter into relationships without thinking about or discussing some of the items contained in this survey. The results can be disasterous.

Students should fill out the survey before class. Put students into groups of 4–6 members, ensuring that there is about a 50/50 mix of males and females in each group. (Discussion in groups of mainly one sex tends to be one-sided and uninteresting.) These group sessions should take about 20–30 minutes.

You should instruct the groups to note which items on the survey had the most agreement and which had the most disagreement. You might also ask them to think about what they learned about their career and marriage expectations.

You might then gather the groups together and ask them to report to the whole class on the items of most agreement and disagreement. This discussion should be quite lively!

Additional Readings

Feldman, D. C., & Weitz, B. A. Career plateaus revisited. (1988). *Journal of Management, 14,* 69–80.

Hall, D. T., & Richter, J. (1990). Career gridlock: Baby boomers hit the wall. *Academy of Management Executive, 4*(3), 7–22.

Howard, A. (1988). Who reaches for the golden handshake? *Academy of Management Executive, 2*(2), 133–144.

Tung, R. L. (1989). Career issues in international assignments. *Academy of Management Executive, 2*(3), 241–244.

■ 10 ■

HELPING, COOPERATION, AND CONFLICT: WORKING WITH OR AGAINST OTHERS IN ORGANIZATIONS

CHAPTER OUTLINE

LEARNING OBJECTIVES

After reading this chapter, you should be able to:
1. Define *prosocial behavior* and describe some of the forms it takes in organizations.
2. Define *citizenship behaviors* and indicate how they are related to perceptions of procedural fairness on the part of organization members.
3. Describe the basic nature of *cooperation* and indicate why it is often replaced in organizations by *competition*.
4. Describe the role of *teams* and *pairing* in promoting cooperation within an organization.

5. Define *conflict* and indicate how it can produce positive as well as negative effects.
6. Describe various styles of managing conflict, and the dimensions that appear to underlie these contrasting styles.
7. List several *interpersonal* and *organizational* causes of conflict.
8. Describe several effective techniques for *managing* conflict, and discuss the *ethical issues* related to such techniques.

Chapter Overview

This chapter deals with issues surrounding decisions to work with or against other members of an organization or group. The chapter begins with a discussion of prosocial behavior in the workplace. Particular attention is paid to organizational citizenship behaviors and whistle-blowing—behaviors of a prosocial nature, both going well beyond the normal call of duty. The chapter then moves on to the topic of cooperation, and discusses individual and organizational factors that generate cooperation rather than conflict. Conflict, the next topic, is presented in terms of the two basic dimensions underlying conflict: distribution and integration. The nature and causes of modern conflict and its effects—positive as well as negative—on organizational behavior are discussed. Finally, the chapter considers several means of effectively managing conflict.

Three special sections appear in this chapter. An OB in Practice (Teamwork: Is It Always a Plus?) discusses the need for training in the development of cooperative systems such as work teams. An International/Multicultural Perspective (Conflict and Face in Five Different Cultures) discusses the influence of cultural differences (individualist-collectivist dimension) on conflict, and choice of conflict resolution strategies. And a Question of Ethics (Styles of Conflict Management: Which Are Best—or Most Appropriate?) discusses the ethical issues associated with each of the five distinct approaches to conflict resolution: avoidance, compromise, collaboration, accommodation, and competition.

The Case in Point (Achieving Cooperation at Johnson Wax) describes how Johnson Wax transformed itself from a company plagued by internal conflict into a highly cooperative, customer-driven business. And the Experiencing Organizational Behavior exercise (Personal Styles of Conflict Management) provides an opportunity for students to diagnose their preferred style of conflict management using a self-report questionnaire.

Lecture and Review Questions

What do we mean by prosocial behaviors in organizations?

Prosocial behaviors are those which benefit others in various ways. There is some debate as to whether there is any behavior that is purely altruistic, but even if the person does expect some type of reward for the behavior, there is still considerable benefit to others. Such behaviors occur in organizations whenever employees assist coworkers with heavy workloads, or help someone who has been absent, or get involved in any tasks that are not part of their jobs. These are all citizenship behaviors. In addition, employees help others with personal problems outside of the job; help customers or clients in ways that go beyond the scope of the job; make suggestions for improvements; or volunteer for extra jobs. It is also possible, however, to engage in a behavior that helps some individual, but actually hurts the organization. Finally, there is whistle-blowing, where employees reveal illegal or improper organizational practices to someone who may be able to correct them. Whistle-blowing is surely a prosocial behavior from the perspective of society, but the situation is more complex from the organization's point of view, since many of the practices that are revealed can be punished with large fines or imprisonment. It is, therefore, crucial to know the employee's motivation in these cases. Where feasible, whistle-blowing that stays within the organization is usually of more benefit to the organization.

What are some individual factors that lead to cooperation instead of competition?

Cooperation describes a situation where two parties work together so that both can gain some valued outcome. Competition describes a situation where one person works to maximize his or her outcomes at the expense of another. The major factors influencing decisions to cooperate instead of compete are the principle of reciprocity, several aspects of communication, and a personal orientation toward working with others. Reciprocity refers to the tendency to treat others as they have treated us. When others have acted competitively toward us, we are likely to respond in a competitive fashion. In fact, due to self-serving biases, we tend to perceive the cooperative behaviors of others as less than they really are and we often tend to undermatch the cooperative behavior of others when it does occur. Open communication also helps cooperation as both parties build personal trust by communicating a belief that cooperation is the best strategy. Communication in the form of threats, on the other hand, tends to engender competition. Finally, not all people are oriented toward cooperation. Some are competitors who generally deal with others by trying to maximize their personal outcomes relative to others. Some people are individualists who seek to maximize personal outcomes regardless of what others do (these people don't care about *beating* someone else; as long as they benefit, they don't care what others do). There are also people who function as equalizers and seek to minimize the differences between their outcomes and the outcomes of others, regardless of the level of outcomes involved. Finally, some people are, by nature, cooperative and they seek to maximize joint outcomes regardless of the behavior of others.

What are some organizational factors that lead to cooperation?

Differences in cooperation across organizations are due, in part, to member differences on the factors identified above. However, there are additional factors that relate to the organization's internal structure and policies. For example, in many organizations, departments are rewarded for surpassing other departments' performances. Such a structure fosters competition, though competition is not necessarily harmful. In other organizations there are interdependent tasks so that no department or unit can complete the task without the cooperation of others. This structure results in greater cooperation. It is also possible for competing organizations to coordinate their effects to attain mutual gains. This interorganizational coordination is most likely when organizations conclude that by joining forces they can compete more effectively against others (such as the case with OPEC). Is is also likely to occur when new, external competitors enter a mature and previously stable market (such as the Japanese entry into the automobile industry). Such coordination is also likely when rapidly changing environmental conditions, such as advances in technology or shifts in government policies, make it difficult for independent organizations ton continue doing business as usual. In such cases, the organizations may enter a merger or they may simply form a consortium where the organizations remain independent, but agree to coordinate their activities through some central consortium management organization.

What is the modern perspective on the nature of conflict?

Conflict is always the result of incompatible aspirations or interests, but there seems to be more to it than that. A model recently proposed by Thomas views conflict as a process that is part of an ongoing relationship between parties. Conflict stems, in part, from the awareness that there is conflict, or incompatible interests and aspirations. Thus, this incompatibility can exist but, if the parties do not recognize it, there will be no conflict. Once the parties are aware of the conflict, they begin to think about and react to it. Emotional responses tend to increase conflict, while rational-instrumental reasoning (consideration of potential costs and benefits) and normative reasoning (consideration of what behavior is appropriate to the situation) tend to reduce the level of conflict. Next, on the basis of these reactions and thoughts, the parties form specific intentions or plans to adopt various strategies during the conflict, and these plans are then translated into actions. These actions then produce reactions by the other party, and the cycle continues.

What are the major organizational causes of conflict?

As noted above, conflict results from the perception of incompatible interests. In organizations, this is usually the result of several factors. The most obvious is competition over scarce and valued resources, where each party seeks to get its share, even if that share is not what really what the party deserves. Ambiguity over responsibility or jurisdiction also leads to conflict. Here, parties are uncertain of who is responsible for performing certain tasks or who has authority in a certain instance. Interdependence also leads to conflict when one party does not feel that the other party is delivering its input in a timely or satisfactory manner. As noted earlier, reward systems that pit parties against each other also lead to conflict. Differentiation within an organization can also lead to conflict.

This refers to the process by which individuals come to identify with a group or unit, and view members of other groups or units as outsiders, leading to an "us versus them" mentality and conflict. Finally, power differentials and differing preferences regarding basic principles of distributive justice (equality versus equity) can contribute to conflict within organizational settings.

What are the major interpersonal causes of organizational conflict?

In addition to the individual differences mentioned earlier, conflicts in organizations are often due to interpersonal problems. For example, some conflict is due to grudges that develop when individuals feel they were made to look silly, or lose face, because of someone else. Conflict can also be the result of faulty attributions. When someone is thwarted by another's efforts conflict arises, especially when the aggrieved party believes the other person acted out of malice, or if no good explanation for the action is forthcoming. Another factor that leads to conflict is faulty communication. Such communication may simply lack clarity, but inappropriate or destructive criticism also leads to conflict. Finally, Type A persons are more likely to become involved in conflict than Type B persons; and persons who are high in self-monitoring are more likely to try to resolve conflict than persons low in self-monitoring.

What are the most important effects of conflict in organizations?

Conflict in organizations can have positive as well as negative effects. Some of the important negative effects include the generation of bad feelings among the persons involved (which can hurt long-term relationships), stress, a breakdown of communications, and a diversion of energies away from behaviors that benefit the organization. In addition, conflict often results in leaders adopting more authoritarian leadership styles as they try to deal with the conflict. Negative stereotyping regarding the "other" group may develop, and, eventually, individuals' identification with their group becomes so strong that it is more difficult to see the other side's perspective and so move toward compromise. There are, however, some positive effects of conflict as well. Conflict can bring issues into the light that have previously been ignored or overlooked, so that solutions can be found. Conflict also motivates people on both sides of an issue to know and understand each other's positions more fully, thus fostering open-mindedness, and leading each side to incorporate aspects of opposing views into their own. Conflict can signal the need for change, making parties more receptive to new procedures and ideas. Also, the quality of decision making can be enhanced by conflict by alerting decision makers to new information that they may have ignored (because of its incompatibility with their initial views). Conflict can enhance motivation by increasing loyalty to the work group and by a closer monitoring of the other party's performance as the group tries to improve that performance. And finally, recent research shows that the free exchange of opposing views that is inherent in cognitive conflict enhances organizational commitment and job satisfaction.

What are some of the methods available for effectively managing conflict?

The key for organizations facing conflict is to manage that conflict so as to minimize the negative effects and maximize the positive ones. The most common method for eliminating and managing organizational conflict is bargaining or negotiation, during which the parties exchange offers, counteroffers, and concessions. If the conflict cannot be resolved through negotiation it could escalate. Negotiations are more likely to be successful when the parties adopt more reasonable bargaining tactics, when the parties focus on the potential benefits of the negotiation process (rather than on what they will have to give up), and when the parties move from a distributive bargaining model (where one side wins and the other side loses) to an integrative model (where both sides can win). Specific tactics for obtaining integrative solutions include *broadening the pie* (finding ways to increase the resources so both sides are satisfied with their share); *nonspecific compensation* (one side gets what it wants and the other side is compensated on an unrelated issue); *logrolling* (each party makes concessions on a low priority issue in exchange for concessions on issues of more importance to them); *cost cutting* (one party gets what it wants, but the costs to the other party are reduced); and *bridging* (where neither party gets what it wants, but a new solution, acceptable to both, is developed).

Another means of managing conflict is third-party intervention. A neutral third party tires to resolve a deadlock between the parties either through mediation (suggesting solutions and helping the negotiation process), arbitration (imposing a solution), or final offer arbitration (where the solution to be imposed is one party's final offer). The induction of superordinate goals is another means of managing conflict. A new goal, common to the two parties, is introduced so that the parties can work together toward this new goal rather than focusing on the conflict. Finally, it is possible to manage conflict by intensifying it. This tactic, known as escalative intervention, involves bringing the conflict to a head, pointing out to the parties other areas where they disagree to broaden the conflict, or encouraging the parties to perceive

hostile intentions in each other's actions. In any case, the parties face mounting tensions so that the continuation of the conflict becomes intolerable to them; then they are motivated to seek a resolution.

Other Teaching Suggestions

1. There are more instances of prosocial behavior in organizations than students might think. Encourage your students to relate instances they have experienced in which one employee went out of his or her way to help someone else or the organization without much clear benefit to him or herself. Next, discuss instances of prosocial behavior in society. All of this might lead to an interesting discussion of whether any behavior is truly altruistic. Does Mother Teresa toil to win a Nobel Prize, to save her soul, or because she thinks it's the right thing to do?

2. The text refers to studies involving the Prisoner's Dilemma game, a major tool in the study of conflict. The basic design stems from the dilemma of a prisoner who can turn in his accomplice or remain quiet. If both prisoners cooperate and neither talks, they will both get light sentences. If, on the other hand, either prisoner talks, he can get off while the other prisoner will face a long prison term; if they both talk, both will face long prison terms. The best strategy is cooperation where no one talks, but that requires a great deal of trust. Either prisoner can adopt a competitive strategy and talk, but that works only as long as the other prisoner doesn't talk. Again, the key is trust. There are many variations on this game, and any one is worth trying in class. There is a variation of this game played by nations regarding their nuclear arsenals that might be worth discussing also.

3. War is probably the ultimate form of interpersonal conflict. Can wars accomplish any good? One might argue that wars of independence do, but the negative effects of this particular form of conflict are more obvious. A discussion of the positive effects of specific wars, and whether these effects justified the costs might be worth developing.

4. Walton and McKersie wrote a book twenty years ago titled "A Behavioral View of Labor Negotiations." It is still a classic in this field. In it, the authors introduce the notions of distributive and integrative bargaining and discuss the tactics for each. They do not argue that all disputes can be made integrative, but they discuss many tactics for trying. The book and the specific tactics and examples they include would be worth sharing with your class.

5. The text briefly mentions final-offer arbitration as an alternative method of third-party intervention. It may deserve more discussion. The logic behind final-offer arbitration is that the parties, knowing their

dispute will be resolved in that way if they cannot resolve it themselves, should be more motivated to find their own solution. Otherwise, since the parties face the possibility that the other party will receive everything they demanded in their final offer, they face strike-like costs. It is interesting to note that contract disputes among professional baseball players are resolved in this way, and the results are published in the newspaper.

Case in Point Notes

Achieving Cooperation at Johnson Wax

This case describes how S. C. Johnson and Son, Inc. (better known as Johnson Wax) dramatically boosted the level of cooperation among its employees through the development and implementation of an integrated, company-wide, computerized information system—Integration of Customer Services Systems (CICSS). The original goal of this project was to completely integrate information about all of Johnson Wax's activities by developing and implementing a high-level information systems architecture (i.e., a single, computerized information system capable of integrating and coordinating information regarding all of the operational activities that Johnson used to manufacture and deliver its products). The project was

launched in 1987. By early 1990, the CICSS project was approaching completion, ahead of schedule and under budget. The CICSS project was a major driving force in reducing the conflict that had plagued the company and instituted a spirit of cooperation.

The details of how cooperation (and reduced conflict) were developed at Johnson Wax are described in the case. The discussion questions that follow the case prompt students to discuss many topics presented in the chapter. Specifically, students are asked to identify the causes of the conflict that originally plagued the company, and then to describe the personal and organizational factors that helped to create such a high level of cooperation at Johnson Wax. Finally, students are asked to explain the role of corporate mission and information technology in promoting cooperation.

Overall, this case provides a rather comprehensive illustration of the various factors associated with cooperation and conflict. To extend the discussion stimulated by this case, consider asking your students if they are aware of other companies that have inadvertently promoted cooperation (or conflict) as a consequence of changing or introducing a new technology into the workplace. Students often response to this question with fascinating, and very illustrative, stories about all aspects of cooperation and conflict.

Additional Case

Savemore Food Store 5116*

The Savemore Corporation is a chain of four hundred retail supermarkets located primarily in the northeastern section of the United States. Store 5116 employs over fifty persons, all of whom live within suburban Portage, New York, where the store is located.

Wally Schultz served as general manager of store 5116 for six years. Last April he was transferred to another store in the chain. At that time the employees were told by the District Manager, Mr. Finnie, that Wally Schultz was being promoted to manage a larger store in another township.

Most of the employees seemed unhappy to lose their old manager. Nearly everyone agreed with the opinion that Schultz was a "good guy to work for." As examples of his desirability as a boss the employees told how Wally had frequently helped the arthritic Negro porter with his floor mopping, how he had shut the store five minutes early each night so that certain employees might catch their busses, of a Christmas party held each year for employees at his own expense, and his general willingness to pitch in. All employees had been on a first-name basis with the manager. About half of them had begun work with the Savemore Corporation when the Portage store was opened.

Source: By John W. Hennessey, Jr., Professor Emeritus, Amos Tuck School of Business Administration, Dartmouth College.

*At the time of the case, the author, a college student, was employed for the summer as a checker and stockboy in store 5116.

Wally Schultz was replaced by Clark Raymond. Raymond, about twenty-five years old, was a graduate of an Ivy League college and had been with Savemore a little over a year. After completion of his six-month training program he served as manager of one of the chain's smaller stores before being advanced to store 5116. In introducing Raymond to the employees, Mr. Finnie stressed his rapid advancement and the profit increase that occurred while Raymond had charge of his last store.

I began my employment in store 5116 early in June. Mr. Raymond was the first person I met in the store, and he impressed me as being more intelligent and efficient than the managers I had worked for in previous summers at other stores. After a brief conversation concerning our respective colleges, he assigned me to a cash register, and I began my duties as a checker and bagger.

In the course of the next month, I began to sense that relationships between Raymond and his employees were somewhat strained. This attitude was particularly evident among the older employees of the store, who had worked in store 5116 since its opening. As we all ate our sandwiches together in the cage (an area about twenty feet square in the cellar fenced in by chicken wire, to be used during coffee breaks and lunch hours), I began to question some of the older employees as to why they disliked Mr. Raymond. Laura Morgan, a fellow checker about forty years old and the mother of two grade-school boys, gave the most specific answers. Her complaints were:

1. Raymond had fired the arthritic Negro porter on the grounds that a porter who "can't mop is no good to the company."
2. Raymond had not employed new help to make up for normal attrition. Because of this, everybody's work load was much heavier than it ever had been before.
3. The new manager made everyone call him "mister . . . he's unfriendly."
4. Raymond didn't pitch in. Wally Schultz had, according to Laura, helped people when they were behind in their work. She said that Schultz had helped her bag on rushed Friday nights when a long line waited at her checkout booth, but "Raymond wouldn't lift a finger if you were dying."
5. Employees were no longer let out early to catch busses. Because of the relative infrequency of this means of transportation, some employees now arrived home up to an hour later.
6. "Young Mr. Know-it-all with his fancy degree . . . takes all the fun out of this place."

Other employees had similar complaints. Gloria, another checker, claimed that ". . . he sends the company nurse to your home every time you call in sick." Margo, a meat wrapper, remarked, "everyone knows how he's having an affair with that new bookkeeper he hired to replace Carol when she quit." Pops Devery, head checker who had been with the chain for over ten years, was perhaps the most vehement of the group. He expressed his views in the following manner: "That new guy's a real louse . . . got a mean streak a mile long. Always trying to cut corners. First it's not enough help, then no overtime, and now, come Saturday mornings, we have to use boxes° for the orders 'til the truck arrives. If it wasn't just a year 'til retirement, I'd leave. Things just aren't what they used to be when Wally was around." The last statement was repeated in different forms by many of the other employees. Hearing all this praise of Wally, I was rather surprised when Mr. Finnie dropped the comment to me one morning that Wally had been demoted for inefficiency, and that no one at store 5116 had been told this. It was important that Mr. Schultz save face, Mr. Finnie told me.

A few days later, on Saturday of the busy weekend preceding the July 4 holiday, store 5116 again ran out of paper bags. However, the delivery truck did not arrive at ten o'clock, and by 10:30 the supply of cardboard cartons was also low. Mr. Raymond put in a hurried call to the warehouse. The men there did not know the whereabouts of the truck but promised to get an emergency supply of bags to us around noon. By eleven o'clock, there were no more containers of any type available, and Mr. Raymond reluctantly locked the doors to all further customers. The twenty checkers and packers remained in their respective booths, chatting among themselves. After a few minutes, Mr. Raymond requested that all retire to the cellar cage because he had a few words for them. As soon as the group was seated

°The truck from the company warehouse brining merchandise for sale and store supplies normally arrived at ten o'clock Saturday mornings. Frequently, the stock of larger paper bags would be temporarily depleted. It was then necessary to pack orders in cardboard cartons until the truck was unloaded.

on the wooden benches in the chicken wire enclosed area, Mr. Raymond began to speak, his back to the cellar stairs. In what appeared to be an angered tone, he began, "I'm out for myself first, Savemore second, the customer third, and you last. The inefficiency of this store has amazed me from the moment I arrived here . . ."

At about this time I noticed Mr. Finnie, the district manager, standing at the head of the cellar stairs. It was not surprising to see him at this time because he usually made three or four unannounced visits to the store each week as part of his regular supervisory procedure. Mr. Raymond, his back turned, had not observed Finnie's entrance.

Mr. Raymond continued, "Contrary to what seems to be the opinion of many of you, the Savemore Corporation is not running a social club here. We're in business for just one thing . . . to make money. One way that we lose money is by closing the store on Saturday morning at eleven o'clock.

Another way that we lose money is by using a 60-pound paper bag to do the job of a 20-pound bag. A 60-pound bag costs us over two cents apiece; a 20-pound bags costs less than a penny. So when you sell a couple of quarts of milk or a loaf of bread, don't use the big bags. Why do you think we have four different sizes anyway? There's no great intelligence or effort required to pick the right size. So do it. This store wouldn't be closed right now if you'd used your common sense. We started out this week with enough bags to last 'til Monday . . . and they would have lasted 'til Monday if you'd only used your brains. This kind of thing doesn't look good for the store, and it doesn't look good for me. Some of you have been bagging for over five years . . . and you oughta be able to do it right by now . . . ." Mr. Raymond paused and then said, "I trust I've made myself clear on this point."

The cage was silent for a moment, and then Pops Devery, the head checker, spoke up, "Just one thing, Mis-tuh Raymond. Things were running pretty well before you came around. When Wally was here we never ran out'a bags. The customers never complained about overloaded bags or the bottoms falling out before you got here. What're you gonna tell somebody when they ask for a couple of extra bags to use in garbage cans? What're you gonna tell somebody when they want their groceries in a bag, and not a box? You gonna tell them the manager's too damn cheap to give 'em bags? Is that what you're gonna tell 'em? No sir, things were never like this when Wally Schultz was around. We never had to apologize for a cheap manager who didn't order enough then. What'a you got to say to that, Mis-tuh Raymond?"

Mr. Raymond, his tone more emphatic, began again, "I've got just one thing to say to that, Mr. Devery, and that's this: Store 5116 never did much better than break even when Schultz was in charge here. I've shown a profit better than the best he ever hit in six years every week since I've been here. You can check that fact in the books upstairs any time you want. If you don't like the way I'm running things around here, there's nobody begging you to stay . . . ."

At this point, Pops Devery interrupted and, looking up the stairs at the district manager, asked, "What about that, Mr. Finnie? You've been around here as long as I have. You told us how Wally got promoted 'cause he was such a good boss. Supposin' you tell this young feller here what a good manager is really like? How about that, Mr. Finnie?"

A rather surprised Mr. Raymond turned around to look up the stairs at Mr. Finnie. The manager of store 5116 and his checkers and packers waited for Mr. Finnie's answer.

Questions

1. Contrast the leadership styles of Schultz and Raymond. Which do you feel is more effective?
2. Explain how leadership style influences organizational climate.
3. What role does the reward system of Savemore play in the establishment of leader-behavior?

Savemore Food Store 5116: Teaching Note

The Savemore Food Store case centers on the changes of employee attitude resulting from the removal of a well-liked but ineffective manager and his replacement with an abrasive younger manager on the move. The new manager's Theory X methods of leadership result in a growing ineffectiveness and hostility on the part of the workers culminating in a final berating of the workers in front of the district manager, Mr. Finnie.

Part I

The new organizational climate and its causes are readily apparent; on the one hand we have Wally Schultz who had served as general manager of the store for six years. During that time a comradery had developed between Wally and his workers. All agreed that Schultz was "a good guy to work for," and numerous examples of Schultz's behavior which brought about this degree of esprit among the employees are in evidence throughout the case, such as his frequent helping of the arthritic janitor or the early closing policies so the employees might catch early busses home.

With Wally's transfer and with his replacement by Clark Raymond we see a radical shift in the organizational climate at Savemore. Raymond is the young and hard-driving manager, bent on maximizing the efficiency of this particular Savemore location at the expense of all other considerations. Financial return has become his chief criterion even if it means bankruptcy in human relations. The changes in climate instituted by Raymond caused a good deal of dysfunctionality in employee morale and are in violation of the behavioral norm set up earlier in the social system under Schultz. Raymond, for example, fired the porter on the grounds that a porter who can't mop is no good to the company; no longer are people allowed to leave early in order to take advantage of public transportation. He has removed himself from the social system that had been established earlier by refusing to share in the work and by insisting that he be addressed as Mr. Raymond. Overall, his actions have had an obvious deleterious effect on the organization.

An additional complication which promises serious consequences centers around Finnie's efforts to save face for Schultz. By explaining to the employees that Schultz has been promoted, he has, in effect, given an organizational blessing to Schultz's management style and has made it doubly difficult for any successor, regardless of who that successor might be. As demonstrated by the head checker, the employees have been led to believe that Schultz's management techniques not only were adequate but that they

earned a promotion for him. This verification not only builds inaccurate expectations on the part of the staff but places Schultz's replacement in an untenable position. He will be held responsible for profits in an unprofitable and static organization.

It can be argued that whoever moved into the position would be virtually crippled by the previous structuring of the situation in the minds of the employees. This situation becomes particularly critical in an organization in which customer relations are of paramount importance. Clark Raymond's leadership style offers another basis for concern on the part of the students studying the Savemore case. The single-dimensional approach to management results in a 9-1 (Blake and Mouton) management style in which the worth of the individuals within the organization is negated and sacrificed to the immediate accomplishment of the task. Raymond's abrasive and yet patronizing attitude allows little opportunity for employee input and has resulted in hard feelings among the Savemore staff.

Raymond's leadership style could be classified as minimal in both consideration and initiating structure. Assuming that consideration and initiating structure are the two chief dimensions used to describe leadership behavior, Clark Raymond falls short in both areas. A leader with high consideration will develop a work atmosphere of mutual trust, respect subordinate ideas, and consider subordinates' feelings. He will also encourage good superior-subordinate rapport and two-way communication. A low consideration score would indicate that the leader was far more impersonal in his dealings with subordinates, a behavior obviously displayed by Raymond. Leaders scoring high in the initiating structure dimension are those who structure their own roles and those of their subordinates toward the attainment of preestablished goals. They are also actively involved in planning work activities, scheduling work, and communicating pertinent information for this "task" dimension. Raymond falls short on this dimension as well, for while he delegates little or not decision-making authority and retains virtually all power in his own centralized position, he has done little to structure his role or those of his subordinates toward the accomplishment of either his organizational or personal goals.

Part II

Often we use this case as a follow-up to a larger class discussion of the organizational climate or leadership styles and resulting behavior in organizations. It serves to illustrate the relationship between the climate or leadership style when one compares employee attitudes across the period of time covered by the case. Schultz and Raymond are individuals obviously located at opposite ends of the "human" dimension of leader behavior. It is interesting to note that while students are frustrated by and quick to condemn the leadership style displayed by Clark Raymond, few will realize the role the organization has in abetting continuation of management and climate of this nature. By holding Raymond alone responsible for bottom-line profit and rewarding him with promotions for achieving those profits regardless of the climate in which they were attained, and by simultaneously demoting Schultz for failure to attain profit in spite of a more attractive and colorful organizational climate, the total Savemore organization has played a major role in the structure of leadership behavior in the organization.

We feel it is important that the students note this fact and that they be able to translate the charge "maximized profits" into a broader, somewhat less-materialistic set of personal objectives for managers.

We have found that the class discussion and participation may proceed for an hour or more and have discovered that most of the "meat" of the conversation takes place in the first twenty-to-thirty minutes, and ordinarily we will seek to limit this discussion to this period of time.

Experiencing Organizational Behavior Notes

Personal Styles of Conflict Management

This exercise allows students to diagnose their preferred style of conflict management using a self-report questionnaire. Complete instructions for filling out the questionnaire are provided in the text. After completing the questionnaire, students are asked to examine their responses for any consistent patterns (this is how the questionnaire is scored). Typically, students diagnose a clear preference for one particular conflict resolution strategy.

While this is understandable, it can be very dysfunctional. Why? Because the effectiveness of each approach to conflict resolution differs, the strategy is contingent on the type of conflict involved. The best approach to conflict management is flexibility, employing the strategy that best fits the particular type of conflict that you are trying to resolve. A discussion of how students should go about becoming flexible provides a useful framework for discussing many of the topics in the chapter.

Additional Experiential Exercise

The Assertiveness Inventory

This instrument has been designed to give you some idea of your level of assertiveness. Assertiveness is not synonymous with aggressiveness—sometimes aggressive people need to become more assertive by constructively channeling their aggressiveness. The results of this inventory are "for your eyes only," and will not be shared with the instructor or anyone else in the class, unless *you* wish to do so.

For each of the statements below, indicate your behavioral approach to the situations described by responding according to the following scale:

1 = behavior never occurs
2 = behavior rarely occurs
3 = behavior sometimes occurs
4 = behavior generally occurs
5 = behavior almost always occurs

Some of the statements are "reverse-scored." That is, for these statements you should score them directly opposite the scale shown above. These statements are indicated by an asterisk (°), and should be scored as follows:

5 = behavior never occurs
4 = behavior rarely occurs
3 = behavior sometimes occurs
2 = behavior generally occurs
1 = behavior almost always occurs

A. Expressing Positive Feelings

____ 1. I give compliments easily and sincerely.
____ 2. I can tell people that I care about them.

° ____ 3. I usually feel critical of others.
° ____ 4. I can think of more negative characteristics of myself that I can positive characteristics.
____ 5. I tell teachers when I like a course.
° ____ 6. It's hard for me to tell my parents and family how much I love them.

B. Expressing Negative Feelings

____ 7. If I get defective merchandise from a store, I can return it easily.
____ 8. If my food comes prepared differently than I ordered it, I send it back.
____ 9. I can disagree with people.
° ____ 10. If there is something I don't like about a course, I usually don't say anything to the teacher, but I do complain to other students.
° ____ 11. If a family member of a close friend is annoying me, I usually pretend not to be bothered.
° ____ 12. I smile even when I am not happy.
° ____ 13. I find it difficult to negotiate prices for purchases, services, or repairs.
° ____ 14. When people cut in line in front of me, I usually let them.

C. Setting Limits

° ____ 15. I have a hard time saying "no."
° ____ 16. I get involved in activities merely because someone I know asked me to.
° ____ 17. If I get invited somewhere and do not want to go, I usually make up a story and beg off.
____ 18. I can say sincerely to people, "No thanks, I am not interested."
____ 19. I know how much I can handle and am careful not to take on too much.

D. Self-Initiative

_____ 20. I think of new projects or activities and then do them.

_____ 21. I can ask a member of the opposite sex for dates.

°_____ 22. I feel left out because not many people invite me places.

_____ 23. I easily initiate conversations with new people.

_____ 24. I have a difficult time meeting new people.

Total Score _____

The Assertiveness Inventory: Teaching Note

This instrument is designed to give students some idea about their general level of assertiveness. It is not designed to be the definite assessment of assertiveness, but should help students see areas in which they have trouble being assertive.

After discussing the scoring of this instrument with your students, you may then lead into strategies designed to enhance their assertiveness.

Scoring Key

100–200 You always stand up for yourself and take initiative, but you may overdo it at times and be aggressive. You may need to practice letting others take charge at times and not always saying everything negative that comes to mind.

61–99 You are probably quite assertive and use appropriate behaviors. You do not often overdo it, so you are rarely aggressive. You usually stand up for your rights, but are respectful of other people at the same time.

24–60 You are too passive and let other people make decisions for you and/or control your life. You need to try not to please others as often and take more initiative in your relationships.

Additional Readings

Brown, A. (1986, April). Labor contract negotiations: Behind the scenes. *Personnel Administrator,* pp. 55–56, 58–60.

Fried, V. H., and Oviatt, B. M. (1989). Michel Porter's missing chapter: The risk of antitrust violations. *Academy of Management Executive,* 3(1), 49–56. (A cautionary note on becoming too competitive.)

Organ, D. W. (1988). *Organizational Citizenship Behavior.* Lexington, MA: Lexington Books.

Perlmutter, H. V., & Heenan, D. A. (1986, March–April). Cooperate to compete globally. *Harvard Business Review,* pp. 136–141.

Walton, R. E., & McKersie, R. B. (1965). *A behavioral theory of labor negotiations.* New York: McGraw-Hill.

◼ 11 ◼

INFLUENCE, POWER, AND POLITICS IN ORGANIZATIONS

CHAPTER OUTLINE

LEARNING OBJECTIVES

After reading this chapter, you should be able to:
1. Distinguish among influence, power, and politics in organizations and describe their role in enhancing social control.
2. Characterize the major varieties of social influence that exist.
3. Describe the conditions under which social influence is used.
4. Identify the five major bases of individual social power and alternative types of individual power.
5. Characterize the conditions under which power is used.
6. Explain the two major approaches to the development of subunit power in organizations (the resource-dependency model and the strategic contingencies model).
7. Describe when and where organizational politics is likely to occur and the forms it is likely to take.
8. Explain the major ethical issues surrounding the uses of power and the enactment of political behavior in organizations.

Chapter Overview

This chapter deals with social influence, power, and politics and discusses the role of each in organizational behavior. The chapter begins by defining social influence (attempts to affect another in a desired fashion), power (the capacity to change the behavior or attitudes of another in a desired fashion), and politics (uses of power that enhance or protect one's own or one's group personal interests), and explains how these concepts and actions are used as control mechanisms in organizations. The chapter then presents in-depth discussions of each of the topics. Social influence tactics are described, with particular attention paid to the contingent approach to social influence—

selecting the influence tactic that best fits the situation. Individual power is then presented by describing French and Raven's typology of power bases (reward, coercive, legitimate, referent, and expert), and the recent expansion to this typology that includes information power, persuasive power, and charisma as additional individual power bases. How these power bases are used is then explained, followed by a discussion of group or subunit power (resource dependency model and the strategic contingencies model). The chapter then moves to a discussion of organizational politics. First, the conditions necessary for political behavior are described, and then various political tactics and games are identified and explained. Several suggestions for limiting the effects of organizational politics are also provided. The chapter ends with a discussion of the ethical implications of organizational politics. Specifically, guidelines for making political behavior ethical and the reasons for unethical behavior are described.

Three special sections appear in this chapter. An International/Multicultural Perspective (Bribery in Nigeria and the United States: Cross-National Differences in the Acceptance of Undue Influence) describes the findings of a study comparing American and Nigerian beliefs about the acceptability of bribery as an influence tactic. An OB in Practice (Empowerment: Shifting the Power Base to Subordinates) describes putting people in charge of what they do, and explains how several noteworthy companies are using empowerment to increase their effectiveness. And a Question of Ethics section (The Ethical Management of Authority: Perspectives from Human Resource Professionals) describes the findings of a study suggesting that self-serving, political pressures are responsible for many of the most unethical practices observed with the human resource management profession.

The Case in Point (CEO Disease: The Use and Abuse of Power) describes the syndrome of abuses committed by CEOs who have become drunk with the power of their position. This case also describes how some CEOs and some cultures prevent the development of CEO disease. The Experiencing Organizational Behavior exercise (Searching for Occupational Differences in the Use of Power) provides students the opportunity to explore differences and similarities in the use of various power bases by members of different professions and occupations.

Lecture and Review Questions

What is social influence and what are the most popular social influence tactics?

Social influence is an attempt to affect another person or persons in a desired fashion. In their research on social influence, Yukl and Falbo identified eight different tactics of social influence and their popularity associated with each tactic. In order of popularity (from most popular to least) are consultation (asking participation in decision making or planning a change), rational persuasion (using logical arguments and facts to persuade another that a desired result will occur), inspirational appeals (arousing enthusiasm by appealing to one's values and ideals), ingratiation (getting someone to do what you want by putting them in a good mood or getting them to like you), coalition (persuading by seeking the assistance of others, or by noting the support of others), pressure (seeking compliance by using demand, threats, or intimidation), upward appeals (noting that the influence request is approved by higher management), and exchange (promising some benefits in exchange for complying with a request). There is some reason to expect that people use influence tactics in a contingent manner. That is, because some influence tactics are more effective in a particular situation than others (e.g., rational persuasion is more effective in influencing a highly participative boss than is coercion), people select influence tactics that best fit the situation at hand.

What are the bases of power available to individuals? Power is the ability to influence others and, according to French and Raven. there are several bases of individual power that make this possible. One is legitimate or formal position power that is derived from a person's position in the formal organization. This is essentially the power someone has over you because he or she is your boss. Usually associated with legitimate power are reward and coercive power. Reward power refers to someone's ability to control valued resources and to offer some reward for compliance with their requests. Coercive power refers to the ability to punish someone who does not comply. Whereas reward power tends to bring people closer to an individual, coercive power tends to drive them further away. Expert power is derived from a person's knowledge or expertise in some area, and may often be the result of knowing how to get things done. Finally, referent power is based on interpersonal attraction, and stems from the fact that people will behave according to the wishes of someone they respect or admire. Recently, additional individual power bases have been added to those identified by French and Raven, These power bases are information power, persuasive power and charisma. Information power refers to the extent to which a supervisor provides a subordinate with the information needed to do the job. Persuasive power is the ability to use facts and logic to present a case persuasively. An charisma refers to an attitude of enthusiasm and optimism that is contagious.

What are the major models used to explain group or subunit power?

The two major models proposed to explain how groups or subunits gain power are the resource dependency model, and the strategic contingencies model. The resource dependency model suggests that groups gain power to the extent that other groups depend on them for resources. Groups which control more resources in an organization are more powerful, although all groups contribute something to the organization and so have some power. The strategic contingencies model is somewhat related by focusing on the extent to which the operations of some subunits might be contingent on the activities of another subunit. Thus, some subunits will be able to control the activities of other groups. Subunits gain this power in several ways: more powerful subunits can reduce the uncertainty faced by other subunits; more powerful subunits perform operations that are central to the organizations's functioning; and more powerful subunits perform activities that are indispensable and non-substitutable within the organization.

What are organizational politics, and how are they played?

Organizational politics are action not officially sanctioned by an organization and taken to influence others in order to meet one's personal goals. Although organizational politics are widespread, they are more likely to occur in some parts of an organization than in others. Specifically, politics tend to occur in situations where there are no clear policies or guidelines, and thus, there is the most ambiguity (as in top management). The basic tactics involved are relatively simple and include: blaming and attacking others when things go wrong; controlling access to information; cultivating a favorable impression; developing a base of support; and aligning with more powerful others. All of these tactics allow one to gain more relative power in the organization. This power can be used to play any one of the following political games: authority games (whether to resist formal authority or to counter resistance to formal authority), power base games (to enhance one's bases of power with subordinates, peers, or superiors), rivalry games (to defeat the other party in the quest for power), and change games (either to correct organizational wrong-doings or to seize control over an organization). Politics and political games are more likely to occur in situations where there is uncertainty, where there are important decisions involving large amounts of scarce resources, where organizational units have conflicting interests, and where organizational units have approximately equal power.

What are the ethical implications of organizational politics?

Organizational ethics refers to the application of moral and ethical standards to the behavior of persons within organizations, so that these standards will act as a restraint on that behavior. Although few people would disagree with this in principle, it is not always clear whether an action is ethical. There are some guidelines, however. Political actions are less likely to be ethical if they promote purely selfish interests, rather than also helping to meet organizational goals. Political activity is less likely to be ethical if it fails to respect the rights of the individuals affected, such as their right to privacy. Finally, political activity is less likely to be ethical if it fails to conform to standards of equity and justice. Unfortunately, there is reason to believe that a considerable amount of unethical behavior and activity takes place in organizations. One reason for this is that organizations often reward behaviors that violate ethical standards, such as stonewalling (withholding information) and passing the buck rather than taking responsibility for one's actions. Another reason is the existence of managerial values that actually undermine integrity. Specifically, many managers think only of the bottom line, without concern for who might suffer as profits are maximized; some managers view others merely as pawns to be used and exploited; and some managers believe that anything is right if the public can be convinced it is right.

Other Teaching Suggestions

1. The text discusses the bases of individual power, and the fact that the more bases available, the easier it is to function as a leader. But not all bases are of equal importance. Think about leaders who have lacked one or more of these and the problems this caused. For example, what about a leader who has considerable legitimate power, as well as reward and coercive power, but all of this power derives from the fact that the leader is the nephew of the company owner. Perhaps your students (or you) have worked for someone for whom you had no respect. This is far more uncomfortable than working for someone who lacks reward or coercive power. In fact, when the legitimate leader lacks referent power, an informal leader often emerges in the group, usually an older worker. During the Vietnam war, there were a number of new second lieutenants who fit the pattern described above, and this presented serious problems. A practice called "fragging" developed, however, and this helped eliminate the problem as well as the officer.

2. One of the interesting things we have learned about powerful people is that, over time, they tend to

think less of the people they are able to influence. Actually, David Kipnis has done some research that suggests that this is true only when the superior feels he or she can bully the subordinate. The leader then comes to hold that person in less esteem and tends to think less of that person's peers as well, making it easier to bully them, too. Some discussion of what people who exercise true power are thinking might be interesting.

3. Group or subunit power was said to derive, in part, from controlling valued resources. One thing that seems to be true of many large organizations is that private secretaries and administrative assistants wield a great deal of power. They control access to powerful people and, therefore, have power themselves. But, even if the person in charge is not powerful, secretaries still wield a great deal of power. Typically, the manager or executive feels it is beneath him or her to be concerned with day-to-day procedures in the organization. Instead, these tasks are delegated to secretaries. Eventually, the only people who know how to requisition supplies or complete the reimbursement form for expenses is the secretary. That is power, and the way to keep it is not to share the information with anyone else. You might ask your students if they are aware of other such power holders.

4. Organizational politics and politics in general are always interesting topics. The best politicians are those who get things done without anyone knowing they're doing it. The only problem is, if you are interested in power, it doesn't result in people perceiving you as powerful. Therefore, every now and then, you must let slip some successful maneuver from the past so others come to recognize the power you really have. This may sound cyclical, but your students should know that office politics are often a way of life, and teachers seldom prepare them for this.

5. Ethics in politics is a hot topic. In 1992 there was a major backlash against politics and professional politicians in the United States, professional politics being considered a perfect example of a situation where everyone is rewarded for violating ethical principles. President Bush was severely criticized for hosting campaign fund raising dinners where guests pay thousands of dollars to attend. It may not be clear that hosting campaign fund raising events is truly unethical, but one must be suspicious about *why* someone would pay so much money just to have a meal with the president. President Bush stated that the fund raising dinners were entirely proper. A growing number of American voters suspected otherwise. In politics, one often gains power by doing favors. If a senator votes for a bill he or she

believes is wrong, is that justified by the fact that he or she will be able to call in the debt when he or she later proposes a different bill that really will be of some benefit? This topic will stimulate discussion among your students.

Case in Point Notes
CEO Disease: The Use and Abuse of Power
This case describes CEO disease—the syndrome of abuses committed by CEOs who have become drunk with the power of their position. This case also describes how some CEOs and some cultures prevent the development of CEO disease. Featured in this case are some of the more notorious victims of CEO disease (Robert Schoellhorn, former CEO of Abbot Laboratories; Walter Connolly, former CEO of the now defunct Bank of New England; and F. Ross Johnson, former CEO of RJR Nabisco) and their assorted, usually extravagant, exploits. An example of CEOs who work to prevent CEO disease are John Scully, CEO of Apple Computer, Robert L. Crandall, CEO of American Airlines, and Chiyoji Misawa, CEO of Misawa Homes (a Japanese construction company). The stories of how each reacts to the power that comes with the office of the chief executive officer is fully described in the case.

Following the case are a set of discussion questions that prompt students to apply what they have learned about social influence, power, and politics to the various stories illustrated in the case. Specifically, students are asked to identify and compare the power base preferences of the CEOs afflicted with CEO disease and the CEOs who have managed to avoid falling victim to the disease. Students are also prompted to consider why Japanese executives are less likely to develop CEO disease as compared to their American counterparts. Finally, students are asked to identify the political tactics and games used by former Abbott CEO Schoellhorn (and what games his heir apparents might have used), and discuss the ethical implications of CEO disease.

This case always generates lively discussion. Students often mention their concerns about the enormously high level of pay CEOs receive in the US and its role as a factor in CEO disease. If this topic comes up, ask your students to consider if high pay is a cause or effect of CEO disease. Also, consider asking your students if they have ever seen CEO disease in person (e.g., a boss, a friend, acquaintance). Stories from students themselves regarding the use of various influences, power, and political strategies provide everyone with an excellent basis for practicing what they have learned from the text.

Bad Chemistry

Sarah Thompson is an intelligent, well-respected chemist in a male-dominated profession. In college, she took as many elective courses in organizational communications as her graduate program would allow. She felt that knowing how to talk to and manage people would be an important asset in her technical field. She was right. In the small company she worked for, she was often praised for her excellent "people skills." But her company needed researchers, not managers. After nine years with this small company, she felt it was time to move on to a company that could offer her career movement into management.

Several months later, Sarah accepted a position with Marion Chemical, a national research and manufacturing company based in Columbus, Ohio. Marion Chemical was known as a mediocre company that tended to jump on bandwagons rather than forge new breakthroughs in the chemical industry. The company intrigued Sarah because of its unique laboratory management structure. In a preliminary interview, she learned that the New Research Lab was dividing into two cooperative teams in an attempt to increase management control over the technical group. The team leaders—chemists—were actually "project coordinators and people problem-solvers." A "Manager of New Research" was the legitimate supervisor of the lab. Sarah was hired as one of the team leaders.

Sarah began her first day at Marion Chemical by meeting Joyce Roberts, the manager of New Research. Sarah was immediately impressed by Joyce because of her dynamic personality and professional, "tailored blue suit" appearance. Sarah though, "Gee, I guess they take management seriously around here. Joyce looks like she is on her way up, and I know it's not easy for a woman to reach the ranks of management in the chemical industry." Joyce briefed Sarah on the market aspects of Marion Chemical and how important it was for their researchers, especially their team leaders, to be innovative. Sarah then asked, "I read that your labs are working on the DZ100 frequencies. What have your studies determined the plasmid characteristics to be?" Joyce repeated the question, then said, "We've determined, uh, that, well, um, I'd rather have the senior member of your team fill you in on the details of that project. Listen, I want you to know that I'm always here to answer your questions or help you out. Your responsibility is to keep your team organized and efficient. I'm here to help you in any way I can. We are all one big team around here." Sarah left the manager's office feeling very good about the open lines of communication in the laboratory.

The next meeting Sarah had was with Conrad King, the other team leader. As they spoke, he was frequently interrupted by phone calls and questions from lab technicians on his team. However, he did not introduce Sarah to any of his team members, even though Sarah thought the two teams would be working cooperatively. Their conversation went like this:

Source: Exerpts from *Casebook for Organizational Communication and Behavior (2 + 2 = 5)* by Allen D. Frank, copyright © 1989 by Holt, Rinehart & Winston, Inc., reprinted by permission of the publisher.

Sarah: So, Conrad, how do you like the idea of teams in the lab?

Conrad: First, I think it's a great opportunity for intelligent lab hermits like us to get into management. That was the major point I stressed when I sold the current management on the team concept. They bought the whole package.

Sarah: You're the one who *sold* them on the idea?

Conrad: Yup. I felt it was about time we got some real management in here. Now I can go ahead and do things that should have been done years ago.

Sarah: Such as . . .

Conrad: Such as making sure that I approve all new research projects and requiring attendance at my weekly update meetings. I've got to be kept informed on everything that goes on around here.

Sarah: How do your new policies affect my team?

Conrad: I would expect your team to honor my policies.

Sarah left Conrad's office feeling confused. What happened to the idea of "one big team?" She questioned her role in the department and felt it would be best to discuss her feelings with the manager, Joyce. In her meeting with Joyce, she began:

Sarah: After meeting Conrad, I'm a bit confused about my role. I thought that he and I were equal. Am I supposed to report to him?

Joyce: Conrad is a wonderful leader. His suggestions have really helped me out here. I trust his judgment. What did he tell you?

Sarah: Well, he told me about some policies that he intended to implement. I get the feeling that he's building his own empire.

Joyce: Yes, Conrad and I discussed the policies. I think they're fine. I also think that you're reading too much into the situation. This lab is running smoothly, and I intend to make sure it stays that way.

Sarah: It seems to me that you're losing power. The long-term success of this lab could be jeopardized if this is the case.

Joyce: Since I've been here, I've brought this lab from disorganization to the organized team approach. That's a great accomplishment. You might find our a little more about us before you jump to conclusions. Everything will be just fine. Let's not make waves, okay?

Sarah left Joyce's office feeling even more confused and a bit helpless. When she got to her office, there was a memo in her basket. It said:

Congratulations Joyce!
Tomorrow we'll have cake and coffee in honor of Joyce Roberts who will be leaving us on Friday. Joyce has been promoted to National Sales Manager because of her success and innovativeness as manager of New Research. In her sixteen-month term here, she has creatively implemented the "team" approach to lab management, making Marion Chemical the only lab in the country to have a completely participative system of lab management!

Sarah was appalled! Sixteen-month term? How could the lab ever make long-term plans if management turnover continued at this pace?

On Monday, Ron Summers was introduced as the next manager of New Research. Sarah studied his background and learned that he had worked as a sales representative with Marion for six years, then became a district sales manager, and then a regional sales manager. He was put on some kind of upward bound list and waited until the right team management position came along so he could make his transition to upper management. She also picked up from the grapevine that anyone who stays for more than two years is considered a loser. "Some joke," she through. "The joke's on us, the researchers."

Sarah decided to hold a team meeting to gather the group's thoughts on lab management. The team's conversation proved interesting.

Sarah: I'd like to get to know each of you better—find out what your interests and goals are. What are your feelings about management in this lab?

Team Member 1: What management? We get a sales manager who hops on our merry-go-round one year and gets off the next. Our managers have no idea what we do.

Team Member 2: I think you're being too harsh. Joyce always made herself available.

Team Member 3: Sure . . . available to talk about personal problems, or to give us a pep talk about how we've got to work together to make breakthroughs in the marketplace. All talk, talk, talk about sales.

Sarah: How about Conrad? What's his role here?

Team Member 3: He's only been here three years, and he's already a team leader. I don't know how he does it, but he seems to know what makes management jump. Last year I tried to get a new piece of equipment in the lab. It would cost Marion about $25,000, but I know it would pay for itself in a few years because we'd save so much time. I couldn't get management to even talk to me about it, so I went to Conrad. He asked me for estimates on how much our lab would save because of the new equipment and what my other arguments were. I know for sure that he made several phone calls to friends he's made in management. He seemed to know which buttons to push and how much information to share with each manager. Before I knew it, I had the equipment.

Team Member 4: Yeah, and remember that Joyce got the award for introducing the new piece of equipment. It sure did increase productivity dramatically! She ended up looking pretty good to upper management.

Sarah: Hmmm. I think I'm getting the picture. How did you feel when Joyce got recognition for your idea?

Team Member 3: Heck, I didn't care about that. I just wanted to get the equipment so I could run an important series of tests on an experiment. My goal isn't to get into management, so I don't want to play all those political games.

Team Member 2: Somebody's got to do it. At least Conrad is a chemist. He understands what we're trying to accomplish. He's really the one running the place.

As she left the team meeting, Sarah thought, "I'm going to keep a close eye on Conrad and on Ron Summers so I can find out what I'm up against."

The following week, one of her team members, Paul Johnson, told Sarah he had discovered a new superplastic that could revolutionize Marion Chemical's market. Sarah enthusiastically shared the news with her team. Each of her team members asked the same question: "Which team will be chosen to investigate the properties of the new superplastic?" Sarah thought, "Paul is on my team, so we will do the investigation. I'd better share the news with Ron Summers."

Sarah met briefly with Ron to tell him that a member of her team had discovered a new superplastic. He congratulated her and Paul, saying, "That's the kind of innovation that will make Marion Chemical a market leader!" He told Sarah he'd get back to her to discuss how they should proceed. He then went into Conrad's office. Ron and Conrad discussed the superplastic.

Ron: I sense from Sarah that the superplastic has great implications for Marion Chemical.

Conrad: Well, Sarah may be a little more enthusiastic than she should be. Now we have to do a lot of investigation. She may not be ready for that.

Ron: What's next?

Conrad: It's critical that Paul be on the investigating team because of his expertise and understanding of the superplastic.

Ron: Now you've got me worried. If this discovery is something big, I want to make sure we do it right. It's important to me.

Conrad: I understand. Listen, I'll take Paul on my team. Then I can get this thing done for you. Ron, it's going to be a big success, you wait and see!

Ron later stopped by Sarah's office and said, "It's all taken care of. Paul will join Conrad's team. Since Conrad has more experience with this kind of thing, I've decided that he should lead the investigation.

Sarah was outraged. She sat in her office fuming and planning her next move.

Questions

1. Consider the forms of power discussed in the chapter. Of the individuals identified in the case, which would you rate high and low on the following forms of power: Expert? Referent? Legitimate? Reward? Coercive? Resource Control? Network?

2. Who at Marion Chemical does the best job of building a power base?

3. What are some positive and negative outcomes resulting from uses of power at Marion Chemical?

Bad Chemistry: Teaching Note

This case gives students a good overview of the sources and uses of power in the workplace. Joyce Roberts (and later Ron Summers) have legitimate power. Their position as Manager of New Research carries with it formal authority (or position power). Joyce used legitimate power to further her career at Marion Chemical. She did little for the teams that worked under her. We do not know much about Ron Summer, except that he seems to be following in Joyce's footsteps. He sees this position as a stepping stone for his future with the company.

1. Consider the forms of power discussed in the chapter. Of the individuals identified in the case, which would you rate high and low on the following forms of power: Expert? Referent? Legitimate? Reward? Coercive? Resource Control? Network?

   Expert power can be seen in Conrad. He also has other sources of power, such as resource control and network centrality, sources of power generally attributed to groups. He has been in his position for only three years, yet he has connections all through Marion Chemical. He was able to get the equipment for a member of a team other than his. Ron Summers deferred to Conrad on the question of reassigning Paul Johnson. Conrad also has an indirect form of reward power. He and his team have been successful, and Joyce has benefitted from that success. Her promotion is a reward, partially attributable to Conrad and his team. The members of Sarah's team seem to think of Conrad as someone having admirable characteristics, and this is a source of referent power.

   It seems obvious that Sarah has little power, Ron perceived her as having little experience, and assigned Paul to Conrad's team. She has not had time to build a network of associates at Marion Chemical.

Team members also have little power, with the exception of Paul Johnson. He has developed a new product that could mean a great deal of success for the company, the New Research Department, and the work team to which he is assigned. Paul has acquired expert power.

2. Who at Marion Chemical dos the best job of building a power base?

   It seems obvious that Conrad has done the best job of building a power base at Marion Chemical. As noted above, Conrad's power stems from a number of sources.

3. What are some positive and negative outcomes resulting from the use of power at Marion Chemical?

   Power is the lubricant that makes organizations function smoothly. It is essential to achieve any organization's goals. Individuals strive for power—it can be a satisfying experience. Power confers status, respect and prestige. However, power can be dysfunctional for organizations. As the saying goes: "Power corrupts, absolute power corrupts absolutely." Power employed to control individuals may be counterproductive to the goals of an organization.

The Labor Contract

George Jensen, chief negotiator for Local 626 of the International Brotherhood of Electrical Workers (IBEW), was not looking forward to the next few weeks. There was little to be optimistic about; negotiations for the new labor contract with Asgood Electronics were to begin on Monday, and the union would undoubtedly be asked to grant wage and benefit concessions to the company.

Asgood Electronics was a major supplier of complex electronic assemblies for the computer industry. However, due to the growth of the personal computer segment of the market, which was not anticipated by product planners at Asgood, company sales and earnings had dramatically fallen over the past eighteen months. The firm was in trouble, and employees were well aware of the situation.

Employee awareness did not necessarily lead to sympathy with the plight of the company. Both the union and Asgood management remembered the results of the last contract negotiations three years ago, a bitter sixty-four day strike that, when settled, did little to resolve the differences between the company and the workers. The issues raised in the negotiation of the previous contract were still fresh in the minds of both parties, and would likely surface during the upcoming negotiations.

Jill Nichols, Manager of Human Resources at Asgood and the firm's chief representative at the bargaining table, was also preparing for the negotiations. Jill remembered the difficulty of the last negotiations, and felt that the union demands were, and remained, totally ridiculous. Thus she did not attempt to hide her feelings in dealing with union representatives. She truly believed that workers would be better off without the union and that the leadership of the union did not accurately reflect the attitudes of the average worker at Asgood.

Local 626 of the IBEW was an important force at Asgood Electronics. Fully 90 percent of the eligible employees belonged to the union, representing some 45 percent of the

Source: By Robert D. Goddard, Appalachian State University.

total work force. Many, if not most, of the union members felt that a strike was unavoidable if the pay and benefit issues were not satisfactorily resolved. the union was in a strong position at Asgood. Operations were impossible without the assembly workers, and they could not be replaced during a strike. George Jensen had conducted a straw vote, and was satisfied that the membership had given him a mandate to seek substantial improvements in both pay and benefits. Many of the employees believed that the recent disclosure of the firm's financial difficulties was a cover to try to "break" the union. They did not trust management, and George believed that Asgood did not really want to reach an equitable agreement with Local 626.

Jill and her team of management negotiators had spent weeks preparing their position, gathering facts and figures to support their case for concessions on the part of the union. However, she felt certain that once the negotiations opened on Monday, cold hard facts would soon give way to hot, emotional arguments. Not only would the union reject requests for concessions, they would seek substantial increases in wages and benefits which might lead to financial ruin for Asgood. Additionally, a strike would have the same disastrous consequences for the company.

It looked like the irresistible force was about to meet the immovable object on Monday!

Questions

1. Do you think George has an accurate understanding of the very real financial difficulties facing Asgood Electronics?
2. Do you think Jill's perception of how well the union's leadership represents members' attitudes is accurate?
3. How does the concept of the superordinate goal provide a possible solution to the dilemma presented above?

The Labor Contract: Teaching Note

This short case provides the student with a small degree of insight into some of the problems of power in negotiation situations. The questions are fairly specific, and can be answered without much deep thinking. You may want to discuss the concept of the superordinate goal in your lecture and how it can be used to channel competitive energies in constructive ways.

You might want to use the case to illustrate the concepts of the *bases of power* that were introduced in the chapter. Ask the students to explain what kind(s) of power George and Jill had in the situation described in the case.

The ideas of political tactics and political games from the text can be interwoven into a discussion of this case. You could ask the students if they can identify any of the political tactics or games described in the text.

The concept of ethics would be harder to bring out with this case, but you could ask the students if they could find examples of the managerial values that might undermine integrity, such as the *bottom line* mentality, the *exploitative* mentality and the *Madison Avenue* mentality.

Experiencing Organizational Behavior Notes

Searching for Occupational Differences in the Use of Power

This exercise provides students the opportunity to explore differences and similarities in the use of various power bases by members of different professions and occupations. Because individual dispositions and work situations are important determinants of the ways people use power, it is likely that people in the same occupation will use power similarly, and that people from different occupations will not. In this

exercise, students are asked to collect data (using a questionnaire provided in the text) from members of difference occupations regarding the power bases that their supervisors use to influence them. Once collected, the results are tabulated in class and analyzed for similarities and differences by occupation.

Included with the instructions for performing the exercise are several points to consider which help students to analyze and interpret their power base data.

Additional Readings

Bartolome, F., & Laurent, A. (1986, November–December). The Manager: Master and servant of power. *Harvard Business Review*, pp. 77–80

Cadbury, A. (1987, September–October). Ethical Managers make their own rules. *Harvard Business Review*, pp. 69–72.

Keys, J. B., & Case, T. L. (1990). How to become an influential manager. *Academy of Management Executive*, 4(4), 38–51.

Nielsen, R. P. (1989). Changing unethical organizational behavior. *Academy of Management Executive*, 1989, 3(2), 123–130.

Philbrick, J. H., & Haas, M. E. (1988). The new management: Is it legal? *Academy of Management Executive*, 2(4), 325–329

∎ 12 ∎

LEADERSHIP: ITS NATURE AND IMPACT IN ORGANIZATIONS

CHAPTER OUTLINE

Special Sections

OB in Practice On the Costs of Arrogance: Or, How *Not* to Lead Effectively

An International Multicultural Perspective Asian and American CEOs: Different Cultures, Different Styles?

OB in Practice Leader Training: Helping Leaders to Polish Up Their Acts

Focus on Research Charisma, Personality, and Presidential Performance: A Retrospective Study

LEARNING OBJECTIVES

After reading this chapter, you should be able to:
1. Define *leadership* and indicate why leading and managing are not always the same.
2. Describe several traits that distinguish leaders from other people.
3. Describe several key dimensions of leader behavior.
4. Indicate whether, and in what ways, male and female leaders differ.
5. Comment on key differences between American and Asian CEOs.
6. Summarize the main points of major theories of leader effectiveness (*contingency theory, normative theory, path-goal theory*).
7. Describe the nature of *transformational* or *charismatic* leadership.
8. Explain why leaders are not always essential to high levels of performance by the groups they lead.
9. Explain why different styles of leadership may be required at different points in the development of work groups.

Chapter Overview

In this chapter leadership, its various forms, and its important influence on organizational behavior are discussed. It begins with a definition of leadership and explains why leadership and management are not the same. The chapter then addresses the role of leader traits and leader behaviors in leader effectiveness. The disappointments associated with early trait research is discussed, as well as recent research findings that show several important trait differences between leaders and other persons. The discussion of leader behaviors focuses on participative versus autocratic leaders, and person- versus production-oriented leaders. The issue of possible differences between female and male leaders is then discussed, followed by an explanation of the complex relationship that exists between leaders and followers, and a description of various types of followers and their effects on leader effectiveness. Next, the major theories of leadership are presented. Specifically, the chapter describes and evaluates (discussing relevant research) Fiedler's contingency theory, normative theory, and path-goal theory. Then the chapter presents a discussion of transformational leadership. Finally, three additional perspectives on leadership are described: the vertical dyad linkage model, substitutes for leadership and situational leadership theory.

Four special sections appear in this chapter. An OB in Practice (On the Costs of Arrogance: Or, How Not to Lead Effectively) identifies arrogance, lack of commitment, and lack of loyalty as key obstacles to leader effectiveness. An International/Multicultural Perspective (Asian and American CEOs: Different Cultures, Different Styles) describes the findings of a study showing important differences between Asian and American chief executive officers. A second OB in Practice (Leader Training: Helping Leaders to Polish Up Their Acts) describes how leaders are learning to improve their people skills. And a Focus on Research (Charisma, Personality, and Presidential Performance: A Retrospective Study) discusses the findings of a research study about charisma among U.S. presidents. This research shows that charismatic leaders do not arise in a social vacuum; rather, they are brought to power by special sets of circumstances.

The Case in Point (Leadership at Levi Strauss) describes the extraordinarily effective leadership practices of transformational leader Robert D. Haas, chairman and CEO of Levi Strauss & Co. The Experiencing Organizational Behavior exercise (In Search of Great Leaders) is designed to demonstrate the importance of special circumstances as a determinant of transformational or charismatic leader effectiveness.

Lecture and Review Questions

What is leadership and why is it different from management?

Leadership is the process whereby one individual influences other group members toward the attainment of defined group or organizational goals. Therefore, leadership is largely concerned with influence as a leader attempts to change attitudes, and hopefully the behavior, of other group members. Although this in-

fluence can be accomplished through coercive tactics, it generally is not. Many managers function as leaders in their jobs, but not all do. Management functions include other activities such as planning, scheduling, and communicating with customers or clients, which do not involve leadership. In fact, not only are there managers who are not leaders, there are also leaders who are not managers.

What traits distinguish leaders from other persons?

The first formal approach to the study of leadership involved searching for traits or individual characteristics that differentiated leaders from followers. Unfortunately, decades of active research about leader traits failed to yield a short, agreed-upon list of key traits shared by all leaders. As a consequence, this line of research dried up and was essentially discontinued by the early 1950s.

Recently, however, there has been a renewed interest in leader traits, and this interest has generated some interesting and worthwhile research. What does this research show? Leaders *do* actually differ from other persons in several important and measurable aspects. Leaders demonstrate a high degree of leader motivation—the desire to influence others. There are two forms of leadership motivation; personalized power motivation and socialized power motivation. Personalized power motivation is the desire to dominate others which often reveals itself in an excessive concern with status. Socialized power motivation is the desire to use power as means to achieve desired, shared goals. Leaders motivated by this form of leadership motivation cooperate with others, develop networks and coalitions, and generally work **with** subordinates rather than try to dominate or control them. Of the two, the socialized power form of leadership motivation is usually far more adaptive for organizations than personalized leadership motivation. Other traits that differentiate leaders from other people are drive (desire for achievement, high energy, initiative and the like), honesty and integrity, cognitive ability (intelligence), self-confidence, knowledge of the business that they are in, creativity, and very important—flexibility (the ability to adapt to the needs of followers and the requirements of the situation).

What are the key dimensions of leader behavior?

Research about leader behavior has been very productive. This type of leadership research—studying what leaders actually do rather than their traits—has generated two general categories of leader behaviors. One category of leader behaviors involves participative and autocratic leaders. Beyond the obvious fact that participative leaders delegate and are open to suggestions while autocratic leaders insist on telling everyone exactly how things are to be done, this approach has gone on to consider four types of leader behavior: directive autocrat (makes all decisions and closely monitors subordinates), permissive autocrat (makes all decisions, but allows latitude in how they are carried out), directive democrat (participative decision making and close supervision), and permissive democrat (participative decision making and latitude). The other major approach to studying leader behavior is concerned with person-oriented leaders and task-oriented leaders. These two dimensions of leader behavior are more commonly known as consideration and initiating structure, and combine to form four leader behavior styles (high or low on each dimension). Although the best style depends a great deal on the situation, the leader who is high on both dimensions usually, has an edge.

Do Male and Female leaders differ?

Several authors have argued that men and women differ in their leadership styles and traits. Author Jan Grant, for example, wrote an article contending that females should stop trying to emulate male qualities such as independence, competitiveness, and analytical thinking, and emphasize, instead, traditionally feminine qualities such as affiliation, cooperativeness, and nurturance. Similar arguments about differences between female and male leaders have been made in other popular books. Is there any validity to these claims that male and female leaders are different? Systematic research (meta-analysis of more than 150 separate research studies of leadership in which comparisons of male and females were possible) on this issue indicates that, in general, female leaders *do not* differ from their male counterparts. Some minor differences were found (e.g., females were found to adopt a more participative decision making style than males), but these differences are smaller in magnitude and less consistent than suggested by sex-role stereotypes.

How important are followers in determining the effectiveness or success of leaders?

Followers are a critical part of leader effectiveness. After all, without followers, there is no such thing as leadership. A recent conceptualization (described in the chapter), identifies four distinct types of followers based on the extent to followers engage in critical thinking and the extent to which they are active or passive toward their jobs and leader. People low on both dimensions are described as *sheep;* they add very little to the leader's performance and may well constitute an obstacle to excellence. Followers who play a more active role, but show little critical thinking are described as *yes people.* In contrast, *alienated people* are critical thinkers, but passive. They may interfere with leader initiatives. Followers who fall in the middle on both dimensions are *survivors;* they neither

add not detract from a leader's success. Finally, *effective followers* are persons who are high on both dimensions; they can think for themselves and carry out tasks with enthusiasm. To the degree that a leader can attract and develop effective followers, he or she is well on the way to success.

What are the major aspects of Fiedler's contingency theory?

Contingency theory suggests a formal system for matching leadership styles with aspects of the situation in order to maximize effectiveness. Fiedler's model classifies leadership styles using an instrument called the least preferred coworker scale (LPC): high LPC leaders tend to be person-oriented, while low LPC leaders tend to be task-oriented. The situation is characterized by three factors: task structure (the extent to which task goals and roles are clearly defined), leader position power (the leader's ability to enforce compliance), and leader-member relations. Situations favor the leader when there are high levels of all three situational factors. According to the theory, low LPC leaders are more successful when situational favorableness is either high or low, while high LPC leaders are more successful in situations between the extremes. Support for the theory has been mixed with more support obtained in laboratory studies than in field studies, and the theory has been criticized for a lack of specificity concerning situational favorableness, and especially for its reliance on the LPC scale to measure leadership styles. Nonetheless, this theory has also been extended to consider the impact of leader cognitive abilities on effectiveness. This extension, known as cognitive resource theory, suggests that leader intelligence has a strong impact on followers *only* if the leader is directive and *only* when stress is low.

What are the major components of the normative theory of leadership?

Vroom and Yetton's normative theory is another attempt to match leadership styles with situations. Here, there are five leadership styles considered, but they vary along the single dimension of participation in decision making. Leadership styles vary from autocratic to group decision with a less extreme autocratic style and two consultative styles in between. The situation in this theory is characterized by a complex set of decision rules that help decide the most appropriate leadership style to be used by the leader. Specifically, the situation is analyzed by the leader's responses to three questions concerning decision quality (Is a high quality decision required? Do I have enough information to make such a decision? Is the problem well structured?), and four questions regarding subordinate acceptance of a decision (Is subordinate acceptance crucial for implementation? Will subordinates accept a decision I make by myself? Do subordinates share organizational goals relevant to this problem? Is conflict likely?). A resulting decision tree and a series of decision rules suggest the most effective leadership style. Research suggests that the recommended style does, in fact, tend to be the most effective.

What are the key components of path-goal theory?

The logic behind House's path-goal theory is that a leader's function is to help subordinates achieve important goals. Specifically, the leader should clarify the nature of the task, reduce obstacles to task accomplishment, and do everything possible to increase the subordinate's perception that effort will lead to performance which will, in turn, be rewarded. When this occurs, there will be increased job satisfaction, motivation, and performance. The theory considers four basic leadership styles: instrumental (focuses on guidance and establishing rules), supportive (focuses on relations among subordinates), participative (the leader consults with subordinates), and achievement-oriented (the leader sets challenging goals for subordinates). The most effective leadership style depends, in part, on the subordinates (high-ability subordinates do best with less structured, more supportive styles while low-ability subordinates require instrumental leaders), and the work environment (instrumental leadership works best with unstructured, non-routine tasks. Research has generally been supportive of the major predictions of path-goal theory and its underlying logic—that the leader must supply what is missing in the situation to make sure that subordinates can accomplish goals.

What is the nature of transformational or charismatic leadership?

Transformational leaders are leaders who generate profound changes in the beliefs, perceptions, values, and actions of their followers. Such leaders have a special relationship with their followers, one in which they can call forth exceptionally high levels of performance, loyalty, and enthusiasm. An important factor in the impressive influence transformational leaders exert over others involves their proposal of an emotion-provoking vision. Other actions by transformational leaders involve framing—defining the purpose of their movement or organization in highly meaningful terms—and willingness to take risks and engage in unconventional actions in order to reach stated goals. Finally, transformational leaders are experts in impression management, and often possess outstanding communication skills.

What is the vertical dyad linkage model of leadership?

The vertical dyad linkage, or VDL, approach focuses on individual leader-subordinate dyads and was origi-

nally proposed by George Graen. This model rejects the notion that leaders act the same way toward all subordinates (an average leadership style approach implied in all the other models), and suggests, instead, that a leader exhibits different leadership styles for each subordinate. Leaders are said to treat trusted, competent subordinates almost as informal assistants, allowing them a great deal of latitude in how to carry out their jobs, while leaders are said to be a great deal more directive with less trusted subordinates. Research has generally supported this view and has found significant differences in productivity, satisfaction, and turnover rates between these two groups of subordinates, often referred to as "in-group members" and "out-group members."

What are substitutes for leadership?

Kerr and Jermier, extending the logic of path-goal theory, suggested that there could be situations where leaders were actually unnecessary. More to the point, they outlined a series of situations where different functions, usually served by leaders, would already be served. For example, if subordinates are knowledgeable, committed, and experienced, there is no need for anyone to direct them on how to get the job done; it is possible to structure jobs so that procedures are self-evident, or technology might drive production to such an extent that employee behavior is irrelevant; strong work norms, coupled with cohesive work groups composed of experienced workers could be productive without any leadership. Although research on this approach has been limited, results have indicated that job performance can be determined by a number of factors that might substitute for effective leadership, and the importance of leaders to work groups may vary considerably across situations.

What are the major aspects of situational leadership theory?

Situational leadership theory, proposed by Hersey and Blanchard, views subordinate maturity as the major determinant of the best leadership style. According to this theory, when subordinate maturity is low (they are inexperienced, perhaps trainees), they require high initiating structure, but little consideration. As they mature (gain more expertise and self-confidence), their need for consideration and support increases and, over time, their need for structure decreases. When they are fully mature (which usually refers to experienced professionals), the best leadership style is one characterized by low levels of both initiating structure and consideration. The research support for the theory has been mixed, but there is enough support to suggest that a leader must be flexible and change styles as subordinates mature on their jobs.

Other Teaching Suggestions

1. A useful way to open any discussion of leadership is to ask students to name leaders or people they think of as leaders. Once they have done this, ask them to tell you why these leaders were or were not successful. Several things tend to happen whenever I ask this of a class. Most people name formal leaders, especially heads of state; the list will be almost exclusively men; someone will mention Adolph Hitler and will probably elicit chuckles. A discussion of someone like Hitler may be particularly interesting; although he was surely a failure as a human being, he was, in fact, a rather successful leader.

2. Mention the major bases of social power, and then discuss which bases the leaders named drew (or draw) on. Note that, typically, more effective leaders have more of these bases of power to draw on than less successful leaders.

3. The trait approach to leadership may not have been the most successful one, but some interesting findings came from this approach. Ask students for their ideas about what traits or characteristics separate leaders from followers. Some of the traits identified in the research were self-confidence, good verbal skills, and intelligence, but leaders were also found to be better dressed, more talkative, older, taller, and more likely to be males. It is interesting to note that these points really are describing a stereotype about ideal leaders. Thus, it should not be surprising that persons possessing these characteristics are more likely to be selected as leaders, but neither is it surprising that these persons don't always make the best leaders.

4. The wisdom of situational approaches to leadership is easy to illustrate, as we think of how different situations demand different leaders. Consider George Patton. Patton seemed to personify the autocratic, egotistical, task-oriented leader who was extremely successful during the war. Contrast this style to that of Omar Bradley, who was much more concerned, participative, and had little ego. There may be some debate about which general was truly more effective during the war but, when WWII ended, the generals also had to be diplomats. Bradley's leadership style was easily adaptable to this new role and, in fact, he had a successful career as a leader in the business world. Patton's style, on the other hand, was all wrong for peace and peacetime alliances. It is, therefore, most fascinating that several books have suggested the jeep accident in which Patton was killed was no accident, but was planned by our government as a way to remove a highly visible leader who could not adapt and whose style was inappropriate for the situation.

5. The centerpiece of Fiedler's model is the LPC scale, yet that was cited as an area of major criticism. Copies of the instrument are available in Fiedler's books on leadership. It would be worth bringing a copy in and having your students complete it. It simply asks for ratings on a series of pairs of adjectives, of the person you least liked working with. Discuss the logic of the scoring. Does it seem reasonable that just because the person you least liked working with was described in negative terms (perhaps that's why he or she was the least liked coworker), you should be a task-oriented leader?

6. The substitutes for leadership approach and the Hersey-Blanchard models may be getting at a lot of the same ideas. Think back to when you learned to drive a car. You needed and sought instructions and direction. As you became more proficient, support was probably what you needed most. Now, assuming you are a competent driver, you don't need a leader at all, and any directions, or even encouragement, might be rather annoying. The same may be true if we think about our parents as leaders, and what we require of them as we get older and more mature.

7. Another interesting approach to the study of leadership is found in the work of Robert Lord and his associates. They have focused on people's prototypes of leaders and how this affects reactions to leaders. That is, most of us have some idea about what leaders should do, and when we encounter people who behave that way, we tend to react more positively and to treat them as leaders. The problem comes when a formal leader does not possess those characteristics. A reference to some of Lord's work is given below, and this might be a line of research worth raising.

Case in Point Notes

Leadership at Levi Strauss

This case describes the leadership practices of transformational leader, Robert D. Haas, chairman and chief executive officer of Levi Strauss & Co. This extraordinarily effective leader is credited with leading Levi Strauss out of the doldrums and into its current leadership position in the clothing industry. How did he do it? As explained in the case, Haas uses a combination of leadership practices. He demonstrates the characteristics of transformational leaders described in the chapter (e.g., he articulates the values of the company in the form of an Aspirations Statement, and leads by example as much as possible). He also employs various leader behaviors described in the chapter (primarily in his interactions with top managers), and insists upon certain leader behaviors being adopted by all of the company's managers. Finally, Haas uses various substitutes for leadership (e.g., LiviLink) as a means of further supporting his leadership efforts.

The discussion questions that follow this case prompt students to analyze Robert D. Haas's leadership practices using the theories presented in the chapter. The case is rather comprehensive in scope, providing students with considerable opportunity to discuss what they have learned about leadership. This case also serves as a useful springboard for launching additional discussion of leadership. Ask students to nominate and describe other leaders who, like Haas, use a combination of leader practices to lead their organizations.

Additional Cases

A Case of Coaching Style

Coach Bob has been coaching the women's soccer team at his university for four years. He does this on a volunteer basis, and is not compensated for his coaching activities. Coach Bob loves the game of soccer and is trying to establish soccer as a varsity sport on the campus. It currently is a club sport, meaning that it is neither officially recognized nor financially supported by the university.

Because women's soccer is not a varsity sport, the coach cannot offer scholarships or other financial incentives to his players. In fact, the players have to come up with money for uniforms, travel expenses, and the like out of their own pockets or by conducting fundraisers (car washes, concession sales at the men's soccer games, etc.). Schedules are arranged with the goal of varsity status always in mind; games are scheduled with other varsity soccer programs in the area or with women's club teams from other universities.

Practices are held after all of the fall varsity programs have had their practice times. This usually means that the women's soccer team is able to obtain use of the only suitable field from 8:30–10:00 P.M., not exactly prime time for most college students. Winter practice times for the indoor season are even worse—from 10:30 P.M. to midnight. Practices consist of skill development, tactics and strategy, and conditioning, and follow a fairly rigid routine.

Women's soccer is a year-round program. The major season is the fall season; thirteen games are scheduled. During the winter season, the team participates in three to four indoor tournaments, each running over a weekend. In the spring, two to three outdoor matches are scheduled. Most of the women participate in all three seasons, although only ten women can be on a roster for the indoor tournaments.

The motivation for these women to participate must come from within, as there are no organizational rewards (scholarships or other recognition) from the university. Showing up for practice and games involves a personal decision by each player. The coach really cannot threaten to withhold that he does not have to give in the first place.

Coach Bob and his players seem to have a good working relationship. Practices are always built around a theme, and although they are physically demanding, there is an element of fun included in each. The players sometimes visit him in his office and discuss things other than soccer. He always holds a party at the end of the spring season and has set aside a big room in his house, complete with kitchen, as a sort of soccer clubhouse.

Questions

1. Using Fiedler's theory, how would you describe the three situational variables: leader-member relations, task structure, and leader position power?

Source: By Robert D. Goddard, Appalachian State University.

2. Given the combination of situational variables described above, what would be the most effective leadership style?
3. According to Fiedler, could Coach Bob change his style of leadership readily? Why or why not?

A Case of Coaching Style: Teaching Note

This case is based on the reality of one author's continuing experience as a volunteer coach. The case fits in nicely with an exposition of the Fiedler model of leadership effectiveness and has not been used anywhere else.

Discussion of this case could begin with a response to the first question—the identification of the three contingency variables. In this case, *leader-member relations* are good. As indicated in the case, the coach and team participate in activities other than soccer. He gives advice to the members of the team on many topics, holds parties for the team, and has made a room in his home available for the team members. Practices are designed with an element of fun, which further enhances this relationship.

The task itself, practices and games, is fairly well-structured. ("Practices consist of skill development, tactics and strategy, and conditioning, and follow a fairly rigid routine.") Schedules are given out at the beginning of the year to each team member, so they know when games and practices will take place. While during the games themselves, conditions will dictate strategy (which some students might interpret to mean that the task is unstructured), overall the goal is to provide a good measure of structure to this task.

Leader position power is poor. As noted above, "The motivation for these women to participate must come from within, as there are no organizational rewards (scholarships or other recognition) from the university. Showing up for practices and games involves a personal decision by each player, the coach really cannot threaten to withhold something that he does not have to give in the first place." Coach Bob cannot really reward (or punish) with organizational outcomes. Rewards for the members of the team are internal; the sense of accomplishment that comes with victory, the social aspects of the team. In fact, if this team ever is granted varsity status, it is expected that some of the women will not go out for the team. Even though this is one of the stated goals of this organization, the forced regimentation of a varsity sport, with more rigid rules and policies, may prove unpalatable to some of these women.

The next point of discussion in this case revolves around student responses to question 2. According to Fiedler, given the combination of situational variables described above and summarized below this situation is quite favorable to the leader.

Leader-Member Relations—Good
Task Structure—High
Leader Position Power—Weak

Coach Bob should, according to these findings, operate from a task orientation, rather than a people orientation. His concern should be with running practices efficiently, scheduling, and devising tactics and strategy for winning matches. He should be concerned with preparation, and then let the girls play their matches with relatively little guidance.

Perhaps the most interesting question is the final one—can a leader change his or her style? According to Fiedler, this is not an easy task. In fact, his conclusion was that it was easier to "engineer the job to fit the person," than attempt to change the leader's basic style. Many of the currently-popular leadership theories suggest just the opposite—that it is relatively easy for a leader to adapt to the situation. This conclusion by Fiedler will undoubtedly raise the most discussion in your classes.

Dick Spencer

After the usual banter when old friends meet for cocktails, the conversation between a couple of university professors and Dick Spencer, a former student who was now a successful businessman, turned to Dick's life as a vice-president of a large manufacturing firm.

"I've made a lot of mistakes, most of which I could live with, but this one series of incidents was so frustrating that I could have cried at the time," Dick said in response to a question, "I really have to laugh at how ridiculous it is now, but at the time I blew mu cork."

Spencer was plant manager of Modrow Company, a Canadian branch of the Tri-American Corporation. Tri-American was a major producer of primary aluminum with integrated operations ranging from the mining of bauxite through the processing to fabrication of aluminum into a variety of products. The company also made and sold refractories and industrial chemicals. The parent company had wholly-owned subsidiaries in 15 different countries.

Tri-American mined bauxite in the Jamaican West Indies and shipped the raw material by commercial vessels to two plants in Louisiana, where it was processed into alumina. the alumina was then shipped to reduction plants in one of three locations for conversion into primary aluminum. Most of the primary aluminum was then moved to the company's fabricating plants for further processing. Fabricated aluminum items included sheet, flat, coil, and corrugated products, siding, and roofing.

Tri-American employed approximately 22,000 people in the total organization. The company was governed by a board of directors that included the chairman, vice-chairman, president, and twelve vice-presidents. However, each of the subsidiaries and branches functioned as an independent unit. The board set general policy, which was then interpreted and applied by the various plant managers. In a sense, the various plants competed with one another as though they were independent companies. The decentralization in organizational structure increased the freedom and authority of the plant managers, but increased the pressure for profitability.

The Modrow branch was located in a border town in Canada. The total work force in Modrow was 1,000. This Canadian subsidiary was primarily a fabricating unit. Its main products were foil and building products such as roofing and siding. Aluminum products were gaining in importance in architectural plans and increased sales were

predicted for this branch. Its location and its stable work force were the most important advantages it possessed.

In anticipation of estimated increases in building product sales, Modrow had recently completed a modernization and expansion project. At the same time, their research and art departments combined talents in developing a series of twelve new patterns of siding which were being introduced to the market. Modernization and pattern development had been costly undertakings, but the expected return on investment made the project feasible. However, the plant manager, who was a Tri-American vice-president, had instituted a campaign to cut expenses wherever possible. In his introductory notice of the campaign, he emphasized that cost reduction would be the personal aim of every employee at Modrow.

Salesman

The plant manager of Modrow, Dick Spencer, was an American who had been transferred to this Canadian branch two years previously, after the start of the modernization plan. Dick had been with Tri-American Company for 14 years, and his progress within the organization was considered spectacular by those who knew him well. Dick had received a Master's degree in Business Administration from a well-known university at the age of 22. Upon graduation he had accepted a job as salesman for Tri-American. During his first year as a salesman, he succeeded in landing a single, large contract which put him near the top of the sales-volume leaders. In discussing his phenomenal rise in the sales volume, several of his fellow salesmen concluded that his looks, charm, and ability on the golf course contributed as much to his success as his knowledge of the business or his ability to sell the products.

The second year of his sales career, he continued to set a fast pace. Although his record set difficult goals for the other salesmen, they considered him a "regular guy," and everyone seemed to enjoy the few occasions when they socialized. However, by the end of the second year of constant travelling and selling, Dick began to experience some doubt about his future.

His constant involvement in business affairs disrupted his marital life and his wife divorced him during his second year with Tri-American. Dick resented her action at first, but gradually seemed to recognize that his career at present depended on his freedom to travel unencumbered. During that second year, he ranged far and wide in his sales territory, and successfully closed several large contracts. None of them was as large as his first year's major sales, but in total volume he again was well up near the top of salesmen for

Source: Adapted from "Dick Spencer," a case prepared and developed by Dr. Margaret Fenn, Graduate School of Business, University of Washington.

the year. Dick's name became well known in the corporate headquarters, and he was spoken of as "the boy to watch."

Dick had met the president of Tri-American during his first year as a salesman at a company conference. After three days of golfing and socializing they developed a relaxed camaraderie considered unusual by those who observed the developing friendship. Although their contacts were infrequent after the conference, their easy relationship seemed to blossom the few times they did meet. Dick's friends kidded him about his ability to make use of his new friendship to promote himself in the company, but Dick brushed aside their jibes and insisted that he'd make it on his own abilities, no someone's coattail.

By the time he was 25, Dick began to suspect that he did not look forward to a life as a salesman for the rest of his career. He talked about his unrest with his friends, and they suggested that he groom himself for sales manager. "You won't make the kind of money you're making from commissions," he was told, "but you will have a foot in the door from an administrative standpoint, and you won't have to travel quite as much as you do now." Dick took their suggestions lightly, and continued to sell the product, but he was aware that he felt dissatisfied and did not seem to get the satisfaction out of his job that he had once enjoyed.

By the end of his third year with the company, Dick was convinced that he wanted a change in direction. As usual, he and the president spent quite a bit of time on the golf course during the annual company sales conference. After their match one day, the president kidded Dick about his game. The conversation drifted back to business, and the president, who seemed to be in a jovial mood, started to kid Dick about his sales ability. In a joking way, he implied that anyone could sell a product as good as Tri-American's, but that it took real "guts and know-how" to make the products. The conversation drifted to other things, but this remark stuck with Dick.

Some time later, Dick approached the president formally with a request for a transfer out of the sales division. The president was surprised and hesitant about this change in career direction for Dick. He recognized the superior sales ability Dick seemed to possess, but was unsure that Dick was willing or able to assume responsibilities in any other division of the organization. Dick sensed the hesitancy, but continued to push his request. Dick later remarked that the president's initial hesitancy convinced him that he needed an opportunity to prove himself in a field other than sales.

Trouble Shooter

Dick was finally transferred back to the home office of the organization and indoctrinated into productive and administrative roles in the company as a special assistant to the senior vice president of production. As a special assistant, Dick was assigned several troubleshooting jobs. He acquitted himself well in this role, but in the process succeeded in gaining a reputation as a ruthless head hunter among the branches where he had performed a series of amputations. His reputation as an amiable, genial, easy-going guy from the sales department was the antithesis of the reputation of a cold, calculating head hunter which he earned in his troubleshooting role. The vice president, who was Dick's boss, was aware of the reputation Dick had earned, but was pleased with the results that were obtained. The faltering

departments Dick had worked in seemed to bloom with new life and energy after Dick's recommended amputations. As a result, the vice president began to sing Dick's praises, and the president began to accept Dick in his new role in the company.

Management Responsibility

About three years after Dick's switch from sales, he was given an assignment as assistant plant manager of an English branch of the company. Dick, who had remarried, moved his wife and family to London, and they attempted to adapt to their new routine. The plant manager was English as were most of the other employees. Dick and his family were accepted with reservations into the community life as well as into the plant life. The difference between British and American philosophy and performance within the plant was marked for Dick who was imbued with modern managerial concepts and methods. Dick's directives from headquarters were to update and upgrade performance in this branch. However, his power and authority were less than those of his superior, so he constantly found himself in the position of having to soft pedal or withhold suggestions that he would have liked to make, or innovations that he would have liked to introduce. After a frustrating year and a half, Dick was suddenly made plant manager of an old British company which had just been purchased by Tri-American. He left his first English assignment with mixed feelings and moved from London to Birmingham.

Plant Manager

As the new plant manager, Dick operated much as he had in his troubleshooting job for the first couple of years of his change from sales to administration. Training and reeducation programs were instituted for all supervisors and managers who survived the initial purge. Methods were studied and simplified or redesigned whenever possible, and new attention was directed toward production which better met the needs of the sales organization. A strong controller helped to straighten out the profit picture through stringent cost control; and by the end of the third year, the company showed a small profit for the first time in many years. Because he felt that this battle was won, Dick requested transfer back to the United States. This request was partially granted when nine months later he was awarded a junior vice president title and was made manager of a subsidiary Canadian plant, Modrow.

Modrow Manager

Prior to Dick's appointment as plant manager at Modrow, extensive plans for plant expansion and improvement had been approved and started. Although he had not been in on the original discussion and plans, he inherited all the problems that accompany large-scale changes in any organization. Construction was slower in completion than originally planned, equipment arrived before the building was finished, employees were upset about the extent of change expected in their work routines with the installation of additional machinery and, in general, morale was at a low ebb.

Various versions of Dick's former activities had preceded him, and on his arrival he was viewed with dubious eyes. The first few months after his arrival were spent in a frenzy of catching up. This entailed constant conferences and meetings, volumes of reading of past reports, becoming acquainted with the civic leaders of the area, and a plethora of dispatches to and from the home office. Costs continued to climb unabated.

By the end of the first year at Modrow, the building program had been completed, although behind schedule, the new equipment installed, and some revamping of cost procedures had been incorporated. The financial picture at this time showed a substantial loss, but since it had been budgeted as a loss, this was not surprising. All managers of the various divisions had worked closely with their supervisors and accountants in planning the budget for the following year, and Dick began to emphasize his personal interest in cost reduction.

As he worked through the first year as plant manager, Dick developed the habit of strolling around the organization. He was apt to leave his office and appear anywhere on the plant floor, in the design offices, at the desk of a purchasing agent or accountant, in the plant cafeteria rather than the executive dining room, or wherever there was activity concerned with Modrow. During his strolls he looked, listened, and became acquainted. If he observed activities that he wanted to talk about, or heard remarks that gave him clues to future action, he did not reveal these at the time. Rather he had a nod, a wave, a smile, for the people near him, but a mental note to talk to his supervisors, managers, and foremen in the future. At first his presence disturbed those who noted him coming and going, but after several exposures to him without any noticeable effect, the workers came to accept his presence and continue their usual activities. Supervisors, managers, and foremen, however, did not feel as comfortable when they saw him in the area.

Their feelings were aptly expressed by the manager of the siding department one day when he was talking to one of his foremen: "I wish to hell he'd stay up in the front office where he belongs. Whoever heard of a plant manager who had time to wander around the plant all the time. Why doesn't he tend to his paper work and let us tend to our business?"

"Don't let him get you down," joked the foreman. "Nothing ever comes of his visits. Maybe he's just lonesome and looking for a friend. You know how these Americans are."

"Well, you may feel that nothing ever comes of his visits, but I don't. I've been called into his office three separate times within the last two months. The heat must really be on from the head office. You know these conferences we have every month where he reviews our financial progress, our building progress, our design progress, etc.? Well, we're not really progressing as fast as we should be. If you ask me we're in for continuing trouble."

In recalling his first year at Modrow, Dick had felt constantly pressured and badgered. He always sensed that the Canadians he worked with resented his presence since he was brought in over the heads of the operating staff. At the same time he felt this subtle resistance from his Canadian workforce, he believed that the president and his friends in the home office were constantly on the alert, waiting for Dick to prove himself or fall flat on his face. Because of the constant pressures and demands of the work, he had literally dumped his family into a new community and had withdrawn into the plant. In the process, he built up a wall of resistance toward the de-

mands of his wife and children who, in turn, felt as though he was abandoning them.

During the course of the conversation with his university friends, he began to recall a series of incidents that probably had resulted from the conflicting pressures. When describing some of these incidents, he continued to emphasize the fact that his attempt to be relaxed and casual had backfired. Laughingly, Dick said, "as you know, both human relations and accounting were my weakest subjects during the Master's program, and yet they were the two fields I felt I needed the most at Modrow at the this time." He described some of the cost procedures that he would have like to incorporate. However, without the support and knowledge furnished by his former controller, he busied himself with details that were unnecessary. One day, as he describes it, he overheard a conversation between two of the accounting staff members with whom he had been working very closely. One of them commented to the other, "For a guy who's a vice president, he sure spends a lot of time breathing down our necks. Why doesn't he simply tell us the kind of systems he would like to try, and let us do the experimenting and work out the budget?" Without commenting on the conversation he overheard, Dick then described himself as attempting to spend less time and be less directive in the accounting department.

Another incident he described which apparently had real meaning for him was one in which he had called a staff conference with his top-level managers. They had been going "hammer and tongs" for better than an hour in his private office, taken off coats, and really rolled up their sleeves. Dick himself had slipped out of his shoes. In the midst of this, his secretary reminded him of an appointment with public officials. Dick had rapidly finished up his conference with his managers, straightened his tie, donned his coat, and had wandered out into the main office in his stocking feet.

Dick fully described several incidents when he had disappointed, frustrated, or confused his wife and family by forgetting birthdays, appointments, dinner engagements, and so on. He seemed to be describing a pattern of behavior which resulted from continuing pressure and frustration. He was setting the scene to describe his baffling and humiliating position in the siding department. In looking back and recalling his activities during this first year, Dick commented on the fact that his frequent wanderings throughout the plant had resulted in nodding acquaintance with the workers, but probably had also resulted in foremen and supervisors spending more time getting ready for his visits and reading meaning into them afterwards than attending to their specific duties. His attempts to know in detail the accounting procedures being used required long hours of concentration and detailed conversations with the accounting staff, which were time-consuming and frustrating for him, as well as for them. His lack of attention to his family life resulted in continued pressure from both wife and family.

The Siding Department Incident

Siding was the product that had been budgeted as a large profit item of Modrow. Aluminum siding was gaining in popularity among both architects and builders because of its possibilities in both decorative and practical uses. Panel sheets of siding were shipped in standard sizes on order; large sheets of the coated siding were cut to specifications in the trim department, packed, and shipped. The trim shop was located near the loading platforms, and Dick often cut through the trim shop on his wanderings through the plant. On one of his frequent trips through the area, he suddenly became aware of the fact that several workers responsible for disposal function were spending countless hours at high-speed saws cutting scraps into specified lengths to fit into scrap barrels. The narrow bands of scrap which resulted from the trim process varied in length from 7 to 27 feet and had to be reduced in size to fit into the disposal barrels. Dick, in his concentration on cost reduction, picked up one of the thin strips, bent it several times and fitted it into the barrel. He tried this with another piece, and it bent very easily. After assuring himself that bending was possible, he walked over to a worker at the saw and asked why he was using the saw when material could easily be bent and fitted into the barrels, resulting in saving time and equipment. The worker's response was, "We've never done it that way, sir. We've always cut it."

Following his plan of not commenting or discussing matters on the floor, but distressed by the reply, Dick returned to his office and asked the manager of the siding department if he could speak to the foreman of the scrap division. The manager said, "Of course, I'll send him up to you in just a minute."

After a short time, the foreman, very agitated at being called to the plant manager's office, appeared. Dick began questioning him about the scrap disposal process and received the standard answer: "We've always done it that way." Dick then proceeded to review cost-cutting objectives. He called for a few pieces of scrap to demonstrate the ease with which it could be bent, and ended what he thought was a satisfactory conversation by requesting the foreman to order heavy-duty gloves for his workers and use the bending process for a trial period of two weeks to check the cost saving possible.

The foreman listened throughout most of this hour's conference, offered several reasons why it wouldn't work, raised some questions about the recordkeeping process for cost purposes, and finally left the office with the forced agreement to try the suggested new method of bending, rather than cutting, for disposal. Although he was immersed in many other problems, his request was forcibly brought home one day as he cut through the scrap area. The workers were using power saws to cut scraps. He called the manager of the siding department and questioned him about the process. The manager explained that each foreman was responsible for his own processes, and since Dick had already talked to the foreman, perhaps he had better talk to him again. When the foreman arrived, Dick began to question him. He received a series of excuses and some explanations of the kinds of problems they were meeting by attempting to bend the scrap material. "I don't care what the problems are," Dick nearly shouted, "when I request a cost-reduction program instituted, I want to see it carried through."

Dick was furious. When the foreman left, he phoned the maintenance department and ordered the removal of the power saws from the scrap area immediately. A short time later, the foreman of the scrap department knocked on Dick's door reporting his astonishment at having maintenance men step into his area and physically remove the saws. Dick reminded the foreman of his request for a trial at cost reduction to no avail, and ended the conversation by saying that the power saws were gone and would not be returned, and the foreman had damned well better learn to get along without them. After a stormy exit by the foreman, Dick congratulated himself on having solved a problem and turned his attention to other matters.

A few days later Dick cut through the trim department and literally stopped to stare. As he described it, he was completely nonplussed to discover gloved workmen using hand shears to cut each piece of scrap.

Questions
1. How would you describe Spencer's leadership style?
2. Is it effective in the Modrow plant? Why or why not?
3. As a behavioral consultant, how might you influence Spencer to change his style?

Dick Spencer: Teaching Note

This case deals with an aggressive and hard-driving mid-level manager and the difficulties he faces when he is transferred and promoted to head up a fabricating subsidiary in a small Canadian border town. The case traces Spencer's career from salesman to vice president in charge of the Modrow plant and details his management approach, culminating in an attempted task change in a medium-size department of the Tri-American Corporation.

Part I

In examining Dick Spencer's style of leadership, the case offers a number of related areas in which the students can match various theories of leadership styles with behavioral consequences on the organizational floor. In each stage of Spencer's career: salesman, trouble shooter, assistant plant manager of the London branch and finally as plant manager of the Modrow facility, Spencer portrays the classic young man on the move—the man intent on scrambling to the top of the ladder regardless of the price.

This case is unique in that it gives the students a long-term look at an individual in terms of the type of leadership styles under examination by the class. The students gain experience in categorizing leadership behavior in terms of its typology, and in understanding how leadership behavior can manifest itself in a particular behavior on the part of the subordinates. This serves to illustrate that, regardless of individual manager's first intentions and desire to accomplish certain goals within the organization, his or her leadership style can prove to be dysfunctional to the overall organizational effectiveness and can, in fact, make it impossible to attain the accomplishments he or she desires.

In dealing with organizational change, the case is more straightforward since if offers a clear example of change initiated at the top and resisted at lower organizational levels. The advantage of this particular case is the knowledge of Dick Spencer's past management style which helps the student better understand the reasons for the attempted change and circumvents that ever-present question, "Why did Dick Spencer do it this way when any fool can see that. . . ." We have found that once you get past the "any fool can see" stage of a case dealing with organizational change, you can move quickly to the particular strengths or weaknesses of the change strategy and beyond that to strategies which might result in the eventual accomplishment of the change itself.

Part II

In dealing with either leadership or organizational change, we tend to begin by asking for a categorization of Dick Spencer and his leadership style in whatever terms are relevant to the class at that point. This case has been used to illustrate concepts as simple as Theories X and Y or coercive styles of leadership, the economic model of man, and even behavioral manifestations of high need for achievement.

Generally we attempt to chart a consensus of class opinion on the board in a four-column matrix.

Career Position	Behavior	Leadership Type	Worker Reaction
1. Salesman			
2. Hatchetman			
3. Assistant Plant Manager (Birmingham)			
4. Plant Manager (Modrow)			
5. Vice President (Modrow)			

By working from left to right we can then directly translate Spencer's behavior as an individual to a specific leadership style and then trace that style to its effects on worker behavior.

A provocative sidetrack of interest to the students is to ask for comments on the lifestyle demanded by the Tri-American Corporation as people are promoted up through the management hierarchy. Most often, students will initially feel that the reason for Spencer's behavior lies within himself, and is perhaps unique to him and to individuals of his type. A bit of prodding (e.g., "If you were the president of Tri-American and promoting people on what you had observed from their behavior, would you promote the Dick Spencers, who obviously are willing to spend tens of extra hours a week at their job sacrificing, to a large extent, out-

side interests and family; or would you promote those who insist on leaving at 5:00 and who insist on placing their family and friends above the organization?").

We do this not with the intent of painting all American businesses with a broad black brush, but instead as an attempt to share with the students the dilemma facing management in large organizations when promotions are given.

We have also found it useful at this point to break the case and undertake a short ten- to fifteen-minute role play where one student takes the role of Dick Spencer immediately after discovering the scrap material incident and another group of four-to-five students play the roles of the foreman and the workmen. From this point, we then attempt to move to a discussion of the particular climate and the atmosphere created in the Modrow plant by Spencer's leadership style and how he might attempt to overcome the social aspects of that style, if indeed that is possible. Additionally, we ask how he might begin to win some semblance of trust and respect from the individuals working under him.

In our opinion the most powerful use of the case comes at this point. Instead of simply speculating on what Dick Spencer might now do to gain that trust, we drop back from consideration of specific points and ask the students if they will, using the Spencer case as an example, list a set of rules and guidelines for themselves for moving into a management position in the organization. The remainder of the class is then spent discussing the lists drawn up by the individual students and attempting to compile one composite list based on overall class opinion.

In using the case strictly as an organizational case, we again go to the initial classification of Dick Spencer's leadership style in each of these jobs and then ask the students to discuss the effects of his attempted change on the organization in Modrow. We then again role play the exercise with the following changes: we first attempt to role play the scrap department situation as Dick Spencer would most likely react. Then, after discussing particular interpersonal behaviors of that situation and how they would influence organizational effects in the future, we ask groups of students to design change strategies and insert them in the role. Finally, the role play is repeated in order to contrast Dick Spencer's traditional style with the change strategies developed by the students. This is obviously a more powerful tool if one has access to videotape in the classroom, for it allows the original situation to be replayed as the changed strategies are discussed.

Experiencing Organizational Behavior Notes

In Search of Great Leaders

This exercise demonstrates the importance of special circumstances as a determinant of transformational leader effectiveness. Students are asked to identify three great leaders, living or from the past. Students are then instructed to explain why they believe these people were great leaders. What did they do? What leadership characteristics did they demonstrate? Once they are finished with their explanations, students are then asked to consider whether the leaders

they identified would have been great leaders at any time in history, in any culture, and in the face of any set of circumstances.

The major point of this exercise is to stimulate students to realize that transformational or charismatic leaders do not arise in a social vacuum, but are brought to power by special sets of circumstances. The vision of any would-be transformational leader must fit the underlying values of followers at a particular point in history if he or she is to be effective.

Additional Experiential Exercise

T-P Leadership Questionnaire

Leadership is very complex. Streams of research resulting from major work in many behavioral sciences have led to agreement on two major dimensions of effective leadership. They are the orientation toward the task and the consideration toward people.

How do you evaluate your own leadership ability? More importantly, in what direction must your own leadership development take you? The T-P Leadership Questionnaire and Profile Sheet should help you to understand more clearly the answers to these questions. There is no correct score for the questionnaire. People vary considerably in their responses.

Nor will this exercise provide you with all of the necessary answers about your abilities as a leader. However, it will serve as a point of departure from which you can become more aware of your present leadership style and your potential impact on group effectiveness.

T-P Leadership Questionnaire

Directions

The following items describe aspects of leadership behavior. Respond to each item according to the way you would most likely act if you were the leader of a work group. Circle whether you would most likely behave in the described way: always (A), frequently (F), occasionally (O), seldom (S), or never (N).

A F O S N   1. I would most likely act as the spokesman of the group.

A F O S N   2. I would encourage overtime work.

A F O S N   3. I would allow members complete freedom in their work.

A F O S N   4. I would encourage the use of uniform procedures.

A F O S N   5. I would permit the members to use their own judgment in solving problems.

A F O S N   6. I would stress being ahead of competing groups.

A F O S N   7. I would speak as a representative of the group.

A F O S N   8. I would needle members for greater effort.

A F O S N   9. I would try out my ideas in the group.

A F O S N   10. I would let the members do their work the way they think best.

A F O S N   11. I would be working hard for a promotion.

A F O S N   12. I would tolerate postponement and uncertainty.

A F O S N   13. I would speak for the group if there were visitors present.

A F O S N   14. I would keep the work moving at a rapid pace.

Source: Copyright © 1974 by the American Educational Research Association. Adapted by permission of the publisher.

A F O S N   15. I would turn the members loose on a job and let them go at it.

A F O S N   16. I would settle conflicts when they occur in the group.

A F O S N   17. I would get swamped by details.

A F O S N   18. I would represent the group outside meetings.

A F O S N   19. I would be reluctant to allow the members any freedom of action.

A F O S N   20. I would decide what should be done and how it should be done.

A F O S N   21. I would push for increased production.

A F O S N   22. I would let some members have authority which I could keep.

A F O S N   23. Things would usually turn out as I had predicted.

A F O S N   24. I would allow the group a high degree of initiative.

A F O S N   25. I would assign group members to particular tasks.

A F O S N   26. I would be willing to make changes.

A F O S N   27. I would ask the members to work harder.

A F O S N   28. I would trust the group to exercise good judgment.

A F O S N   29. I would schedule the work to be done.

A F O S N   30. I would refuse to explain my actions.

A F O S N   31. I would persuade others that my ideas are to their advantage.

A F O S N   32. I would permit the group to set its own pace.

A F O S N   33. I would urge the group to beat its previous record.

A F O S N   34. I would act without consulting the group.

A F O S N   35. I would ask that group members follow standard rules and regulations.

T _____   P _____

T-P Leadership-Style Profile Sheet

Name _____   Group _____

Directions

To determine your style of leadership, mark your score on the concern for task dimension (T) on the left-hand arrow below. Next, move to the right-hand arrow and mark your score on the concern for people dimension (P).

Draw a straight line that intersects the P and T scores. The point at which that line crosses the *shared leadership arrow* indicates your score on that dimension.

Questions

1. Take a look at your score for task (T) versus your score for people (P). Would you make a more successful country club manager? Or a supervisor of a construction crew?

2. Can you list three other managerial positions that might require widely different scores on (T) and (P)?

         Chapter 12

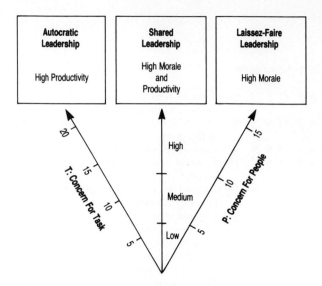

FIGURE 12–1   Shared Leadership Results from Balancing Concern for Task and Concern for People

T-P Leadership Questionnaire: Teaching Note

Objective

To give the student an opportunity to evaluate his or her orientation to task or people.

Procedure

1. Hand out the T-P Leadership Questionnaire without any discussion.
2. Before handing out the scoring keys, briefly discuss some of the possible leadership behaviors resulting from combinations of task and people orientation. Shared leadership is a function of the concerns for task and people (see comments under lecturette).
3. Have each participant score his or her own questionnaire. If you can, duplicate the scoring handout.
4. Have each individual put his or her score on the Profile Sheet.
5. Lead a discussion on the implications of the students' perceptions of their position on the profile.

Scoring Key

The T-P Leadership Questionnaire is scored as follows:

1. Circle the item number for items 8, 12, 17, 18, 19, 30, 34, and 35.
2. Write the number *1* in front of a *circled item number* if you responded S (seldom) or N (never) to that item.
3. Also write the number *1* in front of the *item numbers not circled* if you responded A (always) or F (frequently).
4. Circle the number *1*s which you have written in front of the following items: 3, 5, 8, 10, 15, 18, 19, 22, 24, 26, 28, 30, 32, 34, and 35.
5. *Count the circled number 1s.* This is your score for concern for people. Record your score in the blank following the letter *P* at the end of the questionnaire.
6. *Count uncircled number 1s.* This is your score for concern for task. Record your score in the blank following the letter *T* at the end of the questionnaire.

Follow the directions on the Leadership-Style Profile Sheet. A discussion of implications students attach to their location on the profile sheet would be appropriate.

Variations

1. Let the students predict their final ranking before completing the questionnaire.
2. After completing the questionnaire, let pairs of students predict the other's profile. If unacquainted with one another, suggest they sound each other out by seeing how the other stands on certain questions.
3. Illustrate different profiles through role playing. A classroom situation is one that is familiar with the students modeling different profiles of teacher leadership.

Lecturette

From the work done at Ohio State and Michigan, two behaviors have been singled out as the most important. The concern for task (or initiating structure) is the orientation to "getting the job done." The person with a high concern for task has an eye for organization, planning, and objectives. People become tools to get the job done.

The other behavior is a concern for people. The extreme of this type is often designated "country club management." The needs and whims of the individual are seen, anticipated, and taken care of. A leader with a high concern for people encourages, expresses, mediates, and harmonizes. Shared leadership implies that the leader has a relatively high concern for people and concern for task. This leader recognizes that people are the critical variables in getting the job done and only if the leader creates the climate under which they can grow psychologically will the job get done effectively. Team leadership and the recognition of the interdependence of the leader and follower characterize this leadership.

Additional Readings

Carter, J. (1988, March–April). Jimmy Carter: The Statesman as CEO. *Harvard Business Review,* pp. 62–70.

Conger, J. A. (1989). Leadership: The art of empowering others. *Academy of Management Executive, 3*(1), 17–24.

Conger, J. A. (1991). Inspiring others: The language of leadership. *Academy of Management Executive, 5*(1), 31–45.

Howell, J. M., & Avolio, B. J. (1991). The ethics of charismatic leadership: Submission or liberation? *Academy of Management Executive, 6*(2), 43–54.

Kelley, R. E. (1988, November–December). In praise of followers. *Harvard Business Review,* pp. 142–147.

Lord, R. G. (1985). An information processing approach to social perceptions, leadership, and behavioral measurement in organizations. In B. M. Staw & L. L. Cummings (Eds.), *Research in Organizational Behavior* (Vol. 7, pp. 87–128). Greenwich, CT: JAI Press.

Luthans, F. (1988). Successful vs. effective managers. *Academy of Management Executive, 2*(2), 127–132.

▮ 13 ▮

COMMUNICATION IN ORGANIZATIONS

CHAPTER OUTLINE

LEARNING OBJECTIVES

After reading this chapter, you should be able to:
1. Define the process of communication and describe its major forms.
2. Identify and describe the most prevalent nonverbal communication cues operating in organizations.
3. Distinguish between messages that are best communicated in written and spoken forms.
4. Describe how the formal structure of an organization influences the nature of the communication that occurs within it.
5. Distinguish between centralized and decentralized communication networks with respect to their relative superiority in performing different tasks.
6. Describe how informal patterns of communication operate within organizations.
7. Understand the impact of technology and of the physical layout of offices on communication between people within and between offices.
8. Identify and describe measures that can be taken by individuals and by organizations to improve communication effectiveness.

Chapter Overview

This chapter introduces students to the role of communications in organizational behavior. First, a definition and a working model of communication are presented. This is followed by a discussion of the distinction between formal and informal communications in organizations. The chapter next considers the major influences on organizational communication. Specifically examined are organizational structure, formal and informal communications networks, and the role of technology and office design. Finally, the chapter presents individual strategies for becoming a better communicator and strategies for improving communication on the job.

Three special sections appear in this chapter. An OB in Practice (Layoffs at Middlebury College: How *Not* to Communicate Bad News) describes the insensitive method used by Middlebury College administration to communicate layoffs to seventeen secretarial and clerical employees, some of whom had been working for the college for forty years. The layoffs, ordered by the college's president in response to a budget crisis, were hastily communicated by form letter. This method of communicating so angered the Middlebury community that the president was forced to resign. The botched communication effort illustrates the high cost of failing to fully consider the manner in which negative information is communicated. A Question of Ethics (Privacy Rights and E-Mail: Should Employers Have Access to Employees' Electronic Mailboxes?) discusses the ethical issues related to the rapidly growing use of electronic mail in private organizations. And a Focus on Research (How to Communicate with Employees about a Merger) describes a field experiment comparing the effects of realistic information versus no information about the effects of a forthcoming merger on employees. Employees who received the realistic information (honest, detailed information regarding pending layoffs, transfers, promotions, demotions and the like, using multiple channels of communications) experienced lower uncertainty and were able to better accept and cope with the merger than employees who did not receive realistic information.

The Case in Point (Fixing Communications at General Motors' Saginaw Division) describes how the Saginaw Division used a multifaceted communications approach to instill a sense of trust and openness among its employees, and boosted its productivity and profitability. And the Experiencing Organizational Behavior exercise (Becoming an Active Listener) gives students practice in becoming active listeners.

Lecture and Review Questions

What is meant by communication, and what steps constitute a simple communication model?

Communication is the process through which one person or a group of persons (the sender) transmits some type of information to another person or group of persons (the receiver). This definition suggests that the communication process can be characterized by a model consisting of several steps. First, the sender must have some idea or concept that he or she wants to make known to someone else. Once the sender is motivated to communicate, the information to be transmitted must be put into a form that can be sent to the receiver. This process is known as encoding. The sender next decides on the medium of communication to be used, that is, the exact means by which the message will be transmitted (e.g., written, phone, or face-to-face). The message is then transmitted to the receiver who must then decode the information so that the initial message can be comprehended. Finally, the receiver provides some feedback to the sender regarding the success of the communication and/or simply responds to the message. Despite the apparent simplicity of this model, there are many fac-

tors that can distort the clarity of a message. These factors are referred to as noise. Messages that are poorly encoded or decoded, or channels of communication (mediums) that are too noisy can all reduce communication effectiveness.

What is meant by verbal and nonverbal communication?

Verbal communication refers to the transmission and receipt of ideas using words, and can be either oral or written. In fact, verbal communication is believed to be most effective when oral messages are followed by written ones. Nonverbal communication refers to the transmission and receipt of ideas without the use of words. Among the most prevalent types of nonverbal cues in organizations are: style of dress (wearing *power* suits communicates something much different than wearing jeans), time (people often communicate superior status by making others wait to see them), and space (the arrangement of furniture in an office may communicate openness, while the type of furniture may communicate status). In addition, body-language cues may also communicate feelings and attitudes.

What factors influence manager choice of verbal communication media?

Recent research shows that the choice of a communication media greatly depends on a very important factor—the degree of clarity or ambiguity of the message being sent. In a study of the factors determining the choice of verbal communication media among managers, Daft, Lengel, and Trevino (1987) found that written media (e.g., letters or memos) are preferred for sending clear messages, while oral media (e.g., telephones or face-to-face contact) were preferred for sending ambiguous messages. Apparently, most managers are sensitive to the need to use communications media that allow them to take advantage of the rich avenues for two-way oral communications when necessary, and use the more efficient, one-way, written communications when these are adequate.

What is the role of organizational structure on information flow?

Organizational structure is the formally prescribed pattern of interrelationships existing among various units of an organization. Since most organizations are structured according to some type of hierarchy, with a varying number of levels, it is possible to have upward, downward, and horizontal communication. Downward communication refers to messages sent by those higher in the hierarchy to those at lower levels, and typically consists of instructions, directions, and orders. Downward communication flows from one level to the next, but there is usually some loss of accuracy as it passes through each step. Upward communication flows from lower levels to higher levels in the hierarchy, and usually includes information needed by managers to do their jobs and be aware of the status of projects. Upward communication occurs far less frequently and is often distorted as it rarely includes negative information. Horizontal communication flows laterally, at the same level in the hierarchy and usually includes efforts at coordination with a tendency to be far less formal.

What role do communication networks play in this process?

Communication networks refer to the pattern of communicaton links among the members of a work group or an organization. Research findings suggest that the specific patterns found in an organization can influence both the performance of group members and their satisfaction. One important characteristic of networks is centralization, the extent to which all communications must flow through one specific member. Patterns referred to as *Y* patterns and *Wheel* patterns have a high degree of centralization, while *circle* patterns do not. For simple problems, centralization results in more efficient performance, but decentralized patterns work best for more complex communications and problems. If there is a centralized pattern and the flow of information to the central person becomes too great (information saturation), that person's performance suffers. Regardless of the task or the type of communication, group members report higher levels of satisfaction in decentralized networks, most likely because no one feels left out of the process.

What are the major forms of informal communication in an organization?

In addition to formal channels of communication there are several forms of informal communication in most organizations. In fact, there is reason to believe that employees actually receive more information through informal than through formal means. The basic form of informal communication is known as the *grapevine,* and these usually form around natural contacts in the workplace. They form, in part, as an attempt by employees to make sense of their environments, and they also serve as a safety valve for employees to express concerns and anxieties. Research also indicates that most of the information transmitted through a grapevine is accurate, although any inaccurate information can cause serious problems. The other major form of informal communication is known as the *rumor.* Rumors are generally not true, but are based on speculation and wishful thinking more than facts, and so they are troublesome. Rumors can usually be controlled by the release of accurate information, attempts to discredit the rumor, or encouraging people to think about facts and experiences contrary to the rumor. Despite some problems, the more people involved with the informal communication networks in the organizations, the more power and influence they have, and informal communication can help employees attain formal power. Also, in the scientific community, informal communication is important for the transmittal of scientific knowledge.

What is the role of the work environment in the organizational communication process?

Technology and office design are two aspects of the work environment that can have a profound influence on the communication process. Technology can enhance communication by increasing the number of channels available and by making those channels more accessible. Furthermore, on-line technology has been found to improve office productivity, although it can minimize important contact between managers and their subordinates, and automated technology can make employees feel isolated and dehumanized. A recent form of communication technology is electronic mail (E-mail), a system whereby people use personal computer terminals to send and receive messages from each other. Rapidly growing in its popularity, E-mail is making communication within and between organizations easier than ever before. Electronic transmission of messages appears to be revolutionizing communications by allowing rapid transmission of information, and simultaneous sharing of identical information by people regardless of how widely dispersed they may be. While this technology is also less rich than oral forms of communication, this deficiency appears to be compensated by its efficiency. Office design also has an impact on communication. Open design offices tend to encourage communication, although they remove privacy which can present problems, so partitions are often preferred.

What are some individual and organizational strategies available for improving communications?

There are a number of individual strategies that can help people become better communicators. These include: keeping the language simple, avoiding jargon, and becoming an active, attentive listener. Organizational strategies for improving communications on the job include obtaining feedback (upward communication) through techniques such as employee surveys, suggestion systems (such as a suggestion box), and instituting corporate hotlines where corporate personnel are ready to answer employee questions and listen to their comments, and informal get-togethers rather than meetings to bring together people who do not usually interact because they work at different levels of the organization. In addition, organizations should gauge the flow of communication to prevent overload (potentially through the use of gatekeepers who are responsible for controlling the flow of communication, or queuing), and by employing redundancy (transmitting the same message repeatedly, usually through different channels), and verification (making sure a message was accurately received) to avoid distortion and omission of organizational communication.

Other Teaching Suggestions

1. The chapter present a model of the communication process that includes several steps. Not only is this model useful for understanding the process, it also helps identify those areas where communication can break down. It may be useful to discuss potential problems at each step in the process. For example, if the sender has not really thought about the message to be transmitted, all else is in vain. Most people have received letters or memos that were unintelligible because the sender had failed to really think the message through before transmitting. Even if the message is well formulated, the sender could encode it incorrectly. People who deal with translations of technical material are often troubled by attempts to translate colloquial expressions or figures of speech. The particular channel chosen can also present problems. Phone calls are sometimes cut off (especially international calls) and letters get lost in the mail. There can be similar problems of decoding at the receiver end. Your students might have other examples of problems that lead to a breakdown of communications.

2. Some people are better communicators than others. That is clear, but part of the reason may be due to the individual characteristics of the communicator. For example, individuals tend to be perceived as more effective communicators when they are higher in self-esteem, are more willing to adopt innovations, and are credible (recall the discussion of persuasive communication in chapter 5). Ronald Reagan was known as the "Great Communicator." To what extent did he possess these characteristics and why? George Bush has a much different communication style. Is his style as effective? Why or why not?

3. One of the best ways to illustrate the effectiveness of different communication networks is to arrange groups of students in different patterns and then play "telephone." Begin by whispering a simple message to one person, and have that person whisper it to the next person and so on. How does it come out? Now try it with a more complex message.

4. Oral communication skills probably represent an area where our students receive the least preparation. Whether interviewing for a job, or working as a manager later on, oral presentation skills are critical and yet these skills are ignored. These skills are best developed through practice and feedback. If possible, have students make oral presentations, tape record the presentations, and then have the recordings critiqued by other students. The feedback is invaluable, especially in areas like non-verbal communication. Most of us are simply not aware of the messages we send with our eyes and posture. It is always informative (and often humorous) to examine the non-verbal cues we send.

5. Nonverbal communication is one of the more fascinating topics in this chapter. If you can find a book on body language, bring it in, because there are lots of interesting cues to interpret. But there are also some problems in trying to interpret these cues. Casual gestures are sometimes just that. Much is often made about eye contact as well, but there are real cultural differences in willingness to make eye contact, and there is also the fact that many people are too shy to maintain eye contact. Some of the nonverbal cues discussed are almost funny. For example, there is supposedly a muscle just over the eyes that cannot be controlled and that twitches when we lie. Some people are also concerned about the differences between the way men and women cross their legs and check their fingernails.

6. There is discussion of the effects of technology and office design on communications, but these variables have also been studied from other perspectives. There is literature on human factors in design relating to how dials and gauges should be laid out for machines, how high chairs should be, what kinds of lighting are best for certain tasks, and so forth. It might be interesting to bring in some material on design issues and discuss these from the ergonomic perspective. A textbook on human factors engineering is a good source of information.

7. Personal space is also part of non-verbal communication. This refers to how close (physically) someone can come to us without our feeling uncomfortable. Clearly, the distance we would prefer to maintain is a function of the relationship we have with a person. In fact, observing the distance between two persons as they talk is an excellent way to judge their relationship. What happens when someone comes too close—that is they violate our personal space? Typically, we withdraw from them to re-establish the distance. But such withdrawal is usually interpreted by others as a negative reaction. Think about what happens on a crowded elevator. Strangers violate our space, but there is nowhere to go, so everyone engages in a lot of nervous behavior, and stares up at the lights indicating what floor they're on. It might be interesting to develop this further and discuss other examples of public and private violation of space and how we react to them.

Case in Point Notes

Fixing Communications at General Motors' Saginaw Division

This case describes how General Motors' Saginaw Division in Michigan used a multifaceted communications approach to instill a sense of trust and openness among its employees, and boosted its productivity and profitability. The case opens with a description of what communications at the division used to be. According to Ron Actis, the director of public affairs at General Motors' Saginaw Division, the former communication system was woefully inadequate. Results of a communications survey in 1982 revealed that employees believed the communications system was not working. The survey also showed widespread distrust between labor and management. What did Actis do about it? He knew that if the level of trust were to be increased, a process for prompting management and employees to communicate with each other would have to be developed and implemented. Actis developed a multifaceted communica-

tions system he labeled the Synchronous Communication Process (SCP). SCP consists of educating top management about the advantages and requirements of an effective communications system, upgrading company publications, instituting a video magazine, creating a format for face-to-face meetings between management and employees, and establishing a means of appraising the effectiveness of the entire SCP. The details of each component of Actis's SCP are described in the case. Information regarding the success of the SCP is also provided.

The discussion questions that follow the case take students through a step-by-step analysis of the communications concepts and theories underlying the Synchronous Communication Process (SCP). The rather comprehensive scope of this case provides students with the opportunity to explore numerous types of communication in organizations. To extend discussion beyond this case, ask your students to describe the communications systems of other organizations that they know about.

Additional Case

Who Goofed?

Daniel Cather is the Dean of the College of Business in a major university. His duties encompass many facets of administration including preparing budgets, interviewing prospective faculty, coordinating scheduling of courses, classrooms and faculty, chairing various committees, and fund-raising.

Dean Cather has an Administrative Assistant, Janet Boles, who handles many of the day-to-day activities of the Office of the Dean. Janet has been with the College of Business for about ten years, while Cather has just been hired as Dean. He has been on the job for about a month. His work habits do not coincide with Janet's; he often works until 10:00 PM and comes in to the office around 11:00 AM. He often leaves work to be done on Janet's desk with a brief note of instruction.

On Monday, Janet came into her office to find a pile of work that Dean Cather had prepared over the weekend for her to finish. His note said simply, "Please complete these projects as soon as you can." The major project appeared to be the budget, and she checked the figures that Cather had prepared, then took the budget to the secretarial area, where one of the three secretaries would prepare the final document.

Janet was surprised to find Dean Cather in her office when she arrived for work on Wednesday. When Cather saw Janet he breathed an apparent sigh of relief.

"I've been looking for the budget for half an hour," he said. "Where did you put it?"

Janet explained that she had completed the check of the figures and sent it to the secretaries for typing, and that it

had not been returned yet. She then said that she would check on its progress.

Dean Cather then said, "Good. I'll need eight copies of the budget for the Dean's Advisory Council meeting today at 10. The department chairs will be receiving them, and the vice-president will be briefed on the budget at the meeting."

When Janet called the secretarial area to check on the progress of the budget, she found out that it was not scheduled to be typed until 2:00 that afternoon.

When Janet informed Dean Cather of the schedule, he said that they should go to the secretarial area and try to expedite the budget typing process. When they arrived, the secretary who had the budget agreed to put her other work aside and could have the budget finished by the time of the meeting.

After returning to the Dean's office, Cather expressed his concern about Janet's failure to have the budget finished on time. "On time? Just what do you mean by 'on time'?" she said. "Your note said nothing about when the budget or the other projects were to be completed. Just *look* at it."

When Cather had read the note he said, "I thought so. Right here it says that these projects should be done 'as soon as you can.'"

Janet thought for a moment and then said, "I believe we have what is called 'a failure to communicate.' You think that I made a mistake, and I think that you did not communicate your idea of a deadline adequately."

Source: By Robert D. Goddard, Appalachian State University. All rights reserved.

Questions
1. What went wrong? Which individual made the mistake?
2. How could this situation have been prevented?

Who Goofed? Teaching Note

The problem in this case is a failure to communicate; Janet is correct in her evaluation. What wasn't conveyed in Dean Cather's note was his *meaning*. His "as soon as you can" meant that Janet should complete the budget as her first priority, while she thought he meant when she could get to it. The idea or meaning encoded was not the same idea or meaning decoded.

The case shows that communication problems can be caused by both the sender and the receiver. Neither employed the feedback necessary to ensure the correct transmission of *meaning*.

Experiencing Organization Behavior Notes

Becoming an Active Listener

This exercise gives students the opportunity to practice becoming active listeners. Complete background information and instructions are provided with the exercise. Students are asked to listen actively to a series of statements read by the instructor, and discuss the meaning of each statement, using the guidelines for active listeneing provided in the chapter. Following the exercise, students are asked to respond to several questions prompting them to consider a wide range of concerns involving how people listen.

Additional Experiential Exercise

The Importance of Feedback

How can you be sure that the idea you have been trying to communicate to another person has "gotten through" to that person? How do you go about clarifying what someone else has said to you? Both of these communications episodes should involve the same concept—that of *feedback*.

Feedback is the mechanism that allows the receiver of a message to clarify unclear parts of the message. Conversely, feedback allows the sender of a message to determine if the meaning she or he intended to convey has been comprehended and understood.

This exercise allows your students the opportunity to participate in two communications episodes. One of these episodes involves communication without feedback. In the other, the sender will actively seek feedback from the receivers so that he or she ensures more accurate communication.

Procedure

You should select one individual from your class to act as the *sender* in this exercise. You may choose a class member at random, or you may decide to select the "best communicator" in the class. Ask that person to describe Figure 13–1 to the class, using whatever words she or he wishes, but the sender must employ no hand gestures, nor can the sender accept questions from the class.

The class will be instructed to take out a sheet of paper, and try to reproduce the figure the sender will describe, *exactly as he or she describes it*. (You may wish to provide some incentive for reproducing the figure correctly—an *A* on the pop quiz for the day, for example.) You should tell the class that no one will be allowed to ask questions of the sender.

When everyone is ready, instruct the sender to begin describing Figure 13–1. You should keep a record of the time taken by the sender to complete the description of the figure.

After the sender has completed the description of Figure 13–1, have the class compare their figures with Figure 13–1. One or two in a class of 30 may get the figure completely right—you may have no students correctly reproduce the figure. There will probably be some good-natured kidding of the sender for failing to adequately communicate all of the details of Figure 13–1.

Then, have the sender describe Figure 13–2 to the class. You should instruct the class that they should question the sender on any unclear instructions, or anything they do not understand about the figure being described. Again, keep a record of the time it takes the sender to complete his or her description of Figure 13–2.

Then have the class compare their drawings with Figure 13–2. (You may wish to prepare overhead transparencies of Figures 13–1 and 13–2 in order to show the class what they actually look like.) More than likely, you will have a much higher percentage of the class correctly reproducing Figure 13–2 than did Figure 13–1. You will also find out that it takes much longer for the sender to describe Figure 13–2, with all of the questions/comments being made by the class. You will also find that the level of frustration felt by the class after completing Figure 13–1 was much higher than that felt after completing Figure 13–2.

What is the lesson learned from this exercise? Basically, it is that feedback is important in understanding *meaning*. Communications involves the transfer of *meaning* from one person to others. Message can be recalled, but *meaning* is the important component of communication.

Feedback can also lower the frustration levels of both individuals involved in communications, as illustrated in this exercise. When receivers have the opportunity to clarify, to question, to reassure themselves that they really do understand, then their frustration levels decline. When senders feel that their receivers understand the idea they are trying to convey, their frustration levels also decline.

Source: Adapted from J. Gordon, 1987, *A diagnostic approach to organizational behavior*, Boston: Allyn and Bacon, p. 261.

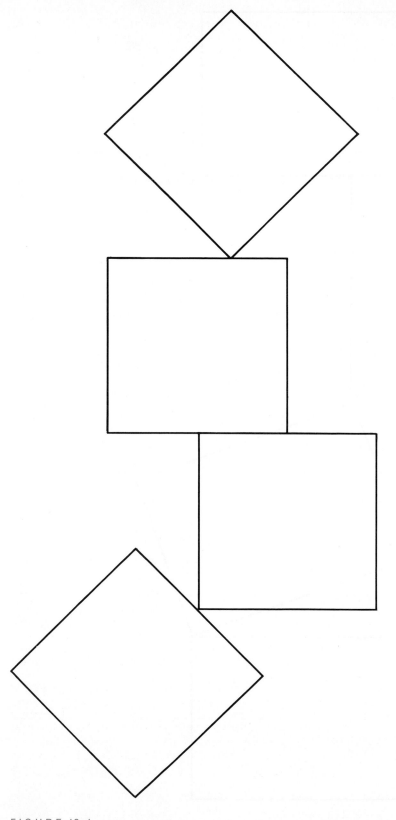

FIGURE 13–1

FIGURE 13–2

Feedback has some costs, as well. One of them is the time involved when feedback is employed. If you were keeping time during the exercise, you found that it probably took the class twice as long to complete Figure 13–2 as it took to complete Figure 13–1. Feedback is time-consuming, and individuals will have to weigh the cost/benefit of

using feedback in their communications. Sometimes when the message being transmitted is one with which the receiver is familiar, not using feedback can be faster and just as accurate. But never assume that the receiver understands the meaning of your communication, just because he or she has heard this message previously.

Additional Readings

Johansen, R., & Bullen, C. (1984, March–April). What to expect from teleconferencing. *Harvard Business Review*, pp. 164–166.

Kiesler, S. (1986, January–February). The hidden messages in computer networks. *Harvard Business Review*, pp. 46–50.

Lengel, R. H., & Daft, R. L. (1988). The selection of communication media as an executive skill. *Academy of Management Executive*, 2(3), 225–232.

Ornstein, S. (1989). The hidden influence of office design. *Academy of Management Executive*, 3(2), 144–147.

∎ 14 ∎

DECISION MAKING IN ORGANIZATIONS

CHAPTER OUTLINE

Organizational Decision Making: Its Basic Nature
> The Traditional, Analytical Model of Decision Making
> An Intuitive Approach to Decision Making: Image Theory
> Varieties of Organizational Decisions

Individual Decision Making in Organizations: An Imperfect Process
> Two Approaches to Individual Decision Making: The Rational-Economic Model and the Administrative Model
> Impediments to Optimal Individual Decisions

Group Decisions: Do Too Many Cooks Spoil the Broth?
> Comparing Group and Individual Decisions: When Are Two (or More) Heads Better Than One?

Obstacles to Quality Group Decisions: Groupthink and Group Polarization
Improving the Effectiveness of Group Decisions: Some Techniques

Special Sections

OB in Practice Undoing Corporate Decisions: Toying Around at Fisher-Price and Taking the Fizzle Out of Coca-Cola

A Question of Ethics Ethical Decisions: The Result of "Bad Apples" in "Bad Barrels"

Focis on Research Training Pilots to Make Decisions about Avoiding Hazardous Weather

LEARNING OBJECTIVES

After reading this chapter, you should be able to:
1. Identify the steps in the traditional, analytic model of decision making.
2. Describe and give examples of the various types of organizational decisions (i.e., *programmed* versus *nonprogrammed,* and decisions made under high and low levels of risk.)
3. Distinguish between the rational-economic model and the administrative model of decision making.
4. Describe the factors that dictate against high-quality individual decisions—both individual, cognitive biases and organizationally induced barriers.

5. Compare the advantages and disadvantages of using groups and individuals to make their decisions in organizations.
6. Describe the conditions under which groups make better decisions than individuals, and the conditions under which individuals make better decisions than groups.
7. Identify the major obstacles to effective group decisions (*groupthink* and *group polarization*).
8. Describe techniques that can be used to improve the quality of group decisions (e.g., the *Delphi technique,* the *nominal group technique,* and *decision training*).

Chapter Overview

This chapter deals with various aspects of decision making in organizations and begins with a discussion of the basic nature of decision making. The traditional view of decision making as a multi-step process through which a problem is identified, objectives are defined, a predecision is made (i.e., a decision about how to make a decision), alternatives are generated and evaluated, an alternative is chosen, implemented, and then followed up, is discussed first. Then image

theory, an alternative view of decision making that claims people will adopt a course of action that best fits their individual principles, current goals, and plans for the future, is explained. The chapter then discusses the distinctions between programmed and nonprogrammed decisions, and certain and uncertain decisions. Next, the rational-economic and the administrative models of individual decision making are presented and contrasted, and several impediments to optimal decision making are described, including cognitive biases—framing and heuristics, the escalation of commitment, and organizational impediments such as time constraints, political pressures, and unethical work environments. The chapter then turns to a comparison of individual and group decision making, noting the circumstances under which each is preferred. Group decision making remains as the focus of the chapter, but the emphasis turns to obstacles of effective group decisions such as groupthink and group polarization. Finally, several recommendations for improving the effectiveness of group decision making are presented. These include the Delphi technique, the nominal groups technique, and issues to be considered in training individuals to perform better as members of groups.

Three special sections appear in this chapter. An OB in Practice (Undoing Corporate Decisions: Toying Around at Fisher-Price and Taking the Fizzle Out of Coca-Cola) describes how two well-known companies undid potentially devastating strategic decisions. The point of this section is that business decisions may not be forever—especially those that do not turn out right. A Question of Ethics (Ethical Decisions: The Result of "Bad Apples" in "Bad Barrels") discusses the results of research showing personal and situational factors that contribute to ethical decision making. The point being, if it is ethical decision making that you want, hire inherently moral people and provide them with a work environment that encourages moral behavior. And a Focus on Research (Training Pilots to Make Decisions about Avoiding Hazardous Weather) discusses the important role that decision making support technology plays in helping airline cockpit crews to make the right decision in critical situations.

The Case in Point (Changing Decision Making at Xerox) describes how Xerox changed the way its employees make decisions, showing the relationship between technology and the company's products. And the Experiencing Organizational Behavior exercise (Are You a Risky Decision Maker? It Depends on Your Frame of Reference) provides students with a chance to see how framing can affect their decision making.

Lecture and Review Questions

What are the steps in the decision-making process?

The decision-making process is usually seen as a series of steps one goes through when trying to solve a problem. The first step is problem identification, which simply involves the recognition and identification of a problem. The next step involves defining the objectives to be met in solving the problem. Any possible solution to the problem will later be evaluated relative to this objective. Next, a predecision is made concerning how to go about making the required decision. That is, a decision is made whether the final decision will be made by a single person or by a group, for example, although some predecisions can now be made by computer through the use of decision support systems. The fourth step is known as alternative generation, and involves proposing a number of potential solutions to the problem. The fifth step calls for evaluating alternative solutions to see which are best, and this is followed by the sixth step in which a choice is made to adopt one of the alternatives. The seventh step involves the implementation of the chosen solution, and the final step is to follow up and monitor the situation in order to determine the solution's effectiveness.

What is the image theory of decision making?

Image theory is an intuitive approach to decision making. According to this view of decision making, people will adopt a course of action that best fits their individual principles, current goals, and plans for the future. They do not necessarily select the best alternative by weighing all available options. Instead, people make decisions in a more automatic, intuitive fashion than traditionally believed.

Specifically, image theory proposes that much decision making involves a 2-step process. The first step is the compatibility test, a comparison of the degree to which a particular course of action is consistent with various images—particularly individual principles, current goals, and plans for the future. If there is any lack of compatibility with respect to any of these considerations, a rejection decision is made. If the compatibility test is passed, then the profitability test is made. That is, people consider the extent to which using various alternative best fit with their values, goals, and plans. The decision is then made to accept to accept the best candidate. These tests are viewed as being made within a certain decision frame—that is, with consideration of meaningful information about the decision context (such as past experiences).

What are the major dimensions of organizational decisions?

The major dimensions along which organizational decisions vary are programmed versus nonprogrammed, and certain versus uncertain. Programmed decisions are routine decisions which are made repeatedly, and which rely on a predetermined course of action. Nonprogrammed decisions are those in which the decision maker faces a unique situation in which solutions are novel. Such decisions are typically made by higher-level personnel, and include strategic decisions that will affect everything the organization does. Certainty refers to the degree of risk involved in the decision. All organizational decisions involve some degree of risk or uncertainty, but the risk involved is a function of the probability of making an incorrect decision. This probability may be based on objective data, or it may simply be a subjective judgement. In general, uncertainty is an undesirable characteristic of a decision; so decision makers attempt to reduce uncertainty, primarily by gathering additional information.

What is the rational-economic model of decision making?

This model assumes that decisions are rational; that is, they maximize the attainment of goals. In this view, the decision-maker recognizes all alternative solutions, accurately and completely evaluates each one, then selects the optimal alternative. These conditions rarely exist, but the model can be viewed as a normative or prescriptive outline of how decisions should be made.

What are the major components of the administrative model of decision making?

The administrative model assumes that, rather than selecting the best solution, decision makers are more likely to select a solution that is good enough. These are called satisficing solutions, and can be contrasted with the optimizing solutions called for in the rational-economic model. In this view, decision-makers do not have the time, nor the cognitive capacity to collect and evaluate all alternatives. Thus, they make rational decisions, but only within the bounds of the alternatives they consider. Furthermore, the cognitive abilities of the decision-makers and the environment in which they operate present a number of impediments to rational decision making that must be recognized. As such, the administrative model is more descriptive than prescriptive.

What are the major impediments to optimal individual decisions?

The major impediments are cognitive biases in decision making, escalation of commitment, and organizationally-imposed time constraints. Cognitive biases refer to the fact that human decision-makers often focus on irrelevant information and fail to consider all the relevant information. Framing is one such systematic bias in the decision-making process. This refers to the fact that people make different decisions based on the way the problem is presented to them, or framed. Heuristics refers to another systematic bias in which decision-makers use simple rules of thumb to guide them through complex alternatives. Two such heuristics are known as the availability heuristic (people tend to make decisions on the basis of information that is readily available), and the representativeness heuristic (people tend to perceive others in a stereotypical way if they appear to be typical representatives of the category to which they belong). Escalation of commitment refers to a bias toward committing more resources to a course of action that has proven to be a failure in the past. Research by Staw and his associates

suggests that this is a result of people trying to justify past decisions, and thus present themselves as rational decision-makers. Finally, organizations introduce impediments of their own by imposing time constraints on decisions. When these constraints are severe, decision-makers are not able to search through all alternatives and are much more likely to rely on heuristics. In addition, political face-saving pressure at work leads decision-makers to adopt alternatives that are best for them, even if they are not best for the organization. And finally, the ethical nature of the work environment seems to exert an important influence on decision making. Even moral people can be led to unethical decision making if the organizational environment supports unethical activity.

When are group decisions superior to individual decisions, and when are individual decisions better?

Group decisions involve bringing together a group of people, which should increase the pool of available talent and ability. The additional personnel also make specialization of labor possible, and group decisions are usually more readily accepted by others since there are several people involved in making the decision. On the other hand, group members also spend time socializing, so group decisons take longer. Also, the effectiveness of group decision making can be hampered by group conflict or intimidation by the group leader. As a result of these factors, groups tend to be most successful when the group is composed of a heterogenous group of people with complementary skills, when ideas are freely communicated, and when good ideas are rapidly accepted. Another important consideration regarding the relative effectiveness of individual versus group decision making is the nature of the decision task. On complex tasks, benefits that go beyond the contribution of what the best group member can do are derived from combining individuals into groups. People can help each other solve complex decision problems not only by pooling their resources, but also by correcting each other's solutions and assisting each other in coming up with ideas. There is also likely to be the intangible synergy created when a group of people help each other and create a climate for success. Even with simple tasks, groups may perform better than individuals as long as the knowledge, skills, and talent that group members bring to the group are sufficient to perform the task. In other words, a group of people who do not know how to perform a simple task is bound to be inferior to an individual who does know how to perform the task—regardless of how many people are included in the group. Research shows that individuals also outperform groups when dealing with poorly structured, creative decision-making tasks. Apparently, even though groups may help to stimulate the creative process, the presence of others in a group inhibits the creativity of individual members by slowing down the process of bringing ideas to fruition. Thus, whether a group makes better decisions than an individual really depends on the nature of the decision-making task.

What are groupthink and group polarization?

When groups become cohesive, members may be unwilling to disrupt the like-mindedness of the group, so they may not be willing to challenge group decisions. When this happens, the group also tends to isolate itself from outside information and ceases to think critically. This phenomenon is known as groupthink and can actually work to discourage the discussion of effective solutions to problems. The major symptoms of groupthink are an illusion of invulnerability, collective rationalization, unquestioned morality, excessive negative stereotyping of others, strong pressure toward conformity, an illusion of unanimity in accepting group decisions, and the existence of self-appointed mind guards who protect the group from negative information. Group polarization refers to the fact that groups tend to make riskier decisions than individuals. This phenomenon is known as the risky shift. Actually, it has been found that groups tend to make decisions that are more extreme on several dimensions. This seems to be due to the fact that, in general, after group discussion, group members tend to shift their individual views in a more extreme direction, resulting in group polarization. Because this can produce more extreme decisions, and riskier decisions, it is potentially quite dangerous.

What are some techniques that have been suggested for improving group decisions?

Several techniques for improving group decisions have been proposed. The Delphi technique involves using a group of experts who work together without ever meeting face-to-face. Each person submits proposed solutions to a leader who compiles the suggestions and looks for a consensus. If there is none, all proposals are returned to all group members for further consideration and a new set of proposals is generated. This process is continued until consensus is obtained. This technique is an effective way of tapping the resources of a group without dealing with conflict or intimidation, but it is quite expensive and time consuming. The nominal group technique calls for members to actually meet, but the meeting is conducted under a strict set of rules. Each member proposes a solution to the group, and other members can only respond with questions of clarification. After all solutions are proposed, each is discussed, and opinions are solicited. When this is done, group members vote on each proposal and the proposal with the highest score (or the lowest rank) is adopted as the group solution. This technique saves time, but is best with simple problems and small groups. It should be noted that the Delphi technique generates the most creative solution and the nominal group technique generates the quickest solutions, but interacting groups produce solutions that gain the greatest acceptance. Finally, it is possible to train individuals to improve group performance by making them aware of and helping them to avoid four problems: hypervigilance (the frantic search for a quick solution), unconflicted adherence (sticking with the first idea someone has regardless of new information), unconflicted change (being too quick to change and adopt new ideas as they come along), and defensive avoidance (avoiding work on the problem at hand).

Other Teaching Suggestions

1. There are also variations on the economic-rational model that might be worth pointing out. The text alludes to one such alternative when it discusses subjective versus objective probability. The alternative model is known as the subjective expected utility (SEU) model, and includes subjective instead of objective probabilities of an outcome occurring, as well as subjective evaluation of the utility of a given outcome. In other words, the decision-maker decides what the outcome is worth to him or her, then estimates the likelihood of obtaining that outcome. The terms are multiplied so that the decision-maker would be unlikely to select an alternative that had a high utility if that outcome had a low subjective probability of occurring. The decision-maker selects the alternative that maximizes this subjective expected utility.

2. Whenever I think about bounded rationality, I think about non-business decisions. Ask your students how many of them are married. Surely there are few decisions we might make that are more important than selecting a mate, so we might expect this to be a case where people are more likely to try to optimize. Yet we clearly do not. We surely do not consider every possible mate, and we don't try to learn everything about the person before we get married. Instead, we satisfice. Think about other examples in day-to-day life where we satisfice rather than maximize our decision making.

3. The text discusses availability and representativeness heuristics. Simon (who developed the administrative model) also discusses a different method of simplifying complex information called "chunking." Since we have limited processing capacity, we can maximize the use of that capacity by consolidating individual bits of information into chunks, and then processing those chunks. Think about the way you remember your social security number (three digits, two digits, four digits) which requires processing three chunks of information rather than nine bits. Simon also found that this is a secret to being a Grand

Master chess player. When I look at a chess board during a game, I try to process every piece and where it is located. A grand master looks at the entire configuration of pieces as one chunk, because the configuration has meaning to someone who plays at that level. This ability not only helps explain the level of grand master play, but also explains the ease with which a grand master can play several games simultaneously and win them all.

4. The text discusses the problems of groupthink and the classic example of the Bay of Pigs invasion. McGraw-Hill has a film that demonstrates groupthink in action, and it is quite insightful, as is the commentary by Janis himself.

5. The NASA moon problem as a classic for studying group decision making. It provides an excellent opportunity to observe group decision making and to compare group and individual decision making. It might even be worth trying to solve the exercise using something like a normal group technique and discussing what problems or advantages that brings.

Case in Point Notes

Changing Decision Making at Xerox

This case describes how Xerox Corporation changed the way its employees thought about the relationship between technology and the company's products. Traditionally, product decisions at Xerox were anchored in terms of xerography, the technology upon which the company was built. Making decisions based on xerography served the Xerox Corporation very well for a number of years, but today's rapidly changing technological environment demanded that Xerox broaden the way its employees think about technology if it was to remain competitive.

How did Xerox change its employees' decision making? Much of the answer has to do with John Brown, Xerox corporate vice president and director of Xerox's research and development group—the Xerox Palo Alto Research Center (PARC). Brown recognized the costs the company was paying by limiting itself to thinking about its products primarily in terms of xerography. So Brown launched a systematic investigation to identify the obstacles that were undermining the decision making processes of Xerox employees. To help him conduct this type of research, he hired social science researchers (anthropologists, sociologists, psychologists, and linguists) to join PARC. His research unveiled several fundamental obstacles that were interfering with employees' ability to better integrate the nonxerographic research produced by PARC into new Xerox products. The case describes each obstacle that Brown discovered (e.g., use of the anchoring heuristic and framing), and the strategies that he used to alter the way Xerox employees make decisions. Information regarding the outcomes of the decision making change effort are also presented.

The discussion questions that follow the case prompt students to discuss many of the topics presented in the chapter. Receiving particular emphasis are individual and organizational impediments to decision making, analysis of the case in terms of image theory, and explaining the theory behind the strategies used by Brown to change employee decision making.

Additional Case

Money: The Root of All Evil

Part I

The Ajax Toy Corporation is a medium-sized firm located in southern Michigan. The firm designs and manufactures toys and games. The wage and salary program of the company operates on a low profile basis; that is, no information on salary ranges in regard to grade classification is given to employees and they are not given minimum, medium, or maximum pay ranges attainable in their present job levels. When employees are formally evaluated each year a merit increase, when given, is usually a small percentage increase, with management retaining any information as to how much money is available for merit increases. When management was asked by employees why merit increases and salaries were handled in this manner, the standard answer was, "It is company policy that this information cannot be given to employees. Only staff personnel have knowledge of this information."

The employees of the Research and Development Department for new products are due for a performance appraisal. Their current minimum and maximum level of wages is from $25,000 to $44,000 per year. These salaries are average for the industry. Last year, the company's conservative wage and salary policies resulted in two of the best people in the department being pirated by Ajax's largest competitor . . . hurting the performance of the Research and Development Department this year. Pirating of employees in other departments has also been a problem for the past two years.

A new Director of Research and Development has recently been hired and management has charged her with proposing recommendations to reduce the pirating of peo-

Source: Adapted from Jack L. Simonetti, *Experiential Exercises and Cases for Human Resource Management.* Copyright © 1987 by Allyn and Bacon. Used with permission.

ple from her department, while also conducting the department's individual performance appraisals and merit distribution. The Manager of Human Resources will later review her ideas against the present system to determine what changes, if any, they may wish to make before the next review period.

Additional information about the Research and Development Department and its employees is as follows:

Roger Ballard: 60 years of age; 20 years experience with Ajax; has had no new ideas during the past year, but works well with others to develop their ideas. Current salary: $44,000 (top of his salary range).

John Connelly: 45 years of age; 10 years with Ajax; is seldom late for work, but doesn't work well with others in the department; was a very good friend of the previous manager; has had one idea this year but it is nowhere near completion. Current salary: $39,000.

David Browing: 32 years of age; four years with Ajax; has had two ideas this year, one of which has been completed; past evaluations have shown him as an average performer, but this year his work has been very good. Current salary: $31,000.

Karen Harding: 24 years of age; was hired 10 months ago to replace one of the pirated employees; has designed two new products which have been completed and are doing very well; has ideas for three more new products; is currently working on these three new ideas with help from Roger; has not received a raise since joining Ajax. Current salary: $25,000.

The director of Research and Development was confidentially informed by the company that she has $12,000 to distribute for use as merit increases. Her recommendation of distribution of the merit dollars requires your approval. As Human Resource Manager, you have just received the following merit increase recommendations from the Director of Research and Development:

1. Roger Ballard . . . $2,000
2. John Connelly . . . $1,000
3. David Browing . . . $4,750
4. Karen Harding . . . $4,250

Questions

1. As Human Resource Manager would you agree with the distribution of the merit money among the four employees by the director of Research and Development?
2. Defend and explain your decision.

Part II

The Director of Research and Development made the following recommendations concerning reducing the number of employees being pirated from her department:

1. Provide employees with information concerning the salary range for their positions, and their level within the range.
2. Automatically increase by $5,000 the range ceiling for any employee who has reached his/her maximum and therefore is no longer eligible for a merit increase.
   or,
3. Eliminate salary ranges altogether.
4. Award merit increases on a percentage rather than a dollar basis.

Questions

As Human Resources Manager, would you:

1. Accept the merit increase policy recommendations as proposed? Why or why not?
2. Recommend different merit increase policy changes other than the ones proposed by the Director of Research and Development? What changes would you make and why?
3. Accept the recommendations for reducing the pirating of people? Why or why not? Which would you accept and which wouldn't you accept? Why?

Money: The Root Of All Evil Teaching Note

In Part I, the questions can be answered by the students in many ways, but the most important learning from this part is in the defense and explanation of their decisions. Did they use the basic decision-making process model discussed in the chapter? Is this a programmed or a non-programmed decision? Was the concept of riskiness addressed? Are the alternatives optimal or satisficing? Is this a decision better made by an individual or by a group? If a group decision is suggested, how might the concept of *groupthink* influence the decision?

Part II asks that the Human Resources Manager consider the R&D Manager's ideas about the merit policy and the fundamental idea of pay secrecy. You may wish to require your students to investigate research on the outcomes of secret pay plans before responding to the questions in Part II. Again, the *justifications* that students prepare for their answers to the questions are more important than their responses to the questions. Improving the individual's decision-making process involves understanding it. The ability to make quality decisions is not something that we are born with; it is acquired through experience and an understanding of the processes by which decisions are made.

Experiencing Organization Behavior Notes

Are You a Risky Decision Maker? It Depends on Your Frame of Reference

This exercise provides students with a chance to see how framing can affect their decision making. A brief review of framing is provided, followed by instruc-

tions for performing the exercise. Students are asked to read two decision situations. The first situation frames decision alternatives in a negative fashion. The second situation frames decision alternatives in a positive perspective. Students are then asked to select their preferred decision alternative for each situation. The alternatives presented in each situation are mathematically identical in their outcome probabilities, yet in all likelihood, students will show a preference for one alternative or another, depending on the manner in which the situation is framed. A debriefing is provided following the exercise as well as a challenge to students to discuss some well-known historical decisions that may have been affected by framing.

Additional Experiential Exercise

The Selection Decision

You are the Human Resource Manager of the Ajax Toy Company, and need to select two Assistant Human Resource Managers to fill recent vacancies. The two individuals who will be promoted need to have all of the managerial skills (technical, conceptual, and human).

Ajax Toy Company is committed to equal opportunity for all workers based on their performance in the work criteria and areas designated below. This information is to be used to make the final decisions.

After you have reviewed the following criteria and data use:

1. The Iterative Selection Procedure.
2. The Weighted Selection Procedure to select the two individuals you would recommend for promotion.

Instructions

1. Iterative Selection Procedure
   a. Eliminate all candidates without enough *seniority* (10 years or more).
   b. Eliminate all candidates with a *Managerial Aptitude Test Score* of less than 80.
   c. Eliminate all candidates whose *Work Attitude* is rated as only Fair or Poor.
   d. Eliminate all candidates whose *Percent of Work Days Absent* is greater than 1.5 percent.
   e. Eliminate all candidates whose *Ability to Make Tough Business Decisions* is rated as only Fair or Poor.
   f. Eliminate all candidates whose *Accuracy of Decisions Made* is rated as only Fair or Poor.
   g. Eliminate all candidates whose *Potential for Advancement* is rated as only Fair or Poor.
   h. Eliminate all candidates whose *Loyalty to Organization* is rated as only Fair or Poor.

Using the Iterative Selection Procedure the positions would be offered to the following two candidates:

1. _____
2. _____

2. The Weighted Selection Procedure
   a. Assign a weight to each criterion.
   b. Rank the candidate's performance on each criterion.
   c. Multiply the ranking by the weight assigned to the criteria for each candidate.
   d. Total the results.

Source: Adapted from Jack L. Simonetti, *Experiential Exercises and Cases for Human Resource Management.* Copyright © 1987 by Allyn and Bacon. Used with permission.

Using the Weighted Selection Procedure the two candidates who would be offered the positions are:

1. _____
2. _____

Biographical Sketches

Steve Walters   34, caucasian, separated, handicapped, one child.
Carlos Sanchez 42, hispanic, married, three children.
Bernard Jones   44, black, married, two children.
Ann Taber   43, caucasian, married, two children.
Pat Mahoney   35, caucasian, divorced, four children.
Judy Nickels   40, black, single, no children.
Don Beemer   46, caucasian, widowed, three children.

Factors Used For Evaluation

Employee: Steve Walters

Seniority with the Company	6 years
Managerial Aptitude Test Score	81
Work Attitude	Poor
Percent of Work Days Absent	2.1
Ability to Make Tough Business Decisions	Fair
Accuracy of Decisions Made	Fair
Potential for Advancement	Fair
Loyalty to Organization	Good

Employee: Carlos Sanchez

Seniority with the Company	11 years
Managerial Aptitude Test Score	83
Work Attitude	Fair
Percent of Work Days Absent	1.2
Ability to Make Tough Business Decisions	Excellent
Accuracy of Decisions Made	Good
Potential for Advancement	Excellent
Loyalty to Organization	Good

Employee: Bernard Jones

Seniority with the Company	14 years
Managerial Aptitude Test Score	78
Work Attitude	Excellent
Percent of Work Days Absent	1.9
Ability to Make Tough Business Decisions	Good
Accuracy of Decisions Made	Excellent
Potential for Advancement	Good
Loyalty to Organization	Excellent

Employee: Ann Taber

Seniority with the Company	12 years
Managerial Aptitude Test Score	79
Work Attitude	Excellent

Percent of Work Days Absent	1.5
Ability to Make Tough Business Decisions	Good
Accuracy of Decisions Made	Excellent
Potential for Advancement	Excellent
Loyalty to Organization	Good

Employee: Pat Mahoney

Seniority with the Company	8 years
Managerial Aptitude Test Score	83
Work Attitude	Fair
Percent of Work Days Absent	1.9
Ability to Make Tough Business Decisions	Fair
Accuracy of Decisions Made	Fair
Potential for Advancement	Fair
Loyalty to Organization	Good

Employee: Judy Nickels

Seniority with the Company	15 years
Managerial Aptitude Test Score	85
Work Attitude	Good
Percent of Work Days Absent	1.4
Ability to Make Tough Business Decisions	Good
Accuracy of Decisions Made	Good
Potential for Advancement	Good
Loyalty to Organization	Excellent

Employee: Don Beemer

Seniority with the Company	13 years
Managerial Aptitude Test Score	89
Work Attitude	Fair
Percent of Work Days Absent	1.2
Ability to Make Tough Business Decisions	Excellent
Accuracy of Decisions Made	Excellent
Potential for Advancement	Good
Loyalty to Organization	Good

Questions

In using the two different selection procedures, answer the following questions:

1. Are the two individuals recommended for promotion the same when using the different procedures?
2. If not, discuss why not.
3. Which selection procedure will assist a Human Resource Manager in making the best possible hiring and/or promotion decisions?
4. Be ready to explain why you weighted the criteria factors the way you did.

Additional Readings

Behling, O., & Eckel, N. L. (1991). Making sense out of intuition. *Academy of Management Executive, 5*(1), 46–54.

Einhorn, H. J., & Hogarth, R. M. (1987, January–February). Decision making: Going forward in reverse. *Harvard Business Review*, pp. 66–69. (A practical discussion of decision making by two of the leading researchers on decision theory.)

Hammond, J. S. (1967, November–December). Better decisions with preference theory. *Harvard Business Review*, pp. 123–126. (Another practical article from a leading scholar.)

Ulvila, J. W., & Brown, R. V. (1982, September–October). Decision analysis comes of age. *Harvard Business Review*, pp. 130–133.

Whyte, G. (1989). Groupthink reconsidered. *Academy of Management Review, 14,* 40–56.

Whyte, G. (1991). Decision failures: Why they occur and how to prevent them. *Academy of Management Executive, 5*(3), 23–31.

The Selection Decision: Teaching Note

This exercise should really generate much discussion in the class. The Iterative Selection Procedure calls for applying each step in the process to all of the candidates, and eliminating those that fail at each step. For example, in the exercise the following candidates would fail at each of the stages below:

1. Iterative Selection Procedure
   a. Eliminate all candidates without enough *seniority* (10 years or more). Eliminate *Walters* and *Mahoney.*
   b. Eliminate all candidates with a *Managerial Aptitude Test Score* of less than 80. *Jones* and *Taber.*
   c. Eliminate all candidates whose *Work Attitude* is rated as only Fair or Poor. *Sanchez* and *Beemer.*
   d. Eliminate all candidates whose *Percent of Work Days Absent* is greater than 1.5 percent. *No one.*
   e. Eliminate all candidates whose *Ability to Make Tough Business Decisions* is rated as only Fair or Poor. *No one.*
   f. Eliminate all candidates whose *Accuracy of Decisions Made* is rated as only Fair or Poor. *No one.*
   g. Eliminate all candidates whose *Potential for Advancement* is rated as only Fair or Poor. *No one.*
   h. Eliminate all candidates whose *Loyalty to Organization* is rated as only Fair or Poor. *No one.*

Once the iterative process has eliminated candidates successively, the only one left who was not disqualified by the process is Nickels.

The obvious problem with a decision rule as inflexible as this is the arbitrary nature of the system. Are any of the qualifying stages more or less important than others? How were the ratings of each candidate completed? How do you define *Work Attitude,* for example?

The problem with the Weighted Selection Procedure is that each student will probably assign different weights to each of the criterion. Then you compound the problem by having the students rank the candidates on each of the criterion. Unless everyone understands the procedure (Can you give equal rankings to candidates who both score "Excellent" on *Potential for Advancement,* for example?) the rankings become less than meaningful. Multiplying the weights and ranks together further muddles the procedure.

This exercise can show that decision rules, while helpful, cannot substitute for good judgment. Don Beemer, who scored "Fair" on *Work Attitude,* would fall out of the running with the Iterative Selection Procedure. He would seem to be a very well-qualified candidate for the position. In fact, his *Work Attitude* may very well improve should he be given the promotion!

∎ 15 ∎

ORGANIZATIONAL STRUCTURE AND DESIGN

CHAPTER OUTLINE

LEARNING OBJECTIVES

After reading this chapter, you should be able to:
1. Explain the basic characteristics of organizational structure revealed in an organization chart (*hierarchy of authority, division of labor, span of control, line versus staff,* and *decentralization*).
2. Describe different approaches to departmentalization—*functional organizations, product organizations,* and *matrix organizations.*
3. Distinguish between *classical* and *neoclassical* approaches to organizational design.
4. Explain how the contemporary approach to organizational design differs from the classical and neoclassical approaches.
5. Describe how an organization's design is influenced by the environment within which the organization operates.
6. Distinguish between *mechanistic organizations* and *organic organizations,* and describe the conditions under which each is most appropriate.
7. Characterize two forms of interorganizational design—*joint ventures* and *conglomerates.*
8. Describe the relationship between organizational design and structure identified in the Woodward studies and in the Aston studies.
9. Explain the implications of *interdependence* on organizational structure.

Chapter Overview

This chapter represents a shift in emphasis from a micro to a macro orientation to organizational behavior; specifically, the issues of organization structure and design and their relationship to organizational environment and technology. The chapter begins by broadly defining organization structure as the formal configuration between individuals and groups with respect to the allocation of tasks, responsibilities, and authority within organizations. Next, the chapter describes the five building blocks of organization structure as represented by an organization chart—hierarchy of authority (summary of reporting relationships), division of labor (the degree to which jobs are specialized), span of control (the number of individuals over which a manager has responsibility), line versus staff positions (jobs permitting direct decision making versus jobs in which advice is given), and decentralization (the degree to which decisions can be made by lower ranking employees as opposed to a few higher ranking individuals). The chapter then shifts to describe the ways in which organizations can be departmentalized, emphasizing functional, product, and matrix organizations. The next major section deals with the process used to coordinate the structural elements of organizations in the most effective manner—organization design. This section opens with a discussion of classical and neoclassical organization theory, followed by descriptions of the contingency approach to organization design, Burns and Stalker's mechanistic and organic organizations, free-form designs, and intraorganizational designs (e.g., joint ventures and conglomerates). The critical role of organizational environment in organization design is discussed throughout this section. The final section of the chapter is devoted to defining technology (small-batch, large-batch, and continuous-process) and explaining its role as a determinant of organization design. Particular emphasis is placed on the findings of the Woodward and Aston studies. This section concludes with a discussion of the types of interdependencies created by technology (Thompson's pooled interdependence, sequential interdependence, and reciprocal interdependence), and the influence of interdependence on organization structure.

Three special sections appear in this chapter. An OB in Practice (Growing Pains Force CDP Publications to Restructure) describes how CDP Publications changed its organization structure to accommodate its growing size. Special emphasis is devoted to changes in the company's hierarchy of authority and shift toward decentralization. An International/Multicultural Perspective (Structuring Organizations for Multinational Operations) defines the multinational corporation and describes how the organization structure of a multinational corporation can change according to the degree to which it is involved in international activities. And a Question of Ethics (Who Takes the Rap for Unethical Corporate Behavior? Camouflaging Immorality within the Web of Organizational Structure) describes how some top officials of organizations hide to avoid accepting responsibility for unethical actions by camouflaging themselves in the veil of a complex organization chart.

The Case in Point (Reorganizing Apple Computer, and Reorganizing It Again . . . and Again) describes the various organization designs that CEO John Sculley has used to organize Apple Computer. This case nicely illustrates how a company struggles to design its organization structure to match the demands of its technology and environment. There is a CNN video (*Apple Computer*) available for use as a supplement to this case. And the Experiencing Organizational Behavior exercise (Mechanistic versus Organic Organizations: Which Do You Prefer?) is a self-assessment tool designed to help students learn about their preferences for either mechanistic or organic organization designs.

Lecture and Review Questions

What are the basic characteristics of organizational structure as revealed in an organization chart?
Organization structure is the formal configuration between individuals and groups with respect to the allocation of tasks, responsibilities, and authority within organizations. The five building blocks of organization structure as represented by an organization structure as represented by an organization chart are hierarchy of authority (summary of reporting relationships), division of labor (the degree to which jobs are specialized), span of control (the number of individuals over which a manager has responsibility), line versus staff positions (jobs permitting direct decision making power versus jobs in which advice is given), and decentralization (the degree to which decisions can be made by lower ranking employees as opposed to a few higher-ranking individuals).

What is meant by function, product, and matrix organizational designs?
Most organizational designs can be classified as falling into one of these three categories. In a functionally designed organization, departments or units are based on specialized functions and are concerned with the performance of specific tasks or activities. All employees involved in the same function (such as accounting) work together and serve the entire organization. In such organizations, interunit cooperation is difficult, integration of functions is impeded, and unit members tend to focus only on their own activities. As a result, innovation is hampered, and it is difficult for the organization to respond to change. A product design includes self-contained units, each consisting of all the necessary functions, but concerned with only a single product line. In essence, each unit is its own organization and can function independently. Organizations designed this way are extremely flexible and adaptable; competition across units is usually healthy; and units are kept to a manageable size. There is duplication of effort and function in each unit, however, and opportunities for advancement may be limited because of the smaller size of each unit. There can be problems of coordination across product lines as well. A matrix design combines elements of functional and product designs. In fact, a product design

is superimposed on a functional design, resulting in a dual system of authority with functional leaders and product leaders, as well as leaders with authority over both who are responsible for maintaining balance. These designs are flexible, allow quick response to environmental changes, and enhance communications. There can be some frustration, however, on the part of employees who must report to two bosses, and one authority system can potentially gain control over the other. The key to success in a matrix organization is constant cooperation.

What is the difference between classical and neoclassical approaches to organization design?

The chief distinction between the classical organizational theorists (such as Max Weber, Frederick Taylor, and Henri Fayol) and the neoclassical theorists (such as Douglas McGregor, Chris Argyris, and Rensis Likert) is the degree of emphasis placed on the need to pay attention to basic human needs to succeed and express oneself when designing organizations. Both camps believed that a universal best way to design organizations existed, but the classical theorists generally ignored human needs and instead focused on ways to maximize organizational efficiency. Inspired in large part by the Hawthorne studies, the neoclassical theorists embraced the idea that organizational effectiveness and efficiency were not the only valid goals of an industrial organization, but employee satisfaction was also important. The concern for employees' needs to succeed and express themselves is a cornerstone of the major neoclassical theories of organization design. Thus, the organizational design implications of neoclassical theory become clear. Specifically, in contrast to the classical approach, calling for organizations to be designed with a rigid, tall hierarchy and narrow span of control (allowing managers to maintain close supervision over their subordinates), the neoclassical approach argues for designing organizations with flat hierarchical structures (minimizing managerial control over subordinates) and a high degree of decentralization (encouraging employees to make their own decisions).

How is an organization's design affected by the environment within which it operates?

The idea that the best design for an organization depends on the nature of the environment in which the organization operates, lies at the heart of modern, contingency approaches to organizational design. Accordingly, it is important to understand what is meant by external environment. Generally speaking, an organization's external environment refers to the sum of all the forces impinging on an organization with which it must deal effectively if it is to survive. These forces include elements of the general environment—the economy, geography, and natural resources, and

elements of the task environment—competitors, customers, work force, and suppliers. A key factor in describing the overall environment of an organization is the degree to which it is subject to change: A stable environment is one in which the elements of the environment do not change, whereas a turbulent environment is one in which the elements of the environment change rapidly. Research has shown that when conditions are stable, mechanistic organizations are effective. A mechanistic organization is one in which people perform specialized jobs, many rigid rules are imposed, and authority is vested in a few top-ranking officials. By contrast, when conditions are turbulent, organic organizations are effective. These are organizations in which jobs tend to be very general, there are few rules, and decisions can be made by lower-level employees. It is important to note, however, that the mechanistic and organic forms are pure types, and organizations can be located in between these two extremes.

What are intraorganizational designs?

Sometimes it is advantageous for parts of different organizations to operate jointly. To coordinate their efforts on such projects, it is necessary to create intraorganizational designs. One common form of intraorganizational design is the joint venture. A joint venture is a type of organizational design in which two or more separate companies legally combine forces to develop and operate a specific business. Among the chief benefits commonly derived from joint ventures are improved technology and economies of scale (e.g., sharing functional operations across organizations). Another intraorganizational design is the conglomerate, a highly diversified organization comprised of entirely unrelated businesses. Organizations form conglomerates to achieve a variety of benefits. The parent company can enjoy the benefits of diversification, thus as one industry languishes, another may excel, allowing the conglomerate to maintain a stable economic position. Conglomerates also provide built-in markets and access to supplies, as companies typically support those organizations within the conglomerate.

What were the major findings of the Woodward studies relating technology to structure and performance?

Woodward found that technology seemed to function as a mediating variable in the relationship between organizational structure and performance. Three major categories of technology were established, allowing firms to be classified according to the complexity of their technology. Small batch and unit production referred to a situation in which production was in limited quantities, made to order according to customer specifications. Large batch and mass production involved highly mechanized production of large quantities of standardized products from which orders were filled on a continuous basis. Continuous process production was the most technologically complex and involved production on a non-stop basis. Woodward found differences in structure across these technological types, but also found differences in the structures of successful firms in each group. Organic management seemed to work best for both small batch and continuous process technologies, while mechanistic management worked best with mass production. Also, she found that span of control, formalization, and centralization tended to be higher in companies employing mass production technologies, while companies using continuous production were the highest on complexity and small batch production was the lowest on complexity. In general, her results indicated that the best structure depends on the technology employed. Subsequent to Woodward's research, another type of technology has been identified. It is known as technical batch production and involves the production of customized, high performance products in small batches, but production is highly automated with computer-controlled machinery. Research involving this additional technology indicates that technical batch production operations tend to have a smaller span of control, more centralization, and more concern with innovation than traditional batch technology operations.

What were the principal findings of the Aston studies?

British researchers at the University of Aston continued to study technology and came to describe technology in terms of three characteristics: automation of equipment (the extent to which work is performed by machines), work-flow rigidity (the extent to which the sequence of steps in production are flexible), and specificity of evaluation (the extent to which work activities can be assessed by quantitative means). These three characteristics were combined to form work-flow integration with high integration indicating high automation, rigid work-flow, and specific evaluation. This line of research found that as work-flow integration increased, so did specialization, standardization, and decentralization. Nonetheless, the final conclusion of these studies was that technology does not always determine structure.

What is the relationship between technology and interdependence as they impact on structure?

Interdependence is the extent to which individuals, departments, or units within a given organization depend on each other for task accomplishment. Work by Thompson explored different types of interdependence and their implications for structure. Pooled interdependence exists when different units are part of the same organization and all contribute to the success of the organization, but each carries out its tasks independently with no work flow between them. Sequential interdependence exists when the output from one unit becomes the input for another. Reciprocal interdependence exists when the output from one unit becomes the input for another and the output from the second unit becomes the input for the first. This is the highest form of interdependence of technology. The need for coordination increases as the level of interdependence increases, as does the need for communications, especially lateral communications. In addition, the structure must allow this greater coordination as interdependence increases.

Other Teaching Suggestions

1. A helpful way of illustrating the different dimensions of structure is to think about examples of organizations that are especially high on each of them. For example, automobile plants are high on specialization, athletic teams are high on formulation of rules, the military has rather long chains of command, a police dispatcher has a broad span of control when assigning cars to calls, and the Catholic Church is such a good example of centralized decision making that Lenin used it as a model for structuring the International Communist Party.

2. We could use the same approach for illustrating different types of organizational structure. Organizations such as General Motors, Proctor and Gamble, and General Foods utilize product designs, while McDonald's, Delta Airlines, and Harley-Davidson utilize functional designs. Examples of matrix designs are less obvious in this country, although German auto parts manufacturers do utilize a matrix design.

3. The notion of trying to control the environment is interesting. The auto industry and, more recently, the microchip industry have both pressured the government to limit Japanese imports, and both the textile and shoe industries have felt threatened by foreign competition and have tried to put restrictions in place. There have been some other approaches as well. Chrysler tried what seemed to be cooptation by putting Douglas Fraser on the board in order to secure the support of their union as they moved toward being competitive once again. Many years ago, movie companies bought the theaters their films would be shown in as a way of controlling markets. This move, and other attempts at acquiring suppliers and/or customers, have been seen, however, as violations of anti-trust laws.

4. We do tend to associate certain technologies with certain types of industries, but there are always

exceptions. For example, when we think of automobile assembly we usually think of assembly lines, but Volvo uses work groups, and Ferrari does a lot of work by hand. Perhaps your class can come up with other examples of one company using different technology than the rest.

Case in Point Notes

Reorganizing Apple Computer, and Reorganizing It Again . . . and Again

As the title suggests, this case about how John Sculley, chief executive officer of Apple Computer, has struggled to find the right organization design for the company—one that meets the demands of the company's technology and environment. The case describes the various organization designs that Sculley has used to organize Apple Computer since he took over leadership of the company in 1983. Among the many organization design issues illustrated in the case is the need to reorganize in response to the organization's growth and maturity—a point of major contention between Sculley and Apple founder Steven Jobs that ultimately led to Jobs leaving the company. Steven Jobs was an ardent advocate of flexible organization design, but John Sculley realized the efficiency benefits to be derived from tightening up the company's structure to make it more mechanistic. The result was Sculley's shifting Apple's structure from a product design to a functional design. The desired efficiencies were obtained, but Apple's rate of new product innovation declined under the functional design. Sculley's response? Shift back towards a more organic structure. This was the beginning of a pattern of back-and-forth organization design shifts, between mechanistic and organic structures, with John Sculley trying to find the perfect design for his organization. The case also illustrates Apple's attempt to use intraorganizational design forms (joint ventures), unfortunately without much success to date.

Overall, this cases touches on numerous aspects of organizational structure and design. The discussion questions that follow the case serve to help students understand the logic of Sculley's organizational design efforts. Rich in its content of organization design issues, this case provides students with valuable insights into the struggle experienced by leaders in their never-ending efforts to find the organization structure that best fits their company's particular technology and environment. At the very least, students should come away from this case a real appreciation for the difficulties inherent in, and the dynamic nature of, organizational designing.

A CNN video is available to accompany this case. This is a video of an interview with Apple CEO John Sculley. One topic discussed during the interview is the difficulty Sculley experienced in telling Steven Jobs that he had to leave Apple. The video also provides additional background on John Sculley and Apple Computer that is helpful to understand the case.

Additional Cases

Jackson Design

Jim Jackson is a young man literally "on the way up." Jim graduated with a degree in accounting from the University of Colorado in June 1982, and went to work for an accounting firm in Denver. He had always been interested in rock climbing and mountaineering, and had been a member of the Rocky Mountain Climbers for three years while in college.

In September 1982, Jim purchased a commercial sewing machine and began to make mountain climbing accessories for himself. He knew what he wanted and found that none of the commercially available products suited his needs and tastes. Specifically, Jim wanted a backpack that was lightweight, but sturdy enough to survive the rigors of rock climbing. He also wanted to make a series of "fanny packs," small pouches to wear around his waist to hold small items of climbing gear. Jim had ideas for other

Source: Based on an in-class film, "The Climber," 1974, courtesy of General Motors Corporation, Detroit, Michigan. Class discussion developed by Robert Goddard, Appalachian State University.

items for rock climbing such as cold-weather clothing that would also stand up to the heavy abrasion encountered during a climb.

Jim constructed the items he wanted and tested them out himself on the rock faces of the nearby mountains. His fellow climbers saw that Jim's climbing accessories were more suited to climbing than those they had purchased (at considerable expense) from the mountaineering stores in the area and from the traditional mail-order outlets. They simply worked better and lasted longer. Jim's friends wanted accessories like his for themselves.

At first, Jim was reluctant to comply with their requests for copies of his climbing accessories. After all, he had a new career as an accountant and that job required him to work long hours. If he spent his free time making climbing accessories for his friends, he would have no time for climbing himself, and he looked forward to getting out of the office and getting "on the rocks." However, he knew that his backpacks and fanny packs were better than those his friends were able to purchase, so he agreed to put together a few for his friends at night after work.

Like many good things, word soon got out in the climbing community of Colorado, and Jim was soon overwhelmed with requests for his climbing accessories. Jim, being the astute business school graduate that he was, saw that there was a need for a set of products that he could fill (his marketing classes were not totally lost on Jim). He began to produce back and fanny packs and designed a single-page brochure describing his products and prices. This brochure was sent to mountaineering stores and climbing clubs in Colorado, and responses started to come in. Jim was really shocked when a large store in Boulder, Colorado, sent him a letter in November 1982, asking if he could produce 100 backpacks and 250 fanny packs by January, 1983. The largest order he had had up to then was a request for two backpacks for a couple in Colorado Springs.

Jim knew he was faced with a decision that would alter the course of his life. Should he quit his good job and become a manufacturer of climbing accessories, or should he give up on this crazy idea of being an entrepreneur? Jim chose the former and resigned his position. With a business plan and this large order in hand, Jim went to a local bank and obtained financing for two more sewing machines. He rented space at a mini-warehouse, set up the three sewing machines, ordered materials, and hired two women on a part-time basis. Jim was in business.

It was a struggle at first. Jim claims now that he learned more in the first six months of business than he did in four years of business school. Of course, the training he received in school helped him understand the kinds of things he should do in order to survive and grow. And grow he did. Over the next two years, Jim moved twice, needing more space for additional sewing machines, storage, and employees. By the beginning of 1985, Jim had five full-time and three part-time employees, and his company, Jackson Design, had reached $225,000 in sales.

However, Jim felt that his sales were reaching a plateau in mountaineering products, and he was looking for additional types of products that could be made on his existing equipment. Since Jim had been raised on a dairy farm, he knew that there was a need for a product that could dispense insecticide, reducing the fly problem that led to diseases and infections in the cattle. After much thought, and a few design failures, Jim came up with a product that would dust the cattle with powdered insecticide as they entered and left the barn. Based on the materials Jim was using in his mountaineering accessories, this item gave Jackson Design a year-round product with wide applicability. Jim was successful in obtaining a patent on his *cattle duster*.

This new product required Jim to take a hard look at his marketing efforts. The traditional promotional outlets for climbing and mountaineering accessories were not suitable for this new agricultural item. Additionally, it was expected that this and other products for the agricultural market would require yet more expansion. Up until this point in time, Jim Jackson had been intimately involved with product design, ordering, production, and marketing and sales for his mountaineering products. He had helped with everything from unloading trucks, running sewing machines, calling customers and prospects, handling the accounting and bookkeeping to sweeping the floors at night.

After promoting the cattle duster in publications aimed at the agricultural market (*Farm Bureau* magazine, rural electric cooperative magazines, etc.), Jackson Design found itself swamped with orders. Jim was forced to reassess his whole organization. He was faced with the prospect of moving again to larger quarters, hiring at least five more sewing machine operators, as well as additional people for the shipping and receiving area. He realized that he could no longer be as involved in the everyday aspects of the business, and that he and Jackson Design were going to have to become more specialized.

Problem

Jackson Design has grown from one employee, Jim Jackson, to a company employing 25 full- and part-time men and women. The product line has expanded from mountaineering and climbing accessories to include agricultural products. All of the business functions—research and product development, marketing, production, finance and accounting, distribution, and management—are currently being handled by Jim Jackson himself. The agricultural product line is expected to expand with the development of new items, while the mountaineering product line has probably reached its growth peak.

Design an organization chart that will fit the requirements of this expanding firm. Keep in mind that Jim Jackson has been a "hands-on" type of manager up to this point, but conditions may force him to reassess his function in the firm.

Jackson Design: Teaching Note

This case represents what happens to a firm that starts out as an idea in one person's mind and its success creates, rather than solves, problems. One of the reasons that many small businesses fail is poor management. What is "poor management"? Is it the failure to properly plan for the future of the firm? Is it the failure to organize the resources and people in the firm properly? Is it the failure to hire and maintain the employees of the firm? Is it the failure to adapt to the political, legal, social, competitive, and customer environments? It can be any or all of the above.

Jackson Design is facing a real problem, and the decisions Jim Jackson makes concerning the proper allocation of people and resources, and the defining and delegation of power, authority, responsibility, and accountability in the firm may make or break the company.

Your students have been asked to: "Design an organization chart that will fit the requirements of this expanding firm. Keep in mind that Jim Jackson has been a 'hands-on' manager up to this point, but conditions may force him to reassess his function in the firm."

There are many possible outcomes from this exercise, and none of them will be the absolutely correct one. However, any organizational chart should consider the external environments and their effects on the firm. Some students may choose a functional design, others a product design, while still others may choose a matrix design. What is important, however, is the *justification* they use for choosing a particular design. One requirement for this exercise should be the preparation of a set of assumptions about Jackson Design and the justification for the organizational design chosen.

Allstar Furniture Company

Joe Davis sat in the lobby of Furniture City Bank waiting for his appointment with Bill Adkins, vice president of commercial lending. Six months ago, Joe borrowed $25,000 to finance the purchase of Starway Woodworking Company, a small furniture manufacturing operation, that he subsequently renamed Allstar Furniture Company. Although the company had been able to meet its first quarterly loan payment, it was now past due on the second, and the bank had requested that Joe come in and discuss the situation.

In addition to missing the loan payment, the company was behind on all of its accounts payable and could no longer purchase materials on credit. Several orders were sitting on the plant floor waiting for completion. Shipping delays were causing customers to take their orders elsewhere. The most pressing situation involved the company payroll account which could fund only one more weekly payroll.

Joe wondered how the condition of the company could have gotten this bad in such a short period of time. He had a gut feeling that his production and financial problems were the direct result of people problems in the plant. Joe was anxious to talk to Bill Adkins, buthe knew he would have to present a specific strategy for remedying the situation before the bank would be willing to provide financial assistance. As he waited, Joe began to recall the events of the past six months.

Background

The company Joe purchased, Starway Woodworking, had been in business for ten years in High Point, North Carolina, an area recognized as a leading furniture manufacturing city. Even though Starway specialized in lower quality furniture frames, it had been a successful business due largely to the efforts of its owner, Buck Johnson. Buck had been in furniture manufacturing all of his life and knew what it took to run a shop on a day-to-day basis.

Buck had an interesting relationship with his employees. During working hours he provided constant guidance and expected his employees to put forth a high level of effort, which they usually did. When the workday ended, however, he tended to look the other way when his employees frequently drank to excess. In fact, Buck had been known to have a few drinks with his employees, and felt that what they did on their off time was their business.

In August 1981, Buck suffered a heart attack and was forced into semi-retirement. Although he hoped to return to the shop on a part-time basis, it was clear that he would not be able to devote the effort that he had previously given the company. As a result, Starway was offered for sale, and Buck notified his employees. His most loyal employees agreed to stay on until the company was sold and clean up any unfinished business.

Joe Davis immediately recognized Starway as an excellent investment opportunity. His position as a vice president of a large furniture company afforded him a comfortable living, but for the past few years he had toyed with the idea of starting up a small family business. After visiting Starway,

Joe reached an agreement with Buck Johnson to purchase the company for $25,000. The conditions of the sale included the retention of any previous employees who wished to stay on and offering employment to Buck, in a supervisory position. Joe felt this was an ideal arrangement since his son and son-in-law were eventually going to manage the business but neither had enough experience to run the plant initially.

Next, Joe had to arrange the financing. After an initial meeting with Bill Adkins, Joe was asked to prepare a loan proposal for the bank's consideration as well as an overall business plan for the company. The basic elements of the plan were as follows:

1. Starway Manufacturing would be renamed Allstar Furniture Company, Incorporated, with Joe Davis holding the stock.
2. Joe Davis would provide the overall management for the company, although he was going to keep his present job and only visit the new company as needed.
3. Greg Davis and Jeff Howard (Joe's son and son-in-law) would provide the day-to-day management of the company, assisted, at least initially, by Buck Johnson, the previous owner.
4. Initial emphasis would be placed on continuing with existing low quality business, but the eventual goal was to ease out of this market into higher quality business. This transition would require skills not presently available in the existing staff.

After reviewing the business plan and the projected financial statements, Bill Adkins agreed that on paper the venture looked good. He was troubled, however, with the proposed management structure. Neither Greg Davis nor Jeff Howard had any direct experience in managing a plant, and with Joe remaining in his present position, the initial success of the company appeared to hinge on Buck Johnson. When Bill voiced his concerns, Joe revealed that he was not totally satisfied in his permanent job and would most likely resign in the near future to work full time at Allstar. The loan was eventually approved, although the bank required that Joe place a second mortgage on his home, in addition to pledging the plant's equipment as collateral.

The New Leadership

Allstar Furniture was incorporated on November 1, 1981. The following Monday, Joe scheduled a meeting for all employees. Also in attendance were Buck Johnson, Greg Davis, and Jeff Howard. During the meeting Joe conveyed the following message:

> Most of you are aware that I am the new owner of this company. You probably have some apprehension about what changes may be in store. First, let me say that each of you can continue to work here if you so desire. Although Buck is not back to 100 percent yet, he will be assisting me on a part-time basis, and I expect things to run pretty much the same as in the past.
>
> I also want to introduce my son, Greg Davis, and my son-in-law, Jeff Howard. They will also be assisting me in running the plant.
>
> As for myself, I will be visiting the plant periodically to monitor our progress. All I ask is that you continue to do your jobs and help us make this transition as smooth as possible.

Source: Adapted from D. Neil Ashworth, *Cases in Management: Examining Critical Incidents.* © 1985, pp. 188–195. Reprinted by permission of Prentice Hall, Inc., Englewood Cliffs, New Jersey.

When the meeting concluded, the employees all agreed to stay on with the company. Most of them were somewhat relieved that there would be no drastic changes and were quite impressed with Joe Davis.

During the next two months, several new accounts were opened and production increased to the point where additional factory workers were hired. Buck was working every morning, and things were running smoothly. Greg and Jeff were spending their time in the various departments, trying to get an overview of the entire operation. Greg had finished one year of college and tended to spend most of his time in the machine room assembly, and shipping/receiving. Jeff, who had a college degree in business, leaned more toward sales, inventory control, and administration.

In early January, Buck's health declined to the point where he was placed back in the hospital for an extended period. At the same time, Allstar landed two new "high-end" accounts. These new orders required high levels of skill and craftsmanship to complete. To gear up for this production, an order was made for a substantial quantity of high quality raw materials, such as prime maple and walnut stock. Several of the employees began to feel uneasy when these materials were delivered. Many had only worked with the lower quality materials Buck had used and had no real experience in making these high quality pieces.

Complicating the situation was the fact that Joe Davis had become extremely busy in his permanent job and was traveling quite a bit. As a result, he was able to visit the plant only rarely.

During the next three months things deteriorated rapidly. A high degree of tension developed in the plant due to the time and quality pressures placed on the employees by the new orders. Overall, a negative attitude toward the high quality work became evident. Jeff overheard the following comments between Eddie and Ron, who had been two of Buck's best employees.

Eddie: I'm getting fed up with this place. This morning Greg jumped on my case because I messed up a pair of walnut chair legs. I told him before I started that I didn't know how to sand walnut.

Ron: I know how you feel. Why do we have to make this hard stuff anyway? Buck always made out okay selling the cheap frames, and there wasn't any pressure. I think Jeff is trying to sell accounts that are over our head.

This low morale led to more serious problems. Some of the workers were coming in with hangovers, and it was affecting their work. Others were not coming in at all. Several oldtimers quit. The tension in the plant seemed to peak a month ago, when Jeff confronted Eddie about his drinking and asked him to go home until he was sober enough to work. Eddie responded by quitting. The following remarks are representative of his comments:

> Ever since Buck got sick again, things have been bad. When he was here we had someone who we could go to with our problems. He knew how to do things right. Now we don't even know who our boss is. Mr. Davis is never here, and no one has shown us how to make those walnut chairs.
>
> We are all drinking more now because there's so much pressure on us. Besides, Buck never came down on us for drinking.

During these few months, production suffered drastically and financial problems grew. Greg and Jeff tried to manage the business as well as they could, but there was a growing conflict, even between them, since they were un-

sure of their exact responsibilities. On several occasions they had disagreed on important decisions. This conflict tended to distort the information that was passed along to Joe, which made it difficult for him to know exactly what was going on at the plant.

Now Joe is in financial trouble and needs a recovery plan. He is sure that Bill Adkins will want evidence that the business can still be successful. What changes can Joe make to support this?

Questions

1. What are the various symptoms that suggest a problem exists at Allstar?
2. What are the major problems that exist within the current framework of Allstar?
3. How could Joe Davis have avoided these problems? What are his existing alternative courses of action?

Allstar Furniture Company: Teaching Note

The Allstar Furniture Company is a classic example of the mismatch between an organization and its internal and external environments. Before Joe Davis purchased the firm, there seemed to be a good fit with the key domains of the external environment:

A. *Industry*—Starway Woodworking, the predecessor of Allstar Furniture, was positioned at the low end of the furniture frame market. It had been in the business for ten years, and had developed successfully in its niche in the industry.
B. *Raw Materials*—Starway built its furniture frames out of pine, an easily-worked wood. The employees were familiar with the materials and were able to work well within the limitations of the materials employed in the process.
C. *Financial Resources*—Over the past ten years, Buck Johnson, the owner of Starway, had been able to work within the limitations of the financial structure created during the formation and operation of the firm. He lived within his limited budget.
D. *Human Resources*—At Starway, Buck did not have the most skilled employees, but they did not have to be, given the requirements of the job. He treated them as equals, overlooking some of their personal problems. There was a good working relationship, built on respect and trust, at Starway Woodworking.
E. *Market*—This refers to the customer demand for the goods and services of a firm. At Starway, the demand was for low-quality pine furniture frames, while Jeff Howard perceived Allstar's market as being more upscale furniture frames.
F. *Government*—This element of the environment did not appear to impact heavily on Starway, nor on Allstar. This is not to say, however, that the various laws and regulations (OSHA, EPA, EEOC, the Federal tax structure, etc.) do not affect firms, but their impact in this case was not discussed.
G. *The Economy*—Again, not much mention of the economy was made in this case, although the dates indicated, the early 1980s, might give a clue as to what might have caused some of the decline in Allstar's fortunes. There was a mild recession occurring in the early 1980s.

H. *Culture*—This dimension refers to the values held in the society where the company operates. The term, "organizational culture," refers to the values held by the management and workers of a firm. Externally, the culture of the society seemed to value (at least in Joe Davis's mind) higher quality furniture, something Starway was not able to provide. Internally, the organizational culture of Starway/Allstar seemed to be work hard on the job and to party hard off the job.

I. *Technology*—the technology required of Starway in creating low-quality pine furniture frames suited the training and abilities of the employees, while the technology of creating upscale walnut and cherry furniture exceeded their abilities, creating problems.

The three key dimensions along which these environmental elements can vary are complexity, stability, and uncertainty. Complexity refers to the number of external elements that are relevant to a firm's operations. Certainly we have seen that in the Allstar Furniture Company, there are quite a few elements of the environment that impact the firm.

Stability refers to the degree to which these elements change over time. In the case of Allstar, the change from a low-quality pine furniture frame operation to a more upscale hardwood furniture operation impacted many of the environmental elements described above. Additionally, the change in management from Buck Johnson to Joe Davis, Jeff Howard, and Greg Davis, did create more instability.

Uncertainty refers to the extent to which the environment is both complex and unstable. This dimension, then, is a combination of complexity and stability. Uncertainty in this case is evident, as are the reactions to uncertainty. Employees quitting, employees with increased drinking and morale problems, financial difficulties, orders being cancelled, excess inventory of materials and supplies, and poor communications between the employees and Greg and Jeff, and between those two and Joe Davis.

Students can use these materials from the chapter to build their responses to the three questions asked. In fact, we have already answered the first two questions. In terms of the third question, "How could Joe Davis have avoided these problems?," students may answer that he should have been more involved in the day-to-day operations of the firm, especially after Buck's decline in health. His absence during these critical three months probably exacerbated the situation, and the lack of experience in Jeff and Greg was evidenced in the firm's rapid decline.

Joe's alternative's seem to be limited. More than likely, he will not be able to continue on the course that has been set by Greg and Jeff. Allstar should concentrate on those aspects of the internal and external environment with which they have a good fit. Given the experience, skills and abilities of the firm's employees, and given the fact that they have had a sound base of customers, Allstar should probably return to what worked for them in the past—building low-quality pine furniture frames. They may be able to sell off the stock of hardwood materials to other furniture manufacturers in the area, and should be able to generate some much-needed working capital.

With this in mind, Joe should then go back to Bill Adkins, the vice president of commercial lending at Furniture City Bank, and present a plan that would have Allstar return to what had worked for them in the past. He should also offer to resign his permanent job and take over management of Allstar on a full-time basis. This should indicate to Bill Adkins that Joe is committed to the success of Allstar.

Experiencing Organizational Behavior Notes

Mechanistic versus Organic Organizations: Which Do You Prefer?

This exercise provides students with a self-assessment tool that helps them to learn about their own preferences for mechanistic or organic organization designs. Students are asked to select one of two alternatives in response to a short list of questions. The questions are designed to measure preferences for various characteristics of mechanistic or organic organizations. Students then score their questionnaires using the scoring instructions provided with the exercise. Their scores provide them with a measure of their preference for either mechanistic or organic organization designs. Following the exercise are several points to consider designed to help students understand the various implications of their preferences. Overall, this exercise not only provides students with important insights as to the types of organizations they may feel most comfortable working at, but the exercise also helps students to understand better the actual dimensions of various organizational designs. Complete instructions are provided with the exercise.

Additional Experiential Exercise

City of Brookside Redesign

Step 1: Review the organizational structure of the City of Brookside shown in IE Figure 15–1.

Source: Adapted from Judith R. Gordon, *A Diagnostic Approach to Organizational Behavior,* 2nd ed. Copyright © 1987 by Allyn and Bacon. Used with permission.

Step 2: Answer the following questions individually, in small groups, or with the entire class.

Description

1. Describe the organization's structure: its division of labor and coordinating mechanisms.

2. What structural paradigms best describe the organization?

Diagnosis

3. Describe the nature of the following contingencies:
   A. goals
   B. environment
   C. technology
   D. work force
   E. size
   F. age
4. How does the organization's structure fit with these contingencies?
5. Is the current design appropriate? Effective?

Prescription

6. What changes should be made?

City of Brookside Redesign: Teaching Note

This exercise asks students to analyze the elements of the external/internal environments that affect a city government. A chart of the present organizational structure is given, and students are asked to analyze and redesign the formal organization. The exercise helps to illustrate the discussion of both internal and external environments.

Step 1: "Review the organizational structure of the City of Brookside shown in Figure 15–1."

Students should review the organizational chart of the City of Brookside. They should examine its structure and assess its appropriateness given various contingencies likely to operate on the City. The instructor may choose to have students complete a written analysis of the City's formal organization at this time. Or the instructor may prefer that students prepare the analysis as they would a case study. To bring the organization to life, students might be given the assignment of interviewing city officials or observing city government in their area. (Time: 15–30 minutes)

Step 2: "Answer the following questions individually, in small groups, or with the entire class."

This step lists a series of guideline questions for use in analyzing and redesigning the formal organization of the City of Brookside. The instructor may choose to have students answer these questions individually and then discuss the questions with the entire class. Alternatively, the students can answer the questions in small groups and then report their answers to the entire class. (Time: 30–60 minutes)

Description

1. Describe the organization's structure: its division of labor and coordinating mechanisms.

   This organization demonstrates relatively extensive horizontal differentiation by functional area and somewhat less vertical differentiation by level of authority. The reorganization relies on all types of coordination. The mayor uses mutual adjustment for coordinating activities with the Board of Councilors. He or she uses direct supervision for coordinating much of the work of various departments. Within the departments, various types

of standardization are used: for example, Purchasing relies on standardization of work processes; the Solicitor relies on standardization of skills; and Recreation relies on standardization of outputs.

2. What structural paradigms best describe the organization?

   This organization seems to be mechanistic and illustrates departmentalization by function. It operates as a hybrid between a machine bureaucracy and a professional bureaucracy.

Diagnosis

3. Describe the nature of the following contingencies:
   A. goals
   B. environment
   C. technology
   D. work force
   E. size
   F. age

   The City's major goal is the provision of services to City residents. Its environment is relatively complex and diverse, yet relatively stable and certain. Recent changes in legislation (the passing of a tax limitation law in the state) created a hostile environment and greater uncertainty than previously; turbulence in the environment likely will increase. The technology varies in different departments, ranging in degree of regulation and sophistication. The work force consists of two groups: highly skilled professionals and less skilled office workers. The City has approximately 100,000 residents; city government employs about 2000 workers. The City has been incorporated for approximately 200 years; the present organization has existed for approximately thirty years.

4. How does the organization's structure fit with these contingencies?

   In general, the fit seems to be fairly good. However, the large span of control of the mayor and the location of the financial departments create problems. Because of the increasing professionalization of the work force and the increasingly turbulent environment faced by city governments, the structure needs to be more organic.

5. Is the current design appropriate? Effective?

   The current design works when the mayor is competent and does not create conflicts with the Board of Councilors. However, the increasing complexity and turbulence of the environment have created problems in this organization. It has used slack resources as one way of combating the problems. Structural redesign that incorporates information-processing mechanisms would be appropriate.

Prescription

6. What changes should be made?

   The following are some changes that could be made. Decentralization of decision making is essential. Further, the span of control of the mayor should probably be reduced. Linking mechanisms between the departments and the Board of Councilors is essential. Some clustering of related departments should occur for planning purposes. More extensive use of computerization is essential. The positioning of the finance department should be assessed.

CITY OF BROOKSIDE
Organizational Chart

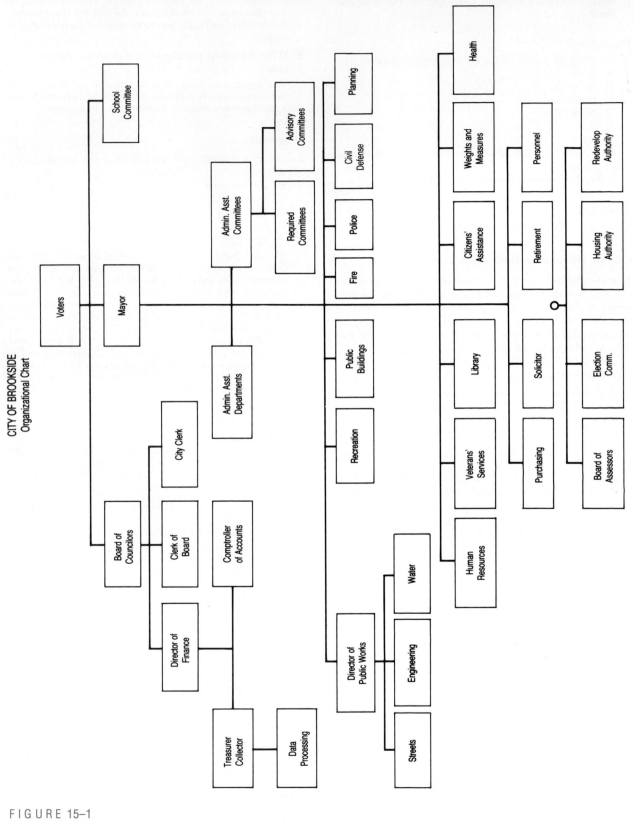

FIGURE 15–1

Additional Readings

Ackoff, R. L. (1989). The circular organization: An update. *Academy of Management Executive, 3*(1), 11–16.

Johnston, R., & Lawrence, P. R. (1988, July–August). Beyond vertical integration: The rise of value adding partnership. *Harvard Business Review,* pp. 94–98.

Lubatkin, M. (1988). Value building mergers: Fact or folklore? *Academy of Management Executive, 2*(4), 295–302.

McCann, J. Design Principles for an innovating company. (1991) *Academy of Management Executive, 5*(2), 76–93.

McQuaid, K. (1981, May–June). The roundtable: Getting results in Washington. *Harvard Business Review,* pp. 114–116.

Ulrich, D., & Wiersama, M. F. (1989). Gaining strategic and organizational capability in a turbulent business environment. *Academy of Management Executive, 3*(2), 115–122.

∎ 16 ∎

ORGANIZATIONAL CHANGE AND DEVELOPMENT

CHAPTER OUTLINE

LEARNING OBJECTIVES

After reading this chapter, you should be able to:
1. Identify the major forces responsible for organizational change.
2. Describe the primary targets of organizational change efforts.
3. Identify the conditions under which organizational change is likely to occur.
4. Explain the major factors making people resistant to organizational change—and some ways of overcoming them.
5. Describe the major techniques of organizational development.
6. Evaluate the effectiveness of organizational development.
7. Debate the idea that organizational development is inherently unethical.
8. Explain the potential cultural barriers to effective organizational development.

Chapter Overview

This chapter deals with the issues relating to change in organizations and discusses the forces behind organizational change. Planned and unplanned internal and external changes are described and illustrated. The basic issues involved in the process of organizational change are introduced; this section focuses on the targets of change, whether the organization is ready for change, factors that determine whether organizational change will be accepted (reasons for resistance to change), and suggestions for overcoming resistance to organizational change. The chapter then turns to the topic of organizational development—the collective term to describe techniques for planning organizational change in order to enhance personal and organizational outcomes. Several major organizational development techniques are described, and some thoughts and research findings concerning the effectiveness of organizational development programs are discussed. The chapter closes with a discussion of two controversial aspects of organizational development. Should organizational development focus on process or results? And is it ethical to use powerful social science techniques in an attempt to change individual attitudes and behaviors?

Three special sections appear in this chapter. A Focus on Research (When Does Strategic Change Occur? A Comparative Study of Executive Team Demographics) describes the findings of a study showing that the demographic make-up of an organization's top executive team is a good predictor of the amount of change that will occur in that organization. Specifically, it was found that more change occurred in organizations whose top team members were younger, better educated, worked less time in their teams and their organizations, were more diverse in educational specialization, and who had more academic training in the sciences compared to those who were opposite along these dimensions. An OB in Practice (Developing Teamwork in the Wilderness: "Mushing" the Way to Group Success) describes how some companies are using mushing—dog sled trips into the Northern wilderness—as a means of developing effective work teams. And an International/Multicultural Perspective (Cultural Barriers to Effective OD Interventions: The Importance of Matching OD Values to National Culture Values) discusses how the effectiveness of organizational development techniques depends in large part on the degree to which they fit the national culture within which they are being applied.

The Case in Point (Transforming the Bell Atlantic Corporation) describes how Bell Atlantic Corporation transformed itself from a rigid bureaucracy into an innovative and entrepreneurial organization. This case is comprehensive in scope, illustrating many topics discussed in the chapter. Also available for use with this case is a CNN video (Bell Atlantic Corporation). And the Experiencing Organizational Behavior exercise (Facing Up to Organizational Change) gives students practice in anticipating and recommending ways to overcome resistance to change.

Lecture and Review Questions

What is meant by the different types of planned and unplanned change in organizations?

Organizational change can be considered as taking four forms: planned internal change, planned external change, unplanned internal change, and unplanned external change. Planned internal change refers to conscious decisions on the part of organizations to change the way they do business or to change the business itself. Examples include changes in the prod-

ucts and services offered (the success of which requires horizontal linkage, or the interaction of the marketing and research departments with each other and the environment), and changes in administrative systems (although there is usually conflict between the administrative and technical cores as to what systems should be replaced). Planned external change refers to changes made in variables that originate outside the organization. Examples include the introduction of new technology (such as computers and robots) and advances in information processing and communications. Unplanned internal change refers to changes that occur not as the result of strategic planning, but in response to other changes within the organization. For example, considerable change is the result of shifts in the demographic composition of the work force (more women and minorities in the work force and an aging work force), and what are called performance gaps (a noticeable discrepancy between observed and desired performance on some dimension). Unplanned external change refers to changes made in response to changing conditions in the external environment. The two most important factors here are government regulation (changes in the minimum wage and imposing or lifting restrictions), and economic competition (the effects of living in a global marketplace with increasing foreign competition).

What are the most common targets of organizational change?

Although there can be many targets of organizational change, three common targets are structure, technology, and people. Changes in structure refer to changes made in specific dimensions of an organization's structure such as changes in the degree of centralization or a move from product-based departments to function-based departments. Changes in technology involve the introduction of technological improvements hoped to enhance effectiveness such as the introduction of robots or better designed tools. Changes in people refer to attempts to change the way people behave. This process is not easy and usually involves three distinct steps: unfreezing (recognition that the current state of affairs is undesirable and in need of change), changing, and refreezing (the changes made are incorporated in the employees' thinking and the organization's operations).

What factors determine when an organization is ready for change and whether change will be accepted?

Even if the need for change in an organization is high and resistance to change is low, there are still other factors that determine an organization's readiness for change. These are: the amount of dissatisfaction with current conditions, the availability of a desirable alternative, and the existence of a plan for achieving that

Chapter 16

alternative. Even if these conditions all exist, the effectiveness of organizational change is largely dependent on overcoming resistance to change. Several key factors have been found to make individuals resistant to change. These are: economic insecurity (the potential threat to one's livelihood), fear of the unknown, threats to social relationships, habit, and failure to recognize the need for change. There are also several organizational factors that lead to a resistance to change, and these are: structural inertia (forces operating on employees to continue performing in the same ways), work group inertia (norms for stability that come from the work group), threats to the existing balance of power, and recollection of previously unsuccessful change efforts. It should be noted that these barriers can be overcome by changing political dynamics, educating the work force on the need for change, involving employees in the change efforts, and rewarding constructive behaviors.

What is organizational development and what are the major types of OD interventions?

Organizational development is a set of social science techniques designed to plan and implement changes in organizations for purposes of enhancing the personal development of individuals and improving the effectiveness of organizational functioning. There are many types of OD interventions including survey feedback, sensitivity training, team building, grid training, quality of work life programs, and management by objectives. Survey feedback involves conducting attitude surveys to discover the strengths and weaknesses within an organization, and presenting the results of the survey to employees in group meetings during which implications are discussed and action plans developed. Sensitivity training invokes discussion sessions in which participants are made aware of their feelings, learn how they are perceived by others, and gain insight into the feelings of others. An expert trainer is required who is responsible for maintaining open and honest communications and for keeping the group together. Team building is an attempt to apply the techniques and rationale of sensitivity training to groups. The process begins when a group recognizes they have a problem and that problem is identified. The problem is then shared with group members in a diagnostic session, followed by the development of an action plan. Grid training is concerned with leadership styles and represents an attempt to foster both a concern for production and a concern for people. The process begins by leaders assessing where they are; then the training tries to move them to the desired style. Quality of work life programs refers to efforts designed to humanize the workplace. These efforts include job restructuring (along the lines of job enrichment) and quality circles (where small groups of volunteers meet regularly to

identify and solve problems related to the quality of work and the conditions under which people perform their jobs). Finally, management by objectives is a process by which goals are jointly decided on by employees and supervisors, action plans are formulated for attaining these goals, the plans are implemented, progress towards the goals is regularly assessed, and evaluation is carried out in terms of whether the goals were reached.

Are organizational development interventions generally effective?

Although the evaluation of OD interventions has produced mixed results, in general, they seem to work. In fact, it is interesting to note that recent data suggest OD efforts are more successful relative to organizational outcomes (increased productivity and profits) than relative to individual outcomes (e.g., job satisfaction). It should also be noted that these interventions are generally more successful with blue-collar workers than with white-collar workers. Also, the effectiveness of any intervention is improved if several interventions are introduced at the same time. Although there have been problems with the design of many of the studies that have attempted to evaluate OD interventions, there is reason to believe that these efforts can be successful if implemented properly.

Is organizational development inherently unethical?

Organizational development applies powerful social science techniques in an attempt to change attitudes and behavior. As such, ethical issues emerge about whether it is just for an organization to try to impose its values on an individual without due consideration of an individual's own values. From the individual's perspective, organizational development is a one-sided approach, as it reflects the imposition of the more powerful organization on the less powerful individual. From this same perspective, organizational development can be considered a form of coercion and manipulation because it fails to provide any free choice on the part of the individual employees. Another ethical concern about organizational development is that it can be misrepresented by management. Management by example can be represented to employees as a means of allowing them greater organizational participation, but in reality be a means of holding individuals responsible for their poor performance and punishing them as a result.

The other side of the ethical debate about the use of organizational development argues that organizational development is no more unethical than the practice of management itself. After all, the very act of taking a job with an organization requires one to submit to the organization's values and the overall values of the society at large. One cannot help but face situations in which others' values are imposed.

Furthermore, organizational development as a collection of social science techniques cannot be either good or evil. It is simply an ethically neutral tool. Whether organizational development is used for good or evil depends on the individual using it.

Which side of the ethical debate is correct? The answer to this question is probably only decided by each of us for ourselves. The only thing that we can be sure of, however, is that from either perspective, because of the power of organizational development techniques to change attitudes and behaviors, it is important that it be used within the context of a strong ethical culture.

Other Teaching Suggestions

1. Technological change is discussed as one of the external forces for organizational change, but it is special in some ways. Changes in technology almost always result in the loss of jobs. Robots may be able to build cars better than people, but what happens to all of the auto workers who used to work the assembly lines? In recent years, several newspapers have endured long strikes (and several have gone out of business) when they tried to introduce computerized typesetting equipment. Organizations usually introduce new technology in order to become more competitive by reducing costs and perhaps increasing quality, but the employees may suffer. This is a topic worth discussing, not only from a humanitarian perspective, but also because affected employees have been known to strike, and even to sabotage the new equipment.

2. Mergers and acquisitions create a major impetus for organizational change. The notification that such a change is about to take place usually sends employees into a panic as they begin to fear for their jobs. Further, there may be a clash of cultures and management styles that requires major adaptation.

Several years ago, R. J. Reynolds acquired General Foods. Reynolds is primarily a tobacco company with most of its operations in the South and is largely non-union. General Foods employees liked to think of themselves as producing healthy (or at least harmless) food products, and they are headquartered in New York with operations worldwide, many of which are unionized. As you can imagine, this acquisition produced a great deal of change in attitudes and caused problems for many General Foods employees.

Case in Point Notes

Transforming the Bell Atlantic Corporation

This case in point describes how Bell Atlantic Corporation transformed itself from a rigid bureaucracy into an innovative and entrepreneurial organization. The case opens with a description of the forces that led Bell Atlantic to realize the need for change (e.g., growing competition in its expanded product line following the break up of "Ma Bell"). The case then goes on to describe Bell Atlantic's overall change plan, detailing each of the change strategies employed (e.g., communication and education, employee involvement, and changes in the reward structure). Finally, the impressive results of the change effort are discussed.

The discussion questions that follow the case prompt students to consider a wide range of issues concerning organizational change, including the internal and external forces pressuring Bell Atlantic to change, the individual and organizational barriers to change at Bell Atlantic, and the change strategies used by Bell Atlantic to overcome resistance to change. Also available as a supplement to this case is a CNN video about Bell Atlantic and its chief executive officer Raymond Smith. This video provides useful background information about the company and its leadership.

Additional Case

Metropolitan Police Department

On July 17, 1988, Verl Iverson, commander of the ninth division of the Metropolitan Police Department (MPD), was trying to figure out some way of motivating the people in his division to wear the new equipment provided by the city as accessories to the basic uniform. For two years, the city and department officials had been trying to institute a change in the accessories to the uniform worn by the city police and had met with much unanticipated resistance from both the old-timers and rookies on the force. Verl had

just had an encounter with Phil Snead, a deputy chief of the department, over the long drawn-out process of changing over to the new equipment. Chief Snead left Verl with an ultimatum: that officers who had not changed over to the new equipment in two weeks should be given an official reprimand including days off without pay.

The New Uniform

In the mid-'80s, the chief of police of the MPD as well as a number of city officials received numerous letters from the public suggesting that the police uniforms worn by the force were outdated and that they gave the policemen a Gestapo look. Being concerned about public image, the chief of police formed a committee and assigned it the task of recommending changes in the uniform to remove the Gestapo look while maintaining the efficiency of the uniform as a piece of equipment. After months of research and evaluation, the committee selected several items of new equipment to be field tested. The results of the field tests, in general, were seen as favorable, and a go-ahead was given to issue the new equipment to academy graduates.

The parts of the uniform that were changed included the hat, the pants belt, and the Sam Browne belt (the belt used to carry handcuffs, holster, and other accessories). The hat was changed to a rounded-top style instead of the old eight-pointed style. The new pants belt had a Velcro fastener instead of the conventional buckle and was lined with Velcro strips on the inside. The new Sam Browne belt was different from the traditional style. Like the pants belt, it was lined with Velcro on the inside; to fasten it to the pants belt, the pants belt was reversed and its exposed Velcro lining was pressed against the Velcro on the reverse side of the Sam Browne. (The old Sam Browne belt was attached to the old pants belt with leather straps.)

The city had gone to considerable expense to make the uniform convey what was thought to be the image of an efficient police officer. It was felt that the removal of the silver belts, the rounding of the crown of the hat, and other minor modifications achieved the goal of obtaining a uniform without the Gestapo look.

Response to the Change

Verl knew that the city officials and high-echelon law enforcement officers who were pushing the change in uniform were committed to the change, and there appeared to be no way to convince them to return to the old-style accessories. All of this had been decided two years ago after heated discussions between the committee and representatives of the law enforcement officers. Verl also knew that many of the officers on the force were opposed to wearing some of the new pieces of equipment.

The opposition to the new gear had been so strong that twice the city had had to postpone the date set for it to be worn by all personnel. Until this point, the city had supplied all new academy graduates with the new equipment and had allowed those who were on the force prior to the introduction of the new pieces to wear what was initially issued them or, in the case of the older officers, what they had purchased themselves.

The opposition to the new equipment was mainly directed at the new pants belt and the new Sam Browne belt. The officers complained that the Velcro cut through the belt loops of their pants, that the Sam Browne belt was uncomfortable, and that it didn't hold up well. Verl knew that many of the old-timers were a little on the heavy side and that the old wide leather belt slipped down comfortably underneath the "overhang" but the new Velcro-lined belt was not as adjustable.

The older officers had voiced the opinion that the new Sam Browne was unsafe. The Sam Browne was an important accessory to a police officer. Almost every piece of equipment was attached to the belt including keys, handcuffs, whistle, and revolver. Each officer had a slightly different way of wearing the Sam Browne. Each could find any piece of equipment in a split second. In emergency and dangerous situations, it was vital that the officer have easy

and quick access to his or her equipment. The old-timers complained that once they had become accustomed to their particular way of carrying equipment on the belt, a change to a new system could cause confusion and delay in an emergency and might cost an officer's life.

The newer officers had also voiced a strong bias against the new belts. After graduating from the academy and beginning service on the force, almost without exception each officer bought the old-style Sam Browne and pants belt and discarded the new ones issued by the city. The younger officers said that the new belt was not worn by anyone but rookies on the force, and that wearing the belts identified a "green" officer both to other officers and to people on the street, who might treat a new cop with less respect than they would an experienced police officer.

During the course of the last two years, the department has tried everything to get the officers to wear the belts, from threats of days off to an animated cartoon showing the benefits of the new equipment. Verl agreed with the points brought up by the officers. He also thought that the equipment change was a waste of time and money. He knew that within a year or two he would retire and that he had reached the highest level he would attain on the force. Nevertheless, he felt a great deal of pressure to get the officers to change. Verl felt that he was in a difficult spot, and he wondered how he could develop a strategy that would satisfy the city council, the chief of police, and the officers in his department.

Questions

1. Why are the officers resisting the effort to introduce the new uniform accessories?
2. What are the forces for change? The forces against change?
3. How could the strategies of "unfreezing," "change," and "refreezing" be employed in this case?

Metropolitan Police Department: Teaching Note

This is a good case illustrating planned external change in an unusual setting. The proposed change in uniform accessories generated heated feelings in those most affected by the change—the officers of the Metropolitan Police Department.

There are many problems that students could identify in this case. First, there is a high level of resistance to the proposed change. The affected officers, for a number of reasons, feel that parts of the old uniform, namely the pants and Sam Browne belts, should not be changed.

Second, the individual who is charged with implementing the change, Verl Iverson, is not committed to the change himself. He is caught in the middle—he does not endorse the proposed new accessories for the uniform, yet he has been told to give official reprimands by Phil Snead.

Third, the imposition of force on those affected by the proposed change by people like Phil Snead generates a counter-force among the officers. More force will only create more counter-force. A classroom discussion of *force-field analysis* might be appropriate at this point, even though the topic is not covered in the text.

Finally, there was little or no consulting of the officers on the change. Some participation in the decision might have lowered the resistance to the change, and even resulted in a uniform having a better combination of features, style, and serviceability for the officers.

Issues

This change in the MPD uniform is based on public image, while the police officers are concerned with the functional and safety aspects of the equipment.

The actual decision-makers—city officials and high echelon law enforcement officers—are removed from the practical issues by virtue of their positions. The officers are experts on the type of equipment that best suits their work.

The change was issued without working with members of the police force. In fact, the committee adopted the changes even though there were heated discussions between the committee and law officers.

Verl is given two choices and supports neither. He must either enforce a change he does not endorse or give official reprimands including days off without pay.

The function of a uniform goes beyond appearance. It is vital to the success or failure of an officer in carrying out his or her duties. There are legitimate concerns regarding safety—would confusion with the new equipment prevent quick action? Does wearing it endanger the officer's life? Also, there are concerns regarding comfort and wear: the new Sam Browne belts are uncomfortable and do not hold up well (pun unintended). Is the uniform's purpose to serve the officer or public appeal?

The rigid position of Phil Snead and his committee members indicates higher concern for enforcing the change than addressing the original concern. In addition, their zealousness may stem from their being publically elected or politically appointed. They may have their own best interests at heart.

The uniform change has been a two-year effort with extended deadlines. The changes has not been enforced, merely prolonged.

New Sam Browne belts indicate an inexperienced officer. This could be a safety concern for a new officer as well as a credibility issue. Rookies who follow regulations face risk and non-member identity. Rookies who break regulations by purchasing and wearing the old Sam Browne belts eliminate the green label and fit in with the other officers.

Verl is caught in the middle. He doesn't agree with Snead and is forced to take a position he doesn't support. He isn't looking to be promoted since he's retiring in a year or two. Since the change has been prolonged for two years already, he may be off the force before it matters.

The attempts of Snead and his committee do not address the concerns of the officers. The threats and the cartoon showing the benefits of the new equipment do not alleviate the concerns of the officers who are directly experiencing both the positive and negative effects.

In order for change to successfully take place, there must be a felt need for change. In this case, the felt need was from outside the system—that is, Phil Snead and the committee. The officers themselves did not feel the need for change.

Note

In the actual situation from which this case was taken, the deputy chief backed down after two weeks. He reported that there was too much time being spent on the change attempt and that the belts were dysfunctional because they wore out the uniforms, were uncomfortable, required the relocation of equipment, and were disliked for aesthetic reasons. In addition, the belts were a symbol of status because they set the young officers apart from the more experienced ones. The new belts were sent back for redesign.

Experiencing Organizational Behavior Notes

Facing Up to Organizational Change
This exercise gives students practice in anticipating and recommending ways to overcome resistance to change. The exercise begins with a brief description of why people are often threatened by the prospect of change. Students are then asked to read three situations and identify likely impediments to change, and ways for overcoming the impediments for each of the situations. Following the case are several points that help students to identify and explain similarities and differences in their responses to each of the three situations.

Additional Experiential Exercise

The Memo

The purpose of this exercise is to give you some first-hand experience in overcoming resistance to change. In preparing the memo described below, try to integrate one or more of the techniques for coping with resistance to change discussed in this chapter.

Susan West is facing one of the more difficult assignments in her career at Second City Bank. The Board of

Directors has just voted to install second-generation automatic teller machines (ATMs), announced by a major computer manufacturer just recently, in the home office location on a six-month trial basis. These new machines have a host of new features not found on the twenty-four-hour bank machines that have been in use for years. The new machines can read signatures on checks, deposit them directly into a customer account, make change (coins and bills), issue travelers' checks, and speak to the customer. They even have a voice recognition feature that allows

Source: By Robert D. Goddard, Appalachian State University.

customers to talk to them, eliminating the need for complicated keyboards or buttons.

Sue realizes that these machines are going to cause problems for the tellers at Second City Bank. Not only can these new machines do what tellers can, they don't need lunch hours, time off for doctor's appointments, and they are never late for work. Tellers at Second City are not going to be happy to hear of the experiment. One of the major fears Sue will have to contand with is the apprehension about the tellers' future with Second City.

Sitting at her desk, Sue is pondering how to handle this delicate situation. The Board of Directors has confirmed that no one will lose his or her job because of these new machines, but that displaced workers will be either reassigned or retrained for other meaningful jobs with Second City. If workers elect to accept neither reassignment nor retraining, the Board assured Susan that every attempt would be made to place them with other financial institutions in the city.

Place yourself in Susan West's shoes, in charge of breaking this news to the employees in the home office of Second City Bank. In the memo, you are to explain the Board's decision to introduce the new teller machines on a six-month trial basis, stressing the financial and service benefits to Second City's customers. Also include in the memo an explanation of the Board's policies of reassignment, retraining, and outplacement. Try to incorporate in your memo some of the tactics for overcoming resistance to change described in this chapter.

Remember, these tellers are probably going to be fearful for their jobs. How can you turn this possible fearful situation into something positive for the tellers? In other words, can you answer their question, "What's in it for me?" What opportunities might this create for the tellers?

The Memo: Teaching Note

This is an example of organizational change that has been triggered by a change in technology. These tellers are faced with the possibility of being displaced by the new ATMs. Changes in work assignments will naturally follow from the change in technology.

Susan West must devise a strategy for introducing the change to those most affected by it—the tellers. There will be fears, naturally, that the tellers will lose their jobs. How Susan handles this situation will have long-term effects on the organization. If she merely states all of the benefits of this new technology to the bank and its customers, the tellers will be flocking to other financial institutions immediately—probably on their lunch hour the day the memo appears. Second City Bank cannot afford to lose its tellers during the trial period—what if the new ATMs don't work out as planned?

Her best strategy would be to heed the suggestion in the last paragraph of this assignment. That is, she needs to turn bad news into good news, if possible. There may be additional personnel needed to process loans, to handle specific customer problems, or to train other Second City branch personnel in the use and maintenance of the new ATMs. There are many possibilities that Susan (and your students) can come up with to answer the question, "What's in it for me?"

Additional Readings

Drucker, P. F. (1988, January–February). The coming of the new organization. *Harvard Business Review*, pp. 45–49.

Hurst, D. K. (1991). Cautionary tales form the Kalahari: How hunters become herders (and may have trouble changing back). *Academy of Management Executive*, (3), 74–86.

Lawrence, P. R. (1969, January–February). How to deal with resistance to change. *Harvard Business Review*, pp. 4–10.

Muczyk, J. P., & Reimann, B. C. (1989). MBO as a complement to effective leadership. *Academy of Management Executive*, 3(2), 131–138.

Seymour, S. (1988, January–February). The case of the willful whistle blower. *Harvard Business Review*, pp. 103–105.

BEHAVIOR IN ORGANIZATIONS

UNDERSTANDING
AND MANAGING
THE HUMAN SIDE
OF WORK

Fourth Edition

Jerald Greenberg
The Ohio State University

Robert A. Baron
Rensselaer Polytechnic Institute

Allyn and Bacon

Boston · London · Toronto · Sydney · Tokyo · Singapore

Copyright © 1993, 1990, 1986, 1983 by Allyn and Bacon
A Division of Simon & Schuster, Inc.
160 Gould Street
Needham Heights, MA 02194

Editor-in-Chief, Behavioral and Social Sciences: Susan Badger
Senior Editorial Assistant: Dana Hayes
Production Coordinator: Deborah Brown
Editorial-Production Service: Sally Stickney
Photo Researcher: Photosynthesis
Cover Administrator: Linda Dickinson
Composition Buyer: Linda Cox
Manufacturing Buyer: Louise Richardson

Library of Congress Cataloging-in-Publication Data

Greenberg, Jerald.
    Behavior in organizations : understanding and managing the human side of work / Jerald Greenberg, Robert A. Baron. — 4th ed.
       p. cm.
    Baron's name appears first on the earlier editions.
    Includes bibliographical references and indexes.
    ISBN 0-205-13697-4
    1. Organizational behavior.   I. Baron, Robert A.   II. Title.
HD58.7.B37   1993
658.3—dc20
                                              92-34952
                                              CIP

Printed in the United States of America

10 9 8 7 6 5 4 3 2 1   98 97 96 95 94 93

Photo Credits

Abbreviations: The Image Bank (TIB), Woodfin Camp and Associates (WCA), Black Star (BS), Photo Researchers, Inc. (PR), Stock Boston (SB), Picture Group (PG), Leo De Wys (LDW), The Stock Market (SM).

Ch. 1: 2: Steve Niedorf/(TIB).   8: Nancy Stafford/(WCA).   18: Fredrik D. Bodin/Offshoot.
Ch. 2: 40: Dilip Mehta/(WCA).   44: Paul Kuroda and W. Campbell/Sygma.   57: Ken Lax/(PR).

Photo Credits continue on page xv, which constitutes an extension of the copyright page.

To Carolyn—

For putting happiness on the menu of my life,
and seasoning it with love.

J. G.

In affectionate memory of Edna—

Source of the little bit of *gypsy* in my soul.

R. A. B.

CONTENTS

iv

C H A P T E R   1 5

ORGANIZATIONAL STRUCTURE AND DESIGN   577

SPECIAL SECTIONS

CN   CASE IN POINT

EXPERIENCING ORGANIZATIONAL BEHAVIOR

C H A P T E R   1 6

ORGANIZATIONAL CHANGE AND DEVELOPMENT   619

SPECIAL SECTIONS

CN   CASE IN POINT

EXPERIENCING ORGANIZATIONAL BEHAVIOR

PREFACE:
IN SEARCH OF THE
IDEAL BALANCE

In a sense, organizational behavior (OB) is a field poised on the fulcrum. On the one hand, it is based on and driven by *research;* it is a discipline that uses highly sophisticated techniques and procedures to study the complex interplay between people and the organizations in which they work. On the other hand, it is also an *applications-oriented* field, one deeply concerned with identifying practical means for enhancing the productivity of individuals and the effectiveness of organizations. In short, OB perpetually seeks the proper balance between these two distinct but complementary orientations and goals.

This search for the point of perfect balance constitutes a major theme of this new edition. In fact, it is a central theme of our efforts to revise and enrich this book. We have continued the strong research tradition that was so well received in previous editions, while at the same time enhancing representation of the practical, applications-oriented side of OB—that is, the many ways in which its findings and principles are used by organizations. How have we attempted to achieve this goal, to accomplish our search for balance? The steps we have taken are described below.

Increased Attention to Applications

To reflect the practical value of organizational behavior more fully, we have instituted several different changes. Together, these serve to illustrate the applications-oriented approach of modern OB.

Greater Use of Examples from Actual Companies   We have liberally sprinkled our discussions of various topics in OB with examples from specific companies (e.g., Anheuser-Busch, Mary Kay Cosmetics, PepsiCo, and Volvo, to name just a few). These examples illustrate the principles and findings being discussed and show how they relate to practical problems and issues faced by functioning organizations—and those working within them.

OB in Practice Sections   Every chapter contains at least one section entitled **OB in Practice.** These sections describe specific ways in which the findings and principles of OB can be—and are being—applied in a wide range of work settings. They expand upon discussions in preceding sections and tie the field of OB firmly to questions and issues faced by operating companies. Some examples follow:

- Avis Employees *Do* Try Harder . . . Because They Own the Company (Chapter 4)
- Dealing with Problem Employees: Managing Wild Ducks, Mavericks, and Other Unruly Types (Chapter 6)
- A Tale of Lost Horizons: Or What Can Happen When a Good Company Goes Bad (Chapter 7)
- Habitual Routine as an Impediment to Group Performance: The Catastrophic Example of Air Florida Flight 90 (Chapter 8)

- Teamwork: Is It Always a Plus? (Chapter 10)
- On the Costs of Arrogance: Or, How *Not* to Lead Effectively (Chapter 12)
- Undoing Corporate Decisions: Toying Around at Fisher-Price and Taking the Fizzle Out of Coca-Cola (Chapter 14)

End-of-Chapter Cases Completely new cases designed to illustrate practical applications of OB have been added. All of these cases focus on specific companies (e.g., Southwest Airlines, Wal-Mart, Levi Strauss, General Motors, Xerox, Apple Computer) and relate the issues they face to topics and findings covered in the text.

Increased Attention to International and Multicultural Issues Many of the most pressing problems faced by organizations today center around the growing *internationalization* of all business activities and the increasing *cultural diversity* of today's work forces. Organizational behavior, as a field, is deeply concerned with such issues. To reflect this fact and to illustrate the many ways in which OB can help modern organizations in their efforts to deal with these matters, we have included an increased number of special sections entitled **An International/Multicultural Perspective.** A few examples follow:

- What Motivates Employees? Work Goals All Over the World (Chapter 4)
- The Stress-Deterrent Effects of Religiosity: Evidence from Israeli Kibbutzim (Chapter 7)
- Race and Career Outcomes in the United States: Different and Still Unequal (Chapter 9)
- Bribery in Nigeria and the United States: Cross-National Differences in the Acceptance of Undue Influence (Chapter 11)
- Asian and American CEOs: Different Cultures, Different Styles? (Chapter 12)
- Structuring Organizations for Multinational Operations (Chapter 15)

Changes in Content

At first glance, the contents for this text appears to be highly similar to that for the preceding edition. Yet, closer examination indicates that, in fact, major changes in content have been made within *each* chapter. Scores of new topics are now included in the text. A small sample of these includes the following: impression management (Chapter 2); the five robust dimensions of personality, positive and negative affectivity, and champions of technological innovation (Chapter 6); stress and personal health: new and effective techniques for stress management (Chapter 7); critical issues in careers in the 1990s (Chapter 9); transformational leadership (Chapter 12); and image theory (Chapter 14);

These changes reflect our strong commitment to keeping the text *current*—having it reflect the latest research, findings, and applications in modern OB. The up-to-dateness of the text is illustrated by the fact that *over 20 percent of the references are from 1990 or later.*

Changes in Special Features

We have already described two of the special features incorporated in the text: the **OB in Practice** and **An International/Multicultural Perspective** sections. Two other types of special sections are also included. The first of these reflects the strong research orientation of the field of OB—and our personal commitment to it. Such sections are entitled **Focus on Research,** and they are designed to accomplish two goals: (1) to describe important new research findings and (2) to illustrate the research process in OB. As indicated by the following list, the topics examined in these sections are highly varied, but all are ones we believe readers will find fascinating:

- What's in a Name? The Origins of Company Reputations (Chapter 2)
- Employee Theft as a Reaction to Underpayment Inequity (Chapter 4)
- Job Satisfaction: Can It Be in the Genes? (Chapter 5)
- Champions of Technological Innovation: Profiling the Agents of a Crucial Form of Organizational Change (Chapter 6)
- Training Pilots to Make Decisions about Avoiding Hazardous Weather (Chapter 14)

The second type of special section, new to this edition, is entitled **A Question of Ethics.** These sections examine the complex ethical issues faced by organizations and individuals in today's business environment. These sections are designed to get readers to think about the moral and legal dilemmas that are part of life in modern organizations and also to illustrate the relevance of OB's findings and principles to such issues. Some examples follow:

- Ethical Obligations to Research Participants (Chapter 1)
- Information about Personality: Is It an Appropriate Basis for Organizational Decisions? (Chapter 6)
- Sexual Harassment: A Pervasive Problem in Work Settings (Chapter 7)
- Styles of Conflict Management: Which Are Best—or Most Appropriate? (Chapter 10)
- Privacy Rights and E-Mail: Should Employers Have Access to Employees' Electronic Mailboxes? (Chapter 13)

Additional Changes

Finally, consistent with our search for the ideal balance, we have made extensive changes in the mix of illustrations in the text and in the chapter-opening stories. Illustrations have been adjusted to include more flowcharts and diagrams and slightly fewer photos. We feel that the new illustrations are more informative than former ones and provide better insights into the nature of the field and the complex processes it seeks to understand.

Similarly, virtually every chapter begins with a new vignette. These fictitious yet true-to-life scenarios have been carefully written to be even more closely tied to the chapter content than in the previous edition and to call clear attention to the practical, applications-oriented side of OB.

Resource Materials for Students

A *Student Study Guide* is available. This guide is designed to help students master the topics and information presented in the text. Among its useful features are detailed learning objectives, definitions of key terms, a variety of review quizzes, further sources of information, and a fill-in-the-blanks guided review.

Resource Materials for Instructors

A wide variety of materials is available for instructors who adopt this book. These include the following:

- Annotated Instructor's Edition
- Instructor's Resource Manual (with test bank and transparency masters)
- CNN Video

■ Video User's Guide
■ Computerized Test Bank

A Balanced Conclusion

Looking back, we can honestly say that we have spared no effort in our attempt to place this new edition of our text on the fulcrum—to attain the ideal balance where research and practice are concerned. In this respect, we have heeded the words of Lord Chesterfield, who wrote

> Aim at perfection in everything, though in most things it is unattainable; however, those who aim at perfection and persevere, will come closer to it than those give it up as unattainable . . .

Whether, and to what extent, we have reached this goal can be judged only by you—our students and colleagues. So, as always, we sincerely invite your input. Please let us know what you like about the book and what features can stand improvement. Such feedback is always welcomed and does not fall on deaf ears. We promise faithfully to take your comments and suggestions to heart and to incorporate them into the next edition.

Jerald Greenberg
Abramowitz Professor of Business Ethics and
    Professor of Organizational Behavior
Department of Management and Human
    Resources
The Ohio State University
Columbus, Ohio 43210

Robert A. Baron (seated)
Chair of the Department of Managerial Policy
    and Organization
Rensselaer Polytechnic Institute
Troy, New York 12180

ACKNOWLEDGMENTS:
SOME WORDS OF THANKS

Writing is a solitary task. Converting authors' words into a book, however, requires the efforts and cooperation of many individuals. In preparing this text, we have been assisted by many dedicated, talented people. We can't possibly thank all of them here, but we do wish to express our appreciation to those whose help has been most valuable.

First, our sincere thanks to our colleagues who read and commented on various portions of the manuscript. Their suggestions were invaluable and helped us in many ways. These reviewers include Mary Kernan (University of Delaware), James McElroy (Iowa State University), Paul Sweeney (Marquette University), Terry Scandura (University of Miami), Rodney Lim (Tulane University), Dan Levi (California Polytechnic University at San Luis Obispo), Taggart Smith (Purdue University), Rabi S. Bhagat (Memphis State University), Richard Grover (University of Southern Maine), Ralph Katerberg (University of Cincinnati), Richard McKinney (Southern Illinois University, Edwardsville), Paula Morrow (Iowa State University), and Shirley Rickert (Indiana University—Purdue University at Fort Wayne). Reviewers of the previous edition include Debra Arvanites (Villanova University), Jane M. Berger (Miami–Dade Community College), Angelo DeNisi (Rutgers University), Maureen Fleming (University of Montana), Hal W. Hendrick (University of Denver), Bruce Kemelgor (University of Louisville), Jack Kondrasuk (University of Portland), Mark Miller (DePaul University), Suzyn Ornstein (Suffolk University), and Charles Regan (Manchester Community College).

Second, we wish to express our appreciation to Susan Badger, our editor at Allyn and Bacon. Her enthusiasm for this project was contagious, and her constant support and good humor certainly helped us bring it to completion in a timely and enjoyable manner.

Third, our sincere thanks go out to the production team at Allyn and Bacon. Although many people were involved in helping make this book so beautiful, we worked most closely with Dana Hayes, Deborah Brown, and Sally Stickney. Their diligence and skill with matters of design, permissions, and illustrations helped us immeasurably throughout the process of preparing this text. Nancy Bell Scott did a very professional job copyediting the text. It was a pleasure to work with such kind and understanding professionals, and we are greatly indebted to them for their contributions. With a team like this behind us—a group that can spot an undotted "i" or an uncrossed "t" from forty paces away—authors cannot help but look good.

Fourth, we wish to thank our colleagues who have provided expert assistance in preparing various features for this book. Rick Grover researched and wrote the very interesting Case in Point features that end each chapter, and he also did a fantastic job with the entire *Instructor's Section* for the *Annotated Instructor's Edition*. Linda Hoopes prepared a very useful *Student Study Guide* to accompany this text. We also wish to thank Jeff Miles for the research assistance he provided and for the truly fascinating "lecture nuggets" he wrote as marginal annotations for the *Annotated Instructor's Edition*.

Finally, Jerald Greenberg wishes to acknowledge the family of the late Irving

Abramowitz for their generous endowment to the Ohio State University, which provided invaluable support during the writing of this book.

To all these truly outstanding people, and to many others too, our warm personal regards.

ORGANIZATIONAL BEHAVIOR: AN INTRODUCTION

CHAPTER OUTLINE

LEARNING OBJECTIVES

After reading this chapter, you should be able to:
1. Describe the focus of the field of organizational
   behavior, including its three basic levels of
   analysis.
2. Characterize the features of the field of organizational behavior today.
3. Outline the historical developments and schools
   of thought leading up to the field of organizational behavior today.
4. Explain why the scientific study of the field of
   organizational behavior is necessary.
5. Describe the role of theory in the pursuit of
   knowledge about organizational behavior.
6. Characterize the major approaches to conducting
   research in the field of organizational behavior.

Flipping on the light switch, Gail Harrington illuminates the scene of her daily frustration—the corporate offices of Kincaid Industries. It is almost 8:00 A.M. on Monday—the beginning of a new workweek for Gail, but one that confronts her with the same old problems she has been experiencing the last several months.

"Good morning, Gail," says Patti Wales as she brushes by her.

"You sure seem chipper," Gail replies as she casts her eyes onto Patti's smiling face.

"I sure am," Patti replies, and questions, "Aren't you?"

"Not at all," Gail offers. "It's the beginning of another workweek, and I don't particularly like it here."

"Things *can* get hectic here," Patti admits aloud, but adds, "It's not really so bad."

Gail just shakes her head. "For me," she replies, "it's not that simple. I really don't like my job. The typing is boring and tedious. The filing hurts my back. Then there's our obnoxious boss, Mr. Flinchman. Basically, I really don't care about what I'm doing. It's all stupid, if you ask me."

"I asked, but I'm almost sorry I did," Patti replies, adding, "Knowing how you feel, I can see why you dread the beginning of the week."

Gail just nods her head in agreement.

"Not for me," Patti continues. "I enjoy what I do and take pride in it. Sending out clearly prepared, accurate price lists isn't exactly glamorous work, but I know that it's important to the company." In a more somber tone, she adds, "Don't get me wrong, though. I'm not saying that everything's perfect for me either."

"What do you mean?" Gail asks as she makes her way over to the coffee maker to begin brewing the morning's first pot of coffee.

"My gripe," Patti responds, "is not that I don't like the work I do, but that they don't always make it easy—or even possible—for you to do it. Take the other day, for example. I was just about to print out and distribute the new price lists for the regional sales meeting when I got a call from Calas in marketing. 'Hold it up,' he said. 'There'll be some last-minute changes!' Meanwhile, of course, Mr. Flinchman was breathing down my neck for the finished list."

"So, why don't you just tell him that Calas asked you to wait?" Gail asks.

"Flinchman hates Calas," Patti replies. "Ever since Calas got promoted over Flinchman, Flinchman has done anything he can to make Calas look bad. So, Flinchman pressured me to get the job done and to not cooperate with Calas. Getting caught up in the middle of their petty feud—now, *that's* what I really dislike."

"Well, I wouldn't put up with that," Gail smirks. "I'd go over his head."

"Whose head, Calas's or Flinchman's?" Patti inquires.

"Either one. Just tell them to let you do your job and stop using you as their political pawn."

"Yeah, sure," Patti answers. "That's easier said than done. There's really no one to talk to. You can't get in to see anyone other than your own supervisor around here. Our department manager isn't even supposed to talk to anyone below Flinchman."

"You're right," Gail agrees. "Remember Beth Anne Cummings? She tried to complain about her supervisor and then mysteriously never showed up again."

"A leave of absence, I think they called it," Patti adds.

"Yeah, an extended vacation at the glamorous unemployment line," chuckles Gail.

They both laugh as they go about their business. Then Mr. Flinchman walks in. "How's my fantastic office staff doing today?" he asks.

Patti and Gail look at each other and smile, but say nothing.

"Now, that's what I like to see—a happy workplace," Flinchman comments. "A happy workplace is a productive workplace. That's what I always say."

If he only knew.

There can be little doubt that something is seriously wrong in the corporate offices of Kincaid Industries. Gail doesn't like or care about the work she does. Patti takes pride in her work but is frustrated by the way she's treated by others and feels helpless about improving the situation. Then there's Mr. Flinchman. Poor Mr. Flinchman doesn't even know that anything's awry in his office. If you think about it, you'll probably realize that things cannot continue this way much longer. The problems of poor motivation and miscommunication, the political games, and the feeling that the system will not change are the ingredients of an organizational disaster waiting to happen. You probably wouldn't be surprised to hear that either Gail or Patti eventually made a serious blunder—or were, at least, blamed for one—or simply quit, leaving Mr. Flinchman without two key staff members.

What causes this situation? It's not that the firm's equipment is faulty or that the technology is antiquated, or even that the economy is troubled. Although such things can—and do—cause problems for companies all the time, the problem at Kincaid centers around *people*. Indeed, such "people problems" are not at all uncommon. They represent a very serious threat to the effective functioning of organizations—not to mention the satisfaction of the people working in them. Even if an organization's equipment and finances are in tip-top shape, people problems can bring a company to its corporate knees. There can be no organizations without people to run them and to work in them (see Figure 1–1 on p. 4). Hence, it makes sense to recognize that "the human side of work" (not coincidentally part of the subtitle of this book) represents an important element of the effective functioning of organizations. It is this people-centered orientation to work that is studied in the field of **organizational behavior** (OB for short).

OB scientists and practitioners study and attempt to solve organizational problems by using the knowledge, findings, and methods of the **behavioral sciences** (e.g., psychology, sociology). In short, OB proposes that applying the scientific approach

FIGURE 1–1

Organizational Behavior: A People-Oriented Field

The functioning of organizations is highly
dependent on the behavior of the people who
work in them, although their relative
contributions are not usually identified as clearly
as they are here. (*Source:* Reprinted by
permission of Leo Cullum.)

of these fields may yield valuable new information about organizations and the
complex processes operating within them. This knowledge can then be used to solve
a wide range of practical problems.

Has this approach succeeded? The pages of this text will, we believe, offer a very
positive answer. In recent decades, OB has developed into a diverse and vigorous
field. At present, it is actively studying virtually every imaginable aspect of organizations and behavior within them.[1] Moreover, the results of this systematic research
have already contributed greatly to making organizations more effective, as well as
better places in which to work.[2] To be frank about our own personal biases, we are
highly optimistic about the potential and actual contributions of OB. We think you
will come to share our optimism as you read this book.

In the remainder of this chapter, we will provide you with the background information you will need for understanding the scope of OB and its potential value
to you in whatever profession or line of work you may pursue. In fact, unless you
become a hermit, you surely will be dealing with other people on the job, and will
benefit from your knowledge of OB. With this in mind, this first chapter is designed
to formally introduce you to the field of OB—its basic characteristics, its history,
and its ways of gathering knowledge (i.e., research methods). First, we will offer a
formal definition of OB, indicating what it is and what it seeks to accomplish. Second,
we will trace the origins of OB from its emergence to its modern form. Third, and
finally, we will consider the methods OB scientists use to carry out one of OB's major
tasks—adding to basic knowledge about organizations and the behavioral processes
operating within them. At this point, we will be ready to move on to the main body
of the text and our primary task: enhancing your understanding of the human side
of work by providing a broad overview of the field of OB and its major findings.

THE FIELD OF ORGANIZATIONAL BEHAVIOR:
A WORKING DEFINITION

We will begin by defining the field and then offer some clarifying comments on it.
Specifically, organizational behavior is *the field that seeks knowledge of all aspects
of behavior in organizational settings through the systematic study of individual,
group, and organizational processes.* The primary goal of this knowledge is to enhance
organizational effectiveness and individual well-being. Because this knowledge is so
complex, several of its key elements warrant clarification and elaboration.

Organizational Behavior and the Scientific Method

Earlier, we noted that the field of organizational behavior rests firmly on the findings and methods of the behavioral sciences. Given this fact, it should not be surprising that modern OB, like these closely related fields, is scientific in orientation. Thus, it seeks increased knowledge through an empirical science-based approach.

Although we will have much more to say about the scientific method later in this chapter, we need to add that not all OB knowledge is gained through rigid adherence to this approach. Most practitioners in the field fully agree that carefully conducted research, performed in accordance with basic scientific principles, is the best single way of adding to our knowledge about behavior in organizations. At the same time, they recognize the complexities of applying such methods in actual organizations, and the limitations this may imply.[3] Further, many believe that important ideas and valuable insights can sometimes be gained through other means (e.g., from the comments of experienced, practicing managers; from information about the conditions present at the time some important event or change occurred).[4] Please don't misunderstand: such sources are *not* viewed as a substitute for the findings of systematic research. There is some feeling, though, that they *can* sometimes be useful as preliminary input and should not be totally ignored. As noted by Paul Lawrence, a well-known researcher in the field, OB accepts the view that qualitative data, too, are sometimes useful, and may supplement purely quantitative data in some instances.[5] In our view, this is an important, enriching aspect of studying OB.

Why is this knowledge important? As we have suggested, many scientists are interested in learning about the behavior of people in organizations for its own sake, simply because it advances scientific understanding in this area. Although many basic scientists are happy to gain insight into "what makes people tick" in organizations, such knowledge often can be put to good practical use. In fact, there is general agreement that knowledge about organizational behavior is potentially valuable insofar as it may be used to enhance both the productive efficiency of organizations *and* the quality of life among those who work in them. That the scientific and applied aspects of OB not only coexist, but also complement each other, should be readily apparent. Indeed, just as knowledge about the properties of physics may be put to use by engineers, and engineering data can be used to test the principles and theories of basic physics, so too are basic knowledge and potential applications closely intertwined in the field of OB.

Individuals, Groups, and Organizations: Three Levels of Analysis

Next, we will address our contention that organizational behavior focuses on three levels of analysis: individuals, groups, and organizations themselves. Why this complexity? To understand behavior in organizational settings, all three levels are essential. To see why, let's consider the opening case on page 2. It illustrates the operation of processes at all three levels. For example, why is Gail uninterested in her job, whereas Patti finds hers interesting and important? Because the attitudes, perceptions, and motivation levels of these employees are certainly involved, it makes sense to study these basic psychological processes. But studying behavior at this level wouldn't tell the whole story. The interpersonal conflict between Calas and Flinchman appears to be hampering Patti's efforts. Obviously, then, some important group dynamics also need to be studied. It's not just the emotional feelings, but the nature of the group interaction, that is critical to our understanding of this situation. Finally, an important aspect of the organization's structure also must be considered when attempting to analyze this situation. Namely, the fact that people are formally discouraged from communicating with those who are not immediately above or below them in the organization is important. Such barriers make people like Patti feel helpless in their attempts to remedy many of the problems they face. Obviously, then, it is essential to study such organizational-level processes when attempting to understand behavior in organizations. On the whole, the story illustrates that a clear understanding of human behavior in organizations requires that three different levels of analysis be used: individual, group, and organizational-level processes.

OB specialists recognize that to understand fully why people think and act as they do in organizational settings, we must acquire information about their reactions as individuals (e.g., their attitudes, perceptions, motives), the groups to which they belong (e.g., communication between them, formal and informal norms affecting their behavior), and the organizations in which they work (e.g., their culture, values, structure; see Figure 1–2). Careful attention to all three levels of analysis is a central theme in modern OB and will be fully reflected throughout this text.

Organizational Behavior: Further Characteristics of the Field

Thus far, we have characterized organizational behavior as a social science field with a basic and applied scientific orientation that studies individuals and groups within, and as they are affected by, organizational settings. Although this is true, additional elements need to be added to the picture of OB we are sketching here to provide an accurate view of the field today.

Organizational Behavior and the Human Resources Model   Suppose you approached a large group of managers working for a diverse group of companies, and asked them to describe their basic views of human nature. What kind of answers would you receive? No doubt, many of the replies would be negative. Some of the managers might even suggest that human beings are basically lazy and irresponsible. Further, they might note that the key task of managers is giving such people direction—keeping them on track, so to speak. This traditional view, known as **Theory X,** has prevailed for centuries and is still with us today.

In contrast, other people in your sample might report a more positive view of human nature. These managers would reject the notion that most people are basically lazy. Instead, they would note that human beings are as capable of working hard and accepting responsibility as they are of "goofing off." What's crucial in determining their reactions is the work environment in which they are placed. If conditions are such that working hard will pay off (i.e., yield rewards they value), *this* is what they'll do. If, instead, conditions are such that effort is not rewarded, it would be foolish to expect much from them. Managers who accept this more optimistic view—known as the **human resources model** or **Theory Y**—might add that the key task for supervisors is assuring that the right conditions exist, *not* "riding herd" on employees and goading them on to hard work.

Which of these perspectives prevails in modern organizational behavior? As you can probably guess, it's the second. Most people working in this field currently believe that employees can indeed demonstrate many desirable behaviors at work, provided appropriate conditions exist.[6] But please note that acceptance of this human resource perspective does *not* imply a Pollyanna-like belief that employees will always, or even usually, act in productive or responsible ways. Rather, it simply recognizes the fact that human beings do indeed respond to their work environments. If these are favorable (e.g., employees are treated fairly and with respect by their managers), they will work hard, become committed to their organizations, and develop many other desirable behaviors. If, in contrast, conditions are negative (e.g.,

Supplementing the distinction between Theory X and Theory Y, management scholar William Ouchi developed Theory Z in an attempt to compare Japanese and U.S. corporations. Ouchi claimed that Japanese corporations are generally more productive than their U.S. counterparts, largely because they guarantee long-term employment, encourage employees' active involvement in decision making, and evaluate performance using a long time frame. Although controversial in some respects, Ouchi's approach was successful in bringing to the attention of contemporary management scholars the importance of studying cross-national differences. [Ouchi, W. G. (1981). *Theory Z*. Reading, MA: Addison-Wesley.]

Test Bank questions 1.5–1.7, 1.46, and 1.56 relate to material on this page.

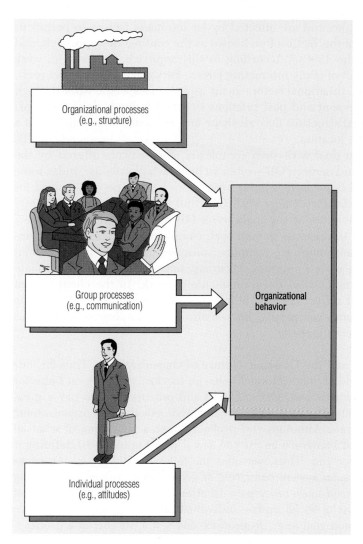

FIGURE 1–2

Organizational Behavior:
Three Levels of Analysis

To fully understand organizational behavior, we must consider processes occurring within individuals, groups, and organizations themselves.

Organizational processes
(e.g., structure)

Group processes
(e.g., communication)

Organizational behavior

Individual processes
(e.g., attitudes)

employees feel exploited, lack confidence in their supervisors), they may adopt far less positive patterns of behavior.

In short, modern OB does not view the world of work through rose-tinted glasses. What it *does* assume is that there are no intrinsic reasons why work settings cannot be pleasant and satisfying or why employees cannot be encouraged to act constructively on the job. In short, it is basically optimistic, but not naive, in its approach to behavior in work settings.

Organizational Behavior and the Contingency Approach: Realizing There Are No Simple Answers   What style of leadership is best? What is the most effective means of motivating employees? What is the best technique for reaching complex decisions? At first glance, these questions may strike you as both intriguing and reasonable; indeed, you might assume that they are close to the core of modern organizational behavior. In fact, there is one basic problem with all of them: they seem to imply the existence of simple, unitary answers. In other words, they suggest that there is indeed *one* best style of leadership, *one* best technique for enhancing motivation, or *one* best procedure for reaching decisions.

Modern OB assumes that such an approach is inaccurate and simplistic. Where behavior in work settings is concerned, there are no simple answers. The processes involved are far too complex and are affected by far too many factors to permit us this luxury. Recognition of this fact is often known as the **contingency approach,** and is a hallmark of OB in the 1990s.[7] According to this approach, behavior in work settings is a complex result of many interacting forces. Personal characteristics (e.g., attitudes, values, beliefs), situational factors (many aspects of a specific work setting), organizational culture, present and past relations between individuals and groups, and existing organizational structure may all shape and influence what happens at a specific time in a specific location.

Because it attempts to deal with such complexity, the answers offered by the contingency approach—and modern OB—often include such phrases as "under some conditions . . . ," or "all other factors being equal. . . ." Some people, hoping for simple "cookbook" formulas for dealing with OB, find such replies disappointing. Indeed, they often grumble about the inability of OB to offer "straight answers." Although we understand the reasons behind such complaints, we feel they are unjustified. People and organizations are complex, so expecting simple answers about them is a bit naive. Even more important, *accuracy*, not simplicity, is the ultimate goal of our attempts to understand the human side of work. In the chapters that follow, therefore, we will reflect the prevailing approach in our field. We will do our best to avoid superfluous complexity, but we also will steer clear of conclusions that are misleading in their simplicity.

Organizational Behavior and the Dynamic Nature of Organizations   Thus far, our characterization of the field of organizational behavior has focused more on behavior than on organizations. Nonetheless, OB scientists and practitioners *do* pay a great deal of attention to the nature of organizations. But what exactly *is* an organization? How would you define one? Although you probably have a good idea of what an organization is, and would recognize one if you saw it (see Figure 1–3), defining it probably isn't that easy for you. Thus, we offer the following definition. An **organization** is *a structured social system consisting of groups and individuals working together to meet some agreed-upon objectives.* In other words, organizations consist of structured combinations of social units—individuals and/or groups—who strive together to attain a common goal (e.g., to produce and sell a product at a profit).

A major assumption made by organizational scholars is that organizations are not static entities, but are dynamic and ever changing. In other words, they view or-

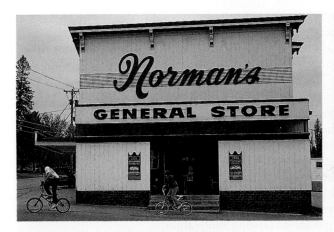

FIGURE 1–3   Which Is an Organization?

The answer is both. Organizations come in different sizes. All are structured social systems consisting of groups and individuals working together to meet some agreed-on objectives.

TABLE 1–1   The Properties of Open Systems

Open systems have properties that allow them to be self-sustaining and permit them to grow and change under appropriate conditions. These same properties distinguish living organisms from inanimate objects.

Property	Explanation
Importation of energy	Energy is imported from the external environment.
Through-put	Open systems transform the energy they import.
Output	Open systems export some product to the external environment.
Cyclical nature	The pattern of energy exchange with the environment is cyclical in nature.
Steady state	The system is maintained in a relatively steady state.
Trend toward differentiation	Open systems tend to become more differentiated and elaborate.
Equifinality	Open systems can reach the same final state from differing initial conditions and in many ways.

Source: Based on suggestions by Katz & Kahn, 1978; see Note 7.

ganizations as **open systems,** that is, as self-sustaining systems that constantly use energy to transform resources from the environment (e.g., raw materials) into output (e.g., a finished product).[8] Table 1–1 outlines some of the properties of open systems. As you can see, open systems receive *input* from the external environment, which they then transform, through internal processes, into *output*. Their exchanges with the environment are cyclic, and throughout the process, they tend to maintain a constant internal state; in short, they are self-sustaining. If successful in these tasks, open systems grow, and tend toward greater internal differentiation (e.g., various components tend to specialize in different functions). Indeed, this description seems to fit many modern organizations. It is also interesting to note that the properties that distinguish open systems from simpler ones (e.g., *control systems* such as the one that regulates the operation of furnaces or air conditioners) are the same properties that distinguish living organisms from inanimate objects. Life, too, is self-sustaining, engages in cyclic exchanges with the external environment, and so on.

A final point: because of its commitment to the practical use of knowledge, OB usually focuses on work-related organizations. For this reason, we will concentrate mainly on such organizations in this text. However, many OB principles and findings apply to organizations generally and may extend beyond the world of work.

Organizational Behavior and the International Perspective   A final characteristic of modern organizational behavior worthy of mention is its growing adoption, in recent years, of an *international perspective*.[9] This shift involves efforts to understand differences between work settings in various nations and the effects these have on both employees and organizations.

If you've ever traveled abroad, you know how different from each other people of various nationalities appear to be. Not only might they dress and speak in a different fashion, but they also may seem to behave and think quite differently. Whether these discrepancies strike you as quaint or curious, real differences do exist between people of different nations. The idea that culture is an important determinant of people's actions and values is clearly an understatement—and a conclusion that has important implications for the study of OB. However, because the scientific study of behavior in organizations first emerged during a period in which the United States was the world's predominant economic power, for many years what we knew about OB was reflected by a uniquely middle-class American perspective.[10] Today, though, the economy is more global in scope and orientation. So many different nations have a grip on the economic state of the world, and so many multinational corporations exist, that the failure to adopt an international perspective would seriously limit the value of OB. Fortunately, we see clear signs that the field is rapidly becoming more international in its approach.[11]

Ricks, Toyne, and Martinez have noted that the international perspective of OB is characterized by its comparative nature—that is, its tendency to examine OB concepts across different nations and cultures.[12] Among the most popular questions asked by scientists in this area are the following: (1) How similar or different are people of different cultures with respect to different types of organizational behavior? and (2) To what extent do OB theories and practices apply across different cultures? Although it is usually very difficult to isolate the unique effects of culture (relative to other variables that might make a difference) when researching comparative cultural questions, many researchers have attempted to do so.[13] Such efforts have proven worthwhile because they have revealed that theories of OB that are "made in the U.S.A." may have limited value when applied to other cultures. This is not to say that all such theories are worthless. They are, in fact, far from it! The point is that simply assuming a unicultural perspective can lead to very misleading results, and incorporating cultural differences into OB research is an effective way of learning about the cultural influences on OB (not to mention, of course, an excellent way of learning about the cultures studied themselves).

Throughout this book, wherever relevant, we will highlight international differences in various aspects of OB (usually in the special section, **An International/ Multicultural Perspective**). For now, we thought you would find it interesting to consider a few of the better-established areas of national differences in the field of OB.[14] For example, whereas Americans usually perceive themselves as able to control the circumstances affecting them, people from other cultures (e.g., fundamentalist Muslims, the Chinese) tend to view their fates as determined by factors beyond their own control, such as God, destiny, social class, or the government.[15] Because people are unlikely to attempt to change factors believed to be beyond their control, they may be reluctant to take action to improve their situation on the job (e.g., by seeking job training). Another example of cross-national differences in OB is rooted in the fact that Americans tend to be highly "individualistic" in their orientation to life (i.e., they value individual accomplishments), whereas people of some European and Asian nations (e.g., China) tend to be more "collectivistic" (i.e., they value contributions to group well-being).[16] Given this difference, it is not surprising that some American theories of motivation (as we will see in chapter 4) tend to emphasize individual achievements, and may be limited when it comes to understanding what motivates people in other cultures (see Figure 1–4). (For another interesting example of cultural differences in OB, see the **International/Multicultural Perspective** section on p. 12.)

ORGANIZATIONAL BEHAVIOR: A HISTORICAL OVERVIEW

In the 1990s, the importance of the human side of work (and organizations) is far from controversial. Most people realize that communication, motivation, cooperation, power, and many other person-based processes play a key role in organizational functioning and success. It is surprising to learn, therefore, that this idea is relatively

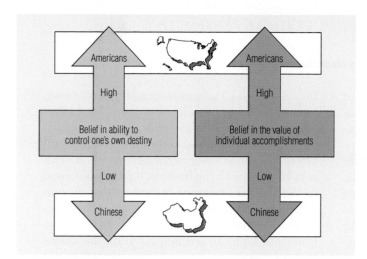

FIGURE 1-4

American Beliefs about Organizations Are Not Universal

People in different cultures hold different organizational values. As summarized in these examples, Americans' beliefs about the ability to control one's own destiny and the value of individual accomplishments tend to be higher than those of people from China. As a result, theories based on American-held beliefs may have limited value when applied to understanding people of different cultures.

new. It took form only during the present century, and did not gain widespread acceptance until recent decades. Why was this the case? How did this idea—which is central to OB—finally emerge? It is on these questions that we will focus next.

Scientific Management: The Roots of Organizational Behavior

How can productivity be improved? This has been a central issue in most organizations since ancient times. In one sense, the emergence of organizational behavior as a distinct field can be traced to efforts to answer this question. To understand why, we must return to the closing decades of the nineteenth century, a period of rapid industrialization and technological change. At that time, the prevailing view of work was much as it had been throughout recorded history. The jobs being performed were what really mattered; the people performing them were much less important. Accordingly, engineers set about the task of applying the new technological knowledge at their disposal to the development of ever more efficient machines. The rationale behind such efforts was straightforward: if the means of production were improved, efficiency, too, would automatically rise.

Only a few pioneering theorists challenged this view. For example, the German psychologist Hugo Münsterberg argued that knowledge of psychology could be applied to the jobs people did to humanize them.[17] Likewise, management writer Mary Parker Follett claimed that organizations could benefit by attempting to recognize employees' needs.[18] These scholars recognized that improving organizational productivity required paying attention to the people who worked in those organizations. This idea seems obvious today, but it wasn't a century ago. At that time, it was typically believed that primarily only new and more efficient machinery enhanced productivity. Because it sometimes did not, however, a growing number of managers reached a new conclusion: although machines and equipment *are* important, they are not all that matter. We must also consider the people who run them.

This idea first became popular in the early part of the twentieth century, and was advanced by influential theorists such as Frank and Lillian Gilbreth. (You classic film buffs may recall a movie about the Gilbreths' large family escapades in the movie *Cheaper by the Dozen*.) However, it was really Frederick W. Taylor (see inside front cover) who unlocked the key to approaching the human side of work by advancing his principles of **scientific management.** From 1878 to 1890, while working as a

AN INTERNATIONAL/MULTICULTURAL PERSPECTIVE

Are the Chinese Motivated to Manage?

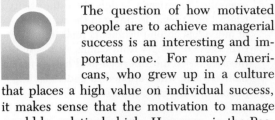

The question of how motivated people are to achieve managerial success is an interesting and important one. For many Americans, who grew up in a culture that places a high value on individual success, it makes sense that the motivation to manage would be relatively high. However, in the People's Republic of China, only recently did the attainment of individual financial success become accepted. In the United States, it has been found that the motivation to manage rises among those in higher positions in an organizational hierarchy, and among those who work in profit-making organizations. After all, profit-making organizations may attract those who are highly motivated to manage because such organizations provide greater opportunities and rewards for doing so (e.g., higher pay, more managerial discretion).[19]

In a recent study, Miner, Chen, and Yu considered whether the same relationships would be found in the People's Republic of China.[20] On the one hand, the investigators reasoned that because strong hierarchical differences within organizations (i.e., recognition of the existence of people at higher and lower levels within an organization's authority structure) are highly valued in China, the motivation to manage should be like it is in the United States. On the other hand, as we noted above, Chinese culture is characterized by a collectivist orientation, one that places a higher value on equality than on individual achievement.[21] Indeed, the Maoist ideology opposes anything elitist. Given these competing cultural forces, the investigators wondered whether the established American-based findings regarding motivation to manage would also be found in China.

To test this idea, a sample of people working in profit-making and nonprofit organizations from Dalian, People's Republic of China, were given a test designed to measure people's motivation to manage. Scoring was based on the way people completed various sentences translated into Chinese from the English language version of the same test. The motivation to manage *was*, in fact, found to be related to job level: higher scores were found among people at higher organizational levels, and lower scores were found among people at lower organizational levels. This is in keeping with the findings typically obtained in the United States, and suggests that despite some cultural tendencies to the contrary, hierarchical systems operate in China. Both Americans and Chinese are motivated by the desire to work their way up to higher organizational levels.

The motivation to manage also was found to be only slightly higher among those in profit-making organizations as opposed to those in nonprofit organizations. This difference, weaker than typically found in the United States, is taken as a reflection that profit-making organizations have existed for only a short time in China, where managers typically have much less discretion than they do in the United States. Not surprisingly, then, the difference between for-profit and not-for-profit organizations is much smaller in China than in the United States. As a result, smaller differences in motivation to manage are to be expected.

Findings such as these provide critical insight into the question of the generalizability of one particular American-derived OB phenomenon. Interestingly, they show that although certain relevant aspects of culture are similar, cross-national differences in organizational phenomena may not be found. However, when differences in cultural values and social conditions exist, the generalizability of OB phenomena discovered in any one culture is likely to be limited. Beyond demonstrating this phenomenon, the present findings may be of critical value to business persons who plan on expanding their horizons into the newly opened capitalistic doors of China. Knowing about the culture of a people cannot help but provide valuable insight into how to interact successfully within that culture.[22] In today's highly competitive international marketplace, such insight may prove to be critical.

foreman at Philadelphia's Midvale Steel Company, Taylor began taking note of the inefficient practices of the employees. For example, noticing that employees often didn't work as hard as they could, he systematically studied many of the jobs and developed standardized ways of performing them. He also changed the pay system so that the employees were paid on a piece-rate basis, thereby rewarding people for the amount of work done rather than the amount of time spent on the job. Such innovations dramatically improved production. Taylor then moved on to other jobs as a management consultant, where he continued developing more efficient ways of working. For example, while at Bethlehem Steel, he redesigned the job of loading and unloading rail cars so that it could be done more efficiently. In 1911, on the heels of the success of his technique, Taylor published his ideas in the book *Principles of Scientific Management*.[23] The work proved to be well accepted by managers and is now recognized as an early classic in the field.

Taylor's book contained two new features that, together, focused attention on employees as well as on their work. First, Taylor suggested that workers should be carefully selected and trained for their jobs. In this respect, he broke with the traditional view that employees are basically interchangeable cogs that can easily be shuffled from job to job. Second, he recognized the importance of motivation in work settings. Indeed, he firmly believed that efforts to raise worker motivation might result in major gains in productivity.[24] His view concerning the basis of such motivation was, by modern standards, quite unsophisticated. Briefly, he assumed that work motivation stems mainly from the desire for monetary gain. Today, in contrast, we realize that people actually seek many goals through their work— everything from enhanced status to personal fulfillment (see chapter 4). Although he was mistaken about the nature of motivation in work settings, Taylor *did* grasp the importance of this key factor. This was certainly a major step forward.

In sum, scientific management was primarily concerned with raising efficiency and output—*not* with enhancing worker satisfaction or morale. But it did begin to recognize the importance of considering people in work settings, especially the abilities, training, and motives of individual employees. This encouraged further attention to the human side of work, and contributed to an intellectual climate that ultimately paved the way for an independent field of OB.

Human Relations: Social Factors in Work Settings

Although scientific management directed some attention to the importance of human behavior at work, it did not go far enough. Good job design and high motivation are indeed important factors where productivity or output is concerned, but performance is also strongly affected by many other factors, including relations among members of work groups, the quality of leadership they receive from supervisors, and their perceptions that they are being treated fairly or unfairly by management.[25] Today, these facts seem so obvious that they hardly bear repeating. In the past, however, this was not the case. In fact, it took some dramatic and unexpected research findings to call the complex, social nature of work and work settings to the attention of practicing managers. The research most directly responsible for this shift is known as the *Hawthorne studies*. Because this research played an important role in the emergence of our field, it is worthy of our attention here.[26]

The Hawthorne Studies: An Overview In the mid 1920s, a series of fairly typical scientific management studies were begun at the Hawthorne plant of the Western Electric Company outside Chicago. One purpose of the research was to determine the impact of level of illumination on worker productivity. Several groups of female employees took part. One group worked in a *control room* where the level of lighting was held constant; another worked in a *test room* where the level of lighting was systematically varied. Results were baffling: productivity increased in *both* locations! Further, there seemed to be no orderly link between level of lighting and performance. Output remained high in the test room even when illumination was reduced to that of moonlight—a level so dim that workers could barely see what they were doing!

Puzzled by these findings, Western Electric officials called in a team of experts headed by Elton Mayo. The results they uncovered contributed to the emergence of an independent field of organizational behavior.[27] In an initial series of studies (known as the *Relay Room experiments*), Mayo and his colleagues examined the impact of thirteen different factors on productivity. These included length of rest pauses, length of workday and workweek, method of payment, place of work, and even a free mid-morning lunch. The participants were again female employees who worked in a special test room. Once more, results were mysterious: productivity increased with almost every change in work conditions. Indeed, even when employees were returned to initial standard conditions, their productivity continued to rise (see Figure 1–5).

As if these findings were not puzzling enough, additional studies soon added to the confusion. For example, in one investigation (known as the *Bank Wiring Room study*), male members of an existing work group were carefully observed by members of the research team. No attempts were made to alter the conditions under which they labored, but they were interviewed by another investigator during nonwork periods. Here, results were quite different from those in the earlier studies. Productivity did *not* rise continuously. On the contrary, it soon became apparent that the employees studied were deliberately restricting their output. This was revealed both by observations of their work behavior (e.g., all men stopped work well before

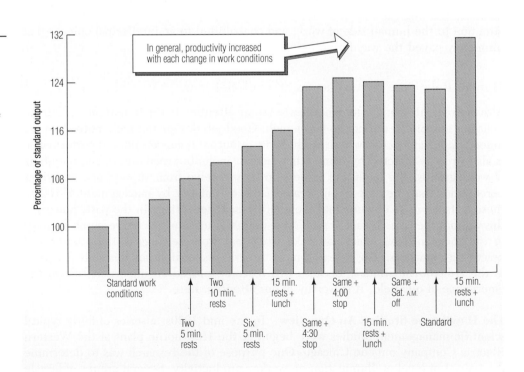

FIGURE 1–5

The Hawthorne Studies: Some Puzzling Results

In one part of the Hawthorne studies, female employees were exposed to several changes in work conditions. Surprisingly, almost every one of these alterations produced an increase in productivity. (Source: Based on data from Roethlisberger & Dickson, 1939; see Note 26.)

quitting time) and by interviews (almost all admitted that they could easily do more if they wished). Why did these people restrict their own output while those in the Relay Room experiments did not? Gradually, Mayo and his colleagues arrived at the following answer: Work settings are actually complex *social systems.* In order to fully comprehend behavior in them, one must understand employees' attitudes, communication between them, and a host of other factors.

Armed with this insight, Mayo and his associates were soon able to interpret the puzzling findings of their research. First, with respect to the Relay Room experiments, productivity rose because people reacted favorably to receiving special attention. In short, they knew they were being studied, and because they enjoyed this attention, their motivation—and also their productivity—rose. In contrast, output was held low in the Bank Wiring Room study because the men in that group feared that high productivity would lead to an increase in the amount they were expected to produce each day, and might even cost some of them their jobs. The result: they established informal rules (*norms*) about behavior on the job—rules that reduced production.

The Hawthorne Studies: Their Implications and Impact   By modern research standards, the Hawthorne studies were seriously flawed. For example, no attempt was made to assure that participants were representative of all the employees in their plant, or all manufacturing personnel generally. As a result, findings could not readily be generalized from the specific groups studied to other groups of employees. Similarly, no efforts were made to assure that the rooms in which participants were tested were identical in all major respects to those in other parts of the plant. As a result, changes in performance could have stemmed from differences in this regard, rather than solely from changes in working conditions (e.g., the level of illumination, length of rest pauses). Also, different groups of employees were exposed to contrasting conditions, or tested in different ways. Thus, all employees in the Relay Room experiments were females, whereas all those in the Bank Wiring Room study were males. Did this factor contribute to the different patterns of findings obtained? From the procedures employed by Mayo and his colleagues, it is impossible to tell. (See the discussion of experimentation on page 26.)

Despite these flaws, the Hawthorne studies exerted several lasting effects relevant to the development of organizational behavior. Together, they underscored the fact that full understanding of behavior in work settings requires knowledge of many factors ignored by scientific management and earlier views—factors relating to complex aspects of human behavior. As recognition of this basic principle grew, a new perspective known as the **human relations approach** took shape.[28] This perspective devoted far more attention to human needs, attitudes, motives, and relationships than did previous ones. In addition, it recognized the fact that lasting gains in productivity and satisfaction can be achieved only through appropriate changes in these and related factors. In this way, it established a close link between the emerging field of OB and several behavioral sciences (e.g., anthropology, psychology, sociology)—a link that has persisted to the present. Although the human relations perspective itself was gradually replaced by even more sophisticated views, several of its ideas and concepts contributed to the emergence and development of OB. Since OB, in turn, has greatly influenced the practices adopted by many organizations, it is clear that the workers in the long-vanished plant outside Chicago probably had greater and more lasting effects on the entire world of work than most of them would ever have dreamed possible.

(Incidentally, we should add that the original topic of the Hawthorne studies—the impact of levels of illumination on productivity—has continued to be the subject of research attention. Studies on this topic suggest that the precise level of illumination best for a given job depends on many factors, such as the nature of the work being performed, other environmental variables such as temperature, and even the color of the walls in the room.[29,30])

Classical Organizational Theory

During the same time that proponents of scientific management got people to begin thinking about the interrelationships between people and their jobs, another approach to managing people emerged. This perspective, known as **classical organizational theory,** focused on the efficient structuring of overall organizations. This is in contrast, of course, to scientific management, which seeks to effectively organize the work of individuals.

Several different theorists are identified with classical organizational theory. Among the first was Henri Fayol, a French industrialist who attributed his managerial success to various principles he developed.[31] Among these are the following:

- A *division of labor* should be used because it allows people to specialize, doing only what they do best.
- Managers should have *authority* over their subordinates, the right to order them to do what's necessary for the organization.
- Lines of authority should be uninterrupted; that is, a *scalar chain* should exist that connects top management to lower-level employees.
- A clearly defined *unity of command*, under which employees receive directions from only one other person, should exist so as to avoid confusion.
- Subordinates should be given *initiative* to formulate and implement their plans.

Although many of these principles are still well accepted today, it is widely recognized that they should not always be applied in exactly the same way. For example, whereas some organizations thrive on a unity-of-command structure, others require that some employees take directions from several different superiors. We will have more to say on this subject when we discuss various types of organizational designs in chapter 15. For now, suffice it to say that current organizational theorists owe a debt of gratitude to Fayol for his pioneering and far-reaching ideas.

Probably the best-known classical organizational theorist is the German sociologist Max Weber. Among other things, Weber is noted for proposing a form of organizational structure well known today—the **bureaucracy.** Weber's idea was that the bureaucracy is the one best way to efficiently organize work in all organizations. The elements of an ideal bureaucracy are summarized in Table 1–2. Weber's "universal" view of bureaucratic structure lies in contrast to more modern approaches to organizational design (see chapter 15), which recognize that different forms of organizational structure may be more or less appropriate in different situations.[32]

When you think about bureaucracies, negative images of inflexible people getting bogged down in red tape probably come to mind. (The term "red tape" is said to have become popular during World War I, when red tape was used on documents from the British government.[33] Given the tendency of national governments to be bureaucratic in structure, it is not surprising that the term "red tape" came to refer to bureaucracies of all types.) Although the bureaucracy may not be a perfect structure for organizing all work, organizational theorists owe a great deal to Weber, many of whose ideas are still considered viable today. Organizations differ widely with respect to their degree of bureaucratization. Some organizations, especially those engaged in a great deal of research and development work (such as Apple Computer during the development of its Macintosh), tend to bear little resemblance to a formal bureaucracy.[34] Others, especially large agencies of the national government, tend to

---

Henri Fayol is also credited with legitimizing the use of horizontal communication linkages within organizations. In the early 1900s, it was customary for communications to flow only up and down (e.g., two employees at equal levels in different departments were not supposed to talk to each other directly, but to send messages to each other indirectly, through their bosses). Fayol recognized the wasted time and effort this practice created and began to encourage horizontal communication between employees at the same level in companies in which he worked. Although we take this practice for granted today, it was not common a century ago. [Fayol, H. (1916). General industrial management (C. Storrs, Trans.). London: Pitman & Sons.]

Not all large organizations are structured bureaucratically. Sears Roebuck is so bureaucratically structured that the formal organizational level of its departments is reflected in their location in the company's headquarters building, Chicago's Sears Tower. Generally, higher ranking departments are located on higher floors. Given that the building is 100 stories tall, there's plenty of room to differentiate between organizational levels. By contrast, the gigantic Wal-Mart chain of

TABLE 1-2 Characteristics of an Ideal Bureaucracy

According to Weber, bureaucracies must possess certain characteristics. Here is a summary of the major defining characteristics of bureaucratic organizations.

Characteristic	Description
Formal rules and regulations	Written guidelines are used to control all employees' behaviors.
Impersonal treatment	Favoritism is to be avoided, and all work relationships are to be based on objective standards.
Division of labor	All duties are divided into specialized tasks and are performed by individuals with the appropriate skills.
Hierarchical structure	Positions are ranked by authority level in clear fashion from lower-level to upper-level ones.
Authority structure	The making of decisions is determined by one's position in the hierarchy; people have authority over those in lower-ranking positions.
Lifelong career commitment	Employment is viewed as a permanent, lifelong obligation on the part of the organization and its employees.
Rationality	The organization is committed to achieving its ends (e.g., profitability) in the most efficient manner possible.

be highly bureaucratic. Despite their reputation, not all bureaucracies are inefficient and unproductive. In fact, one of the most productive American companies currently run, the United Parcel Service, is highly bureaucratic. For a more detailed—and fascinating—look at this example of an effective bureaucracy, see the **OB in Practice** section on page 18.

retail stores is much less bureaucratic. Not only does it have only three different organizational levels, but these are not as clearly distinguished to physically symbolize bureaucratic position. [Needed: Less bureaucracy. (1989, April 12). *USA Today,* p. 14.]

Organizational Behavior in the Modern Era

The realization that behavior in work settings is shaped by a wide range of individual, group, and organizational factors set the stage for the emergence of an independent, science-based field of organizational behavior. And such a field was not long in taking shape. Although no ribbon-cutting ceremonies were held to mark its appearance, significant events suggest that it began to emerge in the 1940s. The first doctoral degree in OB was granted in 1941.[35] The first textbook on this field was published in 1945.[36] By the late 1950s and early 1960s, it was very much a going concern. By that time, active programs of research designed to increase our understanding of key processes such as leadership and motivation were well established, and important studies on the impact of organizational structure and design had already been conducted.[37] (See Figure 1–7 on p. 19 for a summary of some of the key events in the development of OB.)

Unfortunately, the development of scientific investigations into managerial and organizational issues was uneven and unsystematic in the 1940s and 1950s. In response to this state of affairs, the Ford Foundation sponsored a project by economists R. A. Gordon and J. E. Howell in which they carefully analyzed the nature of business education in the United States. They published their findings in 1959, in what became a very influential work known as the *Gordon and Howell report.*[38]

The report recommended that the study of management pay greater attention to basic academic disciplines, especially the social sciences. This advice had an enormous

OB IN PRACTICE

United Parcel Service: The Big Brown Bureaucracy That Really Delivers

Wherever you live in the United States, no doubt you are familiar with those boxy brown delivery vans used by United Parcel Service (UPS). You've seen them on highways and in your neighborhood picking up and delivering packages (about 9 million each weekday) all the time (see Figure 1–6). What you probably don't know is that UPS is a highly bureaucratic organization, and a very profitable one!

As you might imagine, the company uses the latest technology to sort and keep track of the packages it handles. In fact, automatic machines are used in 100 locations to sort from 40,000 to 60,000 packages per hour.[39] However, the heart of the company's operations lies in its bureaucratic structure, initially used by UPS's founder, James E. Casey, who employed principles of scientific management to make the company highly efficient.

For example, there is a strict *division of labor* at UPS. Employees perform their *specialized* jobs, whether they're loaders, drivers, washers (UPS vans are washed inside and out daily), or managers. Moreover, these jobs fall into a clear *hierarchy* with eight levels. These range from washers, at the bottom, to the company president, at the top (by the way, even the president doesn't have a private secretary).

People in all UPS jobs must abide by *strict rules and regulations*. For example, sorters at the large UPS hub near Chicago (Addington, Illinois) are expected to load 500 to 600 packages per hour into vans. Drivers' actions are also routinely scrutinized by supervisors toting digital stopwatches. The actions of delivery drivers are so precisely studied and rigorously enforced that supervisors can usually estimate within six minutes how long it will take drivers to make all their daily stops and return to the garage. In fact, drivers are expected to make their deliveries so quickly that they used to joke that a good driver could get to a stop and back to the van before the seat belt stopped swaying. No wonder some particularly efficient delivery people have been nicknamed "Ace," "Hammer," and "Rocket Shoes."[40]

Finally, all personnel decisions are made strictly according to *merit*, and never on the basis of favoritism. Objective performance standards are set, and those who exceed them are rewarded with raises and promotions. This system encourages excellence: drivers are paid above the industry average, and middle managers' salaries are generously supplemented by stocks and dividends.

This structure has been considered in large part responsible for the financial success and stability of UPS. In existence since 1908 (starting as a local messenger service in Seattle), the company now enjoys net earnings of $700 million annually on revenues of $10 billion, according to recent data.[41] These figures make UPS the most profitable transportation business in the United States. Although several factors doubtlessly contribute to UPS's success, to a great extent, the bureaucratic nature of the company is considered partly responsible. The moral of the story is clear: despite what you might think, the term "bureaucracy" is not necessarily synonymous with "inefficiency."

FIGURE 1–6

United Parcel Service: An Effective Bureaucracy

Despite popular wisdom to the effect that all bureaucracies are inefficient, the bureaucratic design of the United Parcel Service is one key to its success.

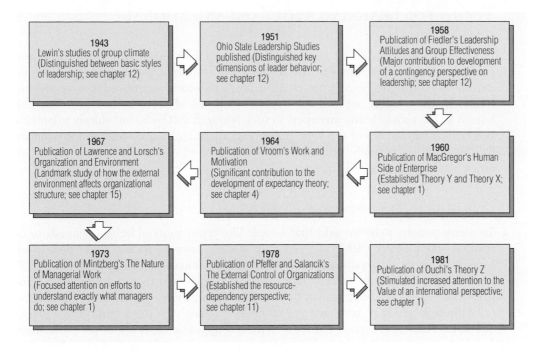

FIGURE 1-7   Major Contributions in the History of Organizational Behavior

The events shown here are among those that have contributed to the development of organizational behavior as an independent field of study. (*Source:* Based on suggestions by Lawrence, 1987; see Note 5.)

influence on business school curricula during the 1960s, and promoted the development of the field of OB. After all, the field draws heavily on the basic social science disciplines recommended for incorporation into business curricula by Gordon and Howell. In sum, by promoting a behavioral approach to the study of organizations, the Gordon and Howell report was responsible for a considerable amount of growth in the field of OB from the 1960s through the 1980s.

Observing the effects of these changes in business curricula in the decades following the Gordon and Howell report, another influential study on the state of management education was conducted by Lyman Porter and Lawrence McKibbin.[42] The *Porter and McKibbin report,* as it has come to be known, published in 1988, recognized the advances made by incorporating social science notions into business curricula, but pushed for further advances in several areas. These include paying greater attention to the effects of the external environment (e.g., society, government, international developments), intensifying consideration of the international aspects of business, noting the ethical implications of business practices, and increasing attention to the growing service and information sectors of business (in contrast to the traditional manufacturing orientation).

Although these recommendations, and other aspects of the Porter and McKibbin report, are considered controversial, OB scientists and practitioners are clearly taking many of these suggestions to heart.[43] Indeed, as you continue reading this book, you will see attention paid to topics such as international differences, ethics, the business environment, and the service sector. These clearly represent areas of growing interest in the field of OB—topics that serve to complement the array of well-established topic areas considered in the field in the years, if not the century, to come.

TOOLS FOR LEARNING ABOUT ORGANIZATIONAL BEHAVIOR: THEORY AND RESEARCH

Organizational behavior, as we have already noted, is essentially scientific in orientation. Thus, in its efforts to add to our knowledge of organizations and behavior within them, it relies heavily on scientific methods widely employed in several other fields. In this section, we will briefly describe some of these techniques. Our goal here is not to turn you into an expert in such research methods, but simply to provide you with a basic grasp of the logic underlying these techniques and an introduction to how they are actually put to use in systematic efforts to understand important aspects of organizational behavior.

Isn't It All Just Common Sense?

To many people, it seems odd that a topic like organizational behavior needs to be studied scientifically. After all, you may already have learned a great deal about human behavior in organizations because of experiences you've had on the job, or by talking to others about their jobs. We're not surprised that you may have some preconceived ideas about human behavior in organizations. It would be difficult not to! Although you may not have yet attained a senior vice presidency at a *Fortune 500* firm, chances are good that you've picked up a few ideas about people at work from jobs you have already had. Besides, there are some things that everybody just takes for granted. For example, consider the idea that happier employees are likely to be more productive than unhappy ones. This makes sense, doesn't it? Well, despite what you may believe—and whatever your past experiences may tell you—this is generally *not* true! In fact, as we will see in chapter 5, people satisfied with their jobs are, in general, no more or less productive than dissatisfied ones. Obviously, here's a case in which your common sense was inconsistent with the findings of systematic, unbiased research into the topic. Moreover, this is not an isolated instance. Commonsense notions about human behavior at work often fail to stand up to scientific scrutiny. To demonstrate this point, we invite you to take the brief self-test we have prepared in the **Experiencing Organizational Behavior** section at the end of this chapter (see pp. 37–38).

A key problem with relying on common sense is that we tend to summarize our collective wisdom in the form of aphorisms that are frequently contradictory. For example, we often hear that "absence makes the heart grow fonder." But we contradict this sentiment when we say, "out of sight, out of mind." Similarly, we hear "three's a crowd" but also "the more, the merrier." Given how contradictory our commonsense knowledge appears to be, it's little wonder that we need to rely on the scientific method.

If we can't trust our common sense to guide us to understanding key aspects of organizations and behavior within them, on what can we rely? This is where scientific research comes into the picture. Although certainly not perfect, the techniques used by researchers in the social sciences can reveal a great deal about OB. Scientific research methods are not designed simply to challenge and debug commonly held assertions about human behavior. Indeed, sometimes research findings may confirm what we already believe to be true. Would that mean that the research was unnecessary? The answer is, emphatically, no! After all, common sense is not the standard against which to gauge the truth about human behavior. Carefully conducted and logically analyzed research studies are used to determine the accuracy of statements about human behavior in organizations. Besides, scientific evidence may reveal a great deal more about the subtle conditions under which various events occur. These would not have been apparent through common sense alone. Hence, reliance on the scientific method is a must for truly understanding human behavior in organizations. Common sense may provide some useful hunches or starting ideas, we agree, but for really understanding exactly what happens and why, there's no substitute for scientific research.

Now that you understand the limitations of common sense as a source of knowledge about OB, you're in a better position to appreciate one of the best-accepted sources of inspiration about OB research—theory.

Test Bank questions 1.33 and 1.73 relate to material on this page.

Theory: An Essential Guide to Organizational Research

Scientists are always talking about theories, and specialists in organizational behavior are no exception. Although OB is in part an applied science, theories still play a large role in the field. That a field is "theoretical" does not mean that it is impractical and out of touch with reality. To the contrary, a theory is simply a useful way of attempting to describe the relationships between concepts. Thus, a theory helps, not hinders, our understanding of the way things work. More formally, we can define a **theory** as *a set of statements about the interrelationships between concepts that allow us to predict and explain various processes and events.* As you might imagine, such statements might be of interest not only to scientists, but to practitioners as well.

Now, to give you a feel for the potential value of theory in OB, let's consider an example. Imagine that we observe the following: when individuals are given concrete goals, their performance on many tasks improves. (We'll return to this topic in detail in chapter 4.) This observation is certainly useful by itself. After all, it allows us to predict what will happen when goals are introduced (performance will increase), and it suggests a useful means for improving performance in a wide range of settings. These two accomplishments—*prediction* and *intervention* (control)—are major goals of science. Yet, the fact that concrete goals enhance performance does not explain *why* this is so. This is where theory enters the picture.

In older fields such as physics or chemistry, theories usually consist of mathematical equations. In OB, however, they generally involve verbal assertions. For example, a theory designed to explain the impact of goals on performance might read: "When individuals are given concrete goals, they know exactly what they are supposed to accomplish. This increases their motivation and helps them to choose the best strategies for reaching the goal. As a result, performance increases."

Note that this theory, like all others, consists of two major parts: several basic concepts (goals, motivation, task strategies), and assertions concerning the relationships between them.

Once a theory has been formulated, a crucial process begins. First, predictions are derived from the theory. These are developed in accordance with basic principles of logic and are known as *hypotheses*. Next, these predictions are tested in actual research. If they are confirmed, confidence in the accuracy of the theory increases. If they are disconfirmed, confidence in the theory may weaken. Then the theory may be altered so as to generate new predictions, and these, in turn, are tested. In short, the process is continuous, involving the free flow of information between a theory, predictions derived from it, and the findings of ongoing research. (See Figure 1–8 on p. 22 for a summary of this process.)

As you might imagine, theories are very useful in the field of OB. In fact, theories serve three useful functions—organizing, summarizing, and guiding. First, theories help *organize* large amounts of data into meaningful propositions. They help make sense out of a complex array of information. Second, these statements help *summarize* what we know about the phenomenon under consideration. Finally, theories suggest important areas of needed research by identifying questions that may not have been otherwise apparent. Hence, theories serve an important *guiding* function. We think you will appreciate these benefits of theories as you come across various ones throughout this book. As you encounter them, you will be able to see how theories organize, summarize, and guide further questions about complex aspects of organizational behavior. You will also see how they help explain behavior in a meaningful fashion. That a theory is only as good as its ability to successfully confirm predictions about behavior will also become clear. In other words, theories must be *testable*. To survive, they must accurately account for the behavior in question.

FIGURE 1–8

Theory: An Important Guide to Research in Organizational Behavior

Once a theory has been formulated, predictions derived from it are tested through direct research. If these are confirmed, confidence in the theory's accuracy increases. If they are disconfirmed, confidence in the theory's accuracy diminishes. Then it may either be modified so as to generate new predictions or, ultimately, be rejected.

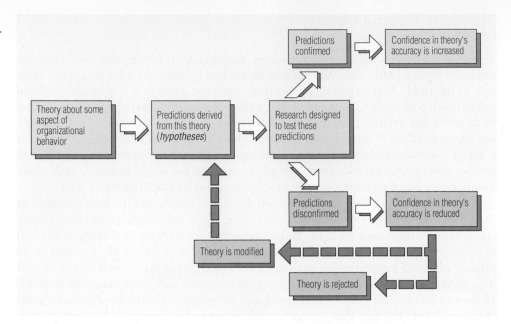

Thus, theories obviously represent a key source of inspiration for research in OB. Much of the research that is conducted either is designed to directly test a theory, or has indirect implications for a theory. Either way, one thing is clear: theories play an important role in guiding research in OB.

Now that you recognize how theories are used in OB research, we are ready to consider the variety of different techniques used by scientists in the field of OB. We believe that such information will prove useful to you in several respects.

First, it will help you to understand the discussions of specific research projects and their findings presented at many points in this text. Second, it will enable you to evaluate the many statements about work-related behavior you are certain to encounter in your future career. Once you know how research on OB *should* be conducted, you will be better able to judge whether such statements rest on relatively firm or shaky foundations. Finally, having a basic grasp of the research methods used in OB will enhance your ability to communicate with persons trained in this field, should you encounter them in your own organization. (This is not at all unlikely; people with advanced training in OB and related fields often work in organizations or are hired as outside consultants to assist with problems relating to employee motivation, organizational conflict, and many other issues.) So, having a working knowledge of the basic research methods used by OB will arm you with one more skill that may prove useful in many ways throughout your own career—even if you're not going to be an OB scientist yourself.

Natural Observation

The simplest, and in some ways most obvious, technique for acquiring information about organizational behavior is **natural observation.** As the phrase suggests, this approach involves spending time in an organization and observing the events and processes that take place within it. For example, suppose an investigator wanted to determine how employees react to a forthcoming merger with another company. Information about this issue could be obtained by visiting the organization in question and observing what employees say and do in the days or weeks prior to the merger.

Further, their behavior could be compared with that during some baseline period, before news of the merger was announced. In a variation of this technique, known as **participant observation,** an investigator could actually be hired by the organization, and then observe it from the inside, as an actual member.[44]

Direct observation of OB offers several obvious advantages. It is applied to actual work settings, and can be used without disrupting normal routines. Further, almost anyone—including people already employed by the organization—can be trained to use it. On the other hand, it suffers from several limitations. Being so close to the daily functioning of the organization may make it difficult for observers to remain impartial; they may become friendly with several people, and be strongly affected by such relationships. Similarly, because most of what takes place in organizations is fairly dull and routine, there is a natural tendency to focus on unusual or unexpected events—with the result that observers' conclusions can be distorted by them. Finally, as we will see in chapter 2, all human beings—even the keenest and most observant— have a limited capacity to notice, process, and store incoming information. Accordingly, observers may miss much that is important and reach conclusions that are biased by their selective sample of information. For these reasons, natural observation is not generally viewed in OB as a basic method for acquiring scientific knowledge about behavior in work settings. Rather, it is seen as a starting point in this process— a basis for insights and ideas that may then be studied by more systematic means.

The Case Method: Generalizing from the Unique

Suppose that in the study of mergers noted above, an investigator decided she would not simply observe employees in the days or weeks prior to a merger. Instead, she would interview them, focus on specific potential changes (e.g., a rise in experienced levels of stress, the initiation of wild rumors), and in general, use a more detailed and systematic approach. Here, she would be using an approach known as the **case method.** The basic idea behind this strategy is that by studying one organization in depth, we can learn much about processes occurring in many others, and so increase our knowledge of organizational behavior. The case method, too, rests on observation of ongoing events and processes. In contrast to natural observation, however, it involves active questioning of employees and other procedures for gaining information about them, their reactions, and their company.

Because it may involve detailed interviews and the use of questionnaires for measuring attitudes and intentions, the case method often yields more quantitative data than natural observation. However, it suffers from some of the same drawbacks (e.g., investigators may become so involved with a particular organization that they lose some of their objectivity). Further, because each organization is in some way unique, findings and principles cannot always be generalized to others. Recognizing this limitation, some scholars have advocated the use of multiple, as opposed to single, case studies for purposes of testing theories.[45] Still, it is widely recognized that case studies can be rich sources of hypotheses, ideas that then need to be subjected to rigorous testing using more objective methods.[46]

Surveys and Correlational Research

In contrast to the largely qualitative research methods we've been discussing thus far, a great deal of organizational research is conducted using more precise, quantitative techniques. Such studies often rely on the use of **surveys**—questionnaires completed by participants in the research project in which they respond to a variety of questions about themselves and their feelings about their jobs and organizations.

How believable are survey results? Even when research is carefully conducted, unintended biases can color the results obtained. Just imagine the serious consequences that may result when people *deliberately* sabotage the results of occupational research. An article appearing in *Ms.* magazine a few years ago asked readers to do just this. As a form of protest against researchers not treating females as seriously as they would males, women were asked to intentionally lie when filling out questionnaires (e.g., reporting that they were a CEO even if they were really a homemaker). [Waring, M. (1990, July–August). Sabotaging their statistics. *Ms.,* pp. 82–83.]

The correlation coefficient was developed by the mathematician Karl Pearson. Its introduction—which allowed scientists to quantify the relationship between variables with great precision—is considered one of the great advances in scientific methodology in the 1900s. Reports of certain correlation coefficients encourage scientists to ask more detailed questions about the causes underlying the

In essence, this approach consists of three major steps: (1) identifying **variables** (aspects of people, organizations, or the environment) that might potentially affect organizational behavior; (2) measuring these variables as precisely as possible; and (3) determining whether they are related to one another in any manner. It would be fair to say that this approach to conducting research is one of the methods most widely used by contemporary OB scientists attempting to gain knowledge about behavior in organizations.

Deciding which variables are the relevant ones is a complex process in which researchers draw on previous research, theories of OB, and even, occasionally, hunches or informal observations. Such variables are typically measured using questionnaires specifically designed to delve into those aspects of people's feelings about their organizations in which the investigator is interested. Finally, the data provided by participants are carefully analyzed by statistical procedures to determine whether these variables are related.

Here, the central question is whether changes in one variable are associated with changes in one or more others. The strength of such relationships is often expressed in terms of **correlation coefficients.** These can vary from -1.00 to $+1.00$; the greater their departure from 0.00, the stronger the relationship between the variables in question. For example, if one variable tends to increase as another rises, this would be reflected in a *positive correlation* (e.g., $+.30$, $+.82$). If, instead, one variable decreases as another increases, this would be reflected in a *negative correlation* (e.g., $-.18$, $-.57$). (See Figure 1–9.) The important thing to keep in mind when interpreting correlation coefficients is that the sign (negative or positive) tells you whether the relationship between the variables measured is either negative or positive, whereas the absolute value of the coefficient (i.e., the number without regard to the sign) tells you how strong the relationship is. Thus, a correlation coefficient of $-.83$ reflects a stronger relationship than one of $+.51$. The $-.83$ merely reflects the fact that more of one variable is associated with *less* of another, whereas the $+.51$ reflects

FIGURE 1–9

Interpreting Positive and Negative Correlations

In a positive correlation, more of Variable A is associated with *more* of Variable B, and vice versa. However, in a negative correlation, more of Variable A is associated with *less* of Variable B.

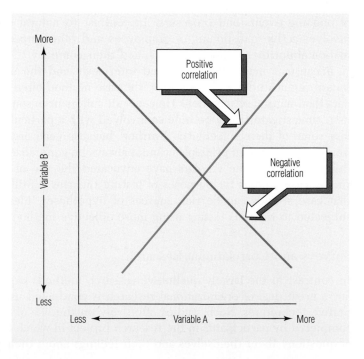

the fact that more of one variable is associated with *more* of another. Of the two sets of relationships described by these numbers, the − .83 is the stronger one (i.e., the two variables measured are more closely related to each other).

Why are correlations useful? The answer is that they can be used to make *predictions*. The stronger the correlation between two variables, the more accurately one can be predicted from the other. Thus, for example, if we discover that job satisfaction and voluntary turnover are strongly correlated in a negative direction (the higher employees' job satisfaction, the lower their rate of quitting), we can predict changes in rate of turnover from changes in employee satisfaction in an accurate manner. Let's look at an example of how the *correlational method* might be used.

Imagine that an OB researcher wanted to gather information on the following possibility: interviewers' moods affect the ratings they assign to the job applicants they interview. Specifically, the researcher has reason to suspect that the more positive the interviewers' moods, the higher the ratings they assign, and that, conversely, the more negative the interviewers' moods, the lower the ratings they assign. Together, these predictions constitute the researcher's **hypothesis**—the as yet untested prediction this person wishes to investigate. How could this issue be examined by means of a correlational study? One possibility is that since the researcher has already identified the variables of interest (interviewer's mood, ratings of applicants), she or he would proceed to the next step: devising ways of measuring these variables. Thus, the researcher might develop a brief rating scale on which interviewers (e.g., persons working in the Human Resources Department of several organizations) report their own current moods. Similarly, the researcher would devise questions for assessing the ratings assigned to job applicants by the interviewers (see Table 1–3 for samples of both measures). He or she would then arrange for a large number of interviewers to complete the mood scales each day, before they begin interviewing applicants, and perhaps at the end of each day as well. The same people would also complete the questionnaire on which they report their ratings of each job candidate. (Of course, no names would be attached to these ratings; the privacy of job applicants would be carefully protected.)

variables they study (e.g., in the United States, there is a .50 correlation between the IQ scores of husbands and those of their wives). [Seligman, D. (1989, September 25). Mr. Correlation speaks. *Fortune*, pp. 251–252.]

TABLE 1–3 Sample Items in Survey Used for Research Purposes

Items such as these might be used to assess interviewers' current moods (left-hand items) and their ratings of job applicants (right-hand items). Information on both factors (variables) would be required in a study concerned with the possible relationship between them.

Please rate your current mood below. (Circle one number for each)

Sad						Happy
1	2	3	4	5	6	7

Bad						Good
1	2	3	4	5	6	7

Tense						Relaxed
1	2	3	4	5	6	7

Please rate the applicant you just interviewed on each of the following dimensions. (Circle one number for each)

Suitability for the position in question

Low						High
1	2	3	4	5	6	7

Motivation

Low						High
1	2	3	4	5	6	7

Background/Experience

Low						High
1	2	3	4	5	6	7

Test Bank questions 1.42–1.43 and 1.74 relate to material on this page.

In the final step, the researcher would apply appropriate statistical procedures to the data collected, to determine whether, in fact, ratings assigned to the job candidates vary with the interviewers' moods. If this analysis yielded a positive correlation (e.g., +.43), evidence supporting the initial hypothesis would be obtained; that is, the more positive the interviewers' moods, the more favorable their ratings tend to be.

Corresponding methods can be applied to virtually any aspect of OB, from leadership effectiveness to the effects of exposure to prolonged job-related stress. Thus, systematic observation is a very valuable research method; indeed, it is one of the most frequently used approaches in OB today. The advantages it offers are both obvious and impressive. This technique can be adapted to almost any topic, can be used in many actual work settings with minimum disruption, and is often quite efficient (a large amount of information can be collected relatively quickly). Further, it can be extended to include many variables at once. For example, in the study mentioned above, such variables as interviewers' years of experience, the level or importance of the job in question, and the gender and age of the applicants could all be included in the study. Through a statistical technique known as **regression analysis,** the extent to which each of these variables is related to ratings of the job applicants, and the extent to which considering each variable adds to our ability to predict such ratings, could be assessed. These are very important techniques and are used frequently in OB research.

Unfortunately, despite such advantages, systematic observation suffers from one important drawback: *the findings it yields are not conclusive with respect to cause-and-effect relationships.* For example, consider the study described above. Suppose that the correlation between interviewers' moods and ratings of job candidates was +.92. Does the existence of this strong relationship indicate that changes in interviewers' moods *cause* changes in their ratings of employees? This seems like a reasonable conclusion, but it is impossible to tell. For example, isn't it also possible that when interviewers are in a good mood, they act in a friendlier manner toward applicants than when they are in a bad mood? This friendly treatment, in turn, might put applicants at ease, helping them perform better during the interview. Thus, it may actually be friendly treatment, not the interviewers' moods themselves, that produces the observed effects. In other words, if interviewers treated applicants in a friendly manner, even if they were *not* in a good mood, these persons might perform better and receive higher ratings (see Figure 1–10). Because of such uncertainty, it is important to avoid interpreting even a strong correlation between two variables as evidence for a direct causal link between them. A cause-and-effect relationship may indeed exist, but a correlation between two variables does not guarantee that this is so. Since establishing such causality is one of the key tasks of science, researchers in OB sometimes turn to another approach that does permit such conclusions to be drawn.

The Experimental Method

The popularity of the **experimental method** is based on the fact that it allows us to establish that one variable directly determines another (rather than their being merely correlated with each other). Both scientists and practitioners are extremely interested in learning about the existence of causal relationships between variables of interest. Such knowledge allows us to predict and explain the various causes of behavior.

Let's consider an example—one following from the research question we posed earlier about the impact of interviewers' moods on their evaluations of job applicants.

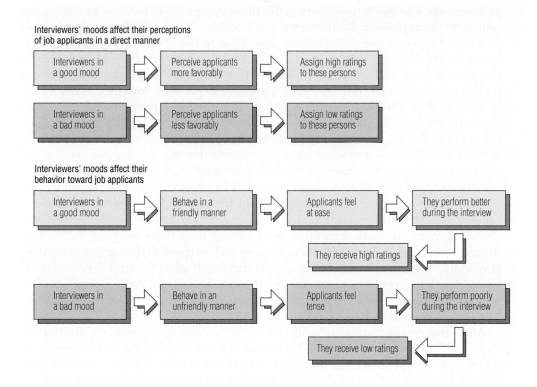

Interviewers' moods affect their perceptions
of job applicants in a direct manner

| Interviewers in a good mood | ⇒ | Perceive applicants more favorably | ⇒ | Assign high ratings to these persons |

| Interviewers in a bad mood | ⇒ | Perceive applicants less favorably | ⇒ | Assign low ratings to these persons |

Interviewers' moods affect their
behavior toward job applicants

| Interviewers in a good mood | ⇒ | Behave in a friendly manner | ⇒ | Applicants feel at ease | ⇒ | They perform better during the interview |

They receive high ratings ⇐

| Interviewers in a bad mood | ⇒ | Behave in an unfriendly manner | ⇒ | Applicants feel tense | ⇒ | They perform poorly during the interview |

They receive low ratings ⇐

FIGURE 1–10   Why Correlation Does Not Guarantee Causation

The fact that interviewers' moods are correlated with the ratings they assign to applicants does not guarantee a direct causal link between these factors. Interviewers' moods may indeed affect their perceptions of applicants directly. However, it is also possible that good and bad moods affect interviewers' behavior toward applicants, and that this factor, *not* mood, is the crucial one. (If this is so, then interviewers who behave in a friendly manner may rate applicants more highly even if they are not in an especially good mood.)

To conduct an experiment on this topic, we could do the following. First, we obtain a group of professional interviewers, selecting them at random from the population of interviewers. For example, we might contact ninety interviewers after selecting their names at random from a directory of professional interviewers published by a trade association. If they agree to participate in the study, we randomly assign one-third of this sample to each of the three different experimental conditions. We then put one group in a good mood (e.g., by giving them information about how well they performed an important task). Another group is put into a bad mood (e.g., by giving them information about how poorly they performed an important task). Finally, a third group receives no information; no attempt is made to alter their moods. This third group is known as a *control group*.

Subjects in all three groups interview one or more job applicants who are, in reality, research assistants. Such persons are carefully trained to behave in a neutral manner, so that what they say and do during the interviews will have minimal impact on the ratings they receive. This gives any effects of the interviewers' moods on such ratings an opportunity to emerge. After each interview is completed, subjects rate the applicants on several dimensions (e.g., their motivation, suitability for the job, intelligence). In a final step, the data collected are subjected to statistical analysis to determine whether interviewers in the three groups do, in fact, assign contrasting ratings to the applicants. If interviewers in a positive mood rate them highest, those in a negative mood rate them lowest, and those in the control group rate them in between (see Figure 1–11), support for the hypothesis under study is obtained. (By the way, several studies quite similar to this imaginary one have actually been performed. In general, their results support the hypothesis described above.[47])

Let's analyze what was done in this simple hypothetical experiment to help explain the basic elements of, and the underlying logic behind, the experimental method. First, recall that we selected subjects from the population and assigned them to one of three conditions on a *random* basis. This means that any interviewer listed in the directory potentially may have been selected for study, and he or she may have been put into any of the three conditions completely by chance. Thus, the possibility that some interviewers may be somehow different from others was minimized. By using *random assignment*, we assured that the interviewers in one condition were not already harsher or more lenient in their ratings than those assigned to another. Because participants were selected at random and assigned to the various conditions at random, any differences between people that might affect the study's results could be assumed to even out across the conditions. This is the logic behind random assignment. Although the use of random assignment in research is not always feasible, it is highly desirable whenever possible.

After the participants were assigned to the various conditions, we altered the states of those in two of the three conditions (except those in the control group, to which nothing was done). The altering of people's states, by giving them information designed to put them in a good or bad mood, is termed *manipulation*. In our example, this was done to determine if people's moods affect their ratings of others. The name given to the variable that was altered in this way is the *independent variable*. An **independent variable** is that variable that is systematically manipulated by the experimenter so as to determine its effects on the behavior of interest. In our example, the interviewer's mood state is the independent variable. The variable that is mea-

F I G U R E   1 – 1 1

Experimentation in Organizational Behavior: A Simple Example

Interviewers placed in a positive mood rate job applicants more favorably than those in a neutral mood. Those placed in a negative mood assign the lowest ratings of all. These findings offer support for the hypothesis that interviewers' moods affect their perception of job applicants. (*Note:* The applicants in this study were accomplices of the researcher, specially trained to behave in the same neutral manner in all cases.)

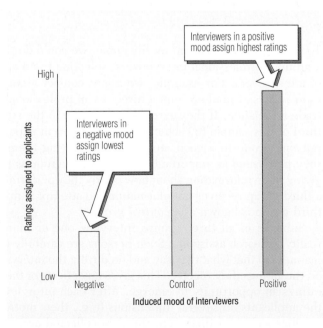

sured, the one influenced by the independent variable, is known as the *dependent variable*. A **dependent variable** is the behavior of interest that is being measured, the behavior that is dependent on the independent variable. In this case, the dependent variables were the ratings of the applicants along various dimensions. By the way, anything that can be measured can be an independent variable or a dependent variable. The choice of what should be manipulated or what should be measured is made by the experimenter on the basis of his or her ideas or interest in certain variables or behaviors (quite often suggested by one or more theories).

The basic logic behind the experimental method is really quite simple, and involves only two major steps: (1) the presence or strength of a factor believed to affect some aspect of organizational behavior is systematically varied, and (2) the effects, if any, of such variations are assessed. The idea behind these steps can also be simply stated: if the factor varied does indeed affect organizational behavior, then people exposed to different levels or amounts of it should also show differences in behavior. For example, exposure to a small amount of the factor in question should result in one level of behavior; exposure to a larger amount should result in a different level; and so on. All experiments are designed to determine the effects of one or more independent variables (variables manipulated by the researcher) on one or more dependent variables (behaviors measured by the researcher).

To conduct experiments properly, all factors other than the independent variable that may influence the behavior in question must be held constant. If the dependent variable differs while no other variables except the independent variables were altered, then we can assume that the independent variable caused the dependent variable. In the example we just considered, we already took one step to help ensure this. Specifically, by randomly assigning participants to conditions, we helped assure that any differences among the interviewers (such as their predispositions toward leniency or harshness) would be equalized. What else besides differences among people might influence the ratings? Many factors might matter, but let's consider some environmental differences. Suppose, for example, that some of the participants were interviewed in very hot or very cold rooms, or that some were hurried and had less time to consider their judgments than others. To the extent that these factors may influence people's ratings (as you might expect they would), it is critical that they be held constant throughout the experiment. Hence, experiments require all the experimental conditions to be kept the same with respect to all variables except the independent variable so that its effects can be determined unambiguously.

As you might imagine, this is often easier said than done. How simple it is to control for the effects of extraneous variables (i.e., factors not of interest to the experimenter) depends, in large part, on where the experiment is conducted. In the field of OB, there are typically two options: experiments can be conducted either in naturalistic organizational settings known as the *field*, or in settings specially created for the study itself, known as the *laboratory* (or *lab*, for short). Let's extend our example. Manipulating interviewers' moods just before they were about to rate real people on the job would be quite difficult. Too many unknowns and uncontrollable factors would be involved. For example, it would be impossible to hold constant across conditions the quality of the people being rated, or the existence of norms to give lenient or harsh ratings. It would also be very awkward and unnatural to induce the moods just before the ratings were to be given (of course, if the mood manipulations were made at the beginning of the day, there would be no control over how much time elapsed until the ratings were given). As a solution, it would be possible to bring people into a lab in which all such factors may be controlled (i.e., kept at a constant level). Although the laboratory certainly offers advantages

Although it has been suggested that business leaders and business researchers work together, such joint efforts may be problematic. For example, some researchers may experience a conflict between their objectivity as scholars and any financial benefit they may gain as a result of claiming certain research findings. To minimize such potential conflicts of interest, some professional journals now require researchers to disclose the sources of their funding and to state that they have no affiliation with or financial interest in the subject matter of their manuscripts. [Williams, S. (1990, April). Should science journals play cop? *Science,* p. 13.]

with respect to control over extraneous variables, it clearly does not mimic real-life conditions, thereby making the results of lab studies subject to questions of *generalizability.* That is, would the same findings occur outside the limited, specific lab setting studied? This is an important question. Because people might not act naturally in the lab (e.g., they know they are being studied, and they may wish to please the experimenter), the results of field studies are considered more realistic and generalizable to other settings. Of course, such realism comes at the cost of lower control over extraneous variables. Thus, whereas lab studies offer greater experimental control, field studies offer greater opportunities to study naturalistic, more generalizable responses (see Figure 1–12). Obviously, important trade-offs must be considered when conducting (or interpreting the results of) laboratory and field experiments.

The experiment, although extremely useful, clearly is not a perfect research tool for studying OB. In fact, no *one* technique is perfect, and scholars recommend using multiple techniques so that their limitations can offset each other. Still, because of its ability to allow us to learn about the variables that cause different types of organizational behavior, the experiment remains an important tool for conducting OB research. As a result, many of the research studies we will consider throughout this text used the experimental method. (Sometimes, the use of experimentation requires altering people's psychological states, or deceiving them in some way. In our example, we systematically attempted to put some people in a good mood and others in a bad

    ## A QUESTION OF ETHICS

Ethical Obligations to Research Participants

 To learn about behavior in organizations, investigators do a lot of probing. They ask questions, observe people, and sometimes put them in unusual situations—all for the sake of science. You may be asking yourself if all this is ethical. This is a very reasonable question, and one we believe you *should* be asking. After all, although researchers need to know things about people, there is clearly a limit to the lengths to which researchers may go in pursuing such knowledge. The obligation to promote scientific knowledge must be balanced by the obligation to treat research participants in a fair and humane manner. Although it would be extremely rare for any research in organizational behavior to cause harm or to expose people to dangerous situations, researchers must be sensitive to more subtle risks (e.g., the potential invasion of one's privacy). With this in mind, we will describe some of the steps that researchers should take to ensure the ethical treatment of their research participants.[48]

First, it is considered appropriate to ensure that people who participate in a research study

are doing so on a *voluntary* basis. Although participants may receive some form of inducement (e.g., a small amount of money or course credit), a reward so large that people feel they have no choice but to participate would be inappropriate (e.g., managers telling their subordinates that they will have to complete a questionnaire if they ever wish to be considered for a raise). In such a case, the inducement would constitute a form of *coercion.* Of course, to make a truly voluntary decision, prospective research participants must be told exactly what will be expected of them before they agree to go along with the study. In other words, they must give *informed consent*—that is, enough information about the research should be given in advance so that people can freely make informed decisions about whether to participate. In the absence of informed consent, truly voluntary participation is not possible.

A second ethical consideration is that deception should be kept to a minimum, but whenever it is necessary, it should be minor and followed by a thorough explanation of the deceit involved. Sometimes, in the course of conducting a lab-

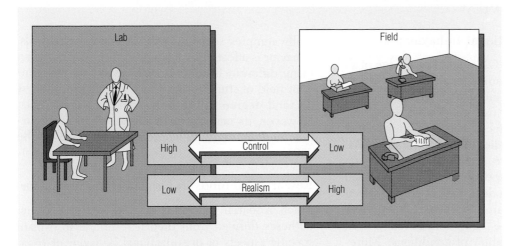

FIGURE 1–12

Trade-offs in Lab and Field Experiments

Organizational behavior researchers may conduct experiments in laboratory or field settings, but each setting has advantages and disadvantages. The lab offers higher control but a lower degree of realism, whereas the field offers lower control but a higher degree of realism.

mood by giving them fictitious information about themselves. Are these practices ethical? For insight into this question, and the ethical aspects of other types of OB research, see the **Question of Ethics** section that starts on the preceding page.)

oratory study, experimenters find it necessary to deceive the research subjects. Consider, for example, the false information about performance given to participants in the hypothetical experiment described earlier. Telling people that they performed worse than expected is a relatively minor deception, whereas it would be a major deception—and a clearly unethical one— to attempt the same manipulation by falsely announcing the death of a loved one. Such a manipulation would certainly be traumatic, and patently unethical. Furthermore, milder deceptions may be acceptable only if it is followed by a thorough *debriefing;* that is, participants should be told exactly how they were deceived and why it was necessary to do so. The deception should be handled in a sensitive, professional manner by the experimenter (e.g., he or she should *not* say, "Ha ha, we really fooled you!"). Investigators owe their research participants a thorough and honest debriefing *anytime* that deception is used in an experiment.

A third ethical imperative is that researchers, whenever possible, should maintain their records so that the identity of no participant can be determined. If you are an employee of a company and a researcher asks you to complete a questionnaire, you may fear that your responses will be shared with company officials, getting you into trouble. Obviously, for an investigator

to collect such data under the guise of a scientific study, and then use it to harm the participant, would be seriously unethical. Although an investigator may share the overall findings of the study with officials of the organization studied, it would be inappropriate to share any one person's responses. Thus, research participants should be assured of *confidentiality* in their responses. That is, only the researchers and no one else should have access to anyone's responses. In fact, whenever possible, the data should be collected on an anonymous basis. When data are collected *anonymously,* no one, even the researcher, can determine the identity of any one participant (e.g., a group of people may complete questionnaires, but do not write their names, or any other identifying information, on them).

Although these are not the only ethical issues to which researchers must be sensitive, they are clearly some of the ones most likely to be encountered in conducting OB research. We think it is important for you to realize that although scientists are interested in collecting data, they must do so within a set of ethical limits. After all, it would indeed be ironic for a social scientist, allegedly concerned with bettering humankind through understanding human behavior, to harm in any way those who are studied for the purpose of deriving this benefit.

SUMMARY AND REVIEW

The Field of Organizational Behavior

Organizational behavior (OB) seeks knowledge of all aspects of behavior in organizational settings through the systematic study of individual, group, and organizational processes. It uses this knowledge to enhance organizational effectiveness and individual well-being. Because it relies on scientific methods, OB provides much more accurate and systematic knowledge about many aspects of work behavior than does common sense. Modern OB is characterized by the belief that people are responsive to their work environments and become highly committed to work under the right combination of conditions. Moreover, the field recognizes that organizations are dynamic, self-sustaining units known as **open systems.** The contemporary approach to OB recognizes that behavior in organizations is not universal; social and cultural differences between people play a large part in understanding organizational behavior.

Development of the Field of Organizational Behavior

OB can trace its roots to work on **scientific management,** which focused on efficient job design. It was strongly affected by the **human relations approach,** which recognized that work settings are actually complex social systems in which individuals' behavior is affected by a complex interplay between many different factors. It emerged as an independent field of study in the 1940s and 1950s (the first doctoral degree in the field was granted in 1941). However, its major growth and adoption of its current multidisciplinary approach took place in the 1960s.

Research Methods in Organizational Behavior

Much research in OB is carried out to test hypotheses derived from **theories**—efforts to explain specific aspects of organizational behavior or organizational processes. In order to acquire accurate information about behavior in organizational settings, OB employs several methods of research. **Natural observation** and the **case method** are generally viewed as starting points—sources of ideas for further study. In **correlational research,** potentially important variables are identified and then measured precisely using **surveys** to determine if they are related to one another in any manner. In the **experimental method,** one or more independent variables are systematically altered by a researcher in order to determine whether such changes affect one or more dependent variables (various measures of interest to organizational scientists).

KEY TERMS

behavioral sciences: Fields such as psychology and sociology that seek knowledge of human behavior and human society through the use of scientific methods.

bureaucracy: An organizational design developed by Max Weber that seeks efficiency by having people perform well-defined jobs within a clear hierarchical authority structure.

case method: A method of research in which one organization is studied in detail in order to establish general principles about organizational behavior or organizational processes.

classical organizational theory: An early approach to studying organizations that focused on the efficient structuring of organizations.

contingency approach: A perspective suggesting that organizational behavior is affected by a very large number of interacting factors.

correlation coefficients: Statistical measures of the extent to which two or more variables are related.

correlational research: A method of research in which variables assumed to affect some area of interest are identified, then carefully measured. These measurements are then subjected to statistical analysis to determine whether (and to what extent) the variables are related to one another.

dependent variable: The variable in an experiment that is measured in order to determine whether it is affected by variations in one or more factors (i.e., independent variables).

experimental method: A method of research in which one or more conditions are systematically varied to determine if such changes have any impact on the behavior of interest.

human relations approach: A perspective on organizational behavior that recognizes the importance of social factors and processes in work settings.

human resources model: A view suggesting that under appropriate circumstances, employees are fully capable of working productively and accepting responsibility.

hypothesis: An as yet unverified prediction concerning relationships between specific variables. Such propositions may be derived from existing theories, or suggested by the findings of previous research or informal observation.

independent variable: The factor in an experiment that is systematically varied by the researcher to determine its effects on behavior (the dependent variable).

natural observation: A method of research in which an investigator observes events and processes occurring in an organization. The observer makes every effort possible to avoid affecting these events or processes by his or her presence.

open systems: Self-sustaining systems that use energy to transform input from the external environment into output, which the systems then return to the environment.

organization: A structured social system consisting of groups and individuals working together to meet some agreed-on objectives.

organizational behavior: The field that seeks increased knowledge of all aspects of behavior in organizational settings through scientific methods.

participant observation: Natural observations of an organization made by individuals who have been hired as employees for the purpose of observing the organization.

regression analysis: Statistical techniques indicating the extent to which each of several variables contributes to accurate predictions of another variable.

scientific management: An early approach to management and organizational behavior emphasizing the importance of effective job design and employee motivation.

surveys: Questionnaires designed to measure some aspect of organizational behavior or organizational functioning.

theory: Efforts made by scientists to explain why various processes or events occur in the way that they do. Theories consist of two major parts: basic concepts, and assertions regarding the relationship between them.

Theory X: A traditional view suggesting that most people in the workplace are lazy and irresponsible, and will work hard only when forced to do so.

Theory Y: See *human resources model.*

variables: Factors (e.g., virtually any aspect of a work setting) that can be assigned different values.

QUESTIONS FOR DISCUSSION

1. How can the field of organizational behavior contribute both to the effectiveness or productivity of organizations *and* to the welfare or well-being of individuals? Is there any inconsistency between these goals?

2. How are organizations affected by the people of whom they are composed? How do organizations shape the behavior, attitudes, and values of individuals within them?

3. What is the contingency approach? How is it reflected in the field of OB?

4. What are the advantages of conducting research using qualitative techniques such as the case method and systematic observation as opposed to quantitative methods such as the correlational approach and the experiment?

5. Suppose you wanted to find out why groups tend to make riskier decisions than individuals. How would you design an experiment to provide information on this issue?

6. Why is theory so important in organizational research?

7. Describe a situation in which an organization might decide to hire a specialist in the field of OB as an outside consultant.

8. What are the ethical considerations involved in conducting research in organizations?

NOTES

1. O'Reilly, C. A., III. (1990). Organizational behavior: Where we've been and where we're going. *Annual Review of Psychology, 42,* 427–458.

2. Schoorman, R. D., & Schneider, B. (Eds.). (1988). *Facilitating work effectiveness.* Lexington, MA: Lexington Books.

3. Schmitt, N. W., & Klimoski, R. J. (1991). *Research methods in human resources management.* Cincinnati, OH: South-Western.

4. Goodman, R. S., & Kruger, E. J. (1988). Data dredging or legitimate research method? Historiography and its potential for management research. *Academy of Management Review, 13,* 315–325.

5. Lawrence, P. R. (1987). Historical development of organizational behavior. In J. W. Lorsch (Ed.), *Handbook of organizational behavior* (pp. 1–9). Englewood Cliffs, NJ: Prentice-Hall.

6. McGregor, D. (1960). *The human side of enterprise.* New York: McGraw-Hill.

7. Katz, D., & Kahn, R. (1978). *The social psychology of organizations.* New York: Wiley.

8. Lawrence, P. R., & Lorsch, J. W. (1967). *Organization and environment.* Homewood, IL: Irwin.

9. Boyacigiller, N. A., & Adler, N. J. (1991). The parochial dinosaur: Organizational science in a global context. *Academy of Management Review, 16,* 262–290.

10. See Note 9.

11. Rosenzweig, P. M., & Singh, J. V. (1991). Organizational environments and the multinational enterprise. *Academy of Management Review, 16,* 340–361.

12. Ricks, D. A., Toyne, B., & Martinez, Z. (1990). Recent developments in international management research. *Journal of Management, 16,* 219–253.

13. Harpaz, I. (1990). The importance of work goals: An international perspective. *Journal of International Business Studies, 21,* 75–93.

14. See Note 9.

15. Adler, N. J., & Jelinek, M. (1986). Is "organization culture" culture bound? *Human Resources Management, 25,* 73–90.

16. Allen, D. B., Miller, E. D., & Nath, R. (1988). North America. In R. Nath (Ed.), *Comparative management* (pp. 23–54). Cambridge, MA: Ballinger.

17. Münsterberg, H. (1913). *Psychology and industrial efficiency.* Boston: Houghton Mifflin.

18. Metcalf, H., & Urwick, L. F. (Eds.). (1942). *Dynamic administration: The collected papers of Mary Parker Follett.* New York: Harper & Row.

19. Miner, J. B., Wachtel, J. B., & Ebrahimi, B. (1989). The managerial motivation of potential managers in the United States and other countries of the world: Implications for national competitiveness and the productivity problem. *Advances in International Comparative Management, 4,* 147–170.

20. Miner, J. B., Chen, C., & Yu, K. C. (1991). Theory testing under adverse conditions: Motivation to manage in the People's Republic of China. *Journal of Applied Psychology, 76,* 343–349.

21. Wall, J. A., Jr. (1990). Managers in the People's Republic of China. *Academy of Management Executive, 4,* 19–32.

22. Black, J. S., Mendenhall, M., & Oddou, G. (1991). Toward a comprehensive model of international adjustment: An integration of multiple theoretical perspectives. *Academy of Management Journal, 16,* 291–317.

23. Taylor, F. W. (1947). *Scientific management.* New York: Harper & Row.

24. Petersen, P. B. (1990). Fighting for a better navy: An attempt at scientific management (1905–1912). *Journal of Management, 16,* 151–166.

25. Greenberg, J. (1990). Organizational justice: Yesterday, today, and tomorrow. *Journal of Management, 16,* 399–432.

26. Roethlisberger, F. J., & Dickson, W. J. (1939). *Management and the worker.* Cambridge, MA: Harvard University Press.

27. See Note 5.

28. See Note 6.

29. Lion, J. S., Richardson, E., & Browne, R. C. (1968).

A study of the performance of industrial inspectors under two kinds of lighting. *Ergonomics, 11,* 23–34.

30. Nelson, T. M., Nilsson, T. H., & Johnson, M. (1984). Interaction of temperature, illuminance and apparent time on sedentary work fatigue. *Ergonomics, 27,* 89–101.

31. Fayol, H. (1949). *General and industrial management.* London: Pitman.

32. Weber, M. (1921). *Theory of social and economic organization* (A. M. Henderson & T. Parsons, Trans.). London: Oxford University Press.

33. Flexner, S. B. (1976). *I hear America talking.* New York: Van Nostrand Reinhold.

34. Scully, J. (1987). *Odyssey: Pepsi to Apple . . . a journey of adventure, ideas, and the future.* New York: Harper & Row.

35. Cited in Lawrence, P. R. (1987). See Note 5. Awarded to George Lombard, Harvard Business School.

36. Gardner, B., & Moore, G. (1945). *Human relations in industry.* Homewood, IL: Irwin.

37. See Note 5.

38. Gordon, R. A., & Howell, J. E. (1959). *Higher education for business.* New York: Columbia University Press.

39. Labich, K. (1988, January 18). Big changes at big brown. *Fortune,* pp. 56–64.

40. Machalaba, D. (1986, April 22). Up to speed: UPS gets deliveries done by driving its workers. *Wall Street Journal,* pp. 1, 14.

41. See Note 39.

42. Porter, L. W., & McKibbin, L. E. (1988). *Management education and development: Drift or thrust into the 21st century.* New York: McGraw-Hill.

43. Cummings, L. L. (1990). Management education drifts into the 21st century. *Academy of Management Executive, 4,* 66–67.

44. Mintzberg, H. (1973). *The nature of managerial work.* New York: Harper & Row.

45. Greenberg, J., & Folger, R. (1988). *Controversial issues in social research methods.* New York: Springer-Verlag.

46. Eisenhardt, K. M. (1989). Building theories from case study research. *Academy of Management Review, 14,* 532–550.

47. Sinclair, R. C. (1988). Mood, categorization breadth, and performance appraisal: The effects of order of information acquisition and affective state on halo, accuracy, information retrieval, and evaluations. *Organizational Behavior and Human Decision Processes, 42,* 22–46.

48. Dane, F. (1990). *Research methods.* Wadsworth, CA: Brooks/Cole.

CASE IN POINT

"How should I go about this research?" That was the question that Alan Honeycutt, president of Honeycutt and Associates, a training and development consulting firm, must have pondered when a client wanted to find out what factors contribute to the success of quality circles—a group-based technique for generating product quality improvement ideas. As an experienced OB researcher, Honeycutt knew that a number of decisions had to be made. What factors should be included in the study? What research method should be used? Who would participate in the study? How would the research data that was collected be analyzed? And, most important, what would Honeycutt discover from doing the research? These are the questions OB researchers typically consider. The following description of Honeycutt's study illustrates how OB research is often done.[1]

In 1982, a Honeycutt client, Hughes Aircraft Company's Space and Communications Group (HAC/SCG), began using quality circles. They were successfully implemented on a small scale, and by 1985 the concept had generated interest throughout the company. At that point, Hughes Aircraft management considered expanding the use of quality circles to other parts of the company. But first they wanted to know what factors contributed to quality-circle success. Management would be better able to target the resources that contribute the most to quality-circle effectiveness.

HAC/SCG managers believed that the success of their quality circles was attributable to the training that members received. Members received four hours of training about the philosophy and practices involved in running quality circles. This training helped members to be more effective in understanding and making suggestions about product-quality problems. Were the managers right?

Honeycutt was appropriately skeptical about the HAC/SCG managers' conclusions. OB research methods had taught him that things in OB are not always what they seem. Other factors, not immediately obvious to the HAC/SCG managers, might also be influencing quality-circle effectiveness. Management support could be the real cause of quality-circle effectiveness. Quality-circle members may have worked hard because they thought the company's management was firmly behind them. Training may have been only a highly visible consequence of management support rather than a causal factor.

Honeycutt knew that he should include other factors that might affect quality-circle effectiveness. He consulted the OB literature, the collective term that researchers use to refer to OB theory and research. By reviewing the OB literature, Honeycutt could find out what other researchers had learned about quality-circle effectiveness. He could then design a study that included not just the single hypothesis derived from the HAC/SCG managers, but also additional hypotheses.

Honeycutt found several factors that might contribute to quality-circle effectiveness. One published study proved especially useful. The study used correlational research to investigate the effects of twenty-one organizational variables on quality-circle effectiveness. Most of the study's variables failed to show any relationship to quality-circle effectiveness, except for three organizational variables. One variable was the degree of training that quality-circle members received regarding quality-circle philosophy and practices—just as HAC/SCG management had suspected. The other two variables were the degree to which participation in quality circles was truly voluntary and the degree to which quality-circle members perceived that management supported the quality-circle concept. Honeycutt was delighted! Being able to build on the results of this study would save lots of time and effort.

Based on his search of the literature and the insights of HAC/SCG management, Honeycutt decided to include member training, voluntary participation, and perceived management support as the major predictor variables. He also chose to do a correlational research study. He would develop a questionnaire to measure study variables and then use statistical techniques to determine which of the study variables were actually related to quality-circle effectiveness.

Honeycutt discussed the research project with Hughes Aircraft management to gain permission to use the company's quality-circle employees as his research sample. Hughes Aircraft management readily agreed to this request.

The next phase was to develop a questionnaire to measure the three predictor variables—member training, voluntary participation, and perceived management support for quality circles—as well as the outcome variable, perceptions of quality-circle effectiveness. Honeycutt wrote a fourteen-item questionnaire that he hoped would accurately measure the predictor and outcome variables. (An item is a question intended to at least partially measure a study variable.) Honeycutt wrote four items for each predictor variable and two items for the outcome variable. For each item, participants were asked to circle a number from 1 to 5. For example, one question, intended to measure the degree to which quality-circle members were volunteers, asked "How much influence did your supervisor or manager have on your joining the quality circle?"[2] Study participants were instructed to respond to this question by circling a number from 1 ("no influence") to 5 ("a lot of influence").

Honeycutt pretested the questionnaire on six divisional quality-circle coordinators to learn if they thought the items were accurate measures of the variables. They agreed that the questionnaire appeared to do a good job measuring the variables. Honeycutt then analyzed the coordinators' responses for level of internal reliability. Internal reliability refers to the relationship (as measured by a correlation coefficient) between questionnaire items that are supposed to measure the same variable. For example, if items one through four of a questionnaire were intended to measure the same variable, then these items should be strongly related to each other (as shown by a high correlation coefficient). A good questionnaire should have a high level of internal reliability. Honeycutt's analysis of the coordinators' responses indicated that the questionnaire did indeed have high internal reliability. Overall, his analysis gave Honeycutt confidence that his questionnaire was an accurate measure of the variables.

Honeycutt then selected eighty-three members of HAC/SCG's quality circles to serve as participants. He distributed the questionnaires to members at the start of their regularly scheduled quality-circle meetings. For each quality circle, he explained the nature of the research and informed members that their responses would remain confidential. He then asked the participants to answer all questions as honestly as possible. Honeycutt observed that it took three to five minutes for study participants to complete the questionnaire. For circle members who were not present at the meeting, Honeycutt mailed the questionnaire with the same explanation and instructions.

After gathering the completed questionnaires, Honeycutt categorized the data according to the four variables. He added the scores for the four questions that measured voluntary participation, the four questions that measured member training, the four questions that measured management support, and the two questions that measured perceptions of quality-circle effectiveness. Honeycutt computed a total score for each variable for the eighty-three questionnaires. He then used a statistical technique called regression analysis to analyze the degree to which scores on each predictor variable were related to quality-circle effectiveness for the sample as a whole. Regression analysis showed member training to be the most powerful predictor of quality-circle effectiveness, followed by management support, which was found to be related to quality-circle effectiveness but to a much lesser degree. Voluntary participation showed no relationship whatsoever to quality-circle effectiveness.

Honeycutt concluded that although no *single* factor entirely explains quality-circle effectiveness, member training—even in relatively small amounts, such as the four hours received by HAC/SCG quality-circle members—has an important influence on the degree to which quality-circle members consider their quality circles to be effective. Says Honeycutt, "A few hours of specific training gave them the confidence to face challenges they may not have been able to handle before, to take on and solve tough problems, and to overcome constraints in the problem-solving process. In this case, a little bit of knowledge was a smart investment at Hughes Aircraft."[3]

As a result of Honeycutt's research, Hughes Aircraft management confirmed their hypothesis that training would be an important dimension for expanding quality circles to other parts of the company. They also learned that by letting their employees know their support of quality circles, they could enhance the ultimate effectiveness of the quality circles.

Does Honeycutt's research study tell us everything we need to know about quality circles? Clearly, it does not. Why did Honeycutt's research fail to find any relationship between voluntary participation and quality-circle effectiveness, whereas the published study did? If member training and management support don't explain all of quality-circle effectiveness, what else does affect it? The HAC/SCG managers seemed to be right about the importance of training to quality-circle effectiveness at Hughes Aircraft, but can we be sure that training will be related to quality-circle effectiveness in other companies too? These and many other questions remain to be answered.

Questions for Discussion

1. What was Honeycutt's motivation for doing research on quality circles? Do you think Honeycutt's motivation is typical of what motivates OB researchers?
2. Why did Honeycutt consult the OB literature? Do you suppose other OB researchers do this, too? Why?
3. Why did Honeycutt go ahead with his research project even after he found a previous study that investigated the same question? In other words, why didn't Honeycutt just rely on the findings of the previous study and save himself all of the time of doing a similar study at Hughes Aircraft?
4. What OB research methods did Honeycutt use in his research? Do you agree with his choice of methods? Why or why not? If you were going to follow up on Honeycutt's research, what research methods would you use? Why?
5. Do you agree with Honeycutt's conclusions? Why or why not? In explaining your answer, indicate the strengths and weaknesses of this type of OB research.

Notes

1. Honeycutt, A. (1989, May). The key to effective quality circles. *Training and Development Journal*, pp. 81–84.
2. See Note 1, p. 82.
3. See Note 1, p. 84.

EXPERIENCING ORGANIZATIONAL BEHAVIOR

Over the years, we have sometimes heard students (and others) remark, "Sure, OB is interesting. But isn't it just common sense? Didn't we know all this stuff before there ever was a field of OB?" If you hold such views, or if you know someone else who does, try the exercise below.

Organizational Behavior versus Common Sense: A Demonstration

Procedure

Read each statement listed below. Then, for each, indicate whether you feel it is true or false. Indicate your answers by inserting a *T* (for True) or an *F* (for False) in the spaces provided. Also, rate your confidence in the correctness of your answer on a seven-point scale (1 = very low confidence; 7 = very high confidence).

1. In most cases, leaders should stick to their decisions once they have made them, even if it appears that these decisions are wrong.
   Answer: _____ Confidence: _____
2. When people work together in groups and know that their individual contributions can't be easily observed, they each tend to put out less effort than when they work on the same task alone.
   Answer: _____ Confidence: _____
3. The best way to stop a rumor is to present convincing evidence against it.
   Answer: _____ Confidence: _____

4. As morale or satisfaction among employees increases in an organization, overall performance almost always rises.
   Answer: _____ Confidence: _____

5. Relatively few top executives show the Type A behavior pattern (extreme competitiveness, time urgency, aggressiveness).
   Answer: _____ Confidence: _____

6. Providing employees with specific goals often interferes with their performance; they resent being told precisely what to do.
   Answer: _____ Confidence: _____

7. In most organizations, the struggle over limited resources is a far more important cause of conflict than other factors such as interpersonal relations among organization members.
   Answer: _____ Confidence: _____

8. In bargaining, the best strategy for maximizing long-term gains is seeking to defeat one's opponent.
   Answer: _____ Confidence: _____

9. Even skilled interviewers are sometimes unable to avoid being influenced in their judgments by factors other than applicants' qualifications.
   Answer: _____ Confidence: _____

10. In general, groups make more accurate and less extreme decisions than individuals.
    Answer: _____ Confidence: _____

11. Most individuals do their best work under conditions of high stress.
    Answer: _____ Confidence: _____

12. In general, women are higher in self-confidence than men and, for this reason, expect greater success in their careers.
    Answer: _____ Confidence: _____

Points to Consider

Our suggested correct answers to these questions are listed below. How did you do? If you are like most students in our classes, you probably missed at least several items. Was your confidence lower on these items than on the others? Perhaps not, because most people think they know more about organizations and behavior in them than they actually do.

Here is another point to consider: the answers listed below really *are* only suggestions. Each of these questions involves complex situations and processes. Thus, in a real sense, there are no simple answers to them. For example, consider question four. Our suggested answer is False, because contrary to what common sense might suggest, research findings indicate that the relationship between job satisfaction and performance is complex. Under some conditions, increments in satisfaction are related to enhanced performance (see chapter 5). Under other conditions, this is not the case. So, in a sense, the most accurate answer to this question is really "It depends."

The same general point could be made about many of the other questions posed above. As we noted earlier, where organizational behavior and organizations are concerned, there really are no simple answers. We hope this exercise helps to emphasize that important point.

Correct Answers: 1 = T, 2 = T, 3 = F, 4 = F, 5 = T, 6 = F, 7 = F, 8 = F, 9 = T, 10 = F, 11 = F, 12 = F

◼ 2 ◼

PERCEPTION: UNDERSTANDING AND EVALUATING OTHERS

CHAPTER OUTLINE

LEARNING OBJECTIVES

After reading this chapter, you should be able to:
1. Define *perception* and explain why it is an active process.
2. Define *social perception* and indicate its relevance to organizational behavior.
3. Explain how we employ *attribution* to understand the causes of others' behavior.
4. Explain various causes of error in social perception such as the *self-serving bias*, *contrast effects*, and *stereotyping*.
5. Describe the process of *impression management*, and indicate how it can influence important aspects of organizational behavior.
6. Indicate how social perception can affect *job interviews*, *performance appraisal*, and *organizational conflict*.

"Come on in, Joe," Heidi Ogden says with a smile to her coworker at Silex, Inc. "We're almost done. I'll be with you in a minute."

Nodding, Joe takes a seat and watches the interaction between Heidi and Josie Reynolds, one of the people in her work group. Josie is fairly new—she's only been with the company eight months. But she's already had one promotion and seems to be well positioned for another.

"Gee, Ms. Ogden," Josie remarks, "I'm really impressed. You sure know your stuff. I hope that someday I'll know as much about the business as you do. But I know that's going to take me a long time!"

"Oh, not so long," Heidi answers modestly. "You're a quick study if I ever saw one."

"But I have such a great teacher!" Josie bubbles over. "Anyone who couldn't learn from you would *really* be in trouble!"

"Thanks, Josie, I appreciate that. But what about those problems with the D-20—any progress?"

"I think so," Josie replies, wrinkling her forehead. "I've got an idea on how we can handle that. But I want your opinion. I mean, I really value your judgment, so I'd like you to tell me if I'm on the right track."

"Well, why don't you bring in your plans when Joe and I are finished. Give us . . . what do you think, Joe? About an hour?"

"Yeah, that should do it," Joe agrees.

"Great!" Josie exclaims with enthusiasm. "That'll give me time to get my ideas together. Thanks so much . . . I really appreciate your helping me. Oh, by the way, I took care of that problem with the air-conditioning. I know you're so busy that you don't have time for that kind of thing."

"I meant to get around to it, but you know how it is these days. Thanks for getting it off my list."

With this, Josie leaves. Once she's gone, Heidi turns to Joe. "Okay, let's get going. Hey, what's with the big grin?"

"Nothing, nothing."

"Come on, Joe, you're not fooling me. You grin like that only when you think you've had one of your big brainstorms. Give!"

"It's just watching that Josie operate. What a number! Can she ever turn it on!"

"Yeah, she's enthusiastic all right. But you've got to give her credit: there's a kid ready to learn."

"Oh, she's ready to learn all right—ready to learn how to jump over ten other people and maybe even get your job."

Now Heidi is no longer smiling. "What do you mean? I don't think she's like that. She's just kind of . . . cheerful, and energetic."

"And *manipulative,* too," Joe adds, shaking his head. "Oh, Ms. Ogden, if only I could be like you! Oh, Ms. Ogden, you're *so* smart! Oh, Ms. Ogden, is there anything else I can do for you? Just name it!"

"So she's impressed—big deal. I'm darn good, and don't you forget it, Joe Carlucci."

"I won't, don't worry. But I just don't like to see someone use every trick in the book to worm her way inside. You'd better watch out: that kind wants something—they always do. And once she's got it, so long, sister!"

"Well, maybe you're right—up to a point," Heidi agrees reluctantly. "But I think she's basically honest, and I don't care what you say—I *like* her. Anyway, dealing with her is my problem, not yours. So let's get going. I don't want to work until eight again tonight."

———————————■———————————

It is often said that "everyone sees the world through different eyes," and as the incident presented above suggests, this idea—by and large—is true. When exposed to the same information, events, or situations, different people often report sharply contrasting reactions or interpretations. Who is correct about Josie: Heidi or Joe? Heidi views her assistant as enthusiastic and cheerful; Joe sees her as manipulative and dishonest. The existence of such differences in perspective underscores the following point: consistent with what common sense suggests, we do *not* know the world around us in a simple or direct manner. Rather, we actively construct a picture or representation of it through an active and complex process. This process is known as **perception,** and it is the major focus of this chapter. Specifically, we will examine perception as *the process through which we select, organize, and interpret information brought to us by our senses in order to understand the world around us.*[1]

Why is perception important to the field of organizational behavior? Because, quite simply, human behavior in any context—including organizational ones—is largely a function of individuals' current interpretations (perceptions) of the events or situations around them. In other words, people don't respond simply to sensory input supplied by their eyes, ears, nose, mouth, and skin: instead, they actively *process* such information cognitively, and then react to the interpretations derived from such processing. Perhaps a few concrete examples will help clarify these points and illustrate the relevance of perception to important organizational processes.

First, consider again the incident described above. How will Heidi react to Josie's flattering remarks, favors, and earnest requests for guidance? This depends, to an important degree, on Heidi's *perception* of such actions. If she views them as stemming from sincere admiration on Josie's part, she may react favorably, with increased liking. If, in contrast, she views these actions as constituting cold-blooded efforts at ingratiation, she may react in an opposite fashion—with anger and irritation.

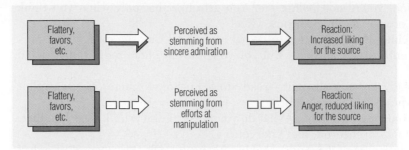

FIGURE 2–1   Perception and Organizational Behavior: An Example

If an individual interprets flattering remarks, favors, and similar actions by another person as a sign of genuine admiration, she may respond with liking for the person who engages in such actions. If, in contrast, she perceives such actions as the basis for manipulation—a setup for future political maneuvers—she may respond in an opposite manner.

Second, in a very different context, imagine that during difficult negotiations, one side offers a concession to the other. How will the opponent react? Again, to a large degree, this depends on how the recipient interprets this action: as a sign of weakness, a genuine effort to reach agreement, or some complex type of trap (see Figure 2–1).

In these and countless other situations, perceptions—interpretations of the external world (and especially other people)—shape the feelings, decisions, and behavior of individuals. Since this principle operates just as strongly in work settings as elsewhere, understanding perception can add appreciably to our grasp of many organizational processes. To increase *your* working knowledge of perception, we will proceed as follows. First, we'll describe several of its basic features—how, in general, it operates. Next, we'll turn to *social perception*, the process through which we attempt to make sense out of the intricate puzzle presented by other people, gaining insight into their traits, motives, and intentions.[2] Third, we'll consider several common *errors* in perception, biases in this process that sometimes lead us seriously astray with respect to important judgments and decisions. Fourth, we'll focus on the process of *impression management*—efforts by individuals to enhance how they appear to others.[3] This is the process that Joe thought was operating in the opening incident, and as we'll soon see, it can have important effects on several aspects of OB. Finally, we'll examine evidence linking perception to three important organizational processes: (1) *employee selection* (job interviews), (2) evaluations of employees' performance (*performance appraisal*), and (3) certain aspects of *organizational conflict*.

PERCEPTION: SOME BASIC FEATURES

At any one moment, we are flooded with input from our various senses. Yet we do not perceive the world as consisting of random collections of colors, sounds, smells, and tastes. On the contrary, we recognize specific objects or people, understand meaningful words and sentences, and notice order and pattern everywhere. These outcomes are due to perception and to the active processing of information it involves. Usually, the construction of a meaningful picture of the world from the raw materials provided by our senses is so automatic that we are hardly aware of its occurrence. Careful study of perception reveals, however, that it actually involves strong tendencies toward *selectivity*.

Attention: Selectivity in Perception

If you've ever been to a noisy party, you are already familiar with the fact that perception is (or at least can be) highly selective. In such settings, you can easily decide to screen out all the voices around you except that of the person to whom you are speaking. This individual's words stand out and make sense; those of all the others blend into a single background buzz. If you then decide that you wish to "tune in" on the conversation of other persons standing nearby, you can do so quite readily. In short, you can shift your *attention* from one person and one conversation to others. In such cases, attention is a conscious process; we decide where to direct it and then do so. In others, however, attention seems to follow a course of its own choosing. For example, many people have great difficulty listening to a dull speaker, no matter how important his or her words. And at other times, we become so absorbed in some activity we are performing (reading a spine-chilling mystery, listening to our favorite kind of music), that we totally fail to notice other events occurring around us—even events that are quite important.

Why is attention important with respect to perception? Because, in a sense, it acts like a filter or gate: only information to which we pay attention can enter our cognitive systems. And only such information, in turn, can contribute to our understanding of the external world. This does not mean, by the way, that we must consciously or purposefully attend to information for it to affect us. Different levels of attention exist, and growing evidence indicates that we can notice, and be affected by, various stimuli even when we can't report, at later times, that we were aware of them.[4] For example, each morning you may comb your hair and brush your teeth while thinking of events totally unrelated to these activities. Clearly, though, your actions while wielding a comb or toothbrush are guided by many stimuli related to these objects and their use. In these and many other cases, we are affected by information from the world around us, or our own actions, without paying careful, conscious attention to them.

A key question with respect to perception is, What factors (other than conscious choice) determine the focus of our attention? Many play a role, but most fall into two major categories.

Personal Influences on Attention: Motives and Attitudes   First, attention is often strongly affected by *personal factors*—ones relating to our current motives and attitudes. For example, imagine that you are attending a dull and tedious meeting. What events do you notice? If it's nearly time for lunch and you skipped breakfast that morning, your attention may be riveted on the smell of cooking food from the nearby company cafeteria. If, instead, you strongly like or dislike the person currently speaking, you may concentrate on his or her words and largely ignore everything else. The basic point is this: in any situation, our attention may, potentially, be directed to a wide range of objects or events. The ones that actually become its focus are usually linked, in some manner, to our motives and attitudes.

External Influences on Attention   Personal factors, however, are only part of the total picture. The focus of our attention is also affected by external factors—various features of events or objects themselves. One such factor is *salience*—the extent to which a given object or event stands out from the others around it. For example, if

Although someone may be working diligently on a task, he or she may continue scanning the environment for important stimuli. For example, an employee's attention can be diverted from the task at hand by hearing the faint whisper of his or her name by a supervisor coming from another conversation across the room. [Davies, D. R., & Taylor, A. (1989). Focusing your attention. In J. G. Beaumont (Ed.), *Brain power: Unlock the power of your mind* (pp. 26–31). New York: Harper & Row.]

all the other people at a conference are wearing dark colors, an individual who appears in bright spring colors will be high in salience and stand out from the crowd. In contrast, if the same person is present at a meeting where most others are also dressed in blues, greens, and yellows, he or she will be low in salience and will not be readily noticed.

Other factors that influence attention include *intensity, size, motion,* and *novelty.* To the extent that a given object or event is large, shows motion, and is unusual or unexpected, it will tend to become the focus of our attention. Advertisers are well aware of these principles and often apply them to ads, commercials, and roadside signs. When used effectively, such features are highly successful in capturing attention; indeed, in combination, they are almost impossible to resist.

Attention and On-the-Job Safety: Reactions to Hazard Warnings

Advertisers use basic principles of attention to promote various products or services, whereas safety experts are concerned with this process from a very different perspective. One task they face is assuring that individuals notice—and pay attention to—warnings concerning various hazards. Efforts to accomplish these goals have generally focused on two aspects of hazard warnings: the *content* of the warning message itself, and various *characteristics* of these messages apart from their meaning. With respect to the content of warning messages, it has been found that some words serve as clearer *signals* of hazards than others. For example, the word *DANGER* is recognized by most people as implying much greater hazard than the words *WARNING* and *CAUTION.* Interestingly, although widely accepted guidelines suggest that *WARNING* refers to more serious hazards than does *CAUTION,* research findings indicate that people interpret both these words as equivalent.[5] In addition, to be effective, hazard warnings should tell what the hazards actually are and should describe the consequences of failure to heed the warning.

Turning to *message characteristics,* existing standards suggest that they should be attention-getting (they should stand out from the background), and that they should be easily understood, concise, and durable—they should be resistant to wear, abuse, and damaging environmental conditions. Hazard warnings that comply with such requirements have generally been found to be more effective in inducing people to act in safe ways than warnings that do not (see Figure 2–2).[6]

On jobs that require constant vigilance, employees' concentration and attention can decline rapidly to dangerous levels after about only thirty to forty-five minutes. To avoid this problem, managers can help increase employees' zattention (and productivity) by scheduling short breaks at least once every hour. [Davies, D. R., & Taylor, A. (1989). Focusing your attention. In J. G. Beaumont (Ed.), *Brain power: Unlock the power of your mind* (pp. 26–31). New York: Harper & Row.]

FIGURE 2–2

Hazard Warnings: Basic Requirements

To be effective, hazard warnings should use appropriate *signal* words and should be concise, attention-getting, and durable. Clearly, the hazard warning on the left meets these criteria more fully than the one on the right.

SOCIAL PERCEPTION: UNDERSTANDING OTHERS

Other people are a central part of our lives, both at work and elsewhere. Bosses, coworkers, subordinates, friends, relatives, lovers—all can (and often do) powerfully influence us in many ways. Given this fact, it is not surprising that we often engage in vigorous attempts to understand the people around us—to figure out the reasons behind their actions, to identify their major traits, to recognize their current emotions and their feelings about us. The benefit of attaining accurate information in these respects is obvious: understanding others is essential for interacting with them effectively. To mention just two examples, you certainly wouldn't want to ask your boss for a favor at a time when he or she is angry and irritable. And if an important customer decided to give her business to a competitor, it would be very important for you to know *why* she did so. Clearly, then, **social perception**—the task of combining, integrating, and interpreting information about others to gain an accurate understanding of them—is important.

Several decades of research on social perception leaves little doubt that it is a complex process. Among its most important components, however, are **attribution**—efforts to identify the causes behind others' behavior, and **social information processing** (or **social cognition**)—cognitive processes that shape the ways in which we sort, store, and later remember information about other people.[7]

Attribution: Identifying the Causes of Others' Behavior

One question we ask repeatedly about other people is "Why?" Why did your boss decide to call a meeting at 4:30 P.M. on Friday? Why did one of your suppliers fail to deliver a major order on time? Why does Randi Helson in Accounting always wait at least a day before returning your calls? In short, one thing we frequently want to know about others is *why* they have acted in certain ways. On closer examination, this question breaks down into two major parts: (1) What are others really like—in other words, what major traits or characteristics do they possess? and (2) Did their actions stem primarily from internal causes (their own traits, motives, values) or primarily from external causes (factors relating to the situation in which they operate)? Research findings suggest that we attempt to answer these two questions in somewhat different ways.[8]

From Acts to Dispositions: Using Others' Behavior as a Guide to Their Traits   Understanding others' major traits can often be very useful. For example, knowing that your opponent in a negotiating session has a reputation for starting with an extreme position but then backing down and making concessions if her opponent stands firm can be very helpful in bargaining with her. Similarly, knowing that one of your subordinates is always punctual, whereas another is usually late, can be quite useful to you in deciding which to send as your representative to an important meeting. But how, precisely, do we go about identifying others' traits? In general, we do so by observing their behavior and then *inferring* their traits from this information.[9]

At first glance, this might seem to be an easy task. Other people are always doing *something*, so we have a rich source of evidence on which to draw. Unfortunately, there are complications to consider. Perhaps the most important is that others sometimes attempt to conceal their major traits, especially if these are generally viewed as undesirable. Thus, employees who are careless, lazy, and unprincipled do their best to hide these facts from view, and will demonstrate them only under conditions where they feel it is safe to do so, or when their "social guard" is down.

Despite such difficulties, we can use several techniques to cut through others' efforts to conceal some of their traits. First, we can focus on their behavior in situations

Test Bank questions 2.7–2.9, 2.47, 2.56, and 2.67 relate to material on this page.

where they do not *have to* behave in a pleasant or socially acceptable manner. It is in precisely such contexts that people often "tip their hand" concerning their basic traits and motives. For example, everyone tends to act courteously toward the company president. But what happens when they are dealing with secretaries or other subordinates? Under these conditions, some will behave in an arrogant, condescending manner. And this, attribution theory suggests, tells us a lot about the kind of person they *really* are.

Similarly, we can learn much by examining behaviors for which there is only one plausible explanation. Many actions people perform can stem from several potential causes. For example, suppose that someone with whom you have an appointment shows up thirty minutes late. There are many possible explanations for such behavior: she got lost, was stuck in traffic, or was detained at her last meeting. Which is correct? It is difficult to tell. But now, suppose you learn from a friend that your tardy visitor actually arrived in the building thirty minutes early, but then went to a nearby coffee shop, where she calmly waited until well past the appointed time. Under these conditions, you would probably conclude that this person was playing some kind of status game with you; after all, no other explanation for her actions seems plausible.

By focusing on these and other unusual aspects of others' behavior, we often *can* gain accurate knowledge of their major traits and characteristics. And this, in turn, is often useful in planning future interactions with them.

Causal Attribution: Another Aspect of the Question "Why?"   Imagine that you observe the following scene. A manager storms into his subordinate's office and proceeds to rake this person over the coals. He shouts, waves his arms in anger, and threatens the subordinate with dire consequences if his work does not improve. After witnessing this incident, what might you conclude? One possibility is that you would attribute the manager's behavior to internal causes, deciding that he has a bad temper, lacks self-control, and is generally ineffective as a supervisor. In fact, this outcome is likely. We seem to have a strong tendency to attribute others' actions to internal factors when strong evidence to the contrary is lacking.

Another possible interpretation of this scene, though, is markedly different. You might conclude that the manager is simply responding to unbearable behavior on the part of the subordinate. In other words, you might guess that this person has provoked the manager repeatedly by refusing to follow his instructions, by very sloppy work, or by an obvious lack of motivation. In this case, you would explain the manager's behavior (and answer the question "Why?") largely in terms of external causes.

In this and many other situations, the conclusions you reach about the relative importance of internal and external causes in shaping others' behavior can have important consequences. If you decide that someone has acted in a specific way because of internal causes (e.g., the person's own nature or personality), you will expect that person to behave in the same manner on future occasions, and may adjust your relations with her or him accordingly. In contrast, if you decide that someone has acted in a specific way because of external causes (e.g., some event or situation in the world around her or him), you will realize that the person's behavior might be very different under other circumstances and you will not expect her or him to act in the same way at other times. How do we choose between these possibilities? A very large body of research findings suggests the following answer.[10]

In our efforts to determine whether another person has acted in some manner because of internal or external causes, we rely on information about three factors. First, we consider the extent to which other people also behave in the same manner;

this is known as *consensus*. Second, we consider the extent to which this person acts in the same manner at other times; this is known as *consistency*. Finally, we consider the extent to which this person behaves in the same manner in other contexts; this is known as *distinctiveness*. (If he or she acts in the same manner in other contexts or situations, distinctiveness is *low*.) Information about these three factors is then combined and forms the basis for our decisions as to the causes behind another's behavior. More precisely, if consensus, consistency, and distinctiveness are all high, we conclude that this person's actions have probably stemmed from *external* causes. (This means that most other people act like this one, that this person behaves in the same manner at other times, and that this person does *not* act in the same manner in other situations or contexts.) In contrast, if consensus and distinctiveness are low, but consistency is high, we conclude that this person's actions probably stemmed from *internal* causes. (Here, most other people do not act like this one, this person acts in the same manner in other situations, and he or she also acts in the same manner at other times.)

Since these comments about causal attribution have been somewhat abstract, let's consider a concrete example to see how the process actually works. Imagine that during an important business lunch, one of the representatives of another company complains about her food, makes critical remarks about the waiter, and indicates strong dislike for the restaurant's decor. Further, imagine that no other member of the group acts in a similar way (consensus is low), you have seen this person act in the same manner at other times (consistency is high), and you have also seen her complain in this fashion in other settings (e.g., during meetings and negotiation sessions; thus, distinctiveness is low). What would you conclude? Probably that her behavior stems from internal causes: she is a "picky" person, difficult to please.

Now, instead, imagine that several other members of the luncheon group also complain about their food and the service (consensus is high), that you have seen this person complain in the same restaurant at other times (consistency is high), but that you have *not* seen her complain in other settings (e.g., at meetings, in other restaurants). In this case, you would probably conclude that her current behavior stems mainly from external causes: the restaurant really *is* inferior in several respects. (See Figure 2–3 on p. 48 for a summary of these contrasting conclusions.)

Do we really think about others, and the causes behind their actions, in this manner? A large body of evidence suggests that we do.[11] However, two additional points should be noted. First, we don't engage in this type of effortful, cognitive work in every situation. Rather, we are most likely to perform it when faced with unexpected actions by others—ones we can't readily or simply explain.[12] Second, in thinking about the causes behind others' behavior, we also frequently consider another dimension in addition to the internal-external one we have just described: whether these causes are *stable* (lasting) or *unstable* (temporary).[13] For example, as we will see in more detail in our later discussion of *performance appraisal*, it is important to know whether a given level of performance stems mainly from temporary causes, such as *effort*, or more stable causes, such as *ability* or *experience*. The former can readily be changed; the latter can be altered only slowly, if at all. That managers do, in fact, pay careful attention to this dimension is suggested by a study carried out by Knowlton and Mitchell.[14] In this laboratory simulation, participants had the task of supervising three subordinates, all of whom were assistants of the researchers. Two of these individuals showed an average level of task performance, whereas the third was either very high or very low in performance. Subjects also received information suggesting that the performance of the standout subordinate stemmed mainly from ability or mainly from effort. The investigators predicted that when later asked to evaluate the performance of all three individuals, subjects would

FIGURE 2–3

Causal Attribution: How It Operates

In determining whether others' behavior stems mainly from internal or external causes, we focus on the three types of information illustrated here.

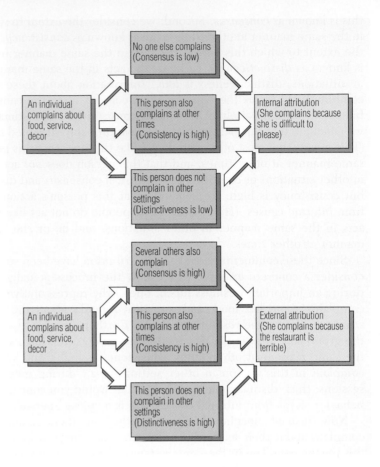

be more extreme in their evaluations of the high- or low-performing subordinate when his behavior seemed to stem mainly from effort rather than from ability. Results offered clear support for this prediction.

In sum, and to put the process of attribution in context, because other people play such an important role in our lives, we often think about them. When we do, one of the key questions we ask is, "Why have they acted in certain ways?" To answer this question, we pay careful attention to certain informative aspects of their behavior—what they say and do. Then, from such information, we infer the answers we seek. Finally, we apply such knowledge (our best-guess understanding of others) to our relations with them. In later sections, we'll return to the question of how such attributions (and other aspects of social perception) play an important role in several organizational processes.

Cognitive Factors in Social Perception

There can be little doubt that understanding others requires considerable mental (cognitive) effort. Making sense out of their behavior, understanding their motives, identifying their key traits—all these activities require detailed thought and careful reasoning. Given this fact, it is clear that in order to understand social perception and the ways in which it shapes our evaluations of others, we must comprehend the many cognitive processes on which it is based. In other words, we must understand the ways in which information about others is sorted or categorized, converted to a form that can be entered into memory (*encoded*), actually stored in our memory systems, and later retrieved and used. Together, these processes are known as *social cognition*, and they have been the subject of a very large amount of research.[15,16] In the remainder of this section, we will call your attention to several key aspects of social cognition—ones that have important implications for practical organizational issues such as appraising job performance.

Schemas: Cognitive Frameworks for Understanding the External World   Have you ever been in a situation where you were flooded with new information—unfamiliar facts, terms, and relationships that seemed to whiz by with little meaning? Almost everyone has had this experience, and most find it disconcerting. These experiences are so bewildering because, in them, we lack *cognitive frameworks* for handling the incoming information. In other words, we have no existing mental categories or knowledge structures into which such input can be entered. The result: the new information seems to float about freely, with no logical connections to other knowledge already at our disposal. And without such mental "anchors," it is often quickly lost.

Fortunately, of course, this is not typical of our daily lives. In general, we *do* possess the kind of cognitive frameworks referred to above. These are known as **schemas,** and they develop gradually, out of our experience with various facets of the world around us.[17] For example, through a wide range of interactions with others, we form *person schemas*—internal frameworks representing various traits that others can possess. Once such schemas have developed, they play an important part in our comprehension of information about coworkers, friends, and any other individuals we encounter. Similarly, we develop *event schemas* (or *scripts*)—internal knowledge frameworks for various types of situations. For example, most people possess an event schema for business meetings. Such schemas suggest that meetings will begin with a call to order, perhaps followed by reading of the minutes from the last meeting. This will be followed by discussion or presentation of various items on the agenda. Then, at some point, the meeting will be brought to a formal close. Event schemas exist for many other events or situations as well.

What effects do schemas have once they are formed? This is the key point of our present discussion. Growing evidence suggests that once these cognitive frameworks take shape, they exert powerful effects on how we handle new information, including information about other people (see Figure 2–4).[18] First, schemas affect *attention*—

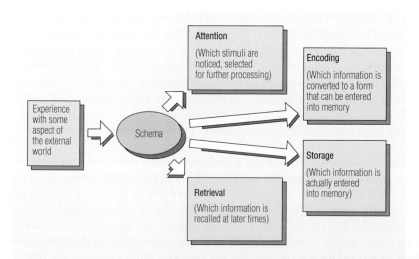

FIGURE 2-4

Schemas: An Overview

Schemas are cognitive frameworks developed through experience. Once formed, they exert powerful effects on attention and on the encoding, storage, and retrieval of information about the external world.

they determine what events or stimuli we notice. In particular, we tend to notice events or actions by others that are inconsistent with existing schemas. For example, if an individual begins to read poetry or to make off-color remarks at a business meeting, we quickly notice such behaviors even if, up to that point, we were almost falling asleep. The unexpected nature of such actions, and their inconsistency with operative schemas, makes them highly attention-getting.

Second, schemas influence what information is entered into memory (*encoded*). Input that is somehow *relevant* to existing schemas often stands a better chance of being retained than information that is totally irrelevant to these internal knowledge structures. And among such input, information that contradicts or is inconsistent with existing schemas is often easier to retain than information that is consistent.[19] The reason for this is that when confronted with input that contradicts our existing knowledge frameworks, we stop and think about it more carefully than we do when information fits with such schemas.[20] The result is that it has a better chance of being entered into memory. For example, consider the case of a subordinate who suddenly turns in a report that is far better than her previous efforts. Many managers would spend much more time puzzling over this unexpectedly good performance than they would spend thinking about a more typical, mediocre report by the same person.

Finally, schemas also shape *retrieval*—they determine what information is recalled from memory in various situations. When, for example, a manager attempts to recall a subordinate's performance in order to rate it on the yearly or semiyearly evaluation form, she is most likely to remember information consistent with her schema for this person—or for the group to which he or she belongs. Thus, if this schema is one that could be described by the label "arrogant, moody people," the manager will remember information consistent with this framework—she will recall instances in which the subordinate was unpleasant or irritable. If, instead, the schema is one that could be labeled "hardworking, cooperative employees," she is likely to remember incidents and actions by the subordinate that fits *this* cognitive framework.

In sum, schemas strongly affect what information about others we notice, what information about them we enter into memory, and what information we recall at later times when we evaluate them in various ways. Clearly, these cognitive frameworks are a key factor in social perception and in its impact on organizational processes.

Schemas and Stereotypes In several later chapters of this book, we will discuss **stereotypes** and their impact in work settings. For example, in chapter 5 we will consider stereotypes relating to gender and in chapter 9 we will comment on stereotypes relating to age. Here, we merely wish to note that stereotypes can be viewed as a special type of schema. They are schemas that relate membership in a particular category to inferred personal attributes. In short, they are cognitive frameworks suggesting that people belonging to particular groups (e.g., women, older employees) all share certain traits or characteristics. Like other schemas, stereotypes strongly affect the interpretation and processing of social information. Information relevant to a particular stereotype is more likely to be noticed than information unrelated to such frameworks. And stereotype-consistent information is often more likely to be remembered than information that is inconsistent. Perhaps a concrete example will be helpful.

Consider a male manager who possesses a well-developed stereotype for women. On one occasion, he observes a female member of his department crying. Because of his gender-related schema (his stereotype), his attention is drawn to this event, and he notices it very clearly. Now, six months later, he is asked to evaluate her performance. Again, the stereotype comes into operation. As a result, he remembers this incident vividly—much more vividly than many other actions that are more directly relevant to job performance. Finally, his memory of this event leads him to

Organizations need to be aware of the unintended stereotypes that may be portrayed in their advertising. For example, several years ago, Quaker Foods was pressured by African-American groups to change its "Aunt Jemima" character that had represented Quaker Foods since 1889. In response to such customer demands, Quaker Foods transformed the character into a sophisticated and modern spokeswoman. [Westerman, M. (1989, March). Death of the Frito Bandito. *American Demographics*, pp. 28–32.]

infer that she is not ready for added responsibility, and he down-rates her for this reason. Other stereotypes operate in a corresponding fashion. Indeed, when such frameworks are strongly established, they have powerful and general effects on our perceptions of others. As we will soon see, this, in turn, can have important implications for key organizational processes. (For information about how we perceive organizations, see the **Focus on Research** section on pp. 52–53.)

WHEN SOCIAL PERCEPTION FAILS: ERRORS IN OUR EFFORTS TO UNDERSTAND OTHERS

Have you ever failed to notice a STOP sign? Has the moon ever appeared to you to be much larger when near the horizon than when overhead? If so, you already know that our perceptions of the physical world are often incorrect. For some reason, we interpret the information brought to us by our senses incorrectly, and so arrive at false conclusions. If perception can encounter such difficulties with respect to the physical world, it is hardly surprising that it can fail—and fail badly—with respect to interpretations of other people. We will now describe several types of errors relating to the process of social perception that are both common and potentially destructive.

Errors in Attribution

When we described *attribution,* our comments implied that it is a highly rational process—one in which we use all information at our disposal to identify the causes of others' behavior. Usually, this is the case; attribution *is* logical and accurate in many respects. However, it is also subject to several forms of bias that can generate serious errors in our thinking about other people.

We have already mentioned one of these—our tendency to explain others' actions in terms of internal rather than external causes. In other words, we perceive others as behaving as they do because they possess certain traits or dispositions. The many external factors that may also affect their behavior tend to be ignored, or at least downplayed. This tendency is so strong and general that it has sometimes been termed the **fundamental attribution error.**[21] Its presence seems to derive from the fact that it is easier to explain others' actions in terms of discrete traits than in terms of a complex pattern of situational factors that might also have affected their actions. Unfortunately, this type of attributional error can be quite damaging. It leads us to expect greater consistency in others' behavior than we should; then we are surprised and chagrined when they act "out of character" in some new situation, and this can contribute to tension and conflict.

A second type of attributional error involves our tendency to attribute success or other positive outcomes to internal causes (our own admirable qualities!) but failure or other negative outcomes to external causes (factors beyond our control). This is known as the **self-serving bias,** a very common tendency. As a concrete example of this form of error, consider the case of an individual who submits a report to his boss, only to receive harsh criticism of it. How will he explain her comments? The chances are good that he will do so in terms of external factors—his boss's unrealistic standards, her failure to *really* understand the report, and so on. But what if, instead, he receives high praise for the report? He will likely explain this outcome in terms of internal factors, such as his own talent, effort, and diligence.

Interestingly, recent findings indicate that females are less likely to demonstrate the self-serving bias than males.[22] At first, this might sound like a plus for women: after all, they are less likely to make an important form of attributional error than men. In fact, however, quite the opposite may be true. A reluctance to explain away failures in terms of external causes, and a corresponding hesitancy to take personal credit for successes, may operate to lower women's self-esteem, and so work against them in many contexts (see chapter 5 for further discussion of this point).

What accounts for the self-serving bias? Two factors seem to play a role. First, the self-serving bias allows us to protect or enhance our self-esteem. If we are responsible for positive outcomes but are not to blame for negative ones, our feelings about our own worth may be bolstered. Second, the self-serving bias permits us to

 FOCUS ON RESEARCH

What's in a Name? The Origins of Company Reputations

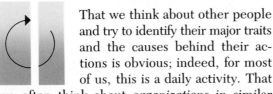 That we think about other people and try to identify their major traits and the causes behind their actions is obvious; indeed, for most of us, this is a daily activity. That we often think about *organizations* in similar ways, however, is just as obvious. For example, we attach labels such as *aggressive, dynamic, reliable,* or *old-fashioned* to individual companies on the basis of their past actions. Together, such perceptions form the basis for their *reputations*—overall evaluations of the companies' success, competence, and future prospects.[23] A positive reputation can be a valuable asset for organizations. For example, it may enable them to charge higher prices than competitors, to gain favorable treatment in capital markets, and to attract desirable employees.[24] Conversely, an unfavorable reputation may place organizations at a distinct disadvantage relative to competitors in all these respects. Cultivating and maintaining a favorable reputation, then, is an activity few companies can afford to ignore. But what factors contribute to such reputations—to the public's perceptions of organizations? A major study by Fombrun and Shanley offers revealing answers to this question.[25]

These researchers hypothesized that company reputations are based on a wide range of factors or *signals*. These include *market signals,* such as recent market performance and dividend policy; *accounting signals,* such as profitability and risk (variation in return on investment); *institutional signals,* such as ownership of the company's stock by financial institutions and its

contributions to social programs; visibility in *mass media;* and *strategy signals,* such as the extent to which the company is differentiated from competitors and its policies concerning diversification in its product line(s).

To examine the role of these and other factors in company reputations, Fombrun and Shanley examined their effects on the replies of more than 8,000 executives who responded to a *Fortune* survey in which they were asked to rate the reputations of 292 corporations. The executives rated these companies on a number of different dimensions, including quality of management, quality of products or services, long-term investment value, innovativeness, financial soundness, and ability to attract, develop, and keep talented people. Measures of each potential predictor of company reputation were obtained from relevant sources. For example, economic performance was assessed in terms of the prior year's return on invested capital, whereas market risk was measured in terms of beta coefficients—an index of variation in stock prices. Institutional ownership was assessed directly in terms of the percentage of all outstanding shares held by institutions (e.g., pension funds, mutual funds, and so on), and media exposure was measured in terms of the number of articles about each company in major business publications. Differentiation from competitors was assessed in terms of advertising expenditures (adjusted for company size) and charitable contributions. Diversification was assessed in terms of data from standard sources relating to this factor (COMPUSTAT).

enhance our public image—to look good to others. Regardless of its precise origins, this type of attributional error is quite common and can be the cause of much interpersonal friction. For example, it may lead each member of a work group to take more credit for success and to blame others for failure to a greater extent than is justified. And it may lead subordinates to view their performance appraisals as unfairly harsh even when their managers view them as quite lenient. In these and many other contexts, the effects of the self-serving bias can be both harmful and serious.

Results indicated that many of the factors identified by Fombrun and Shanley did in fact predict the favorableness of the companies' reputations. Specifically, as shown in Figure 2–5, profitability, advertising intensity, and company size all exerted positive effects on reputation, whereas accounting risk (assessed by variation in return on invested capital during a nine-year period) had a strong negative effect. Similarly, institutional ownership, low dividend yield, and involvement in social concerns exerted positive effects on reputation, whereas a high degree of unrelated product diversification produced a negative impact. Finally, and contrary to initial predictions, increasing exposure in the mass media did *not* enhance companies' reputations. In fact, for highly diversified firms, the opposite was true: the greater the media exposure, the lower their reputations. Since fully 87 percent of the examined articles contained positive content, these effects did *not* seem to reflect the fact that media reports present mainly unfavorable information about organizations. An alternative possibility is that the public reacts negatively to all forms of publicity, perhaps because of concerns about the impact of close public scrutiny on a company's future performance. Whatever the basis for this finding, media exposure appears not to be the unmixed blessing that many executives believe.

In sum, company reputations apparently rest on many different factors—some largely economic, and others less tied to financial results. Influencing the public's perception of all these variables is clearly a complicated task. However, given the important benefits that can flow from a favorable reputation, the task is one that few organizations can afford to ignore.

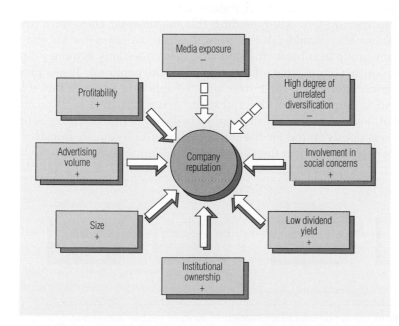

FIGURE 2–5

Company Reputations: Key Factors

As shown here, company reputations derive from a wide range of factors.

Halo Effects: When Overall Impressions Shape Specific Judgments

Have you ever heard the phrase "Love is blind"? It refers to the fact that when individuals are in love, they often lose all ability to evaluate the object of their affection in an accurate, impartial manner. Unfortunately, those in love are not the only ones to fall victim to such effects. Once we form an overall impression of another person, this general reaction often has powerful effects on our judgments of his or her specific traits or performances. These tendencies are collectively known as **halo effects,** and can be either positive or negative. If our impression of another person is favorable, we tend to see everything he or she does or says in a positive light (a favorable halo). If our overall impression is unfavorable, we tend to perceive all of this person's words and actions in a negative manner (a "rusty halo" or "horns" effect).

Another way to think of halo effects in organizational settings is in terms of inflated correlations between various dimensions on which performance is rated. In other words, when the performance of specific employees is rated on several dimensions, halo effects tend to inflate the correlations between these dimensions.[26] Thus, it appears that performance on the various dimensions is more closely linked than is actually the case. In practical terms, this means that people rated high on some dimensions tend to be rated high on others, even if they don't really deserve these ratings. Conversely, people rated low on some dimensions tend to be rated low on others, too. We should add that recent evidence indicates that such effects occur only when the dimensions being rated are, in fact, *not* closely related. When they are highly correlated, halo effects do not seem to inflate them any further. Still, regardless of the precise form they take, there is general agreement on one point: when they occur, halo effects reduce accuracy—they interfere with the task of appraising individuals' performance accurately.[27] (See Figure 2–6 for an overview of the nature and impact of halo effects.)

An intriguing demonstration of the impact of halo effects on important organizational processes is provided by a study conducted by Binning and his colleagues.[28] In this investigation, male and female subjects were provided with information designed to induce either a favorable or unfavorable impression of a job applicant's suitability for a specific job. After reading this information, they were asked to generate questions they would ask this person during an interview for the job in question. A new group of subjects then divided these questions into ones designed to seek either positive or negative information about the applicant. It was predicted that subjects given information suggesting that the applicant was well suited for the job would tend to formulate positive questions—ones designed to confirm their favorable initial impression. In contrast, subjects given information suggesting that the applicant was poorly suited for the job would tend to formulate negative questions—ones designed to confirm their negative initial impression. These predictions

FIGURE 2–6   Halo Effects: Their Basic Nature

Halo effects occur when our overall evaluation of another person affects our judgments of this person with respect to specific traits or dimensions. Halo effects can be positive or negative.

Test Bank questions 2.25 and 2.62 relate to material on this page.

were generally confirmed. The only exception was that when subjects expected to interview an individual of the other gender, they formulated more positive questions for a low-suitability than a high-suitability applicant. This unexpected finding might have stemmed from the fact that in such cases, subjects used positive questions as a form of impression management—to enhance their own attractiveness to the other-gender interviewee.

Although the study conducted by Binning et al. was not specifically designed to study the impact of halo effects, its findings can be interpreted as consistent with the impact of this type of bias. In this context, they suggest that halo effects can operate in a disturbing self-fulfilling manner. Once they exist, they shape interactions between the persons involved so that they tend to be confirmed.

Similar-to-Me Effects

It is a well-established principle in the behavioral sciences that individuals tend to like others who are similar to themselves better than others who are dissimilar. Since we tend to evaluate people we like more favorably than people we dislike (refer to our discussion of halo effects above), it seems reasonable to expect that perceived similarity might operate as an additional source of perceptual error or bias in organizational settings. In fact, this appears to be the case. The higher the perceived similarity between supervisors and their subordinates, the higher the performance ratings they assign to one another.[29] Thus, similarity, or the **similar-to-me effect,** as it is often termed, constitutes another potential source of bias with respect to social perception.

Actually, three distinct types of similarity seem to exert such influences, so perhaps a better term would be similar-to-me effects. The first of these, *perceived similarity,* refers to the extent to which people in a given work setting believe that they share a similar outlook, values, and work habits. The second, termed *perceptual congruence*, focuses more directly on work-related behaviors. It involves the degree to which subordinates and supervisors hold similar views about the factors important in receiving merit pay raises. In other words, such similarity reflects the extent to which subordinates and their supervisors agree about what, precisely, constitutes good performance. A third type of similarity, *demographic similarity*, relates to the extent to which supervisors and subordinates resemble one another in terms of race, age, educational level, and years of experience.

That all three types of similarity play an important part in organizations is indicated by a recent study conducted by Turban and Jones.[30] These researchers asked subordinates and supervisors at a large rehabilitation center to provide information on each of the three types of similarity mentioned above. In addition, subordinates reported their level of satisfaction with their jobs and the organization, whereas supervisors provided overall ratings of their subordinates' performance. When these factors were correlated, each type of similarity was found to be significantly related to both subordinate job satisfaction and performance.

These findings, and those of related studies, suggest that subordinates who are similar to their supervisors in several respects may have an unfair advantage over those who are not. Correspondingly, supervisors who are perceived as similar by their subordinates may also gain an advantage. We should add, however, that these effects may constitute more than the operation of yet another form of perceptual bias. Additional findings gathered by Turban and Jones indicate that subordinates have greater trust and confidence in supervisors they perceive as similar to themselves than in those they perceive as dissimilar. This suggests that perceived similarity among the people in a work group may contribute to positive relationships between them. This factor, not merely perceptual bias, may account for the higher evaluations

People tend to prefer others who are similar to themselves—especially those others who are physically attractive. Recently, scientists have analyzed the component features of attractive people. They found that those believed to be most attractive were *not* blessed with rare physical beauty, but had features representative of the mathematical average of all facial features in a particular population. Apparently, being "average" might not be so bad after all. [Bower, B. (1990, May 12). Average attractions: Psychologists break down the essence of physical beauty. *Science News*, pp. 298–299.]

assigned by supervisors to similar subordinates. In sum, although it is important to guard against similar-to-me effects when they operate to distort accurate evaluations of performance, increasing perceived similarity between supervisors and their subordinates may yield actual benefits that should not be overlooked. (For more information on the potential benefits of similarity in work settings, see the **International/Multicultural Perspective** section below.)

Stereotypes: Fitting Others into Cognitive Molds of Our Own Making

A final type of error in perceiving others is one we have already described: the operation of stereotypes. As you may recall, these are schemas that suggest that membership in a particular group or category is associated with possession of various traits. One result of stereotypes is that people holding them tend to perceive all members of various groups (especially ones other than their own) as being very much alike (as sharing the same traits and behaviors). And in many cases, these shared traits are seen as largely negative.[31]

You are probably already quite familiar with the nature and impact of some stereotypes—ones relating to race, gender, and age. These have been the subject of a great deal of concern and attention in recent years, as efforts to overcome their negative effects in work settings, and in society generally, have been instituted. However, you may not be as aware of the existence of several other stereotypes that

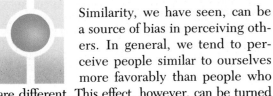

AN INTERNATIONAL/MULTICULTURAL PERSPECTIVE

In Search of Diversity: Matching Work Force to Customer Base at Kinney Shoes

Similarity, we have seen, can be a source of bias in perceiving others. In general, we tend to perceive people similar to ourselves more favorably than people who are different. This effect, however, can be turned to good purpose in another context: efforts by many companies in the United States to reflect the cultural diversity of the customers they serve. One impressive example of such efforts is provided by Kinney Shoes, a national chain that operates more than 4,000 stores selling footwear and accessories from coast to coast.[32]

"At Kinney, we recognize that everyone isn't the same. Therefore, we're concentrating on treating these differences fairly," says John Kozlowski, the company's senior vice president of human resources. Putting this principle into practice involves special efforts to hire sales staff similar in ethnic and cultural background to the customers they assist. This involves combating the notion that all successful sales personnel will fit into a single mold—for example, that they

must speak standard, accent-free English (see Figure 2–7). Instead, the company concentrates on recruiting and hiring the best talent in the area of each store. "We stress that talent is color- and gender-blind and culture-neutral," says Bob Jacinto, director of Kinney's Office of Fair Employment Practice. And he adds, "America isn't sameness anymore. New York City is a majority minority city. California will be a majority minority state by the year 2000. To assume we're a homogeneous work force that is northern European–based is a fallacy."

But Kinney does more than simply concentrate on hiring qualified people from a wide range of cultural backgrounds. It also conducts workshops and seminars designed to help employees appreciate and understand cultural differences and the special problems of women and minorities. Through the discussion of how people from different backgrounds may perceive a given situation in contrasting terms, employees' sensitivity to such matters is increased. For example, one situation covered in the workshops involves

also have powerful effects on key organizational processes. Extremely common are the stereotypes held by individuals trained in various professions or occupations about individuals in other professions or occupations. For example, accountants may be heard to remark, "Oh, you know what those scientist types are like . . . they haven't the slightest idea of keeping track of costs." Conversely, scientists in a research and development unit may state, "Those people in accounting can drive you nuts; all they ever do is worry about those #$%!& forms!" Stereotypes also often exist with respect to departments or work groups. Thus, people in Maintenance may stereotype those in Production; people in Marketing may stereotype those in Engineering; and so on. Obviously, to the extent that various groups in an organization hold stereotypes of one another, communication may suffer and the likelihood of conflict may increase. We'll return to such effects in more detail in chapter 13.

Why do stereotypes exist? Several factors, all relating to the basic ways in which we process information about others, seem to play a part. First, as human beings, we seem to possess a basic tendency to divide the world into two social categories: *us* and *them*. Moreover, people we perceive as outside our own group are viewed as being more similar to one another than people in our own group. In other words, because we have less information about them, we tend to lump them all together, and see them as quite homogeneous.[33] Second, stereotypes seem to derive, in part, from our tendency to do as little cognitive work as possible in thinking about other people.[34] If, by assigning individuals to particular groups, we can assume that we know much about them (their major traits, how they tend to act), we save the tedious

the case of a supervisor publicly praising an employee. If this person is of European descent, that may be an appropriate course of action: such praise is viewed in largely positive terms. But if the person is, say, a Native American, he or she may be greatly embarrassed by such praise and find it an unpleasant experience.

Kinney feels that the knowledge and skills gained in this program, known in the company as *Workforce 2000*, enhance employees' abilities to work together and to serve the company's customer base. In addition, the program pro-

vides other benefits, such as smoothing the disruptions that often follow when promising managers are moved from one area of the country to another—for example, from a rural setting in Iowa or Idaho to an urban one such as Chicago or New York.

As Jacinto sums it up, "Any issues that are issues for the U.S. population in general certainly will be manifested in our corporation. Unfortunately, we've found so few other retailers who are making this type of effort that it's shocking. I say 'Good, we have the advantage here. . . .'"

FIGURE 2–7

Reflecting Cultural Diversity: A Key Task for U.S. Corporations

At Kinney Shoes, Inc., special efforts are currently under way to reflect the ethnic and cultural diversity of customers in the backgrounds of the company's sales staff.

work of understanding them as individuals. Apparently, this shortcut to social perception is too tempting to resist in many cases.

Whatever their origins, stereotypes can exert powerful effects on several aspects of organizational behavior, from performance appraisals to conflict. Thus, they are certainly one potential source of error with important practical consequences.

IMPRESSION MANAGEMENT: THE FINE ART OF LOOKING GOOD

The desire to make favorable impressions on others is virtually universal. Few people are willing to give up on this task as readily as the person in Figure 2–8. On the contrary, most of us engage in active efforts to control how we appear to others—and in particular, to appear in the best or most favorable light possible. This process is known as **impression management,** and considerable evidence indicates that being able to perform it successfully can be a major plus for individuals' careers.[35] For example, existing impressions of employees strongly affect evaluations of their performance.[36] And such effects tend to persist even in the face of contradictory information, so that evaluations of people viewed as poor performers tend to rise relatively slowly if their performance improves, whereas evaluations of people viewed as good performers tend to drop relatively slowly if their track records deteriorate. Only if changes in performance are attributed by raters to internal causes (ability, effort) do comparatively rapid shifts in evaluations occur.[37]

In the remainder of this discussion, we'll first examine some of the tactics individuals use for creating favorable impressions on others and then consider the impact of impression management on several forms of organizational behavior.

Impression Management: Specific Tactics

What steps do people take to manage or control the impressions others form about them? And which of these steps are actually effective in producing such outcomes? Systematic research on these issues has revealed some intriguing answers.[38]

It appears that specific tactics can be divided into two major groups known, respectively, as *self-enhancing* and *other-enhancing* behaviors. Included in the first category are actions that focus on enhancing the personal appeal of the individual

FIGURE 2–8

Impression Management: How *Not* to Do It

Few people would present themselves in this manner for a job interview. On the contrary, most engage in active efforts to enhance the impressions they make on others. (*Source:* Drawing by Stan Hunt; © 1983 The New Yorker Magazine, Inc.)

"I'd just like to say, sir, that I always make a bad first impression."

Test Bank questions 2.53, 2.64, and 2.72 relate to material on this page.

engaging in impression management. Many of these tactics involve efforts to improve one's appearance through dress and personal grooming. Such tactics have been the focus of many popular books (e.g., *Dress for Success* and its many offshoots), and existing evidence indicates that such efforts are often effective, at least up to a point.[39] For example, it has been found that when women dress in a professional manner (business suit or dress, subdued jewelry), they are evaluated more favorably for management positions than when they dress in a more traditionally feminine manner (patterned dresses, large or dangling jewelry).[40] Similarly, other research indicates that although a small amount of perfume or cologne is viewed as acceptable in a business setting, a highly noticeable level is not, and may generate negative reactions to the wearer.[41]

Perhaps the most intriguing self-enhancing tactic uncovered to date involves requests for feedback from others as a form of impression management.[42] At first glance, asking for feedback might appear to have little connection to efforts at impression management, but in fact the two are sometimes closely linked. First, it is clear that in most organizations, seeking advice and guidance about one's work is viewed favorably; after all, how can people improve if they don't have such input at their disposal? Thus, the mere act of inviting feedback can boost one's image. As noted by Morrison and Bies, however, even more important are the *when, whom,* and *how* of feedback-seeking behavior.[43] In other words, the trick, from the point of view of enhancing one's image, is knowing when to ask for feedback, whom to ask, and how to pose such requests. In terms of when to ask, it is usually better to request feedback after a positive event (e.g., a good performance) than after a negative one (e.g., a poor performance). With respect to whom to ask, it is often more advantageous to seek feedback from high-status, powerful people within an organization than from low-status, low-power people—especially, again, after a favorable performance.

The question of how to ask for feedback is somewhat more complicated and involves the use of several different, but related, tactics. All involve providing the target person with cues suggesting how the request for feedback should be interpreted. For example, to increase one's responsibility for a favorable outcome, a feedback seeker can use *entitlement*—making such statements as "I really knocked myself out on this project—what do you think of it?" To reduce responsibility for a negative outcome, in contrast, a feedback seeker might use an *excuse:* "That new competitor is really gouging and using unfair tactics. But taking that into account, what do you think of our figures this quarter?" A third tactic—*enhancement*—involves presenting a request for feedback along with statements of positive reactions from others: "Harry and Kawanda really *loved* this idea; what do you think of it?" In these and many other ways, individuals can use requests for feedback more as a tactic for bolstering their own image than as one for improving their performance.

Additional self-enhancing tactics include statements about one's experience and competence, name-dropping (claiming acquaintance with well-known, high-status people), relatively rapid speech (which conveys the impression of intelligence or verbal quickness), and, sometimes, self-deprecating comments—ones suggestive of a reasonable amount of modesty.

Other-enhancing tactics include strategies such as flattery: undeserved praise of target people, agreement with their views or opinions, showing a high degree of interest in them, and demonstrating liking or approval of them, either verbally or nonverbally (through smiles, nods, and similar actions)—are all in widespread use. An additional tactic involves doing favors for others—favors considerably smaller than the ones impression managers want in return.

Do such tactics work? A growing body of evidence suggests that if used with skill and care, they do. For example, in one laboratory study on this topic, Godfrey, Jones, and Lord asked pairs of strangers to carry on two brief conversations with

Although creating a good impression is important, top executives try not to be overly concerned about what others think of them. Instead, they recommend that people strike a balance between worrying about self-presentation and the information presented by others. People often perform better when they concentrate not only on what they are communicating to others, but also on the information these people are presenting to them. [Stone, J. (1988, April). Second thoughts on first impressions: Are they really so important? *Glamour,* p. 120.]

each other.[44] After the first conversation, one person in each pair was asked to try to make the other person like him or her as much as possible. The others were not given such instructions. After the second conversation, participants in the study rated each other on a number of dimensions. In addition, two trained raters coded and analyzed videotapes of the conversations. Results indicated that participants told to ingratiate themselves with their partners succeeded in doing so: they were rated as more likable by these persons after the second conversation than after the first. Further, some of the factors behind this success were apparent in the videotapes. The persons engaging in impression management reduced the amount of time they spoke, and listened to their partners more. They also showed more agreement with these persons from the first to the second conversation. In contrast, participants who were not instructed to engage in impression management did not demonstrate such changes.

In sum, impression management is a process in which most people engage on various occasions. It involves a wide range of different tactics, but all are directed toward a single common goal: inducing positive feelings, reactions, and attributions toward the impression managers among the target persons. And, it appears, impression management *works:* it often produces the kinds of effects its users desire.

Impression Management and Organizational Behavior

That many people in work settings use impression management is apparent. But do such tactics have any effect on important aspects of organizational behavior? A skeptic might argue that since almost everyone is familiar with such strategies, their impact would be blunted or minimized in most situations. However, a growing body of empirical evidence suggests that such conclusions are unwarranted; in fact, impression management appears to influence a wide range of organizational processes.

First, consider its effects on performance appraisals. Several studies indicate that various tactics of impression management do influence this crucial aspect of organizational reward systems.[45] Specifically, after working with subordinates who engage or do not engage in impression management tactics (e.g., self- and other-enhancing actions, offers of favors), supervisors rate those who engage in impression management more favorably than those who do not. In addition, they tend to engage in friendlier and more open communication with those who have used impression management than with those who have not.

Second, consider the impact of impression management tactics on the quality of subordinate-supervisor exchanges.[46] Recent findings indicate that subordinates who engage in impression management are liked more by their supervisors, and that such liking, in turn, enhances the quality of their exchanges.

Third, efforts at impression management may also influence the nature and pattern of information about important organizational events that subordinates provide to their supervisors. This fact—and additional revealing information about the conditions that encourage or discourage the use of impression management tactics by subordinates—has been reported by Fandt and Ferris in a well-conducted laboratory study.[47]

In this study, customer service employees in a telecommunications corporation were asked to make decisions concerning a series of realistic customer service problems (e.g., a power failure on a hot summer afternoon). After reading each scenario, they made a decision about how to proceed, and then documented their decisions by writing a brief report to their supervisors and by selecting information items from a list of precoded items, to include a brief oral report to their supervisors. In order to determine the impact of two situational factors on participants' tendencies to engage in impression management, they performed these tasks under conditions of (1) high or low *accountability*—they were informed that they would be responsible for the outcomes that resulted or that they would not be held responsible for such outcomes, and (2) high or low *ambiguity*—either they knew their supervisors' decision in a similar past situation or they did not receive such information. Fandt and Ferris predicted that the tendency to engage in impression management would be strongest under conditions of high accountability and low ambiguity. They felt this would occur because under these circumstances, participants would feel most responsible for the outcomes produced and would also know how their supervisor had acted in similar situations in the past—their past policy preferences.

The extent to which participants engaged in impression management was measured in two ways. First, their written reports were content-analyzed to determine how much information of four types they transmitted to their supervisors: (1) positive information—information reflecting favorably on their decision process; (2) negative information—reflecting unfavorably on their decision process; (3) open information—accepting of responsibility; and (4) defensive information—serving to shift responsibility or cover any mistakes. Second, the extent to which they selected items for their oral presentations previously coded as positive, negative, open, and defensive was assessed. Investigators assumed that the more positive and defensive information participants transmitted to their supervisors but the less negative and open information they transmitted, the greater their tendencies to engage in impression management.

Results offered support for the major prediction: participants were indeed more likely to transmit more positive and defensive and less negative and open pieces of information in the high accountability–low ambiguity condition than in any other (see Figure 2–9). This was true for both measures of impression management.

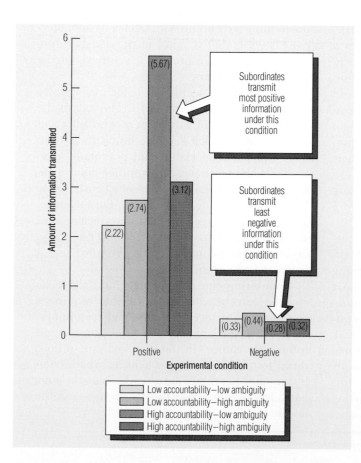

FIGURE 2–9

Impression Management and Subordinate-Supervisor Communication

Customer service employees in a telecommunications company were most likely to engage in impression management when transmitting information to their supervisors under conditions of high accountability and low ambiguity. Under these circumstances, they transmitted more positive and defensive information, and less negative and open information, than was true under any other conditions of accountability and ambiguity. (*Source:* Based on data from Fandt & Ferris, 1990; see Note 47.)

These findings suggest that in order to place themselves in a favorable light, individuals may sometimes screen the information they transmit to supervisors. The result: these people receive a distorted view of various situations—an outcome with potentially serious consequences for them and the organization. (See the **OB in Practice** section below for more information on this issue.)

In sum, impression management appears to be an important process in many organizational settings. Efforts by individuals to create favorable impressions in others frequently occur—and often succeed. To the extent that they do, they can produce distortions in crucial organizational processes such as performance appraisal, feed-

 OB IN PRACTICE

Escaping the Echo Chamber: Or, How to Counter the MUM Effect

 Almost no one enjoys the task of transmitting bad news. (We say "almost" because, of course, a few people do seem to relish such assignments.) In fact, most people shy away so strongly from the role of "bearer of ill tidings" that this tendency has its own name: the **MUM effect.** This refers, especially, to the reluctance of subordinates to transmit negative information to their bosses. Although the MUM effect is completely understandable, it poses a real danger to organizations. If top managers in a company become insulated from bad news and from negative feedback about their ideas and policies, they stand a good chance of living in what some describe as the *echo chamber*—an environment in which all they hear is repetition of their own ideas and agreement with their views. As Andrall Pearson, former president of PepsiCo, puts it, "Once you get a guy making decisions without access to information from competing sources, after a while he's dead."[48]

What can be done to prevent such outcomes—to get managers out of the echo chamber so that they know what's really happening in their organization and get a chance to hear objections to their ideas? One simple solution involves appointing someone as the *devil's advocate*, a role in which the person's assigned task is to object to the majority view. More formal procedures are used by Anheuser-Busch for its top policy-making committee. Whenever this committee considers a major initiative—making a big expenditure, getting into or leaving a busi-

ness—it assigns specific teams to argue for each side of the question. Sometimes there are two teams, sometimes three. Each team has the task of marshaling all the arguments and evidence it can for a specific view. And usually, members of the teams are specifically chosen to be in favor of a position other than the one for which they must argue. Pat Stokes, a senior executive at Anheuser-Busch, comments that through this procedure "we end up with decisions and alternatives we hadn't thought of previously"—positions that often represent a synthesis of the competing positions.

Another useful technique is for managers to keep their personal staffs small. This avoids the "helpful" actions of gatekeepers who filter out negative information—and so help to seal their bosses into a comfortable, but potentially dangerous, echo chamber. Still another point managers should remember is this: at all costs, avoid "killing" the bearer of ill tidings. Do this once, and you may never hear bad news again; after all, who wants to put their career on the line in order to make people who don't want to hear it listen to bad news?

Countering the MUM effect and the echo chamber can be a difficult task that requires a combination of several contrasting techniques. The stakes are high, however, so there seems to be little choice. In the final analysis, it boils down to a choice between hearing what's comforting and hearing what's true. Over the long haul, few organizations can afford to select the former.

Test Bank questions 2.32 and 2.65 relate to material on this page.

back-seeking behavior, subordinate-supervisor exchanges, and the transmission of information about decisions. From this perspective, further efforts to understand the nature and impact of impressions management would appear to be well worthwhile.

SOCIAL PERCEPTION AND ORGANIZATIONAL BEHAVIOR: ITS ROLE IN JOB INTERVIEWS, PERFORMANCE APPRAISAL, AND ORGANIZATIONAL CONFLICT

In the preceding discussions of social perception, we have repeatedly referred to the impact of this process on important forms of organizational behavior. In this final section, we'll focus directly on this topic. In particular, we'll consider some of the ways in which the processes and errors described can, and often do, affect employee selection, evaluation of their performance, and even the occurrence of organizational conflict.

Social Perception and Job Interviews

Despite concerns about their fairness and validity, *employment interviews* are still widely used by organizations in the recruitment and selection of employees.[49] Since such interviews involve first meetings between two strangers, social perception—efforts by each to understand the other—is clearly an important part of the process. Further, there can be little doubt that the perceptions (*first impressions*) of each applicant formed by interviewers play a major role in the decisions and evaluations they assign to these persons. What factors or aspects of social perception are important in this respect? Recent research has identified several.

Nonverbal Cues   One such factor involves the nonverbal cues emitted by job candidates. In general, the more positive the cues transmitted by applicants, the higher the ratings they receive from interviewers.[50] For example, in one study of such effects, male and female subjects conducted simulated interviews with another person, who played the role of an applicant for an entry-level management job.[51] In fact, the applicant was an accomplice, specially trained to behave in one of two ways. In one condition, she emitted many positive nonverbal cues (e.g., she smiled frequently, maintained a high level of eye contact with the interviewer). In another condition, she behaved in a more neutral manner and did not emit such positive nonverbal cues. After the interview, subjects rated the applicant on several dimensions relating to her qualifications for the job (e.g., her motivation, potential for success) and her personal traits (friendliness, likableness, intelligence). Results indicated that she received higher ratings on most of these dimensions when she had previously demonstrated many positive nonverbal cues than when she had shown relatively neutral behavior.

Other findings, however, suggest that emitting a high level of nonverbal cues does not always succeed in generating positive reactions among interviewers. For example, when information about applicants' qualifications is also available, this factor seems predominant. In other words, apparent qualifications exert much stronger effects on the ratings that applicants receive than the nature of their nonverbal behavior.[52] Further, when applicants with poor credentials emit many nonverbal cues, they seem to be down-rated relative to ones who do not engage in such behavior. Perhaps this is because interviewers attribute such actions to efforts, by these applicants, to shift attention away from their poor qualifications. Whatever the reason, emitting a high level of positive nonverbal cues can clearly sometimes backfire and produce effects opposite the ones intended. The best strategy for applicants to follow, therefore, seems to be this: by all means, practice effective nonverbal behavior, and try to use it to your advantage during an interview. But for best results, combine it with clear evidence of competence and excellent qualifications.

Stereotypes   Earlier we noted that stereotypes can exert strong effects on our perceptions of others. Do these cognitive frameworks also play a role in job interviews? Again, growing evidence suggests that they do. Although several different stereotypes have been studied in this regard, the ones usually viewed as most important, and which have received the most attention, are those relating to gender: *sex role stereotypes.*

Such stereotypes suggest that members of the two genders possess different characteristics. For example, according to these stereotypes, males tend to be forceful, assertive, and decisive, and females tend to be passive, emotional, and indecisive. We should hasten to note that such stereotypes have, by and large, been proven false: differences between the genders in such traits are nonexistent, or at least much smaller than sex role stereotypes suggest.[53] This does not prevent them from affecting social perception, however. Several studies have found that under conditions where limited information about job applicants is available, interviewers tend to assign lower ratings to females than to males. The reason does not seem to lie mainly in direct prejudice against females. Rather, characteristics attributed to men by sex role stereotypes seem more appropriate for various jobs (especially managerial ones) than the characteristics attributed to women. In other words, evaluators assign higher ratings to males because they are seen (falsely) as being more suited to various positions than females.

Although such results are disturbing, they have usually been reported in situations where interviewers have little information about applicants. Fortunately, in many real contexts, this is not the case: interviewers receive a considerable amount of information about applicants' previous experience, training, and background. Under these conditions, the effects of sex role stereotypes do appear to be somewhat weaker and less consistent.[54] Thus, although sex role stereotypes still exist and influence perceptions of males and females in several contexts, their impact on the outcome of interviews is often less than laboratory studies on this topic seemed to suggest.

Social Perception and Performance Appraisal

One of the most important processes in any organization is the evaluation of performance. Accurate **performance appraisal** is crucial to effective personnel decisions—determining which employees should receive raises, promotions, bonuses, and other rewards, and which ones, perhaps, should be dismissed. Ideally, performance appraisal should be a totally rational process—one in which completely accurate evaluators use highly valid measures to assign ratings to individual employees. As you can readily guess, however, this ideal is far easier to describe than attain. Many complexities exist with respect to designing valid measures of performance. For example, if they are to be useful, such measures should reflect *all* important aspects of performance, but should *not* include unrelated or irrelevant behaviors.[55] Similarly, such measures must be presented in a format that raters can easily understand and use.

In addition, human beings are definitely *not* completely accurate in the role of evaluator. We possess a limited capacity to process, store, and retrieve information. Further, our perceptions or interpretations of information relating to performance appear to be subject to many extraneous influences. It is on these factors that we will now focus.

Despite the fact that the stereotypes of male and female employees are changing in the United States, they are still prevalent in some other countries. For example, in China, although women are usually the best students, they are routinely given lower grades so that men will be at the top of the classes. In addition, Chinese organizations often pass over women and hire men with poorer grades as candidates for the most desirable jobs. Such discriminatory practices serve to reinforce sexist stereotypes. [Doder, D. (1989, April 24). The old sexism in the new China. *U.S. News & World Report,* pp. 36–38.]

Test Bank questions 2.38–2.40 relate to material on this page.

Performance Appraisal and Expectations Imagine that you are a manager faced with the task of evaluating the performance of two of your subordinates. Your expectations for one were quite high; you anticipated that she would do very well. Your expectations for the other were low; you predicted that his work would be average at best. Now, looking at the records and searching your own memory, you conclude that both have been average. Do you assign different ratings to each? A completely rational rater would not. Since the two employees show similar levels of performance, they should receive similar ratings. In fact, however, this does not seem to be the way most evaluators operate. Because the first employee has disconfirmed your predictions whereas the second has not, you might actually assign lower ratings to the former. No one likes to be wrong, and the negative feelings generated by discovering that your predictions failed might well spill over to influence your perceptions, and evaluations, of the first individual. That such effects actually occur in respect to real performance appraisals is indicated in a study by Hogan.[56]

In this investigation, supervisors in a large bank were asked to indicate how well they expected their two newest tellers to do on the job. Then, four months later, they rated the actual performance of these individuals. Results indicated that when their expectations were disconfirmed, the supervisors rated the tellers lower than when these expectations were confirmed. In other words, these managers assigned lower ratings to tellers who performed either better or worse than they predicted than to tellers whose performance matched their earlier predictions. (These comparisons were made with actual level of performance held constant through statistical means.)

These findings have unsettling implications, especially for people who expend extra effort on the job and do better than their supervisors expect. Apparently, such unanticipated increments in performance may sometimes result in *lower* rather than higher performance appraisals. Does this mean that employees are locked into whatever level of performance their managers expect? Not necessarily. Perhaps effects such as the ones noted by Hogan can be avoided if managers realize that their predictions failed simply because a new element entered the equation—increased motivation on the part of a subordinate. In any case, the effect of prior expectations on performance ratings emphasizes the fact noted earlier: human beings are definitely *not* totally rational or accurate evaluators. On the contrary, our behavior in this role can be strongly affected by many factors that shape our perceptions of others but that, presumably, should not be part of the process.

Performance Appraisal and Attributions Now, imagine once again that you are a manager faced with the task of evaluating two subordinates. As before, these employees demonstrate similar, average levels of performance. However, you also know that one is a very talented individual, with a great deal of experience, who is coasting along, putting a minimum of effort into her work. The other is a new and inexperienced person with less obvious talent, but a penchant for hard work: he does his very best every day. Would you assign equal ratings to the two people? Perhaps; but it is also quite possible that you will give higher ratings to the latter person. The reason is clear: hard work and effort seem more deserving of credit (and reward) than underutilized talent. In other words, you might assign different ratings to these two persons because although their actual levels of performance are similar, the *reasons behind* their performance are sharply different. In short, *attributions* often play an important role in performance appraisal. Do practicing managers actually behave in this fashion? Research findings suggest that they do. In some cases, at least, they assign higher ratings to subordinates whose performance seems to stem from high motivation and effort than to subordinates whose similar performance stems mainly from talent or past experience.[57]

FIGURE 2-10

Managers' Attributions for Good and Poor Performance by Subordinates

Managers were more likely to attribute excellent performance by subordinates to internal causes (e.g., effort, ability) if these people were members of their *ingroup* than if they were members of their *outgroup*. Corresponding differences did not appear in attributions to external causes (e.g., luck, task difficulty), however. (*Source:* Based on data from Heneman, Greenberger, & Anonyuo, 1989; see Note 58.)

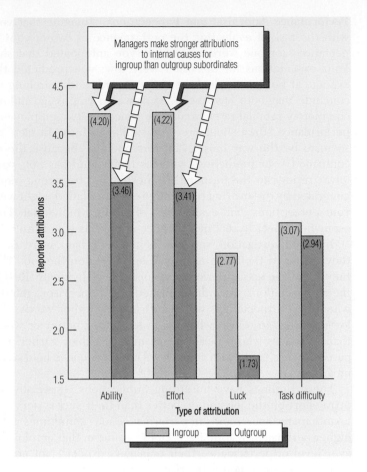

Another way in which attributions influence performance appraisal involves interpretations, by managers, of poor or excellent performance by people they like (those in their *ingroup*) and people they dislike (those in their *outgroup*). Given our tendency to evaluate people we like favorably, it seems likely that managers will attribute excellent performance by people in their ingroup to internal factors such as effort or ability to a greater extent than identical performance by people in their outgroup. Conversely, managers might attribute poor performance by people in their ingroup to external factors such as luck or task difficulty to a greater extent than identical performance by people in their outgroup. To test these predictions, Heneman, Greenberger, and Anonyuo conducted a study in which almost 200 supervisors named their single favorite and least favorite subordinates.[58] Then the supervisors were asked to describe critical incidents in which the performance of each of these persons exceeded or fell short of established standards. Finally, in each case, they were asked to rate the extent to which their subordinates' performance stemmed from the following factors: ability, effort, luck, and task difficulty.

Results indicated that, as expected, managers attributed effective performance to internal factors to a greater extent for ingroup than outgroup members (see Figure 2–10). Contrary to predictions, however, they did not attribute ineffective performance to external factors to a greater extent for ingroup than for outgroup members. These latter findings may have stemmed, in part, from the fact that when asked to think about *critical* incidents of good and poor performance, managers may have focused on internal causes and paid much less attention to external factors. Thus, significant findings failed to appear for this measure. Whatever the ultimate explanation, results did lend support to the contention that managers' attributions concerning excellent performance by subordinates are influenced by more than just performance alone: they are also affected by managers' relationships with these subordinates.

Social Perception and Organizational Conflict

During the course of normal working activities, individuals sometimes engage in actions that disappoint or offend others. When they do, a spiral of annoyance, anger, and desire for revenge may be initiated—a cycle that may lead ultimately to costly instances of *organizational conflict*.[59] Since we will consider the causes and effects of such conflict in detail in chapter 10, we will not examine these topics here. Instead, we merely wish to point out that attributions often play a crucial role in organizational conflict. This can occur in several different ways, but perhaps the most important involves individuals' interpretations of seemingly provocative actions by others. Are such actions perceived as stemming from internal causes such as conscious desires to harm the recipient in some way? Or are they, instead, viewed as stemming from external causes—factors beyond the actor's control? Research findings indicate that attributions concerning provocative actions strongly determine reactions to them.[60]

For example, consider a study conducted by Shapiro.[61] In this investigation (the results of which are summarized in Figure 2–11), subjects played the role of an inventor or a marketer of a new computer program. Their task was to persuade another person, who played the role of loan officer at a bank, to grant them a student

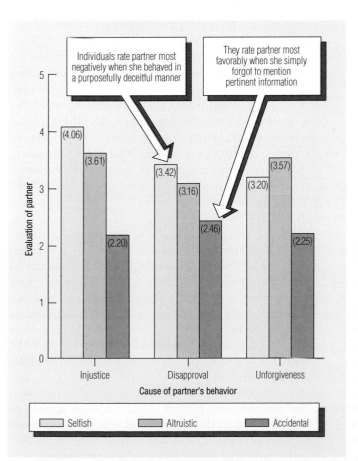

FIGURE 2–11

Attributions and Reactions to Provocative Actions

Subjects reported more negative reactions to a partner when she acted in a purposely deceitful manner than when she withheld information from a loan examiner by accident. They reacted most negatively when their partner acted in a deceitful manner for selfish reasons. These findings call attention to the importance of attributions concerning the causes of provocative actions in determining reactions to such behaviors. (*Source:* Based on data from Shapiro, in press; see Note 61.)

Test Bank questions 2.45 and 2.75 relate to material on this page.

One of the hottest selling executive toys is subliminal tapes—audio tapes containing self-improvement messages hidden underneath soothing music. The messages supposedly operate below the level of conscious perception and are touted to help increase productivity, reduce conflict, and enable people to do such things as lose weight and stop smoking. Despite these claims, recent scientific evidence has shown that these claims are completely groundless. The real message is not disguised at all: buyer beware! [Krajick, K. (1990, July 30). Sound too good to be true? Behind the boom in subliminal tapes. *Newsweek*, pp. 60–61.]

loan to proceed with the project. Subjects worked in teams, and, presumably, each would have a chance to meet with the loan officer. In reality, both subjects were informed that their partner had gone first, and were then provided with a note from the loan officer indicating that he had rejected their request because their partner had been deceitful. This information also provided an explanation for their partner's behavior, and this was systematically varied to indicate that this person had lied either *selfishly* (to maximize her own gains), *altruistically* (to maximize the joint outcomes of both people by increasing the chances of the loan being approved), or *unintentionally* (she had forgotten to include some crucial information). After receiving this information, subjects rated the extent to which they viewed their partner as dishonest, they felt cheated by this person, and they forgave their partner for her deceitful actions. Results indicated that, as predicted, subjects reported the more negatively to their partner when she was purposely deceitful than when she was accidentally deceitful, and most negatively of all when she acted deceitfully for selfish rather than altruistic reasons.

In sum, attributions do indeed influence a wide range of organizational behavior—from appraisal of job applicants and subordinates on the one hand through the occurrence and intensity of organizational conflict on the other. In these and many other instances, what other people say or do is not all that matters; our interpretations of the *causes* of their actions, too, are often crucial.

SUMMARY AND REVIEW

Basic Aspects of Perception

Perception is the process through which we select, organize, and interpret information brought to us by our senses. Perception is *selective*—we tend to notice some stimuli while largely ignoring others. This fact is often taken into careful account in the design of controls and displays (e.g., the cockpits of airplanes), and in the design of *hazard warnings*—messages and labels warning individuals that some substance or process is potentially harmful.

Social Perception: Perceiving Other People

In our efforts to understand other people, we often focus on the task of comprehending the causes behind their behavior—a process known as **attribution.** We accomplish this task by focusing on certain aspects of their behavior (e.g., actions that are unusual, or for which there is only one plausible cause). To determine whether a person's actions stem mainly from internal or external causes, we consider three types of information about his or her behavior: (1) *consensus*—whether other persons act in a similar manner; (2) *consistency*—whether this person acts in the same manner in a given situation across time; and (3) *distinctiveness*—whether this person acted in a similar manner in other situations.

Social perception can also be viewed as a *cognitive process* in which individuals notice, encode, store, and later retrieve information about others. Such information processing is often strongly affected by **schemas**—cognitive frameworks for understanding the world around us. Once established, schemas may determine which information we notice, which information is entered into memory, and which is later remembered. Schemas play a key role in **stereotypes**—cognitive frameworks that relate membership in specific groups to the possession of various traits or characteristics.

Errors in Social Perception

Social perception is subject to several sources of error. The **self-serving bias** involves our tendency to attribute positive outcomes to internal causes (our own traits), but negative outcomes to external factors. **Halo effects** occur when our overall impression of another person affects perceptions of his or her individual traits or behaviors. We also tend to like and evaluate more positively people who are similar to ourselves (the **similar-to-me effect**). This tendency can be a source of error in social perception, but can also have beneficial effects when applied to efforts to match the cultural and ethnic backgrounds of sales personnel to the customers they serve. Another potential source of error is **stereotypes.**

Impression Management: The Fine Art of Looking Good

Individuals often engage in efforts to create favorable impressions on others; this process, **impression management,** is very common in organizational settings. Among the tactics used to manage impressions are *self-enhancing* strategies, such as efforts to improve one's appearance through dress and grooming, name-dropping, and even self-deprecating, modesty-demonstrating statements. In addition, individuals often use *feedback-seeking* behavior as a means of enhancing their personal image.

Additional tactics of impression management involve *other-enhancing* strategies. These include flattery of target people, agreement with their views or opinions, showing a high degree of interest in them, and demonstrating liking or approval of them, either verbally or nonverbally (through smiles, nods, and similar actions), and doing favors for them. Impression management influences a wide range of organizational processes. These include performance appraisal, the quality of subordinate-supervisor exchanges, and the transmission of information about decisions from subordinates to their supervisors.

Social Perception and Organizational Behavior

Social perception plays an important role in several forms of organizational behavior. It affects the outcomes of job interviews, where the ratings assigned to applicants are often influenced by such factors as the nonverbal cues they emit and by various stereotypes. It also influences *performance appraisal.* Here, evaluations of others' performance can be affected by expectations about them, perceived similarity between raters and ratees, and attributions concerning the causes behind good or poor performance. Social perception also plays a role in *organizational conflict.* Attributions concerning the causes behind seemingly provocative actions can strongly determine reactions to such behaviors, and the level of conflict that follows their occurrence.

KEY TERMS

attribution: The process through which individuals attempt to determine the causes behind others' behavior.

fundamental attribution error: The tendency to attribute others' actions to internal causes (e.g., their traits) while largely ignoring external factors that may have also influenced such behavior.

halo effects: The tendency for the overall impressions of others to affect objective evaluations of their specific traits. (Alternatively, the perception of spuriously elevated correlations between various traits being rated or evaluated.)

impression management: Efforts by individuals to improve how they appear to others.

MUM effect: The reluctance of subordinates to transmit negative information or feedback to their supervisors.

perception: The process through which we select, organize, and interpret information gathered by our senses in order to understand the world around us.

performance appraisal: The process of evaluating employee performance on various work-related dimensions.

schemas: Cognitive frameworks developed through experience that affect the way in which information about the external world is noticed, encoded, stored, and remembered.

self-serving bias: A form of attributional error in which individuals attribute successes to internal causes (their own traits), but attribute failure to external factors beyond their control.

similar-to-me effect: The tendency of raters to assign higher evaluations to ratees who are similar to themselves in various respects (e.g., in terms of attitudes, demographic factors).

social information processing (or **social cognition**): The process through which social information is sorted, stored, and retrieved from memory.

social perception: The process through which individuals attempt to combine, integrate, and interpret information about others.

stereotypes: Beliefs that all members of specific groups share similar negative traits and behaviors.

QUESTIONS FOR DISCUSSION

1. What do various visual illusions tell us about the nature of perception?

2. In what work-related contexts is it important to be able to determine whether others' behavior stems primarily from internal or external causes?

3. Schemas can't be seen or measured directly. Given this fact, how can we obtain evidence for the existence of such cognitive frameworks?

4. How can the self-serving bias serve as a potential cause of friction and conflict in organizations?

5. It is often said that all stereotypes contain a grain of truth. Do you think this is correct? If so, why?

6. On the basis of information provided in this chapter, how should individuals prepare for important job interviews?

7. What techniques can individuals use to improve the impression they make on others?

NOTES

1. Schiffmann, H. R. (1990). *Sensation and perception: An integrated approach* (3rd ed.). New York: Wiley.

2. Baron, R. A., & Byrne, D. (1991). *Social psychology: Understanding human interaction* (6th ed.). Boston: Allyn & Bacon.

3. Liden, R. C., & Mitchell, T. R. (1988). Ingratiatory behaviors in organizational settings. *Academy of Management Review, 13,* 572–587.

4. Cohen, J. D., Dunbar, K., & McClelland, J. L. (1990). On the control of automatic processes: A parallel distributed processing account of the Stroop effect. *Psychological Review, 97,* 332–361.

5. Wogalter, M. S., & Silver, N. C. (1990). Arousal strength of signal words. *Forensic Reports, 3,* 407–420.

6. Wogalter, M. S., & Young, S. L. (1991). Behavioral compliance in voice and print warnings. *Ergonomics, 39,* 79–89.

7. Ross, M., & Fletcher, G. J. O. (1985). *Attribution and social perception.* In G. Lindzey & E. Aronson (Eds.), *Handbook of social psychology* (2nd ed.). New York: Random House.

8. See Note 7.

9. See Note 7.

10. Kelley, H. H., & Michela, J. L. (1980). Attribution theory and research. *Annual Review of Psychology, 31,* 457–501.

11. Harvey, J. H., & Weary, G. H. (1981). *Perspectives on attributional processes.* Dubuque, IA: Brown.

12. Hansen, R. D. (1980). Common sense attribution. *Journal of Personality and Social Psychology, 39,* 996–1009.

13. Weiner, B. (1985). An attributional theory of achievement motivation and motivation. *Psychological Review, 82,* 548–573.

14. Knowlton, W. A., Jr., & Mitchell, T. R. (1980). Effects of causal attributions on a supervisor's evaluation of subordinate performance. *Journal of Applied Psychology, 65,* 459–466.

15. Fiske, S. T., & Taylor, S. E. (1991). *Social cognition* (2nd ed.). Reading, MA: Addison-Wesley.

16. Srull, T. K., & Wyer, R. S. (1988). *Advances in social cognition.* Hillsdale, NJ: Erlbaum.

17. See Note 16.

18. Bodenhausen, G. V. (1988). Stereotypic biases in social decision making and memory: Testing process models of stereotype use. *Journal of Personality and Social Psychology, 55,* 726–736.

19. See Note 15.

20. O'Sullivan, C., & Durso, F. T. (1984). Effects of schema-incongruent information on memory for stereotypical attributes. *Journal of Personality and Social Psychology, 47,* 55–70.

21. Mullen, B., & Riordan, C. A. (1988). Self-serving attributions for performance in naturalistic settings: A meta-analytic review. *Journal of Applied Social Psychology, 18,* 3–22.

22. Maass, A., & Volpato, C. (1989). Gender differences in self-serving attributions about sexual experiences. *Journal of Applied Social Psychology, 19,* 517–542.

23. Wilson, R. (1985). Reputations in games and markets. In A. E. Roth (Ed.), *Game-theoretic models of bargaining* (pp. 65–84). New York: Cambridge University Press.

24. Fombrun, C., & Shanley, M. (1990). What's in a name? Reputation building and corporate strategy. *Academy of Management Journal, 33,* 233–258.

25. See Note 24.

26. Murphy, K. R., & Reynolds, D. H. (1988). Does true halo affect observed halo? *Journal of Applied Psychology, 73,* 235–238.

27. Fisicaro, S. A. (1988). A reexamination of the relation between halo errors and accuracy. *Journal of Applied Psychology, 73,* 239–244.

28. Binning, J. H., Goldstein, M. A., Garcia, M. F., & Scattaregia, J. H. (1988). Effects of preinterview impressions on questioning strategies in same- and opposite-sex employment interviews. *Journal of Applied Psychology, 73,* 30–37.

29. Pulakos, E. D., & Wexley, K. N. (1983). The relationship among perceptual similarity, sex, and performance ratings in manager-subordinate dyads. *Academy of Management Journal, 26,* 129–139.

30. Turban, D. B., & Jones, A. P. (1988). Supervisor-subordinate similarity: Types, effects, and mechanisms. *Journal of Applied Psychology, 73,* 228–234.

31. Santora, J. E. (1991). Kinney shoe steps into diversity. *Personnel Journal, 70,* 72–77.

32. Ainlay, S. C., Becker, G., & Coleman, L. (Eds.). (1986). *The dilemma of difference.* New York: Plenum.

33. Linville, P. W., Fischer, G. W., & Salovey, P. (1989). Perceived distributions of the characteristics of in-group and out-group members: Empirical evidence and a computer simulation. *Journal of Personality and Social Psychology, 42,* 193–211.

34. See Note 16.

35. Giacalone, R. A., & Rosenfeld, P. (Eds.). (1990). *Impression management in the organization.* Hillsdale, NJ: Erlbaum.

36. Smither, J. W., Reilly, R. R., & Buda, R. (1988). Effect of prior performance ratings on present performance: Contrast versus assimilation revisited. *Journal of Applied Psychology, 73,* 487–496.

37. Hanges, P. J., Braverman, E. P., & Rentsch, J. R. (1991). Changes in raters' perceptions of subordinates: A catastrophe model. *Journal of Applied Psychology, 76,* 878–888.

38. Baron, R. A. (1989). Impression management by applicants during employment interviews: The "too much of a good thing" effect. In R. W. Eder & G. R. Ferris (Eds.), *The employment interview: Theory, research, and practice.* Newbury Park, CA: Sage.

39. Molloy, J. T. (1975). *Dress for success.* New York: Warner.

40. Forsythe, S., Drake, M. F., & Cox, C. E. (1985). Influence of applicant's dress on interviewer's selection decisions. *Journal of Applied Psychology, 70,* 374–378.

41. Baron, R. A. (1986). Self-presentation in job interviews: When there can be "too much of a good thing." *Journal of Applied Social Psychology 16,* 16–28.

42. Ashford, S. J., & Tsui, A. S. (in press). Self-regulation for managerial effectiveness: The role of active feedback seeking. *Academy of Management Journal.*

43. Morrison, E. W., & Bies, R. J. (1991). Impression management in the feedback-seeking process: A literature review and research agenda. *Academy of Management Review, 16,* 322–341.

44. Godfrey, D. K., Jones, E. E., & Lord, C. G. (1986). Self-promotion is not ingratiating. *Journal of Personality and Social Psychology, 50,* 106–115.

45. Wayne, S. J., & Kacmar, K. M. (1991). The effects of impression management on the performance appraisal process. *Organizational Behavior and Human Decision Processes, 48,* 70–88.

46. Wayne, S. J., & Ferris, G. R. (1990). Influence tactics, affect, and exchange quality in supervisor-subordinate interactions: A laboratory experiment and field study. *Journal of Applied Psychology, 75,* 487–499.

47. Fandt, P. M., & Ferris, G. M. (1990). The management of information and impressions: When employees behave opportunistically. *Organizational Behavior and Human Decision Processes, 45,* 140–158.

48. Kiechel, W., III. (1990, June 18). How to escape the echo chamber. *Fortune,* pp. 129–130.

49. Arvey, R. D., & Campion, J. E. (1982). The employment interview: A summary and review of recent research. *Personnel Psychology, 35,* 281–322.

50. Rasmussen, K. G., Jr. (1984). Nonverbal behavior, verbal behavior, résumé credentials, and selection interview outcomes. *Journal of Applied Psychology, 69,* 551–556.

51. See Note 41.

52. Riggio, R. E., & Throckmorton, B. (1988). The relative effect of verbal and nonverbal behavior, appearance, and social skills on valuations made in hiring interviews. *Journal of Applied Social Psychology, 18,* 331–348.

53. Powell, G. N. (1990). One more time: Do female and male managers differ? *Academy of Management Executive, 4,* 68–75.

54. Tosi, H. L., & Einbender, S. W. (1985). The effects of type and amount of information in sex discrimination research: A meta-analysis. *Academy of Management Journal, 28,* 712–723.

55. Saal, F. E., & Knight, P. A. (1988). *Industrial/organizational psychology: Science and practice.* Pacific Grove, CA: Brooks/Cole.

56. Hogan, E. A. (1987). Effects of prior expectations on performance ratings: A longitudinal study. *Academy of Management Journal, 30,* 354–368.

57. Mitchell, T. R., Green, S. G., & Wood, R. S. (1982). An attributional model of leadership and the poor performing subordinate: Development and validation. In B. M. Staw & L. L. Cummings (Eds.), *Research in organizational behavior* (Vol. 3). Greenwich, CT: JAI Press.

58. Heneman, R. L., Greenberger, D. B., & Anonyuo, C. (1989). Attributions and exchanges: The effects of interpersonal factors on the diagnosis of employee performance. *Academy of Management Journal, 32,* 466–476.

59. Thomas, K. W. (1992). Conflict and negotiation processes in organizations. In M. D. Dunnette (Ed.), *Handbook of industrial and organizational psychology* (2nd ed.). Palo Alto, CA: Consulting Psychologists Press.

60. Baron, R. A. (1990). Attributions and organizational conflict. In S. Graham & V. Folkes (Eds.), *Attribution theory: Applications to achievement, mental health, and interpersonal conflict* (pp. 185–204). Hillsdale, NJ: Erlbaum.

61. Shapiro, D. L. (in press). Has the conflict-mitigating effect of explanations been overestimated? An examination of explanations' effects under circumstances of exposed deceit. *Administrative Science Quarterly.*

Team-Based Performance Appraisal at Digital Equipment Corporation

When the Customer Support Center of Digital Equipment Corporation began using self-managed work teams, it was faced with the problem of how to appraise the performance of team members. How do you make sound performance appraisal decisions for employees working in self-managed teams? In addition, this program, started at the company's Colorado Springs, Colorado, facility, was a pilot program not used in other divisions throughout the company. All eyes were focused on the outcome of this division's experiment.

A company known for being on the cutting edge of technology, Digital sought to develop a cutting-edge technique for doing performance appraisal in groups. The company adopted a team-based, participatory performance appraisal process as described Carol Norman, a Digital systems specialist, and Robert Zawacki, an organizational behavior expert.[1]

Digital's self-managed teams are composed of up to forty members. Each team is assigned one management consultant who advises on matters of organizational and group processes. Each team is responsible for developing and maintaining itself. Team members interview and select prospective coworkers and handle all scheduling—work activities, vacations, training time, and leaves. Team members are also responsible for appraising the performance of their team as a whole (group process and the like) and of individual members.

Digital's team-based performance appraisal system is radically different from performance appraisal in traditional organizations, which is routinely conducted by an employee's supervisor. The team approach to performance appraisal incorporates tactics that fit the participatory nature of team functioning.

The team-based performance appraisal process relies heavily on both self-evaluation and peer evaluation. At Digital, a typical team-based performance appraisal involves gathering input from every person on the team, which is passed on to a performance appraisal committee that reviews and organizes it. Finally, the committee feeds back the performance information to the person being appraised. In this manner, peer assessments provide the team, Digital, and each team member with a multirater assessment of his or her performance.

To avoid contaminating performance appraisal with information not pertinent to performance, each team prepares an extensive job description for each team member. The job description identifies the critical features of team-member performance, thereby allowing the performance appraisal committee to review only how well a team member does his or her job. The job description also serves a valuable motivational purpose by clearly stating the group's performance expectations for each team member.

The performance appraisal process begins when the person to be evaluated (the evaluee) is notified by electronic mail that a performance appraisal will be conducted in thirty days. The evaluee selects a fellow team member to chair the appraisal committee—the person selected is expected to be the evaluee's advocate. Two other team members are randomly selected to join the committee, and the team's management consultant serves as the final member of the performance appraisal committee.

Once the committee is formed, the evaluee prepares a preliminary self-appraisal of his or her achievements during the previous year. This report is sent to all other team members, who use the report as the basis for making comments about the evaluee's performance (peer evaluations). The committee then collects all team-member comments, reviews and organizes the input, and sends a copy of the total input to the evaluee.

During the input collection and organizing phase, the committee screens comments and opinions for "harsh or blatantly inaccurate verbiage."[2] The committees routinely screen to reduce the likelihood that evaluees will be exposed to information that may cause them to react negatively to feedback. The goal of the performance appraisal committee is to create a supportive and nurturing development and performance enhancement process.

The next step is for the evaluee to prepare a complete self-appraisal report of his or her performance. This report is given to the appraisal committee. The committee reviews the self-appraisal, as well as the comments of team members, and then meets with the evaluee to discuss the evaluee's performance and to establish the evaluee's goals for the coming year.

The chair of the committee prepares a summary report of the findings and recommendations. The report is signed by committee members and the evaluee and forwarded to the personnel department for record keeping and any action deemed appropriate.

How well does the team-based performance appraisal system work for Digital's Customer Support Center? According to Norman and Zawacki, team-member productivity has significantly increased. Member commitment to the team has also risen. Not only do team members have an important say in how their performance is evaluated, but they are also empowered by the process to contribute to the formulation of their goals for the next year. Thus, every team member not only comes to understand the group's expectations, but the group's and the evaluee's expectations become highly integrated through the interactive appraisal process.

The team-based approach to performance appraisal has some distinct advantages over the supervisor-appraiser approach. The information gathered by the team is more reliable because it comes from coworkers, who are in the best position to observe the evaluee's performance. Also, team members believe that the observations of their peers are more accurate than those of someone in a supervisory position. They trust their coworkers' perceptions. Evaluees seem more willing to accept suggestions for change when they come from other team members.

Another significant advantage of using a team-based approach is multiple appraisers. Any single appraiser is vulnerable to perceptual biases. At Digital an evaluee has up to forty appraisers, so the perceptual biases of a single person are minimized.

On the down side, the team-based performance appraisal process is very time-consuming. "A typical performance appraisal can take a minimum of forty team hours in input alone, provided each individual spends one hour on every performance appraisal."[3] Also, the comments by team members can still contain perceptual biases. Team members were found to be prone to the halo effect, strictness, and leniency biases. Recognizing the potential for perceptual biases, Digital provides all team members with training to recognize and avoid perceptual pitfalls in the performance appraisal process.

Being appraised by fellow team members can be threatening, especially for new team members. To minimize threatening feelings, group expectations are described in detail during interviews with prospective team members. These realistic job previews help to reduce any gap that may exist between perceived job activities and reality.

The team-based performance appraisal system has worked well for Digital's Customer Support Center. Productivity and commitment of team members are up. Management is so impressed by the success of the approach that it is looking at other, nonteam areas to see if self-evaluation and peer evaluation can be used throughout the company.

Questions for Discussion

1. Describe the perceptual processes involved in appraising another person's performance.
2. How does Digital's team-based performance appraisal process reduce the perceptual errors discussed in the text?
3. Digital's team-based performance appraisal process uses a combination of self-evaluation and peer evaluation. What perceptual biases are likely to affect self-appraisals? How about peer evaluations?
4. Why do Digital team members have so much confidence in the evaluative comments of their fellow team members?
5. The performance appraisal committee screens the comments of the evaluee's coworkers for harsh and inaccurate verbiage. Based on what you have learned about perception, do you think this is a good idea? Explain why or why not.

Notes

1. Norman, C. A., & Zawacki, R. A. (1991, September). Team appraisals—Team approach. *Personnel*, pp. 101–104.
2. See Note 1, p. 104.
3. See Note 1, p. 104.

The All-Too-Powerful Impact of Stereotypes

Most people are well aware of the existence of stereotypes. They realize that in the past, negative stereotypes were responsible for unfair treatment of women and minority group members in many work settings. At the same time, though, most people do not recognize the existence and potentially powerful impact of a wide range of other stereotypes. This exercise is designed to demonstrate the fact that your own thinking (enlightened as it may be) can be affected by various stereotypes, even if you think you are an eminently fair-minded and unbiased person. Follow the directions below for some firsthand insights into such effects.

Procedure

Rate the members of the following groups on each of the following dimensions. (Circle one number for each characteristic.)

Investment Bankers

Liberal						Conservative
1	2	3	4	5	6	7
Intelligent						Unintelligent
1	2	3	4	5	6	7
Greedy						Generous
1	2	3	4	5	6	7
Dull						Interesting
1	2	3	4	5	6	7

Engineers

Liberal						Conservative
1	2	3	4	5	6	7
Intelligent						Unintelligent
1	2	3	4	5	6	7
Greedy						Generous
1	2	3	4	5	6	7
Dull						Interesting
1	2	3	4	5	6	7

Professors

Liberal						Conservative
1	2	3	4	5	6	7
Intelligent						Unintelligent
1	2	3	4	5	6	7
Greedy						Generous
1	2	3	4	5	6	7
Dull						Interesting
1	2	3	4	5	6	7

Points to Consider

Did your ratings of the various groups differ? If you are like most people, they probably did. For example, you probably rated investment bankers as more conservative and less interesting than professors. Moreover—and this is an important point—your ratings may well have differed *even if you do not know members of these various professions personally.*

The point of this exercise is straightforward. We hold stereotypes concerning the supposed traits or characteristics of many different groups. Furthermore, such beliefs are so pervasive that we are often unaware of their existence until, as in this demonstration, they are called into action. Given the widespread existence of stereotypes and their potential effects on important organizational processes, it is important to be aware of them and to try to resist their influence. If you choose, instead, to ignore them, you may well fall victim to serious errors in perceiving others.

■ 3 ■

LEARNING:
ADAPTING TO THE
WORLD OF WORK

LEARNING OBJECTIVES

After reading this chapter, you should be able to:
1. Understand the concept of learning and how it applies to the study of behavior in organizations.
2. Identify and describe the three major approaches to learning and how they apply to understanding organizational behavior.
3. Name and distinguish between various schedules of reinforcement.
4. Appreciate how principles of reinforcement may be used in organizational behavior management programs to improve organizational functioning.
5. Understand the principles of learning that make organizational training effective.
6. Describe the conditions necessary for discipline to be effectively used in organizations.

It is 4:00 A.M., that special time of day reserved for only a few, such as security guards and all-night disc jockeys. For Natalie Pearson, not only is her workday just beginning, but so is her career as a pastry chef. The Acacia Tree restaurant is considered by those in the know to be the current in-spot for trendy cuisine. Natalie knows she is lucky to get a job here, even as an assistant, right after graduating from culinary school.

She is, of course, in awe of Executive Pastry Chef Marc Tallmadge, the man whose photos have adorned the pages of the many magazine features about him she has seen. Now, instead of posing next to elaborate dessert masterpieces, he is standing in front of his crew, clipboard in hand, giving out the day's assignments.

"Natalie," he commands, "you'll be helping Pierre today. He's already in the pastry cooler, so check with him."

"Sure, Marc," she replies. With this, all of a sudden, a hush falls over the group.

Not having any hint as to what is wrong, and not wanting to ask, she simply asks, "Where's the pastry cooler?"

"Down past the dish line, across from the pantry." Marc points, as the others fight to hold back their giggling.

Natalie approaches the huge stainless-steel door of the pastry cooler and yanks it open. There is Pierre, a stocky pastry chef, counting trays of rolls. "*Dix-huit, dix-neuf, . . .*" he counts aloud in French. Seeing Natalie out of the corner of one eye, he motions to her to wait with one hand, while he continues counting with the other.

"*Oui,*" he says a moment later, as he finishes his task.

"You must be Pierre. I'm Natalie Pearson. Marc sent me over to help you."

"Oh yes," he replies in a thick French accent, "I was expecting you."

Eager to get to work, Natalie inquires, "What do you want me to do?"

Pierre is quick to reply. "First," he says, "you should know never to call the chef by his first name. Out of respect, we call him Chef, or Chef Tallmadge. But never just Marc!"

"Oh no!" Natalie cringes. "I just called him Marc in front of the whole crew. No wonder they all got so quiet."

"Because it's your first day, it'll be okay, but you'll not want to do that again," Pierre cautions.

As Natalie shakes her head, Pierre changes his tone. "Enough of that," he says. "Now, let's get to work. For your first job, I'll need you to help me with tonight's desserts. So, please melt the dark chocolate for the glaze for the ganache torte. While it's melting, you can chop the cashews for the cashew crunch tart. Okay?"

"No problem," Natalie replies with great confidence, although she is still very nervous on her first day. She has heard all about these desserts; they're legendary in town. Now she's helping to prepare them.

She rummages around the cooler, finds some chocolate and some nuts, and carries them back to her station. Grabbing a knife from the rack, she chops the chocolate into meltable-size chunks and places them into a saucepan over the heat. She then begins chopping the nuts, when Pierre looks over to see what's going on.

"*Mon dieu!*" he yells. He often speaks his native language in times of stress. "What are you doing? You don't sauté the chocolate, you melt it—using a double boiler!"

"I know that," Natalie explains. "I'm just so nervous I forgot." As she reaches for the stove to remove the pan, Pierre sees the nuts she was chopping.

"What's this?" he asks, trying to hold back his anger.

"You said you wanted the cashews chopped, didn't you?" Natalie replies.

"That's right," answers Pierre. "So why are you chopping almonds?"

"Oh, I'm not getting off to a very good start," says Natalie in disgust. "I really *do* know this stuff. You can ask any of my teachers. It's just that I'm overwhelmed on my first day."

"C'mon, Natalie, let's get a cup of coffee and calm down a bit," Pierre counsels. "I know there's a lot for you to learn on your first day, and it can be confusing."

Natalie begins to feel better as she and Pierre reach the coffee table. They continue talking as she prepares the coffee for both of them.

"Regular?" she asks, as she fixes the coffee.

"But of course," replies Pierre, now smiling and speaking in a reassuring tone. This pleasant moment is not to last, however, as they take their first sips.

"Yech!" exclaims Pierre, spitting his first sip of coffee into the air. Natalie is more restrained as she struggles not to mimic Pierre's reaction.

The two of them look down at the table, their eyes scanning for the spoon Natalie used. There is it, resting in a bowl of salt instead of a bowl of sugar!

Just as Natalie begins to wish she had never showed up for work this day, Pierre offers her some backhanded reassurance.

"Don't worry, Natalie," he remarks. "From here, things can only get better."

Poor Natalie. It's certainly easy to relate to the frustration she must be feeling. She unknowingly showed disrespect to her boss, scorched the chocolate, chopped the wrong nuts, and topped it all off by treating herself and Pierre to a mouthful of salty coffee—all within the first few minutes of her new job. What a way to begin a new career! However, it seems as if Pierre isn't too worried about Natalie. He probably realizes that she has a great deal to learn, and the first few days (not to mention the first few minutes) of a new job can be overwhelming for anyone. By what names or titles should people be addressed? What techniques and ingredients should be used to prepare various dishes? With a little experience, Natalie will surely acquire the skills and knowledge she needs to function properly on the job. Whether we're talking about learning social skills, such as what to call the boss, or learning job skills, such as how to prepare a dessert, the basic processes of learning are the same (see Figure 3–1). As we will show in this chapter, **learning** is a fundamental process relevant to many aspects of organizational behavior.[1]

FIGURE 3–1

Learning: A Basic Process in Organizations

As demonstrated by these examples, the process of learning takes many different forms within organizations.

Although you most likely already have a good idea of what learning is, a formal definition of the term probably isn't easy to imagine. Because it's so crucial to carving out the domain of this chapter, we will offer such a definition. Specifically, we define learning as *a relatively permanent change in behavior occurring as a result of experience.*[2] Despite its great simplicity, several aspects of this definition bear pointing out. First, it's clear that learning requires that some kind of change occur. Second, this change must be more than just temporary. Finally, it must be the result of experience—that is, continued contact with the world around us. Given this definition, we cannot say that short-lived performance changes on the job, such as those due to illness or fatigue, represent the result of learning. Learning is a difficult concept to grasp because it cannot be directly observed. Instead, it has to be inferred on the basis of relatively permanent changes in behavior. In our opening story, Natalie is in the early stages of learning lots of things about her new job—what to call the boss, how to prepare the desserts, and so on. As Natalie gains more experience on the job, we'll surely see changes in the way she behaves. Eventually, she will no longer call her boss Marc, and no longer prepare the chocolate glaze using the incorrect method. Then, clearly, Natalie will have learned.

As you might imagine, hardly any process is more basic to human functioning than learning. Not only is it responsible for acquiring new job skills, as we have seen, but it is also involved in attaining other vital, but informal, information, such as who really has the power in an organization, how to get things done most effectively, and even what kinds of things you can get away with doing when no one's watching. Because the process is so basic to human functioning, we have chosen to cover it very early in this book. Our treatment of the learning process will begin by reviewing the most prominent theories of learning advanced in the social sciences. Then we will apply this information by examining some of the ways principles of learning are used to manage effective organizational behavior—both maintaining desirable behaviors and reducing undesirable behaviors. Specifically, we will show how the sound application of learning principles can be a key to the effective management of people in organizations. (To operate effectively, organizations often rely on the learning process—usually by teaching employees ways to improve their job performance. However, some organizations have found that their effective functioning depends on the effectiveness of their clients' learning. For a closer look at this interesting phenomenon, see the **OB in Practice** section below.)

THEORIES OF LEARNING: AN OVERVIEW

During this past century, several different theoretical approaches have been taken toward understanding learning. Each one explains the learning process in a different way and focuses on the learning of different types of behaviors. Because they are so

 OB IN PRACTICE

Becoming Profitable by Teaching Customers Their Business

Most of the time, we think about learning as a way of improving ourselves—gaining new skills as a means of becoming more productive. These days, many companies are seeking a different approach to improving business, one that represents the flip side of the coin—educating customers. The rationale is simple: as customers learn to improve the way they conduct business, the market is improved for their suppliers. Indeed, many of today's companies have found that educating their customers is an effective way to make it to the top.[3]

Consider the case of Archery Center International (ACI), a successful wholesale distributor of archery equipment that saw its annual sales grow from $540,000 in 1985 to $3.8 million in 1990. The company attributes a large part of that growth to a move it took to instruct its dealers in the fundamentals of business (frequently, retailers in this industry know more about bow hunting than commerce). With this in mind, ACI's chief executive officer, Sheila West, decided in 1985 to stage a trade show for its customers one weekend—a "Pow Wow" in which seminars were given on topics of interest to them. To Ms. West's delight, the Pow Wow was a huge success, and each subsequent year the event has grown larger and has attracted more dealers. They attend seminars devoted to topics such as pricing, tax laws, and related issues of interest to small dealers. The result has been great for ACI. Their customers have become more suc-cessful, thereby creating more of a need for ACI's products. Of course, in exchange for the good-will ACI creates by hosting the seminars, the dealers are more than glad to do business with them.

The customer education approach has been used successfully by other companies as well. Here is a sampling:

- **Harrisville Designs, Inc.** (a $3 million manufacturer of yarns and looms) twice a year educates small groups of retailers about the yarn business.
- **Hearing Technology, Inc.** (a $6 million hearing-aid manufacturer) holds seminars for medical practitioners and hearing practitioners on topics such as personnel development and office management.
- **Skyline Displays, Inc.** (a $45 million manufacturer of portable displays for trade shows) teaches its customers effective techniques for exhibiting at trade shows.

Although what these companies are doing can be costly, customer education tends to more than pay for itself in terms of new and repeat business. What it does for customer loyalty is especially effective. The idea is that an educated customer is a good, loyal customer, one who is in a better position to appreciate the company's product. As these examples show, business success requires educating not only the people in one's own company, but one's customers as well.

relevant to understanding behavior in organizations, we will review the three major approaches to learning: *classical conditioning*, *operant conditioning*, and *observational learning*.

Classical Conditioning: Learning by Association

Imagine, if you will, the following situation. You've always disliked the smell of paint; it makes you sick. After many years of hard work, you've just been promoted to a junior executive position. You now have the power, the prestige, and the fancy office to go with it. Only one problem: the maintenance crew just repainted your newly assigned office, and it's making you ill. The aroma nauseates you for the first few days it lingers in the air. Then a funny thing happens. Even though the smell is gone after a few days, you have associated the way the office looks and nausea. Now you feel sick whenever you enter your office. Is this any way for a new executive to act? Actually, it's not at all strange. You're merely the victim of a very strong and well-known type of learning known as **classical conditioning.**

This type of learning was discovered by the Russian physiologist Ivan Pavlov at the beginning of the twentieth century.[4] You are probably already familiar with Pavlov's discoveries concerning a dog's salivation in response to a bell. Pavlov noted that a certain stimulus (known as an *unconditioned stimulus*), such as food, would elicit a naturally occurring reflexive response (known as an *unconditioned response*), such as salivation. Over time, if that unconditioned stimulus was paired with another, neutral stimulus (known as a *conditioned stimulus*), such as a bell, that stimulus would come to elicit a response similar to the naturally occurring, unconditioned response (known as a *conditioned response*)— in this case, salivation. This process of classical conditioning—also known as **Pavlovian conditioning,** after the scientist who first studied it—takes advantage of the natural tendency for some stimuli to elicit some responses automatically, reflexively. By repeatedly pairing an unconditioned stimulus with another, neutral one, that previously neutral stimulus eventually brings about the same response as the original stimulus. Recently, scientists have noted that this conditioning occurs as a result of a set of cognitive processes. Specifically, as the conditioning proceeds, people respond to the conditioned stimulus because they develop an *expectancy* that it will be followed by the unconditioned stimulus.[5] Just think of how it whets your appetite when you merely see the name and description of your favorite food. Reading the words makes you think about the food, which triggers your appetite. A summary of the classical conditioning process is shown in Figure 3–2 (see p. 82). The example on the left shows the process in operation for Pavlov's dogs; the example on the right shows the process in operation in the case of the foul-smelling office.

The process of classical conditioning may help explain a variety of organizational behaviors. For example, workers who have witnessed dangerous industrial accidents after certain warning lights have gone on may be expected to feel fear the next time those lights begin to flash. As another illustration, imagine that you have just been praised by your boss, making you feel good, while standing in front of a new employee unfamiliar to you. Now, whenever you see that new employee, you will associate him or her with the praise you received, and will likely feel good once again. In fact, research has shown that the classical conditioning process actually does operate in this manner in organizations. Specifically, it has been found that we tend to like, and evaluate highly, coworkers we associate with praise we have received ourselves.[6]

Although classical conditioning explains some types of learning in organizations, its usefulness is limited. It deals only with behaviors that are *reflexive* in nature— that is, they are involuntary and occur automatically. The illness experienced at the

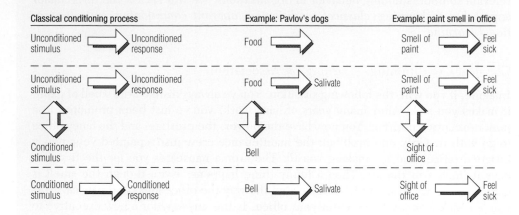

FIGURE 3-2   The Classical Conditioning Process: An Overview

The process of classical conditioning is based on the tendency of some naturally occurring stimulus (the *unconditioned stimulus*) to elicit a reflexive response (the *unconditioned response*). By pairing a previously neutral stimulus (the *conditioned stimulus*) with the unconditioned stimulus, it will eventually elicit a response similar to the unconditioned response (known as a *conditioned response*).

formerly smelly office, the fear experienced in response to the warning light, and, of course, the salivation of Pavlov's dogs are all examples of simple reflexive behaviors. Of course, many behaviors learned on the job are far too complex to be explained in terms of classical conditioning. The next type of learning we will describe, operant conditioning, better explains how we acquire more complex forms of behavior.

Operant Conditioning: Learning through Rewards and Punishments

Imagine you are a copywriter working at an advertising agency. The vice president just assigned you to an important new account. If you can write the perfect radio script and get it in on time, the company stands a chance of gaining a lot of future business. Knowing it's important, you stay up all night working on it. The next day you present it and . . . finish the ending yourself. Either the client loves it, and your grateful boss gives you a large raise and a promotion, *or* the client hates it, and your angry boss gives you two weeks' severance pay and fires you. Regardless of how the story ends, one thing is certain: whatever you do in this situation, you will be sure to either do it again (if it succeeds), or avoid doing it again (if it fails).

This story nicely illustrates an important principle of **operant conditioning** (also known as **instrumental conditioning**)—namely, that our behavior usually produces consequences. If our actions have pleasant effects, then we will be more likely to repeat them in the future. If, however, our actions have unpleasant effects, we are less likely to repeat them in the future. This phenomenon, known as the **Law of Effect,** is fundamental to operant conditioning.[7] As you may know, our knowledge of the operant conditioning process comes from the work of the famous social scientist B. F. Skinner. Skinner's pioneering research (initially with animals, although also with humans—including his own daughter) has shown us that it is through the connections between our actions and their consequences that we learn to behave in certain ways.[8] See the summary of this process and the example shown in Figure 3–3.

One thing we learn is to engage in behaviors that have positive results, actions that are pleasurable. For example, employees may find it pleasant and desirable to receive monetary bonuses, paid vacations, praise and recognition, and awards. The process by which people learn to perform acts leading to desirable outcomes is known as **positive reinforcement.** Whatever response led to the occurrence of these positive events is likely to occur again, thus strengthening the response. For a reward to serve as a positive reinforcer, it must be made contingent on the specific behavior sought. An employee may be rewarded for his or her good attendance by receipt of a monetary bonus. But that bonus is a positive reinforcer only when it is clearly tied to the desired behavior. Employees who do not perceive a link between the good attendance record and the reward will not be reinforced for their good attendance. Consider the example that opened this section, in which you were an advertising copywriter. If your script is well received, you will probably try that same approach on another campaign. The fact that it was positively reinforced—that is, linked to desired rewards—"teaches" you to make that same response again.

Sometimes we learn to perform acts because they permit us to avoid undesirable consequences. Unpleasant events, such as reprimands, rejection, probation, demotion, and termination, are some of the consequences faced for certain actions in the workplace. The process by which people learn to perform acts leading to the avoidance of such undesirable consequences is known as **negative reinforcement,** or **avoidance.** Whatever response led to the termination of these undesirable events is likely to occur again, thus strengthening that response. For example, imagine that you are involved in a very boring business meeting. When you can no longer stand it, you begin to gather your belongings and recommend breaking for lunch. As everyone concurs and begins to get up, it appears that you have escaped the boredom you faced. You were negatively reinforced for your act of recommending a lunch break, and you will be likely to do the same thing again the next time you are involved in a boring meeting. You learned how to avoid the aversive situation.

Thus far, we have identified responses that are strengthened because they either lead to positive consequences or the termination of negative consequences. However, the connection between a behavior and its consequences is not always strengthened; the link also may be weakened. This is what happens in the case of **punishment.** Punishment involves presenting an undesirable or aversive consequence in response to an unwanted behavior. A behavior accompanied by an undesirable outcome is less likely to occur again if the person eventually learns that the negative consequences

Parents should be extremely careful when punishing their children, because the link between adult psychological problems as a result of severe punishment in childhood is well documented. A large, random sample of adults in St. Louis revealed that 56 percent of people diagnosed as depressed and 43 percent of those who were alcoholics suffered severe punishment from their parents when they were children. In contrast, only 18 percent of individuals classified as healthy were punished when they were young. Managers as well as parents should use punishment only sparingly. [Jordan, N. (1989, June). Spare the rod, spare the child. *Psychology Today,* p. 16.]

FIGURE 3–3

The Operant Conditioning Process: An Overview

The basic premise of operant conditioning is that people learn by connecting the consequences of their behavior with the behavior itself. In the example shown here, the manager's praise for the subordinate increases the subordinate's tendency to perform the job properly in the future. Learning occurs by providing the appropriate antecedent and consequent conditions.

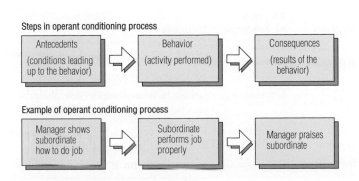

Steps in operant conditioning process

Antecedents (conditions leading up to the behavior) ⇨ Behavior (activity performed) ⇨ Consequences (results of the behavior)

Example of operant conditioning process

Manager shows subordinate how to do job ⇨ Subordinate performs job properly ⇨ Manager praises subordinate

are contingent on the behavior. For example, if you are chastised by your boss for taking long coffee breaks, you are considered punished for this action, weakening your tendency to repeat it in the future. Note that punishment is *not* the same as negative reinforcement. Whereas negative reinforcement *removes* an aversive stimulus, thereby increasing the strength of the response that led to its removal, punishment *applies* an aversive stimulus, thereby decreasing the strength of the response that led to its presentation.

The link between a behavior and its consequences may also be weakened via the process of **extinction.** When a response that was once rewarded is no longer rewarded, it tends to weaken; it will gradually die out, or be *extinguished.* Suppose that for many months you and the members of your weekly planning group met in your office for breakfast, and, being a congenial host, you supplied the doughnuts. Your colleagues always thanked you for the doughnuts, and jealously fought over favorite kinds (i.e., you were positively reinforced through their social approval). Now, however, your colleagues are realizing that they may have eaten too many doughnuts and have all begun dieting. This time, when you open the box of doughnuts, nobody says anything. The doughnuts are tempting, but your colleagues' willpower prevails and the doughnuts remain in the box, uneaten. If this happens a few more times, you will no longer bother to purchase doughnuts. Your once-rewarded behavior is no longer rewarded and will eventually die out. This is the process of extinction.

The various relationships between a person's behavior and the consequences resulting from that behavior—*positive reinforcement, negative reinforcement, punishment,* and *extinction*—are known collectively as **contingencies of reinforcement.** The four contingencies discussed are summarized in Table 3–1. As we will see, these contingencies have very important effects on many types of organizational behavior. Selectively reinforcing (either positively or negatively), punishing, and extinguishing behaviors are very effective tools for managing employees. (For an example of the way operant techniques may be applied to enhancing performance, read the **Focus on Research** section on the next page. The research described shows that successful task performance is related to some of the basic steps in the operant conditioning process described in Figure 3–3).

TABLE 3–1   Contingencies of Reinforcement: A Summary

The four reinforcement contingencies may be defined in terms of the presentation or withdrawal of a pleasant or unpleasant stimulus. Positively or negatively reinforced behaviors are strengthened; punished or extinguished behaviors are weakened.

Stimulus Presented or Withdrawn	Desirability of Stimulus	Name of Contingency	Strength of Response	Example
Presented	Pleasant	**Positive reinforcement**	Increases	Praise from a supervisor encourages continuing the praised behavior
	Unpleasant	**Punishment**	Decreases	Criticism from a supervisor discourages enacting the punished behavior
Withdrawn	Pleasant	**Extinction**	Decreases	Failing to praise a helpful act reduces the odds of helping in the future
	Unpleasant	**Negative reinforcement**	Increases	Future criticism is avoided by doing whatever the supervisor wants

FOCUS ON RESEARCH

Testing an Operant Model among Sailboat Race Teams

Successful operant conditioning requires that people maintain a keen awareness of the behaviors of interest and the consequences of performing them. This is critical because unless these things are done, it is impossible to use rewards effectively to bring about desired behaviors. For managers to be effective, they must regularly monitor their subordinates' performance (e.g., observe how well they are doing) and manage their consequences (e.g., provide feedback). When managers gather little information about their subordinates' performance and/or fail to take appropriate actions, they are bound to be ineffective.

In an ingenious test of these ideas, Komaki, Desselles, and Bowman stationed trained observers aboard each of ten J-24 sailboats engaged in a fleet racing competition.[9] The observers' job was to note the occurrence of certain types of remarks made by the skippers to their crew members. Of greatest interest to us were those remarks dealing with

- **Monitoring**—remarks for collecting performance information (e.g., "Ready to put the chute up yet?")
- **Consequences**—remarks indicating knowledge of performance (e.g., "No, grab the chute. Faster. Now.")

The investigators hypothesized that the effectiveness of a team leader will be based on how often he or she provides information regarding monitoring and consequences.

To test this hypothesis, they randomly assigned observers to watch the series of six races in which nineteen different skippers participated. During the races, the observers were stationed in the cabin areas, approximately ten feet from the skippers. Using special coding sheets, they recorded exactly what each skipper said and did every fifteen seconds. These ratings were compared to each skipper's effectiveness—measured in terms of the number of points obtained per race (where one point was awarded for coming in first place, two points for second, and so on).

The results were then analyzed by correlating the frequency of the skippers' monitor comments and their consequence comments with their effectiveness ratings. For both measures, the results were as hypothesized. The more skippers gathered performance information, the more effective they were ($r = -.51$), and the more they indicated knowledge about their crew members' performance, the more effective they were ($r = -.47$). (Note that both correlation coefficients were negative because success was measured so that *lower* scores reflected better performance.) These findings help underscore a very important point about operant conditioning. Namely, for supervisors to be successful in influencing the behavior of their subordinates, they must closely monitor and provide feedback about that performance. The more information about performance is collected and shared with subordinates, the more effectively they perform.

Observational Learning: Learning by Modeling Others

Although operant conditioning is based on the idea that we engage in behaviors for which we are directly reinforced, many of the things we learn—especially on the job—are not directly reinforced. For example, imagine that you're new to the job. On your first day, you see many of your coworkers complimenting your boss on his attire—"Nice suit, Mr. Johnson, looks good." Each time someone says something flattering, the boss stops at his or her desk, smiles, and acts friendly. They're reinforced for complimenting the boss by his return of social approval. Chances are, by observing this, you, too, will eventually say something nice to the boss, hoping to

Test Bank questions 3.61 and 3.69 relate to material on this page.

receive similar social approval. Although you may not have experienced it directly, you would expect those consequences in return for your actions on the basis of what you've observed happening to others.

This example describes another kind of learning, known as **observational learning,** or **modeling.** It occurs when one person acquires new information or behaviors *vicariously*—that is, by observing what happens to others.[10] The person whose behavior is imitated is called the *model.* For someone to learn by observing a model, several processes must occur. (See Figure 3–4.)

First, the learner must pay careful *attention* to the model. Learning will be most effective when models get the attention of others. Models can purposely call attention to themselves in order to facilitate learning. When one worker trains another on the job, he or she may call attention to job performance by asking the trainee to "pay attention, and watch carefully." Second, workers must have good *retention* of the model's actions. The person learning to do the job must be able to develop some verbal description or mental image of the model's actions in order to remember them. If the learner can imagine himself or herself behaving just as the model did— a process known as *symbolic rehearsal*—then learning will be facilitated. Third, there must be some *behavioral reproduction* of the model's behavior. Unless workers are capable of doing just what the model does, they do not have any hope of being able to learn observationally from that model. Of course, the ability to reproduce many observed behaviors may be quite limited initially, but can improve with practice. Finally, workers must have some *motivation* to learn from the model. We don't emulate every behavior we see, but focus on those we have some reason or incentive to match—such as actions for which others are rewarded.

Interestingly, in observational learning, the learning process is controlled by the learners themselves. What you learn is, of course, based on what you observe and desire to learn. The more you observe others and carefully attend to what happens to them, the more you can learn from them. You can reward yourself by carefully imitating the successful behavior of others. In many cases, the desire to feel that you have successfully taught yourself something constitutes the only reward received. For example, one of the authors knows someone who used to work for a large

FIGURE 3–4

Observational Learning: An Overview

The process of observational learning requires that an observer pay attention to and remember a model's behavior. By observing what the model did and rehearsing those actions, the observer may learn to imitate the model, but only if the observer is motivated to do so (i.e., if the model was rewarded for behaving as observed).

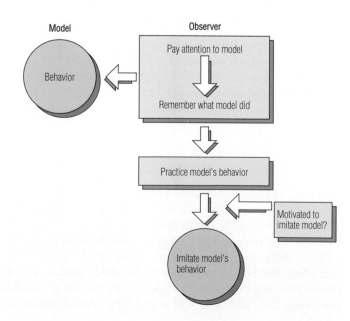

FIGURE 3–5

Observational Learning: Learning by Watching and Doing

Many job skills are learned through the process of observation. The young apprentices shown here can learn a great deal by watching and trying to imitate their more experienced coworker.

commercial bakery, making some of the company's delicious candy products. Every day she observed the pastry chefs working nearby as they made their elaborate cakes and tarts. She diligently watched them mix the various ingredients and bake, assemble, and decorate the cakes. In time, she learned to make them herself, just by watching and practicing on her own. Today, she makes them very well. She was not directly reinforced by rewards offered on the job, but by her own self-approval (feeling good about acquiring her new baking skills).

A great deal of what is learned about how to behave in organizations can clearly be explained as the result of observational learning (see Figure 3–5).[11] On the job, observational learning occurs both formally and informally. As we will see, observational learning is a key part of many formal job instruction training programs.[12] Workers given a chance to observe experts doing their jobs, followed by an opportunity to practice the desired skills, and feedback on their work, tend to be very effectively trained. Of course, observational learning also occurs in a very informal, uncalculated manner. Workers who experience the norms and traditions of their organizations, and who subsequently incorporate these into their own behavior, have also learned through observation. In chapter 9, we will show that observational learning is responsible, in part, for the ways new employees are socialized into their organizations (i.e., how they "learn the ropes") and how they come to appreciate their organization's traditions and ways of doing things (i.e., its culture).

REINFORCING DESIRABLE ORGANIZATIONAL BEHAVIORS

One of the most useful purposes of learning in organizations is assuring that desirable job behaviors (e.g., high-quality performance, safe job behavior, high attendance) are developed and maintained. As we have just discussed, an effective mechanism for getting people (and animals, too) to behave in a desired fashion is reinforcement. A **reinforcer** is any event (e.g., a pay raise, praise) that increases the probability of the behavior preceding it. For example, praising an employee for superb performance on a special project positively reinforces the employee's good work. In other words,

Social learning plays an important role in the success of college freshmen. Undergraduate students are more likely to succeed when they study together, meet frequently with their advisors, and enroll in at least one small class every term than when they do not have these kinds of one-on-one contact with others. Students who learn from each other (such as by watching, helping, and practicing solving problems together) are more successful than those who try to make it through school on their own. [DePalma, A. (1991, November 6). How undergraduates can succeed: Study together, and in small classes. *The New York Times*, p. B8(N).]

FIGURE 3–6   Praise: An Important Organizational Reward

A compliment can be an effective source of reinforcement among people working in organizations. Although a compliment *may,* in fact, be more affordable than cash, it will be effective only when given in response to desired behaviors. (*Source:* © King Features Syndicate, Inc.)

it increases the chance that he or she will do just as well the next time a similar project comes along (see Figure 3–6).

For reinforcement to be effective, it must be properly administered—which is easier said than done. Indeed, companies sometimes make the mistake of inadvertently reinforcing the very behaviors they wish to eliminate (e.g., some companies may reinforce the wasting of money by raising the budgets of departments that spent all their money the previous year).[13] On the other hand, proper use of a reinforcer, such as a supervisor's praise, is credited for saving one large company, Emery Air Freight, $3 million in a three-year period.[14] Management's recognition of and praise for good employee performance lowered turnover and improved productivity, resulting in Emery's dramatic financial gain. Another company, Autodesk, Inc. (a Sausalito, California, software maker), instituted a monthly bonus system that rewarded employees for being highly productive and reducing errors.[15] Before the bonus system began in 1985, employees worked a lot of unnecessary overtime and the error rate was quite high. After all, they were rewarded for *how long* they worked, not *how well* they did. By 1990, only five years after the bonus plan began, the benefits were quite dramatic. Specifically, although the company's sales increased almost tenfold, and its error rate all but disappeared, its employee base only doubled, and production workers received 10 to 15 percent higher pay than they would have had they still been paid on an hourly basis. Clearly, both the company management *and* its employees themselves greatly benefited by the use of this bonus plan. As these examples demonstrate, the use of reinforcement may have dramatic effects on the functioning of organizations and the people working within them.

Obviously, it is important to examine how to use reinforcement effectively in organizations. Our consideration of this topic will focus on two different approaches for systematically reinforcing desired behavior in organizations: *organizational behavior management* programs and *training* programs. Before examining these practical applications, we will take a closer look at the important issue of how reinforcements are administered, patterns better known as **schedules of reinforcement.**

Schedules of Reinforcement: Patterns of Administering Rewards

Although rewards may help reinforce desirable behavior, rewarding employees for everything they do that may be worthy of reward is not always practical (or, as we will see, advisable). Rewarding *every* desired response made is called **continuous reinforcement.** Unlike an animal learning to perform a trick, people on the job are rarely reinforced continuously. Instead, organizational rewards tend to be administered following **partial** (or **intermittent**) **reinforcement** schedules—that is, rewards are administered intermittently, with some desired responses reinforced and some not. Four varieties of partial reinforcement schedules have direct application to organizations.[16]

1. **Fixed interval schedules** are those in which reinforcement is administered the first time the desired behavior occurs after a specific amount of time has passed. For example, the practice of issuing paychecks each Friday at 3:00 P.M. or receiving pay raises once a year on the anniversary date of hiring are good examples of fixed interval schedules. In both instances, the rewards are administered on a regular, fixed basis. Fixed interval schedules are not especially effective in maintaining desired job performance. For example, clerical workers who know that their boss will pass by their desks every day at 11:30 A.M. will make sure they are working hard at that time, and will surely avoid taking an early lunch. However, without the boss around to praise or reprimand at other times, they will be less likely to work as hard because they know that positive reinforcement or punishment will not be forthcoming.

2. **Variable interval schedules** are those in which a variable amount of time (based on some average amount) must elapse between the administration of reinforcements. For example, a bank auditor who pays surprise visits to the various branch offices on an average of every eight weeks (e.g., visits may be six weeks apart one time, and ten weeks apart another) to check their books is using a variable interval schedule. So too is a boss who passes the desks of his or her employees at unannounced times once a day—perhaps 9:30 A.M. on Monday, but 4:30 P.M. on Tuesday. Because the staff members in both examples cannot tell exactly when they may be rewarded, they will tend to perform well for a relatively long period. They may slack off after they have been reinforced, but they cannot stay that way for long because they don't know how long they'll have to wait until they are reinforced again. It may be sooner than they think.

3. **Fixed ratio schedules** are those in which reinforcement is administered the first time the desired behavior occurs after a specific number of such actions have been performed. For example, migrant farm workers are often paid a certain amount based on the number of boxes or pounds of fruit or vegetables they pick. In fact, any type of *piecework pay system* constitutes a fixed ratio schedule of reinforcement. As another example, employees may know that they will receive a monetary bonus and/or praise from their boss each time they exceed a certain level of production or sales. Immediately after receiving the reinforcement, work may slack off, but it will then pick up again as workers approach the next performance level at which the reinforcement is administered.

4. **Variable ratio schedules** are those in which a variable number of desired responses (based on some average amount) must elapse between the administration of reinforcements. For example, a salesperson might receive a sizable bonus every time an average of twenty sales are made, but sometimes the bonus may be given after only fifteen sales, sometimes after twenty sales exactly, and others after twenty-five. As a result of not knowing how many desired responses are necessary in order to be rewarded, salespeople may work diligently in the hope of being reinforced for their next successful job performance. A classic example of the effectiveness of variable ratio schedules is playing slot machines. Since these devices pay off after a variable number of plays, the gambler can never tell whether the next coin inserted and pull of the handle will hit the jackpot. It is this lack of knowledge about what will happen that makes the variable ratio schedule so effective in maintaining performance.

Test Bank questions 3.21–3.25, 3.52, 3.62–3.63, and 3.70–3.72 relate to material on this page.

As we have described them here, the various schedules of reinforcement have a number of important similarities and differences. We have summarized these in Table 3–2. As you review this table, keep in mind that these schedules of reinforcement represent "pure" forms. Used in practice, however, many reinforcement schedules may be combined, thereby making complex new schedules. For example, a company's promotion policy may require that promotions be given only after a fixed interval of time has passed (e.g., five years of job experience) *and* a fixed amount of successful performance is demonstrated (e.g., $1 million in sales). In such a case, the reward (the promotion) is based on both a fixed interval and fixed ratio schedule. Whether they operate separately or in conjunction with one another, different schedules of reinforcement can exert strong influences on organizational behavior.

Research has shown that people perform quite differently in response to various schedules of reinforcement. For example, Saari and Latham compared the job performance of beaver trappers working for a paper products company in the Pacific Northwest who were paid under different schedules of reinforcement.[17] Before the study began, the trappers were paid a flat rate of $7 per hour, regardless of their job performance (i.e., their reward was administered *noncontingent* on performance). The experiment augmented their base salary in one of two ways contingent on their job performance—following either a continuous reinforcement schedule or a variable ratio schedule. Those receiving continuous reinforcement were paid $1 for each beaver they caught. Those on a variable ratio schedule were given $4 whenever they caught a beaver *and* then twice correctly predicted an odd or even outcome on two consecutive rolls of a pair of dice. Because the chance of making these predictions correctly is one in four, the workers paid on a variable ratio basis had, over time, the opportunity to earn the same amount of money as their coworkers paid $1 per beaver caught. Despite this, those paid using the variable ratio schedule were over 70 percent more productive than those paid according to a continuous reinforcement schedule. (By the way, you may find it interesting to know that the trappers went along with these unusual pay plans because they supplemented the base pay normally received.) After either contingent pay plan was introduced, the level of productivity almost doubled (see Figure 3–7).

Some employees are more willing than others to wait for rewards they have earned. Whereas some people desire immediate praise after performing well, others are more willing to "delay gratification." The capacity to delay gratification appears to be based on the degree to which, as a child, one was immediately rewarded by his or her parents or was forced to wait for rewards. It is not yet known if it is possible for supervisors to alter subordinates' willingness to delay gratification for those employees not forced to wait for gratification as children. [Mischel, W., Shoda, Y., & Rodriguez, M. L. (1989, May). Delay of gratification in children. *Science, 244,* 933–937.]

T A B L E 3 – 2   Schedules of Reinforcement: A Summary

The four schedules of reinforcement summarized here represent different ways of systematically administering reinforcements intermittently (i.e., according to a partial reinforcement schedule).

Schedule of Reinforcement	Description	Example
Fixed interval	Rewards given after a constant amount of time has passed	Paycheck given the same time each week
Variable interval	Rewards given after a variable amount of time has passed	Bank auditor visits branch offices an average of once every eight weeks, but not on a fixed schedule
Fixed ratio	Rewards given after a constant number of actions performed	Pay of $1 is given for every five boxes of fruit picked and packed
Variable ratio	Rewards given after a variable number of actions performed	A slot machine pays a jackpot, on average, one time per million plays

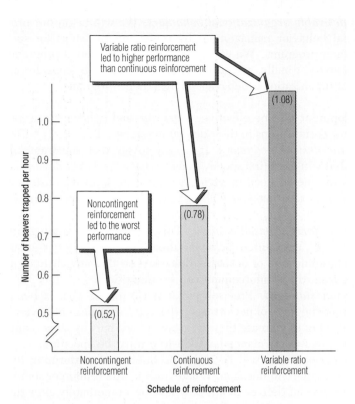

Number of beavers trapped per hour

Variable ratio reinforcement led to higher performance than continuous reinforcement

(1.08)

Noncontingent reinforcement led to the worst performance

(0.78)

(0.52)

Noncontingent reinforcement | Continuous reinforcement | Variable ratio reinforcement

Schedule of reinforcement

FIGURE 3–7

The Effectiveness of Variable Ratio Schedules: An Experimental Demonstration

An experiment compared the job performance of beaver trappers originally paid on a noncontingent (flat salary) basis with their performance after a contingent pay schedule (either a continuous reinforcement schedule or a variable ratio schedule) was introduced. As the results described here show, making pay contingent on performance improved individual productivity. The improvement when payment was made on a variable ratio schedule was greater than when payment was made on a continuous reinforcement schedule. (*Source:* Based on data in Saari & Latham, 1982; see Note 17.)

Findings such as these provide a good example of the effectiveness of contingent reinforcement, especially variable ratio schedules of reinforcement. In general, research has found that many kinds of organizational rewards (e.g., praise, time off) made contingent on the performance of specific desirable behaviors (i.e., employees paid according to ratio schedules) tend to be effective in raising performance. In contrast, rewards contingent on the passage of time (i.e., interval schedules) tend to be less effective in enhancing performance.[18] Certainly, this makes sense. You would probably find yourself working harder if your pay raises were based on how productive you were than you would if you knew that the same pay raise was automatically forthcoming regardless of your productivity. As a result, it is not surprising that many previously hardworking employees tend to become less productive when pay plans that make their pay contingent on job performance (known as *merit-pay* plans, or *pay-for-performance* plans) are eliminated in favor of systems in which raises are given on the basis of seniority.[19]

Organizational Behavior Management: Positively Reinforcing Desirable Organizational Behaviors

Earlier, in describing operant conditioning, we noted that it is the consequences of our behavior that determine whether we repeat or abandon it. Behaviors that are rewarded tend to be strengthened, repeated in the future. Accordingly, we can administer rewards selectively to help reinforce behaviors that we wish repeated in the future. This is the basic principle behind **organizational behavior management** (also known as **organizational behavior modification,** or more simply, **OB Mod**). Organizational behavior management may be defined as *the systematic application of positive reinforcement principles in organizational settings for the purpose of* *raising the incidence of desirable organizational behaviors.* We will begin our presentation of organizational behavior management by reviewing the steps for successfully implementing such programs. We will then discuss some actual programs that have been used in industry. Finally, we will conclude this section by considering the ethical implications of organizational behavior management programs.

Steps in Program Development   To be effective, organizational behavior management programs must follow certain steps in their development (see Table 3–3).[20] The first step is to *pinpoint the desired behaviors.* It is easy to say that you want job performance to improve, but you must first specify exactly what aspect of performance you want changed. For example, instead of saying you wish to improve customer service, it would be better to say that you will answer your customers' inquiries more quickly.

The second step is to *perform a baseline audit.* This involves determining the rate at which the desirable (i.e., pinpointed) behavior already occurs. It is, of course, necessary to identify the baseline rate of desirable behaviors so that any changes in these behaviors resulting from the reinforcement can be identified.

Third, *define a criterion standard.* Precisely what performance goal is being sought? What will constitute the level of performance desired from your employees? For example, do you want them to increase their wearing of hard hats by 20 percent, 40 percent, or more? The exact performance level desired must be specified.

Fourth, *choose a reinforcer.* What will be the consequence of performing the desired behavior? This is an important decision. Whatever it is, the reinforcer should be something that supervisors can deliver in a timely fashion immediately after the desired behavior. After all, for a reward to reinforce behavior, the connection between the desired behavior and the reward must be made. Praise is commonly used as a reinforcement in many organizational management programs. So too are rewards such as time off from work, small gifts, and the like.

Next, it is considered useful to *selectively reward desired behaviors that approximate the criterion standard.* In other words, it would speed the learning process if employees were reinforced for improving their behavior in the general direction of the desired standard. The process of selectively reinforcing behaviors approaching

TABLE 3–3   Developing an Organizational Behavior Management Program: Some Basic Steps

The general steps of an organizational behavior management program are listed here, along with an example of how each step may be applied in the case of improving secretaries' typing speed.

Step	Example
1. Pinpoint the desired behavior	Improve typing speed
2. Perform a baseline audit	Currently typing at 50 wpm
3. Define criterion standard	Desired typing speed is 65 wpm
4. Select a reinforcer	Praise improvements in typing speed
5. Selectively reward desired behaviors approximating the goal, until it is reached	Praise when performance improves to 55 wpm, again at 60 wpm, and again when the goal of 65 wpm is met
6. Periodically reevaluate	Monitor typing for changes in performance; alter goal and/or administer new reinforcers as needed

the goal is known as **shaping.** For example, imagine that the baseline rate of wearing safety goggles on the job is 62 percent, and you wish to raise it to 95 percent. After a few days, the rate of wearing the goggles increases to 71 percent. Although the desired rate has not been met, it has improved, and the employees should be praised for moving in the right direction. Saying "I'm really glad to see you're wearing your goggles; keep it up" would surely help. (Although this may sound hokey to you, subordinates tend to be quite sensitive to the praise they receive from their superiors, and may find such remarks highly reinforcing.) Then you would give more praise only when the rate of goggles-wearing has increased more and more until the desired goal is reached.

Finally, after the desired goal has been attained, it would be useful to *periodically reevaluate the program.* Is the goal behavior still performed? Are the rewards still working? To expect some changes in these events over time is not unusual. As a result, it is important to audit the behavior in question. Without careful monitoring, the behaviors you worked so hard to develop may change.

Organizational Behavior Management in Action: Some Examples   Research has shown that principles of reinforcement have been used effectively to improve a variety of organizational behaviors.[21] The technique has been used in a wide range of organizations, such as Michigan Bell, United Airlines, Chase Manhattan Bank, IBM, Procter & Gamble, and General Electric, to cite just a few well-known companies.[22]

As one example of an effective organizational behavior management program, let's consider the bonus system used by the city of Detroit to improve the performance of its garbage collectors in the early 1970s.[23] The city was interested in reducing the costs of its refuse collection operation and, with the cooperation of the unions involved, instituted a bonus system to reward the workers for increased efficiency. The plan established a pool of savings based on reductions in the number of hours worked, reductions in overtime costs, the percentage of routes completed on schedule, and the cleanliness of the routes serviced. The city and the refuse workers agreed to split the savings on a fifty–fifty basis. The program was considered a great success, because improvements were found on all the criterion measures. Everyone benefited: in 1974, the city saved $1,654,000; each employee received a bonus of $350; and citizen complaints decreased markedly.

Another successful example of an organizational behavior management plan in operation can be found at Diamond International of Palmer, Massachusetts, a plant with 325 employees that manufactures Styrofoam egg cartons.[24] In response to sluggish productivity and strained relations with employees, a simple but elegant and effective reinforcement system has been put into place. Any employee working for a full year without an industrial accident is given twenty points. Perfect attendance is given another twenty-five points. Once a year, the points are totaled. When workers reach 100 points, they get a blue nylon jacket with the company's logo and a patch indicating their membership in the "100 Club." Workers earning over 100 points receive extra rewards. For example, in exchange for 500 points, workers can select a blender, a set of cookware, a wall clock, or a pine cribbage board. Although the workers can well afford these inexpensive prizes, they recognize these items as tokens of appreciation. This plan has helped improve things at Diamond International dramatically. Compared with before the reinforcement program was initiated, productivity improved 16.5 percent, quality-related errors were reduced 40 percent, grievances decreased 72 percent, and time lost due to industrial accidents was lowered by 43.7 percent. The result of all of this has been over $1 million in gross financial benefits. Needless to say, here is an example of a very simple and very effective organizational behavior management program.

The exact form that shaping may take is not the same in all countries. For example, students in China are taught through a method called "teaching by holding one's hand." Specifically, they are taught how to master exact motions, such as those involved in writing, painting, and sculpture, by the instructor, who literally holds the students' hands. In the United States, by contrast, children are more likely to be taught by a process that allows them to explore, experience, and learn on their own. Teachers help students to learn techniques, but students are typically free to develop and experiment on their own with guidance from their teachers. [Gardner, H. (1989, December). Learning, Chinese-style. *Psychology Today*, pp. 54–56.]

TABLE 3–4   Organizational Behavior Management Programs: Some Success Stories

Although not all organizational behavior management programs are as successful as the ones summarized here, many have been extremely effective in bringing about improvements in desired behaviors.

Company	Reinforcers Used	Results
General Electric	Praise and constructive reinforcement	Productivity increased, cost savings resulted
Weyerhaeuser Co.	Contingent pay, and praise/recognition	Productivity increased in most work groups (18–33 percent)
B. F. Goodrich Chemical Co.	Praise and recognition	Production increased over 300 percent
Connecticut General Life Insurance Co.	Time off based on performance	Chronic absenteeism and lateness drastically reduced
General Mills	Praise and feedback for meeting objectives	Sales increased

Sources: Based on Hamner & Hamner, 1976, Note 22; and Frederiksen, 1982, Note 18.

These are only a few examples of many effective organizational behavior management programs that have been employed (for a summary of several others, see Table 3–4). Although other programs may have brought about less spectacular results, most organizational behavior management programs have been quite successful. Research has found such programs to be effective in improving the quantity and quality of performance, reducing absenteeism, improving employee safety, reducing waste and theft, and improving customer service.[25]

Before concluding this section, we should note that not all reinforcement contingencies need to be administered by supervisors. Some theorists and practitioners, inspired by the observational learning approach, have recognized that employees may be able to improve their own behavior by rewarding themselves appropriately.[26] The key is for employees to catch themselves performing correctly, and to praise or somehow otherwise reward themselves for doing so. One recommendation for doing this is that employees carefully observe and keep a record of their own job performance. Individuals must systematically monitor their performance (e.g., words per minute typed) to recognize and feel good about improvements. Through observation, and trial and error, improvements in performance may be noted. Once this happens, people can reward themselves. They may, for example, praise themselves, or allow themselves to put off doing a less preferred job. Although the effectiveness of such *self-managed reinforcement plans* has yet to be firmly established, they represent an interesting new direction for the field of organizational behavior management. If nothing else, such research shows that the management of organizational behavior may be the result of not only operant conditioning principles, but observational learning principles as well.

Organizational Behavior Modification: Is It Ethical? Despite their apparent effectiveness—or perhaps because of it—organizational behavior management programs have generated some criticism. One of the primary criticisms is that such programs tend to be too demeaning, manipulative, and "controlling" of human behavior, and as such are unethical.[27] Although we encourage you to make up your own mind on this issue, it is certainly important to put a few key issues in perspective.

No doubt, positive reinforcement is a form of manipulation, but, as Skinner reminds us, we are all constantly influencing (hence, manipulating) each other, and such impact is inevitable. Therefore, the key question is *not* whether we influence each other through our actions, but whether such influence is constructive.[28] In the case of organizations, the proper use of reinforcements may improve profitability not only for the organizations involved, but for employees as well. This is certainly true in the studies we have reviewed here. A manager somehow misusing reinforcement contingencies to control employees in inappropriate ways is probably rare. Indeed, most employees would not allow this to happen, making the manager's questionable actions self-defeating. Thus, we believe that organizational behavior management is, like any other technique used in the social sciences, inherently neutral. It is only as "good" or "evil" as the person using it.

Thus far, we have been relatively vague about the processes through which employees learn to perform the skills needed to do their jobs. Systematic efforts at establishing needed job skills are referred to as *training*.

Training: Learning and Developing Necessary Job Skills

Probably the most obvious use to which principles of learning may be applied in organizations is **training**—that is, the process by which people systematically acquire and improve the skills and abilities needed to better their job performance.[29] Just as the classroom training you are receiving in school is designed to give you the skills needed to function in life (and perhaps a profession), the training of employees is designed to prepare them to operate effectively on their jobs. Training may be used not only to prepare newly hired employees to meet the challenges of the jobs they are about to face, but also to upgrade and refine the skills of existing employees. Sometimes people are trained to perform specific jobs, and sometimes they are trained in skills that are not immediately useful, but which may prove valuable at some later time. In either case, good training programs focus on meeting the needs of employees and their organizations, preparing them for jobs that need to be done—both now and in the future.

Training is an extensive, ongoing activity in many organizations. Consider, for example, data reported by the Carnegie Foundation showing that U.S. industrial corporations spend more than $40 billion annually on employee training.[30] IBM alone reportedly spends $1 billion annually on training.[31] Obviously, training is a process in which organizations invest a great deal of resources, hoping to enable their employees to function in a manner that maximizes their usefulness to the organization.

Training programs take many different forms. These range from the most simple, "show and tell" approach of job instruction training to very complicated simulation devices used off the job (such as those used to train pilots and astronauts). In Table 3–5 (see p. 96), we identify and summarize some of the training programs most commonly used today. Please review this table carefully. We think you'll find it interesting to see the range of methods used to train people to do their jobs. As you review the table, note that the most effective training programs rely on more than one of these techniques. Indeed, because no one method is perfect, several methods are often used together to maximize the effectiveness of training. The idea behind this is that any one training method may be more effective in getting people to learn one aspect of the job better than another. So using several different approaches together may be most helpful in reaching the goal of training—getting the trainee's

Although women and minorities are making inroads into all levels of business, most of the executive training is still going to white males. In M.B.A. programs, typically paid for by students themselves, about 30 percent of the students are women. However, in executive education programs, which are typically paid for by employers, women and minorities make up only a tiny percentage of those trained. For example, recently only 3 percent of the people enrolled in Stanford's executive education programs were women. [Executive education is too white and too male. (1991, October 28). *Business Week,* p. 150.]

TABLE 3-5   Training Techniques: A Summary of Some Popular Methods

As shown here, employee training can take many forms, some very simple and others quite elaborate. The techniques may be distinguished with respect to whether the training takes place on the job or off the job.

Training Method	Description
On-the-Job Methods	
Apprenticeship programs	An inexperienced trainee works alongside a senior coworker for a certain number of years; often accompanied by formal classroom training; used to train skilled trade workers (e.g., carpenters, electricians)
Job instruction training	Trainees are told about the job, instructed on how to do it, allowed to try out the job, given feedback, and then permitted to work on their own (with someone nearby to help, if needed)
Off-the-Job Methods	
Films/video presentations	Complex procedures not easily demonstrated in person may be shown on film or videotape; because questions cannot be asked, presentations are often used in conjunction with a live lecture by a knowledgeable trainer
Simulations	Simulations may range from the most simple procedures, such as cases and role-playing exercises used to train managers in interpersonal skills, to the most complex computer-assisted simulations used to train astronauts for space flights

performance up to the desired level as quickly as possible. Any one technique is effective because it incorporates more of one principle of effective learning than another; a good training program can use multiple methods, thereby assuring that several learning principles are incorporated into the training.

If you try to recall the factors that have helped you learn various skills, such as how to study, drive, or use a word processor, you probably can appreciate some of the principles that help make training effective. Four major principles are most relevant.

1. **Participation.** For training to be effective, trainees must be actively involved, performing the desired skills. It is well established that people learn more quickly—and tend to retain their learned skills—when they actively participate in learning. For example, when learning to swim, there is no substitute for getting in the water and actually moving your arms and legs. The principle of participation applies to learning cognitive skills just as it does to learning motor skills. Students who listen attentively in class, think about the material, take notes, and get involved in discussions prove to be more effective learners than those who just sit passively.

2. **Repetition.** If you know the adage "Practice makes perfect," you are well aware of the benefits of repetition on learning. Indeed, that learning is facilitated by repeating the desired behaviors is well established. If you've ever tried to learn a poem or the script of a play, you probably already know that constantly repeating the material helps you learn it. After all, this is probably how you learned the multiplication table and the alphabet! In learning many job skills, we know that practice makes perfect. We also know that practice is more effective when spread out over time than when all lumped together. When practice periods are too long, learning

can suffer from fatigue, whereas learning a little bit at a time allows the material to sink in. The question of exactly how long one should practice and how long one should rest depends on many factors, such as the nature of the task and the ability of the person performing it.[32] So it's not possible to give you a simple answer regarding how long one should practice a task and how long one should rest in order to achieve the maximum benefits of repetition. Despite this complexity, however, the major conclusion is simple: practice spaced repeatedly over time is more effective in promoting learning over the long term than is practice crammed into long periods without rest. (If you've ever crammed all night for an exam, you are probably already aware that you would have learned more and retained the material longer had you studied a little bit of the material each night during the last week!)

3. **Transfer of training.** For training to be most effective, what is learned during training must be applied to the job. In fact, the more closely a training program matches the demands of the job, the more effective the training will be.[33] This is the principle behind the elaborate simulation devices used in the training of combat pilots and astronauts. By using sophisticated computer-based techniques to carefully simulate real flight conditions, trainees can learn what it is like to manipulate their craft safely, without actually risking their lives and expensive equipment. Naturally, training that is any less elaborate in the degree to which it simulates the actual work environment (e.g., a home computer flight-simulation game) is less effective. The basic idea is that what is learned during training sessions can be transferred to the job itself. The same principle applies as well to more down-to-earth jobs. For example, suppose you learn to operate a cash register or a computer while in trade school, and later have to operate such equipment on your job. To the extent that the equipment used during training is similar to that used in the actual job itself, we may expect that more of the training will transfer to the actual job.

4. **Feedback.** No learning of any type can be effective without feedback—that is, knowledge of the results of one's actions. Feedback provides information on the effectiveness of one's training.[34] Unless you learn what you're doing well and what you need to correct, you will probably not be able to improve your skills. If you've ever tried to play golf, shoot at a target, or pitch a baseball, you know only too well how important feedback can be to your training. In these cases, knowing that the golf ball, arrow, or baseball went too far to the right or left, for example, is critical for you to correct your actions next time. In the absence of such knowledge, your training will certainly be considerably less effective. The same thing applies in any class you take. Test grades gauge the effectiveness of your classroom training; they provide feedback about how well you're doing so that appropriate actions can be taken to improve. The same principle applies to the training of employees on the job. For example, people being trained as word processing operators must know exactly how many correct words they have entered per minute to judge whether they have improved.

In sum, these four principles—*participation, repetition, transfer of training,* and *feedback*—are the key to the effectiveness of any training program. The most effective training programs are those that incorporate as many of these principles as possible. (As we noted earlier, employees can be trained in just about any aspect of the job deemed relevant by officials of the organization. In recent times, organizations have discovered that it is not sufficient to train employees only in areas such as technical skills and general managerial skills, but that it is also necessary to supplement this training in new areas of need, such as business ethics. For a closer look at how one major company is attempting to train its employees to be more sensitive to ethical issues, see the **Question of Ethics** section on p. 98.)

Training employees will be a critical activity for managers through the end of the decade. By the year 2000, employees with below average job skills will be acceptable only on 27 percent of the jobs performed, compared to 40 percent now. In addition, 41 percent of all jobs will require average or better skills, compared to 24 percent of the jobs now. Managers will need to find innovative ways to train and retrain employees. [Johnston, B. (1988). *Workforce 2000.* Washington, DC: U.S. Government Printing Office.]

A QUESTION OF ETHICS

Learning to Be Ethical: Citicorp Employees Play the Work Ethic Game

 "If you're immoral, you're immoral; that's just the way you are, and nobody's ever going to change you." Statements of this type are not unusual; some individuals believe that you cannot train people to be more ethical than they already are. In recent years, however, this fatalistic outlook has been challenged by experts who counter that people *can* be trained in matters of business ethics.[35] Specifically, many businesses have trained employees to recognize the moral aspects of the decisions confronting them, to become more aware of their moral obligations, and to consider various ethical points of view.[36] The basic idea is very simple: as ethical scandals fill the pages of our daily newspapers, those charged with immoral conduct tend to falter, whereas those who maintain high moral practices tend to succeed. In short, if good ethics makes for good business, training employees to be ethical makes sense.[37]

This is the idea behind a novel training tool used by Citicorp to communicate ethical practices to its 90,000 worldwide employees.[38] It's called The Work Ethic, a board and card game that presents teams of players with ethical dilemmas (e.g., insider trading, conflicts of interest) and awards them points based on their selection of one of four predetermined solutions.

To paraphrase, one of the scenarios used goes something like this. You are to imagine that you are a corporate recruiter for your organization. A vice president asks you to find a new position for a manager who you know is a poor performer. This puts you in a difficult situation. The vice president wants this poor performer out of her department within a few months, but you cannot afford to anger the vice president because your own success depends on having good rapport with her. What would you do in this situation? You must discuss each of the following alternatives, and then select one:

1. Insist that the manager be counseled on his performance before he is transferred.
2. Say nothing about the manager's poor performance when presenting him for another job.
3. Refuse to get involved in transferring the manager.
4. Be frank about the manager's performance problems when presenting him for another job.

The idea of the game is to encourage dialogue. In this case, for example, there are many issues to discuss. It certainly is not easy to tell a superior that you will do what she wants only with a condition attached (in this case, arranging the transfer if the problem manager is counseled). Yet, that solution (1) merits the most points, twenty. Solution 2 receives minus-ten points, solution 3 rates zero points, and solution 4 is awarded ten points. If these point assignments don't happen to reflect what you might think would be the right thing to do, don't be alarmed. It doesn't mean you are unethical. The game is *supposed to* generate disagreement. In fact, players can disagree formally with preprinted answers by taking their cases to an appeals board made up of four of Citicorp's senior managers.

By engaging in dialogues created by the game, participants receive a clear message that senior management at Citicorp is *very* serious about ethics. Similarly, the company's policy to encourage employees to speak out on ethical matters without fear of censure is reaffirmed.

Specific ethical issues that reflect the varied activities of Citicorp's employees have been developed. For example, the game includes questions that address diverse matters such as credit card collections, recruiting, law, trading, international money management, and the like. The game has been played by 30,000 to 40,000 Citicorp employees in at least fifty-four nations, where it has been translated into the local languages. Obviously, Citicorp is very optimistic about the use of this training tool. To quote Kate Nelson, the head of communication for corporate human resources, "You can't overstate the importance of talking about ethics whether it's in a corporation or in our personal lives. Without training, even well-meaning employees can make bad decisions."[39]

DISCIPLINE: ELIMINATING UNDESIRABLE ORGANIZATIONAL BEHAVIORS

Thus far, this chapter has focused on ways to reinforce desirable organizational behaviors. Although getting employees to behave appropriately is very important, getting them to stop behaving in some undesirable ways is sometimes also necessary. Indeed, it is not too difficult to imagine how problems like absenteeism, lateness, and drug and alcohol addiction cost companies vast sums of money.[40] Managing such problems involves the use of **discipline**—the systematic administration of punishment. As you may recall from our earlier discussion, punishment is the process through which an undesirable outcome follows the performance of an unwanted behavior, thereby reducing the strength of that behavior. It is important to keep in mind that an unpleasant stimulus is not by itself a punishment; an unpleasant stimulus may be considered a punishment only when it suppresses an unwanted behavior.

Our discussion of discipline will focus on two important issues. First, we will review the various ways disciplinary measures are used in organizations. We will then discuss the factors that make discipline effective.

The Uses of Discipline

Disciplining problem employees in one form or another is a common practice in organizations. In fact, a survey of 100 organizations found that discipline, or the threat of discipline, was used by 83 percent of the companies in response to undesirable behaviors.[41] Although some believe punishment produces undesirable side effects (such as aggression and withdrawal), the process is commonly used in organizations in one form or another.[42] Many types of disciplinary problems exist in organizations, some of a personal nature (e.g., alcoholism, emotional disorders), and others more directly job related (e.g., incompetence and insubordination).[43] Although some of these problems may be temporary and others more chronic, they are likely to have profound effects on the whole organization (e.g., poor morale, decreases in production, interpersonal conflict), and are therefore frequently punished. In fact, organizations that neglect systematically punishing the inappropriate actions of its employees run a serious risk of failing. For example, insiders have noted that the demise of the once-successful brokerage firm E. F. Hutton can be attributed to the fact that no one in top management was ever punished for making poor decisions.[44]

Disciplinary actions in organizations vary greatly. At one extreme, they may be very formal, such as written warnings that become part of the employee's permanent record. At the other extreme, they may be quite informal and low-key, such as friendly reminders and off-the-record discussions between supervisors and their problem subordinates. An interesting field study by Beyer and Trice reported the frequency with which different types of disciplinary actions were taken by a large sample of managers in dealing with their problem subordinates (a large proportion of whom had alcohol addiction problems).[45] Specifically, they found that 95 percent of the managers first discussed the problem informally with their subordinates, with most of the discussions covering both constructive topics (e.g., ways to get help with their problems) and confrontational topics (e.g., possible disciplinary steps, and the effects on their work record). More formal, and more punitive, written warnings were given by 49 percent of the managers. Suspension without pay (for an average of four days) was used by 27 percent of the managers. Finally, only 3 percent fired the problem workers.

The large organization studied in this research used punishment *progressively*— that is, starting mildly, and then increasing in severity with each successive infraction. This is the idea behind **progressive discipline**—the practice of basing punishment

Managers are currently experimenting with different types of discipline. One type, "team discipline," places the responsibility for disciplining employees in the hands of one's fellow work-group members. It is not nearly as effective to have a supervisor "chew out" an employee as it is to have members of one's work group confront the problem person. When one's colleagues shake their heads in disapproval and say "You really let us down," the impact is likely to be profound. [Kiechel, W., III. (1990, May 7). How to discipline in the modern age. *Fortune*, pp. 179–180.]

on the frequency and severity of the infraction.[46] For example, for some offenses, such as unauthorized absences or tardiness, a progressive discipline program might begin by giving the employee an informal spoken warning. Then, with the next offense, the employee would have a formal meeting with his or her supervisors and be given a more formal spoken warning. A third offense would result in a formal written warning that becomes part of the employee's personnel record. Fourth offenses would result in several days' suspension without pay. Finally, if the problem continued after all this, the employee would be dismissed. For more serious offenses, such as gambling, the program would eliminate some of the more preliminary, informal disciplinary actions and begin with a formal written warning. The most serious offenses, such as stealing, falsifying information, or destroying company property, would result in immediate dismissal. Companies using progressive disciplinary programs can adjust the punishments given to reflect how serious they believe the infraction is. They can also publicize their punishment rules in company handbooks in order to communicate to their employees the kinds of behaviors they will not tolerate.

As you might imagine, managers may be predisposed toward using different disciplinary measures and corrective actions in response to different employee problems. A survey of managers from 100 companies located throughout the United States asked what techniques they used in dealing with four crucial problems—alcoholism, use of marijuana, use of hard drugs, and serious emotional illness.[47] The results (summarized in Figure 3–8) show that employees with alcohol problems were likely to be disciplined and counseled rather than discharged, whereas those using hard drugs were more often discharged. Such findings reveal a great deal about the extent

FIGURE 3–8

Corporate Reactions to Employees' Problems

Survey results show that companies are likely to take different disciplinary actions for the different personal problems of its employees. The relative use of various actions is shown for four serious employee problems. (*Source:* Based on data reported by Miner & Brewer, 1976; see Note 41.)

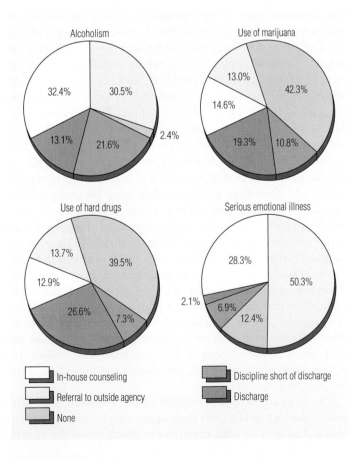

to which managers believe they can and should do something about their subordinates' various personal problems. Companies appear to be willing to help employees eliminate their serious personal problems, but, at the same time, reserve the most serious disciplinary actions for incidents in which these personal problems directly result in poor job performance.[48]

Of course, not all inappropriate actions are punished all the time. There are several reasons for this.[49] For one, many supervisors may feel constrained against using punishment, either because of limitations imposed on them by labor unions or by their lack of formal organizational authority. It is sometimes easier for managers to just sit back and hope the undesirable behavior will go away—especially when they feel their hands are tied. Sometimes supervisors believe their use of punishment is not supported by company policy. Punishment is most likely to be used when organizations support the use of disciplinary actions through specific programs outlining the appropriate actions to take.[50]

As we have shown here, managers may be willing to use some forms of punishment under the appropriate circumstances. Obviously, the use of punishment as an effective managerial tool requires much care.

The Impact of Discipline: What Makes Punishment Effective?

Punishing others is a tricky business, at best. Those who administer punishment may dislike doing so, much as those who are disciplined dislike being punished. Although it might not be exactly accurate for the punishment giver to tell the person being punished that "this is going to hurt me more than it hurts you," it is safe to assume that few of us enjoy making others feel bad—even if it's for their own good. One reason supervisors find administering punishment so undesirable is that they anticipate the strong negative emotional reactions the punished individual may display. They may also fear revenge or retaliation on the part of the disciplined employee (e.g., industrial sabotage). Fortunately, much of the research and theory on the use of punishment has pointed to some ways to avoid these problems and, at the same time, to make punishment an effective method of eliminating undesirable organizational behaviors. Our presentation will focus on several very useful principles for effectively administering punishment.[51]

Principle 1: Deliver punishment immediately after the undesired response occurs. When the undesirable consequence is delivered immediately after the undesirable behavior occurs, people are more likely to make the connection between the two events. The undesirable consequence will serve as a punishment, thereby reducing the probability of the unwanted behavior. The more time that separates the undesirable behavior and its consequences, the weaker the association between them will be. So, for example, supervisors should immediately show their disapproval to employees who arrive for work two hours late. The same disapproval given later in the day would surely be less effective in reducing subsequent tardiness.

Principle 2: Give moderate levels of punishment—nothing too high or low. Punishment that is too weak (e.g., rolling your eyes to show disapproval when someone makes an error) is unlikely to work, because employees may easily get used to the mildly undesirable consequences. On the other hand, punishment that is too intense (e.g., immediate dismissal) is unlikely to work, because other employees are likely to reject it as unfair and inhumane, and may resign. For these reasons, it is important that the progressive discipline programs described earlier in this chapter do not start with punishments that are too weak or too strong.

Test Bank questions 3.42, 3.55, and 3.75 relate to material on this page.

Principle 3: Punish the undesirable action, not the person. The employees' undesirable acts, not the individuals themselves, should be punished. Indeed, this must be communicated clearly to the people involved. A supervisor should not feel uneasy about disciplining a coworker with whom he or she has developed a friendship. Good punishment is impersonal. It should not be treated as an act of revenge or a chance to vent frustrations. When discipline is handled impersonally, the punished person is less likely to feel humiliated, and, as a result, the administrator is less likely to be the victim of revenge. To punish impersonally, supervisors should focus their remarks on the employee's behavior instead of his or her personality. For example, in response to a tardy employee, a supervisor should *avoid* saying something like "Sam, your kind of laziness and irresponsibility will not be tolerated around here. You better show up on time, or else!" It would be much better to say, "Sam, lateness costs this company a lot of money each year. All employees are expected to help us by showing up on time."

Principle 4: Use punishment consistently—all the time, for all employees. Unlike the intermittent schedules that so effectively reinforce desirable behaviors, punishment is most effective when administered according to a continuous reinforcement schedule. *Every* undesired response should be punished every time it occurs. The manager who, out of a sense of kindness, turns a blind eye to an infraction may be doing more harm than good by inadvertently reinforcing an undesirable behavior. Consistency is also important in punishing all employees. Everyone who commits the same infraction should be punished the same way by any of the supervisors in charge. Fairness demands that supervisors show no favoritism. If one supervisor is very lenient, and another very harsh, the subordinates will learn to avoid not the undesirable behavior, but the harsh supervisor! Similarly, discipline that is believed to be uneven, the result of not being "in" with the supervisor, will not work because it does not link the disciplinary actions to the undesired behavior.

Principle 5: Clearly communicate the reasons for the punishment given. Making clear exactly what behaviors led to what disciplinary actions greatly facilitates the effectiveness of punishment. Clearly communicated explanations can only help strengthen the connection between the behavior and its consequences. Wise managers use their opportunities to communicate with subordinates to make clear that the punishment being given constitutes not revenge, but an attempt to eliminate an unwanted behavior (which, of course, it is). Communicating information about poor performance in a personal interview is a good idea. To make such interviews as effective as possible, managers should follow several steps (see the summary in Figure 3–9).[52]

In the first step of the interview, the supervisor should refer to any past disciplinary meetings that have occurred. In the second step, she or he should identify exactly what problem was noted and seek an explanation from the employee. Naturally, blaming an employee for a problem that remains out of his or her control would be a mistake. In fact, the supervisor should avoid assigning any blame at all, but simply point out exactly what behaviors led to what negative consequences. In the third step, the supervisor can give a warning. It should, of course, fall within the supervisor's authority. Just as important, the warning should be carefully tied to specific performance problems, and a written record should be made of this agreement. It's also a good idea to explain that the rule is being enforced fairly—namely, that all others who have broken the same rule are punished the same way. In the fourth step, the supervisor should seek a commitment from the employee. In other words, the supervisor and the employee should agree on some plan of attack that documents the change required of the disciplined employee. In the fifth and final step, a follow-

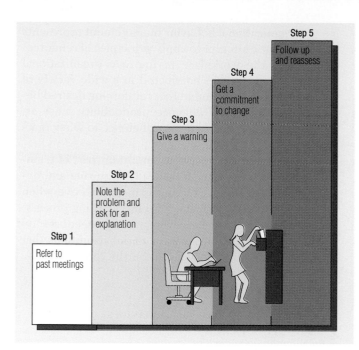

FIGURE 3-9

Steps of a Disciplinary
Interview

It's never easy to
communicate a
performance problem.
Following these steps
helps ensure that the
problem is identified
and that the
consequences for failing
to improve are made
clear. (*Source:* Based on
suggestions by Lussier,
1990; see Note 52.)

up meeting should be scheduled in which the same problematic behavior, if any,
will be reassessed. In many cases, the employee's knowledge that the supervisor
will follow up on the problem will be a strong deterrent.

Principle 6: Be careful not to follow punishment with noncontingent rewards.
Imagine that you are a supervisor who has just written a formal letter of discipline
in reaction to a serious infraction of the rules by a particular subordinate. The
disciplined employee is feeling very low, which makes you feel remorseful. Feeling
bad, you reduce your guilt by telling the worker he can take the rest of the day off
with pay. Although this may make you feel better, it poses a serious problem. You
have inadvertently rewarded the person for the unwanted behavior. His serious
infraction was punished by the letter, but rewarded by the time off. As a result, the
effect of the punishment may be greatly diminished. More seriously, such an action
sends the wrong message to the other employees. Soon, they too learn that they can
get you to give them time off if they display the proper degree of dejection. For
punishment to be most effective, a supervisor must not inadvertently reward undesirable behaviors.

If, after reading all this, you are thinking that it is truly difficult to properly
administer rewards and punishments in organizations, you have reached the same
conclusion as experts in the field of organizational learning.[53] Indeed, one of the key
skills that makes some managers so effective is their ability to influence others by
properly administering rewards and punishments.

SUMMARY AND REVIEW

Theories of Learning

The concept of **learning** refers to a relatively permanent change in behavior occurring as a result of
experience. One theory of learning, **classical conditioning,** explains the learning of automatic, reflex-

ive behaviors in terms of pairing a previously neutral
stimulus (*conditioned stimulus*) with a stimulus (*unconditioned stimulus*) that naturally elicits a certain
response (*unconditioned response*). After pairing the

conditioned stimulus with the unconditioned stimulus, the conditioned stimulus comes to elicit a response similar to the unconditioned response (known as a *conditioned response*).

In the **operant conditioning** approach, individuals learn to perform actions based on the consequences of those actions. Stimuli that increase the probability of the behaviors preceding it are known as **reinforcers.** Reinforcement may be either *positive,* if it is based on the presentation of a desirable outcome, or *negative,* if it is based on the withdrawal of an unwanted outcome. The probability of certain responses can be decreased if an unpleasant outcome results (**punishment**), or if a pleasant outcome is withdrawn (**extinction**).

Observational learning involves learning by modeling the behavior of others. By paying attention to and rehearsing the behaviors of others, we can learn vicariously, that is, through the model's experiences.

Learning Desirable Organizational Behaviors

The rules for systematically applying reinforcements are known as **schedules of reinforcement.** These may either be *continuous,* in which every desired response is rewarded, or *partial,* in which case not all desired responses are reinforced. Behavior may be rewarded on the basis of a fixed or variable number of desired acts performed (*fixed ratio* and *variable ratio* schedules, respectively), or after the passage of a fixed or variable amount of time (*fixed interval* and *variable interval* schedules, respectively).

Organizational behavior management represents a systematic attempt to apply principles of reinforcement to the workplace to improve organizational functioning. Studies conducted in a wide variety of organizations have found that reinforcing desired behaviors can greatly enhance productivity, raise attendance rates, and improve adherence to safety practices.

Reinforcement is also an important part of **training,** the process of systematically acquiring and developing job skills. Training is most effective when trainees actively participate in the learning process, repeat the desired behaviors, receive feedback on their performance, and learn under conditions that closely resemble those found on the job.

Reducing Undesirable Behaviors Through Discipline

Discipline, the systematic application of punishment, is widely practiced in organizations in forms ranging from the very mild and informal (e.g., displays of disapproval) to the very severe and formal (e.g., suspension without pay, or even termination).

The effects of discipline are most beneficial when punishment is applied immediately after the undesired activity, moderately severe, focused on the undesirable action instead of the person, applied consistently over time and for all employees, clearly explained and communicated, and not weakened by the use of inadvertent rewards.

KEY TERMS

avoidance: See *negative reinforcement.*

classical conditioning: The form of learning in which a stimulus, initially not capable of eliciting a specific response, is paired with another that can elicit this reaction. As a result of such pairings, the first stimulus gradually acquires the capacity to elicit reactions similar to those elicited by the second stimulus.

contingencies of reinforcement: The various relationships between one's behavior and the consequences of that behavior—positive reinforcement, negative reinforcement, punishment, and extinction.

continuous reinforcement: A schedule of reinforcement in which all desired behaviors are reinforced.

discipline: The process of systematically administering punishments.

extinction: The process through which responses that are no longer reinforced tend to gradually diminish in strength.

fixed interval schedules: Schedules of reinforcement that dictate that after a reinforcement is administered, a fixed period of time must elapse before another response can be reinforced.

fixed ratio schedules: Schedules of reinforcement in which a fixed number of responses must be performed before reinforcement is administered.

instrumental conditioning: See *operant conditioning.*

Law of Effect: The basic law of operant conditioning, which operates on the observation that behaviors with desirable consequences are strengthened and behaviors with undesirable consequences are weakened.

learning: A relatively permanent change in behavior occurring as a result of experience.

modeling: See *observational learning.*

negative reinforcement: The process by which people learn to perform acts that lead to the removal of undesired events.

observational learning: The form of learning in which people acquire new behaviors by systematically observing the things that happen to others.

operant conditioning: The form of learning according to which people associate the consequences of their actions with the actions themselves. Behaviors with positive consequences are acquired; behaviors with negative consequences tend to be eliminated.

organizational behavior management: The practice of systematically reinforcing desirable organizational behaviors through operant conditioning and observational learning principles.

organizational behavior modification (OB Mod): See *organizational behavior management.*

partial (or **intermittent**) **reinforcement:** A schedule of reinforcement in which only some desired behaviors are reinforced. Types include fixed interval, variable interval, fixed ratio, and variable ratio.

Pavlovian conditioning: See *classical conditioning.*

positive reinforcement: The process by which people learn to perform behaviors that lead to the presentation of desired outcomes (i.e., rewards).

progressive discipline: The practice of gradually increasing the severity of punishments for employees who exhibit unacceptable job behavior.

punishment: Decreasing undesirable behavior by following it with undesirable consequences.

reinforcer: Any event that increases the probability of the behavior that preceded it.

schedules of reinforcement: Rules governing the timing and frequency of the administration of reinforcement.

shaping: The process of selectively reinforcing behaviors that approach a desired goal behavior.

training: The process of systematically teaching employees to acquire and improve job related skills and knowledge.

variable interval schedules: Schedules of reinforcement that dictate that after one reinforcement is administered, a variable period of time (based on some average value) must elapse before another response can be reinforced.

variable ratio schedules: Schedules of reinforcement in which a variable number of responses (based on some average value) must be performed before reinforcement is administered.

QUESTIONS FOR DISCUSSION

1. Describe the concept of learning and discuss the ways it is applied in the field of organizational behavior.

2. Give an example of learning occurring in organizations that exemplifies each of the following: classical conditioning, operant conditioning, and observational learning.

3. Describe four different schedules of reinforcement and give an example of how each may be used in organizations.

4. What is organizational behavior management? Describe the principles of learning that make this practice effective.

5. Describe the principles needed to institute an effective training program in organizations.

6. What are the advantages and disadvantages of using discipline in organizational settings?

NOTES

1. Weiss, H. M. (1990). Learning theory in industrial/organizational psychology. In M. D. Dunnette and L. M. Hough (Eds.), *Handbook of industrial and organizational psychology* (2nd ed., Vol. 1, pp. 171–222). Palo Alto, CA: Consulting Psychologists Press.

2. Atkinson, R. C., Herrnstein, R. J., Lindzey, G., & Luce, R. D. (Eds.). (1988). *Steven's handbook of experimental psychology* (2nd ed., Vol. 2). New York: Wiley.

3. Finegan, J. (1990, October). Reach out and teach someone. *Inc.*, pp. 112–114, 118, 120, 124.

4. Pavlov, I. P. (1927). *Conditioned reflexes* (G. V. Anrep, Trans.). London: Oxford University Press.

5. Hall, J. F. (1989). *Learning and memory.* Boston: Allyn & Bacon.

6. Scott, W. E., & Podsakoff, P. M. (1985). *Behavioral principles in the practice of management.* New York: Wiley.

7. Thorndike, E. L. (1911). *Animal intelligence.* New York: Macmillan.

8. Skinner, B. F. (1969). *Contingencies of reinforcement.* New York: Appleton-Century-Crofts.

9. Komaki, J. L., Desselles, M. L., & Bowman, E. D. (1989). Definitely not a breeze: Extending an operant model of effective supervision to teams. *Journal of Applied Psychology, 74,* 522–529.

10. Bandura, A. (1986). *Social foundations of thought and action: A social cognitive theory.* Englewood Cliffs, NJ: Prentice-Hall.

11. Manz, C. C., & Sims, H. P., Jr. (1981). Vicarious learning: The influence of modeling on organizational behavior. *Academy of Management Review, 6,* 105–113.

12. Goldstein, I. L. (1991). Training in work organizations. In M. D. Dunnette and L. M. Hough (Eds.), *Hand-*

book of industrial and organizational psychology (2nd ed., Vol. 2, pp. 507–620). Palo Alto, CA: Consulting Psychologists Press.

13. Kerr, S. (1975). On the folly of rewarding A while hoping for B. *Academy of Management Journal, 18,* 769–783.

14. Anonymous. (1973). At Emery Air Freight: Positive reinforcement boosts performance. *Organizational Dynamics, 1*(3), 41–50.

15. Anonymous. (1991, March). You get what you pay for. *Inc.,* p. 92.

16. Luthans, F., & Kreitner, R. (1985). *Organizational behavior modification and beyond.* Glenview, IL: Scott, Foresman.

17. Saari, L. M., & Latham, G. P. (1982). Employee reactions to continuous and variable ratio reinforcement schedules involving a monetary incentive. *Journal of Applied Psychology, 67,* 506–508.

18. Frederiksen, L. W. (1982). *Handbook of organizational behavior management.* New York: Wiley.

19. Heneman, R. L. (1992). *Merit pay.* Reading, MA: Addison-Wesley.

20. Miller, L. (1978). *Behavior management.* New York: Wiley.

21. O'Hara, K., Johnson, C. M., & Beehr, T. A. (1985). Organizational behavior management in the private sector. A review of empirical research and recommendations for further investigation. *Academy of Management Review, 10,* 848–864.

22. Hamner, W. C., & Hamner, E. P. (1976). Behavior modification on the bottom line. *Organizational Dynamics, 4*(4), 8–21.

23. See Note 20.

24. Anonymous. (1985, May 15). Hot 100: A million dollar incentive plan. *Business Week,* p. 52.

25. See Note 20.

26. Kreitner, R., & Luthans, F. (1984). A social learning approach to behavioral management: Radical behaviorists "mellowing out." *Organizational Dynamics, 12*(3), 14–19.

27. Ashby, E. (1967, February 2). Can education be machine made? *New Scientist,* pp. 18–22.

28. Skinner, B. F. (1972). *Beyond freedom and dignity.* New York: Knopf.

29. See Note 12.

30. Eurich, N. P. (1985). *Corporate classrooms.* Princeton, NJ: Carnegie Foundation.

31. Sellers, P. (1988, June 6). How IBM teaches techies to sell. *Fortune,* pp. 141–142, 146.

32. See Note 1.

33. Baldwin, T. T., & Ford, J. K. (1988). Transfer of training: A review and directions for future research. *Personnel Psychology, 41,* 63–105.

34. Ilgen, D. R., & Moore, C. F. (1987). Types and choices of performance feedback. *Journal of Applied Psychology, 72,* 401–406.

35. Nagorski, Z. (1989, February 12). Yes, Socrates, ethics can be taught. *New York Times,* p. F2.

36. Harrington, S. J. (1991). What corporate America is teaching about ethics. *Academy of Management Executive, 5,* 21–30.

37. Etzioni, A. (1989, February 12). Good ethics is good business—really. *New York Times,* p. F2.

38. Ireland, K. (1991). The ethics game. *Personnel Journal, 31*(3), 72, 74–75.

39. See Note 38.

40. Morin, W. J., & Yorks, L. (1990). *Dismissal.* New York: Drake Beam Morin.

41. Miner, J. B., & Brewer, J. F. (1976). The management of ineffective performance. In M. D. Dunnette (Ed.), *The handbook of industrial/organizational psychology* (pp. 995–1029). Chicago: Rand McNally.

42. Katz, D., & Kahn, R. L. (1978). *The social psychology of organizations* (2nd ed.). New York: Wiley.

43. O'Reilly, C. A., III, & Weitz, B. A. (1980). Managing marginal employees: The use of warnings and dismissals. *Administrative Science Quarterly, 25,* 467–484.

44. Fromson, B. D. (1988, February 29). The slow death of E. F. Hutton. *Fortune,* pp. 82–84, 86, 88.

45. Beyer, J. M., & Trice, H. M. (1984). A field study of the use and perceived effects of discipline in controlling work performance. *Academy of Management Journal, 27,* 743–764.

46. Oberle, R. L. (1978). Administering disciplinary actions. *Personnel Journal, 18*(3), 30–33.

47. See Note 41.

48. Podsakoff, P. M. (1982). Determinants of a supervisor's use of rewards and punishments: A literature review and suggestions for further research. *Organizational Behavior and Human Performance, 29,* 58–83.

49. Arvey, R. D., & Jones, A. P. (1985). The use of discipline in organizational settings: A framework for future research. In L. L. Cummings & B. M. Staw (Eds.), *Research in organizational behavior* (Vol. 7, pp. 367–408). Greenwich, CT: JAI Press.

50. See Note 43.

51. Arvey, R. D., & Ivancevich, J. M. (1980). Punishment in organizations: A review, propositions, and research suggestions. *Academy of Management Review, 5,* 123–132.

52. Lussier, R. H. (1990, August). A discipline model for increasing performance. *Supervisory Management,* pp. 6–7.

53. See Note 2.

CASE IN POINT

Times are tough, and bosses are turning up the heat on their employees. Once used as a last resort, coercion and punishment are becoming the learning strategies of choice for a growing number of managers. CEOs are being pressured by stockholders to increase profits. Companies like IBM are restructuring to remain competitive. Employees have a lot to learn to become more competitive, and top management has decided to use "get-tough" tactics to get them to change—or leave.[1]

At Westcon, an East Chester, New York, distributor of computer products and support services, CEO Tom Dolan uses the "Norman Schwarzkopf approach" to motivate employees to change their ways.[2] Dolan wants his employees to be more competitive and customer-service oriented. Drawing upon his experience as a Marine lieutenant, Dolan orders employees to change and change immediately. His approach to employees is to tell them in no uncertain terms that they *will* pay more attention to serving customer wants and needs or they will be fired. Dolan is convinced that increasing customer service is the key to Westcon's competitive survival, and he believes that getting tough with his employees is the best way to achieve his goal.

At Grey Advertising, CEO Ed Vick is relying on punishment, too. Brought in to turn the ad agency around, Vick emphasizes the importance of employees having a strong work ethic. Anyone who doesn't stack up to his idea of a strong work ethic risks being fired. "In difficult times you need to find people with the right work ethic. People who don't show that ethic—you've got to get rid of them."[3]

At IBM, the atmosphere has changed from benevolent to blistering. CEO John Akers believes that IBM employees have become too complacent. Facing declining profits and eroding market share, Akers uses a "get-tough" strategy to get his point across. Says Akers, "Our people have to be competitive, and if they can't change fast enough, as fast as our industry . . . good-bye."[4]

Akers's get-tough policy is in sharp contrast to IBM's tradition of providing employees with considerable comforts.[5] For example, IBM employees have come to rely on the company's no-layoff policy. But Akers's recent threats and increased firings have caused IBM employees to seriously question whether the no-layoff policy means very much.

IBM's tradition of offering generous severance benefits may be changing, too. Employees who are targeted to leave the company had better leave when Akers suggests that they leave or face harsh consequences. IBM's new severance program gives exiting employees two weeks of pay for every year that he or she has worked for IBM. *But*, targeted employees who refuse to leave the company are now told that they are likely to face pay cuts and eventual firing—known as MIA (management-initiated attrition). Even the employees who do eventually agree to IBM's severance deal will suffer if they pass up their first chance to leave. Instead of two weeks for each year worked, employees who are slow to leave receive only one week of severance pay per year worked. Akers's message is clear: Do it my way or face punishing consequences!

IBM is changing its vacation practices, too. Traditionally, IBM employees could carry over earned vacation time from one year to the next, which resulted in the company having to pay retiring employees substantial sums of money for their unused vacation time. IBM now requires employees to use their vacation during the year it is awarded. However, one un-intended consequence of this change in policy is that now so many employees are taking Mondays and Fridays off—for long weekends—that most meetings can be scheduled only during the middle of the week.

Things are getting tough for IBM, and Akers believes that there is no time to waste in changing the way the company does business. IBM's market share of the computer industry is shrinking—from 37 percent in 1983 to about 23 percent in 1991. By making IBM more competitive, Akers believes he can regain lost market share. Also, Akers knows that his time at IBM is running short. He is a couple of years away from IBM's mandatory retirement age of sixty. If he is to firmly establish his legacy, he knows he needs to change things fast, and to him the best way to do this is to get tough.

Akers's sense of urgency is evident in recent comments he made to managers: "I used to think my job as a sales rep was at risk if I lost a sale. Tell them [IBM employees] theirs is at risk if they lose. I'm sick and tired of visiting plants to hear nothing but great things about quality and cycle time—and then to visit customers who tell me of problems. If the people in labs and plants miss deadlines . . . tell them their job is on the line, too. The tension is not high enough in the business—everyone is too damn comfortable at a time when the business is in crisis."[6]

What has all this tough action produced? At Westcon, several longtime employees found Dolan's approach too heavy-handed and left the company. But others didn't seem to object. Says Dolan, "Those who remained became invigorated."[7]

At Grey Advertising, Ed Vick's get-tough tactics don't seem to be working. Since Vick took over as CEO, the ad agency has lost two huge accounts—Frito Lay and Subaru. It is not clear if the loss of these accounts was due to Vick's punishing tactics, but questions about the long-term effects of punishment on the agency's employees are now being asked.

And what has happened at IBM? Many IBM employees think that Akers's tactics are undermining employee morale. One telling message left by an IBM employee on the company's electronic mail network says that CEO Akers is "out of touch if he thinks that the tension level within IBM is not high enough. From where I sit, it's so high that management is paralyzed."[8]

Rank-and-file IBM workers think Akers and top management are being too hard on employees and not hard enough on themselves. Says one employee, "I think it is time that the people at the top accepted some part of the responsibility for our present problems. I don't see any sign of that happening."[9]

At all three companies, the get-tough approach toward employees is taking its toll. Some managers worry that valuable employees may eventually become so discouraged and dissatisfied by the browbeating that they will resign. There is also concern that employees performing poorly may resort to sabotaging company property rather than improving their performance or quitting. Managers are feeling the effects of the get-tough approach, too. Bitter outbursts are becoming commonplace in manager meetings and executive suites, and the sense of teamwork that companies have tried to build in recent years is eroding under the force of increasingly coercive management tactics.

Says Karen Berg, a management consultant with CommCore, Inc., "The Marine approach might be just what employees need. But probably before you escalate to the Uzi stage, you've got to know your people very well. The risk is demoralizing them."[10]

David Nadler, CEO of Delta Consulting Group, also cautions against relying too much on "beating" employees into shape. Says Nadler, "If all you do is create pain and get people worked up, and you don't tell them what to do, then it could backfire. People get defensive and angry at you, the CEO."[11]

Questions for Discussion

1. What operant contingencies are being used by CEOs Dolan, Vick, and Akers?
2. How effective is the "get-tough" approach to learning likely to be for the companies in this case? Is there a difference between the short-term and long-term effectiveness of this approach? Why?
3. When IBM stopped allowing its employees to defer earned vacation time from year to year, what operant contingency was it using? In terms of operant conditioning, why did IBM employees start taking Mondays and Fridays off? Using the basic steps in organizational behavior management, how would you stop vacation-deferring behavior without suffering the dysfunctional effects of employees taking Mondays and Fridays off?
4. If you were a CEO feeling enormous pressure to change the way your employees did their work, what learning strategies would you use? Why?

Notes

1. Stern, G. (1991, June 18). As the going gets tougher, more bosses are getting tough with their workers. *Wall Street Journal*, pp. B1 and B12.
2. See Note 1, p. B1.

3. See Note 1, p. B1.
4. Carroll, P. B. (1991, May 29). Akers to IBM employees. Wake up! *Wall Street Journal*, pp. B1 and B4.
5. Carroll, P. B. (1991, May 23). IBM wants its managers to encourage certain workers to leave the company. *Wall Street Journal*, p. A4.
6. See Note 1, p. B1.
7. See Note 1, p. B1.
8. See Note 4, p. B4.
9. See Note 4, p. B1.
10. See Note 1, p. B12.
11. See Note 1, p. B12.

EXPERIENCING ORGANIZATIONAL BEHAVIOR

In this chapter, we've shown how the process of reinforcement is responsible for shaping many aspects of behavior in organizations (see pages 87–97). It is important to be aware that social factors such as personal approval may serve as potent *positive reinforcers*, in addition to more formal organizational rewards such as pay. In fact, showing approval—smiling or nodding in agreement—is a particularly effective way of encouraging others to keep talking about a topic. After all, the reward of social approval increases the probability that people will repeat the rewarded behavior. This exercise is designed to demonstrate this phenomenon.

The Reinforcing Value of Social Approval

Procedure

1. Members of the class should divide into teams of two (if there's an odd number of students, a team of three may form). One member of each pair will be an *interviewer*, and the other an *observer* (two students may be observers in teams of three). The observer should have access to a digital watch, or one with a sweep second hand.

2. Each team should go to a nearby location on campus where students congregate socially, such as a lounge or cafeteria. Members of each team should approach a person unknown to either of them and introduce themselves. (The person approached should be alone and not look busy.) Ask that individual if he or she would mind answering a few questions about his or her preferences for current television shows. Tell the interviewee that it's for a class project in [your professor's name]'s class. If the person approached declines, politely excuse yourself. If the person agrees, thank him or her and explain that the observer will be taking notes. The interviewer begins by asking the interviewee what his or her favorite TV show is.

3. The interviewer should respond positively to some of the interviewee's remarks and neutrally to others. Positive reactions include smiles, head nods, and expressions of agreement. Neutral reactions include showing no emotion, and simply saying "Uh huh" or "Yes, I see." (For example, the interviewee may say, "Well, I really like 'The Tonight Show,' " in response to which the interviewer may respond positively, smiling and agreeing. After the interviewee finishes speaking, the interviewer may ask, "Tell me about any other show you like." As the interviewee responds, the interviewer should now act neutrally.) The interviewer continues to respond positively to some reactions and neutrally to others for about five to ten minutes (or until the interviewee expresses disinterest).

4. The observer should keep track of the amount of time the interviewee spends talking about specific shows based on whether the interviewer reacted positively or neutrally. Simply note (a) the show discussed, (b) the interviewer's reaction to the topic (positive or neutral), and (c) the amount of time the interviewee spent talking about that topic.

5. After completing the interview, thank the interviewee and return to class. If the interviewees express any interest or curiosity, explain the project to them.

6. With the instructor recording the data reported by the observers in each team, compute the average length of time (in seconds) the interviewees spoke in response to the interviewers' positive and neutral reactions.

Points to Consider

1. What differences, if any, were observed in the amount of time interviewees spent talking about TV shows for which they received positive social approval compared to those for which no approval was given?

2. Were these findings similar or different for each of the various interviewer-observer pairs? What do you think this means?

3. What do you think would have happened had the interviewers acted negatively with respect to the topic instead of neutrally?

4. What safeguards were incorporated into the procedure to ensure the ethical treatment of the participants in this exercise?

5. Explain specifically how the process of reinforcement operated in the social interactions observed.

6. Do you think social approval serves as a reinforcer of behavior in organizations? Explain why or why not.

■ 4 ■

MOTIVATION IN ORGANIZATIONS

CHAPTER OUTLINE

LEARNING OBJECTIVES

After reading this chapter, you should be able to:
1. Define *motivation* and explain its importance in the field of organizational behavior.
2. Describe *need hierarchy theory* and what it recommends about improving motivation in organizations.
3. Identify and explain the conditions through which *goal setting* can be used to improve job performance.
4. Explain *equity theory* and some of the research designed to test its basic tenets.
5. Describe the components of *expectancy theory* and their interrelationships.
6. Distinguish between *job enlargement* and *job enrichment* as techniques for motivating employees by redesigning jobs.
7. Describe the various components of the *job characteristics model*.

Ted Nelson and Nate Stern have almost completed their first year's work as the *Gazette's* cub reporters. Because they were hired at the same time and write the same kinds of stories, people tend to think of them as being alike. However, their conversation, this Friday afternoon before the long Labor Day weekend, reveals a fundamental difference between them.

"Yeah, just a few minutes, and I'll be out of here," says Ted with a huge grin. "I'll be on my way to three fabulous days with Laurie at a cottage on the shore."

"Sounds great," Nate replies, "but I'll be spending most of that time researching possible fraud in the mayor's office. I heard this rumor, and I have to check it out, especially so close to election day."

"You must be crazy, Nate," Ted says in amazement. As he begins cleaning up his desk, he adds, "Why don't you and Pam join us for the weekend? No phones, no VDTs, no city editors breathing down your neck for a story—just a little sun, surf, and relaxation."

Nate smiles. "Thanks for the offer," he says. "It's tempting, but I promised myself that I'd use this slow period to do that research. After all, it can be a big story, and I want to break it!"

"You know," Ted confides, "I've always wondered why you work so hard. We make the same money—and not much of it, at that! As I figure it, why bust your tail? Chances are good that all your research will only lead you down a blind alley anyway. Besides, if the story's any good, you just know they're gonna yank it from you and give it to one of the big shots."

"I'm not trying to prove anything," replies Nate. "It's just that I like what I'm doing, and it's important to me to do a good job. I take pride in my stories. Sometimes, doing a good one means making sacrifices."

"I suppose this is one of them?" Ted asks.

"Exactly," Nate answers.

This talk makes Ted a little defensive. "Don't get me wrong," he says, "I like my work. It's just that I'm not willing to give up my whole life for it."

"That's a good approach, I suppose," says Nate, nodding his head in approval. "Still, you do your thing, and I'll do mine."

With this, Ted gets up, approaches the door, and says good-bye to everyone. "Don't work too hard, now," he chuckles as he looks back at Nate.

By the time Nate can reply "I won't," Ted is out the door. Now Nate begins to wonder: *Should I be taking it easier?*

As Ted enters the elevator, he also questions himself: *Maybe I'm a goof-off, and I should be working harder.*

These ideas flicker no longer than the flame of a candle about to go out, and both men drop their thoughts and go about their separate ways. For two young reporters thought to be so much alike by their colleagues, they certainly are very different. Yet, they are alike in one respect: they both agree to disagree with each other about the role of work in their lives.

Do you know people like Ted and Nate? Perhaps you can relate to one of them. What makes Ted more interested in taking time off than in working, and Nate more interested in working than in playing? What is it about them that explains this difference? Or, just as important, we may ask: what is it about the way managers behave, or the way a job is structured, that creates such crucial differences between people? There always seem to be some people who watch the clock while others keep their shoulders to the wheel (see Figure 4–1). Understanding these differences is one of the most important tasks confronting the field of organizational behavior. In great part, the underlying issue has to do with *motivation*, this chapter's theme.

As we noted in chapter 1, the field of OB is concerned with both understanding human behavior in organizations and applying that knowledge toward improving job performance and employees' quality of life. Nowhere in the field are these goals more clearly realized than in the study of motivation. Indeed, we are interested in asking both theoretical questions, such as "*What* motivates people, and *why?*" and applied questions, such as "*How* can this knowledge be put to practical use?" Hence, our focus will be both on theories of motivation and on practical application of those

Early clock-watchers

FIGURE 4–1

Motivation: An Important Aspect of Organizational Behavior

It's usually easy to find some people who are highly motivated to perform their jobs well, and others who prefer to slack off. The study of motivation provides insight into the conditions under which each of these outcomes is likely to occur. (*Source:* The Far Side Cartoon by Gary Larson is reprinted by permission of Universal Press Syndicate.)

theories. The theories and conceptualizations we will consider represent the major approaches to the topic of motivation currently studied.[1] Our look at each one will focus on what the theory says, the research bearing on it, and its practical implications. We think that with this approach you will develop a solid understanding of the importance of motivation as a topic of interest to organizational scientists. However, before turning to these theories and applications, we will begin by taking a closer look at the concept of motivation and the role of motivation in the work ethic.

THE NATURE OF MOTIVATION IN ORGANIZATIONS

On the basis of what we've said so far, you should not be surprised to hear that motivation is one of the most important and widely studied topics in the field of organizational behavior.[2] To help us better understand and appreciate what is known in this field, we will explore some very important basic issues about motivation in organizations. First, however, we need to define the concept of motivation and explain its role in organizational behavior.

Motivation: A Definition

Although motivation is a broad and complex concept, organizational scientists have agreed on its basic characteristics.[3] We define **motivation** as *the set of processes that arouse, direct, and maintain human behavior toward attaining a goal.* Obviously, this definition requires some elaboration. The diagram in Figure 4–2 will help guide our explanation.

The first part of our definition deals with *arousal.* This has to do with the drive behind behavior, the energy behind our actions. A hungry person may be aroused to seek food, and a lonely person may be aroused to seek companionship. People are also concerned about meeting various needs in organizations. Besides being interested in making money, workers are also interested in making a good impression on their supervisors and coworkers. Clearly, the drive to attain these various goals (i.e., the reduction of hunger, the reduction of loneliness, and making a good impression on others) constitutes a major part of the definition of motivation.

But, as our definition implies, motivation is more than just the drive behind behavior; it also involves the *direction* behavior takes. People make choices about how to meet their goals. The hungry person, for example, may decide between having a can of soup at home, going out for a fast-food hamburger, or perhaps splurging on a trendy meal at the popular Chez Yuppie. Likewise, the lonely person may choose to seek the company of various friends in order to feel less lonely. Even an employee trying to please his or her supervisor may select from among various options: doing the supervisor a special favor, working extra hard on an important project, or complimenting the supervisor on his or her good work. Each of these activities has something in common—they represent some of the possible choices

The Japanese construction giant Kajima has found a unique way to arouse workers: scented air is pumped through the ventilation system of its headquarters. In the morning, employees smell fresh lemons to help fire them up. At noon, the scent of roses calms them so that they can enjoy lunch. Late in the afternoon, woody tree-trunk oils fill the air to help keep people motivated to the end of the day. [Solo, S. (1989, February 27). Scents to make you work harder. *Fortune*, p. 8.]

FIGURE 4–2

The Components of Motivation

The process of motivation involves the arousal, direction, and maintenance of behavior toward a goal.

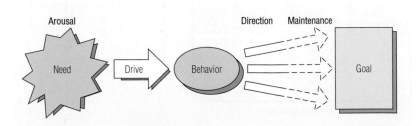

people make to direct their efforts at attaining some goal. These intentional choices are an important part of the concept of motivation.

The final part of our definition deals with *maintaining* behavior directed toward meeting a goal. Such persistence is important. The hungry or lonely person who gives up on the way to seeking his or her goals will surely not be fulfilled. Workers who do not maintain their actions toward meeting their goals (e.g., writers who type a few pages and then goof off the rest of the day) cannot be considered motivated.

To summarize, motivation requires all three components: the arousal, direction, and maintenance of goal-directed behavior. An analogy may help tie these components together. Imagine that you are driving down a road on your way home. The arousal part of motivation is like the energy created by the car's fuel and drive systems (e.g., the engine). The direction component is like the steering wheel, taking you along the chosen road. Finally, the maintenance aspect of the definition is the persistence that keeps you going until you arrive home—your goal.

Now that we've defined motivation, two important points arise. First, *motivation and job performance are not synonymous*. In fact, along with an individual's natural skills and the abilities acquired on the job, motivation is just one of several determinants of job performance. Indeed, managers have to be careful about diagnosing a subordinate's sagging performance as a problem of motivation. Although it is all too easy to do so, poor performance can be caused by poor training, inadequate equipment, or many other factors unrelated to motivation. A second key point is that *motivation is multifaceted*. In other words, employees may have several motives operating at once, which can be problematic when motives conflict. This might happen, for example, when an employee in a manufacturing plant is motivated to please his or her foreman by being very productive, but is also motivated to avoid antagonizing his or her coworkers by being more productive than they are.

These examples clearly show that motivation is a complex and important concept in the field of organizational behavior. This complexity creates challenges for the theories of motivation used in the field. Before turning to these theories, however, we will further set the stage for them by examining the role of motivation in the work ethic.

Motivation and the Work Ethic

Throughout history, views about the meaning and importance of work have shifted dramatically.[4] In ancient Rome, for example, work was considered a vulgar and degrading activity. According to the Roman writer Cato the Elder, "The best principle of management is to treat both slaves and animals well enough to give them the strength to work hard."[5] As civilization developed, so did more positive feelings about work. By the Middle Ages, a tradition espousing the virtues of hard work was firmly established. Following the teachings of Judeo-Christian philosophers (such as Luther and Calvin), beliefs in the value of work eventually became a cherished tradition in American society. Reflecting this view in modern times, former U.S. president Richard M. Nixon once proclaimed, "Labor is good in itself. A man or woman at work . . . becomes a better person by virtue of the act of working."[6]

Despite such inspiring words, many observers of American business trends have attributed problems of sagging production to a general lack of motivation within the work force.[7] However, to claim that today's employees are poorly motivated would be misleading. After all, survey findings report that most Americans would continue to work even if they didn't need the money.[8] Although money is certainly important to people, they are motivated to attain many other goals as well. Today's work force of "baby boomers" (persons born in the years immediately after World War II), raised in a prosperous society, grew up expecting a more comfortable and more leisurely life than that of their parents, who worked just to survive during the depression of the late 1920s and the 1930s. Because of technological advances that took the drudgery out of many jobs, today's workers are motivated by the prospect of performing jobs that are interesting and challenging—not just jobs that pay well. As a result, problems of motivation may be difficult to identify because of the wide variety of rewards that workers may be motivated to achieve. (Although we have been talking here about American work values, the **International/Multicultural Perspective** section below shows how the cultural traditions of various nations are important in influencing the work values of their citizens.)

NEED THEORIES

The first conceptualizations of motivation we will consider are the most basic: theories that explain motivation on the job in terms of the satisfaction of basic human needs. Indeed, organizational scholars have paid a great deal of attention to the idea that

AN INTERNATIONAL/MULTICULTURAL PERSPECTIVE

What Motivates Employees? Work Goals All Over the World

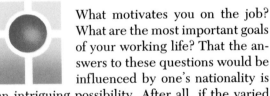

What motivates you on the job? What are the most important goals of your working life? That the answers to these questions would be influenced by one's nationality is an intriguing possibility. After all, if the varied social, political, and religious beliefs of people in different nations influence work values, it follows that people in different countries would be motivated by different work goals. Testing this reasoning, Itzhak Harpaz conducted a survey in which 8,192 randomly selected people in the labor force of seven different nations (Belgium, Great Britain, West Germany, Israel, Japan, the Netherlands, and the United States) were asked to identify their most important work goals.[9] Specifically, they were asked to rank-order from most important to least important each of the following:

- Opportunity to learn new things
- Good interpersonal relations with others
- Good opportunity for promotion
- Convenient work hours
- A great deal of variety
- Doing interesting work (work you really like)
- High amount of job security
- Good match between personal abilities and job requirements

- Good pay
- Pleasant working conditions
- Considerable autonomy (freedom to decide how to do the work)

The results of the survey were very interesting. Investigators observed a very high degree of agreement among people from the various nations surveyed (see Figure 4–3). Specifically, by a wide margin, the paramount work goal was found to be "interesting work." In fact, people in four of the seven nations identified this as the most important goal, and people in the remaining three rated it second or third. Immediately behind in popularity were "good pay" and "good interpersonal relations with others." The lowest-ranked goal, by a wide margin, was "opportunity for promotion." Of the eleven goals studied, this one ranked either tenth or last in all of the nations studied, except Israel, where it also ranked low (eighth). (This is not to say, of course, that it is an unimportant goal, but it is considered less important than the others.)

These findings are interesting in several respects. First, they reveal that the goals people are motivated to seek in their jobs are remarkably similar within the seven highly industrialized countries studied. Of course, because the survey did not include people in other nations,

---

people are motivated to use their jobs as mechanisms for satisfying their needs. Probably the best-known conceptualization of human needs in organizations has been proposed by Maslow.[10]

Maslow's Need Hierarchy Theory

Abraham Maslow was a clinical psychologist who introduced a theory of personal adjustment, known as **need hierarchy theory,** based on his observations of patients throughout the years. His premise was that if people grow up in an environment in which their needs are not met, they will be unlikely to function as healthy, well-adjusted individuals. Much of the popularity of Maslow's approach is based on applying this same idea in organizations; that is, unless people get their needs met on the job, they will not function as effectively as possible.

Specifically, Maslow theorized that people have five types of need, and that these are activated in a *hierarchical* manner. This means that the needs are aroused in a specific order from lowest to highest, and that the lowest-order need must be fulfilled

especially less industrialized ones, how generalizable and universal the findings may be cannot be determined. Yet, such a great deal of agreement among people working in very different cultures is quite impressive. Obviously, despite the existence of national differences with respect to economic and social conditions, there is widespread agreement about the relative importance of different work goals. Given this conclusion, it is not surprising that variables related to interesting work and pay consistently emerge (albeit in different forms) in the various theories of motivation we will consider.

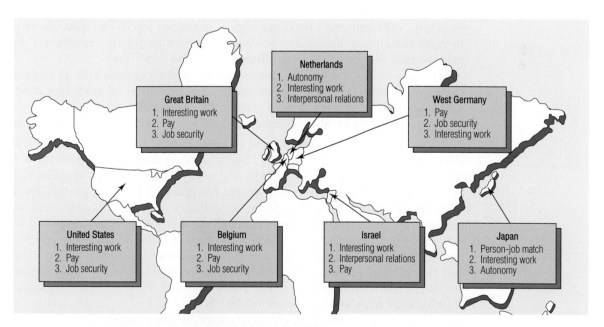

FIGURE 4–3   What Motivates Workers? An International View

Survey research assessing the predominant work goals of more than 8,000 workers in seven nations found considerable agreement that the two most important motivating factors were *interesting work* and *pay*. (*Source:* Based on data in Harpaz, 1990; see Note 9.)

FIGURE 4-4

Need Theories: A Comparison

The five needs identified by Maslow's need hierarchy theory correspond to the three needs of Alderfer's ERG theory. However, Maslow's theory specifies that needs are activated in order from lowest level to highest level, whereas Alderfer's theory specifies that needs can be activated in any order.

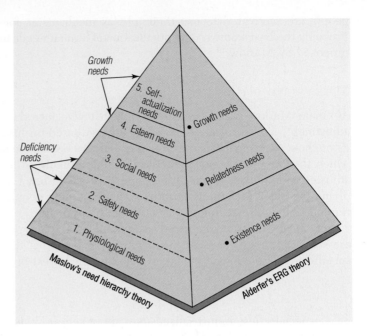

before the next highest order need is triggered, and so on. The five major categories of need are listed on the left side of Figure 4–4. Please refer to this diagram as a summary of the needs as we describe them here.

1. *Physiological needs* are the lowest-order, most basic needs specified by Maslow. These refer to satisfying fundamental biological drives such as the need for food, air, water, and shelter. To satisfy such needs, organizations must provide employees with a salary that allows them to afford adequate living conditions (e.g., food and shelter). Similarly, sufficient rest breaks are also an important job feature that allows people to meet their physiological needs. More and more frequently, companies are providing exercise and physical fitness programs for their employees—50,000 American and 1,000 Canadian businesses by one recent count.[11] Providing such facilities may also be recognized as an attempt to help employees stay healthy by satisfying their physiological needs. After all, people who are too hungry or too ill to work will hardly be able to make much of a contribution to their companies.

2. *Safety needs,* the second level of need in Maslow's hierarchy, are activated after physiological needs are met. Safety needs refers to the need for a secure environment, free from threats of physical or psychological harm. Organizations can do many things to help satisfy safety needs. For example, they may provide employees with life and health insurance plans, opportunity for payroll savings, and security forces (e.g., police and fire protection staff) that enable people to perform without fear of harm. Similarly, jobs that provide tenure (such as teaching) and no-layoff agreements enhance psychological security, and may be viewed as promoting the satisfaction of employees' safety needs. To help provide security from variability in business cycles, IBM has, in recent years, changed the way it pays its sales force, shifting away from uncertain commissions in favor of a more secure salary.[12] Such a plan is intended, in part, to help satisfy workers' safety needs.

3. *Social needs* represent the third level of need specified by Maslow. These are theorized to be activated after both physiological and safety needs are met. Social needs refers to the need to be affiliative—to have friends, to be loved and accepted by other people. To help meet social needs, organizations may encourage participation in social events, such as office picnics or parties. Company bowling or softball

Test Bank questions 4.8, 4.10–4.12, 4.47, and 4.57 relate to material on this page.

leagues also provide an opportunity for meeting social needs. Country club memberships provide good opportunities for top executives to engage in valuable "networking" with their fellow executives while meeting their social needs. Earlier, we mentioned that physical fitness programs can help satisfy physiological needs. Of course, they help satisfy social needs, too. Indeed, working out or playing sports with coworkers provides an excellent opportunity to develop friendships. Research has shown that social needs are especially likely to be aroused under conditions in which "organizational uncertainty" exists, such as when the possibility of a merger threatens job security.[13] Under such conditions employees may be likely to seek their coworkers' company to gather information about what's going on.

Taken together as a group, physiological needs, safety needs, and social needs are known as *deficiency needs.* Maslow's idea was that if these needs aren't met, an individual will fail to develop into a healthy person, both physically and psychologically. In contrast, the next two highest-order needs—the ones at the top of the hierarchy—are known as *growth needs.* Gratification of these needs is said to help a person grow and develop to his or her fullest potential.

4. *Esteem needs* are the fourth level of need. These refer to a person's need to develop self-respect and to gain the approval of others. The desires to achieve success, have prestige, and be recognized by others all fall into this category. Companies do many things to satisfy their employees' esteem needs. They may, for example, have awards banquets to recognize distinguished achievements. Printing articles in company newsletters describing an employee's success, giving keys to the executive washroom, assigning private parking spaces, and posting signs identifying the "employee of the month" are all examples of things that can be done to satisfy esteem needs. For a summary of what some companies are doing to satisfy the esteem needs of their employees, see Table 4–1.[14]

TABLE 4–1   Recognizing Employees' Contributions: What Some Companies Are Doing

Many creative ways can be found to recognize the valued contributions of employees, thereby satisfying their esteem needs. Summarized here are some ingenious tactics practiced by three companies.

Company	Practice
United Electric Controls Company (Watertown, MA)	The company's Valued Ideas Program presents $100 at an awards ceremony to employees whose ideas for improvement are implemented. People submitting suggestions that are not used are eligible to receive prizes (e.g., tickets to sports events) at a monthly drawing. (See end-of-chapter Case in Point.)
GTE Data Services (Temple Terrace, FL)	Employees who develop ways of improving customer satisfaction or business performance are nominated for awards. The big award is a four-day first-class vacation, $500, a plaque, and recognition in the company magazine.
Temps & Company (Washington, DC)	To reward employees for taking risks, a prize of $100 is given to the manager who makes the most significant blunder. By encouraging people to discuss their mistakes freely, the plan has enabled the company to implement needed improvements.

Source: Based on information in Gunsch, 1991; see Note 14.

According to a recent survey, a growing number of employees in Western nations are seeking self-actualization rather than traditional measures of success, such as security, promotions, and high pay. For example, 26 percent of U.S. employees, 15 percent of British employees, and 14 percent of German employees want to work only for organizations that encourage creativity and flexibility. These individuals also seek self-actualization off their jobs (through their families and hobbies) as well as on their jobs. [Plummer, J. T. (1989, January–February). Changing values. *The Futurist*, pp. 8–13.]

5. *Self-actualization needs* are found at the top of Maslow's hierarchy. These are the needs aroused only after all the lower-order needs have been met. **Self-actualization** refers to the need for self-fulfillment—the desire to become all that one is capable of being, developing one's potential. By working at their maximum creative potential, employees who are self-actualized can be extremely valuable assets to their organizations. Individuals who have self-actualized are working at their peak and represent the most effective use of an organization's human resources.

Research testing Maslow's theory has supported the distinction between deficiency needs and growth needs. Unfortunately, the research has shown that not all employees are able to satisfy their higher-order needs on the job. For example, Porter found that whereas lower-level managers were able to satisfy only their deficiency needs on the job, managers from the higher echelons of organizations were able to satisfy both their deficiency and growth needs.[15] An interesting study by Betz also examined the extent to which different groups' needs are met—specifically, housewives and women who work outside the home.[16] Betz found that full-time homemakers had higher levels of deficiency needs than married women employed outside the home. Presumably, this was because they did not have a job through which these needs could be fulfilled. It was also found that the growth needs of working women were higher than those of full-time homemakers, presumably because their deficiency needs were already satisfied on the job. This evidence is clearly consistent with Maslow's ideas about the satisfaction of deficiency needs prior to growth needs.

Despite such general evidence, Maslow's theory has not received a great deal of support with respect to the specific notions it proposes—namely, the exact needs that exist and the order in which they are activated.[17] Many researchers have failed to confirm that there are only five basic categories of need. Also, these needs haven't been found to be activated in the exact order specified by Maslow.

Alderfer's ERG Theory

In response to these criticisms, an alternative formulation has been proposed by Clayton Alderfer.[18] This approach, known as **ERG theory,** is much simpler than Maslow's. Alderfer specifies not only that there are three types of need instead of five, but also that these are not necessarily activated in any specific order. In fact, Alderfer postulates that any need may be activated at any time.

The three needs specified by *ERG theory* are the needs for *existence*, *relatedness*, and *growth*. *Existence* needs correspond to Maslow's psyiological needs and safety needs. *Relatedness* needs correspond to Maslow's social needs, the need for meaningful social relationships. Finally, *growth* needs correspond to the esteem needs and self-actualization needs in Maslow's theory—the need for developing one's potential. A summary of Maslow's need hierarchy theory and the corresponding needs identified by Alderfer's ERG theory is shown in Figure 4–4.

Clearly, ERG theory is much less restrictive than Maslow's need hierarchy theory. Its advantage is that it fits better with research evidence suggesting that although basic categories of need do exist, they are not exactly as specified by Maslow.[19] Despite the fact that need theorists are not in complete agreement about the exact number of needs that exist and the relationships between them, they do agree that satisfying human needs is an important part of motivating behavior on the job.

Practical Applications of Need Theories

Probably the greatest value of need theories lies in the practical implications they have for management. In particular, the theories are important insofar as they suggest specific things that managers can do to help their subordinates become self-actualized. Because a self-actualized employee is more likely to work at his or her maximum creative potential, it makes sense to help people achieve this goal by meeting some of their needs. Here are some things that can be (or are being) done.

1. To help meet physiological needs, companies obviously need to pay their employees sufficient wages to have food to eat and a roof over their heads. We also mentioned that providing employees with exercise facilities helps maintain a healthy work force, thereby satisfying physiological needs. Recently, some organizations have found another way to encourage healthful behavior among their employees. Companies such as Hershey Foods Corporation, U-Haul (in Phoenix, Arizona), and Southern California Edison Company are just a few that give insurance rebates or charge extra premiums to employees with good health habits (e.g., moderately active nonsmokers who are not overweight and who have normal cholesterol and blood pressure levels).[20] For example, Hershey employees meeting a healthy profile can save as much as $360 per year on their health insurance premiums, whereas those with an unhealthy lifestyle may be charged as much as $1,404 in additional premiums. No doubt such a plan provides quite an incentive for employees to help the company help them meet their physiological needs.

2. Companies can also help meet employees' security needs. Although economic factors prevent companies from guaranteeing most employees total job security, something can be done to soften the blow of getting laid off. More and more organizations are providing *outplacement services*.[21] Specifically, they provide necessary counseling and assistance to help a laid-off employee secure a new position elsewhere. Employees' knowledge that such assistance is available, if needed, helps reduce the negative emotional aspects of job insecurity.

3. To help fulfill esteem needs, companies can recognize the achievements of successful employees and reward them with a symbolic gesture. We already mentioned various awards, such as "employee of the month." Recipients and their coworkers should know exactly what special behavior is being rewarded. If the award is too general or vague (e.g., "best attitude"), it might not have the reinforcing effect intended. In fact, it might just make others angry, feeling that they, too, could have received the honor. Thus, rewards given to enhance self-esteem should be clearly tied to a desired activity. When the award is bestowed in public, it is certainly important for everyone to agree that the award is well earned and appropriate.

To conclude, need theories represent a potentially useful approach to understanding motivation in organizations. These theories reflect the major ways in which human needs are involved in explaining motivation in work organizations. We will now move on to a related concept—goals.

According to a survey of twenty large corporations, 71 percent of insurance claims come from only 8.4 percent of the employees. As a result, some companies, such as U-Haul International, are getting tough with their staff members who don't stay in good health. As a disincentive for continuing bad health habits, U-Haul has recently begun to dock employees $10 per paycheck for smoking or for being overweight or underweight. [Garland, S. B. (1990, May 21). Health care costs: Trying to cool the fever. *Business Week*, pp. 46–47.]

GOAL-SETTING THEORY

Just as people are motivated to satisfy their needs on the job, they are also motivated to strive for and attain goals. In fact, the process of setting goals is one of the most important motivational forces operating on people in organizations.[22] We will describe a prominent theory of **goal setting** and then review research findings revealing techniques for setting goals in a manner that maximizes performance.

Locke and Latham's Goal-Setting Theory

Suppose that you are performing a task, such as word processing, when a performance goal is assigned. You are now expected, for example, to input 70 words per minute (wpm) instead of the 60 wpm you've been doing all along. Would you work hard to meet this goal, or would you simply give up? Some insight into the question of how people respond to assigned goals is provided by a model proposed by Locke and Latham.[23] They claim that an assigned goal influences a person's beliefs about being able to perform the task (referred to as "self-efficacy") and his or her personal goals. (We will have more to say about the concept of self-efficacy in chapter 6.) Both of these factors, in turn, influence performance. A summary of these steps appears in diagrammatic form in Figure 4–5.

The basic idea behind Locke and Latham's theory is that a goal serves as a motivator because it causes people to compare their present capacity to perform with that required to succeed at the goal. To the extent that people believe they will fall short of a goal, they will feel dissatisfied, and will work harder to attain the goal so long as they believe it is possible for them to do so. Having a goal may enhance performance because the goal makes clear exactly what type and level of performance is expected. Goals also help improve performance because they provide information about how well one is performing a task. For example, an experiment by Vance and Colella revealed that the opportunity to compare one's own performance with assigned goals enhanced acceptance of the goals and performance on the task (at least until the goal became too difficult).[24]

The model also claims that assigned goals will lead to the acceptance of those goals as personal goals. In other words, they will be accepted as one's own. Indeed, recent research by Klein has shown that people will be more committed to a goal to the extent that they desire to attain the goal and believe they have a reasonable chance of doing so.[25] Likewise, the more one believes he or she is capable of meeting the goal, the more likely that person is to accept the goal as his or her own.[26]

Finally, the model claims that beliefs about both self-efficacy and personal goals influence task performance. This makes sense insofar as people are willing to exert greater effort when they believe they are capable of succeeding than when they believe their efforts will be in vain.[27] Moreover, goals that are not personally accepted will have little capacity to guide behavior.

In general, Locke and Latham's model of goal setting has been supported by several studies.[28] However, the most practical benefits of research can be seen in various studies focusing on the content of goals themselves. In other words, these studies ask the question, "How should goals be set to enhance performance?"

Practical Conclusions of Goal-Setting Research

Because researchers have been actively involved in studying the goal-setting process for many years, it is possible to summarize their findings in the form of principles. These represent very practical guidelines that practicing managers can use to enhance motivation.

Assign specific goals.   Probably the best-established finding of research on goal setting is that people perform at higher levels when asked to meet a specifically high performance goal than when simply asked to "do your best," or when no goal at all is assigned.[29] Employees tend to find specific goals quite challenging, and are motivated to try to meet them—not only to fulfill management's expectations, but also to convince themselves that they have performed well. The quest to attain specific goals has been shown to have beneficial effects on employees' job behaviors in several organizations. Research conducted at Parkdale Mills, Inc., provides a particularly dramatic demonstration of this principle. Before the goal-setting program began, the employees in this organization had an average attendance rate of 86 percent. As part of the goal-setting program, they agreed to raise their average attendance rate to 93 percent. Each day an attendance chart was kept so employees could be kept informed

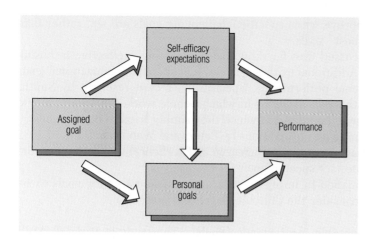

FIGURE 4–5

Locke and Latham's Model of Goal Setting

According to Locke and Latham's goal-setting model, assigned goals influence beliefs about performing a task (self-efficacy expectations) and encourage the acceptance of those goals as personal goals. Both of these factors, in turn, influence performance. (*Source:* Based on suggestions in Locke & Latham, 1990, see Note 22; and Earley & Lituchy, 1991, see Note 28.)

of their progress toward meeting their goal. Within four weeks of setting this goal, they not only met it, but surpassed it—averaging 94.3 percent attendance for the nine weeks following the goal setting.[30]

Similar results were found in another field study, this one involving crews of loggers who hauled logs from a forest to the company's sawmill.[31] Before the study, the loggers tended to load the trucks to only about 60 percent of their legal weight capacity. Then a specific goal was set, challenging them to load the trucks to 94 percent of their capacity before driving to the plant. Not only was the specific goal effective in raising performance to the goal level in just a few weeks, but the effects were long-lasting as well. In fact, the loggers were found to sustain this level of performance as long as seven years later. (Apparently, loading the trucks to 94 percent of their legal weight capacity became an accepted group practice—what we will describe in chapter 8 as a group norm.) Just as impressive were the financial savings the company realized as a result of eliminating wasted trips. Specifically, the company's accountants estimated that $250,000 was saved in the first nine months alone!

The results of these two studies are typical of many that have found task performance to improve in response to the setting of specific goals.[32] For a graph showing the results of a typical goal-setting study, see Figure 4–6. As this figure shows,

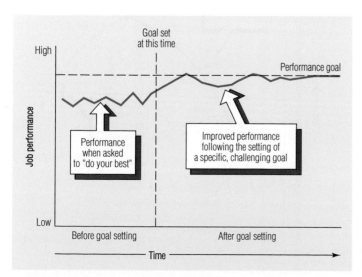

FIGURE 4–6

Typical Effects of Goal Setting

Many studies have shown that relative to general, "do your best" goals, job performance is enhanced by the setting of specific, challenging goals. In time, performance rises to meet specific performance goals.

performance tends to improve when specific, challenging goals are set, rather than more general, "do your best" goals.

The studies we've discussed thus far show that goal setting is effective in raising individual performance. Additional evidence shows that specific organizational goals help enhance organizational performance. Specifically, recent research by Smith, Locke, and Barry found that organizations in which people worked to meet specific goals were more productive than those in which they simply tried to do their best.[33] Such evidence is consistent with observations by Peters and Waterman (in their 1982 best-selling popular management book, *In Search of Excellence*) suggesting that the most productive companies set specific goals for themselves.[34]

Of course, for performance to improve, it is not sufficient just for goals to be specific. One must also consider the difficulty level of these goals.

Assign difficult, but acceptable, performance goals.   The study at Parkdale Mills demonstrated the effectiveness of assigning specific goals. But note also that the goal the organization set was a difficult one. A goal must be difficult and challenging as well as specific for it to raise performance. People work harder to reach higher goals, as long as these are within the limits of their capability. However, as goals become too difficult, performance drops because people reject the goals as unrealistic (see Figure 4–7).[35] For example, you may work much harder in a class that challenges your ability than in one that is very easy, but you would probably give up if the only way of getting an A were to get perfect scores on all papers and exams. As Figure 4–7 suggests, a professor who sets such an impossible goal would not be motivating students to do their best.

The same phenomenon has been found in industry. At a General Electric manufacturing plant, specific goals were set for productivity and cost reduction. Those goals perceived as challenging, but possible, led to improved performance. However, those goals perceived as unattainable led to decreased performance.[36] Given this, an important question arises as to how to set goals that enhance employees' commitment.

FIGURE 4–7

Job Performance: It Depends on the Acceptance of Difficult Goals

Research and theory on goal setting suggests that people will accept and work hard to attain difficult goals, until they reach the limits of their capabilities. However, as goals become too difficult, they may be rejected, and performance will suffer. (*Source:* Adapted from Locke & Latham, 1984; see Note 35.)

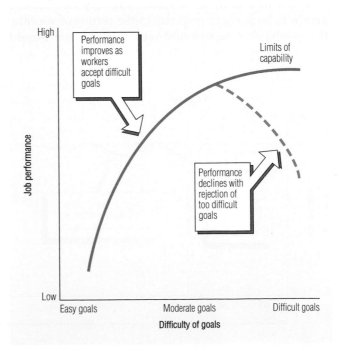

After all, as Figure 4–7 shows, the higher the goal workers will accept, the more productive they will be.[37]

One obvious way of enhancing goal acceptance is to *involve workers in the goal-setting process*. Research on workers' participation in goal setting has been quite extensive and, over the years, has yielded mixed results. Recently, however, investigators have agreed that participation in goal setting may enhance job performance more than goals assigned by others.[38] Specifically, it has been found that employees tend to perform at higher levels when they are allowed to participate freely in setting their own performance goals than when their supervisors tell them what goals to meet.[39] Participation in the goal-setting process may be helpful not only because it ensures that employees understand and appreciate the goals, but also because it makes them more committed to attaining these goals. After all, people are unlikely to reject as unreasonable any goals they have had a voice in creating. Also, possibly because workers have more direct knowledge about what it takes to do a job than their supervisors, they are likely to come up with goals that are acceptably high, but not so high as to be rejected as unreasonable.

Sometimes, it is impractical to involve employees in the goal-setting process, so other techniques may be used to enhance goal acceptance. One such approach involves using *psychological contracts* to make people more committed to attaining their goals. By getting employees to publicly commit themselves to attaining a goal, their acceptance of that goal and their likelihood of attaining it are increased.

Acceptance of difficult goals can also be enhanced through *supervisory support*. Subordinates can hardly be expected to strive to attain goals that their own supervisors don't seem to care about. Research has shown that when a boss gives his or her subordinates confidence about their abilities, the employees tend to set higher goals, which, of course, leads to higher levels of performance.[40] One form of support is giving people recognition for meeting their goals. Employees at IBM specifically identify the support and personal recognition they receive from their supervisors as an important part of what keeps them working toward their goals.[41]

One very simple and direct technique for enhancing acceptance of goals involves *explaining the logic behind goal setting*. Because employees may be threatened or intimidated by the imposition of goals, several suggestions for getting them to accept goals have been offered.[42] First, it is necessary to explain how goals were set (such as through past performance), so that people don't feel they are being taken advantage of. Second, the effects of the program on employees' pay should be clearly explained. For example, that salaried personnel's pay will not be reduced if they fail to meet the goals should be explained. The financial benefits of the program for those paid on a piece-rate basis should also be explained. Finally, involvement in goal-setting programs should be voluntary, and this should be explained to workers. Goal setting will not work if the employees reject the goals and suspect the management of tricking them. With this in mind, a few well-chosen words of reassurance may be useful in getting employees to accept goals.

Provide feedback concerning goal attainment.   The final principle of goal setting we will mention is an obvious one (although too often it is not followed in practice). Just as golfers need feedback about where their ball is going when they hit it in order to improve their swing, workers need feedback about how closely they are approaching their performance goals in order to meet them.

The importance of combining feedback and goal setting has been shown in a recent field study examining the effects of goal setting on occupational safety.[43] The participants were employees working in various shops of a manufacturing plant. Before and after safety goals were set, various employee behaviors were observed. From these, judgments were made of the percentage of employees performing their jobs

Recent research has found how very effective employee participation programs can be. For example, productivity was found to be 5 percent to 10 percent higher in firms that have profit-sharing plans (i.e., firms that reward employees for their contributions to corporate success) than those that do not have them. A review of fifteen studies shows that in every case there is a positive relationship between profit-sharing programs and employee productivity. [Blinder, A. S. (1989, April 17). Want to boost productivity? Try giving workers a say. *Business Week*, p. 10.]

in a completely safe manner. During the ten weeks before goal setting began, about 65 percent of the workers performed their jobs safely. Then, after a difficult but attainable goal of 95 percent safe behavior was set, the safety rate rose to over 80 percent—an improvement, but still shy of the goal. Only after the goal setting was accompanied by feedback about safety was the goal actually met.

A very ambitious recent study of different units in the U.S. Air Force showed that feedback and goal setting together helped improve performance for work groups (as opposed to individuals).[44] The job effectiveness index (a measure of the extent to which expectations were met or exceeded) of five different groups was measured repeatedly over a two-year period. During the first nine months, a baseline measure of effectiveness was taken that could be used to compare the relative impact of feedback and goal setting. Then the groups received feedback for five months (monthly reports explaining how well they performed on various performance measures). After five months of feedback, the groups began the goal-setting phase of the study. During this time, the crew members set goals for themselves with respect to their performance on various measures. Then, for the last five months, in addition to the feedback and goal setting, an incentive (time off from work) was made available to crew members who met their goals. The relative effectiveness of the crews during each phase of the study is shown in Figure 4–8.

As Figure 4–8 clearly shows, feedback and goal setting dramatically increased group effectiveness. Group feedback improved performance approximately 50 percent over the baseline level. The addition of group goal setting improved it 75 percent over baseline. These findings show that the combination of goal setting and feedback helps raise the effectiveness of group performance. Groups that know how well they're doing and have a target goal to shoot for tend to perform very well. Providing incentives, however, improved performance only negligibly. The real incentive seems to be meeting the challenge of performing up to the level of the goal.

Feedback is clearly a necessary element of the goal-setting process, and different kinds of feedback are possible. Recent research by Earley, Northcraft, Lee, and

Goal Setting and Feedback: Most Effective When Combined

Research on U.S. Air Force crews over a two-year period showed that feedback enhanced performance relative to baseline levels of group effectiveness, and that the addition of goal setting enhanced it even more. After feedback and goal setting were used, the introduction of incentives had negligible additional impact on effectiveness. (Based on data in Pritchard, Jones, Roth, Stuebing, & Ekeberg, 1988; see Note 44.)

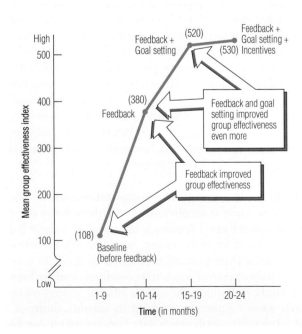

Lituchy found that two different kinds of feedback were *both* effective in enhancing performance: *outcome feedback*—information about the consequences of one's actions; and *process feedback*—information about ways to improve task performance.[45] This distinction may be best understood using an example from baseball. Telling a batter that he or she hit three foul balls in a row would be an example of outcome feedback. However, suggesting that the batter choke up on the bat would be an example of process feedback. Obviously, both types of feedback are useful, but process feedback is especially helpful in getting people to understand *how* to improve. In fact, it has been noted that 65 percent of the verbal comments made during practice by John Wooden, the highly successful former basketball coach of UCLA, were specific statements about what the players were doing, its effects, and how to improve in the future.[46] This observation provides a further example of the beneficial effects of feedback on task performance.

In sum, goal setting is a very effective tool managers can use to motivate subordinates. Setting specific, acceptably difficult goals and providing feedback about progress toward the goal greatly enhance motivation and job performance.

EQUITY THEORY

The theories we've described thus far are based on the operation of completely individual processes—the activation of needs, and the responses to goals. The next approach to motivation we will consider, **equity theory,** is also an individual-based theory, but one that adds a social component. Specifically, equity theory views motivation from the perspective of the social comparisons people make among themselves. It proposes that individuals are motivated to maintain fair, or "equitable," relationships among themselves and to change those relationships that are unfair, or "inequitable."[47] The ways in which this is done has been a topic of considerable interest in the field of organizational behavior. Equity theory is concerned with people's motivation to escape the negative feelings that result from being treated unfairly on their jobs. Such feelings may result when people engage in the process of *social comparison* (i.e., when they compare themselves to others).

Adams's Equity Theory

The major version of equity theory studied by organizational scientists was proposed by J. Stacy Adams, in his "theory of inequity," or, as it is better known, *equity theory.* Specifically, equity theory proposes that people make social comparisons between themselves and others with respect to two variables—*outcomes* and *inputs.* **Outcomes** refer to the things workers believe they and others get out of their jobs, including pay, fringe benefits, and prestige. **Inputs** refer to the contributions employees believe they and others make to their jobs, including the amount of time worked, the amount of effort expended, the number of units produced, and the qualifications brought to the job. Note that equity theory is concerned with outcomes and inputs as they are *perceived* by the people involved, *not* necessarily as they actually are. Not surprisingly, therefore, workers may disagree about what constitutes equity and inequity on the job.

Equity theory states that people compare their outcomes and inputs to those of others in the form of a ratio. Specifically, they compare the ratio of their own outcomes/inputs to the ratio of other people's outcomes/inputs. As shown in Figure 4–9 (see p. 128), these comparisons can result in any of three states: *overpayment, underpayment,* or *equitable payment.*

FIGURE 4–9

Equity Theory: An Overview

To judge equity or inequity, people compare the ratios of their own outcomes/inputs to the corresponding ratios of others. The resulting states—overpayment inequity, underpayment inequity, and equitable payment—and their associated emotional responses are summarized here.

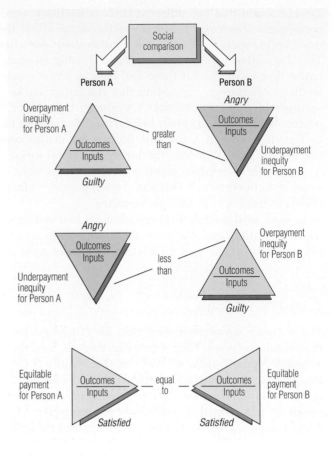

- **Overpayment inequity** occurs when someone's outcome/input is *greater than* the corresponding ratio of another person with whom that person compares himself or herself. People who are overpaid are theorized to feel *guilty*.
- **Underpayment inequity** occurs when someone's outcome/input ratio is *less than* the corresponding ratio of another with whom that person compares himself or herself. People who are underpaid are theorized to feel *angry*.
- **Equitable payment** occurs when someone's outcome/input ratio is *equal to* the corresponding ratio of another person with whom that person compares himself or herself. People who are equitably paid are theorized to feel *satisfied*.

To help us understand what equity theory predicts, suppose that Jack and Ray work alongside each other on an assembly line, doing the same job. Both men have the same degree of experience, training, and education (i.e., their inputs are identical). However, while Jack is paid $500 per week, Ray is paid only $350 per week (i.e., Jack's outcomes are greater than Ray's). How will they feel when they talk to each other one day and learn of this situation? According to equity theory, Jack may be considered overpaid, and would be expected to feel guilty, whereas Ray may be considered underpaid, and would be expected to feel angry.

According to equity theory, people are motivated to escape these negative emotional states of anger and guilt. Equity theory recognizes several ways of resolving inequitable states (see the summary in Table 4–2). In our example, Jack and Ray can do several things to redress the inequity and feel satisfied. For instance, Ray, or any other underpaid person, may respond by lowering his inputs. He may not

TABLE 4-2   Possible Reactions to Inequity: A Summary

People can respond to overpayment and underpayment inequities in behavioral and/or psychological ways. A few of these are summarized here. These reactions help change the perceived *inequities* into a state of perceived *equity*.

Type of Inequity	Type of Reaction	
	Behavioral (What you can *do* is . . .)	Psychological (What you can *think* is . . .)
Overpayment inequity	Raise your inputs (e.g., work harder), or lower your outcomes (e.g., work through a paid vacation)	Convince yourself that your outcomes are deserved based on your inputs (e.g., rationalize that you work harder than others and so you deserve more pay)
Underpayment inequity	Lower your inputs (e.g., reduce effort), or raise your outcomes (e.g., get a raise in pay)	Convince yourself that others' inputs are really higher than your own (e.g., rationalize that the comparison worker is really more qualified and so deserves higher outcomes)

work as hard, arriving at work late, leaving early, taking longer breaks, doing less work, or performing lower-quality work. In an extreme case, he may even quit his job. He may also attempt to raise his outcomes, asking the boss for a raise, or even taking home company property (such as tools or office supplies). All these examples may be considered *behavioral* reactions to inequity because they represent things people can do to change their existing inputs or outcomes.

In addition to these behavioral reactions to underpayment inequity, some *psychological* reactions are likely. Given that many people feel uncomfortable stealing from their employers (as they should) or would be unwilling to restrict their productivity or to ask for a raise, they may resort to resolving the inequity by changing the way they think about the situation. Because equity theory deals with perceptions of fairness or unfairness, it is reasonable to expect that inequitable states may be redressed effectively by merely thinking about the circumstances differently. For example, underpaid people may attempt to rationalize that others' inputs are really higher than their own, thereby convincing themselves that the others' high outcomes are justified. One recent study even found that workers who received a 6 percent pay cut rationalized that their pay was still equitable by coming to think of their work environments in more favorable terms.[48] So by coming to perceive the situation as equitable, people can effectively reduce their inequity distress.

An analogous set of behavioral and psychological reactions can be identified for overpayment inequity. Specifically, a salaried employee who feels underpaid may raise his or her inputs by working harder or for more hours. Similarly, employees who lower their own outcomes by not taking advantage of company-provided fringe benefits may be seen as redressing an overpayment inequity. In addition, overpaid persons may readily convince themselves psychologically that they are really worth their higher outcomes by virtue of their superior inputs. People who receive substantial pay raises may not feel distressed about it at all because they rationalize that the raise is warranted on the basis of their superior inputs, and therefore does not constitute an inequity.

A growing business concern has been the overpayment of CEOs. Whereas employees' wages declined in the 1980s, the salaries of CEOs soared. Corporate profits in the United States increased by only 5 percent between 1977 and 1987, whereas the salaries and bonuses of CEOs rose by 220 percent. The average CEO earned ninety-three times more than the average employee. [Naylor, T. H. (1990, May 30–June 6). Redefining corporate motivation. *The Christian Century*, pp. 566–570.]

Research has generally supported the theory's claim that people will respond to overpayment and underpayment inequities in the ways just described.[49] In one of the most ambitious tests of equity theory, Pritchard, Dunnette, and Jorgenson hired male clerical workers to work part-time over a two-week period.[50] In their simulated company, the experimenters manipulated the equity or inequity of the payment their employees received. *Overpaid* employees were told the pay they received was higher than that of others doing the same work. *Underpaid* employees were told their pay was lower than that of others doing the same work. *Equitably paid* employees were told the pay they received was equal to that of others doing the same work. The results of the study were consistent with equity theory: people who were overpaid were more productive than those who were equitably paid; and people who were underpaid were less productive than those who were equitably paid. Moreover, both overpaid and underpaid employees reported being more dissatisfied with their jobs than those who were equitably paid. Thus, the people participating in this study behaved precisely as equity theory predicted.

In recent years, conditions of underpayment have been created by **two-tier wage structures**—payment systems in which newer employees are paid less than employees hired at an earlier time to do the same work. Such a wage structure can be considered inequitable because it pays newer employees a lower starting salary than earlier hired, equally qualified people doing the same job. Not surprisingly, research has shown that employees hired into the lower-wage tier reported their payment to be less fair than that of those in the upper tier.[51] Lower-paid employees also express great dissatisfaction. One Los Angeles supermarket clerk, paid about half as much as an earlier-hired coworker, said, "It stinks. They're paying us lower wages for the same work."[52] Not only are they unhappy, but underpaid personnel tend to refuse work assignments, and to quit their jobs. For example, after institution of a two-tier wage structure, two-thirds of the lower-paid employees at the Giant Food supermarket chain quit their jobs during the first three months. Even the proposal of a two-tier pay structure in the mid-1980s caused United Airline pilots to go on strike. This is not surprising, since a two-tier wage system instituted by American Airlines in 1985 virtually cut in half the amount DC-10 pilots would be paid at the top of their careers—a difference of over \$64,000 per year![53] Although two-tier wage systems are set up to help companies save money, employees' negative reactions to them clearly may make them costlier than ever imagined.

So far we have been discussing only how changes in performance level can reflect feelings of inequity. However, people may also react to feelings of inequity in other ways. For example, in the **Focus on Research** section on pages 132–133, we will describe a study showing that people respond to feelings of underpayment by stealing from their employers.

Applying Equity Theory: Some Motivational Tips

Compared to their counterparts in other countries, U.S. employees may feel underpaid when it comes to the amount of time off they receive per year. For example, on average, U.S. employees work 40 hours per week and get 11 holidays and 12 days of paid vacation per year. British employees work 39-hour weeks and get 8 paid holidays and 25 days of paid

Before concluding this section, we will summarize its main points by briefly pointing out some useful practical suggestions for motivating employees that equity theory makes. First, because people who are underpaid tend to respond in a counterproductive fashion, such as by lowering their performance or stealing from their employers, *underpayment should be avoided*. On the other hand, although overpaid employees may improve their performance, the effects are only temporary. Besides, when one employee is overpaid (and raises his or her performance), chances are good that others who work with that person will feel underpaid (and lower their performance), thereby yielding a net reduction in productivity. Thus, it is reasonable to recommend that *overpayment should be avoided*. Taken together, these guidelines lead to the conclusion that managers should strive to treat all employees equitably.

We realize, of course, that this may be easier said than done. Part of the difficulty resides in the fact that feelings of equity and inequity are based on perceptions that people have, and these aren't always easy to control (as we discussed in chapter 2). One approach that may help is to *be open and honest about outcomes and inputs.* People tend to overestimate how much their superiors are paid, and therefore tend to feel that their own pay is not as high as it should be.[54] If information about pay is shared, inequitable feelings may not result. Finally, we recommend that *managers should present information about outcomes and inputs in a thorough and socially sensitive manner.* Not only may doing so take some of the sting out of receiving undesirable outcomes (such as layoffs), but it also enhances the manager's image as a fair person.[55]

EXPECTANCY THEORY

Of the theories we have examined thus far, *expectancy theory* is the broadest in scope. Instead of focusing on individual needs, goals, or social comparisons as the previously described theories have done, **expectancy theory** looks at the role of motivation in the overall work environment. In essence, the theory asserts that people are motivated to work when they expect they will be able to achieve the things they want from their jobs. Expectancy theory characterizes people as rational beings who think about what they have to do to be rewarded and how much the reward means to them before they perform their jobs. But, as we will see, the theory doesn't just focus on what people think—it also recognizes that these thoughts combine with other aspects of the organizational environment to influence job performance.

Basic Elements of Expectancy Theory

Before describing expectancy theory in more detail, we should note that it has been presented in many different forms—including the important pioneering work of Vroom[56] and of Porter and Lawler.[57] However, the differences between the various versions of expectancy theory need not concern us; we will describe it in its most general form.

Expectancy theory specifies that motivation is the result of three different types of beliefs that people have. These are known as

1. **Expectancy**—the belief that one's effort will result in performance
2. **Instrumentality**—the belief that one's performance will be rewarded
3. **Valence**—the perceived value of the rewards to the recipient

Sometimes, employees believe that putting forth a great deal of effort will result in getting a lot accomplished. However, in other cases, hard work will have little effect on how much gets done. For example, an employee operating a faulty piece of equipment may have a very low *expectancy* that his or her efforts will lead to high levels of performance. Someone working under such conditions probably would not continue to exert much effort.

Even if an employee works hard and performs at a high level, motivation may falter if that performance is not suitably rewarded by the organization—that is, if the performance is not perceived as *instrumental* in bringing about the rewards. So, for example, a worker who is extremely productive may be poorly motivated to perform if he or she has already reached the top level of pay given by the company.

Finally, even if employees receive rewards based on their performance, they may be poorly motivated if those so-called rewards have a low *valence* to them. Someone who doesn't care about the rewards offered by the organization is not motivated to

vacation. By law, French employees work 39-hour weeks and receive 8 paid holidays, and they get 25½ days of paid vacation. Germans work 38-hour weeks and get 10 holidays and 30 days of paid vacation per year. Employees in Japan work 42-hour weeks and get 22 holidays and 16 days of vacation, although they rarely take their vacation time, choosing to work instead. [You must be very busy. (1990, August 20). *Time*, p. 82.]

Executives have recently begun to realize that efforts to motivate and improve the productivity of poor performers can be hampered if these employees expect to be fired regardless of their efforts to improve. Managers who have shifted to a "no firing" policy have found that removing expectations of termination drastically improves productivity and morale. [Jaffe, A. (1989, August). Firing: There's (almost) always a better way. *Psychology Today*, pp. 68–69.]

attempt to attain them. For example, a multimillionaire would probably be poorly motivated to work for a reward of $100, whereas a person of more modest means would probably perceive that reward as being extremely valuable. Keep in mind that almost anything can have some positive valence to employees. For example, executives at LensCrafters (the $600 million chain of eyeglass shops) offer a highly unique but valued reward to their store managers who reach stated sales and service targets—a chance to throw a pie in the face of field managers.[58] The point is simple: almost any reward—financial or otherwise—can enhance motivation if it almost any reward—financial or otherwise—can enhance motivation if it is valued.

Expectancy theory claims that motivation is a multiplicative function of all three components. This means that higher levels of motivation will result when valence,

FOCUS ON RESEARCH

Employee Theft as a Reaction to Underpayment Inequity

 Imagine yourself in the following situation. You're an employee of a manufacturing firm during an economic recession. The company has lost some large contracts and now finds itself in a temporary cash flow crisis. Rather than laying off any employees, company officials decide that the best way to weather the storm is to impose a 15 percent pay cut for all employees for a period of ten weeks. Naturally, you'd feel displeased, and inequitably treated. After all, you would now be underpaid relative to the pay you received earlier. However, in such a situation, you may feel reluctant to lower your work performance because you may not want to call negative attention to yourself and risk getting fired. Still, you feel angry about your pay cut. What might you do? A recent study by Greenberg found that people in this same exact underpayment inequity situation found an ingenious way to raise their outcomes—they stole from their employer.[59] Although it's unethical to do so, stealing may be an effective way of restoring equity with an employer who has underpaid you. Not only might it raise your outcomes (especially if you're stealing something of value to you), but it also represents a way of retaliating against those who have caused you some harm.

The research was conducted in three manufacturing plants. In one, there was no need for a pay cut, and it was business as usual; this was the *control group*. The other two plants were similar to the control group in that they employed people with similar backgrounds to do the same types of manufacturing jobs. The pay cuts in these two plants were handled in very different ways. In one of the plants (chosen at random), employees received a very thorough and sensitive explanation of their pay cut. In this *adequate explanation condition*, they were given a detailed financial accounting justifying the need for the pay cuts, and they were shown a considerable amount of remorse and sympathy over their fate. By contrast, employees in the *inadequate explanation condition*, the other plant, were given only the most superficial information about the necessity for the pay cuts, and this information was presented in a highly uncaring fashion. The researcher wanted to see how the explanations would influence the amount of employee theft that occurred. Theft rates were measured using a standardized formula to account for otherwise unaccounted-for inventory losses. Inventory was taken weekly by company officials who were unaware of the study. Measures of theft were taken over thirty consecutive weeks—ten weeks before the pay cut, ten weeks during the pay cut period, and ten weeks after normal pay was reinstated.

Was the pay cut responsible for raises in employee theft? Did the amount of theft differ according to the explanation given? The answers are revealed by the data summarized in Figure 4–10. Before the pay cut, the level of theft was quite low, and about the same in all three groups. Then, once the pay cut occurred, the theft rate went up—moderately for those given an ade-

instrumentality, and expectancy are all high than when they are all low. The multiplicative assumption of the theory also implies that if any one of the components is zero, the overall level of motivation will be zero. So, even if an employee believes that her effort will result in performance, which will result in reward, motivation may be zero if the valence of the reward she expects to receive is zero. Figure 4–11 (see p. 134) summarizes the definitions of expectancy theory components and shows their interrelationships.

Figure 4–11 also shows that expectancy theory assumes that motivation is not equivalent to job performance, but is only one of several determinants of job performance. In particular, the theory assumes that *skills and abilities* also contribute to a person's job performance. It is no secret that some people are better suited to

quate explanation, but dramatically (twice as much!) in the inadequate explanation plant. Interestingly, once normal pay levels were reestablished, theft rates returned to their regular, low levels.

Obviously, the findings were quite dramatic. Not only did theft result from underpayment, as equity theory suggests, but also the *amount* of theft was found to be affected by the explanation given for the underpayment. Whereas a thorough, sensitive explanation made people more accepting of the underpayment, and less

extreme in their reactions to it, a superficial, insensitive explanation encouraged people to fully express their dissatisfaction by stealing. These findings make it clear that feelings of inequity are influenced not only by the balance of outcomes and inputs between them, as equity theory suggests, but also by the way people are treated by others. Indeed, treating others in a kind, sensitive manner has been shown to be an effective way of getting people to accept many of the different inequities they may expect to encounter on the job.

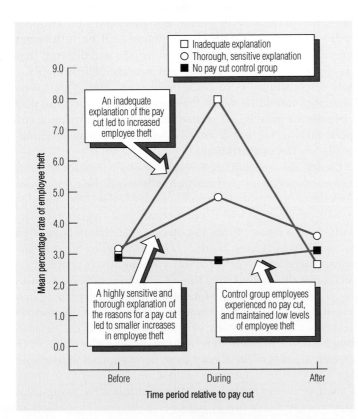

An inadequate explanation of the pay cut led to increased employee theft

A highly sensitive and thorough explanation of the reasons for a pay cut led to smaller increases in employee theft

Control group employees experienced no pay cut, and maintained low levels of employee theft

□ Inadequate explanation
○ Thorough, sensitive explanation
■ No pay cut control group

Mean percentage rate of employee theft

Time period relative to pay cut

Before — During — After

FIGURE 4–10

Underpayment Inequity as a Cause of Employee Theft

A field experiment by Greenberg showed that employees who experienced a temporary cut in their pay stole more from their employers during the time of the pay cut than did similar employees who experienced no pay cut. Theft was greater when the reasons for the pay cut were not adequately explained and little social sensitivity was shown. However, providing a highly sensitive and thorough explanation for the pay cut led to smaller increases in employee theft. (*Source:* Based on Greenberg, 1990; see Note 59.)

FIGURE 4–11

Expectancy Theory: An Overview

According to *expectancy theory,* motivation is the product of three types of beliefs: expectancy (effort will result in performance) × instrumentality (performance will result in rewards) × valence of rewards (the perceived value of the rewards). It also recognizes that motivation is only one of several factors responsible for job performance.

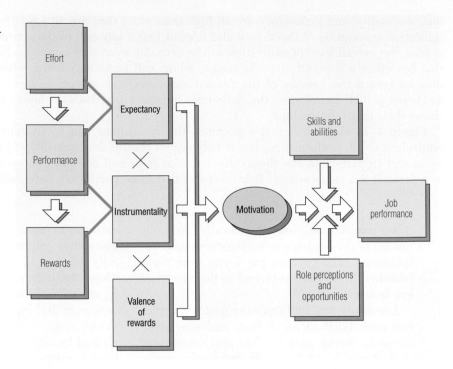

perform their jobs than others by virtue of the unique characteristics and special skills or abilities they bring to their jobs. For example, a tall, strong, well-coordinated person is likely to make a better professional basketball player than a very short, weak, uncoordinated one, even if the shorter person is highly motivated to succeed.

Expectancy theory also recognizes that job performance will be influenced by people's *role perceptions.* How well workers perform their jobs will depend, in part, on what they believe is expected of them. An assistant manager, for example, may believe her primary job responsibility is to train employees. But if the manager believes the assistant manager should be doing the paperwork instead, she may be seen as performing her job inadequately. Of course, such poor performance results *not* necessarily from poor motivation, but from misunderstandings concerning the role one is expected to play in the organization.

Finally, expectancy theory also recognizes the role of *opportunities to perform* one's job. Even the best employees may perform at low levels if their opportunities are limited. The work of salespeople provides a good example. Even the most highly motivated salesperson will perform poorly if opportunities are restricted—if the available inventory is very low (as is sometimes the case among certain popular cars), or if the customers are unable to afford the product (as is sometimes the case among salespeople whose territories are heavily populated by unemployed people).

It is important to recognize that expectancy theory views motivation as just one of several determinants of job performance. Motivation, combined with a person's skills and abilities, role perceptions, and opportunities, influences job performance.

Expectancy theory has generated a great deal of research and has been successfully applied to understanding behavior in many different organizational settings.[60] However, although some specific aspects of the theory have been supported (particularly the impact of expectancy and instrumentality on motivation),[61] others have not (such as the contribution of valence to motivation, and the multiplicative assumption).[62] Despite this mixed support, expectancy theory has been a dominant approach to the field of organizational motivation.

Practical Applications of Expectancy Theory

Probably the primary reason for expectancy theory's popularity is the many useful suggestions it makes for practicing managers. As we describe these below, you can refer to the summary of major points in Table 4–3.

One important suggestion is to *clarify people's expectancies that their effort will lead to performance.* Motivation may be enhanced by training employees to do their jobs more efficiently, thereby achieving higher levels of performance from their efforts. It may also be possible to enhance effort–performance expectancies by following employee's suggestions about ways to change their jobs. To the extent that employees are aware of problems in their jobs that interfere with their performance, attempting to alleviate these problems may help them perform more efficiently. In essence, what we are saying is, *make the desired performance attainable.* Make clear to people what is expected of them *and* make it possible for them to attain that level of performance.

A second practical suggestion from expectancy theory is to *clearly link valued rewards and performance.* Using the terminology of expectancy theory, managers should attempt to enhance their subordinates' beliefs about instrumentality—that is, make clear to them exactly what job behaviors will lead to what rewards. To the extent that it is possible for employees to be paid in ways directly linked to their performance—such as through piece-rate incentive systems or sales commission plans—expectancy theory specifies that it would be effective to do so because this would enhance beliefs about instrumentality. Indeed, a great deal of research has shown that performance increases can result from carefully implemented merit systems—frequently referred to as **pay-for-performance** systems.[63] One note of caution: not only should managers lead their employees to believe that their performance will be rewarded in a certain way, but they should also accurately follow up—that is, actually pay them in the stated way.[64] Enhancing instrumentality beliefs is effective only insofar as these beliefs are borne out in actual practice.

Finally, one of the most obvious practical suggestions from expectancy theory is to *administer rewards that are positively valent to employees.* The carrot at the end of the stick must be a tasty one, according to the theory, for it to have potential as a motivator. These days, when the composition of the work force is changing with increasing numbers of unmarried parents and single people working, it would be a mistake to assume that all employees care about having the same rewards made available to them by their companies. Some might recognize the incentive value of a pay raise, whereas others might prefer additional vacation days, improved insurance

TABLE 4–3   How to Motivate Employees: Some Suggestions from Expectancy Theory

Expectancy theory makes some specific recommendations for enhancing motivation. Various organizational practices can help implement these recommendations. A few are summarized here.

Recommendation	Corresponding Practice
Clarify the expectation that working hard will improve job performance	Design jobs so as to make the desired performance more attainable
Clearly link valued rewards to the job performance needed to attain them	Institute a *pay-for-performance* plan, paying for meritorious work
Administer rewards that have a high positive valence to workers	Use a *cafeteria-style benefit plan*, allowing workers to select the fringe benefits they most value

Test Bank questions 4.35–4.36 relate to material on this page.

benefits, or day-care facilities for children. With this in mind, more and more companies are instituting **cafeteria-style benefit plans**—incentive systems through which employees select their fringe benefits from a menu of available alternatives. Given that fringe benefits represent an average of 37 percent of payroll costs, more and more companies are recognizing the value of administering them flexibly.[65] For example, Primerica (previously known as American Can) has had a flexible benefit plan since 1978—one that is reportedly very successful. According to one report, almost 95 percent of the company's 8,000 salaried employees believed that the plan allowed them to select benefits that were most valuable to them.[66] The success of these plans suggests that making highly valent rewards available to employees may be an effective motivational technique.

CREATING JOBS THAT MOTIVATE

The final approach to motivation we will consider is the largest in scope because it is directed at changing the very nature of the work performed. The idea behind **job design** is that motivation can be enhanced by making the jobs people do more appealing to them. The roots of this idea can be traced back to the early part of this century when Frederick W. Taylor attempted to stimulate productivity by analyzing the minute motions involved in work tasks to discover the most efficient ways of performing them. This approach, known as **scientific management,** was intended to make work highly efficient (recall our discussion of scientific management in chapter 1). Unfortunately, however, it also made many jobs highly routine and monotonous. The problem with this, of course, is that people who are bored with their jobs tend to be absent or to quit.[67] As a result, motivational practitioners have sought ways of designing jobs that are simultaneously efficient and pleasant.

Several contemporary approaches to task design seek to motivate people in more humane, and effective, ways than scientific management. These approaches motivate people by designing jobs that are more involving. Our discussion will focus on two approaches to job design popular in the 1950s and 1960s—*job enlargement* and *job enrichment*—as well as an approach introduced and studied in the 1970s and 1980s that is still popular today—the *job characteristics model.*

Job Enlargement and Job Enrichment

One of the first modern ways of motivating people in organizations was to redesign jobs according to the principles of **job enlargement.** This refers to the practice of expanding the content of a job by increasing the number of different tasks performed at the same level. For example, if an employee on an automobile assembly line normally has the job of tightening the lugs on the left rear wheel of the car as it rolls down the assembly line, that job may be enlarged by requiring him or her to now tighten the lugs on all four wheels. As a result, the individual now performs a greater number of tasks, but they are all at the same low level of difficulty and require very little responsibility. Adding to jobs in this fashion is said to increase the *horizontal job loading*, that is, the number of tasks performed at the same level of skill and responsibility. Jobs with greater horizontal loadings have more variety because they include more tasks to perform. However, the tasks all provide an identical level of responsibility and control over the work itself.

In contrast to job enlargement, **job enrichment** gives employees not only more jobs to do, but more tasks to perform at a higher level. Job enrichment refers to the practice of giving employees the opportunity to have greater responsibility and to take greater control over how to do their jobs. Because people performing enriched

To help motivate employees, Taco Bell encourages both lateral movement across divisions and the broadcasting of job openings. For example, a Taco Bell benefits manager can take on the additional responsibilities of recruiting new employees and planning their activities. [Weber, J. (1990, December 10). Farewell fast track: Promotions and raises are scarcer—so what will energize managers? *Business Week,* pp. 192–200.]

jobs have increased opportunities to work at higher levels, the job enrichment process is said to increase the job's *vertical job loading*. (Incidentally, we should note that the idea of job enrichment was developed by Frederick Herzberg. Because Herzberg's theory focuses heavily on the determinants of job satisfaction, we have reserved discussion of it until chapter 5.) For a summary of the differences between job enlargement and job enrichment, see Figure 4–12. Job enlargement and job enrichment programs have been used at some of the largest companies in the United States, including IBM, AT&T, General Foods, Procter & Gamble, and others.

Most of the research examining the effectiveness of job enlargement plans has been anecdotal. However, a recently completed investigation by Campion and McClelland carefully studied the impact of a job enlargement program instituted at a large financial services company.[68] The unenlarged jobs had different employees perform separate paperwork tasks such as preparing, sorting, coding, and keypunching various forms. The enlarged jobs combined these various functions into larger jobs performed by the same people. Although it was found to be more difficult and expensive to train employees to perform the enlarged jobs than the separate jobs, important benefits were associated with enlarged jobs. Namely, employees expressed greater job satisfaction and less boredom. And because one person followed the whole job all the way through, greater opportunity to correct errors resulted. Not surprisingly, customers were then more satisfied with the work performed. Obviously, these benefits are quite impressive.

Similar positive effects have been noted in studies of job enrichment. Probably the most carefully studied job enrichment program was the one developed by Volvo, the Swedish auto manufacturer. In response to serious labor problems in the late 1960s, such as strikes and high rates of absenteeism and turnover, the company's new president, Pehr Gyllenhammar, introduced job enrichment in its assembly plant in the southern Swedish town of Kalmar.[69] Cars were assembled by twenty-five groups of approximately fifteen to twenty-five workers who were each responsible for one part of the car's assembly (e.g., engine assembly, electrical system). In contrast to the usual assembly line method of manufacturing cars, Volvo's work groups were

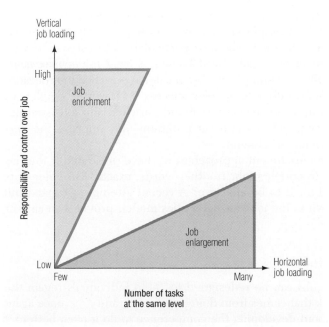

FIGURE 4–12

Job Enlargement and Job Enrichment: Comparing Two Traditional Approaches to Job Design

Designing jobs by increasing the number of tasks performed at the same level (horizontal job loading) is referred to as *job enlargement*. Designing jobs by increasing workers' responsibility and control over their jobs (vertical job loading) is referred to as *job enrichment*.

set up so they could freely plan, organize, and inspect their own work. In time, the workers became more satisfied with their jobs and the plant experienced a significant reduction in turnover and absenteeism. Although it was more costly to manufacture cars this way, the resulting increases in quality and improvements in worker relations enhanced the company's commitment to job enrichment programs.

Even though job enrichment was well received at Volvo, it is important to ask whether job enlargement and enrichment plans succeed generally. The support for job enlargement is mostly anecdotal. There are more case studies than good empirical investigations supporting the effectiveness of job enlargement programs. Job enrichment has been the subject of more rigorous empirical investigations, but here, too, critics have found the evidence in support of its effectiveness questionable.[70] In other words, although enlargement and enrichment programs are often reported to be effective, the scientific evidence for their effectiveness is not all that compelling.

Without detailing the specific problems with the studies on job enlargement and enrichment programs and their findings, let's review some of the problems that have been identified with establishing such programs. One obvious problem is the *difficulty of implementation*. Clearly, to redesign existing physical plants so as to enrich many jobs would be expensive. Also, the technology required to perform some jobs makes it difficult, if not impossible, to do them differently. It is perhaps for these reasons that formal job enrichment plans remain quite atypical in the United States. In one survey of 125 industrial firms, only five reported attempts to institute formal job enrichment programs.[71]

In addition to these economic and technical impediments, there's a human impediment—the problem of *lack of acceptance*, particularly among unionized employees. To quote one AFL-CIO leader, "If you want to enrich the job, enrich the paycheck. . . . That's the kind of job enrichment unions believe in."[72] But not all employees want the added responsibility that goes along with performing enriched jobs, as is demonstrated nicely in one study in which six auto workers from Detroit worked in Sweden as engine assemblers in a Saab plant. In Sweden, enriched jobs are typical, and the auto workers at Saab exercise a great deal of freedom and responsibility in deciding how to perform their jobs. After a month, five out of the six Americans reported preferring their traditional assembly line jobs. In the words of one of the workers, "If I've got to bust my a _ _ to be meaningful, forget it; I'd rather be monotonous."[73] Clearly, enriched jobs might not be for everyone.

Given this, we may ask which employees respond most positively to enriched jobs. A recent study found that individuals who were particularly interested in striving to be successful in their lives (a personality trait known as *need for achievement*, which we will discuss more fully in chapter 6) worked harder at enriched jobs because such jobs provided more opportunities to achieve success.[74] However, employees who were less concerned about achieving success found enriched jobs a frustrating, dissatisfying experience. In sum, job enrichment programs may improve the performance only of those who seek enrichment.

One problem with the job enrichment approach as we have presented it thus far is that it fails to specify *how* to enrich a job. In other words, exactly *what* elements of a job need to be enriched for it to be effective? A recent attempt to expand the idea of job enrichment, known as the **job characteristics model**, provides an answer to this important question.

The Job Characteristics Model

This approach assumes that jobs can be redesigned to "help individuals regain the chance to experience the kick that comes from doing a job well, and . . . once again *care* about their work and about developing the competence to do it even better."[75]

According to Jack Hoffman, an executive at General Electric, this is what his company is trying to do. Specifically,

> What we're all trying to do is get every person feeling important about his or her job, whether they sweep the floor, drive screws in a unit, interact with customers, coordinate in a certain area or are an individual contributor. What we know is that people want more out of a job than that paycheck. They want a feeling of input.[76]

This is what the job characteristics model is all about. It helps identify how jobs can be designed to give workers those feelings of importance to which Hoffman refers. In particular, the job characteristics model specifies that enriching certain elements of jobs is effective in altering people's psychological states in a manner that enhances their work effectiveness.[77]

Specifically, the model identifies five *core job dimensions* that help create three *critical psychological states*, leading, in turn, to several beneficial outcomes for individuals and the organizations employing them (see Figure 4–13). Three job dimensions—skill variety, task identity, and task significance—contribute to a task's experienced meaningfulness. Let's take a closer look at them.

■ *Skill variety* refers to the extent to which a job requires a number of different activities using several of the employee's skills and talents. For example, a secretary with high skill variety may have to perform many different tasks (take dictation, do word processing, use both manual and electronic filing systems, answer the telephone, and welcome visitors to the office).

■ *Task identity* refers to the extent to which a job requires completing a whole piece of work from beginning to end. For example, tailors will have high task identity if they do everything related to making a whole suit (measure the client, select the fabric, cut and sew it, refit the customer, and alter it as needed).

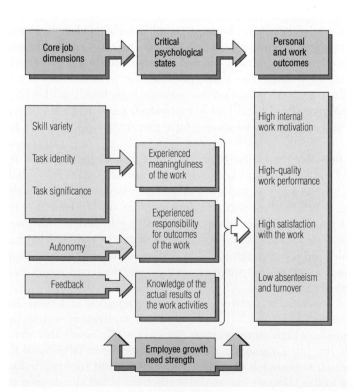

FIGURE 4–13

The Job Characteristics Model: An Overview

The *job characteristics model* stipulates that certain *core job dimensions* create *critical psychological states,* which in turn lead to several beneficial *personal and work outcomes.* The model recognizes that these relationships are strongest among employees who are high in the personality dimension of *growth need strength.* (*Source:* Adapted from Hackman & Oldham, 1980; see Note 77.)

- *Task significance* refers to the degree of impact the job is believed to have on other people, either within the organization or in the world at large. Consider, for example, the high task significance of medical researchers working to find a cure for a serious disease.

These three factors contribute to a task's *experienced meaningfulness*. According to the job characteristics model, a task is considered meaningful if it is experienced as important, valuable, and worthwhile.

The job characteristics model identifies two additional core job dimensions. One of these is autonomy.

- *Autonomy* refers to the extent to which an employee has the freedom and discretion to plan, schedule, and carry out the job as desired. For example, a furniture repair person may act highly autonomously by freely scheduling his or her day's work, and by freely deciding how to tackle each repair job confronted.

Autonomous jobs are said to make workers feel *personally responsible and accountable for the work* they perform. They are free to decide what to do and how to do it, so they feel more responsible for the results, good or bad. The fifth core job dimension is feedback.

- *Feedback* refers to the extent to which the job allows people to have information about the effectiveness of their performance. For example, telemarketing representatives regularly receive information about how many calls they made per day and the number and value of the sales made.

Effective feedback gives employees *knowledge of the results of their work*. When a job is designed to provide people with information about the effects of their actions, they are better able to develop an understanding of how effectively they have performed. Such knowledge helps improve the effectiveness of job performance.

The job characteristics model specifies that the three critical psychological states (experienced meaningfulness, responsibility for outcomes, and knowledge of results) affect various personal and work outcomes—namely, people's feelings of motivation, the quality of work performed, satisfaction with work, and absenteeism and turnover. The higher the experienced meaningfulness of work, responsibility for the work performed, and knowledge of results, the more positive the personal and work benefits will be. When they perform jobs that incorporate high levels of the five core job dimensions, employees should feel highly motivated, perform high-quality work, be highly satisfied with their jobs, be absent infrequently, and be unlikely to resign from their jobs.

We should also note that the model is theorized to be especially effective in describing the behavior of individuals who are high in *growth need strength*—that is, people who have a high need for personal growth and development. Individuals not particularly interested in personal growth and development are not expected to experience the theorized psychological reactions to the core job dimensions nor, consequently, to enjoy the beneficial personal and work outcomes predicted by the model.[78] With this variable, the job characteristics model recognizes the important limitation of job enrichment noted in the previous section: not everyone wants and benefits from enriched jobs.

Based on the proposed relationship between the core dimensions and their associated psychological reactions, the model claims that job motivation would be highest when jobs performed are high on the various dimensions. To assess this idea, a questionnaire known as the Job Diagnostic Survey (JDS) has been developed to measure the degree to which various job characteristics are present in a particular job.[79] Based on responses to the JDS, we can make predictions about the degree to which a job motivates the people who perform it. This is done using an index known as the **motivating potential score (MPS),** computed as follows:

$$MPS = \frac{\text{Skill variety} + \text{Task identity} + \text{Task significance}}{3} \times \text{Autonomy} \times \text{Feedback}$$

The MPS is a summary index of a job's potential for motivating workers. The higher the MPS for any given job, the greater the likelihood of experiencing the beneficial personal and work outcomes specified by the job characteristics model. Knowing a job's MPS helps one identify jobs that might benefit by being redesigned.

The job characteristics model has been the focus of many empirical tests, most of which suggest that the model identifies some effective ways of enriching jobs.[80] One study conducted among a group of South African clerical workers found particularly strong support for many aspects of the model.[81] The jobs of employees in some of the offices in this organization were enriched according to the suggestions of the job characteristics model. Specifically, the employees were given the opportunity to (1) choose what kinds of tasks they would perform (high skill variety), (2) perform the entire job (high task identity), (3) receive instructions regarding how their job fit into the organization as a whole (high task significance), (4) freely set their own schedules and inspect their own work (high autonomy), and (5) keep records of their daily productivity (high feedback). Another group of clerical workers, equivalent in all respects except that their jobs were not enriched, served as a control group.

After employees performed the newly designed jobs for six months, comparisons were made between them and their counterparts in the control group. With respect to most of the outcomes specified by the model, individuals performing the redesigned jobs showed superior results. Questionnaire measures found them feeling more internally motivated and more satisfied with their jobs. Furthermore, objective measures found lower rates of absenteeism and turnover among employees performing the enriched jobs. The only outcome predicted by the model that was not found to differ was actual work performance; performance quality was *not* significantly higher for employees performing the enriched jobs compared to those performing the traditional jobs. This result is typical of those found in many other studies. Enriching jobs appears to have much greater impact on job attitudes and beliefs than on actual job performance—and this is especially true of individuals who are high in growth need strength.[82] Considering the many factors that enter into determining job performance (as discussed in connection with expectancy theory), this finding should not be too surprising. (We will discuss the relationship between job attitudes and performance more thoroughly in chapter 5.)

Practical Suggestions for Applying the Job Characteristics Model

The job characteristics model specifies several things that can be done to redesign jobs to enhance their motivating potential.[83] We summarize these in the form of general principles in Table 4–4 (see p. 142).

Principle 1: Combine tasks.   Have employees perform an entire job (e.g., manufacture a product) instead of having several different people perform various parts of the job. Doing so helps provide greater skill variety and task identity.

Principle 2: Form natural work units.   Distribute work so that employees are identified with the jobs they've done. For example, one word processing operator can prepare an entire report, instead of several different operators completing parts of the report. Designing the job this way enhances task identity and task significance.

T A B L E 4 – 4   Enriching Jobs: Some Suggestions from the Job Characteristics Model

The *job characteristics model* specifies several ways jobs can be designed to incorporate the core job dimensions responsible for enhancing motivation and performance. A few are listed here.

Principle of Job Design	Core Job Dimensions Incorporated
1. Combine jobs, enabling workers to perform the entire job	Skill variety Task identity
2. Form natural work units, allowing workers to be identified with their work	Task identity Task significance
3. Establish client relationships, allowing providers of a service to meet the recipients	Skill variety Autonomy Feedback
4. Load jobs vertically, allowing greater responsibility and control over work	Autonomy
5. Open feedback channels, giving workers knowledge of the results of their work	Feedback

Source: Based on information in Hackman, 1976; see Note 75.

Principle 3: Establish client relationships.   Set up jobs so that the person performing a service (such as an auto mechanic) comes into contact with the recipient of the service (such as the car owner). Jobs designed in this manner not only help the employee by providing job feedback, but also provide skill variety (talking to customers in addition to working on cars) and enhance autonomy (by giving people the freedom to manage their own relationships with clients).

Principle 4: Load jobs vertically.   As we described earlier, loading a job vertically involves giving people greater responsibility for their jobs. Taking responsibility and control over job performance away from managers and giving it to their subordinates increases the level of autonomy the jobs offer these lower-level employees.

Principle 5: Open feedback channels.   Employees may receive many different types of feedback, and jobs should be designed to offer as many as possible.[84] Customers, supervisors, and coworkers can provide feedback. Cues about job performance can also be provided by the job itself, using various indexes such as the number of words correctly typed per minute, the dollar total of the day's sales, and so on. The more feedback channels used, the more accurate a picture people will have of how well they're doing, and the more motivated they will be to improve.

Despite these specific suggestions, implementing job enrichment programs is not easy. As mentioned earlier, people attempting to enrich jobs face many obstacles related to technical limitations and resistance to change from the work force. (The situation is clearly different, however, when jobs are changed in the ultimate vertical manner—that is, by giving employees ownership of the company. Naturally, employees who own their company will feel very high degrees of responsibility for their actions. For a closer examination of the motivating effects of employee ownership in one particular company, see the following **OB in Practice** section.)

OB IN PRACTICE

Avis Employees *Do* Try Harder . . . Because They Own the Company

"We try harder" goes the old advertising slogan once used by Avis, the giant car-rental company. The phrase signified the willingness of Avis employees to surpass the service of its larger rival in the business, Hertz. That may have been decades ago, but since 1987, Avis employees have tried even harder than before. The reason is simple: the employees own the company (see Figure 4–14).

According to the job characteristics model, employees will be motivated to perform well when they believe that their work contributions are meaningful and important. You can expect people to recognize immediately the value of their work when they are part owners of the company. Avis employees participate in an *employee stock ownership plan (ESOP).*[85] ESOPs work like this: The ESOP borrows money to buy the company, which is held by a trustee who represents the eventual shareholders. As the company pays off its debt, all employees receive shares of the company in proportion to their pay (up to a $30,000 per year federal limit). After fifteen to eighteen years, all 24 million shares of Avis will be owned by its employees. An employee must remain at Avis for his or her shares to be vested. Employees leaving the company after five years must sell their shares back to the trust, which sells them to new employees.

Part of the effectiveness of ESOPs lies in their eligibility for certain income tax advantages. Despite the benefits, ESOPs do not work unless they enhance workers' motivation. At Avis, the concept clearly works. Analysts have noted that since Avis's ESOP went into effect, the morale of its employees has improved dramatically, and its customers have noticed the improvement. Employees now make many more suggestions (and follow up on them!) and work harder than ever to improve performance standards. Avis employees are actively involved in all aspects of company functioning, and the company changes its operations as a result. In fact, changes ranging from billing procedures to baby seats have been credited to management's active attention to employees' suggestions.

Recent research by Katherine Klein suggests that Avis's success with its ESOP is not at all atypical.[86] Her survey of more than 3,800 employees participating in thirty-seven ESOPs revealed that responses to these programs were very positive. Specifically, employees in such plans tended to be highly satisfied with their jobs, highly committed to their companies, and unlikely to quit—especially when the plans were well run and profitable. The key is for management to be highly committed to employee ownership, and for the company to communicate clear and thorough information about how the plan is working. On the basis of such research, it is safe to conclude that ESOPs represent a form of organizational management that has great potential to effectively motivate employees.

FIGURE 4–14

Company Owners at Work at Avis

Whether they're auto mechanics, cleaners, or service assistants, Avis employees are highly motivated to perform at a high level because they collectively own the company.

SUMMARY AND REVIEW

The Nature of Motivation

Motivation is concerned with the set of processes that arouse, direct, and maintain behavior toward a goal. It is not equivalent to job performance, but is one of several determinants of job performance. Today's work ethic motivates people to seek interesting and challenging jobs, instead of just money.

Need Theories

Maslow's **need hierarchy theory** postulates that people have five types of need, activated in a specific order from the most basic, lowest-level need (physiological needs) to the highest-level need (need for self-actualization). Although this theory has not been supported by rigorous scientific studies, it has been quite useful in suggesting several ways of satisfying employees' needs on the job.

Goal-Setting Theory

Locke and Latham's **goal setting theory** claims that an assigned goal influences a person's beliefs about being able to perform the task (referred to as self-efficacy) and his or her personal goals. Both of these factors, in turn, influence performance. Research has shown that people will improve their performance when specific, acceptably difficult goals are set and feedback about task performance is provided. The task of selecting goals that are acceptable to employees may be facilitated by allowing employees to participate in the goal-setting process.

Equity Theory

Adams's **equity theory** claims that people desire to attain an equitable balance between the ratios of their work rewards (outcomes) and their job contributions (inputs) and the corresponding ratios of comparison others. Inequitable states of overpayment and underpayment are undesirable, motivating people to try to attain equitable conditions. Responses to inequity may be either behavioral or psychological.

Expectancy Theory

Expectancy theory recognizes that motivation is the product of a person's beliefs about **expectancy** (effort will lead to performance), **instrumentality** (performance will result in reward), and **valence** (the perceived value of the rewards). In conjunction with skills, abilities, role perceptions, and opportunities, motivation contributes to job performance.

Job Design

An effective organizational level technique for motivating people is the designing or redesigning of jobs. **Job design** techniques include **job enlargement** (performing more tasks at the same level) and **job enrichment** (giving people greater responsibility and control over their jobs). The **job characteristics model**, a currently popular approach to enriching jobs, identifies the specific job dimensions that should be enriched (skill variety, task identity, task significance, autonomy, and feedback), and relates these to the critical psychological states influenced by including these dimensions on a job. These psychological states will, in turn, lead to certain beneficial outcomes for both individual employees (e.g., job satisfaction) and the organization (e.g., reduced absenteeism and turnover).

KEY TERMS

cafeteria-style benefit plans: Incentive systems in which employees have an opportunity to select the fringe benefits they want from a menu of available alternatives.

equitable payment: The state in which one person's outcome/input ratio is equivalent to that of another person with whom this individual compares himself or herself.

equity theory: The theory stating that people strive to maintain ratios of their own outcomes (rewards) to their own inputs (contributions) that are equal to the outcome/input ratios of others with whom they compare themselves.

ERG theory: An alternative to Maslow's *need hierarchy theory* proposed by Alderfer, which asserts that there are three basic human needs—existence, relatedness, and growth.

expectancy: The beliefs that people hold regarding the extent to which their efforts will influence their performance.

expectancy theory: The theory that asserts that motivation is based on people's beliefs about the probability that effort will lead to performance (*expectancy*), multiplied by the probability that performance will lead to reward (*instrumentality*), multiplied by the perceived value of the reward (*valence*).

goal setting: The process of determining specific levels of performance for workers to attain.

inputs: People's contributions to their jobs, such as their experience, qualifications, or the amount of time worked.

instrumentality: An individual's belief regarding the likelihood of being rewarded in accord with his or her own level of performance.

job characteristics model: An approach taken by organizations toward job enrichment, which specifies that five *core job dimensions* (skill variety, task identity, task significance, autonomy, and job feedback) produce critical psychological states that lead to beneficial outcomes for individuals (e.g., high job satisfaction) and the organization (e.g., high performance).

job design: An approach to motivation suggesting that jobs can be created so as to motivate people. (See *job enlargement, job enrichment,* and the *job characteristics model.*)

job enlargement: The practice of expanding the content of a job to include more variety and a greater number of tasks at the same level.

job enrichment: The practice of giving employees a high degree of control over their work, from planning and organization, through implementing the jobs and evaluating the results.

motivating potential score (MPS): A mathematical index describing the degree to which a job is designed so as to motivate people, as suggested by the *job characteristics model.* It is computed on the basis of responses to a questionnaire known as the Job Diagnostic Survey (JDS). The higher the MPS, the more motivating a job is; the lower the MPS, the more the job may stand to benefit from redesign.

motivation: The set of processes that arouse, direct, and maintain human behavior toward attaining a goal.

need hierarchy theory: Maslow's theory that there are five human needs (physiological, safety, social, esteem, and self-actualization) and that these are arranged in such a way that lower, more basic needs must be satisfied before higher-level needs become activated.

outcomes: The rewards employees receive from their jobs, such as salary and recognition.

overpayment inequity: The condition, resulting in feelings of guilt, in which the ratio of one's outcomes/inputs is greater than the corresponding ratio of another person against whom that person compares himself or herself.

pay-for-performance: A payment system in which employees are paid differentially, based on the quantity and quality of their job performance (i.e., *merit pay*). Pay-for-performance plans strengthen *instrumentality* beliefs.

scientific management: An early approach to motivation in which jobs were redesigned to make them simpler and more efficient, although highly routine and monotonous.

self-actualization: The need to discover who we are and to develop ourselves to the fullest potential.

two-tier wage structures: Payment systems in which newer employees are paid less than employees hired at earlier times to do the same work.

underpayment inequity: The condition, resulting in feelings of anger, in which the ratio of one's outcomes/inputs is less than the corresponding ratio of another person against whom that person compares himself or herself.

valence: The value a person places on the rewards he or she expects to receive from an organization.

QUESTIONS FOR DISCUSSION

1. Define the concept of motivation and describe how this topic is relevant to the field of organizational behavior.

2. Characterize the importance placed on work as a life value at different periods in history. What is the predominant belief about the role of work as a life value in today's society?

3. Maslow's need hierarchy theory specifies several ways to satisfy people's needs on the job. Identify each of the five need categories specified by Maslow, and for each one describe something that can be done on the job to enhance need satisfaction.

4. According to equity theory, how might an individual who is overpaid feel and behave? What might such a person do to alleviate this inequity? How about someone who is underpaid?

5. Imagine a student who performs poorly on an exam and then claims to the instructor, "I tried." According to expectancy theory, what other factors can account for performance besides motivation?

6. Compare and contrast the role of money as a motivator as characterized by need theory, equity theory, and expectancy theory.

7. Imagine that you are establishing a goal-setting program for an organization. Describe the way goals should be set and some of the factors that will make the program effective. What hurdles would have to be overcome?

8. Think of a job with which you are familiar, and describe specific things that can be done to enrich the job using the core job dimensions identified by the job characteristics model. What obstacles would have to be overcome to apply the model to this particular job?

NOTES

1. Kanfer, R. (1990). Motivational theory and industrial and organizational psychology. In M. D. Dunnette & L. M. Hough (Eds.), *Handbook of industrial and organizational psychology* (2nd ed., Vol. 1, pp. 75–170). Palo Alto, CA: Consulting Psychologists Press.

2. Steers, R. M., & Porter, L. W. (Eds.). (1989). *Motivation and work behavior* (5th ed.). New York: McGraw-Hill.

3. Landy, F. J., & Becker, W. S. (1987). Motivation theory reconsidered. In L. L. Cummings & B. M. Staw (Eds.), *Research in organizational behavior* (Vol. 9, pp. 1–38). Greenwich, CT: JAI Press.

4. Furnham, A. (1989). *The Protestant work ethic: The psychology of work beliefs and behaviours.* London: Routledge.

5. Grant, M. (1960). *The world of Rome* (p. 112). London: Weidenfeld and Nocolson.

6. *Newsweek* (1971, October 18). p. 31.

7. Nord, W. R., Brief, A. P., Atieh, J. M., & Doherty, E. M. (1988). Work values and the conduct of organizational behavior. In B. M. Staw & L. L. Cummings (Eds.), *Research in organizational behavior* (Vol. 10, pp. 1–42). Greenwich, CT: JAI Press.

8. Work still a labor of love. (1981, April 20). *The Columbus Dispatch*, p. 1.

9. Harpaz, I. (1990). The importance of work goals: An international perspective. *Journal of International Business Studies, 21*, 75–93.

10. Maslow, A. H. (1970). *Motivation and personality* (2nd ed.). New York: Harper & Row.

11. Falkenberg, L. E. (1987). Employee fitness programs: Their impact on the employee and the organization. *Academy of Management Review, 12*, 511–522.

12. Byrne, J. A. (1984, January 30). Motivating Willy Loman. *Forbes*, p. 91.

13. Veroff, J., Reuman, D., & Feld, S. (1984). Motives in American men and women across the life span. *Developmental Psychology, 20*, 1142–1158.

14. Gunsch, D. (1991). Award programs at work. *Personnel Journal, 23*(4), 85–89.

15. Porter, L. W. (1961). A study of perceived need satisfaction in bottom and middle management jobs. *Journal of Applied Psychology, 45*, 1–10.

16. Betz, E. L. (1982). Need fulfillment in the career development of women. *Journal of Vocational Behavior, 20*, 53–66.

17. Wahba, M. A., & Bridwell, L. G. (1976). Maslow reconsidered: A review of research on the need hierarchy theory. *Organizational Behavior and Human Performance, 15*, 212–240.

18. Alderfer, C. P. (1972). *Existence, relatedness, and growth.* New York: Free Press.

19. Salancik, G. R., & Pfeffer, J. (1977). An examination of need-satisfaction models of job satisfaction. *Administrative Science Quarterly, 22*, 427–456.

20. Miller, A., & Bradburn, E. (1991, July 1). Shape up—or else! *Newsweek*, pp. 42–43.

21. Morin, W. J., & Yorks, L. (1990). *Dismissal.* New York: Drake, Beam, Morin.

22. Locke, E. A., & Latham, G. P. (1990). *A theory of goal setting and task performance.* New York: Prentice-Hall.

23. Wood, R. A., & Locke, E. A. (1990). Goal setting and strategy effects on complex tasks. In B. M. Staw & L. L. Cummings (Eds.), *Research in organizational behavior* (Vol. 12, pp. 73–110). Greenwich, CT: JAI Press.

24. Vance, R. J., & Colella, A. (1990). Effects of two types of feedback on goal acceptance and personal goals. *Journal of Applied Psychology, 75*, 68–76.

25. Klein, H. J. (1991). Further evidence on the relationship between goal setting and expectancy theories. *Organizational Behavior and Human Decision Processes, 49*, 230–257.

26. Wood, R. E., & Bandura, A. (1989). Social cognitive theory of organizational management. *Academy of Management Review, 14*, 361–384.

27. Meyer, J. P., & Gellatly, I. R. (1988). Perceived performance norm as a mediator in the effect of assigned goal on personal and task performance. *Journal of Applied Psychology, 73*, 410–420.

28. Earley, P. C., & Lituchy, T. R. (1991). Delineating goal and efficacy effects: A test of three models. *Journal of Applied Psychology, 76*, 81–98.

29. Latham, G. P., & Lee, T. W. (1986). Goal setting. In E. A. Locke (Ed.), *Generalizing from laboratory to field settings* (pp. 100–117). Lexington, MA: Lexington Books.

30. Miller, L. (1978). *Behavior management: The new science of managing people at work.* New York: Wiley.

31. Latham, G. P., & Locke, E. (1979). Goal setting—a motivational technique that works. *Organizational Dynamics, 8*(2), 68–80.

32. Locke, E. A., Latham, G. P. (1984). *Goal setting: A motivational technique that works!* Englewood Cliffs, NJ: Prentice-Hall.

33. Smith, K. G., Locke, E. A., & Barry, D. (1990). Goal setting, planning, and organizational performance: An experimental simulation. *Organizational Behavior and Human Decision Processes, 46*, 118–134.

34. Peters, T. J., & Waterman, R. H., Jr. (1982). *In search of excellence.* New York: Harper & Row.

35. Locke, E. A., & Latham, G. P. (1984). *Goal setting for individuals, groups, and organizations.* Chicago: Science Research Associates.

36. Stedry, A. C., & Kay, E. (1964). *The effects of goal difficulty on performance.* General Electric Company, Behavioral Research Service.

37. See Note 36.

38. Locke, E. A., Latham, G. P., & Erez, M. (1988). The determinants of goal commitment. *Academy of Management Review, 13*, 23–39.

39. Latham, G. P., Erez, M., & Locke, E. A. (1988). Resolving scientific disputes by the joint design of crucial experiments by the antagonists: Application to the Erez–Latham dispute regarding participation in goal setting. *Journal of Applied Psychology, 73,* 753–772.

40. Latham, G. P., & Saari, L. M. (1979). Importance of supportive relationships in goal setting. *Journal of Applied Psychology, 64,* 151–156.

41. Chase, S. (1982, April 8). Life at IBM. *Wall Street Journal,* p. 1.

42. See Note 31.

43. Chhokar, J. S., & Wallin, J. A. (1984). A field study of the effects of feedback frequency on performance. *Journal of Applied Psychology, 69,* 524–530.

44. Pritchard, R. D., Jones, S. D., Roth, P. L., Stuebing, K. K., & Ekeberg, S. E. (1988). Effects of group feedback, goal setting, and incentives on organizational productivity. *Journal of Applied Psychology, 73,* 337– 358.

45. Earley, P. C., Northcraft, G. B., Lee, C., & Lituchy, T. R. (1990). Impact of process and outcome feedback on the relation of goal setting to task performance. *Academy of Management Journal, 33,* 87–105.

46. Thwarp, R. G., & Gallimore, R. (1976, January). What a coach can tell a teacher. *Psychology Today,* pp. 75–78.

47. Adams, J. S. (1965). Inequity in social exchange. In L. Berkowitz (Ed.), *Advances in experimental social psychology* (Vol. 2, pp. 267–299). New York: Academic Press.

48. Greenberg, J. (1989). Cognitive re-evaluation of outcomes in response to underpayment inequity. *Academy of Management Journal, 32,* 174–184.

49. Greenberg, J. (1987). A taxonomy of organizational justice theories. *Academy of Management Review, 12,* 9–22.

50. Pritchard, R. D., Dunnette, M. D., & Jorgenson, D. O. (1972). Effects of perceptions of equity and inequity on worker performance and satisfaction. *Journal of Applied Psychology, 57,* 75–94.

51. Martin, J. E., & Peterson, M. M. (1987). Two-tier wage structures: Implications for equity theory. *Academy of Management Journal, 30,* 297–315.

52. Ross, I. (1985, April 29). Employers win big on the move to two-tier contracts. *Fortune,* pp. 82–92.

53. See Note 52.

54. Lawler, E. E., III. (1967). Secrecy about management compensation: Are there hidden costs? *Organizational Behavior and Human Performance, 2,* 182–189.

55. Greenberg, J. (1992). The social side of fairness: Interpersonal and informational classes of organizational justice. In R. Cropanzano (Ed.), *Justice in the workplace: Approaching fairness in human resource management.* Hillsdale, NJ: Erlbaum.

56. Vroom, V. H. (1964). *Work and motivation.* New York: Wiley.

57. Porter, L. W., & Lawler, E. E. (1968). *Managerial attitudes and performance.* Homewood, IL: Irwin.

58. Motivating on the cheap. (1991, April). *Inc.,* p. 14.

59. Greenberg, J. (1990). Employee theft as a reaction to underpayment inequity: The hidden cost of pay cuts. *Journal of Applied Psychology, 75,* 561–568.

60. Mitchell, T. R. (1983). Expectancy-value models in organizational psychology. In N. Feather (Ed.), *Expectancy, incentive, and action* (pp. 293–314). Hillsdale, NJ: Erlbaum.

61. Miller, L. E., & Grush, J. E. (1988). Improving predictions in expectancy theory research: Effects of personality, expectancies, and norms. *Academy of Management Journal, 31,* 107–122.

62. Harrell, A., & Stahl, M. (1986). Additive information processing and the relationship between expectancy of success and motivational force. *Academy of Management Journal, 29,* 424–433.

63. Miceli, M. P., Jung, I., Near, J. P., & Greenberger, D. B. (1991). Predictors and outcomes of reactions to pay-for-performance plans. *Journal of Applied Psychology, 76,* 508–521.

64. Markham, S. E. (1988). Pay-for-performance dilemma revisited: Empirical example of the importance of group effects. *Journal of Applied Psychology, 73,* 172–180.

65. Foegen, J. H. (1982, October 18). Fringe benefits are being diversified too. *Industry Week,* pp. 56–58.

66. Zippo, M. (1982). Flexible benefits: Just the beginning. *Personnel Journal, 17*(4), 56–58.

67. Griffin, R. W. (1987). Toward an integrated theory of task design. In L. L. Cummings & B. M. Staw (Eds.), *Research in organizational behavior* (Vol. 9, pp. 79–120). Greenwich, CT: JAI Press.

68. Campion, M. A., & McClelland, C. L. (1991). Interdisciplinary examination of the costs and benefits of enlarged jobs: A job design quasi-experiment. *Journal of Applied Psychology, 76,* 186–198.

69. Gyllenhammar, P. G. (1977). *People at work.* Reading, MA: Addison-Wesley.

70. Fein, M. (1974, Winter). Job enrichment: A reevaluation. *Sloan Management Review,* pp. 69–99.

71. Luthans, F., & Rief, W. E. (1974). Job enrichment: Long on theory, short on practice. *Organizational Dynamics, 2,* 30–43.

72. Winpisinger, W. (1973, February). Job satisfaction: A union response. *AFL–CIO American Federationist,* pp. 8–10.

73. Goldman, R. B. (1976). *A work experiment: Six Americans in a Swedish plant.* New York: Ford Foundation.

74. Steers, R. M., & Spencer, D. G. (1977). The role of achievement motivation in job design. *Journal of Applied Psychology, 62,* 472–479.

75. Hackman, J. R. (1976). Work design: In J. R. Hackman & J. L. Suttle (Eds.), *Improving life at work* (p. 103). Santa Monica, CA: Goodyear.

76. Ropp, K. (1987, October). Candid conversations. *Personnel Administrator,* p. 49.

77. Hackman, J. R., & Oldham, G. R. (1980). *Work redesign.* Reading, MA: Addison-Wesley.

78. Graen, G. B., Scandura, T. A., & Graen, M. R. (1986). A field experimental test of the moderating effects of growth need strength on productivity. *Journal of Applied Psychology, 71,* 484–491.

79. Hackman, J. R., & Oldham, G. R. (1976). Motivation through the design of work: Test of a theory. *Organizational Behavior and Human Performance, 16,* 250–279.

80. Fried, Y., & Ferris, G. R. (1987). The validity of the job characteristics model: A review and meta-analysis. *Personnel Psychology, 40,* 287–322.

81. Orpen, C. (1979). The effects of job enrichment on employee satisfaction, motivation, involvement, and performance: A field experiment. *Human Relations, 32,* 189–217.

82. Loher, B. T., Noe, R. A., Moeller, N. L., & Fitzgerald, M. P. (1985). A meta-analysis of the relation of job characteristics to job satisfaction. *Journal of Applied Psychology, 70,* 280–289.

83. See Note 76.

84. Ilgen, D. R., & Moore, C. F. (1987). Types and choices of performance feedback. *Journal of Applied Psychology, 72,* 401–406.

85. Kirkpatrick, D. (1988, December 5). How the workers run Avis better. *Fortune,* pp. 103, 106, 110, 114.

86. Klein, K. J. (1987). Employee stock ownership and employee attitudes: A test of three models. *Journal of Applied Psychology, 72,* 319–322.

CASE IN POINT

Motivation through Employee Involvement at United Electric Controls

"You reach a point where you can't go back but also don't like where you are. It's scary," says David Reis, president of United Electric Controls Company,[1] describing the process that transformed his company from a tired old factory into a vibrant, competitive manufacturing business.[2] David and his older brother Robert own this sixty-year-old manufacturer of industrial temperature and pressure controls. Located in Watertown, Massachusetts, United Electric had grown to symbolize the outmoded American factory. Antiquated technology and deeply entrenched autocratic management practices brought the company to the brink of failure in 1987. Today, United Electric is a thriving, profitable $36 million company. What happened? How did David and Robert Reis transform this faltering company into a world-class organization?

United Electric's success required a complete transformation. State-of-the-art Japanese operational techniques such as *pokayoke* (a quality-control system based on the philosophy of correcting mistakes at the point where they are made, rather than at the end of the production process) and *kanban* (a highly efficient inventory-control system) were implemented. These improvements were important, but the critical element was allowing United Electric's 350 employees to decide how their work should be done. Management asked employees to look at how they do their jobs and come up with ideas for doing them better.

United Electric set up three programs to collect employee ideas. The Valued-Ideas Program invites employees to submit their ideas to management by way of a suggestion box. As an incentive, employees are given $100 in cash for each usable idea they submit (up to a maximum of ten usable ideas per person per year). Even ideas not found to be usable are valued.

The second program is the Action Center Program, an employee-started group created to solve a particular work problem. Action centers, which meet during regular work hours, stay together just long enough to solve the problem at hand (usually several weeks). Employees must get management's approval to start an action center, but management rarely objects. During the first month following the announcement of the Action Center Program, more than forty action centers were created.

The third employee-involvement program is the Cause-and-Effect Diagram with the Addition of Cards (CEDAC). Employee groups are created to diagnose the causes of particularly bewildering problems. These groups use a problem-analysis technique that calls for group members to brainstorm about possible causes of a problem, write them down on cards, and then systematically investigate each cause until the most likely one is identified. CEDAC groups usually stay together for a long time, requiring several months to complete their tasks.

"Over and over again you hear about empowering employees. You know intuitively that it's the thing to do."[3] But moving from autocratic management to employee involvement was not easy for the Reis brothers. The hard part, according to Robert Reis, wasn't recognizing that United Electric had to change its management practices, but having the courage to let go. Mirroring Robert's comments, David Reis says that at times management felt like "throwing in the towel."[4] But United Electric stuck with it, and today the company has an entirely new look and feel.

Employees suggested hundreds of ideas for improving the way work is done, and United Electric's once-monotonous environment now pulsates with excitement. Many ideas have been successfully implemented. A visitor to the factory sees what can best be described as a hodgepodge of homemade technological gadgetry. According to Joshua Hyatt, a writer for *Inc.* magazine, "Everywhere, it seems, workers are using devices that they themselves invented—to work faster or test more accurately or track materials more closely."[5] Employees are doing their jobs their own way. Everything fits together to create a sense of excitement and productivity. Hyatt observes, "At times employees seem engaged in sleight of hand as they spin shelves of fixtures that rest on lazy Susans, or slide out worktables that are cleverly stored, trundle bed style, underneath tabletops."[6] The process of improvement is not over. Gladys Appleby, a twenty-two-year employee, says, "There's always a way to do something better. We always thought of things [before]. But there was nobody to listen to our ideas. Now there is."[7]

Among the numerous employee inventions is Bob Comeau's "machines on wheels." Bob is manager of the wiring department. Prior to acting on his idea, Bob's job required him to carry fifty-pound spools of wire, on an as-needed basis, to each of his cutting, measuring, and stripping machines. Bob claimed that lifting them was painful and time-consuming, and that his back was killing him. Noticing that Robert and David Reis were actually implementing the work improvement suggestions of other employees, Bob decided it was time to figure out a way to prevent his backaches. His first idea was to create a rack with wheels on it that could hold all thirty-five spools of wire he used in his work. He could then roll the rack from machine to machine as various types of wire were needed. As he experimented with this idea, he concluded that the rolling rack was too dangerous. Even with as few as six spools, the rack was heavy, and prone to tipping over and potentially hurting someone.

Although frustrated by the failure of his rolling rack idea, Bob was hooked on the notion that there must be a better way to do his job. Then it hit him—why not put the cutting, measuring, and stripping machines on wheels and move them to the wire spools? Bob built a permanent rack for the thirty-five wire spools and mounted each of the machines onto wheels. The "rolling machines" were stable, and Bob's problem was solved. Bob's success inspired him to change other jobs in his department as well, substantially boosting productivity.

The motivation and creativity stimulated by the Reises' decision are impressive. But employees care about the productivity and competitiveness of United Electric for other reasons, too. In 1987, employees felt the pain of watching their profit-sharing bonuses disappear. They were also well aware of United Electric's dwindling profits. They knew that they would soon be without jobs if something didn't change. Moreover, since the start of the employee-involvement programs, employees have earned substantial financial rewards for initiating and implementing productivity improvement ideas. In 1989, employees offered 500 ideas for improving United Electric. During 1990, nearly 1,000 ideas were suggested. Roughly two-thirds of these ideas were actually implemented, costing United Electric well over $50,000 in employee bonuses. In addition, for their idea contributions in action center and CEDAC groups, employees have won numerous prizes such as sports tickets and vacation trips.

Is it worth it? David Reis thinks so: "The improvements we get in return far exceed the amount we invest."[8] On-time delivery has gone from 65 to 95 percent. Bob Comeau's wiring department now produces more with a staff of two than it did with seven. An idea to eliminate just one sheet of paper from the materials requisition process saves $6,000 per year. How have employees been affected by United Electric's involvement programs? Their self-esteem and morale are way up. They now have a sense of ownership in the company.

Before United Electric introduced its employee-involvement programs, it was losing money on sales of $28 million. Today, sales are up nearly 30 percent and United Electric is earning substantial profits. The effect of employee involvement is best summed up by an employee's remark: "With fewer employees, we're spitting out more production than we ever did."

Questions for Discussion

1. How do you explain the success of United Electric's employee-involvement program in terms of need theory? Expectancy theory? Goal-setting theory? Job enrichment theory?
2. All employee ideas, regardless of usability, are recognized in some way at United Electric. Why does United Electric do this?
3. When Bob Comeau became frustrated by the failure of his rolling rack idea, he didn't give up. Why do you think he was motivated to try another idea?
4. At United Electric, a variety of incentives are offered to employees to encourage productivity improvement ideas. What are they? Is it wise to use a combination of incentives? Why?
5. According to David Reis, once the process of letting employees take control of how they do their work begins, you can't go back. Why does Reis believe you can't go back? Why is the process of employee involvement scary to him?

Notes

1. Hyatt, J. (1991, May). Ideas at work. *Inc.*, p. 59.
2. Hyatt, J. (1991, May). Ideas at work. *Inc.*, pp. 59–66.
3. See Note 1.
4. See Note 1.
5. See Note 1.
6. See Note 2, pp. 59–60.
7. See Note 2, p. 60.
8. See Note 2, p. 66.

EXPERIENCING ORGANIZATIONAL BEHAVIOR

The effectiveness of goal setting as a motivational technique has been well established. Setting goals that are specific, and difficult but acceptable, and providing feedback on their attainment, improves job performance (see pages 121–127). As this exercise demonstrates, you can apply these same guidelines to improving your own personal productivity.

Goal Setting and Personal Productivity

Procedure

1. Think of a task you need to perform before the next class meeting. The task should be one for which performance can be measured. Some good examples would be studying a certain subject, writing a term paper, or making improvements in your living quarters.

2. Set specific goals for performing this task, goals that challenge you but are possible to achieve. Make sure the goals are such that progress toward attaining them can be measured. For example, it is appropriate to set the goal of studying two chapters in your history text in the next forty-eight hours. However, the goal of "working harder to improve myself" is much too general.

3. Share your goals with your classmates. Through discussion, help everyone set goals that are specific, measurable, and difficult but acceptable.

4. Once it is clear that everyone has set a specific goal, agree to try to meet these goals and report back to the class on your progress at the next class meeting.

5. During the next class session, take turns reporting on your experiences in meeting your goals. Did you meet your goals? Exactly how well did you do? Do you think setting the goals was helpful? What factors interfered with goal setting?

Points to Consider

1. How many students succeeded in meeting their goals? How many failed? What factors do you believe distinguish between those who succeeded and those who failed?

2. What could have been done to make the unsuccessful students more successful? Did the goals they set for themselves prove too easy or too difficult? Was it possible to measure their goal attainment?

3. On what other tasks might you be able to successfully apply goal-setting principles?

4. Do you think people are capable of setting their own performance goals, or should they obtain the help of others?

5. Do you think social approval serves as a reinforcer of behavior in organizations? Explain why or why not.

5

WORK-RELATED ATTITUDES: THEIR NATURE AND IMPACT

CHAPTER OUTLINE

Attitudes: Their Basic Nature
Components of Attitudes and a Definition
A Note on the Role of Attitudes in
Organizational Behavior
**Changing Attitudes: A Critical Task in
Organizational Behavior**
Changing Others' Attitudes: Two Major
Determinants of Persuasion
Changing Our Own Attitudes: The Cognitive
Dissonance Phenomenon
Job Satisfaction: Attitudes toward One's Job
How Prevalent Is Job Satisfaction? Do People
Really Like Their Work?
Measuring Job Satisfaction: Assessing Reactions
to Work
Theories of Job Satisfaction
Job Satisfaction: Its Principal Causes
Job Satisfaction: Its Major Effects

**Organizational Commitment: Feelings of
Attachment toward Organizations**
Organizational Commitment: Its Major Types
Factors Influencing Organizational Commitment
Organizational Commitment: Its Major Effects
Prejudice: Negative Attitudes toward Others
Prejudice: Its Role in Organizations
Sexism: Prejudice Based on Gender

Special Sections

Focus on Research   Job Satisfaction: Can It Be in
the Genes?

OB in Practice   Organizational Commitment in the
Magic Kingdom

Focus on Research   Physical Attractiveness and
M.B.A.s' Salaries: Beauty Pays Off

LEARNING OBJECTIVES

After reading this chapter, you should be able to:
1. Identify and describe the major components of
attitudes.
2. Define what attitudes are, and describe their
role in the study of organizational behavior.
3. Describe the major ways of changing someone
else's attitudes.
4. Describe the process of *cognitive dissonance*,
and how it leads people to change their own
attitudes.

5. Identify and describe two major theories of job
satisfaction, and techniques for measuring it.
6. Explain the major causes and consequences of
job satisfaction.
7. Describe the major types of organizational
commitment.
8. Describe the major causes and consequences of
organizational commitment.
9. Define the prejudice of sexism, and discuss its
underlying causes.

I just can't believe it," Mitch Atwater sighs with obvious disdain, as he plops himself down onto a chair in the break room at Pepper Imports.

"What's the matter, Mitch?" Becky Samuels inquires, as she reads the annoyed look on his face.

"Oh, it's that Jack Pepper again," Mitch replies. "Ever since the big boss hired his son to manage the place, he's been on my back. Now he wants me to supervise the monthly inventory. Not only do I hate doing that, but we have to do it on a Friday afternoon this time—right before my weekend getaway."

"Ouch!" exclaims Larry Ramos, as he enters the break room and joins Mitch and Becky. "That happened to me once, and it wasn't any fun. You want to get out of town, and all you get to do is count boxes."

"That's what I mean, Becky," Mitch continues. "Ramos, here, knows what it's like. Who wants to be shouting 'item 485-G, six pieces' when you could be relaxing somewhere?"

"I know that," Becky answers, "but you know that inventory *has* to be done, and as a floor manager, you have to take your turn eventually. Unless we do a careful inventory, we really don't know what we have to sell and what we need to order. Besides, they need to do it for tax reasons."

"Don't get me wrong," Mitch defends himself. "I know *why* it has to be done. It's just that I don't like doing it."

At this, Larry Ramos begins to laugh. Mitch feels better, realizing Larry is on his side.

This really angers Becky. "Look, you guys," she pleads, "it's that kind of selfish attitude that makes life hard on everyone around here. There's a job to be done, and you just have to do it. There are lots of things I have to do that I might not like, but I just pitch in and do it. It's for the good of the company. Just think—what's good for the company is good for you. After all, if Pepper Imports falters, you'll be looking for a new job."

"Yeah," Larry Ramos pitches in, "and with your attitude, you wouldn't get a good letter of recommendation."

"You should talk," Mitch interrupts. "Now you're taking her side?"

With this, Becky's frustration begins to show. "Okay, okay, guys. Calm down. I didn't mean to get you all upset."

"I know that," Larry replies. "It's just that I know what Mitch is talking about. Work is only part of my life. Basically, I like what I do on the job, but I don't always want to be doing it. There are just too many other things in life. You can't blame him for that, Becky."

"Of course," Becky says, and cautions, "Don't get me wrong. It's just that I've been around here for fifteen years, and I've seen the company grow from nothing to a really big, successful operation. I worked hard to make that happen, so I don't like it when I hear about people not wanting to put anything extra into their work. Maybe I'm nuts, but that's what I think."

"Maybe so," Mitch replies, as they all laugh.

People seldom feel neutral about the things they encounter in the world around them. We all have different feelings about the people, events, objects, and activities we experience; everyone has likes and dislikes, aversions and preferences. Given that work constitutes a large part of most people's lives, it shouldn't be surprising that work is frequently the object of such positive and negative reactions. Indeed, our *work-related attitudes* can be quite strong. You probably know people like those portrayed in our opening incident who are strongly committed to their jobs (Becky) and who are less concerned about what they are doing on the job (Mitch). These feelings—*attitudes*, as they are called—are important to understand for several reasons. Not only do they constitute an important part of the quality of life experienced on the job, but they are also related to key aspects of organizational behavior, such as job performance, absenteeism, and turnover (see Figure 5–1).

Because work-related attitudes are important—both for the individuals who have them and for the organizations in which these people work—we will consider them in detail in this chapter. First, we will describe the general nature of attitudes, explaining what they are. Second, we will focus on an important practical issue— namely, how attitudes can be changed. In the remainder of the chapter, we will

FIGURE 5–1

Attitudes: An Important Aspect of Organizational Behavior

The attitudes that people have about their jobs influence not only the quality of their work life, but also the nature of their job performance on many key dimensions (e.g., performance, turnover).

take a closer look at several specific types of work-related attitudes. We'll start with *job satisfaction*—essentially, people's positive or negative feelings about their jobs.[1] Specifically, we will describe some of the major factors contributing to feelings of satisfaction and dissatisfaction with one's work, and then consider the consequences of such reactions on organizational behavior. Building on this, we will turn to another important work-related attitude—*organizational commitment*. This has to do with people's feelings about the organizations for which they work—the degree to which they identify with the organizations that employ them.[2] Finally, we will turn to a special type of attitude with which you are probably (unfortunately!) already somewhat familiar—*prejudice*. This involves negative views about others who fall into certain categories, such as women, minority groups, older people, and the differently abled, to mention just a few.[3] As we will see, such attitudes can have a seriously disruptive impact—not only on people's lives, but on the effective functioning of organizations and of society as a whole.

ATTITUDES: THEIR BASIC NATURE

Earlier, we noted that attitudes involve our reactions to various aspects of the world— our reactions to people, objects, activities, and ideas. We will now take a closer look at exactly what's involved in this process. Specifically, we will identify the components from which attitudes are created and offer a more formal definition of an attitude. Then we will follow up by noting the special role that attitudes play in the field of organizational behavior.

Components of Attitudes and a Definition

Suppose we ask you how you feel about your job. You may say that you really enjoy doing it, you believe it's important work, and you fully intend to keep on doing it in the future. Or you may say that you truly hate everything about it, you believe it is menial and boring, and you want to look for a new job. In either case, you've expressed an attitude. Whether or not they are expressed as clearly as in these examples, attitudes are widely agreed to consist of three major components—an evaluative component, a cognitive component, and a behavioral component.[4] Let's take a look at each.

Do you have a positive or negative feeling toward your boss, your coworkers, your pay, your day off, the pension plan? The *evaluative component* of an attitude reflects how you feel about it, your liking or disliking of these, or any other focal items or events on the job. Attitudes also consist of things you know, or believe to be the case, about your job (or any object). You may, for example, believe a coworker is paid more than you, or you may believe that your boss is very knowledgeable about her job skills. These beliefs—whether based on fact or simply unfounded rumor—comprise the *cognitive component* of attitudes. Finally, suppose you believe your boss is a crook (cognitive component) and you really don't enjoy the work you're doing (evaluative component). More than likely, this would predispose you to quit and seek a new job. Attitudes, then, also have a *behavioral component*—a predisposition to act in a certain way. Note that this refers to an intention to act in a certain way. Whether or not one acts in a manner consistent with this intention will depend on many other factors. In our example, the person dissatisfied with his or her job may intend to get a new one, but might not do so because the economy is poor, or because there are other aspects of the work environment that are positively valued. Thus, it is important to recognize that a behavioral intention is not necessarily predictive of one's actual behavior.

FIGURE 5–2

Attitudes: Three Basic Components

Attitudes are composed of the three components shown here: the *evaluative* component, the *cognitive* component, and the *behavioral* component.

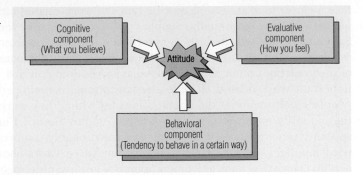

By putting these three components together, we can define **attitudes** (see Figure 5–2) as *relatively stable clusters of feelings, beliefs, and behavioral predispositions (intentions directed toward some specific abstract or concrete object).*[5] The phrase "relatively stable" is part of the definition of attitudes because we are referring to something that is not fleeting and that, once formed, tends to persist. Indeed, as we will describe in the next section, changing attitudes may require considerable effort.

When we speak about **work-related attitudes,** then, we are talking about those lasting feelings, beliefs, and behavioral tendencies toward various aspects of the job itself, the setting in which the work is conducted, and/or the people involved. Thus, we may have attitudes that focus on supervisors, subordinates, customers, competitors, specific tasks, company policies, new equipment, reward systems, the entire organization, or virtually any other aspect of work you can name. As you might imagine, people can—and often do—hold well-developed attitudes toward these, and countless other, focal objects and events related to their jobs.

A Note on the Role of Attitudes in Organizational Behavior

Why are work-related attitudes important in the field of organizational behavior? The answer relates to the two major goals of the field we identified in chapter 1—improving the quality of working life, and improving the functioning of organizations. By studying work-related attitudes, we have a good opportunity to help improve them, thereby making people feel better about the jobs they perform.

Job-related attitudes may also be associated with key aspects of OB—such as task performance, absence from work, and voluntary turnover. This is not to say that attitudes are the only (or even the most important) determinant of these behaviors, or even that they are a direct cause. Consider, for example, what might happen in an organization in which most of the employees hold strongly negative attitudes toward their jobs. Although you might expect the rate of voluntary turnover to be high in such a situation, this would not necessarily be the case *if* the economy is soft and new jobs are difficult to find. In such a situation, the link between the work-related attitude and voluntary turnover may be weak—or, more precisely, qualified by the nature of the economy. However, such dissatisfaction might express itself in other ways, such as reluctance to provide extra help to one's coworkers, or unwillingness to say good things about the company to a prospective employee. In other words, the link between job-related attitudes and behaviors may be complex. Not only might different situations dictate the effects of attitudes on behaviors, but the effects might be different on different types of behavior.

In view of this, keep the following basic principle in mind as you read this chapter: work-related attitudes exist, they are held by people in most settings, and they are related to many different aspects of OB. Their impact varies greatly across situations, however, and their effects might not be apparent to the same degree in all contexts at all times. As you come to see the complex relationships between work-related attitudes and job behaviors later in this chapter, you will be clearly reminded of this basic principle.

CHANGING ATTITUDES: A CRITICAL TASK IN ORGANIZATIONAL BEHAVIOR

Given the important role that work-related attitudes play in organizations, it may be worthwhile to understand how attitudes can be changed. Changing attitudes can be a valuable task for two obvious reasons. First, there is a potential connection between attitudes and various aspects of job performance (e.g., turnover and absenteeism). Indeed, as we will detail in chapter 16, a basic assumption of the notion of *organizational development* is that organizational functioning may be improved through planned attempts to change employees' attitudes and behavior. For now, however, we will concentrate on the basics of the attitude change process—when and how it occurs.

A second reason that we may want to change work-related attitudes is to improve those attitudes themselves. For example, employees would certainly enjoy more positive feelings when they have generally positive attitudes toward their jobs than when they have negative attitudes. It's important to remember that work-related attitudes may be a key aspect of the quality of life people experience on the job, and that creating positive attitudes may be a desirable end in itself.

Changing Others' Attitudes: Two Major Determinants of Persuasion

Imagine that your boss asks you to work overtime to complete a project in time for a critical presentation at tomorrow's board meeting. Or suppose you're watching a TV commercial touting the healthful benefits of a new breakfast cereal. Although these two situations don't appear, at first, to have much in common, they share one key element—both are appeals to change your attitudes. In fact, although you probably don't think about it much, you are likely to be constantly bombarded by attempts to change your attitudes. Although the form of such appeals may very greatly, it is clear that attempts at **persuasion** are common in organizations.

In the persuasion process, a target person (the individual whose attitude is to be changed) is given a message (either written or spoken) in which the information presented is designed to change his or her attitude. The process involves two basic elements—the *communicator* (the person doing the persuading) and the *communication* (the specific content of the message itself).[6] Refer to the summary of these factors appearing in Figure 5–3 (see p. 158) as we describe them below.

Communicators: What Makes Them Persuasive? Research has shown that several key factors are associated with the effectiveness of communicators in changing attitudes. For example, effective communicators tend to be *individuals we like*. Indeed, because we tend to ignore those whom we dislike, such people are unlikely to be effective agents of attitude change. Not surprisingly, effective persuaders also tend to be people who *present themselves in a smooth, eloquent style,* who speak fast and

The ancient Greeks believed there were three basic ways of persuading people to adapt a new point of view: using logical arguments (*logos*), using an effective and persuasive speaker (*ethos*), and using arguments that sway the emotions of the audience (*pathos*). Interestingly, researchers have confirmed the effectiveness of these approaches. [Golden, J. L., Berquist, G. F., & Coleman, W. E. (1978). *The rhetoric of Western thought*. Dubuque, IA: Kendall/Hunt.]

The Attitude Change Process: Its Major Determinants

Several factors make persuasive appeals more effective. These generally fall into two categories: characteristics of the *communicator* **(the person delivering an appeal), and characteristics of the** *communication* **(the message itself).**

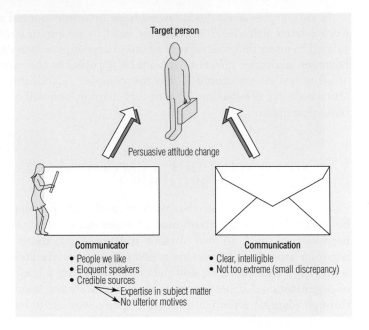

Target person

Persuasive attitude change

Communicator
- People we like
- Eloquent speakers
- Credible sources
  → Expertise in subject matter
  → No ulterior motives

Communication
- Clear, intelligible
- Not too extreme (small discrepancy)

convincingly (as opposed to slowly and with hesitation).[7] Thus, contrary to the popular belief that fast-talking people are untrustworthy, people generally find these individuals to be especially believable!

In addition, a third characteristic has been identified as probably the single most important determinant of one's persuasive capacity—a person's *credibility*. This refers to the extent to which an individual seems trustworthy or believable. The more credible a person is believed to be, the more effective he or she will be in changing attitudes.

Given this, we may ask what determines credibility. First, credibility is determined by an individual's apparent level of *expertise*.[8] Indeed, it has been shown that the more we believe someone knows what he or she is talking about, the more likely that person is to be able to change a target's attitudes, compared with another who appears to be less expert on the topic. Thus, if we are going to be persuaded, it will most likely be by someone who we believe knows a great deal about the topic under consideration. After all, why should we be persuaded by one who doesn't know any more than we do? As you may have noted, advertisers are aware of—and use—this fact when they portray experts to present information about their products (e.g., people who have played the role of doctors on TV are often believed to be knowledgeable about medical issues, and are often used to sell medications).

Another determinant of credibility is the *communicator's apparent motives*. Research has shown that people who have little to gain from changing our views are usually more influential than ones who stand to gain by effectively changing another's attitude.[9] Consider, for example, the approach taken by Lee Iacocca, the successful CEO of the often-troubled Chrysler Corporation. When Iacocca criticizes the management practices of American auto companies, as he has done, his cohorts (executives at Ford and General Motors) may be expected to take seriously what he has to say, and to be influenced by his remarks. After all, his criticisms are clearly aimed at himself, too, and may not be mistaken as self-serving puffery that should be ignored. By contrast, were a similar attack to come from the head of the United Autoworkers

Union, the remarks might be discounted because they are believed to reflect the interests of someone who has something to gain by changing your attitudes. In other words, a persuasive communicator is someone who has no vested interest in the situation and, therefore, has no apparent reason to misrepresent himself or herself for purposes of changing someone's attitude.

Communications: What Makes a Message Persuasive?   Thus far, we have concentrated on characteristics of the person delivering the message, but have said nothing about the message itself, the *content*. Obviously, this factor is very important in determining the impact of attitude change appeals. What are the characteristics of a persuasive message? There are several.

First, the message should be presented in a manner, and at a level, that is *clear and intelligible* to the targets (the persons to whom the message is being sent). The reason is obvious—unless messages are understood, they have little or no chance of changing one's attitudes. Unfortunately, people in business settings too often fail to take this basic fact into account. People—particularly those with technical expertise— commonly "talk over the heads" of their colleagues at meetings, or when specifically trying to change attitudes during a presentation. As a result, the audience may completely miss the point that's being made, rendering the attitude change attempt ineffective.

A second factor that determines the persuasiveness of messages is how different they are from the views already held by the target persons—that is, the *size of the attitude discrepancy*. Sometimes people are asked to change their attitudes completely, moving from being totally against something to being totally for it (e.g., from pro-life to pro-choice on the abortion debate). At other times, people are asked to change their attitudes only a little, or a moderate amount (e.g., from being completely in favor of forced retirement for elderly workers to being only moderately in favor of it). As you might imagine, it is easier to change attitudes when the change represents a small discrepancy from the individuals' initially held opinions than when the discrepancy is larger.[10] This is, in large part, due to the tendency people have to dismiss highly discrepant views as unreasonable and unworthy of their consideration, whereas more moderate views are not believed to be unreasonable and are not rejected out of hand.

We could readily continue with this discussion, for many different factors seem to influence the process of persuasion. Instead, though, we'd like to note that recent research on this process has taken a somewhat different path. Instead of asking "What kinds of messages produce the most attitude change?" recent studies have focused on the following issue: "What cognitive processes determine whether someone will or will not be persuaded?" In other words, efforts have been made to tie the process of persuasion more closely to current knowledge about human cognition generally, and *social cognition*—the manner in which we process, store, and remember social information.[11] Since we already considered social cognition in our discussion of perception, we won't return to it here. However, we should note that research conducted within this perspective suggests that people exposed to persuasive messages actively attempt to process the information these contain. They extract the key points and relate them to information already at their disposal. They remember facts and information that agree or disagree with the persuasive message, and formulate these into arguments for and against its accuracy.[12] Whether, and to what extent, they then alter their attitudes depends on the relative weight of these self-generated arguments and the extent to which information in the persuasive message is consistent with their existing cognitive frameworks *(schemas)*. (See Figure 5–4 on p. 160 for

FIGURE 5-4

Persuasion: A Cognitive
Perspective

The *cognitive approach* to
persuasion suggests that it is
an active process in which
individuals take into account
information contained in
persuasive messages.

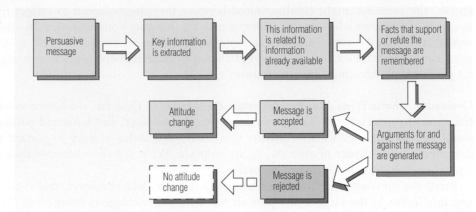

an overview of this process.) In short, persuasion appears to be an *active* process involving a great deal of cognitive effort, not one in which target people are passively changed by convincing external messages.

Changing Our Own Attitudes: The Cognitive Dissonance Phenomenon

Suppose that as graduation approaches, a college student receives two job offers. After much agonizing, she selects one. Will her attitudes toward the two companies now change? If she is like most people, they may. After the student accepts one of the two jobs, she may find that her evaluation of this position, and the company that offered it, has improved: it now seems better than it did initially, before the decision was reached. Conversely, she may find that her attitude toward the rejected firm has become less favorable. The same process occurs after other kinds of decisions, too. Whether individuals choose among cars, schools, jobs, or courses of action, they often experience a positive shift in attitudes toward the chosen alternative, and a negative shift in attitudes toward the others. Why? The answer seems to lie in a process known as **cognitive dissonance.**[13]

In simple terms, dissonance refers to the fact that human beings dislike inconsistency. When we say one thing but do another, or discover that one attitude we hold is inconsistent with another that we also accept, an unpleasant state of *dissonance* arises. We notice the inconsistency between our words and deeds, or between our various attitudes, and react negatively. As the above example suggests, dissonance is also generated by many decisions. When we choose one alternative, we must necessarily forgo the benefits of others. As a result, *postdecision dissonance* arises.

Many factors determine the magnitude of dissonance and the precise ways in which we seek to reduce it. Since our attitudes are usually easier to change than our behavior, cognitive dissonance often leads to attitude change. We've already noted how this occurs following decisions: chosen alternatives are enhanced, whereas rejected ones are derogated. In other cases, we may change our attitudes to bring them into line with our overt actions, or alter one attitude to make it more consistent with others.

For example, suppose that you believe quite strongly in affirmative action (special efforts to hire and promote members of minority groups who have previously been the victims of discrimination). At the same time, you also believe in promotion on the basis of merit. No problems arise until, one day, a person from a minority group is promoted over one of your close friends at work, even though your friend has more experience and is better qualified in several ways. Confronted with this situation, you experience dissonance: your two attitudes are inconsistent. What happens next? The chances are good that one or the other of these views will change. You may become less favorable toward affirmative action or less supportive of promotions-by-merit (see Figure 5–5).

Because it is an unpleasant state most people wish to reduce, dissonance can be used as an important entering wedge for persuasion.[14] If would-be persuaders can place individuals in a situation where they will experience dissonance unless they alter their attitudes in desired directions, considerable success is possible. In organizations, tactics based on dissonance are applied in many contexts. One of the most important of these is their use by people favoring the adoption of some plan or course of action. Such individuals often concentrate their efforts on getting decision makers in their organization to make an initial, tentative commitment to the plan. They realize that once this is done, the decision makers may become quite reluctant to pull out and reverse their choices, even if initial results are negative. Dissonance appears to be one of several factors involved in the reluctance to cut one's losses. In situations where an initial investment in some course of action has been made, but outcomes are negative, the individuals involved realize that they chose this plan voluntarily, and hold at least mildly positive attitudes about it. Yet, such views are inconsistent with the knowledge that the plan is not succeeding. This results in dissonance, which can be reduced in either of two ways: pulling out and cutting their losses, or concluding that the plan *will* work if given enough time or if more resources are invested in it. Because one's beliefs are easier to change than one's behavior, the latter tendency often prevails, with the result that what started out as a very tentative commitment grows stronger and stronger over time—just as the persuaders originally intended. (Such effects, sometimes known as *escalation of commitment*, will be covered in more detail in chapter 14.)

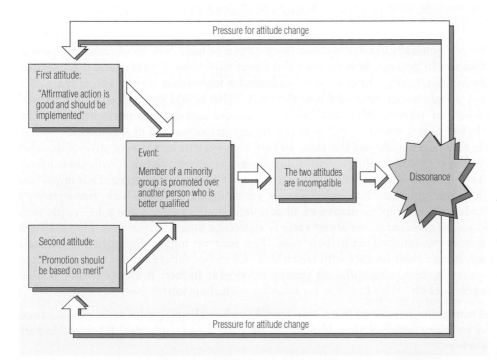

FIGURE 5–5

Cognitive Dissonance as a Source of Attitude Change

When individuals notice that two of their attitudes are inconsistent, an unpleasant state of *dissonance* occurs. This generates pressures to change one, or perhaps both, of the attitudes.

In sum, the induction of dissonance can be a powerful tactic of persuasion. In fact, as noted in the heading of this section, under the right conditions, people experiencing this unpleasant cognitive state become virtual allies of those who wish to persuade them by generating internal pressures to change their own attitudes!

JOB SATISFACTION: ATTITUDES TOWARD ONE'S JOB

In general, employees in the United States are more satisfied with their work than are their counterparts in the nations of the European Community and Japan. According to recent survey findings, the percentage of U.S. employees who report feeling very satisfied with their work is 43 percent—a higher figure than obtained among European employees (28 percent) and Japanese employees (17 percent). [Tetzeli, R. (1991, November 4). Office woes East and West. *Fortune*, p. 14.]

The work we do plays a dominant role in most people's lives. Our work not only occupies more of our time than any other single activity, but also provides the economic basis for our lifestyles, and constitutes a central aspect of who we are, how we define ourselves as individuals. Given this importance, it should not be surprising that people hold strong attitudes toward their jobs. Indeed, most people can tell you all about how they feel about their jobs (e.g., "I really dislike what I do"), the things they believe about it (e.g., "I think the work is really important for the people of our community"), and their behavioral intentions toward it (e.g., "I'm going to look for another position"). In other words, people hold various attitudes toward their jobs, attitudes that are specifically referred to as **job satisfaction**—the topic of the next section of this chapter. Formally, we may define job satisfaction as *individuals' cognitive, affective, and evaluative reactions toward their jobs*.[15]

In taking a closer look at job satisfaction, we will address several major issues. For example, we will consider how job satisfaction is measured. We will also describe theories of job satisfaction, attempts to address how the process of job satisfaction works. Next, we will review the major factors that are responsible for making people satisfied or dissatisfied with their jobs. Then, finally, we will consider the principal effects of job satisfaction on various aspects of organizational behavior. Before considering these topics, however, we will begin by considering a very basic question: are people generally satisfied with their jobs?

How Prevalent Is Job Satisfaction? Do People Really Like Their Work?

Have you generally liked or disliked the jobs you've had? Now think about the people you know. In general, how do they feel about their jobs? Approaching the question more systematically, suppose you conducted a large-scale survey asking many different people in different jobs how they felt. What would you expect to find? Based on frequent reports about problems of turnover and sagging performance in the workplace, most would expect to find widespread evidence of dissatisfaction.[16] However, this is generally *not* the case. In fact, surveys conducted over several decades have found that 80 to 90 percent of people *are* relatively satisfied with their jobs.

As you might imagine, the complete picture is a bit more complex. One important trend is that although the general level of job satisfaction is quite high, these positive attitudes are not representative of all people and all aspects of the job. People may hold vastly different views about various aspects of their job. For example, although they may be satisfied with their pay, they may be highly dissatisfied with their supervisor or their contact with coworkers. Likewise, different levels of job satisfaction may occur among different groups of people. In fact, it occurs within several specific pockets. Who tends to be satisfied with their job?[17]

■ White-collar personnel (e.g., managerial, technical, and professional people) tend to be more satisfied than blue-collar personnel (e.g., physical laborers, factory workers).

■ Older people, those with more job seniority, tend to be more satisfied with their jobs than younger, less experienced people. (This shouldn't be surprising. After all, people who are highly dissatisfied with their jobs may be expected to leave them if they can. Moreover, according to cognitive dissonance theory, the longer one stays on a job, the more one feels compelled to justify his or her tenure by seeing the job in a positive light.)

■ In general, women and members of minority groups tend to be more dissatisfied with their jobs than men and members of majority groups. (However, although barriers to acceptance are far from completely removed, it is clear that as acceptance of such individuals in the work force improves, they will be likely to experience greater levels of satisfaction.)

Not only may certain groups of people be more satisfied with their jobs than others, but in addition some individuals are likely to be either consistently satisfied or consistently dissatisfied with their jobs. In fact, you're probably well acquainted with individuals who always like their jobs—no matter what they are—and others who are chronically dissatisfied. The main idea is this: job satisfaction is a relatively stable *disposition*, a characteristic of individuals that stays with them across situations (we will have more to say about such characteristics in chapter 6).

Recent research has shown that some people are, in fact, predisposed to "negative affect," to report feeling distressed and uncomfortable in the absence of any objective source of stress, and that these individuals tend to be dissatisfied with their jobs.[18] The notion that job satisfaction may be dispositional in nature is an intriguing finding from a fascinating study by Staw and Ross.[19] Their survey of more than 5,000 men who changed jobs between 1969 and 1971 found that expressions of job satisfaction were relatively stable (in fact, they were correlated .33). Despite different jobs, people satisfied or dissatisfied in 1969 also tended to be satisfied or dissatisfied in 1971. In view of this, that there is a generally strong relationship between levels of job satisfaction and life satisfaction is not at all surprising.[20] People who generally like their jobs also generally like their lives. Hence, the disposition toward positive or negative affect tends to cut across various attitudes in our lives. (What accounts for this stability in levels of job satisfaction? For compelling evidence of a rather surprising nature, read the **Focus on Research** section on p. 164.)

There is another reason why older workers, particularly those over fifty, tend to be more satisfied with their jobs than are younger workers. Older people grew up during the Great Depression of the late 1920s and 1930s, a period when times were hard, and having any job at all was welcomed. As a result of having these early harsh economic experiences, today's older people are not likely to be as particular about their jobs as their younger counterparts. Those who never experienced the Depression grew up in a period of relative affluence and economic expansion. Knowing only good times, they tend to have relatively high expectations about what they desire from their jobs. [Job satisfaction: Based on generation, not class. (1989, November–December). *Society,* pp. 2–3.]

Measuring Job Satisfaction: Assessing Reactions to Work

Attitudes are certainly real, but they are not directly visible. People do not go about proclaiming their views to everyone they meet. On the contrary, they usually keep their attitudes about politics, religion, and other matters largely to themselves. Attitudes about work are no exception to this general rule. Most people express these views openly only to a small group of friends or relatives—certainly *not* to all of their supervisors or subordinates. For this reason, measuring job satisfaction is a more difficult task than you might initially guess. Several techniques for assessing this important aspect of work environments do exist, however. Among the most useful are *rating scales* or *questionnaires*, *critical incidents*, and *interviews*.

Rating Scales and Questionnaires: Measuring Job Satisfaction through Self-Report   The most common approach to measuring job satisfaction involves the use of special rating scales or questionnaires. In this method, employees are asked to complete special forms on which they report their current reactions to their jobs. A number of scales have been developed for this purpose, and they vary greatly in form and scope. For example, one that is very popular, the **Job Descriptive Index**

FOCUS ON RESEARCH

Job Satisfaction: Can It Be in the Genes?

We usually think of job satisfaction as a situational attitude. Thus, it reflects how someone feels about a particular job at a particular time. However, given recent evidence that job satisfaction appears to be, at least in part, a dispositional characteristic, it is reasonable to ask what accounts for this stability. A study by Arvey and his associates suggests that the answer is, to some extent, genetics.[21]

The researchers measured the current level of job satisfaction experienced by thirty-four pairs of monozygotic twins who were separated at an early age and then reared apart (see Figure 5–6). Given that such individuals share an identical genetic makeup, but have different backgrounds, the extent to which their attitudes are correlated provides an estimate of the degree to which the attitude is genetically determined. The investigators found that genetics accounted for approximately 30 percent of the job satisfaction between the twins—a significant, but not overwhelming, figure. Apparently, as is the case with many other kinds of attitudes and behaviors, *both* nature and nurture are involved in job satisfaction, albeit to different degrees.

The considerable overlap in the nature of the jobs held by the twins was a particularly interesting finding of this study. They tended to hold jobs that matched their siblings' with respect to key job dimensions such as motor skill requirements, complexity, and physical demands. In other words, the tendency to seek and remain in certain jobs appears to be, in part, inherited. The finding that job satisfaction is somewhat the result of genetic factors is important. Probably the major implication is that certain programmatic efforts at raising levels of job satisfaction (such as by making the work environment more interesting, as we have seen in chapter 4) may be limited by a "genetic ceiling." People might be made somewhat more satisfied by changing certain aspects of the jobs performed, but only up to a point limited by inherited tendencies.

FIGURE 5–6

Monozygotic Twins: Useful for Studying Effects of Genetics

Research using twins has shown that approximately 30 percent of job satisfaction is dispositional in nature—an inherited predisposition to like or dislike one's job.

(JDI), presents individuals with lists of adjectives and asks them to indicate whether each does or does not describe a particular aspect of their work.[22] They do so by placing a *Y* for "yes," an *N* for "no," or a *?* for "undecided" next to each adjective. One interesting feature of this scale is that it measures reactions to five distinct aspects of jobs: the work itself, pay, promotional opportunities, supervision, and people (coworkers).

Another widely used measure of job satisfaction is the **Minnesota Satisfaction Questionnaire (MSQ).** On this scale, individuals rate the extent to which they are satisfied with various aspects of their present job (e.g., their degree of responsibility, opportunities for advancement, pay).[23] Such ratings range from "not at all satisfied" through "extremely satisfied." Obviously, the higher the ratings individuals report, the greater their satisfaction with various aspects of their jobs.

Other scales focus in more detail on specific facets of job satisfaction. For example, as its name suggests, the **Pay Satisfaction Questionnaire (PSQ)** is primarily concerned with attitudes about various aspects of pay. A recent study by Scarpello, Huber, and Vandenberg indicates that this scale measures individuals' reactions to *pay level* (how much they actually receive), *raises, pay structure and administration* (how pay is allocated by rank and how it is actually distributed to employees—weekly, monthly, and so on), and *benefits* (sick leave, vacations, insurance, and so on).[24] Items similar to those used on the JDI, MSQ, and PSQ are shown in Table 5–1.

An important advantage of rating scales is that they can be completed quickly and efficiently by large numbers of people. Another benefit is that because they have already been administered to many thousands of individuals, average scores for people in many kinds of jobs and many types of organizations are available. Thus, it is possible to compare the scores of people in a given company with these, and obtain a measure of *relative* satisfaction—very useful information in many cases. However, there is a key problem with such scales. As is true with all self-report measures, the usefulness of the results obtained depends on the respondents' honesty, as well as their ability to report accurately on their feelings. (Since these are some-times unclear, a certain degree of error can be introduced into the measurement process.) To the extent that cooperation from respondents is lacking, and they are unable to identify and describe their own reactions, the findings obtained with such questionnaires can be misleading.

TABLE 5–1   Items Similar to Those on Popular Job Satisfaction Questionnaires

The items shown here are similar to those used on three popular measures of job satisfaction. (Note: The items shown are *not* identical to ones on the actual scales.)

Job Description Index (JDI)	Minnesota Satisfaction Questionnaire (MSQ)	Pay Satisfaction Questionnaire (PSQ)
Enter "Yes," "No," or "?" for each description or word below.	Indicate the extent to which you are satisfied with each aspect of your present job. Enter one number next to each aspect.	Indicate the extent to which you are satisfied with each aspect of your present pay. Enter one number next to each aspect.
Work itself: ___ Routine ___ Satisfactory ___ Good	1 = Extremely dissatisfied	1 = Extremely dissatisfied
Promotions: ___ Dead-end job ___ Few promotions ___ Good opportunity for promotion	2 = Not satisfied 3 = Neither satisfied nor dissatisfied 4 = Satisfied 5 = Extremely satisfied	2 = Not satisfied 3 = Neither satisfied nor dissatisfied 4 = Satisfied 5 = Extremely satisfied
	___ Utilization of your abilities ___ Authority ___ Company policies and practices ___ Independence ___ Supervision–human relations	Items measuring satisfaction with *pay level:* ___ My current pay ___ Size of my salary Items measuring satisfaction with *raises:* ___ Typical raises ___ How raises are determined

Source: Based on items from the JDI, MSQ, and PSQ; see Notes 22, 23, and 24.

Critical Incidents and Job Satisfaction   A second technique for assessing job satisfaction is the **critical incident procedure.** Here, individuals describe incidents relating to their work that they found especially satisfying or dissatisfying. Their replies are then carefully examined to uncover underlying themes and reactions. For example, if many employees mentioned on-the-job situations in which they felt physically uncomfortable this would suggest that the factor of physical comfort plays an important role in job satisfaction.

Interviews and Other Face-to-Face Meetings   Additional techniques for assessing job satisfaction involve interviews with employees, and what have sometimes been termed *confrontation meetings*. Interviews permit a more detailed exploration of employees' attitudes than questionnaires and are sometimes useful for this reason. In addition, they may sometimes provide revealing insights into the causes of job satisfaction and work-related attitudes. For example, in one recent study, Sutton and Callahan used interviews to study the effects on employees of their organizations' filing for protection under Chapter 11 of the Federal Bankruptcy Code.[25] These interviews provided intriguing information on how this event affected participants' attitudes toward their jobs and toward their organizations. In confrontation meetings, employees are invited to "lay it on the line," to discuss their major complaints and concerns with management. If such sessions are conducted skillfully, problems that adversely affect job satisfaction, but which might otherwise remain hidden, can be brought out into the open. Then steps to correct or eliminate them can be developed.

Theories of Job Satisfaction

What makes some people satisfied with their jobs and others highly dissatisfied? In other words, what underlying processes account for people's feelings of job satisfaction? Insight into these important questions is provided by various theories of job satisfaction. We will describe two of the most influential approaches—Herzberg's *two-factor theory* and Locke's *value theory*.

Herzberg's Two-Factor Theory   One well-known theory of job satisfaction is Frederick Herzberg's **two-factor theory** (also known as **motivator-hygiene theory**). This conceptualization focuses on the following question: do job satisfaction and dissatisfaction stem from the same conditions, or are they actually the result of different sets of factors?[26] Common sense suggests that both reactions derive from common causes. Certain factors produce job satisfaction when they are present, but feelings of dissatisfaction when they are absent. According to Herzberg, however, this is not the case. His two-factor theory contends that job satisfaction and dissatisfaction actually derive from contrasting sources. You may find it interesting to learn how Herzberg first reached this surprising conclusion.

He began by conducting a study in which more than 200 engineers and accountants were asked to describe times when they felt especially satisfied or dissatisfied with their jobs.[27] Thus, he used the *critical incident* technique described above. Careful analysis of their answers yielded the following pattern of results. When describing incidents in which they felt dissatisfied, many people mentioned conditions surrounding their jobs rather than the work itself. For instance, they commented on factors such as physical working conditions, pay, security, the quality of supervision they received, company policies, and their social relations with others at work. To the extent that these conditions were positive, feelings of dissatisfaction were prevented. Because such factors prevented negative reactions, Herzberg termed them *hygienes* or *maintenance factors*. In contrast, when describing incidents in which they felt especially satisfied or happy with their jobs, respondents often mentioned factors relating more directly to the work they performed or to outcomes deriving

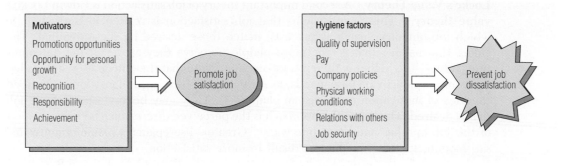

FIGURE 5–7   Herzberg's Two-Factor Theory

Herzberg's *two-factor theory* suggests that job satisfaction and job dissatisfaction stem from different sets of factors. These are labeled *motivators* and *hygienes,* respectively.

from it. They commented on the nature of their jobs and daily tasks, achievement in them, promotion opportunities, recognition from management, increased responsibility, and the chance for personal growth. Because such factors contributed to positive attitudes (i.e., job satisfaction), Herzberg labeled them *motivators.* (See Figure 5–7 for a summary of the factors he identified as motivators and hygienes.) As you can see, these factors are closely related to the *growth needs* specified by Maslow's theory of motivation (refer to chapter 4). Thus, Herzberg's theory suggests that job satisfaction stems from the satisfaction of higher-level needs. Similarly, job dissatisfaction is related to conditions that fail to satisfy lower-level needs (social needs, physiological needs).

Has research supported the accuracy of the two-factor theory? Unfortunately, results have been mixed. Some studies have yielded results consistent with the theory's central claim that job satisfaction and dissatisfaction stem from different factors. For example, in one study, conducted by Machungawa and Schmitt, several hundred employees in a developing nation (Zambia) described times when they worked exceptionally hard or when they put little effort into their work.[28] Careful analysis of these incidents indicated that positive attitudes and high effort were related to factors similar to Herzberg's motivators (e.g., opportunities for advancement or personal growth). Conversely, negative attitudes and low effort were linked to factors similar to hygienes (e.g., perceived fairness in organizational practices, physical work conditions).

Several other studies, however, found that factors labeled as hygienes and motivators exerted strong effects on *both* satisfaction and dissatisfaction.[29] Such findings are contrary to the theory's basic assertion that these positive and negative attitudes stem from distinct clusters of variables.

In view of such evidence, Herzberg's theory should be seen as an intriguing, but unverified, framework for understanding job satisfaction. This is not to say, however, that it has been of little value. First, as noted by Landy, although the theory does not seem useful in predicting employee satisfaction and motivation, it does seem to provide a useful framework for describing the conditions people find satisfying and dissatisfying. Second, the theory has called attention to the important role in job satisfaction of factors such as the opportunity for personal growth, recognition, and increased responsibility. Attention to such factors, in turn, has stimulated much work on *job enlargement* and *job enrichment*—discussed in chapter 4. In this way, Herzberg's theory has contributed much to the field of organizational behavior, despite the lack of clear support for some of its key predictions.

Test Bank questions 5.28 and 5.60 relate to material on this page.

Locke's Value Theory   A second important theory of job satisfaction is Edwin Locke's **value theory.**[30] This theory claims that job satisfaction is related to the extent to which job outcomes (such as rewards) match those desired by the individual. The closer the match—that is, the more people perceive they are receiving outcomes they value—the higher is their job satisfaction. Note that the outcomes people value may not necessarily be basic needs, as reflected in Herzberg's theory (or in the need theories of motivation described in chapter 4). They may be any aspect of the job that is desired. The key to this approach is the perceived *discrepancy* between aspects of the job one has and those one wants. Greater discrepancies result in more dissatisfaction, lesser discrepancies result in more satisfaction.

Evidence for this claim may be found in a study by Rice, McFarlin, and Bennett.[31] Using a questionnaire, these investigators measured how much of various job facets—such as pay, hours worked, commuting time, and promotion opportunities—a diverse group of employees wanted and how much they felt they already had. They also measured how satisfied the respondents were with each of these job facets. As shown in Figure 5–8, an interesting trend emerged. The aspects of the job about which respondents experienced the greatest discrepancies were the ones with which they were most dissatisfied, and those with which they experienced the smallest discrepancies were the ones with which they were most satisfied.

An interesting implication of this theory is that it calls attention to the aspects of the job that need to be changed for job satisfaction to result. Specifically, the theory suggests that these aspects might not be the same ones for all people, but any valued aspects of the job about which people perceive serious discrepancies. By emphasizing values, Locke's theory suggests that job satisfaction may be derived from *many* factors. In this respect, it is fully consistent with the findings of research on the causes of job satisfaction—the topic to which we will now turn.

Job Satisfaction: Its Principal Causes

Despite the limited capacity of theories of job satisfaction to provide a comprehensive overview of its causes, research designed to identify the factors that might influence job satisfaction attitudes has been quite successful. Indeed, many of the conditions that lead individuals to hold positive or negative views of their job have been identified. This is a diverse list, but the major factors fall into two broad categories: (1) those relating to organizational policies and the nature of the job performed, and (2) those relating to the personal characteristics of the employees themselves.

Another key determinant of employee satisfaction is unionization. Research has shown that unionized workers are less satisfied with their jobs than are nonunionized workers. However, unionized workers are more satisfied with the levels of pay they receive and with their job security than are nonunionized workers. [Meng, R. (1990). The relationship between unions and job satisfaction. *Applied Economics, 22,* 1635–1648.]

Organizational Determinants of Job Satisfaction   What organizational policies and procedures, and what elements of the work itself, are related to job satisfaction? Several key determinants have been identified.

First, we know that the organization's *reward system* is highly related to job satisfaction. This refers to how pay and promotions are distributed. Are people paid adequately and fairly relative to others? Indeed, research has found that satisfaction is enhanced by the use of pay systems believed to be fair—with respect to both the level of compensation received and the mechanisms used to determine that pay.[32] Consider, for example, a study by Berkowitz and his associates in which a random sample of several hundred people were interviewed about their current job satisfaction.[33] The single best predictor of job satisfaction was found to be the belief that one is treated in a fair and equitable manner. (As you will recall from chapter 4, perceptions of equity also represent a key source of job motivation.)

A second organizationally based determinant of job satisfaction is *perceived quality of supervision.* Specifically, studies have determined that satisfaction tends to be high when people believe their supervisors are competent, have their best interests

Test Bank questions 5.29 and 5.61 relate to material on this page.

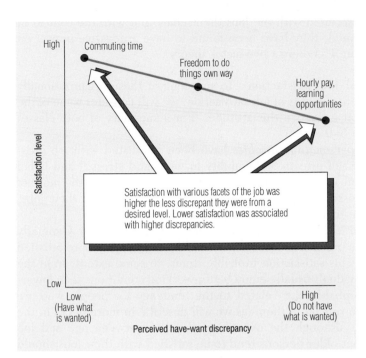

FIGURE 5–8

Job Satisfaction: A Function of Discrepancies between What You Have and What You Want

Consistent with Locke's *value theory,* research has shown that people's satisfaction with various aspects of their jobs is based on the degree to which there is a discrepancy between how much they have and how much they want of that job factor. Satisfaction is higher when discrepancies are smaller. (*Source:* Based on data provided by Rice, McFarlin, & Bennett, 1989; see Note 31.)

in mind, and treat them with dignity and respect. By contrast, satisfaction tends to be lower among those who believe they receive poorer-quality supervision—specifically, by superiors believed to be incompetent, selfish, and uncaring.[34]

Third, we know that job satisfaction is related to the *decentralization of power.* As we will discuss later in this book—in the contexts of power (chapter 11), decision making (chapter 14), and organizational design (chapter 15)—decentralization refers to the degree to which the capacity to make decisions resides in many people as opposed to just one (central) person. When power is decentralized, many people are allowed to make decisions and people can freely participate in decision making. Such situations tend to promote job satisfaction.[35] By contrast, when decision-making authority is concentrated in the hands of just a few, people tend to believe that they are relatively powerless and, not surprisingly, feel dissatisfied.

A fourth determinant is level of *work and social stimulation.* People tend to be most satisfied with jobs that provide them with an overall work load and level of variety that are not so low as to be boring and not so high as to be overwhelming and unduly challenging.[36] Recent research by Wright has shown that this factor applies mostly to individuals who see their jobs as a career (e.g., those who desire promotion and have a long-term orientation) as opposed to those who see the position as a temporary, short-term one.[37] By contrast, those who do not have a career orientation tend to be most satisfied not by aspects of the work, but by pleasant social conditions (e.g., lots of friends) on the job. This is not surprising, because only those who really care about their careers would be expected to find satisfaction in the work they do. Indeed, research has shown that job satisfaction tends to be higher the more one is committed to attaining work-related goals.[38] (This also should not be surprising in view of the job characteristics model's inclusion of the variable *growth need strength* as a factor qualifying the extent to which various job characteristics enhance many key variables, including job satisfaction; see chapter 4.)

A fifth determinant of job satisfaction is *pleasant working conditions.* Research has shown that job satisfaction is reduced by overcrowded conditions, and dark noisy environments with extreme temperatures and poor air quality.[39] Although these factors are not directly associated with the jobs themselves, but with the context in which the work is performed, they have been found to have a negative impact on job satisfaction (challenging Herzberg's two-factor theory).

Personal Determinants of Job Satisfaction   To supplement these organizationally related and job-related determinants of job satisfaction, we will consider some of the major personal factors that influence this attitude. (For a summary of both classes of factors, refer to Figure 5–9.)

First, many different *personality variables* have been associated with job satisfaction. Among these are self-esteem,[40] the ability to withstand stress,[41] and belief in the ability to control one's own outcomes.[42] Research has shown that the more of these variables people possess, the more satisfied they will feel about their jobs. (We will have much more to say about these variables in chapter 6.)

Second, job satisfaction is related to organizational status and seniority. Generally speaking, the higher one's position in an organizational hierarchy, the more satisfied that individual will be.[43] This satisfaction probably stems, to some extent, from the fact that higher-level individuals usually enjoy better working conditions than lower-level individuals. It is probably also related to the tendency for people who are satisfied with their jobs to remain in them (as we will describe in more detail in the next section). Therefore, although the overall relationship between age and job satisfaction is complex, that older persons tend to be satisfied with their jobs should not be surprising.[44]

Third, and finally, job satisfaction has been found to be related to one's *general life satisfaction*. The more people are satisfied with aspects of their lives unrelated to the job, the more they also tend to be satisfied with their jobs.[45] Although the research on the relationship between work and nonwork satisfaction has not been completely consistent, the most recent investigations have found the relationship to be especially strong. Tait, Padgett, and Baldwin have argued that this is the result of the growing tendency for work to play a central role in the lives of women.[46] As work takes on an increasingly significant role in the lives of women, satisfaction with the job and satisfaction with life itself become more strongly associated.

To summarize, a broad array of both personal and job-related variables are associated with job satisfaction. Although some of these variables are consistent with

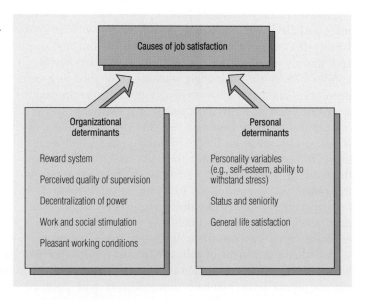

FIGURE 5–9

Job Satisfaction: Two Primary Causes

Based on many research studies, two principal causes of job satisfaction have been found— *organizational* causes and *personal* causes. Several examples of each are shown here.

established theoretical statements, others either are at odds with such views or fail to be taken into consideration by them. As a whole, these lines of investigation take a critical step toward the dual goals of studying job satisfaction and improving the quality of working life as well as the functioning of organizations.

Job Satisfaction: Its Major Effects

In discussing the success or failure of specific organizations, practicing managers (and many others) often refer to the important influence of *employee morale*. They suggest that successful organizations are ones in which morale is high, whereas those that fail are ones in which morale is low. Is this actually the case? In other words, does job satisfaction really exert strong effects on important aspects of organizational behavior? In general, the answer appears to be "yes." As we will soon note, job satisfaction among employees does affect many aspects of OB. Note, however, that this relationship is far from simple or direct. As we stated earlier, attitudes *do* affect behavior in many instances, but this is not always the case. Sometimes their impact is blocked by external factors or conditions. And attitudes are most likely to shape overt actions when they are specific and strong; they are far less likely to produce such effects when they are general or weak. Thus, it would be naive to expect the impact of job satisfaction to be readily visible in all situations and contexts. Having offered this cautionary note, we will now summarize current evidence concerning the ways in which these work-related attitudes influence behavior in work settings.

Job Satisfaction, Absenteeism, and Turnover   Consider two employees. Both hate to get up early in the morning and dislike commuting very much. However, one likes her job, whereas the other dislikes it. Which person is more likely to call in sick or miss work for other reasons? The answer is obvious: the one who dislikes her job. That job satisfaction affects absence from work is indicated by the findings of many different studies. In general, the lower individuals' satisfaction with their jobs, the more likely they are to be absent from work.[47] As you might well guess, though, the strength of this relationship is modest rather than strong. This is because job satisfaction is just one of many different factors influencing employees' decisions to report or not report to work.

Similar findings have also been obtained with respect to voluntary turnover. The lower individuals' level of satisfaction with their jobs, the more likely they are to resign and seek other opportunities. Again, the strength of this relationship is modest, and for similar reasons.[48] Many factors relating to individuals, their jobs, and economic conditions shape decisions to move from one job to another. Several of the factors affecting voluntary turnover are described in a model of this process proposed by Mobley and his associates.[49] According to this model, job dissatisfaction leads employees to think about the possibility of quitting. This, in turn, leads to the decision to begin searching for another job. If this search is successful, the individual next develops definite intentions either to quit or to remain on the job. These intentions are then reflected in concrete actions (actually quitting or remaining in the organization; see Figure 5–10 on p. 172 for a summary of this process).

The suggestion that economic conditions, and hence the success of an initial search for alternative jobs, exert a strong impact on voluntary turnover is supported by the findings of a study by Carsten and Spector.[50] These researchers examined the results of a large number of previous studies concerned with turnover. For each, they contacted the people who had conducted the study and determined the precise dates during which data had been collected. Then Carsten and Spector obtained data on the unemployment rates prevailing at those times. They predicted that the relationship between job satisfaction and turnover would be stronger at times when

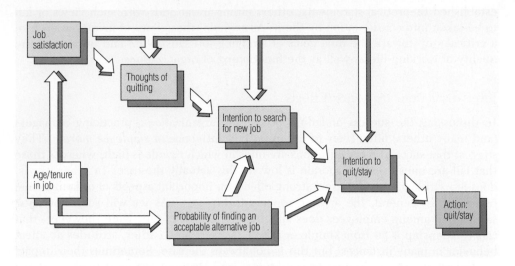

FIGURE 5-10   Voluntary Turnover: An Overview

According to a model proposed by Mobley and his associates, voluntary turnover involves a complex process: low levels of job satisfaction begin a process in which individuals first think about quitting, then search for another job, and finally form intentions to quit or stay in their present job. At several steps in this process, the probability of finding an acceptable alternative job plays a key role. (*Source:* Based on suggestions by Mobley, Horner, & Hollingsworth, 1978; see Note 49.)

unemployment was low than at times when it was high. When unemployment was low, they reasoned, individuals would perceive many opportunities for other jobs. Thus, the lower their satisfaction, the more likely they would be to leave their current positions. In contrast, when unemployment was high, individuals would realize that they could not readily find other positions. As a result, they would tend to remain in their current jobs regardless of their satisfaction with them. In short, poor economic conditions would serve as an external factor preventing job satisfaction from affecting overt, work-related behavior (see Figure 5–11). Results confirmed these predictions.

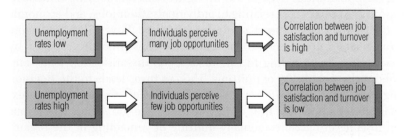

FIGURE 5-11   Job Satisfaction, Economic Conditions, and Turnover

When unemployment rates are low, individuals perceive many opportunities for other jobs. Thus, their level of job satisfaction is a good predictor of turnover (whether they will remain in their current jobs or seek others). In contrast, when unemployment rates are high, individuals perceive few opportunities for other jobs. Under these conditions, job satisfaction is not a good predictor of turnover. (*Source:* Based on suggestions by Carsten & Spector, 1987; see Note 50.)

Test Bank questions 5.34 and 5.62 relate to material on this page.

The higher the unemployment rates were, the lower the correlation between job satisfaction and turnover.

We should add that factors known to affect job satisfaction have also been found to affect voluntary turnover. For example, in their study of the impact of physical aspects of work settings on job satisfaction, Oldham and Fried also measured turnover among participants.[51] They found that poor physical conditions (e.g., few office enclosures, low levels of illumination) were related to increased turnover. These and other findings suggest that factors that reduce job satisfaction often increase turnover as well. Although this finding does not, by itself, indicate that low job satisfaction is a direct cause of turnover, it is consistent with other evidence suggesting that this is the case.

Job Satisfaction and Task Performance   Many managers seem to operate according to the belief that "happy workers are productive workers." Is this really the case? Is job satisfaction directly linked to task performance or productivity? Some evidence suggests that this is so. In a recent review of studies concerned with the impact of participation in decision making on both job satisfaction and productivity, Miller and Monge found evidence that the opportunity to participate in decision making increases job satisfaction and that such positive attitudes, in turn, facilitate productivity.[52] However, other findings suggest that the overall picture is more complex. In many studies, job satisfaction has been found to have little, if any, effect on task performance. Why is this the case? Several possibilities exist.

First, in many work settings, there is little room for large changes in performance. Jobs are structured so that the people holding them *must* maintain at least some minimum level of performance. If they do not, they cannot retain their jobs. Further, there is often little leeway for *exceeding* these minimum standards. Even if an individual increases his or her own output, this may have no impact because needed input from other employees, who have not increased their effort, is lacking. The result: an individual who, because of high job satisfaction, increases his or her output may soon find that he or she has little to do! In such cases, even very high levels of job satisfaction have little effect on overall productivity.

Second, job satisfaction and productivity may actually not be directly linked. Rather, any apparent relationship between them may stem from the fact that both are related to a third factor—receipt of various rewards. As suggested by Porter and Lawler, the situation may be as follows.[53] Past levels of performance lead to the receipt of both extrinsic rewards (e.g., pay, promotions) and intrinsic rewards (e.g., feelings of accomplishment). If employees judge these rewards to be fair, they may come to perceive a link between their performance and these outcomes. This, in turn, may have two effects. First, it may encourage high levels of effort and, thus, good performance. Second, it may lead to high levels of job satisfaction. In short, high productivity and high job satisfaction may both stem from the same conditions. These two factors themselves, however, may not be directly linked.

For these and other reasons, job satisfaction may not be directly related to performance in many contexts. We should note, however, that this conclusion may hold true only with respect to "standard" measures of performance. That is, job satisfaction does not, by itself, strongly affect the quantity or quality of employees' output. However, it may well influence other aspects of their on-the-job behavior. For example, it may affect **organizational citizenship behaviors.**[54] These are actions by individuals that enhance social relationships and cooperation within an organization (e.g., offering help to coworkers when it is requested; demonstrating a cheerful, cooperative attitude; protecting or conserving the organization's resources; tolerating temporary inconveniences without complaint). Such actions may contribute to the smooth and effective functioning of organizations without showing up directly in monthly summaries of output or sales. Presumably, the higher the individuals' satisfaction with their jobs, the more likely they will be to engage in such actions.

Evidence for precisely such a relationship has been reported by Bateman and Organ.[55] These investigators asked supervisors at a large university to rate their subordinates in terms of their tendency to engage in the type of citizenship behaviors described above. At the same time, the employees reported on their own level of job satisfaction by completing the Job Descriptive Index. Results indicated that there was indeed a positive relationship between reported satisfaction and rated citizenship behaviors. The higher the subjects' job satisfaction, the higher the citizenship ratings they received from their supervisors.

These findings suggest that in answer to the question "Are job satisfaction and performance linked?" we should first respond, "What kind of performance do you have in mind?" For many traditional indices of job performance, a link between positive work attitudes and performance may exist but be difficult to demonstrate. For other aspects of performance such as citizenship behaviors, it may be somewhat stronger, or at least easier to observe.

ORGANIZATIONAL COMMITMENT: FEELINGS OF ATTACHMENT TOWARD ORGANIZATIONS

One of the best ways for an organization to develop a committed work force is for it to demonstrate its commitment to its employees. This can be accomplished by developing policies and programs that are responsive to the needs of the workers. As an example, the recent actions of Hewlett-Packard reflect its commitment to its employees' well-being. Recently, in response to harsh economic times, the company was forced to cut labor costs. Instead of laying off 10 percent of the work force, it was decided to have all employees work 10 percent less in exchange for 10 percent less pay. [Verespej, M. A. (1990, July 16). Where people come first. *Industry Week,* pp. 22–32.]

Have you ever known someone who loved his work but hated the company that employed him? Conversely, have you ever known anyone who hated her job, but felt strong loyalty toward her company? If you have encountered individuals of either type, you are already aware of an important fact: positive or negative feelings about one's job are only part of the total picture where work-related attitudes are concerned. In addition to holding such views, individuals often also possess positive or negative attitudes toward their entire organization. Such attitudes, usually termed **organizational commitment,** reflect the extent to which an individual identifies with and is involved with his or her organization and is unwilling to leave it. As you might imagine, many factors are believed to cause organizational commitment, and the different levels of commitment have many important consequences. Before we consider these various causes and consequences of organizational commitment, we will begin by taking a closer look at the major varieties of organizational commitment that exist.

Organizational Commitment: Its Major Types

Historically, two conceptualizations of organizational commitment—the *side-bets orientation* and the individual-organizational *goal congruence orientation*—have dominated.[56] Becker's **side-bets orientation** focuses on the accumulated investments an individual stands to lose if he or she leaves the organization.[57] The idea is that over time, leaving an organization becomes more costly because people fear losing what they have invested in the organization and become concerned that they cannot replace these things. For example, people may be unwilling to leave their jobs because they are concerned about being perceived as "job hoppers" and stake their reputation for stability on remaining in their present jobs (hence, they make a "side-bet" on some aspect of themselves on continued organizational membership). The individual-organizational **goal congruence orientation** focuses on the extent to which individuals identifying with an organization have personal goals that are in keeping with those of the organization. This approach, popularized by Porter and his associates, reflects people's willingness to accept and work toward meeting organizational goals.[58] It views organizational commitment as the result of three factors: (1) acceptance of the organization's goals and values, (2) willingness to help the organization achieve its goals, and (3) the desire to remain within the organization.

As researchers began to study organizational commitment from each of these two perspectives, it became clear that neither approach was ideal[59] and that both provided important insight into organizational commitment.[60] As a result, Meyer, Allen, and Gellatly have proposed that *both* orientations are valid, and that there are really two different kinds of organizational commitment—*continuance commitment* and *affective commitment*.[61] **Continuance commitment,** related to the side-bets approach, refers to the strength of a person's tendency to need to continue working for an organization (because he or she cannot afford to do otherwise). **Affective commitment,** similar to the goal congruence approach, refers to the strength of a person's desire to continue working for an organization (because he or she agrees with it, and wants to do so). Questionnaires measuring both types of commitment have been developed.[62] Table 5–2 shows items similar to those used to measure each kind of commitment.

Using measures such as those shown in Table 5–2, researchers, in addition to finding that *both* kinds of commitment are important, have shown that they reflect different causes and effects of organizational commitment. For example, Allen and Meyer have found that whereas affective commitment was associated with work experiences that make people feel competent, continuance commitment was associated with concern about losing one's job benefits.[63] Overall, many variables have been found to be associated with one norm of commitment or another—either as its causes or its consequences. We will now turn to the task of summarizing some of the major causes and effects of organizational commitment.

Factors Influencing Organizational Commitment

As our discussion thus far has suggested, many possible determinants of organizational commitment exist. We will review these now.

Research has shown that organizational commitment is affected by various *job characteristics*.[64] For example, it has been found that commitment tends to be greater when people have high levels of responsibility over the jobs they perform, and lower when people suffer limited opportunities for promotion. Organizational commitment

TABLE 5–2 Organizational Commitment: How Is It Measured?

Questionnaire items similar to those shown here are used to measure the two major aspects of organizational commitment—*continuance commitment* and *affective commitment*. The more strongly people endorse each item, the more strongly they are expressing the type of commitment associated with it.

Continuance Commitment Items	Affective Commitment Items
1. At this point, I stay in my job because I have to more than because I want to.	1. I feel I strongly belong to my organization.
2. Leaving my job would entail a lot of personal sacrifice.	2. I feel I am emotionally connected to the organization in which I work.
3. I don't have any other choice but to stay in my present job.	3. I feel like I'm a part of the family at my organization.
4. Too much of my life would be disrupted if I left my present job.	4. I'd be very pleased to spend the rest of my life working for this organization.

Source: Based on items from McGee & Ford, 1987; see Note 62.

Test Bank questions 5.40–5.42, 5.53, and 5.63–5.64 relate to material on this page.

also tends to be higher among those who believe that their jobs possess high amounts of those enriching characteristics associated with high levels of motivation (i.e., the "motivation potential score" discussed in chapter 4).[65] Jobs having these characteristics are likely to strengthen workers' feelings of attachment to them.

Second, organizational commitment is affected by the existence of *alternative employment opportunities*. As you might expect, the greater the perceived chances of finding another job, the lower an individual's commitment (particularly continuance commitment) tends to be.[66]

Various *personal characteristics* also influence organizational commitment. For example, workers who are older and more experienced in their jobs tend to be more committed to those jobs than those who are less experienced. (This makes sense according to the side-bets approach because more senior people may have more invested in their jobs than newer employees.) Interestingly, for many years it was also found that women tend to be less committed to their jobs than men. This makes sense insofar as the less involving, lower-level jobs that women were often required to perform were unlikely to trigger any especially strong attraction to the job. As time has passed, however, women have become more likely to work in higher-level, more gratifying jobs. As this trend has unfolded, gender differences in organizational commitment have disappeared.[67]

Finally, perceptions of commitment are likely to be related to an organization's *treatment of newcomers*. As we will describe in detail in chapter 9, organizations can do various things to help new employees learn the ropes and become productive members of their organizations. Such treatment also influences organizational commitment. For example, a study by Caldwell, Chatman, and O'Reilly has found that organizational commitment was influenced by the organizations' use of rigorous recruitment methods and strong, clear organizational value systems.[68] These factors make a great deal of sense. The more an organization invests in someone by strongly trying to hire that person, the more that individual is likely to return the investment of energy by expressing feelings of commitment to the organization. Moreover, the more clearly an organization's values are expressed, the more strongly those who endorse those values may feel toward the organization (the goal congruence perspective); those who do not agree with the organization are likely to be more certain of this assessment, and to seek alternative opportunities for employment.

Organizational Commitment: Its Major Effects

The prediction that people who feel deeply committed to their organizations will behave differently at work from those who do not seems reasonable. And, despite very complex findings, considerable evidence supports this suggestion.[69] Organizational commitment appears to greatly affect several key aspects of work behavior.

First, generally speaking, studies have found that high levels of organizational commitment tend to be associated with *low levels of absenteeism and turnover*.[70] Indeed, more committed individuals are less likely to look for new jobs than less committed ones. However, this relationship is far from simple, and it may be qualified by numerous aspects of the way the research is conducted.[71]

Second, organizational commitment is associated with *high levels of willingness to share and make sacrifices*.[72] It should not be surprising that these types of organizational citizenship behaviors are related to commitment inasmuch as we can expect those who are most committed to their organizations to be those who give most generously of themselves.

Finally, organizational commitment has *positive personal consequences*. Although one might expect commitment to an organization would detract from one's personal life (based on the idea that it would be costly in terms of time and emotional invest-

Today's employees are less committed to their organizations than were those of past generations. Twenty years ago an employee who had less than five years of tenure with an organization was considered disloyal and unreliable (short tenure "looked bad"). Today, however, it is not uncommon, and much better accepted, for people to change jobs much more frequently—even every two to three years. Such "job hopping" is the result of people attempting to find more advanced positions as they become experienced, but find limited opportunities for advancement in their present jobs. In addition, as more and more companies fail, mass layoffs occur, causing people to seek new jobs—perhaps sooner than they had desired. [McKenna, J. F. (1990, May 7). The bounties of the mutiny. *Industry Week*, pp. 11–13.]

ment), recent research by Romzek suggests otherwise.[73] Her survey of public employees' work attitudes suggests that those who were most strongly attached to their organizations tended to enjoy highly successful careers and pleasant nonwork lives.

Taking all these findings into account, steps designed to generate high levels of organizational commitment among employees seem well worthwhile. A committed work force, it appears, is indeed a stable and productive one. This is not to suggest that organizational commitment cannot have potential costs, however. While highly committed employees may work hard and remain on the job, they may also be resistant to change. Such people may be strongly committed to existing ways of handling various tasks, and to existing organizational culture. This commitment may prove costly in the face of shifting conditions that dictate the need for major change. Still, high levels of organizational commitment are often beneficial and should be fostered in most situations. (For an excellent example of what one major company is doing to promote organizational commitment among its employees, see the **OB in Practice** section on pp. 178–179.)

PREJUDICE: NEGATIVE ATTITUDES TOWARD OTHERS

Most people would agree that the warning "Don't jump to conclusions" is good advice. Yet, where reactions to other people are concerned, this advice is often ignored. Individuals often *do* jump to conclusions about others. They often base important judgments about the people they meet on their ethnic background, race, gender, or age. Even worse, such judgments are usually negative in nature. People assume that another person possesses undesirable traits simply because he or she fits within a specific social category. These reactions are termed **prejudice.** More precisely, prejudice can be defined as *negative attitudes toward the members of specific groups based solely on their membership in those groups.*[74] As this definition implies, people are often quick to jump to conclusions about what others are like, and they do so on the basis of limited information (see Figure 5–12).

Prejudicial attitudes are potentially problematic because they predispose people toward behaving in ways consistent with these attitudes. For example, someone who does not like members of a certain minority group might be expected to treat such

"At least on paper, you're pretty impressive."

FIGURE 5–12

Jumping to Conclusions about Others: A Potential Source of Prejudice

Prejudices are formed on the basis of limited information about others—information that is often untrue or incomplete. (*Source:* Drawing by Koren; © 1991 The New Yorker Magazine, Inc.)

Test Bank questions 5.44 and 5.65 relate to material on this page.

people in a manner than reflects those negative feelings. Such actions are referred to as *discriminatory acts* (or simply *discrimination*) because they treat different people in different ways. The key thing to keep in mind is this: prejudice is a negative attitude, and discrimination is the behavior that follows from it (the behavioral expression of that attitude).

Prejudice: Its Role in Organizations

Prejudice has serious implications for society as a whole. Indeed, recent decades have been marked by vigorous efforts in many nations to eliminate the harmful effects of such attitudes. In addition, prejudice can, and does, play a role in organizations and organizational behavior. First, where such reactions exist, they may be the cause of friction or conflict. If specific people hold negative attitudes toward others simply because of differences in their personal background, training, or professional identification, they may have difficulty working together. This can have truly devastating effects on cooperation and efficiency.

Second, prejudice may have adverse effects on the careers of people who are the target of such attitudes. These individuals may encounter various forms of discrim-

 OB IN PRACTICE

Organizational Commitment in the Magic Kingdom

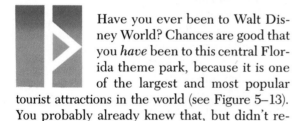 Have you ever been to Walt Disney World? Chances are good that you *have* been to this central Florida theme park, because it is one of the largest and most popular tourist attractions in the world (see Figure 5–13). You probably already knew that, but didn't realize the scope of it. "The Magic Kingdom," as it is called, employs over 25,000 people in 1,100 different jobs, serves more than 25 million customers a year, and takes in about $1 billion annually.[75] Given the gigantic scale of this operation, it is particularly impressive that the company is well known for its highly satisfied

FIGURE 5–13

Walt Disney World: The Magic Kingdom Is a Magical Place to Work

Central Florida's Walt Disney World is one of the most successful tourist attractions in the world and one of the best places to work in the United States. This is in large part because of the company's successful efforts at promoting organizational commitment.

ination—some overt, some quite subtle—with respect to hiring, promotion, pay, and appraisal of their work. Third, organizations themselves may suffer greatly from such practices. If talented individuals are overlooked or passed over simply because of their membership in certain groups, the organizations involved may suffer a loss of precious human resources—a loss few can afford.

Most research on the impact of prejudice in work settings has focused on *racism*, prejudice based on race, and *sexism*, prejudice based on gender.[76] But other forms of prejudice are also relevant to OB. For example, prejudice based on *age* is all too common. Laws in the United States and elsewhere have done much to counter the negative impact of such attitudes on older employees, but such reactions continue to exist in more subtle forms. For example, within a given organization, there are often clear beliefs about the appropriate age range for individuals occupying various positions. Thus, it may be implicitly assumed that first-line managers should be in their late twenties or early thirties, department heads should be in their mid-thirties to mid-forties, and vice presidents should be at least forty.[77] Given such beliefs, individuals who attain a given position sooner than expected may benefit from an age-related halo, whereas those who attain it later than anticipated, or who remain in a position longer than expected, may be evaluated negatively.

and committed work force. In fact, the company has been identified as one of the best ones to work for in the United States.[78]

What does the company do to promote these positive attitudes? It begins at the hiring stage. As part of the orientation process, new Disney employees are given extensive training about the operation of the park and its traditions. (We will have more to say about new-employee socialization in chapter 9.) They are made to feel excited about what they'll be doing and are thoroughly briefed on the company's philosophy and way of doing things. For example, employees are considered "cast members" because they are all playing a part in a continuous show for their "Guests" (with a capital G)—*not* customers. The concern for promoting employee commitment doesn't end with a formal training session, but is incorporated into the day-to-day interaction between managers and cast members. Specifically, management is encouraged to treat all employees in a way that (1) shares company goals and information, (2) reinforces Disney values and traditions, and (3) creates a legacy for the employees. In the words of Doug Cody, a senior manager, "Relevant information in an effective medium on a timely basis gives employees pride, morale, and a sense of belonging."[79]

As you might imagine, the company does still more to make its employees feel strongly committed to it. For example, 60 to 80 percent of higher-level positions at Disney World are filled from within, thereby giving employees good hope for advancement (and strengthening their commitment to the company). The company also gives employees responsibility over Guest relations, safety, and the like. Because responsibility for these key functions is shared, employees are more committed to succeeding at them (recall our discussion of goal setting in chapter 4). In addition, employees are rewarded for their contributions with awards such as "Cast Member of the Month" (or "Quarter" or "Year"). Through the company's "I Have an Idea" program, a very large award—$10,000—is given to the employee who submits the best original idea to management for improving park operations.

To make sure that its efforts at promoting organizational commitment are on target, the company regularly surveys all its cast members (using formal open-ended and multiple-choice questionnaires) and conducts small group interviews with them. Even those who leave the company (as is inevitable, despite high levels of commitment) are interviewed to find out how they felt about working there. Information collected from these sources is used to spot problems and improve the attitudes of future employees. Given how well Walt Disney World seems to be doing, such efforts are clearly very effective. It's obviously the sound application of organizational behavior principles, and not fairy dust, that makes the Magical Kingdom such a magical place to work!

Many other forms of prejudice exist as well. As we noted in chapter 2, individuals in various departments or occupational groups often perceive people in other departments or occupations as "all alike," mainly in negative ways. ("You know how engineers are!" "All those design people are a little flaky.") All of these reactions are worthy of attention, but the form of prejudice that has received the most attention in OB in recent years is sexism. Prejudice based on gender continues to be the focus of legislative, political, and research interest.

Sexism: Prejudice Based on Gender

Change—and at an increasingly rapid pace—was certainly the slogan of the 1970s and 1980s. Organizations have been no exception to this trend, and they, too, have altered in many ways. One of the most dramatic shifts they have experienced involves the entry (or reentry) into the work force of vast numbers of women. A large majority of adult females now work full-time in the United States and other Western nations. And they do not occupy only relatively low level jobs: growing numbers have moved into responsible managerial positions. Currently, more than 30 percent of managers in the United States are females, compared to less than 10 percent twenty years ago. Despite such change, however, disparities in average salary remain, and as Steinberg and Shapiro have noted, "Women populate corporations but they rarely run them."[80] They are not, as yet, fully represented in higher managerial ranks. Why is this the case? Given the existence of legislation banning discrimination based on gender, this factor no longer seems central. Another possibility is that sufficient time has not yet passed for women to move into senior management–level positions. To some extent, this is probably true: overt barriers against female advancement have disappeared (or at least decreased) only quite recently. Careful research on this question, however, also points to other potential causes—subtle, but often powerful, forces that continue to operate against women in many work settings.

The Role of Sex Role Stereotypes Once such force involves the persistence of traditional views about the characteristics supposedly possessed by men and women. Such views (often known as *sex role stereotypes*) suggest that males tend to be aggressive, forceful, persistent, and decisive, whereas females tend to be passive, submissive, dependent, and emotional. Growing evidence indicates that such differences are largely false: males and females do not differ as consistently or to as large a degree in these ways as sex role stereotypes suggest.[81] Yet, such beliefs persist, and continue to play a role in organizational settings. One reason for this is that the traits attributed to males by these stereotypes seem consistent with managerial success, whereas the traits attributed to females seem inconsistent with such success.[82] The result: females are *perceived* as being less suited for managerial positions, even when they possess the appropriate credentials for them.

Evidence for the operation of such sex role stereotypes has been obtained by Heilman and her colleagues in a series of related studies.[83] These experiments repeatedly found that females are perceived as being less suited for jobs traditionally filled by males, and that any characteristics that serve to emphasize or activate female sex role stereotypes tend to intensify such negative effects. For example, females who are physically attractive are perceived as being more feminine and therefore less suited for managerial roles than females who are less physically attractive. Interestingly, the impact of sex role stereotypes can be countered if clear evidence for a woman's ability or competence is provided. In such cases, females applying for traditionally male dominated jobs (e.g., sports photographer) actually receive *higher* ratings than males.[84] Apparently, this is so because they are perceived as a special subgroup—one that is even more competent than males for such jobs. In general,

Organizational discrimination against women is, unfortunately, alive and well—and may be seen in many ways. First, very few women in the United States hold top executive positions. In fact, in the largest U.S. corporations, only 3 out of every 100 top executives are women. This low percentage has not changed appreciably in the last ten years. [Saltzman, A. (1991, July 17). Trouble at the top. *U.S. News & World Report,* pp. 40–48.] Second, women tend to be barred from some of the country's most prestigious golf clubs, where members of the "old boy network" make some of the biggest business deals. Interestingly, although U.S. federal tax laws preclude discrimination on the basis of race or nationality (for fear of losing tax-exempt status), no such laws prevent clubs from banning female members. Such discriminatory practices create a serious barrier to success for women. [MacLean, P. A. (1991, April). Tee'd off: Women golfers learning that swinging a club can be easier than joining one. *Women's Sports & Fitness,* pp. 43–48.]

though, traditional sex role stereotypes tend to operate against success and advancement by women in work settings.

The Role of Expectations   Another factor impeding advancement by females in at least some work settings involves their expectations. In general, women seem to hold lower expectations of their careers than men. For example, among recent business graduates, females expect to receive lower starting and peak salaries than males. Several factors probably contribute to such differences (e.g., the fact that females specialize in lower-paying areas than do males; their observation that on average, females do, in fact, tend to earn less than males in most organizations). Whatever the basis, it is a general rule in life that people tend to get what they expect. Thus, the lower expectations held by females may be one factor operating against them in many instances.

The Role of Self-Confidence   Confidence is often said to be the single best predictor of success. People who expect to succeed often do; those who expect to fail find that these predictions, too, are confirmed. Unfortunately, women tend to express lower self-confidence than men in many achievement situations. Thus, the fact that they have not as yet attained full equality with men in many work settings may stem, at least in part, from this factor. Evidence suggesting that this is indeed the case has been reported by McCarty.[85]

In a laboratory study on this issue, she asked male and female students to work on tasks involving creativity. Subjects performed three such tasks (devising unique uses for ordinary objects such as a pencil or wire hanger) and received feedback about their performance on each one. Some learned that they had done very well (positive feedback), others were told that they had done quite poorly (negative feedback), and still others received no feedback whatsoever. Subjects were asked to rate their self-confidence both before working on the tasks and again after receiving feedback. As you can see from Figure 5–14, women reported lower levels of self-

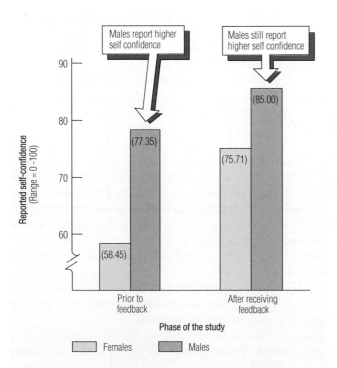

FIGURE 5–14

Feedback and Self-Confidence among Males and Females

Females reported lower self-confidence than males before receiving feedback about their performance. After receiving positive feedback, their self-confidence increased but was still lower than that of males. (Only data for the positive feedback condition are shown.) (*Source:* Based on data from McCarty, 1986; see Note 85.)

FOCUS ON RESEARCH

Physical Attractiveness and M.B.A.s' Salaries: Beauty Pays Off

Beauty, it is often said, is in the eye of the beholder. But what are the effects of being perceived as physically attractive? Are those who are perceived as attractive any more or less successful on the job than those who are less attractive? Recent research has found that people are, in fact, biased against those who are generally perceived to be unattractive.[86] This is particularly important because unlike other forms of prejudice—such as those based on gender, race, and age—unattractiveness is not protected by any legislation.

One of the most dramatic effects of the bias in favor of attractive people has been shown in a recent study by Frieze, Olson, and Russell.[87] These investigators had four raters (two of each gender) judge the attractiveness of a large group of former M.B.A. students appearing in yearbook photos (the scale ranged from 1 = very unattractive, to 5 = very attractive). Then the people pictured were contacted and asked to complete a questionnaire revealing information about their salary history.

The connection between salaries and attractiveness rating was quite strong—and very interesting. Specifically, starting salaries for men, but not for women, were found to be related to their attractiveness. In fact, men who were rated as attractive (4 and above) had starting salaries

of $2,200 more than those believed to be unattractive (2 and under). As time went on, these differences became even greater! Both attractive men and women currently (in 1983) had higher salaries than their unattractive counterparts (see Figure 5–15). For men, each rating scale unit of attractiveness was found to be worth $2,600 per year (thus, those rated 2 received about $5,200 per year less than those rated 4). For women, the relationship was identical, although the figures were slightly lower—each unit was worth about $2,100 per year. Thus, women rated 2 received about $4,200 per year less than those rated 4. These findings are particularly dramatic when one takes into account that these are 1983 figures, and they represent a larger proportion of the overall salaries than they would given today's higher salaries.

These findings provide clear evidence of a bias against unattractive people (or in favor of attractive people) in the workplace. However, *why* these results occur is not clear. One possibility is that attractive people are believed to be more competent and, therefore, worth more. Attractive people also may have more self-confidence and project a more successful image of themselves. Of course, both factors may be operating, with each accounting for some degree of the observed effect.

We believe it is important to caution that al-

confidence before working on the tasks. More important, although positive feedback increased their self-confidence, it did not eliminate the difference in favor of men; women continued to report lower self-confidence throughout the study. Interestingly, men who received no feedback during the study reported self-confidence as high as that of women who had received positive feedback.

Together, these findings suggest that positive feedback about task performance may be especially important for women. Even in its absence, men express relatively high degrees of self-confidence. However, women report similar levels of confidence only when receiving encouraging feedback. This is a point managers who wish to foster advancement among women would do well to consider.

Regardless of the status of gender-based discrimination, the existence of other sources of prejudice is well established. For a closer look at another particularly

though one's attractiveness might account for one's salary to some extent, clearly other factors are involved. For example, one's experience and level of performance are critical determinants of one's salary and should not be discounted. Those seeking higher salaries would be better advised to improve their job skills rather than their appearance, because these factors are likely to be more important (except in jobs such as modeling, for which attractiveness *is* a job requirement). Still, the conclusion is clear: like gender, race, and age, physical attractiveness constitutes another source of bias in the workplace—and, one that is reflected in wage discrimination. Attractive individuals tend to enjoy a real salary advantage over unattractive ones.

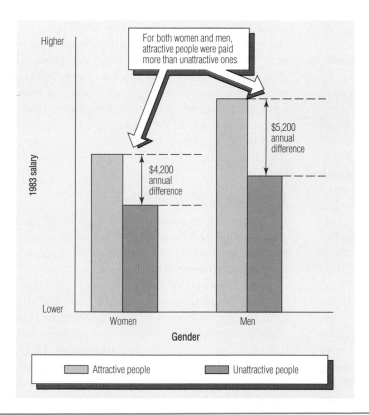

FIGURE 5–15

Physical Unattractiveness: A Co$tly Bias

Recent research shows that both attractive men and attractive women are paid higher salaries than their unattractive counterparts. (*Source:* Based on data from Frieze, Olson, & Russell, 1991; see Note 87.)

interesting type of prejudice—and potentially costly discrimination—on the job, refer to the **Focus on Research** section that begins on the preceding page.

SUMMARY AND REVIEW

The Nature of Attitudes

Attitudes are stable clusters of feelings, beliefs, and behavior tendencies directed toward some aspect of the external world. **Work-related attitudes** involve such reactions toward various aspects of work settings or the people in them. Attitudes are most likely to affect behavior when they are specific and intense, and when external factors do not block their impact.

Changing Attitudes

Efforts to change attitudes often involve **persuasion,** a process in which one individual attempts to change the attitudes of one or more others through written, spoken, or taped messages. The success of persuasion in altering attitudes depends on several characteristics of the person who delivers such messages and the content and form of the messages delivered.

When individuals discover that two attitudes they hold are inconsistent, or that their attitudes and their behavior are inconsistent, an unpleasant state of **cognitive dissonance** results. This produces pressure to alter either the attitudes or the behaviors involved.

Job Satisfaction

Job satisfaction involves positive or negative attitudes toward one's work. Such attitudes can be measured by rating scales and questionnaires such as the JDI or MSQ, or by asking individuals to describe instances relating to their work that they found especially satisfying or dissatisfying (the **critical incident procedure**).

According to Herzberg's **two-factor theory,** job satisfaction and dissatisfaction stem from different factors. Evidence for the accuracy of this theory has been mixed at best. Locke's **value theory** suggests that job satisfaction reflects the apparent match between the outcomes individuals desire from their jobs (what they *value*) and what they believe they are actually receiving.

Job satisfaction is affected by many factors relating to organizational policies and procedures, specific aspects of jobs and work settings, and personal characteristics of employees. Most people report being at least moderately satisfied with their current jobs. However, these high levels of satisfaction may be more apparent than real. Job satisfaction affects important aspects of organizational behavior, such as absenteeism and voluntary turnover. Its impact on task performance is less certain, but some evidence indicates that it may have an effect on **organizational citizenship behaviors.**

Organizational Commitment

There are two kinds of **organizational commitment.** One is **continuance commitment**—the strength of a person's tendency to continue working for an organization because he or she has to and cannot afford to do otherwise. The other is **affective commitment**—the strength of a person's tendency to continue working for an organization because he or she agrees with its goals and orientation, and desires to stay with it. Organizational commitment stems from many different factors (e.g., the level of responsibility or autonomy connected with a given job, employee ownership of the company). It affects several aspects of organizational behavior (e.g., absenteeism, turnover).

Prejudice in Work Settings

Prejudice refers to negative attitudes toward the members of specific groups. Forms of prejudice especially relevant to work settings involve those based on *age, race,* or *gender.*

Large numbers of women have entered the work force in recent decades, yet they have not attained full equality with men in terms of pay or levels of responsibility. Such differences may stem, in part, from overt discrimination against females. However, they seem to result primarily from several forces operating against women in organizations. These include *sex role stereotypes,* and lower *expectations* and *self-confidence* among women.

KEY TERMS

affective commitment: The strength of a person's desire to work for an organization because he or she agrees with it and wants to do so. (See *goal congruence orientation.*)

attitudes: Stable clusters of feelings, beliefs, and behavioral intentions toward specific aspects of the external world.

cognitive dissonance: An unpleasant state that occurs when individuals notice inconsistencies between various attitudes they hold, or between such attitudes and their behavior.

continuance commitment: The strength of a person's desire to continue working for an organization because he or she needs to do so and cannot afford to do otherwise. (See *side-bets orientation.*)

critical incident procedure: A technique for measuring job satisfaction in which employees describe incidents relating to their work that they find especially satisfying or dissatisfying.

goal congruence orientation: An approach to organizational commitment according to which the degree of agreement between an individual's personal goals and those of the organization is a determinant of organizational commitment. (See *affective commitment.*)

Job Descriptive Index (JDI): A rating scale for assessing job satisfaction. Individuals respond to this questionnaire by indicating whether various adjectives describe aspects of their work.

job satisfaction: Positive or negative attitudes held by individuals toward their jobs.

Minnesota Satisfaction Questionnaire (MSQ): A rating scale for assessing job satisfaction. Individuals completing this scale indicate the extent to which they are satisfied with various aspects of their jobs.

motivator-hygiene theory: See *two-factor theory*.

organizational citizenship behaviors: Actions by employees that contribute to the smooth functioning of their organization, but which are not part of their formal job requirements (e.g., helping others, giving advice).

organizational commitment: The extent to which an individual identifies with and is involved with his or her organization and/or is unwilling to leave it. (See *affective commitment* and *continuance commitment*.)

Pay Satisfaction Questionnaire (PSQ): A questionnaire designed to assess employees' level of satisfaction with various aspects of their pay (e.g., its overall level, raises, benefits).

persuasion: A process in which one or more individuals attempt to alter the attitudes of others.

prejudice: Negative attitudes toward the members of specific groups, based solely on the fact that they are members of those groups. Prejudice can be based on age, gender, race, and even occupation or profession.

side-bets orientation: The view of organizational commitment that focuses on the accumulated investments an individual stands to lose if he or she leaves the organization. (See *continuance commitment*.)

two-factor theory (of job satisfaction): A theory, devised by Herzberg, suggesting that satisfaction and dissatisfaction stem from different groups of variables (*motivators* and *hygienes*, respectively).

value theory (of job satisfaction): A theory, devised by Locke, suggesting that job satisfaction depends primarily on the match between the outcomes individuals value in their jobs and their perceptions about the availability of such outcomes.

work-related attitudes: Attitudes relating to any aspect of work or work settings.

QUESTIONS FOR DISCUSSION

1. How is *persuasion* used in organizations? Does using this process contribute to career success?

2. After making decisions, individuals often come up with many reasons supporting their choices. How does cognitive dissonance explain this common tendency?

3. Suppose that as a manager, you wanted to enhance job satisfaction among your subordinates. What steps might you take to accomplish this goal?

4. Most people indicate that they are reasonably satisfied with their jobs. Why? How might we go about determining whether such satisfaction is real or only apparent?

5. Voluntary withdrawal is a costly problem for many companies. What steps might be taken to reduce the incidence of this decision by valued employees?

6. In what ways can high levels of organizational commitment among employees actually lead to negative outcomes for their company?

7. Do you think we will ever reach the point at which the proportion of top executives who are female equals the proportion of females in the general population? Why or why not?

NOTES

1. Locke, E. A. (1976). The nature and causes of job satisfaction. In M. D. Dunnette (Ed.), *Handbook of industrial and organizational psychology* (pp. 1297–1350). Chicago: Rand McNally.

2. Mowday, R. T., Steers, R. M., & Porter, L. W. (1979). The measurement of organizational commitment. *Journal of Vocational Behavior, 14*, 224–247.

3. Stone, E. F., Stone, D. L., & Dipboye, R. L. (1991). Stigmas in organizations: Race, handicaps, and physical unattractiveness. In K. Kelley (Ed.), *Issues, theory and research in industrial/organizational psychology* (pp. 385–457). Amsterdam: Elsevier Science Publishers.

4. McGuire, W. J. (1985). Attitudes and attitude change. In G. Lindzey & E. Aronson (Eds.), *Handbook of social psychology* (3rd ed.) (Vol. 2, pp. 233–346). New York: Random House.

5. See Note 4.

6. Petty, R. E., & Cacioppo, J. T. (1984). *Attitudes and persuasion: Central and peripheral routes to persuasion.* New York: Springer-Verlag.

7. Miller, N., Maruyama, G., Beaber, R. J., & Valone, K. (1976). Speed of speech and persuasion. *Journal of Personality and Social Psychology, 34*, 615–624.

8. Moscovici, S. (1985). Social influence and conformity. In G. Lindzey & E. Aronson (Eds.), *Handbook of social psychology* (3rd ed., Vol. 2, pp. 347–412). New York: Random House.

9. Walster, E., & Festinger, L. (1962). The effectiveness

of "overheard" persuasive communications. *Journal of Abnormal and Social Psychology, 65,* 395–402.

10. See Note 4.

11. Wyer, R. S., & Srull, T. K. (1984). *Handbook of social cognition.* Hillsdale, NJ: Erlbaum.

12. See Note 4.

13. Festinger, L. (1957). *A theory of cognitive dissonance.* Evanston, IL: Row, Peterson.

14. See Note 6.

15. See Note 1.

16. Quinn, R. P., & Staines, G. L. (1979). *The 1977 quality of employment survey.* Ann Arbor: Institute for Social Research.

17. Weaver, C. N. (1980) Job satisfaction in the United States in the 1970s. *Journal of Applied Psychology, 65,* 364–367.

18. Levin, I., & Stokes, J. P. (1989). Dispositional approach to job satisfaction: Role of negative affectivity. *Journal of Applied Psychology, 74,* 752–758.

19. Staw, B. M., & Ross, J. (1985). Stability in the midst of change: A dispositional approach to job attitudes. *Journal of Applied Psychology, 70,* 56–77.

20. Tait, M., Padgett, M., & Baldwin, T. T. (1989). Job and life satisfaction: A reevaluation of the strength of the relationship and gender effects as a function of the date of the study. *Journal of Applied Psychology, 74,* 502–507.

21. Arvey, R. D., Bouchard, T. J., Jr., Segal, N. L., & Abraham, L. M. (1989). Job satisfaction: Environmental and genetic components. *Journal of Applied Psychology, 74,* 187–192.

22. Smith, P. C., Kendall, L. M., & Hulin, C. L. (1969). *The measurement of satisfaction in work and retirement.* Chicago: Rand McNally.

23. Weiss, D. J., Dawis, R. V., England, G. W., & Lofquist, L. H. (1967). *Manual for the Minnesota Satisfaction Questionnaire* (Minnesota Studies on Vocational Rehabilitation, Vol. 22). Minneapolis: Industrial Relations Center, Work Adjustment Project, University of Minnesota.

24. Scarpello, V., Huber, V., & Vandenberg, R. J. (1988). Compensation satisfaction: Its measurement and dimensionality. *Journal of Applied Psychology, 73,* 163–171.

25. Sutton, R. I., & Callahan, A. L. (1987). The stigma of bankruptcy: Spoiled organizational image and its management. *Academy of Management Journal, 30,* 405–436.

26. Herzberg, E. (1966). *Work and the nature of man.* Cleveland: World.

27. Herzberg, E. (1964). The motivation-hygiene concept and problems of manpower. *Personnel Administrator, 27,* 3–7.

28. Machungawa, P. D., & Schmitt, N. (1983). Work motivation in a developing country. *Journal of Applied Psychology, 68,* 31–42.

29. Landy, F. J. (1985). *Psychology of work behavior* (3rd ed.). Homewood, IL: Dorsey Press.

30. See Note 1.

31. Rice, R. W., McFarlin, D. B., & Bennett, D. E. (1989). Standards of comparison and job satisfaction. *Journal of Applied Psychology, 74,* 591–598.

32. Miceli, M. P., and Lane, M. C. (1991). Antecedents of pay satisfaction: A review and extension. In K. Rowland & G. R. Ferris (Eds.), *Research in personnel and human resources management* (Vol. 9, pp. 235–309). Greenwich, CT: JAI Press.

33. Berkowitz, L., Fraser, C., Treasure, F. P., & Cochran, S. (1987). Pay equity, job gratifications, and comparisons in pay satisfaction. *Journal of Applied Psychology, 27,* 544–551.

34. Trempe, J., Rigny, A. J., & Haccoun, R. R. (1985). Subordinate satisfaction with male and female managers: Role of perceived supervisory influence. *Journal of Applied Psychology, 70,* 44–47.

35. Locke, E. A., & Schweiger, D. M. (1979). Participation in decision-making: One more look. In B. M. Staw & L. L. Cummings (Eds.), *Research in Organizational Behavior* (Vol. 1, pp. 265–339). Greenwich, CT: JAI Press.

36. Curry, J. P., Wakefield, D. S., Price, J. L., & Mueller, C. W. (1986). On the causal ordering of job satisfaction and organizational commitment. *Academy of Management Journal, 29,* 847–858.

37. Wright, P. L. (1990). Teller job satisfaction and organization commitment as they relate to career orientations. *Human Relations, 43,* 369–381.

38. Hackman, J. R., & Oldham, G. R. (1976). Motivation through the design of work: Test of a theory. *Organizational Behavior and Human Performance, 16,* 250–279.

39. Sundstrom, E. (1986). *Workplaces.* New York: Cambridge University Press.

40. See Note 1.

41. Scheier, M. F., Weintraub, J. K., & Carver, C. S. (1986). Coping with stress: Divergent strategies of optimists and pessimists. *Journal of Personality and Social Psychology, 51,* 1257–1264.

42. Andrisani, P. J., & Nestel, C. (1976). Internal-external control as a contributor to and outcome of work experience. *Journal of Applied Psychology, 61,* 156–165.

43. Near, J. P., Smith, C. A., Rice, R. W., & Hunt, R. G. (1984). A comparison of work and non-work predictors of life satisfaction. *Academy of Management Journal, 27,* 33–42.

44. Zeitz, G. (1990). Age and work satisfaction in a government agency: A situational perspective. *Human Relations, 43,* 419–438.

45. See Note 1.

46. See Note 20.

47. Porter, L. W., & Steers, R. M. (1973). Organizational work and personal factors in employee turnover and absenteeism. *Psychological Bulletin, 80,* 151–176.

48. Mowday, R. T., Koberg, C. S., & McArthur, A. W. (1984). The psychology of the withdrawal process: A cross-validational test of Mobley's intermediate linkages model

of turnover in two samples. *Academy of Management Journal, 27,* 79–94.

49. Mobley, W. H., Horner, S. O., & Hollingsworth, A. T. (1978). An evaluation of precursors of hospital employee turnover. *Journal of Applied Psychology, 63,* 408–414.

50. Carsten, J. M., & Spector, P. E. (1987). Unemployment, job satisfaction, and employee turnover: A meta-analytic test of the Muchinsky model. *Journal of Applied Psychology, 72,* 374–381.

51. Oldham, G. R., & Fried, Y. (1987). Employee reactions to workspace characteristics. *Journal of Applied Psychology, 72,* 75–80.

52. Miller, K. I., & Monge, P. R. (1986). Participation, satisfaction, and productivity: A meta-analytic review. *Academy of Management Journal, 29,* 727–753.

53. Porter, L. W., & Lawler, E. E., III (1968). *Managerial attitudes and performance.* Homewood, IL: Dorsey Press.

54. Organ, D. W. (1988). *Organizational citizenship behavior.* Lexington, MA: Lexington Books.

55. Bateman, T. S., & Organ, D. W. (1983). Job satisfaction and the good soldier: The relationships between affect and employee "citizenship." *Academy of Management Journal, 26,* 587–595.

56. Reichers, A. E. (1985). A review and reconceptualization of organizational commitment. *Academy of Management Review, 10,* 465–476.

57. Becker, H. S. (1960). Notes on the concept of commitment. *American Journal of Sociology, 66,* 32–40.

58. Porter, L. W., Steers, R. M., Mowday, R. T., & Boulian, P. V. (1974). Organizational commitment, job satisfaction, and turnover among psychiatric technicians. *Journal of Applied Psychology, 59,* 603–609.

59. Mathieu, J. E., & Zajoc, D. M. (1990). A review and meta-analysis of the antecedents, correlates, and consequences of organizational commitment. *Psychological Bulletin, 108,* 171–194.

60. Cohen, A., & Lowenberg, G. (1990). A re-examination of the side-bet theory as applied to organizational commitment: A meta-analysis. *Human Relations, 43,* 1015–1050.

61. Meyer, J. P., Allen, N. J., & Gellatly, I. R. (1990). Affective and continuance commitment to the organization: Evaluation of measures and analysis of concurrent and time-lagged relations. *Journal of Applied Psychology, 75,* 710–720.

62. McGee, G. W., & Ford, R. C. (1987). Two (or more?) dimensions of organizational commitment: Reexamination of the affective and continuance commitment scales. *Journal of Applied Psychology, 72,* 638–641.

63. Allen, N. J., & Meyer, J. P. (1990). The measurement and antecedents of affective, continuance, and normative commitment to the organization. *Journal of Occupational Psychology, 63,* 1–18.

64. See Note 36.

65. Mathiew, J. E., & Hamel, K. (1989). A causal model of the antecedents of organizational commitment among professionals and nonprofessionals. *Journal of Vocational Behavior, 34,* 299–317.

66. Caldwell, D. F., Chatman, J. A., & O'Reilly, C. A. (1990). Building organizational commitment: A multifirm study. *Journal of Occupational Psychology, 63,* 245–261.

67. Bruning, N. A., & Snyder, R. A. (1983). Sex and position as predictors of organizational commitment. *Academy of Management Journal, 26,* 485–491.

68. See Note 56.

69. Randall, D. M. (1990). The consequences of organizational commitment. Methodological investigation. *Journal of Organizational Behavior, 11,* 361–378.

70. Shore, L. M., & Martin, H. J. (1989). Job satisfaction and organizational commitment in relation to work performance and turnover intentions. *Human Relations, 42,* 625–638.

71. Huselid, M. A., & Day, N. E. (1991). Organizational commitment, job involvement, and turnover: A substantive and methodological analysis. *Journal of Applied Psychology, 76,* 380–391.

72. Randall, D. M., Fedor, D. B., & Longenecker, C. O. (1990). The behavioral expression of organizational commitment. *Journal of Vocational Behavior, 36,* 210–224.

73. Romzek, B. S. (1989). Personal consequences of employee commitment. *Academy of Management Journal, 39,* 649–661.

74. Stephan, W. G. (1985). Intergroup relations. In G. Lindzey & E. Aronson (Eds.), *Handbook of social psychology* (3rd ed.). New York: Random House.

75. Blocklyn, P. L. (1988, December). Making magic: The Disney approach to people management. *Personnel, 65,* 28–35.

76. Hess, B. B., & Feree, M. M. (Eds.). (1988). *Analyzing gender: A handbook of social science research.* Newbury Park, CA: Sage.

77. Lawrence, B. S. (1988). New wrinkles in the theory of age: Demography, norms, and performance ratings. *Academy of Management Journal, 31,* 309–337.

78. Levering, R., Moskowitz, M., & Katz, M. (1984). *The 100 best companies to work for in America.* Reading, MA: Addison-Wesley.

79. See Note 1.

80. Steinberg, R., & Shapiro, S. (1982). Sex differences in personality traits of female and male master of business administration students. *Journal of Applied Psychology, 67,* 306–310.

81. Heilman, M. E., & Martell, R. F. (1986). Exposure to successful women: Antidote to sex discrimination in applicant screening decisions? *Organizational Behavior and Human Decision Processes, 37,* 376–390.

82. Heilman, M. E., Block, C. J., Martell, R. F., & Simon, M. C. (1989). Has anything changed? Current char-

acterizations of men, women, and managers. *Journal of Applied Psychology, 74,* 935–942.

83. Heilman, M. E., Martell, R. F., & Simon, M. C. (1988). The vagaries of sex bias: Conditions regulating the undervaluation, equivaluation, and overvaluation of female job applicants. *Organizational Behavior and Human Decision Processes, 41,* 98–110.

84. Major, B., & Konar, E. (1984). An investigation of sex differences in pay expectations and their possible causes. *Academy of Management Journal, 27,* 777–792.

85. McCarty, P. A. (1986). Effects of feedback on the self-confidence of men and women. *Academy of Management Journal, 29,* 840–847.

86. Morrow, P. C. (1990). Physical attractiveness and selection decision making. *Journal of Management, 16,* 45–60.

87. Frieze, I. H., Olson, J. E., & Russell, J. (1991). Attractiveness and income for men and women in management. *Journal of Applied Social Psychology, 21,* 1039–1057.

CASE IN POINT

Attitude Is Everything at Southwest Airlines

A CNN video is available to accompany this case. Additional information can be found in the CNN Video User's Guide.

"Fun is a stimulant to people. They enjoy their work more and work more productively,"[1] says Herb Kelleher, chief executive officer at Southwest Airlines. Kelleher credits the enormous success of Southwest Airlines to the positive attitude of its employees.[2] And he works—and plays—hard to maintain that attitude.

Southwest Airlines is a relative newcomer to the airline industry. Launched in 1971 with four planes providing service to Dallas, Houston, and San Antonio, Southwest now flies 120 planes to thirty-two cities all around the country. It has a solid record of profits and, as of 1991, was the eighth-largest airline in the United States. Southwest has accomplished so much in twenty years partly because of the "work hard, play hard" attitude instilled in its employees.

Southwest offers very frequent, short-distance flights at low fares. It does this by capitalizing on operational efficiencies to stay lean. Because all of its flights are short distances, Southwest needs only one type of aircraft; its entire fleet is composed of Boeing 737s, a medium-range jet. This practice saves in maintenance, training, and parts inventory costs.

But Southwest owes most of its success to the productivity of its employees. Everyone at Southwest chips in to do whatever needs to be done. Airplanes are cleaned only once per day. Flight attendants and pilots pick up trash between flights, allowing Southwest to lead the industry in turnaround time between flights—less than fifteen minutes on 80 percent of its flights.

Southwest resists overhiring during good times so it can avoid layoffs when times are tough. Lean staffing means everyone works hard. But hard work doesn't get in the way of having a good time.

Herb Kelleher believes that good customer service depends largely on a high level of esprit de corps. Kelleher wants Southwest employees, and its customers, to have fun. "I've always felt that there's no reason that work has to be suffused with seriousness, that professionalism can be worn lightly."[3]

Kelleher goes out of his way to make sure everyone has fun. The dress code is informal and comfortable. Attendants wear shorts, casual shirts, and sneakers. On-board antics are encouraged—the zanier, the better. Passenger safety briefings are often delivered in a rap beat, and the comments from the cockpit crew often border on the outrageous. One example from a Southwest pilot: "As soon as y'all set both cheeks on your seats, we can get this ol' bird moving."[4] And Kelleher does his share of clowning around, too. Whether flying on Easter dressed up as the Easter Bunny or visiting with maintenance employees in the middle of the night dressed in drag—à la Klinger of the "M*A*S*H" television series—Kelleher loves to have fun.

Extremely selective in whom it hires, Southwest looks for people who like other people, who enjoy providing the best service possible, and who have a real zest for living. According to Kelleher, "We draft great attitudes. If you don't have a good attitude, we don't want you, no matter how skilled you are. We can change skill levels through training. We can't change attitude."[5]

Does this emphasis on hiring people with great attitudes and keeping these people happy pay off? Southwest employees and customers think so. The productivity of its employees has made Southwest the lowest-cost company in the airline industry, 15 percent lower than its next-lowest-cost competitor, American Airlines. Southwest makes more money per revenue dollar earned than any of its competitors. Customer satisfaction is very high, as is employee job satisfaction. Southwest's relationships with its employee unions are cooperative, and it has one of the lowest levels of employee turnover in the industry.

Illustrative of the high level of employee commitment to Southwest is the "Fuel from the Heart" program. When Iraq invaded Kuwait in 1990, jet fuel prices skyrocketed. Without Kelleher's knowing anything about it, one-third of Southwest's 8,600 employees volunteered a portion of their pay to buy fuel for the airline. Kelleher first learned of the program when employees presented him with a "Fuel from the Heart" banner, signed by all of the employees who had contributed.

The financial help was appreciated, but Kelleher was moved the most by the demonstration of the positive attitude that prevails at Southwest Airlines. Says Kelleher, "It indicated that the spirit of Southwest Airlines was alive."[6]

Questions for Discussion

1. Herb Kelleher attributes Southwest's performance to the attitudes of its employees. To what extent does evidence support the existence of such an attitude-behavior link? Explain your answer.
2. What factors affect employee job satisfaction at Southwest Airlines?
3. How is job satisfaction related to performance at Southwest Airlines?
4. Why is employee turnover so low at Southwest Airlines?
5. Why does Southwest Airlines enjoy such a positive relationship with its unions, when so many other airlines seem to have antagonistic relations with unions?
6. Would you like to work at Southwest Airlines? Why?

Notes

1. Chakravarty, S. N. (1991, September 16). Hit 'em hardest with the mostest. *Forbes*, p. 48.
2. Chakravarty, S. N. (1991, September 16). Hit 'em hardest with the mostest. *Forbes*, pp. 48–53.
3. See Note 2, p. 50.
4. See Note 2, p. 51.
5. See Note 2, p. 51.
6. See Note 2, p. 50.

**Getting What
You Expect:
Anticipated
Compensation of
Women and Men**

Despite efforts to eliminate differences in pay for women and men, a gender gap persists in this respect. Currently, women's average salaries are still considerably lower than men's. Many factors probably contribute to this state of affairs. Because of past sexual discrimination, women have filled many jobs—especially higher-level ones—for shorter periods than their male counterparts. Further, women have often been encouraged to enter lower-paying fields or occupations. Yet another factor that contributes to the present gender gap is that women hold lower expectations with respect to both starting and highest career salaries than men. You can demonstrate this difference for yourself by following the instructions below.

Procedure

Ask five to ten classmates of each gender to answer the following questions. (To avoid bias, it would be best to work only with individuals who have *not* yet had a course in organizational behavior.)

1. What *starting salary* do you expect to receive on your first full-time job?
2. What will be the *highest salary* you will receive during your career? (Estimate in terms of current salary levels.)
3. How long will it be (in years and months) before you receive your first *major* promotion?
4. What field or occupation do you plan to enter after graduation?

Points to Consider

After you have collected data from all respondents, add the figures for males and females separately, and compare the means (averages) on each question. In all likelihood, you will find that females report somewhat lower expectations than males. Why? One possibility is that many females plan to enter fields offering relatively lower pay. Another possibility is that these expectations simply reflect current conditions: females recognize that they actually receive lower pay, on average, than males. Can you think of other reasons for these differences in expectations? Will they disappear in the future as efforts to eliminate sexism continue?

◼ 6 ◼

PERSONALITY: INDIVIDUAL DIFFERENCES AND ORGANIZATIONAL BEHAVIOR

CHAPTER OUTLINE

Personality: Its Basic Nature
Personality and Organizational Behavior

Work-Related Aspects of Personality
The Five Robust Dimensions of Personality: A Look at the Big Picture
The Type A Behavior Pattern: Its Effects on Task Performance and Interpersonal Relations
Machiavellianism: Using Others on the Way to Success
Locus of Control: Perceived Control over One's Outcomes and Fate
Self-Monitoring: Public Image versus Private Reality
Self-Efficacy: Beliefs in One's Ability to Perform Various Tasks
Self-Esteem: The Importance of Self-Evaluations
Positive and Negative Affectivity: Stable Tendencies to Feel Good or Bad at Work

Measuring Personality: Some Basic Methods
Objective Tests: Assessing Personality through Self-Report

Projective Techniques: Ambiguous Stimuli and Personality Assessment

Special Sections

An International/Multicultural Perspective Type A's and Type B's on the Job: Evidence from Two Different Cultures

OB in Practice Dealing with Problem Employees: Managing Wild Ducks, Mavericks, and Other Unruly Types

Focus on Research Champions of Technological Innovation: Profiling the Agents of a Crucial Form of Organizational Change

A Question of Ethics Information about Personality: Is It an Appropriate Basis for Organizational Decisions?

LEARNING OBJECTIVES

After reading this chapter, you should be able to:
1. Define *personality* and explain its importance to the field of organizational behavior.
2. Identify the *five robust dimensions* of personality, and indicate how they relate to various aspects of job performance.
3. Describe the following personality characteristics and indicate their relevance to important forms of organizational behavior: *self-monitoring, Machiavellianism, locus of control, positive affectivity,* and *negative affectivity.*

4. List the major traits of *innovation champions,* people who play a key role in their organization's adoption of technological innovations.
5. Describe the characteristics of *problem employees,* including *wild ducks,* or *mavericks,* and indicate how managers can best cope with such people.
6. Explain how personality is measured, and be able to comment on the ethical issues involved in the use of such information in organizations.

So what do we do now?" Ken Borzymowski asks, shaking his head in despair. "Li's not working out, that's obvious." Li-Ching Chen, one of the rising young stars in the company, has been attempting to run a new company operation.

"Yeah, I agree," Ken's friend and coworker Donna Sassman replies. "And I can't figure it out. If I ever saw someone who looked like the right person for the job, it's Li. But now that he's out there, it's a disaster. If I have to listen to one more complaint from Joe Cachaza, I'm going to scream!"

"I know, I've been getting hit with the shock waves, too," says Ken. "But what I can't figure out is *why* he's such a bomb. On paper, he looks great: he's got all the know-how, and that project in Texas should have made this one seem like a snap."

"Well, as near as I can figure it, it's just one of those cases of 'oil and water don't mix,'" Donna concludes. "There are some real *wild ducks* working on this project, and they just don't like Li's 'do-it-by-the-book' approach. You know how he is. . . ."

"Right. When I worked with him, at least ten times a day he'd say 'First, Step 1, *then* Step 2'—but it worked; he really got things organized."

"I know, if anyone can make order out of chaos, it's Li. But somehow, that's not the right style this time around. This project is too fluid—too up in the air. What it needs, I can see now, is someone willing to take more risks."

"Hmph! If that's right, then we sent the wrong guy. Li's no gambler. He likes to be pretty certain before he makes a move." Chuckling, Ken continues, "I'll just *bet* he ruffled some feathers once he arrived."

"And what he didn't ruffle, he trimmed," adds Donna. "And you know those maverick types, they want to fly *free!*"

"Okay, okay, so hindsight wins again," Ken laments. "Now, great geniuses that we are, we can see that we made a mistake. Li's a great guy with a bright future, but this wasn't the right spot for him. But that doesn't solve our problem. I repeat: *What do we do now?*"

"Oil and water don't mix." Is that the right explanation for Li's difficulties in his new role? Is he failing in his current assignment because his personal style is somehow out of synch with that of the *wild ducks* he's been asked to manage? If that's really the case, then there's an important message in this story for the field of organizational behavior: the traits or characteristics people possess and carry around with them from situation to situation really *do* matter. Put another way, traits that equip an individual for success in one context don't necessarily guarantee success in another situation. And woe to the organization that fails to pay attention to such factors! Such individual differences—known, together, as *personality*—are the focus of this chapter. We will begin by considering the basic nature of personality, defining this term more precisely, and examining what it implies and how it may be related to important aspects of OB. Then, we will turn to several aspects of personality that have been found to be related to behavior in work settings. Finally, we will examine some of the major ways in which personality is measured. This is an important issue, for unless personality can be assessed accurately, its usefulness in predicting—and understanding—OB will be quite limited.

PERSONALITY: ITS BASIC NATURE

If our experience with other people tells us anything, it is this: they are all *unique* and, at least to a degree, they are all *consistent*. Each possesses a unique pattern of traits and characteristics not fully duplicated in any other person, and these traits or characteristics are fairly stable over time. Thus, if someone you know is dependable, friendly, optimistic, and intelligent today, that person probably showed these traits in the past and will likely continue to show them in the future.[1] Moreover, he or she will tend to show them (emphasize the word *tend*) in many different situations as well as over time. Together, these two facts form the basis for a useful working definition of **personality:** it is the unique and relatively stable pattern of behavior, thoughts, and emotions shown by individuals.[2] Personality refers to the lasting ways in which a given person is different from all others.

Do you find this definition reasonable? Probably so. Most people accept the view that human beings possess specific traits (tendencies to think and act in certain ways) and that these traits are fairly constant over time. You may be surprised to learn, therefore, that until quite recently, a heated controversy existed in the behavioral sciences over the accuracy of these beliefs.

On one side of this debate were scientists who contended that people do *not* possess lasting traits.[3] According to these researchers (whom we might term the "antipersonality" camp), behavior is shaped largely by external factors or conditions. Thus, we should not expect people to behave consistently at different times or in different settings. Indeed, our belief that they do is largely an illusion stemming from the fact that we *want* to perceive such consistency—it makes our task of predicting others' actions easier.

On the other side of the controversy were scientists who held, equally strongly, that stable traits *do* exist, and that these lead individuals to behave consistently at different times and in many settings. Which of these views has prevailed? As you can guess from the presence of this chapter, the latter one. The weight of scientific opinion has swung strongly toward the view that individual behavior *does* often stem, at least in part, from stable traits or characteristics. Several lines of evidence offer support for this conclusion.

First, in a number of recent studies, the behavior of individuals has been studied for extended periods of time (months or even years). The result: a great deal of consistency with respect to basic aspects of personality has been observed.[4]

The term *personality* is derived from the Latin word for mask. Ancient philosophers thought of personality as the mask that people wear in public. [Smith, D. R., & Williamson, L. K. (1981). *Interpersonal communication: Rules, roles, strategies, and games.* Dubuque, IA: Wm. C. Brown.] Traditionally, psychologists have believed that personality was firmly established by the age of five or six years. Today, however, it is recognized that significant life experiences (e.g., encountering a serious conflict with another, forming a close personal relationship) may contribute to changing personality throughout one's life span. [Segal, J., & Segal, Z. (1989, June). Do kids ever change? *Parents*, p. 212.]

Test Bank questions 6.1–6.2, 6.56, and 6.66 relate to material on this page.

FIGURE 6-1

Personality and Situational Constraints

Strong situational constraints may overwhelm differences in personality between individuals so that they behave in much the same manner (lower panel). When such pressures are absent, however, differences in personality may be reflected in contrasting modes of behavior (upper panel).

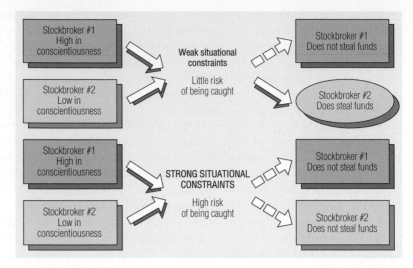

Second, other research indicates that individuals' behavior does indeed reflect their stable traits whenever this is feasible—in situations where these personal tendencies are not overwhelmed by powerful situational factors.[5] As an illustration of this point, consider the following situation. Two stockbrokers work for the same company, and both discover that by a slight change in the computer programs they are using, they can divert huge amounts of money into their own personal accounts. One stockbroker is very high in *conscientiousness*—the tendency to be responsible, be thorough, and behave ethically; the other is quite low in this dimension. Will they act in different ways? Perhaps. Imagine, first, that the funds can be transferred quickly, and that there is little risk that anyone will notice this illegal action for a long time. Under these conditions, the broker low in conscientiousness may well yield to temptation, transfer the funds—and make a rapid exit! The broker who is high in conscientiousness, however, may well resist the temptation to make a quick, but illegal, profit. Now, in contrast, imagine that transferring the funds is a relatively slow process, requiring several weeks, and that frequent audits of the company's books take place on an unpredictable schedule. Under these conditions, both brokers may refrain from enriching their own accounts. This is because powerful *situational constraints* are operating—constraints that prevent the large differences in the two brokers' personalities from being reflected in their behavior (see Figure 6–1). In sum, personality *is* important in determining individual behavior, but only in contexts where external pressures do not overwhelm such differences.

Personality and Organizational Behavior

Most people find personality an intriguing topic. They are aware that human beings differ in many ways and that these differences are important in everyday life. But how relevant is knowledge about personality and other individual differences to the field of organizational behavior? In other words, does knowing something about personality really contribute to our understanding of behavior in organizational settings and to the goals described in chapter 1: enhancing both productivity *and* the quality of working life? An ongoing, heated debate about this issue continues in OB—a debate in which some researchers have dismissed personality and other individual difference factors as unimportant, and have even described their impact as something of a mirage! However, we believe that existing evidence actually offers a convincing case for the view that such factors do, indeed, matter. In a sense, the remainder of this chapter, in which we will present evidence for the impact of various aspects of personality on key aspects of OB, provides support for this conclusion. But from a more general perspective, we can take a step back from this issue and ask the following, more basic question: does the degree of fit between individuals' personal characteristics and the demands of their jobs predict actual job performance? In other words, do people whose unique patterns of skills, experience, and traits closely match the requirements of their jobs perform better than those whose patterns do not? Evidence that they do would provide a strong argument for including individual differences within the scope of OB. In fact, several recent studies actually provide such evidence. Perhaps the clearest findings in this respect have been reported in a series of investigations carried out by Caldwell and O'Reilly.[6]

The basic approach adopted in these studies was as follows. First, individuals familiar with specific jobs were interviewed to identify the skills and characteristics necessary to perform the jobs well. Next, the lists of competencies identified were presented to other people expert in the jobs for validation. These individuals checked to make sure the items on the list were indeed required for the job, and reworded descriptions to improve their clarity. Third, individuals actually performing the jobs in question were asked to indicate how important for good job performance each of the skills and other characteristics on the list were. They did this by sorting them into nine piles, ranging from unimportant to very important. In a fourth step, another group of people holding the jobs in question were asked to indicate the extent to which each of the critical set of skills or characteristics was characteristic of themselves. In two final steps, the extent to which individuals' self-descriptions matched the profile of skills and characteristics required by their jobs was determined, and then this information was used to predict important work-related outcomes such as performance and job satisfaction (see Figure 6–2 for an overview of these procedures).

Caldwell and O'Reilly applied this basic method to a wide range of jobs and employees; their samples included production supervisors in a large consumer products company, claims adjustment supervisors in a large insurance company, managers in a large public utility, computer equipment sales managers, and secretaries at a major university. As might be expected, a wide range of different skills and characteristics were identified as being crucial for success in these jobs. For example, for managers in the public utility, characteristics such as the ability to build trust with subordinates and respond to others' ideas and suggestions nondefensively were identified as crucial. In contrast, for computer equipment sales managers, the ability

It is important to keep in mind that there are no inherently good or bad personality types for all employees. Instead, differences in individual styles make some people more or less appropriate for performing certain types of jobs. [Webb, B. (1990, June 15). Type-casting: Life with Myers-Briggs. *Library Journal*, pp. 32–37.]

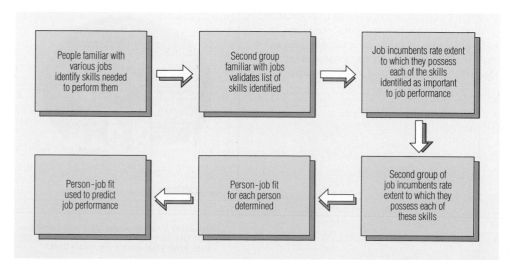

FIGURE 6–2

Investigating the Impact of Person-Job Fit on Performance

To study the impact of person-job fit on job performance, Caldwell and O'Reilly followed the steps shown here. (*Source:* Based on Caldwell & O'Reilly, 1990; see Note 6.)

to set challenging personal goals emerged as a key characteristic. Despite such differences, results were clear: in all cases, the higher the **person-job fit** (the stronger the correlation between participants' skills and characteristics and the requirements of their jobs), the better their job performance. Moreover, this was true regardless of whether performance was measured by means of performance ratings or of objective measures such as sales. In addition, the study involving secretaries found that the closer the person-job fit, the higher the job satisfaction reported by employees.

As noted by Caldwell and O'Reilly, these findings offer support for the importance of considering individual difference variables in efforts to enhance both productivity and job satisfaction. The closer the fit between individuals' personal traits and the requirements of their jobs, it appears, the better they perform and the more positive their work-related attitudes. Clearly, then, efforts to maximize the degree of person-job fit by means of careful selection and job assignments may yield substantial practical benefits in many different settings.

WORK-RELATED ASPECTS OF PERSONALITY

We trust you are now convinced—as we are—that individual differences do matter, and that searching for relationships between personality and key aspects of organizational behavior makes sense. But *what* facets of personality are most relevant? Most research has focused on this question. In this section, therefore, we will identify several traits or characteristics that have been found to have an important bearing on behavior in work settings.

The Five Robust Dimensions of Personality: A Look at the Big Picture

As suggested by Figure 6–3, individuals differ in countless ways. Indeed, in one classic study concerned with personality, it was found that fully *17,953* different words in English referred to specific traits.[7] And even when words with similar meanings were combined, a total of 171 distinct traits remained. Does this mean

FIGURE 6–3

GOOD NEWS • BAD NEWS

Personality: One OB-Relevant Dimension

Individuals differ along a seemingly limitless number of dimensions, and many of these are relevant to organizational behavior. The individual shown here, for example, has an exceptionally high need for achievement. (*Source:* © Tribune Media Services, Inc.)

"...and after the takeover you will become head of the largest company in the world, but *still* you won't be satisfied."

that efforts to relate aspects of personality to important forms of organizational be-havior must consider a huge number of separate characteristics? Fortunately, the answer appears to be "no." Sophisticated research points to the conclusion that there may be a much smaller number of key dimensions to consider. In fact, five central dimensions now appear to underlie all of the others.[8] Because these dimensions emerge so often in so many diverse research projects, they are often described as the **five robust dimensions** of personality. These dimensions can be described as follows:

1. **Extraversion/introversion.** A dimension ranging from sociable, talkative, asser-tive, and active at one end to retiring, sober, reserved, and cautious at the other.

2. **Agreeableness.** A dimension ranging from good-natured, gentle, cooperative, forgiving, and hopeful at one end to irritable, ruthless, suspicious, uncooperative, and inflexible at the other.

3. **Conscientiousness.** A dimension ranging from careful, thorough, responsible, organized, self-disciplined, and scrupulous at one end to irresponsible, disorga-nized, lacking in self-discipline, and unscrupulous at the other.

4. **Emotional stability.** A dimension ranging from anxious, depressed, angry, emo-tional, insecure, and excitable at one end to calm, enthusiastic, poised, and secure at the other.

5. **Openness to experience.** A dimension ranging from imaginative, sensitive, in-tellectual, and polished at one end to down-to-earth, insensitive, narrow, crude, and simple at the other.

That these five dimensions of personality are related to important aspects of OB is indicated by the results of a recent review of all pertinent literature carried out by Barrick and Mount.[9] These researchers examined the results of more than 200 separate studies in which one or more of the five robust dimensions were related to job performance. The studies were divided into ones that included five different occupational groups: (1) professionals (e.g., engineers, architects, attorneys, doctors, accountants), (2) police, (3) managers, (4) sales, and (5) skilled/semiskilled employees. Measures of job-related performance included job proficiency (performance ratings), training proficiency (performance during training programs), and personnel data (salary, turnover, tenure in current job). Barrick and Mount predicted that two dimensions—conscientiousness and emotional stability—would be valid predictors of job performance for all jobs and all criteria, but that extraversion and agreeableness would predict job performance only for jobs in which interpersonal factors are im-portant: sales and managerial positions. Finally, they predicted that openness to experience would be related to training proficiency.

Results offered partial support for all these hypotheses. First, conscientiousness was indeed a valid predictor of performance for all jobs and all types of measures (performance ratings, training proficiency, personnel data). However, contrary to predictions, emotional stability was not an effective predictor of performance. Sec-ond, extraversion predicted performance in managerial and sales positions; however, agreeableness was not related to job performance in these occupations. Finally, as expected, openness to experience did predict training proficiency.

Why did emotional stability fail to predict job performance? Perhaps, Barrick and Mount argue, because only individuals who are fairly high on this measure retain their jobs; thus, there is a restricted range on this variable among employed people. Similarly, agreeableness may have failed to predict job performance because most work settings require at least a minimum level of cooperativeness and flexibility. Again, the range on this dimension may be quite limited, thus attenuating its use-fulness as a predictor of job performance.

In general, introverts learn more efficiently and per-form monotonous tasks more efficiently than extro-verts. This happens mostly because introverts demand less external stimulation (and therefore are less likely to be dis-tracted by others) than ex-troverts (who are more likely to seek attention from the people around them). To compensate for this, managers may help extroverts learn by provid-ing them with highly stim-ulating projects. [Benton, D. (1989). Does the body control the mind? In J. G. Beaumont (Ed.), *Brain power: Unlock the power of your mind* (pp. 186–193). New York: Harper & Row.]

Although the findings of this research are not conclusive, they do indicate that across hundreds of studies conducted with people holding a wide range of jobs, several of the robust dimensions of personality are indeed closely linked to performance. Thus, with further refinement, measures of where individuals stand on these dimensions may prove useful in helping to predict their ultimate success in specific employment settings.

The Type A Behavior Pattern: Its Effects on Task Performance and Interpersonal Relations

Think about all the people you know. Can you name one who always seems to be in a hurry, is extremely competitive, and is often irritable? Now, in contrast, try to name one who shows the opposite pattern—someone who is relaxed, not very competitive, and easygoing in relations with others. The persons you now have in mind represent extremes on one key dimension of personality. The first individual would be labeled **Type A,** and the second would be labeled **Type B.**[10] People classified as Type A show high levels of competitiveness, irritability, and time urgency (they are always in a hurry). In addition, they demonstrate certain stylistic patterns, such as loud and accelerated speech, and a tendency to respond very quickly in many contexts (e.g., during conversations they often begin speaking before others are through). People classified as Type B show an opposite pattern. Individuals are classified as Type A or Type B on the basis of their responses to the Jenkins Activity Survey, a personality test designed to measure these patterns, or on the basis of their reactions during a special type of structured interview.

As you can probably guess, the differences between Type A and Type B individuals have important implications for their behavior in work settings. The most central of these involve differences in their personal health, their performance on many tasks, and their relations with others. Because we will consider the impact of the Type A behavior pattern on health—especially on reactions to stress—in detail in chapter 7, we will focus on the remaining two issues here.

The Type A Pattern and Task Performance   Given their high level of competitiveness, it seems reasonable to expect that Type A's will work harder at various tasks than other people, and will perform at higher levels. In fact, however, the situation turns out to be more complex than this. On the one hand, Type A's *do* tend to work faster on many tasks than Type B's, even when no pressure or deadline is involved. Similarly, they are able to get more done in the presence of distractions.[11] And Type A's often seek more challenge in their work and daily lives than type B's. For example, when given a choice, they select more difficult tasks than Type B's.[12]

Surprisingly, though, Type A's do not *always* perform better than Type B's. For example, Type A's frequently do poorly on tasks requiring patience or careful, considered judgment. They are simply in too much of a hurry to complete such work in an effective manner. More important, surveys reveal that most members of *top* management are Type B, not Type A. Several factors probably contribute to this pattern. First, it is possible that Type A's simply don't last long enough to rise to the highest management levels—the health risks noted above tend to remove them from contention at a relatively early age! Second, the impatient, always-in-a-hurry style of Type A's is generally incompatible with the decision-making role of top-level executives. Finally, the impatient, hostile style of Type A's may irritate the people around them—a factor that can adversely affect their chances for promotion.

In sum, available evidence suggests that Type A's tend to do better than Type B's on some tasks—especially ones involving time pressure or solitary work. However, they may actually do *worse* than Type B's on tasks involving complex judgment, accuracy rather than speed, and working as part of a team. Thus, neither pattern appears to have an overall edge. Rather, the nature of the tasks being performed will usually determine whether Type A's or Type B's tend to excel. (Is the Type A–Type B dimension relevant to task performance in various cultures, or is its impact restricted to Western nations such as the United States? For evidence on this issue, see the **International/Multicultural Perspective** section on pp. 200–201.)

The Type A Pattern and Interpersonal Relations   In addition to differences in personal health and task performance, Type A and Type B individuals also demonstrate contrasting styles of interpersonal behavior. First, because they are always in a hurry, Type A's tend to become impatient with other people, and frequently grow angry if someone delays them in any way. Second, when given a choice, Type A's prefer to work by themselves rather than with others. They are definitely loners— not team players. Third, Type A's are more irritable and aggressive than Type B's. They lose their tempers more frequently, and are more likely to lash out at others for even slight provocations.[13] As a result of these tendencies, Type A's report becoming involved in more conflicts at work than Type B's. In one recent study on this issue, Baron asked managers at a large food-processing company to indicate the frequency with which they experience conflict with subordinates, peers, and supervisors.[14] As you can see from Figure 6–4, those classified as Type A reported a significantly higher frequency of conflict than those classified as Type B or those who did not fall clearly into one or the other of these two groups. In sum, several characteristics of Type A's seem to get them into more than their share of interpersonal difficulties at work.

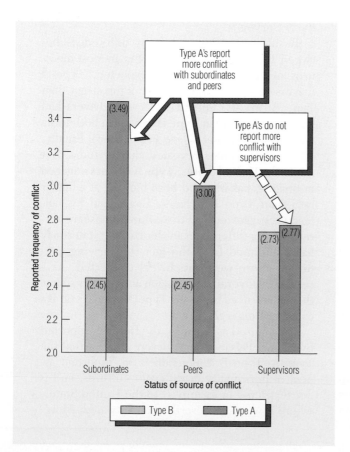

FIGURE 6–4

Conflict and the Type A Behavior Pattern

Type A managers reported a higher incidence of conflict with peers and subordinates than did Type B managers. However, they did not report a higher incidence of conflict with supervisors than did Type B managers. (*Source:* Based on data from Baron, 1989; see Note 14.)

Machiavellianism: Using Others on the Way to Success

In 1513 the Italian philosopher Niccolo Machiavelli published a book entitled *The Prince.* In it, he outlined a ruthless strategy, now known as **Machiavellianism,** for seizing and holding political power. The main thrust of his approach was simple: other people can be readily used or manipulated by sticking to a few basic rules. Among the guiding principles he recommended were the following: (1) never show humility—arrogance is far more effective when dealing with others; (2) morality and ethics are for the weak—powerful people feel free to lie, cheat, and deceive whenever this suits their purpose; and (3) it is much better to be feared than loved. In general, Machiavelli urged those who desired power to adopt a totally pragmatic approach to life. Let others be swayed by considerations of friendship, loyalty, or fair play, he suggested; a truly successful leader should always be above such factors. In short, he or she should be willing to do *whatever it takes to get his or her way.*

That the ideas Machiavelli proposed are still very much with us is clear—and unsettling. In fact, they are readily visible in many books that have made their way onto the best-seller lists in recent years—books that describe similar self-centered

AN INTERNATIONAL/MULTICULTURAL PERSPECTIVE

Type A's and Type B's on the Job:
Evidence from Two Different Cultures

Do people classified as Type A or Type B behave in similar ways around the world? And are such differences visible in their on-the-job behavior? Evidence reported by Evans, Palsane, and Carrere suggests that the answer to both questions is "yes."[15] These researchers studied the performance of urban bus drivers in two sharply contrasting cultures—the United States and India. They chose this particular occupation because it is known to be quite stressful, and they reasoned that differences between Type A's and Type B's would be readily visible in this context.

To compare the Type A and Type B drivers, Evans and his associates examined three sources of data. First, they asked drivers in both categories (Type A's and Type B's) to rate the stressfulness of their work on a specific day. Second, they obtained records of each driver's prior accidents, absences, and official reprimands. Finally, they asked trained raters to ride on the drivers' buses and record the frequency with which they blew their horns, passed other vehicles, and stepped on their brakes. (The drivers were classified as being Type A or Type B on

the basis of their responses to the Jenkins Activity Survey.)

Results revealed consistent differences between Type A and Type B drivers on most measures in both countries. As expected, Type A drivers reported higher levels of job stress than Type B drivers. Similarly, Type A drivers had more accidents than Type B drivers in both India and the United States (see Figure 6–5). Finally, direct observations revealed that in India, but not in the United States, Type A drivers engaged in braking, passing, and horn-blowing at a higher rate than Type B drivers. Evans and his colleagues suggested that the failure to observe corresponding differences in the United States may have stemmed from the fact that driving conditions there were much less congested. As a result, the overall rate of such actions was so low that differences between Type A's and Type B's could not emerge.

Considered as a whole, the findings reported by Evans, Palsane, and Carrere suggest that the Type A–Type B dimension is an important aspect of personality in different cultures, and is not restricted in its impact to the United States, where it was first described and studied. More-

strategies for gaining power and success. The popularity of such books suggests that people are as fascinated today by the tactics Machiavelli described as they were more than four centuries ago. But are these strategies really put to actual use? Are there individuals who choose to live by the ruthless, self-serving creed Machiavelli proposed? The answer appears to be "yes." When large numbers of people complete a test designed to measure acceptance of Machiavelli's suggestions (the *Mach scale*), many receive very high scores.[16] Thus, people with a Machiavellian orientation (often called *High Machs*) are quite common. Indeed, you are almost certain to encounter them during your own career. Since this is so, it is useful to know two things about them: (1) how they operate—how, precisely, they manage to manipulate others for their own gain; and (2) how you can defend yourself against them.

High Machs: Their Preferred Strategies   Influence, as noted in chapter 11, is a central fact of life in modern organizations. Many people direct a great deal of time and effort to persuading others to accept their views or recommendations. Yet few are as effective in accomplishing this task as High Machs. What accounts for their success in this respect? Several factors seem to play a role. First, High Machs follow

over, their results indicate that this aspect of personality can affect several forms of on-the-job behavior. In view of this evidence, the Type A–Type B dimension clearly has important implications both for organizations and for the field of organizational behavior.

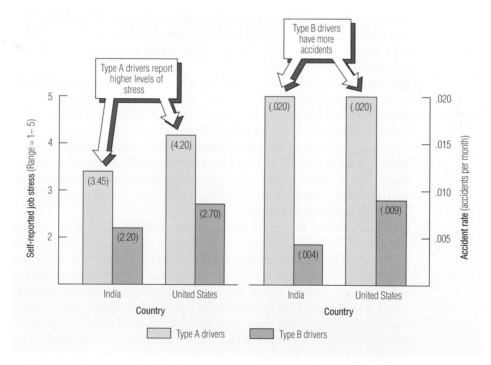

FIGURE 6–5   Type A Behavior and Job Performance in Two Cultures

Type A bus drivers reported higher levels of job stress and became involved in more accidents than Type B bus drivers. This was true in both the United States and India. (*Source:* Based on data from Evans, Palsane, & Carrere, 1987; see Note 15.)

Machiavelli's advice about being *pragmatic*. As far as they are concerned, any means is justified so long as it helps them toward their goals. Thus, they are perfectly willing to lie, cheat, play "dirty tricks," or engage in virtually any actions that succeed. Second, High Machs often possess characteristics associated with successful persuasion, including confidence, eloquence, and competence. These traits, combined with their pure pragmatism, can be quite devastating. Third, High Machs are often very adept at choosing situations in which their preferred tactics are most likely to work. Such situations include those in which they can interact with the persons they intend to manipulate face-to-face, in which there are few clear rules, and in which others' emotions are running high. Since High Machs never let their "hearts rule their heads," they can take full advantage of the fact that others' emotions make them especially vulnerable to manipulation.[17] Finally, High Machs are skilled at various political maneuvers, such as forming coalitions with others. And as you might expect, in these coalitions, most of the advantages are theirs.

High Machs: How to Protect Yourself against Them   Given their lack of concern for the welfare of other people, and their seeming lack of conscience, High Machs are wily adversaries indeed. Yet, there *are* strategies for protecting yourself against them. Here are several that may prove useful.

- **Expose them to others.** One reason High Machs often get away with breaking promises, lying, and using "dirty tricks" is that in many cases, their victims choose to remain silent. This is hardly surprising; few people wish to call attention to the fact that they have been cheated or manipulated. Unfortunately, this understandable desire to protect one's ego plays directly into the High Machs' hands, leaving them free to repeat the process. One effective means of dealing with them involves exposing their unprincipled behavior. Once their actions are made public within an organization, High Machs may find it much harder to use their manipulative tactics on future occasions.

- **Pay attention to what others do, not what they say.** High Machs are often masters at deception. They frequently succeed in convincing other people that they have their best interests at heart, just when they (the High Machs) are busy cutting the ground out from under them. Although it is often difficult to see through such maneuvers, focusing on what others *do* rather than on what they *say* may help. If their actions suggest that they are cold-bloodedly manipulating the people around them, even while loudly proclaiming commitment to such principles as loyalty and fair play, chances are good that they are Machiavellian in orientation and should be carefully avoided.

- **Avoid situations that give High Machs an edge.** To assure their success, High Machs prefer to operate in certain types of situations—ones in which others' emotions run high and in which others are uncertain about how to proceed. The reason for this preference is simple: High Machs realize that under such conditions, many people will be distracted and less likely to recognize the fact that they are being manipulated for someone else's gain. It is usually wise, therefore, to avoid such situations. And if this is not possible, at least refrain from making important decisions or commitments at that time. Such restraint may make it harder for High Machs to use you for their own benefit.

Together, these points may help you avoid falling under the spell—and into the clutches—of unprincipled, pragmatic High Machs. Given the presence of at least some High Machs in most organizations, and the dangers they pose to the unwary, it is worth keeping these suggestions, and the existence of this unsettling aspect of personality, firmly in mind.

Test Bank questions 6.15–6.16 and 6.18 relate to material on this page.

Locus of Control: Perceived Control over One's Outcomes and Fate

Before going any further, answer the questions in Table 6–1. How did you respond to these items? If you chose (a) for most, you probably believe that there is a direct link between your own actions and the kind of outcomes you experience. You feel that, by and large, you can influence your own fate: what you do in most situations really matters. If, instead, you selected (b) for most items, you probably feel that there is a weaker or less direct relationship between your own actions and the outcomes you obtain. You believe that forces beyond your direct control (e.g., luck, fate, others' actions) often have strong effects on your life.[18]

The items in Table 6–1 are similar to ones on a test designed to measure this dimension—generally known as **locus of control**.[19] At one extreme are *Internals*, people who believe that their outcomes stem mainly from their own actions. At the other are *Externals*, individuals who believe that much of what happens to them is the result of external causes beyond their direct control. As you can probably guess, most people fall somewhere in between, and are neither very high nor very low on this characteristic.

Locus of control is related to several important aspects of organizational behavior. First, and perhaps most important, the stronger individuals' beliefs in internal control, the stronger their tendencies to perceive direct links between their effort and their performance, and their performance and various rewards.[20] As we noted in chapter 4, such expectancies often play a key role in motivation, so differences with respect to locus of control can be reflected in differences in work motivation and task performance. Perhaps as a result of these tendencies, Internals tend to be more successful in their careers than Externals. They hold higher-level jobs, are promoted more quickly, and earn more money.[21] In addition, Internals report higher satisfaction with their jobs and seem to cope better with high levels of stress than Externals.[22] Taking all these findings into account, it seems clear that from the point of view of organizations, Internals often make better employees than Externals. Thus, this may be one factor worth considering when making decisions relating to hiring or promotion.

TABLE 6–1   Measuring Locus of Control

The items shown here are similar to ones appearing on an inventory designed to measure one important aspect of personality—*locus of control*.

For each item below, indicate whether you feel that choice (a) or choice (b) is closer to your own beliefs.

1. (a) I am the master of my fate.
   (b) A great deal of what happens to me is probably a matter of choice.

2. (a) Promotions are earned through hard work and persistence.
   (b) Making a lot of money is largely a matter of getting the right breaks.

3. (a) People like me can change the course of world affairs if we make ourselves heard.
   (b) It is only wishful thinking to believe that we can really influence what happens in society at large.

4. (a) In my experience, I have noticed that there is usually a direct connection between how hard I study and the grades I get.
   (b) Many times the reactions of professors seem haphazard to me.

5. (a) Getting along with people is a skill that must be practiced.
   (b) It is almost impossible to figure out how to please some people.

Test Bank questions 6.20–6.25, 6.50, 6.60, and 6.70 relate to material on this page.

One final point: locus of control, like many other personality characteristics or dimensions, is definitely open to change. When individuals find themselves in situations where good performance is both recognized and rewarded, even those initially holding strong beliefs in external locus of control tend to shift toward a more internal orientation. This is one more reason why careful attention to establishing effective reward systems is important for all organizations and managers.

Self-Monitoring: Public Image versus Private Reality

Consider the following question: to what extent do you behave differently with different groups of people or in different situations? Answering may be difficult, for most individuals do adjust their behavior in this respect to some degree. For example, most behave somewhat differently when interacting with subordinates from when interacting with their bosses. Yet, considerable individual differences in this tendency also seem to exist. At one extreme are people who readily adjust their own behavior so as to produce positive reactions in others. They are known as *high self-monitors*, and their actions are usually guided by the requirements of a given situation. As high self-monitors themselves report, they are indeed "different with different persons and in different situations."[23] At the other end of this dimension of **self-monitoring** are people who seem less aware of or concerned with their impact on others. Their actions usually reflect their inner feelings and attitudes, and they are less likely to change or adjust in each new context.

At this point, we should note that self-monitoring actually involves three major, and somewhat distinct, tendencies. One is the willingness to be the center of attention—a tendency to behave in outgoing, extraverted ways. (This is closely related to the social skill of emotional expressiveness.) A second tendency reflects individuals' sensitivity to the reactions of others. Finally, a third involves individuals' ability (and willingness) to adjust their behavior so as to induce positive reactions in others.

Whatever the precise components or skills involved in self-monitoring, individual differences along this dimension (which can be measured by any of several tests) are related to important aspects of organizational behavior. First, high self-monitors are often more effective than low self-monitors in jobs that require *boundary spanning*—communicating and interacting with different groups of people who, because of contrasting goals, training, or skills, "speak different languages."[24] Since they can readily adjust their actions to the norms, expectations, and styles of each group, high self-monitors are more successful in dealing with them, and this improves their performance. Boundary-spanning roles are very important in most organizations, so assigning people high in self-monitoring to such positions can yield substantial benefits.

Second, self-monitoring appears to be related to performance in other tasks or roles, especially ones requiring clear communication. In one recent study concerned with this relationship, Larkin asked college students to think of the best or worst instructor they had ever had.[25] When they rated these individuals in terms of self-monitoring, clear differences emerged: the best teachers were rated much higher (see Figure 6–6). In a follow-up study, Larkin asked participants to imagine that they were going to tutor two students, one very tense and nervous, and the other overconfident. Subjects then rated the extent to which they felt they could change their teaching style to fit the needs of each individual. As predicted, people who were high in self-monitoring reported greater flexibility than those who were low in self-monitoring (see Figure 6–6).

Test Bank questions 6.26–6.28, 6.30–6.31, 6.51, 6.61, and 6.71 relate to material on this page.

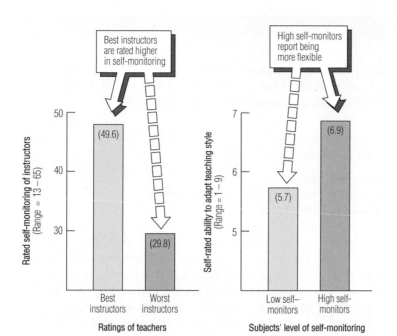

FIGURE 6-6

Self-Monitoring and Teaching Excellence

College students rated their best instructors as higher in self-monitoring than their worst instructors. In addition, students high in self-monitoring reported greater flexibility than students low in self-monitoring in their own teaching styles while serving as tutors. (*Source:* Based on data from Larkin, 1987; see Note 25.)

Third, self-monitoring appears to be related to the use of several different techniques of *impression management* (recall our discussion of this topic in chapter 2).[26] In particular, recent findings reported by Fandt and Ferris indicate that high self-monitors are more likely than low self-monitors to try to create a favorable impression on their managers through manipulation or "filtering" of the information they transmit upward.[27] As noted in chapter 2, Fandt and Ferris asked customer service employees in a telecommunications corporation to make decisions concerning realistic customer service problems (e.g., power failures on a hot summer afternoon). Participants decided how to proceed in these situations and then wrote a brief report justifying these decisions to their supervisors. Under conditions of high accountability (they were told that they would be responsible for the results of their decisions), subjects high in self-monitoring transmitted more positive information (information reflecting favorably on their decision process) and more defensive information (information that shifted the blame for mistakes to others) than people low in self-monitoring. Thus, high self-monitors engaged in impression management to a greater extent than low self-monitors.

Finally, self-monitoring is also related to certain aspects of organizational conflict. People high in self-monitoring report stronger tendencies to resolve conflicts through collaboration or compromise, and weaker tendencies to resolve conflicts through avoidance or competition, than people low in self-monitoring. In sum, they seem to approach conflicts in a more conciliatory manner, and with greater concern for long-range solutions, than low self-monitors. (We will consider organizational conflict in more detail in chapter 10).

In light of all these findings, it seems clear that self-monitoring is an aspect of personality with important implications for understanding organizational behavior. (For information on people who are, in some respects, the opposite of those high in self-monitoring, see the **OB in Practice** section on pp. 206–207.)

Self-Efficacy: Beliefs in One's Ability to Perform Various Tasks

Suppose that two individuals are assigned the same task by their supervisor, and that each must work on it alone. One is confident of her ability to carry it out successfully, and the other has serious doubts on this score. Which person is more

 OB IN PRACTICE

Dealing with Problem Employees: Managing Wild Ducks, Mavericks, and Other Unruly Types

Ask any manager: "Do you have any problem subordinates?" and the answer is likely to be an emphatic *"Yes!"*—followed by a deep sigh. Almost everyone who has managed has had to deal with individuals they found difficult, at best, and downright impossible, at worst. Here is how some managers describe the problem subordinates in *their* organizations:

"Talking to that man is like talking to a rock! I know he's very bright . . . but he must have been brought up in a test tube. He never smiles and it's impossible to carry on a normal conversation with him. He intimidates . . . most people by just staring at them."

"He seems to be unplugged from the socket. I mean, . . . he seems to be disconnected from the realities of his job. He tells me things that make no sense whatsoever and I really can't rely on him to complete a job of any importance. If he weren't so close to retirement age I might do something—maybe put a bomb under his chair?"[28]

Although problem employees come in an almost limitless number of forms, many—perhaps most—can be described in terms of two major dimensions: (1) ability to work well with others, and (2) performance (above or below expectations). Together, these dimensions generate the quadrants shown in Figure 6–7. In the upper left-hand section are employees who perform

FIGURE 6–7

Classifying Problem Subordinates: One Useful Framework

Problem subordinates can be classified in terms of where they fall with respect to two dimensions: ability to work well with others and job performance. (*Source:* Based on suggestions by Veiga, 1988; see Note 28.)

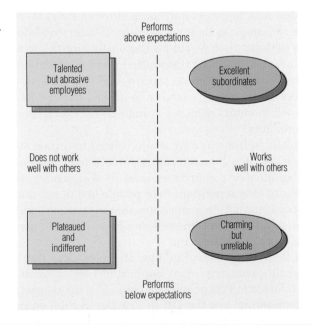

likely to succeed? Assuming that all other factors (e.g., differences in their ability or motivation) are held constant, it is reasonable to predict that the first will do better. She is higher in what has been termed **self-efficacy**—belief in one's capability to perform a specific task.[29]

When considered in the context of a given task, self-efficacy is not, strictly speaking, an aspect of personality. However, individuals seem to acquire general expec-

well, but do not get along with others. In the lower left-hand quadrant are ones who neither perform well nor work effectively with others. The lower right-hand section contains subordinates who do get along well with others, but perform below expectations. Finally, in the upper right-hand quadrant are nonproblem employees: they work well with others *and* perform up to expectations.

Not included in this chart are employees often described as *wild ducks* or *mavericks*. These are people who are high in creativity and provide many of the best new ideas in an organization. At the same time, however, they are highly independent and often downright abrasive to the people around them. They definitely are *not* team players, and they don't mind stepping on multiple toes in the process of getting their ideas accepted. As Robert Bramson, president of Bramson, Parlette, Harrison, & Associates, puts it: "Most mavericks are too good to fire, but they're very hard to live with. Still, without them, executives tend to hire 'for comfort'—they hire a staff that thinks the way they do; they all see the same world. The problem is that they leave out a whole piece of the world and their decisions become too biased and narrow."[30]

How can managers cope with problem employees, wild ducks or otherwise? According to John Veiga, the answer is to confront these people directly, and early in the process. Veiga remarks: "Problematic individuals cannot be handled with kid gloves or in a detached counseling-like way. . . . The goal is to clarify the unwanted behaviors and the consequences. . . . This is no time to offer a 'positive sandwich'—praise followed by criticism, followed by praise again—because most subordinates are smart enough to perceive its contents as baloney."[31]

It is also important, Veiga contends, for managers to recognize the part they have played in creating the problem or allowing it to continue.

Few people enjoy dealing with problem subordinates, so they tend to shy away from the painful task of giving them helpful feedback. This may minimize difficulties in the short run, but is almost certain to magnify them in the long run. Dealing with problem subordinates head on and early on is the best, if not the most comfortable, strategy to adopt.

But what about mavericks and wild ducks? Can these highly independent people be induced to behave as team players, at least part of the time? "Yes," say several experts. The crucial point seems to be convincing them that there are limits to their independence, without, at the same time, restricting them so much that their creativity suffers. As Lester Tobias of Nordli, Wilson Associates, puts it, "It's a really dynamic situation. The maverick can't be excellent if he allows himself to be forced into a linear mode of thinking and behaving."[32] At the same time, organizations cannot allow mavericks or wild ducks to fly off in any direction they choose. Brian Moore, general manager of Hewlett-Packard's Manufacturing Systems Group, comments: "You don't want disruption in the execution phase. Mavericks have to be able to play with the team. Otherwise, they don't last too long."[33] So the trick to managing mavericks, and to getting wild ducks to fly in formation, is to give them sufficient freedom to develop their ideas and contribute original modes of thought to their companies, but to restrain them from excesses that can prove disruptive. Attaining this balance, although often difficult, may be well worth the effort. Without creative thinkers, organizations tend to stagnate. Moreover, as noted by Edward Mandt, vice president for personnel at Maccabees Mutual Life Insurance Company, "The true maverick is our intellectual conscience, maybe our social conscience, too."[34] What organization, in the complex world of the 1990s, can afford to be without such people?

tations concerning their ability to perform a wide range of tasks in many different contexts. Such generalized beliefs about self-efficacy are stable over time, and can reasonably be viewed as another important dimension along which individuals differ in a consistent, stable manner.

How do feelings of self-efficacy develop? According to Bandura, the leading expert on this factor, they develop partly through *direct experiences*, in which individuals perform various tasks and receive feedback on their success, and partly through *vicarious experiences*, in which they observe others performing various tasks and attaining varying levels of success at them.[35] Whatever their precise source, beliefs about self-efficacy appear to exert strong effects on task performance. The stronger individuals' beliefs that they can perform successfully, the higher their performance actually tends to be.

Not surprisingly, research on self-efficacy suggests that it is closely related to work motivation in many settings (see chapter 4). First, feelings of self-efficacy influence the difficulty of goals chosen by individuals. The higher self-efficacy, the more difficult and challenging such goals tend to be.[36] Second, self-efficacy may moderate reactions to various types of feedback. Individuals high in self-efficacy may respond to negative feedback (information suggesting that they are not reaching their goals or meeting established standards of performance) with increased effort and motivation. In contrast, those low in self-efficacy may give up and reduce their motivation in the face of such feedback.[37] Interestingly, a recent study by Baron suggests that feedback that is *destructive* (e.g., inconsiderate in tone, general rather than specific, contains threats) reduces both feelings of self-efficacy and self-set goals.[38] Thus, such feedback—which is often delivered by managers when they become angry with subordinates and lose their tempers—may have lasting, negative effects on motivation.

Self-efficacy is a relatively new topic of study in organizational behavior, but has already been identified as having important implications for several processes.[39] First, given its role in motivation, it may affect performance on many different tasks. Second, it may play a role in training of employees and in career counseling with them (see chapter 9). Low self-efficacy with respect to specific tasks may help pinpoint areas in which additional skills or training are needed. And more general performance problems may be traced, ultimately, to generalized, low levels of this factor. Third, self-efficacy may be related to reactions to performance appraisals. As noted above, individuals high in self-efficacy may respond to negative feedback in more constructive ways than those low in self-efficacy. Finally, low self-efficacy may pose an internal barrier to advancement by some members of previously disadvantaged minority groups. Such individuals may doubt their own ability to perform certain tasks. This, in turn, may actually reduce their performance in these areas. To the extent that this is so, self-efficacy may be an important factor to consider in efforts to overcome the harmful effects of prejudice and discrimination.

Self-Esteem: The Importance of Self-Evaluations

Beliefs about one's ability to perform specific tasks are an important part of the *self-concept*—individuals' conceptions of their own abilities, traits, and skills. Yet, they are only a small portion of this concept. Another important aspect concerns **self-esteem**—the extent to which people hold positive or negative views about themselves. People high in self-esteem evaluate themselves favorably—they believe that they possess many desirable traits and qualities. In contrast, people low in self-esteem evaluate themselves unfavorably—they conclude that they are lacking in important respects, and that they possess characteristics that others find unappealing. Do such feelings affect behavior in organizational settings? Considerable evidence indicates that they do.[40]

First, people high in self-esteem often report higher levels of job satisfaction and motivation than those low in self-esteem. Second, they actually perform at higher levels on some tasks and in some settings. Third, and perhaps even more unsettling, individuals high in self-esteem are more successful in identifying, and then obtaining, appropriate jobs. Evidence pointing to such conclusions is provided by a study conducted by Ellis and Taylor.[41]

These researchers asked business school seniors to complete several questionnaires. Some of these provided measures of subjects' self-esteem, whereas others yielded evidence on the nature and success of subjects' job searches (e.g., the sources of information they used, the number of job offers they actually received). In addition, ratings of participants by organizational recruiters who had interviewed them were obtained. Ellis and Taylor predicted that individuals low in self-esteem would generally conduct less adequate job searches and attain less favorable results than those high in self-esteem. Specifically, they expected that the lower subjects' self-esteem, the less likely they would be to use informal sources of information (e.g., friends, relatives), the fewer offers they would receive, and the lower the ratings they would get from interviewers. Results supported all of these hypotheses. Thus, low self-esteem appeared to be quite costly for these young individuals about to launch their careers.

Although our comments so far sound somewhat discouraging, we can conclude on a more positive note. Low self-esteem can indeed be damaging to individuals' careers, but it *can* be changed. Several practical techniques for enhancing self-esteem, and thereby countering its negative effects, exist. For example, it has been found that one serious problem faced by low self-esteem individuals is their tendency to show a pattern of attributions opposite to that of most others. Instead of demonstrating the kind of *self-serving bias* we described in chapter 2, in which successes are attributed largely to internal causes (their own sterling qualities), but failures are attributed to external ones, low self-esteem people show opposite tendencies. They often blame themselves for failures, and refuse to take credit for success (see Figure 6–8). Training designed to reverse these tendencies can help boost both the confi-

Having low self-esteem and being overly critical of one's physical appearance are major factors that contribute to the prevalence of the disease bulimia. This body-racking binge-and-purge eating disorder is currently occurring at alarming rates among successful corporate women. [Heyn, D. (1989, August). Body hate. *Ms.,* pp. 35–36.]

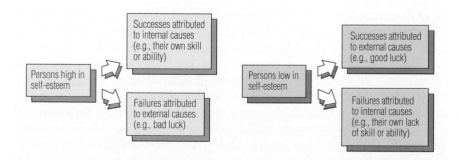

FIGURE 6–8 Self-Esteem and Attributions for Successes and Failures

People low in self-esteem often demonstrate a pattern of attributions for successes and failures opposite to that of people high in self-esteem. They blame themselves for negative outcomes and refuse to take credit for positive ones.

Test Bank questions 6.38–6.39 and 6.54 relate to material on this page.

dence and later performance of low self-esteem people.[42] Other techniques include exposing low self-esteem people to positive feedback or success, and helping them overcome the feelings of depression and hopelessness from which they often suffer. Through such procedures, the harmful effects of a negative self-image can be reduced. Then both individuals and the organizations in which they work can reap important benefits.

Positive and Negative Affectivity: Stable Tendencies to Feel Good or Bad at Work

Moods, as we all know, fluctuate rapidly—and often widely—during the course of a single day. Favorable feedback from their boss causes most people to experience strong positive feelings, whereas harsh criticism produces the opposite reaction. Superimposed on such temporary shifts in affective *state* are more lasting tendencies to experience positive or negative feelings (affect). In other words, individuals differ, and differ consistently, in the tendencies to experience positive and negative affect.[43] People high in the trait of **positive affectivity** tend to have an overall sense of well-being, to see themselves as pleasurably and effectively engaged, and to experience positive emotional states. In contrast, those high in the trait of **negative affectivity** tend to hold negative views of themselves and others, to interpret ambiguous stimuli negatively, and to experience negative emotional states. Do such differences in characteristic levels of mood play any role in organizational behavior? Recent studies by George indicate that they do.[44]

In what is perhaps the most revealing of these investigations to date, George asked salespeople working in a large department store to complete measures of positive and negative affectivity.[45] She then used these individual scores to determine the *affective tone* of the work groups to which these people belonged. Affective tone was defined as the typical or consistent level of affective reactions within a group. George reasoned that affective tone would vary from work group to work group because, in part, people with similar personalities will tend to be attracted to, selected by, and retained by such groups.[46]

Going one step farther, George then argued that the affective tone of work groups would influence their members' willingness to engage in prosocial behavior—in this case, willingness to help customers—and their rates of absence (how often group members are absent from work). Results indicated that negative affective tone was indeed a significant predictor of prosocial behavior by group members: the greater the amount of negative affect, the less willing they were to assist customers. Surprisingly, positive affective tone was not a significant predictor of helping. However, the higher the positive affective tone of the work groups, the lower their absence rate.

Together, these findings support the view that not only do various aspects of personality influence the attitudes and behavior of individuals at work, they may shape the nature—and hence performance—of work groups as well. This possibility is suggested by a theory known as the **attraction-selection-attrition framework**.[47] According to this theory, people with similar personalities will tend to be attracted to one another and so tend to form groups. The groups then tend to select persons whose personality traits match those of people who are already members. In most cases, only people who share such characteristics will be retained as members. In this manner, George and others contend, aspects of individual personality can, and often do, influence the nature and functioning of groups (see Figure 6–9). Given the wide range of tasks carried out by groups in most organizations, and recent emphasis on *team-building* and related techniques, such links between personality

Although it is natural for people to experience both positive and negative moods, top executives have rosier perspectives than most employees. As a group, overall they tend to remain optimistic and positive regardless of the situation confronting them. It is interesting to consider the possibility that such inherent optimism is responsible for the success they have achieved. [Seligman, M. E. P. (1991). *Learned optimism.* New York: Knopf.]

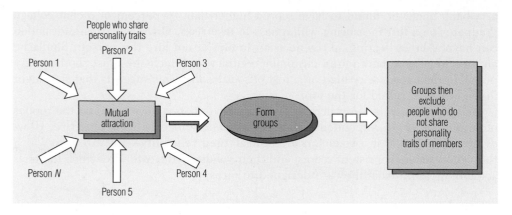

FIGURE 6-9   The Attraction-Selection-Attrition Framework

The *attraction-selection-attrition framework* suggests that people with similar personalities are attracted to one another and tend to form groups. Then they admit and retain only individuals who share these traits. (*Source:* Based on suggestions by Schneider, 1987; see Note 47.)

and group performance should definitely *not* be overlooked.[48] (For a discussion of another way in which the characteristics of individuals can have major importance for entire organizations as well as work groups, see the **Focus on Research** section on pp. 212–213.)

MEASURING PERSONALITY: SOME BASIC METHODS

Physical traits such as height and weight can be measured directly, through appropriate devices. Various aspects of personality, however, cannot be assessed in the same manner. There are no rulers for measuring self-confidence, no thermometers for assessing dependability or ambition, and no scales for estimating integrity. How can differences among individuals on these and many other important dimensions be quantified? Several methods exist for accomplishing this task. The most important of these are known, respectively, as *objective tests* and *projective techniques*.

Objective Tests: Assessing Personality through Self-Report

Objective tests such as *inventories* and *questionnaires* are by far the most widely used method for assessing personality. These consist of a series of questions or statements to which individuals respond in various ways. For example, a questionnaire may ask respondents to indicate whether each of a set of statements is true or false about themselves, the extent to which they agree or disagree with various sentences, or which of each pair of named activities they prefer. Their answers are then scored by means of special keys and compared with the scores obtained by hundreds, or even thousands, of other people who have taken the test previously. In this way, an individual's relative standing on the trait or traits being measured can be determined. For example, an individual applying for a job as a loan officer at a bank might be found to have scored higher than 90 percent of recent college graduates on a test measuring willingness to take risks. Obviously, this information can have a direct bearing on the decision to hire or not hire this person. Similarly, an individual seeking a job in customer relations, in which she must soothe angry people, might score very high on a test of social skills. This suggests that she might indeed be well suited for the job.

Because such tests use concrete items and have scoring keys based on the replies of large numbers of respondents, they are often described as being *objective*. However, as with any test, two factors are crucial: their **reliability**—the extent to which they yield stable, consistent scores; and their **validity**—the extent to which the tests actually measure what they are designed to measure.

 FOCUS ON RESEARCH

Champions of Technological Innovation: Profiling the Agents of a Crucial Form of Organizational Change

Although assessing the times in which one lives is always difficult—we are simply too involved to make accurate judgments—we are now undoubtedly in an unparalleled period of rapid technological change. Further, it seems clear that only individuals and organizations capable of adapting to such change can look forward to successful careers and continued, profitable existence, respectively. Yet, resistance to technological change is a fact of organizational life.[49] As we will discuss in more detail in chapter 16, many people—and sometimes entire organizations—seem to dig in their heels and resist when confronted with change. Because such resistance can prove devastatingly costly, overcoming it is crucial in many situations, and individuals who emerge as active and enthusiastic promoters of technological change often play a pivotal role. They are often described as **champions of technological innovation** or *change*, and efforts to identify them, and to determine why and how they play this role, have continued for several decades.[50] Only recently, however, has a relatively clear picture of how such people operate begun to emerge. In this respect, research conducted by Howell and Higgins is especially informative.[51, 52]

These researchers propose that *champions of change* possess personal characteristics that suit them for this role. These traits, in turn, lead

them to adopt styles of leadership and influence tactics that, together, permit such individuals to overcome resistance to technological innovations and get them adopted by their organization. What personal characteristics qualify individuals for the role of champions of change? Again, Howell and Higgins offer some intriguing insights.[53]

In this investigation, the researchers first identified eighty-five organizations that had recently implemented a technological innovation. They then interviewed executives in these companies to identify champions of innovation. The champions, in turn, were interviewed to obtain more information on their role in winning acceptance for the innovations. Finally, both champions and nonchampions completed measures designed to assess a wide range of personality traits, their leadership behaviors, and the specific tactics they used to try to influence others in their organizations.

Results indicated that champions of change did differ from other people in several aspects of personality. They were significantly higher in the inclination to take risks. In addition, champions tended to be higher than nonchampions in innovativeness (the tendency to develop novel solutions to problems) and achievement (the desire to accomplish difficult tasks).

These personality traits, in turn, lead champions of change to adopt a *transformational lead-*

With respect to reliability, a test would obviously be useless if a person taking it on two separate occasions obtained markedly different scores. Unless it is assumed that their standing with respect to the traits being measured changed greatly over time, such results would suggest that the test itself is flawed. Similarly, a test designed to measure a single aspect of personality would be useless if it were found that items on it were unrelated to one another and, in fact, appeared to measure several different traits. Much is known about the factors that determine the reliability of personality tests, so constructing ones with high levels of reliability is usually not a serious problem.

Establishing a test's *validity*, however, is often far more complex. The issue of validity involves the question of whether, and to what extent, a given test measures

ership style—a style of leadership in which they attempted to inspire others through emotional appeals, and through vivid images of the beneficial changes that would follow adoption of the technological innovations. (We will discuss such leadership in more detail in chapter 12.) Finally, champions reported using a wider range of influence tactics, and using them more frequently, than nonchampions. In sum, the model proposed by Howell and Higgins was supported: champions of technological innovation do seem to possess traits that lead them to adopt styles of leadership and tactics of influence that, together, encourage their emergence as champions of change, and actually produce the shifts they desire (see Figure 6–10).

Given the importance of such champions in modern organizations, a final question remains: what can be done to encourage their emergence—and success? Howell and Higgins offer several concrete suggestions. First, top management must indicate its support of both in-

novativeness and risk taking; without such support, it is difficult indeed for champions to operate. Second, these messages must be backed up with visible recognition for creative ideas. In other words, champions of change must *not* go unrewarded. Third, champions should be given the freedom they need to pursue innovations. This means that they must be granted considerable autonomy and diverse career experiences within the organization. Finally, top management must be willing to run interference for innovation champions, removing roadblocks from their path and protecting them from the fallout of political infighting. Through these and related steps, top management in an organization can "champion the champions," and encourage an organizational culture promotive of innovation. Then both champions and their organizations may survive and prosper in the uncertain but ever changing environment we know as the modern business world.

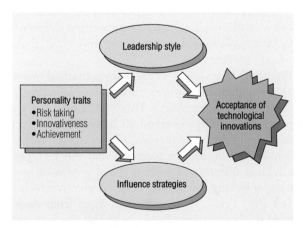

FIGURE 6–10

The Traits and Behavior of Champions of Technological Innovation

Champions of technological innovation possess specific traits, such as the inclination to take risks, that suit them for this role. These traits lead them to adopt influence techniques and leadership styles that assist them in winning acceptance for technological innovations. (*Source:* Based on suggestions by Howell & Higgins, 1991; see Note 51.)

what it purports to measure. Establishing validity usually involves demonstrating that the scores on a test are related to, or can predict, some other measure of the trait in question. For example, consider a test designed to measure the desire for high levels of excitement or stimulation. If the test is valid, then the higher people score on it, the more likely they should be to do things such as (1) drive sports cars, (2) engage in sport parachute-jumping, mountain climbing, or similar exciting activities, and (3) seek change and challenge in their careers. If people who score high on the test do indeed engage in these activities to a greater extent than people who score low, we might conclude, albeit tentatively, that the test does measure the desire for excitement. But which of these activities is most closely related to this aspect of personality? It is difficult to tell, so if high scorers on the test show some of these activities more than others, we are left with a degree of uncertainty concerning the test's validity. Also, all of these behaviors may reflect the operation of other variables as well. For example, people might drive sports cars partly because doing so enhances their status; thus, such behavior might indicate status-seeking as well as excitement-seeking tendencies. Similarly, individuals may seek challenge in their careers because they are ambitious, not merely out of a preference for high levels of stimulation. Because of these and many other complexities, establishing the validity of any objective measure of personality is a difficult task. The conservative rule, then, is to question the validity of *all* tests of personality unless they are accompanied by convincing evidence that they really do measure what they claim to measure.

Having made these points, we should note that all of the traits considered in this chapter are measured by tests known to be both reliable and valid. Thus, you can be confident that the findings we have discussed are based on important dimensions of personality, and are definitely *not* the mirages referred to in some critiques of the value of studying individual differences in organizational settings.[54]

Projective Techniques: Ambiguous Stimuli and Personality Assessment

Look at the drawing in Figure 6–11. What is happening in this picture? Now, consider the following questions: Would your interpretation differ from those of other people? And would this reveal anything about differences between your personality and others'? Another means for measuring personality assumes that the answer to both questions is "yes." Briefly, such **projective techniques** assume that if different people are exposed to ambiguous stimuli, each will report something different. The pattern of these differences, in turn, will reveal much about important aspects of personality.

Actually, the illustration in Figure 6–11 is similar to the ones contained in a widely used test designed to measure individual differences in achievement and power motivation, the *Thematic Apperception Test* or *TAT*.[55] This test consists of a series of ambiguous drawings, and people taking it are asked to make up a story about each. These are carefully analyzed for certain basic themes, in accordance with highly specific scoring procedures. Considerable evidence suggests that the TAT provides valuable information about individual differences with respect to several personal motives. However, such evidence is lacking for several other projective techniques (e.g., the famous *Rorschach Ink Blot Test*). Thus, scores derived from such tests should be interpreted with a great deal of caution. Please note, by the way, that the task of scoring and interpreting projective tests is complex. It should be performed

Projective measures of personality are so called because they enable the people completing them to project themselves into the ambiguous situations depicted in the tests. They are like a blank canvas onto which individuals cast the images of themselves for experts to interpret. [Walker, C. E. (1991). *Clinical psychology: Historical and research foundations*. New York: Plenum.]

FIGURE 6-11

Projective Techniques for Measuring
Personality: An Example

Drawings similar to the one in this photo are used in one popular projective technique for measuring personality—the *TAT*. (*Source:* From Robert J. Gregory, *Psychological Testing: History, Principles, and Applications*. Copyright © 1992 by Allyn and Bacon. Reprinted with permission.)

only by individuals who have had extensive training in such procedures. (Is it ethical for organizations to use information about personality for personnel decisions? For discussion of this issue, see the **Question of Ethics** section on pp. 216–217.)

SUMMARY AND REVIEW

The Nature of Personality

Personality refers to the unique but stable set of characteristics and behaviors that set each individual apart from others. Personality influences behavior unless it is overwhelmed by strong situational constraints. Growing evidence indicates that personality and other individual difference factors can affect many aspects of organizational behavior. For example, the higher the **person-job fit**—the stronger the correlation between individuals' skills and characteristics and the requirements of their jobs—the better their job performance.

Work-Related Aspects of Personality

Many aspects of personality are especially relevant to organizational behavior. Several of the **five robust dimensions** of personality—especially conscientiousness, extraversion, and openness to experience—influence both job performance and job satisfaction. People demonstrating the **Type A** behavior pattern perform better than **Type B** individuals on some tasks (e.g., ones requiring speed) but worse on others (e.g., tasks requiring considered judgment). Type A's lose their tempers more often than Type B's and, as a result, are involved in more instances of organizational conflict.

Individuals who adopt a manipulative approach to their relations with others are sometimes described as being high in **Machiavellianism.** They are not influenced by considerations of loyalty, friendship, or ethics. They simply do whatever is needed to get their way or to win.

People high in **self-monitoring** are expressive, are concerned with making good impressions on others, and can adapt their behavior to match requirements of a given situation. High self-monitors are more effective boundary spanners than low self-monitors, and are rated as being better teachers by many students. In addition, high self-monitors tend to use various tactics of *impression management* more frequently than low self-monitors.

Individuals who believe that they possess the capability of performing various tasks—people high in **self-efficacy**—often achieve higher levels of performance than people lacking in such confidence. Individuals high in **self-esteem** have positive feelings about themselves and their characteristics. They often report higher job satisfaction, perform at higher levels, and generally conduct better job searches than people low in self-esteem.

A QUESTION OF ETHICS

Information about Personality: Is It an Appropriate Basis for Organizational Decisions?

Personality is a fascinating topic. Almost everyone is interested in other people, and insights into the characteristics that make them unique are intriguing, to say the least. Further, many aspects of personality appear to be related to important forms of organizational behavior. It is hardly surprising then, that some organizations have sought to use information about the personality in various ways—for example, in selecting employees, deciding who is and who is not suitable for various jobs. Although we fully understand the temptation to engage in such actions, exercising a healthy degree of caution in doing so is important for several reasons.

First, some measures of personality are of doubtful *reliability* and *validity*. The scores they yield are not stable, and that they actually measure what they claim to measure is not clear. For example, consider the **Myers-Briggs Type Indicator.**[56] This test ostensibly measures aspects of individuals' cognitive styles—how they think about the world. Scores on it are used to classify people along several different dimensions: introverted or extraverted, sensing or intuitive (relying on sensations or intuition), thinking or feeling (relying on cognition or emotions), and perceiving or judging (responding to the world without evaluating it versus making various judgments). Presumably, various patterns of these tendencies make individuals especially suited for certain jobs. For example, individuals classified as *sensation-thinking* are assumed to

be thorough, logical, and practical—and would make good CPAs or safety engineers. In contrast, people classified as *intuitive-feeling* are charismatic and sociable; they would be expected to succeed in public relations or in human resource management (see Table 6–2).

The Myers-Briggs test has been used by many major corporations, including Apple Computer, Exxon, and General Electric. In fact, more than 2 million people take it each year in the United States alone. Yet—and here is the crucial point— *there is virtually no hard evidence for its validity!* Millions of people take the test, receive scores on it, and interpret these as revealing important information about their cognitive styles, despite the fact that no convincing basis exists for assuming that the test really measures what it claims to measure. Clearly, until such evidence is attained, important ethical issues remain concerning the continued promotion and use of this test, and many others for which firm validation evidence is lacking.

Second, even when measures of personality are both reliable and valid, relationships between the traits they assess and organizational behavior are often complex. For example, as we noted earlier, Type A individuals do not always perform better than Type B people—the nature of the tasks in question and several other factors determine which of these groups has an edge. In such cases, simple generalizations are unwarranted. Thus, information about this and many other aspects of personality must be interpreted with care.

Although moods fluctuate frequently throughout the day, individuals also have stable tendencies to experience positive or negative affect. These tendencies are known, respectively, as **positive affectivity** and **negative affectivity**. Recent findings indicate that these characteristics are related both to prosocial behavior at work and to frequency of absences.

Champions of technological innovation differ from other people with respect to several characteristics. They are higher in risk taking and tend to be higher in innovativeness and the desire for achievement. These characteristics lead them to adopt leadership styles and influence tactics that, together, assist them in gaining acceptance for technological innovations.

TABLE 6-2   Dimensions of the Myers-Briggs Type Indicator

Scores on the *Myers-Briggs Type Indicator* are used to categorize individuals in terms of their cognitive style. As shown here, certain styles are assumed to suit individuals for specific kinds of jobs. However, very little evidence concerning the *validity* of this test currently exists.

Sensation-Thinking	Sensation-Feeling	Intuitive-Thinking	Intuitive-Feeling
Traits	*Traits*	*Traits*	*Traits*
Logical	Responsible	Independent	Charismatic
Thorough	Committed	Creative	Sociable
Practical	Conscientious	Critical	
Occupations	*Occupations*	*Occupations*	*Occupations*
Auditor	Union negotiator	Lawyer	Human resource manager
Quality-control supervisor	Social worker	Professor	Politician
Safety engineer	Psychologist	Systems analyst	Public relations

Third, when using information about personality, it is all too easy to fall into the trap of allowing the labels we assign to specific persons to influence our perceptions of them. In other words, once we have labeled someone as being a Machiavellian, as being low in self-esteem, or as being a high self-monitor, the label may color our perceptions of everything he or she says or does. The result: that person (and we) are locked into these categories, even if they are false.

Fourth, information about personality is often complex and requires considerable interpretation. It is crucial, therefore, that people charged with this task have sufficient training and expertise to accomplish it. All too often, unfortunately, this is not the case. Many personality tests are heavily promoted as being simple to use and easy to interpret. The result: such tests are often administered by people who lack the training and knowledge needed to select appropriate tests and fully interpret the results. In a sense, the situation is akin to one in which people without medical training attempt to decipher the results of complex blood tests. Clearly, situations of this type raise unsettling ethical questions.

For all of these reasons, it is important to exercise caution in the use of information about others' personalities. Such information can indeed be revealing, but should be employed only when three conditions are met: (1) the information itself is accurate (the tests used to obtain it are reliable and valid), (2) it has direct bearing on performance or other key aspects of organizational behavior, and (3) the individuals who interpret and use such information have sufficient training and experience to do so adequately. If uncertainty exists with respect to *any* of these conditions, the best course of action is a conservative one: refrain from using such information for organizational purposes.

Measuring Personality

Personality is often assessed by means of *inventories* and *questionnaires* in which individuals answer various questions about themselves. It is sometimes also measured by means of **projective techniques.** Here individuals respond to ambiguous stimuli. The responses they provide are assumed to reflect their underlying traits or motives. In order to be useful, various measures of personality must be *reliable* and *valid.* Unfortunately, little evidence exists for the reliability or validity of several widely used personality scales, such as *Myers-Briggs Type Indicator.* This fact raises complex ethical issues concerning the use of information about personality for organizational purposes.

KEY TERMS

attraction-selection-attrition framework: A theory suggesting that people with similar personality traits tend to form groups. The groups then tend to select and retain only individuals whose personality traits match those of existing members.

champions of technological innovation: Individuals in an organization who play a crucial role in the acceptance of technological innovations.

five robust dimensions: Five basic dimensions of personality that are assumed to underlie many specific traits.

locus of control: The extent to which individuals believe that their outcomes are determined by their own actions (*Internals*) or by factors beyond their direct control (*Externals*).

Machiavellianism: A personality trait involving willingness to manipulate others for one's own purposes.

Myers-Briggs Type Indicator: A test designed to measure several aspects of cognitive style, such as the extent to which individuals rely on sensation versus intuition, or thinking versus feeling.

negative affectivity: The tendency to experience negative moods and feelings in a wide range of settings and under many different conditions.

objective tests: Questionnaires and inventories designed to measure various aspects of personality.

person-job fit: The extent to which individuals possess the competencies and traits required for performance of specific jobs.

personality: The unique and relatively stable pattern of behavior, thoughts, and emotions shown by individuals.

positive affectivity: The tendency to experience positive moods and feelings in a wide range of settings and under many different conditions.

projective techniques: Methods for measuring personality in which individuals respond to ambiguous stimuli. Their responses ostensibly provide insight into their major traits.

reliability: The extent to which a test yields consistent scores on various occasions, and the extent to which all of its items measure the same construct.

self-efficacy: Individuals' beliefs concerning their ability to perform specific tasks successfully.

self-esteem: Individuals' evaluations of their own traits and behavior.

self-monitoring: An aspect of personality involving individuals' sensitivity to the reactions of others, their ability to manage their own expressive behavior so as to induce positive reactions in others, and their willingness to serve as the center of others' attention.

Type A (behavior pattern): A pattern of behavior involving high levels of competitiveness, time urgency, and irritability.

Type B (behavior pattern): A pattern of behavior opposite to that shown by Type A individuals.

validity: The extent to which a test actually measures what it purports to measure.

QUESTIONS FOR DISCUSSION

1. Why do individuals with contrasting personalities often act in similar ways in a given situation?

2. When you meet someone for the first time, what basic dimensions of this person's personality might be readily visible in his or her actions?

3. Suppose you had to choose one of two persons for a middle management position. One is Type A and the other is Type B. Which would you select? Why?

4. Imagine that one group of employees who work under your supervision always seems to be "down." They complain a lot and generally seem to be in a negative mood. What steps might you take to change this situation?

5. On the basis of the information contained in this chapter, do you believe that some individuals are really "born

to be led" whereas others are "born to follow"? Why or why not?

6. Suppose that you wanted to select someone in your organization to help win acceptance for adoption of a new form of technology. What characteristics would you look for in choosing a person to "champion" this cause?

7. Do you think that all human beings, even those living in very different cultures, differ in terms of the same set of personality traits? If so, what might these basic traits be?

8. Under what conditions would you be willing to use information about others' personalities to make organizational decisions about them—for example, whether they should be promoted to specific jobs?

NOTES

1. Burger, J. M. (1990). *Personality* (2nd ed.). Belmont, CA: Wadsworth.

2. Buss, D. M., & Cantor, N. (Eds.). (1989). *Personality psychology: Recent trends and emerging directions.* New York: Springer-Verlag.

3. Mischel, W. (1985). *Personality: Lost or found? Identifying when individual differences make a difference.* Paper presented at the meeting of the American Psychological Association, Los Angeles.

4. Tice, D. M. (1989). Metatraits: Interitem variance as

personality assessment. In D. M. Buss & N. Cantor (Eds.), *Personality psychology: Recent trends and emerging directions*. New York: Springer-Verlag.

5. Epstein, S., & O'Brien, E. J. (1985). The person-situation debate in historical and current perspective. *Psychological Bulletin, 98*, 513–537.

6. Caldwell, D. F., & O'Reilly, C. A., III. (1990). Measuring person-job fit with a profile-comparison process. *Journal of Applied Psychology, 75*, 648–657.

7. Allport, G. W., & Odbert, H. S. (1936). Trait names: A psycholexical study. *Psychological Monographs, 47*, 211.

8. Digman, J. M. (1980). Personality structure: Emergence of the five-factor model. *Annual Review of Psychology, 41*, 417–440.

9. Barrick, M. R., & Mount, M. K. (1991). The big five personality dimensions and job performance: A meta-analysis. *Personnel Psychology, 44*, 1–26.

10. Friedman, M., & Rosenman, R. H. (1974). *Type A behavior and your heart*. New York: Knopf.

11. Glass, D. C. (1977). *Behavior patterns, stress, and coronary disease*. Hillsdale, NJ: Erlbaum.

12. Holmes, D. S., McGilley, B. M., & Houston, B. K. (1984). Task-related arousal of Type A and Type B persons: Level of challenge and response specificity. *Journal of Personality and Social Psychology, 46*, 1322–1327.

13. Holmes, D. S., & Will, M. J. (1985). Expression of interpersonal aggression by angered and nonangered persons with the Type A and Type B behavior patterns. *Journal of Personality and Social Psychology, 48*, 723–727.

14. Baron, R. A. (1989). Personality and organizational conflict: Effects of the type A behavior pattern and self-monitoring. *Organizational Behavior and Human Decision Processes, 44*, 281–297.

15. Evans, G. W., Palsane, M. N., & Carrere, S. (1987). Type A behavior and occupational stress: A cross-cultural study of blue collar workers. *Journal of Personality and Social Psychology, 52*, 1002–1007.

16. Christie, R., & Geis, F. L. (1970). *Studies in Machiavellianism*. New York: Academic Press.

17. See Note 16.

18. Rotter, J. B. (1975). Some problems and misconceptions related to the construct of internal versus external control of reinforcement. *Journal of Consulting and Clinical Psychology, 43*, 56–67.

19. Rotter, J. B. (1982). *The development and applications of social learning theory: Selected papers*. New York: Praeger.

20. Szilagyi, A. D., Jr., & Sims, H. P., Jr. (1975). Locus of control and expectancies across multiple organizational levels. *Journal of Applied Psychology, 60*, 156–165.

21. Andriasni, P. J., & Nestel, C. (1976). Internal-external control as a contributor to and outcome of work experience. *Journal of Applied Psychology, 61*, 156–165.

22. Anderson, C. R. (1977). Locus of control, coping behaviors, and performance in a stress setting: A longitudinal study. *Journal of Applied Psychology, 62*, 446–451.

23. Snyder, M. (1987). *Public appearances/Private realities: The psychology of self-monitoring*. New York: Freeman.

24. Caldwell, D. F., & O'Reilly, C. A., III. (1982). Boundary spanning and individual performance: The impact of self-monitoring. *Journal of Applied Psychology, 67*, 124–127.

25. Larkin, J. E. (1987). Are good teachers perceived as high self-monitors? *Personality and Social Psychology Bulletin, 23*, 64–72.

26. Liden, R. C., & Mitchell, T. R. (1988). Ingratiatory behaviors in organizational settings. *Academy of Management Review, 13*, 572–587.

27. Fandt, P. M., & Ferris, G. M. (1990). The management of information and impressions: When employees behave opportunistically. *Organizational Behavior and Human Decision Processes, 45*, 140–158.

28. Veiga, J. H. (1988). Face your problem subordinates now! *Academy of Management Executive, 2*, 145–152.

29. Bandura, A. (1986). *Social cognitive theory*. Englewood Cliffs, NJ: Prentice-Hall.

30. Patterson, W. P. (1987). Managing the maverick: Or . . . how to get a "wild duck" to fly in formation. *Human Resources, 23*, March 9, 25–28.

31. See Note 28.

32. See Note 30.

33. See Note 30.

34. See Note 30.

35. Bandura, A. (1977). *Social learning theory*. Englewood Cliffs, NJ: Prentice-Hall.

36. Locke, E. A., Frederick, E., Lee, C., & Bobko, P. (1984). The effect of self-efficacy, goals, and task strategies on task performance. *Journal of Applied Psychology, 69*, 241–252.

37. Bandura, A., & Cervone, D. (1986). Differential engagement of self-reactive influence in cognitively-based motivation. *Organizational Behavior and Human Decision Processes, 38*, 92–113.

38. Baron, R. A. (1988). Negative effects of destructive criticism: Impact on conflict, self-efficacy, and task performance. *Journal of Applied Psychology, 73*, 199–207.

39. Wood, R., Bandura, A., & Bailey, T. (1990). Mechanisms governing organizational performance in complex decision-making environments. *Organizational Behavior and Human Decision Processes, 46*, 181–201.

40. Brockner, J. (1988). *Self-esteem at work*. New York: Lexington Books.

41. Ellis, R. A., & Taylor, M. S. (1983). Role of self-esteem within the job search process. *Journal of Applied Psychology, 68*, 632–640.

42. Brockner, J., & Guare, J. (1983). Improving the performance of low self-esteem individuals: An attributional approach. *Academy of Management Journal, 36*, 642–656.

43. Watson, D., & Clark, L. A. (1984). Negative affectivity: The disposition to experience aversive emotional states. *Psychological Bulletin, 98*, 219–235.

44. George, J. (1989). Mood and absence. *Journal of Applied Psychology, 74*, 317–324.

45. George, J. M. (1990). Personality, affect, and behavior in groups. *Journal of Applied Psychology, 75*, 107–116.

46. Schneider, B. (1983). Work climates: An interactionist perspective. In N. W. Feimer & E. S. Geller (Eds.), *Environmental psychology: Directions and perspectives*. New York: Praeger.

47. Schneider, B. (1987). The people make the place. *Personnel Psychology, 40*, 437–453.

48. Tjosvold, D. (1989). *Managing conflict*. Minneapolis: Team Media.

49. Morgan, G. (1988). *Riding the waves of change*. San Francisco: Jossey-Bass.

50. Schon, D. A. (1963). Champions for radical new inventions. *Harvard Business Review, 41*, 77–86.

51. Howell, J. M., & Higgins, C. A. (1991). Champions of change: Identifying, understanding, and supporting champions of technological innovations. *Organizational Dynamics*, 40–55.

52. Howell, J. M., & Higgins, C. A. (1990). Champions of technological innovation. *Administrative Quarterly, 35*, 317–341.

53. See Note 52.

54. Davis-Blake, A., & Pfeffer, J. (1989). Just a mirage: The search for dispositional effects in organizational research. *Academy of Management Review, 14*, 385–400.

55. McClelland, D. C. (1961). *The achieving society*. Princeton, NJ: Van Nostrand.

56. Myers-Briggs Type Indicator. (1987). Palo Alto, CA: Consulting Psychologists Press.

CASE IN POINT

The Personality Behind Wal-Mart

He is the richest man in America and he couldn't care less.* He is Sam Moore Walton, founder and CEO of the Wal-Mart Corporation—America's biggest retailer. Wal-Mart currently operates almost 2,000 stores and opens more than 150 new ones each year. The stores, which offer a wide range of merchandise (drugs, cosmetics, and other household products) at cut-rate prices, are so efficiently run that the opening of one in a new community is often the death knell for many local "Mom-and-Pop" operations.

John Huey of *Fortune* recently spent a few days visiting numerous Wal-Mart stores with Sam Walton. This is what he observed of this interesting and driven man.[1]

Sam Walton has achieved enough wealth and success to do just about anything he wants to do. So what *does* he do? He spends most of his time crisscrossing the country visiting his 345,000 "associates"—Wal-Mart's term for employees—to make sure that they are still running his stores his way—the Wal-Mart way. His remaining time is spent pursuing his other passion—hunting quail. Walton estimates that he devotes about four months each year to this passion, often mixing quail hunting and business.

Walton has a history of achieving. Growing up in Missouri, he was the youngest Eagle scout in the state. In high school, he was president of the student council and quarterbacked his school's football team to a state championship. He served as an officer in the army and has earned a reputation for being a fiercely competitive tennis player. Sam Walton seems to succeed at just about everything he takes on.

Walton believes in his abilities and is not afraid to take risks. He founded his first Wal-Mart store in Bentonville, Arkansas, when he was forty-four years old. He had considerable experience as a small-town retailer, having worked for other retailers and having previously owned a very successful Ben Franklin store. Walton borrowed heavily from almost every bank

*Sam Moore Walton died on April 5, 1992, losing his two-year struggle with bone cancer. His forty-seven-year-old son, S. Robson ("Rob") Walton, has been appointed by Wal-Mart's board of directors as their new chairman.

in Arkansas. In its early years, Wal-Mart was so highly leveraged by debt that sometimes Walton had to get a new loan just to meet payments on his other loans. Wal-Mart's beginnings were filled with risk, but Walton's gamble has paid off. Today, Wal-Mart boasts annual sales in the neighborhood of $40 billion.

Walton loves to fly. He says of flying, "I like the challenge. But mostly I like the independence of being able to go where I want to when I want to—in a hurry."[2] Like most things Walton tackles, his landings are well practiced and perfect.

Walton is a shrewd businessman—always looking for a good deal. He takes pride in the fact that he bought the twin-prop Cessna he currently flies secondhand from a bankrupt investment banker. If you meet him in one of his stores, he's likely to show you a bag of candy or some other piece of merchandise that he managed to get for a particularly good price. Although today Wal-Mart employs 165 buyers, it wasn't too long ago that Walton did much of the buying himself.

Walton believes in keeping overhead low. During his barnstorming around the country to visit Wal-Mart stores, he stays at medium-priced hotels like Ramada Inn and Holiday Inn. He doesn't have a backup pilot, any personal assistants, or limousines. He never lets a seat go empty on his airplane either. He takes buyers from headquarters along with him on his trips to show them what Wal-Mart is really all about.

Walton insists that buyers get out of the office to see what happens to the goods they buy. And he wants them to hear firsthand any complaints his associates and customers may have. He is especially concerned about the feelings of *"Sam's favorite folks*—the hourly employees who stock the shelves and wait on the customers."[3] Walton is very conscientious. When one of his "favorite folks" has a complaint, he expects it to be resolved—and fast.

Walton loves to compete. During a visit to a new Super Wal-Mart store—one that sells a full line of grocery products in addition to its regular merchandise—Walton noticed that milk, eggs, and numerous other grocery items were priced very low. Asked why this was so, the store manager said that they were in the middle of a price war with a local Kroger grocery store. Walton removed his "Sam" name badge and trademark Wal-Mart baseball hat and proceeded to do some shopping at Kroger. He noticed that their milk was priced 10¢ per gallon less than Wal-Mart's. By the time his plane lifted off that evening—off to another store—the price of milk at the Super Wal-Mart store was 10¢ per gallon less than at Kroger's.

Walton works hard and believes in self-sacrifice for the good of the company. This billionaire still gets up every Saturday at 3:00 A.M. to look over the weekly sales reports. He expects all of his employees to give Wal-Mart the same level of dedication and effort that he does. To encourage commitment, Walton gives every Wal-Mart associate ownership in the company. Wal-Mart has profit sharing, incentive programs, and stock-option programs—all tied to the success of Wal-Mart.

Walton created the "store within a store" concept to push the idea that associates own Wal-Mart. Associates are provided with all the financial information regarding their departments. They get sales and cost data so they always know their overhead, markups, and profits, which lets them track their performance. With this information, they see how doing things the Wal-Mart way results in profits. Within Wal-Mart guidelines, department heads run their departments as their own stores, and they directly benefit from their store within a store's success.

Walton is a planner with an eye for specifics. When he arrives at a store—usually with less than an hour's notice, sometimes without any notice at all—he gathers all of the store's department heads together to review their thirty-, sixty-, and ninety-day plans. Walton then goes around the store to ask associates how business is going. He asks for specifics and that's what he gets. For example, when Walton asked a Wal-Mart pharmacist how well a particular brand of baby oil was selling, the pharmacist's immediate response was that the product was the department's VPI (volume producing item). Never passing up an opportunity to recognize a job well done—or a good idea—Walton immediately pulled out his pocket tape recorder and noted "I'm here in Memphis at store 950, and Georgie has done a real fine thing with this endcap display of Equate Baby Oil. I'd like to try this everywhere."[4]

Before Walton left Memphis store 950, he took the time to recognize its associates for surpassing their recent sales goals and to challenge them to continue their good work. Knowing how important specific goals are, he leaves with a challenge to boost sales by 10 percent—2 percent more than their already recognized performance. As a final act, Walton leads his associates in the Wal-Mart cheer: " 'Give me a W, give me an A,' and so on."[5]

Perhaps most revealing of his personality is Walton's enormous devotion to Wal-Mart even as he is fighting incurable bone cancer. This seventy-three-year-old man recognizes his own mortality, but he doesn't dwell on it. Looking back on his life, he says he wouldn't change a thing about it. He is determined to live out his life doing what he does best—merchandising in the most competitive way he can. Says Walton, "This is still the most important thing I do, going around to the stores, and I'd rather do it than anything I know of. I learn a lot about who's doing good things in the office, and I also see things that need fixing, and I help fix them."[6]

After spending a few days with Walton, Huey concludes that aside from his incredible energy, willingness to take risks, and ever-present optimism, Walton's real secret of success is his ability and determination to maintain his focus. Walton single-mindedly focuses on making Wal-Mart a better merchandiser. His focus is evident in everything he does.

Questions for Discussion

1. Describe Sam Walton using the five robust dimensions of personality.
2. How does Walton's personality affect his performance?
3. Walton is said to possess traits consistent with the transformational leadership style—the style typically adopted by champions of change. Which of Walton's personality characteristics are typical of champions of innovation?
4. Does Walton have a Type A or Type B personality?
5. What is Walton's level of self-esteem? What is his level of locus of control?
6. Considering your own personality, would you get along with Sam Walton? In other words, do people with similar personalities get along better (i.e., which is true: birds of a feather gather together; or opposites attract)?

Notes

1. Huey, J. (1991, September 23). America's most successful merchant. *Fortune*, pp. 46–59.
2. See Note 1, p. 46.
3. See Note 1, p. 48.
4. See Note 1, p. 50.
5. See Note 1, p. 54.
6. See Note 1, p. 50.

Machiavellianism in Action: The $10 Game

That we frequently encounter people who are high in *Machiavellianism*—a willingness to manipulate others for their own gain—is obvious. Generally, however, such people are quite adept at concealing their ruthless, self-centered approach to life, at least in the short run. The result? High Machiavellians are often not recognized as such by others and so can continue to operate without interference—and with impunity.

The exercise described below offers a means of observing such people in action—an opportunity to see just how they "do their thing" where manipulating others is concerned. To perform this exercise, you need three people. It is especially useful to try to arrange conditions so that one of these individuals is someone you suspect is a high Machiavellian whereas the others are lower on this dimension.

Follow the instructions below, and be sure to observe the actions of all three individuals carefully as the situation unfolds.

Procedure

The materials you will need are ten index cards or slips of paper. Then read the following instructions to the participants: "Imagine that these index cards are real money; each slip represents $1. The rules of the game are simple: this money will belong to *any two people who can agree on how to divide it*. When I give the signal, you can begin. You are free to make any arrangements you wish and to proceed in any fashion you'd like."

Now, place the index cards or slips of paper on a table in front of the three individuals. Then continue, reading the following sentence: "Remember: the money will belong to any two people in each group who can agree on how to divide it."

Allow the individuals involved to negotiate for five minutes, or until two of them reach an agreement. Note that this agreement will, of necessity, exclude the third person.

Points to Consider

1. What happened in the game? Did two of the people form a coalition, thus excluding the third participant?
2. What was this agreement like? Did the two people who reached it decide to divide the money equally? If not, how did they divide it?
3. How was the agreement reached? Did one person push for a coalition more strongly than the other two? What did she or he say that finally won the cooperation of another participant?
4. Was the person you suspected of being high in Machiavellianism part of the team that agreed to divide the money between them? If so, did this person receive more than her or his partner?
5. What would *you* have done in this situation?

7

STRESS:
ITS NATURE,
IMPACT, AND
MANAGEMENT

CHAPTER OUTLINE

Special Sections

LEARNING OBJECTIVES

After reading this chapter, you should be able to:
1. Define stress in terms of its physiological, behavioral, and cognitive components.
2. Describe several major work-related causes of stress and several personal factors that also contribute to stress in organizational settings.
3. Describe the impact of stress on personal health, task performance, and decision making.
4. Define burnout, describe its major components, and indicate why it occurs.

5. Explain how reactions to stress are affected by several personal characteristics, such as optimism, hardiness, and the Type A behavior pattern.
6. Describe physiological, behavioral, and cognitive techniques individuals can use to manage their own stress.
7. Describe several techniques that organizations can use to help manage stress among their employees.

S o, Mr. Nakao, what seems to be the problem?"

"I don't know, doctor," Joe Nakao replies, shaking his head. "I just don't feel like myself lately. When I come home from the office I'm totally exhausted. Some days it seems as though I hardly have the energy to push the button for the elevator. And I'm not sleeping like I usually do. I have a lot of trouble falling asleep, and then when I do, I wake up four, maybe five, times during the night. That never happened to me before."

"Hmm," Dr. Williams murmurs, stroking his chin. "Anything else?"

"Yeah. This past six months I've had about three colds. One of them was really bad—kept me out of the office for four days. I can't figure it out; I *never* get sick. Before this year, I can't even remember the last time I missed more than a day of work at one time. And my digestion's been bothering me, too. Usually, I can eat just about anything. But lately, when I eat spicy foods, I get a burning sensation. Sometimes it's real bad."

"Well, let's have a look at you," Dr. Williams comments. For the next thirty minutes, there's mostly silence in the room, as he conducts a thorough physical examination. When he's done, he says: "Okay, you can get dressed now. I'll see you in my office right away."

Joe dresses hurriedly, and then enters the doctor's office. A couple of minutes later, Dr. Williams arrives and takes a seat.

"Well, Joe, I don't think there's anything seriously wrong with you—at least not *yet*," he remarks. "All of your symptoms seem to be related to one thing: stress. Your pulse is irregular, your blood pressure is up from what it usually is, and I see that you've lost some weight. Altogether, it looks to me like the effects of stress. Is this an especially stressful time for you?"

"I'll say!" Joe answers emphatically. "I don't know if I ever mentioned it, but I work for the government, and two months ago we had a big cut in our budget—the biggest ever. I mean, they slashed us eighty percent—can you believe it? Eighty percent!"

"And you're upset about that?"

"Yeah, but that's only part of it. See, my job involves reviewing grant proposals from scientists all over the country, to decide whose research gets supported. After these cuts, there's not much left to support *any* research. So all day long all I do is say 'No.' And a lot of these people are my friends. Can you imagine what it's like to tell someone who's been working on a project for ten years that suddenly there's no money, and that they have to close up shop?" At this Joe shudders visibly. "It's awful!"

"Do you have to do that sort of thing every day?"

"Absolutely. Some days, that's just about *all* I do—give people bad news."

"And there's nothing you can do about the situation?"

"No, nothing, except maybe try to stretch what little money's left to as many people as I can."

"So you really *are* under a lot of stress at work."

"I guess so," Joe answers, shaking his head. Then, after a brief hesitation, he continues. "But that's really not all of it, I guess. My wife and I . . . we're not getting along like we used to. We moved here from out West, and she really hates Washington. She's never gotten used to all the heat in the summer. And she misses her friends. Anyway, she's been kind of depressed, and I probably haven't been as understanding as I should have been. So we fight a lot. It's gotten so that I get kind of a sinking feeling in the pit of my stomach when I reach for the handle on the front door. I never know what to expect."

At this point, Dr. Williams interrupts. "You don't have to go on, Joe, I get the picture. And I do think we've pinpointed your problem. You're just under too much stress. I'm going to give you a mild muscle relaxant to calm you down a little. That ought to help your sleep. I also think you should try some exercise—you know, jogging, swimming—almost anything that will give you a chance to work out some of your tension. That really *can* help. And here's a little pamphlet on ways of handling stress. It has some pretty good tips in it."

"Do you really think that's what's wrong with me, doctor? I know stress isn't good for you, but could it really be the reason I feel like I do?"

"Absolutely," Dr. Williams responds with conviction. "All the evidence I've seen indicates that stress is one of the worst things around where personal health is concerned. You wouldn't believe some of the papers I've read on the subject. No, I'm certain that all your problems are stress related. Anyway, let's go ahead on that assumption. Why don't you try some of the things I've suggested and come back in, let's say, about six weeks. If you're not feeling any better by then, we'll do some more tests. But believe me: I think we've got the problem identified. Now, it's really up to *you* to do something about it."

Have you ever felt like Joe Nakao—that you were right on the edge of being overwhelmed by events in your life that you could not control and with which you might not be able to cope? If so, you are already familiar with *stress*—the main focus of this chapter. Unfortunately, stress is an all-too-common part of life in the 1990s, something few individuals can avoid. Moreover, stress is costly for both organizations and individuals. Growing evidence suggests that high levels of stress adversely affect physical health, psychological well-being, and many aspects of task performance.[1]

Given such effects, stress is a topic of considerable importance to the field of organizational behavior. In this chapter, we will consider it in detail. First, we will examine the *basic nature* of stress—what it is and its major components. Next, we will turn to its *major causes*—factors in work settings and life generally that tend to induce high levels of stress. Third, we will examine the impact of stress—its effects on health, task performance, and other aspects of work-related behavior. Finally, we will examine procedures for *managing stress*—techniques that individuals and organizations can employ to help reduce stress or counter its adverse effects.

STRESS: ITS BASIC NATURE

When asked to describe their own experiences with stress, many people emphasize its emotional nature. They refer to stress largely as an unpleasant subjective state accompanied by high levels of arousal. To a degree, such descriptions are accurate: stress does indeed involve a subjective, emotional component. However, experts on this subject now agree that this is only part of the total picture. Full understanding of stress and its many effects must involve attention to three related issues.

First, consider the *physiological aspects* of stress. According to Selye, a leading expert on this topic, these can be divided into several distinct stages.[2] When confronted with any threat to our safety or well-being, we experience an immediate and vigorous *alarm reaction*. Arousal rises quickly to high levels, and many physiological changes that prepare our bodies for strenuous activity (either flight or combat) take place. This initial reaction is soon replaced by a second stage known as *resistance*. Here, activation remains relatively high, but drops to levels that are more sustainable over relatively long periods of time. If stress persists, the body's resources may become depleted and a final stage known as *exhaustion* occurs. At this point, the ability to cope (at least physically) decreases sharply, and severe biological damage may result if stress persists. (See Figure 7–1 for a summary of these physiological reactions.)

Second, to fully understand stress, one must consider the external events or stimuli that induce it—the nature of various **stressors.** What is it about these stimuli that produces stress? What do they have in common? No final answers to such questions currently exist, but many stressful events appear to share the following properties: (1) they are so intense, in some respects, that they produce a state of *overload*—we

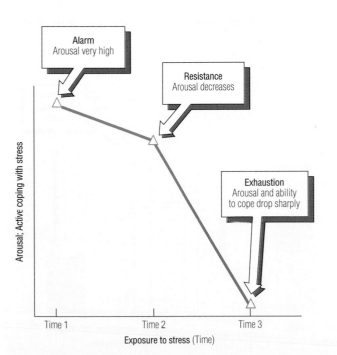

FIGURE 7–1

Physiological Reactions to Stress

When we are exposed to stress, several physiological changes occur. First, we experience a vigorous *alarm reaction*. This is followed by a stage of *resistance* in which we actively seek to cope with the source of stress. If stress persists, a final stage of *exhaustion* may occur, in which our ability to cope with stress drops to a low level. (*Source:* Based on suggestions by Selye, 1976; see Note 2.)

Alarm
Arousal very high

Resistance
Arousal decreases

Exhaustion
Arousal and ability to cope drop sharply

Arousal; Active coping with stress

Time 1   Time 2   Time 3

Exposure to stress (Time)

can no longer adapt to them; (2) they evoke simultaneous incompatible tendencies (e.g., urges to both approach and avoid some object or activity); and (3) they are uncontrollable—outside our ability to change or influence.

Finally, and perhaps most important of all, stress involves the operation of several cognitive factors. Perhaps the most central of these is individuals' *cognitive appraisal* of a given situation or potential stressor.[3] In simple terms, stress occurs only to the extent that the individuals involved perceive (1) that the situation is somehow threatening to their important goals, and (2) that they will be unable to cope with these potential dangers or demands—that the situation is, in essence, beyond their control. In short, stress does not simply shape our thoughts; in many cases, it derives from and is strongly affected by them.

Direct evidence for the important role of cognitive factors in the occurrence and magnitude of stress is provided by an informative study conducted recently by Evans and Carrere.[4] These researchers hypothesized that bus drivers in urban areas would experience increasing stress as traffic congestion on the routes increased. Moreover, such stress would stem primarily from the fact that as traffic congestion increased, drivers would experience a reduced sense of control over their jobs. Such feelings of reduced personal control would reflect the fact that as traffic congestion increases, drivers' ability to regulate their speed to stay on schedule, and to change lanes as needed to pick up passengers, is greatly reduced.

To test the hypothesized mediating role of perceived job control, Evans and Carrere measured the amount of stress experienced by drivers through physiological means: the amount of adrenaline and noradrenaline in their urine. (Stress is known to increase the concentration of these substances.) In addition, drivers answered a questionnaire designed to assess their feelings of personal control over their jobs (e.g., "To what extent does your job allow you a lot of freedom as to how you do your work?"). Traffic congestion was calculated from records on traffic volume at various times during the day, for each driver's route. Results offered strong support for the view that perceived control over one's job plays an important role in the level of stress experienced by urban bus drivers. As shown in Figure 7–2, the drivers' perceived control over their jobs dropped as traffic congestion increased, whereas physiological signs of stress (urine concentrations of noradrenaline) rose sharply.

FIGURE 7–2

Job Stress and Perceived Control

Urban bus drivers' levels of stress rose with rising traffic congestion. Further, as traffic congestion increased, their perceived control over their jobs decreased. These findings are consistent with the view that perceived job control often plays an important role in work-related stress. (*Source:* Based on data from Evans & Carrere, 1991; see Note 4.)

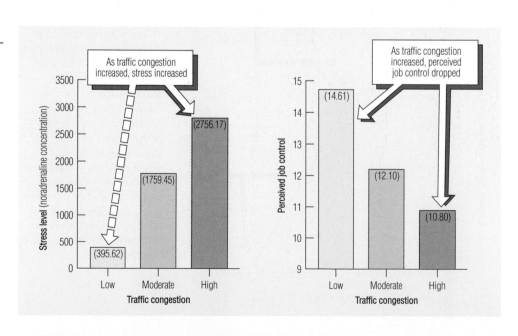

Test Bank questions 7.5–7.6 relate to material on this page.

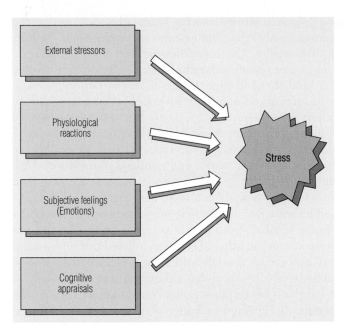

FIGURE 7–3

Basic Components of Stress

To fully understand stress, we must take into account the emotional, physiological, and cognitive reactions it involves, and the external conditions that contribute to its occurrence.

These results, and those of several other studies, indicate that perceived job control is indeed an important factor determining stress for many jobs.[5]

To understand the nature of stress, therefore, it is necessary to consider the emotional and physiological reactions it involves, the external conditions that produce it, and the cognitive processes that play a role in its occurrence (see Figure 7–3). Taking all these factors into account, we can define **stress** as *a pattern of emotional states and physiological reactions occurring in situations where individuals perceive threats to their important goals which they may be unable to meet.*[6] In short, stress occurs when people feel, rightly or wrongly, that they may soon be overwhelmed by events or circumstances that exceed their personal resources.

STRESS: ITS MAJOR CAUSES

What factors contribute to stress in work settings? Unfortunately, the list is a long one. As we will soon see, many different conditions play a role. Moreover, these factors are not independent in their effects. For example, the presence of one stressor may intensify reactions to one or more others. For purposes of this discussion, however, we will consider each major cause of work-related stress separately. In addition, for purposes of clarity, we will divide these factors into two major categories: those relating directly to organizations or jobs, and those relating to other aspects of individuals' lives.

Work-Related Causes of Stress

As anyone who has been employed well knows, work settings are often highly stressful environments. Yet, that they vary greatly in this respect is also clear. Some jobs and organizations expose individuals to high levels of stress on a regular basis. In contrast, others involve much lower levels and frequency of stress. What factors account for these differences? What are the major causes of stress in organizational contexts? A complete answer to this question is beyond the scope of this chapter. However, several of the most important sources of stress in the workplace are described below.

A bank teller's job is particularly stressful. This stress is largely because of the ever-growing threat of being robbed at gunpoint. At Wells Fargo Bank alone, the number of robberies in the first quarter of 1991 increased 37 percent. In response to this alarming statistic, Wells Fargo established a formal program of psychological counseling designed to help those employees who have been involved in a robbery. [Farnham, A. (1991, October 7). Who beats stress best—And how. *Fortune*, pp. 71–86.]

Occupational Demands: Some Jobs Are More Stressful Than Others   Consider the following jobs: production manager, librarian, emergency room physician, janitor, firefighter, college professor, airline pilot. Do they differ in degree of stressfulness? Obviously, they do. Some, such as emergency room physician, firefighter, and airline pilot, expose the people who hold them to high levels of stress. Others, such as college professor, janitor, and librarian, do not. This basic fact—that some jobs are much more stressful than others—has been confirmed by the results of a careful survey involving more than 130 different occupations.[7] Results of this survey indicate that several jobs (e.g., physician, officer manager, foreman, waitress or waiter) are quite high in stress. In contrast, others (e.g., maid, craft workers, farm laborer) are much lower in this regard. But what, precisely, makes some jobs more stressful than others? A partial answer is provided by a study conducted by Shaw and Riskind.[8]

These researchers reviewed information about the levels of stress experienced by people holding a very wide range of jobs—from executive and architect on the one hand to secretary and factory worker on the other. Then they related this information about stressfulness to various aspects of the jobs. Results indicated that several features of jobs are indeed related to the levels of stress they generate. For example, the greater the extent to which a given job requires (1) making decisions, (2) constant monitoring of devices or materials, (3) repeated exchange of information with others, (4) unpleasant physical conditions, and (5) performing unstructured rather than structured tasks, the more stressful the job tends to be. Moreover—and this is the most important point—such relationships were found to be quite general in nature. Thus, the greater the extent to which virtually *any* job possesses these characteristics, the higher the level of stress it produces among individuals holding it, regardless of the specific tasks being performed. This is certainly a point worth considering when planning a career or choosing between potential jobs (see the discussion of these topics in chapter 9).

Role Conflict: Stress from Conflicting Demands   Consider the following situation. Because she has done excellent work for several years, a young chemist is promoted to the position of Assistant Director for Research. In her new role, she must oversee numerous projects being carried out in her company's laboratories. As a member of her organization's management team, she must try to assure that these projects are completed in a timely and cost-efficient manner, and that they contribute to the company's stated goals (e.g., the development of new products). Now, however, one of the scientists in her department informs her that he has uncovered an interesting new phenomenon. It is not directly related to the work he is doing, but he feels it is exciting, scientifically, and should be pursued. What does the Assistant Director do? Her job seems to require that she discourage the scientist from going off on a tangent, spending company time and money on topics not directly related to his work. Yet, as a chemist, she fully appreciates the potential scientific value of his discovery.

As you can see, this may be an unpleasant and potentially stressful situation for the young woman in question. She is experiencing **role conflict**—conflicting demands from her obligations as Assistant Director for Research and her professional identity as a chemist. Unfortunately, role conflict is common in many work settings. Most people fulfill several roles in their lives and, as a result, frequently find that the demands of one role conflict with the demands of another. Perhaps the most disturbing conflicts of this type involve the conflicting demands of the employee and parent roles. Growing evidence indicates that such role conflict is a major cause of stress for many individuals, and especially for females.[9] Working mothers report that they must engage frequently in *role juggling*—rapidly switching from one role and one type of activity to another. (See chapter 8 for more information about roles.)

This pattern, in turn, is often highly stressful for them. A recent study by Williams, Suls, Alliger, Learner, and Choie provides direct evidence for this conclusion.[10]

This investigation employed a novel technique known as *experience sampling*. In this procedure, individuals wear a small device that signals them, at random times during the day, to enter their current activity on a special form. Participants in the study conducted by Williams et al. were working mothers, who agreed to enter their current activities on a form when signaled to do so between the hours of 8:00 A.M. and 10:00 P.M. on each of eight consecutive days. Participants indicated whether they were engaged in solitary work-related activities, group work-related activities, household or family-related activities, social activities, or other types of activities (e.g., shopping). They also indicated whether, during the past thirty minutes, they had found it necessary to juggle two or more tasks at once, and they described the nature of these tasks. Finally, participants rated their current moods, and their enjoyment of their current tasks.

Results indicated that the greater the amount of role juggling experienced by participants, the lower their enjoyment of reported tasks. Similarly, the greater their degree of role juggling, the more negative their current moods. Although stress was not measured directly, these results do imply that role juggling is a demanding chore, one that places a heavy drain on individuals' personal resources. Indeed, Williams and his colleagues interpret their findings as suggesting that role juggling is a stressor— one that increases demands on individuals' cognitive capacities to the point at which considerable psychological strain occurs.[11]

Do these findings indicate that role conflict, or role juggling, inevitably produces stress and the adverse effects associated with it? Other evidence indicates that this is not necessarily so. For example, Newton and Keenan reported that the adverse effects of role conflict are less pronounced in work settings characterized by friendliness and social support than in work settings where such conditions are lacking.[12] These findings suggest that although a degree of role conflict is probably unavoidable in many contexts, its contribution to overall levels of stress can be countered by other, positive conditions.

Role Ambiguity: Stress from Uncertainty   Even if individuals avoid the stress associated with role conflict, however, they may still encounter an even more common source of job-related stress: **role ambiguity.** This occurs when people are uncertain about several matters relating to their jobs: the scope of their responsibilities, what's expected of them, how to divide their time between various duties. Most people dislike such uncertainty and find it quite stressful, but it is often unavoidable. Thus, role ambiguity is quite common. In fact, 35 to 60 percent of employees surveyed report experiencing it to some degree.[13] Clearly, then, it is one major cause of stress in many work settings.

Overload and Underload: Doing Too Much or Too Little   When the phrase "work-related stress" is mentioned, most people envision scenes in which employees are asked to do too much—more work than they can handle in a given period of time. In fact, this image is often correct, for such *overload* is one important cause of stress in many work settings. A distinction should be made, however, between **quantitative overload**—situations in which individuals are asked to do more work than they can complete in a specific period of time; and **qualitative overload**—employees' belief that they lack the required skills or abilities to perform a given job. Both types of overload are unpleasant, and research findings suggest that both can lead to high levels of stress.[14]

Yet, overload is only part of the total picture. Although being asked to do too much can be stressful, so can being asked to do too little. In fact, there seems to be

The effects of overload are particularly prominent in Japan, where many employees have suffered from *karoshi*, or "death from overwork." These individuals are literally killing themselves trying to complete more work than they can physically handle. Unfortunately, the number of people who die from over-

Test Bank questions 7.10–7.12, 7.49, 7.58–7.59, and 7.68 relate to material on this page.

work is expected to rise. In a recent study, 40 percent of the Japanese employees surveyed said that they feared that overwork might kill them, but few planned to do anything about it. [Impoco, J. (1991, March 18). Dying to work. *U.S. News & World Report,* p. 24.]

considerable truth in the following statement: "The hardest job in the world is doing nothing—you can't take a break." *Underload* leads to boredom and monotony. Since these reactions are quite unpleasant, underload, too, can be stressful. Again, there is a distinction between **quantitative underload** and **qualitative underload.** Quantitative underload refers to the boredom that results when employees have so little to do that they find themselves sitting around much of the time. In contrast, qualitative underload refers to the lack of mental stimulation that accompanies many routine, repetitive jobs. (See Figure 7–4 for an overview of the nature of these various types of overload and underload.)

Responsibility for Others: A Heavy Burden Division of responsibility occurs in every organization. Some people deal primarily with the physical side of the business (e.g., obtaining supplies, directing production, maintaining equipment), others focus mainly on financial matters (e.g., budgets, taxes, accounting), and still others— usually supervisors or managers—deal primarily with people. Do the levels of stress associated with these contrasting roles differ? Research suggests that they do. In general, individuals who are responsible for other people—who must motivate them, reward or punish them, communicate with them—experience higher levels of stress than individuals who handle other organizational functions.[15] Such people are more likely to report feelings of tension and anxiety, and are actually more likely to show overt symptoms of stress such as ulcers or hypertension, than their counterparts in finance or supply. The reasons behind this difference are complex, so only two are

FIGURE 7–4

Overload and Underload

Both *overload* and *underload* can be sources of stress at work. Two distinct patterns— quantitative and qualitative—exist for each.

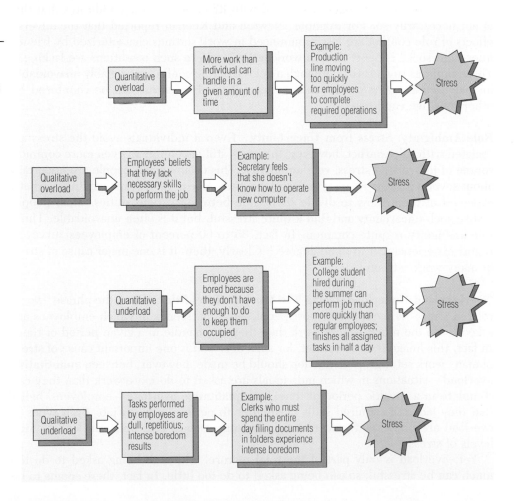

mentioned here. First, it is managers who must, ultimately, confront the human costs of organizational policies and decisions. For example, they must deliver negative feedback and then witness the distress it often generates. Second, it is their task to deal with the many frictions that are a normal part of human relations at work. This involves listening to endless complaints, mediating disputes, promoting cooperation, and exercising leadership. All of these tasks are demanding and can contribute to the total burden of stress experienced by managers.

Lack of Social Support: The Costs of Isolation   According to one old saying, "Misery loves company." In the context of stress, this statement implies that if we have to face stressful conditions, it's better to do so along with others (and with their support) rather than alone. Many people accept this view as correct. When confronted with stress, they seek support and comfort from others. Does this strategy actually work? In general, the answer seems to be "yes." When individuals believe they have the friendship and support of others at work, their ability to resist the adverse effects of stress seems to increase. For example, in one investigation on this topic, Oullette-Kobasa and Pucetti studied managers at a large public utility who were experiencing high levels of stress.[16] They found that the managers who felt they had the support of their immediate supervisors reported fewer physical symptoms associated with stress than managers who did not feel that they enjoyed such support.

How does social support help individuals deal with stress? Several mechanisms may play a role. First, having friends to turn to in times of difficulty may help individuals perceive stressful events as less threatening and more under their control than would otherwise be the case. Second, friends can often suggest useful strategies for dealing with sources of stress. Third, they can help reduce the negative feelings that often accompany exposure to stressful events.

Lack of Participation in Decisions: Helplessness Strikes Again   As we have noted several times, most people want to feel that they have at least some control over their own fate. The opposite belief—that we are helpless pawns tossed about by forces beyond our control—is disturbing. Unfortunately, one factor contributing to such feelings is common in work settings: lack of participation by employees in decisions affecting their jobs. Most people feel that they know a good deal about their work. Thus, when they are prevented from offering input into decisions concerning them, they feel left out and unable to control their own outcomes. The result: they experience considerable stress. In general, then, permitting employees to participate in decisions that affect their jobs seems to be a wise strategy. Not only does it enhance their work-related attitudes, it helps counter an important source of work-related stress as well. (For information on another, and highly unsettling, cause of stress in work settings, see the **Question of Ethics** section on pp. 234–236.)

Other Work-Related Sources of Stress: Appraisals, Working Conditions, and Change   The factors described above appear to be among the most important sources of stress in organizations, but several others are also worthy of mention. Perhaps the most important of these is the process of **performance appraisal**. Being evaluated by their supervisors is a highly stressful experience for many people; after all, the stakes are high (their future career is on the line), and the possibility of negative feedback is real. For this reason, it is important that such appraisals be conducted in as calm, rational, and fair a manner as possible. This often involves considerable preparation on the part of the manager *and* the individuals being evaluated (e.g., exactly what aspects of performance will be considered, and what form evaluations will take, should be decided in advance). The effort invested in such tasks is well worthwhile, though, for the annual or semiannual performance appraisal can be a major source of stress in most organizations.

A QUESTION OF ETHICS

Sexual Harassment: A Pervasive Problem in Work Settings

 Patricia Kidd sensed she faced trouble when her new boss, Mr. Carter, began complimenting her, in a very personal way, on her looks. And these comments did not occur in a sexual vacuum: her boss also kept pictures of nude women on the wall of his office. In subsequent conversations, Carter told Ms. Kidd that women who reached the top in District of Columbia government (where they both worked) "got there on their backs." Then he started calling her at home and propositioning her. The situation came to its ultimate conclusion when, the day after the office Christmas party, Carter called Ms. Kidd at the office from a hotel a block away and told her to come join him. When she refused, he threatened to fire her if she did not come. Ms. Kidd, a single mother with two dependent children, submitted. From that point on, he continued his campaign of *sexual harassment,* insisting that she dine with him; and on several occasions, he took her to his house, where they again had sexual relations. Disgusted and dismayed by this intolerable situation, Ms. Kidd filed a formal complaint against Carter. Her initial complaint was dismissed, but she persisted, filing a personal suit against him. Finally, with the aid of several witnesses, and telephone logs confirming Carter's calls to her from the hotel, Ms. Kidd obtained some measure of justice: a jury awarded her $300,000 in damages.

Although this case is extreme, there can be little doubt that sexual harassment, directed primarily at women, is an all-too-common problem in many work settings. Indeed, when asked in a recent poll conducted jointly by the *New York Times* and CBS News whether they had ever been the object of sexual advances, propositions, or unwanted sexual discussions from men who supervise them, fully *30 percent* of the women polled answered "yes." And this is not a one-sided perception: when asked if they had ever said or done something at work that could be construed by a female colleague as harassment, fully 50 percent of the men polled indicated that they had.[17] So **sexual harassment,** generally defined as unwanted contact or communication of a sexual nature, is indeed a frequent occurrence in the world of work.[18] (See Figure 7–5 for more information about the prevalence of sexual harassment.)[19]

Is such harassment more common today than in the past? Some statistics seem to suggest that it is. The number of complaints filed by employees rose from 4,272 in 1981 to almost 6,000 by 1990. Whether this is due to an actual increase in the incidence of sexual harassment or merely to greater reporting of its occurrence is impossible to say. Certainly, media attention to this problem has increased tremendously, especially during the U.S. Senate hearings in 1991 concerning Supreme Court nominee Clarence Thomas. As you may recall, Judge Thomas was accused of sexual harassment by Anita Hill, a former subordinate. Although Professor Hill's charges were never conclusively proven, they did raise public consciousness of this problem to new heights. In any event, it is clear that for every case of sexual harassment reported, many more go *un*reported. Indeed, only 10 percent of women who report having experienced sexual harassment indicate that they actually reported the incident.[20]

Certainly, sexual harassment raises important ethical issues. On the one hand, the occurrence of such behavior in work settings indicates that organizations have a strong responsibility to do everything in their power to prevent harassment from occurring and to deal with it firmly when it takes place.[21] This means developing and clearly stating formal policies concerning sexual harassment. Such policies should describe what constitutes sexual harassment, and should draw the line in this respect *very* conservatively. Ethics, as well as legal considerations, dictate that there should be virtually no tolerance of this type of behavior. Similarly, organizations must state clear policies concerning the potential penalties for sexual harassment and adopt mecha-

---

A CNN video is available to accompany this section. Additional information can be found in the CNN Video User's Guide.

Test Bank questions 7.17 and 7.69 relate to material on this page.

nisms for assuring that these are enacted. Research findings indicate that individuals who sexually harass one fellow employee often harass others as well. It is crucial, therefore, that when instances of sexual harassment come to light they be dealt with quickly and firmly. The policy adopted by AT&T (presented in Figure 7–6 on p. 236) provides a good model for an explicit policy on sexual harassment. Notice how clearly and precisely it defines actions that can be considered sexual harassment and the penalties that may be invoked against employees who engage in such practices.

The other side of the ethical coin involves the responsibilities of fellow employees who are not themselves the victims of sexual harassment. Sexual harassment is so stressful and disturbing to its victims, and so destructive both to the victims and to their companies, that such a case is definitely *not* one in which bystanders can stand idly by. On the contrary, people who witness sexual harassment must resist the temptation to avoid "getting involved," and join together with victims to take a firm stand against this problem. Indeed, in cases where victims are too intimidated to take action themselves, ethical

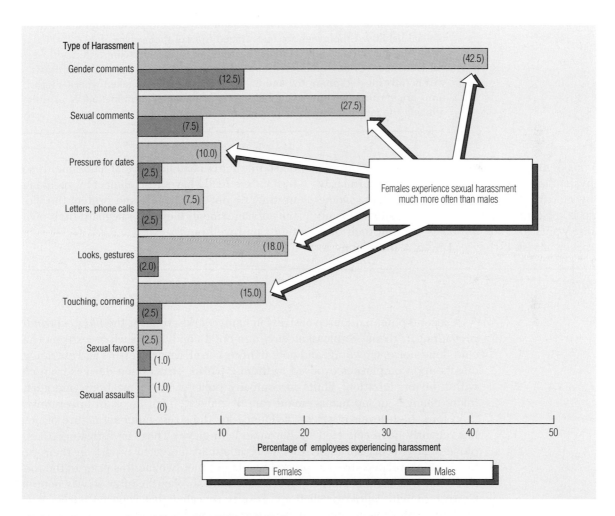

FIGURE 7–5   Sexual Harassment in Work Settings

As shown here, recent surveys indicate that various forms of sexual harassment are disturbingly common in work settings. (*Source:* Based on data from Niven, 1992; see Note 19.)

AT&T's sexual harassment policy prohibits sexual harassment in the workplace, whether committed by supervisory or nonsupervisory personnel. Specifically, no supervisor shall threaten to insinuate, either explicitly or implicitly, that an employee's submission to or rejection of sexual advances will in any way influence any personnel decision regarding that employee's employment, wages, advancement, assigned duties, shifts, or any other condition of employment or career development.

Other sexually harassing conduct in the workplace that may create an offensive work environment, whether it be in the form of physical or verbal harassment, and regardless of whether committed by supervisory or nonsupervisory personnel, is also prohibited. This includes, but is not limited to, repeated offensive or unwelcome sexual flirtations, advances, propositions, continual or repeated verbal abuse of a sexual nature, graphic verbal commentaries about an individual's body, sexually degrading words used to describe an individual, and the display in the workplace of sexually suggestive objects or pictures.

Sexual harassment in the workplace by any employee will result in disciplinary action up to and including dismissal and may lead to personal legal and financial liability. Employees are encouraged to avail themselves of AT&T's internal Equal Opportunity complaint procedure if they are confronted with sexual harassment or any prohibited form of harassment. Such internal complaints will be investigated promptly, and corrective action will be taken where allegations are verified. No employee will suffer retaliation or intimidation as a result of using the internal complaint procedure.

considerations virtually require that responsible bystanders intervene on their behalf—primarily by alerting the appropriate authorities. Doing so is, of course, difficult in many situations: no one wants to "rock the boat" and put their own career at risk if they can help it. But failing to do so implicitly condones sexual harassment, so bystanders really have little choice: by speaking up they do not simply help and protect the victims of harassment; they also safeguard their own rights and well-being.

A second potential source of stress in many work settings is the *physical conditions* prevailing in them. Unpleasant environmental conditions such as extreme heat or cold, loud noise, crowding, and poor lighting can all act as stressors and exert negative effects upon employees exposed to them.[22] Third, stress often derives from *change* within an organization. Shifts in company policies, reorganizations, mergers, and major changes in top management can all generate high levels of uncertainty and, therefore, high levels of stress. Evidence for the stress-inducing nature of mergers has recently been collected by Baron and Bingley.[23] These investigators asked employees in two organizations that were about to merge to report on their current levels of job-related stress at several points in time: two months prior to the merger, one month after the merger took place, and six months after it was completed. Consistent with initial predictions, results revealed that reported stress rose immediately after the merger, but then decreased with the passage of time, presumably because necessary adjustments were completed.

Do Some Employees Carry Their Own Stress with Them? So far in this discussion we have focused on factors present in work settings that induce stress among people exposed to them. This is certainly appropriate, for a large body of evidence indicates that stress is indeed generated by specific external conditions. There is another aspect of this picture, however, and we would be remiss if we neglected to mention it. Although working conditions certainly do influence the level of stress experienced by employees, it is also true that stress is influenced by personal factors. In other words, to some extent, specific people seem to carry their own stress around with them, and tend to experience fairly high levels of stress no matter where they work. Evidence for this conclusion has been reported by Nelson and Sutton in a carefully conducted longitudinal study—one that assessed the levels of stress experienced by a group of individuals over a nine-month period.[24]

Participants in the study were newcomers to three organizations. These individuals completed measures dealing with their style of coping with stress (*problem-focused:* taking steps to cope directly with the causes of stress; *emotion-focused:* release of feelings to reduce tension; or *appraisal-focused:* considering various alternatives for handling the problem) and the level of distress they experienced (physical symptoms related to stress). They completed these measures on three separate occasions: (1) prior to the first day of work, (2) six months later, and (3) nine months later. The investigators predicted that problem-focused coping and appraisal-focused coping would be negatively related to distress, whereas emotion-focused coping would be positively related to distress. None of these hypotheses was confirmed. However, it was also predicted—and found—that the greater the level of distress reported by subjects before joining the organization, the greater the level of distress they would report nine months later. In other words, individuals joined the organization with a specific level of distress and, nine months later, generally showed a similar level of distress.

As noted by Nelson and Sutton, these findings suggest that "individuals bring into a job a large proportion of the [stress-related] symptoms they experience on the job."[25] Thus, some stress at work may reflect personal dispositions and tendencies as much as conditions actually prevailing in an organization. What characteristics might be involved? One possibility, noted by Nelson and Sutton, is *negative affectivity*—the tendency to experience negative affect, which we discussed in chapter 6.[26] Whatever the precise basis, some people appear to carry relatively high (or low) levels of stress around with them, and tend to show these levels in a wide range of work environments. We'll return to this point later when we consider several different techniques individuals can use to manage their own stress.

Personal (Life-Related) Causes of Stress

Although work is clearly one of the most important activities in many people's lives, it is far from the only activity. Most individuals have a full and varied life outside the workplace as well as within it. Given this fact, it is not surprising that events outside work settings often generate stress that persists and is carried back to work the next day. Many events or experiences contribute to life-related stress—everything from family squabbles to leaking roofs to cars that won't start on cold mornings. Most, however, seem to fit under two broad categories: *major stressful life events* and *daily hassles*.[27]

Stressful Life Events   Death of a spouse, divorce, injury to one's child, a stock market crash, failure in school, unwanted pregnancy—unless an individual leads a truly charmed life, he or she is likely to experience traumatic events or changes like these at some point. What are the effects of such events? This question was first studied by Holmes and Rahe, who asked large groups of people to assign arbitrary points (from 1 to 100) to various life events according to how much readjustment

T A B L E   7 – 1   Stressful Life Events

When asked to assign arbitrary points (1–100) to various life events according to the degree of readjustment they required, a large group of individuals provided the values shown here. The higher the numbers shown, the more stressful the events listed.

Event	Relative Stressfulness
Death of a spouse	100
Divorce	73
Marital separation	65
Jail term	63
Death of a close family member	63
Personal injury or illness	53
Marriage	50
Fired from job	47
Retirement	45
Pregnancy	40
Death of a close friend	37
Son or daughter leaving home	29
Trouble with in-laws	28
Trouble with boss	23
Change in residence	20
Vacation	13
Christmas	12
Minor violations of the law	11

Source: Based on data from Holmes & Masuda, 1974; see Note 29.

each had required.[28] Holmes and Rahe reasoned that the greater the number of points assigned to a given event, the more stressful it was for the people experiencing it.

Some of the values assigned by subjects to various stressful life events are shown in Table 7–1. As you can see, the highest numbers were assigned to serious events such as death of a spouse, divorce, or marital separation. In contrast, smaller numbers of points were assigned to such events as change in residence, vacation, or minor violations of the law (e.g., receiving a speeding ticket).

Going further, Holmes and Rahe then related the total number of points accumulated by individuals during a single year to changes in their personal health. The dramatic results they attained did much to stir interest in the effects of stress among scientists in several different fields. The greater the number of "stress points" people accumulated, the greater their likelihood of becoming seriously ill. For example, in one study on this topic, Holmes and Masuda asked patients at a university medical center to report all significant life changes (events) during the past eighteen months.[29] People who experienced events totaling 300 points or more showed a much higher incidence of illness during the next nine months than those with 200 points or less (49 percent versus 9 percent).

At this point, we should note that this seemingly simple relationship between stress and health is complicated by large individual differences in the ability to withstand the impact of stress. Some people suffer ill effects after exposure to a few mildly stressful events, whereas others remain healthy even after prolonged exposure to high levels of stress; they are described as being *stress-resistant* or *hardy*. We'll return to such differences below. For the moment, we merely wish to emphasize that in general, the greater the number of stressful life events experienced by individuals, the greater the likelihood that their subsequent health will suffer in some manner.

The Hassles of Daily Life   Traumatic life events such as the ones studied by Holmes and Rahe, although clearly very stressful, are relatively rare. Many people live for years, or even decades, without experiencing any of them. Does this mean that such individuals live their lives in a serene lake of tranquillity? Hardly. Daily life is filled with countless minor sources of stress that seem to make up for their relatively low intensity by their high frequency of occurrence. That such *daily hassles* are an important cause of stress is suggested by the findings of several studies by Lazarus and his colleagues.[30] These researchers have developed a *Hassles Scale* on which individuals indicate the extent to which they have been "hassled" by common events during the past month. As shown in Table 7–2, items included in this scale deal with a wide range of everyday events (e.g., having too many things to do at once, shopping, concerns about money). Scores on the Hassles Scale developed by Lazarus, or on other, similar scales, are positively related to self-reported stress. The more hassles individuals report experiencing, the greater the stress they feel. In addition, scores on the scales designed to measure the minor irritants of everyday life are also related to psychological symptoms: the more hassles people experience, the poorer their psychological well-being. Finally, scores on such scales are also linked to physical health. The more hassles people experience, the larger the number of symptoms and minor ailments they report having.[31]

In sum, although traumatic life events such as the death of a loved one or the loss of one's job are stressful and have adverse effects on health, the minor hassles of daily life—perhaps because of their frequent, repetitive nature—may sometimes

TABLE 7–2   Daily Hassles as a Source of Stress

The everyday events and concerns shown here are ones many people describe as common sources of stress.

Type of Problem	Examples
Household hassles	Preparing meals Shopping
Time pressure hassles	Too many things to do Too many responsibilities
Inner concern hassles	Being lonely Fear of confrontation
Environmental hassles	Neighborhood deterioration Noise Crime
Financial responsibility	Concerns about owing money Financial responsibility for someone who doesn't live with you

Source: Based on information in DeLongis et al., 1985; see Note 27.

Test Bank questions 7.22 and 7.71 relate to material on this page.

prove even more crucial in this respect. Whatever their relative importance, both traumatic life events and daily hassles are important sources of stress for many people. And since the stress generated is often carried into their jobs by the individuals involved, these factors are certainly worth noting in this discussion of stress and its impact in work settings.

Total Life Stress: The Combined Picture   In the preceding discussion of sources of stress, we separated stressors related to work and those related to personal life events. This distinction reflects the fact that research on stressors often focuses on one or the other of these two major categories. But from the individual's point of view, work-related stress and life-related stress often seem to combine into a seamless—and potentially overwhelming—pattern of adversity. Is work going poorly? Are there many seemingly impossible deadlines to meet? Are one's boss or one's coworkers "acting up"? Then, it often seems, this is also the time for problems with one's children, one's relatives, or one's spouse. And is it *now,* when one is already feeling overloaded, that the furnace, car, or refrigerator begins making funny sounds— or quits working altogether!

The usefulness of adopting a broad approach in which work-related and personal causes of stress are combined into the construct of **total negative life stress** is suggested by the fact that such total stress is a better predictor of negative organizational outcomes (e.g., reduced job satisfaction and organizational commitment, increased turnover intentions) than either work-related or personal stressors alone.[32] So, where stress as actually experienced by individuals is concerned, no hard-and-fast boundaries exist between what happens at work and what happens at home. On the contrary, these two spheres of life are intertwined in many ways, so that added insights into the nature and impact of stress can often be gained by considering the two together as a unified whole.

STRESS: SOME MAJOR EFFECTS

By now, we're sure you are convinced of two facts: (1) stress stems from many sources, and (2) it exerts important effects on the people who experience it. What may not yet be apparent, though, is just how powerful and far-reaching such effects can be. We illustrated some of these effects in the story at the beginning of this chapter, where stress was, apparently, undermining the health of a vigorous young man. Such effects of stress on personal health are clearly very important, but systematic research indicates that stress can influence us in other ways as well. Specifically, it can also affect our psychological well-being, our performance on many tasks, and even the accuracy of our decisions. We will now describe several of these effects in more detail.

Stress and Health: The Silent Killer

How strong is the link between stress and personal health? According to medical experts, very strong indeed. In fact, some authorities estimate that stress plays some role in anywhere from 50 to 70 percent of all forms of physical illness.[33] Moreover, included in these figures are some of the most serious and life-threatening ailments known to medical science. To list just a few, stress has been implicated in the occurrence of heart disease, high blood pressure, hardening of the arteries, ulcers, and even diabetes.

In addition to its role in such *degenerative diseases*, growing evidence indicates that stress may also play a major role in *infectious diseases*—diseases that are caused by the introduction, into our bodies, of an infectious agent such as bacteria or viruses. Many studies indicate that exposure to high levels of stress increases susceptibility to diseases such as upper respiratory infections, herpesvirus infections, and various bacterial infections.[34] Some of these studies employ what is known as *prospective methodology*. In such research, the level of stress experienced by individuals at one point is related to their health at later times. Many studies of this type indicate that the rate of infectious illness does indeed increase following high-stress episodes. Still other investigations employ an approach in which healthy volunteers (emphasize the word *volunteers*) are purposely exposed to disease-causing agents, and to either stressful or nonstressful conditions. Results indicate that those exposed to stressful conditions do tend to develop the illness in question more frequently.[35]

How can stress increase susceptibility to infectious disease? A model proposed recently by Cohen and Williamson suggests that several mechanisms may play a role. According to this model, stress may influence the immune system by affecting hormonal balance within the body or the neural mechanisms that regulate various aspects of the immune system (e.g., production of white blood cells). Similarly, stress may influence health practices and coping through social contact; these, in turn, may alter rate of exposure to disease-causing organisms (see Figure 7–7). Whatever the precise mechanism, existing evidence does suggest that stress can play a significant role in the occurrence, and course, of many infectious diseases. (For additional evidence concerning the adverse effects of stress, see the **OB in Practice** section on pp. 242–243.)

Stress and Task Performance

At one time in the past, the relationship between stress and performance on many tasks was generally believed to be *curvilinear*, so that, at first, increments in stress (from none to low or moderate levels) were energizing and so led to improved

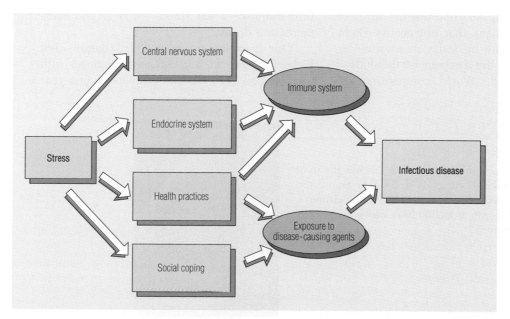

FIGURE 7–7

Stress and Infectious Disease: One Model

According to a model proposed by Cohen and Williamson, stress may increase susceptibility to infectious diseases through several different mechanisms. (*Source:* Based on suggestions by Cohen & Williamson, 1991; see Note 34.)

Job performance may be enhanced when stress levels are reduced by clarifying work expectations. Interestingly, this happens even among jobs that are not thought of as being particularly stressful. For example, it has been found that college professors produce more and better research when they are given specific information about what is expected of them than when no such information is provided. [Graham, C. W. (1989). Increased research performance through reduced stress and improved human well-being. *Society of Research Administrators Journal, 21*(3), 35–39.]

performance. Beyond some point, however, additional increments in stress were assumed to be distracting or to interfere with performance in other ways. Thus, at high or very high levels of stress, performance would actually fall.

Although this relationship may hold true under some conditions, growing evidence suggests that stress exerts mainly negative effects on task performance. In other words, performance can be disrupted even by relatively low levels of stress. Evidence pointing to this conclusion is provided in a study conducted by Motowidlo, Packard, and Manning.[36] These researchers asked a large group of nurses to describe their own levels of work-related stress. Ratings of their actual job performance were then obtained from supervisors or coworkers. Results indicated that the higher the nurses' feelings of stress, the lower their job performance. In other words, there was no evidence for initial increments in performance as the curvilinear hypothesis suggests.

These findings, and those of several other studies, indicate that in many real-life settings, performance may be reduced even by low or moderate levels of stress. Why is this the case? Shouldn't the activation produced by moderate levels of stress facilitate performance in many situations? Although this possibility remains, and may apply in some situations (see below), several reasons exist for expecting even moderate levels of stress to interfere with task performance. First, even relatively mild stress

   OB IN PRACTICE

A Tale of Lost Horizons: Or What Can Happen When a Good Company Goes Bad

Once, not so long ago, Pan American Airlines was the most glamorous company in a glamorous industry. As late as the 1970s, Pan Am had more flights to more international destinations than any other U.S. airline (see Figure 7–8). So great was the allure of a job with the company that prospective flight attendants would line up a day in advance for interviews. But then the company hit the skids—and hit them hard. World competition in-

creased, unions escalated their demands, and management, quite frankly, made mistakes. The result: passenger traffic fell, profits evaporated, and almost before it knew what had happened, the company was teetering on the brink of bankruptcy. The result for many of Pan Am's long-time employees was stress—in large and ever-increasing doses.[37]

"Our lives are up in the air," commented Richard Laskowski, a maintenance engineer with the company. He was laid off twice in one year

FIGURE 7–8

Pan Am: The Glory Days

For several decades, Pan Am was the most glamorous company in a highly glamorous industry. Then, in the 1970s, the airline went into a decline from which it never recovered.

can be distracting. Individuals experiencing it may focus on the unpleasant feelings and emotions stress involves rather than on the task at hand. The result: their performance suffers. Second, prolonged or repeated exposure to even mild levels of stress may have harmful effects on health, and this may interfere with effective performance. Finally, a large body of research indicates that as arousal increases, task performance may at first rise, but at some point begins to fall. The precise location of this *inflection point* (the point at which the direction of the function reverses) seems to depend, to an important extent, on the complexity of the task being performed. The greater the complexity, the lower the levels of arousal at which a downturn in performance occurs. Are the tasks performed by today's employees more complex than those in the past? Many observers contend that they are. For this reason, too, even relatively mild levels of stress may interfere with performance in today's complex world of work.

Having said all this, we must note that there are exceptions to the general rule that stress interferes with task performance. First, some individuals, at least, do seem to "rise to the occasion" and turn in exceptional performances at times of high stress. This may result from the fact that they are truly expert in the tasks being performed, so that the inflection point in the arousal-performance function described

alone, and finally had had enough: "Everything is terrible. I'm leaving this business. It's too shaky," he remarked. The effects of exposure to high levels of stress stemming from the company's uncertain future were easy to see. Absenteeism rose, and the number of employees seeking help for marital and financial problems skyrocketed. Headaches, insomnia, digestive problems, depression—these were a few of the problems reported by growing numbers of Pan Am employees as they wrestled with the problems of being the last people on what appeared to be a rapidly sinking ship.

Perhaps the most dramatic incident related to the stress of seeing jobs they had held for decades vanish in the crosscurrents of international competition involved John Doig, a Pan Am flight engineer instructor from Mineola, New York. Distraught over the imminent loss of his job, he shot himself in the chest. "He took Pan Am's demise really hard," his daughter says. "He loved that airline." Although other factors, too, were no doubt involved in Doig's suicide, depression over the fate of his beloved company was certainly a contributing factor.

To help employees cope with an ever-worsening situation, Pan Am conducted a series of management classes. Not to be outdone, Pan Am employees tried to help each other, and the company, in various ways. One retired Pan Am

pilot, Everard Bierer, even donated $400,000 of his own savings to help the company avoid bankruptcy. But all these efforts failed, and Pan Am filed for Chapter 11 bankruptcy in February 1991. In March, when it appeared that sale of the company's London routes to United Airlines might be blocked, employees panicked and medical claims jumped sharply.

The effects of Pan Am's plight, and the stress it produced, were also seen in the cockpit, where stress took a toll on pilot performance—and hence on safety. As John McCann, Pan Am's medical director, put it: "Stress is off the scale" and it "affects our flight safety. We have an accident waiting to happen."

Unfortunately, this particular story has a distressing ending. In 1991, Delta Airlines offered to purchase Pan Am. This increased the chances that many Pan Am employees at least would retain their jobs. But then several months later, Delta backed out of the deal, citing Pan Am's deteriorating performance as the reason for this change of heart. The result: Pan Am ceased operations, thus confirming the worst fears of its thousands of employees. The only silver lining to this cloudy ending is that the long-suffering Pan Am employees no longer have to face one continuing, major source of stress: wondering whether their company will survive and whether they will continue to hold jobs with it.

FIGURE 7–9

Outstanding Performance under Conditions of High Stress

Some people perform at very high levels even in the presence of high levels of stress. This may reflect the fact that they are highly expert in the tasks in question and perceive them as a challenge rather than as a threat.

previously is very high (see Figure 7–9). Alternatively, people who are exceptionally skilled at a given task may cognitively appraise even very high levels of stress as a *challenge* rather than a *threat*. As we noted earlier, stress exerts adverse effects primarily when it is viewed in the latter terms.

Second, large individual differences seem to exist with respect to the impact of stress on task performance. As your own experience may suggest, some individuals do indeed seem to thrive on stress: they actively seek arousal and high levels of sensation or stimulation. For such people, stress is exhilarating and may improve their performance. In contrast, other people react in an opposite manner. They seek to avoid arousal and high levels of sensation. Such individuals find stress upsetting, and it may interfere with their performance on many tasks.

So, taking available evidence into account, the most reasonable conclusion we can offer concerning stress and task performance is as follows: In many situations, stress can indeed interfere with performance. However, its precise effects depend on several different factors (e.g., complexity of the task being performed, personal characteristics of the individuals involved, their previous experience with this task). In view of such complexities, generalizations about the impact of stress on task performance should be made with considerable caution.

Stress and Decision Making: Some Costs and Some Benefits The mixed pattern we have presented so far also seems to apply to an especially important type of activity performed by managers: *decision making*. We'll consider this topic in detail in chapter 14, so here our interest is primarily in the impact of stress on decisions.

The *costs* referred to in the heading above refer mainly to adverse effects of stress on the quality of decision making. Existing evidence indicates that when people make decisions under high-stress conditions, they tend to make more errors than they do at other times. Moreover, the process through which decisions are reached, as well as the decisions themselves, seems to suffer. When making decisions under high levels of stress, people often tend to show *premature closure*—they make their decisions before examining all available choices. And they tend to adopt *nonsystematic scanning*—they examine the available choices in a less systematic manner than they do under lower levels of stress.[38] Clearly, then, decision making seems to suffer in several important respects when people must operate in high-stress environments.

High levels of stress also seem to exact important costs with respect to decisions by groups as well as by individuals. Several studies indicate that when organizations confront stressful conditions, they tend to centralize authority and to assign decision making to higher levels of the organization.[39] Since a lack of participation in decision making is positively related to stress and negatively related to acceptance of the decisions once they are reached, these tendencies toward centralization can prove costly. On the other side of the coin, however, high levels of stress also seem to provide certain benefits where group decision making is concerned. Some evidence suggests that under high-stress conditions, leaders actually show greater responsiveness to inputs from subordinates, and so adopt a more egalitarian approach to decision making. Evidence for precisely such effects is provided by a recent study conducted by Driskell and Salas.[40]

These researchers had students at a naval technical school work with a fictitious partner on a task involving visual judgments. (The partner was shown only on videotape and was not actually present.) Some students performed this task under high stress: they were told that tear gas might be introduced into the room; others performed under low stress—no mention of tear gas was made. Another aspect of the study involved students' status relative to their partner's. In one condition he outranked them, and in the other they outranked him. Thus, their own status was either low or high relative to the partner. There were no correct answers to the task, so the main question was: How would subjects respond to disagreements with their partner, which were programmed into the situation? Would they change their judgments on the task to match his, or "stick to their guns"? Driskell and Salas predicted that subjects would be more likely to defer to their partner when he was higher in status than themselves. However, they also predicted that high stress would increase participants' responsiveness to input from their partner, regardless of his apparent status. As shown in Figure 7–10 (see p. 246), this is precisely what happened. The students were more likely to change their answers to agree with those of their partner under high stress than under low stress.

What accounts for this tendency? One possibility is that people's desire for task-relevant information increases under high-stress conditions, thus increasing their tendency to accept input from others. Another is that under high stress, people's desire to diffuse responsibility—to share responsibility for incorrect decisions with others—increases. This leads them to pay more careful attention to others' opinions. Whatever the process involved, it seems clear that stress can influence decision making in several different ways and that in certain contexts, at least, some of these effects can be beneficial.

Burnout: Stress and Psychological Adjustment

Most jobs involve some degree of stress. Yet, somehow, the people performing them manage to cope; they continue to function despite their daily encounters with various stressors. Some individuals, though, are not so fortunate. Over time, they seem to be worn down (or out) by repeated exposure to stress. Such people are often described as suffering from *burnout,* and they demonstrate several distinct characteristics.[41]

Test Bank questions 7.28–7.29, 7.53, and 7.62 relate to material on this page.

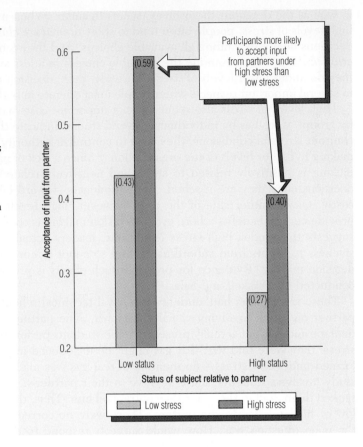

FIGURE 7–10

Effects of Stress on Group Decision Making

High stress increased the tendency of students at a naval technical school to accept input from their partners. Moreover, this was true when the students were higher in status than their partners as well as when they were lower in status. (*Source:* Based on data from Driskell & Salas, 1991; see Note 40.)

The term *burnout* was first used to describe social workers who entered the profession because they thought they could change the world. At a certain point some of them realized that the problems of their clients were so overwhelming that they could never achieve the goals they had brought with them into the profession. As a result of using up their reserves of energy and enthusiasm, the social workers couldn't function any longer and were called "burned out." [Failing, P. (1989, May). Gloom at the top. *Art-News*, pp. 126–131.]

First, victims of burnout suffer from *physical exhaustion*. They have low energy and feel tired much of the time. In addition, they report many symptoms of physical strain such as frequent headaches, nausea, poor sleep, and changes in eating habits (e.g., loss of appetite). Second, they experience *emotional exhaustion*. Depression, feelings of helplessness, and feelings of being trapped in one's job are all part of the picture. Third, people suffering from burnout often demonstrate a pattern of *mental* or *attitudinal exhaustion*, often known as *depersonalization*. They become cynical about others, tend to treat them as objects rather than as people, and hold negative attitudes toward them. In addition, they tend to derogate themselves, their jobs, their organizations, and even life in general. To put it simply, they come to view the world around them through dark gray rather than rose-colored glasses. Finally, they often report feelings of *low personal accomplishment*. People suffering from burnout conclude that they haven't been able to accomplish much in the past, and assume that they probably won't succeed in the future, either. In sum, **burnout** can be defined as a syndrome of emotional, physical, and mental exhaustion coupled with feelings of low self-esteem or low self-efficacy, resulting from prolonged exposure to intense stress. That these factors actually provide an accurate description of burnout is indicated by the findings of recent studies, conducted with large numbers of managerial and nonmanagerial employees.[42] (See Figure 7–11 for a summary of the major components of the burnout syndrome.)

Burnout: Some Major Causes   What are the causes of burnout? As we have already noted, the primary factor appears to be prolonged exposure to stress. However, other variables also play a role. In particular, a number of conditions within an organization plus several personal characteristics seem to determine whether, and to what degree, specific individuals experience burnout.[43] For example, job conditions implying that one's efforts are useless, ineffective, or unappreciated seem to contribute to burnout.[44] Under such conditions, individuals develop the feelings of low personal accomplishment that are an important part of burnout. Similarly, poor opportunities for promotion and the presence of inflexible rules and procedures lead employees to feel that they are trapped in an unfair system and contribute to the development of negative views about their jobs.[45] One of the most important factors contributing to burnout is the *leadership style* used by employees' supervisors.

Evidence concerning this relationship has been reported by Seltzer and Numerof.[46] These researchers asked more than 800 M.B.A. students to report on their own levels of burnout, the leadership style of their supervisors, and several other factors (e.g., their position within their organization, their age, marital status). Results indicated that the lower the amount of consideration demonstrated by their supervisors (i.e., the lower their concern with employees' welfare or with maintaining friendly relations with them), the higher employees' reported levels of burnout. Among the other variables studied, only marital status exerted significant effects: married individuals reported lower levels of burnout than those who were single. (We will return to the impact of various styles of leadership in chapter 12.)

Burnout: Its Major Effects Whatever the precise causes of burnout, once it develops it has important consequences. First, it may lead individuals to seek new jobs or careers. In one study concerned with the impact of burnout, Jackson, Schwab, and Schuler asked several hundred teachers to complete a questionnaire designed to measure burnout and to report on the extent to which they would prefer to be in another job or career.[47] As expected, the greater the teachers' degree of burnout, the more likely they were to prefer another job and to be actively considering a change of occupation. Second, people suffering from burnout may seek administrative roles where they can hide from jobs they have grown to hate behind huge piles of forms. Although this pattern certainly occurs, it appears to be relatively rare. Most victims of burnout seem either to change jobs or to withdraw psychologically and mark time until retirement.

Job burnout regularly occurs at three specific times of crisis during employees' working lives. Burnout may initially occur during the first two years of employment, as people learn that they cannot do what they once expected to do on their jobs. Another round of burnout is likely to strike during the fifth year on the job. At this stage, once employees have had considerable job experience they may begin to feel bored and in need of new challenges. Finally, burnout often occurs about two-thirds of the way through an individual's working life, a symptom of midcareer crisis. During this time of people's careers, they may begin to question what they should be doing with the rest of their working lives. [How to prevent on-the-job burnout. (1991, December). *USA Today Magazine*, p. 4.]

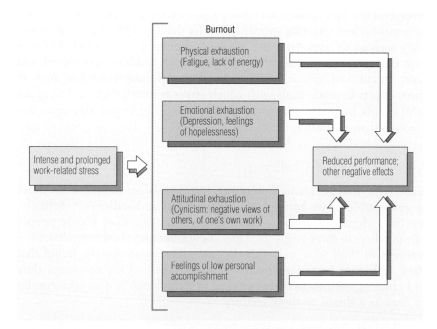

FIGURE 7-11

Major Components of Burnout

When people are exposed to high levels of stress over prolonged periods of time, they may experience *burnout*. This syndrome involves physical, mental, and attitudinal exhaustion, plus feelings of low personal accomplishment. (*Source:* Based on suggestions by Maslach, 1982; see Note 41.)

Burnout

Physical exhaustion (Fatigue, lack of energy)

Emotional exhaustion (Depression, feelings of hopelessness)

Intense and prolonged work-related stress

Reduced performance; other negative effects

Attitudinal exhaustion (Cynicism: negative views of others, of one's own work)

Feelings of low personal accomplishment

Burnout: Can It Be Reversed?   Before concluding, we should comment briefly on one final question: can burnout be reversed? Fortunately, growing evidence suggests that it can. With appropriate help, victims of burnout can recover from their physical and psychological exhaustion. If ongoing stress is reduced, if burnout victims gain added support from friends and coworkers, and if they cultivate hobbies and other outside interests, at least some people, it appears, can return to positive attitudes and renewed productivity. Such results can be attained, however, only through active efforts designed to overcome burnout and to change the conditions from which it develops.

INDIVIDUAL DIFFERENCES IN RESISTANCE TO STRESS

A recent study found that pregnant employees were particularly at risk for suffering stress-related problems. Pregnant women in high-stress jobs were found to produce high levels of catecholamines, the so-called fight-or-flight hormones. As a result of these hormone secretions, the women were more likely to have premature labor and low-birthweight babies. Thus, it would seem that high-stress jobs may be especially dangerous for pregnant women. [Fackelmann, K. A. (1991, March 16). Job stress: A risk for pregnant workers? *Science News,* p. 165.]

There can be little doubt that individuals differ greatly in their resistance to stress. Some suffer ill effects after exposure to brief periods of relatively mild stress, whereas others are able to function effectively even after prolonged exposure to much higher levels of stress. How do such people differ? Research on this topic suggests that several personal tendencies or dispositions are crucial.

Optimism: A Buffer against Stress

One personal factor that seems to play an important role in determining resistance to stress is the familiar dimension of *optimism-pessimism*. Optimists, of course, are people who see the glass as half full; they are hopeful in their outlook on life, interpret a wide range of situations in a positive light, and tend to expect favorable outcomes and results. Pessimists, in contrast, are people who see the glass as half empty; they interpret many situations negatively, and expect unfavorable outcomes and results. Recent studies indicate that, as you might well guess, optimists are much more stress resistant than pessimists. For example, optimists are much less likely than pessimists to report physical illness and symptoms during highly stressful periods such as final exams.[48]

Additional findings help explain why. Optimists and pessimists seem to adopt sharply contrasting tactics for coping with stress. Optimists concentrate on *problem-focused coping*—making and enacting specific plans for dealing with sources of stress. In addition, they seek *social support*—the advice and help of friends and others— and refrain from engaging in other activities until current problems are solved and stress is reduced. In contrast, pessimists tend to adopt different strategies, such as giving up in their efforts to reach goals with which stress is interfering, and denying that the stressful events have even occurred.[49] Obviously, the former strategies are often more effective than the latter.

Hardiness: Viewing Stress as Challenge

Although traditional stress-reducing techniques encourage people to slow down and relax, research has found that being "tough" (i.e., facing problems head-on) may be an even more effective strategy for coping with stress.

A second characteristic that seems to distinguish stress-resistant people from those who are more susceptible to its harmful effects is known as **hardiness**.[50] Actually, this term refers to a cluster of characteristics rather than just one. Hardy people seem to differ from others in three respects. They show higher levels of *commitment*— deeper involvement in their jobs and other life activities; *control*—the belief that they can, in fact, influence important events in their lives and the outcomes they experience; and *challenge*—they perceive change as a challenge and an opportunity to grow rather than as a threat to their security.

Test Bank questions 7.34–7.36, 7.54, and 7.74 relate to material on this page.

Together, these characteristics tend to arm hardy persons with high resistance to stress. For example, in one study on this topic, Oullette-Kobasa and Pucetti asked executives at a larger public utility to complete questionnaires designed to measure their level of hardiness, the number of stressful life events they had recently experienced, and their current health.[51] Results indicated that people classified as high in hardiness did indeed report better health than those low in hardiness, even when they had recently encountered major stressful life changes. Similar results have been reported in several other studies with people from different occupations (e.g., nurses, lawyers, police officers).[52] Together, such findings suggest that hardiness is a useful concept for understanding the impact of stress. However, recent evidence suggests that commitment and a sense of control are the most important components of hardiness.[53] Thus, further research concerned with this personal dimension and its role in resistance to stress should focus primarily on these aspects.

The Type A Behavior Pattern Revisited

In chapter 6, we noted that people who demonstrate the Type A behavior pattern seem to respond more strongly than others to various forms of stress. Specifically, they show higher levels of arousal in the presence of stress than Type B's. Here we note that not only do Type A's react more strongly to stress, but they also seem to actually invite it. Specifically, they tend to behave in ways that increase their work load and generate conditions most people would describe as stressful. Direct evidence for such effects has been reported by Kirmeyer and Biggers, in a study of civilian radio dispatchers in police departments.[54] These researchers had seventy-two dispatchers complete a standard measure of Type A behavior (the Jenkins Activity Survey). Then they observed their behavior on the job during several work shifts. As predicted, these observations revealed that the higher the dispatchers scored on the Type A dimension, the more likely they were to initiate work, to engage in and complete more work, and to divide their attention between two or more simultaneous tasks. As Kirmeyer and Biggers put it, "By their actions Type A's not only constructed for themselves a highly demanding work environment but also created conditions likely to evoke a driven, time-urgent, and impatient behavioral style."[55] Clearly, this is one more reason why individuals who demonstrate the Type A pattern should take steps to modify their behavior: doing so may be extremely beneficial to their health!

Although the Type A behavior pattern has often been viewed as a unitary dimension, recent studies indicate that it consists of several distinct components.[56] The most important of these involve the Type A's *achievement strivings*—the tendencies of Type A's to take their work seriously, and to expend great effort on it; and the Type A's *impatience-irritability*. The first of these components is linked to performance on many tasks, whereas the second is more closely related to the adverse health effects described above. Thus, when considering the Type A pattern, examination of the impact of these two components separately makes good sense. That they do have differential effects on key aspects of organizational behavior is indicated by the results of a study conducted by Bluen, Barling, and Burns.[57]

These researchers had all the life insurance brokers working in the Johannesburg, South Africa, region complete measures of Type A achievement strivings (AS) and impatience-irritability (II). In addition, participants completed questionnaires designed to assess their overall job satisfaction and their current feelings of depression. Finally, the researchers gathered information on the number of policies sold by each agent during a recent twelve-month period. They predicted that the AS component would be related to job performance (number of policies sold) and to job satisfaction, but unrelated to depression. In contrast, they predicted that the II component would

Some people are naturally "tougher" than others, although anyone can work to increase this tendency. To become "tougher," people can actively seek out stressful situations and practice confronting them directly. [Miller, L. (1989, December). To beat stress: Don't relax: Get tough. *Psychology Today*, pp. 62–63.]

be linked to depression, unrelated to policies sold, and negatively related to job satisfaction. All these predictions were confirmed.

These findings indicate that the Type A pattern should not be viewed as a single characteristic. To understand this pattern and its relationships to stress, job performance, and personal health, we should view it as consisting of distinct components. As found by Bluen, Barling, and Burns, these components often have contrasting effects on different aspects of organizational behavior.

Tension Discharge Rate

Nearly everyone experiences some degree of pressure or stress at work—this is a fact of life in modern organizations. However, individuals differ greatly in terms of how they handle such feelings at the end of the day. Some seem capable of leaving tension behind when they head for home. In contrast, others take it with them as excess psychological baggage. Which group is more likely to suffer harmful effects from exposure to stress? Obviously, the latter. That this is indeed the case, and that individual differences in *tension discharge rate* really matter, is indicated by a study conducted by Matteson and Ivancevich.[58] These researchers had several hundred medical technologists complete two questionnaires. One measured **tension discharge rate**—the rate at which individuals dissipated their job-related tensions at the end of the day. The second measured several aspects of personal health (e.g., the total number of health problems the technologists had experienced during the past six months). When they compared responses to these two questionnaires, the investigators found that people low in tension discharge rate (those who carried stress home with them at the end of the day) did indeed report poorer health than those high in tension discharge rate. These findings suggest that the ability to leave one's worries behind at the end of the day can be very beneficial where resisting the harmful impact of stress is concerned. Thus, this is an additional determining factor in the ultimate impact of work-related stress. (For more evidence on personal characteristics that can moderate the impact of stress on personal health, see the **International/Multicultural Perspective** section on the following page.)

Coping Styles: Problem-Focused and Emotion-Focused

In our earlier discussion of optimism, we noted that one reason optimists seem better able to cope with stress than do pessimists is that optimists are more likely to engage in *problem-focused coping*—direct efforts to deal with, understand, and overcome current causes of stress. Here, we wish to expand on this point briefly by noting that a considerable body of evidence indicates that such problem-focused coping is generally superior in moderating the adverse effects of stress than an alternative approach—one often described as *emotion-focused coping*. Emotion-focused coping centers around efforts to reduce or manage the emotional distress resulting from stress and often involves strategies such as refusing to recognize painful realities, convincing oneself that things could be worse, or—perhaps more self-destructively—masking the distress with alcohol and other drugs. Findings reported by Baghat, Allie, and Ford indicate that problem-focused coping is far more effective than emotion-focused coping in reducing the adverse effects of both work-related and life-related stress.[61] Thus, where the ability to withstand the potentially damaging effects of stress is concerned, it is not simply personal characteristics or traits that matter: the style of coping with stress that individuals adopt also plays a crucial role.

Test Bank questions 7.38 and 7.64 relate to material on this page.

AN INTERNATIONAL/MULTICULTURAL PERSPECTIVE

The Stress-Deterrent Effects of Religiosity: Evidence from Israeli Kibbutzim

Religion is, of course, a highly personal issue. Individuals' beliefs about the existence and nature of a creator, the relationship of humanity to such a being, the ultimate meaning of life, and many other questions are matters of personal belief and personal conscience. It has long been thought, however, that holding religious beliefs, whatever their form, may provide individuals with some protection against the ravages of significant, stressful life events such as those listed near the top of Table 7–1 (see p. 238). Presumably, this might be so for several reasons. For example, some people suggest that religion provides individuals with much-needed social support when adversity strikes, or that it deters them from engaging in practices such as excessive use of alcohol that may impair their health and reduce resistance to stress.[59] Do such benefits actually occur? And if so, are they related to personal religious beliefs or to being part of a religious community? Evidence on these issues has recently been provided by Anson and her colleagues in a study of people living in Israeli kibbutzim.

Two kibbutzim were selected for study, one that was religious in orientation and one that was nonreligious. In all other respects, such as age and gender of their members, the two kibbutzim were virtually identical. Participants at the two kibbutzim completed a measure on which they reported on the occurrence of recent stressful life events, including divorce, marital separation, death of a loved one, and so on. In addition, they rated their personal health and reported on recent illnesses and disabilities. Finally, they rated their own religious commitment and religious practices.

Results were clear. For members of the nonreligious kibbutz, the greater the frequency of stressful life events, the stronger the members' psychological distress and the greater the adverse effects on their health. For members of the religious kibbutz, however, the impact of stressful life events was much reduced. In other words, being part of a religious community *did* seem to buffer the potentially harmful impact of stress. Interestingly, similar effects were *not* found for personal religiosity. In other words, holding personal religious beliefs and engaging in private religious practices did not seem to protect individuals from the ill effects of stress in the same manner as did being part of a religious community.

Why does belonging to a religious community buffer the adverse effects of stressful life events? Anson and her colleagues suggest that it may relate to the characteristic of *hardiness*. Presumably, belonging to such a community offers individuals a foundation for commitment—the belief that one's life has a purpose and does, ultimately, make sense. Whatever the underlying factors, belonging to a community that makes religion a key part of its functioning seems to yield important physical and health-related benefits as well as ones of a more spiritual nature.

MANAGING STRESS: SOME USEFUL TACTICS

Stress stems from so many different factors and conditions that to eliminate it entirely from our lives is probably impossible. What both individuals and organizations *can* do, however, is take steps to reduce its intensity and minimize its harmful effects—to *cope* with stress when it occurs. Several strategies for attaining these goals exist. Here, we will consider these under two major headings: techniques individuals can apply themselves and techniques requiring interventions by organizations.

Test Bank questions 7.39 and 7.40 relate to material on this page.

Personal Approaches to Stress Management: Tactics That Work

What steps can people take to protect themselves against the adverse effects of stress? Many exist, and as suggested by Figure 7–12, they are highly varied. However, most fall into one of three major categories: physiological, cognitive, and behavioral approaches.

Researchers have found that people can lower their blood-pressure levels and other bodily responses to stress merely by owning a pet. Although dogs had the greatest relaxing and calming effects on people, other pets, such as cats and birds, were also good stress reducers. It was also found that the soothing effects of pets occurred only among people who were comfortable around animals. For those who were uncomfortable around animals, exposure to pets *increased* stress. [Bower, B. (1991, November 2). Stress goes to the dogs. *Science News*, p. 285.]

Physiological Techniques Many procedures for managing stress focus on physiological/biological changes that can enhance our resistance to stress. These include improving our diet and nutrition, increasing our physical fitness, and learning specific procedures for substituting relaxation for the tension that often accompanies stress.

With respect to nutrition, growing evidence indicates that reduced intake of salt and saturated fats, and increased consumption of fiber- and vitamin-rich fruits and vegetables, are steps that can greatly increase the body's ability to cope with the physiological effects of stress.[62] Although making significant changes in eating habits can be difficult—and require a large amount of will power!—the benefits attained can certainly justify such efforts.

Turning to physical fitness, existing evidence suggests that people who exercise regularly obtain many benefits closely related to resistance of the adverse effects of stress. For example, fitness reduces both the incidence of cardiovascular illness and the death rate from such diseases. Similarly, physical fitness lowers blood pressure, an important factor in many aspects of personal health. Perhaps the most convincing evidence for the stress-buffering effects of physical fitness is that reported recently by Brown.[63] He measured the physical fitness of college undergraduates by observing their performance on an exercise bicycle; the increase in their pulse rate after riding the bicycle provided a direct measure of the students' fitness. In addition, he obtained both self-reports of recent illnesses from participants and reports of recent stressful life events. Finally, an objective measure of their health was obtained from records at the university health center. Results indicated that for people low in physical fitness, high stress led to increased visits to the university health center for physical illness. Among those high in physical fitness, however, increased stress did *not* produce a similar deterioration in health (see Figure 7–13). In sum, people who were physically fit appeared to be less vulnerable to the adverse effects of life stress than those who were less fit.

Additional techniques for managing stress involve learning to relax in the face of such conditions. This can be accomplished through **relaxation training**, in which

FIGURE 7–12   Personal Stress Management: One Technique

People use many different techniques to manage their stress. Do you think the one shown here is really effective? (*Source:* Cathy cartoon is reprinted by permission of Universal Press Syndicate.)

Test Bank question 7.41 relates to material on this page.

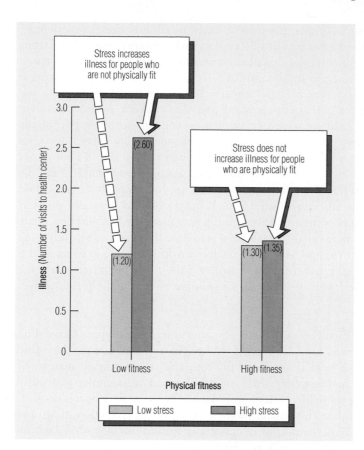

FIGURE 7–13

Physical Fitness, Resistance to Stress, and Personal Health

Students who were physically fit showed little increase in frequency of illness when exposed to high levels of stress. In contrast, students who were not physically fit showed a much larger increase in illness. (*Source:* Based on data from Brown, 1991; see Note 63.)

individuals learn how to first tense and then relax their own muscles. In this way, they become familiar with the difference between these two states, and can learn to induce varying degrees of relaxation when they feel that they are becoming too tense.

A related technique, **meditation,** involves learning to clear one's mind of external thoughts, often by repeating a single syllable or *mantra* over and over again. This, in turn, induces a relaxed state incompatible with feelings of stress.

Cognitive Techniques   Quick—answer honestly: do you worry too much? Surveys indicate that almost 90 percent of all people answer "yes."[64] Most of us, then, feel that we spend too much time worrying about various problems. The key issue, however, is not the sheer volume of worry; rather, it is *what* we tend to worry about. In many cases, people worry about things that are really quite unimportant and not directly under their control. Needless to say, to the extent that we can stop wasting cognitive effort in this fashion, we can each help manage our own stress. An exercise dealing with this topic is included at the end of this chapter; completing it may be well worth your while.

Excessive worrying is not the only thing we do that contributes to our own stress, however. In addition, we often engage in what some stress-management experts describe as *inappropriate self-talk*.[65] This involves telling ourselves over and over how horrible and unbearable it will be if we fail, if we are not perfect, or if everyone we meet does not like us. Such thoughts seem ludicrous when spelled out in the pages of a book, but considerable evidence indicates that most people entertain them at least occasionally. Unfortunately, they can add to personal levels of stress, as individuals *awfulize* or *catastrophize* over the horrors of not being successful, perfect, or loved. Fortunately, such thinking can be readily modified. For many people, merely recognizing that they have implicitly accepted such irrational and self-defeating beliefs is sufficient to produce beneficial change and increased resistance to stress.

Perhaps the guiding principle in all cognitive techniques for managing stress is this: it is essential to realize that we can't always change the world around us, but we *can* change our reactions to it. In other words, we don't have to permit ourselves to worry excessively over things we can't change or control, to allow potentially irritating situations to drive us up the wall, or to engage in hopeless quests for perfection. Instead, we can actively decide to avoid such reactions and choose *not* to become upset when things don't go our own way. Perhaps one simple example will illustrate the main point. Imagine that you are on your way to an important meeting when you become stuck in a traffic jam. What do you do? How do you feel? One possibility is that you become frustrated, and worry ceaselessly about being late for the meeting. Another, more adaptive reaction is to note that you can't do anything about the situation and to remind yourself that the world won't come to an end if you are late for the meeting. By exercising control over their own cognitive reactions, individuals can reduce the levels of stress they experience—and so help themselves in many different ways.

Behavioral Techniques   Finally, several stress management techniques focused on changing our overt behavior are also useful. When faced with events they find stressful, people can often help themselves to stem the rising tide of anxiety by adopting actions that are *incompatible* with such feelings. For example, instead of allowing their speech to become increasingly rapid and intense as they become upset, they can consciously modulate this aspect of their behavior. A reduction in arousal and tension may result. This technique is especially helpful for Type A's, whose always-in-a-hurry style tends to magnify reactions to stress in many situations.

Similarly, when confronted with rising tension, people can consciously choose to insert a brief period of delay (sometimes known as *time-out*). This can involve taking a short break, going to the nearest restroom to splash cold water on one's face, or any other action that yields a few moments of breathing space. Such actions interrupt the cycle of ever-rising tension that accompanies stress, and can help to restore equilibrium and the feeling of being at least partly in control of ongoing events.

Still another behavioral technique for stress control involves building pleasure into one's life. Many people—especially Type A's—try to crowd so much into their schedules that little or no time is left for relaxation or pursuing hobbies. This is unfortunate, for even short vacations or short periods of time spent pursuing activities one really enjoys can go a long way toward alleviating the adverse effects of stress. So, in short, it is important for people to be kind to themselves, at least occasionally, if they wish to avoid the potential dangers of "living on the edge" where stress is concerned.

Organization-Based Strategies for Managing Stress

Although individuals can increase their own resistance to stress, they cannot, by themselves, eliminate many of its causes from their work environments. For this reason, organizations, too, can play a key role in stress management. They can adopt changes in their internal structure and procedures, or alter the nature of jobs, to reduce stress among employees.

Changes in Organizational Structure and Function   Several changes in organizational policy and function are useful in reducing job-related stress. First, such benefits can sometimes be gained by *decentralization*—a process in which authority is spread

Management consultants advise employees to avoid stress by refraining from overscheduling themselves (i.e., squeezing too much into an already full work schedule). They recommend that people leave some work time unscheduled by keeping white space on their calendars. This open time can be used to handle problems that come up unexpectedly during the day or to permit people to take a brief break every now and then, both of which can help reduce stress. [Kiechell, W., III. (1991, April 8). Overscheduled, and not loving it. *Fortune*, pp. 105–107.]

Managers may be effective in lowering sources of stress created by work environments (e.g., excess illumination and noise). For example, they may have to ask some employees to refrain from talking so that others can concentrate on their jobs. They may also provide shades to dim bright lights

more widely throughout an organization. This reduces feelings of helplessness among employees, and so reduces their overall level of stress. Second, employees can be afforded greater participation in decisions, especially ones involving their jobs. As we noted earlier, the lack of opportunities for such input can be a major source of stress. Third, steps can be taken to assure that performance appraisals and the distribution of organizational rewards are as fair as possible. To the extent that individuals perceive that these matters are being handled in a reasonable manner, the stress relating to them can be significantly reduced.

Changes in the Nature of Specific Jobs   Careful attention to the nature of specific jobs can also reduce stress. For example, the stress resulting from boring, repetitive tasks can be lessened through *job enlargement*—efforts to broaden the scope of the activities they involve. At the very least, supervisors can try to put some variety into tasks that are by nature dull and repetitive, and to give employees opportunities to socialize with one another. This is precisely the approach taken by Maids International, a franchised house-cleaning service operating in the United States.[66] The company cannot afford the high turnover rates traditional in this industry, so they have attempted to improve conditions—and reduce stress—for employees in many different ways. As Dan Bishop, CEO of Maids International, comments: "We focused the whole concept of the company on the labor. Fatigue and boredom are what burn people out. We tried to eliminate them." To accomplish this task, the company tries to train employees in efficient ways of doing various cleaning jobs so that the amount of effort required is reduced. And time for socializing is built into the schedule during the drives between customers' houses. The result: employees stay on the job for an average of nine months versus an industry average of less than five months. Finally, important causes of stress can be removed through eliminating hazardous or unpleasant working conditions.

Employee Fitness Programs   Another method of enhancing employees' ability to resist stress is **employee fitness programs.** These are programs, run and funded by organizations, to improve the physical fitness of their employees.[67] Such programs are based, in part, on the evidence reviewed above, suggesting that improved physical fitness increases individuals' resistance to the adverse effects of stress. However, their growing popularity also derives from findings suggesting that physical fitness reduces absenteeism and enhances productivity, plus other evidence suggesting that employee fitness programs contribute to commitment and other positive attitudes among employees (see chapter 4).[68] (These latter benefits stem from the fact that employees perceive company-sponsored fitness programs as a sign that the organization is truly concerned about their welfare.) Given these important benefits, it is not at all surprising that such programs have grown in popularity and are now widespread throughout many different industries; indeed more than 50,000 are currently in operation in the United States.[69]

that may otherwise cause headaches and induce stress. [Beware excessive sound and light. (1991, August). *USA Today Magazine,* p. 91.]

SUMMARY AND REVIEW

The Basic Nature of Stress

Stress is a pattern of emotional states and physiological reactions occurring in situations where individuals perceive threats to their important goals, which they feel they may be unable to meet. To fully understand stress, we must consider the emotional and physiological reactions it involves, the external factors that produce it, and the cognitive processes that play a role in its occurrence. With respect to cognitive factors, *cognitive appraisals* and fear of loss of control appear to be of central importance.

Major Causes of Stress

Stress in work settings stems from many different factors. Several are directly related to jobs and organizations, and include occupational demands, role conflict, role ambiguity, responsibility for others, underload and overload, and lack of social support. One especially unsettling cause of work-related stress is **sexual harassment**—unwanted sexual contact or communication. Other sources of work-related stress include performance appraisals and physical working conditions. Some evidence indicates that individuals bring relatively high or low levels of stress with them into their jobs.

Stress also stems from events and situations arising outside work settings. *Stressful life events* such as divorce or death of a close relative are an important source of stress. Stress also stems from the *hassles of daily life*—milder but more frequent events that strain individuals' resources.

Effects of Stress

Stress exerts adverse effects on health. It has been linked to the occurrence of *degenerative diseases* such as heart disease, high blood pressure, hardening of the arteries, ulcers, and even diabetes. In addition, growing evidence indicates that exposure to high levels of stress may increase susceptibility to *infectious diseases*, such as upper respiratory infections and herpesvirus infections.

Stress influences the performance of many tasks. The precise impact is difficult to predict, however, and seems to depend on the complexity of the task in question and an individual's previous experience with it. In general, it appears that even relatively mild levels of stress can interfere with task performance under a wide range of conditions.

Stress also influences decision making. With respect to individual decisions, high levels of stress appear to reduce the quality or accuracy of decisions. Stress also interferes with the process of decision making, producing such effects as premature closure and nonsystematic scanning of available options. In the case of group decisions, recent evidence indicates that stress may increase the responsiveness of both leaders and subordinates to input from others. This can sometimes lead to a more egalitarian style of decision making.

Prolonged exposure to stress can lead to **burnout**—a syndrome consisting of physical, emotional, and mental exhaustion, plus intense feelings of low personal accomplishment. Burnout is affected by several different factors, but one of the most important appears to be leaders' personal style.

Individual Differences in Resistance to Stress

Large individual differences exist in ability to resist the adverse effects of stress. *Optimists* are better able to cope with stress than *pessimists*. People high in **hardiness,** a combination of high commitment, feelings of personal control, and the tendency to perceive change as a challenge rather than a threat, are better able to resist the effects of stress than those low in hardiness. Type A individuals are more susceptible to the impact of stress than are Type B's, partly because they show greater physiological reactions to stress and partly because they behave in ways that expose them to high levels of stress. People who are able to leave stress at the office, those high in **tension discharge rate,** are less affected by stress than those who carry it home with them. Belonging to a religious community seems to buffer or moderate the adverse effects of stress.

Stress-Management Techniques

Personal approaches to managing stress involve *physiological, cognitive,* and *behavioral techniques.* Physiological techniques include improvements in nutrition and physical fitness, **relaxation training,** and **meditation.** Cognitive techniques include worry control (worrying only about things that are important and under one's control) and avoiding inappropriate self-talk. Behavioral techniques involve actions such as modulating the intensity of one's speech or actions, and taking brief time-out periods away from stress-inducing situations.

Organization-based strategies for managing stress include changes in organizational structure, job enlargement, and **employee fitness programs.**

KEY TERMS

burnout: A syndrome that results from prolonged exposure to stress. It consists of physical, emotional, and mental exhaustion, plus feelings of a lack of personal accomplishment.

employee fitness programs: Organization-sponsored programs designed to enhance the physical fitness of employees.

hardiness: A combination of traits (commitment to one's

work, a sense of personal control, the ability to view change as a challenge rather than as a threat) that assists individuals in resisting the harmful effects of stress.

meditation: A technique for inducing relaxation in which individuals clear disturbing thoughts from their minds by repeating a single syllable (*mantra*).

performance appraisal: The process through which individuals' job performance is evaluated and feedback about this is provided to them.

qualitative overload: The belief among employees that they lack the skills or abilities needed to perform their jobs.

qualitative underload: The lack of mental stimulation that accompanies many routine, repetitive jobs.

quantitative overload: A situation in which individuals are required to do more work than they can actually accomplish in a given period of time.

quantitative underload: A situation in which individuals have so little to do that they spend much of their time doing nothing.

relaxation training: Procedures through which individuals learn to relax in order to reduce anxiety or stress.

role ambiguity: Uncertainty among employees about the key requirements of their jobs and how they should divide their time between various tasks.

role conflict: Incompatible demands made on an individual by different groups or persons.

sexual harassment: Unwanted contact or communication of a sexual nature.

stress: A pattern of emotional states and physiological reactions occurring in situations where individuals perceive threats to their important goals that they feel unable to meet.

stressors: Various factors in the external environment that induce stress among people exposed to them.

tension discharge rate: The rate at which individuals rid themselves of work-related tension at the end of the day. People high in *tension discharge rate* leave such tensions at the office, whereas those low in this characteristic tend to bring them home.

total negative life stress: The combined stress stemming from work-related and personal causes of stress.

QUESTIONS FOR DISCUSSION

1. Two individuals exposed to the same situation may experience sharply contrasting levels of stress. Why?

2. Suppose you are considering a new job. What factors will you examine closely to determine how stressful the new position might be?

3. Imagine that you are exposed to high levels of stress over a prolonged period of time. What effect might this have on your personal health—in particular, on the likelihood that you will catch a cold or the flu?

4. Suppose you are faced with the task of choosing employees for a high-stress job. What personal characteristics will you seek in the people you hire? What characteristics will you try to avoid?

5. Imagine that you are faced with the task of developing a written company policy concerning sexual harassment—one that will be distributed to all employees. What points should be included in this policy?

6. What kind of things do you say silently to yourself when you are irritated or frustrated that actually increase the level of stress you experience? What different thoughts would help you to manage stress in such situations?

7. What role does the sense of personal control over one's job play in work-related stress?

8. Stress-related illnesses often prove very costly to organizations in terms of employee absence and the costs of administering health insurance plans. What steps can companies take to reduce stress among their employees and these associated costs?

NOTES

1. Kahn, R. (1992). Stress and behavior in work settings. In M. D. Dunnette (Ed.), *Handbook of industrial organizational psychology* (2nd ed.). Palo Alto, CA: Consulting Psychologists Press.

2. Selye, H. (1976). *Stress in health and disease.* Boston: Butterworths.

3. Lazarus, R. S., & Folkman, S. (1984). *Stress, appraisal, and coping.* New York: Springer-Verlag.

4. Evans, G. W., & Carrere, S. (1991). Traffic congestion, perceived control, and psychophysiological stress among urban bus drivers. *Journal of Applied Psychology, 76,* 658–663.

5. Schaefler, M., Street, S., Singer, J., & Baum, A. (1988). Effects of control on the stress reactions of commuters. *Journal of Applied Social Psychology, 18,* 944–957.

6. McGrath, J. E. (1976). Stress and behavior in organizations. In M. D. Dunnette (Ed.), *Handbook of industrial and organizational psychology.* Chicago: Rand McNally.

7. National Institute for Occupational Safety and Health, Department of Health, Education, and Welfare. (1978). Washington, D.C.: Government Printing Office.

8. Shaw, J. B., and Riskind, J. H. (1983). Predicting job stress using data from the position analysis questionnaire. *Journal of Applied Psychology, 68,* 253–261.

9. Newton, T. J., & Keenan, A. (1987). Role stress reexamined: An investigation of role stress predictors. *Organizational Behavior and Human Decision Processes, 40,* 346–368.

10. Williams, K. J., Sula, J., Alliger, G. M., Learner, S. M., & Choie, K. W. (1991). Multiple role juggling and daily mood states in working mothers: An experience sampling study. *Journal of Applied Psychology, 76,* 664–674.

11. See Note 10.

12. See Note 9.

13. See Note 6.

14. French, J. R. P., & Caplan, R. D. (1972). Organizational stress and individual strain. In A. J. Morrow (Ed.), *The failure of success.* New York: Amacom.

15. McClean, A. A. (1980). *Work stress.* Reading, MA: Addison-Wesley.

16. Oullette-Kobasa, S. C., & Pucetti, M. C. (1983). Personality and social resources in stress resistance. *Journal of Personality and Social Psychology, 45,* 839–850.

17. Kolbert, E. (1991, October 10). Sexual harassment at work is pervasive. *New York Times,* pp. A1, A17.

18. Strom, S. (1991, October 20). Harassment rules often not pushed. *New York Times,* pp. A1, A22.

19. Niven, D. (1992, March–April). The case of hidden harassment. *Harvard Business Review,* 12–23.

20. Gutek, B., Nakamura, C. Y., Ganart, M., Handschumacher, J. W., & Russell, D. (1980). Sexuality and the workplace. *Basic and Applied Social Psychology, 1,* 255–265.

21. Terpstra, D. E., & Baker, D. D. (1988). Outcomes of sexual harassment charges. *Academy of Management Journal, 31,* 185–194.

22. Oldham, G. R., & Fried, Y. (1987). Employee reactions to workspace characteristics. *Journal of Applied Psychology, 72,* 75–80.

23. Baron, R. A., & Bingley, J. (1988). *Effects of a merger on work-related attitudes, stereotyping, and conflict.* Paper presented at the meeting of the Eastern Psychological Association, Boston.

24. Nelson, D. L., & Sutton, C. (1990). Chronic work stress and coping: A longitudinal study and suggested new directions. *Academy of Management Journal, 33,* 859–869.

25. See Note 24.

26. See Note 24.

27. George, J. M. (1990). Personality, affect, and behavior in groups. *Journal of Applied Psychology, 75,* 107–116.

28. Holmes, T. H., & Rahe, R. H. (1967). Social readjustment rating scale. *Journal of Psychosomatic Research, 11,* 213–218.

29. Holmes, T. H., & Masuda, M. (1974). Life change and illness susceptibility. In B. S. Dohrenwend & B. P. Dohrenwend (Eds.), *Stressful life events: Their nature and effects* (pp. 45–72). New York: Wiley.

30. Lazarus, R. S., & Folkman, S. (1984). *Stress, appraisal, and coping.* New York: Springer-Verlag.

31. DeLongis, A., Coyne, J. C., Dakof, G., Folkman, S., & Lazarus, R. S. (1982). Relationships of daily hassles, uplifts and major life events to health status. *Health Psychology, 1,* 119–136.

32. Baghat, R. S., McQuaid, S. J., Lindholm, H., & Segovis, J. (1985). Total life stress: A multimethod validation of the construct and its effects on organizationally valued outcomes and withdrawal behaviors. *Journal of Applied Psychology, 70,* 202–214.

33. Frese, M. (1985). Stress at work and psychosomatic complaints: A causal interpretation. *Journal of Applied Psychology, 70,* 314–328.

34. Cohen, S., & Williamson, G. M. (1991). Stress and infectious disease in humans. *Psychological Bulletin, 109,* 5–24.

35. Totman, R., Kiff, J., Reed, S. E., & Craig, H. W. (1980). Predicting experimental colds in volunteers from different measures of recent life stress. *Journal of Psychosomatic Research, 24,* 155–163.

36. Motowidlo, S. J., Packard, J. S., & Manning, M. R. (1986). Occupational stress: Its causes and consequences for job performance. *Journal of Applied Psychology, 71,* 618–629.

37. Pulley, B. (1991, September 16). A grand tradition can make a fall that much harder. *Wall Street Journal,* pp. A1, A11.

38. Keinan, G. (1987). Decision making under stress: Scanning of alternatives under controllable and uncontrollable threats. *Journal of Personality and Social Psychology, 52,* 638–644.

39. Staw, B. M., Sandelands, L. E., & Dutton, J. E. (1981). Threat-rigidity effects in organizational behavior: A multi-level analysis. *Administrative Science Quarterly, 26,* 501–524.

40. Driskell, J. E., & Salas, E. (1991). Group decision making under stress. *Journal of Applied Psychology, 76,* 473–478.

41. Maslach, C. (1982). *Burnout: The cost of caring.* Englewood Cliffs, NJ: Prentice-Hall.

42. Lee, R. T., & Ashforth, B. E. (1990). On the meaning of Maslach's three dimensions of burnout. *Journal of Applied Psychology, 75,* 743–747.

43. Golombiewski, R. T., Ninzenrider, R. F., & Stevenson, J. G. (1986). *Stress in organizations: Toward a phase model of burnout.* New York: Praeger.

44. Pines, A. M., Aronson, E., & Kafry, D. (1981). *Burnout: From tedium to personal growth.* New York: Freeman.

45. Gaines, J., & Jermier, J. M. (1983). Emotional exhaustion in high stress organizations. *Academy of Management Journal, 31,* 567–586.

46. Seltzer, J., & Numerof, R. E. (1986). Supervisory leadership and subordinate burnout. *Academy of Management Journal, 31,* 439–446.

47. Jackson, S. E., Schwab, R. L., & Schuler, R. S. (1986). Toward an understanding of the burnout phenomenon. *Journal of Applied Psychology, 71,* 630–640.

48. Scheier, M. F., & Carver, C. S. (1985). Optimism, coping, and health: Assessment and implications of generalized outcome expectancies. *Health Psychology, 4,* 219–247.

49. Scheier, M. F., Weintraub, J. K., & Carver, C. S. (1986). Coping with stress: Divergent strategies of optimists and pessimists. *Journal of Personality and Social Psychology, 51,* 1257–1264.

50. Kobasa, S. C. (1982). The hardy personality: Toward a social psychology of stress and health. In G. E. Sanders & J. Suls (Eds.), *Social psychology of health and illness.* Hillsdale, NJ: Erlbaum.

51. See Note 16.

52. Rich, V. L., & Rich, A. R. (1985). *Personality hardiness and burnout in female staff nurses.* Paper presented at the annual meeting of the American Psychological Association, Los Angeles.

53. Hull, J. G., Van Treuren, R. R., & Virnelli, S. (1987). Hardiness and health: A critique and alternative approach. *Journal of Personality and Social Psychology, 53,* 518–530.

54. Kirmeyer, S. L., & Biggers, K. (1988). Environmental demand and demand engendering behavior: An observational analysis of the Type A pattern. *Journal of Personality and Social Psychology, 54,* 997–1005.

55. See Note 54, p. 1003.

56. Edwards, J. R., & Baglioni, A. J., Jr. (1991). Relationship between Type A behavior pattern and mental and physical symptoms: A comparison of global and component measures. *Journal of Applied Psychology, 76,* 276–290.

57. Bluen, S. D., Barling, J., & Burns, W. (1990). Predicting sales performance, job satisfaction, and depression by using the achievement strivings and impatience-irritability dimensions of Type A behavior. *Journal of Applied Psychology, 75,* 212–216.

58. Matteson, M. T., & Ivancevich, J. M. (1983). Note on tension discharge rate as an employee health status predictor. *Academy of Management Journal, 26,* 540–545.

59. Idler, E. L. (1987). Religious involvement and the health of the elderly: Some hypotheses and an initial test. *Social Forces, 66,* 226–238.

60. Anson, L., Carmel, S., Bonneh, D. Y., Levenson, A., & Maoz, B. (1991). Recent life events, religiosity, and health: An individual or collective effect. *Human Relations, 43,* 1051–1066.

61. Baghat, R. S., Allie, S. M., & Ford, D. L., Jr. (1991). Organizational stress, personal life stress and symptoms of life strains: An inquiry into the moderating role of styles of coping. In P. L. Perrewe (Ed.), *Handbook of job stress.* Special issue of *Journal of Social Behavior and Personality, 6,* 163–184.

62. See Note 15.

63. Brown, J. D. (1991). Staying fit and staying well: Physical fitness as a moderator of life stress. *Journal of Personality and Social Psychology, 60,* 555–561.

64. Roskies, E. (1987). *Stress management for the healthy Type A.* New York: Guilford.

65. Weisinger, H. (1985). *Anger workout book.* New York: Quill.

66. Stewart, T. A. (1990, October 22). Do you push your people too hard? *Fortune,* pp. 121, 124, 128.

67. Falkenberg, L. E. (1987). Employee fitness programs: Their impact on the employee and the organization. *Academy of Management Review, 12,* 511–522.

68. Shephard, R. J., Cox, M., & Corey, P. (1981). Fitness program: Its effect on workers' performance. *Journal of Occupational Medicine, 23,* 359–363.

69. See Note 67.

**Stressed Out at
Nordstrom Stores**

They call themselves "Nervous Nordies." They regularly limp into the offices of employment counselors like Alice Snyder, who describes Nervous Nordies as "suffering from ulcers, colitis, hives and hand tremors."[1] They are victims of stress—from working under incredible pressure as salesclerks for the Seattle-based Nordstrom Stores—the nationwide chain of upscale department stores known for their outstanding customer service and profitability.

Nordstrom's sales floors are a shopper's delight. Musicians provide background music while salespeople compete to provide the utmost in customer service. But behind the scenes—in the back rooms—lies the real work world of the Nordstrom salesclerks (or Nordies, as they refer to themselves). Covering the back-room walls are posters shouting slogans such as "Make your goal," "Don't let us down," "Be the top Pacesetter," and performance charts and sales-contest standings.[2] Salesclerks rush from one place to another, desperate to get back to the customer, pamper him or her as much as possible, and hope for a sale. Sales volume is everything at Nordstrom. High sales mean recognition and contest wins. Let your sales drop, and you are terminated.

Nordstrom uses a combination of base pay and sales commission to compensate its employees. Its base pay is one of the highest in the retail industry—nearly $10 per hour. Once salesclerks reach a specified minimum level of sales (the sales quota), they work on a sales commission. Under the sales commission plan, it is possible for Nordstrom salesclerks to earn as much as $80,000 per year.

The sales performance chart is central to the life of every Nordstrom salesclerk. Every payday employees gather around the chart to see where they stand relative to their coworkers. All salesclerks are ranked according to their latest sales-per-hour performance record. A red line is drawn to mark the level of sales that management believes is acceptable. If your name appears above the red line, you're safe. If your name drops below the red line, you're likely to be fired.

Nordies have developed a number of ways to make sure that their numbers stay high. One method—encouraged by Nordstrom management—is to punch off the time clock before working on any activity not directly related to selling, such as restocking the shelves, making customer deliveries, or writing thank you notes to customers. They are warned that if they fail to punch off the time clock, the hours it takes to do these nonselling parts of their job will "dilute their critical sales-per-hour performance. A low SPH is grounds for dismissal."[3]

Nordstrom employees must smile whenever they are in sales areas. Nordstrom regularly conducts smiling contests. Managers take pictures of employees and then select the employee who smiles the most. The winning picture is posted on the lunchroom wall. Nordstrom hires secret shoppers to monitor salesclerk demeanor. Getting caught with a frown earns demerits that can lead to termination.

Nordies often resort to "sharking" to keep their jobs. Sharking refers to the predatory tactics and scams that salesclerks use to steal customers away from coworkers. Nordstrom employees are coming forward with tales of salesclerks monopolizing the cash register so other employees can't ring up sales, making deals with noncommission salesclerks to use their code numbers when ringing up sales, and even stealing the code numbers of rival salesclerks and assigning the rival's code number to returned merchandise (salesclerk commissions on returned merchandise are deducted from their pay and their sales-per-hour rating). Nordstrom employees have gone as far as setting up a coworker to get fired if it allows them to get ahead. Consider the case of Cindy Nelson, the number-one salesclerk in a Bellevue, Washington, Nordstrom store. Not able to outsell Nelson, the number-two and number-three salesclerks conspired with other coworkers to start a complaint-letter campaign against Nelson. These employees sent several *unsigned* complaint letters to Nelson's manager, accusing Nelson of stealing customers and the like. Shortly after receiving the letters, her manager confronted Nelson with the accusations. Nelson asked to see the letters, but her manager refused her request, saying they weren't any of her business. The manager fired Nelson based on the accusations alleged in the anonymous letters.

Working at Nordstrom involves a fair degree of role ambiguity and conflict. The management by innuendo that characterizes Nordstrom's management practices contributes to confusion about what the sales job really encompasses. Confusion is particularly likely among new employees. For example, employees must often attend Saturday morning department meetings. When they try to punch in on the time clock, they see a sign that reads "Do not punch the clock." Employees who ask about the sign are told that the clock is broken. And if they try to write the hours that they work during the department meetings on their time cards, then their hand-written hours are simply crossed off by payroll personnel. They are left in a state of confusion until they figure out that Nordstrom never had any intention of paying them to attend the so-called mandatory meetings.

The Nordstrom employee manual doesn't answer employee questions either. The employee manual consists of a single statement: "Use your good judgment in all situations."[4] Nordstrom used to have a twenty-page employee manual outlining job expectations, and grounds and procedures for termination. But so many ex-employees used the manual as the basis for proving their wrongful discharge suits that Jim Nordstrom, co-chairman of the company, ordered the manual to be revised. Says Nordstrom, "Our wrongful termination problems have gone way down since we got rid of that darn handbook."[5] Now Nordstrom employees are largely left to guess when and on what grounds they might be fired.

Many Nordstrom employees claim that the company's atmosphere is threatening. A cosmetics manager in one of Nordstrom's California stores wrote a memo considered typical of the numerous edicts that Nordies receive. After outlining a lengthy list of sales goals for cosmetics-counter employees to achieve, the manager wrote, "In the next sixty days if any of these areas are not met to our expectations you will be terminated."[6] In other communications, employees are told that even one sick day in three months is excessive and indicates a lack of dedication to the job. Again, there is considerable inconsistency in the communications issued by Nordstrom management. The end result is a threatening *and* confusing work environment.

What are the effects of working under such high pressure? For some employees, illness is their "reward." Long hours are the rule. Nordies often work twelve- to fifteen-hour days and seven to ten days without a break. And Jim Nordstrom is fond of telling employees that he doesn't think they work hard enough.

Employees respond to the job stress in a variety of ways. Some develop ulcers, others have nervous breakdowns, and many others finally quit. As one longtime employee says, "The girls around me were dropping like flies. Everyone was always in tears. You feel like an absolute nothing working for them."[7] Another employee, complaining about the work hours, says that "before you know it, your whole life is Nordstrom. But you couldn't complain, because then your manager would schedule you for the bad hours, your sales-per-hour would fall and the next thing you know, you're out the door."[8] Both these employees, consistent high performers, eventually quit their jobs at Nordstrom for better jobs (higher pay and far fewer hours)—one after developing an ulcer and working twenty-two days straight without a break; the other out of sheer exhaustion.

And how about the big money that salesclerks are supposed to be earning? Very few Nordstrom employees ever get rich. Of the 1,500 Nordstrom employees (out of 30,000 employees) represented by a union (United Food and Commercial Workers), only 7 are making more than $40,000 per year. Any employee who fails to meet the sales quota necessary to be on a commission basis more than a few times is fired. Overall though, Nordstrom salesclerks do earn considerably more on average ($20,000 to $24,000 per year) than typical retail workers nationwide (about $12,000 per year).

Some Nordstrom employees flourish under this Darwinian incentive system. Says Pat McCarthy, a twenty-year Nordstrom employee who does earn $80,000 in sales commissions per year, "It's really a people job which I love. Every year my sales have gotten progressively better."[9] Another happy salesclerk says, "Here at Nordstrom, I feel that I can be the best that I can be. While other retailers give you a book of rules, when I came here, Nordstrom gave me one with only one rule: Use your best judgment. That's because they want me to be my own boss."[10]

Although the company has an admirable reputation for customer service, which has contributed to the company's profitability line, their practices have also incurred some significant costs. Those unionized sales personnel have filed 500 complaints with their union against the company for unfair labor practices as of 1990. So many Nordstrom employees volunteered to provide evidence against Nordstrom that the union started an 800 hotline to handle the complaints. Union leaders believe that it won't be long before many of Nordstrom's other stores become unionized, too.

The State of Washington Department of Labor and Industries has also taken action against Nordstrom for its unfair labor practices. The agency found Nordstrom guilty of not paying employees for overtime worked and not paying for extra work activities that they were forced to perform off the clock. The agency has ordered Nordstrom to pay back wages that will total more than $30 million.

Nordstrom may well be at an important crossroads. The high-pressure tactics that seem to have helped Nordstrom achieve its envied position in the retail industry may, in the long run, undermine its ability to provide its most valuable selling point—outstanding customer service. Some Wall Street analysts fear that stressed-out employees, and their success in winning back wages in the Washington State Department of Labor and Industries decision, threaten to destroy Nordstrom's ability to continue to provide its hallmark standard of customer service.[11] Also, some Nordies are beginning to question Nordstrom's commitment to customer service. Says one stressed-out Nordie, "In the end, really serving the customer, being an All-Star, meant nothing; if you had low sales per hour, you were forced out."[12]

Questions for Discussion

1. What are the work-related causes of stress at Nordstrom Stores?
2. What are the effects of stress on Nordstrom employees?
3. Why do some employees thrive under Nordstrom's management practices whereas other employees experience stress?
4. Why are Wall Street analysts concerned about the level of stress felt by Nordstrom employees? Based on what you have learned from the text, do you believe that their concerns are justified? Explain your answer.

Notes

1. Faludi, S. C. (1990, February 20). At Nordstrom Stores, service comes first—But at a big price. *Wall Street Journal*, p. A1.
2. See Note 1, pp. A1 and A16.
3. See Note 1, p. A16.
4. See Note 1, p. A16.
5. See Note 1, p. A16.
6. See Note 1, p. A16.
7. See Note 1, p. A16.
8. See Note 1, p. A16.
9. See Note 1, p. A16.
10. See Note 1, p. A16.
11. Schwadel, F. (1990, February 20). Nordstrom to post its first decline in annual profit. *Wall Street Journal*, p. A16.
12. See Note 1, p. A16.

EXPERIENCING ORGANIZATIONAL BEHAVIOR

Procedure

List all the things you worry about below—big things/issues, little things/issues—anything that causes you concern or makes you uneasy. Your worries can be about *any* aspect of your life. Common categories of things that people worry about include the following:

Personal health and well-being
Success; career-related issues
Immediate and extended family
Finances
Job-related concerns
Community-related issues (e.g., taxes, politics, schools)
Trivia (all the little things that bother you)

Classifying Worries: Are They Really Necessary?

Now that you have completed your worry list, classify the top ten items on your list by placing each of them in *one* of the four boxes below as follows:

If a worry is *important* and *can be controlled,* place it in Box 1.
If a worry is *important* and *cannot be controlled,* place it in Box 2.
If a worry is *not important* and *can be controlled,* place it in Box 3.
If a worry is *not important* and *cannot be controlled,* place it in Box 4.

	Can Be Controlled	**Cannot Be Controlled**
Important	Box 1	Box 2
Not Important	Box 3	Box 4

Did you include any items in Box 2, 3, or 4? If so, do you think you should be worrying about these issues? If so, why? If not, why?

Points to Consider

1. In your opinion, why do people worry about things they can't control?
2. Does worrying have any positive effects? Or is it always counterproductive?
3. Why do some people worry so much more than others?
4. Can you think of any specific aspects of personality that might be related to excessive worry?
5. What can *you* do to reduce your own needless worrying?

■ 8 ■

GROUP DYNAMICS: UNDERSTANDING GROUPS AT WORK

CHAPTER OUTLINE

Groups at Work: Their Basic Nature
    What Is a Group? A Working Definition
    Types of Groups within Organizations
    Why Do People Join Groups?
    How Do Groups Develop?
The Structure of Work Groups
    Roles: The Many Hats We Wear
    Norms: A Group's Unspoken Rules
    Status: The Prestige of Group Membership
    Cohesiveness: Getting the "Team Spirit"
Task Performance: Working with and around Others
    Social Facilitation: Individual Performance in the Presence of Others
    Social Loafing: "Free Riding" When Working with Others

Performance on Other Types of Group Tasks

Special Sections

Focus on Research   Choosing to Work Alone or in Groups: Experimental Evidence

An International/Multicultural Perspective   The Norms of Working Relationships: A Cross-National Comparison

OB in Practice   Habitual Routines as an Impediment to Group Performance: The Catastrophic Example of Air Florida Flight 90

LEARNING OBJECTIVES

After reading this chapter, you should be able to:
1. Define what a group is and distinguish it from other collections of people.
2. Identify different types of groups operating within organizations and understand how they develop.
3. Describe the different roles played by individuals within organizations.
4. Understand what norms are and how they develop within work groups.
5. Distinguish between different types of status and explain how each influences organizational behavior.
6. Identify the causes and consequences of group cohesiveness within organizations.
7. Describe the phenomenon of social facilitation and explain various reasons for its occurrence.
8. Describe the social loafing effect and some ways of overcoming it.
9. Distinguish between additive, compensatory, disjunctive, and conjunctive groups, and summarize how well they perform relative to individuals working alone.

J ust how heavy a unit do you think they'll go for?" asks Derek Simmons, manager of the Research and Development team at Psi-Clone Computers, a small microcomputer manufacturer. He is referring to the weight of the new notebook computer they have been talking about developing—one that would be so light and so inexpensive that everyone, they hope, would carry one around with them.

Cindy Delhurst, a production specialist on the team, is quick to answer: "The competition's just got them down from six pounds to a little over three. But I think that to make a splash, we'll have to shoot for a pound or less."

"I can just see the ad campaign for it now," says Ted Hughes, the engineering rep on the team, " 'the one-pounder, from Psi-Clone.' "

"Or, better yet," interjects Derek, " 'now, fit the power of a Psi-Clone in the palm of your hand.' "

"That's okay," says Cindy, "but the real winner would be, 'weighing in at just one pound, the heavyweight computing champ, Psi-Clone.' "

Everyone laughs and nods their heads, when Derek offers a sobering reminder. "Remember, folks, we're not in marketing. We've got to develop the product before we can sell it."

Quick to get back to the point, Ted asks, "Well, are we agreed that we're shooting to create the lightweight champ, or should we ask marketing to test the concept more thoroughly before we develop it?"

"Need I remind you of Bill Fisher's memo?" Cindy asks as she fishes through a large stack of papers. No one seems to know what she's talking about.

"Here, I found it," she says. "In his memo to us dated two months ago, he asked us to begin work on 'the lightest notebook computer ever made' because his department's research says we can sell it—*if* the price is right."

"That's an awfully big 'if,' I think," Derek responds. "Maybe the technology exists, but I'm not so sure. For one thing, the new plastics we'll have to develop won't come cheaply. We're not talking about miniaturizing standard off-the-shelf parts, but starting from scratch with new materials—stuff that will have to be tested for heat endurance, tensile strength, the works!"

"We'll need special new batteries, too," says Cindy. "Lithium, I suppose, but I'll check with our suppliers."

"Let's get focused," Ted Hughes remarks. "What we need to do is break the project down into its component parts and assign one or two people to each part."

"I agree," nods Derek. "We'll need research in plastics, chip miniaturization, microassembly techniques, disk drive and storage design, display technology, power supplies, you name it."

Thinking about this, Cindy begins to question the project. "It's really a gigantic job—one that would take a long time, many years, given our limited resources," she says. "As a company, are we really positioned to take on such a project? I, for one, am not so sure."

"Certainly, it *is* a departure from our usual clone philosophy," Ted notes. "Maybe we should just follow our usual path by letting one of the big guys develop the technology and then improving on it. That's been our real strength as a company. Maybe we shouldn't stray from it."

"So what are you proposing, Ted?" Cindy interjects.

"I'm not proposing anything," Ted answers. "I'm just thinking aloud, asking a question."

Sensing frustration in the ranks, Derek comes to the rescue. "Okay, calm down," he says. "We're not getting anywhere on this. Let me see where we stand. Fisher asked us to work on this project two months ago, and we're only now considering that as a department, a company, we're not quite up to the task. Given that kind of inefficiency, I suppose we're really *not* ready to do the job."

Silence fills the room as Derek stands up. "I'll talk to Fisher about it directly," he says, "first thing tomorrow. But now I think we can all stand a little morale booster. C'mon, team, we're going out for lunch, and the tab's on me."

Immediately, the mood changes as everyone stands up and smiles. "Well, Derek," says Ted, "you found a way to get us processing like Psi-Clones after all."

———————————— ■ ————————————

What can be said about how Psi-Clone's research and development team is operating? One obvious conclusion is that there's no strong sense of direction or coordination; people are considering moving in different directions without knowing what's best for the company. Despite this haphazard approach, we can also see a strong concern for the company and its goals; everyone wants to do the right thing for Psi-Clone. The team members also clearly share camaraderie; they're all concerned—perhaps even oversensitive—about what the others think. They have a great deal of say in what goes on, yet they're willing to accept their manager's direction to look into the issues they face. Their willingness to overlook their differences and go to lunch together tells us something about the positive feelings they have about each other. Given these dynamics, it would be interesting to see how well the team does its work. Will the company benefit by having specialists in several areas combine their resources? How will the team grow and develop? These questions are all basic to the topic of *group dynamics*, the focus of this chapter.

Group dynamics focuses on the nature of groups—the variables governing their formation and development, their structure, and their interrelationships with individuals, other groups, and the organizations within which they exist.[1] Given how prevalent groups are in organizations, the importance of the topic of group dynamics in the field of organizational behavior is easy to appreciate. Because groups exist in all types of social settings, the study of group dynamics has a long history in the social sciences—including OB.[2] In fact, it has been said that the study of groups "does not 'belong' to any one of the recognized social sciences alone. It is the common property of all."[3] Our presentation of group dynamics will be derived from work in the fields of psychology, sociology, communication, and anthropology, and applied to the domain of work organizations.

Many key aspects of group dynamics interest scientists and practitioners concerned with OB. Specifically, we will focus on how groups are structured, the dynamics of their operation, and the forces that keep them together. We will then examine group performance, first exploring how individuals are influenced by the presence of groups, and finally reviewing the performance of different types of work group. Before proceeding with these topics, however, we will take a closer look at some basic issues involving the nature of groups themselves.

GROUPS AT WORK: THEIR BASIC NATURE

To understand the dynamics of groups and their influence on individual and organizational functioning, we must begin by addressing some basic questions—namely, what is a group, what types of groups exist, and how do groups come into being?

What Is a Group? A Working Definition

Imagine three people waiting in line at the cashier's stand at a supermarket. Now compare them to Derek, Cindy, and Ted, the three characters in our opening story. Which collection would you consider to be a "group"? Although in our everyday language we may refer to the people waiting in line as a group, they are clearly *not* a group in the same sense as our three characters at Psi-Clone. Obviously, a group is more than simply a collection of people. But what exactly makes a group a group?

Social scientists have formally defined a **group** as *a collection of two or more interacting individuals with a stable pattern of relationships between them who share common goals and who perceive themselves as being a group.*[4] To help us examine this definition more closely, we have portrayed it visually in Figure 8–1.

One of the most obvious characteristics of a group is that it is composed of *two or more people in social interaction.* In other words, the members of a group must have some influence on each other. The interaction between the parties may be either verbal (such as sharing strategies for a corporate takeover) or nonverbal (such as exchanging smiles in the hallway), but the parties must have some impact on each other to be considered a group.

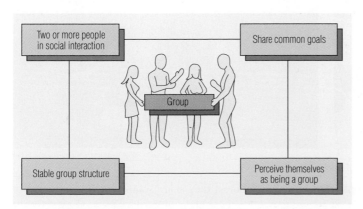

FIGURE 8–1

A Group: Its Defining Characteristics

The four major criteria for determining the existence of a group are summarized here. As shown, in a group there must be two or more people in social interaction who share common goals, have a stable group structure, and perceive themselves as being a group.

Test Bank questions 8.1, 8.46, and 8.66 relate to material on this page.

A group must also possess a *stable structure*. Although groups can and often do change, there must be some stable relationships between the members that keep a group together and functioning as a unit. A collection of people that constantly changes (e.g., the collection of people inside an office waiting room at any one time) cannot be thought of as a group. For a group, some greater stability would be required.

A third characteristic of a group is that its members *share common goals*. Groups often form because of some common interest or goal that individuals could not realize alone. For example, a sports team is a group that may be sustained by the mutual interest of its members in winning a championship. The members share this dream and work together to bring it to reality.

Finally, to be a group, the *individual members must perceive themselves as a group*. Groups are composed of people who recognize each other as a member of their group and can distinguish these individuals from nonmembers. The members of a board of governors or a bowling team, for example, know who is in their group and who is not. In contrast, shoppers in a checkout line probably don't recognize each other as members of a group. Although they stand physically close to each other and may interact, they have little in common (except, perhaps, a shared interest in reaching the end of the line) and fail to identify themselves with the others in the line.

By defining groups in terms of these four characteristics, we have identified a group as a very special collection of individuals. As we shall see, these characteristics are responsible for the very important effects groups have on organizational behavior. To better understand these effects, we will now review the wide variety of groups that operate within organizations.

Types of Groups within Organizations

What do the following have in common: a company softball team, four guys getting together for their Thursday night poker game, the board of directors of a large corporation, and the three-person cockpit crew of a commercial airliner? As you probably guessed, the answer is that they are all groups (see the photos in Figure 8–2). As these examples illustrate, many different types of groups exist in organizations.

FIGURE 8–2   Groups at Work: Two Examples

Despite the differences between the collections of people shown in these photos, they share something in common: each is a group.

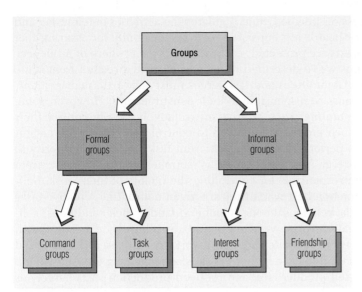

FIGURE 8-3

Varieties of Groups in Organizations

Many different kinds of group may be identified within organizations. For example, distinctions may be made between formal groups (such as command groups and task groups) and informal groups (such as interest groups and friendship groups).

Formal Groups   Perhaps the most basic way of identifying types of groups is to distinguish between *formal groups* and *informal groups* (see Figure 8–3). **Formal groups** are created by the organization and are intentionally designed to direct its members toward some important organizational goal. One type of formal group is referred to as a *command group*—a group determined by the connections between individuals who are a formal part of the organization (i.e., those who exercise legitimate command over others). For example, a command group may be formed by the vice president of marketing for a large organization who gathers together her regional marketing directors from around the country to hear their ideas on a new national advertising campaign. The point is that command groups are determined by the organization's rules regarding who reports to whom, and usually consist of a supervisor and his or her subordinates.

A formal organizational group may also be formed around some specific task. Such a group is referred to as a *task group*. Unlike command groups, a task group may be composed of individuals with some special interest or expertise in a specific area regardless of their positions in the organizational hierarchy. For example, a company may have a committee on equal employment opportunities whose members monitor the fair hiring practices of the organization. It may be composed of personnel specialists, corporate vice presidents, and workers from the shop floor. Whether they are permanent committees, known as *standing committees*, or temporary ones formed for special purposes (such as a committee formed to recommend solutions to a parking problem), known as *ad hoc committees* or *task forces*, task groups are common in organizations.

Two very special types of formal organizational groups are *boards* and *commissions*. Boards consist of people who are either elected or appointed to manage some entity. Typically, they are responsible for taking into account the interests of those who selected them (i.e., their constituents). For example, a board of directors is chosen by the stockholders of a corporation to manage its operations. Similarly, school boards are selected to direct the educational activities of a community's schools in a manner consistent with its goals and values.

Although similar to boards in their operation, *commissions* tend to operate in the government sector. You may be familiar with the Securities and Exchange Commission, the body that oversees the operations of the stock market, or the Federal

Teams and task forces, two common types of organizational groups, are different from each other in several key areas—specifically, their permanence, composition, and underlying function. A team is a relatively permanent group, whereas a task force is temporary, and ad hoc in nature. Also, whereas teams are usually composed of people of relatively similar ranks, task forces tend to be made up of people from a wider variety of organizational ranks and departments. Finally, teams tend to work on an entire product or service (e.g., developing a new software package), whereas task forces tend to deal with specific organizational problems or issues (e.g., establishing a

corporate smoking policy).
[Hoerr, J. (1989, February
20). Is teamwork a man-
agement plot? Mostly not.
Business Week, p. 70;
Kiechel, W., III. (1991,
January 28). The art of
the corporate task force.
Fortune, p. 104.]

Communications Commission, the body that regulates the activities of television and radio stations. Both these boards are entrusted with responsibility for assuring that the general public's interests are protected, each within its own sphere of influence.

All of the formal groups we've described thus far must take direction from some outside person or group. Committees and task forces must answer to management, and boards and commissions are responsible to their constituencies. However, some groups, known as *self-regulating work groups*, are relatively free to control their own work. Members of such groups are allowed to control their own work assignments, are encouraged to perform a variety of different tasks, have the authority to do the job as they wish (e.g., purchase necessary supplies and equipment, train employees), and are even responsible for controlling the quality of their work. Self-regulated work groups function best when they are given nonroutine, creative tasks to perform and have cordial relations among members. Under such conditions, self-regulated work groups have proven very successful. Specifically, compared with groups that are not allowed to regulate their own work, recent research has found that self-regulated groups tend to have higher job satisfaction among their members, reduced turnover, increased productivity, and reduced production costs (largely as a result of implementing the innovations recommended by the groups).[5] Such findings—based on recent research in work groups as diverse as coal miners, aviation workers, scientists and engineers, garment workers, schoolteachers, and others— suggest that self-regulated work groups may hold a promising future in many organizations.

Informal Groups   Of course, not all groups found in organizations are as formal as those we've identified thus far. Informal groups also commonly develop. **Informal groups** develop naturally among an organization's personnel without any direction from the management of the organization within which they operate. One key factor in the formation of informal groups is a common interest shared by its members. People who get together to satisfy a common interest may be said to have formed an *interest group*. For example, a group of employees who band together to seek union representation, or to march together to protest their company's pollution of the environment, may be called an interest group. The common goal sought by members of an interest group may unite workers at many different organizational levels. The key factor is that membership in an interest group is voluntary—it is not forced by the organization, but encouraged by the expression of common interests.

Of course, sometimes the interests that bind individuals together are far more diffuse. Groups may develop out of a common interest in participating in sports, or going to the movies, or just getting together to talk. These kinds of informal group are known as *friendship groups*. A group of coworkers who hang out together during lunch may also bowl or play cards together after work. Friendship groups extend beyond the workplace because they provide opportunities for satisfying the social needs of workers that are so important to their well-being (as you may recall from our discussion of Maslow's need hierarchy theory in chapter 4).

Informal work groups are an important part of life in organizations. Although they develop without the direct encouragement of management, friendships often originate out of formal organizational contact. For example, three employees working along side each other on the assembly line may get to talking and discover their mutual interest in basketball, and may decide to shoot baskets, or perhaps go to games together after work. Interestingly, such informal friendship groups can have very beneficial effects on organizational functioning.

In fact, one of the oldest established findings in the field of group dynamics is that being part of a desirable work group can help promote job satisfaction. This was demonstrated forty years ago by Van Zelst's study of carpenters and bricklayers working on a housing development.[6] During the first five months of the job, the men got to learn all about each other by being assigned many different coworkers by their supervisors. Then they were allowed to work in groups of those they liked best. This new arrangement resulted in a greatly reduced rate of turnover and a drop in the cost of building the housing development. Among the greatest benefits were the personal gains experienced by the workers themselves. To quote one of the workers, "The work is a lot more interesting when you've got a buddy working with you. You certainly like it a lot better anyway."[7]

As this study shows, both formal and informal group contact are important determinants of behavior in organizations. Now that we know what types of groups exist, we can turn our attention to the question of why people join groups.

Why Do People Join Groups?

Have you ever joined a fraternity or sorority, or any other campus club or organization? On the job, have you ever been a member of a committee working on ways to solve organizational problems? If you answered "yes" to either of these questions, then you're probably implicitly aware of many of the reasons people join groups. Several key explanations can be identified—and, as you might imagine, more than one motive can prompt a person to join a given group. As we review these below, you may find it useful to review the summary in Table 8–1.

No doubt you have heard that there is "safety in numbers." Indeed, people often join groups because they seek the *security* provided by group membership. Whether we're talking about the anxiety of being alone, fear of making an important decision without the benefit of others' input, or the possibility of being embarrassed about one's remarks, most of us want to be protected from external threats, real or imagined. That's where groups come in. Historically, the basic need to band together for protection against aversive management practices has been, in large part, responsible for the growth of labor unions.

As implied by this example, many groups form because of the *mutual benefits* they can provide members. One such benefit is economic self-interest. Professional associations, such as the American Medical Association or the American Bar Asso-

TABLE 8–1   Why Do People Join Groups? Some Major Reasons

People become members of groups for a variety of different reasons. Any one or more of the following may explain why people join groups.

Reason	Explanation
Security	Groups provide safety in numbers, protection against a common enemy
Mutual benefits	By joining together, group members can work to ensure the attainment of shared goals and benefits
Need to be social	Groups satisfy the basic need to be with others
Self-esteem	Membership in certain groups provides people with opportunities to feel good about their accomplishments
Mutual self-interest	Banding together, people can share their mutual interests (such as hobbies)
Physical proximity	People join groups because they come into contact with each other and discover they have something in common

ciation, exist, in part, because of the assistance they provide their constituents in lobbying government officials for legislation that favors their mutual economic interests.

This is not to say that groups are always designed to promote some instrumental good; indeed, they also exist because they appeal to a basic psychological *need to be social*. As we already discussed in the context of Maslow's need hierarchy theory (in chapter 4), people are social animals; they have a basic need to interact with others. Groups provide good opportunities for friendships to develop—hence, for social needs to be fulfilled.

Again, as suggested by Maslow, people have a basic desire for their *self-esteem* to be fulfilled. Group memberships can be a very effective way of gaining self-esteem. For example, if a group to which one belongs is successful (such as a sports team that wins a championship), the self-esteem of all members (and supporters) may be boosted. Similarly, election to membership in an exclusive group (e.g., a national honor society) will surely raise one's self-esteem.

What do a high school band, a stamp-collecting club, and a debating team have in common? They all exist for the purpose of satisfying the *mutual self-interest* of their members. Recent years have seen the growth of many computer-user groups across many communities. Groups of this type help people meet their mutual needs by sharing a common interest or hobby. By coming together to form such groups, people can more effectively enjoy activities that are less satisfying alone.

Finally, people often form groups because of their *physical proximity* to each other. Think about friendships you've formed with neighbors simply because you live next to each other and come into contact with one another. Although being physically close to someone doesn't ensure that a group will form, research suggests that social networks may form when the environment puts people in close contact with one another.[8] Imagine, for example, two sets of executive offices designed like the ones shown in Figure 8–4. Compare the private offices and secretaries arranged in a straight line (as shown on the upper left) with those arranged in a circular fashion around a shared secretary in the middle (as shown in the lower configuration). In which arrangement is contact by the executives more likely to occur? As you might

> Physical proximity is important for establishing interactive groups.
> Managers can make sure that office furniture is arranged in a manner that facilitates rather than discourages the potential formation of groups. One approach to arranging people and furniture that has become popular over the last ten years is using

FIGURE 8–4

Office Architecture: A Possible Determinant of Group Formation

In which of the two office designs shown here are the executives more likely to come into contact with each other? Because they share a common secretary, those in the lower configuration are more likely to meet. Once people meet, they may learn that they have common interests, and may form a group. Note that meeting others does not automatically lead to formation of a group. Architectural design merely serves to bring people into contact with one another.

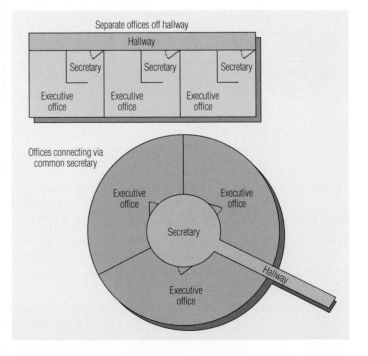

guess, the arrangement on the lower right will be more likely to bring the office occupants into contact with each other. Hence, they will be more likely to meet, to discuss their common interests, and to form friendship groups. We might expect to see them go out to lunch together. This does not preclude the possibility that groups will also form among those who are physically separated. Indeed, people with common interests, or who work in the same department, may seek each other's company despite their spatial separation in the work facility. So, for example, we may find that members of a command group located throughout an office building still meet and operate as a group despite their usual physical distance from each other. Spatial factors can play an important role in stimulating the creation of groups.

As we have shown, people join groups for many different reasons. However, people don't *always* work in groups; they sometimes work alone. Clearly, although groups hold some attraction for people, they are not always the preferred form in which to work. (For a closer look at the conditions under which people choose to work in groups or alone, see the **Focus on Research** section on pp. 274–275.)

How Do Groups Develop?

Now that we know *why* people join groups, let's consider *how* groups form. We will consider the natural stages through which groups develop and some guidelines for assembling groups in the most effective manner.

Stages of Group Development   Just as infants develop in certain ways during their first months of life, groups also show relatively stable signs of maturation and development.[9] One popular theory identifies five distinct stages through which groups develop.[10] As we describe these below, you may want to review our summary of the five stages shown in Table 8–2.

The first stage of group development is known as *forming.* During this stage of group development, the members get acquainted with each other. They establish the ground rules by trying to find out what behaviors are acceptable, with respect to both the job (how productive they are expected to be) and interpersonal relations (who's really in charge). During the forming stage, people tend to be a bit confused

a series of interlocking cubicles, called "cattle stalls." Although this technique is flexible and allows for better group interaction than standard offices, it does not provide any privacy for employees and is difficult to wire for rapidly changing office technology. As a result, designers have started arranging people in "clusters" or "neighborhoods," with each group of people having its own copy and conference rooms around a central staircase. These office clusters maintain the desired flexibility and relaxed feel that enhances group formation, but they are easier to wire for technology and provide more privacy than a sea of workstations. [Gordon, B. (1991, March 25). Office interior design evolves as work combinations change. *The Business Journal—Portland,* pp. 18–19.]

TABLE 8–2   The Five Stages of Group Development

As outlined in this model, groups go through several stages of development.

Stage	Primary Characteristic
1. Forming	Members get to know each other and seek to establish ground rules
2. Storming	Members come to resist control of group leaders and show hostility
3. Norming	Members work together, developing close relationships and feelings of camaraderie
4. Performing	Group members work toward getting their job done
5. Adjourning	Groups may disband either after meeting their goals or because members leave

Source: Based on information in Tuckman & Jensen, 1977; see Note 10.

Test Bank questions 8.49, 8.58, and 8.68 relate to material on this page.

and uncertain about how to act in the group and how beneficial it will be to become a member of the group. Once the individuals come to think of themselves as members of a group, the forming stage is complete.

The second stage of group development is referred to as *storming*. As the name implies, this stage is characterized by a high degree of conflict within the group. Members come to resist the control of the group's leaders and show hostility toward

 FOCUS ON RESEARCH

Choosing to Work Alone or in Groups: Experimental Evidence

Imagine that you are presented with a task to perform—such as changing the oil in a car or cooking a meal—and that you must do it at a high level of proficiency. Would you prefer to perform the task alone, or would you prefer to do it with the help of another?

When considering this question, people usually take into account their own expertise and capacity to perform the task alone. When you don't believe you can perform a task well, you might prefer to take on a partner, but when you believe you can already do the task, your need for the partner is less. In the latter case, the partner would add only a social benefit (i.e., provide company), but would not help you perform the task any better. How proficient one expects to be at a task depends on many considerations, among them the sex-type of the task—that is, whether the task is more likely to be performed by men (such as repairing a car) or by women (such as sewing a dress). We would expect that people of both genders expect to perform better—and not seek a partner—on those tasks in which they believe they have greater expertise. Thus, men would expect to perform better on masculine-type tasks, and women would expect to perform better on feminine-type tasks. (Of course, these judgments rely on social stereotypes, yet they may be accurate insofar as they describe overall differences between the interests of the vast majority of men and women in a given culture.) As a result, they may be expected to prefer to perform such tasks alone rather than with the benefit of another.

An interesting study by Vancouver and Ilgen tested these ideas.[11] Specifically, they asked col-

lege men and women how interested they would be in performing several different tasks either alone or with a partner. The tasks were established in advance as either masculine (such as building a tool shed) or feminine (such as designing a store window), but equally difficult to perform. How did the sex-type of the job affect the preference to perform the task alone or in groups? The results are shown in Figure 8–5.

As shown in Figure 8–5, people preferred performing tasks in groups when those tasks were ones with which they were relatively unfamiliar (i.e., sex-incongruent tasks). However, for tasks with which the parties were generally more familiar (i.e., sex-congruent tasks), the preference for group interaction was lower. Although these findings emerged overall, the differences were generally greater among women than men. This is in large part because men generally perceive themselves as being more competent than do women. (Note that we're *not* saying that men are any more competent than women, but that men are generally more confident of their own capabilities than are women.)

Of course, the desire to work in groups depends not only on expected task success, but also on one's general need for social interaction, the desire to have contact with others. Vancouver and Ilgen also assessed this in their study. Specifically, they found that although females were generally more interested in affiliating with others than were men, no significant correlation was found between one's affiliative needs (measured using a paper-and-pencil personality inventory; see chapter 6) and the desire to work with another person. The desire to work with others, at least in the cases studied, appears more strongly accounted for by the need to find a

each other. If these conflicts are not resolved and group members withdraw, the group may disband. However, as conflicts are resolved and the group's leadership is accepted, the storming stage is complete.

The third stage of group development is known as *norming*. During this stage, the group becomes most cohesive and identification as a member of the group becomes greatest. Close relationships develop, shared feelings become common,

qualified partner than by the general need to be with other people.

These findings are important because they suggest that someone's willingness to work with others may be a more complicated matter than ever suspected. It is determined, in part, by factors such as one's gender, the sex-based nature of the task, one's own capacity to perform the task successfully, and one's need for social interaction. And the issue may become even more complicated in the future. Consider, for

example, that the sex-type of many jobs is changing (as men enter traditionally feminine fields and women enter traditionally masculine fields). Given such trends, the decision to work with others will probably be less strongly related to the sex-type of the job performed. As fewer tasks become reliably linked to gender-related competence, we might expect competency judgments to become less predictable on the basis of congruence between one's gender and the sex-type of the task in question.

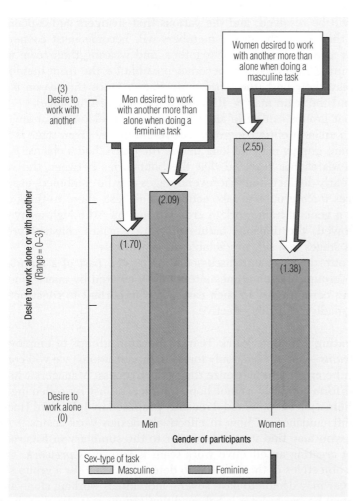

FIGURE 8–5

Working Together versus Alone: Experimental Evidence

Vancouver and Ilgen asked men and women how much they desired to do various masculine-type tasks (e.g., fixing a car) and feminine-type tasks (e.g., cooking a meal) either alone or with another person. They found that people more strongly desired to work in groups when the sex-type of the task was incongruent with their gender than when it was congruent. The assumed lower familiarity with sex-incongruent tasks encouraged people (especially women) to seek the benefits of having a partner. (*Source:* Based on data reported by Vancouver & Ilgen, 1989; see Note 11.)

and a keen interest in finding mutually agreeable solutions develops. Feelings of camaraderie and shared responsibility for the group's activities are heightened. The norming stage is complete when the members of the group come to accept a common set of expectations that constitutes an acceptable way of doing things.

The fourth stage is known as *performing*. During this stage, questions about group relationships and leadership have been resolved and the group is ready to work. Having fully developed, the group may now devote its energy to getting the job done—the group's good relations and acceptance of the leadership helps the group perform well.

Recognizing that not all groups last forever, the final stage is known as *adjourning*. Groups may cease to exist because they have met their goals and are no longer needed (such as an ad hoc group created to raise money for a charity project), in which case the end is abrupt. In other cases, groups may adjourn gradually, as the group disintegrates, either because members leave or because the norms that have developed are no longer effective for the group.

To help illustrate these various stages, imagine that you have just joined your university's football team. At first, you and the other rookies feel each other out. You watch to see who plays best, who helps the team most, who seems to take charge, and the like (the forming stage). Then you may see a battle over choice of first-string positions, and the offensive and defensive captains slots (the storming stage). Soon, this will be resolved, and the various first-stringers and captains will be established. At this stage, the group members will become most cooperative, working together as a team, hanging out together, and wearing their team jackets on campus (the norming stage). Now it becomes possible for the team members to work together to play their best (the performing stage). Once the season is over, players graduate, and the team may be disbanded (the adjourning stage).

Keep in mind that groups can be in any one stage of development at any given time. Moreover, the amount of time a group may spend in any given stage is highly variable. In fact, some groups may fail long before they have had a chance to work together. Recent research has revealed that the boundaries between the various stages may not be clearly distinct, and that several stages may be combined, especially as deadline pressures force groups to take action.[12] It is best, then, to think of this five-stage model as a general framework of group formation. Although many of the stages may be followed, the dynamic nature of groups makes constant progress through the various stages in a set, predictable order unlikely.

The stages of group development discussed thus far are part of a natural progression. However, groups are sometimes intentionally created by management for the purpose of doing certain jobs. In such cases, it is important to construct work groups that can be made maximally effective.

Guidelines for Creating Effective Work Teams   Because groups of employees—often called *work teams*—are so commonly found in organizations, we will consider how such teams can be created to maximize their effectiveness. Managers who want a work group to perform properly cannot hope for success just by collecting some people and giving them a job to do. A model recently proposed by J. Richard Hackman provides some useful guidance on how to effectively design work teams.[13] As we present this model, you may find it useful to refer to the summary in Figure 8–6.

The first stage of creating an effective work team is known as *prework*. One of the most important objectives of this phase is to determine whether a group should be created. A manager may decide to have several individuals working alone answer to him, or a group may be created if it is believed that groups may develop the most creative and insightful ways to get things done. In considering this, it is important

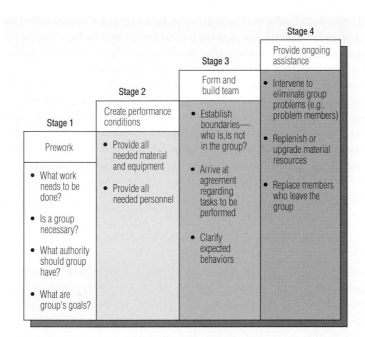

FIGURE 8-6

Stages of Creating Effective Work Teams

Rather than just throwing groups together and allowing them to perform, managers can take several steps to ensure the success of work teams. Four important steps are outlined here. (*Source:* Based on information in Hackman, 1987; see Note 13.)

to note exactly what work needs to be done. The group's objectives must be established, and an inventory of the skills needed to do the job should be made. In addition, decisions should be made in advance about what authority the group should have. They may just be advisory to the manager, or they may be given full responsibility and authority for executing their task (i.e., self-regulating). Such basic decisions constitute the prework stage of team formation.

Building on this, stage two involves *creating performance conditions.* In this stage, managers are to ensure that the group has the proper conditions under which to carry out its work. Resources necessary for the group's success should be provided. This involves both material resources (e.g., tools, equipment, and money) and human resources (e.g., the appropriate blend of skilled professionals). Unless managers help create the proper conditions for group success, they are passively allowing the possibility of failure.

Stage three involves *forming and building the team.* Three things can be done to help a work team get off to a good start. First, managers should *form boundaries*—clearly establish who is and who is not a member of the group. As strange as it may seem, membership in many work groups is often left unclear. Reducing such ambiguity can help avoid confusion and frustration. Second, members must *accept the task to perform.* Sometimes, group members have different ideas about what their group is expected to do. All group members must agree on what should be done and how the various duties will be subdivided for the group to function most effectively. Third, managers must *clarify expected behaviors*—make perfectly clear those tasks for which their subordinates will be responsible. Will they be responsible for monitoring and planning their own work? If so, such expectations should be spelled out explicitly.

Finally, once a group is functioning, supervisors should *provide ongoing assistance.* Although once groups start operating they often guide themselves, managers may be able to help by providing opportunities for the group to eliminate problems and perform even better. For example, disruptive group members may be either counseled or replaced. Similarly, material resources may have to be replenished or upgraded. Although it may be unwise for a manager to intervene in the successful affairs of a group that has taken on its own life, it also may be unwise to neglect opportunities to help a group improve and learn from its experiences.

Most likely, as you ponder these suggestions, you will recognize the considerable managerial skill and hard work it takes to create and manage work teams. However, as managers learn these skills, and as group members have successful experiences as members of effective work teams, the deliberate steps outlined above may become second nature to all concerned. As Hackman concludes, "When that stage is reached, the considerable investment required to learn how to use work teams well can pay substantial dividends—in work effectiveness and in the quality of the experience of both managers and group members."[14]

THE STRUCTURE OF WORK GROUPS

As noted earlier, one of the key characteristics of a group is its stable structure. When social scientists use the term **group structure,** they are referring to the interrelationships between the individuals constituting a group, the guidelines to group behavior that make group functioning orderly and predictable. The structure of a group has been likened to the interrelationship between the planets in our solar system.[15] Just as we may learn about the solar system by studying the interrelationship between the planets, we may learn about groups by studying the relationships between the people constituting them. In this section, we will describe four different aspects of group structure: the various parts played by group members *(roles)*, the rules and expectations that develop within groups *(norms)*, the prestige of group membership *(status)*, and the members' sense of belonging *(cohesiveness)*.

Roles: The Many Hats We Wear

One of the primary structural elements of groups is the members' tendency to play specific roles in group interaction. Social scientists use the term *role* in much the same way as a director of a play would refer to the character who plays a part. Indeed, the part one plays in the overall group structure is what we mean by a role. More formally, we may define a **role** as the typical behaviors that characterize a person in a social context.[16]

In organizations, many roles are assigned by virtue of an individual's position within an organization. For example, a boss may be expected to give orders, and a teacher may be expected to lecture and to give exams. Typically, these are formally prescribed in the person's job description or the company's policy manual. For example, the president of the United States (whose role assignments largely come from the U.S. Constitution) makes foreign policy decisions, attempts to improve the American economy, and so on—all behaviors expected of the person occupying that office. These are behaviors expected of the person playing that role, the person referred to as the *role incumbent*. When a new president takes office, that person assumes the same role and has the same powers as the previous president. The same behaviors are expected of whomever is occupying the role. Although the specific behaviors of individual presidents may vary, the fact remains that certain behaviors are expected of role incumbents (referred to as *role expectations*).

The role incumbent's recognition of the expectations of his or her role helps avoid the social disorganization that would surely result if clear role expectations did not exist. Sometimes, however, workers may be confused about the things that are expected of them on the job, such as their level of authority or their responsibility.

Such *role ambiguity,* as it is called, is typically experienced by new members of organizations who have not had much of a chance to "learn the ropes," and often results in job dissatisfaction, a lack of commitment to the organization, and an interest in leaving the job.[17]

Role Differentiation: Specialized Functions of Group Members   As work groups and social groups develop, the various group members come to play different roles in the social structure—a process referred to as **role differentiation.** The emergence of different roles in groups is a naturally occurring process. Think of committees to which you may have belonged. Was there one member who joked and made people feel better, and another member who worked hard to get the group to focus on the issue at hand? These examples of differentiated roles are typical of role behaviors that emerge in groups. Organizations, for example, often have their "office comedian" who makes everyone laugh, or the "company gossip" who shares others' secrets, or the "grand old man" who tells newcomers the stories about the company's "good old days." Group researchers long ago found that one person emerges who more than anyone else helps the group reach its goal.[18] Such a person is said to play the *task-oriented* role. In addition, another group member may emerge who is quite supportive and nurturant, someone who makes everyone else feel good. Such a person is said to play a *socioemotional* (or *relations-oriented*) role. Still others may be recognized for the things they do for themselves, often at the expense of the group—individuals recognized for playing a *self-oriented* role.

Many specific role behaviors can fall into one or another of these categories. Some of these more specific subroles are listed in Table 8–3. Although this simple distinction will help us understand some of the roles found in work groups, we should note that more complex conceptualizations have been proposed, including one that identifies as many as twenty-six different roles.[19] These efforts at understanding role differentiation, regardless of how simple or complex the distinctions may be, help

Today's managers note that new employees have surprisingly little experience working together with others in groups. As a result, such individuals often have to be specifically trained how to work effectively with other group members. One of the best potential opportunities for employees to learn how to work in groups is for them to get involved in group projects while in college classes. These in-class experiences in cooperating with others are recognized as an invaluable source of training. Students who get to practice group skills in college tend to effectively adapt to group tasks encountered on the job. [Comer, J. P. (1991, October). Learning to cooperate. *Parent's Magazine,* p. 171.]

T A B L E 8 – 3   Some Roles Commonly Played by Group Members

Organizational roles may be differentiated into *task-oriented, relations-oriented* (or *socioemotional*), and *self-oriented* roles—each of which has several subroles. A number of these are shown here.

Task-Oriented Roles	Relations-Oriented Roles	Self-Oriented Roles
Initiator-Contributors Recommend new solutions to group problems	*Harmonizers* Mediate group conflicts	*Blockers* Act stubborn and resistant to the group
Information seekers Attempt to obtain the necessary facts	*Compromisers* Shift own opinions to create group harmony	*Recognition Seekers* Call attention to their own achievements
Opinion givers Share own opinions with others	*Encouragers* Praise and encourage others	*Dominators* Assert authority by manipulating the group
Energizers Stimulate the group into action whenever interest drops	*Expediters* Suggest ways the groups can operate more smoothly	*Avoiders* Maintain distance, isolate themselves from fellow group members

Source: Based on Benne & Sheats, 1948; see Note 18.

Test Bank questions 8.24–8.27, 8.51, and 8.60 relate to material on this page.

make the point that similarities between groups may be recognized by the common roles members play.

By carefully analyzing the roles played by people in the work context, we can understand the factors influencing the jobs that people do. As an example, let's consider a fascinating study conducted by Rafaeli analyzing the role of cashiers in Israeli supermarkets.[20] Her analysis was based on three data-collection methods: systematic observations of the interactions between cashiers and customers (by trained observers hidden from view), observations while working as a cashier (i.e., the "participant-observer" method), and extensive interviews with cashiers and customers (see Table 8–4). Using these techniques, several interesting things were found

TABLE 8–4   Strategies Used to Gain Control by Israeli Supermarket Cashiers: Multiple Sources of Data

Research has shown that Israeli supermarket cashiers engage in four major strategies aimed at maintaining control over the way they do their jobs. Summarized here is evidence from three different sources of data that show the operation of each strategy.

	Source of Data		
Strategies	**Unstructured Observations**	**Participant Observation**	**Interviews**
Ignoring	Cashiers focus their eyes on the cash register, avoid eye contact with customers if they can.	Trainer told observer: "Sometimes they say really nasty things about how you should do your work. I think you should ignore them because there is no end to such comments."	"When they tell me what to do, like how many earrings to wear, and I don't want to do it, I simply ignore them and don't listen."
Rejecting	No evidence noted.	Cashiers label customers who request continuous monitoring of prices entered "pests" and "naggers."	"He is paying for the merchandise. He is not paying my salary. Why does he think he can tell me what to do?"
Reacting	Customer was angry that cashier had to "waste" time looking for a code, started yelling. Cashier tried to calm him down by saying, "Why do you have to yell? Why do you have to talk like that?"	A customer said, "In America, all the cashiers smile." Cashier replied: "So go to America. What do you want from me?"	"After a customer has rushed me through his purchases I love to sit back, cross my arms, watch him, and let everyone see how *he* is wasting everyone's time now."
Engaging	Cashier to customer: "Now if you smile, everything will be OK." Cashiers ask customers to put produce on scale.	Cashier keeps customers busy by telling them what to do: "You can take the bread, now pack the oranges, I typed the coffee."	"If I see that they are upset I might sing. I don't sing that well but it makes them laugh and forget they were angry."

Source: From Rafaeli, 1989; see Note 20. Reprinted by permission of the *Academy of Management Journal* and the author.

about the cashier's job. The most immediate influence on the cashiers was the customers (with whom they spent approximately 78 percent of their time). A less immediate but more formal source of influence was from managers (with whom they spent only about 13 percent of their time). In their relationships with customers and store management, cashiers often felt that they were being challenged, and worked hard at controlling the way they did things. For example, the cashiers generally resented someone else—such as customers, or even managers—telling them how to do their jobs (despite the fact that managers were expected to do so!). As a result, they tended to develop strategies for effectively maintaining control over what they did. These were *ignoring*, taking no action; *rejecting*, thinking about the other's lack of legitimate control; *reacting*, showing one's displeasure; and *engaging*, keeping others busy so they cannot attempt to exercise control. Table 8–4 summarizes some of the ways the cashiers used these strategies, as identified through each of the data-collection techniques. As this research reveals, Israeli supermarket cashiers often feel threatened about the power they wield, and respond in many ways to the struggle to maintain control over their jobs. Clearly, in-depth studies such as this reveal a great deal about the thoughts and behaviors of various role incumbents.

Role Conflict: Competing Demands from the Roles We Play   Researchers in the field of organizational behavior have expressed a great deal of interest in the concept of **role conflict**—the idea that the appropriate behaviors for enacting one role may be inconsistent with the appropriate behaviors for enacting another role or other requirements of the same role. That a person's various role requirements may conflict shouldn't be surprising, given the many roles people play—employee, friend, and family member, to name just a few (see chapter 7).

Although many types of role conflict exist, the two most common are *interrole* conflict and *intrarole* conflict.[21] These are summarized in Figure 8–7. **Interrole conflict** refers to the incompatible demands made on someone playing two or more roles. A common example is when a friendship develops between a supervisor and his or her subordinates. What a supervisor may be expected to do as a boss (e.g., be tough) may conflict with the behaviors expected as a friend (e.g., be sympathetic). As a result, fulfilling the demands of both roles simultaneously may be difficult.

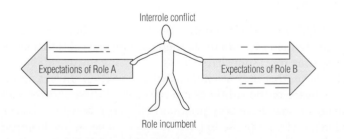

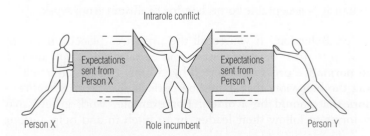

FIGURE 8–7

Role Conflict: Two Sources

Two major sources of role conflict are summarized here. In *interrole conflict*, there are different sets of expectations on a person playing more than one role. In *intrarole conflict*, there are different sets of expectations sent from different persons to someone playing one role.

Another common interrole conflict is created by the simultaneous demands of fulfilling work role obligations and family role obligations. Although in recent years the focus of such conflict has been on women, it is now clear that conflicting role obligations between work and family life (i.e., between one's roles as an employee, a spouse, and a parent) cause problems for men as well.[22] Indeed, as we will note later in this section, such conflicts can have a variety of serious consequences for both work life and family life.

Employees also may experience **intrarole conflict,** in which there are contradictory demands within a single role as viewed by different members of the group (referred to as *role senders*). A good example is the dual set of expectations faced by foremen. As members of their work groups, foremen are expected to be loyal to their fellow group members, which may be difficult given that upper management may expect them to support corporate interests as well. Intrarole conflict can also stem from ambiguities inherent in the positions held by role incumbents.[23] If what a person occupying a given role is expected to do isn't clear, different people expect different things of a role incumbent, thereby creating intrarole conflict.

Research has revealed a variety of negative consequences resulting from role conflict, including job dissatisfaction, poor group performance, and the rejection of other group members.[24] One study of interrole conflict has found that the more managers and their subordinates disagreed about a subordinate's role expectations, the more the subordinate experienced work-related stress and uncertainty about the possibility of promotion (see chapter 7).[25] A particularly important focus of recent research on role conflict has been the contradictory demands made on workers by their jobs and their families, a common problem faced by members of today's dual-career families. For example, in one study, Cooke and Rousseau examined the role conflicts experienced by 200 teachers.[26] The researchers found that the more teachers experienced conflicts between their roles as teachers and family members (such as taking home extra work to do), the more they reported feeling work overload (difficulty having enough time to get their work done) and high role conflict (interference between job demands and freetime activities), and the more they showed symptoms of physical and psychological strain. These findings clearly demonstrate how role conflicts can have a severe negative impact on workers' job performance as well as on their personal well-being.

Norms: A Group's Unspoken Rules

One feature of groups that enhances their orderly functioning is the existence of group *norms*. **Norms** may be defined as generally agreed on informal rules that guide group members' behavior.[27] They represent shared ways of viewing the world. Norms differ from organizational rules in that they are *not* formal and written. In fact, group members may not even be aware of the subtle group norms that exist and regulate their behavior. Yet, these norms may have very profound effects on behavior. Norms tend to regulate the behavior of groups in important ways, such as by fostering workers' honesty and loyalty to the company, establishing the appropriate ways to dress, and dictating when it is acceptable to be late for or absent from work.

Normative Influences on Behavior   If you recall the pressures placed on you by your peers as you grew up to dress or wear your hair in certain styles, you are well aware of the profound normative pressures exerted by groups. Norms can be either *prescriptive*—dictating the behaviors that should be performed—or *proscriptive*—dictating the behaviors that should be avoided. For example, work groups may develop prescriptive norms to follow their leader, or to pitch in and help a group

Norms are especially important when it comes to conducting business in cross-cultural situations. It is dangerous to assume that the unspoken rules followed in one culture are the same as those followed in another culture. For example, whereas most Americans feel it is appropriate (within limits) to tell jokes and make sarcastic remarks while in business meetings, strict norms dictate against these behaviors in Japan. In addition, in Japan the accepted norm is to allow the host to pick the topic

member who needs assistance. They may also develop proscriptive norms to avoid arriving at work late, or to refrain from blowing the whistle on each other.

Sometimes the pressure to conform to norms is subtle, as in the dirty looks that might be given a manager by his peers for going to lunch with one of the assembly line workers. Other times, normative pressures may be quite severe, as when one production worker strikes another because he is performing at too high a level, thereby making his coworkers look bad. In fact, as shown in Figure 8–8, employees may receive approval for behaving within a normatively acceptable range, but receive displays of disapproval for exceeding these limits in either direction.[28] Although curves of this type may take different shapes for different organizational behaviors (such as norms regarding absenteeism and attempts to exert influence on group members), group norms create potent pressures to behave in whatever way the group deems acceptable.

An experiment by Mitchell, Rothman, and Liden illustrates the impact of normative pressures on work performance.[29] These investigators hired college students to place lids on ice cream containers. The employees in one condition faced a wall chart revealing the alleged productivity of others doing the same job. Employees in another condition were provided with the same productivity information, but in the form of actually seeing the work performed by another. It was found that the participants in the study were more likely to match the production levels of other workers (i.e., to confirm the observed performance norm set by others) than to match summary data presented in chart form. People apparently felt the pressure to match the demonstrated performance level of others, thereby providing an excellent illustration of the impact of social norms on job performance.

Research has shown that norms influence not only people's productivity, but also the subtle ways they go about doing their jobs. For example, in a naturalistic observation study, Sutton studied the norms that existed within a large collection agency regarding the emotions collection agents are supposed to display when talking to debtors over the phone.[30] For example, a norm mandates that bill collectors should convey a sense of urgency when talking to debtors (i.e., to show high arousal with a hint of irritation). By displaying this demeanor, bill collectors operate effectively. Sutton found that this norm was reflected in the way the organization selected prospective employees (e.g., by looking for "intensity" and "aggressiveness" in pro-

of conversation, even if that means not talking about business at all. [Holden, T., & Woolley, S. (1989, October 2). The delicate art of doing business in Japan. *Business Week*, p. 120.]

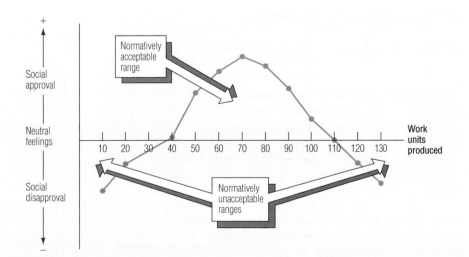

FIGURE 8–8

Norms: Defining Socially Acceptable Work Behavior

Employees often experience normative pressures to perform within a socially acceptable range. Performance higher than or lower than this range is socially disapproved. (*Source:* Based on Nadler, Hackman, & Lawler, 1979; see Note 28.)

spective hires), trained them to do their jobs (e.g., explaining that an "urgent" and "concerned" style was appropriate), and rewarded them on the job (e.g., by praising them for displaying the properly urgent emotional style). As you might imagine, some people would have difficulty adhering to such a norm because they may feel sensitive to the debtor's plight and communicate these emotions. To guard against this behavior (and jeopardizing their effectiveness), bill collectors were trained in techniques that helped them maintain the proper level of emotional detachment. This study clearly demonstrates the importance of work norms in regulating key aspects of work-related behavior.

The Development of Norms   The question of how group norms develop has been of considerable interest to organizational researchers.[31] An insightful analysis of the way norms develop in work groups has been presented by Feldman.[32] Table 8–5 summarizes the four steps in this model.

First, norms develop because of *precedents set over time*. Whatever behaviors emerge at a first group meeting will usually set the standard for how that group is to operate. Initial group patterns of behavior frequently become normative, such as where people sit, and how formal or informal the meeting will be. Such routines help establish a predictable, orderly interaction pattern.

Similarly, norms develop because of *carryovers from other situations*. Group members usually draw from their previous experiences to guide their behaviors in new situations. The norms governing professional behavior apply here. For example, the norm for a physician to behave ethically and to exercise a pleasant bedside manner is generalizable from one hospital to another. Thus, a doctor changing hospitals can expect the same norms of professionalism to preside in the new setting. Such carryover norms can assist in making interaction easier in new social situations. Carryover norms mean that there may be fewer new norms to learn, thereby enhancing the ease of social interaction. Demonstrating the prevalence of carryover norms,

T A B L E 8 – 5   Norms: How Do They Develop?

This table summarizes four ways in which group norms can develop.

Basis of Norm Development	Example
1. Precedents set over time	Seating location of each group member around a table
2. Carryovers from other situations	Professional standards of conduct
3. Explicit statements from others	Working a certain way because you are told "that's how we do it around here"
4. Critical events in group history	After the organization suffers a loss due to one person's divulging company secrets, a norm develops to maintain secrecy

Source: Based on Feldman, 1984; see Note 32.

Bettenhausen and Murnighan performed a study in which they put together new groups of bargainers composed of individuals whose previous groups had developed strong norms to bargain in a certain way.[33] They found that the behaviors people brought to their new groups were in keeping with the norms of their previous groups. Clearly, group norms may carry over from one situation to another.

Sometimes norms also develop in response to an *explicit statement by a superior or a coworker*. Newcomers to groups quickly "learn the ropes" when one of their coworkers tells them "That's the way we do it around here." The explanation is an explicit statement of the norms; it describes what one should do or avoid doing to be accepted by the group. Sometimes the explicit statement of group norms represents the accepted desires of a powerful group member, such as a supervisor. If a supervisor wants reports prepared in a certain way, or expects a certain degree of formality or informality in addressing others, norms may develop to adopt these standards. The socialization of new group members frequently requires learning group norms by listening to more experienced group members.[34]

Finally, group norms may develop out of *critical events in the group's history*. If an employee releases an important organizational secret to a competitor, causing a loss to the company, a norm to maintain secrecy may develop out of this incident. In a similar manner, a professional group that decides to censure the inappropriate behavior of one of its members (e.g., a member of Congress who accepts a bribe, a physician who uses poor medical judgment) may be seen as acting to reaffirm its commitment to the violated norm. Both incidents represent critical events that help either establish or reaffirm a group norm.

Although some group norms may be unique to the individuals involved, others are more widely accepted. For example, the norms to "play fairly" and to "not steal" are widely accepted throughout society. Are some norms about the treatment of others widely accepted across different organizations? For a closer look at this question, and at the extent to which different work norms exist within different nations, see the **International/Multicultural Perspective** section on p. 286.

Status: The Prestige of Group Membership

Have you ever been attracted to a group because of the prestige accorded its members? You may have wanted to join a certain fraternity or sorority on your campus because it is highly regarded by the students. Aspiring members of street gangs long for the day they can wear their gang's "colors" in the streets. No doubt, members of Super-Bowl-winning football teams proudly sport their Super Bowl rings to identify themselves as members of a championship team. Clearly, one potential reward of group membership is the status associated with being in that group. Even within social groups, different members are accorded different levels of prestige. Fraternity and sorority officers, gang leaders, and team captains, for example, may well be recognized as more important members of their respective groups. This is the idea behind **status**—the relative social position or rank given to groups or group members by others.[35]

Formal and Informal Status   Within most organizations, status may be recognized as both formal and informal in nature. *Formal status* refers to attempts to differentiate between the degrees of formal authority given employees by an organization. This is typically accomplished through the use of *status symbols*—objects reflecting the position of an individual within an organization's hierarchy. Some examples of status symbols include job titles (e.g., "Director"); perquisites, or "perks," (e.g., a reserved parking space); the opportunity to do desirable and highly regarded work (e.g.,

People in groups, such as organizations and universities, often display a logo or emblem in team or company colors as a way of expressing their status of membership, or liking of specific groups. One such item that people have been wearing for almost 150 years is the baseball cap. Baseball hats were first made out of straw and were worn by the Knickerbockers, a team that many consider to be the first organized baseball team, in Hoboken, New Jersey, in 1846. Besides caps, you are likely to see students on college campuses wearing university logo T-shirts in sup-

AN INTERNATIONAL/MULTICULTURAL PERSPECTIVE

The Norms of Working Relationships: A Cross-National Comparison

Are some norms regarding work-related behavior so critical to the effective functioning of organizations that they have become standard across different organizations? According to a questionnaire study by Henderson and Argyle, the answer is "yes."[36] These researchers asked a diverse sample of people in the United Kingdom to indicate the norms that they believed govern work relationships. They found that there were two main types of work norms: those regarding *maintenance* (e.g., minimizing conflict), such as "Do not disclose secrets" and "Do not criticize others in public," and those regarding *reward* (e.g., providing desired outcomes), such as "Cooperate with others" and "Use initiative." They also found that different rules predominated in different types of relationships. Specifically, when dealing with supervisors, people are expected to follow rules such as "plan work efficiently" and "keep others informed." When dealing with subordinates, people are expected to abide by the guidelines "Don't hesitate to question" and "Use initiative." Finally, when dealing with peers, people are expected to adhere to the norms "Accept a fair share of the work" and "Help when asked."

Remember, these findings reflected the commonly found norms among people in the United Kingdom. Would the same results occur in other countries? Given that cultural values and the nature of work differ in other nations, it is logical to assume that feelings about work norms may differ among people in different nations. A follow-up study asked identical questions (translated, of course) to people in Italy, Japan, and Hong Kong. Only a few national differences were found, but these were very interesting, usually distinguishing the Japanese from the people of the other cultures studied. Here are some of the highlights:

- People in Japan indicated that it was not acceptable for them to display their emotions to their peers or superiors.
- The Japanese believed that it was least appropriate to show submissiveness when dealing with subordinates.
- Japanese people believed it was inappropriate to display any concern about their subordinates' well-being.

Overall, these findings reflect the general tendency for Japanese people to emphasize saving face and avoid showing their vulnerability to others (see chapter 10). Given these general cultural norms, we are not surprised to find that work-related norms reflect deep-rooted cultural differences. To the extent that work norms are maintained because they ease social functioning, it makes sense that work-related norms reflect the general cultural values of the people adopting them.

---

port of their schools (or even other schools). [Why wear a baseball cap? (1989, July 3). *The New York Times*, p. 31(L).]

serving on important committees); and luxurious working conditions (e.g., a large, private office that is lavishly decorated).[37] (For an example, see Figure 8–9.)

Status symbols help groups in many ways.[38] For one, such symbols serve to remind organizational members of their relative roles, thereby reducing uncertainty and providing stability to the social order (e.g., your small desk reminds you that you are an Indian, not a chief). In addition, they provide assurance of the various rewards available to those who perform at a superior level (e.g., maybe one day I'll have the key to the executive washroom). They also provide a sense of identification by reminding members of the group's values (e.g., a gang's jacket may remind its wearer of his expected loyalty and boldness). It is, therefore, not surprising that organizations do much to reinforce formal status through the use of status symbols.

Systems of *informal status* within organizations are also widespread. These refer to the prestige accorded individuals with certain characteristics that are not formally dictated by the organization. For example, employees who are older and more experienced may be perceived as higher in status by their coworkers. Those who have certain special skills (such as the home-run hitters on a baseball team) also may be regarded as having higher status than others. The lower value generally placed on the work of women and members of minority groups, however unfortunate, can also be considered an example of informal status in operation.[39]

Status is not fixed or tangible. Like beauty, status is in the eye of the beholder. It is conferred on those who hold it in the case of both formal and informal status. If members of an organization fail to recognize certain positions or certain jobs as being more important than others, those who hold them are unlikely to receive different amounts of status because of this. Informal status is also in the eye of the beholder. For example, employees who do not value the greater experience of a coworker with seniority would probably not show that person any special deference. Our point is simple: status differences exist only when status dimensions are recognized and valued by others.

The Influence of Status on Organizational Behavior   One of the best-established findings in the study of group dynamics is that higher-status people tend to be more influential than lower-status people. This phenomenon may be seen in a classic study of decision making in three-man bomber crews.[40] After the crews had difficulty solving a problem, the experimenter planted clues to the solution with either a low-status group member (the tail gunner) or a high-status group member (the pilot). It was found that the solutions offered by the pilots were far more likely to be adopted than the same solutions presented by the tail gunners. Apparently, the greater status accorded the pilots (because they tended to be more experienced and hold higher military ranks) was responsible for the greater influence they wielded. Similar findings have been obtained in analyses of jury deliberations. Research in this area has shown that members of juries having high-status jobs (such as professional people) tend to exert greater influence over their fellow jurors than others holding lower occupational status.[41]

"Instead of the bigger desk you requested, which might have led to resentment and envy among your colleagues, we are giving you a more ornate one, which we hope will merely lead to muffled mirth."

FIGURE 8-9

Desk Size: One Sign of Status in Many Organizations

As shown here, status symbols such as desk size help reflect the level of influence a person has within an organization. (*Source:* Reprinted with permission of the artist J. B. Handelsman and Ralph Guild, Interep Radio Store.)

Status differences are also largely responsible for the way people communicate with each other. For example, people of lower status are likely to address those of higher status by their titles, such as "General," or "Mr. President," or "Doctor," whereas less formality—using only first names—is commonly found in addressing people of lower status.[42] Similarly, people prefer communicating with others of equal status, and are uncomfortable communicating with others of much higher or much lower status levels.[43] However, when people of unequal status do communicate, it is usually considered more acceptable for the higher-status person to initiate the conversation. This phenomenon is demonstrated clearly in a classic study by Whyte.[44] Observing the interaction between waitresses (considered lower status) and chefs (considered higher status), Whyte found that conflicts emerged when the waitresses passed their orders directly to the chefs. The chefs resented the initiation of action from the lower-status waitresses. Then, after an "order wheel" was installed, the waitresses simply attached their orders to it, thereby allowing the chefs to take the orders whenever they were ready. Higher-status individuals no longer had to respond to the actions of lower-status individuals, eliminating considerable conflict. Such findings are typical of the tendency for people of higher status to expect to influence others rather than to be influenced by them.

Cohesiveness: Getting the "Team Spirit"

Team members who work well together can develop a camaraderie or an esprit de corps (French for "group spirit"). When group spirit is high, group performance may benefit. A group of employees at the General Mills company worked so well together making Oatmeal Crisp cereal that they improved their group's productivity by 40 percent. The employees felt that they couldn't have accomplished this feat without the team spirit they had developed while working together. [Dumaine, B. (1990, May 7). Who needs a boss? *Fortune*, pp. 52–60.]

One very obvious determinant of any group's structure is its *cohesiveness*. We may define **cohesiveness** as the pressures group members face to remain part of their groups. Highly cohesive work groups are ones in which the members are attracted to each other, accept the group's goals, and help work toward meeting them. In very uncohesive groups, the members dislike each other and may even work at cross-purposes.[45] In essence, cohesiveness refers to a "we" feeling, an "esprit de corps," a sense of "belonging" to a group.

What Makes a Group Cohesive?   Several important factors have been shown to influence the extent to which group members tend to "stick together." One such factor involves the *severity of initiation into the group*. Research has shown that the greater the difficulty people overcome to become a member of a group, the more cohesive the group will be.[46] To understand this, consider how highly cohesive certain groups may be that you have worked hard to join. Was it particularly difficult to "make the cut" on your sports team? Were you accepted into an extremely competitive school? Indeed, the rigorous requirements for gaining entry into elite groups such as the most prestigious medical schools and military training schools may well be responsible for the high degree of camaraderie found in such groups. Having "passed the test" tends to keep individuals together, and separates them from those who are unwilling or unable to "pay the price" of admission.

Group cohesion also tends to be strengthened under conditions of *high external threat or competition*. When workers face a "common enemy," they tend to draw together. Such cohesion not only makes workers feel safer and better protected, but also aids them by encouraging them to work closely together and coordinate their efforts toward the common enemy (see the photo in Figure 8–10). Under such conditions, petty disagreements that may have caused dissension within groups tend to be put aside so that a coordinated attack on the enemy can be mobilized.

Sherif and his associates clearly demonstrated the dynamics of such a situation in a classic study of eleven- and twelve-year-old boys attending camp.[47] When they first arrived at camp, the boys were divided into two groups living in separate cottages. During the first few weeks, the members of each group worked together on projects that required high degrees of cooperation within the group (e.g., pre-

FIGURE 8-10

External Threat: A Source of Group Cohesion

As demonstrated by the example shown here, the presence of a common enemy can help foster feelings of cohesiveness within groups.

paring dinner required one boy to get firewood, another to mix soft drinks, another to make hamburgers). Soon, feelings of cohesiveness developed, and the groups gave themselves names to establish their identities—the "Rattlers" and the "Eagles." Next, a meeting was arranged between the two groups, and they soon challenged each other to various competitive events. Rapidly, they became enemies, not only fighting each other on the playing field, but also raiding each other's cottages and having food fights.

At this point, an interesting observation was made: the more the Rattlers and the Eagles fought each other, the more cooperative the members of each group became toward each other, and the greater degree of cohesiveness they experienced. Reasoning that the imposition of an enemy strengthened the animosity between the groups and the cohesiveness within them, Sherif attempted to bring the two groups together by presenting them with a common enemy. Various catastrophes were staged that forced the two groups to work together. For example, a breakdown in the camp's plumbing system required the boys to form a bucket brigade. On another occasion, the breakdown of a truck forced them to band together, pushing to help start it. In both cases, the boys from both groups worked together to oppose their common threats and felt cohesive as a single unit—now they were operating as members of the same camp, not as opposing subgroups within that camp. However, as soon as the problems were solved and the common enemy disappeared, the groups reverted to the much lower levels of cohesiveness that existed before the common external threat. This fascinating study provides solid evidence of the extent to which a common external threat can help high degrees of cohesiveness develop within groups.

Research has also shown that the cohesiveness of groups is established by several additional factors.[48] For one, cohesiveness generally tends to be greater the more time group members spend together. Obviously, limited interaction cannot help but interfere with opportunities to develop bonds between group members. Similarly, cohesiveness tends to be greater in smaller groups. Generally speaking, groups that are too large make it difficult for members to interact and, therefore, for cohesiveness to reach a high level. Finally, because "nothing succeeds like success," groups with a history of success tend to be highly cohesive. It is often said that "everyone loves a winner," and the success of a group tends to help unite its members as they rally around their success. For this reason, employees tend to be loyal to successful companies, and members of winning athletic teams tend to want not to be traded away from them. As summarized on the left side of Figure 8–11 (see p. 290), these are among many factors that contribute to the cohesiveness of a group.

FIGURE 8–11

Group Cohesiveness: Its
Causes and Consequences

As summarized here,
several factors contribute
to a group's cohesiveness.
High levels of cohesiveness
may have both positive and
negative consequences.

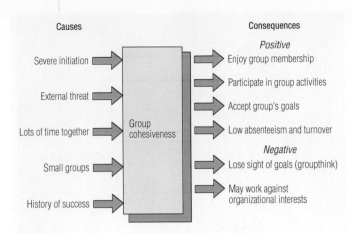

The Benefits and Costs of Cohesive Groups   Although we often hear about the
benefits of highly cohesive groups, the consequences of cohesiveness are not always
positive. In fact, research has shown both positive and negative effects of cohesiveness
(see the summary on the right side of Figure 8–11).

On the positive side, people are known to enjoy belonging to highly cohesive
groups. Members of closely knit work groups participate more fully in their group's
activities, more readily accept their group's goals, and are absent from their jobs less
often than members of less cohesive groups.[49] Not surprisingly, cohesive groups tend
to work together quite well and are sometimes exceptionally productive. In fact,
research has shown that high levels of group cohesiveness tend to be associated with
low levels of voluntary turnover.[50] People's willingness to work together quite well
and to conform to the group's norms is often responsible for their success, and their
willingness to stay with the group.[51]

However, the tendency for members of highly cohesive groups to go along with
their fellow members' wishes sometimes has negative consequences for the ultimate
group product. Consider, for example, the actions of the highly cohesive Committee
to Re-elect President Nixon preceding the 1972 presidential election. The Watergate
conspirators were a highly cohesive group—so cohesive that they were blinded to
the possibility that they were committing illegal and unethical acts. Poor decisions
resulting from too high a level of cohesiveness reflect a phenomenon known as
groupthink.[52] Groupthink occurs when a group is so cohesive that its members
potentially lose sight of its ultimate goals for fear of disrupting the group itself.
(Because of the negative impact of groupthink on the quality of group decisions, we
will discuss this phenomenon in greater detail in the context of decision making in
chapter 14.)

Group cohesion can influence productivity in many other ways. It makes sense
that after a group experiences success its members will feel more committed to each
other. Similarly, we might expect a cohesive group to work well together and to
achieve a high level of success. However, a work group whose members are strongly
committed to each other does not necessarily perform well within the organization.[53]
For example, if a group's goals are contrary to the organization's goals, a highly
cohesive group may actually do a great deal of harm to an organization. Highly
cohesive workers who conspire to sabotage their employers are a good example.
Apparently, group cohesiveness can have either positive or negative effects on
performance.

One of the first studies to look at the relationship between group cohesion and
organizational productivity was conducted in the early 1950s by Stanley Seashore.[54]

The participants in this experiment were employees of a manufacturing plant who formed over 200 small work groups. They completed questionnaires measuring the degree of cohesiveness of their work groups, which were then compared with job performance over a three-month period. It was found that high cohesiveness was associated with high productivity when group members felt that management supported them, but low productivity when management threatened them. This implies that a cohesive work group may be successful only if what it is doing goes along with management's wishes.

More recently, a study conducted at a public utility revealed that in highly cohesive groups a supportive managerial style was related to higher performance, but not in weakly cohesive groups.[55] A similar tendency for high performance levels to be associated with highly cohesive groups operating under a supportive managerial atmosphere was found in a study of soldiers in the Israeli army.[56] It appears, then, that there is no simple relationship between group cohesion and job performance. Our summary of these studies in Figure 8–12 shows that a cohesive group *can* enhance productivity, but *only* when the manager's style supports the group's efforts. If a group of workers bands together but finds that its efforts are not supported by the company's management, it will perform poorly. Cohesion can aid productivity as long as superiors and subordinates are not operating in opposition to each other. Organizations may well benefit by the existence of cohesive groups, but only when the groups and the organizations are working together.

TASK PERFORMANCE: WORKING WITH AND AROUND OTHERS

Now that we have reviewed the basic elements of group structure, we are prepared to examine an aspect of group dynamics most relevant to the field of organizational behavior—the effects of groups on performance. We will consider this issue from two different perspectives. First, we will look at the influence of the presence of a group on individual performance. Then we will consider how well different types of groups perform as a whole.

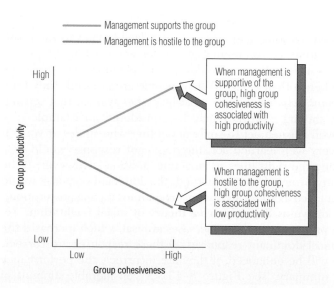

FIGURE 8–12

Group Cohesion and Productivity: Mediating Effects of Management

Several studies have shown that the relationship between group performance and group cohesiveness depends on management's support for and acceptance of the group. Greater cohesion is associated with greater productivity when management is supportive of the group, and less productivity when management is hostile to the group.

Social Facilitation: Individual Performance in the Presence of Others

Imagine that you have been studying drama for five years and you are now ready for your first acting audition in front of some Hollywood producers. You have been rehearsing diligently for several months, getting ready for the part. Now you are no longer alone at home with your script in front of you. Your name is announced, and silence fills the auditorium as you walk to the front of the stage. How will you perform now that you are in front of an audience? Will you freeze, forgetting the lines you studied so intensely when you practiced alone? Or will the audience spur you on to your best performance yet? In other words, what impact will the presence of the audience have on your behavior?

Almost a century ago, this same question was asked by a bicycling enthusiast named Norman Triplett, who put his skills as a social scientist to work to find an answer.[57] Triplett noticed that cyclists invariably achieved faster times when they raced against others than when they raced alone, against the clock. Intrigued by these observations, he conducted a laboratory experiment in which children, either alone or in pairs, played a game requiring them to turn a fishing reel as fast as possible. Just as he had observed at the bicycle track, Triplett found that the children performed the task better when they were in the presence of another person than when they were alone.

As other scientists began studying the effects of the presence of an audience or of *coactors* (people working separately on the same task at the same time in each other's presence) on individual performance, they did not always find that performance improved, as Triplett noted. In fact, sometimes they found that people did worse when performing a task in the presence of others than when alone. This tendency for the presence of others to enhance an individual's performance at times and to impair it at other times became known as **social facilitation.** (Although the word "facilitation" implies improvements in task performance, scientists use the term *social facilitation* to refer to both performance improvements and decrements stemming from the presence of others.) For many years, scientists were confused about the seemingly contradictory effects of others' presence on task performance. Then, in the mid-1960s, Robert Zajonc proposed a model that accounted for the apparent inconsistency in the findings regarding social facilitation.[58] Zajonc's model offered a simple, yet elegant, explanation of when others' presence would help and when it would hinder performance.

A Model of Social Facilitation   Zajonc reasoned that social facilitation was the result of the heightened emotional arousal (e.g., feelings of tension and excitement) people experience when in the presence of others. (Wouldn't you feel more tension playing the piano in front of an audience than alone?) When people are aroused, they tend to perform the most *dominant response*—their most likely behavior in that setting. (Returning the smile of a smiling coworker may be considered an example of a dominant act; it is a very well learned act to smile at another who smiles at you.) If someone is performing a very well learned act, the dominant response would be a correct one (such as speaking the right lines in an acting audition). However, if the behavior in question is relatively novel, newly learned, the dominant response would be expected to be incorrect (such as speaking the incorrect lines during an audition). Together, these ideas are known as Zajonc's **drive theory of social facilitation.** According to this theory, the presence of others increases arousal, which increases the tendency to perform the most dominant responses. If these responses are correct, the resulting performance will be enhanced; if they are incorrect, the performance will be impaired. (For a summary, see Figure 8–13.) A considerable amount of

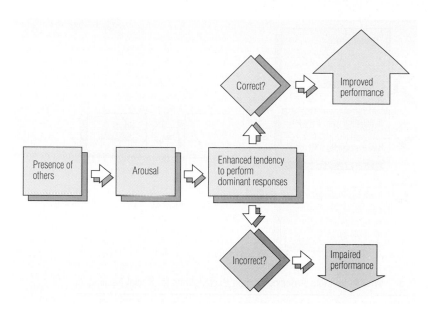

FIGURE 8–13

Social Facilitation: A Drive Theory Approach

The *drive theory of social facilitation* states that the presence of others is arousing. Such increased arousal enhances the tendency to perform the most dominant (i.e., strongest) responses. If these are correct, performance will be improved, but if these are incorrect, performance will be impaired.

research has shown support for this theory: people (and lower animals, too) perform better on a task in the presence of others if that task is very well learned, but poorer if it is not well learned.[59]

Why Are Others Arousing? Some Possible Explanations   Although it is well established that dominant responses—whether correct or incorrect—are enhanced by the presence of others, investigators disagree about exactly *why* these effects occur. Several perspectives have been offered (for a summary, see Figure 8–14 on p. 294).

As we have already explained, Zajonc proposed that the presence of others makes people feel aroused. According to Zajonc, this arousal results simply because the others are there, what he calls their "mere presence." He uses the term *compresence* to refer to the presence of others and the innately arousing effect that it has.[60]

Other scientists have modified Zajonc's approach, claiming that the arousal resulting from others' presence is not due to the fact that others are simply there, but that these others can potentially evaluate the person.[61] Their major idea is that social facilitation results from **evaluation apprehension**—the fear of being evaluated or judged by another person. Indeed, people may be aroused by performing a task in the presence of others because of their concern over what those others might think of them. For example, a concert pianist may suffer evaluation apprehension when he or she is concerned about the reactions of music critics seated in the audience. Likewise, industrial workers may suffer evaluation apprehension when they are worried about what their boss thinks of their work.

Does social facilitation occur simply because other people are present, or because those others can evaluate our performance? Although both of these factors may be involved, a third possibility is suggested by the **distraction-conflict model** proposed by R. S. Baron.[62] This model recognizes that the presence of others creates a conflict between paying attention to others and paying attention to the task at hand. The conflict created by these tendencies leads to increased arousal (which, in turn, leads to social facilitation, as shown in Figure 8.14). If you've ever tried doing a homework assignment while your friends or family watch TV nearby, you're probably already aware of the conflict that competing demands for your attention can create. Such conflicts tend to be arousing, and lead to social facilitation. Growing evidence suggests that the distraction-conflict model accounts for social facilitation within work groups.[63]

One context in which people often express their lack of desire to be evaluated is the formal performance evaluation (PE). PEs have been called a "no-win" situation in both the private and public sectors. During PEs, managers believe it is their duty to provide employees with feedback about their performance and to motivate them to improve their performance. Unfortunately, many managers fail to tell their subordinates all of the things that they have been doing right, instead focusing only on the negative. Employees, on the other hand, would like PEs to be an occasion in which they re-

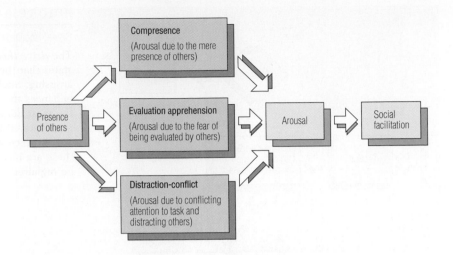

FIGURE 8-14   Why Are Others Arousing? Three Explanations for Social Facilitation

Theorists studying social facilitation have identified three different explanations for the arousing effects of the presence of others. The *compresence* explanation says that arousal is a natural reaction to the mere presence of others. The *evaluation apprehension* explanation says that arousal follows from the fear of being evaluated by others. Finally, the *distraction-conflict model* says that arousal is due to the conflict between paying attention to the task and to the distracting effects of others.

ceive promotions or pay raises. Often they merely receive criticism about their job performance. As a result, many bosses and those working under them dread these PEs. [Glen, R. M. (1990). Performance appraisal: An unnerving yet useful process. *Public Personnel Management, 19*, 1–9.]

However promising the distraction-conflict model may be in explaining social facilitation, it is certainly true that all the explanations noted provide some important insights into the social facilitation process. Although the processes underlying social facilitation are somewhat unclear, the effect itself may have a profound influence on organizational behavior.

Social Loafing: "Free Riding" When Working with Others

Thus far, our discussion has focused on tasks in which people work in the presence of others to produce an individual result. Although many such tasks are performed in organizations (e.g., typists working in a typing pool), not all tasks fall into this category. Other jobs in which group members work together to produce a group product are done in organizations. On many group tasks, the individual contributions of the group members are added together to form the group's product. Such tasks are considered **additive tasks,** and include activities such as several people combining their efforts to stuff envelopes for a political campaign, or several people working together to mow a lawn or shovel snow off a driveway.

The Phenomenon of Social Loafing   When people know that their work will be combined with that of others, an interesting thing often happens: they stop working as hard as they did as individuals, appearing to let others do their work for them, going on a "free ride." As suggested by the old saying "Many hands make light the work," a group of people would be expected to be more productive than any one individual. Five people raking leaves would get more work done than only one person, as you might expect, but generally *not* five times more! This effect was first noted over fifty years ago by a German scientist named Ringlemann, who compared the amount of force exerted by different size groups of people pulling on a rope. Specifically, he found that one person pulling on a rope alone exerted an average of 63 kilograms of force. However, in groups of three, the per-person force dropped to 53 kilograms, and in groups of eight it was reduced to only 31 kilograms per person—less than half the effort exerted by people working alone! In short, the greater the number of people working together on the task, the less effort each one put forth—an effect known as **social loafing.** This effect is portrayed graphically in Figure 8–15.

The phenomenon of social loafing has been studied extensively in recent years by Latané and his associates. In one of their earliest experiments, groups of students were asked to perform a very simple additive task—to clap and cheer as loudly as they could.[64] The participants were told that the experimenter was interested in seeing how much noise people could make in social settings. Comparisons were made between the amount of noise produced by one person relative to groups of two and six persons. Although more people made more noise, the amount of noise made per person dropped dramatically as the group size increased. Pairs of people made 82 percent as much noise as individuals working alone, and groups of six produced only 74 percent as much noise. Such findings clearly demonstrate the social loafing effect.

The phenomenon of social loafing may be explained by **social impact theory.**[65] According to this theory, the impact of any social force acting on a group is divided equally among its members. The larger the size of the group, the less the impact of the force on any one member. In the study noted above, the participants faced external pressure to make as much noise as possible. The more people present, the less pressure each person faced to perform well. That is, the responsibility for doing the job was diffused over more people when the size of the group increased. As a result, each group member felt less responsible for behaving appropriately, and social loafing occurred.

Although feeling less responsible for an outcome is clearly one factor responsible for the social loafing phenomenon, the effect may also result from other experiences likely to arise among people performing their jobs. For example, people may also engage in social loafing because they feel that the presence of others makes their contributions less needed—that is, more dispensable. Demonstrating this phenomenon, Weldon and Mustari had college students perform a judgment task (e.g., assessing the desirability of a job as the basis of describing it to potential applicants) and told them either that they were the only ones performing the task or that their

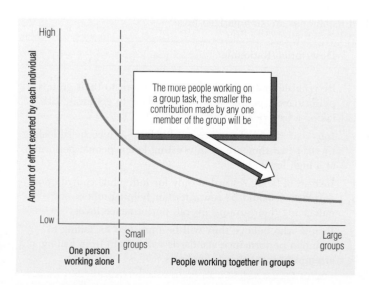

FIGURE 8–15

Social Loafing: Its General Form

According to the *social loafing* effect, when individuals work together on an additive task, the more people contributing to the group's task, the less effort each individual will exert.

judgments would be one of two or one of sixteen judgments used to make a final assessment.[66] The experimenters reasoned that people who believed their judgments would be one of many would take their jobs less seriously, spending less time on the task and making less complex judgments. In fact, this is exactly what they found. The larger the size of the group, the more dispensable people believed their judgments were and the less complex their judgments were. These data strongly support the idea that social loafing occurs because people believe that in larger groups their contributions are less necessary than when working alone.

Overcoming Social Loafing: Some Strategies   Obviously, the tendency for people to reduce their effort when working with others could be a serious problem in organizations. Fortunately, some research has shown that the tendency for social loafing to occur can be overcome. Some suggestions for attaining this goal are summarized in Table 8–6.

A possible antidote to social loafing is to *make each performer identifiable*. Social loafing may occur when people feel they can get away with "taking it easy"—namely, under conditions in which each individual's contributions cannot be determined. A variety of studies on the practice of "public posting" support this idea.[67] This research has found that when each individual's contribution to a task is displayed where it can be seen by others (e.g., weekly sales figures posted on a chart), people are less likely to slack off than when only overall group (or companywide) performance is made available. In other words, the more one's individual contribution to a group effort is highlighted, the more pressure each person feels to make a group contribution. Thus, social loafing can be overcome if one's contributions to an additive task are identified. Potential social loafers are not likely to loaf if they believe they may get caught.

Another way to overcome social loafing is to *make work tasks more involving*. Recent research has revealed that people are unlikely to go along for a free ride when the task they are performing is believed to be highly involving and important.[68] To help in this regard, it has been suggested that managers should *reward individuals for contributing to their group's performance*.[69] Instead of the usual practice of

Social loafing may also be eliminated by group pressure on an individual to increase performance. On most group tasks, the majority of the members can be expected to perform up to standards. However, some individuals might not perform as well as they could, but instead ride on the benefits of the other hard-working members of the group; such people are often called "shirkers," "loafers," or "free-riders." Thus, managers are usually asked to watch groups and make sure that all members perform adequately. However, rather than relying on managers to monitor performance, the groups can be given the freedom and responsibility to perform this function themselves. Researchers have found that group performance actually improves when groups are allowed to monitor their own performance levels and even get rid of group members who are loafing on the job, compared to groups in which managers monitor performance levels. [Dumaine, B. (1990, May 7). Who needs a boss? *Fortune*, pp. 52–60.]

TABLE 8–6   Overcoming Social Loafing: Some Recommendations

Because of the potentially detrimental effects of social loafing on organizational productivity, several tactics for minimizing or eliminating its impact have been noted. Some of the best established techniques are summarized here.

Recommendation	Description/Rationale
Make workers identifiable	By pointing out individuals' contributions to their groups' performance, people would be unlikely to get away with taking a free ride
Make work more involving	Jobs that are involving are not likely to induce social loafing; the fact that they are so interesting keeps people performing at a high level
Reward individuals for their contributions to their group	Instead of being rewarded only for individual contributions, employees should be rewarded for helping others, for enhancing their groups' overall performance level
Threaten punishment	People who believe they will be punished for failing to maintain performance standards will refrain from loafing and attempt to meet those standards

rewarding employees for their individual performance, rewarding them for their contributions to a group effort (e.g., giving all salespeople in a territory a bonus if they jointly exceed their sales goal) may help them focus more on collective concerns and less on individualistic concerns. In doing so, people would be expected to become more sensitive to the performance of their work groups. This is important, of course, in that the success of an organization is more likely to be influenced by the collective efforts of groups than by the individual contributions of any one member.

A third mechanism for overcoming social loafing is to *use punishment threats*. To the extent that performance decrements may be controlled by threatening to punish the individuals slacking off, it may be possible to reduce social loafing. This effect was demonstrated in a recent experiment by Miles and Greenberg.[70] The participants in this study were members of high school swim teams who swam either alone or in relay races during practice sessions. In some conditions, the coach threatened the team by telling them that everyone would have to swim "penalty laps" if anyone on the team failed to meet a specified difficult time for swimming 100 yards freestyle. In a control group, no punishment threats were issued. How did the punishment threats influence task performance? As shown in Figure 8–16, people swam faster alone than as part of relay teams when no punishment was threatened, thereby confirming the social loafing effect. However, when punishment threats were made, group performance increased, thereby eliminating the social loafing effect. Note that

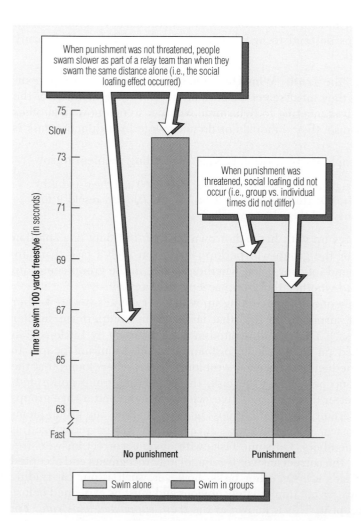

When punishment was not threatened, people swam slower as part of a relay team than when they swam the same distance alone (i.e., the social loafing effect occurred)

When punishment was threatened, social loafing did not occur (i.e., group vs. individual times did not differ)

Time to swim 100 yards freestyle (in seconds)

No punishment   Punishment

Swim alone   Swim in groups

FIGURE 8–16

Using Punishment to Eliminate Social Loafing: An Experimental Demonstration Using Swimmers

High school swim team members swam 100 yards freestyle faster when they swam alone than when they swam the same distance as part of a four-person relay team. However, when they were punished with penalty laps for failing to meet a prescribed time, the *social loafing* effect disappeared. (*Source:* Based on data from Miles & Greenberg, in press; see Note 70.)

the punishment threats were effective in this study because the swimmers were used to being punished by their coaches by having to swim laps. The same results might not hold in cases in which the use of punishment is atypical and not considered appropriate. Although punishment threats reduced social loafing in this context, its use in other settings may be less effective.

Performance on Other Types of Group Tasks

The phenomenon of social loafing has been demonstrated to occur on additive tasks—as described earlier, those in which the individual contributions of group members are added together. However, groups may perform other types of tasks, each of which has its own unique characteristics.

Compensatory Tasks: The Benefits of Compromise   On some tasks, the inputs of various group members are averaged together to create a single group outcome. These are known as **compensatory tasks.** The resulting compromise solution is referred to as *compensatory* because one person's judgments may compensate for another's. Imagine that a group of people is attempting to judge the temperature of the room the group is in. As you might expect, the judgments made by some group members that are incorrect in one direction (e.g., too high) may be offset by the judgments of others that are incorrect in the other direction (e.g., too low). As a result, more accurate decisions would be made by averaging the decisions of everyone in the group than by most individual members. Several studies have found that on compensatory tasks groups *do* tend to make more accurate judgments than many individual group members.[71]

Disjunctive Tasks: When "the Truth" Wins Out   On **disjunctive tasks,** group members cannot compromise; they must select a solution offered by one member of the group. A group of executives meeting to determine whether to merge with another company cannot compromise; they either do or do not merge. A disjunctive task is of the "either-or" variety.

Suppose a group of people is given the following car-trading problem to solve:

> A used car salesman bought a car from one customer for $3,000 and then sold it to another customer for $4,000. He then bought it back for $5,000 and resold it for $6,000. How much money did the salesman make?

Each group member comes up with his or her own answer, but only one solution can be accepted. Whether the group will perform better on such a task than any single individual will depend, of course, on whether anyone in the group comes up with the right answer, *and* whether the group accepts that answer.

Because the odds of any one person coming up with the right answer are higher in larger groups it is not surprising to find that larger groups outperform smaller groups on disjunctive tasks.[72] This was illustrated in a recent study by Littlepage in which participants worked on solving logic problems, a task requiring people to compile clues and make deductions to solve a problem.[73] Researchers found that the larger the size of the group performing the task, the better the group performed. Thus, groups of ten did better than groups of five, who in turn did better than groups of two. However, an important qualification must be kept in mind: one group member's having the right answer does not always mean that it will be recognized as correct by other group members. On some tasks with obvious correct answers (referred to as *Eureka* tasks), the correct answer is immediately recognized and accepted by the group (Eureka, that's it!). On other tasks, however, such as our car-trading problem, the correct answer is not immediately obvious and must be explained before the group is likely to accept it. This is known as the *truth supported wins rule.* For the correct answer to be taken as the group's answer, that answer not only must be obtained, but also must be supported by the group. On a Eureka task, the truth usually wins out, giving the advantage to the group over most individuals. However, on the other, less obvious tasks, any potential group advantage is less certain.

(By the way, the answer to our car-trading problem: the salesman made $2,000.)

Conjunctive Tasks: Slowed Down by the "Weakest Link" Tasks in which a group's performance is limited by the performance of the worst-performing member are referred to as **conjunctive tasks.** For example, a group of mountain climbers can move no faster than the speed of the slowest-moving member of the expedition. Similarly, the effectiveness of a pit crew of an auto racing team is limited by the time it takes to perform the most time-consuming task (e.g., changing the tires or filling the gas tank).

That most individuals will do better than a group on a conjunctive task should be readily apparent. Imagine a group of people filling sandbags and passing them to each other in a line, attempting to secure a crumbling retaining wall. If any one person consistently drops the bags or otherwise falters, the group will be probably far *less* effective with than without this person. In such a situation, the group is forced to adjust its performance downward to the level of the poorest performer.

In some cases, such as an expedition of mountain climbers whose safety is ensured by slowing the pace to accommodate the slowest climber, the lower performance of conjunctive groups may not be problematic. However, most work organizations can hardly afford to be slowed down by an ineffective team member. If any one individual proves so inept that his or her group suffers, that person may be fired, or face so much social pressure from group members that he or she may resign. As an analogy, the final assembly of an automobile can be no faster than the speed at which the various subassemblies are manufactured. Some auto manufacturing plants are closed when they are plagued by technical problems or labor stoppages. Similarly, the construction of an entire building often must come to a standstill when just one of the construction unions goes on strike.

Some Final Considerations In Figure 8–17, we have graphed the likely effects of task type on group performance. On some tasks (e.g., additive tasks), groups may

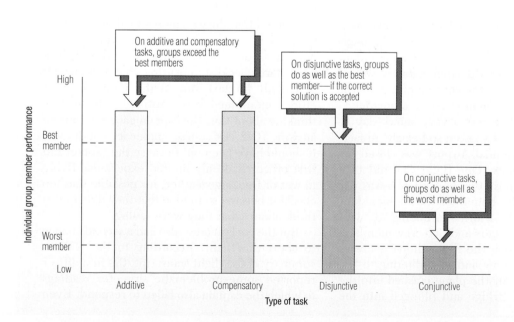

FIGURE 8–17

Group versus Individual Productivity: The Influence of Task Type

As summarized here, how effectively groups perform relative to individuals depends on the type of task performed. (*Source:* Based on suggestions by Steiner, 1976; see Note 71.)

Test Bank question 8.45 relates to material on this page.

be expected to outperform individual group members, although on others (e.g., conjunctive tasks) the average individual would outperform the group. Accordingly, answers to questions about the relative productivity of individuals and groups would depend to a great extent on the nature of the tasks the group is performing.

Of course, the picture is far more complex than suggested by this graph. For example, although the social loafing effect makes individuals inefficient on additive tasks, groups performing additive tasks tend to do better than individuals at an overall level because several people are contributing to the overall outcome. Also, whether the group's decision on a disjunctive task is as good as the best individual judgment depends on the group's willingness to accept that answer. Obviously, the topic of group performance is very complex, and we have only begun to scratch its surface in this chapter. You will find issues of group productivity appearing elsewhere in this book, particularly in our discussions of communication (chapter 13), power (chapter 11), and decision making (chapter 14).

The aspects of task performance that we have been examining are those that focus on the unique characteristics of groups. This is not to say, however, that group performance is not also subject to the same determinants as individual performance.

 OB IN PRACTICE

Habitual Routines as an Impediment to Group Performance: The Catastrophic Example of Air Florida Flight 90

Have you ever found yourself doing something wrong and explaining it by saying, "It's just a habit"? For example, if you're used to driving a car with a manual transmission, you may at first find your left foot reaching for the clutch pedal when driving a rented car with an automatic transmission. You're used to a certain behavioral routine when driving, a complex array of behaviors known as a habit that is the source of the mistake. Although this common example involves an individual habit, work groups may develop habits as well.[74] As highlighted below, the consequences of such routinized group behaviors can be dramatic.

January 13, 1982, was a very snowy day in Washington, D.C. It snowed so heavily, in fact, that the city's National Airport was closed for intermittent periods. One flight that did take off—although almost two hours late—was Air Florida's Flight 90, bound for the sunnier skies of Fort Lauderdale, Florida, a Boeing 737 with seventy-four passengers and five crew members on board. However, the flight didn't get very far. Heavy with snow and ice adhering to the aircraft, at 4:01 P.M. the plane crashed into the busy 14th Street Bridge and plunged into the icy Potomac River. Later that year, the National Transportation and Safety Board (NTSB) found that the accident was due to the flight crew's failure to use anti-icing devices, despite indications that such measures were necessary, and the captain's failure to cancel the takeoff despite instrument readings that weren't right.[75]

Further analyzing what was said in the cockpit at the time of the accident, Gersick and Hackman noted that the captain responded according to routine even though conditions were far from normal.[76] For example, when going through the after-start checklist, ensuring that the aircraft was ready for taxi, one of the items the first officer mentioned was "Anti-ice?" Instead of thinking about this, the captain gave the routine answer, "Off." Of course, under icy conditions, it should have been *on*! Because the captain and first officer had only limited experience flying in wet or freezing weather, it's possible that the checklist became so routine that they didn't even think about what they were saying.

But the cockpit crew also had a second chance to abort the flight. According to the NTSB's summary of the flight transcript, the first officer reported some problematic altimeter readings to which the captain also failed to respond. Even

For example, just as individuals might make mistakes because they "get into ruts," so too may group members develop highly routinized behaviors. As illustrated in the **OB in Practice** section that begins on the preceding page, the effects of some types of routinized group behaviors may be quite severe.

SUMMARY AND REVIEW

The Nature of Groups

A **group** is defined as a collection of two or more interacting individuals with a stable pattern of relationships between them who share common goals and who perceive themselves as being a group. Within organizations, there are two major classes of groups—*formal groups* and *informal groups*. Groups often develop by going through five principal stages—*forming, storming, norming, performing,* and *adjourning.*

Group Structure

The structure of work groups (i.e., the pattern of interrelationships between the individuals constituting a group; the guidelines of group behavior that

when the first officer said, "Look at that thing, that doesn't seem right," the captain did nothing to break the routine and continued with the takeoff. The entire takeoff procedure may have become so routine for the cockpit crew that nobody responded to the indications that something out of the ordinary needed to be done (namely, aborting the takeoff).

Although this incident is an extreme example of what can happen when flight operations become too routinized, it is—unfortunately—not unusual. Indeed, an investigation by the National Aeronautics and Space Administration (NASA) identified over sixty accidents occurring between 1968 and 1976 in which a significant cause was poor coordination among crew members.[77] Part of the problem is that informal norms develop within crews that discourage pilots from following all the formal policies of their airlines. For example, an airline captain under pressure to meet on-time performance standards may encourage lower-ranking crew members to take shortcuts, and these pressures may be more influential than any "by the book" policies established by the airlines.[78] Another aspect of the problem is that the development of routines may interfere with effective cockpit performance even when crew members intend to follow formally prescribed procedures. Simply put, strongly developed group routines may divert group members' attention away from important aspects of the task at hand. Clearly, that's part of what went on in the Air Florida case.

Given this, we might ask: what can be done to help groups break out of habitual routines? Gersick and Hackman offer several recommendations. First, they note that people must recognize the need to change. Certainly, a critical incident such as the Air Florida crash might be an effective way to shock crews into realizing the consequences of not changing their ways. Redesigning the nature of the crew's task, such as changing what's on the checklist and when the checklist is reviewed, might also be helpful. Such changes may force people to pay greater attention to what they're doing and break routines. A similar source of change may come from altering work group membership. To the extent that different captains and first officers work together, idiosyncratic routines may be less likely to develop. As you can see, there are several possible ways to break routines and thereby minimize the problems caused by the lack of attention to critical detail.

It is difficult to tell whether such practices ultimately will be effective. After all, routines help people perform complex tasks with ease and predictability. To eliminate them completely could cause even more problems. Obviously, the trick is to get groups to avoid the routines that are most susceptible to problems without losing the high task efficiency they offer. As researchers continue to delve into this topic, we are optimistic that a practical way to avoid the problems of routines, while realizing their benefits, will emerge.

make group functioning orderly and predictable) is determined by four key factors. **Roles** represent the typical pattern of behavior in a specific social context. Roles are often differentiated into *task-oriented* roles (concerned about getting the job done), *socioemotional* roles (concerned about the social climate of the group), and *self-oriented* roles (concerned about one's own well-being). Roles often place conflicting demands on people, such as between the competing demands placed on someone playing different roles (i.e., **interrole conflict**) or the contradictory demands placed on someone within a certain role (i.e., **intrarole conflict**).

Norms, a set of generally agreed on informal rules, have profound effects on dictating the variety and quantity of organizational behaviors performed. **Status,** a person's prestige ranking within a group, represents another structural element of groups. It may be either formal or informal, and in either case dictates the nature of communication and social influence within groups.

A final element of group structure is **cohesiveness,** the pressures faced by group members to remain in their groups. Group cohesiveness is created by several factors, including severe group initiations and the presence of external threats. Although highly cohesive groups may perform better than noncohesive groups, this is not always the case. Cohesiveness aids performance if the group's goals are consistent with management's interests.

Task Performance

Individual productivity is influenced by the presence of other group members. Sometimes, a person's performance improves in the presence of others (when the job they do is well learned), and sometimes performance declines in the presence of others (when the job is novel). This phenomenon is known as **social facilitation.** These effects have been attributed to the *mere presence* of others, the **evaluation apprehension** caused by others, and the conflicting tendencies to pay attention to others versus the task at hand (i.e., the **distraction-conflict model**).

Group productivity is affected by the type of task performed. On **additive tasks,** where each member's individual contributions are combined, **social loafing** occurs. According to this phenomenon, the more people who work on a task, the less each group member contributes to it. On **compensatory tasks,** the judgments made by the group members are averaged together, and groups tend to do better than the average individual group member. On **disjunctive tasks,** one solution to a problem must be accepted. So long as one group member comes up with the answer and convinces others of its correctness, the group will do as well as the best individual. On **conjunctive tasks,** the group can do no better than the poorest group member. As a result, groups tend to perform worse than the average individual group member.

KEY TERMS

additive tasks: Types of group tasks in which the coordinated efforts of several people are added together to form the group's product.

cohesiveness: The pressures on group members to remain a part of the group.

compensatory tasks: Particular group tasks in which the average of all members' contributions is taken as the group's product.

conjunctive tasks: Types of group tasks in which the performance of the poorest member is taken as the group's product.

disjunctive tasks: Types of group tasks in which only one member's judgment is taken as the group's product.

distraction-conflict model: A conceptualization explaining social facilitation in terms of the tendency for others' presence to cause a conflict between directing attention to others versus directing attention to the task at hand.

drive theory of social facilitation: The theory according to which the presence of others increases arousal, which increases people's tendencies to perform the dominant response. If that response is well learned, performance

will improve, but if it is novel, performance will be impaired.

evaluation apprehension: The fear of being evaluated or judged by another person, which accounts for the arousing effect of others' presence.

formal groups: Groups that are created by the organization, intentionally designed to direct its members toward some organizational goal.

group: A collection of two or more interacting individuals who maintain stable patterns of relationships, share common goals, and perceive themselves as being a group.

group dynamics: The social science field focusing on the nature of groups—the factors governing their formation and development, the elements of their structure, and their interrelationships with individuals, other groups, and organizations.

group structure: The pattern of interrelationships between the individuals constituting a group; the guidelines of group behavior that make group functioning orderly and predictable.

informal groups: Groups that develop naturally among people, without any direction from the organization within which they operate.

interrole conflict: The incompatible demands made on someone playing two or more different roles.

intrarole conflict: The contradictory demands made on one person, by virtue of the different sets of expectations imposed on that person by others.

norms: Generally agreed on informal rules that guide group members' behavior.

role: The typical behaviors that characterize a person in a specific social context.

role conflict: A condition that results when the appropriate behaviors for enacting one role are inconsistent with the appropriate behaviors for enacting another role (see *interrole conflict*) or other requirements of the same role (see *intrarole conflict*).

role differentiation: The tendency for various specialized roles to emerge as groups develop.

social facilitation: The tendency for the presence of others sometimes to enhance an individual's performance and at other times to impair it.

social impact theory: The theory that explains *social loafing* in terms of the diffused responsibility for doing what is expected of each member of a group. The larger the size of a group, the less each member is influenced by the social forces acting on the group.

social loafing: The tendency for group members to exert less individual effort on an additive task as the size of the group increases.

status: The relative prestige, social position, or rank given to groups or individuals by others.

QUESTIONS FOR DISCUSSION

1. Define what a *group* is. Would you say that a collection of people waiting in line at a movie theater constitutes a group? Why or why not?

2. Within organizations, some groups are *formal* and others are *informal*. Distinguish between these two types of group and give an example of each within any organization with which you are familiar.

3. Identify the stages of *group development* noted in the text, and apply them to any group to which you belong. Do all the stages apply?

4. Distinguish among *task-oriented*, *relations-oriented*, and *self-oriented* roles within groups. Give an account of someone playing each of these roles within any groups with which you are familiar.

5. Four factors are responsible for *norm development*. Identify these and give an example of each one.

6. How do differences in formal or informal *status* influence the way people behave in organizations?

7. Argue for or against the following statement: *Group cohesiveness* aids the attainment of organizational goals.

8. Imagine that you are about to go on stage to give a solo piano recital. How would the phenomenon of *social facilitation* explain your likely performance?

9. Describe some conditions existing within organizations that may lead to the *social loafing* effect, and some steps that can be taken to overcome it.

10. Compare and contrast how well groups may be expected to perform tasks that are *additive*, *compensatory*, *disjunctive*, and *conjunctive*. Give an example of each kind of group task.

NOTES

1. Cartwright, D., & Zander, A. (1968). Origins of group dynamics. In D. Cartwright & A. Zander (Eds.), *Group dynamics: Research and theory* (pp. 3–21). New York: Harper & Row.

2. Bettenhausen, K. L. (1991). Five years of group research: What we have learned and what needs to be addressed. *Journal of Management, 17,* 345–381.

3. Hare, A. P., Borgatta, E. F., & Bales, R. F. (1955). *Small groups: Studies in social interaction* (p. vi). New York: Knopf.

4. Forsyth, D. L. (1983). *An introduction to group dynamics.* Monterey, CA: Brooks/Cole.

5. Pearce, J. A., II, & Ravlin, E. C. (1987). The design and activation of self-regulating work groups. *Human Relations, 40,* 751–782.

6. Van Zelst, R. H. (1952). Sociometrically selected work teams increase production. *Personnel Psychology, 5,* 175–185.

7. See Note 6, p. 183.

8. Festinger, L., Schachter, S., & Back, K. (1950). *Social pressures in informal groups: A study of human factors in housing.* New York: Harper.

9. Long, S. (1984). Early integration in groups: "A group to join and a group to create." *Human Relations, 37,* 311–332.

10. Tuckman, B. W., & Jensen, M. A. (1977). Stages of small group development revisited. *Group and Organization Studies, 2,* 419–427.

11. Vancouver, J. B., & Ilgen, D. R. (1989). Effects of interpersonal orientation and the sex-type of the task on

choosing to work alone or in groups. *Journal of Applied Psychology, 74,* 927–934.

12. Gersick, C. J. G. (1988). Time and transition in work teams: Toward a new model of group development. *Academy of Management Journal, 31,* 9–41.

13. Hackman, J. R. (1987). The design of work teams. In J. W. Lorsch (Ed.), *Handbook of organizational behavior* (pp. 315–342). Englewood Cliffs, NJ: Prentice-Hall.

14. See Note 13, p. 338.

15. See Note 4.

16. Biddle, B. J. (1979). *Role theory: Expectations, identities, and behavior.* New York: Academic Press.

17. Jackson, S. E., & Schuler, R. S. (1985). A meta-analysis and conceptual critique of research on role ambiguity and role conflict in work settings. *Organizational Behavior and Human Decision Processes, 36,* 16–78.

18. Benne, K. D., & Sheats, P. (1948). Functional roles of group members. *Journal of Social Issues, 4,* 41–49.

19. Bales, R. F. (1980). *SYMLOG case study kit.* New York: Free Press.

20. Rafaeli, A. (1989). When cashiers meet customers: An analysis of the role of supermarket cashiers. *Academy of Management Journal, 32,* 245–273.

21. Katz, D., & Kahn, R. L. (1978). *The social psychology of organizations* (2nd ed.). New York: Wiley.

22. Leinster, C. (1988, April 25). The young exec as superdad. *Fortune,* pp. 233–234, 238, 242.

23. Pearce, J. L. (1981). Bringing some clarity to role ambiguity research. *Academy of Management Review, 6,* 665–674.

24. Van Sell, M., Brief, A. P., & Schuler, R. S. (1981). Role conflict and role ambiguity: Integration of the literature and directions for future research. *Human Relations, 34,* 43–71.

25. Berger-Gross, V., & Kraut, A. I. (1984). "Great expectations": A no-conflict explanation of role conflict. *Journal of Applied Psychology, 69,* 261–271.

26. Cooke, R. A., & Rousseau, D. M. (1984). Stress and strain from family roles and work-role expectations. *Journal of Applied Psychology, 69,* 252–260.

27. Hackman, J. R. (1991). Group influences on individuals in organizations. In M. D. Dunnette (Ed.), *Handbook of industrial/organizational psychology* (2nd ed.). Palo Alto, CA: Consulting Psychologists Press.

28. Nadler, D., Hackman, J. R., & Lawler, E. E., III. (1979). *Managing organizational behavior.* Boston: Little, Brown.

29. Mitchell, T. R., Rothman, M., & Liden, R. C. (1985). Effects of normative information on task performance. *Journal of Applied Psychology, 70,* 48–55.

30. Sutton, R. I. (1991). Maintaining norms about expressed emotions: The case of bill collectors. *Administrative Science Quarterly, 36,* 245–268.

31. Bettenhausen, K., & Murnighan, J. K. (1985). The emergence of norms in competitive decision-making groups. *Administrative Science Quarterly, 30,* 350–372.

32. Feldman, D. C. (1984). The development and enforcement of group norms. *Academy of Management Review, 9,* 47–53.

33. Bettenhausen, K. L., & Murnighan, J. K. (1991). The development of an intragroup norm and the effects of interpersonal and structural challenges. *Administrative Science Quarterly, 36,* 20–35.

34. Wanous, J. P., Reichers, A. E., & Malik, S. D. (1984). Organizational socialization and group development: Toward an integrative perspective. *Academy of Management Review, 9,* 670–683.

35. Wilson, S. (1978). *Informal groups: An introduction.* Englewood Cliffs, NJ: Prentice-Hall.

36. Henderson, M., & Argyle, M. (1986). The informal rules of working relationships. *Journal of Occupational Behavior, 7,* 259–275.

37. Greenberg, J. (1988). Equity and workplace status: A field experiment. *Journal of Applied Psychology, 73,* 606–613.

38. Stryker, S., & Macke, A. S. (1978). Status inconsistency and role conflict. In R. H. Turner, J. Coleman, & R. C. Fox (Eds.), *Annual review of sociology* (Vol. 4, pp. 57–90). Palo Alto, CA: Annual Reviews.

39. Jackson, L. A., & Grabski, S. V. (1988). Perceptions of fair pay and the gender wage gap. *Journal of Applied Social Psychology, 18,* 606–625.

40. Torrance, E. P. (1954). Some consequences of power differences on decision making in permanent and temporary three-man groups. *Research Studies, Washington State College, 22,* 130–140.

41. Greenberg, J. (1976). The role of seating position in group interaction: A review, with applications for group trainers. *Group and Organization Studies, 1,* 310–327.

42. McLaughlin, M. L., Cody, M. J., & Rosenstein, N. E. (1983). Account sequences in conversations between strangers. *Communication Monographs, 50,* 102–125.

43. Luft, J. (1984). *Group processes* (3rd ed.). Palo Alto, CA: Mayfield Publishing.

44. Whyte, W. F. (1948). *Human relations in the restaurant industry.* New York: McGraw-Hill.

45. Hare, A. P. (1976). *Handbook of small group research* (2nd ed.). New York: Free Press.

46. Aronson, E., & Mills, J. (1959). The effects of severity of initiation on liking for a group. *Journal of Abnormal and Social Psychology, 59,* 177–181.

47. Sherif, M., Harvey, O. J., White, B. J., Hood, W. R., & Sherif, C. W. (1961). *Intergroup cooperation and competition: The Robber's Cave experiment.* Norman, OK: University Book Exchange.

48. See Note 4.

49. Cartwright, D. (1968). The nature of group cohesiveness. In D. Cartwright & A. Zander (Eds.), *Group dynamics: Research and theory* (3rd ed.)(pp. 91–109). New York: Harper & Row.

50. George, J. M., & Bettenhausen, K. (1990). Understanding prosocial behavior, sales performance, and turn-

over: A group-level analysis in a service context. *Journal of Applied Psychology, 75,* 698–709.

51. Shaw, M. E. (1981). *Group dynamics: The dynamics of small group behavior* (3rd ed.). New York: McGraw-Hill.

52. Janis, I. L. (1982). *Groupthink: Psychological studies of policy decisions and fiascos* (2nd ed.). Boston: Houghton Mifflin.

53. Douglas, T. (1983). *Groups: Understanding people gathered together.* New York: Tavistock.

54. Seashore, S. E. (1954). *Group cohesiveness in the industrial work group.* Ann Arbor, MI: Institute for Social Research.

55. Schreischeim, J. F. (1980). The social context of leader-subordinate relations: An investigation of the effects of group cohesiveness. *Journal of Applied Psychology, 65,* 183–194.

56. Tziner, A., & Vardi, Y. (1982). Effects of command style and group cohesiveness on the performance effectiveness of self-selected tank crews. *Journal of Applied Psychology, 67,* 769–775.

57. Triplett, N. (1898). The dynamogenic factor in pacemaking and competition. *American Journal of Psychology, 9,* 507–533.

58. Zajonc, R. B. (1965). Social facilitation. *Science, 149,* 269–274.

59. Bond, C. F., Jr., & Titus, L. J. (1983). Social facilitation: A meta-analysis of 241 studies. *Psychological Bulletin, 94,* 265–292.

60. Zajonc, R. B. (1980). Compresence. In P. B. Paulus (Ed.), *Psychology of group influence* (pp. 35–60). Hillsdale, NJ: Erlbaum.

61. Cottrell, N. B. (1972). Social facilitation. In C. G. McClintock (Ed.), *Experimental social psychology* (pp. 214–241). New York: Holt, Rinehart & Winston.

62. Baron, R. S. (1986). Distraction-conflict theory: Progress and problems. In L. Berkowitz (Ed.), *Advances in experimental social psychology* (Vol. 19, pp. 1–40). New York: Academic Press.

63. Ferris, G., & Rowland, K. (1983). Social facilitation effects on behavioral and perceptual task performance measures. *Group and Organization Studies, 8,* 421–438.

64. Latané, B., Williams, K., & Harkins, S. (1979). Many hands make light the work: The causes and consequences of social loafing. *Journal of Personality and Social Psychology, 37,* 822–832.

65. Latané, B., & Nida, S. (1980). Social impact theory and group influence: A social engineering perspective. In P. B. Paulus (Ed.), *Psychology of group influence* (pp. 3–34). Hillsdale, NJ: Erlbaum.

66. Weldon, E., & Mustari, E. L. (1988). Felt dispensability in groups of coactors: The effects of shared responsibility and explicit anonymity on cognitive effort. *Organizational Behavior and Human Decision Processes, 41,* 330–351.

67. Nordstrom, R., Lorenzi, P., & Hall, R. V. (1990). A review of public posting of performance feedback in work settings. *Journal of Organizational Behavior Management, 11,* 101–123.

68. Brickner, M. A., Harkins, S. G., & Ostrom, T. M. (1986). Effects of personal involvement: Thought-provoking implications for social loafing. *Journal of Personality and Social Psychology, 51,* 763–769.

69. Albanese, R., & Van Fleet, D. D. (1985). Rational behavior in groups: The free-riding tendency. *Academy of Management Review, 10,* 244–255.

70. Miles, J. A., & Greenberg, J. (in press). Using punishment threats to attenuate social loafing effects among swimmers. *Organizational Behavior and Human Decision Processes.*

71. Steiner, I. D. (1976). Task-performing groups. In J. W. Thibaut, J. T. Spence, & R. C. Carson (Eds.), *Contemporary topics in social psychology* (pp. 393–422). Morristown, NJ: General Learning Press.

72. Steiner, I. D. (1972). *Group processes and productivity.* New York: Academic Press.

73. Littlepage, G. E. (1991). Effects of group size and task characteristics on group performance: A test of Steiner's model. *Personality and Social Psychology Bulletin, 17,* 449–456.

74. Gersick, C. J. G., & Hackman, J. R. (1990). Habitual routines in task-performing groups. *Organizational Behavior and Human Decision Processes, 47,* 65–97.

75. National Transportation and Safety Board. (1982). *Aircraft accident report* (NTSB Report No. AAR-82-8). Washington, DC: NTSB Bureau of Accident Investigation.

76. See Note 74.

77. Cooper, G. E., White, M. D., & Lauber, J. K. (Eds.). (1980). *Resource management on the flight deck: Proceedings of a NASA/industry workshop* (NASA Conference Publication No. 2120). Moffett Field, CA: NASA-Ames Research Center.

78. Gregorich, S. E., Helmreich, R. L., & Wilhelm, J. A. (1990). The structure of cockpit management attitudes. *Journal of Applied Psychology, 75,* 682–690.

Making Teams Work at Monsanto

"I'd like to be able to say we had a grand plan, but the fact is we backed into it."[1] So says personnel manager Paul Ward as he describes how Monsanto Corporation's Pensacola, Florida, plant introduced self-managed teams into its workplace.[2]

Monsanto invested heavily in its Pensacola chemical and nylon manufacturing plant, originally built in 1953, turning it into the corporation's largest facility. By 1985, $1 billion had been sunk into the plant. The result of this enormous investment was a marvelous physical facility, but disappointing profits.

Monsanto management responded by trimming its product line and eliminating 1,133 of the plant's 4,290 jobs. One strategy Monsanto used was to offer attractive early retirement programs. More than half of the plant's 163 foremen retired early. This left plant management with a unique opportunity: hire new foremen to resume its traditional method of operations, or try something entirely different. They chose to do something radically different.

First-line managers (or foremen) often resist the introduction of self-managed teams out of fear that their jobs will be eliminated. Their fears are understandable because self-managed teams assume responsibility and authority for making decisions once relegated to management (e.g., foremen). With over half of its foremen gone, corporate and plant management recognized that this was a perfect time to try self-managed teams. Impressed by the success of self-managed teams at its smaller plants, Monsanto executives introduced self-managed teams at its Pensacola facility in 1986.

Each work team is composed of ten to twelve employees. Team members have complete responsibility for managing themselves. They decide who joins their team. Every team member interviews and rank-orders prospective teammates. And Monsanto top management does not interfere.

Team members are also responsible for making all job assignments. As a group, they decide what must be done and when it needs to be done; and they then schedule work accordingly. If the team decides overtime is necessary, they work it. They purchase everything they need to operate and make all production decisions.

If problems arise, team members are responsible for solving them. If safety or product quality is threatened, team members have the authority to shut down production and correct the problem. Teams have full authority to deal directly with suppliers to buy whatever is needed to solve problems.

Team success is measured by each team's productivity, an incentive to keep costs down. Teams are evaluated on their product quality and safety, too. If the team performs poorly, everyone on the team is affected. Monsanto wants employees to judge their success or failure in terms of how well their team as a whole performs.

Each team has a team leader chosen by the team members. The team leader is responsible for monitoring the group processes and bringing up any problems that arise (e.g., decreases in members' cooperation and productivity problems). Team leaders are paid a small premium to perform their job. Members may take turns being team leader. The job may go to the most experienced member of the team. Regardless of the approach used, the team members have the responsibility and authority to choose their own team leader.

Monsanto's shift to self-managed teams dramatically changed the nature of supervisory work at the Pensacola plant. Team members make decisions that used to be the responsibility of the foremen, who are now trainers. They teach team members how to make decisions. They typically assist teams during the day shift only; the teams are entirely on their own during the second and third shifts. The role of the trainer is limited to offering advice instead of actually making operational decisions.

Team building can be very stressful for all involved. At the heart of the self-management concept is self-policing. Team members exert pressure on each other to conform to group norms, values, and beliefs. Not everyone wants the added responsibility that self-managed teams require. Some workers shirk responsibility in an attempt to undermine implementation of teams. According to a consultant Monsanto hired to review the plant's progress, some of the plant's teams were failing to adequately appraise the performance of their members. Team members were failing to continuously evaluate their processes to improve their performance. For some employees, assuming decision-making responsibility, managing coworkers, and being managed by coworkers involves a lot of stress—stress that some employees attempt to avoid.[3]

A lot of training is required to teach employees how to build and operate within teams. Such efforts are not only expensive, but also very time-consuming. Plant manager Lee Hebert says employees spend 5 to 10 percent of their work time learning the new skills necessary to work as a team. (This percentage is actually lower than the 15 to 20 percent that team-building experts suggest businesses plan on during the first three years of team building.[4]) Monsanto's Pensacola plant is five years into the process.

Plant employees also find training to be distracting, since the time spent in training is time taken away from normal operational activities. It is frustrating to get up and running, only to have everything interrupted by having to participate in training. Apparently, team building requires substantial short-term costs to achieve long-term productivity benefits.

As anticipated, shifting from traditional management to self-managed teams was, and continues to be, an anxiety-producing experience for the plant's foremen. The foremen saw their traditional responsibilities shift and feared for their jobs.

Self-managed work teams did endanger the traditional supervisory jobs. Although the traditional job of foreman was transformed to the job of trainer, the plant does not require as many trainers as it did foremen. And other managers, above the level of foreman, have found reason to fear for their jobs, too. The Pensacola plant has reduced its layers of management from seven (before self-managed teams) to four in 1991. Lee Hebert plans to eliminate one more layer of management in the near future.

Some managers have responded to their fears by deliberately attempting to undermine the effectiveness of team-building efforts. For example, some managers refuse to provide team members with sufficient authority to effectively self-manage, thus slowing progress in successfully implementing teams throughout the plant. Important information and guidance can also be withheld by managers.

Monsanto learned that its human resource management practices had to be radically changed. Its traditional human resource management practices had been focused primarily on promoting *individual* achievement. One type of human resource management change that Monsanto believes is necessary to foster teamwork is to put plant workers on salary rather than pay them on an hourly basis. Management wants to directly link team performance with compensation. Once in place, employee compensation will be a combination of straight salary and profit-sharing bonus, with the bonus based entirely on the performance of the team as a whole (as defined by its contribution to the profitability of the plant). Hebert hopes that employees will feel that their efforts to improve productivity are fairly rewarded—a major concern among many employees.

Another chronic problem is confusion about team goals. Because Monsanto's involvement with self-managed teams grew out of happenstance rather than a deliberate strategic plan, the teams didn't have a clear understanding of their goals. Training and development in group processes and team building are helping, but even after five years the goals of various teams are still not clear. According to one of Monsanto's consultants, "Overall, they hadn't clearly distinguished between product teams, shift teams, management teams, quality improvement teams, and so on, by clearly defining terms and goals."[5]

Monsanto's Pensacola plant is not unionized. Monsanto executives believe that not having to deal with unions has been an advantage in implementing self-managed teams. They may be right. Some union officials argue that the self-managing aspect of teams is really just an extension of top-management control over labor (workers perform the same supervisory jobs that managers used to do but without any additional compensation). And even more disconcerting for some critics is the cross-training inherent in self-managed teams. Team members must be able to do whatever job needs to be done. Some critics fear that teams will make workers interchangeable, and therefore more expendable.[6]

But not all union people fear self-managed teams. Union supporters of the concept remind critics that unions were the driving force behind the team movement in Europe. The self-managing aspect of teams like those at Monsanto represents a shift in the direction of more, rather than less, worker control in the management of companies. The increased worker control—and in turn, value to company success—can actually increase job security, not threaten it.[7]

Despite the problems, Monsanto's use of self-managed work teams has yielded impressive benefits. Today, the plant is operating at the highest levels of productivity and safety in its history, and top executives are planning to institute self-managed teams throughout the company worldwide.

Monsanto's experience at its Pensacola plant reveals the importance of careful planning when shifting to self-managed teams as a primary operational strategy. Because of its chance beginning, the plant's goals and human resource management practices developed reactively rather than proactively. The consequence is that as of 1991, Monsanto management believed that another three years would be required before the team approach would become fully operational. As Monsanto management has learned, building fully operational self-managed teams is a difficult and costly process—but one worth the investment.

Questions for Discussion

1. What type of group is the self-managed team used by Monsanto's Pensacola plant? According to the text, what are the characteristics of this type of group?
2. According to the text, what stages of group development must self-managed teams go through to become productive?
3. The team-building process at the Pensacola plant has been stressful. Why? Which stage of group development is likely to be most stressful for the members of the Pensacola plant's self-managed teams?
4. Some of the foremen and managers at the Pensacola plant are attempting to undermine the implementation of self-managed groups. Why?
5. Members of Monsanto's self-managed teams select their own leaders. What is the team leader's role? How does the method used to select a team leader affect the behavior of team members?
6. What factors influence the level of cohesion in the Pensacola plant's self-managed teams?
7. Would you like to work in a self-managed team? Why or why not?

Notes

1. Feder, B. J. (1991, June 25). Work teams: Not all teamwork. *New York Times*, p. D1.
2. See Note 1, pp. D1 and D6.
3. See Note 1.
4. See Note 1.
5. See Note 1, p. D6.
6. See Note 1.
7. See Note 1.

EXPERIENCING ORGANIZATIONAL BEHAVIOR

The greater the number of people contributing to your group's task output, the less your individual productivity is likely to be. This phenomenon, known as *social loafing*, can have serious adverse influences on group performance (see pp. 294–298). The following exercise is designed to demonstrate this effect.

Procedure

1. Select an additive task that may be conveniently performed in class. For example, you may form groups whose members combine their individual contributions to any of the following tasks: (1) copying entries from a telephone book onto index cards, (b) counting the number of sheets in a large stack of paper, or (c) folding letters and inserting them into envelopes.

2. Perform the task for ten minutes, in groups of different sizes. Try to do your best. Select one person at random to perform the task alone. Combine the remaining students into groups of two, three, four, and so on until the largest possible group is formed (remaining students can simply be included in the largest group). Make random selections by drawing names written on folded slips of paper.

3. After ten minutes, count the number of units you have produced (be it entries copied, sheets counted, letters folded and inserted, or whatever output results from the task performed).

4. Each group computes the average number of units produced by its individual members.

5. At the board, the instructor will record this information in graph form, plotting the average number of units produced per individual (on the vertical axis) as a function of the size of the individuals' work group (on the horizontal axis).

Points to Consider

1. Did the general pattern of performance obtained reveal the social loafing effect? What basis is there for this conclusion?
2. If you did not find evidence for the social loafing effect, why do you think this happened? Might it have been because you expected it to occur and refrained from the natural tendency to lower your individual performance in groups? To test this possibility, repeat the exercise using participants who do not know about this phenomenon. Compare the results.
3. How did members of different size groups feel about the contributions they were making to the task they performed? Specifically, did members of larger groups feel more dispensable, or that they could easily get away with doing less?
4. What could have been done to counteract any "free riding" that may have occurred in this demonstration?

■ 9 ■

THE COURSE OF WORKING LIFE: ORGANIZATIONAL CULTURE, SOCIALIZATION, AND CAREERS

CHAPTER OUTLINE

LEARNING OBJECTIVES

After reading this chapter, you should be able to:

1. Define the term *organizational culture,* and indicate how such culture develops and how it can be changed.

2. Describe some of the ways in which organizational culture affects both individuals and the effectiveness of entire organizations.

3. Define the term *organizational socialization* and indicate how this process takes place in organizations.

4. Distinguish between individualized and institutionalized tactics of socialization, and indicate how these affect innovativeness and commitment among employees.

5. Summarize the potential advantages and disad-

vantages to both parties of *mentor-protégé* relationships, and describe the impact of early mentorship on protégés' later career development.

6. Describe important issues individuals confront in the early, middle, and later stages of their careers, and indicate how people today determine whether their careers are on track.

7. Describe the effects of work-family conflict, and indicate how these effects differ for females and males.

8. Indicate how unemployment affects the psychological and physical health of the people who experience it.

So how's life?" Josi Ortiz says with a smile as she joins her friend Maura Riley at a booth in their favorite lunchtime spot.

"I'd like to be able to say 'Fine, just fine,'" Maura replies, looking dejected, "but it wouldn't be true."

"Wow!" Josi comments. "You do look down. Come on, give . . . what's up?"

"Oh, I guess it's a lot of things all together," Maura remarks, shaking her head. "I told you that my mother has gotten a lot worse lately. She just can't seem to cope. That means trips over there at least every week—sometimes twice a week."

"And that's, what, two hours each way?" Josi asks.

"At least; when the traffic's bad, it's more like two and a half or three. And that comes on top of all these big projects Bob Loring keeps piling on me."

"But I thought you *wanted* more responsibility—more challenge?" Josi asks, seemingly puzzled.

"Yeah, I do. He's really being nice and doing me a favor. The only way to get ahead in my company is to get noticed, and the kind of projects he's giving me will sure do that. He's really looking out for my future. But now, on top of everything else, Toni's been acting up." (Toni is Maura's thirteen-year-old daughter.)

"What's she up to these days?"

"Oh, you know teenagers. When she gets out of school, she goes down to this hangout. I wouldn't mind if the kids were her age, but some of them are a lot older. Sometimes she isn't even back when I get home from work at 7:00 or 7:30. And when I tell her I don't want her hanging out there, she gets so rebellious—you know, tears, door slamming, the works."

"Don't I ever! My two are just the same. So what's wrong with your husband— can't he help? It sounds to me as though you can sure use it."

"I guess so, but Todd's under a lot of pressure, too, these days. His company's not doing so well and they've cut lots of people. Just last week Ron Metchnik, one of Todd's best friends, got the ax; he was really upset. The last thing Todd can afford to do right now is slow down. And the cuts have meant lots more travel, too. Honestly,

I don't think he's been home more than ten days in the past month. He tries to help with the house when he's there, but you know how men are. Mostly, I'd rather do it myself than try to teach him!"

At this, the two friends laugh. But all too quickly, Maura's smile fades from her face. "I don't know, Josi, some days, it all seems like too much. I've been thinking about quitting my job, maybe taking part-time work somewhere. We need the money, but, I don't know, we could probably cut back."

Josi is shocked: "What! And give up everything you've worked so hard to get? Don't even *think* about it. I know how much that job means to you. Look, I know that things are rough right now, but try to stick it out a little longer; they're bound to get better. After all, people like you don't come along everyday, you know. So come on, let's order lunch. I'm starved!"

Maura perks up, and putting their cares aside for the moment, the two friends bury their heads in the menus.

———————————■———————————

No one ever said life would be easy, but in the 1990s, it sometimes seems—for millions of people like Maura and Josi—to border on the unmanageable with its competing demands of family and work, the growing uncertainties of a world economy rife with international competition, the changes produced by an increasingly diverse work force; no, for most of us, life is certainly not "a bowl of cherries."[1]

Faced with these and other complexities, many people express nostalgia for the simpler times and more predictable lifestyles of the past. And in some respects, life *was* simpler in earlier decades. Until well into the current century, for example, most people spent the majority, if not all, of their working years in a single organization. They entered a company after finishing their formal education and remained with it until retirement—or at least for long periods of time. Although this pattern persists in a few nations today, it is definitely not the rule in many others. In the United States and most other Western nations, increasing numbers of people work for multiple organizations during the course of their careers, sometimes changing not only their jobs but their occupations as well.[2]

Further, in the past, two-career families—very much the norm in most developed nations today—were relatively rare. Instead, an older pattern prevailed in which men worked outside the home as the principal family breadwinner and women worked full-time as homemakers. At present, such family arrangements are uncommon. Indeed, current figures indicate that in the United States *less than 7 percent of all households* fit this pattern.[3]

Taking note of such trends and shifts, organizational behavior researchers have focused increasing attention on what might be termed *the course of working life*— changes and challenges individuals encounter during the forty to fifty years that constitute their working careers. As we will soon note, many of these changes center around the task of adjusting to life in a new organization—learning the ropes in a new work setting, so to speak. Such adjustments, in turn, involve two important issues: **organizational culture**—the shared beliefs, expectations, and values held by members of a given organization and to which all newcomers must adjust[4]; and **organizational socialization**—the process through which new employees make such adjustments and become fully functioning members of their organizations.[5]

In this chapter, we will consider both of these topics. We will then turn to several aspects of **careers**—the sequence of jobs, roles, and positions individuals hold during their working lives.[6] Here, we will examine some of the key issues individuals face during early, middle, and late stages of their careers. In addition, we will examine the relationship between such issues and changes related to physical and social development during our adult years—various *life stages* through which most people move. Finally, we will consider several issues currently affecting the course of working life for many people. These include *work-family conflict*—competing pressures from work and family; the adverse effects of *unemployment;* and the role of *race and ethnic factors* in career development.[7,8]

ORGANIZATIONAL CULTURE: ITS ORIGINS, NATURE, AND EFFECTS

Anyone who has worked in several different organizations knows that each is unique. Even organizations concerned with the same activities or that provide similar products or services can be very different places in which to work. One reason for this is obvious: different organizations are composed of different individuals. Since these individuals are unique in many respects, it is not at all surprising that this uniqueness is mirrored in the organizations themselves. This is only part of the total picture, however. In many organizations, employees are a constantly changing cast of characters—old ones leave and new ones join with considerable frequency. Despite such shifts, however, the organizations themselves alter slowly, if at all. In fact, it is often the new employees who change rather than the organization. In a sense, then, organizations have an existence of their own, quite apart from the people of which they are composed. They may remain relatively stable in many respects even in the face of high rates of turnover.

What accounts for such stability? One answer involves the impact of **organizational culture**—a cognitive framework consisting of attitudes, values, behavioral norms, and expectations shared by organization members.[9,10] Once established, these beliefs, expectancies, and values tend to persist unless relatively dramatic events, such as radical shifts in the external environment or a merger or acquisition, intervene.

An organization's culture often has dramatic effects on the actions of its members. Culture specifies *norms*, formal or informal rules governing behavior in various situations. (Norms are considered in more detail in chapter 8.) These may apply to virtually every aspect of the organization's activities, from specifying who should communicate with whom, and in what style, to how rewards will be distributed, and even to corporate strategy (e.g., views about the relative importance of price leadership versus product quality). In short, an organization's culture is often a powerful force determining how it operates and how it performs (see Figure 9–1).

"Lambert, we don't celebrate the fiscal year here at Polk, Hendershott & Samuels."

FIGURE 9–1

Organizational Culture in Operation

As shown here, *organizational culture* exerts important effects on many aspects of organizational behavior. (*Source:* Drawing by Chas. Addams; © 1981 The New Yorker Magazine, Inc.)

At this point, we should pause briefly to clarify an important issue. Our comments so far seem to suggest that each organization has a single culture—one set of shared values, beliefs, and expectations. In fact, this is rarely the case. Research findings suggest that several *subcultures* based on occupational, professional, or functional divisions usually exist within any large organization.[11] In short, people belonging to different fields or who work in departments with different functions often share more attitudes and values with others in their own fields or work units than they do with people in other sections of the organization. It is important to keep this fact in mind when considering organizational culture and its effects.

Now that we have defined culture and commented on its importance, we will consider several basic questions relating to it: (1) How and why does it originate? (2) What are its major effects? and (3) Why and how does it change?

Organizational Culture: Its Origins

Why do many individuals within an organization (or, at least, within its major divisions) share basic attitudes, values, and expectations? Several factors contribute to this state of affairs and hence to the emergence of organizational culture.

First, organizational culture may be traced, at least in part, to the founders of the company. These individuals often possess dynamic personalities, strong values, and a clear vision of how the organization should operate. Since they are on the scene first, and play a key role in hiring initial staff, their attitudes and values are readily transmitted to new employees. The result: these views become the accepted ones in the organization, and persist as long as the founders are on the scene, or even longer. For example, Debbi Fields, the founder of Mrs. Fields' Cookies (a chain of cookie stores found in many shopping malls), believes strongly in the motivation and ability of employees to do a good job. As a result, she has designed the operations of her stores to provide employees with a considerable amount of autonomy, and with opportunities to use their own initiative to generate goodwill among customers. These attitudes permeate the entire company and are a part of its basic culture.

It is an intriguing notion that the culture of any organization is likely to be influenced by the culture of the nation within which it operates. In general, the culture of U.S. firms tends to differ from the culture of Japanese firms in ways that reflect the underlying cultural differences between these two peoples. Whereas U.S. firms tend to pay higher wages in exchange for average working hours and limited job security, Japanese firms tend to pay lower wages in exchange for longer working hours and greater job security. In recent years, both U.S. and Japanese firms have begun doing business in Malaysia, a country whose people prefer higher pay and shorter working hours. As a result, the Malaysians have been generally uncomfortable working for

Second, organizational culture often develops out of an organization's experience with the external environment.[12] Every organization must find a niche for itself in its industry and in the marketplace. As it struggles to do so in its early days, it may find that some values and practices work better for it than others. For example, one company may determine that delivering defect-free products is its strong point; by doing so, it can build a core of solid customers who prefer it to competing businesses. As a result, the organization may gradually acquire a deep, shared commitment to high quality. In contrast, another company may find that selling products of moderate quality, but at attractive prices, works best for it. The result: a dominant value centering around *price leadership* takes shape. In these and countless other ways, an organization's culture is shaped by its interaction with the external environment.

Third, organizational culture develops out of contact between groups of individuals within an organization. To a large extent, culture involves shared interpretations of events and actions on the part of organization members. In short, organizational culture reflects the fact that they assign similar meaning to various events and actions—that they come to perceive the key aspects of the world, those relevant to the organization's work, in a similar manner (refer to our discussion of perception in chapter 2). But does repeated interaction between organization members actually lead them to share perceptions or interpretations of the external world? A sophisticated study conducted by Rentsch provides direct evidence for this view.[13]

In this investigation, members of an accounting firm were first interviewed and asked to describe their organization—what events take place in it, why these events occur, and so on. On the basis of these interviews, fifteen frequently occurring events

Test Bank questions 9.4–9.6 and 9.47 relate to material on this page.

were identified, along with nine adjectives used by participants to describe them. A few of the events were as follows: (1) Account executives allocate billable work to team members; (2) The team concept is employed here; (3) Staff and partners are to be reviewed every six months; (4) Timeliness is important here; and (5) Partners sometimes play golf in the afternoon. Adjectives used by members of the firm in describing these events included professional/nonprofessional, stressful/relaxed, planful/unorganized, fair/unfair, and team oriented/individually competitive.

Participants then completed questionnaires in which they indicated the extent to which the fifteen events were similar to one another, and rated each event in terms of the nine adjective dimensions. They also indicated the extent to which they, personally, interacted with all other members of the organization. This last set of data was used to identify various *interaction groups*—groups of people within the organization who interacted regularly with one another.

Rentsch's major predictions were straightforward: people belonging to various interaction groups would perceive organizational events in a similar manner to a greater extent than people belonging to different interaction groups. In other words, people who interacted with one another on a regular basis would come to perceive key aspects of their working world in similar terms, whereas those who did not interact regularly would come to perceive the same events differently. Results offered strong support for these predictions (see Figure 9–2).

These findings suggest that shared meanings or interpretations—a key ingredient in organizational culture—do derive, at least in part, from shared experiences and from the experience of working together. Moreover, this same process seems to play a role in the development of organizational subcultures, as groups of employees who usually work together develop views somewhat different from those of other groups of employees about what is happening in their company and of the meaning of such events. These findings have several practical applications. First, because different groups within an organization have somewhat different cultures, interventions designed to change job performance or work-related attitudes through shifts in culture should be *customized* for each important group. Second, if shared expectations and values are desired across an organization, steps should be taken to increase contact and interaction between various groups—perhaps through job rotation (refer to our discussion of this topic in chapter 3). Finally, Rentsch's findings point to the fact that sometimes, seemingly small events can carry big messages. For example, in Rentsch's research, one of the events described most frequently by organization members was

either U.S. or Japanese firms that operate in Malaysia. [Sanger, D. E. (1991 December 5). Working for the Japanese, job stability, but longer hours. *The New York Times*, p. D22(L).]

One of the most effective mechanisms used by a company to communicate its culture to its employees is the sharing of stories, myths, and legends about the organization. In fact, one expert claims that "a good company uses its oral legacy to embellish its history and focus its aspirations." One reason stories are likely to be so effective is that people are more likely to remember them than they are to remember formal, written policies. With this in mind, some companies intentionally provide opportuni-

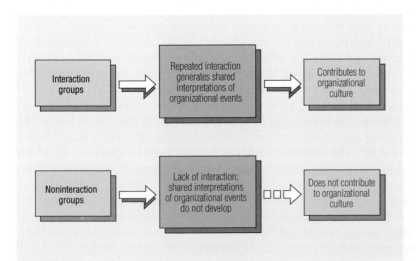

FIGURE 9–2

Organizational Culture as Shared Meanings

Organization members who interacted with one another on a regular basis came to share interpretations of organizational events. Those who did not interact with one another did not share such interpretations. According to Rentsch (1991; see Note 13), such shared meanings or interpretations are an important component of organizational culture.

Test Bank question 9.7 relates to material on this page.

ties for stories to be told (and for myths to be created). For example, the Saturn automobile corporation compiles videotapes of employees telling stories about outstanding customer service and teamwork, and distributes these throughout the company in the form of a weekly news show. In doing so, this new organization (with only a limited history) can help promote the elements of its culture that it deems most valuable. [Deutsch, C. H. (1991, October 13). The parables of corporate culture. *The New York Times*, p. F25(L).]

"Partners sometimes play golf in the afternoon." Senior partners in the company were shocked to discover that this activity, which they viewed as relatively trivial, received so much attention from others. In retrospect, however, they realized that it conveyed important meanings to other employees—meanings such as "Only senior partners have any privileges around here," or "Whatever people say, status is really important." We will return to this point in our discussion of efforts to change organizational culture; for now we simply note that where organizational culture is concerned, the adage "Actions speak louder than words" seems to be highly accurate.

Organizational Culture: Its Major Effects

Because it involves shared values, attitudes, and expectations, organizational culture exerts many effects on individuals and on organizational processes. With respect to organization members, culture generates strong if often subtle pressures to *go along*—to think and act in ways that are consistent with the existing culture. Thus, if an organization's culture stresses a cooperative relationship between management and labor, dealings between these groups will tend to be courteous and amicable. If, instead, the organization's culture decrees an adversarial relationship, dealings between them will probably take on a very different tone. Similarly, if an organization's culture stresses the importance of product quality and excellent service to customers, these individuals will generally find their complaints handled politely and efficiently. If, instead, the organization's culture stresses high output as a primary goal, customers seeking service may find themselves on a much rockier road. An organization's culture can strongly affect everything from the way employees dress, and the amount of time allowed to elapse before meetings begin, to the speed with which people are promoted and the nature of any profit-sharing or bonus plans adopted.

Turning to the impact of culture on organizational processes, much research has focused on the possibility of a link between culture and performance.[14] One view is that in order to influence performance, organizational culture must be *strong*—approval or disapproval must be expressed to those who act in ways consistent or inconsistent with the culture, respectively, and there must be widespread agreement on values among organizational members.[15] Only if these conditions prevail, researchers believe, will a link between organizational culture and performance be observed. Some evidence supports this contention. For example, Dennison reported that corporations with cultural values favoring participation by employees in decision making and other activities generate a return on investment twice as great as that of corporations lacking this value.[16] Similarly, in their best-selling book, *In Search of Excellence*, Peters and Waterman reported that possession of a "strong" culture characterized eighty highly successful firms in the United States.[17] Although such studies are intriguing and make for stimulating reading, recent reviews by Saffold as well as Siehl and Martin suggest that they do not as yet provide compelling evidence for a clear link between culture and performance.[18,19]

Another approach to this issue, however, appears to offer a useful resolution. In a recent paper, O'Reilly, Chatman, and Caldwell suggest that the crucial link in the chain between organizational culture and organizational performance may involve *person-organization fit*—the extent to which the values held by specific individuals match those of their organization's culture.[20] The better this fit, the investigators predicted, the more beneficial the outcomes. Specifically, the closer the person-organization fit with respect to cultural values, the stronger employees' organizational commitment, the higher their job satisfaction, the lower their intention to leave, and the lower their actual rate of voluntary turnover. By extension, then, the better the person-organization fit across an organization, the more effective its overall performance.

Test Bank question 9.8 relates to material on this page.

To test this important hypothesis, O'Reilly and his colleagues first asked hundreds of individuals from eight different organizations to complete a questionnaire designed to measure the values of their companies (the *Organizational Culture Profile*). Among the values measured by this instrument are orientation toward outcomes or results, attention to detail, innovation and risk taking, emphasis on growth, and collaborative and team orientation. Next, the same participants reported on their own values—the extent to which various values were important to them. In a third step, the closeness of fit between individuals' values and those of their organizations (person-organization fit) was assessed. Finally, the researchers related closeness of person-organization fit to measures of organizational commitment, job satisfaction, intentions to leave, and records of actual turnover during a two-year period.

O'Reilly and his colleagues predicted that the closer the person-organization fit, the more positive the outcomes that would be observed. Results offered strong support for this general hypothesis. First, the closer the person-organization fit, the higher individuals' normative commitment—commitment based on acceptance of the organization's values—and the higher their expressed job satisfaction. Second, the higher the person-organization fit, the lower participants' intentions to leave their organizations. Finally, when participants were divided into groups with relatively high and low person-organization fit, those for whom fit was high were indeed less likely to quit their jobs over a two-year period than those for whom fit was low (see Figure 9–3). In fact, people in the first category would be predicted to stay on the job about twice as long as those in the second, poor-fit category.

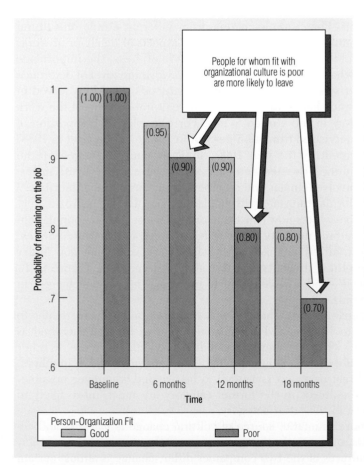

FIGURE 9–3

Person-Organization Fit and Voluntary Turnover

Individuals whose values closely matched those of their organization's culture were less likely to voluntarily quit their jobs than were individuals whose values did not closely match those of their organization's culture. (*Source:* Based on data from O'Reilly, Chatman, & Caldwell, 1991; see Note 20.)

These findings have important implications both for individuals and for organizations. First, they suggest that people seeking employment should examine carefully the prevailing culture of an organization before deciding to join it. If they don't, they run the risk of finding themselves in a situation where their own values and those of their company clash. Second, these findings also suggest that organizations should focus on attracting individuals whose values match their own. This involves identifying key aspects of organizational culture, communicating these to prospective employees, and selecting those for whom the person-organization fit is best. Considerable effort may be involved in completing these tasks. Given that high levels of person-organization fit can contribute to commitment, satisfaction, and low rates of turnover among employees, however, the effort appears to be well spent.

Organizational Culture: Why and How It Changes

Our earlier comments about the relative stability of organizational culture may have left you wondering about the following questions: If culture tends to be so stable, why and how does it ever change? Why isn't it simply passed from one generation of organizational members to the next in a totally static manner? The basic answer, of course, is that the world in which an organization operates changes. External events such as shifts in market conditions, new technology, altered government policies, and many other factors change over time and may necessitate corresponding changes in an organization's mode of doing business—and hence in its internal culture.

Similarly, over time, the people entering an organization may differ in important ways from those already in it, and these differences may impinge on the existing culture of the organization. For example, people from different ethnic or cultural backgrounds may have contrasting views about various aspects of behavior at work. For instance, they may hold contrasting views about style of dress, the importance of being on time (or even what constitutes "on time" behavior), the level of deference one should show to higher status people, and even what foods should be served in the company cafeteria. Rapid change in the ethnic and cultural makeup of the work force is currently under way in the United States. For example, the proportion of females in the work force increased from 40.5 percent in 1976 to 45 percent in 1988, and will move to 47.5 percent by the year 2000. Similarly, only 15 percent of the growth in the labor force during the next ten years will involve native white males; most of the increase will involve females and members of various ethnic minorities.[21] One final statistic: in California, the state with the largest population (approximately 30 million at present), native whites now constitute only 57 percent of the population; by 2000, there will be no ethnic majority in the state. In short, in the United States, and in several other industrialized nations, nothing short of a revolution is now under way with respect to the ethnic diversity of national work forces (see Figure 9–4). Such shifts have produced—and will continue to produce—important changes in the cultures of many organizations.

Yet another factor contributing to change in an organization's culture relates to culture itself. According to Wilkins and Dyer, some cultures may be classified as change-oriented in nature, whereas others are stability-oriented.[22] In some, in other words, change is viewed as a desirable outcome to be actively encouraged; in others, change is viewed as a threat or a necessary evil to be avoided whenever possible. Obviously, organizational cultures in the former category are much more likely to alter over time than those in the latter category.

Another, and even more dramatic, source of cultural change is *mergers* and *acquisitions*. In such events, one organization purchases or otherwise absorbs another. To the extent that the cultures of the two companies differ, change is almost certain

FIGURE 9-4

Ethnic Diversity in the
Workplace

Ethnic diversity among
the work force is
increasing dramatically
in the United States and
many other nations.

to occur. A classic example of this process, and the cultural clashes it often produces, is provided by the merger of Nabisco, Inc., a producer of cookies and other baked goods famous for such brands as Fig Newtons and Oreos, with RJ Reynolds, Inc., a major producer of tobacco products.

Nabisco was headquartered in New York, and its executives were known for a fast-paced life in which perks such as corporate jets, penthouse apartments, and lavish, all-night parties featured prominently. Yet, company employees prided themselves on the "American-as-apple-pie" image of Nabisco, and valued the high degree of autonomy in performing their jobs that Nabisco management permitted. RJ Reynolds, headquartered in Winston-Salem, North Carolina, had a strikingly different culture. It was characterized by a strong work ethic, much less autonomy for employees, and a deep commitment to its local community and to philanthropic activities. Corporate jets, penthouse apartments, and lavish parties were definitely *not* features of RJ Reynolds' corporate life.

When the two companies, with their sharply different cultures, actually merged, sparks flew. Nabisco executives chafed under the tighter controls imposed by Tylee Wilson, chief executive officer of Reynolds. As some put it, "You have to raise your hand to go to the bathroom!" The fact that their company was not afforded the level of independence within the new corporation promised before the merger upset many Nabisco employees. The result: within a year, bitter internal feuds erupted. These resulted in a takeover of the new company by Ross Johnson, CEO of Nabisco. Once in power, he quickly purged the company of virtually all former Reynolds executives and moved the headquarters to Atlanta. Now, years later, the merged organization still suffers from decreased productivity in some units, increased turnover, and strong internal divisions. When organizational cultures collide, the changes that follow can be wrenching.

Finally, cultural change may result from conscious decisions to alter the internal structure of basic operations of an organization. Once such decisions are reached, many practices in the company that both reflect and contribute to its culture may change. For example, the company may adopt different criteria for recruiting newcomers or promoting current employees. Similarly, managers may be directed to focus their attention on different goals from those in the past. As these shifts take place, new norms governing preferred or acceptable behavior emerge, and attitudes and values supporting these norms may take shape. The result may be a considerable shift in existing culture. (How do various operating companies seek to alter their own cultures? For information on this important issue, see the **OB in Practice** section on pp. 320–321.)

Given that organizational mergers and acquisitions are so widespread, it is likely that many employees will have to face changes in corporate culture during their working lives. In 1990, 3,400 U.S. firms were involved in mergers, affecting some 800,000 employees. Because newly formed companies often have norms and values that differ from the original parent companies, employees may combat changes in culture. As a result, the employees may be left not knowing how or where they fit into the new organization, or what behaviors are expected of them. To help alleviate employees' fears of the unknown, managers should work with them to help reduce uncertainties they have about their places in the new organization. [Galosy, J. R. (1990, April). The human factor in mergers and acquisitions. *Training & Development Journal*, pp. 90–93.]

ORGANIZATIONAL SOCIALIZATION: THE PROCESS OF JOINING UP

Think back over the jobs you have held in recent years. Can you recall your feelings and reactions during the first few days (or weeks) on each? If so, you probably remember that these were uncomfortable periods. As a new employee, you were suddenly confronted with a work environment that was different in many respects from the one you had just left. Most, if not all, of the people around you were strangers, and you had to begin the process of getting to know them—and their personal quirks—from scratch. Unless your job was identical to one you had performed before, you also had to learn new procedures, skills, and operations relating to it. You had to acquire working knowledge of the policies, practices, and procedures in force in your new organization, so that you would know how to carry out your work assignments in accordance with them. And you had to begin forming an image of the organization's culture—its values, style, and approach to doing business. In short, you had to *learn the ropes*.

Successfully completing these complex tasks is clearly important to the future

 OB IN PRACTICE

Creating a New Organizational Culture: Some Practical Steps

Change rarely comes easily. If you've ever attempted to lose or gain weight, begin a program of exercise, or switch from one software program to another, you already recognize this fact on a personal level. If it's often difficult to change our own behavior in a specific area of life, imagine how difficult it may be to alter the culture—the shared values, beliefs, attitudes, expectancies—of an entire organization. This daunting task has caused many top managers to throw their hands up in despair, as history and established practices work to defeat their efforts to produce desirable change—even change that might help to keep their companies alive.

In recent years, however, some practical, and effective, steps for altering organizational culture have been devised. Perhaps the best way of illustrating these is to examine how they have been applied by several distinct companies. Let's begin with Du Pont, and its "Adopt a Customer" program. Du Pont CEO John Wollard believes that "nothing is worthwhile unless it touches the customer." But how to overcome a lack of concern with customer satisfaction among Du Pont's blue-collar workers? One approach has been to encourage blue-collar employees to visit a specific customer once a month, in order to find out the customer's needs and complaints. The worker becomes the customer's representative on the factory floor, and works with other Du Pont employees to solve problems relating to product quality and delivery schedules. In a sense, these employees *adopt* one of the company's customers, and try to represent their needs throughout the manufacturing process. The result: Du Pont is now permeated with a new value—the view that customers really do come first.

Next, consider Walt Disney Corporation. For several years after its famous and talented founder died, the company was, seemingly, haunted by his ghost. Every time a major decision arose, top management would ask, "What would Walt say?" "What would Walt do?" The results were catastrophic: the company failed to adjust its products to radical changes in the marketplace and soon acquired a reputation for producing dull, stodgy films that bored children as well as adults. In a sense, the company found itself a prisoner of its own history. What could be done to break loose and change the organization's culture? CEO Michael Eisner made a radical decision: he literally cleared the boards of managers who had worked with Walt Disney, bringing in a new crew of people who, in most cases, had never met the company's founder. These people

performance of virtually any new employee. In other words, the speed and ease with which individuals learn the ropes in organizations they have recently joined are crucial from both the individual's and organization's point of view. This process is known as **organizational socialization.** More formally, it can be defined as *the process through which individuals are transformed from outsiders to participating, effective members of organizations.*[23] In a sense, a *career* can be viewed as consisting of a series of socialization experiences, as an individual moves into new organizations or new positions in his or her present one. Thus, understanding organizational socialization is important to understanding several aspects of careers and career development.

In this section, therefore, we will consider several key aspects of such socialization. First, we will describe the basic stages of socialization—steps through which most people pass en route to becoming full members of their organization and work groups. Next, we will consider various techniques used by organizations to help smooth new employees' passage through this difficult process, and some of the effects these produce. Finally, we will consider the role of *mentors*—older and more experienced coworkers—in the socialization process.

created a culture that was more adventurous and willing to take necessary risks. The result: Disney was revitalized and quickly moved to record profits.

As a third example, consider how Sharp, Inc., a major Japanese manufacturer of electronics equipment, has sought to make the company more innovative. Japanese managers, as you probably know, often fret over the fact that the cultures of their organizations do not foster innovation; rather, reflecting values prevalent in the wider national culture, they tend to encourage teamwork and an incremental approach to product design.[24] To alter such values, Sharp rewards people who develop useful innovations by placing them on a special *Gold Badge* project team—a team that reports directly to the company president. Team members enjoy high status and many privileges—and other employees envy them. The result: Sharp's culture has changed to place greater emphasis on innovativeness.

What do all these tactics have in common? According to people who have studied changing organizational cultures, several basic points. Perhaps the most important is this: you can't change culture with words alone; rather, concrete actions are needed. To get blue-collar employees interested in product quality, have them visit customers to hear their side of the equation, as is done at Du Pont; to induce employees to be more innovative, reward such efforts handsomely—and make them part of the basic values of the company. With respect to changing cor-porate culture, in short, actions really *do* speak louder than words.

Another important point involves understanding the present culture. One cannot, after all, map a course to desired change without knowing the present location. Third, successful change efforts require strong support from top management. Unless these key players really believe that change is possible and that all employees have the capacity to contribute to the process, it simply won't happen. Fourth, successful efforts to change organizational culture recognize that the process is likely to be a slow one involving years, not months. People don't, after all, adopt and reject values with ease, so patience and a long-term perspective are important. Finally, cultural change must involve all levels of the organization. Top management can initiate the process and guide it, but unless employees at all levels buy in, nothing much will happen. This returns us to the first point above: words or policies alone won't produce change in an organization's culture. Change will be accomplished only when top management takes specific actions designed to encourage the process.

In summary, change in organizational culture *is* possible. Like all worthwhile change, the process is apt to be long and difficult. If the course is well charted, however, the gains achieved may more than offset these costs. In today's increasingly competitive world, there is simply no choice for many organizations. Change or vanish—those are the only options.

Test Bank questions 9.12–9.13, 9.57, and 9.68 relate to material on this page.

Major Stages in the Socialization Process

In one sense, organizational socialization is a continuous process—one that begins before individuals actually arrive on the scene and proceeds for weeks or months after their entry. The process can be divided into three basic periods, which are often marked by discrete events signifying their beginning and their end. These have been described by Feldman as the stages of *getting in, breaking in,* and *settling in.*[25]

Getting In: Anticipatory Socialization   Before individuals actually join an organization, they usually know quite a bit about it. Such information, which is the basis for expectations concerning what the organization and their specific jobs will be like, is obtained from several sources. In many cases, friends or relatives already working for the organization provide it. They can offer a wealth of information (not all of it accurate!) that strongly colors the perceptions and expectations of new recruits.

Second, individuals often acquire information about an organization from professional journals, magazine and newspaper articles, its annual reports, and other formal sources.

Third, and perhaps most important, potential employees gain information from the organization's *recruitment procedures.* Since competition for top-notch employees is always intense, successful recruitment of them usually involves a skilled combination of salesmanship and diplomacy. Recruiters tend to describe their companies in glowing terms, glossing over internal problems and emphasizing positive features. The result is that potential employees receive an unrealistically positive impression about what working in them will be like. When new employees actually arrive on the job and find that their expectations are not met, disappointment, dissatisfaction, and even resentment about being misled can follow. Such reactions, in turn, can contribute to high rates of turnover, low organizational commitment, and other negative outcomes.[26]

In extreme cases, the reactions experienced by employees discovering that conditions in the organization are not what they expected can take the form of **entry shock**—strong feelings of dismay, confusion, and disillusionment.[27] For example, consider the reactions of a new college graduate who enters an organization with high hopes and positive expectations. Much to her chagrin, she finds that conditions are not at all what she expected. Her supervisor seems to have little interest in her; contrary to expectations formed during her interview, she discovers that her input is rarely invited and that she has little role in decision making. The work she is asked to perform is far less stimulating than she anticipated, and in contrast to conditions in college, where she received feedback from her professors on a regular basis, she now receives input only on relatively rare occasions. Finally, she is disillusioned to learn that promotions, raises, and other rewards are distributed largely on the basis of organizational politics—not strictly on the basis of merit, as she assumed. Hit with this unsettling combination of disappointments, she rapidly loses interest in her work and decides to begin another job search as soon as possible.

Can such reactions be avoided, or at least reduced? One useful technique for doing so is **realistic job previews**—providing job applicants with accurate descriptions of the jobs they will perform and the organizations they will enter.[28] Growing evidence suggests that people exposed to such previews later report higher satisfaction and show lower turnover than those who receive glowing—but often misleading—information about the companies in question. In particular, realistic job previews designed to counter overoptimistic *and* overpessimistic expectations tend to produce more satisfied employees, and ones less likely to quit their jobs, than less realistic previews.[29]

Test Bank questions 9.15–9.20, 9.49, 9.58, 9.60, and 9.69 relate to material on this page.

Breaking In: The Encounter Stage   The second major stage in organizational socialization begins when individuals actually assume their new duties. During this stage, they face several key tasks. First, they must master the skills required by their new jobs. Second, they must become oriented to the practices and procedures of the organization. This often involves unlearning old habits or behaviors and acquiring new ones, for coworkers quickly tire of hearing a new recruit say, "That's not how we did it where I worked before." Third, new members of an organization must establish good social relations with other members of their work group. They must get to know these people and gain their acceptance. Only when they do can they become full members of the team. It is during the encounter stage that formal *training and orientation programs* are conducted. These are designed to help individuals accomplish the tasks described above. We will comment further on the nature of such programs below.

How, precisely, do newcomers obtain needed information about their organizations? According to Miller and Jablin, who have studied this process in detail, they do so in many different ways.[30] In particular, they use techniques such as direct questions, indirect questions (e.g., hinting), observing others, and disguised conversations, in which they conceal their efforts to obtain information behind such tactics as joking and self-disclosure. An overview of the information-seeking tactics that newcomers use is presented in Table 9–1.

Settling In: The Metamorphosis Stage   Sometime after an individual enters an organization, he or she attains full member status. Depending on the type and length of the training program used, this entry may be marked by a formal ceremony or may be quite informal. In the former case, individuals may attend a dinner, reception, or graduation exercise at which they exchange their temporary, provisional title (e.g., trainee, apprentice) for a more permanent one. Alternatively, they may receive a concrete sign of their new status (e.g., the key to the executive washroom, a pass to the executive dining room, a permanent identity badge). In other cases, especially when training has been short or informal, full acceptance into the work group may not be marked by any specific ceremony. Instead, it may be acknowledged by informal

TABLE 9 – 1   Information-Seeking Tactics Used by Newcomers

Newcomers to organizations use the tactics listed here to obtain desired information.

Information-Seeking Tactic	Description
Overt questions	Direct requests for information
Indirect questions	Hints, noninterrogative questions
Third parties	Information sought from coworkers, others
Testing limits	Create situation to which sources of information must respond; their responses provide desired information
Disguising conversations	Disguise information-seeking attempts as natural part of conversations
Observing	Observing information sources' behavior
Surveillance	Retrospectively attempting to interpret behavior of information sources

Source: Based on suggestions by Miller & Jablin, 1991; see Note 30.

Test Bank questions 9.21–9.24 and 9.61 relate to material on this page.

actions, such as being invited to lunch by coworkers or being assigned a seat at their table in the dining room.

Whatever form it takes, the settling-in phase of socialization marks important shifts both for individuals and for organizations. Employees now make permanent adjustments to their jobs (e.g., they resolve conflicting demands between their jobs and their personal lives). And organizations now treat them as if they will be long-term members of the work team rather than temporary fill-ins.

Organizational Socialization: How It Occurs

Most organizations have some type of program or procedure designed to help new employees adjust to their new jobs. However, as you might expect, these programs differ in many respects. According to Van Maanen and Schein, researchers who have studied the process in great detail, most of the differences involve the dimensions shown in Table 9–2.[31]

First, socialization programs differ in terms of whether newcomers are socialized individually or in groups. The former approach is often adopted by organizations that hire people all through the year at different times. The latter is adopted by organizations that hire groups of workers at specific times. For example, one of the authors underwent a collective socialization program when he entered a large federal agency. He and other new recruits were sent to a resort where they participated in a five-day-long formal program designed to orient them to their new positions and responsibilities.

Second, socialization can be *formal*, as in the program just mentioned, or *informal*, involving on-the-job experiences. Formal programs are generally used when new employees are quite unfamiliar with their new roles or in connection with complex jobs. Informal ones are often used when employees already know much about their positions, or when their jobs are simple.

Third, socialization can be *sequential*, involving a process in which recruits obtain full membership in the organization by passing through a series of concrete steps or stages (e.g., they may be designated as trainees, apprentices, assistants, and so on,

Most organizations have brief, formal "orientation" programs that allow new employees to learn about the organization, including its formal rules, regulations, history, and even its myths and legends. Although many colleges used to have very short, often cursory, orientations for entering freshmen, the growing dropout rate has encouraged these institutions to develop longer and more in-depth orientation programs. For example, to increase student retention, Bard College now offers intense orientation sessions that cover such broad topics as sexuality, substance abuse, and harassment. Just as these longer orientations have been used successfully by colleges to retain students, organizations might also benefit by providing this same type of intensive program to help retain new employees. [DePalma, A. (1991, August 28). As life changes, so does freshman orientation. *The New York Times*, p. D19(L).]

TABLE 9–2   Basic Dimensions of Organizational Socialization

Programs of organizational socialization can vary along each of the dimensions listed here.

Dimension	Explanation
Individual–Group	Are newcomers socialized individually or as part of groups of trainees?
Informal–Formal	Is training formal or on-the-job?
Sequential–Nonsequential	Do newcomers progress toward full-member status one step at a time, or do they become members as soon as orientation is over?
Serial–Disjunctive	Is training conducted by members of the organization or by others?
Investiture–Divestiture	Does training seek to affirm the self-confidence of newcomers or reduce it?
Fixed–Variable	Do newcomers know or not know when their probationary period will end?

Source: Based on suggestions by Van Maanen & Schein, 1979; see Note 31.

as they complete specific periods of time with the organization). In contrast, social-ization can be *nonsequential*. Here, newcomers receive full member status as soon as orientation and training are completed.

A fourth dimension involves the question of whether newcomers are trained by experienced members of the group (*serial* training) or by people who do not belong to the organization itself (*disjunctive*). In the latter type of training, professionals with special expertise are hired for this specific purpose.

Fifth, socialization programs often differ with respect to whether they are designed to affirm the ability and self-confidence of recruits (*investiture programs*) or to strip away their feelings of self-confidence so that they will be in a better state to accept new roles and patterns of behavior (*divestiture programs*). The former process is often used with high-level recruits. Since these people were hired on the basis of their credentials and expertise, their new organizations don't want to change them. On the contrary, their entry is meant to be as smooth and pleasant as possible.

In contrast, divestiture programs are designed to strip away certain characteristics or attitudes that new recruits bring with them to the new organization. Such tactics are often applied to people entering military service, professional or graduate school, or college-level sports. The goal is to "shake them up," so they more readily surrender any current attitudes and behaviors they brought with them that are counter-pro-ductive from their new organization's point of view. For example, medical and profes-sional schools, faced with newcomers who have experienced a great deal of previous academic success, load these new students with extremely heavy programs to make them painfully aware of their own limitations and of the demands of their new roles.

Finally, socialization programs differ in terms of whether newcomers know in advance when their probationary period will end (*fixed programs*), or do not know when they will gain full acceptance (*variable programs*).

Recently, Jones has suggested that the six dimensions discussed above actually reflect a single underlying dimension: *institutionalized versus individualized* social-ization.[32] Institutionalized socialization involves procedures in which all newcomers move through a formal, shared initiation process involving a fixed sequence of steps. Role models (current employees) are provided, and socialization confirms the new-comers' identity and self-confidence (investiture). In contrast, individualized social-ization is characterized by informal, individually tailored procedures, on-the-job training, and divestiture, in which newcomers' identities are disconfirmed rather than enhanced. Both types are widely used, but, as we will shortly see, they have somewhat different effects on newcomers and their later performance.

Effects of Contrasting Socialization Tactics   As we have just noted, the procedures used by organizations to socialize their new recruits differ in many ways. Given the scope of these differences, it seems only reasonable to expect that these contrasting tactics might yield different patterns of behavior or performance among newcomers. In fact, this appears to be the case. For example, consider an informative study conducted by Allen and Meyer.[33]

These researchers suggested that the two kinds of socialization procedures de-scribed above—institutionalized versus individualized—might be related to impor-tant aspects of employees' behavior: (1) their **role orientation** with respect to their jobs—whether they adopted an *innovative* perspective in which they were willing to alter various aspects of their jobs, or a *custodial* perspective in which they were unwilling to make such alterations, and (2) their level of organizational commitment. Drawing on previous research, Allen and Meyer predicted that institutionalized socialization procedures would increase organizational commitment but reduce em-ployees' tendency to adopt an innovative perspective. In contrast, individualized socialization practices would reduce organizational commitment, but foster an innovative perspective. The rationale behind these predictions was as follows. Institutionalized socialization procedures, which expose all newcomers to shared experiences and enhance their self-confidence, increase organizational commitment to a greater extent than individualized procedures. Correspondingly, because of their fixed, formal nature, institutionalized socialization procedures foster a custodial, "don't-rock-the-boat" approach among newcomers, while individualized procedures encourage a higher level of job innovation.

To test these predictions, recent graduates of an M.B.A. program were asked to complete measures describing the socialization practices used by the organizations they had recently joined, as well as to report on the extent to which they had changed procedures for doing their jobs (whether they adopted a custodial or innovative role orientation). They also completed a measure of organizational commitment. Participants completed the last two of these measures twice—six months after graduation and twelve months after graduation—to determine whether the effects of contrasting socialization practices changed over time.

Results offered clear support for both major predictions. As expected, institutionalized tactics of socialization promoted a custodial orientation among participants, whereas individualized tactics encouraged an innovative orientation (see Figure 9–5). Institutionalized tactics were also associated with higher levels of organizational commitment, whereas individualized procedures were associated with lower levels of commitment. Both effects were observed at twelve months as well as at six months; however, they were somewhat stronger on the first than on the second occasion.

These findings point to two important conclusions with practical implications for organizations. First, the socialization practices adopted by a company have important, and relatively lasting, effects on the behavior and orientation of newcomers. Second, no single type of socialization practice is best. Rather, different approaches yield contrasting outcomes that, depending on the needs of a particular organization, are more or less desirable. For example, an organization wishing to instill high levels of commitment among its new recruits might find institutionalized practices preferable to individualized ones. In contrast, an organization wishing to foster an innovative

FIGURE 9–5

Organizational Socialization: Effects on Employees' Role Orientation

Individualized tactics of socialization encourage an innovative orientation among employees. In contrast, institutionalized tactics seem to encourage high levels of organizational commitment. (*Source:* Based on suggestions by Allen & Meyer, 1990; see Note 33.)

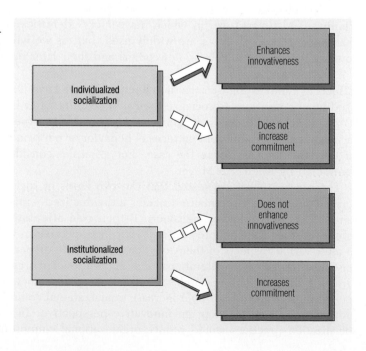

orientation among newcomers would probably prefer individualized procedures. Of course, as Allen and Meyer note, it may be possible to combine elements of both approaches to foster high levels of commitment *and* high levels of innovativeness. In any case, these and other findings suggest that what organizations do to teach newcomers the ropes can have lasting effects on their performance and attitudes. Thus, careful attention to the nature of these procedures, and their potential effects, seems well worthwhile.

Mentors and Socialization

In many fields, young and inexperienced individuals learn much from older, more experienced ones. Thus, in medicine and law, interns learn from established physicians and attorneys; in science, graduate students acquire a broad range of knowledge and skills from the researchers under whose guidance they work. Does the same process of *mentorship* operate in work settings? A growing body of evidence suggests that it does.[34] Young and relatively inexperienced employees often report that they have learned a great deal from a **mentor**—an older and more experienced employee who advises, counsels, and otherwise enhances their personal development.

Research on the nature of such relationships suggests that mentors do many things for their protégés. They provide much-needed emotional support and confidence. They advance the protégé's career by nominating him or her for promotions, and by providing opportunities for the protégé to demonstrate his or her competence. They suggest useful strategies for achieving work objectives, ones protégés might not generate for themselves. They bring the protégé to the attention of top management—a necessary first step for advancement. Finally, they protect protégés from the repercussions of errors, and help them avoid situations that may be risky for their careers.

Of course, these potential gains are offset by possible risks or hazards. Protégés who hitch their wagon to a falling rather than a rising star may find their own careers in danger when their mentors suffer setbacks. Indeed, in some cases they may find themselves without a job if a purge follows defeat in a political struggle (see chapter 11). In addition, mentors are only human, so not all the advice they supply is helpful. And there is always the danger that protégés will become so dependent on their mentors that their development as self-reliant individuals able to accept authority and responsibility is slowed.

Although our comments so far might suggest that mentors are totally selfless people—benefactors who want little or nothing in return—this is not actually the case.[35] Mentors expect several things from protégés. First, they expect their protégés to turn in hard work and effort on assigned tasks. Second, they expect them to be loyal supporters within the organization; after all, they are now members of the mentor's team! Third, mentors may gain recognition from others in the company for helping to nurture young talent, and can bask in the reflected glory of any success gained by their protégés. Finally, they may reap psychological benefits from feeling needed, and from a sense of accomplishment in helping the younger generation. (See Figure 9–6 on p. 328 for an overview of the potential benefits and dangers to both parties of mentor-protégé relationships.)

Other findings suggest that mentor-protégé pairs do not form at random. Mentors are usually older than their protégés (by about eight to fifteen years). They tend to be people with considerable power and status within their companies. As a result, they can assist rising young stars without feeling threatened. How do mentors select their protégés? Existing evidence suggests that they are impressed with a young employee's initial performance, or find interacting with him or her easy and pleasant. This may be because mentor and protégé share similar attitudes and backgrounds,

Although we usually think of mentoring as a process that goes on within organizations to develop current employees, it also might be used to develop potential future generations of employees. In a recent project conducted in the Washington, D.C., area, almost 600 employees of the U.S. Department of Labor volunteered to mentor nearby school children by showing them what it's like to go to work each day to earn a living. Because these children came from disadvantaged families, they may not have otherwise been exposed to this process that most of us take for granted. The mentoring may therefore provide an effective early learning experience for these disadvantaged children. [Mentoring. (1991, March). *Education Digest,* p. 55.]

FIGURE 9-6

Potential Gains and Losses Resulting from Mentoring

Mentor-protégé relationships yield important benefits to both parties. However, as indicated here, such relationships also contain elements of risk on both sides.

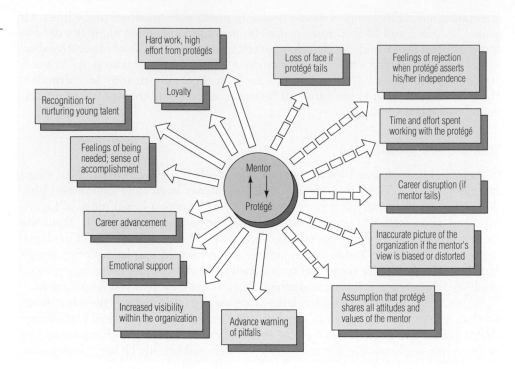

or because protégés are socially skilled and clearly transmit their desire for an experienced tutor. In still other cases, would-be protégés approach potential mentors and actively ask for help or attempt to initiate a relationship in other ways.

Most human relationships develop over time, and mentorship is no exception. In fact, most mentor-protégé relationships seem to pass through several distinct phases.[36] The first, known as *initiation*, lasts from six months to a year and represents the period during which the relationship gets started and takes on importance for both parties. The second phase, known as *cultivation*, may last from two to five years. During this time, the bond between mentor and protégé deepens, and the young individual may make rapid career strides because of the skilled assistance he or she is receiving. The third stage, *separation*, begins when the protégé feels it is time to assert independence and strike out on his or her own, or when there is some externally produced change in the role relationships (e.g., the protégé is promoted; the mentor is transferred). Separation can also occur if the mentor feels unable to continue providing support and guidance to the protégé (e.g., if the mentor is experiencing physical illness or psychological problems). This phase can be quite stressful if the mentor resents the protégé's growing independence, or if the protégé feels that the mentor has withdrawn support and guidance prematurely. If separation is successful, the relationship may enter a final stage termed *redefinition*. Here, both persons perceive their bond primarily as one of friendship. They come to treat one another as equals, and the roles of mentor and protégé may fade away completely. However, the mentor may continue to take pride in the accomplishments of the former protégé, and this person may continue to feel a debt of gratitude toward the former mentor.

At this point, we note that not all mentor-protégé relationships involve the intense, long-term relationship we have described so far. Existing evidence suggests that in addition to such *primary* mentoring, another, less intense form known as *secondary* mentoring also exists.[37] Mentoring of this latter type is shorter and less intense, and tends to focus more directly on career-related issues than on personal and psychological ones. In addition, young employees may receive assistance from several

Test Bank questions 9.35–9.36 and 9.52 relate to material on this page.

different mentors rather than from only one, as is usually the case in primary mentoring. Such mentoring is probably more common than primary mentoring, but it, too, can have important beneficial effects on the careers of protégés. This is illustrated clearly by a study conducted by Whitely, Dougherty, and Dreher.[38]

These researchers predicted that with other variables that also influence success held constant (variables such as the areas in which individuals work—finance, sales, marketing, technical; the size of their companies; the number of hours they work each week), experience with mentors would still contribute to individuals' early career progress. In addition, they predicted that individuals' socioeconomic status would *moderate* the relationship between mentoring and career progress. In other words, having had one or more secondary mentors would be more beneficial to people with relatively high socioeconomic status than to those with relatively low socioeconomic status. This prediction was based on the suggestion that most mentors are high in socioeconomic status and so would find it easier to form strong bonds with protégés who shared their background.

To examine the accuracy of these predictions, Whitely, Dougherty, and Dreher asked currently employed individuals holding M.B.A. or bachelor's degrees in business to indicate the number of promotions they had obtained since graduation and their current total compensation. In addition, participants reported on the socioeconomic backgrounds of their families and the extent to which they had experienced mentoring during their early careers. Finally, they provided information on factors such as the size of their companies, the field of their present job, and the number of hours they worked each week.

Results indicated that with all these other factors held constant, the more mentoring individuals had received, the more promotions they earned and the higher their current compensation. In addition, and also as expected, the beneficial effects of mentoring occurred primarily for people from relatively high socioeconomic backgrounds. Only for this group was amount of mentoring a significant predictor of promotions and compensation. For people from low socioeconomic backgrounds, in contrast, other factors, such as number of years of work experience, were more closely related to promotions and earnings (see Figure 9–7).

These results are both encouraging and discouraging. On one hand, they suggest that mentoring can significantly enhance the early careers of individuals fortunate enough to obtain such help. On the other hand, they also indicate that people from

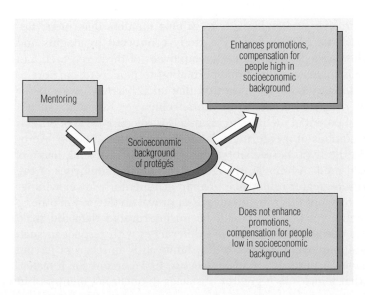

FIGURE 9–7

Socioeconomic Status and the Benefits of Mentoring

Recent evidence suggests that the beneficial effects of mentoring for individuals' careers are stronger for people from high socioeconomic backgrounds than for those from relatively low socioeconomic backgrounds. (*Source:* Based on findings reported by Whitely, Dougherty, & Dreher, 1991; see Note 38.)

Test Bank question 9.37 relates to material on this page.

relatively underprivileged backgrounds are less likely to reap such benefits. Whitely and his colleagues found no difference in the *amount* of mentoring received by people from contrasting backgrounds. Thus, these findings do not seem to derive from the fact that people from lower socioeconomic backgrounds simply receive less mentoring. Why, then, do they benefit from such help to a lesser degree? One possibility may involve differences in the focus of mentoring activities received by the two groups. People from high socioeconomic backgrounds may receive mentoring directed toward enhancing their careers—efforts by mentors to make them visible, to sponsor them and their ideas, and so on. In contrast, people from lower socioeconomic backgrounds may receive mentoring directed, at least in part, to their social and emotional needs—to help them overcome low self-confidence and fit into a social world with which they are relatively unfamiliar.[39] To the extent that this is the case, it is not surprising that mentoring has a stronger effect on career outcomes such as promotions and compensation for people from high as opposed to low socioeconomic backgrounds. Whatever the basis, mentoring is clearly not equally beneficial, or beneficial in the same ways, for all groups of employees. In these times of increasing diversity in the work force, this issue deserves careful attention.

Gender Differences and Mentoring   Recent evidence suggests that some of the early claims for the powerful benefits of mentorship were probably somewhat overstated.[40] Still, having an experienced, powerful mentor does seem helpful in many situations and gives at least some young people an important edge. Unfortunately, this conclusion has unsettling implications for women, who often seem to have less access to suitable mentors than men do. Several factors contribute to this state of affairs.[41] First, there are simply fewer senior female executives available to serve as mentors for young female employees. Second, females have fewer formal and informal opportunities than men do for developing mentoring relationships. They lack access to informal settings such as clubs and sports activities where mentor-protégé relationships take shape. And since they tend to occupy relatively low-level positions in many organizations, they simply do not have much contact with higher status people who might serve as potential mentors. Finally, women may fear that efforts to obtain male mentors will be misinterpreted by other organization members as sexual advances. On the other side of the coin, potential male mentors may shy away from establishing mentorship relationships with female employees for much the same reason, or simply because they view such relationships as more complex than ones with male subordinates.[42]

Do women actually perceive greater barriers to gaining mentors than men? Revealing evidence on this issue is provided by a study conducted by Ragins and Cotton.[43] These researchers asked more than 800 employees of three research and development organizations to answer questions pertaining to perceived barriers to obtaining a mentor. Preliminary analyses indicated that such barriers came under several major categories: restricted access to mentors, reluctance to initiate such a relationship, willingness of potential mentors to assume this role, approval of others, and potential misinterpretations of mentoring relationships by other people. Additional findings confirmed the hypothesis that women would perceive such barriers to be stronger than would men. As shown in Figure 9–8, female employees of the three organizations reported greater reluctance to approach mentors, lower willingness of potential mentors to adopt this role, greater disapproval on the part of others, and greater fear that such a relationship would be misinterpreted than did male employees. Interestingly, despite these perceived differences with respect to such barriers, male and female employees did not differ significantly in terms of having actually obtained mentors: 55 percent for males versus 49.5 percent for females. These findings suggest that females face greater obstacles to obtaining mentors but

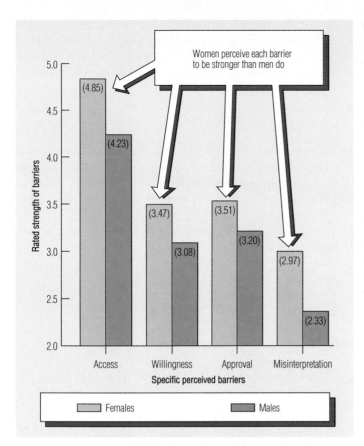

FIGURE 9–8

Gender Differences in
Perceived Barriers to
Mentorship

As shown here, women
perceive stronger
barriers to obtaining a
mentor at work than do
men. Such differences
exist with respect to
several barriers to
mentorship. (Higher
numbers indicate
stronger perceived
barriers.) (*Source:* Based
on data from Ragins &
Cotton, 1991; see Note
42.)

exert extra effort to overcome these barriers. If this is actually the case, then this
may constitute another subtle barrier to achievement by females in work settings.
Clearly, organizations should take active steps to lessen gender differences in access
to mentors so that the dice do not remain loaded against females with respect to this
important process.

CAREERS: HOW WORK AND WORK EXPERIENCES CHANGE THROUGHOUT LIFE

"Change," it is often said, "is the only constant." Where the course of working life
is concerned, this comment certainly seems accurate. During their working years
(which typically fill from four to five decades), most individuals experience major
shifts with respect to their work. The tasks they perform, the status they enjoy, the
roles they play, their geographic location, the compensation they receive—all these
features of working life, plus many others, can alter radically as the decades slip by.
Together, such changes constitute an individual's **career**. More formally, careers can
be defined as *the sequence of attitudes and behaviors associated with work-related
activities experienced by individuals over the span of their working lives.*[44]

Although work-related changes are certainly important, they are only part of the
total picture. As individuals move through various stages or portions of their careers,
they are also moving from one stage of life to another. Youth is replaced by maturity,
which gives way to middle age, and so on. This inexorable movement through the
life span, and the changes in family obligations and personal relationships it brings,
is often closely linked to changes in individuals' careers. Thus, isolation of one of
these topics (careers) from the other (development during adult life) is impossible.

Recognizing this fact, we will call attention to the links between careers and life events and change at several points. Such an approach is consistent with recent research on the course of individual careers (**career development**), and also with the major theme of this entire chapter: change throughout the course of working life.[45]

When people change careers, they often do so because they feel that their work is not particularly meaningful or satisfying. This encourages them to seek careers that *are* motivating and fulfilling. A growing number of professionals have found this fulfillment by leaving their former occupations and

Career Changes: Basic Dimensions

All careers are unique, but viewed from the perspective of an outside observer, most seem to develop along three basic dimensions.[46] First, careers often involve *vertical movement*—promotions up the hierarchy within an organization. Of course, different individuals working in different settings experience vertical movement at tremendously different rates.

Second, careers often involve *horizontal movement*. This reflects changes in specific job functions or, more rarely, in major fields or specialties. For example, people

 OB IN PRACTICE

Is Your Career on Track? Changing Perspectives on Personal Progress

If you are reading this book, it is a good bet that you are concerned about your future career—and about making progress in it. Members of the *counterculture*, after all, don't usually enroll in courses focused on behavior in work settings. But how does one go about judging success with respect to one's career? In the past, such judgments seemed relatively simple: career success was evaluated in terms of the speed with which individuals rose through the ranks. How many promotions they obtained, and at what ages, were the guiding principles. And closely linked to such matters was the issue of compensation. An old rule, used by many people in the 1960s and 1970s, was "A successful person is one whose salary equals his or her age × $1,000." Inflation has made that rule obsolete, but the principle remains clear: success in one's career was judged in terms of a few concrete criteria.

Now the picture has changed radically. First, promotions in many organizations are much rarer and harder to come by than was true in the past. Today's "lean and mean" organizations cannot afford a large number of managerial levels. As a result, opportunities for promotion have been reduced, and people are staying at the same level longer than ever before. Consider Susan Doten, manager of marketing in Quaker Oats'

pet food division. Doten moved quickly through six jobs in nine years. But then she reached a level above which the managerial pyramid flattened out considerably. As she puts it: "I will hang out at this level for a lot longer than I hung out at the lower levels. There are about thirteen marketing directors in U.S. grocery products, then only four vice presidents of marketing at the next level." And projections suggest that this promotion squeeze will tighten even more in the years ahead: by the year 2000, most large companies will probably have half as many management levels as they have today.[48]

Reductions in the number of promotions available indicate that increasing numbers of people will find it necessary to accept *lateral moves*—changes in jobs that do not carry greater responsibility, status, or pay. Such moves can be very beneficial, however. By accepting them, individuals can learn more about the business and expand the scope of their personal networks. Also, by shifting to another job—and another promotion track—people may increase the number of upward moves available to them. Consider the experience of Anne Pol, an employee of Pitney Bowes. Five years ago, she left a senior position in human resources to accept a position within her company as a plant manager. This gave her the operating experience she needed to be considered for higher-level jobs at

trained in engineering often shift from working as practicing engineers into management or administrative roles. Similarly, individuals who start out in marketing may move into sales or vice versa. In recent years, growing numbers of people have been willing to make such a horizontal move, even though it may involve a considerable amount of retraining.[47] Presumably, this trend reflects society's growing interest in self-fulfillment through one's work.

Finally, careers also involve what Schein terms *radial movement*, toward the inner circle of management in an organization. Such movement often follows vertical movement (i.e., promotion), but not always. For example, an individual may receive a promotion that moves her out of the central office, where real power resides, and into a branch or subsidiary operation. The promotion is real, but the individual is now farther away from the organization's inner circle than before. (How do people determine whether their careers are on track—whether they are making the kind of progress they want to make? For some insight into this issue, see the **OB in Practice** section that starts on the preceding page.)

becoming teachers. Given recent increases in teachers' salaries and efforts to speed up the certification process, the shift into teaching has become a reality for many formerly dissatisfied professionals. Most of the professionals who have made this career change report that they were unhappy with their former jobs and wanted to do something more satisfying, such as helping a student make it through high school. [Tifft, S. (1989, February 13). The lure of the classroom. *Time*, p. 69]

Pitney Bowes. After a stint in manufacturing, she returned to take the top job in personnel—but only with the guarantee that she could go back to operations later. Recently, she moved again, this time to a position as vice president for manufacturing operations. In Pol's case, then, several lateral moves did pay off.

Perhaps an even more dramatic shift related to judging career success, and one attached primarily to the baby-boom generation, involves a willingness to trade off earnings for more time with one's family or simply for feelings of inner fulfillment. In other words, increasing numbers of people are judging their own success in terms of personal happiness rather than high earnings and other outward signs of achievement. As

Philip Seiden, an IBM physicist who voluntarily left a senior management position at IBM to concentrate on basic research, puts it: "If you haven't made it in society's eyes, who cares? Have you made it in your own eyes? That's what really matters. If you're happy, why do more? To satisfy your mother-in-law?"[49]

So, as Table 9–3 indicates, today's managers evaluate their own success, and the status of their careers, quite differently from managers of previous decades. Whether such changes are good or bad is, of course, in the eye of the beholder. But at the very least, they do seem to reflect the enormous shifts that have occurred in society in recent years, and that in itself can be viewed as a plus.

TABLE 9–3   Career Success: Then and Now

The criteria individuals apply to judge the success of their careers have changed sharply in recent years.

How Career Success Was Judged in the Past	How Career Success Is Judged Now
All career moves must be upward	Lateral moves can be desirable
Promotions within two years	Jobs last considerably longer
Success means job security	Success means inner fulfillment
Good pay = age × $1,000	Good pay package includes equity stake and/or profit sharing
Work week is forty hours; evenings and weekends for family	Work lasts until job is done

Source: Based on suggestions by Kirkpatrick, 1990; see Note 48.

Test Bank question 9.40 relates to material on this page.

Career Development and Life Stages

At the same time that careers develop along the dimensions noted above, they also seem to move through repeated cycles of stability and change.[50] Soon after an individual has been hired or promoted to a new position, a stage of *career growth* occurs. During this period, individuals consolidate their recent gains by acquiring the new skills and information needed to perform their current jobs effectively. As this process is completed, they enter a stage of *stabilization,* in which they are performing their jobs to their fullest capacity and things are on a (temporary) even keel. This is followed by a period of *transition,* in which individuals prepare themselves, psychologically, for their next move upward. During this period, they anticipate the demands of their next career stage and get ready to meet them. When the expected promotion arrives, the cycle starts over again. In short, the careers of many individuals are marked by a process in which they grow into each new position, become acclimated to it, and then begin preparations for the next step on the ladder (see Figure 9–9).

Crosscutting this cycle are important critical choice points that most people face in their career planning. These are age-related and occur for different individuals at different points on the cycle of growth, stabilization, and transition noted above.[51]

The first of these critical age-related choice points arises at about age thirty, when many people confront a number of decisions that are either irreversible or difficult to change. Should they marry? Start a family? Stick with their present career or seek another one? Make career or family central in their lives? Such issues must be faced and resolved, and the decisions individuals make with respect to each will strongly affect the remainder of their lives.

The second occurs during the early forties. At this time, individuals must decide whether to have a last child—or any—before, biologically, it is too late. Perhaps even more important, this is the period during which most people first come face to face with their own mortality. Signs of age become more obvious, and many individuals undergo a subtle shift in perceptions of their own life span. Prior to age forty, most think in terms of how long they have lived—their current age. After forty, an increasing proportion begin to think in terms of how many years they have left until retirement, or until death. That many people must now confront the limits of their careers adds to the stress of this mid-life period. They can see with increasing clarity just how far they can realistically expect to go, and by what margin they will fall short of attaining cherished dreams and hopes of glory. In the light of such conclusions, they must decide to remain with the same organization or strike out on new career paths different from the ones they originally charted. Time, it seems, is running out, and this may be the last opportunity for initiating radical change.

The final critical choice point occurs as individuals move into their late fifties. The key question here is, how should they spend the rest of their lives? Should they become deeply involved in the lives of children and grandchildren, or remain focused on their own lives and activities? Should they remain active at work or begin a gradual process of withdrawal? Should they move out of their current home (which may be

FIGURE 9–9

The Career Change Cycle

Careers often move through repeated cycles of *career growth, stabilization,* and *transition.*

Career growth	Stabilization	Transition
Acquisition of new skills and information needed for current job	Current job is being performed to fullest capacity	Preparation for next career move

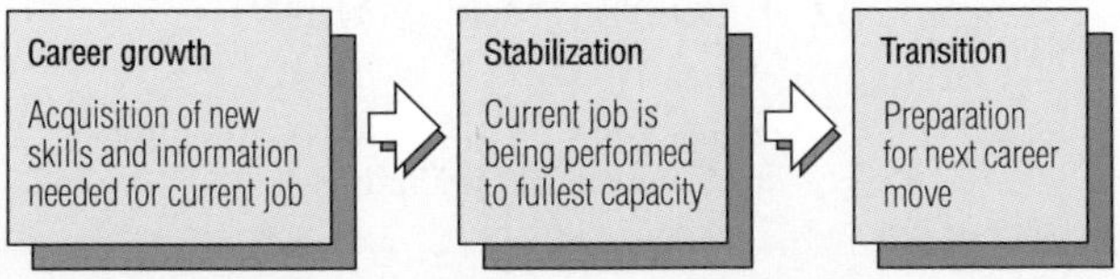

Test Bank questions 9.41–9.42, 9.53, and 9.73 relate to material on this page.

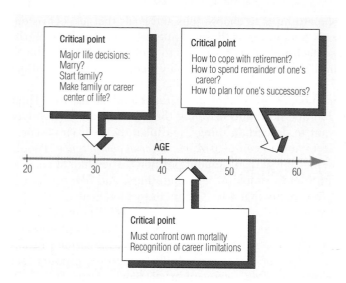

FIGURE 9–10

Critical Choice Points during Adult Life

Change occurs throughout life. However, research findings suggest that several critical choice points are especially stressful for many people. These occur at about age thirty, in the early forties, and again in the late fifties.

far too large now that their children are grown)? What kind of retirement do they want, and how should they plan for it? Questions such as these must be answered as individuals begin seriously contemplating the end of their own careers and their coming *retirement.* (See Figure 9–10 for a summary of these key life choice points.)

Clearly, age-related factors in individuals' lives have an important bearing on their careers. The proverbial *biological clock* is indeed always running, and individuals must take it carefully into account as they map the course of their careers, and weigh the responsibilities of families and other interests against the demands of their jobs and professions.

Career Issues: Early, Middle, and Late

At different points in life, we face different issues or problems. The twenties are a time of getting started—choosing a career, getting established in it, selecting a mate. For many people, the thirties bring rising family responsibilities, as they start or add to their families. The forties bring a mid-life crisis for at least some individuals, as they realize that they are now as close to the end as to the beginning, and come to terms with the fact that they will never achieve many of their youthful dreams. And so the process continues: different concerns and problems during different decades of life.

In a corresponding manner, different stages of our careers are also marked by contrasting issues. Because these are often divided into issues relating to *early, middle,* and *late* career stages, we will consider them in this way here.

Early Career Issues Perhaps the key task faced by individuals during their early careers is *career planning.* This is when most of us must map the course of our future careers, deciding what types of jobs and activities we will pursue in the decades that follow. How do we make such decisions? What factors lead us to select one path over all the others? One intriguing answer is provided by the concept of *career anchors,* first proposed by Schein.[52] According to Schein, an expert on careers and career development, by the time individuals enter their early thirties, most have fairly clear ideas or *self-perceptions* of their talents and abilities, needs and motives, and attitudes and values. Together, these self-perceptions come to guide and stabilize

Starting a career often begins with getting a college degree. But choosing a field of study is often difficult. For example, 60 percent of the students who entered science, math, or engineering programs in U.S. colleges as undergraduates changed their minds and switched to other majors. This high dropout rate was a concern for the National Science Foundation, which conducted a study to determine the reasons for it. The study revealed some surprising findings. The "switchers" and "nonswitchers" were equally as talented and hard working. However, the difference between them was that the switchers did not have the kind of support available to them (e.g., study support groups) to help them get over the rough spots that the nonswitchers did. Thus, people may change their fields of study because of the lack of needed support available rather than their underlying ability or interest. [Cipra, B. (1991, October 18). They'd rather switch than fight. *Science, 254,* 370–371.]

a person's career, as he or she attempts to choose jobs and goals that are consistent with these basic characteristics. Schein terms these self-perceptions **career anchors,** because they tend to firmly attach individuals' careers to their underlying abilities, needs, and values. Everyone has such anchors, but they may take several distinct forms.

For some people, career anchors are *technical* or *functional* in nature. Their primary concern in making job decisions and mapping their future careers involves the *content* of work. They want to do certain things, and plan their careers accordingly. For a second group, career anchors emphasize *managerial competence.* People in this category want to attain high-level management positions. They like to analyze and solve difficult business problems, enjoy influencing others, and like exercising power. Thus, they choose career paths that will lead them to such goals.

A third group is primarily concerned with *security* and *stability.* Their search for security often leads them to enter large, stable companies, and long-term employment with a single firm. A fourth group, in contrast, emphasizes *creativity* or *entrepreneurship* in career plans. Such people want to build or create a product that is unique and of their own devising. They are good at starting and running small companies but, like Mitch Kapor of Lotus Development fame, they may choose to leave when these organizations become too large and bureaucratic in nature. Finally, some individuals emphasize *autonomy* and *independence.* They want to be free of external constraints, and prefer to work at their own pace and set their own goals. Such people often select careers in academia and professional writing, or prefer to run their own small businesses. (See Figure 9–11 for a summary of these different career anchors.)

Although the task of identifying their abilities, motives, and values is important, it is hardly the only issue individuals face during the early portion of their careers. In addition, they must confront relatively frequent *job changes*—ones stemming from transfers and promotions. Although such changes can be beneficial to individuals' careers, they involve considerable costs, both for organizations and for the people involved. Individuals who are transferred or promoted are expected to "hit the floor running"—to demonstrate high performance from the very start. Further, such demands occur just when they must establish new networks of social support, learn new skills, and eliminate old patterns of behavior and attitudes no longer

FIGURE 9–11

Career Anchors

Individuals' perceptions of their own abilities, motives, and values often serve as *career anchors.* People attempt to choose jobs and goals consistent with these characteristics. Career anchors often emphasize one or more of the factors shown here. (*Source:* Based on suggestions by Schein, 1978; see Note 50.)

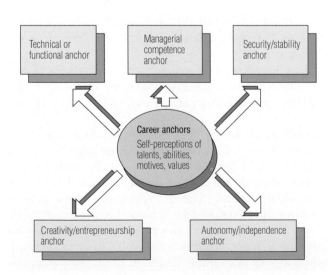

appropriate to their new position. Clearly, this is an unsettling combination of events, but one that must be handled successfully if individuals are to stay on track with respect to their own career plans.

One hazard faced by at least some people early in their careers is also worth noting—a danger described by Lewicki as **organizational seduction.**[53] This refers to situations in which the promise of rapid promotions and raises encourages young employees to make career moves that are actually against their best long-term interests. How do organizations "seduce" talented individuals into making such decisions? According to Lewicki, through a combination of challenging, stimulating work, extremely pleasant work environments, and many opportunities to fulfill rising status needs (e.g., they are provided with memberships in prestigious clubs, invited to meetings with top management). If they succumb to such inducement, individuals become deeply committed to the organization—so much so that they are willing to sacrifice virtually all other aspects of their lives to their work, and experience intense guilt if they even think about leaving. The costs of allowing oneself to fall into this trap can be high, so young and ambitious people should be on guard against doing so unless they have carefully considered all the costs and ramifications.

Middle Career Issues   As we noted earlier, age forty marks the end of the dream for many people. At this point, they realize they will never go as far as they had hoped and will never fulfill many of their fondest dreams.[54] At the same time, people in this age group find that because they have already risen to fairly high-level positions within their organizations, fewer and fewer promotions are available for them. As if this were not enough, when they glance back over their shoulders they see hordes of ambitious younger people, more energetic and better trained (technically) than themselves, pushing up from behind. No wonder many people find turning forty an unsettling experience!

The key issue facing individuals in the middle part of their careers is this: since I can't get where I really hoped to be, what can I do instead? Some people, of course, answer this question by retreating into cynicism and apathy. As we saw in chapter 7, they experience *burnout* and become liabilities to themselves and to their companies. Fortunately, however, there are other, more constructive ways of handling this dilemma.

First, individuals can choose to become *mentors*. In fact, at this stage in their careers they are expected to assume such a role in many organizations. Since we have already described the satisfactions and benefits of serving as a mentor, there's no need to elaborate on this career path here.

Second, individuals at this stage of their careers can remain active in their work, but expand their interests so that they no longer focus exclusively on their jobs. This can involve a conscious decision to spend more time with their families, the development of new hobbies, and related actions. People who choose this route forgo some of the potential that may remain in their careers. However, they derive adequate satisfaction from other sources, and so remain personally happy and emotionally secure.

Another, and related, issue many people face in mid-career is the discovery that they have reached a **career plateau.**[55] In short, they find that they have arrived at a point from which they are unlikely to gain further promotions or be given increased responsibility and authority. They are at a virtual dead end in their careers. What leads to this state of affairs? Potentially, several factors. First, as noted earlier, some individuals consciously choose to put a brake on their own careers. They may not wish to take on added responsibility, or they don't want to leave a particular geographic region. Others find themselves part of a two-career family, and wish to maximize joint outcomes for both members. People in these categories can retain a high level of performance, even though they have little chance of advancement. For others, however, entry onto a career plateau is less voluntary. They may have failed to keep up with developments in their fields, and so no longer possess the skills and knowledge required for further promotions. Alternatively, they may find themselves in a company suffering from slow growth or no growth at all. Such a pattern severely restricts the number of promotions available, and traps at least some organization members in their present jobs.

Fortunately, involuntary career plateaus do not have to be permanent. By recognizing the need for change and taking such steps as seeking retraining, developing alternate roles within the organization (e.g., serving as a mentor), or actually moving to another job, some people, at least, can escape from such dead ends and the malaise that often accompanies them. To help employees cope with such problems and plan effectively for the development of their own careers, many organizations have established **career management programs**.

Late Career Issues   Studs Terkel once suggested, somewhat tongue-in-cheek, that there are five distinct stages to careers.[56] He summarized these by the following statements:

> "Who is this guy, John Fortune?"
> "Gee, it would be great if we could get that guy, what's his name?"
> "If we could only get John Fortune."
> "I'd like to get a young John Fortune."
> "Who's John Fortune?"

These statements suggest that with careers, as with almost anything else, what goes up usually, at some point, also comes down. This is the key issue most individuals face in the later years of their careers. Many find that they have indeed gone as far as they can go, and have either accomplished key goals or will never be able to achieve them. They must also come to terms with the fact that, like their physical energies, their power and influence within the organization are beginning to wane.

Yet another, related problem faced by older employees is that they increasingly become the subject of negative stereotypes. Typically, they are viewed as being less productive, efficient, motivated, and capable of working under pressure than younger people. And such stereotypes persist despite strong evidence that they are inaccurate. Indeed, one recent review of previous research on the relationship between age and job performance suggests that older workers (perhaps because of their greater experience) are actually *more* productive than younger ones![57] Still, the stereotypes remain and are a fact of life for many individuals as they approach the end of their careers.

Another late career issue for many people is *job succession*—who will take over when they retire? Few people who have spent years building up a business or department take this matter lightly. They want someone to follow in their footsteps who shares their values and will maintain the standards they have established. What sort of successors should they seek in order to attain these goals? The results of an intriguing study by McCall and Lombardo offer some tentative answers.[58]

These researchers interviewed top executives and human resource managers in several large corporations. The goal of the project was uncovering differences between managers who made it to the top and were perceived as highly successful and those whose careers were somehow derailed along the way. Results indicated that highly successful people—ones most of us would choose as current leaders or as future successors—possess a mixed bag of desirable characteristics. They are bright, ana-

Lack of adequate succession planning is a problem plaguing business. Of the 15 million businesses in America, 90 percent of them are family owned and managed. Unfortunately, the average family-owned business has a life expectancy of only twenty-four years (the amount of time the founder is able to work). Only one-third of all family businesses successfully pass the reins on to the next generation

lytical thinkers who are highly motivated for success, but maintain a good sense of humor and are skilled in dealing with others. They work hard and expect high commitment and effort from others, but are also diplomatic and avoid confrontations whenever possible. Obviously, identifying such people is an important goal for all organizations, and is especially crucial for top managers as they begin the search for an excellent successor.

Another issue individuals face late in their careers is coming to terms with retirement. This involves a gradual reorientation away from their careers and work toward the leisure-time activities that will become dominant during retirement. In addition, it should involve careful planning to meet the special challenges faced by retired workers—a loss of social contact with many friends, reduced feelings of accomplishment, reduced earnings. Fortunately, growing evidence suggests that if individuals take the time to prepare for such factors, the end of their working years can be a new beginning. It can mark entry into a period of renewed personal growth and fulfillment, rather than merely signaling inevitable decline. (Existing evidence suggests that most people, regardless of their gender or ethnic background, face the kinds of issues described above as they move through various stages of their careers. But it is also clear that not all groups attain equal career outcomes. See the **International/Multicultural Perspective** section on pp. 340–341 for information on this issue.)

Careers in the 1990s: Some Critical Current Issues

Although organizations often seem to be worlds unto themselves, they do not exist in a social vacuum. On the contrary, they closely mirror events and trends occurring in the societies around them. We have already commented, in this chapter and elsewhere, on the far-reaching effects on organizations of increasing ethnic diversity in the work force. But this is only one way in which the everchanging patterns of modern societies affect organizations and the people working in them. In this final section, we will examine two important issues with major implications for the lives and careers of tens of millions of individuals: the strains and inner conflicts that often result from *two-career families*, and the potentially devastating effects of increased rates of *unemployment*.

Two-Career Families: When Work and Home Collide   Earlier in this chapter, we noted that the proportion of females in the work force has risen sharply in the past three decades. The causes behind this shift are complex, including economic factors (continued inflation and the need for additional family income) and social ones (increasing motivation to pursue careers on the part of many women). Whatever the causes, however, the facts are clear: in most families, including families with young children, both parents are now employed on a full-time basis.[59] The traditional pattern, in which males are the primary breadwinners and females remain at home to care for children and complete various household chores, has all but vanished in many industrialized nations.

The benefits of this shift are obvious: increased family income and enhanced opportunities for women. The costs, however, are also readily apparent. With both parents working, child care becomes a key issue. Further, with both parents absent from the home for many hours each day and the obligations of competing schedules, opportunities for family gatherings and interactions are sharply reduced. Needless to say, such difficulties are even greater for single-parent families—another growing household pattern in the United States and elsewhere.

These effects do not flow merely from work to family life, however; rather, this is very much a two-way street, in which obligations and roles at home can—and

(after the founder leaves), and only 15 percent of the businesses last long enough to see the founder's grandchildren take over. The use of adequate succession plans could drastically improve these survival rates for family-owned businesses. [Cohen, G. (1990, July 9). Why you can't keep it all in the family. *U.S. News & World Report,* pp. 36–37; Warner, J. (1991, September 30). Nothing succeeds like a succession plan. *Business* Week, pp. 126–127.]

often do—affect performance at work. In the past, most individuals (especially men) tended to put their careers ahead of their family obligations. If their jobs called, they answered, even if it meant neglecting various aspects of home and family life. Now, however, the picture is changing. An increasing number of employees are putting the needs of their families on a par with—or even ahead of—those of their careers.[60] This trend is especially visible among employees in their twenties, who have watched older colleagues, older brothers and sisters, or even their own parents struggle with

AN INTERNATIONAL/MULTICULTURAL PERSPECTIVE

Race and Career Outcomes in the United States: Different and Still Unequal

 First, the good news: the number of black people occupying managerial positions in the United States has risen substantially in recent years. In the 1970s, only about 3 percent of all managers were black; by the 1990s, this figure had doubled, to more than 6 percent.[61] In this sense, at least, black people have made visible, concrete progress. Now for the bad news: blacks occupying managerial positions continue to experience less favorable career outcomes than whites. They often receive lower performance evaluations than whites, and higher proportions of blacks than whites are stuck at career plateaus. What accounts for such outcomes? One answer involves what several authors have termed **treatment discrimination**.[62] In such discrimination, people belonging to minority groups receive fewer rewards, resources, or opportunities on the job than do others. Thus, they are not denied access to managerial jobs; but once in them, they are held back from attaining success by poorer treatment and reduced opportunities. We hasten to add that such treatment discrimination is not necessarily intentional; it may sometimes arise because other organization members, being unfamiliar with blacks, feel somewhat uncomfortable around them. Alternatively, treatment discrimination may occur because some people hold unfavorable implicit assumptions about blacks and other minority group members. In other words, they believe that such people are not capable of excellent work, even while supporting efforts to hire and promote them.

Is treatment discrimination a reality? Does it contribute to the poorer career outcomes experienced by blacks in the United States? A recent study by Greenhaus, Parasuraman, and Wormley examined these issues.[63] In this investigation, several hundred black managers and white managers provided information on their organizational experiences. Their supervisors also provided job evaluations for these managers and ratings of their promotability. Finally, the number of years the managers had occupied their present positions was used to assess the extent to which they had reached career plateaus.

Greenhaus and his colleagues proposed a model in which race exerted its effects on career outcomes through its impact on managers' organizational experiences (see Figure 9–12). In other words, they expected that the effects of race on career outcomes would be indirect, operating through the mechanism of contrasting organizational experiences. Some support for this model was obtained. Race did influence ratings of promotability indirectly, through its impact on job discretion and two aspects of job performance evaluations. And as the model predicted, blacks did perceive themselves as having less discretion in their jobs and reported lower organizational acceptance than whites. However, in general, race seemed to exert *direct* rather than indirect effects on career outcomes. In other words, blacks were more likely to be at career plateaus, to report lower career satisfaction, and to receive lower job performance evaluations quite aside from the impact of poorer organizational experiences.

this problem. As a result, recruiters now find that they are often quizzed carefully by prospective employees about their organizations' policies concerning flexible scheduling, time off to care for ailing relatives, and child-care facilities. As Christian Kjeldsen, a vice president at Johnson & Johnson, puts it, "Work and family policies are now being viewed as a competitive tool. That wasn't the case five years ago."[64]

In response to these new demands, many organizations have established new policies designed to assist employees in balancing work and family obligations. As

What do these findings mean? One possibility is that experiences prior to entering the organization, such as poorer educational opportunities, contribute to the reduced career outcomes of blacks. Such differences may serve as handicaps for black managers, interfering with their climb up the corporate ladder. Another possibility is that race differences in job performance evaluations stem from bias in the rating process itself rather than from actual differences in the performance of blacks and whites. To the extent that such bias exists, it, too, may reduce the career outcomes of black managers.

Whatever the precise explanation, it is clear that although blacks have gained entry to an increasing number of responsible, managerial jobs, their outcomes in these positions are by no means equal to those of whites. Equality of *opportunity*, of course, does not imply a guarantee of equality of *outcome*. In organizations, as in life, rewards must go to those who contribute most and achieve the highest levels of performance. But the fact that black managers continue to experience poorer career outcomes than white managers is disturbing, and should be addressed with care. Is equality of opportunity in U.S. organizations a reality or merely an illusion? This is a complex question with no simple answers. Clearly, however, merely hiring blacks and other minorities as managers is only one step in the right direction. Unless such people are then assured equal opportunities to grow and develop, the process can quickly turn into an empty sham—one in which hopes are raised only to be quickly dashed. The moral for all organizations, therefore, is as follows: take vigorous steps to assure that *all* employees have the kind of experiences that will help them reach their fullest potential.

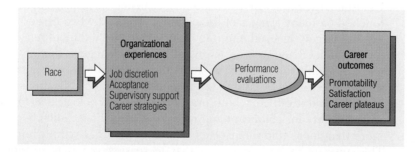

FIGURE 9–12   Race, Organizational Experiences, and Career Outcomes

One model seeking to explain the poorer career outcomes experienced by black managers in the United States suggests that these effects occur because of *treatment discrimination*—less favorable organizational experiences for black managers. However, research designed to test this model suggests that race may actually affect career outcomes in a more direct fashion. (*Source:* Based on suggestions by Greenhaus, Parasuraman, & Wormley, 1990; see Note 63.)

TABLE 9–4   "Family-Friendly" Policies

An increasing number of organizations are establishing policies designed to relieve some of the burdens faced by two-career families and single parents.

Company	Programs
Johnson & Johnson	Family care leave; child care; community child-care centers and subsidies
IBM	Flexible scheduling; leaves of absence; work-at-home programs; funds to improve quality of child care
Aetna Life & Casualty	Job sharing; part-time work; flexible hours; school-holiday program; work at home
Corning	Child care; part-time work; summer camps; after-school programs

Source: Information reported by Shellenbarger, 1991; see Note 60.

shown in Table 9–4, these policies are varied in form, and touch on aspects of working life such as flexible scheduling, job sharing, and child-care facilities. Increasingly, companies that do not provide such benefits are finding it difficult to compete for the best employees. Thus, the trend is clear: the days when young parents were willing to sacrifice virtually all aspects and joys of family life on the altar of their careers are coming to a close. A new generation of young employees, having witnessed such sacrifices themselves, has drawn the line; and woe to the organizations that do not recognize this.

Gender Differences in Work-Family Conflict   Our discussion up to this point has touched on many aspects of the difficulties faced by two-career (or two-job) families, but has largely ignored one important point: these difficulties do not fall with equal weight on men and women. Growing evidence suggests that in the struggle between work and family obligations, women often suffer even more than men.[65] Many women seem quite willing to assume the responsibilities and obligations of a full-time career, but they find it difficult, both practically and psychologically, to give up the primary responsibility for child care and managing many household chores. The result: they, more than men, find themselves having to perform two full-time jobs instead of one. This appears to be one reason that increasing numbers of female executives are withdrawing from the work force; they simply find it impossible to continue to meet both sets of obligations as they grow somewhat older.[66]

Direct evidence for the suggestion that women find conflict between work and family obligations somewhat more stressful than men is provided by a study conducted by Duxbury and Higgins.[67] They had several hundred male and female managers complete a questionnaire that assessed the degree to which they experienced work conflict (incompatible pressures at work), work expectations (demands of their jobs), family conflict (incompatible pressures at home), family expectations (demands of their family roles), and work-family conflict (interrole conflict in which role pressures from work and family domains are incompatible). The researchers predicted that in some cases, relationships between these variables would be stronger for men than for women, whereas in others the reverse would be true. As shown in Table 9–5, the general predictions were confirmed. For example, work conflict was a better predictor of family conflict for men than for women; this suggests that for men, tensions and pressures at work spilled over, more easily, into tensions and conflict at home. In contrast, family conflict was a stronger determinant of work-family conflict for women than for men. For women, competing pressures at home played a larger role in generating conflict between experienced work and family obligations. In short, the burdens of juggling work obligations and family obligations appear to take an important toll on both genders. However, in some respects, females seem to bear the brunt of such problems.

Unemployment: Adverse Effects of a Disturbing Trend   Unemployment is far from a new problem; economic recessions and depressions have occurred with unsettling regularity for at least the past several centuries—with predictable effects on the availability of jobs. What seems to be new to the present decade, however, is the extent to which unemployment now affects white-collar as well as blue-collar employees. Unemployment among managers and others with technical educations appears to be on the rise. And some experts predict that this trend will continue, so that by the year 2000, many organizations will have only half the number of managers on their payrolls that they have at present.[68]

We have already considered some of the effects of unemployment in chapter 7, where we noted that being confronted with an impending layoff—or even the possibility that one's job is no longer secure—is a major cause of work-related stress.[69] Such people often feel betrayed and deserted by their organizations, especially if they are longtime employees who have spent much of their working careers with a single company. Here, we add that the effects on *survivors*—those employees who remain after downsizing or other types of layoff—are also often distressing. In a series of studies on this issue, Brockner, Davy, and Carter have found that following layoffs, survivors often experience an unsettling mixture of guilt and anxiety.[70] The guilt arises from the belief that it is somehow unfair that they have retained their jobs whereas others, who are equally talented and motivated, have been fired. In

Unemployment is a problem that is difficult to combat because it is tied to the production levels of the entire country. For example, it takes about a 1 percent growth in the gross national product (GNP) of the United States to reduce the unemployment rate by one-third of 1 percent. Thus, as the GNP is only expected to increase at less than 3 percent in the coming years, the level of unemployment may not change very much during this period. [Pomice, E., & Hawkins, D. (1991, June 17). The misery continues. *U.S. News & World Report*, pp. 50–53.]

TABLE 9–5   Gender Differences in Work-Family Conflict

As predicted, women and men experience conflict between work demands or expectations and family demands or expectations differentially. In some cases, relationships between work and family-related factors are stronger for females, whereas in others such relationships are stronger for males.

Relationships Stronger for Women	Relationships Stronger for Men
Work involvement and work-family conflict	Family involvement and work-family conflict
Family expectations and work-family conflict	Work expectations and work-family conflict
Family conflict and work-family conflict	Work conflict and family conflict
Quality of working life and life satisfaction	Quality of family life and work-family conflict
	Quality of family life and life satisfaction

Source: Based on data from Duxbury & Higgins, 1991; see Note 67.

short, survivors often feel *overrewarded* relative to their less fortunate coworkers. The anxiety, of course, involves the belief that they will soon be next. As Richard Leifer, one researcher who has studied the effects of downsizing on employees, puts it: "There's a survivor syndrome. People who are left feel guilt, for example, and anxiety that it's going to happen again."[71] Management often contributes to such feelings, failing to communicate to employees the overall plan for downsizing or plant closings. Because these people are left in the dark about the final goals, they often imagine the worst—scenarios and final outcomes that are actually more negative than those planned by the company. The result: people the organization wants to retain begin to leave, too, rather than face the high levels of stress generated by uncertainty about the future of their jobs.

The negative effects of unemployment are perhaps most clearly illustrated by longitudinal research conducted by Winefield and his colleagues.[72] In a series of investigations, these researchers followed hundreds of recent graduates in Australia for an eight-year period. At various points during this interval, participants in the study completed questionnaires designed to measure their self-esteem, feelings of depression, negative affect, and general health. Subjects also reported on whether they were unemployed, and the extent to which they found their jobs satisfactory.

Results indicated that as expected, unemployment had many negative effects on these young people (see Figure 9–13). Unemployed individuals, and also those who reported being dissatisfied with their jobs, reported lower self-esteem, greater depression, more negative affect, and poorer personal health than those who were employed in jobs with which they were quite satisfied. Additional findings indicated that these differences increased over time, primarily because people employed in

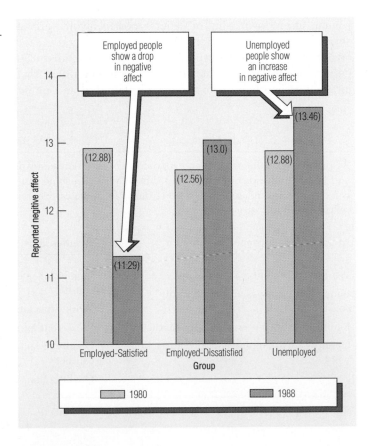

FIGURE 9–13

Adverse Effects of Unemployment

Individuals who reported being satisfactorily employed showed improvements in self-esteem, psychological well-being, and personal health over time. In contrast, people who were unemployed or who reported being dissatisfied with their jobs did not demonstrate such improvements. (*Source:* Based on data from Winefield, Winefield, Tiggemann, & Goldney, 1991; see Note 72.)

jobs they liked showed gains with respect to most of these measures, whereas those who were unemployed, or employed in jobs they disliked, did not. In other words, the two groups diverged over time because being satisfactorily employed led to enhanced well-being and functioning. These findings are consistent with several theories of personal development suggesting that one key stage of early adulthood is finding a satisfactory personal identity through one's job or career.[73]

Additional findings reported by other researchers indicate that the negative effects of unemployment are stronger for people who show strong *commitment to work*—people for whom the desire to be engaged in paid employment is high.[74] Apparently, for such people to find, quite suddenly, that one of the central anchors of their lives has been severed is especially devastating. Unfortunately, it is precisely such work-oriented people who are most valuable to their organizations.

In sum, rising rates of unemployment in many industrialized countries pose a serious challenge to the health and well-being of individual employees, and to the productivity of organizations. Since unemployment results from cycles and factors beyond the control of organizations—perhaps beyond the control of governments as well—this problem is likely to persist in the years ahead. However, enlightened management can help to ease the pain of downsizing and other reductions in staff through several different steps: engaging in open, accurate communication with employees, running effective outplacement programs, explaining the criteria for choosing those who will go and those who will remain. By following such steps, organizations may reduce negative reactions on the part of survivors, and so increase the chances of attaining the goals they seek through reductions in work force: lowered costs and enhanced productivity.

SUMMARY AND REVIEW

Organizational Culture

The shared beliefs, attitudes, values, and expectations held by individuals in an organization constitute its **organizational culture**. Organizational culture involves shared meanings—interpretations of organizational events and actions. Organizational culture influences important processes such as commitment, job satisfaction, intentions to leave, and voluntary turnover. Such effects appear to be mediated by the degree of *person-organization fit*, the extent to which an organization's culture reflects values held by individual employees.

Organizational Socialization

The process through which newcomers learn the ropes in their organizations and become full-fledged members is known as **organizational socialization**. This process involves three distinct stages known, respectively, as *getting in*, *breaking in*, and *settling in*. **Realistic job previews** during recruitment of newcomers help them avoid unrealistically optimistic or pessimistic expectations about their future jobs. *Individualized socialization* tactics, which are infor-

mal and tailored to specific newcomers, appear to enhance an innovative perspective on jobs. In contrast, *institutionalized socialization* tactics, in which all newcomers pass through formal and identical procedures, seem to contribute to later commitment on the part of these people. **A mentor**, a more experienced employee who provides support and instruction to newcomers, often plays an important role in protégés' careers. The benefits of mentorship appear to be stronger for people from high than from low socioeconomic backgrounds.

Careers

The sequence of occupations and jobs individuals hold during their working lives constitutes their **career**. Most careers develop *vertically*, through promotions; *horizontally*, through different jobs or functions; and *radially*, toward inner circles of power within an organization. Crucial points in career planning coincide with movement through important life stages. Individuals face somewhat different issues at different stages of their careers. Important early career issues involve the establishment of **career anchors, job changes,** and **organizational seduction**.

Middle career issues involve coming to terms with the fact that all of one's hopes will not be realized, and the possibility of a **career plateau**. Late career issues involve accepting reduced power and influence, choosing one's successors, and preparing for retirement. Although the proportion of managers in the United States who are black has increased in recent years, recent evidence indicates that such people experience less favorable career outcomes than others. This appears to be due, at least in part, to **treatment discrimination**—less positive work experiences and opportunities. The careers of millions of people are currently affected by *work-family conflict*—incompatible pressures from work and family obligations, often generated by *two-career* (or two-job) *families*. Another issue currently affecting millions of people is that of growing rates of *unemployment* among white-collar as well as blue-collar employees. Growing evidence indicates that unemployment exerts adverse effects on self-esteem and physical health and produces tendencies toward depression.

KEY TERMS

career: The sequence of attitudes and behaviors associated with work-related activities experienced by individuals over the span of their working lives.

career anchors: Individuals' self-perceptions of their own abilities, motives, and values, and their efforts to choose jobs or careers consistent with these self-perceptions.

career development: The pattern of changes that occur during an individual's career.

career management (assistance) programs: Organization-sponsored programs designed to assist individuals in planning their careers.

career plateau: A point in a career from which an individual is unlikely to gain further promotions or receive increased responsibility.

entry shock: The confusion and disorientation experienced by many newcomers to an organization.

mentor: An older and more experienced employee who offers advice, assistance, and protection to a younger and less experienced one.

organizational culture: The shared attitudes, values, and expectations held by members of a given organization.

organizational seduction: A process through which an organization obtains extremely high levels of effort and commitment from young employees by providing them with highly attractive benefits (e.g., pleasant working conditions, opportunities to enhance their status).

organizational socialization: The process through which newcomers to an organization are converted to full-fledged members who share its major values and understand its policies and procedures.

realistic job previews: Accurate information concerning conditions within an organization, provided to potential employees prior to their decision to join the organization.

role orientation: The extent to which employees are willing to change various aspects of their jobs (an *innovative orientation*) or are unwilling to change aspects of their jobs (a *custodial orientation*).

treatment discrimination: Treatment under which people belonging to minority groups receive fewer rewards, resources, or opportunities on the job than do others. Such discrimination can function even when *access discrimination* (access to various jobs) has largely been eliminated.

QUESTIONS FOR DISCUSSION

1. It is often said that the founders of a company continue to influence it long after they have retired or departed for other reasons. Is this true? Why or why not?

2. What effects are likely to follow when two organizations with sharply different cultures merge?

3. Imagine that you are planning an orientation program for new employees of your company. What major points will you try to incorporate?

4. Most successful executives report that they had one or more mentors during their careers. Do you think having a mentor is necessary for success? If so, why? If not, why?

5. How can you determine whether your own career is, or is not, on track? What factors are most important to you in measuring your own success?

6. An increasing proportion of managers in the United States come from various minority groups. Such people continue to experience poorer career outcomes than others, however. Why do you think this occurs? What can be done to change the situation?

7. Some evidence indicates that in two-career or two-job families, women experience more conflict than men between work obligations and family obligations. Do you think this is true? If so, why? If not, why?

8. Suppose that after working for a company for several years, you learn that it is downsizing and you will probably lose your job. How do you react? What will you do? Now suppose you learn that you are one of the lucky people: you will get to keep your job. How do you react now? What feelings are you likely to experience?

NOTES

1. Miller, W. H. (1991, May 6). A new perspective for tomorrow's workforce. *Industry Week*, pp. 7–9.

2. Feldman, D. C. (1988). *Managing careers in organizations*. Glenview, IL: Scott, Foresman.

3. Nieva, V. (1988). Work and family linkages. In B. Gutek, A. Stromberg, & L. Larwood (Eds.), *Women and work* (Vol. 3, pp. 162–191). Newbury Park, CA: Sage.

4. Rousseau, D. (1990). Quantitative assessment of organizational culture: the case for multiple measures. In B. Schneider (Ed.), *Frontiers of industrial and organizational psychology* (Vol. 3, pp. 153–192). San Francisco: Jossey-Bass.

5. Wanous, J. P., Reichers, A. E., & Malik, S. D. (1984). Organizational socialization and group development: Toward an integrative perspective. *Academy of Management Review, 9*, 670–683.

6. Hall, D. T. (1987). Careers and socialization. *Journal of Management, 13*, 301–321.

7. Greenhaus, J., Bedeain, A., & Mossholder, K. (1987). Work experiences, job performance, and feelings of personal and family well-being. *Journal of Vocational Behavior, 31*, 200–215.

8. Winefield, A. H., & Tiggemann, M. (1990). Employment status and psychological well-being: A longitudinal study. *Journal of Applied Psychology, 75*, 455–459.

9. See Note 4.

10. Schneider, B., & Rentsch, J. (1988). Managing climates and cultures: A futures perspective. In J. Hage (Ed.), *Futures of organizations* (pp. 181–200). Lexington, MA: Lexington Books.

11. Schein, E. H. (1985). How culture forms, develops, and changes. In R. H. Kilmann, M. J. Saxton, & R. Serpa (Eds.), *Gaining control of the corporate culture* (pp. 17–43). San Francisco: Jossey-Bass.

12. See Note 11.

13. Rentsch, J. R. (1991). Climate and culture: Interaction and qualitative differences in organizational meanings. *Journal of Applied Psychology, 75*, 668–681.

14. Wiener, Y. (1988). Forms of value systems: A focus on organizational effectiveness and cultural change and maintenance. *Academy of Management Review, 13*, 534–545.

15. Saffold, G. S., III (1988). Culture traits, strength, and organizational performance: Moving beyond "strong" culture. *Academy of Management Review, 13*, 546–558.

16. Dennison, D. (1984). Bringing corporate culture to the bottom line. *Organizational Dynamics, 13*, 5–22.

17. Peters, T. J., & Waterman, R. H. (1982). *In search of excellence*. New York: Harper & Row.

18. See Note 15.

19. Siehl, C., & Martin, J. (1988). *Organizational culture: A key to financial performance?* (Research Paper Series, No. 998.) Stanford, CA: Stanford University, Graduate School of Business.

20. O'Reilly, C. A., III, Chatman, J., & Caldwell, D. F. (1991). People and organizational culture: A profile comparison approach to assessing person-organization fit. *Academy of Management Journal, 34*, 487–516.

21. See Note 1.

22. Wilkins, A. L., & Dyer, W. G., Jr. (1988). Toward culturally sensitive theories of culture change. *Academy of Management Review, 13*, 522–533.

23. Feldman, J. C. (1976). A contingency theory of socialization. *Administrative Science Quarterly, 21*, 433–452.

24. Dumaine, B. (1990, January 15). Creating a new company culture. *Fortune*, pp. 127–134.

25. Feldman, J. C. (1980). A socialization process that helps new recruits succeed. *Personnel, 57*, 11–23.

26. Wanous, J. P. (1981). *Organizational entry*. Reading, MA: Addison-Wesley.

27. Louis, M. R. (1980). Surprise and sense making: What newcomers experience in entering unfamiliar organizational settings. *Administrative Science Quarterly, 25*, 226–251.

28. Wanous, J. P. (1983). The entry of newcomers into organizations. In J. R. Hackman, E. E. Lawler, & L. W. Porter (Eds.), *Perspectives on behavior in organizations* (2nd ed., pp. 126–135). New York: McGraw-Hill.

29. Meglino, B. M., DeNisi, A. S., Youngblood, S. A., & Williams, K. J. (1988). Effects of realistic job previews: A comparison using an enhancement and a reduction preview. *Journal of Applied Psychology, 73*, 259–266.

30. Miller, V. D., & Jablin, F. M. (1991). Information seeking during organizational entry: Influences, tactics, and a model of the process. *Academy of Management Review, 16*, 92–120.

31. Van Maanen, J., & Schein, E. H. (1979). Toward a theory of organizational socialization. In B. Staw (Ed.), *Research in organizational behavior* (Vol. 1, pp. 209–264). Greenwich, CT: JAI Press.

32. Jones, G. R. (1986). Socialization tactics, self-efficacy, and newcomers' adjustments to organizations. *Academy of Management Journal, 29*, 262–279.

33. Allen, N. J., & Meyer, J. P. (1990). Organizational socialization tactics: A longitudinal analysis of links to newcomers' commitment and role orientation. *Academy of Management Journal, 33*, 847–858.

34. Kram, K. E. (1985). *Mentoring at work: Developmental relationships in organizational life*. Glenview, IL: Scott, Foresman.

35. Burke, R. J. (1984). Mentors in organizations. *Group and Organization Studies, 9*, 353–472.

36. Kram, K. E. (1983). Phases of the mentor relationship. *Academy of Management Journal, 26*, 608–625.

37. Zey, M. (1984). *The mentor connection*. Homewood, IL: Dow Jones–Irwin.

38. Whitely, W., Dougherty, T. W., & Dreher, G. F. (1991). Relationship of career mentoring and socioeconomic origin to managers' and professionals' early career

progress. *Academy of Management Journal, 34,* 331–351.

39. See Note 38.

40. Hurley, D. (1988). The mentor mystique. *Psychology Today, 22*(5), 38–43.

41. Noe, R. A. (1988). Women and mentoring: A review and research agenda. *Academy of Management Review, 13,* 65–78.

42. Ragins, B. R., & Cotton, J. L. (1991). Easier said than done: Gender differences in perceived barriers to gaining a mentor. *Academy of Management Journal, 34,* 939–951.

43. See Note 42.

44. Hall, D. T. (1976). *Careers in organizations.* Pacific Palisades, CA: Goodyear Publishing.

45. Hall, D. T. (1986). Career development in organizations: Where do we go from here? In D. T. Hall & Assocs. (Eds.), *Career development in organizations* (pp. 332–351). San Francisco: Jossey-Bass.

46. See Note 45.

47. Schein, E. H. (1971). The individual, the organization, and the career: A conceptual scheme. *Journal of Applied Behavioral Science, 7,* 401–421.

48. Kirkpatrick, D. (1990, July 2). Is your career on track? *Fortune,* pp. 39–48.

49. See Note 48.

50. Schein, E. H. (1978). *Career dynamics: Matching individual and organizational needs.* Reading, MA: Addison-Wesley.

51. Levinson, D. J. (1986). A conception of adult development. *American Psychologist, 41,* 3–13.

52. See Note 50.

53. Lewicki, R. J. (1981). Organizational seduction: Building commitment to organizations. *Organizational Dynamics, 10,* 5–22.

54. Dalton, G. W., Thompson, P. H., & Price, R. (1977). Career stages: A model of professional careers in organizations. *Organizational Dynamics,* 19–42.

55. Ference, T. P., Stoner, J. A. F., & Warren, E. K. (1977). Managing the career plateau. *Academy of Management Review, 2,* 602–612.

56. Terkel, S. (1974). *Working.* New York: Pantheon.

57. Waldman, D. A., & Avolio, B. J. (1986). A meta-analysis of age differences in job performance. *Journal of Applied Psychology, 71,* 33–38.

58. McCall, M. W., Jr., & Lombardo, M. M. (1983). What makes a top executive? *Psychology Today, 16*(20), 26–31.

59. Piotrowski, C. S., Rapoport, R. N., & Rapoport, R.

(1987). Families and work. In M. Sussman & S. Steinmetz (Eds.), *Handbook of marriage and the family* (pp. 251–283). New York: Plenum.

60. Shellenbarger, S. (1991, November 15). More job seekers put family needs first. *Wall Street Journal,* pp. B1, B12.

61. Williams, L. (1987, July 14). For the black professional, the obstacles remain. *New York Times,* p. A16.

62. Ilgen, D. R., & Youtz, M. A. (1986). Factors affecting the evaluation and development of minorities in organizations. In K. Rowland & G. Ferris (Eds.), *Research in personnel and human resource management: A research annual* (pp. 307–337). Greenwich, CT: JAI Press.

63. Greenhaus, J. H., Parasuraman, S., & Wormley, W. M. (1990). Effects of race on organizational experiences, job performance, evaluations, and career outcomes. *Academy of Management Journal, 33,* 64–86.

64. See Note 60.

65. Voydanoff, P. (1987). *Work and family life.* Newbury Park, CA: Sage.

66. See Note 60.

67. Duxbury, L. E., & Higgins, C. A. (1991). Gender differences in work-family conflict. *Journal of Applied Psychology, 76,* 60–74.

68. See Note 1.

69. Anderson, E. (1991, October 20). Layoffs take a toll on employees who remain. *Schenectady Gazette,* pp. C1, C2.

70. Brockner, J., Davy, J., & Carter, C. (1986). Layoffs, self-esteem, and survivor guilt: Motivational, affective, and attitudinal consequences. *Academy of Management Journal, 26,* 642–656.

71. See Note 69.

72. Winefield, A. H., Winefield, H. R., Tiggemann, M., & Goldney, R. D. (1991). A longitudinal study of the psychological effects of unemployment and unsatisfactory employment on young adults. *Journal of Applied Psychology, 76,* 424–431.

73. Erikson, E. H. (1956). The problem of ego identity. *Journal of American Psychoanalytic Association, 4,* 56–121.

74. Jackson, P. R., Stafford, E. M., Banks, M. H., & Warr, P. B. (1983). Unemployment and psychological distress in young people: The moderating role of employment commitment. *Journal of Applied Psychology, 68,* 525–535.

CASE IN POINT

"Getting your self-esteem from money, power and control is diminishing," says a psychologist who counsels managers who are finding themselves out of work in the 1990s.[1] Mergers, acquisitions, and the continued pressure to downsize in an attempt to reduce costs and become more competitive are causing U.S. companies to drastically cut their management ranks.

For these unemployed managers, finding a similar management position at another company is not likely. Most U.S. companies are cutting management jobs. There are more managers looking for work than U.S. industry can possibly absorb.[2] James Swalow, a vice president for A. T. Kearney management consultants, agrees: "A lot of people will walk out of these management positions and never see these kinds of jobs again."[3]

William Morin of Drake Beam Morin—an outplacement company that helps laid-off managers find new jobs and launch new careers—describes losing your job this way: "When you lose your job, even if it's in mass or as an individual, it's a loss of self-esteem, you're upset, you're angry, it's a sense of being out-of-control."[4] These managers have spent years working their way up the organizational hierarchy, only to find the hierarchy is being dismantled and their traditional management skills (directing and controlling) are no longer needed.

Being one of an army of unemployed managers looking for work is hard on a person's sense of self-esteem. Says one displaced manager, a former division president and a victim of a corporate takeover, the job market is "full of people like me. And it's getting cold and rude out there. Right now it's rare that you even hear back from your inquiries. That's what is so discouraging and disappointing. They are not even courteous enough to reject you."[5] It doesn't take long before displaced managers realize that the day of the traditional boss is dying, and the need to shift career strategies is becoming ever more apparent.

What do displaced managers do? James Cabrera, president of Drake Beam Morin, argues that managers must stop relying on the corporation to take care of them and start taking responsibility for their own careers. Losing your job gives you the opportunity to take control of your career. William Morin describes the silver lining (the benefits) of losing a job: "You really get in touch with yourself. A lot of people say they get in touch with their families, they get in touch with reality again, they are not servicing that god called the corporation anymore and they can kind of look inward, reattach to values and feelings and emotions they haven't had in years."[6]

Edgar Schein, a prominent career development expert, developed the concept of *career anchors*, the set of self-perceptions about values, preferences, abilities, and motives that serve to guide people into certain careers.[7] People are attracted to careers that match their career anchor. For example, some people are attracted to careers that offer autonomy and independence. Others look for careers that provide opportunities to express creativity and entrepreneurship. The traditional U.S. corporate management position has typically attracted people who seek careers that allow them to fulfill their career anchor—to exercise power and influence over other people. With companies changing, people attracted to the traditional corporate manager career are finding fewer and fewer jobs available. These people need to identify their niche, and then modify their career to fit the niche.

John Huey, a writer for *Fortune* magazine, investigated the job pursuits of displaced managers.[8] His research revealed several career paths. The first path is the traditional one—compete for one of the shrinking number of remaining corporate management jobs. *But*, the managers who land such jobs are finding out that even the nature of the traditional corporate management job is changing. Says Huey, the corporate management job of the 1990s means "you will have to transform yourself from an overseer into a doer, from a boss into a team leader or maybe just a team player."[9] Will the new corporate manager find his or her career anchor fulfilled by this new type of corporate management role? There is clearly reason for doubt. If the job changes too much, these people may have to change their career anchor, or explore new careers that provide them with the career anchor fulfillment they once found as corporate managers.

Changing Management Careers in the 1990s?

A CNN video is available to accompany this case. Additional information can be found in the CNN Video User's Guide.

Another career path managers are pursuing is to become a general manager in a small company. Bill Wendell, a longtime corporate marketing manager for several Fortune 500 companies, saw the downsizing that was going on and started looking for a job in a small company. He sought to become a big fish in a small pond. He wanted to find a management position that would demand a wide range of his manager skills. He took the job of vice president of marketing for Success Business Industries, a 300-employee office supplies company.

Wendell's career has changed dramatically. At large corporations, Wendell's job was much more specialized. At Success Business Industries, he is involved in all aspects of marketing activities. In previous corporate jobs, he had a lot of professional and administrative support. Gone is his support staff. "The major difference day to day is how much more I have to do myself."[10] His new job involves the responsibilities he had with his previous corporate work (and a whole lot more), but now he does everything himself. Wendell has become much more of a doer than an overseer.

Was changing careers worth all of the extra work? Wendell thinks it has been. In spite of the longer hours, he has a much greater sense of responsibility and satisfaction than he ever experienced in a large corporation. "In the big companies I never had the feeling that my efforts contributed directly to anybody's well-being except my own. Here I know that their livelihood depends on our success together . . . so much is within my influence."[11]

Other displaced managers shift careers from manager to entrepreneur. Michael Bressler, a forty-six-year-old veteran of several large corporations, saw his vice president of marketing job vanish with his employer's bankruptcy. After months of looking for a similar management position, he realized that he didn't really want to be a manager anymore. In fact, he decided that he no longer wanted to work for someone else. He wanted to create something himself. "I made a decision that I didn't want anybody else telling me when I could or couldn't work. So I set out to develop a business plan and execute it."[12] Bressler founded Affiliated Graphics, a company that helps businesses find printing services that best match their needs. Running his own company takes a lot of work (working nights and weekends is the norm rather than the exception), and he admits that he has made plenty of mistakes along the way. But all in all, he believes his career change was a good move. "What I like about it is being able to execute a business without having to go through layers of approval."[13]

Another popular career path for many displaced managers is consulting, also known as contract management. According to A. T. Kearney management consultants, contract management is one of the fastest growing areas of manager employment in the United States. As consultants, managers hire themselves out to companies on a contract basis. They manage a project until it is finished and then move on to another client. According to Steve Weiss, a futurist who helps identify emerging trends for several Fortune 500 companies, the corporation of the future will rely heavily on consultants. These corporations will maintain a lean management core but will buy, on a temporary basis, whatever management expertise they need. This emerging industry promises to be a major source of jobs for managers who are seeing their traditional jobs disappear.

Some displaced managers decide to leave the field of management altogether. Lorton Trent opted out of management following a twenty-five-year management career with Texas Instruments. At age fifty-seven, Trent was "encouraged" to take advantage of Texas Instrument's early retirement program. His knee-jerk response was to look for another management position. Trent quickly learned that his old management job wasn't out there anymore. While searching the job ads, he noticed a teaching position at Southern Methodist University in the mechanical-engineering laboratory. He applied for and got the job. How does he find the change? He likes it—a lot! He has discovered a sense of meaning and fulfillment that was lacking in his work as a manager. "Here I've gotten an opportunity to pass along to students my knowledge of the real engineering world. . . . I'm really enthusiastic about it."[14]

In summary, displaced managers are reevaluating their career anchors and taking action to redirect their careers by redefining the manager job as team leader or team player, jumping to a smaller pond, becoming a consultant or entrepreneur, or finding something outside of managing. In a world of corporate restructuring, this type of career shifting is well on its way to becoming the norm rather than the exception.

Questions for Discussion

1. Using the three basic dimensions of career change discussed in the text (i.e., vertical, horizontal, and radial), describe each of the career changes illustrated in the case.
2. What career anchors are illustrated by the career paths discussed in the case (e.g., redefined management job in a large corporation, entrepreneur, teacher, general manager in a small company)?
3. What is your career anchor? Suppose that you were a displaced manager. Would you pursue one of the career options presented in the case? Which one? Why? Would you prefer to pursue another career path? If so, what career path would you pursue? Why?

Notes

1. O'Reilly, B. (1992, January 27). Preparing for leaner times. *Fortune*, p. 40.
2. See Note 1, pp. 40–47.
3. Huey, J. (1992, January 27). Where will managers go? *Fortune*, p. 50.
4. Schuch, B. (1991, October 28). William Morin of Drake Beam Morin, Inc., *Pinnacle*.
5. See Note 3, p. 52.
6. See Note 4.
7. Schein, E. H. (1978). *Career dynamics: Matching individual and organizational needs.* Reading, MA: Addison-Wesley.
8. See Note 3, pp. 50–60.
9. See Note 3, p. 51.
10. See Note 3, p. 51.
11. See Note 3, p. 52.
12. See Note 3, p. 52.
13. See Note 3, p. 52.
14. See Note 3, p. 60.

**Personal Values
Throughout Life**

Many people believe that once they are adults, they undergo little change aside from physical aging. They assume, often without question, that their goals and values will remain largely unaltered as the decades come and go. Is this really so? To gather some firsthand evidence on this issue, complete the exercise described below.

Procedure

First, list the three personal goals you are currently seeking that are most important to you. Think carefully, and list only the ones you value most.

1.
2.
3.

Now, try to remember the personal goals that were most important to you five years ago. List them below.

1.
2.
3.

Finally, imagine yourself ten years from now. What personal goals will be most important to you then? List these below.

1.
2.
3.

Points to Consider

Did you notice any shifts in your major personal goals? If you are like most people, you probably did. Studies of how people change and develop over time suggest that many undergo major shifts in their goals, values, and beliefs during the fifty, sixty, or more years they spend as adults. Shifts in goals and values, in turn, often have profound effects on careers. For example, individuals who highly value such goals as status and wealth early in their careers often find that these goals lose much of their appeal as they grow older. Later in life, these people report that other goals, such as happiness, good health, or peace of mind, have replaced their earlier ones.

Will you, too, change in these ways? Only time, and your own experience, can reveal the answer. But awareness that most people continue to change during their adult years is important for planning your own career and for managing the careers of people who will work under your supervision.

■ 10 ■

HELPING, COOPERATION, AND CONFLICT: WORKING WITH OR AGAINST OTHERS IN ORGANIZATIONS

CHAPTER OUTLINE

Prosocial Behavior: Helping Others at Work
Organizational Citizenship Behaviors: Beyond the Call of Duty
Cooperation: Mutual Assistance in Work Settings
Individual Factors and Cooperation
Organizational Factors and Cooperation
Conflict: Its Nature and Causes
Integration and Distribution: The Basic Dimensions of Conflict
Conflict: A Modern Perspective
Conflict: Its Major Causes
Conflict: Its Major Effects
Conflict: The Negative Side
Conflict: The Positive Side
Conflict: Its Effective Management
Bargaining: The Universal Process

Third-Party Intervention: Help from the Outside
The Induction of Superordinate Goals
Escalative Interventions: Intensifying Conflicts to Resolve Them

Special Sections

OB in Practice   Teamwork: Is It Always a Plus?

An International/Multicultural Perspective
Conflict and Face in Five Different Cultures

A Question of Ethics   Styles of Conflict Management: Which Are Best—or Most Appropriate?

LEARNING OBJECTIVES

After reading this chapter, you should be able to:

1. Define *prosocial behavior* and describe some of the forms it takes in organizations.
2. Define *citizenship behaviors* and indicate how they are related to perceptions of procedural fairness on the part of organization members.
3. Describe the basic nature of *cooperation* and indicate why it is often replaced in organizations by *competition*.
4. Describe the role of *teams* and *pairing* in promoting cooperation within an organization.

5. Define *conflict* and indicate how it can produce positive as well as negative effects.
6. Describe various styles of managing conflict, and the dimensions that appear to underlie these contrasting styles.
7. List several *interpersonal* and *organizational* causes of conflict.
8. Describe several effective techniques for *managing* conflict, and discuss the *ethical issues* related to such techniques.

isten, kid," Art Grady says to his young assistant, Lotisha James. "You've got to have the killer instinct in these situations. I mean, you go for the jugular, see?"

"I don't know, Art," Lotisha responds. "Don't you think that when you do, you take a chance on . . . I don't know . . . missing something? Some way to work things out?"

"Baloney!" Art practically shouts. "I'm telling you: in this world, you don't get what you deserve—you get what you *negotiate*, and the only way to negotiate is by blasting them right at the start. Let 'em know that you're not going to be a pushover."

"I can see how that's a good strategy," Lotisha answers, "I really can. And I know that it works for you. But sometimes, I think, you've got to try to take the other side's point of view. I mean, don't we have to deal with these people again? And if we make them mad, won't it be harder to work with them next time around?"

"What are you, some kind of New Age weirdo?" Art asks, a puzzled look on his face. "Is that the kind of stuff they dish out in business school these days? Well, let me tell you, it doesn't cut it. If you don't beat up on your opponents, they're sure as heck going to beat up on you. Never give 'em a chance to get their balance: that's my motto. And when they're down, hit 'em hard! Winning—that's all that matters."

"Okay, okay," Lotisha murmurs, "don't get all worked up about it. I see what you mean. But let me give you an example of what's bothering me."

"Yeah, please do," Art replies.

"Today we concentrated mainly on delivery date. And you did a great job of knocking them down on that one. But we've still got to get an agreement on the design work. Are we going to pick up the costs or will they? And what about maintenance? They claim the schedule we're proposing means extra people on the maintenance end. Where do we stand on that one?"

"I'll tell you where: we're going to beat them down on every point that comes up. Heck, I only just started on 'em today."

"But Art, suppose for a minute that we decided to give in to them a little on the design work. It's pretty minimal from our point of view. And then, maybe if we give up a little there, we can get even more from them on the delivery date, and that's what we really care about. What do you think? Anyway, I keep reminding myself that this whole situation is kind of all in the family—I mean, they're one of our subsidiaries, right? Why do we have to knock them senseless when we're all part of the same company?"

"Because, my young friend," Art comments, acid dripping from his words, "I don't care *what* you say: the more they get, the less we get, and vice versa. It's us against them, and I'm never going to see it any other way. So get that mush out of your head; we've got a job to do, and it wouldn't matter to me if we were negotiating against your mother. *We're going to win!*"

———————————————■———————————————

Does this situation strike you as strange? It should, for Art and Lotisha are negotiating over several issues with people *from their own company*. This means that in the final analysis, they and their opponent are *interdependent:* what happens to one side affects what happens to the other. After all, if one part of the company does extremely well at the expense of another, the organization itself gains little, if anything. In fact, the ill will and resentment generated may prove so costly that ultimately everyone loses. A much better approach would be for the two sides to *cooperate* to attain an ideal solution. In that case, both will benefit and the adage "A rising tide floats all boats" may apply.

In all work settings, *cooperation*—a mutual sharing of benefits—clearly should be the guiding principle. Departments, divisions, units, and individuals should coordinate their efforts and work together as effectively as possible to maximize the attainment of shared organizational goals—the kind of situation shown in Figure 10–1.[1]

Yet, as you probably already know, reality often falls short of this ideal—far short. Instead of benevolent places filled with the spirit of mutual assistance, organizations are just as likely to be places dominated by indifference, needless competition, smoldering feuds, and even open conflict. Why is this so? What factors lead individuals and groups to work against one another when they should, by all rational

CATHY   **By Cathy Guisewite**

FIGURE 10–1   Coordination of Effort in Organizations

As suggested by this cartoon, coordination takes many different forms in organizations. (*Source:* Cathy cartoon is reprinted by permission of Universal Press Syndicate.)

standards, be cooperating? And what steps can be taken to tip the balance away from such reactions and toward higher levels of coordination? We will focus on these and related questions in this chapter. Specifically, we will examine three major processes related to the extent to which individuals or groups in an organization work with, or against, one another. The first of these is *prosocial behavior*—actions by individuals or groups that assist others within the organization with no requirement that the recipients return the favor. The second is *cooperation*—mutual, two-way assistance between individuals or groups. The third, and in some ways most disturbing, is *conflict*—a process resulting from actions by groups or individuals that are perceived by others as having negative effects on their important interests.[2,3] We will now review current knowledge relating to each of these processes.

PROSOCIAL BEHAVIOR: HELPING OTHERS AT WORK

Is there such a thing as pure altruism—actions by one person that benefit one or more others under conditions in which the donor expects absolutely, positively nothing in return? Philosophers have long puzzled over this question. More recently, social scientists have entered the debate.[4] That their research casts considerable doubt on the existence of totally selfless helping is disappointing. Close examination of many instances in which individuals offer aid to others in a seemingly altruistic manner reveals that even in such cases, donors anticipate *some* form of compensation for their assistance. This return on their investment can be quite subtle (e.g., feelings of self-satisfaction resulting from the knowledge that they have acted benevolently; elimination of the negative emotions produced by exposure to others in need of assistance).[5] Yet, such gains are certainly real, and seem to provide at least a portion of the motivation behind seemingly altruistic acts. This is not to imply that instances of pure altruism cannot exist. A strong case can be made for the presence of such behavior in some contexts (e.g., self-sacrifice by parents for their children or by lovers for the objects of their affection). At the least, though, pure, selfless altruism seems to be far rarer and much more difficult to identify than people once assumed.

Regardless of whether such altruism exists, one fact is clear: human beings do frequently engage in **prosocial behavior**. They perform many actions that benefit others in various ways. Is such behavior common in work settings? Absolutely. As noted recently by Brief and Motowidlo, many types of prosocial behavior occur in functioning organizations.[6] First, and most obviously, individuals who work together often assist each other with job-related matters. They pitch in and help those who have been absent, assist those experiencing especially heavy work loads, and take on tasks that are not necessarily part of their own jobs. In short, they demonstrate the kind of organizational *citizenship* behaviors we described in chapter 5.

Second, employees often assist coworkers with personal matters not directly related to their jobs. They provide emotional support, assist them with family matters, and generally offer a sympathetic ear for personal problems and difficulties. A third form of prosocial behavior that organizational members often show involves providing services or products to people outside the organization with whom they do business (e.g., customers). Here, actions such as helping customers choose the right product for their needs or providing necessary service or information are part of the total picture. Additional forms of prosocial behavior involve suggestions for procedural or administrative improvements, putting forth extra effort on the job, volunteering for additional work assignments, and representing the organization favorably to outsiders (e.g., saying positive things about it, its products, or its services).

Test Bank questions 10.1–10.2 relate to material on this page.

All of the prosocial actions we have considered so far benefit an organization either directly or indirectly. Note, however, that not all prosocial behaviors produce such effects. In some cases, individuals engage in actions that benefit specific people but reflect negatively on the functioning of the organization itself. For example, consider employees who falsify records to conceal disapproved activities by friends; who offer special, costly deals to preferred customers; or who hire or promote people they know are unqualified for such rewards, but with whom they have some special relationship. Such people are certainly behaving in a prosocial manner toward specific individuals—the beneficiaries of their actions. Yet, they are certainly *not* contributing to the well-being of their organizations.

Other complexities are introduced into the equation by activities such as **whistle-blowing**—cases in which employees reveal an improper or illegal organizational practice to someone who may be able to correct it.[7] Is this a prosocial action? From the point of view of society, it usually is. The actions of whistle-blowers can protect the health, safety, or economic security of the general public. For example, an employee of a large bank who reports risky or illegal practices to an appropriate regulatory agency may protect thousands of depositors from large financial losses, or at least from considerable delay in recovering their savings. Similarly, an individual who blows the whistle on illegal dumping of toxic chemicals by his or her company may save many people from serious illness.

From the point of view of the organizations involved, however, the situation is more complex. First, whether such actions are or are not prosocial in nature depends on the motivation underlying them. If a whistle-blower benefits from his or her actions while the organization suffers, it is reasonable to conclude that the whistle-blower did not intend to help the company. In such cases, whistle-blowing cannot be viewed as prosocial with respect to the organization. Second, much depends on how such whistle-blowing is carried out. If the potentially damaging information is revealed first to people in authority *within* the organization who can take appropriate corrective actions, whistle-blowing is reasonably viewed as prosocial. If the information is offered first to people outside the organization, however, negative effects will probably follow, and such actions are not prosocial, at least from the organization's point of view. For example, one large brokerage house in the United States convicted of insider trading and related practices had to pay fines and damages totaling $650,000,000 when its illegal activities were made known to the Securities and Exchange Commission.

Whistle-blowing actions in any given company must be examined from the perspective of the motives underlying their performance and their ultimate effects before they can be classified as prosocial or not.

Organizational Citizenship Behaviors: Beyond the Call of Duty

In chapter 5, we noted that high levels of job satisfaction tend to promote **organizational citizenship behaviors (OCB)**—actions by individuals that are discretionary (e.g., voluntary), not related to the formal reward system of the organization, and not included in their formal job description. Such behaviors include showing courtesy to others, being conscientious in work-related tasks, being a "good sport" about extra work assignments or duties, and generally protecting the organization's resources and property.[8] In addition, of course, a central component of citizenship behaviors is offering help to others *without* the expectation of immediate reciprocity on the part of the individuals receiving such aid. Growing evidence suggests that occurrence of organizational citizenship behaviors enhances the pleasantness of work settings,

Although blowing the whistle on illegal activities seems like a noble and righteous activity, employees are often reluctant to do it for several reasons, such as fear of losing their jobs or fear of retaliation from other workers. In addition, merely telling the authorities about wrongdoing is no guarantee that something will be done about the questionable behavior. For example, even when auditors from Price Waterhouse uncovered evidence that the Bank of Credit and Commerce International (known as BCCI) was laundering drug money, the regulatory authorities did not act immediately, but waited until the proof of wrongdoing was overwhelming. [Young, A. (1991, September). Blowing the whistle on corporate fraud. *The Accountant's Magazine*, pp. 4–6.]

and can contribute to increased performance and efficiency.[9] This, in turn, suggests an important question: what steps can organizations take to enhance such actions among employees? The answer seems to involve efforts to enhance feelings of being treated *fairly* on the part of organization members.[10] Apparently, to the extent that individuals feel they are being treated fairly by their organizations in several different ways, the likelihood that they will engage in OCB increases. A study conducted recently by Moorman demonstrated this relationship convincingly.[11]

In this investigation, several hundred employees of two different manufacturing companies completed questionnaires designed to measure the frequency with which they engaged in OCB, as well as their current levels of job satisfaction. Other items on the questionnaire assessed participants' feelings about several kinds of perceived justice: *distributive justice*—the extent to which rewards are perceived as being related to performance; *procedural justice*—the extent to which formal procedures for distributing available rewards are perceived as being fair; and *interactional justice*—the extent to which these procedures are carried out in a courteous, considerate manner.[12] Moorman predicted that perceptions of organizational justice would enhance both OCB and job satisfaction, and that perceptions of procedural justice would enhance perceptions of distributive justice. As shown in Figure 10–2, all of these predictions were confirmed. In short, perceived fairness seems to be a key factor in the occurrence of OCB. Given the importance most people attach to being treated fairly, this is hardly surprising. (Refer to our discussion of fairness in chapter 3.)

Interestingly, the results of this study also suggested that *interactional justice* played the most central role in encouraging citizenship behaviors. The greater the extent to which employees felt that their supervisors had applied the formal procedures for distributing rewards in a fair and courteous manner, the greater the incidence of citizenship behavior. This finding is consistent with a growing body of evidence indicating that interactional justice is often the most important kind where individual employees are concerned. Fortunately, such justice is also often the easiest type for managers to provide. Distribution of raises and other benefits, and the formal procedures for allocating rewards, are often outside an individual manager's control. Treating subordinates in a fair and considerate manner, however, is not. Thus, the moral for managers wishing to encourage OCB behaviors is clear: do everything in your power to build interactional justice into dealings with your subordinates. The benefits of doing so can be quite substantial.

FIGURE 10–2

Perceived Justice and Organizational Citizenship Behaviors

Perceptions of being treated fairly by their organization seem to play a key role in employees' willingness to engage in organizational citizenship behaviors. *Interactional justice*—the extent to which formal procedures are carried out with courtesy and consideration—seems to be especially important in this respect. In addition, perceptions of being treated fairly contribute to increased job satisfaction. (*Source:* Based on data from Moorman, 1991; see Note 11.)

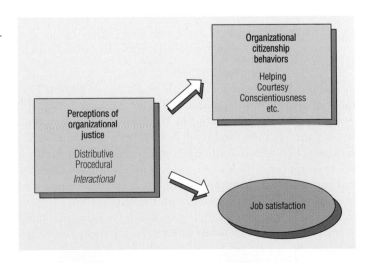

COOPERATION: MUTUAL ASSISTANCE IN WORK SETTINGS

In prosocial behavior, people engage in actions designed to benefit other individuals, groups, or the entire organization. As we have already noted, such actions are fairly common in work settings and take many forms. Although prosocial behavior is frequent another pattern known as **cooperation** is probably even more widespread.[13] Here, assistance is mutual, and two or more individuals or groups work together to enhance progress toward shared goals. Such cooperation is a basic form of coordination in many work settings. To mention just a few examples, it occurs when several computer experts work together to debug a faulty program, when employees on a loading dock pool their physical efforts to lift a heavy package, and when members of a special project team consisting of experts from several different backgrounds combine their skills to develop a new product or service. In all these cases, the underlying principle is much the same: the persons, groups, or units involved coordinate their actions to reach goals or levels of performance they could not attain alone. Then, once the mutually desired goals are reached, the benefits are shared among the participants in some agreed-on manner. The result: cooperation yields positive outcomes for all concerned.

The obvious benefits of this pattern raise a basic question: why, if it is so useful, does it often fail to develop? Why don't people, groups, or units seeking the same (or at least similar) goals always join forces? Several factors account for the puzzling lack of coordination, but by far the most important is this: cooperation simply cannot develop in many situations because the goals sought by the individuals or groups involved cannot be shared. For example, two people seeking the same job or promotion cannot join forces to attain it—the reward can go to only one. Similarly, if two companies are courting the same potential merger candidate, only one can succeed; it makes little sense for them to work together to assure that a merger does in fact take place, since only one will enjoy the benefits of this transaction.

In cases such as these, an alternative form of behavior known as **competition** often develops. Here, each person, group, or unit strives to maximize its individual gains, often at the expense of others. Indeed, as noted by Tjosvold, each side tends to view gains and losses by the other side as linked, so that their "wins" constitute the other side's "losses," and vice versa.[14] In some contexts, competition is both natural and understandable. People and departments do have to compete for scarce organizational resources and rewards. And organizations themselves must compete in the marketplace for supplies, government contracts, customers, and market share (see Figure 10–3 on p. 360). In many instances, however, competition is *not* dictated by current conditions, and cooperation might develop instead. For example, consider the story at the start of this chapter. Couldn't Art have followed Lotisha's advice and made concessions on some issues to maximize the joint outcomes for both sides? After all, he was dealing with a subsidiary of his own company. Why, then, did he choose head-on competition? As we suggested, the answer is complex and involves many factors. To acquaint you with some of these, we will now focus on the following question: what factors serve to tip the balance toward cooperation or competition in situations where either pattern is possible? As we will soon note, both individual and organizational factors play a role.

Individual Factors and Cooperation

Several factors affecting the tendency to cooperate seem to function primarily through their impact on individuals. They influence the perceptions and reactions of specific people, and in this manner shape individuals' decisions with respect to cooperating

Cooperative arrangements are especially difficult to maintain when they involve parties from different countries. Such arrangements are commonly seen in the form of joint ventures, partnerships, and strategic alliances, such as Germany's Daimler-Benz and Japan's Mitsubishi in electronics, as well as France's Renault and Sweden's Volvo in automobiles. However, such alliances are difficult to operate and manage, and only about half of them succeed. Among the problems of maintaining these international cooperatives are differences in cultural values regarding norms of trust and fairness in social exchange. [Rules of engagement. (1990, Summer). *Multinational Business,* pp. 66–67.]

FIGURE 10-3   Competition: A Basic Fact of Life for Most Organizations

Organizations must compete with one another for market share, scarce supplies, and many other resources.

or competing with others. Among the most important of these are the principle of *reciprocity*, several aspects of *communication*, and the *personal orientation* toward working with others held by individuals.

Reciprocity: Reacting to Others' Behavior   Throughout life, we are urged to follow the "Golden Rule"—to do unto others as we would have others do unto us. Despite such exhortations, we usually behave differently. Most people tend to treat others not as they would prefer to be treated, but rather as *they* have been treated in the past, either by these individuals or by others. In short, most individuals follow the principle of **reciprocity** much of the time. This tendency to behave toward others as they have acted toward us is quite powerful. We can observe it in actions as diverse as attraction, where individuals tend to like others who express positive feelings toward them, and aggression, where "an eye for an eye and a tooth for a tooth" seems to prevail.[15] The choice between cooperation and competition is no exception to this powerful rule. When others act in a competitive manner, we usually respond with mistrust and efforts to defeat them. In contrast, if they behave cooperatively, we usually do the same.

The tendency to reciprocate cooperation is not perfect, however. In judging others' level of cooperation and adjusting our response to it, we often fall prey to the same type of *self-serving bias* described in chapter 2: we perceive others' level of cooperation as lower than it really is, and our own level of cooperation as somewhat higher than reality would dictate. The result: in our dealings with others, we tend to *undermatch* the level of cooperation they demonstrate.[16]

This tendency aside, reciprocity does appear to be the guiding principle of cooperation. The key task in establishing coordination in organizations, then, seems to be getting it started. Once individuals, groups, or units have begun to cooperate,

Test Bank questions 10.16–10.18, 10.48, and 10.58 relate to material on this page.

the process may be largely self-sustaining. To encourage cooperation, therefore, managers should do everything possible to get the process under way. After it begins, the obvious benefits cooperation confers, plus powerful tendencies toward reciprocity, may well maintain it at high levels.

Communication: Potential Benefits, Potential Costs   Where cooperation could potentially develop but does not, its absence is often blamed on a "failure to communicate." People suggest that better or more frequent contact between the individuals or groups involved might have facilitated coordination. Is this suggestion accurate? In one sense, it is. Some forms of communication do indeed seem to increase interpersonal trust, and so to enhance actual cooperation. For example, an open exchange of views may convince all parties that working together is the best strategy, and that a fair division of responsibilities and rewards is possible. Similarly, unless some minimal level of communication exists, close coordination of work activities may be impossible; after all, each individual or group will have little idea of what the others are doing.

Not all types of communication yield such beneficial outcomes, however. In fact, research findings indicate that at least one type of contact between individuals or groups—communication involving the use of *threats*—can reduce rather than encourage cooperation.

Threats take many different forms, but they typically involve statements suggesting that negative consequences will be delivered if the recipient does not behave in a certain manner or refrains from acting in a certain manner. For example, a manager may warn her subordinate that if he continues to tie up the phones with personal calls, his phone privileges will be revoked. Similarly, during negotiations, representatives from one company may inform those from another that they will end the current discussions unless one of their requests is met. Although the use of such tactics is tempting, they often produce mixed effects at best. In many cases, they anger recipients, stiffening their resolve to resist. Even when threats appear to succeed and produce immediate yielding or surrender, they may leave a residue of resentment that can return later to haunt those who issued them. And of course, threats often stimulate counterthreats and create a damaging spiral that can lead, ultimately, to open and costly conflict. A clear example of such effects is provided in a laboratory study conducted by Youngs.[17]

In this study, female students played a special type of game against an opponent who issued either few or many threats and whose threats, when delivered, were either small or large in magnitude. In this game, both players were asked to choose, on a number of occasions, between two options. If both selected Option 1 (the cooperative choice), each player won two points. (Points could be converted into money prizes at the end of the game.) If both selected Option 2 (the competitive choice), each lost two points. If a mixed pattern of choices occurred (one player selected Option 1 and the other Option 2), the player choosing Option 1 lost six points, and the player choosing Option 2 gained six points. This type of game has often been used in laboratory research on cooperation, for despite its obvious artificiality, it confronts players with a situation reminiscent of many real-life contexts: pressures toward both cooperation and competition exist, and operate concurrently. As you might guess, people who participate in such games soon become highly involved in them and do their best to outscore their opponents.

In Youngs's study, at various points during the game, either participants or their opponents (but not both simultaneously) were allowed to send "warning messages" requesting that the other player select Option 1 (the cooperative choice). These

In many cases, cooperation between managers and subordinates could be enhanced if employees were given a chance to tell their managers about their current problems or concerns. Unfortunately, most managers don't give their employees any such opportunity. In fact, studies have shown that throughout the 1980s only about 8 percent of companies had a formal policy or program through which employees could officially voice their concerns to their managers. If managers were willing to be more open, then cooperation between employees and managers might be greatly enhanced. [Lee, C. (1990, April). Talking back to the boss. *Training*, pp. 29–35.]

messages served as threats, for in them the players could indicate the number of points they would subtract from their opponent's score if she did not comply. In reality, the participants' opponent was fictitious, and was programmed by Youngs to issue either many or relatively few threats (on 50 percent of the game trials or 100 percent of these trials), and to issue threats of relatively small magnitude (losses of eight to twelve points to the subject) or of relatively large magnitude (losses of sixteen to twenty points).

Youngs predicted that, consistent with the reciprocity principle described earlier, players in the game would generally tend to match the level of threat they received from their opponent, and this was indeed the case. Participants issued more threats when they received many rather than few threats from their opponent, and they issued larger threats when their opponent used large rather than small ones. In addition, the overall level of cooperation during the game was low; participants chose the cooperative option only 33 percent of the time when the opponent did not send a threat.

These findings, plus those of many other studies, suggest that threats are a very poor means of enhancing cooperation in a wide range of settings. Although they may succeed in obtaining concessions and compliance in the short run, they tend to interfere with establishment of long-term, lasting patterns of coordination. For this reason, as well as several others we will describe in a later section (see page 376), threats appear to be one type of communication that managers should avoid on most occasions.

Personal Orientations and Cooperation   Think about the many people you have known during your life. Can you remember ones who were highly competitive—individuals who viewed most situations as contests in which they, or someone else, would triumph? In contrast, can you recall others who were highly cooperative—people who preferred to minimize differences between their own performance or outcomes and those of others? You probably have little difficulty in bringing examples of both types to mind, for people differ greatly in their tendencies to cooperate or compete. Such differences, in turn, seem to reflect contrasting perspectives toward working with others—perspectives that individuals carry with them from situation to situation and over relatively long periods of time.[18] Both tendencies vary along continuous dimensions (from very low to very high), but research findings suggest that many, if not most, people fall into one of four distinct categories.

First, a sizable proportion are **competitors**—people whose primary motive is doing better than others—beating them in open competition. Indeed, in extreme cases competitors prefer negative outcomes that exceed those of their opponents to positive ones that are less than those attained by others. Second, some people are concerned almost exclusively with maximizing their own gains. Such **individualists** have little interest in the outcomes of others, and don't really care whether others do better or worse than themselves. Their major focus is simply on gaining as much as possible in every situation. Third, a relatively small number of people can be classified as **cooperators.** These individuals are primarily concerned with maximizing *joint outcomes*—the total received by themselves and others. They want everyone they work with to be satisfied with their rewards, and do not wish to beat or defeat them. Finally, a few people can be described as **equalizers**. Their major goal is minimizing differences between their own performance or outcomes and those of others. In short, they wish to assure that everyone they work with receives the same basic results. (See Figure 10–4 for an overview of the motives of these four types of people.)

At this point we should note that while many individuals seem to fall into one of these categories, others demonstrate a mixture of these perspectives. Substantial

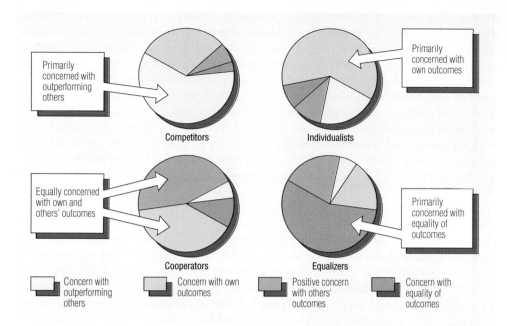

FIGURE 10-4

Personal Orientations
toward Working with Others

As shown here,
individuals with
different orientations
toward working with
others demonstrate
sharply contrasting
patterns of motives.
These differences, in
turn, influence their
behavior in a wide
range of situations.

numbers seem to combine an individualistic orientation with a competitive one: they want to do as well as they can, but are also interested in surpassing others when possible. Similarly, some people combine an individualistic orientation with a desire for equality. They want to do as well as they can, but don't want their outcomes to get too far out of line with those of others.

How common is each of these patterns? In other words, are there more competitors or cooperators? Do mixed patterns outnumber the simple ones? A study by Knight and Dubro provides information on this issue.[19] These researchers asked a large group of individuals (both males and females) to complete several tasks designed to reveal their orientation toward working with others. Results indicated that substantial proportions of the participants fell into each of the categories mentioned above. However, the pattern of these preferences differed somewhat for men and women. Among males, the single largest group was competitors; fully one-third showed this orientation, whereas another 18 percent showed an individualistic pattern. In contrast, among females, the single largest group was cooperators (about 20 percent), followed closely by competitors (about 15 percent). Only a relatively small proportion of each gender could be classified as equalizers.

As you might suspect, people showing different perspectives toward working with others tend to behave quite differently.[20] Competitors frequently attempt to exploit the people around them, and cooperate only when they see no other choice. In contrast, cooperators prefer friendly ties with coworkers, and would rather work with them than against them. Individualists are flexible—they choose whatever strategy will succeed in a given situation. In addition, they often prefer to work alone, concentrating solely on their own outcomes rather than those of others. People with a mixed orientation are harder to predict; they often oscillate or adopt intermediate approaches in working with others.

From a practical point of view, managers should recognize the existence of these different patterns and should guard against assuming that all individuals are similar in their approach to exchange relations. Further, they should realize that such differences are relevant to several key personnel decisions (e.g., hiring, promotion, work assignments). For example, people with a competitive orientation may be highly effective in situations in which representatives of several organizations must compete against one another. However, they may wreak havoc in contexts requiring prolonged teamwork. In contrast, cooperators may shine as team players, but do poorly in some types of negotiations. Equalizers may excel in positions requiring the fair distribution of resources among various groups (e.g., scheduling space or equipment). But they may run into serious problems if, as managers, they must evaluate the performance of subordinates and recommend differential raises or promotions for them. In summary, individual differences with respect to such orientations are important and can affect performance in a wide range of positions.

Organizational Factors and Cooperation

That organizations differ greatly in their internal levels of cooperation is obvious. Some—typically those that are quite successful—demonstrate a high degree of cooperation between their various units or departments.[21] Others—typically those that are *not* highly successful—show a lower level of such behavior. What accounts for these differences? We have already provided part of the answer: cooperation within an organization is affected by several factors relating primarily to individuals (e.g., communication, individual perspectives or preferences). In addition, several factors relating to an organization's internal structure and function play a role.

The reward system greatly determines whether or not people will help each other. For example, at one time in Switzerland, students had to pass two national exams in order to practice medicine. Because there was no limit on the number of students who could pass, students were not competing against each other, creating no reason for them to refrain from helping each other. By contrast, in the United States, where severe competition often exists between students trying to get into the most desirable programs in colleges and universities, cooperation is not at all likely. [Davidson, J. (1990, Spring). Competition is healthy if approached correctly—and unhealthy if it isn't. *Management Quarterly,* pp. 42–43.]

Reward Systems and Organizational Structure   Imagine the following situation. A large insurance company has two major divisions: Consumer Underwriting (which issues policies for individuals) and Commercial Underwriting (which issues policies for businesses). The company has a major bonus system, and each year sizable bonuses are distributed to individuals in the division that is more profitable. This results in a high degree of competition between the units. At first glance, this might seem beneficial. However, it leads to situations in which sales personnel from one division actively interfere with the efforts of sales personnel from the other division. For example, while working hard to win a multimillion-dollar policy with a large manufacturing concern, agents from the Commercial Underwriting division actually discourage top management within this company from seeking individual life and property policies from their company; after all, this will contribute to the sales of their archrival, Consumer Underwriting. And the opposite pattern is true as well. Agents for the consumer division discourage large clients from seeking policies for their businesses from the commercial division.

Although this might seem to be an extreme case, it reflects conditions that are all too common in many organizations. Reward systems are often "winner-take-all" in form. This fact, coupled with internal differentiation, tends to reduce coordination between units or divisions, as each seeks to maximize its own rewards. This is not to imply that such internal competition is necessarily bad or counterproductive—far from it. Still, managers should assure that it does not reach a level where it hinders the functioning and success of the entire organization.

Interdependence among Employees: The Nature of Specific Jobs   Imagine two organizations. In the first, the major tasks performed by employees can be completed alone; there is no need for individuals to work closely with others. In the second, the tasks performed by employees cannot be completed alone; they must work together closely to do their jobs. In which organization will higher levels of coop-

Test Bank questions 10.24–10.26 and 10.68 relate to material on this page.

eration develop? The answer is obvious: in the second. The reason for this difference, too, is apparent. The level of cooperation attained is determined by the nature of the work performed. The greater the degree of interdependence among employees, the higher cooperation among them tends to be. This relationship has been verified in research studies, so it appears to be a useful principle to keep in mind.[22] (Is close coordination among employees always beneficial? For a discussion of this issue, see the **OB in Practice** section on pp. 366–367.)

Conflict: its nature and causes

If prosocial behavior and cooperation constitute one end of a continuum describing how individuals and groups work together in organizations, **conflict** certainly lies at the other end. This term has many meanings and has been used to refer to events ranging from the inner turmoil produced by competing needs or desires (inner conflict) to open violence between entire societies (warfare). In the context of organizational behavior, however, conflict refers primarily to instances in which units or individuals within an organization work *against* rather than with one another.[23] More formally, according to one widely accepted definition, conflict is a process in which one party perceives that another party has taken some action that will exert negative effects on its major interests, or is about to take such action. In other words, the key elements in conflict seem to include (1) opposing interests between individuals or groups, (2) recognition of such opposition, (3) the belief by each side that the other will thwart (or has already thwarted) these interests, and (4) actions that actually produce such thwarting (see Figure 10–5).

Unfortunately, conflict, defined in this manner, is all too common in modern organizations. Moreover, its effects are far too costly to ignore. Practicing managers report that they spend approximately *20 percent of their time* dealing with conflict and its impact.[24] And the smoldering resentment and broken relationships that are the aftermath of many conflicts can persist for months or even years, continuing to exact a major toll in precious human resources long after the situation that initiated the conflict is merely a memory. For these and related reasons, **organizational conflict** is an important topic for the field of OB, and one deserving of our careful attention. In the remainder of this section, we will provide an overview of current knowledge about this costly process. First, we will examine two basic dimensions that seem to underlie many forms of conflict. Second, we will describe a recent, sophisticated model of conflict—one that helps place this process within a broader

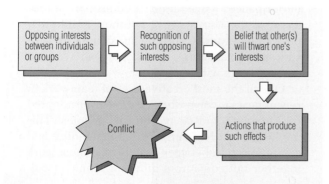

FIGURE 10-5

The Nature of Organizational Conflict

Conflict involves opposing or incompatible interests between groups or individuals, recognition of these opposing interests, and the belief by both sides that their adversary has acted, or will soon act, to thwart their important interests. (*Source:* Based on suggestions by Thomas, 1992; see Note 3.)

context of both organizational and individual processes. Then we will examine many causes of conflict and several of its major effects. Finally, we will focus on tactics for resolving or *managing* organizational conflict—procedures for maximizing its potential benefits while minimizing its potential, and all too obvious, adverse effects.

Integration and Distribution: The Basic Dimensions of Conflict

Answer this question quickly: In your dealings with other people, to what extent do you focus on your own interests—on maximizing *your* outcomes? And to what extent do you focus on *their* interests—on assuring that they are treated fairly, or that the

 OB IN PRACTICE

Teamwork: Is It Always a Plus?

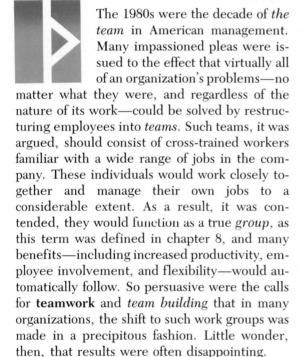

The 1980s were the decade of *the team* in American management. Many impassioned pleas were issued to the effect that virtually all of an organization's problems—no matter what they were, and regardless of the nature of its work—could be solved by restructuring employees into *teams*. Such teams, it was argued, should consist of cross-trained workers familiar with a wide range of jobs in the company. These individuals would work closely together and manage their own jobs to a considerable extent. As a result, it was contended, they would function as a true *group*, as this term was defined in chapter 8, and many benefits—including increased productivity, employee involvement, and flexibility—would automatically follow. So persuasive were the calls for **teamwork** and *team building* that in many organizations, the shift to such work groups was made in a precipitous fashion. Little wonder, then, that results were often disappointing.

Now the issue of teams is being reexamined—and this time more systematically. As David Luther, head of quality programs at Corning, Inc., puts it, "Teams get to be teams by learning to be teams. Training in teamwork is required."[25] He goes on to remark that the need to belong is indeed powerful in human behavior, and it can be put to good purpose in teamwork. "What gives a team richness, texture, and ultimately resourcefulness," he says, "is the diversity of its members and an artful linking of their diverse

gifts." In other words, teams can't be formed in a random or haphazard manner; rather, they should be composed of individuals with complementary skills. And teams begin to function as teams only after they have completed a period of learning—a period of group formation, if you will. (Again, recall our discussion of this topic in chapter 8.)

When do teams work, adding something over and above more traditional work groups? Experts on this issue agree that teamwork is beneficial primarily for tasks that involve a high degree of interdependence among separate jobs. In contrast, jobs involving little uncertainty and little technology-based interdependence can be handled through older and more traditional approaches.

Another problem with teams is that often, when organizations switch to this format, they fail to make corresponding adjustments in compensation systems. If work is carried out by teams, then rewards, too, must be tied to team performance. As Gerald E. Ledford, Jr., a professor at the University of Southern California, puts it: "Rewards must be in alignment with strategy or structure, or people will work in crosscurrents with each other."[26]

One of the most creative uses of teamwork in recent years involves the *Pairs Program* adopted by Monsanto and many other companies. This method is used to enhance understanding and communication between people who must work together but come from different ethnic or cul-

size of the available "pie" (whatever it is) is maximized for all concerned? These questions are difficult to answer accurately, because most cultures have strong norms against pure selfishness—concern purely with one's own outcomes. Yet, the temptation to pursue one's own interests is strong and hard to resist in many situations. (Recall the views stated by Art in the chapter-opening story.) Several basic models of conflict take careful note of these facts, suggesting that conflict, as an organizational or interpersonal process, can best be understood in terms of two key dimensions: **distribution**—concern with one's own outcomes; and **integration**—concern with the outcomes of others. A large body of research evidence indicates that these dimensions are important and that, moreover, they are largely independent. Thus, in a given

tural backgrounds.[27] When a dispute or misunderstanding between such individuals occurs, a *Pair* that mirrors the racial and ethnic backgrounds of the people involved, plus their educational level and experience, is called in for consultation. Pairs have received intensive training on how cultural backgrounds shape attitudes, and their job is to determine whether disputes stem from racism, sexism, and other forms of bias, or merely from contrasting roles. The program appears to be highly successful in many instances. For example, in one case, a black engineer felt that his boss, a white marketing manager, questioned everything he did because of racist attitudes. A Pair concluded, however, that the difficulties the engineer and his boss were experiencing were mainly due to a clash of perspectives, which often occurs be-

tween engineers and marketing experts (see Figure 10–6).

In this and many other cases, Monsanto and other companies have used specially trained teams of employees to "head trouble off at the pass" and enhance communication within the organization. The training that Pair members receive—and then share with other organization members—sometimes produces profound changes. As one participant from an Alcoa, Inc., program describes it: "I no longer let my seven-year-old tell ethnic jokes or call something stupid or ugly when in fact it is just different. The training changes how you deal with people everywhere." In sum, the Pairs Program appears to be a highly successful application of one basic team principle: people working together *can* often solve problems they cannot solve alone.

FIGURE 10–6   The Pairs Technique: One Valuable Application of Teamwork

Disputes between people of different ethnic or cultural backgrounds can sometimes be settled in an amicable fashion by trained teams, known as *Pairs*. Pairs match the individuals involved in the dispute in several respects—ethnic background, training, and amount of experience. Thus, they are in a good position to determine the actual causes of the dispute and to recommend beneficial resolutions.

FIGURE 10–7

Basic Styles of Resolving Conflict

Different approaches to resolving conflict reflect two underlying dimensions present in most conflict situations: concern with one's own outcomes and concern with the outcomes of others. For example, competition reflects high concern with one's own interests but low concern with the interests of others. In contrast, accommodation reflects high concern with others' interests but relatively low concern with one's own interests.

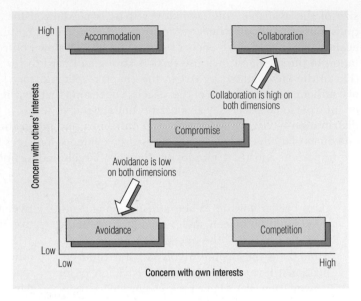

situation, it is possible to pursue actions that are high in both distribution and integration, low in both dimensions, or high in one and low in the other.[28] In fact, various combinations of these motives underlie five distinct styles of handling conflict with others: *competing, collaborating, avoiding, accommodating,* and *compromising.*[29]

Figure 10–7 illustrates the position of each of these styles with respect to integration and distribution. *Compromise,* which involves splitting issues down the middle, is in the middle on both dimensions: it reflects moderate degrees of concern with one's own interests and the interests of others. In contrast, *competition* represents a style of conflict resolution reflecting high concern with one's own interests but low concern with the interests of others. *Avoidance* is a style reflecting low standing on both dimensions, whereas *collaboration*—seeking maximum outcomes for both sides—is high on both dimensions. *Accommodation*—giving others whatever they want—is low in distribution but high in integration.

Several researchers have designed questionnaires to measure personal preferences for these contrasting styles of conflict resolution—for example, the Killmann-Thomas *Management of Differences* (MODE) questionnaire, and the *Rahim Organizational Conflict Inventory* (ROCI).[30,31] Recent studies suggest that these questionnaires do indeed measure styles of conflict resolution related to the dimensions of integration and distribution. Moreover, the various styles appear to represent points on these dimensions close to the ones shown in Figure 10–7. Recent evidence indicates that avoiding and accommodating may be more similar than anticipated, perhaps because both involve distinctly nonconfrontational modes of behavior.[32] In addition, the two most popular scales (the MODE and the ROCI) appear to require further refinement to distinguish more clearly between certain styles of conflict resolution: competing and collaborating in the case of the MODE, and compromising and collaborating in the case of the ROCI. These distinct styles are not discriminated by scores on these scales as cleanly as one might wish.[33] In general, however, it appears that conflict can indeed be understood in terms of the dimensions of *integration* and *distribution* and that major styles or approaches to resolving conflict represent distinct points along these two dimensions. (Do people from different cultures prefer contrasting styles of resolving conflicts? And do they show different levels of concern with others' and their own interests? For information on these intriguing possibilities, see the **International/Multicultural Perspective** section on pp. 370–371.)

Conflict: A Modern Perspective

Opposing interests, it is widely agreed, lie at the core of most conflicts. Indeed, it makes little sense to use the term *conflict* in the absence of incompatible interests or aspirations. Yet conflict involves much more than this. Bitter disputes often erupt in situations where the interests of the two sides are *not* clearly opposed. In other cases, conflict fails to develop despite deep divisions between potential adversaries. Such situations suggest that a full understanding of conflict will require much more than mere identification of opposing interests. Many other factors relating to the thoughts, feelings, and actions of the people involved enter into the picture and must be carefully considered. How, then, should we conceive of organizational conflict? A model proposed recently by Thomas offers one intriguing answer.[34]

According to Thomas, it is important to view conflict as a *process*—a complex series of events over time that both *reflect* external conditions and, in turn, *affect* them. More specifically, Thomas notes that conflict episodes between individuals or groups stem from preceding events and conditions, and produce results and outcomes. In other words, conflict is part of a continuing, ongoing relationship between two or more parties, not an isolated event that can be considered in and of itself. What, then, are the key elements in this continuing process? Thomas calls attention to several.

The first is *awareness of the conflict*. Thomas suggests that conflicts are, to a large extent, in the eye of the beholder—they occur only when the parties involved recognize the existence of opposing interests. This, of course, is why conflict sometimes fails to emerge when outside observers notice deep divisions between potential opponents. The parties themselves do not notice (or care to notice!) these conditions, and if they do not, conflict remains only a possibility.

Second, once aware of the conflict, both parties experience emotional reactions to it and think about it in various ways. These emotions and thoughts are crucial to the course of the developing conflict. For example, if the emotional reactions of one or both sides include anger and resentment from past wrongs or from contemplated future ones, the conflict is likely to be intense. If such reactions are absent, or if other emotions (e.g., fear over the potential costs) are dominant, it may be of lower intensity and develop quite differently. Similarly, the parties' reasoning concerning the conflict can have profound effects on its form and ultimate resolution. Here, both *rational-instrumental reasoning* (e.g., thoughts concerning potential costs and benefits, the conflict's bearing on major goals) and *normative reasoning* (e.g., concerns about what is appropriate in the situation or how others would react) are important.

Third, on the basis of such thoughts and emotions, individuals formulate specific *intentions*—plans to adopt various strategies during the conflict. These may be quite general (e.g., plans to adopt a conciliatory, cooperative approach) or quite specific (e.g., decisions to follow specific bargaining tactics).

In the next step, such intentions are translated into actual behavior. These actions then elicit some response from the opposite side, and the process recycles. That is, the opponent's reactions affect current thoughts and feelings about the conflict,

AN INTERNATIONAL/MULTICULTURAL PERSPECTIVE

Conflict and Face in Five Different Cultures

Cultures differ in many ways, but one factor that appears to have important implications for conflict and how it is handled is known as the **individualistic-collectivistic dimension.**[35] Individualistic cultures tend to value individual goals over group goals, and individual rights and needs over collective responsibilities and obligations. Examples include the United States, Australia, and many European countries. Collectivistic cultures, in contrast, tend to value group goals over individual goals, and collective needs over individual needs or rights. Cultures classified as collectivistic include China, Korea, and many other Asian countries.

What does this individualistic-collectivistic dimension have to do with conflict and approaches to its resolution? A theory proposed recently by Ting-Toomey and her colleagues suggests two important links.[36] First, according to this theory, people from collectivistic cultures would be expected to show greater concern than people from individualistic cultures with *others' face*—with efforts to maintain others' self-respect and personal image. This means that they would avoid humiliating their opponents by making them look foolish in front of others, and would try to give them an "out"—a good excuse for negative performances or outcomes. (Again, recall Art's approach to negotiations from the chapter-opening story. Clearly, he is very low on concern with others' face.) In contrast, people from individualistic cultures would be expected to show greater concern with *self-face*—with protecting or enhancing their own image and self-respect.

Ting-Toomey's theory also predicts that people from individualistic cultures would tend to use more dominating strategies (e.g., competition) and more integrative strategies (collaboration) to manage conflict, whereas people from collectivistic cultures would tend to use more obliging (e.g., accommodation) or avoidance-oriented tactics.

To test these predictions, Ting-Toomey and her colleagues conducted several studies comparing the conflict-handling tactics of people from various cultures.[37] In the most recent of these, seven researchers from five different countries asked almost 1,000 students at various universities in the United States, Japan, China, Korea, and Taiwan to complete questionnaires designed to measure their concern with maintaining their own face and that of their opponent in a conflict situation. In addition, the students completed the ROCI-II measure of preferences for each of five distinct modes of resolving interpersonal conflicts (dominating, obliging, integrating, avoiding, and compromising). Results offered strong support for Ting-Toomey's theory, and for the view that culture plays an important role in conflict-handling actions.

First, with respect to maintaining their own and others' face, participants from China, Korea, and Taiwan all reported more concern with maintaining others' face in conflict situations than did participants from the United States. Turning to maintenance of self-face, participants from Japan reported the highest concern, and those from Korea reported the lowest concern. Participants from the United States, China, and Taiwan were intermediate in this respect.

Significant cultural differences also emerged with respect to preferences for various modes of handling conflict. As expected, U.S. participants reported significantly greater preference for dominating than did those from Japan and Korea. They also reported stronger preference for integrating than did those from Japan. Highest scores on obliging and avoiding were earned by participants from Taiwan and China, and those from the United States and Korea showed the lowest scores (refer to Figure 10–8).

In sum, it was found in this study and in several others that cultural factors do indeed play a key role in conflict situations. People from collectivistic cultures tend to show more concern with protecting or maintaining their opponent's face than do people from individualistic cultures. And those from individualistic cultures tend to show stronger preferences for resolving conflicts through dominating and integrating approaches, whereas people from collectivistic cultures tend

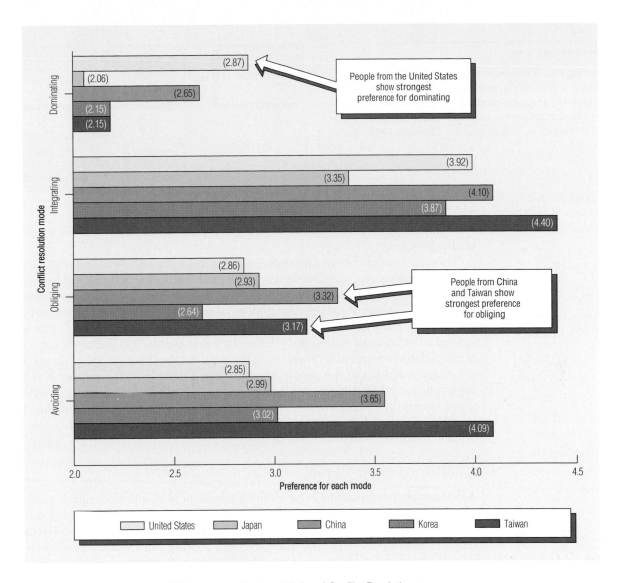

People from the United States show strongest preference for dominating

People from China and Taiwan show strongest preference for obliging

United States   Japan   China   Korea   Taiwan

FIGURE 10–8   Cultural Differences in Preferred Modes of Conflict Resolution

As shown here, people from *individualistic* cultures such as the United States showed stronger preferences than people from *collectivistic* cultures such as China and Taiwan for resolving conflicts through dominating. In contrast, people from collectivistic cultures showed stronger preferences for resolving conflicts through obliging and avoiding. (*Source:* Based on data from Ting-Toomey et al., 1991; see Note 37.)

to prefer strategies based more on obliging and avoiding. This is not to imply, of course, that cultural factors are all-powerful; on the contrary, all individuals, regardless of their cultural background, may adopt any approach to resolving specific conflicts, and may differ greatly, as individuals, in their concern for their own and others' face. But culture does appear to form an important backdrop for conflict, so efforts to understand this important process—and how best to manage it—should certainly take cultural factors into account. To the extent that cultural influences are ignored or overlooked, the picture of conflict that emerges from ongoing research will remain incomplete.

FIGURE 10–9

Conflict: A Modern View

According to a framework proposed by Thomas, conflict is a complex process involving the thoughts and emotions of participants, their intentions to behave in certain ways, and their overt actions. (*Source:* Based on suggestions by Thomas, 1992; see Note 3.)

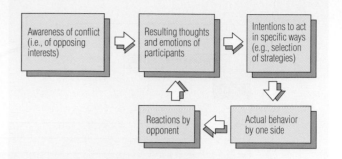

intentions concerning further behavior, and so on. (See Figure 10–9 for a summary of this process.)

Thomas's model of organizational conflict is quite sophisticated and rests on a firm basis of empirical research. However, there can be little doubt that it will be modified in the years ahead as additional information about conflict and its components accumulates. Perhaps its main contribution, then, is that it calls attention to the following important facts: (1) organizational conflict is an ongoing *process* that occurs against a backdrop of continuing relationships and events; it is definitely not a short-term, isolated occurrence; (2) such conflict involves the thoughts, perceptions, memories, and emotions of the people involved; these must be taken into account in any complete model of organizational conflict; and (3) conflict stems from a very wide range of conditions and events—ones relating to individuals and ones relating to the structure, norms, and functioning of organizations. It is to these factors—the major causes of conflict—that we turn next.

Conflict: Its Major Causes

As we noted above, conflict involves the presence or perception of opposing interests. Yet this condition, by itself, is neither a necessary nor a sufficient condition for the occurrence of actual conflict. Open confrontations sometimes fail to develop despite the existence of incompatible interests. And conflict does often emerge when opposing interests are not present, or when, at least, ambiguity exists. Clearly, then, many factors and conditions contribute to its occurrence. These can be divided into two major groups: factors relating to organizational structure or functioning, and factors relating to interpersonal relations.

Organizational Causes of Conflict   Perhaps the most obvious organization-based cause of conflict is *competition over scarce resources.* No organization has unlimited resources, and conflicts often arise over the division or distribution of space, money, equipment, or personnel. Unfortunately, such conflicts are often intensified by the *self-serving bias* described in chapter 2. Each side tends to inflate its contribution to the organization, and therefore its fair share of available resources. The result can be intense, prolonged conflict.

Two closely related factors involve *ambiguity over responsibility* or *jurisdiction.* In the former case, groups or individuals within an organization are uncertain as to who is responsible for performing various tasks or duties. As a result, each involved party disclaims responsibility, and conflict can develop over this issue. In the latter instance, uncertainty exists over who has jurisdiction or authority. Disputes over this issue, too, can be intense.

A third organizational factor that often plays a role in conflict is *interdependence* and events stemming from it. In most organizations, various units, groups, and

The accepted conflict level in an organization is usually determined by the person in charge, such as the CEO. If the CEO screams, abuses people, and doesn't listen to other people's opinions, then this attitude will be reflected by other employees down the line, because lower-level managers tend to emulate the behavior of their superiors. So if managers want their employees to handle conflict in a certain manner, they should set an example for their subordinates to follow. [Weinstein, S. (1990, May). Conflicts: The good, the bad, and the ugly. *Progressive Grocer,* pp. 88–92.]

individuals must depend on others for performance of their own jobs. They receive input from others and cannot proceed without it. When input is delayed or delivered in an incomplete or unsatisfactory form, strong conflict may result. This is hardly surprising; groups or individuals faced with this situation perceive (and rightly so) that their major goals are being blocked or interfered with by others. Little wonder that they then retaliate in kind and that productive work may grind to a halt (or at least slow appreciably) in the spiraling conflict that follows.

We have already described yet another organization-based cause of conflict: *reward systems*. When such systems pit one unit or group against another (as is often the case), a degree of conflict is practically guaranteed. This is especially likely if the people involved perceive the system as somehow unfair or biased.[38] In such instances, the groups that fail to attain important benefits (e.g., bonuses, raises) may experience resentment, and unnecessary conflict may be the next step in the process.

Conflict is sometimes also a by-product of *differentiation* within an organization. As organizations grow and develop, many experience a trend toward an increasing number of departments or divisions. Individuals working in these groups become socialized to them, and tend to accept their norms and values. As they come to identify with these work groups, their perceptions of other organization members may alter. They view people outside their units as different, less worthy, and less competent than those within it. At the same time, they tend to overvalue their own unit and the people within it. Ultimately, this process may encourage costly conflicts. After all, if individuals in each department or unit are fiercely loyal to their own turf, they may lose sight of shared organizational goals and tend to focus, instead, on pursuing their own self-interests.

Increasing differentiation within an organization encourages individuals within it to divide it into "us" (members of our own group) and "them" (people outside it), and this, in turn, can be a contributing factor in the initiation of conflict. (See Figure 10–10 for a summary of the organization-based causes of conflict discussed in this section.)

Finally, as noted recently by Kabanoff, conflict can stem from *power* relationships between organization members.[39] Kabanoff states that in organizations, as in other settings, a continuous tension exists between the norms of *equity*—the belief that organization members should be rewarded in terms of their relative contributions; and *equality*—the belief that everyone should receive the same or similar outcomes, at least in certain respects. These rules are often applied to different kinds of outcome. For example, equity is applied to raises, bonuses, and other tangible rewards. In

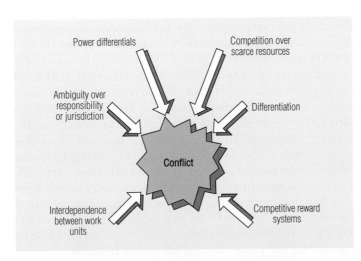

FIGURE 10–10

Organizational Causes of Conflict

Several organization-based factors contribute to the occurrence of conflict in work settings.

Test Bank question 10.36 relates to material on this page.

contrast, equality is applied to such socioemotional outcomes as courteous treatment, friendliness, and so on.

Kabanoff reasons that the greater the power differential between any two organizational members, the greater their acceptance of equity as the distributive rule governing their relationship. As a result, the likelihood of overt conflict over distribution of available rewards decreases. However, at the same time, the low-power individuals may experience feelings of frustration and decreased involvement in the relationship—reactions sometimes described as *nondirected conflict*. So, in a sense, organizations face something of a trade-off where power differentials and conflict are concerned. High-power differentials in organizational relationships tend to minimize clear cognitions of injustice on the part of the less powerful parties, and so also reduce the likelihood of overt conflict over reward distributions. At the same time, however, such differentials give rise to a kind of smoldering discontent, which may translate into nondirected conflict. Whatever the precise outcomes, Kabanoff's theory calls attention to the fact that both power differentials and basic principles of distributive justice can contribute to conflict in organizational settings.

Interpersonal Causes of Organizational Conflict   In the past, most research on organizational conflict focused on the type of organizational causes noted above. More recently, however, attention has been drawn to the possibility that in many instances, costly organizational conflicts stem as much (or perhaps more) from interpersonal factors—relations between specific individuals—as from organizational structure or underlying conflicts of interest. First, consider the impact of lasting *grudges*. When people are angered by others, and especially when they are made to "lose face" (to look foolish publicly), they may develop strong negative attitudes toward the individuals responsible for these outcomes. The result: they spend considerable time and effort planning or actually seeking revenge for these wrongs. Unfortunately, such grudges can persist for years, with obvious negative effects for the organizations or work groups involved.

Second, conflict often stems from (or is intensified by) *faulty attributions*—errors concerning the causes behind others' behavior. When individuals find that their interests have been thwarted by another person, they generally try to determine *why* this person acted in the way he or she did. Was it malevolence—a desire to harm them or give them a hard time? Or did the provoker's actions stem from factors beyond his or her control? A growing body of evidence suggests that when people reach the former conclusion, anger and subsequent conflict are more likely and more intense than when they reach the latter conclusion.[40] For example, in one study on this issue, Baron had students engage in simulated negotiations with another person (actually an accomplice).[41] Both individuals played the role of executives representing different departments within a large organization; they bargained over the division of $1,000,000 in surplus funds between their respective departments. The accomplice adopted a very confrontational stance, demanding fully $800,000 out of $1,000,000 in available funds for his or her own department, and offered only two small concessions during the negotiations. As the bargaining proceeded, the accomplice made several statements indicating that he or she had been ordered to behave in this "tough" manner by his or her constituents. In other words, the accomplice adopted a bargaining tactic often described as the "my hands are tied" strategy. In one condition, participants received information suggesting these claims were true (the opponent appeared to be *sincere* in his or her statements); in another, they learned that these claims were false (the opponent appeared to be *insincere*). As predicted, participants reported more negative reactions to the accomplice, and stronger tendencies to avoid and compete with this person on future occasions, when they learned that he or she had misrepresented the causes behind his or her behavior.

Test Bank questions 10.37 and 10.52 relate to material on this page.

In related research, Bies, Shapiro, and their colleagues have examined the role of *explanations* or **causal accounts** in reactions to potentially conflict-inducing actions by others.[42,43] The results of these studies indicate that the explanations individuals provide for provocative, conflict-inducing actions play an important role in whether, and to what extent, conflict actually occurs. The more adequate these explanations and the more sincere they are perceived to be, the lower individuals' anger and disapproval of the people who engage in actions such as refusing requests or delivering bad news. But precisely what aspects of an explanation lead recipients to view it as adequate or inadequate? A series of studies conducted by Shapiro, Buttner, and Barry offers revealing insights into this issue.[44]

In one of these studies, undergraduate business students were presented with a scenario in which a student who received a failing grade requested an explanation from the professor. Several aspects of the professor's response were systematically varied to study the effects of these factors on subjects' perceptions of the explanation's adequacy. One factor involved the apparent *sincerity* of the professor's explanation. In the high-sincerity condition, the professor responded with a letter in which he addressed the student personally, expressed concern, and offered to help. In the low-sincerity condition, subjects received a memo that addressed the student by social security number and excluded expressions of concern. A second factor varied was the *specificity* of the explanation. In the high-specificity condition, a clear explanation of how the grade was reached was provided; in the low-specificity condition, no information of this type was included. A third factor was the *severity* of the outcome produced. In the high-outcome-severity condition, the student would not be able to graduate on time because of the failing grade. In the low-outcome-severity condition, in contrast, the failing grade would not interfere with graduation.

After reading a scenario in which each factor was either high or low, participants in the study rated the adequacy of the professor's explanation to the student. Consistent with previous findings, results indicated that students viewed the explanation as more adequate in the high-sincerity and high-specificity conditions than in the low-sincerity and low-specificity conditions. Perhaps even more important, the three factors varied in the study (sincerity, specificity, and outcome severity) interacted in influencing ratings of the explanation's adequacy. When severity of outcome was low, high sincerity and high specificity increased an explanation's perceived adequacy. When severity of outcome was high, however, sincerity did *not* increase perceived adequacy when the explanation was also high in specificity (see Figure 10–11 on p. 376). Why did sincerity fail to yield beneficial effects under these conditions? Perhaps, Shapiro and her colleagues suggest, because in this situation sincerity represented a kind of overkill. When an explanation is specific and detailed, adding statements designed to convey interpersonal sensitivity may backfire and create an impression of *insincerity*, as in the adage "He/she doth protest too much."[45] Whether or not this was the case, the findings obtained by Shapiro and her colleagues, plus those reported by other researchers, indicate that several characteristics of explanations do indeed determine their perceived adequacy. And, as noted above, the more adequate an explanation for a provocative action, the less likely that action is to initiate conflict between the individuals involved.

A third interpersonal factor of considerable importance in generating organizational conflict might be termed *faulty communication*. This refers to the fact that individuals often communicate with others in a way that angers or annoys them, even though it is not their intention to do so. Faulty communication often involves a lack of clarity—for example, a manager is certain that she communicated her wishes clearly to a subordinate, but the subordinate is confused about what he is supposed to do. When the manager later finds that the task has not been completed, she is annoyed. The subordinate, in turn, is angered by what he considers unfair treatment.

FIGURE 10–11

Explanations for Provocative Actions: What Makes Them
Seem Adequate?

Explanations that were *specific* and seemed *sincere*
were generally rated as more adequate than
explanations that were not specific and seemed
insincere. However, sincerity produced beneficial
effects only when the importance of the outcomes
involved was relatively low. When importance was
high, adding statements designed to create the
impression of sincerity did not enhance apparent
adequacy of explanations—perhaps because this
constituted overkill in the specific situation studied.
(*Source:* Based on data from Shapiro, Buttner, &
Barry, in press; see Note 43.)

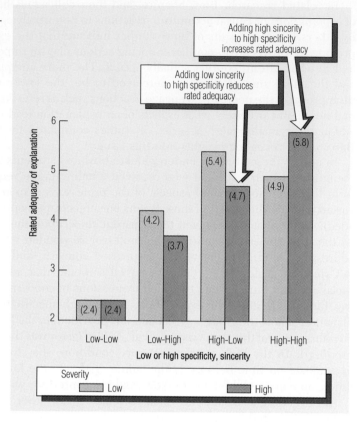

In other cases, conflict involves inappropriate *criticism*—negative feedback delivered
in a manner that angers the recipient instead of helping this person to do a better
job. What makes criticism *constructive* rather than *destructive*? Research findings
point to the factors shown in Table 10–1.[46,47] We're sure that none of the factors
listed there will surprise you: after all, we have all been on the receiving end of
criticism, and know that negative feedback that is delivered in a considerate and
timely manner, does not contain threats, and does not make unflattering attributions
about the causes behind our behavior or performance is far preferable to criticism
that is harsh, contains threats, and so on. The following facts are surprising, however.
First, although most people understand these basic principles, they often find it
difficult to follow them in their dealings with subordinates, coworkers, friends, and
family. Most individuals are reluctant to deliver negative feedback to others. As a
result, they make no comment—until the problem becomes so great, or their anger
and irritation so strong, that they can no longer hold their tempers in check. What
follows is an angry outburst, unlikely to adhere to the simple rules for constructive
criticism listed above.[48]

Second, as you might expect from our discussion of social perception in chapter
2, we often show a strong *self-serving bias* with respect to criticism. In other words,
we tend to perceive criticism that we deliver as more fair, designed to help, more
appropriate, and more deserved than criticism we receive. Such effects have been
reported in several recent studies.[49] In one of these, managers from several different
companies described incidents in which they had given criticism to another person
and in which they had received criticism themselves. For each incident, they rated

TABLE 10-1 Constructive versus Destructive Criticism

The factors listed here distinguish *constructive* criticism (negative feedback that may be accepted by the recipient and improve his or her performance) from *destructive* criticism (negative feedback likely to be rejected by the recipient and unlikely to improve his or her performance).

Constructive Criticism	Destructive Criticism
Considerate—protects self-esteem of recipient	Inconsiderate—harsh, sarcastic, biting
Does not contain threats	Contains threats
Timely—occurs as soon as possible after the poor/inadequate performance	Not timely—occurs after inappropriate delay
Does not attribute poor performance to internal causes	Attributes poor performance to internal causes (e.g., lack of effort, motivation, ability)
Specific—focuses on aspects of performance that were inadequate	General—a sweeping condemnation of performance
Focuses on performance, not on the recipient	Focuses on the recipient—his or her personal characteristics
Offers concrete suggestions for improvement	Offers no concrete suggestions for improvement
Motivated by desire to help the recipient improve	Motivated by anger, desire to assert dominance over recipient, desire for revenge, and so on

Source: Based on suggestions by Weisinger, 1989, & Baron, 1990; see Notes 45, 46.

the criticism they delivered or received on a number of different dimensions. As predicted, they rated criticism they delivered more favorably than criticism they received in several respects. For example, they reported that criticism they delivered stemmed more from a desire to help the recipient than criticism they received, and that criticism they delivered was more fair than criticism they received (see Figure 10–12 on p. 378). This self-serving bias, in turn, leads individuals to conclude that they do a better job of delivering criticism than is actually the case. The result: they devote little or no effort to doing a better job in this important process.

Finally, several personal characteristics, too, seem to play a role in organizational conflict. For example, Type A individuals report becoming involved in conflict with others more frequently than Type B people (refer to our discussion of this characteristic in chapter 6).[50] Conversely, people who are high in *self-monitoring* (ones who are highly aware of how others are reacting to them) report resolving conflict in more productive ways (e.g., through collaboration or compromise) than those who are low in self-monitoring.[51]

In summary, considerable evidence suggests that conflict in work settings often stems from relations between individuals and from their personal characteristics, as well as from underlying structural (organization-based) factors. At first glance, this finding might appear to be quite pessimistic in its implications for the reduction or management of such conflict; after all, it adds several potential causes to those that have traditionally been viewed as important. In fact, however, it can actually be interpreted as quite optimistic. Interpersonal behavior, and even many personal

FIGURE 10–12

The Self-Serving Bias in Negative Feedback

Managers rated criticism (negative feedback) they had delivered to others as being more fair and as stemming more from a desire to help the recipient than was true for criticism they received from others. (*Source:* Baron, in press; see Note 48.)

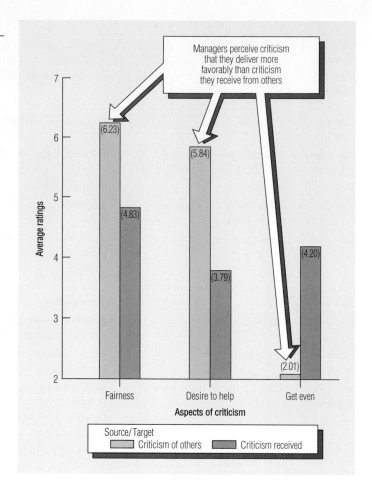

characteristics, can readily be modified. Indeed, in many cases, these may be easier to change than organizational structure, and easier to modify than built-in underlying conflicts of interest. For this reason, understanding the interpersonal causes of organizational conflict may offer important, practical benefits.

CONFLICT: ITS MAJOR EFFECTS

In everyday speech, the term *conflict* has strong negative connotations. It seems to imply anger, direct confrontations, and harsh, damaging behavior. In fact, however, conflict in work settings actually operates like the proverbial "double-edged sword." Depending on why it occurs and how it develops, it can yield beneficial as well as harmful effects.

Conflict: The Negative Side

Conflict can easily get out of hand when the rewards involved are large. A growing problem in international business has been corporate espionage, or spying on competitors.

Some of the negative effects produced by conflict are too obvious to require much comment. For example, it often produces strong negative emotions and thus can be quite stressful. Conflict frequently interferes with communication between individuals, groups, or divisions. In this way, it can all but eliminate coordination between them. Third, it diverts attention and needed energies away from major tasks and

Test Bank questions 10.41, 10.53, and 10.72 relate to material on this page.

efforts to attain key organizational goals. In all these ways, conflict can seriously interfere with organizational effectiveness.

Other negative effects of conflict are somewhat more subtle and are sometimes easily overlooked. First, it has been found that conflict between groups often encourages their leaders to shift from participative to authoritarian styles.[52] The reason for this is as follows: Groups experiencing stress require firm direction. Recognizing this fact, their leaders adopt more controlling tactics when conflict develops. As a result of such changes, groups experiencing conflict tend to provide less pleasant work environments than ones not faced with this type of stress.

Second, conflict increases the tendency of both sides to engage in negative stereotyping. As we noted earlier, the members of opposing groups or units tend to emphasize the differences between them. These differences are interpreted in a negative light, so that each side views the other in increasingly unfavorable terms.

Finally, conflict leads each side to close ranks and emphasize loyalty to their own department or group. Anyone who suggests, even tentatively, that the other side's position has some merit is viewed as a traitor and is strongly censured. As a result, it becomes increasingly difficult for opponents to take each other's perspective—a development that sharply reduces the likelihood of an effective resolution of their differences,[53] and increases the likelihood of *groupthink* (see chapter 14).

Conflict: The Positive Side

The picture is not entirely bleak, however. Although conflict often has a disruptive impact on organizations, it can, under some conditions, also yield important benefits.[54] First, conflict serves to bring problems that have previously been ignored out into the open; since recognition of problems is a necessary first step to their solution, conflict can sometimes be useful in this way. Second, conflict motivates people on both sides of an issue to know and understand each other's positions more fully. As noted by Tjosvold, this can foster open-mindedness and lead each side to incorporate aspects of the opposing views into their own.[55]

Third, conflict often encourages the consideration of new ideas and approaches, facilitating innovation and change. This is so because once open conflict erupts, an organization or work unit simply cannot continue with "business as usual." The need for hard decisions, new policies, major shifts in personnel, or even a new internal structure is driven home, and appropriate change may then follow.

Fourth, growing evidence suggests that conflict can lead to better decisions. When decision makers receive information incompatible with their views—which is often the case when conflict exists—they tend to make better judgments and reach more adequate decisions than when controversy does not exist.[56]

Fifth, conflict enhances group loyalty, increasing motivation and performance within the groups or units involved. Each strives to attain higher levels of excellence to outdo its rival, and if not carried too far, such efforts can have beneficial effects.

Finally, recent findings indicate that conflict, especially *cognitive conflict*, in which opposing views are brought out into the open and fully discussed, can enhance organizational commitment.[57] In contrast, to the extent that such discussion is blocked and a free exchange of opposing views is not permitted to occur, job satisfaction may be reduced.[58]

In summary, conflict can actually contribute to organizational effectiveness. Note, however, that benefits occur *only* when conflict is carefully managed and does not get out of control. If conflict is permitted to become extreme, rationality—and the potential benefits described above—may vanish in a haze of intense negative emo-

For example, an investigation found that the French intelligence agency Direction Generale de la Securite Exterieure had recruited spies in the European branches of IBM and Texas Instruments. The spies were monitoring and intercepting electronic communication about research and marketing, and sending the messages to the French computer manufacturer Compagnie des Machines Bull. Experts have forecasted that the use of corporate espionage will continue in the future. [Peterzell, J. (1990, May 28). When "friends" become moles. *Time,* p. 50.]

FIGURE 10–13

Positive Effects of Conflict

Contrary to popular belief, conflict can produce a number of beneficial effects. The most important of these are shown here.

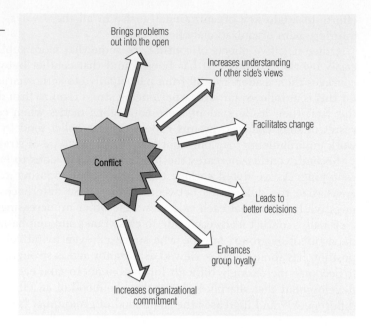

tions. Assuming that such dangers are avoided, however, existing evidence suggests that conflict can indeed often play a constructive role in many organizations. (Please see Figure 10–13 for an overview of the potential positive effects of conflict.)

CONFLICT: ITS EFFECTIVE MANAGEMENT

If conflict can indeed yield benefits as well as costs, the key task organizations face with respect to this process is *managing* its occurrence. In short, the overall goal should not be to eliminate conflict; instead, it should be to adopt procedures for maximizing its potential benefits while minimizing its potential costs. Fortunately, a number of approaches have been found useful in this regard. Several of these will now be reviewed.

Bargaining: The Universal Process

In a recent survey, 82 percent of negotiators reported that the tactics used in negotiation settings raised serious ethical questions. For example, negotiators who were surveyed felt it was "somewhat ethical" to pay off friends and associates to get information about the opposition, to make threats to harm opponents, and to make hollow promises to obtain the cooperation of former opponents. It is curious that these questionable practices are believed to be

By far the most common strategy for resolving organizational conflicts, and therefore for managing them effectively, is **bargaining** or **negotiation**.[59] In this process, opposing sides to a dispute exchange offers, counteroffers, and concessions, either directly or through representatives. If the process is successful, a solution acceptable to both sides is attained and the conflict is effectively resolved, perhaps with "extras" such as enhanced understanding and improved relations between the two sides. If, instead, bargaining is unsuccessful, costly deadlock may result and the conflict may intensify. What factors determine which of these outcomes occurs? Given the importance of bargaining, and its occurrence in virtually all spheres of life, this question has been the subject of intensive study for decades. The answer that has emerged from such research would fill several volumes, so we can do no more than touch on it briefly here. If you are particularly interested in this topic, please refer to recent volumes by Sheppard, Bazerman, and Lewicki, or Lewicki and Litterer.[60,61]

One group of factors that strongly affects the outcomes of negotiations involves the specific tactics adopted by bargainers. Many of these are designed to reduce opponents' aspirations—to convince them that they have little chance of reaching their goals and should, instead, accept offers that are actually quite favorable to the side proposing them. Many specific strategies can be used for this purpose. For example, one side can suggest that it has other potential partners and will withdraw from the current negotiations if its proposals are not accepted. Similarly, one party to a dispute can claim that its break-even point is much lower than it really is—a procedure known as the "big lie" technique.[62] If the other side accepts this information, it may make sizable concessions. Third, the course of negotiations and final settlements are often strongly affected by the nature of initial offers. Relatively extreme offers seem to put strong pressure on opponents to make concessions, resulting in settlements favorable to the side adopting such positions.[63] On the other hand, if initial offers are too extreme, opponents may be angered and decide to seek other negotiating partners.

A second group of factors that determines the nature and outcomes of bargaining involves the cognitive set or focus adopted by negotiators. Several studies suggest that when bargainers adopt a *positive frame*—focusing on the potential benefits of negotiations and of the settlements that may result—bargaining is facilitated. In contrast, when they adopt a *negative frame*—focusing on potential losses or costs—bargaining is impaired.[64] In short, expectations or cognitive sets shape reality, determining the nature and course of actual bargaining.

A third aspect of negotiations that plays an important role in this process is the *perceptions* of the people involved.[65] Recent studies by Thompson and his colleagues reveal that negotiators enter bargaining situations with important misperceptions about the situation. In particular, they seem to begin with the view that their own interests and those of the other side are entirely incompatible—the **incompatibility error**. This, of course, causes them to overlook interests that are actually compatible. In addition, they tend to begin with the view, often false, that the other party places the same importance or priority that they do on each issue, a tendency known as the **fixed-sum error**. Both of these assumptions are false and often prevent bargainers from obtaining an agreement that is maximally beneficial to both sides.

Fortunately, these misperceptions concerning interests and priorities do change during the course of negotiations, fading over time, often within the first few minutes of negotiations.[66] And experienced negotiators are less likely to fall prey to such errors than inexperienced ones.[67] However, many negotiators retain these false perceptions even over prolonged periods of bargaining, with the result that both parties experience lower payoffs than would otherwise be true. As might be expected, the smaller such errors in perception—the more accurate bargainers' perceptions of each other's outcomes are—the higher the joint payoffs obtained by both sides.[68] Clearly, then, steps designed to improve the accuracy of negotiators' perceptions of the situation they face and each other's interests and priorities can go a long way toward enhancing the outcomes of this process. Such steps may include training negotiators to seek information from each other during negotiations instead of clinging to their initial assumptions, and making them aware of the *fixed-sum* and *incompatibility errors* described above.

Perhaps the single most important factor determining the success of negotiations in producing settlements satisfactory to both sides, however, involves participants' overall orientation toward this process. Almost three decades ago, Walton and McKersie pointed out that people taking part in negotiations can approach such discussions from either of two distinct perspectives.[69] On the one hand, they can view negotiations as "win-lose" *(distributive)* situations in which gains by one side are necessarily linked with losses for the other. On the other hand, people can approach negotiations as potential "win-win" situations—ones in which the interests of the two sides are not

ethical in the context of negotiation ("all's fair—or at least ethical—in love and war"). [Heger, K. (1989, September). One communicator's gold star is another's scarlet letter. *IABC Communication World*, pp. 34–36.]

necessarily incompatible and in which the potential gains of both can be maximized. Not all situations offer the potential for such agreements, but many that at first glance seem to involve simple head-on clashes between the two sides do, in fact, provide such possibilities. If participants are willing to explore all options carefully, and exert the effort required to identify creative potential solutions, they can attain **integrative agreements**—ones that offer greater joint benefits than simple compromise (splitting all differences down the middle).

How can such integrative agreements be attained? Pruitt and his colleagues suggest the possibilities summarized in Table 10–2.[70] As you can see, these involve several distinct tactics. In *nonspecific compensation*, one side receives certain benefits and the other is compensated for providing these in some unrelated manner (e.g., by concessions on some other issue). In *logrolling*, each side makes concessions on relatively unimportant issues to attain concessions on issues it views as more central to its needs. For example, consider a dispute between scientists and management in a research department of a large organization. The scientists want to be free to order any equipment they want, to pursue projects they feel are important, and to do as little paperwork as possible. Management wants to hold costs to a minimum, wants the scientists to pursue only company-chosen projects, and requires many reports and forms. Under the strategy of logrolling, the scientists might agree to do more paperwork (a relatively unimportant issue to them, but one that is very important to management), and to pay more attention to costs (another issue of great importance to management). However, they would gain more freedom to pursue at least some projects of their own choosing (a central issue to the scientists).

Research findings suggest that when disputing parties strive for integrative agreements, joint outcomes do indeed increase. Moreover, the nature of their discussions changes. *Contentious tactics* such as threats or taking unyielding positions decrease, and the open exchange of accurate information between the two sides increases. Thus, not only does integrative bargaining increase the outcomes of both sides—it may enhance their relationships, too. Given such benefits, it seems clear that encouraging such an approach to negotiations is one highly effective strategy for managing real or potential conflicts.

TABLE 10–2   Techniques for Reaching Integrative Agreements

Several strategies can be useful in attaining *integrative agreements* in bargaining.

Type of Agreement	Description
Broadening the pie	Available resources are broadened so that both sides can obtain their major goals
Nonspecific compensation	One side gets what it wants; the other is compensated on an unrelated issue
Logrolling	Each party makes concessions on low-priority issues in exchange for concessions on issues that are of higher value to it
Cost cutting	One party gets what it desires, and the costs to the other party are reduced or eliminated
Bridging	Neither party gets its initial demands, but a new option that satisfies the major interests of both sides is developed

Source: Based on suggestions by Pruitt and his colleagues, 1983; see Note 70.

Third-Party Intervention: Help from the Outside

Despite the best efforts of both sides, negotiations sometimes deadlock. When they do, the aid of a third party, someone not directly involved in the dispute, is often sought. Such *third-party intervention* can take many forms, but the most common are **mediation** and **arbitration.** In mediation, the third party attempts, through various tactics, to facilitate voluntary agreements between the disputants. Mediators have no formal power and cannot impose an agreement on the two sides. Instead, they seek to clarify the issues involved and enhance communication between the opponents. Mediators sometimes offer specific recommendations for compromise or integrative solutions; in other cases, they merely guide disputants toward developing such solutions themselves. Their role is primarily that of *facilitator*—helping the two sides toward agreements they both find acceptable.

In contrast, *arbitrators* do have the power to impose (or at least strongly recommend) the terms of an agreement. In *binding arbitration*, the two sides agree in advance to accept these terms. In *voluntary arbitration*, though, the two sides retain the freedom to reject the recommended agreement (although the personal stature and expertise of the arbitrator may make it difficult for them to do so). In *conventional arbitration*, the arbitrator can offer any package of terms he or she wishes. However, in *final offer arbitration*, the arbitrator merely chooses between final offers made by the disputants.

Both mediation and arbitration can be helpful in resolving organizational conflicts. However, both suffer from certain drawbacks. Because it requires voluntary compliance by the disputing parties, mediation often proves ineffective. Indeed, it may simply serve to underscore the depth of the differences between the two sides. Arbitration suffers from several potential problems. First, it may exert a *chilling effect* on negotiations, bringing voluntary progress to a halt. Since both sides know the arbitrator will resolve the dispute for them, they see little point in engaging in serious bargaining, which, after all, is hard work. Second, one or both sides may come to suspect that the arbitrator is biased. The result: disputants become increasingly reluctant to agree to arbitration. Finally, there is some indication that commitment to arbitrated settlements is weaker than that to directly negotiated ones.

In most instances, mediation and arbitration are relatively formal procedures involving the services of people from outside an organization. Are they also used by practicing managers to resolve disputes between individuals under their authority? Research by Sheppard suggests that this is not usually the case.[71] Sheppard asked a large number of practicing managers to describe how they intervened in disputes between their subordinates. Careful analysis of their replies indicated that managers usually adopt one of three approaches in such situations, and none of these closely resembles traditional mediation. In the first and most common form, managers actively question both sides about the nature of the dispute and their opposing positions. Then they impose a solution that they believe will meet the needs of both sides.

In a second approach, managers don't actively question both sides—they simply listen to their respective points of view and then impose a solution. Finally, in a third pattern, managers make a quick, informal diagnosis of the nature of the conflict. After doing so, they tell both sides to negotiate directly with each other and reach a solution, warning them that if they don't succeed, the manager will impose one. Why are these approaches different from standard mediation or arbitration? Many factors probably play a role, but two seem most important. First, time constraints are often intense in such situations. Conflict between subordinates must be quickly resolved, so little opportunity exists for the institution of formal procedures. Second,

Companies are increasingly turning to alternate dispute-resolution systems as a means of avoiding costly litigation. For example, internal corporate mediation has proven particularly effective in resolving disputes before they reach the stage of arbitration or litigation. In three years, the A. L. Williams Company handled 2,000 disputes through a mediation specialist. All of the disputes were resolved to the mutual satisfaction of the participants. Using mediators has virtually eliminated the need for the company to go to court, thereby saving a tremendous amount of money while keeping employees satisfied. [Conti, A. J., & Cohn, J. C. (1988, Spring). An internal corporate mediation program. *Employment Relations Today*, pp. 56–61.]

managers have established relationships with the people involved. Thus, their approach to resolving conflicts between subordinates must occur within this context. Whatever the precise factors involved, it is clear that managers often seek to resolve conflicts between their subordinates in ways other than standard mediation or arbitration.

The Induction of Superordinate Goals

At several points in this chapter, we have noted that individuals often divide the world into two opposing camps: *us* and *them*. They perceive members of their own group as quite different from, and usually better than, people belonging to other groups. These dual tendencies to magnify the differences between one's own group and others and to disparage outsiders are very powerful and are as common in organizations as in other settings.[72] Further, they seem to play a central role in many conflicts between various departments, divisions, and work groups. How can they be countered? One answer, suggested by research findings, is through the induction of **superordinate goals**—ones that tie the interests of the two sides together. The basic idea behind this approach is simple: by inducing both parties to a conflict to focus on and work toward common objectives, the barriers between them—ones that interfere with communication, coordination, and agreement—can be weakened. Then the chances for cooperation rather than conflict are enhanced.

Escalative Interventions: Intensifying Conflicts to Resolve Them

Perhaps the most intriguing approach to managing organizational conflict suggested in recent years is one that seems, at first glance, to fly in the face of common sense. This approach, known as **escalative intervention,** seeks to intensify existing conflicts as a means of resolving them and attaining several related goals as well.[73] The reasoning behind this strategy is as follows: increasing the intensity of a conflict brings matters to a head. The underlying causes of friction or disagreement are clarified, and the motivation to search for effective, integrative solutions is increased. Then, instead of continuing to smolder beneath the surface, conflicts emerge into the open and can be resolved to the satisfaction of those involved.

According to Van de Vliert, several tactics can be used to intensify ongoing conflicts.[74] First, steps may be taken to add to the existing causes of conflict. For example, present channels of communication may be blocked, or the incompatibility of various goals can be emphasized. Similarly, various barriers to open conflict can be removed or lessened (e.g., direct contacts between the opposing sides can be increased; both sides may be urged to express negative feelings about one another). Second, the range of issues on which the conflict is based can be extended by calling attention to additional matters about which the disputants disagree. Third, additional parties can be added to the conflict, thus fueling its scope or intensity. In a fourth strategy, actions that serve to escalate the conflict can be encouraged (e.g., one side is urged to prove to the other that it is right, or to cause the other to lose face). Finally, the two sides may be encouraged to perceive hostile intentions in each other's actions, or to express strong disapproval of one another's proposals.

To the extent that such tactics succeed, ongoing conflict is intensified. Thus, strong pressures toward reaching a resolution are generated, and several benefits may follow. First, and most important, faced with mounting tension and a situation that is fast becoming intolerable, the two sides may increase their efforts to reach effective, integrative agreements. In addition, other benefits, such as the stimulation

Sometimes organizational conflicts are intensified by one side or the other. For example, Mobil Oil was recently in a conflict with *The Wall Street Journal.* Mobil was upset with the paper for printing unfavorable stories about the company. To retaliate, Mobil escalated the conflict by blocking all channels of communication with the paper by withholding all press releases from it (thereby putting the paper at a competitive disadvantage). Although Mobil's tactics sent a clear message to the newspaper, public relations experts do not recommend such escalating actions inasmuch as they can hamper future relations between the parties involved. [Doll, B. (1991, May). Avoiding culture conflict. *Public Relations Journal,* pp. 22–25.]

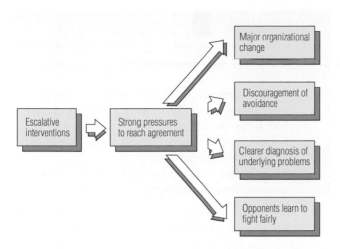

FIGURE 10-14

Reducing Conflict through Escalative Interventions

In some instances, increasing the intensity of ongoing conflicts can be a useful technique. Several potential benefits of such procedures are shown here. (*Source:* Based on suggestions by Van de Vliert, 1985; see Note 74.)

of major change, discouragement of avoidance behaviors, and a clearer diagnosis of underlying problems within an organization, may also result (see Figure 10–14). However, these favorable outcomes are certainly *not* guaranteed. They follow only when the individuals managing such an intensification of conflict are skilled in this task and are able to direct the growing tensions and friction into constructive channels.

Is it actually possible to direct escalating conflicts in this fashion? Research evidence suggests that it is, and that escalative interventions are indeed helpful in several contexts (e.g., in marital disputes as well as organizational ones). Thus, in this context, there appears to be a favorable trade-off between controlled, temporary escalation of conflict and its effective long-term management. (Efforts to manage conflict raise complex ethical issues. For a discussion of these, see the **Question of Ethics** section on pp. 386–387.)

SUMMARY AND REVIEW

Prosocial Organizational Behavior

Individuals often engage in **prosocial behavior** in work settings, performing actions that benefit others in the organization. For example, they may assist others with their jobs or with personal matters and provide suggestions for procedural or administrative improvements. Recent findings indicate that **organizational citizenship behaviors**—discretionary actions by individuals that aid their organization or people in it—are fostered by the individuals' feeling that they are being treated fairly by the organization.

Cooperation and Competition

Cooperation involves mutual assistance or coordination between two or more persons or groups. Its occurrence in work settings is affected by several factors relating to individuals (e.g., strong tenden-

cies toward **reciprocity,** communication, personal orientations and preferences). It is also affected by several organizational factors (e.g., reward systems, interdependence among employees). **Teamwork**—an important form of cooperation—can yield major benefits for organizations. However, it requires a careful process of *team building,* and is primarily beneficial with respect to tasks that involve a high degree of interdependence between separate jobs.

Conflict: Its Nature and Causes

Conflict is a process that begins when one person or group perceives that another person or group has taken or is about to take some action inconsistent with the perceiver's major interests. Conflict situations involve two basic dimensions: *distribution*—concern with one's own outcomes; and *integration*—

A QUESTION OF ETHICS

Styles of Conflict Management: Which Are Best—or Most Appropriate?

 Throughout this discussion of conflict, we have repeatedly referred to five distinct styles of or approaches to conflict resolution: avoiding, compromising, collaborating (integrating), accommodating (obliging), and competing (dominating). From a practical point of view, each of these different styles clearly can be useful under certain circumstances. This is relatively easy to see with respect to approaches such as collaborating or compromising, but it is true even for approaches such as avoidance and accommodation. For example, consider a situation in which the costs of direct confrontation are very high. Here, avoiding the issue—and the people involved—may be the best course of action, at least temporarily. Similarly, accommodating may be an appropriate strategy in long-term relationships if the individual who accommodates hopes to gain various benefits in the future. In summary, all of the approaches to conflict resolution we have considered can, and do, have their place.

But what of *ethical issues* relating to the use of these strategies? Are any to be preferred on the basis of ethical principles rather than pure pragmatism? This issue has recently been addressed by Rahim, Garrett, and Buntzman in thoughtful analysis.[75] Rahim and his colleagues begin with the assumption that the appropriateness of any given style of conflict management can be determined, ethically, on the basis of three criteria:

1. Its contribution to the common good of the organization—what Rahim and his colleagues describe as the organization's *proper end:* the good of its members in light of the functions the organization seeks to perform

2. Satisfaction of more general social needs—those of the larger society

3. Fulfillment of the moral and ethical needs of organizational members

On the basis of these criteria, Rahim, Garrett, and Buntzman propose that each style of conflict resolution can be viewed as appropriate or inappropriate in specific situations. Let's consider these styles one at a time.

First, and perhaps easiest, is *collaboration* (integration). According to Rahim and his colleagues, it is almost always an ethical approach. This is so because collaboration treats all participants with maximum respect and is, ultimately, consistent with the organization's proper end. Only if leaders lose sight of the organization's legitimate interests and surround themselves with people who focus on narrow self-interest can collaboration pose ethical dilemmas.

Accommodation can be ethically inappropriate when a subordinate obliges a superior who is incompetent or out of touch with the organization's proper end. In such cases, refusal to comply and even whistle-blowing are more appropriate actions. *Competition* (dominating), too, can be unethical, if it becomes exploitative and ignores the legitimate needs and goals of the opponent or one's subordinates. In other words, competition becomes unethical when it goes too far.

Like the other approaches, *avoidance* is often an appropriate reaction to real or potential conflicts. However, it can be unethical when it stems

concern with others' outcomes. Contrasting styles or approaches to resolving conflict, such as *competition, collaboration, avoidance, accommodation,* and *compromise,* reflect specific points along these dimensions. Cultures vary along the **individualistic-collectivistic dimension.** Cultures that are relatively individualistic emphasize the goals and rights of individuals; those that are collectivistic emphasize group goals and responsibilities. People from individualistic cultures such as the United States prefer to resolve conflicts through competitive and integrative strategies; people from collectivistic cultures such as China and Korea prefer to handle conflicts through accommodation and avoidance.

Modern theories of conflict emphasize that it is a process and involves the perceptions, thoughts,

from a desire to evade actions that are morally required but personally unpleasant—for example, providing negative feedback to a subordinate in need of such information. Finally, *compromise*, although ethical in many contexts, can be unethical if the demands of one's opponent are morally wrong. In such cases, reaching a compromise is inappropriate. For example, compromising with another organization member over the amount of toxic chemical wastes to be dumped into a nearby lake is ethically wrong: such a compromise is inconsistent with the organization's proper end *and* with the moral responsibilities of the individuals involved.

An overview of the reasoning presented by Rahim, Garrett, and Buntzman concerning each conflict resolution mode is presented in Table 10–3. As you can see, except for collaboration, each of the major approaches can be ethical and appropriate or unethical and inappropriate, depending on specific circumstances. In answer to the question posed in the title of this section, then, no conflict-management approach is always best or most ethical. Rather, this is a complex judgment that must take into account the given situation and the specific set of circumstances.

TABLE 10–3   Conflict Management Styles: Ethical Issues

Different modes of resolving conflict can be viewed as ethical or unethical under different conditions.

Conflict Style	Ethical	Unethical
Collaboration (integrating)	In almost all cases	Rarely
Accommodation (obliging)	By subordinates	When subordinates ignore own needs
		When superior's decisions are contrary to organization's proper end
Competition (dominating)	When this supports organization's proper end	Exploitation of others
	When this includes concern for subordinates	
Avoidance	When other issues are of greater importance	If motive is to avoid unpleasant but correct course of action
	When current confrontation would be very costly	
Compromise	When interests are truly conflicting	When there is a correct course or decision

Source: Based on suggestions by Rahim, Garrett, & Buntzman, in press; see Note 75.

feelings, and intentions of all participants. **Organizational conflict** stems from both organization-based and interpersonal factors. Included in the first category are competition over scarce resources, ambiguity over responsibility or jurisdiction, interdependence, reward systems that pit people or units against one another, and power differentials. Included in the second category are attributional errors,

faulty communication, and personal characteristics such as the Type A behavior pattern.

The Effects and Management of Conflict

Although conflict often exerts negative effects on organizations, interfering with communication and coordination, it sometimes produces positive outcomes. These include bringing problems out into the open, enhanced understanding of each other's positions among adversaries, increased consideration of new ideas, better decisions, and increased organizational commitment. Thus, the key task with respect to conflict is managing its occurrence, not eliminating it entirely. Several tactics are useful in this regard.

Bargaining or **negotiation** is the most common procedure for resolving organizational conflicts. Many factors influence the course and outcomes of bar-

gaining, including specific tactics used by participants, their perceptions of each other's interests and priorities, and their overall approach to bargaining—"win-lose" or "win-win." *Third-party interventions* such as **mediation** and **arbitration** can also prove helpful in resolving conflicts. Another approach involves the induction of **superordinate goals**—ones shared by both sides. Finally, conflict can sometimes be resolved through **escalative intervention**—actions that temporarily intensify current conflicts to resolve them more effectively.

KEY TERMS

arbitration: A form of third-party intervention in disputes in which the intervening person has the power to determine the terms of an agreement.

bargaining: A process in which two or more parties in a dispute exchange offers, counteroffers, and concessions in an effort to attain a mutually acceptable agreement.

causal accounts: Explanations offered for provocative, conflict-inducing actions such as refusing legitimate requests.

competition: A process in which individuals or groups seek to attain desired goals at the expense of others seeking the same goals.

competitors: Individuals who are primarily concerned with exceeding the outcomes of others.

conflict: See *organizational conflict.*

cooperation: A process in which individuals or groups work together to attain shared goals.

cooperators: Individuals who are primarily concerned with maximizing joint outcomes.

distribution: A basic dimension of conflict situations, referring to the extent to which individuals show concern for their own outcomes.

equalizers: Individuals primarily concerned with assuring equality of outcomes among all people who work together on joint projects.

escalative intervention: A technique for managing conflict that seeks to increase conflict as a means of resolving it effectively.

fixed-sum error: The perception on the part of bargainers that the other party places the same importance or priority as they do on each issue.

incompatibility error: The perception on the part of bargainers that their own interests and that of the other side are completely incompatible.

individualistic-collectivistic dimension: The extent to which a given culture emphasizes individual goals and rights or group goals and collective responsibilities and obligations. Cultures that emphasize individual goals and rights are termed *individualistic,* whereas those that emphasize group goals and collective responsibilities are termed *collectivistic.*

individualists: People primarily concerned with maximizing their own outcomes.

integration: A basic dimension of conflict situations, referring to the extent to which individuals show concern for others' outcomes.

integrative agreements: Agreements between negotiators that maximize the joint outcomes of all parties.

mediation: A form of third-party intervention in disputes in which the intervener does not have the authority to dictate an agreement. Mediators simply attempt to enhance communication between opposing sides and to provide conditions that will facilitate acceptable agreements.

negotiation: See *bargaining.*

organizational citizenship behaviors (OCB): Discretionary behaviors by individuals that aid their organizations and that are not related to the formal reward system or their formal job description.

organizational conflict: A process that begins when individuals or groups perceive that others have taken or will soon take actions incompatible with their own major interests. Conflict involves awareness of opposing interests, the thoughts and emotions of all involved parties, their strategies and intentions, and their overt actions.

prosocial behavior: Actions that benefit others within an organization. Such behaviors may or may not benefit the organization as well.

reciprocity: The principle that we should treat others as they have treated us in the past.

superordinate goals: Goals shared by the parties in a conflict or dispute.

teamwork: Close cooperation between cross-trained employees who are familiar with a wide range of jobs in their organization.

whistle-blowing: One form of *prosocial behavior* in organizations. Whistle-blowing involves calling attention to actions or practices that are inconsistent with established organizational norms or policies.

QUESTIONS FOR DISCUSSION

1. What kinds of *organizational citizenship behaviors* have you observed in your own work experience? Why, if individuals receive no direct benefit for engaging in such actions, do they ever perform them?

2. When, in your experience, do *teams* contribute to performance? Can teams ever detract from performance or productivity?

3. Under what conditions does communication enhance cooperation? Under what conditions does it interfere with cooperation?

4. For what kind of jobs would highly competitive people be best? For what kind of jobs would very cooperative people be a better choice?

5. Do you think that consistent individual differences exist with respect to the preferred mode of resolving conflicts? In other words, do some people consistently prefer competition, others collaboration, still others avoidance, and so on?

6. "Conflict doesn't exist until it is recognized by the parties involved." Do you agree with this statement? If so, why? If not, why?

7. When you engage in provocative actions—ones that could potentially anger other people and initiate conflict—do you ever attempt to defuse their annoyance by offering explanations for your actions? If so, what are these explanations like? Do they succeed?

8. The downside of conflict is obvious, but growing evidence indicates that it has an upside as well. Have you ever experienced positive results from a conflict? If so, why do you think such effects occurred?

9. Many people approach bargaining as a "win-lose" situation. Why is a "win-win" approach often better?

NOTES

1. Deutsch, M. (1990). Sixty years of conflict. *International Journal of Conflict Management, 1,* 237–263.

2. Pondy, L. R. (1967). Organizational conflict: Concepts and models. *Administrative Science Quarterly, 12,* 296–320.

3. Thomas, K. W. (1992). Conflict and negotiation processes in organizations. In M. D. Dunnette (Ed.), *Handbook of industrial and organizational psychology* (2nd ed.). Palo Alto, CA: Consulting Psychologists Press.

4. Eisenberg, N. (1985). *Altruistic emotion, cognition, and behavior.* Hillsdale, NJ: Erlbaum.

5. Dovidio, J. F., Allen, J. L., & Schroeder, D. A. (1990). Specificity of empathy-induced helping: Evidence for altruistic motivation. *Journal of Personality and Social Psychology, 59,* 249–260.

6. Brief, A. P., & Motowidlo, S. J. (1986). Prosocial organizational behaviors. *Academy of Management Review, 4,* 710–725.

7. Dozier, J. B., & Miceli, M. P. (1985). Potential predictors of whistle-blowing: A prosocial behavior perspective. *Academy of Management Review, 11,* 823–836.

8. Organ, D. W. (1988). *Organizational citizenship behavior: The good soldier syndrome.* Lexington, MA: Lexington Books.

9. Organ, D. W. (1990). The motivational basis of organizational citizenship behavior. In B. M. Staw & L. L. Cummings (Eds.), *Research in organizational behavior* (Vol. 12, pp. 43–72). Greenwich, CT: JAI Press.

10. Konovsky, M. A., & Folger, R. (1991). The effects of procedure and distributive justice on organizational citizenship behavior. Unpublished manuscript, A. B. Freeman School of Business, Tulane University.

11. Moorman, R. H. (1991). Relationship between organizational justice and organizational citizenship behaviors: Do fairness perceptions influence employee citizenship? *Journal of Applied Psychology, 76,* 845–855.

12. Tyler, T. R., & Bies, R. J. (1990). Beyond formal procedures: The interpersonal context of procedural justice. In J. S. Carroll (Ed.), *Applied social psychology in business settings* (pp. 77–98). Hillsdale, NJ: Erlbaum.

13. Forsyth, D. R. (1983). *An introduction to group dynamics.* Monterey, CA: Brooks/Cole.

14. Tjosvold, D. (1986). *Working together to get things done.* Lexington, MA: Lexington Books.

15. Gouldner, A. W. (1960). The norm of reciprocity: A preliminary statement. *American Sociological Review, 25,* 161–178.

16. Youngs, G. A., Jr. (1986). Patterns of threat and punishment reciprocity in a conflict setting. *Journal of Personality and Social Psychology, 51,* 541–546.

17. See Note 16.

18. Knight, G. P., & Dubro, A. F. (1984). Cooperative, competitive, and individualistic social values: An individualized regression and clustering approach. *Journal of Personality and Social Psychology, 46,* 98–105.

19. See Note 18.

20. Kuhlman, D. M., & Marshello, A. F. J. (1975). Individual differences in game motivation as moderators of preprogrammed strategy effects in prisoner's dilemma. *Journal of Personality and Social Psychology, 32,* 922–932.

21. Peters, T. J., & Waterman, R. H., Jr. (1982). *In search of excellence: Lessons from America's best-run companies.* New York: Warner Books.

22. Cheng, J. L. (1983). Interdependence and coordination in organizations: A role-system analysis. *Academy of Management Journal, 26,* 156–162.

23. See Note 3.

24. Thomas, K. W., & Schmidt, W. H. (1976). A survey

of managerial interests with respect to conflict. *Academy of Management Journal, 10,* 315–318.

25. Cox, A. (1991, January 7). The homework behind teamwork. *Industry Week,* pp. 21–23.

26. Verespez, M. A. (1990, June 18). Yea, teams? Not always. *Industry Week,* pp. 184–185.

27. Deutsch, C. H. (1991, September 1). Pairing up for better understanding. *New York Times,* p. 23.

28. Walton, R. E., & McKersie, R. B. (1965). *A behavioral theory of labor negotiations: An analysis of a social interaction system.* New York: McGraw-Hill.

29. Thomas, K. W. (1976). Conflict and conflict management. In M. D. Dunnette (Ed.), *Handbook of industrial and organizational psychology* (pp. 889–935). Chicago: Rand McNally.

30. Kilmann, R. H., & Thomas, K. W. (1977). Developing a forced-choice measure of conflict-handling behavior: The "MODE" instrument. *Educational and Psychological Measurement, 37,* 309–325.

31. Rahim, M. A. (1983). A measure of styles of handling interpersonal conflict. *Academy of Management Journal, 26,* 368–376.

32. Van de Vliert, E., & Kabanoff, B. (1990). Toward theory-based measures of conflict management. *Academy of Management Journal, 33,* 199–209.

33. Van de Vliert, E. (1992). Support for the integration-distribution model of conflict behaviors. Unpublished manuscript, University of Groningen, Netherlands.

34. See Note 3.

35. Hofstede, G. (1980). *Culture's consequences: International differences in work-related values.* Beverly Hills, CA: Sage.

36. Ting-Toomey, S. (1988). Intercultural conflict styles: A face-negotiation theory. In Y. Kim & W. Gudykunst (Eds.), *Theories in intercultural communication* (pp. 213–235). Newbury Park, CA: Sage.

37. Ting-Toomey, S., Gao, G., Trubisky, P., Yang, Z., Kim, H. S., Lin, S. L., & Nishids, T. (1991). Culture, face maintenance, and styles of handling interpersonal conflict: A study in five cultures. *International Journal of Conflict Management, 2,* 275–296.

38. Greenberg, J. (1987). A taxonomy of organizational justice theories. *Academy of Management Review, 12,* 9–22.

39. Kabanoff, B. (1991). Equity, equality, power, and conflict. *Academy of Management Review, 16,* 416–441.

40. Johnson, T. E., & Rule, B. G. (1986). Mitigating circumstance information, censure, and aggression. *Journal of Personality and Social Psychology, 50,* 537–542.

41. Baron, R. A. (1988). Attributions and organizational conflict: The mediating role of apparent sincerity. *Organizational Behavior and Human Decision Processes, 41,* 111–127.

42. Bies, R. J., Shapiro, D. L., & Cummings, L. L. (1988). Causal accounts and managing organizational conflict: Is it enough to say it's not my fault? *Communication Research, 15,* 381–399.

43. Shapiro, D. L., Buttner, E. H., & Barry, B. (in press). Explanations: What factors enhance their perceived adequacy? *Organizational Behavior and Human Decision Processes.*

44. See Note 43.

45. Weisinger, H. (1989). *The critical edge.* Boston: Little, Brown.

46. Baron, R. A. (1990). Countering the effects of destructive criticism: The relative efficacy of four potential interventions. *Journal of Applied Psychology, 75,* 235–245.

47. Larson, J. R., Jr. (1989). The dynamic interplay between employees' feedback-seeking strategies and supervisors' delivery of performance feedback. *Academy of Management Review, 14,* 408–422.

48. Baron, R. A. (in press). Criticism (informal negative feedback) as a source of perceived unfairness in organizations: Effects, mechanisms, and countermeasures. In R. Cropanzano (Ed.), *Justice in the workplace: Approaching fairness in human resource management.* Hillsdale, NJ: Erlbaum.

49. Baron, R. A. (1989). Personality and organizational conflict: Effects of the Type A behavior pattern and self-monitoring. *Organizational Behavior and Human Decision Processes, 44,* 281–297.

50. See Note 49.

51. See Note 49.

52. Fodor, E. M. (1976). Group stress, authoritarian style of control and use of power. *Journal of Applied Psychology, 61,* 313–318.

53. Blake, R. R., & Mouton, J. S. (1984). *Solving costly organizational conflicts.* San Francisco: Jossey-Bass.

54. Baron, R. A. (1991). Positive effects of conflict: A cognitive perspective. *Employee Rights and Responsibilities Journal, 4,* 25–36.

55. Tjosvold, D. (1985). Implications of controversy research for management. *Journal of Management, 11,* 21–37.

56. Schwenk, C. R., & Cosier, R. A. (1980). Effects of the expert, devil's advocate, and dialectical inquiry methods of prediction performance. *Organizational Behavior and Human Performance, 26,* 409–424.

57. Cosier, R. A., & Dalton, D. R. (1990). Positive effects of conflict: A field assessment. *International Journal of Conflict Management, 1,* 81–92.

58. See Note 57.

59. Lewicki, R. J., & Litterer, J. A. (1985). *Negotiation.* Homewood, IL: Irwin.

60. Sheppard, B. H., Bazerman, M. H., & Lewicki, R. J. (Eds.). (1990). *Research in negotiation in organizations* (Vol. 2). Greenwich, CT: JAI Press.

61. See Note 59.

62. Chertkoff, J. M., & Baird, S. L. (1971). Applicability of the big lie technique and the last clear change doctrine to bargaining. *Journal of Personality and Social Psychology, 20,* 298–303.

63. Chertkoff, J. M., & Conley, M. (1967). Opening offer and frequency of concessions as bargaining strategies.

Journal of Personality and Social Psychology, 7, 181–185.

64. Huber, V. L., Neale, M. A., & Northcraft, G. G. (1987). Decision bias and personnel selection strategies. *Organizational Behavior and Human Decision Processes, 40,* 136–147.

65. Thompson, L., & Hastie, R. (1990). Social perception in negotiation. *Organizational Behavior and Human Decision Processes, 47,* 98–123.

66. See Note 65.

67. Thompson, L. (1990). An examination of naive and experienced negotiators. *Journal of Personality and Social Psychology, 59,* 82–90.

68. Thompson, L., & Hastie, R. (1990). Judgment tasks and biases in negotiation. In B. H. Sheppard, M. H. Bazerman, & R. J. Lewicki (Eds.), *Research in negotiation in organizations* (Vol. 2). Greenwich, CT: JAI Press.

69. See Note 28.

70. Pruitt, D. G., Carnevale, J. D., Ben-Yoav, O., Nochajski, T. H., & Van Slyck, M. R. (1983). Incentives for cooperation in integrative bargaining. In R. Tietz, *Aspiration levels in bargaining and economic decision making.* Berlin: Springer-Verlag.

71. Sheppard, B. H. (1984). Third party conflict intervention: A procedural framework. In B. Staw & L. Cummings (Eds.), *Research in organizational behavior* (Vol. 6, pp. 141–190). Greenwich, CT: JAI Press.

72. Fiske, S. T., & Taylor, S. E. (1984). *Social cognition.* Reading, MA: Addison-Wesley.

73. Van de Vliert, E. (1984). Conflict: Prevention and escalation. In P. J. D. Drenth, H. Thierry, P. J. Willems, & C. J. de Wolff (Eds.), *Handbook of work and organizational psychology.* New York: Wiley.

74. Van de Vliert, E. (1985). Escalative intervention in small-group conflicts. *Journal of Applied Behavioral Science, 21,* 19–36.

75. Rahim, M. A., Garrett, J. E., & Buntzman, G. F. (in press). Ethics of managing interpersonal conflict in organizations. *Journal of Business Ethics.*

CASE IN POINT

You must develop "a spirit of cooperation. Without it, the best technology and methods would have failed."[1] So says Cory Mason, senior information services manager for S. C. Johnson and Son (known as Johnson Wax), describing how the company successfully transformed itself into an organization driven to provide customer satisfaction.

Achieving Cooperation at Johnson Wax

Johnson Wax, located in Racine, Wisconsin, has been in business for over a hundred years. The company is privately owned and continues to be led by the family of its founder, Samuel C. Johnson. The company has estimated earnings in excess of $2.5 billion and has long enjoyed a leadership position in the household products industry.[2]

Like many other U.S. companies of its size, Johnson Wax realized during the 1980s that if it was to be competitive, it had to improve its level of customer satisfaction. The company conducted customer-satisfaction studies that produced the same strong message: become better at anticipating and resolving customer needs.

To become customer-oriented, the U.S. Consumer Products Division of Johnson Wax initiated the Computer Integration of Customer Service Systems project (CICSS). The goal was to integrate information about all of Johnson Wax's activities by developing and implementing a high-level information system capable of integrating and coordinating information regarding all of the operational activities that Johnson Wax used to manufacture and deliver its products. Launched in 1987, by early 1990, the CICSS project was approaching completion, "ahead of schedule and under its $5 million budget."[3] The project was a major force in the transformation of Johnson Wax into a customer-oriented company. How did it do this? Largely by reducing or eliminating the conflict that had plagued the company and by instituting instead a spirit of cooperation.

From the start, it was apparent to Johnson Wax management that the company was not as efficient or as customer-focused as it should be. Numerous basic mistakes in customer billing and product shipping were common. And as shown by its own customer-satisfaction studies, the company was not proactive enough in anticipating customer needs.

The major challenge was to develop cooperation between the operational departments of the company. According to Dave Henry, vice president in charge of the newly formed Customer Service and Logistics department (a product of the CICSS project), "No one was really focusing on customer needs. Finance, manufacturing, distribution, sales and marketing each had a job to do and each did that job to meet its own objectives."[4] The company had no unifying mission. Each organizational department acted to advance its own self-interests rather than the common interests of the company.

Employees of one department did not perceive themselves as interdependent with employees of other departments. When it came to the customer, there was considerable ambiguity among employees as to who had responsibility for customer satisfaction. If the topic of customer service came up at all, employees from different departments simply used the concept of customer satisfaction as leverage to increase the amount of company resources that flowed into their particular departments. Furthermore, each department had its own information system and data bases. Johnson Wax had no single, unifying information system to track its product manufacturing and delivery process from order entry to customer delivery. The only way anyone in the company could learn of a mistake in product manufacture or delivery was if a customer complained.

It was clear that the level of cooperation among departments had to improve dramatically. Johnson Wax management believed that the place to start was to develop an integrated information system to track the company's production and delivery activities. The system would then be used to support efforts to improve customer satisfaction.

The CICSS project was launched. A steering committee, made up of the vice presidents from all departments, was formed and charged with the task of determining how the new information system should be designed, implemented, and used to foster a spirit of cooperation among departments and employees.

Cory Mason was selected to lead the CICSS project. For Mason, the most important aspect of the job was to reduce or eliminate existing conflicts (e.g., between operating departments) and to foster a spirit of cooperation sufficient to bring everyone together in an integrated effort to provide the highest level of customer satisfaction possible. Mason was the right person for the job. He had extensive experience at Johnson Wax (eighteen years in various project management and technical roles), and he was known to have a team-oriented philosophy. Mason was also a very good communicator. His open, honest, and nonthreatening approach to communicating earned him the trust he needed to develop cooperation among CICSS team members. And he understood the give and take necessary to get things done when real differences exist between various departments and people.

Mason first formed a tactical team composed of himself, the director of the customer service department, and the director of the logistics department. The team mapped all of the "business functions involved in the entire customer service life cycle and their interrelationships. The team then developed a high-level systems architecture identifying the interconnection of systems, the information flows and the applications needed."[5]

Based on the new systems architecture, the team formulated a plan to reengineer all of Johnson Wax's business functions into a highly interdependent, customer-satisfaction-driven network. The plan was approved and the company's once *independent* departments were about to become entirely *interdependent* on each other to accomplish their work. Every department and employee was to "seek differentiation by focusing on the customer and on service. The individual priorities of individual organizational units had to be secondary to that goal."[6]

But how was Mason going to get everyone to cooperate to make Johnson Wax's overriding goal a reality? Mason formed a set of teams to implement the reengineering of the company's organizational units, based on the new information-systems architecture. To enhance each team's credibility with the end users, Mason included employees from the departments that would be affected by the system as members of the implementation teams.

Mason soon ran into problems. The members of one of his implementation teams became embroiled in conflict. The team consisted of information-systems employees and employees from the client services department. Because the client services employees would be the ultimate users of the system, they were assigned to help design the information system's computer menu screens. Information-systems employees developed various screens and client services employees decided what changes should be made to make the screens more user-friendly. From the start, the information-systems employees "didn't like being told how to design screens by the client service people."[7]

The team completed its work in 1988. The finished product was an absolute failure! The information system was loaded with programming errors and basic design flaws. Says the team's leader, "we really couldn't bring it off because the team still wasn't singing out of the same hymnal."[8] But out of the team's failure came the seeds of the team's ultimate success. The members of the team had seen firsthand the product of their conflict—a highly sophisticated and complicated information-system *failure*. The team members came to realize that if they ever hoped to succeed they had no choice but to stop fighting and start cooperating. They went back to work, cooperated, and succeeded.

Mason's CICSS implementation teams went on to successfully reengineer Johnson Wax's organizational departments. Throughout the process, Mason and his team leaders insisted that all decision making be guided by a cross-functional perspective, focusing on the business as a whole rather than any single organizational unit. Johnson Wax's senior management created a new functional department to oversee and maintain the newly learned cooperative behavior—the Customer Service and Logistics department. It is responsible for overseeing the entire customer service process—from order entry to the delivery of products to the customer.

How is Johnson Wax doing now? The level of customer service is much improved. Any problems that occur are quickly recognized and resolved—*before* they get to the customer. Employees are working *together* to enhance customer satisfaction. And Johnson Wax management uses the company's new system to track customer-use patterns to anticipate the future needs of its customers. But the best is really yet to come. As vice president Dave Henry says, "We have the foundation in place now to be proactive."[9]

Questions for Discussion

1. Before the "spirit of cooperation" was achieved at Johnson Wax, what factors contributed to conflict among the different organizational departments of the company?
2. Cory Mason is credited with getting Johnson Wax employees to cooperate with each other. What individual characteristics does Mason have that helped him to develop a spirit of cooperation?
3. What organizational tactics did Johnson Wax management use to foster a spirit of cooperation?
4. The mission of Johnson Wax is "to seek differentiation by focusing on the customer and on service."[10] According to the text, what type of conflict management tactic does Johnson Wax's mission illustrate?
5. Johnson Wax relied heavily on using its integrative information system to promote cooperation among the company's departments and employees. How does an integrated information system affect the level of cooperation in this case?

Notes

1. Pantages, A. (1990, March 15). The new order at Johnson Wax. *Datamation*, p. 103.
2. See Note 1, pp. 103–106.
3. See Note 1.
4. See Note 1, p. 104.
5. See Note 1, pp. 104–105.
6. See Note 1, p. 105.
7. See Note 1, p. 106.
8. See Note 1, p. 106.
9. See Note 1, p. 106.
10. See Note 1, p. 105.

**Personal Styles
of Conflict
Management**

Conflict with others is a common and probably inescapable part of life. Given this fact, an important task we all face is *managing* conflict effectively when it arises. How do *you* deal with such situations? What is your preferred mode of handling disagreements and conflicts with others? For some insight into this important issue, follow the instructions below.

Procedure

First, recall three recent events in which you have experienced conflict with other people. Describe each briefly below, and then answer the following questions for each.

Incident #1

To what extent did you try to resolve this conflict through *avoidance*—sidestepping the issue, withdrawing from the situaton?

	Did Not Do This						Did Do This
	1	2	3	4	5	6	7

To what extent did you try to resolve this conflict through *accommodation*—giving in to the other person, yielding to his or her point of view?

	Did Not Do This						Did Do This
	1	2	3	4	5	6	7

To what extent did you try to resolve this conflict through *competition*—trying to win, standing up for your rights or views?

	Did Not Do This						Did Do This
	1	2	3	4	5	6	7

To what extent did you try to resolve this conflict through *compromise*—finding the middle ground between your position and the other person's?

	Did Not Do This						Did Do This
	1	2	3	4	5	6	7

To what extent did you try to resolve this conflict through *collaboration*—working with the other person to find some solution that would satisfy both of your basic needs or concerns?

	Did Not Do This						Did Do This
	1	2	3	4	5	6	7

Incident #2

To what extent did you try to resolve this conflict through *avoidance*—sidestepping the issue, withdrawing from the situation?

	Did Not Do This						Did Do This
	1	2	3	4	5	6	7

To what extent did you try to resolve this conflict through *accommodation*—giving in to the other person, yielding to his or her point of view?

```
        Did Not                          Did Do
        Do This                          This
          1       2       3       4       5       6       7
```

To what extent did you try to resolve this conflict through *competition*—trying to win, standing up for your rights or views?

```
        Did Not                          Did Do
        Do This                          This
          1       2       3       4       5       6       7
```

To what extent did you try to resolve this conflict through *compromise*—finding the middle ground between your position and the other person's?

```
        Did Not                          Did Do
        Do This                          This
          1       2       3       4       5       6       7
```

To what extent did you try to resolve this conflict through *collaboration*—working with the other person to find some solution that would satisfy both of your basic needs or concerns?

```
        Did Not                          Did Do
        Do This                          This
          1       2       3       4       5       6       7
```

Incident #3

To what extent did you try to resolve this conflict through *avoidance*—sidestepping the issue, withdrawing from the situation?

```
        Did Not                          Did Do
        Do This                          This
          1       2       3       4       5       6       7
```

To what extent did you try to resolve this conflict through *accommodation*—giving in to the other person, yielding to his or her point of view?

```
        Did Not                          Did Do
        Do This                          This
          1       2       3       4       5       6       7
```

To what extent did you try to resolve this conflict through *competition*—trying to win, standing up for your rights or views?

```
        Did Not                          Did Do
        Do This                          This
          1       2       3       4       5       6       7
```

To what extent did you try to resolve this conflict through *compromise*—finding the middle ground between your position and the other person's?

```
        Did Not                          Did Do
        Do This                          This
          1       2       3       4       5       6       7
```

To what extent did you try to resolve this conflict through *collaboration*—working with the other person to find some solution that would satisfy both of your basic needs or concerns?

```
        Did Not                          Did Do
        Do This                          This
          1       2       3       4       5       6       7
```

Points to Consider

Now examine your reactions in all three situations. Do you notice any consistencies? Did you tend to prefer one basic mode of resolving conflict over the others? Research on this topic suggests that many people possess relatively clear preferences in this regard: they tend to approach many conflict situations in a similar manner. Although such preferences are understandable, they can cause serious difficulties. Each conflict situation we encounter is, to some extent, unique. Thus, the most adaptive approach is probably one emphasizing *flexibility:* choose the approach that best fits the current circumstances. Keeping this point firmly in mind may help you to manage conflicts more effectively.

∎ 11 ∎

INFLUENCE, POWER, AND POLITICS IN ORGANIZATIONS

CHAPTER OUTLINE

LEARNING OBJECTIVES

After reading this chapter, you should be able to:

1. Distinguish among influence, power, and politics in organizations and describe their role in enhancing social control.
2. Characterize the major varieties of social influence that exist.
3. Describe the conditions under which social influence is used.
4. Identify the five major bases of individual social power and alternative types of individual power.
5. Characterize the conditions under which power is used.

6. Explain the two major approaches to the development of subunit power in organizations (the resource-dependency model and the strategic contingencies model).
7. Describe when and where organizational politics is likely to occur and the forms it is likely to take.
8. Explain the major ethical issues surrounding the uses of power and the enactment of political behavior in organizations.

A lthough only three years old, Ameri-Claim has become the state's largest processor of health insurance claims for self-insured companies. Todd Wright, the entrepreneurial guiding spirit of the company, remains its president and chief executive officer despite widespread acknowledgment that Jack Forest, the vice president of operations, really calls the shots.

Todd and Jack are talking in the hallway after a board meeting, when Lou Chen, the service director, passes by. "Hey, Lou," says Todd, "Jack and I were just talking about the new call-menuing system for the customer service 800-lines."

"Press one to enter the conversation," Lou jokes as he joins Todd and Jack. "Actually, I've been putting together some notes on that topic."

Sensing that he is no longer needed, Todd nods and says, "I'll let you guys get down to business." As he begins walking away from Lou and Jack, he adds, "Besides, it's almost time for my golf game. I hate to miss a tee time at the club."

Lou and Jack just smile as Todd walks away. "While you're here, Lou," says Jack, "come down to my office. I want to talk to you about something."

Curious about Jack's mysterious invitation, Lou nods and says, "Let's do it," as they head down the hall to Jack's office.

When they arrive, Lou is immediately drawn to a comfortable leather chair in front of Jack's gigantic desk. "Nice place you got here, Jack," Lou comments as he looks around Jack's spacious office, decorated with the most tasteful pieces of modern art.

"I like it," Jack is quick to reply. "It goes with the territory. You know, VPs here do quite well for themselves."

"I can see that," says Lou, raising his eyes. "But no one can say you don't deserve it; you've really done a lot here."

"Thanks, Lou," replies Jack, as he moves closer to Lou, sitting on the corner of his desk. "That means a great deal coming from you."

"I really mean it," says Lou.

Jack sees this as his cue to get to the question he has on his mind. Boldly, he looks back at Lou and asks, "Do you like me enough to support my move to the presidency and CEO?"

"Now that's what I call getting to the point," Lou replies. "But what about Todd? Is he thinking of stepping down?"

"No, not yet," Jack answers. "But he just might, *if* he thought his position was vulnerable because enough of us failed to support him on the board. I happen to know that a lot of the execs around here are interested in having me in the driver's seat instead of Todd."

"But, Jack," Lou points out, "Todd brought us both aboard and really helped us. I can't exactly stab him in the back."

"Don't think of it like that," Jack replies. "We both know I can do a better job. After all, I've been the one who's really made a difference here in the last two years, not Todd."

Lou listens attentively and nods, replying, "I suppose you're right, but still. . . ."

Jack quickly interrupts Lou and tries to comfort him. "It isn't exactly as if he'd be thrown out into the street," he says. "We'd reach a very generous settlement with him, and then take this company where it's never been. I'm talking national, providing Ameri-Claim services in all fifty states. That's a leap Todd would never make. I have the company's best interests in mind. So, what do you think?"

"I'd find that kind of move very exciting, Jack," Lou says, but reiterates, "I'm not certain I like the idea of a palace coup."

"Well, you *do* like this office, don't you?" Jack asks.

"Just what do you mean?" Lou inquires.

"Do I have to spell it out for you?" Before Lou can answer, Jack continues, "As CEO, I'd need good people like you in VP positions. In fact, it's my position, and I have this office in mind for you, Lou. Besides, I don't forget those who supported me on my way to the top."

"Well, Jack," says Lou, "you've given me a lot to think about."

"That's all I can ask," says Jack as he stands up and extends his hand to Lou. "We don't need any rash judgments around here," he says as he squeezes Lou's hand firmly, adding, "especially not from new VPs."

———————————————— ■ ————————————————

Do you have any doubt that Jack Forest eventually will be successful in his quest to oust Todd Wright and take over control of Ameri-Claim? Jack is highly regarded by others for his expertise, and he's hardly shy about his ambitions. In fact, given the promotion he's promising Lou Chen, it might be difficult for Lou to refrain from throwing his support Jack's way. At the heart of the impending struggle between Jack and Todd is an interest in **power**—the formal capacity to control others and the company. Jack's efforts at courting Lou's support represent attempts at **social influence**—attempts to persuade another to behave as desired. These influence attempts appear to reflect Jack's ambitious organizational aspirations, activities designed to protect his self-interests, known as **organizational politics.**

Although our story about Ameri-Claim is fictitious, it illustrates some dynamics of power and politics that are not uncommon in organizations. For example, in a power struggle at Apple Computer in the early 1980s, Steven Jobs, the company's founder, was forced to resign from the board of directors after losing the support of John Sculley, the executive Jobs had hired earlier to help the company out of trouble.[1] Indeed, Sculley saw trouble in the company, but mostly in those divisions of it managed by Jobs (including the then-fledgling Macintosh division), so it was goodbye to Jobs, forced out by the very person he hired to help him. As you might imagine, this was quite an acrimonious power struggle.[2] This incident illustrates a basic fact of organizational life: people seek to control the actions of others, to successfully influence their behavior (see Figure 11–1 on p. 400). Although very few

FIGURE 11–1

Power: Frequently Sought in Organizations

People who have power over others can exert formal influence over them and hope to be successful in controlling their behavior. (*Source:* Drawing by Stevenson; © 1990 The New Yorker Magazine, Inc.)

"Let's face it—I'm a bit of a control freak."

of us encounter power struggles at such stratospheric organizational echelons, efforts at seeking control over others are commonplace at all levels within organizations.

Given the central place of influence, power, and politics in organizational functioning, we will devote this chapter to examining the nature of social influence processes within organizations, sources of power that provide opportunities for influence, and the political activities of those who seek to attain power. Specifically, we will take a look at the tactics used to influence others in organizations. Then we will examine how power is attained—both by individuals and by organizational subunits—and how that power is used. Following this, we will examine the political mechanisms used to gain power—what they are and when they occur. We also will pay special attention to the ethical aspects of power and politics; activities of this nature may be of questionable morality due to their potentially adverse effects on others. Before turning to these topics, however, we will begin by carefully distinguishing among the concepts of influence, power, and politics from the related notion of control in organizations.

ORGANIZATIONAL INFLUENCE, POWER, AND POLITICS AS MECHANISMS OF CONTROL

Imagine that you are a supervisor heading a group of a dozen staff members working on an important new project for your company. Tomorrow is the day you're supposed to make a big presentation to company officials, but the report isn't quite ready. If only several staff members will work a few hours extra, the job will be done on time. Unfortunately, a company party is scheduled for tonight and nobody wants to work late. Question: What can you do to persuade some of your staff to work late and complete the job? In other words, how will you attempt to influence their behavior?

The concept of **social influence** refers to *attempts (whether successful or unsuccessful) to affect another in a desired fashion.* It may be said that we have influenced someone to the extent that our behavior has had an effect—even if unintended—on that person. Although we may attempt to affect another's behavior in a certain fashion, our attempts may be unsuccessful. This would not mean, however, that we did not influence the person, just that we did not influence him or her successfully.

Test Bank questions 11.1 and 11.46 relate to material on this page.

To illustrate this point, let's return to our example of a boss needing people to work overtime on party night. Imagine that you see the boss coming out of her office, and you expect her to ask you to work overtime. Uninterested in doing so, you walk away from your desk in the hope that the boss has not seen you and will ask someone else instead. In this case, can we say that the boss influenced you? Although she was unsuccessful, she clearly *did* have an effect on you (after all, you ran away from her). Thus, we can say that the boss influenced you. However, we cannot say that the boss controlled your behavior. For that to be true, the boss would have to be successful in bringing about the effects desired—in this case, to convince you to stay and work overtime. If the influence attempt were successful, we would say that the boss exercised control over you. Thus, **control** refers to those attempts to influence another that bring about desired results. If your boss tracked you down and explained the situation to you, causing you to stay and work (as she desires you to do), we would say that she influenced you successfully—she controlled you. Thus, social influence represents actions that have any effect on another, whereas control represents only those actions that have the desired effect. For an illustration of this distinction, see the left portion of Figure 11–2.

Where do power and politics fit in? As illustrated in the center portion of Figure 11–2, **power** refers to the potential to control another. More formally, it is *the capacity to change the behavior or attitudes of another in a desired fashion.*[3] In contrast with social influence (actions that affect others), the related concept of power refers to the *capacity* to have a desired effect on others. As we will detail in the next section, there are several different sources of such power. For now, however, assume that the boss has power over you by virtue of her access to considerable resources that enable her to reward you with raises (in exchange for being cooperative) or punish you by not supporting your promotion (if you refrain from pitching in). These represent the formal actions the supervisor can take to attempt to influence you successfully; they are the sources of power.

Often, when people exercise their power, they take into account their own individual interests. For example, the supervisor in our story may be motivated by an interest in promoting—or at least saving—her own career by making sure that the report gets done on time. This is not to say that she might not also recognize the

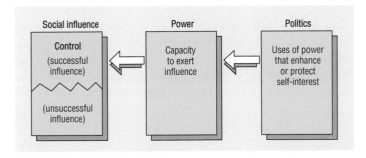

FIGURE 11–2   Relationship among Social Influence, Control, Power, and Politics

When someone attempts to get another to act in a desired fashion, that person is seeking to *influence* the other. Those successful influence attempts are known as *control*. The capacity to exert influence over another is known as *power*. Uses of power that enhance or protect one's self-interest are known as *politics*.

value of the report to the company. It's just that her actions are motivated primarily by her own selfish concerns. The actions taken to satisfy these concerns reflect **organizational politics** (see the right portion of Figure 11–2). This term refers to *uses of power that enhance or protect one's own or one's group's personal interests.*[4] Later in this chapter, we will describe many varieties of political actions; people can use their power in a number of ways to protect their personal interests in organizations.

Now that we have clarified the role of influence, power, and politics as mechanisms for controlling others in organizations, we are in a good position to take a closer look at the social influence process in organizations. In the next section, we will examine some of the most widely used social influence techniques and review some of the ways influence is used in organizations.

SOCIAL INFLUENCE: HAVING AN IMPACT ON OTHERS

By what means do you persuade others to fulfill your wishes? Are you straightforward and tell people what you want them to do, or are you more inclined to emphasize why they should do what you say and what will happen to them if they do not do so? Is it your style to pressure people, or to convince them to do what you want by getting them to like you? Regardless of your answers, you are confronting the challenge of *social influence*—getting others to do what you want.

It is widely acknowledged that successful managers are those who are quite adept at influencing others.[5] We will summarize the social influence techniques used, and then review when and how people use their influence over others.

Tactics of Social Influence

In recent years, researchers have examined the tactics people use to influence each other in organizations. Specifically, they have questioned people on the job about how they get others—bosses, peers, and subordinates—to do what they want them to do.[6] Recently, an investigation by Yukl and Falbe found that eight major tactics were used.[7] These are identified and summarized in Table 11–1. Some techniques were more popular than others; they are presented in order from those most often used to those least often used. As you can see, the open, highly consultative techniques were used most frequently, whereas the more highly coercive tactics were used less often.

Yukl and Falbe found only minor differences in the rank ordering of influence techniques as a function of who was being influenced. Thus, people did not differentiate between their peers, bosses, and subordinates in terms of the social influence tactics they used. Whatever techniques they were inclined to use, they were more or less equally inclined to use on others regardless of their relative level in the organization.

Putting Influence Tactics to Work

These findings do not necessarily imply, however, that all people will always use the same influence tactics. In fact, research has shown that people's choice of an influence tactic takes into account the reaction they anticipate from the person being influenced. Specifically, research findings indicate that people attempting to influence their bosses used upward appeals and ingratiation when they believed their bosses were inclined to be highly authoritarian, but used rational persuasion when they believed their bosses were highly participative.[8] These findings make sense if you imagine that influence requires a highly coercive action (such as appealing to one's superior) to influence an authoritarian boss, whereas a participative boss might

Why are some people more successful than others at influencing people? Researchers have found that there may be a physiological explanation. A study at UCLA's Neuropsychiatric Institute has found that males who wield power have high levels of the neurotransmitter serotonin circulating in their bloodstreams. In fact, males in powerful positions had almost twice as much serotonin as those without power. Interestingly, the serotonin levels of males who lost power dropped to those of males who never had power to begin with. It is not yet known whether having power causes the increase in serotonin, or if one's level of serotonin influences one's attainment of power. [Stein, K. (1985, July). The biology of power plays. *Omni*, pp. 68–72.]

Test Bank question 11.5 relates to material on this page.

TABLE 11–1   The Most Popular Social Influence Techniques

Research by Yukl and Falbe identified eight different tactics of social influence. Shown, in order from most popular (rank 1) to least popular (rank 8), are the various tactics and a description of each one.

Rank	Tactic	Description
1	Consultation	Asking for participation in decision making or planning a change
2	Rational persuasion	Using logical arguments and facts to persuade another that a desired result will occur
3	Inspirational appeals	Arousing enthusiasm by appealing to one's values and ideals
4	Ingratiation	Getting someone to do what you want by putting her in a good mood or getting her to like you
5	Coalition	Persuading by seeking the assistance of others, or by noting the support of others
6	Pressure	Seeking compliance by using demands, threats, or intimidation
7	Upward appeals	Noting that the influence request is approved by higher management
8	Exchange	Promising some benefits in exchange for complying with a request

Source: Based on Yukl & Falbe, 1990; see Note 7.

be more amenable to learning about a rational argument. Although these findings are somewhat tentative, they are important because they suggest that people's use of power is a function of not simply their own characteristics, but also their beliefs about the likely effects of their actions.

To the extent that influence techniques take into account the reactions of others, it can be said that a *contingency approach* to social influence is being followed. Given the widespread use of contingency approaches to leadership we will see in chapter 12, it makes sense that such an orientation holds promise for understanding social influence. However, because it has not yet been extensively studied, this kind of approach still must be considered tentative.

As you might imagine, the social influence tactics we've discussed can be effective in changing people's behavior. Typically, we think of such techniques as helpful in bringing about behavior that is adaptive to oneself and helpful to the organization. Returning to our overtime example, it certainly would be helpful to your boss and the organization as a whole for you to work overtime. Doing so would also benefit you to the extent that you are credited for your last-minute contribution (indeed, a good manager would remember and reward you for your efforts). However, because people are typically part of many different social groups, they may confront several conflicting sources of social power, some that may be negative. For instance, recent research has shown that adolescents' use of alcohol and tobacco is directly linked to the extent to which they are influenced by their peers.[9] This is both because they are directly affected by peers who pressure them into using these substances and because they already believe that the majority of their peers use them. Obviously, peer influence can exert powerful effects on behavior.

This study found that boys and girls were equally susceptible to social influence from peers. The findings are in keeping with additional research with adults in

Test Bank questions 11.6–11.8, 11.47, 11.57, and 11.67 relate to material on this page.

organizational settings in which gender differences were also not found in either the way men and women use social influence or the types of influence tactics to which men and women are subjected.[10,11] Findings such as these suggest the possible existence of a set of consensually held (i.e., widely agreed-on) beliefs about what constitutes appropriate ways of influencing others. Generally speaking, more open, consultative techniques are believed to be more appropriate than more coercive techniques.[12] Thus, even if members of one gender would be predisposed to use

AN INTERNATIONAL/MULTICULTURAL PERSPECTIVE

Bribery in Nigeria and the United States: Cross-National Differences in the Acceptance of Undue Influence

 Exchange is a widely accepted form of social influence. Reciprocity ("You do something for me, and I'll do something for you") represents one of its most common forms of exchange. However, pressure to reciprocate sometimes can be forced in a one-sided manner, as in the case of *bribery:* "If you want me to do something for you, I demand that you do something for me." As such, bribery represents what is commonly considered "exerting undue influence."

Is bribery always considered inappropriate, or is it sometimes accepted by people from different cultures? In the United States, the *Foreign Corrupt Practices Act* makes it illegal for Americans to bribe officials of foreign governments. In Germany, however, bribery is so well accepted as a business practice that bribes represent legitimate tax-deductible business expenses.[13] Such evidence suggests that cross-national differences exist in the acceptance of bribes as appropriate business practices. (Such differences do not necessarily reflect dissimilarities in the inherent morality of people from various nations. Instead, they simply may reflect cultural differences in people's willingness to tolerate and accept a widespread activity as inevitable.)

To look at cross-national differences in people's reactions to bribery, Tsalikis and Nwachukwu conducted a study in which samples of Americans and Nigerians described their reactions to various hypothetical situations involving people from their own and the other country being offered a bribe or being forced to pay a bribe.[14] The situations described also differed with respect to whether the bribe came from someone from the same nation or from a foreigner, and whether the foreign business person convinced the native person to take the bribe, or the native business person convinced the foreign person to take the bribe. After reading the various scenarios, the participants indicated their acceptance of the business person's activities on a variety of rating scales that, taken together, reflect acceptance of the action as ethical.

Several interesting findings emerged with respect to areas within which Americans and Nigerians both agreed and disagreed. For example, both Americans and Nigerians agreed that it was unethical for business people to offer bribes, but less so if the bribe was made to a foreign official than to a native. Similarly, attempts to bribe a native official were much less accepted when they came from a foreigner than from a native (again, regardless of the country involved). An analogous set of results emerged on the issue of payment of bribes. Specifically, people from both cultures accepted as somewhat ethical the payment of bribes to foreign officials by native business people. It was considered much less ethical for a foreign business person to be forced to pay a bribe to a native official.

In addition to these similarities, some key differences were found between Americans and Nigerians with respect to bribery by people from their own cultures. For example, as summarized in Figure 11–3, Americans believed that it was more unethical for business people to *offer* bribes to others than did Nigerians. Analogous results were found on questions dealing with the ethicality of paying a bribe that is demanded. Again, Nigerians perceived the *payment* of bribes demanded by others to be more ethical than did Americans. These findings are in keeping with

different influence tactics from those of the opposite gender, the existence of such norms about using influence appropriately might override any predisposition to influence others based on gender differences alone. (In addition to the prospect of gender differences, it is also an interesting possibility that the use of influence techniques might differ as a function of culture. For a closer look at cross-national differences in one important influence technique, see the **International/Multicultural Perspective** section that begins on the preceding page.)

the tendency for Nigerians to be more accepting than Americans of the use of bribes as a legitimate aspect of business life.

Despite the tendency for Nigerians to excuse bribery within their own country more than Americans, no evidence of their acceptance of bribery by foreign officials emerged. Nigerians believed it was unethical for people from foreign countries to bribe Nigerian officials. In other words, there is a clear double standard for bribes: they're acceptable from other Nigerians, but not

acceptable from foreigners. As you might imagine, such knowledge may be very valuable to people doing business in Nigeria. A bribe they see a Nigerian giving another Nigerian may not be well accepted when it comes from a foreigner. This study suggests that in the case of Nigeria, at least, the adage "When in Rome, do as the Romans do" should be changed to "When in Nigeria, the Nigerians don't want you to do as the Nigerians do."

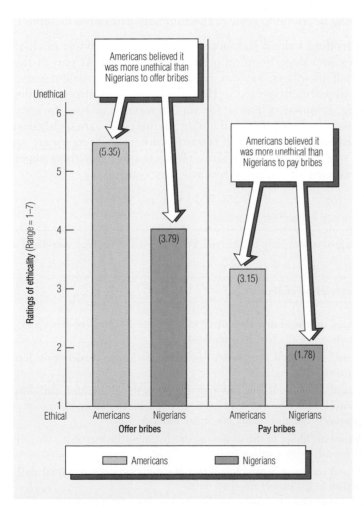

FIGURE 11–3

How Ethical Is It to Offer or Pay Bribes? Differences between Americans and Nigerians

Research has shown that Americans believe it is more unethical than do Nigerians either to offer bribes to another or to pay bribes to another to receive a favorable business outcome. These findings reflect the fact that Nigerians are more accepting of bribery as a form of influence in business transactions. (*Source:* Based on data reported by Tsalikis & Nwachukwu, 1991; see Note 14.)

Obviously, we have a great deal to learn about how and when people attempt to influence others. We will now turn our attention to one of the greatest determinants of influence—social power. To the extent that one has power over another, that person has the capacity to control the other's behavior.

INDIVIDUAL POWER: A BASIS FOR INFLUENCE

Historically, although men have been able to wield power directly because of their access to resources, women have gained power indirectly, such as through cajoling or flattery. Because women were barred from most professions, they were able to align themselves with power only by being married to a powerful man or by being born into a powerful family. In addition, most of the role models of powerful women were usually evil and wicked, such as the poisoner Lucrezia Borgia and Shakespeare's Lady Macbeth. Because women are now beginning to enter occupations at all organizational levels, they can now enjoy their own power rather than have to exert power indirectly through men and family members. [Dowd, M. (1991, November). Power: Are women afraid of it—or beyond it? *Working Woman,* pp. 96–99.]

As defined earlier, *power* involves the potential to influence others—both the things they do and the ways they feel about something. In this section, we will focus on the individual bases of power, that is, factors that give people the capacity to control others successfully. It is an inevitable fact of organizational life that some individuals can boast a greater capacity to influence people successfully than others. Within organizations, the distribution of power is typically unequal. Why is this so? What sources of power do people have at their disposal?

Five Bases of Individual Power

Answers to these questions are provided in a classic framework developed by French and Raven.[15] This work identifies five different bases of social power derived from the characteristics individuals possess and the nature of the relationships between individuals with and without power. As we describe each of these interpersonal sources of power, it may be useful to refer to the summary presented in Table 11–2.

Reward Power: Controlling Valued Resources   Imagine a supervisor in charge of twenty-five employees in a department of a large organization. As part of her job she is free to hire staff members, set pay raises, control work assignments, and prepare budgets for department projects. How this kind of control over desired resources can provide a source of power for this supervisor is easy to see. The resources at her disposal—access to jobs and money, in this case—are highly desired. Individuals with the capacity to control the rewards workers will receive are said to have **reward power** over them. Subordinates often comply with their superiors' wishes in hopes of receiving the valuable rewards they control.

TABLE 11–2   Individuals' Power: Five Major Bases

Individuals' power in organizations may be derived from any of the sources identified and described here.

Type of Power	Description of Base
Reward power	Based on the ability to control valued organizational rewards and resources (e.g., pay, information)
Coercive power	Based on control over various punishments (e.g., suspensions, formal reprimands)
Legitimate power	Based on the belief that an individual has the recognized authority to control others by virtue of his or her organizational position (e.g., the person is a high-ranking corporate official)
Referent power	Based on liking of the power-holder by subordinates (e.g., the superior is friends with a subordinate)
Expert power	Based on the accepted belief that the individual has a valued skill or ability (e.g., expert medical skills)

Source: Based on French and Raven, 1959; see Note 15.

Test Bank questions 11.10 and 11.48 relate to material on this page.

The rewards at a manager's disposal may be tangible, such as raises, promotions, and time off, or intangible, such as praise and recognition. In either case, access to these resources often forms a source of individual power in organizations. Indeed, managers have been known to complain that the inability to control any important resources in their organizations leaves them powerless figureheads. This is especially likely in the case of first-line supervisors, who often find themselves responsible for the actions of others but severely restricted by the incentives they can offer others for following their orders.[16] Keep in mind (based on our discussion of the concepts of *reinforcement* in chapter 3 and *valence* in chapter 4) that resources may enhance one's power only to the extent that they are actually desired by the recipients. You also may recall from chapter 3 that to be effective in changing people's behavior, rewards must be closely tied to the desired behavior. Thus, whereas access to valued resources may enhance a manager's power base, the manager must administer them properly to be effective. Having resources at one's disposal and using them appropriately are obviously two different things.

Coercive Power: Controlling Punishments   In addition to controlling desired resources, managers often control the punishments of others—a capacity known as **coercive power.** Subordinates may do what their superior desires because they fear the superior will punish them if they do not. Punishments may include pay cuts, demotions, suspension without pay, formal reprimands, undesirable work assignments, and the like. As in the case of reward power, punishments are effective only if used properly. In chapter 3, we noted that punishments may have undesirable side effects if they are too harsh or inconsistently administered (in extreme cases, employees may even rebel against an overly harsh supervisor by organizing their colleagues in protest or by quitting their jobs).[17] Regardless, the capacity to administer punishment represents an important source of power in organizations.

Legitimate Power: Recognized Organizational Authority   What would happen in your class if you learned that one of your classmates would be making the decisions about the final course grades? Someone might stand up and question this, asking, "Who is *he* to make those decisions?" If so, the speaker would be challenging the legitimacy of that individual's power. However, if the professor announced that she would be determining the final grades herself, probably no one would raise any questions. The difference between these two situations has to do with **legitimate power**—the recognized right of individuals to exercise authority over others because of their position in an organizational hierarchy. Students recognize the accepted authority of professors to determine their grades (i.e., professors have legitimate power in this regard), but reject as illegitimate the power of their classmates to make these same decisions.

Usually, legitimate power is derived from an individual's formal rank or position. Organizational members are likely to accept attempts to influence their behavior based on the fact that one has a higher position (see Figure 11–4 on p. 408). This does not mean, however, that the higher-ranking individual can legitimately control all aspects of others' behavior. Managers have authority over only those aspects of others' behavior that fall under their accepted areas of organizational responsibility. For example, whereas secretaries may recognize the legitimate authority of their bosses to ask them to file and prepare office correspondence, they may reject as illegitimate a boss's request to type his son's homework papers. Similarly, a plant manager may accept the authority of a vice president of production who directs him to increase inventories of certain items, but may question the authority of the very same order voiced by the vice president of finance. The key point is that legitimate authority applies only to the range of behaviors that are recognized and accepted as legitimate by the parties involved.

Test Bank questions 11.11–11.14 and 11.58 relate to material on this page.

FIGURE 11-4

Legitimate Power: Control
Based on Formal Authority

One source of social power, *legitimate power,* is based on the idea that members of an organization recognize and accept the formal authority of individuals who have higher-ranking positions within the organizational hierarchy.

Referent Power: Control Based on Admiration   "Joe, we go back over twenty years in this company, and I consider you a good friend. I'm in kind of a bind right now, and I could sure use your help. You see, what happened is. . . ." Joe is most certainly being set up to help the speaker, who is relying on the fact that he and Joe have a long-standing friendship. Out of his allegiance to that relationship and his liking and admiration for the speaker, Joe probably feels obligated to go along with whatever is being asked. Individuals who are liked and respected by others can get them to alter their actions in accord with their directives—a type of influence known as **referent power.** Senior managers who possess desirable qualities and good reputations may find that they have referent power over younger managers who identify with them and wish to emulate them. Similarly, sports heroes and popular movie stars often have referent power over their admiring fans (a fact advertisers often capitalize on when they employ these individuals as spokespersons to endorse their products).

Expert Power: Control Based on Skills and Knowledge   If a foreman tells one of his machine shop workers to readjust the settings on a certain piece of equipment, that person may well do it because he believes that the foreman is expert in the operation of the machine. To the extent that a subordinate recognizes a superior's advanced skill or knowledge and follows his orders because he realizes that the superior knows what's best, that superior is said to have **expert power.** The running of organizations often relies on experts who must be consulted frequently, and whose advice must be followed if an organization is to survive. The power of various experts is usually very narrowly defined, limited to the scope of their expertise. Accountants may have expert power when it comes to corporate taxes and investments, whereas market researchers may have expert power when it comes to deciding what type of advertising to use for a new product. Recent research has revealed that within teams of health care professionals (e.g., nurses, occupational therapists), the physician tends to hold the most power—in part a result of the high level of professional expertise they are believed to possess.[18]

Expert power can be a very successful way of influencing others in organizations. After all, it would be difficult to justify not following the directives of a trained professional who is better equipped than you are to know what to do. Thus, problems often develop when younger, less experienced employees are given responsibility for a work crew. Until they prove themselves with a record of success, many employees find it difficult to exercise power over others. By the same token, the recognized expertise of many managers and the extreme power they wield as a result makes them highly sought after as employees.

Measuring Individual Power Bases and an Alternative Conceptualization

How can researchers tell what kinds of power people use? They ask them—but asking questions about the kinds of power people use is easier said than done. In fact, scholars have recently criticized the way power has been measured in several previous studies.[19] A questionnaire developed by Hinkin and Schriesheim appears to have improved on the limitations of the previous efforts.[20] People completing the scale are asked to describe how closely various statements describe their own supervisors' behaviors. Four items measure each of the five bases of power identified by French and Raven. Participants complete the scale by indicating how much they agree that each item describes the way their supervisors treat their subordinates. The questionnaire is then scored by summing the degrees of agreement with the four items reflecting each scale. By collecting several such measures for a particular supervisor, scientists can gauge the relative degree to which that supervisor is recognized by his or her subordinates for using various types of power. For a look at items similar to those developed by Hinkin and Schriesheim, see Table 11–3.

TABLE 11-3   What Kinds of Power Do You Use?

Scientists use tests similar to this one to measure people's beliefs about their supervisors' power. To complete the test, follow the directions below. To score, add your responses to numbers 1 and 3. This measures your beliefs about your supervisor's *reward power*. The sum of numbers 2 and 4 measures *coercive power*. The sum of numbers 5 and 7 measures *legitimate power*. The sum of numbers 6 and 9 measures *expert power*. Finally, the sum of numbers 8 and 10 measures *referent power*. Although the questionnaire is incomplete and items presented are not exactly the same as the ones actually used, this will give you a good idea of how social scientists measure individual power in organizations.

Directions: Indicate how strongly you agree or disagree that each of the following statements accurately describes *your supervisor*. Answer by using the following numbers: 1 = strongly disagree; 2 = disagree; 3 = neither agree nor disagree; 4 = agree; and 5 = strongly agree.

My supervisor can

_____   1. See that I get a raise

_____   2. Give me jobs I dislike

_____   3. Make sure I get the promotion I desire

_____   4. Make my work life miserable

_____   5. Explain my responsibilities

_____   6. Give me good advice on getting the job done

_____   7. Understand the tasks I have to accomplish

_____   8. Make me feel good

_____   9. Give me the benefit of his or her technical know-how

_____ 10. Get me to feel important

Source: Based on Hinkin and Schriesheim, 1989; see Note 20.

FIGURE 11–5

An Alternative Conceptualization of Individual Power

Recently, Yukl and Falbe have noted that individual power is best conceptualized as having two major dimensions—*position power* and *personal power*—each of which has four distinct power bases. This conceptualization builds on and extends French and Raven's original view of five power bases. (*Source:* Based on Yukl & Falbe, 1991; see Note 21.)

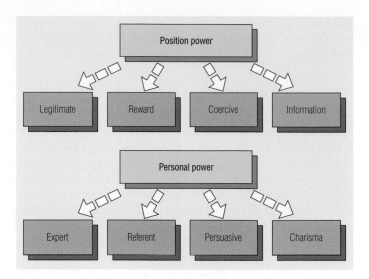

By design, questionnaire items such as these tap French and Raven's five bases of social power. Unfortunately, this conceptualization, although frequently cited, has not been subject to much empirical verification. Are there really only five bases of social power that people use? A recent exploratory study by Yukl and Falbe reveals that although evidence exists for the five bases of power already identified, there appear to be three more, for a total of eight.[21] What's more, these bases of power reflect two basic underlying dimensions. Refer to the summary of this alternative view of power in Figure 11–5 as we describe it in more detail below.

One broad dimension, referred to as **position power,** has to do with *power based on one's formal position in an organization.* It includes three of the five bases of power we've identified so far—legitimate power, reward power, and coercive power—and a new one, **information power.** This refers to *the extent to which a supervisor provides a subordinate with the information needed to do the job.*

The other broad dimension is known as **personal power.** This refers to *the power that one derives because of his or her individual qualities or characteristics.* It includes two of the French and Raven power bases—expert power and referent power—plus two more, *persuasive power* and *charisma.* **Persuasive power** refers to *the ability to use facts and logic to present a case persuasively.* In contrast, **charisma** is more elusive—namely, *an attitude of enthusiasm and optimism that is contagious.* (Note that this use of the term is similar to the way it will be used to refer to a characteristic of a leader in chapter 12.)

This alternative approach is obviously a bit more thorough and complex than the original conceptualization proposed by French and Raven more than thirty years ago. Although the evidence is promising that it provides a very thorough and accurate view of the types of power that exist within organizations, it is still too soon to tell whether this approach is really any better than the original. If you think more about the conceptualization, you may realize that a clearer distinction is needed between the somewhat similar notions of referent power and charisma, as well as between expert power and information power. Similarly, position power and legitimate power also appear to be closely related. Given how important these notions are in explaining behavior in organizations, efforts at clarifying distinctions between various sources of power would prove worthwhile. Fortunately, because researchers are actively investigating this topic, conceptual clarification and evidence regarding the value of various approaches to understanding individual power bases will probably be forthcoming.

Individual Power: How Is It Used?

As researchers take on the challenge of distinguishing among the various bases of individual power, one consideration facing them is the widespread overlap in the ways people use power. Only sometimes is a single source of power used; indeed, it is recognized that the various power bases are closely related to each other.[22] For example, consider that the more someone uses coercive power, the less that person will be liked, and hence, the lower his or her referent power will be. Similarly, managers who have expert power are also likely to have legitimate power because their directing others within the field of expertise is accepted. In addition, the higher someone's organizational position, the more legitimate power that person has, which is usually accompanied by greater opportunities to use reward and coercion.[23] Clearly, then, the various bases of power should not be thought of as completely separate and distinct from each other. They are often used together in varying combinations.

What bases of power do people prefer to use? Although the answer to this question is quite complex, research has shown that people prefer using expert power most and their coercive power least often.[24] These findings are limited to the power bases we've identified thus far. However, when we broaden the question and ask people to report exactly sources of power they have on their jobs, a fascinating picture emerges. Figure 11–6 depicts the results of a survey in which 216 CEOs of American corporations were asked to rank-order the importance of a series of specific sources of power.[25] The figures indicate the percentage of executives who included that source of power among their top three choices. These findings indicate not only that top executives rely on a broad range of powers, but also that they base these powers on

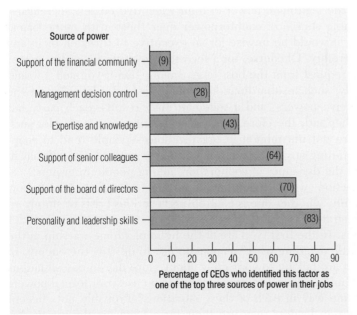

FIGURE 11–6

American CEOs: What Are Their Power Bases?

A survey of more than 200 American CEOs revealed that they obtained their power primarily through the support of others at different levels throughout the organization. (*Source:* Based on data appearing in Stewart, 1989; see Note 25.)

support from people located in a host of other places throughout their organizations. Interestingly, when asked about how much power they currently had compared to ten years ago, only 19 percent said they now had more power. Thirty-six percent indicated that they had the same amount of power, and the largest group, 42 percent, indicated that they had less power.

A potentially important determinant of the use of power that is not taken into account by such findings is the notion that people's personalities differentially predispose them toward using power in different ways. In chapter 6, we described several personality characteristics of individuals who are likely to be related to the use of power. Most notably, the trait of *Machiavellianism* is relevant here. People who score high on this trait are likely to use whatever power they have at their disposal to manipulate others.

Despite possible differences between individuals with respect to power, certain situational factors can greatly influence the use of various power tactics. One has to do with the target of influence attempts—that is, who is being influenced. Although many different forms of power tend to be used to influence subordinates, research has shown that expert power is the preferred form used to influence peers and superiors.[26] After all, it is almost always appropriate to try to get others to go along with you if you justify your attempt on the basis of your expertise. In contrast, coercive tactics tend to be frowned on in general, and are especially inappropriate when one is attempting to influence a higher-ranking person.[27] Influencing superiors is tricky because of the *counterpower* they have. When attempting to influence another who is believed to have no power at his or her disposal, one doesn't have to worry about fear of retaliation. When dealing with an individual with considerably greater power, however, one can do little other than simply comply with that more powerful person.

However, the situation is complicated by the fact that one may have higher power on one dimension, and another may have higher power on another dimension. Consider, for example, the case of some secretaries who have acquired power because they have been with their companies for many years. They know the ropes and can get things done for you if they want, or they can get you hopelessly bogged down in red tape. Their expert knowledge gives them a great sense of power over others. Although they may lack the legitimate power of their executive bosses, secretaries' expertise can be a valuable source of counterpower over those with more formal powers. For this reason, it would be unwise for an executive to threaten or in any way coerce his or her secretary. Of course, for a secretary to abuse his or her power by ignoring a legitimate request from the boss (e.g., saying "Do it yourself") would also be unwise. Naturally, such insubordination is likely to lead a boss to test the limits of his or her coercive powers, and a stalemate may result—each party has some power over the other and, therefore, may be reluctant to use it. Under such circumstances—which are not uncommon in organizations—people tend to cooperate with each other, limiting any imbalances in influence options. (Recall that in chapter 10 we discussed the dynamics of cooperation among people in groups.)

Before closing this section, we note another important factor that dictates how people use power—namely, whether one is confronting a serious crisis or simply an everyday matter. To illustrate this point, imagine that you are a naval commander in two different situations. In the first, you are at the helm of a huge warship in the middle of a ferocious battle deciding what weapons to use to destroy the enemy. In the second situation, you are talking to your crew about more day-to-day situations such as what the cook should prepare for dinner. Would you use your formal powers as commander in the same way in each of these situations? Probably not. Recent research suggests that group leaders may use their formal powers differently depending on whether their group is facing a crisis situation.

A recent investigation by Mulder and his associates surveyed the use of different powers by the managers of a bank in the Netherlands.[28] They were given a questionnaire asking them to describe the behaviors of their immediate supervisors in either a crisis situation or an everyday, noncrisis situation. (The executives were asked to think of crisis and noncrisis situations that actually occurred within their departments.) Among the types of power studied in the questionnaire were two of the bases of power identified by French and Raven that we noted earlier—*expert power* and *referent power*. Were the managers surveyed more likely to report that their supervisors used these forms of power under crisis or noncrisis situations? The answer is shown in Figure 11–7.

As Figure 11–7 reveals, both expert power and referent power were more likely to be used in crisis situations than everyday situations. Apparently, when crises occurred, such formal powers were relied on to get things done. However, everyday situations were not as likely to call for reliance on formal powers to manage. How, then, do superiors go about managing under noncrisis situations? The investigators found that under these circumstances supervisors relied instead on *open consultation* with their subordinates. This refers to the tendency for managers to resolve problems by talking them out with their subordinates, and allowing themselves to be persuaded by subordinates' arguments. Supervisors using this approach do not use the power they could claim over subordinates, but instead treat them as equals.

These findings point to some important conclusions regarding the use of power in organizations. Most important, they suggest that having power and using it are two different things. Just because a manager has certain powers at his or her disposal does not mean that they will be used automatically. Managers may prefer to rely on more open, two-way communication with their subordinates when dealing with everyday situations, in which using their influence would be unnecessarily severe. However, when crisis situations dictate the need for more formal powers, managers are not reluctant to use the powers at their disposal. Accordingly, it is important to keep in mind that managers' use of power is likely to be based on the situations they

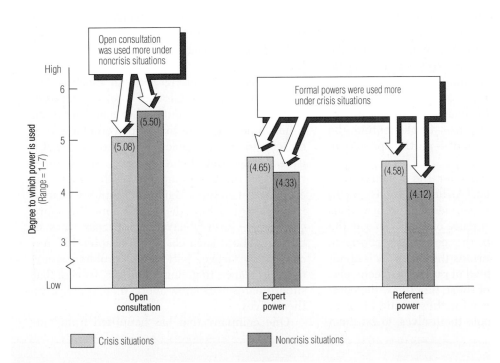

FIGURE 11–7

Power Use under Crisis and Noncrisis Conditions: An Experimental Comparison

When asked to report the types of power they used in crisis situations, Dutch bank managers noted using either their *expert power* or their *referent power*. Under noncrisis situations, in contrast, they reported a preference for openly consulting with their subordinates. (*Source:* Based on data reported by Mulder, de Jong, Koppelaar, & Verhage, 1986; see Note 28.)

Test Bank question 11.22 relates to material on this page.

face. (A similar point will be made in chapter 12 about the most effective leadership style for a given situation.)

One intriguing aspect of these findings is that the typical (noncrisis) way of influencing others was to openly consult with them. When a supervisor consults with a subordinate, he or she is sharing power with that person, allowing the individual to have a voice in how things are done. Some managers believe in completely giving subordinates the opportunities to make decisions, that is, giving them power—or, as it is known, *empowering* them. (For a closer look at the *empowerment* process, see the **OB in Practice** section below.)

GROUP OR SUBUNIT POWER: STRUCTURAL DETERMINANTS

Groups of consumers can gain power by using boycotts, or organized bans on purchases of products made by organizations. In the early 1990s, some 250 national, regional, and local boycotts were in effect

Thus far, this chapter has examined the uses of power by individuals. However, in organizations, not only people acting alone, but also groups, wield power. Organizations are frequently divided into *subunits* given responsibility for different functions such as finance, human resource management, marketing, and research and devel-

 OB IN PRACTICE

Empowerment: Shifting the Power Base to Subordinates

The traditional approach to management is autocratic. Supervisors gain power, in large part, because of their superior position along a vertical hierarchy. Although not always made explicit, coercion is the name of the game, and the threat of getting fired for fouling up looms large in the minds of employees. Although this approach may have worked well in the 1950s, several experts claim that today's business environment requires people who can face the challenges of a rapidly changing world. According to management consultant Peter Block, this requires implementing the process of **empowerment**—putting people in charge of what they do.[29]

As an example, consider the organizational chart at Scandinavian Airline Systems (SAS), where the customer service and reservations people—*not* the company officials—are at the top. This represents the company's efforts to communicate how serious the company is about these functions. Instead of putting someone else in power in charge of these functions, the company allows the power for these critical jobs to reside within the people themselves, to get them

to take responsibility for their own actions. Empowering means thinking of supervisors as consultants, giving major responsibilities to the people who do the jobs themselves. As Block put it, "The challenge for managers trying to empower their staffs—and themselves—is to see every act as a catalyst for change. It's just not true that you have to be at the top, or have angels at the top, to change a way of doing business. It's up to you."[30]

An executive who agrees with Block is Andrew S. Grove, the CEO of Intel Corporation (the $3.1 billion computer chip manufacturer), although he points out that empowerment is very difficult to put into practice. He says it's "not a natural approach for managers. Many were trained in old-line companies with a more hierarchical structure. Major philosophical change is necessary before they can adopt the more democratic form."[31] (We will discuss ways of bringing about such change in chapter 16.) According to Grove, part of the problem stems from resistance to giving up power, fearing that subordinates will know more than supervisors themselves.

One company that has benefited from em-

opment. The formal departments devoted to these various organizational activities often must direct the activities of other groups, requiring them to have power. What are the sources of such power? By what means do formal organizational groups successfully control the actions of other groups? Two theoretical models have been proposed to answer these questions—the *resource-dependency model* and the *strategic contingencies model*. Our review of these approaches will help identify the factors responsible for subunit power and describe how they operate.

The Resource-Dependency Model: Controlling Critical Resources

It is not difficult to think of an organization as a complex set of subunits that are constantly exchanging resources with each other. By this, we mean that formal organizational departments may be both giving to and receiving from other departments such valued commodities as money, personnel, equipment, supplies, and information. These critical resources are necessary for the successful operation of organizations.

against various organizations. One of the most successful recent boycotts was against the H.J. Heinz Company, when consumer groups stopped buying Star-Kist tuna as a protest against the company's killing of dolphins in its tuna nets. Although most boycotts do not appreciably affect sales levels, as was the case with the tuna boycott, they create a lot of negative publicity. In this way, groups can often successfully influence the behavior of the organizations. [Rodkin, D. (1991, July/August). Boycott power. *Mother Jones*, pp. 18–19.]

powering employees is Howard Miller, Inc. (a $793 million office furniture manufacturer).[32] The culture at Howard Miller is rich in participation and democracy. Employees are expected to participate with managers in discussions involving production as well as corporate direction, and the environment is highly egalitarian. Indeed, the company has practiced participative management since 1950 and strongly promotes the values of this practice through stories told to new hires. It's safe to say that at Howard Miller, empowerment is a way of life. CEO Richard H. Ruch attributes much of the company's success to this approach to management.

Another beneficial effect of empowerment (specifically, low employee absenteeism) has been found in a Volvo manufacturing plant in Sweden.[33] Here, automobile workers routinely handle the traditional managerial duties of scheduling, quality control, and hiring. They also can discuss problems with top company officials instead of supervisors who are usually quite limited in their power to correct things. (In Sweden, the law requires employees to have a considerable amount of input into the way their jobs are done.) At Howard Miller, where empowerment is an integral part of the culture, and at Volvo, where empowerment is the law, it is not surprising that the plan is so easily practiced.

Would empowerment work as well under conditions in which a shift occurs from tradi-

tional downward managerial power to total empowerment of subordinates? It certainly would be very difficult. Some progress can be made by having managers participate with and listen to others (instead of just telling them what to do). Andrew Grove acknowledges that this isn't likely to be easy, but says that it's probably worth the effort.

This empirical question has, unfortunately, received scant research attention. An important study by Leana, conducted in an insurance company, revealed that more claims were processed at lower cost when supervisors delegated power to their subordinates than under the more traditional system under which the supervisor retains power.[34] Apparently, in this case, empowering the subordinates helped them do their jobs better. The extent to which empowering other types of employee in other situations is also effective remains to be determined through systematic research. Moreover, we need to be able to explain *why* empowering works. Is it because it somehow energizes people to do their best by giving them more responsibility for their work (see chapter 4), or simply because it removes an unnecessary layer of hierarchy from an overburdened decision-making structure? Such questions need to be addressed if we are to understand the role of empowerment in organizations.

Test Bank questions 11.50 and 11.70 relate to material on this page.

FIGURE 11-8

Power between Subunits: The
Resource-Dependency Model

The *resource-dependency model* of organizational power explains that subunits acquire power when they control critical resources needed by other subunits. In the example shown here, the Accounting Department would be considered more powerful than either the Production Department or the Marketing Department.

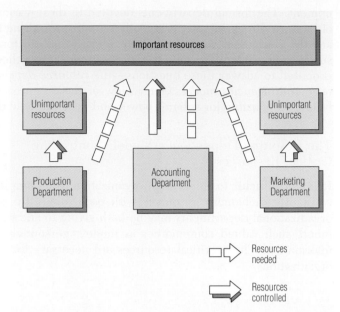

Various subunits often depend on others for such resources. Imagine, for example, a large organization that develops, produces, and sells its products. The Sales Department provides financial resources that enable the Research and Development Department to come up with new products. Of course, it cannot do so effectively without information from the Marketing Department about what consumers are interested in buying and how much they would be willing to pay. The Production Department has to do its part by manufacturing the goods on time, but only if the Purchasing Department can supply the needed raw materials—and at a price the Finance Department accepts as permitting the company to turn a profit. It is easy to see how the various organizational subunits are involved in a complex set of interrelationships with others. To the extent that one subunit controls the resources on which another subunit depends, it may be said to have power over it. After all, controlling resources allows groups to successfully influence the actions of other groups. Subunits that control more resources than others may be considered more powerful in the organization. Indeed, such imbalances, or *asymmetries*, in the pattern of resource dependencies occur normally in organizations. The more one group depends on another for needed resources, the less power it has (see Figure 11–8).

In proposing their **resource-dependency model,** Pfeffer and Salancik note that a subunit's power is based on the degree to which it controls the resources required by other subunits.[35] Thus, although all subunits may contribute something to an organization, the most powerful ones are those that contribute the most important resources. Controlling the resources other departments need puts a subunit in a better position to bargain for the resources it requires. To illustrate this point, let's consider an important study by Salancik and Pfeffer.[36] Within a university, the various academic departments may be very unequal with respect to the power they possess. For example, some may have more students, be more prestigious in their national reputation, receive greater grant support, and have more representatives on important university committees than others. As such, they would be expected to have greater control over valued resources. This was found to be the case within the large state university studied by Salancik and Pfeffer. The more powerful departments proved to be those that were most successful in gaining scarce and valued resources from the university (e.g., funds for graduate student fellowships, faculty research grants, and summer faculty fellowships). As a result, they became even more powerful, suggesting that within organizations, the rich subunits get richer.

A question follows from this conclusion: How do various organizational subunits come to be more powerful to begin with? That is, why might certain departments come to control the most resources when an organization is newly formed? Insight into this question is provided by Boeker's fascinating study of the semiconductor industry in California.[37] Boeker used personal interviews, market research data, and archival records as the main sources of data for this investigation. Results indicated that two main factors accounted for how much power an organizational subunit had: (1) the period within which the company was founded, and (2) the background of the entrepreneur starting the company. For example, because research and development functions were critical among the earliest semiconductor firms (founded 1958–1966, when semiconductors were new), this department had the most power among the oldest firms. Hence, the importance of the area of corporate activity at the time the company began dictated the relative power of that area years later (in 1985, when the study was done). It also was found that the most powerful organizational subunits tended to be those that represented the founder's area of expertise (see Figure 11–9). Thus, for example, the Marketing and Sales departments of companies founded by experts in marketing and sales tended to have the greatest amounts of power. This research provides an important missing link in our understanding of the attainment of subunit power within organizations.

The resource-dependency model suggests that a key determinant of subunit power is the control of valued resources. However, as we will now illustrate, it is not only control over resources that dictates organizational power, but also control over the activities of other subunits.

FIGURE 11–9   Company Founders: Important Influences on Subunit Power

Research has shown that the functional areas within which company founders specialize tend to be the ones that have the most power. For example, Henry Ford, the founder of Ford Motor Company (left), was a specialist in manufacturing technology—still a powerful department at Ford. William Gates, the founder of Microsoft (right), is a specialist in developing computer software products—still a powerful department at Microsoft.

The Strategic Contingencies Model: Power through Dependence

The Accounting Department of a company might be expected to have responsibility over the approval or disapproval of funds requested by various departments. If it does, its actions greatly affect the activities of other units, who depend on its decisions—that is, other departments' operations are *contingent* on what the Accounting Department does. To the extent that a department is able to control the relative power of various organizational subunits by virtue of its actions, it is said to have control over *strategic contingencies*. For example, if the Accounting Department consistently approved the budget requests of the Production Department but rejected the budget requests of the Marketing Department, it would be making the Production Department more powerful.

Where do the strategic contingencies lie within organizations? In a classic study, Lawrence and Lorsch found out that power was distributed in different departments in different industries.[38] They found that within successful firms, the strategic contingencies were controlled by the departments that were most important for organizational success. For example, within the food-processing industry, where it was critical for new products to be developed and sold, successful firms had strategic contingencies controlled by the Sales and Research departments. In the container-manufacturing field, where the timely delivery of high-quality goods is a critical determinant of organizational success, successful firms placed most of the decision-making power in the Sales and Production departments. Thus, successful firms focused the control over strategic contingencies within the subunits most responsible for their organization's success.

What factors give subunits control over strategic contingencies? The **strategic contingencies model** of Hickson and his associates suggests several key considerations.[39] Refer to the summary of these factors in Figure 11–10.

Power may be enhanced by subunits that can help *reduce the levels of uncertainty* faced by others. Any department that can shed light on the uncertain situations organizations may face (e.g., those regarding future markets, government regulation, availability of needed supplies, financial security) can be expected to wield the most organizational power. Accordingly, the balance of power within organizations may

FIGURE 11–10

Strategic Contingencies Model: Identifying Sources of Subunit Power

The *strategic contingencies model* explains intraorganizational power in terms of the capacity of some subunits to control the actions of others. Subunit power may be enhanced by the factors shown here.

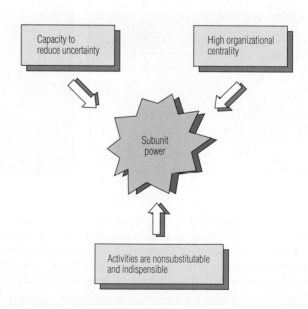

be expected to change as organizational conditions change. Consider, for example, changes that have taken place over the years in public utility companies. Studying the strategic contingencies in such organizations, Miles noted that a shift has occurred.[40] When public utilities first began, the engineers tended to wield the most power. But now that these companies have matured and face problems of litigation and governmental regulation (particularly over nuclear power), the power has shifted to lawyers. A similar shift toward the power of the Legal Department has occurred in recent years in the area of human resource management, where a complex set of laws and governmental regulations have created a great deal of uncertainty for organizations. Powerful subunits are those that can help reduce organizational uncertainty.

That more powerful subunits are ones that have a *high degree of centrality in the organization* has also been established. Some organizational subunits perform functions that are more central, and others, more peripheral. For example, some departments—such as Accounting—may have to be consulted by most others before any action can be taken, giving them a central position in their organizations. Centrality is also high when a unit's duties have an immediate effect on an organization. For example, the effects would be much more dramatic on an auto manufacturer if the production lines stopped than if market research activities ceased. The central connection of some departments to organizational success dictates the power they wield.

Third, a subunit controls power when its *activities are nonsubstitutable and indispensible.* If any group can perform a certain function, subunits responsible for controlling that function may not be particularly powerful. In a hospital, for example, personnel in Surgery are certainly more indispensable than personnel in Maintenance because fewer individuals have the skills needed to perform their department's duties. Because an organization can easily replace some employees with others either within or outside it, subunits composed of individuals who are most easily replaced tend to wield very little organizational power.

The strategic contingencies model has been tested and supported in several organizational studies.[41] For example, one investigation conducted in several companies found that a subunit's power within an organization was higher when it could reduce uncertainty, occupied a central place in the work flow, and performed functions that other subunits could not perform.[42] The strategic contingencies model should be considered a valuable source of information about the factors that influence the power of subunits within organizations.

ORGANIZATIONAL POLITICS: POWER IN ACTION

Our discussion of power focused on the *potential* to influence others successfully. When this potential is realized, put into action to accomplish desired goals, we are no longer talking about power, but **politics**.[43] It is quite easy to imagine situations in which someone does something to accomplish his or her own goals, which do not necessarily agree with the goals of the organization (Jack's behavior in our story on page 398 provides a good example). This is what **organizational politics** is all about— *actions not officially sanctioned (approved) by an organization taken to influence others to meet one's personal goals.*[44] Our definition of organizational politics incorporates the three major elements of definitions of this construct that Drory and Romm identified.[45] Specifically, it takes into account (1) one person influencing another, (2) using political means, (3) such that the interests of the parties conflict with one another.

If you think we're describing something that is a bit selfish and appears to be an abuse of organizational power, you are correct. Organizational politics *does* involve placing one's self-interests above the interests of the organization. Indeed, this element of using power to foster one's own interests distinguishes organizational politics from uses of power that are approved and accepted by organizations.

Organizational Politics: Where Does It Occur?

There can be little doubt that organizational politics is widespread. A survey of managers by Gandz and Murray revealed that political activities in organizations is one of the most common topics of conversation among employees.[46] However, political activity is not equally likely to occur throughout all parts of organizations.[47]

The Gandz and Murray survey showed that the most likely areas of political activity were those in which clear policies were nonexistent or lacking, such as interdepartmental coordination, promotions and transfers, and delegation of authority. However, when it came to organizational activities that had clearly defined rules and regulations, such as hiring and disciplinary policies, political activities were lowest. A survey of organizational political practices by Allen and his associates revealed similar findings.[48] Specifically, organizational politics was perceived to be greatest in subunits (such as boards of directors and members of the marketing staff) that followed poorly defined policies, whereas political activity was perceived to be lowest in areas (such as production and accounting) in which clearly defined policies existed. Similarly, because of the inherently high levels of ambiguity associated with human resource management tasks (such as personnel selection and performance appraisal), political behavior is likely to occur when these functions are being performed.[49] Together, these findings help make an important point: *political activity is likely to occur in the face of ambiguity.* When there are clear-cut rules about what to do, it is unlikely that people will be able to abuse their power by taking political action. However, when people face highly novel and ambiguous situations in which the rules guiding them are unclear, it is easy to imagine how political behavior results.

Where in the organization is the political climate most active? In other words, at what organizational levels do people believe the most political activities are likely to occur? As shown in Figure 11–11, Gandz and Murray found that organizations were perceived as more political at the higher levels, and less political at the lower managerial and nonmanagerial levels of the organization.[50] Apparently, politics is most likely to occur at the top, where, of course, the stakes are highest and power may corrupt.

Political Tactics: Gaining the Power Advantage

Holding power can be a determinant of one's identity, and losing that power can be a challenge to that identity—and the way one is treated by others. First Lady Barbara Bush is reported to have told her husband that if he did not win the presidential election in 1988 and if he insisted upon driving away from the White House in their own car, she was not going to go with him. She was not going to ride in a car driven by a man who had not driven for eight years (i.e., while he was

To understand organizational politics, one must recognize the various forms political behavior can take in organizations. In other words, what are the techniques of organizational politics? When this question was asked of a group of managers surveyed by Allen and his associates, five techniques were identified as being used most often.[51]

1. **Blaming and attacking others.** One of the most popularly used tactics of organizational politics involves blaming and attacking others when bad things happen. A commonly used political tactic is finding a *scapegoat,* someone who could take the blame for some failure or wrongdoing. A supervisor, for example, may explain that the failure of a sales plan she designed was based on the serious mistakes of one of her subordinates—even if this is not entirely true. Explaining that "it's his fault," that is, making another "take the fall" for an undesirable event, gets the real culprit "off the hook" for it. Finding a scapegoat can allow the politically astute individual to avoid (or at least minimize) association with the negative situation. Although this practice may raise serious ethical questions, it goes on quite frequently in organizations.

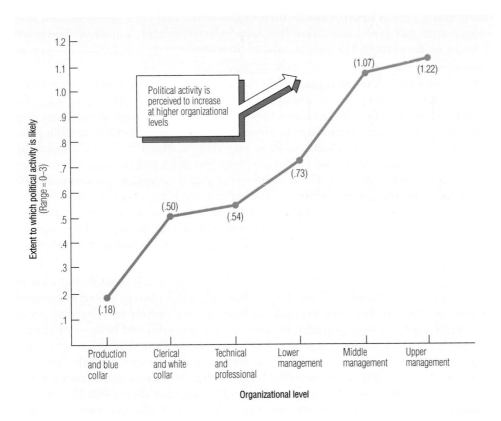

FIGURE 11–11

Organizational Politics:
More Likely at the Top

Survey research has
shown that employees
believe political activity
is more likely to occur
at higher organizational
levels (where the
guiding rules are more
ambiguous and the
stakes are higher) than
at lower levels. (*Source:*
Based on data reported
by Gandz & Murray,
1980; see Note 44.)

2. **Controlling access to information.** As we will note in chapter 13, information
is the lifeblood of organizations. Therefore, controlling who knows and doesn't know
certain things is one of the most important ways to exercise power in organizations.
Although outright lying and falsifying information may be used only rarely in organizations (in part because of the consequences of getting caught), there are other
ways of controlling information to enhance one's organizational position. For example,
you might (1) withhold information that makes you look bad (e.g., negative sales
information), (2) avoid contact with those who may ask for information you would
prefer not to disclose, (3) be very selective in the information you disclose, or (4)
overwhelm others with information that may not be completely relevant. These are
all ways to control the nature and degree of information people have at their disposal.
Such information control can be critical. A recent analysis of the organizational
restructuring of AT&T's Phone Stores revealed that control was transferred through
the effective manipulation, distortion, and creation of information.[52] A vice president's
secret plan to feed incomplete and inaccurate information to the CEO was responsible
for that vice president's winning control over the stores.

3. **Cultivating a favorable impression.** People interested in enhancing their organizational control commonly engage in some degree of image building—an attempt
to enhance the goodness their impressions on others. Such efforts may take many
forms, such as (1) "dressing for success" (as will be discussed in chapter 13), (2)
associating oneself with the successful accomplishments of others (or, in extreme
cases, taking credit for others' successes), or (3) simply drawing attention to one's
own successes and positive characteristics.[53] With this in mind, Ferris and King
recently identified those who worked hard to fit into their organizations as *organizational chameleons.*[54] Such individuals figure out what behaviors they believe are

vice president). [Kayden,
X. (1990, March/April).
Losing power. *The Ameri-
can Enterprise,* pp. 12–
13.]

considered generally appropriate in their organization, and then go out of their way to make sure that others are aware that they behaved in such a manner. These are all ways of developing the "right image" to enhance one's individual power in organizations.

4. **Developing a base of support.** For successful influencing of others, it is often useful to gain the support of others within the organization. Managers may, for example, lobby for their ideas before they officially present them at meetings, ensuring that others are committed to them in advance and thereby avoiding the embarrassment of public rejection. They may also "scatter IOUs" throughout the organization by doing favors for others who may feel obligated to repay them in the form of supporting their ideas. The norm of *reciprocity* is very strong in organizations, as evidenced by the popular phrases "You scratch my back, and I'll scratch yours" and "One good turn deserves another." After all, when someone does a favor for you, you may say, "I owe you one," suggesting that you are aware of the obligation to reciprocate that favor. "Calling in" favors is a well-established and widely used mechanism for developing organizational power.

5. **Aligning oneself with more powerful others.** One of the most direct ways to gain power is by connecting oneself with more powerful others. There are several ways to accomplish this. For example, a lower-power person may become more powerful if she has a very powerful mentor, a more powerful and better-established person who can look out for and protect her interests (recall our discussion of mentor-protégé relationships in chapter 9). As another example, people may also agree in advance to form *coalitions*—groups that band together to achieve some common goal (e.g., overthrowing a current corporate CEO). Research has shown that the banding together of relatively powerless groups is one of the most effective ways they have to gain organizational power.[55] Two relatively powerless individuals or groups may become stronger if they agree to act together, forming a coalition. People may also align themselves with more powerful others by giving them "positive strokes" in the hope of getting more powerful people to like them and help them—a process known as *ingratiation*.[56] Agreeing with someone more powerful may be an effective way of getting that person to consider you an ally. Such an alliance, of course, may prove indispensible when you are looking for support within an organization. To summarize, having a powerful mentor, forming coalitions, and using ingratiation are all potentially effective ways of gaining power by aligning oneself with others.

The techniques of organizational politics noted here are just some of the many available means of gaining power in organizations.[57] That there are so many techniques has led organizational scientists to view political behavior as a collection of games going on in a multiring circus. The idea is that many people or groups may be trying to influence many other people or groups simultaneously—as in playing a game. What, then, are the political games that unfold in organizations?

Playing Political Games in Organizations

One expert in the field of organizational power and politics, Henry Mintzberg, has identified four major categories of political games.[58] As we describe them, refer to our summary in Table 11–4.

1. **Authority games.** Some games are played to resist authority—*insurgency games*. Others are played to counter such resistance to authority—*counterinsurgency games*. Insurgency can take forms ranging from quite mild (such as intentionally not doing what is asked) to very severe (such as organizing workers to mutiny or sabotage their

TABLE 11-4   Political Games: A Summary of Some Examples

Many political games are played in organizations, each involving different individuals playing for different political goals.

Game	Typical Major Players	Purpose
Authority Games		
Insurgency game	Lower-level managers	To resist formal authority
Counterinsurgency game	Upper-level managers	To counter resistance to formal authority
Power Base Games		
Sponsorship game	Any subordinate employee	To enhance base of power with superiors
Alliance game	Line managers	To enhance base of power with peers
Empire building	Line managers	To enhance base of power with subordinates
Rivalry Games		
Line vs. staff game	Line managers and staff personnel	To defeat each other in the quest for power
Rival camps game	Any groups at the same level	To defeat each other in the quest for power
Change Games		
Whistle-blowing game	Lower-level operators	To correct organizational wrongdoings
Young Turks game	Upper-level managers	To seize control over the organization

Source: Adapted from Mintzberg, 1983; see Note 5.

workplaces). Companies may try to fight back with counterinsurgency moves. One way they may do so is by invoking stricter authority and control over subordinates. Often unproductive for both sides, such games frequently give way to the more adaptive techniques of bargaining and negotiation discussed in chapter 10.

2. **Power base games.** These games are played to enhance the degree and breadth of one's organizational power. For example, the *sponsorship game* is played with superiors. It involves attaching oneself to a rising or established star in return for a piece of the action. A relatively unpowerful subordinate, for example, may agree to help a more established person (such as his boss) by loyally supporting him in exchange for getting advice and information from him, as well as some of his power and prestige. Both benefit as a result. Similar games may be played among peers, such as the *alliance game*. Here, workers at the same level agree in advance to mutually support each other, gaining strength by increasing their joint size and power.

One of the riskiest power base games is known as *empire building*. In this game, an individual or group attempts to become more powerful by gaining responsibility for more and more important organizational decisions. Indeed, a subunit may increase its power by attempting to gain control over budgets, space, equipment, or any other scarce and desired organizational resource.

Test Bank questions 11.37 and 11.64 relate to material on this page.

3. **Rivalry games.** Some political games are designed to weaken one's opponents. For example, in the *line versus staff game* managers on the "line," who are responsible for the operation of an organizational unit, clash with those on "staff," who are supposed to provide needed advice and information. For example, a foreman on an assembly line may attempt to ignore the advice from a corporate legal specialist about how to treat one of his production workers, thereby rendering the staff specialist less powerful. (We will have more to say about the distinction between "line" and "staff" positions in chapter 15.) Another rivalry game is the *rival camps game*, in which groups or individuals with differing points of view attempt to reduce each other's power. For example, an organization's Production Department may favor the goals of stability and efficiency, whereas the Marketing Department may favor the goals of growth and customer service. The result may be that each side attempts to cultivate the favor of those allies who can support it and who are less sensitive to the other side's interests. Of course, because organizational success requires the various organizational subunits to work in concert with each other, such rivalries are considered potentially disruptive to organizational functioning. One side or the other may win from time to time, but the organization loses as a result.

4. **Change games.** Several different games are played to create organizational change. For example, in the *whistle-blowing game* an organizational member secretly reports some organizational wrongdoing to a higher authority in the hope of righting the wrong and bringing about change. (We discussed the phenomenon of whistle-blowing in chapter 10). A game played for much higher stakes is known as the *young Turks game*. In it, camps of rebel workers seek to overthrow the existing leadership of an organization—a most extreme form of insurgency. The change sought by people playing this game is not minor, but far-reaching and permanent. In government terms, they are seeking a "coup d'état."

Some political activities may readily coexist with organizational interests (e.g., the sponsorship game), whereas others are clearly antagonistic to organizational interests (e.g., the young Turks game). As such games are played out, it becomes apparent that although political activity may sometimes have little effect on organizations, more often it is quite harmful.[59] Now that we know what types of behavior reflect political activity in organizations, we are prepared to consider the conditions under which such behaviors take place.

When Does Political Action Occur?

Imagine the following situation. You are the director of a large charitable organization that administers funds supporting many charitable projects (e.g., saving endangered animals, providing shelter to the homeless). A wealthy philanthropist dies, and his will leaves your organization $1 million to be spent in any desired manner. Hearing of this generous bequest, the directors of the various charitable groups are all interested in obtaining as much of this money as possible to support their projects. Several aspects of this situation make it liable to trigger political activity.[60]

First, this situation is fraught with *uncertainty;* it is not obvious where the money should be spent. If the organization has no clearly prescribed priorities about how to spend its monies, various groups might very well try to get their share by any means possible. Second, this is clearly a matter in which there is an *important decision involving large amounts of scarce resources*. If the size of the gift were much smaller, say $500, or if it involved something trivial or readily available, such as paper clips, the incentive for political action would probably be weak.

The different groups in our example each have *conflicting goals and interests*. The save-our-wildlife group is intent on serving its interests; the shelter-for-the-

Organizations may attempt to increase their political power by forming political action committees (PACs). Using PACs, managers of corporations can pool their political contributions, sending their money off in a lump sum to the political candidates of their choice, who will support the views of their organizations. In re-

homeless group has very different interests. The differing goals make political activity likely. Finally, note that this situation is potentially politically active because the different charitable groups are all approximately *equal in power*. If there were a highly asymmetrical balance of power (with one group having a lot more control over resources than others), political action would be futile because the most powerful group would simply make the decision.

As shown in Figure 11–12, political behavior is likely to occur when (1) uncertainty exists, (2) large amounts of scarce resources are at stake, (3) organizational units (individuals or groups) have conflicting interests, or (4) the organizational units have approximately equal power.

Politics in Human Resource Management   If you think about these conditions, you won't be surprised that political behavior often centers around key human resource management activities such as performance appraisal, personnel selection, and compensation decisions.[61] For example, given that there is often a certain amount of ambiguity associated with evaluating another's performance, and that such evaluations might cultivate certain images of oneself, it follows that performance ratings may be recognized as more of a reflection of the rater's interest in promoting a certain image of himself than an interest in accurately evaluating another's behavior.[62,63] Similarly, when making personnel decisions, people are at least as much concerned about the implications of their hires for their own ideal careers (e.g., will this person support me or make me look bad?) as they are concerned about doing what's best for the organization.[64] Finally, pay raise decisions have been shown to be politically motivated. Specifically, in a management simulation exercise, Bartol and Martin found that managers gave the highest raises to individuals who threatened to complain if they didn't get a substantial raise, particularly if it were known that these people had political connections within the organization.[65] Taken together, these findings suggest that the very nature of human resource management activities in organizations makes them prime candidates for activities within which organizational politics are likely to be activated.

Politics and the Organizational Life Span   The conditions leading to political activities are likely to differ as a function of the stage of an organization's life. Hence, contrasting degrees and types of political activity are expected. Organizations can

cent years, PACs have been particularly effective in keeping incumbents in office and blocking new candidates from attaining office. Although PACs have enabled organizations to have considerable influence in political affairs, their underlying ethics have been questioned, leading to the possibility of some type of regulatory legislation. [Novack, J. (1989, February 20). Influence for sale. *Forbes*, pp. 108–109.]

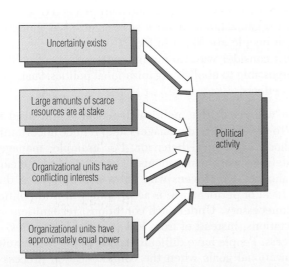

FIGURE 11–12

What Triggers Political Activity in Organizations? A Summary

Several conditions are likely to stimulate political activity within organizations. A few of the key conditions are shown here.

be distinguished quite simply as those that are just being started by entrepreneurs (the *birth and early growth* stage), those that are fully developed (the *maturity* stage), and those that face decline and dissolution (the *decline or redevelopment* stage). As Gray and Ariss explain, different types of political activity are likely to occur during these various stages of an organization's life.[66]

When an organization is newly begun, it may have little or no structure and be guided by the philosophy of the founder. During this stage, the entrepreneur gains political power by presenting his or her ideas as rational to the employees, who accept this person's image of the corporate mission. The founder usually has complete access to information and makes decisions based on his or her own values. Explaining these decisions to subordinates is a way of inculcating these values to others in the organization, and thereby exercising power over them. Political activity is not particularly likely during this stage.

However, as organizations mature and become more complex, they tend to grow and to departmentalize, creating conditions in which the vested interests of different groups are likely to conflict. Political means may be used to gain an advantage in such a situation. Indeed, it is likely that the full range of political activities noted earlier will be employed when organizations are mature (e.g., forming coalitions, using information). It is particularly interesting to note that when organizations begin to decline, subunits may be quite insecure and the need for political action may be great as people and groups compete for the power to control (and perhaps turn around) the organization. A period of decline reflects a time of great uncertainty, and thus a period in which political activity is likely to be quite intense. For example, Hannan and Freeman found that staff members employed in California school districts experiencing decline tended to have more intense competitive interactions and were at odds with each other more than members of similar organizations during periods of growth.[67] Clearly, the use of political practices in organizations is likely to be affected by its degree of maturity.

Coping with Organizational Politics: Some Techniques

Given how fundamental the need for power appears to be among people, and how differences in power between employees are basic to organizations, it is safe to say that organizational politics is inevitable. This is not good news, however, as many of the effects of organizational politics are quite negative. Indeed, lowered corporate morale and diversion from key organizational goals (as employees pay closer attention to planning their attacks on others than to doing their jobs) are expected to result from political activity. The more organizational politics is recognized as going on, the less trust and more alienation people are likely to feel.[68]

In view of this, managers must consider ways to minimize the effects of political behavior. Although it may be impossible to abolish organizational politics, managers can do several things to limit its effects.

- **Clarify job expectations.** You will recall that political behavior is nurtured by highly ambiguous conditions. To the extent that managers help reduce uncertainty, they can minimize the likelihood of political behavior. For example, managers should give very clear, well-defined work assignments. They should also clearly explain how work will be evaluated. Employees who know precisely what they are supposed to do and what level of performance is acceptable will find political games to assert their power unnecessary. Under such conditions, recognition will come from meeting job expectations, instead of from less acceptable avenues.
- **Open the communication process.** People have difficulty trying to foster their own goals at the expense of organizational goals when the communication process is

open to scrutiny by all. Compare, for example, a department manager who makes budget allocation decisions in a highly open fashion (announced to all) and one who makes the same decisions in secret. When decisions are not openly shared and communicated to all, conditions are ideal for unscrupulous individuals to abuse their power. Decisions that can be monitored by all are unlikely to allow any one individual to gain excessive control over desired resources.

- **Be a good role model.** It is well established that higher-level personnel set the standards by which lower-level employees operate. As a result, any manager who is openly political in her use of power is likely to create a climate in which her subordinates behave the same way. Engaging in dirty political tricks teaches subordinates not only that such tactics are appropriate, but also that they are the desired way of operating within the organization. Managers will certainly find it difficult to constrain the political actions of their subordinates unless they set a clear example of honest and reasonable treatment of others in their own behavior.

- **Do not turn a blind eye to game players.** Suppose you see one of your subordinates attempting to gain power over another by taking credit for that individual's work. Immediately confront this individual and do not ignore what he did. If the person believes he can get away with it, he will try to do so. What's worse, if he suspects that you are aware of what he did, but didn't do anything about it, you are indirectly reinforcing his unethical political behavior—showing him that he can get away with it.

In conclusion, it is important for practicing managers to realize that because power differences are basic to organizations, attempts to gain power advantages through political maneuvers are to be expected. However, a critical aspect of a manager's job is to redirect these political activities away from any threats to the integrity of the organization. Although expecting to eliminate dirty political tricks would be unrealistic, we believe the suggestions offered here provide some useful guidelines for minimizing their impact.

THE ETHICAL IMPLICATIONS OF ORGANIZATIONAL POLITICS

Probably one of the most important effects of organizational power is that it invites corruption. Indeed, the more power an individual has at his or her disposal, the more tempted that person is to use that power toward some immoral or unethical purpose.[69] Obviously, then, the potential is quite real for powerful individuals and organizations to abuse their power and to behave unethically. Because such behaviors are negatively regarded, the most politically astute individuals—including politicians themselves—often attempt to present themselves in a highly ethical manner.

Unfortunately, the potential to behave unethically is too frequently realized. Consider, for example, how greed overtook concerns about human welfare when the Manville Corporation suppressed evidence that asbestos inhalation was killing its employees, or when Ford failed to correct a known defect that made its Pinto vulnerable to gas tank explosions following low speed rear-end collisions.[70] Companies that dump dangerous medical waste materials into our rivers and oceans also appear to favor their own interests over public safety and welfare. Although these examples are better known than many others, they do not appear to be unusual. In fact, the story they tell may be far more typical than we would like, as one expert estimates that about two-thirds of the 500 largest American corporations have been involved in one form of illegal behavior or another.[71] Given the scope of the problems associated with unethical organizational behaviors, we will focus on the ethical aspects of politics in the final section of this chapter.

What do CEOs do when they suspect unethical behavior among their ranks? One way such companies as Unisys, Rockwell International, and Martin Marietta have combated internal wrongdoings has been to hire an independent outside law firm to conduct an internal investigation of the company. In the case of Martin Marietta, the investigation revealed that employees had been padding costs, causing the company to have to make a settlement with the U.S. Justice Department. Because any evidence revealed in such independent internal investigations may be used against the company, organizations are reconsidering the merits of such investigations. [Fanning, D. (1989, February 6). Beware the boomerang. *Forbes*, pp. 66–67.]

Political Behavior: What Makes It Ethical?

Although there are obviously no clear-cut ways to identify whether a certain organizational action is ethical, Velasquez and his associates suggest some useful guidelines.[72] For a summary of the central questions associated with assessing the ethics of political behavior, see Figure 11–13.

As a first consideration, we may ask: *will the political tactics promote purely selfish interests, or will they also help meet organizational goals?* If only one's personal, selfish interests are nurtured by a political action, it may be considered unethical. Usually, political activity fails to benefit organizational goals, but not always. Suppose, for example, that a group of top corporate executives is consistently making bad decisions that are leading the organization down the road to ruin. Would it be unethical in such a case to use political tactics to try to remove the power-holders from their positions? Probably not. In fact, political actions designed to benefit the organization as a whole (as long as they are legal) may be justified as appropriate and highly ethical. After all, they are in the best interest of the entire organization.

A second question in considering the ethics of organizational politics is: *does the political activity respect the rights of the individuals affected?* Generally speaking, actions that violate basic human rights are, of course, considered unethical. For example, dirty political tricks that rely on espionage techniques (such as wiretapping) are not only illegal, but also unethical in that they violate the affected individual's *right to privacy.* However, as you may know, police agencies are sometimes permitted by law to use methods that violate privacy rights under circumstances in which the greater good of the community at large is at stake. It is not easy, of course, to weigh the relative benefits of an individual's right to privacy against the greater societal good. Indeed, making such decisions involves a potential misuse of power in itself. It is because of this that society often entrusts such decisions to high courts charged with the responsibility for considering both individual rights and the rights and benefits of the community at large.

FIGURE 11–13

Guidelines for Determining
Ethical Action

Although assessing the ethicality of a behavior is complex, answers to the three questions shown here can provide a good indication. The flow chart shows the path that must be taken to achieve ethical action.

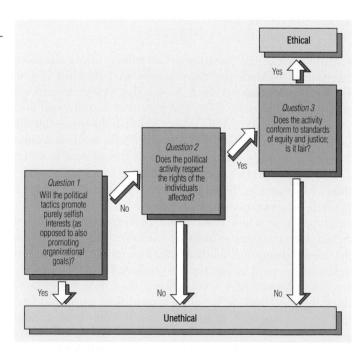

Velasquez and his associates also identified a third consideration in assessing the ethics of political action: *does the activity conform to standards of equity and justice; is it fair?* Any political behavior that unfairly benefits one party over another may be considered unethical. Paying one person more than another similarly qualified person is one example (as you may recall from our discussion of *equity theory* in chapter 4). Standards regarding the fair treatment of individuals are often unclear. Not surprisingly, more powerful individuals often use their power to convince others (and themselves!) that they are taking action in the name of justice. That is, they seek to implement seemingly fair rules that benefit themselves at the expense of others.[73] This, of course, represents an abuse of power. However, we must sometimes consider instances in which violating standards of justice may be considered appropriate. For example, it has been found that managers may sometimes give poorly performing employees higher pay than they deserve in the hope of stimulating them to work at higher levels.[74] Although the principle of equity is violated in this case (people should be paid in proportion to their job contributions), the manager may argue that the employee and the organization benefit as a result. Of course, the result may be considered unfair to the other individuals who are not so generously treated. Obviously, we will not be able to settle this complex issue here. Our point is that although ethical behavior involves adhering to standards of justice, there may be instances in which violations of these standards may be considered ethically acceptable.

As you can probably tell by now, most matters involving the resolution of moral and ethical issues are quite complex. Each time a political strategy is considered, its potential effects should be evaluated in terms of the questions outlined here. If the practice appears to be ethical based on these considerations, it may be acceptable in that situation. If ethical questions arise, however, alternative actions should be seriously considered. Unfortunately, many unethical political practices are followed in organizations despite their obvious violations of moral standards. We will now consider some of the underlying reasons for this.

Why Does Unethical Behavior Occur in Organizations? Prevailing Political Norms

As noted earlier in this chapter, unethical organizational practices are embarrassingly commonplace. It is easy to define practices such as dumping chemical wastes into rivers, insider trading on Wall Street, and overcharging the government for Medicaid services as morally wrong. Yet these and many other unethical practices go on almost routinely in many organizations. Why is this so? In other words, what accounts for the unethical actions of people within organizations?

One answer to this question is based on the idea that *organizations often reward behaviors that violate ethical standards*. Consider, for example, how many business executives are expected to deal in bribes and payoffs, and how good corporate citizens blowing the whistle on organizational wrongdoings may fear being punished for their actions (refer to our discussion of whistle-blowing in chapter 10). Jansen and Von Glinow explain that organizations tend to develop *counternorms*—accepted organizational practices that are contrary to prevailing ethical standards. Some of these are summarized in Figure 11–14 on p. 430.

The top of Figure 11–14 identifies being open and honest as a prevailing ethical norm. Indeed, governmental regulations requiring full disclosure and freedom of information reinforce society's values toward openness and honesty. Within organizations, however, it is often considered not only acceptable, but desirable, to be much

FIGURE 11-14

FIGURE 11-14

Societal Norms versus
Organizational Counternorms:
An Ethical Conflict

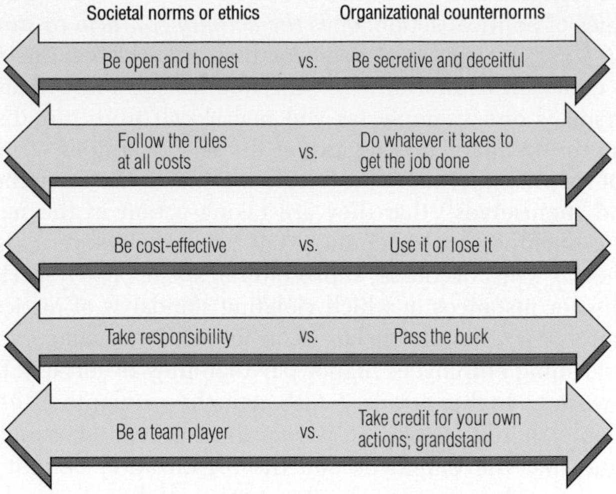

	Societal norms or ethics		Organizational counternorms
	Be open and honest	vs.	Be secretive and deceitful
	Follow the rules at all costs	vs.	Do whatever it takes to get the job done
	Be cost-effective	vs.	Use it or lose it
	Take responsibility	vs.	Pass the buck
	Be a team player	vs.	Take credit for your own actions; grandstand

more secretive and deceitful. The practice of *stonewalling*—willingly hiding relevant information—is quite common. One reason is that organizations may actually punish those who are too open and honest. Consider, for example, the disclosure that B. F. Goodrich rewarded employees who falsified data on the quality of aircraft brakes to win certification.[76] Similarly, it has been reported that executives at Metropolitan Edison encouraged employees to withhold information from the press about the Three Mile Island nuclear accident.[77] In both incidents, the counternorms of secrecy and deceitfulness were accepted and supported by the organization.

As you can see from Figure 11–14, many other organizational counternorms promote morally and ethically questionable practices. That these practices are commonly rewarded and accepted suggests that organizations may be operating within a world that dictates its own set of accepted rules. This reasoning suggests a second answer to the question of why organizations act unethically—namely, because *managerial values exist that undermine integrity.* In a recent analysis of executive integrity, Wolfe explains that managers have developed some ways of thinking (of which they may be quite unaware) that foster unethical behavior.[78]

One culprit is referred to as the **bottom line mentality.** This line of thinking supports financial success as the only value to be considered. It promotes short-term solutions that are immediately financially sound, despite the fact that they cause problems for others within the organization or for the organization as a whole. It promotes an unrealistic belief that everything boils down to a monetary game. As such, rules of morality are merely obstacles, impediments along the way to bottom line financial success.

Wolfe also notes that managers tend to rely on an **exploitative mentality**—a view that encourages "using" people in a way that promotes stereotypes and undermines empathy and compassion. This highly selfish perspective sacrifices concern for others in favor of benefits to one's own immediate interests. In addition, there is a **Madison Avenue mentality**—a perspective suggesting that anything is right if the public can be convinced that it's right. The idea is that executives may be more concerned about their actions appearing ethical than about their legitimate morality—a public relations–guided mentality. This kind of thinking leads some companies to hide their unethical actions (by dumping their toxic wastes under cover of night, for instance) or to otherwise justify them by attempting to explain them as completely acceptable.

Recognizing the problems associated with these various orientations is not difficult. Their overemphasis on short-term monetary gain may lead to decisions that not only hurt individuals in the long run, but also threaten the very existence of organizations themselves. Although an organization may make an immediate profit by cutting corners, exploiting people, and convincing others that they have behaved appropriately, whether such practices are in the long-term best interest of organizations is questionable. Just as people are learning that they cannot continue to exploit their natural environments forever without paying a cost (e.g., depletion of natural resources, hazards allegedly caused by openings in the earth's ozone layer), the same may apply to business environments as well. Indeed, society appears to be increasingly less tolerant of organizations that continue to violate moral standards in the name of short-term profit.[79]

It has even been argued that when organizations continue to behave unethically, they may actually find that doing so is not profitable in the long run. Consumers who find the well-publicized unethical actions of various companies objectionable may cast their votes for greater social responsibility by not patronizing those organizations.[80] The tendency for dubious ethical practices to be commonplace may be changing—but only time will tell. (One effective means of tracking ethical values in organizations is to conduct surveys tapping perceptions of ethical practices in organizations. According to the results of one recent survey, self-serving, political pressures appear to be responsible for many of the most unethical practices within one important realm of organizational functioning—human resource management. For a review of these findings, see the **Question of Ethics** section on pp. 432–433.)

SUMMARY AND REVIEW

Influence

When someone attempts to affect another in a desired fashion, that person is said to be using **social influence.** If this influence attempt is successful, that individual will have exercised **control** over the other. People generally prefer to use open, consultative forms of influence rather than coercive methods.

Organizational Power

The concept of **power** refers to the capacity to change the behavior or attitudes of others in a desired manner. Power may reside within individuals, and five bases of individual social power have been identified. **Reward power** and **coercive power** refer to an individual's capacity to control valued rewards and punishments, respectively. **Legitimate power** is the recognized authority that an individual has by virtue of his or her organizational position. **Referent power** is a source of control based on the fact that an individual is liked and admired by others. Finally, **expert power** refers to the power an individual has

because he or she is recognized as having superior knowledge, skill, or expertise in some valued area. An alternative conceptualization of power distinguishes between **position power**—power based on one's formal organizational position—and **personal power**—power derived from one's individual qualities or characteristics. Research has shown that differences in the use of power depend not only on individual characteristics (e.g., personality) but also on the specific situations faced (e.g., facing others who have counterpower).

Power may also reside within work groups, or subunits. The **resource-dependency model** asserts that power resides within the subunits that control the greatest share of valued organizational resources. The **strategic contingencies model** explains power in terms of a subunit's capacity to control the activities of other subunits. Such power may be enhanced by the capacity to reduce the level of uncertainty experienced by another unit, having a central position within the organization, or performing functions that other units cannot perform.

A QUESTION OF ETHICS

**The Ethical Management of Authority: Perspectives from
Human Resource Professionals**

 A sure sign of someone's authority in an organization is the capacity to "pull strings," to get things done in a manner that goes outside normal organizational channels. Consider, for example, someone who may tell you, "I have a friend at that company who owes me a favor, so I'll get him to hire you for that job you want." Although such practices are not uncommon, a recent survey has shown that hiring decisions made to fulfill a favor are considered unethical because they are not based on job performance.

More than 1,000 professionals in the field of human resource management were recently surveyed concerning their feelings about the ethics of various managerial practices.[81] Interestingly, among the ethical situations considered most serious were several practices that dealt with political activities reflecting an abuse of power. These included practices such as "making personnel decisions based on favoritism instead of job performance" and "basing differences in pay on friendship." In fact, these were the two most frequently cited types of unethical situation faced by human resource managers (with almost 31 percent of the sample indicating that each was among *the* most serious violations). Another type of unethical political behavior (indicated as being most serious by over 23 percent of the sample) was "making arrangements with vendors or consulting agencies leading to personal gain." As shown in Figure 11–15, these actions are in addition to various other types of unethical behavior that represent bias, but that are clearly not so self-serving as to constitute political acts.

Given that so many critical ethics violations appear to be politically motivated, self-serving actions, it is not surprising that these happened to be the very behaviors that managers had the greatest difficulty addressing. In fact, only about half of the managers surveyed reported having any success in minimizing a problem such as hiring based on favoritism. The very fact that such behaviors benefit oneself makes them difficult to eliminate. In contrast, it is easier to combat unethical behaviors based on insensitivity (e.g., lack of attention to privacy) because these serve no beneficial functions for the person doing the violating.

Managers tend to be relatively unaware of the political biases underlying their unethical actions, however. Instead, they attribute their actions to the attitudes and behaviors of senior management. Specifically, whereas only 10 percent of the study participants attributed unethical behaviors to political pressures, 56 percent attributed unethical behaviors to the attitudes and behaviors of senior management. They blamed top management most frequently for instances of unethical behavior, but they also recognized that top management of organizations tends to be committed to ethical conduct. Despite such commitment, company officials tend to overlook the capacity of human resource managers to help promote their company's ethical values. Too often, they tend to concentrate on using human resource managers for maintaining

Organizational Politics

Behaving in a manner that is not officially approved by an organization to meet one's own goals by influencing others is known as **organizational politics.** Such activities typically occur under ambiguous conditions (such as in areas of organizational functioning in which clear rules are lacking). Political tactics may include blaming and attacking others, controlling access to information, cultivating a favorable impression, developing an internal base of support, and aligning oneself with more powerful others. This may involve the playing of political games, such as asserting one's authority, enhancing one's power base, attacking one's rivals, and trying to foster organizational change. Such actions typically occur under conditions in which organizational uncertainty exists, important decisions involving large amounts of

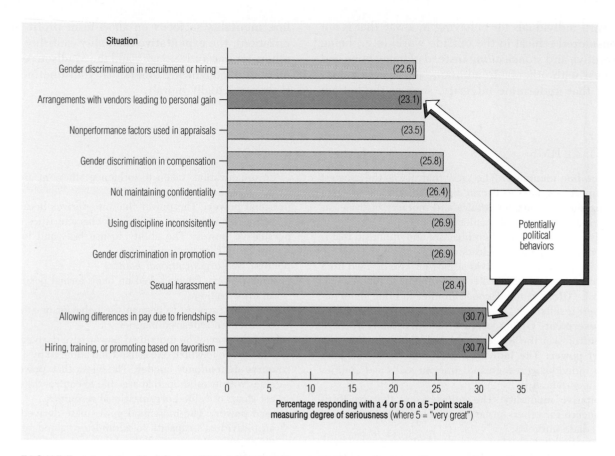

Situation

- Gender discrimination in recruitment or hiring — (22.6)
- Arrangements with vendors leading to personal gain — (23.1)
- Nonperformance factors used in appraisals — (23.5)
- Gender discrimination in compensation — (25.8)
- Not maintaining confidentiality — (26.4)
- Using discipline inconsisitently — (26.9)
- Gender discrimination in promotion — (26.9)
- Sexual harassment — (28.4)
- Allowing differences in pay due to friendships — (30.7)
- Hiring, training, or promoting based on favoritism — (30.7)

Potentially political behaviors

0   5   10   15   20   25   30   35

Percentage responding with a 4 or 5 on a 5-point scale measuring degree of seriousness (where 5 = "very great")

FIGURE 11–15   Most Serious Ethical Situations Reported by Human Resource Managers: Survey Results

Recent survey results show that among the most widely reported sources of unethical behavior noted by human resource managers are those dealing with political behaviors (i.e., those that benefit oneself as opposed to the organization). (*Source:* Based on data reported by the Commerce Clearing House, 1991; see Note 81.)

up-to-date legal information about personnel matters. But, ethics goes well beyond mere compliance with the law, and society expects companies to go well beyond the ethical minimums. For these reasons—not to mention the long-term success of companies themselves—it is essential for human resource officials to help institute policies that encourage basing personnel-related decisions on job performance instead of on favoritism.

scarce resources are made, and the groups involved have conflicting interests but are approximately equal in power. Specifically, political activity is expected to be high when it comes to matters of human resource management and during an organization's mature stage of development (as opposed to its early and declining stages). The effects of organizational politics can be limited by practices such as clarifying job expectations, opening the communication pro-cess, being a good role model, and not turning a blind eye to game players.

Although there are exceptions, political behavior may be considered ethical to the extent that it fosters organizational interests over individual greed, respects the rights of individuals, and conforms to prevailing standards of justice and fair play. Unethical behavior occurs in organizations for several reasons. For one, organizations develop *counternorms* that

Test Bank question 11.45 relates to material on this page.

reward individuals for behaving in a way that is not considered ethical in the outside world (e.g., being secretive and *stonewalling* instead of being open and honest with others). In addition, managerial values exist that undermine integrity, such as the **bottom line mentality** (a focus on short-term profit maximization), the **exploitative mentality** (selfishly using others for one's advantage), and the **Madison Avenue mentality** (convincing others that your unethical actions are actually moral).

Key terms

bottom line mentality: The view that places the greatest importance on short-term financial gains of an organization. It considers ethics and morality obstacles as being in the path of financial gain.

charisma: An attitude of enthusiasm and optimism that is contagious; an aura of leadership.

coercive power: The individual power base derived from the capacity to administer punishment to others.

control: Attempts to influence another to bring about desired results.

empowerment: Giving people the opportunity to have control over the way they do their jobs.

expert power: The individual power base derived from an individual's recognized superior skills and abilities in a certain area.

exploitative mentality: The selfish view that sacrifices concern for others in favor of an individual's own immediate interests.

information power: The extent to which a supervisor provides a subordinate with the information needed to do the job.

legitimate power: The individual power base derived from one's position in an organizational hierarchy; the accepted authority of one's position.

Madison Avenue mentality: The view suggesting that anything is right if others can be convinced that it's right; a public relations–guided morality.

organizational politics: Actions not officially approved by an organization, taken to influence others in order to meet one's personal goals.

personal power: The power that one derives because of his or her individual qualities or characteristics.

persuasive power: The ability to use facts and logic to present a case persuasively.

politics: See *organizational politics*.

position power: Power based on one's formal position in an organization.

power: The capacity to change the behavior or attitudes of others in a desired manner.

referent power: The individual power base derived from the degree to which one is liked and admired by others.

resource-dependency model: The view that power resides within subunits that are able to control the greatest share of valued organizational resources.

reward power: The individual power base derived from an individual's capacity to administer valued rewards to others.

social influence: Attempts to affect another in a desired fashion.

strategic contingencies model: A view explaining power in terms of a subunit's capacity to control the activities of other subunits. A subunit's power is enhanced when (1) it can reduce the level of uncertainty experienced by other subunits, (2) it occupies a central position in the organization, and (3) its activities are highly indispensible to the organization.

Questions for discussion

1. Suppose your professor asks you to redo a homework assignment. Explain the various bases of individual social power he or she may use to influence your behavior in this situation.

2. Using the *resource-dependency model* and the *strategic contingencies model* as the basis for your analysis, describe the relative power differences between groups in any organization with which you are familiar.

3. Suppose you are a corporate official on the lookout for places within your organization where political behavior is likely to occur. What places and conditions would you look for? Explain your answer.

4. Describe the political tactics and tricks that one person may use to gain a power advantage over another in an organization.

5. Although it might not be possible to completely eliminate organizational politics, it might be possible to effectively manage political activity. Describe some of the things that can be done to cope with organizational politics.

6. Suppose you're the manager of a human resources department. Are political activities more likely or less likely to take place in your department compared to other departments? Why? What form might these actions be expected to take?

7. Explain why an organization's ethical norms may differ from ethical standards existing in the outside world.

8. Argue for or against this statement: The use of power in organizations is unethical.

NOTES

1. O'Reilly, B. (1988, January 4). Growing Apple anew for the business market. *Fortune*, pp. 36–37.

2. Scully, J. (1987). *Odyssey: Pepsi to Apple . . . a journey of adventure, ideas, and the future.* New York: Harper & Row.

3. Cobb, A. T. (1984). An episodic model of power: Toward an integration of theory and research. *Academy of Management Review, 9,* 482–493.

4. Mayes, B. T., & Allen, R. T. (1977). Toward a definition of organizational politics. *Academy of Management Review, 2,* 672–678.

5. Mintzberg, H. (1983). *Power in and around organizations.* Englewood Cliffs, NJ: Prentice-Hall.

6. Schriesheim, C. A., & Hinkin, T. R. (1990). Influence tactics used by subordinates: A theoretical and empirical analysis and refinement of the Kipnis, Schmidt, and Wilkinson Subscales. *Journal of Applied Psychology, 75,* 246–257.

7. Yukl, G., & Falbe, C. M. (1990). Influence tactics and objectives in upward, downward, and lateral influence attempts. *Journal of Applied Psychology, 75,* 132–140.

8. Ansari, M. A., & Kapoor, A. (1987). Organizational context and upward influence tactics. *Organizational Behavior and Human Decision Processes, 40,* 39–49.

9. Graham, J. W., Marks, G., & Hansen, W. B. (1991). Social influence processes affecting adolescent substance abuse. *Journal of Applied Psychology, 76,* 291–298.

10. Dreher, G. F., Dougherty, T. W., & Whitely, W. (1989). Influence tactics and salary attainment: A gender-specific analysis. *Sex Roles, 23,* 535–550.

11. Izraeli, D. N. (1987). Sex effects in the evaluation of influence tactics. *Journal of Occupational Behaviour, 12,* 79–86.

12. Offermann, L. R. (1990). Power and leadership in organizations. *American Psychologist, 45,* 179–189.

13. Johnson, H. L. (1985). Bribery in international markets: Diagnosis, clarification, and remedy. *Journal of Business Ethics, 4,* 447–455.

14. Tsalikis, J., & Nwachukwu, O. (1991). A comparison of Nigerian to American views of bribery and extortion in international commerce. *Journal of Business Ethics, 10,* 85–98.

15. French, J. R. P., & Raven, B. (1959). The bases of social power. In D. Cartwright (Ed.), *Studies in social power* (pp. 150–167). Ann Arbor, MI: Institute for Social Research, University of Michigan.

16. Kanter, R. M. (1979). Power failure in management circuits. *Harvard Business Review, 57,* 65–75.

17. Arvey, R. E., & Jones, A. P. (1985). The use of discipline in organizational settings: A framework for future research. In L. L. Cummings & B. M. Staw (Eds.), *Research in organizational behavior* (Vol. 7, pp. 367–408). Greenwich, CT: JAI Press.

18. Fiorelli, J. S. (1988). Power in work groups: Team member's perspective. *Human Relations, 41,* 1–12.

19. Schriesheim, C. A., Hinkin, T. R., & Podsakoff, P. M. (1991). Can ipsative and single-item measures produce erroneous results in field studies of French and Raven's (1959) five bases of power? An empirical investigation. *Journal of Applied Psychology, 76,* 106–114.

20. Hinkin, T. R., & Schriesheim, C. A. (1989). Development and application of new scales to measure the French and Raven (1959) bases of social power. *Journal of Applied Psychology, 74,* 561–567.

21. Yukl, G., & Falbe, C. M. (1991). Importance of different power sources in downward and lateral relations. *Journal of Applied Psychology, 76,* 416–423.

22. Podsakoff, P. M., & Schriesheim, C. A. (1985). Field studies of French and Raven's bases of power: Critique, re-analysis, and suggestions for future research. *Psychological Bulletin, 97,* 387–411.

23. Huber, V. L. (1981). The sources, uses, and conservation of managerial power. *Personnel, 51*(4), 62–67.

24. Kipnis, D., Schmidt, S. M., Swaffin-Smith, C., & Wilkinson, I. (1984, Winter). Patterns of managerial influence: Shotgun managers, tacticians, and bystanders. *Organizational Dynamics,* 58–67.

25. Stewart, T. (1989, November 6). CEOs see clout shifting. *Fortune,* p. 66.

26. Kahn, R. L., Wolfe, D. M., Quinn, R. P., Snoek, J. D., & Rosenthal, R. A. (1964). *Organizational stress: Studies in role conflict and ambiguity.* New York: Wiley.

27. See Note 22.

28. Mulder, M., de Jong, R. D., Koppelaar, L., & Verhage, J. (1986). Power, situation, and leaders' effectiveness: An organizational field study. *Journal of Applied Psychology, 71,* 566–570.

29. Block, P. (1990, July). How to be the new kind of manager. *Working Woman,* pp. 51–54.

30. See Note 29.

31. Grove, A. S. (1991, February). The perils of empowerment. *Working Woman,* pp. 20–22.

32. See Note 29.

33. See Note 29.

34. Leana, C. R. (1987). Power relinquishment versus power sharing: Theoretical clarification and empirical comparison of delegation and participation. *Journal of Applied Psychology, 72,* 228–233.

35. Pfeffer, J., & Salancik, G. (1978). *The external control of organizations.* New York: Harper & Row.

36. Salancik, G., & Pfeffer, J. (1974). The bases and uses of power in organizational decision-making. *Administrative Science Quarterly, 19*, 453–473.

37. Boeker, W. (1989). The development and institutionalization of subunit power in organizations. *Administrative Science Quarterly, 34*, 388–410.

38. Lawrence, P. R., & Lorsch, J. W. (1967). *Organization and environment*. Cambridge, MA: Harvard University Press.

39. Hickson, D. J., Astley, W. G., Butler, R. J., & Wilson, D. C. (1981). Organization as power. In L. L. Cummings & B. M. Staw (Eds.), *Research in organizational behavior* (Vol. 4, pp. 151–196). Greenwich, CT: JAI Press.

40. Miles, R. H. (1980). *Macro organizational behavior*. Glenview, IL: Scott, Foresman.

41. Saunders, C. S., & Scarmell, R. (1982). Intraorganizational distributions of power: Replication research. *Academy of Management Journal, 25*, 192–200.

42. Hinings, C. R., Hickson, D. J., Pennings, J. M., & Schneck, R. E. (1974). Structural conditions of intraorganizational power. *Academy of Management Journal, 19*, 22–44.

43. See Note 4.

44. Gandz, J., & Murray, V. V. (1980). The experience of workplace politics. *Academy of Management Journal, 23*, 237–251.

45. Drory, A., & Romm, T. (1990). The definition of organizational politics: A review. *Human Relations, 43*, 1133–1154.

46. See Note 44.

47. Ferris, G. R., & King, T. R. (in press). Politics in human resources decisions: A walk on the dark side. *Organizational Dynamics*.

48. Allen, R. W., Madison, D. L., Porter, L. W., Renwick, P. A., & Mayes, B. T. (1979). Organizational politics: Tactics and characteristics of its actors. *California Management Review, 22*, 77–83.

49. See Note 47.

50. See Note 44.

51. See Note 28.

52. Feldman, S. P. (1988). Secrecy, information, and politics: An essay in organizational decision making. *Human Relations, 41*, 73–90.

53. Greenberg, J. (1990). Looking fair vs. being fair: Managing impressions of organizational justice. In B. M. Staw & L. L. Cummings (Eds.), *Research in organizational behavior* (Vol. 12, pp. 111–157). Greenwich, CT: JAI Press.

54. See Note 47.

55. Welsh, M. A., & Slusher, E. A. (1986). Organizational design as a context for political activity. *Administrative Science Quarterly, 31*, 389–402.

56. Liden, R. C., & Mitchell, T. R. (1988). Ingratiatory behaviors in organizational settings. *Academy of Management Review, 13*, 572–587.

57. Vredenburgh, D. J., & Maurer, J. G. (1984). A process framework for organizational politics. *Human Relations, 37*, 47–66.

58. See Note 5.

59. Madison, D. L., Allen, R. W., Porter, L. W., Renwick, P. A., & Mayes, B. T. (1980). Organizational politics: An exploration of managers' perceptions. *Human Relations, 33*, 79–100.

60. Pfeffer, J. (1981). *Power in organizations*. Boston: Pitman.

61. Ferris, G. R., & Kacmar, K. M. (in press). Perceptions of organizational politics. *Journal of Management*.

62. Wayne, S. J., & Ferris, G. R. (1990). Influence tactics, affect, and exchange quality in supervisor-subordinate interactions. *Journal of Applied Psychology, 75*, 487–499.

63. Greenberg, J. (1991). Motivation to inflate performance ratings: Perceptual bias or response bias? *Motivation and Emotion, 15*, 81–98.

64. See Note 47.

65. Bartol, K. M., & Martin, D. C. (1990). When politics pays: Factors influencing managerial compensation decisions. *Personnel Psychology, 43*, 599–614.

66. Gray, B., & Ariss, S. S. (1985). Politics and strategic change across organizational life cycles. *Academy of Management Review, 10*, 707–723.

67. Hannan, M. T., & Freeman, J. H. (1978). Internal politics of growth and decline. In M. W. Meyer (Ed.), *Environment and organizations* (pp. 177–199). San Francisco: Jossey-Bass.

68. Kumar, P., & Ghadially, R. (1989). Organizational politics and its effects on members of organizations. *Human Relations, 42*, 305–314.

69. Kipnis, D. (1976). *The powerholders*. Chicago: University of Chicago Press.

70. Buchholz, R. A. (1989). *Fundamental concepts and problems in business ethics*. Englewood Cliffs, NJ: Prentice-Hall.

71. Gellerman, S. W. (1986, July–August). Why "good" managers make bad ethical choices. *Harvard Business Review*, pp. 85–90.

72. Velasquez, M., Moberg, D. J., & Cavanaugh, G. F. (1983). Organizational statesmanship and dirty politics: Ethical guidelines for the organizational politician. *Organizational Dynamics, 11*, 65–79.

73. See Note 53.

74. Greenberg, J. (1982). Approaching equity and avoiding inequity in groups and organizations. In J. Greenberg & R. L. Cohen (Eds.), *Equity and justice in social behavior* (pp. 389–435). New York: Academic Press.

75. Jansen, E., & Von Glinow, M. A. (1985). Ethical ambivalence and organizational reward systems. *Academy of Management Review, 10*, 814–822.

76. Vandevier, K. (1978). The aircraft brake scandal: A cautionary tale in which the moral is unpleasant. In A. G. Athos & J. J. Babarro (Eds.), *Interpersonal behavior: Communication and understanding relationships* (pp. 529–540). Englewood Cliffs, NJ: Prentice-Hall.

77. Gray, M., & Rosen, I. (1982). *The warning*. New York: Norton.

78. Wolfe, D. M. (1988). Is there integrity in the bottom

line: Managing obstacles to executive integrity. In S. Srivastava (Ed.), *Executive integrity: The search for high human values in organizational life* (pp. 140–171). San Francisco: Jossey-Bass.

79. Buchholz, R. A. (1989). *Fundamental concepts and problems in business ethics.* Englewood Cliffs, NJ: Prentice-Hall.

80. Murray, K. B., & Montanari, J. R. (1986). Strategic management of the socially responsible firm: Integrating management and marketing theory. *Academy of Management Review, 11,* 815–827.

81. Commerce Clearing House. (1991, June 26). *1991 SHRM/CCH survey.* Chicago: Author.

CASE IN POINT

What do the former chief executive officers of Abbott Laboratories, RJR Nabisco, and the now bankrupt Bank of New England have in common? They each became so drunk with power that they developed a malady called CEO (chief executive officer) disease.[1]

CEO Disease: The Use and Abuse of Power

The symptoms of CEO disease are very evident. Bosses afflicted with this disease are slow to make decisions. They do not seem to understand or care about the business anymore. They regard themselves as invincible and refuse to admit making mistakes. They surround themselves with yes-men. They get upset if employees don't stand up when they enter the room. They brutalize anyone who disagrees with or criticizes their actions. They spend nearly all of their time outside the company—serving on boards of directors and playing the role of statesperson—all for the purpose of enhancing their own personal fame and fortune. They are self-indulgent, draining the companies' resources by buying all sorts of luxuries. CEOs with this disease have the biggest and most ornate headquarters buildings, the largest and most lavish fleets of corporate jets. And worst of all, bosses with CEO disease won't leave. They try to undermine and destroy any heirs apparent who threaten to take their jobs. They can cost their companies millions of dollars in golden parachute payments or lawsuit settlements; or they may even drive their companies into bankruptcy.

How do once hardworking, diligent, responsible people develop CEO disease? Robert Schoellhorn, CEO of Abbott Laboratories from 1979 to 1990, was ousted by his board of directors. Having worked for American Cyanamid for twenty-six years, Schoellhorn joined Abbott in 1973. He achieved an impressive management record, and in 1979 he was promoted to CEO. During his first years as CEO, Abbott achieved substantial profits. Then things began to change. Schoellhorn began to attribute the company's success exclusively to his leadership. In his mind, Abbott was his private fiefdom. Schoellhorn had succumbed to the temptations and delusions of power.

John Sculley, the CEO of Apple Corporation, says, "Too many people treat CEOs as some kind of exalted, omnipotent leader. The real danger is that you start believing that stuff."[2] Unlike nearly everyone else in the corporate world, CEOs enjoy an enormous amount of power that is largely unchecked. They rarely undergo any formal performance appraisal, and they discover that in most instances they have the power to make decisions without being challenged. They look around and see the rich array of perks that come with the job. Some CEOs become intoxicated with power.

Schoellhorn's presence and advice were sought by fellow CEOs. This attention further supported his delusion that he was solely responsible for Abbott's success. By the mid-1980s, Schoellhorn demonstrated nearly all of the symptoms of CEO disease. He was away from the office 70 percent to 80 percent of the time. In 1985, he divorced his wife and married his former secretary. Together, they spent millions of company dollars to buy two corporate jets. Abbott employees dubbed the two jets "his and hers" because the jets were used exclusively by the Schoellhorns.

"The primary agenda of Bob Schoellhorn was preserving his own power and eliminating his competition. He was addicted to the power and the privilege of the office."[3] This statement from a current Abbott executive suggests the manner in which a CEO drunk with power behaves. To protect his position, Schoellhorn surrounded himself with yes-men. Three heirs apparent who dared to challenge him were fired. To maintain his image as a capable leader and to shore up company earnings, Schoellhorn undermined the long-term viability of Abbott by cutting research and development budgets.

Schoellhorn's reign finally ended when his wife hired a stripper to perform at his sixtieth birthday party. His fellow executives and their spouses were outraged. Combined with his ouster of the third heir apparent, this event was too much for the board of directors, who fired Schoellhorn in March 1990. Schoellhorn sued and eventually received a $5.2 million out-of-court settlement. Abbott paid a lot of money to get rid of Schoellhorn, but their actions saved the company from ruin.

Other companies have not acted in time. Walter Connolly, former CEO of the Bank of New England (BNE), drove his organization into the ground with his attempts to protect his power position. A former supervisor of U.S. Marine drill instructors, Connolly completely dominated the Bank of New England. He surrounded himself with yes-men and brutally harassed anyone who dared to criticize him. The culture that Connolly developed at BNE became known as "WWW—Whatever Walter Wants."[4] He involved BNE in numerous land development projects, often without consulting BNE loan personnel. When the bottom fell out of the Northeast real estate market, BNE was stuck with $1.2 billion in bad loans. Connolly was fired by his board of directors. Unfortunately, the board's action was too late. On January 6, 1991, the government seized BNE.

At RJR Nabisco, F. Ross Johnson carried greed and excess to new heights. He bought ten corporate planes and hired twenty-six corporate pilots. He built a palatial hangar. "Adjacent to the hangar is a three story building, complete with marble floors, inlaid mahogany walls, and a roomy atrium with a Japanese garden."[5] In a bold attempt to enrich himself, he tried to take Nabisco private using a leveraged buyout. He failed and was ultimately ousted. But Johnson's departure cost Nabisco $53.8 million.

John Sculley of Apple Computer avoids CEO disease by taking sabbaticals. He uses these times away to reacquaint himself with the fact that the powers that come with the CEO title are not his own, but belong to the company. Other highly successful CEOs establish management philosophies that protect them from becoming enamored with power. F. Kenneth Iverson, CEO of Nucor Steel Corporation, says, "Reduce any difference between management and anyone else at the company—destroy corporate hierarchy."[6] Nucor's corporate headquarters consist of a mere half a floor of a four-story building located in Charlotte, North Carolina. For business lunches, Iverson walks with his executives across the street to a shopping center deli. Nucor doesn't own any corporate aircraft, and all Nucor executives, including Iverson, fly coach. Nucor hasn't had a loss in twenty-five years. It is one of the most profitable companies in the steel industry, and its 1990 earnings were up 30 percent to $75 million on sales of $1.5 billion.

Robert L. Crandall, CEO of American Airlines, lives by a management philosophy similar to Iverson's. He avoids perks, and he keeps communication channels open. He hosts an annual conference at which he and senior management meet with employees to share ideas and concerns about the business. And he doesn't hire yes-men. These actions allow Crandall to stay in touch with what's going on in the company and to avoid letting the power of his position go to his head.

Culture also can help to prevent CEO disease. Japanese CEOs rarely become intoxicated with power. Why? Japanese culture is different from U.S. culture in ways that inhibit CEOs from abusing their power. Consider the case of Chiyoji Misawa, CEO of Misawa Homes. In

1990, Misawa Homes won its first U.S. contract, to build houses for a San Francisco–area resort. CEO Misawa was delighted to have penetrated the U.S. housing market and looked forward to competing for additional U.S. contracts. But he was abruptly stopped. His employees didn't share his enthusiasm for building in the United States and quashed his plans for future bidding. Deferring to the wishes of the group is the norm in Japan. Says Misawa, "I can decide I want to do something, but if I don't have employee support it won't work."[7] In Japanese culture, CEOs are expected to maintain harmony between their personal desires and the concerns of the group. Moreover, the behavior of Japanese CEOs is closely monitored by their boards of directors. In Japan, CEOs earn seven to ten times the salary of blue-collar workers. In the United States, CEOs earn eighty-five times the salary of blue-collar workers.

The power that comes with the CEO job can be so intoxicating that it can cause CEO disease. Companies such as Abbott, Nabisco, and the Bank of New England have suffered the ravages of this dangerous malady, but they could have immunized themselves against it. Companies that work to minimize status differences in the workplace and keep communication channels open are well on their way to staying healthy.

Questions for Discussion

1. Identify the bases of power used by Schoellhorn, Connolly, and Johnson. Which power base did each of these CEOs use the most?
2. Are the bases of power for CEOs who have CEO disease different from those for CEOs like Sculley, Iverson, and Crandall, who don't have the disease?
3. How do the power bases of Japanese CEOs compare to the power bases of U.S. CEOs?
4. What political tactics did Schoellhorn, Connolly, and Johnson use?
5. Schoellhorn fired three heirs apparent. What political games could these heirs apparent have played to avoid being fired? What political games could they have played to take control of Abbott away from Schoellhorn?
6. What are the ethical implications of CEO disease? How can CEO disease be prevented? Do the same things that prevent CEO disease promote ethical behavior? How?

Notes

1. Byrne, J. A., Symonds, W. C., & Siler, J. F. (1991, April 1). CEO disease. *Business Week*, pp. 52–60.
2. See Note 1, p. 52.
3. See Note 1, p. 55.
4. See Note 1, p. 58.
5. See Note 1, p. 54.
6. Byrne, J. A., & Symonds, W. C. (1991, April 1). The best bosses avoid the pitfalls of power. *Business Week*, p. 59.
7. Miller, K. L. (1991, April 1). How Japan vaccinates its CEOs. *Business Week*, p. 60.

EXPERIENCING ORGANIZATIONAL BEHAVIOR

Searching for Occupational Differences in the Use of Power

Different individual predispositions and work situations are responsible for the ways people use power. If one assumes some commonalities among people in various professions, it may follow that people in the same profession use power similarly and that people within different professions use power differently. This exercise explores such a possibility.

Procedure

1. Based on class discussion, identify members of various professions whom students in the class know well enough to survey. Try to find different professions whose members can be approached by several different class members (about five different professions whose members can be surveyed by ten different students would be ideal). For example, several class members may have access to people working in church organizations or in the military, or to teachers or nurses.

2. Type and copy the questionnaire shown in Table 11–3 (on page 409). Have each student in the class give the questionnaire to people in the assigned groups, specifying that they are to describe their immediate supervisors. (Make sure that all local Institutional Review Board permissions are granted and that students have permission from appropriate organizational officials to administer the questionnaire. It usually helps to simply have students ask permission of an official of an organization whom they already know.)

3. When students return to class with their questionnaires, tabulate the uses of each of the five sources of power by people in each profession tapped. It would help to summarize the data as follows (adding as many professions as needed):

Type of Power	Profession 1	Profession 2	Profession 3
Reward			
Coercive			
Referent			
Legitimate			
Expert			

In each cell, insert the mean scores (following the scoring directions) for that type of power within that profession, using the data collected by all students who surveyed individuals in that profession.

Points to Consider

1. Did people from different professions use power differently? For each profession, what type of power was highest and lowest? For each type of power, what professions scored highest and lowest?
2. Were there any logical connections between the use of power and the stereotypes of the professions? For example, were kindergarten teachers higher in reward power, whereas law officers were higher in coercive power?
3. Discuss the possible reasons for the results. For example, are the stereotypes consistent with reality concerning the use of power?
4. What could have been done differently to improve this demonstration?

■ 12 ■

LEADERSHIP: ITS NATURE AND IMPACT IN ORGANIZATIONS

CHAPTER OUTLINE

Special Sections

LEARNING OBJECTIVES

After reading this chapter, you should be able to:
1. Define *leadership* and indicate why leading and managing are not always the same.
2. Describe several traits that distinguish leaders from other people.
3. Describe several key dimensions of leader behavior.
4. Indicate whether, and in what ways, male and female leaders differ.
5. Comment on key differences between American and Asian CEOs.
6. Summarize the main points of major theories of leader effectiveness (*contingency theory, normative theory, path-goal theory*).
7. Describe the nature of *transformational* or *charismatic* leadership.
8. Explain why leaders are not always essential to high levels of performance by the groups they lead.
9. Explain why different styles of leadership may be required at different points in the development of work groups.

A s he steps into their bedroom, Henry Williams notices that his wife, Tanisha, is singing—again.

"*I found my thr-i-l-l on blueberry h-i-l-l . . .*" Tanisha is belting it out with gusto.

"Ow, come on, Tani," Henry pleads, "it's so early! Do you have to sing at 7:00 A.M.?"

"What are you, some kind of grouch?" she replies, laughing. "You'd think a husband would be happy to hear his wife sing."

"I am, I am . . . usually. But not at this time of the morning. And anyway, what's making you so happy these days?"

"You, you big strong hunk of man!" Tanisha gushes, grabbing her husband around the waist.

"Natch," Henry answers, hugging her back. "But besides that, what else is making you bubble over with all this joy-of-living so suddenly?"

"I guess I'm feeling good because for the first time in years, I'm really enjoying my job." Tanisha is vice president for marketing at IED, Inc., a leading manufacturer of air filtration equipment. IED was recently purchased by a much larger company, Airodyne Corporation, and as a result, there have been many changes.

"You really like your new boss, don't you?" Henry asks.

"You bet!" Tanisha replies with feeling. "She's the greatest. You don't get to work for someone like Sandra Lawton every day, you know."

"But what's so great about her?" Henry asks. "I mean, I know she's real efficient and that she's got her eye on you for a juicy promotion, but that wouldn't be enough to make you sing every morning."

"No, it wouldn't. It's a lot more than that. Hm . . . I don't really know how to put it into words. But let me give you a 'for instance.' Tuesday, we had another one of those meetings for V.P.'s. And did she ever turn it on. After listening to her, everyone—and I do mean *everyone*—was all fired up. We went out of there *believing* that we can be the best; number one in every market we enter."

"So she's confident—big deal. Most people who get to the top are that way," Henry comments.

"Right, but it's more than that. She's got . . . I don't know . . . maybe *vision* is the right word. When she describes where we're going, you can almost see it there in front of you. And there's something else that's maybe even more important. She doesn't just talk about being number one and making more profits. She sort of gives the whole business a meaning. Before she came, I figured that we were selling air filters. Nice, but no big deal. Now, I see it differently: we're helping people live and work in better environments—ones that are healthier and more productive. With Sandra, you really get the big picture."

"So, that's what's making you sing every morning?"

"That's a big part of it. These days, I really enjoy going to work; I feel like I'm part of something big and exciting, and, I don't know, it sort of makes it all fall into place."

"Okay, woman," Henry comments, laughing, "since you're feeling so together, how about planting one big kiss right here, just to show how much you missed your old husband while he was out of town last week."

If you surveyed 100 executives working in a wide variety of jobs and asked them to name the single most important factor in determining organizational success, chances are good that many would reply "effective leadership." This answer reflects the existence of a strong and general belief, in the world of business, that leadership is a key ingredient in corporate effectiveness. And this view is by no means restricted to organizations; many people assume that leadership also plays a central role in politics, sports, and many other human activities.

Is this view justified? Do leaders really play such a crucial role in shaping the fortunes of organizations? More than fifty years of research on this topic suggest that they do.[1] Effective leadership, it appears, is indeed a key factor in organizational success. Given this fact and its relevance to the field of organizational behavior, it seems appropriate for us to consider the topic of *leadership* in some detail. In this chapter, therefore, we will summarize current information about this complex process. One review of research on leadership published a few years ago cited more than 5,000 separate articles and books on this topic, so there is obviously quite a lot of ground to cover.[2]

To make the task of summarizing this wealth of information more manageable, we will proceed as follows. First, we will consider some basic points about leadership—what it is and why being a leader is not necessarily synonymous with being a manager. Second, we will examine two basic views of leadership, one focusing primarily on the *traits* of leaders, and the other focusing primarily on their *behaviors*. In this context, we will consider the question of whether female and male leaders differ in style or behavior. Third, we will examine several major theories of *leader effectiveness*—contrasting views concerning the factors that determine the extent to which leaders are effective or ineffective in their important role. After that, we will examine a topic that has received increasing attention in recent years: *transformational* or *charismatic* leadership. These terms refer to instances in which leaders exert profound effects on their followers, primarily by proposing, and winning support for, *visions* of what an organization can or should be. Finally, we will examine several additional perspectives that provide other insights into the nature and function of the process of leadership.

LEADERSHIP: ITS BASIC NATURE

In one sense, at least, **leadership** resembles love: it is something most people feel they can recognize, but often find difficult to define. What, precisely, is it? And how does being a leader differ from being a manager? We will now focus on these questions.

Leadership: A Working Definition

Imagine that you accepted a new job and entered a new work group. How would you recognize its **leader?** One possibility, of course, is through the formal titles and assigned roles each person in the group holds. In short, the individual designated as department head or project manager would be the one you would identify as the group's leader. But imagine that during several staff meetings, you noticed that this person was really not the most influential. Although she or he held the formal authority, these meetings were actually dominated by another person, who, ostensibly, was the top person's subordinate. What would you conclude about leadership then? Probably that the real leader of the group was the person who actually ran things—not the one with the fancy title and the apparent authority.

In many cases, of course, the disparity we have just described does not exist. The individual possessing the greatest amount of formal authority is also the most influential. In some situations, however, this is not so. And in such cases, we typically identify the person who actually exercises the most influence over the group as its leader. These facts point to the following working definition of leadership—one accepted by many experts on this topic: *leadership is the process whereby one individual influences other group members toward the attainment of defined group or organizational goals.*[3]

Note that according to this definition, leadership is primarily a process involving *influence*—one in which a leader changes the actions or attitudes of several group members or subordinates. As we saw in chapter 11, many techniques for exerting such influence exist, ranging from relatively *coercive* ones—the recipient has little choice but to do what is requested; to relatively *noncoercive* ones—the recipient can choose to accept or reject the influence offered. In general, *leadership* refers to the use of relatively noncoercive influence techniques. This implies that leadership rests, at least in part, on positive feelings between leaders and their subordinates. In other words, subordinates accept influence from leaders because they respect, like, or admire them—not simply because they hold positions of formal authority.[4] As you can easily see, this makes sense, for when we describe a leader as being effective, we generally assume that positive feelings of loyalty and commitment on the part of subordinates are part of the total picture.

The definition presented above also suggests that leadership involves the exercise of influence for a purpose—to attain defined group or organizational goals. In other words, leaders focus on altering those actions or attitudes of their subordinates that are related to specific goals; they are far less concerned with altering actions or attitudes that are irrelevant to such goals.

Finally, note that our definition, by emphasizing the central role of influence, implies that leadership is really something of a two-way street. Leaders do indeed influence subordinates in various ways. But since influence and power are always reciprocal in nature, at least to a degree, they do not operate in social isolation. On the contrary, leaders are often influenced, in turn, by their subordinates. After all, one can't lead without followers!

Leaders and Managers: Related, But Not Necessarily Identical, Roles In everyday speech, the terms *leader* and *manager* are often used almost interchangeably. Although we understand the temptation to do so, we believe that the two terms should be clearly distinguished. Many managers, of course, do function as leaders according to our definition: they exert influence over subordinates to attain organizational goals. However, others do *not* function in this manner. Their jobs require that they devote most of their time to other management activities—planning, processing information, communicating with customers or suppliers, and so on. Such people are not leaders in the sense noted earlier. Indeed, they might reject the view that they are leaders.

Conversely, many people who are leaders are not managers. They operate in contexts outside the world of business and do not perform the basic functions usually associated with managerial roles (e.g., organizing, controlling, planning).

In summary, although some managers are indeed leaders, others are not, so there is no necessary or automatic link between the two roles (see Figure 12–1). Therefore, we will distinguish clearly between these two terms in the remainder of this chapter and throughout this text.

LEADER TRAITS AND LEADER BEHAVIORS

At one time or another, most people have daydreams about being a leader. They have fantasies of taking charge of large groups and being viewed with great awe and respect. Despite the prevalence of such daydreams, however, relatively few individuals convert them into reality by becoming actual leaders. Further, among these, only a small proportion are considered effective in this role. This fact raises an intriguing question: what sets such individuals apart from most others? Why, in short, do some people, but not others, become effective leaders? Many answers have been proposed, but two have received the most attention. These perspectives suggest, respectively, that effective leadership is largely a function of either the *traits* possessed by individuals, or the patterns of *behavior* they demonstrate.[5,6]

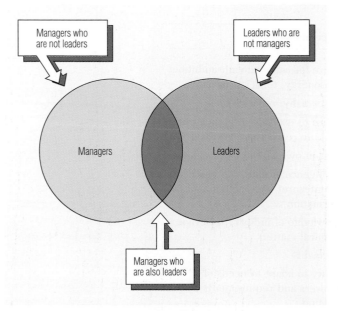

FIGURE 12–1

Managers and Leaders: Not Necessarily Identical

Although some managers act as leaders, others do not. Further, not all leaders are managers. For these reasons, it is useful to distinguish clearly between the two terms.

The Trait Approach: Leadership and Personal Characteristics

Those individuals who rise to the top of their organizations are not necessarily the best businesspeople. It used to be that the CEO of a company became its leader because he or she was remarkably knowledgeable in a specific functional area, such as production or marketing. Today, however, given the increasing politicalization of the marketplace and other institutional changes, business leaders are required to be able to speak well, handle the media, field questions from consumers and interest groups, and listen with dignity at congressional hearings, to name just a few requisite skills. Because not everyone is capable of developing all of these required leader behaviors, trade-offs may be accepted. As a result, it is possible that someone who seems only modestly knowledgeable about his or her company's operations might end up being its leader. [Sowell, T. (1991, May 27). A flaw in leadership. *Forbes*, pp. 74–75.]

Are some people born to lead? Common sense suggests that this is so. Great leaders of the past such as Alexander the Great, Queen Elizabeth I, and Abraham Lincoln do seem to differ from ordinary human beings in several respects. For example, they all seem to have possessed high levels of ambition coupled with clear visions of precisely where they wanted to go. To a lesser degree, even leaders lacking in such history-shaping fame seem different from their followers. Top executives, some politicians, and even sports heroes or heroines often seem to possess an aura that sets them apart from others. On the basis of such observations, early researchers interested in leadership formulated a view known as the **great person theory.** According to this approach, great leaders possess key traits that set them apart from most other human beings. Further, the theory contends that these traits remain stable over time and across different groups. Thus, it suggests that all great leaders share these characteristics regardless of when and where they lived, or the precise role in history they fulfilled.

Certainly, these are intriguing suggestions, and seem to fit quite well with our own informal experience. You will probably be surprised to learn, therefore, that they have *not* been strongly confirmed. Decades of active research (most conducted prior to 1950) failed to yield a short, agreed-on list of key traits shared by all leaders.[7] A few consistent findings did emerge (e.g., leaders tend to be slightly taller and more intelligent than their followers), but these were hardly dramatic in nature or in scope.[8] Indeed, the overall results of this persistent search for traits associated with leadership were so disappointing that most investigators gave up in despair and reached the following conclusion: leaders simply do not differ from followers in clear and consistent ways.

TABLE 12–1   Characteristics of Successful Leaders

Research findings indicate that successful leaders demonstrate the traits listed here.

Trait or Characteristic	Description
Drive	Desire for achievement; ambition; high energy; tenacity; initiative
Honesty and integrity	Trustworthy; reliable; open
Leadership motivation	Desire to exercise influence over others to reach shared goals
Self-confidence	Trust in own abilities
Cognitive ability	Intelligence; ability to integrate and interpret large amounts of information
Knowledge of the business	Knowledge of industry, relevant technical matters
Creativity	Originality
Flexibility	Ability to adapt to needs of followers and requirements of situation

Test Bank questions 12.5, 12.7, 12.48, 12.57, and 12.67 relate to material on this page.

Until quite recently, this conclusion was widely accepted as true. Now, however, it has been called into question by a growing body of evidence indicating that leaders *do* actually differ from other people in several important—and measurable—respects. After reviewing a large number of studies on this issue, Kirkpatrick and Locke recently reached the conclusion that traits do matter—that certain traits, together with other factors, contribute to leaders' success in business settings.[9] What are these traits? A summary of those identified as most important by Kirkpatrick and Locke, plus commentary on their basic nature, is presented in Table 12–1. You will readily recognize and understand most of these characteristics (drive, honesty and integrity, self-confidence). However, others seem to require further clarification.

Consider, first, what Kirkpatrick and Locke term **leadership motivation.** This refers to leaders' desire to influence others and—in essence—to lead. Such motivation, however, can take two distinct forms. On the one hand, it may cause leaders to seek power as an end in itself. Leaders who demonstrate such *personalized power motivation* wish to dominate others, and their desire to do so is often reflected in an excessive concern with status (see Figure 12–2). In contrast, leadership motivation can cause leaders to seek power as a means to achieve desired, shared goals. Leaders who evidence such *socialized power motivation* cooperate with others, develop networks and coalitions, and generally work with subordinates rather than trying to dominate or control them. Needless to say, this type of leadership motivation is usually far more adaptive for organizations than personalized leadership motivation.

With respect to *cognitive ability*, it appears that effective leaders must be intelligent and capable of integrating and interpreting large amounts of information. However, mental genius does not seem to be necessary and may, in some cases, prove detrimental.[10]

Do you know who you're talking to, Buster? Your're talking to the guy with the biggest desk, biggest chair, longest drapes, and highest ceiling in the business!"

FIGURE 12–2

Leadership Motivation Gone Astray

When motivation to influence others is *personalized,* it often focuses on a desire to dominate. This, in turn, can lead to the emphasis on status illustrated here. (*Source:* Drawing by Dana Fradon; © 1981 The New Yorker Magazine, Inc.)

Although the list of traits in Table 12–1 is relatively complete, recent findings call attention to another characteristic that seems to play a crucial role in effective leadership. This trait, perhaps best described as *flexibility*, refers to the ability of leaders to recognize what actions are required in a given situation and then to act accordingly. Evidence for the importance of such flexibility is provided by an ingenious laboratory simulation conducted by Zaccaro, Foti, and Kenny.[11]

These researchers investigated the role of flexibility in leader emergence in small task-performing groups. They arranged for groups of students who were unacquainted with one another to work on several different tasks. The tasks chosen were known to require different styles of leadership, so it was possible to determine whether the individuals who emerged as leaders in these groups actually adopted a style of leadership appropriate for each task. For example, one task employed involved brainstorming about the issue "Should children with AIDS be allowed to attend school?" Previous research indicated that this task required a leadership style focused on maintaining good interpersonal relations between group members. In contrast, another task involved constructing "moon tents" by folding paper. This task required a leadership style that emphasized production. The same people did not work together on each task; rather, group members were rotated, so that new groups were formed for each task.

After completing a given task, group members rated each other's behaviors on several leadership dimensions (e.g., efforts at persuasion, emphasis on production). In addition, they rated each other in terms of acting as a leader. Results offered support for the view that flexibility plays a key role in leader emergence. First, there was a strong tendency for the same people to be perceived as leaders across the four tasks used and across the many different groups. Second, these individuals did show flexibility, matching their leadership style (as shown by specific behaviors) to the requirements of the task being performed. For example, they showed a high level of concern with interpersonal relations when this was required, but a high level of concern with production when that was required. And the greater their degree of flexibility, the higher the leadership ratings these individuals received from other group members. In short, flexibility—the ability to match one's style and behavior to the needs of followers and demands of the situation—may be an important trait in effective leadership.

In summary, recent evidence seems to necessitate some revision in the widely accepted view that leaders do not differ from other people with respect to specific traits. As noted by Kirkpatrick and Locke,

> Regardless of whether leaders are born or made . . . it is unequivocally clear that *leaders are not like other people.* Leaders do not have to be great men or women by being intellectual geniuses or omniscient prophets to succeed, but they do need to have the "right stuff" and this stuff is not equally present in all people. Leadership is a demanding, unrelenting job with enormous pressures and grave responsibilities. It would be a profound disservice to leaders to suggest that they are ordinary people who happened to be in the right place at the right time. . . . In the realm of leadership (and in every other realm), the individual does matter.[12]

(For information on one trait that may interfere with leaders' effectiveness, see the **OB in Practice** section on the following page.)

Leader Behavior: Some Key Dimensions

When the search for a small list of key traits distinguishing leaders from followers or effective leaders from ineffective ones failed, researchers turned their attention to another possibility: perhaps the differences they sought would be apparent with

OB IN PRACTICE

On the Costs of Arrogance: Or, How *Not* to Lead Effectively

Quick: what one characteristic in others is most likely to make you angry and set your teeth on edge? If you answered *arrogance,* you are in good company, for research findings indicate that most people find this trait very objectionable in others.[13] What is arrogance? Primarily, it is the tendency to look down at others—to belittle their efforts or accomplishments. In extreme forms, it involves the view that others are so inferior and pathetic that they can probably never accomplish anything worth considering.

Unfortunately, arrogance is far from rare in many organizations. In addition to angering or infuriating those exposed to it, it also seems to take a large toll on those who demonstrate it.[14] This is clearly illustrated by the experience of PepsiCo, a leading soft-drink producer in the United States. Wayne D. Calloway, chief executive officer of PepsiCo, is convinced that arrogance is the number-one reason why gifted young managers fail to live up to their potential. As Calloway puts it, "Arrogance is the illegitimate child of confidence and pride. Arrogance is the idea that not only can you never miss shooting a duck, but no one else can ever hit one."[15] Arrogance, Calloway contends, places a roadblock on the path to success because it prevents those who show it from becoming part of the team—and teamwork is what's needed in many settings in today's business world.

Two other traits that also bode ill for young executives' success and interfere with their leadership potential are lack of commitment and lack of loyalty. By lack of commitment, Calloway does not mean a reluctance to work long hours or make personal sacrifices. Rather, he means "an unwillingness to commit to a goal that's bigger than they are—to keep coming at a problem even after failing, until they finally come up with a solution." Loyalty means a willingness to put a larger cause—the company or team performance—above one's own personal interests. "If an executive doesn't have this concept of loyalty, what eventually starts to creep through is pettiness, constant complaints and excuses, cutting down co-workers, and finally acrobatics to cover his/her backside to avoid getting blamed for mistakes. It all adds up to mediocre performance at best—destructive behavior at worst."

So at Pepsico, at least, the young managers who rise to leadership positions are the ones who avoid the trap of arrogance while demonstrating teamwork, commitment, and loyalty. And Calloway believes that these characteristics are needed for success in many other companies as well. As he remarks, "Truly successful businesses are never dominated by arrogant, dishonest types for long. They may succeed for a short time . . . , but over a long time victory goes to people who work hard, are consistent, fair, open, and candid."

---

respect to concrete *behaviors.* In other words, it seemed possible that effective and ineffective leaders differ not primarily with respect to specific traits, but rather with respect to their approaches to or styles of leadership. Research designed to investigate this possibility was much more successful, and added appreciably to our understanding of how leaders behave and how their actions affect their followers.

Participative versus Autocratic Leaders: From Directive Autocrats to Permissive Democrats   Think about the different bosses you have had in your life or career. Can you remember one who wanted to control virtually everything—someone who made all the decisions, told people precisely what to do, and wanted, quite literally, to run the entire show? In contrast, can you recall a boss or supervisor who allowed employees greater freedom and responsibility—someone who invited their input before making decisions, was open to suggestions, and allowed them to carry out

Although autocratic leaders have a bad reputation for bullying people, they are making a comeback. One reason for their popularity is that many attempts to implement autonomous work groups have been unsuccessful, largely because some people don't like the extra responsibility that follows from democratic, self-managed leadership. Many employees take comfort in simply following their manager's orders, without having to make any decisions themselves. Although not for everyone, some employees work best following autocratic leaders. [Smither, R. D. (1991, November). The return of the authoritarian manager. *Training*, pp. 40–44.]

various tasks in their own way? If so, you already have firsthand experience with two sharply contrasting styles of leadership: **autocratic** and **participative.**

In the past, these styles were viewed as endpoints along a single continuum. However, as noted recently by Muczyk and Reimann, they actually seem to involve two separate dimensions.[16] The first is the extent to which leaders permit subordinates to take part in decisions; this is the *autocratic-democratic* dimension. The second involves the extent to which leaders direct the activities of subordinates and tell them how to carry out their jobs; this is the *permissive-directive* dimension. Combining these two variables yields four possible patterns, which Muczyk and Reimann label (1) directive autocrat, (2) permissive autocrat, (3) directive democrat, and (4) permissive democrat. (These patterns are described in Table 12–2.) Although any attempt to divide human beings into discrete categories raises thorny issues, these patterns do seem to make good sense; many managers adopt a leadership style that fits, at least roughly, within one.

But given that leaders differ along these two dimensions and can, as a result, be classified as falling into one of the four patterns listed above, do any of them have a clear-cut edge? In short, is one pattern superior to the others in many, if not most, situations? Existing evidence suggests that this is doubtful. All four styles seem to involve a mixed pattern of advantages and disadvantages. Moreover—and this is the crucial point—the relative success of each depends heavily on conditions existing within a given organization and its specific stage of development. For example, consider managers who might be described as *directive autocrats*. Such people make decisions without consulting subordinates and supervise subordinates' work activities very closely. It is tempting to view such a pattern as undesirable (it runs counter to the value of personal freedom), but this approach may actually be highly successful in some settings (e.g., when employees are inexperienced or underqualified for their jobs; when subordinates adopt an adversarial stance toward management and must be closely supervised).

In contrast, consider the case of *permissive autocrats* (leaders who combine permissive supervision with an autocratic style of making decisions). This pattern may be useful in dealing with employees who have a high level of technical skill and want

TABLE 12–2   Contrasting Styles of Leadership

According to Muczyk and Reimann, leaders often adopt one of the four distinct styles described here.

Leadership Style or Type	Description
Directive autocrat	Makes decisions unilaterally; closely supervises activities of subordinates
Permissive autocrat	Makes decisions unilaterally; allows subordinates considerable latitude in carrying out assigned tasks
Directive democrat	Makes decisions participatively; closely supervises activities of subordinates
Permissive democrat	Makes decisions participatively; allows subordinates considerable latitude in carrying out assigned tasks

Source: Based on suggestions by Muczyk & Reimann, 1987; see Note 16.

Test Bank questions 12.10–12.12 and 12.58 relate to material on this page.

to be left alone to manage their own jobs (e.g., scientists, engineers, computer programmers), but who have little desire to participate in routine decision making. The remaining two patterns (directive democrat and permissive democrat) are also most suited to specific organizational conditions. The key task for leaders, then, is to match their own style to the needs of their organization, and to change as these needs shift and evolve. What happens when leaders in organizations lack such flexibility? Actual events in one company—People Express—are instructive.

Don Burr, the founder and CEO of this airline, had a very clear managerial style: he was a highly permissive democrat. He involved employees in many aspects of decision making, and emphasized autonomy in work activities. Indeed, he felt that everyone at People Express should be viewed as a "manager." This management style worked well while the company was young, but as it grew and increased in complexity, such practices created mounting difficulties. New employees were not necessarily as committed as older ones, so permissive supervision was ineffective with them. And as decisions increased in both complexity and number, a participative approach became less and less appropriate. Unfortunately, top management was reluctant to alter its style; after all, it seemed to have been instrumental in the company's early success. This poor match between the style of top leaders and changing external conditions seems to have contributed (along with many other factors) to People Express's mounting problems. Losses rose until finally the company was purchased by Texas Air, whose CEO, Frank Lorenzo, favored a much more directive leadership style.

To conclude, no single leadership style is best under all conditions and in all situations.[17] However, recognizing the importance of differences in this respect can be a constructive first step toward assuring that the style most suited to a given set of conditions is, in fact, adopted.

Person-Oriented versus Production-Oriented Leaders: Consideration versus Initiating Structure Think again about all the bosses you have had in your career. Divide these into two categories: those who were relatively effective and those who were relatively ineffective. How do the two groups differ? If you think about this issue carefully, your answers are likely to take one of two forms. First, you might reply, "My effective bosses helped me to get the job done. They gave me advice, answered my questions, and let me know exactly what was expected of me. My ineffective bosses didn't do this." Second, you might answer, "My effective bosses seemed to care about me as a person. They were friendly, listened to me when I had problems or questions, and seemed to help me toward my personal goals. My ineffective bosses didn't do this."

A large body of research, much of it gathered at the University of Michigan by Likert and his colleagues[18] and at Ohio State University by Stogdill and his associates,[19] suggests that leaders do differ greatly along these dimensions. Those high on the first, known as **initiating structure,** are mainly concerned with production and focus primarily on getting the job done. They engage in actions such as organizing work, inducing subordinates to follow rules, setting goals, and making leader and subordinate roles explicit. In contrast, other leaders are lower on this dimension and show less tendency to engage in these actions.

Leaders high on the second dimension, known as **consideration,** are primarily concerned with establishing good relations with their subordinates and being liked by them. They engage in actions such as doing favors for subordinates, explaining things to them, and assuring their welfare. Others, in contrast, are low on this dimension and don't really care much about how they get along with subordinates.

At first glance, you might assume that these two dimensions (initiating structure and consideration) are closely linked. You might guess that people high on one must,

One of the best ways of establishing good relations with subordinates and gaining their respect as a leader is to be fair, honest, and consistent in dealing with them. Fairness in the treatment of employees is a cornerstone of effective leadership. Employees respect and appreciate leaders who treat them with dignity, consideration, and simple honesty. Credibility comes from "walk what you talk," or the consistency that leaders demonstrate between their words and actions. Following these steps can help leaders establish better relationships with employees. [Axley, S. R. (1990, September/October). The practical qualities of effective leaders. *Industrial Management*, pp. 29–30.]

Test Bank questions 12.13–12.14, 12.50, and 12.59 relate to material on this page.

FIGURE 12-3

Key Dimensions of Leader Behavior

Leaders' behavior can vary from low to high with respect to *consideration* (person-orientation) and with respect to *initiating structure* (task-orientation). Patterns of leader behavior produced by variations along these two dimensions are illustrated here. Leaders high on both dimensions are often most effective, but this depends on the specific situation.

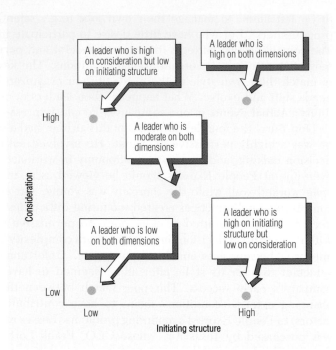

necessarily, be low on the other. In fact, this is not the case. The two dimensions actually seem to be largely independent.[20] Thus, a leader may be high on both concern with production and concern for people, high on one of these dimensions and low on the other, moderate on one and high on the other, and so on (see Figure 12-3). Is any one of these possible patterns best?

Careful study indicates that this is a complex issue, for production-oriented and people-oriented leadership styles both offer a mixed pattern of pluses and minuses. With respect to showing consideration (high concern with people and human relations), the major benefits are improved group atmosphere and morale.[21] However, since leaders high on this dimension are reluctant to act in a directive manner toward subordinates and often shy away from presenting them with negative feedback, productivity sometimes suffers. Regarding initiating structure (high concern with production), efficiency and performance are indeed sometimes enhanced by this leadership style. If leaders focus entirely on production, however, employees may soon conclude that no one cares about them or their welfare. Then work-related attitudes such as job satisfaction and organizational commitment may suffer.

Having said all this and pointed out the complexities, we add that one specific pattern may indeed have an edge in many settings. This is a pattern in which leaders demonstrate high concern with both people and production.[22] As we will see in chapter 16, encouraging such an approach (known as *team management*) is the goal of a popular form of organizational development, *grid training*.[23] A laboratory simulation carried out by Tjosvold illustrates the potential benefits of this pattern.[24]

In this experiment, male and female students first worked with another person on a problem (rank-ordering the survival value of items available after a plane crash). Subjects played the role of a subordinate, while another individual—actually an accomplice—served as their manager. During this period, the accomplice either behaved in a manner indicative of high concern with productivity (e.g., he or she told subjects precisely what to do; praised and criticized their performance) or showed low concern with productivity. In addition, the accomplice either demonstrated personal warmth (e.g., maintained a high level of eye contact with subjects and showed a friendly facial expression) or demonstrated personal coldness. Following completion of the first task, the accomplice asked subjects to work on a second task and then left the room, explaining that he or she had other work to perform at the moment. Tjosvold predicted that both variations in the accomplice's behavior would influence subjects' performance on this second task (which involved arithmetic and work problems). Specifically, Tjosvold hypothesized that subjects would work hardest when the leader was both warm and showed high concern with productivity, but would exert least effort when the leader was warm and showed low concern with productivity. (They would feel most free to goof off under the latter condition.) Results confirmed both predictions. In addition, subjects generally had more favorable impressions of the leader when this person acted in a warm and friendly manner than when he or she behaved in a cold and aloof fashion. They liked the leader more and expressed greater willingness to work with this person again.

These findings suggest that contrary to what common sense might suggest, high concern with people (showing consideration) and high concern with productivity (initiating structure) are *not* incompatible. On the contrary, skillful leaders can combine these orientations in their overall style to produce favorable results. Thus, although no one leadership style is best, leaders who combine these two concerns may often have an important edge over leaders who show only one or the other.

Gender Differences in Leadership: Do Male and Female Leaders Differ?

The year 1970 is less than a quarter of a century in the past. Yet, if you visited work settings in that year and compared them to those of the present, you would notice one dramatic difference. In 1970, only about 15 percent of all managers were females; in the 1990s, this figure has risen to more than 40 percent.[25] As females have moved in ever increasing numbers into management positions—and into leadership—an intriguing question has repeatedly arisen: do female and male managers differ in their style or approach to leadership? Some authors suggest that they do. For example, in a well-known and controversial article, Jan Grant contended that females should stop trying to emulate male qualities such as independence, competitiveness, and analytic thinking.[26] Instead, she suggested, they should place greater emphasis on traditionally feminine qualities such as affiliation, cooperativeness, and nurturance. Similar suggestions regarding actual or potential differences between female and male leaders have been offered by other authors in popular, but somewhat controversial, books.[27] Are these claims valid? Do male and female leaders really differ? Systematic research on this issue suggests that, in general, they do not.[28] Although female and male leaders do appear to differ in a few respects, these differences are smaller in magnitude, and fewer in number, than widely held sex-role stereotypes suggest. Perhaps the most comprehensive evidence on this issue is that reported recently by Eagly and Johnson.[29]

These researchers examined the results of more than 150 separate studies of leadership in which comparisons between females and males were possible. They performed this task by means of a highly sophisticated technique known as *meta-analysis*, a statistical procedure for evaluating the effects of one or more variables across many different studies. Three types of investigation were included in the analysis: *laboratory studies* (in which participants interacted with a stranger), *assessment studies* (in which measures of subjects' leadership style were obtained), and *organizational studies* (in which leadership behavior in actual organizations was as-

If both men and women have similar leadership styles, and both are capable of being effective leaders, why are there so few women business leaders today? One explanation appears to involve gender differences in perceptions of the situations facing women on the job. A study by Russell Reynolds Associates found that only 2 percent of male leaders believe that women experience any hostility from their supervisors. In contrast, 67 percent of female leaders reported that such hostility exists. Additionally, whereas 75 percent of male leaders believe their firms actively encourage the development of female leaders, 67 percent of women believe that women are *not* being developed as leaders. It is an intriguing possibility that such perceptual differences are, to some extent, responsible for the

Test Bank questions 12.15–12.16 and 12.69 relate to material on this page.

underrepresentation of female leaders in today's organizations. [Enslow, B.
(1991, April). Why women
follow. *Across the Board*,
p. 21.]

sessed). Eagly and Johnson reasoned that any differences between males and females would be more apparent in the first two types of study than in the third type. This would be the case because in actual organizations, leadership roles would require similar behavior from males and females. As a result, any differences between them would tend to disappear. In laboratory and assessment studies, in contrast, differences between males and females would not be reduced by such role requirements.

Potential differences between male and female leaders were examined with respect to several dimensions we have already considered: (1) showing consideration, (2) initiating structure, and (3) participative versus autocratic decision-making style. Sex-role stereotypes suggest that female leaders might show more concern with inter-personal relations and tend to make decisions in a more participative manner than male leaders. Results, however, offered only weak support for such beliefs. Few significant findings emerged on showing consideration and initiating structure. In laboratory studies, females were slightly higher than males on both dimensions. In organizational studies, no differences on these dimensions were observed.

Regarding decision-making style, females did appear to adopt a more democratic or participative style than males; moreover, this was true across all three groups of studies (laboratory simulations, assessment studies, and organizational studies). What accounts for this difference? One possibility, of course, is that female leaders *are* more concerned than males with interpersonal relations, and realize that permitting subordinates to offer input into decisions is one way of maintaining good relations with them.[30] Another possibility, suggested by Johnson and Eagly, is that women are higher than men in interpersonal skills. Such superiority, in turn, may make it easier for them to adopt a decision-making approach involving considerable give-and-take with subordinates. Whatever the precise basis for this difference, the overall findings of the meta-analysis conducted by Johnson and Eagly suggest that female and male leaders may indeed differ in some respects, but that these differences are smaller in magnitude and less consistent than sex-role stereotypes suggest (see Figure 12–4).

FIGURE 12–4   Male and Female Leaders: Any Differences Are Small

Existing evidence indicates that male and female leaders behave in very much the same manner. Female leaders appear to favor participative decision making to a greater extent than males, but in most other respects, both groups of leaders are quite similar.

Additional studies conducted by other researchers point to the same general conclusions. Thus, as noted by Powell,

> Organizations should not assume that male and female managers differ in personal qualities. . . . There is little reason to believe that either women or men make superior managers, or that women and men are different types of managers. Instead, there are likely to be excellent, average, and poor managerial performers within each sex. Success in today's highly competitive marketplace calls for organizations to make best use of the talent available to them. To do this, they need to identify, develop, encourage, and promote the most effective managers, regardless of sex.[31]

Although female and male leaders do not appear to differ appreciably in behavior or style, other evidence indicates that important differences may exist between leaders in different cultures. (For information on these differences, see the **International/Multicultural Perspective** section on pp. 456–457.)

Leaders and Followers: A Complex, Reciprocal Relationship

Throughout this discussion, we have focused on *leaders*—their traits and their behaviors. Followers, by and large, have been ignored. But note: in a crucial sense, followers are the essence of leadership. Without them, there really is no such thing as leadership. As Lee put it, "Without followers leaders cannot lead. . . . Without followers, even John Wayne becomes a solitary hero, or, given the right script, a comic figure, posturing on an empty stage."[32]

The importance of followers, and the complex, reciprocal relationship between leaders and followers, is widely recognized by organizational researchers. Indeed, major theories of leadership such as those we will consider in the next section note—either explicitly or implicitly—that leadership is really a two-way street. Leaders do indeed exert influence on followers, altering their attitudes, perceptions, actions, and goals. At the same time, however, followers influence leaders. In fact, as we noted earlier, research findings suggest that successful leaders are people who are adept at recognizing the requirements of a given situation and the needs of their followers and then adjusting their own behavior accordingly.[33] Moreover, many studies make clear that a complex give-and-take relationship exists between the perceptions, goals, needs, and traits of followers and the corresponding perceptions, goals, needs, and actions of leaders (see Figure 12–5). Again, this theme will be echoed in our later discussion of current theories of leadership.

How important are followers in determining the effectiveness or success of leaders? A growing number of experts believe that they are crucial. For example, Lee suggests that effective followers—ones who are enthusiastic, intelligent, and self-reliant—are essential to leaders' success in many different contexts.[34] To be effective, however, followers must be *empowered* by leaders; they must be given a say in making decisions

Negative connotations are often associated with the term *follower* (e.g., being a sheep). However, being an effective leader requires knowing all about following, for the ultimate leader must also be a follower. After all, the best leaders are those who most effectively serve the needs of their subordinates. Because leaders have power over people, they are accountable to them, making them followers as well. Additionally, people who are leaders in some situations (e.g., the CEO of an organization) may be followers in other situations (e.g., when in court). [Lee, C. (1991, January). Followership: The essence of leadership. *Training*, pp. 27–35.]

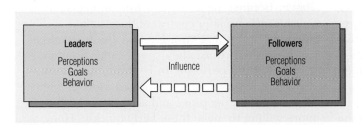

FIGURE 12–5

Leadership as a Two-Way Street

Leaders influence the perceptions, goals, and behavior of followers, but followers also shape the perceptions, goals, and behavior of leaders. Thus, leadership is actually very much a two-way street involving reciprocal influence.

Test Bank questions 12.18 and 12.70 relate to material on this page.

about how their jobs are designed and how their work is conducted. Such participation enhances their morale, engages their commitment, and improves their performance.[35] Just as leaders differ in many respects, followers, too, vary in many ways. Two dimensions, however, appear to be crucial: the extent to which they show

 ## *AN INTERNATIONAL/MULTICULTURAL PERSPECTIVE*

Asian and American CEOs: Different Cultures, Different Styles?

T. Fujisawa, the cofounder of Honda Corporation, once stated, "Japanese and American management are 95 percent the same, and differ in all important respects." By this insightful comment, he meant that because of basic requirements of the modern business world, all organizations, whatever their location, *must* be similar in many ways. Yet, they may still differ in some respects that reflect the contrasting values and beliefs of the cultures in which they operate. Do such differences exist in the leadership styles of top Asian and American managers? Growing evidence indicates that they do.[36] Some of the most revealing information on this issue has been reported by Doktor in comparative studies of the CEOs of U.S., Japanese, Korean, and Hong Kong companies.[37]

Doktor suggests that cultural values determine how people perceive the nature of their jobs and their interpretation of various tasks and work-related situations. A very strong value in Japanese culture, he contends, is the perception that Japan is one organic entity. Thus, what affects one part of the society is perceived by top managers as potentially affecting many other parts as well. Because of this view, Japanese business leaders perceive their corporate decisions in a very broad context that takes into account the decisions' consequences for segments of society beyond their companies. Doktor notes that Korean culture is somewhat similar, but also places a stronger emphasis on authority and a top-down decision-making process. Hong Kong presents a mixed picture, since in that culture, traditional Chinese values emphasizing mutual influences between various aspects of society are combined with Western beliefs that place a high value on individuality and independence. In the United States, in contrast, decisions are viewed in a somewhat narrower context, focused on the organization, its needs, and its goals.

How might these contrasting cultural values and beliefs influence the leadership style of Asian and American CEOs? To find out, Doktor compared the workdays of CEOs in Japan, Korea, Hong Kong, and the United States. The comparisons yielded revealing findings. First, consider the amount of time spent by these leaders working alone (e.g., desk work, telephone communications) versus working with others (scheduled and unscheduled meetings). Here, few large differences emerged. In each country, CEOs spend approximately 25 percent of their workdays in solo tasks and 75 percent in group tasks. But now consider the *duration* of each task performed by the CEOs. In the United States, almost half of all tasks filled nine minutes or less of the leaders' time. In Japan and Korea, in contrast, only 10 percent and 14 percent of tasks were so brief. As might be expected, Hong Kong was in between with a figure of 37 percent. The reverse pattern, of course, appeared for tasks requiring more than sixty minutes; American managers spent only 10 percent of their time on such activities, whereas Japanese and Korean managers spent much more of their time on such tasks (see Figure 12–6). So a clear pattern of differences emerged. American managers spend their days moving between many tasks of relatively short duration, and Japanese and Korean managers divide their days into a smaller number of longer segments and tasks.

These differences, Doktor notes, are entirely consistent with the cultural factors mentioned above. Because Japanese and Korean managers consider the broader context of their actions and decisions, they feel strongly that these should not be rushed; thus, they spend more time on each task they perform. In contrast, American managers adopt a more restricted view of the impact of their decisions and actions, and so are more willing to make these fairly quickly. Hong Kong managers, working within a mixed cultural

these theories differ sharply in their content, terminology, and scope. Yet, all are linked by two common themes. First, all adopt a *contingency approach* to this complex topic. All recognize that there is no single preferred style of leadership, and that the key task of organizational behavior researchers is determining which leadership styles will prove most effective under which specific conditions. Second, all are concerned with the issue of *leader effectiveness*. They seek to identify the conditions and factors that determine whether, and to what degree, leaders will enhance the performance and satisfaction of their subordinates.

Many theories of leadership exist, but three have probably received the most attention within OB. These are Fiedler's *contingency theory*,[39] Vroom and Yetton's *normative theory*,[40] and House's *path-goal theory*.[41] We will now describe each of these theories.

Fiedler's Contingency Theory: Matching Leaders and Tasks

Leadership does not occur in a social or environmental vacuum. Rather, leaders attempt to exert their influence on group members within the context of specific situations. Since these can vary greatly along many different dimensions, it is only reasonable to expect that no single style or approach to leadership will always be best. Rather, as we have already noted, the most effective strategy will probably vary from one situation to another.

Acceptance of this fact lies at the core of the **contingency theory,** a theory of leader effectiveness developed by Fiedler.[42] The term is certainly appropriate, for the theory's central assumption is as follows: a leader's contribution to successful performance by his or her group is determined both by the leader's traits and by various features of the situation. To fully understand leader effectiveness, both types of factors must be considered.

With respect to characteristics possessed by leaders, Fiedler identifies *esteem (liking) for least preferred coworker* (LPC for short) as most important. This refers to a leader's tendency to evaluate the person with whom she or he has found it most difficult to work in a favorable or unfavorable manner. Leaders who perceive this person in negative terms (low LPC leaders) seem primarily concerned with attaining successful task performance. In contrast, those who perceive their least preferred coworker in a positive light (high LPC leaders) seem mainly concerned with establishing good relations with subordinates. (As you can see, this dimension is related to two aspects of leader behavior described previously: initiating structure and showing consideration. These dimensions appear over and over again in systematic studies of leadership. Thus, there seem to be firm grounds for viewing them as basic aspects of this process.)

Which type of leader—low LPC or high LPC—is more effective? Fiedler's answer is: it depends. And what it depends on is several situational factors. Specifically, Fiedler suggests that whether low LPC or high LPC leaders are more effective depends on the degree to which the situation is *favorable* to the leader—provides this person with *control* over subordinates. This, in turn, is determined largely by three factors: (1) the nature of the leader's relations with group members (the extent to which he or she enjoys their support and loyalty), (2) the degree of structure in the task being performed (the extent to which task goals and subordinates' roles are clearly defined), and (3) the leader's position power (his or her ability to enforce compliance by subordinates). Combining these three factors, the leader's situational control can range from very high (positive relations with group members, a highly structured task, high position power) to very low (negative relations, an unstructured task, low position power).

To return to the central question: when are different types of leader most effective? Fiedler suggests that low LPC leaders (ones who are task-oriented) are superior to high LPC leaders (ones who are relations- or people-oriented) when situational control is *either* very low or high. In contrast, high LPC leaders have an edge when situational control falls within the moderate range (refer to Figure 12–8).

The reasoning behind these predictions is as follows: under conditions of *low* situational control, groups need considerable guidance and direction to accomplish their tasks. Since low LPC leaders are more likely to provide structure than high LPC leaders, they will usually be superior in such cases. Similarly, low LPC leaders also have an edge under conditions that offer the leader a *high* degree of situational control. Here, low LPC leaders realize that conditions are very good, and that successful task performance is virtually assured. As a result, they turn their attention to improving relations with subordinates, and often adopt a relaxed "hands off" style. Subordinates appreciate such treatment, and performance and morale are both enhanced. In contrast, high LPC leaders, feeling that they already enjoy good relations with their subordinates, may shift their attention to task performance. Their attempts to provide guidance may then be perceived by subordinates as needless meddling, with the result that performance is impaired.

Turning to situations offering the leader *moderate* situational control, conditions are mixed, and attention to good interpersonal relations is often needed. High LPC leaders, with their intrinsic interest in people, often have an important advantage in such cases. In contrast, low LPC leaders, who continue to focus on task performance, may become even more autocratic and directive. The negative reactions of subordinates to such behaviors may then have detrimental effects on performance.

To repeat: Fiedler's theory predicts that low LPC (task-oriented) leaders will be more effective than high LPC (relations-oriented) leaders under conditions of either low or high situational control. In contrast, high LPC leaders will have an edge under conditions in which situational control is moderate.

FIGURE 12–8

Contingency Theory: Its Basic Predictions

Fiedler's *contingency theory* predicts that low LPC leaders (ones who are primarily task-oriented) will be superior in performance to high LPC leaders (ones who are primarily people-oriented) when situational control is either very low or high. The opposite is true when situational control is moderate.

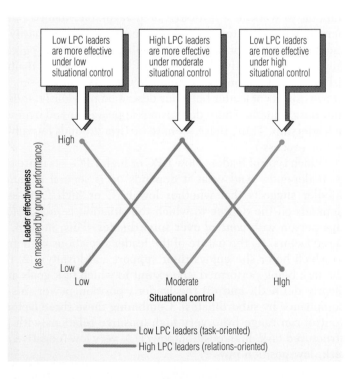

Contingency Theory: Its Current Status   Because it directs attention to characteristics of leaders, situational factors, and reactions among subordinates, Fiedler's theory is fully consistent with the modern view of leadership described earlier. Where any scientific theory is concerned, however, the ultimate question must be: how does it fare when put to actual test? For the contingency theory, the answer appears to be "moderately well." One review of more than 170 studies undertaken to test various aspects of Fiedler's theory indicates that most obtained positive results.[43] For example, consider one such study by Chemers and his colleagues.[44]

These investigators reasoned that leaders whose personal style did not match the conditions in their groups (i.e., low LPC leaders with moderate situational control, high LPC leaders with high or low degrees of control) would experience greater job-related stress than leaders whose personal style matched these conditions (i.e., low LPC leaders with high or low control, high LPC leaders with moderate control). To test this hypothesis, Chemers and his associates had administrators at a large university complete questionnaires designed to measure their degree of situational control, their standing on the LPC dimension (high or low), and the level of job stress they experienced. Results offered support for the initial hypothesis. Leaders whose personal style did not match the level of situational control they enjoyed reported greater stress than those whose personal style matched this factor.

Although the results are encouraging and lend support to the theory, not all findings have been consistent with it. In fact, a more recent review suggests that although laboratory studies have tended to support Fiedler's view, field investigations (carried out with existing groups operating in a wide range of contexts) have not been as favorable.[45] Such investigations have sometimes yielded results contrary to what contingency theory would predict. In addition, the theory has been criticized on several important grounds. For example, a degree of ambiguity exists with respect to classifying specific situations along the dimension of situational control. Unless situations can be accurately classified as very low, low, moderate, and so on in this regard, predictions concerning leader effectiveness are difficult to make. Similarly, some critics have questioned the adequacy of the questionnaire used to assess leaders' standing on the LPC dimension. In particular, the reliability of this measure does not seem to be as high as that of other widely used tests.[46]

Taking such criticisms plus existing evidence into account, the following tentative conclusion seems warranted: contingency theory has indeed added to our understanding of key aspects of leadership and leadership effectiveness. However, several questions about its accuracy remain and require further, detailed attention. Therefore, it should be viewed more as a theory still undergoing development and refinement than as one that offers a fully valid framework for understanding leader effectiveness.

Normative Theory: Decision Making and Leader Effectiveness

One of the major tasks performed by leaders is making decisions. Indeed, one defining characteristic of leadership positions is that they are where "the buck finally stops" and concrete actions must be taken. Since the decisions reached by leaders often have far-reaching effects on their subordinates, one major determinant of leader effectiveness clearly is the adequacy with which they perform this key task. Leaders who make good decisions will be more effective in the long run than leaders who make bad ones. We will consider various strategies leaders (and others) can employ to maximize their chances of making good decisions in chapter 14. Here we will focus on a different, but equally important, question: in reaching decisions, how should leaders behave with respect to their subordinates? Specifically, how much

TABLE 12-3   Potential Strategies for Making Decisions

According to Vroom and Yetton, in making decisions leaders often adopt one of the five basic strategies described here.

Decision Strategy	Description
AI (Autocratic)	Leader solves problem or makes decision unilaterally, using available information
AII (Autocratic)	Leader obtains necessary information from subordinates but then makes decision unilaterally
CI (Consultative)	Leader shares the problem with subordinates individually, but then makes decision unilaterally
CII (Consultative)	Leader shares problem with subordinates in group meeting but then makes decision unilaterally
GII (Group decision)	Leader shares problem with subordinates in a group meeting; decision is reached through discussion to consensus

participation should leaders invite from them? As we noted earlier, participation in decision making is an important variable in many organizational settings—one with implications for job satisfaction, stress, and productivity. Thus, the manner in which leaders handle this issue can be crucial in determining their effectiveness.

But how much participation in decisions by subordinates should leaders allow? Perhaps the most useful answer to this question is provided by the **normative theory** developed by Vroom and Yetton.[47] After careful study of available evidence, these researchers concluded that leaders often adopt one of five distinct methods for reaching decisions. These are summarized in Table 12–3, and as you can see, they cover the entire range from decisions made solely by the leader in a totally autocratic manner through ones that are fully participative.

Are any of these approaches strongly preferable to the others? Vroom and Yetton suggest not. Just as there is no single best style of leadership, there is no single best strategy for making decisions. Each pattern offers its own mixture of benefits and costs. For example, decisions reached through participative means stand a better chance of gaining support and acceptance among subordinates. However, such decisions require a great deal of time—often, more time than a leader or organization can afford. Similarly, decisions reached autocratically (by the leader alone) can be made more rapidly and efficiently. But such an approach can generate resentment among followers and encounter difficulties with respect to actual implementation. According to Vroom and Yetton, then, a major task faced by leaders is selecting the specific decision-making approach that will maximize potential benefits but minimize potential costs. How can this be done? Again, they offer specific suggestions.

Vroom and Yetton propose that leaders should attempt to select the best approach (or at least eliminate ones that are not useful) by answering several basic questions about the situation. These relate primarily to the *quality* of the decision—the extent to which it will affect important group processes such as communication or production; and to *acceptance* of the decision—the degree of commitment among subordinates needed for its implementation. For example, with respect to decision quality, a leader should ask questions such as: Is a high-quality decision required? Do I have enough information to make such a decision? Is the problem well structured? With respect to decision acceptance, he or she should ask: Is it crucial for effective implementation that subordinates accept the decision? Do subordinates share the organizational goals that will be reached through solution of this problem?

According to the normative model, answering such questions, and applying specific rules such as those shown in Table 12–4, eliminates some of the potential approaches to reaching a given decision. Those that remain constitute a feasible set that can, potentially, be used to reach the necessary decision.

To simplify this process, Vroom and Yetton recommend using a decision tree such as the one shown in Figure 12–9 on p. 464. To apply this diagram, a manager begins on the left side and responds, in turn, to the questions listed under each letter (A, B, C, and so on). As the manager replies to each question, the set of feasible approaches narrows. For example, imagine that the manager's answers are as follows:

Question A: Yes—a high-quality decision is needed.
Question B: No—the leader does not have sufficient information to make a high-quality decision alone.
Question C: No—the problem is not structured.
Question D: Yes—acceptance by subordinates is crucial to implementation.
Question E: No—if the leader makes the decision alone, it may not be accepted by subordinates.
Question F: No—subordinates do not share organizational goals.
Question G: Yes—conflict among subordinates is likely to result from the decision.

TABLE 12–4   Decision Rules in Normative Theory

By applying the rules shown here, leaders can eliminate decision-making strategies that are likely to prove ineffective in a given situation, and select those likely to be most effective.

Rules Designed to Protect Decision Quality

Leader Information Rule   If the quality of the decision is important and you do not have enough information or expertise to solve the problem alone, eliminate an autocratic style.

Goal Congruence Rule   If the quality of the decision is important and subordinates are not likely to make the right decision, rule out the highly participative style.

Unstructured Problem Rule   If the quality of the decision is important but you lack sufficient information and expertise *and* the problem is unstructured, eliminate the autocratic leadership styles.

Rules Designed to Protect Decision Acceptance

Acceptance Rule   If acceptance by subordinates is crucial for effective implementation, eliminate the autocratic styles.

Conflict Rule   If acceptance by subordinates is crucial for effective implementation, and they hold conflicting opinions over the means of achieving some objective, eliminate autocratic styles.

Fairness Rule   If the quality of the decision is unimportant but acceptance *is* important, use the most participatory style.

Acceptance Priority Rule   If acceptance is critical and not certain to result from autocratic decisions, and if subordinates are not motivated to achieve the organization's goals, use a highly participative style.

FIGURE 12-9

Choosing the Most Effective Decision-Making Strategy

By answering the questions listed here and tracing a path through this *decision tree*, leaders can identify the most effective approaches to making decisions in a specific situation. Note: the path suggested by the answers to questions A through G (see page 463) is shown by the orange-colored triangles. (*Source:* Based on suggestions by Vroom & Yetton, 1973; see Note 40.)

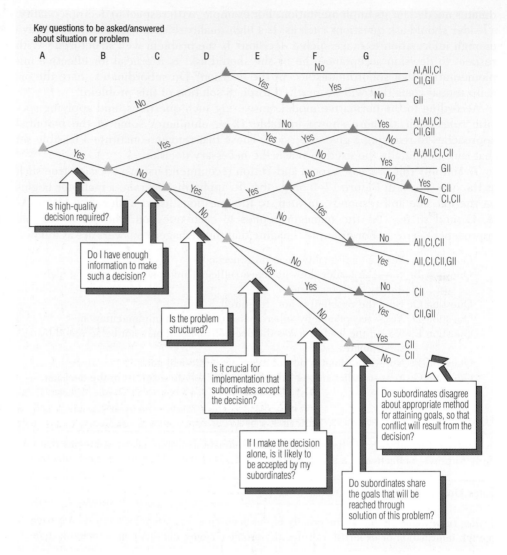

As you can see, these replies lead to the conclusion that only one decision-making approach is feasible: full participation by subordinates. (The path leading to this conclusion is shown in orange in Figure 12–9.) Of course, different answers to any of the seven key questions would have led to different conclusions.

The Vroom and Yetton model is highly appealing for several reasons. It takes full account of the importance of subordinate participation in decisions and offers leaders clear guidance for choosing among various methods for reaching decisions. As with any theory, though, the key question remains: Is it valid? Are its suggestions concerning the most effective style of decision making under various conditions really accurate? The results of several studies designed to test the model have been encouraging.

First, it has been found that practicing managers rate their own past decisions as more successful when they are based on procedures falling within the set of feasible options identified by the model than when they fall outside this set of methods.[48] Second, when small groups of subjects reach decisions through methods falling within the feasible set identified by the model, these decisions are judged to be more effective by outside raters than when they are made through other methods.[49] Finally, store managers who made decisions in accordance with the basic principles of the model (even without formal training in its use) run more profitable operations than managers who do not seem to function in this manner.

Together, these findings suggest that the Vroom and Yetton model offers important insights into a key aspect of leader effectiveness. Note, however, that other research findings suggest the need for adjustments in the theory. First, findings reported by Heilman and her colleagues suggest that most people prefer a participative approach to decision making even under conditions where the model recommends a more autocratic approach.[50] Second, leaders and subordinates seem to differ in their re- actions to various methods for reaching decisions. Leaders tend to prefer those methods suggested by the normative model in a given situation, whereas subordinates tend to prefer participative strategies in all cases.[51] Third, certain characteristics of leaders may play a key role in determining the relative effectiveness of various decision strategies.[52] For example, it appears that in situations involving conflicting opinions, only managers who are relatively high in conflict-handling skills should use the kind of participative decision-making strategy recommended by the Vroom and Yetton model. When managers are low in conflict-handling skills, in contrast, they obtain better results with a relatively autocratic style, even though this is not predicted by the model. Finally, recent evidence reported by Field and House indicates that the Vroom and Yetton model predicts the perceived effectiveness of decisions among managers, but not necessarily among their subordinates.[53]

These researchers asked both managers and their subordinates to report their reactions to a recent decision made by the managers. Participants described the process used by the managers to make the decision (the various decision strategies listed in the Vroom and Yetton model), and their perceptions of the extent to which the decisions were accepted and were effective. Results indicated that managers and their subordinates generally agreed in their perceptions of the decision processes used by the managers, and also with respect to the effectiveness of these decisions. Tests of the Vroom and Yetton model revealed that when managers used one of the decision strategies identified as appropriate by the model, they rated these decisions as more effective than when they adopted a decision strategy *not* identified by the model. This finding offered support for the validity of the Vroom and Yetton model. However, similar results were not obtained for subordinates. They did not rate their managers' decisions as more effective when made in accordance with strategies identified by the model than when they were not (see Figure 12–10 on p. 466).

Why did data from subordinates fail to confirm the Vroom and Yetton model? Field and House suggest that the contrasting roles of subordinates and managers may account, in part, for this finding. Subordinates appear to have a strong aversion to autocratic decision-making strategies, even when these are predicted by the model to be most effective. This, in turn, may reflect subordinates' strong desire to have a say in decisions affecting their jobs. Whatever the precise mechanism, the Vroom and Yetton model seems more applicable, in certain respects, to managers than to subordinates.

To conclude, existing evidence suggests that the normative theory offers useful guidelines to leaders for choosing the most effective approach to decision making. However, adjustments in the model seem necessary, to take account of strong, general preferences for participative procedures, differences in the perspectives of leaders and subordinates, and the personal skills or traits of leaders. With such modifications, the Vroom and Yetton model may prove very helpful in our efforts to understand this key aspect of leader effectiveness.

Test Bank question 12.36 relates to material on this page.

FIGURE 12-10

Evidence Concerning the Validity of Normative Theory

When managers used one of the decision strategies identified as appropriate by normative theory, they rated these decisions as more effective than was true when they adopted a decision strategy not identified by the model. These findings were not replicated with subordinates, however. They did not rate managers' decisions as more effective when they were made by means of strategies consistent with normative theory. (*Source:* Based on data from Field and House, 1990; see Note 53.)

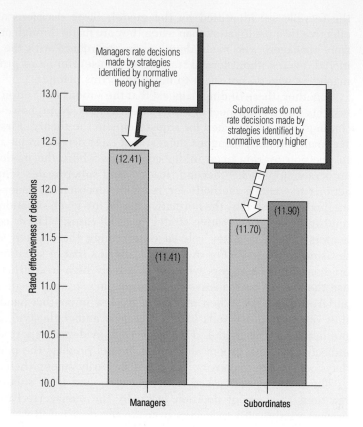

Path-Goal Theory: Leaders as Guides to Valued Goals

Suppose you conducted an informal survey in which you asked 100 people to indicate what they expect from their leaders. What kind of answers would you receive? Although they would vary greatly, one common theme you might uncover would be, "I expect my leader to *help*—to assist me in reaching goals I feel are important."

This basic idea plays a central role in House's **path-goal theory** of leadership.[54] In general terms, the theory contends that subordinates will react favorably to a leader only to the extent that they perceive this person as helping them progress toward various goals by clarifying actual paths to such rewards. More specifically, the theory contends that actions by a leader that clarify the nature of tasks and reduce or eliminate obstacles will increase perceptions on the part of subordinates that working hard will lead to good performance and that good performance, in turn, will be recognized and rewarded. Under such conditions, House suggests, job satisfaction, motivation, and actual performance will all be enhanced. (As you can see, this path-goal theory of leadership is closely related to expectancy theory; refer to our discussion of this theory in chapter 4.)

How, precisely, can leaders best accomplish these tasks? The answer, as in other modern views of leadership, is "It depends." And what it depends on is a complex interaction between key aspects of *leader behavior* and certain *contingency* factors. With respect to leader behavior, path-goal theory suggests that leaders can adopt four basic styles:

- **Instrumental** (directive): an approach focused on providing specific guidance, establishing work schedules and rules

- **Supportive:** a style focused on establishing good relations with subordinates and satisfying their needs
- **Participative:** a pattern in which the leader consults with subordinates, permitting them to participate in decisions
- **Achievement-oriented:** an approach in which the leader sets challenging goals and seeks improvements in performance

By the way, these styles are not mutually exclusive; in fact, the same leader can adopt them at different times and in different situations. Indeed, showing such flexibility is one important aspect of an effective leader.

Which of these contrasting styles is best for maximizing subordinate satisfaction and motivation? This depends on the *contingency factors* mentioned above. First, the style of choice is strongly affected by several *characteristics of subordinates*. For example, if followers are high in ability, an instrumental style of leadership may be unnecessary; instead, a less structured, supportive one may be preferable. On the other hand, if subordinates are low in ability, the opposite may be true; such people need considerable guidance to help them attain their goals. Similarly, people high in need for affiliation (close, friendly ties with others) may strongly prefer a supportive or participative style of leadership. Those high in the need for achievement may strongly prefer an achievement-oriented leader.

Second, the most effective leadership style also depends on several aspects of *work environments*. For example, path-goal theory predicts that when tasks are unstructured and nonroutine, an instrumental approach by the leader may be best; much clarification and guidance are needed. However, when tasks are structured and highly routine, such leadership may actually get in the way of good performance, and may be resented by subordinates who think the leader is engaging in unnecessary meddling. (See Figure 12–11 for an overview of all these aspects of path-goal theory.)

Path-goal theory has been subjected to empirical testing in several studies.[55] In general, results have been consistent with major predictions derived from the theory, although not uniformly so. Thus, at present, path-goal theory appears to be another framework offering valuable insights into leadership and the many factors that determine the degree to which individual leaders are successful in this role. (Can leaders be trained to be more effective? For information on this important topic, see the **OB in Practice** section on pp. 468–469.)

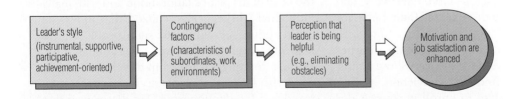

FIGURE 12–11 Path-Goal Theory: An Overview

According to *path-goal theory*, perceptions among employees that leaders are helping them to reach valued goals enhance both employees' motivation and job satisfaction. Such perceptions, in turn, are encouraged when a leader's style is consistent with the needs and characteristics of subordinates (e.g., their level of experience, achievement motivation) and aspects of the work environment (e.g., requirements of the tasks being performed). (*Source:* Based on suggestions by House and Baetz, 1978; see Note 41.)

TRANSFORMATIONAL LEADERSHIP: LEADERSHIP THROUGH VISION AND CHARISMA

In the darkest days of the Depression, the United States seemed poised on the brink of social chaos. With millions out of work and the economy in an apparently endless decline, despair was, seemingly, out of control. Through his inspiring speeches ("The only thing we have to fear is fear itself . . .") and vigorous actions, President Franklin D. Roosevelt pulled the nation back from the edge of violence and saved the grand American experiment in political democracy.

In the 1970s, Chrysler Corporation was being written off by many analysts of the automobile industry with a single word: "Terminal." One man, however, refused to accept this economic verdict. Instead, Lee Iacocca launched a concerted campaign to win government loan guarantees for Chrysler, and so continued survival for the company. Through example—his famous $1 salary—and exhortation, he rallied Chrysler's tens of thousands of employees to unheard-of levels of effort and sacrifice,

 OB IN PRACTICE

Leader Training: Helping Leaders to Polish Up Their Acts

What single trait or characteristic is most crucial to a leader's success? If you answered *people skills* or something similar, many experts would contend that you are on the right track. There is a growing consensus that in practical terms, the most important skill a leader can possess is the ability to get along well with others.[56] As Lawrence A. Weinbach, CEO of Arthur Anderson, Inc., puts it, "Pure technical knowledge is only going to get you to a point. Beyond that, interpersonal skills become critical." Can such skills be taught? In other words, can leaders learn to "read" others more accurately, to communicate more effectively, and to polish up the rough edges of their behavior or personalities to smooth their interactions with others? An increasing number of companies believe that they can. And they are willing to put their resources behind this conviction, paying for their top executives to enroll in courses designed to accomplish precisely these goals.

Perhaps the most famous of these programs is the one conducted by the *Center for Creative Leadership* in Greensboro, North Carolina. At the center's Executive Development Program, executives from many different companies and backgrounds work hard to develop the improved interpersonal skills they believe will help them toward their career goals. This program, and many others like it, employs a wide range of techniques to enhance participants' understanding of their own behavior—how they are perceived by others—as well as specific interpersonal skills, such as communication, conflict resolution, and even how to manage their own tempers (see Figure 12–12).[57]

Consider the case of Robert Siddall, a plant manager for Bethlehem Steel Corporation. He was an aggressive and sometimes abrasive leader who found himself involved in many clashes with the head of his plant's labor union and with many individual workers. He realized that unless he could reduce or eliminate such problems, his hopes for career advancement might be dashed. While attending a leadership development program, he learned that his style was too structured and too domineering. He discovered that he often ignored others and showed little respect for their views. After mastering these and related skills, he now gets along much better with subordinates. His performance ratings have improved, and his employees now refer to him as the "New Bob." When he slips into his old shoot-

and saved the day. Chrysler survived, prospered, and paid back all its loans, thus establishing a new chapter in the annals of government-industry cooperation in the United States.

World history and the history of organizations are replete with similar examples. Through the ages, some leaders have had extraordinary success in generating profound changes in the beliefs, perceptions, values, and actions of their followers (see Figure 12–13 on p. 470). Indeed, it is not extreme to suggest that such people have often served as key agents of social change, transforming entire societies through their words and actions.[58] Individuals who accomplish such feats are often described as **transformational** or **charismatic leaders,** and the terms seem fitting. They do indeed transform social, political, or economic reality; and they do seem to possess unusual and special skills that equip them for this task. (The word "charisma" means "gift" in Greek.) What personal characteristics make certain leaders charismatic? How do such leaders exert their profound effects on many other people? Systematic research on this issue has begun to yield some intriguing answers to these and related questions.

Although the success of charismatic leaders has been touted by the media, charismatic leaders may be successful only under certain conditions. They may even be detrimental to an organization under

from-the-temper approach, they chide him by saying "Old Bob, Old Bob" over and over again.

Similarly, consider the experience of Richard S. Helrich, director of marketing for a division of American Cyanamid Company. He always perceived himself as an enlightened manager who delegated responsibility to his subordinates and encouraged them to set their own deadlines. "I thought I had the perfect style," he remarks. But while attending a leadership development program, he discovered that he was viewed by subordinates and superiors as too aloof and as lacking in communication skills. "I was devastated," Helrich notes in describing his reactions to this feedback. After completing the program,

he made special efforts to become more involved in subordinates' projects and overcame his aloofness, improving his communication style noticeably. The result: his relations with subordinates improved to the point where projects that previously took six or seven months to complete were now completed in three.

Many other executives report similar changes and benefits. Where interpersonal skills are concerned, in short, it *does* seem possible to teach "old dogs"—highly experienced leaders—new tricks. The final result may be substantial gains both for the individuals involved and for their companies.

FIGURE 12–12

Learning More Effective Interpersonal Skills

To be effective, leaders need excellent *interpersonal* skills. Such skills can be acquired through participation in special training programs.

other conditions. For example, although many charismatic leaders are excellent at helping companies through various crises, once the crisis is over, the charismatic leader is often ineffective at managing the company on a routine, day-to-day basis. For example, Jeffrey Campbell, chairman of Burger King from 1983 to 1987, was able to orchestrate a miraculous turnaround of the company by reversing declining market shares and eroding margins. However, once the company was back on track, Campbell was unable to handle the more mundane chores of routine management. Charismatic leadership may not be well suited to situations in which organizations are already performing well in a stable, noncrisis environment. [Machan, D. (1989, January 23). The charisma merchants. *Forbes*, pp. 100–101.]

FIGURE 12–13   Transformational Leaders through History

Over the centuries, some leaders have exerted a profound impact on their own societies—and in some cases, on the entire world. Two of these *transformational leaders*, Abraham Lincoln and Martin Luther King, Jr., are shown here.

The Basic Nature of Charisma: Traits or Relationships?

At first glance, it is tempting to assume that transformational or charismatic leaders are special by virtue of the possession of certain traits; in other words, such leadership might be understood as an extension of the *great person theory* described earlier in this chapter.[59] Although traits may well play a role in transformational leadership, the belief that it makes more sense to view such leadership as involving a special type of *relationship* between leaders and their followers is growing.[60] Within this framework, charismatic leadership rests more on specific types of reaction by followers than on traits possessed by leaders. Such reactions include (1) levels of performance beyond those that would normally be expected,[61] (2) high levels of devotion, loyalty, and reverence toward the leader,[62] (3) enthusiasm for and excitement about the leader and the leader's ideas, and (4) a willingness on the part of subordinates to sacrifice their own personal interests for the sake of a larger collective goal.[63] In short, transformational or charismatic leadership involves a special kind of leader-follower relationship, in which the leader can, in the words of one author, "make ordinary people do extraordinary things in the face of adversity."[64]

The Behavior of Transformational Leaders

Can transformational leaders go too far? Many of the world's most infamous transformational leaders have believed themselves to be rulers by "divine right" and have had their followers worship them, including Alexander the Great, France's Louis XIV, Hitler, Hirohito, Stalin, Muammar Qaddafi, and Saddam Hussein, to name just a few. Although these leaders sometimes started

But what, precisely, do transformational or charismatic leaders do to generate this kind of relationship with their subordinates? Studies designed to answer this question point to the following general conclusion: such leaders gain the capacity to exert profound influence over others through many different tactics.

First, and perhaps most important, transformational leaders propose a *vision*. They describe, usually in vivid, emotion-provoking terms, an image of what their nation, group, or organization could—and should—become. The leader described in the story at the start of this chapter operated in this fashion, providing a stirring vision that engaged the energies and enthusiasm of many people in her company. A more dramatic example is provided by the words of Martin Luther King, in his famous "I Have a Dream" speech:

Test Bank questions 12.40 and 12.74 relate to material on this page.

So I say to you, my friends, that even though we must face the difficulties of today and tomorrow, I still have a dream. It is a dream deeply rooted in the American dream that one day this nation will rise up and live out the true meaning of its creed—we hold these truths to be self-evident, that all men are created equal. This will be the day when all of God's children will be able to sing with new meaning 'my country 'tis of thee, sweet land of liberty. . . .'

But transformational leaders do not simply describe a dream or vision; they also offer a clear road map for attaining it; they tell their followers, in straightforward terms, how to get from here to there. This too seems crucial, for a vision that appears perpetually out of reach is unlikely to motivate people to try to attain it.

Third, transformational leaders engage in what Conger terms *framing:* they define the purpose of their movement or organization in a way that gives meaning and purpose to whatever actions they are requesting from followers.[65] Perhaps the nature of framing is best illustrated by the well-known tale of two stonecutters working on a cathedral in the Middle Ages. When asked what they are doing, one replies, "Why, cutting this stone, of course." The other replies, "Building the world's most beautiful temple to the glory of God." Which person would be more likely to expend greater effort? The answer is obvious. In the business world, transformational leaders frame the activities of their organizations in ways that give them added meaning and that tie them closely to the accepted values of society. Consider Mary Kay Ash's words in describing her company, Mary Kay Cosmetics: "My objective was just to help women. It was not to make a tremendous amount of sales. I want women to earn money commensurate with men. I want them to be paid on the basis of what they have between their ears and their brains and not because they are male or female."

Imagine if, instead, she had stated: "My objective was to increase our sales by 25 percent annually, so that in five years we'd become the third- or fourth-largest company in the business. In that way, we'd provide an excellent return to shareholders and build the value of our company's stock." Would you, as a Mary Kay representative, work as hard for these goals and this vision as for the one Ash actually expressed? We suspect not.

In addition, transformational leaders often show greater-than-average willingness to take risks and engage in unconventional actions to reach their stated goals. To help thwart the coup that threatened the budding democracy of his nation, Boris Yeltsin rushed to the Russian Parliament, where he stood on top of a tank and pleaded with troops sent there by the new hard-liners to withdraw. By this high-risk behavior, he demonstrated his deep commitment to the forces of reform.

Other qualities shown by transformational leaders include expressing high levels of self-confidence; showing a high degree of concern for their followers' needs; demonstrating excellent communication skills, such as the ability to "read" others' reactions quickly and accurately; and a stirring personal style. Finally, transformational leaders are often masters of *impression management*, engaging in many tactics designed to enhance their attractiveness and appeal to others. When these forms of behavior are added to the captivating and exciting visions they propound, the tremendous impact of transformational or charismatic leaders begins to come sharply into focus. Their influence, it appears, does not stem from the possession of semi-magical traits; rather, it is a logical result of a complex cluster of behaviors and techniques. In the final analysis, however, the essence of transformational leadership does appear to rest on the ability of such people to inspire others, through their words, their vision, and their actions. As Conger puts it, "If you as a leader can make an appealing dream seem like tomorrow's reality, your subordinates will freely choose to follow you."[66] (For additional information on charismatic leadership and its potential role in the effectiveness of American presidents, see the **Focus on Research** section on pp. 472–473.)

out with worthwhile visions, they let their power go to their heads and became dictators who believed the myths that they created to inspire followers. Unfortunately, most of the followers of these treacherous leaders realized only too late that they had created a monster who had total control over them—someone more interested in serving his own selfish interests than those of his followers. [Bratman, F. (1990, November 2). Cult of personality. *Scholastic Update*, pp. 8–9.]

ADDITIONAL PERSPECTIVES ON LEADERSHIP: THE VERTICAL DYAD LINKAGE MODEL, THE ATTRIBUTION APPROACH, SUBSTITUTES FOR LEADERSHIP, AND SITUATIONAL LEADERSHIP THEORY

Executives are currently marveling at a new type of leadership that continually seems to raise expectations, called *TQM,* or *Total Quality Management.* At the core of TQM is the relentless pursuit of continu-

Because it is widely viewed as a central organizational process, leadership has long been the subject of extensive study in organizational behavior. Yet, recent years seem to have brought an acceleration in both the scope and the volume of such work. In this final section, we will review several of the newer perspectives that have grown out of this research. Each is unique, but together they add appreciably to our understanding of the nature and impact of leadership.

 FOCUS ON RESEARCH

Charisma, Personality, and Presidential Performance: A Retrospective Study

 Charismatic leaders play an important role in the fortunes of many business organizations, but their potential impact on another type of organization—duly constituted governments—is, in several respects, even more dramatic. A strong argument can be made that through their actions in the political arena, charismatic or transformational leaders have shaped and reshaped the course of human history. But what, precisely, are such people like? What are their traits and motives? What situations encourage their emergence? And are they actually more effective than other types of leader? Revealing answers to these and related questions have recently been provided by an ingenious study conducted by House, Spangler, and Woycke.[67]

These researchers focused on charisma among American presidents. They reasoned that certain motives—a high need for power coupled with a strong tendency to employ such power for social rather than personal goals—would be positively related to charismatic behavior on the part of presidents. Such charismatic behavior, in turn, would be linked to presidential performance. House and his colleagues further reasoned that political crises would call forth or encourage charismatic behavior among presidents and that, in general, charismatic behavior would be more prevalent among recent presidents than ones from previous centuries. This would be the case partly because of the increas-

ing frequency of political and world crises (which would encourage charismatic behavior), and partly because of changing conceptions of the nature of the presidency—a shift away from the early ideal of a restrained statesman toward a view of presidents as active visionaries.

To test these predictions, House, Spangler, and Woycke adopted complex and highly sophisticated procedures. They obtained measures of the power needs of thirty-one U.S. presidents from an analysis of the content of their speeches. Such written documents can be readily scored for the amount of power-related images or ideas they contain.[68] To measure the presidents' charismatic behavior, they examined biographies to determine the extent to which these leaders demonstrated high levels of self-confidence, strong ideological convictions, high expectations of followers, and high levels of confidence in subordinates. All of these characteristics have been found to be associated with a charismatic style of leadership.[69] Political crises were assessed through historical records, and included events such as declaration of war by the United States, financial panics, rebellions and uprisings, and so on. Finally, measures of presidential performance were obtained from ratings of presidential prestige, strength of action, and greatness provided by a large number of American historians.

Analysis of this complex set of data provided strong support for the model of charisma, personality, and presidential performance de-

The Vertical Dyad Linkage Model: The Importance of Leader-Follower Exchanges

Do leaders treat all their subordinates in the same manner? Informal observation suggests that, clearly, they do not. Yet many theories of leadership tend to ignore this fact. They discuss leadership style or behavior in terms that suggest similar actions toward all subordinates. The importance of potential differences in this respect is brought into sharp focus by the **vertical dyad linkage (VDL)** model developed by Dansereau, Graen, and Haga.[70]

This theory suggests that leaders form distinct exchange relationships with each of their subordinates. Within these exchange relationships, leaders offer valued outcomes such as advice, support, inviting input into decisions, and open communi-

ous improvement of both an organization and its members. To make TQM work, leaders try to facilitate participation, involvement, and contributions of all employees. Continual training, along with accountability and responsibility for all employees, is also involved. Leaders try to help all employees understand how and why the organization works, including keeping

scribed above. As expected, need for power and activity inhibition successfully predicted presidents' level of charismatic behavior. Similarly, charismatic behaviors were positively related to ratings of presidential performance. Crises, too, were linked in a positive manner to behavioral charisma; they did seem to call forth this style of leadership. Finally, charismatic behavior did in fact increase with time, so that it was more prevalent among recent presidents than ones from early days of the republic (see Figure 12–14).

These findings have important implications for organizations. First, they suggest that individuals' potential for charismatic or transformational leadership may be identified, perhaps at a relatively early age, from study of their personality profiles. Those high in need for power and activity inhibition appear to be more likely candidates for this role than those lower in these

motives. Second, charismatic leaders appear more likely to emerge—and most likely to succeed—in situations that call for a combination of highly involved leadership and high levels of emotional commitment from followers in the pursuit of visionary or ideological goals. Situations requiring more routine or pragmatic actions, in contrast, are ones in which charismatic leaders are likely to prove ineffective or dysfunctional.[71] Finally, charismatic leaders are more likely to emerge under conditions of crisis than at other times. The overall message is clear: charismatic leaders do not arise in a social vacuum; rather, they are brought to power by special sets of circumstances. Given the rapid pace of change in the modern business world and the complex challenges faced by many organizations, the times indeed seem ripe for leaders who lead by vision, enthusiasm, and confidence—in a word, charisma.

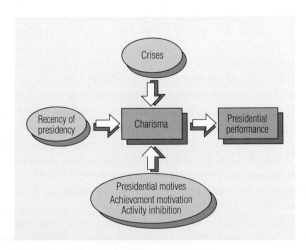

FIGURE 12–14

Personality, Political Crises, Charisma, and Presidential Effectiveness

Evidence gathered in a study conducted by House, Spangler, and Woycke indicates that certain traits or motives on the part of U.S. presidents encourage them to adopt a charismatic style. Such behavior is also fostered by political crises and by the recency with which the presidents have held office. Charismatic behaviors, in turn, are linked to ratings of presidential effectiveness. (*Source:* Based on data from House, Spangler, & Woycke, 1991; see Note 60.)

no secrets about the organization from employees. For TQM to succeed, organizations must establish small-scale plans that focus on specific quality improvements. One such TQM success story occurred at Stone Construction Equipment, Inc., which moved from fifth to first in its field in the world. [Day, C. R., Jr. (1992, January 6). Quality: Make it a matter of policy. *Industry Week*, p. 46.; Fuchsberg, G. (1992, May 14). Quality programs show shoddy results. *The Wall Street Journal*, p. B1.]

cation, and subordinates reciprocate with increased commitment, loyalty, and effort. Although leaders form such relationships with all of their subordinates, the nature of these dyadic exchanges can differ sharply. At one extreme, the leader holds positive views about a subordinate, who, in turn, feels that the leader understands his or her problems, appreciates his or her potential, and is willing to offer help and support when these are needed. At the other end of the continuum, the leader holds negative views about the subordinate, who, in turn, has little faith or confidence in the leader. According to the VDL model, such differences in the quality of leader-member relations can have powerful effects on the performance, job satisfaction, and even career development of subordinates.[72]

To the extent that this is true—and a growing body of research evidence suggests that it is—the next question is obvious: can any steps be taken to improve individual leader-member relations? The answer appears to be "yes." For example, in one study on this topic, supervisors in a large government department underwent special training designed to equip them with skills that would help them establish positive relations with subordinates.[73] Before and again after the training was completed, the subordinates of these individuals completed questionnaires on which they rated the quality of their relationship with their supervisor, their satisfaction with his or her leadership, and their satisfaction with their jobs. Results indicated that the special training did indeed help: subordinates reported higher satisfaction and better relations with their leaders after the leaders had completed the training. In addition, as VDL theory suggests, the gains in these respects were greater for subordinates who initially reported poor relations with their supervisors than for those who initially reported good relations.

These findings, and those of related studies, suggest that attention to the relations (dyadic exchanges) between leaders and specific followers can be very useful. Such relations, it seems, vary greatly even within relatively small work groups. And their nature can strongly affect the morale, commitment, and performance of employees. Helping leaders to improve such relations, therefore, can be of practical value in several respects.

The Attribution Approach: Leaders' Explanations of Followers' Behavior

As we have just seen, leaders' relationships with individual subordinates can play an important role in determining the performance and satisfaction of these individuals. One specific aspect of such exchanges serves as focus of another contemporary perspective on leadership—the *attribution approach*.[74] This theory emphasizes the role of leaders' *attributions* concerning the causes behind followers' behavior—especially, in work settings, the causes of their current *performance*. The reasoning behind the attribution approach is closely related to that which we described in chapter 2, in our discussion of the role of attributions in performance appraisal.

Leaders observe the performance of their followers and then attempt to understand why this behavior met, exceeded, or failed to meet their expectations. Since poor performance often poses greater difficulties than effective performance, leaders are more likely to engage in a careful attributional analysis when confronted with the former. When they are, they examine the three kinds of information described in chapter 2 (consensus, distinctiveness, and consistency), and on the basis of such information form an initial judgment as to whether followers' performance stemmed from internal causes (e.g., low effort, commitment, or ability) or external causes (factors beyond their control, such as faulty equipment, unrealistic deadlines, or illness). Then, on the basis of such attributions, they formulate specific actions designed to change the present situation, and perhaps improve followers' performance. Attribution theory suggests that such actions are determined, at least in part, by leaders' explanations of followers' behavior. For example, if they perceive poor performance as stemming from a lack of required materials or equipment, they may focus on providing such items. If, instead, they perceive poor performance as stemming mainly from a lack of effort, they may reprimand, transfer, or terminate the person involved.

Evidence for the accuracy of these predictions has been reported in several studies.[75] In perhaps the best known of these, Mitchell and Wood presented nursing supervisors with brief accounts of errors committed by nurses.[76] The incidents suggested that the errors stemmed either from internal causes (lack of effort or ability) or from external causes (e.g., overdemanding work environment). After reading about the incidents, supervisors indicated what kind of action they would be likely to take in each situation. Results showed that they were more likely to direct corrective action toward the nurses when they perceived the errors as stemming from internal causes, but more likely to direct action toward the environment when they perceived the errors as stemming from external factors.

In summary, the attribution approach suggests that leaders' behavior often reflects their attributions concerning the actions and performance of followers. Leadership, then, lies as much in the perceptions of the people who exercise such influence as in the perceptions of those who confer the right to wield it over them.

Substitutes for Leadership

Throughout this chapter, we have emphasized that leaders are important. Their style, actions, and degree of effectiveness all exert major effects on subordinates and, ultimately, on organizations. In many cases, this is certainly true. Yet, almost everyone has observed or been part of groups in which the designated leaders actually had little influence—groups in which these people were mere figureheads with little impact on subordinates. One explanation for such situations involves the characteristics of the leaders in question: they are simply weak and unsuited for their jobs. Another, and in some ways more intriguing, possibility is as follows: in some contexts, other factors may actually *substitute* for a leader's influence, making it superfluous. This is known as the **substitutes for leadership** approach.

According to a framework developed by Kerr and Jermier, many different variables can produce such effects.[77] First, a high level of knowledge, commitment, or experience on the part of subordinates may make it unnecessary for anyone to tell them what to do or how to proceed. Second, jobs themselves may be structured in ways that make direction and influence from a leader redundant. Third, work norms and strong feelings of cohesion among employees may directly affect job performance and render the presence of a leader unnecessary. Fourth, the technology associated with certain jobs may strongly determine the decisions and actions of people performing them, and so leave little room for input from a leader.

Evidence for these assertions has been obtained in several recent studies. For example, in an investigation conducted by Sheridan, Vredenburgh, and Abelson, nurses' job performance (as rated by their supervisors) was more strongly affected by many factors that might, potentially, serve as substitutes for leadership (e.g., the type of technology available, group norms concerning the quality of care) than by their supervisors' leadership style or behavior.[78]

If leaders are superfluous in many situations, why has this fact often been overlooked? One possibility, suggested by Meindl and Ehrlich, is that we have a strong tendency to romanticize leadership—to perceive it as more important and more closely linked to performance in many contexts than it actually is.[79] To test this suggestion, Meindl and Ehrlich presented M.B.A. students with information about an imaginary firm, including a five-year summary of selected indicators of its performance (e.g., total sales, profit margins, net earnings, stock price). Attached to these data was a paragraph describing the firm's key operating strengths. The content of this paragraph was varied, so that four different groups of subjects received four different versions. These attributed the firm's performance to its top-level management team, the quality of its employees, changing patterns of consumer needs and preferences, or federal regulatory policies, respectively.

After reading one of these paragraphs and examining other information about the firm, subjects rated two aspects of its overall performance: profitability and risk. Meindl and Ehrlich reasoned that because of the tendency to overestimate the importance of leadership, subjects would rate the firm more favorably when its performance was attributed to top-level management than when it was attributed to any of the other factors. As you can see in Figure 12–15, this was precisely what occurred. The imaginary company was rated as higher in profitability and lower in risk when subjects had read the leadership-based paragraph than when they had read any of the others.

These findings, plus others obtained by the same researchers, help explain why leaders are often viewed as important and necessary even when, to a large degree, they are superfluous. Note: this in no way implies that leaders are usually unimportant. On the contrary, they often *do* play a key role in work groups and organizations. However, because this is not always so, their necessity should never be taken for granted.

Situational Leadership Theory: Follower Maturity and Leadership Style

Consider an organization with a stable work force. As time passes, many people—including leaders and their subordinates—will work together for years or even decades. Since change is indeed the only constant for human beings, these individuals and their relationships will alter over time. One such change involves increasing maturity on the part of subordinates. As subordinates grow older and obtain more job-related experience, they will become more mature in many respects. Will such shifts be reflected in their need for various types of leadership? According to a theory proposed by Hersey and Blanchard, they will.[80] In a view known as **situational leadership theory,** these authors propose the following sequence. Initially, when subordinates' maturity is relatively low, their need for directive actions by the leader (initiating structure) will be high. Later, as they master their jobs, their need for emotional support (showing consideration) will increase. Finally, as they attain full maturity, the need for this, too, will decrease. Then supervisory actions by their leader will become superfluous in many respects.

Are these assertions about the changing course of leadership requirements over time accurate? Situational leadership theory is quite new, so little evidence about it currently exists.[81] However, a study conducted by Vecchio offers at least some support for its usefulness.[82] In this investigation, Vecchio had several hundred high school teachers complete questionnaires designed to measure their perceptions of their leaders' (principals) behavior. Specifically, teachers indicated the extent to which the principals engaged in initiating structure and showing consideration. They also reported on the quality of their exchanges with their principals and on their satisfaction with their principals' leadership. The principals also took part in the study. They rated the maturity and job performance of the teachers working under their supervision.

In determining which style of leadership is the most appropriate, one can look as far back as the dawn of humanity for an answer. In one of the oldest professions, that of sheepherder, there was said to be two types of leaders: one who walked behind his sheep and drove them; and another who walked in front of his sheep and led them. When the leader walked behind the sheep, they became resentful, listless, and apathetic. They lost all drive and were unhappy and neurotic. But when the leader walked in front of the sheep, they were more positive. They could look ahead and use their initiative and individuality. As such, they could thrive, innovate, and grow. When trying to determine what type of leadership style is best to use, it may be useful to think of the analogy of the shepherd pointing out a new direction for the flock. [Batten, J. (1991, August). Real leadership is the answer. *Manage,* pp. 24–27.]

Test Bank question 12.45 relates to material on this page.

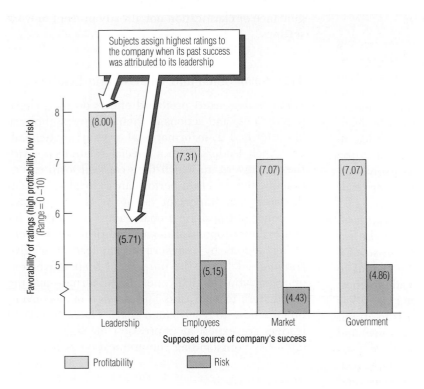

FIGURE 12-15

Leadership: Evidence that We Overestimate Its Importance

People who received information suggesting that an imaginary company's past success was attributable to its top management rated the company more favorably (higher in profitability, lower in risk) than those who received information suggesting that the identical record had stemmed from other causes. These findings offer support for the view that we tend to *romanticize* leadership, overestimating its impact in many situations. (*Source:* Based on data from Meindl and Ehrlich, 1987; see Note 79.)

Situational leadership theory predicts that subordinates will demonstrate the highest performance and express the greatest satisfaction when their leader's style matches their own level of maturity. To test this prediction, Vecchio divided the teachers into two groups: those whose leader's style matched their level of maturity and those whose leader's style did not match. Then he compared the performance and self-rated satisfaction of teachers in the two groups. Consistent with predictions derived from the theory, teachers in the first category generally reported higher satisfaction, and received higher performance ratings, than those in the latter. However, these findings were clearest for teachers who were relatively low in maturity; they did not occur among those who were high in maturity.

Taken together, these findings suggest that situational leadership theory may be most applicable to newly hired employees—ones who require a high degree of structuring from their supervisors—and least applicable to more experienced, and more mature, individuals. Whatever its ultimate fate, the theory does emphasize an important fact: a style of leadership that is adaptive and successful at one point in time may not necessarily be so at others. Thus, once more, we are left with the same basic message for leaders or would-be leaders: *flexibility* is, perhaps, the most effective route to success.

SUMMARY AND REVIEW

Leadership: Some Basic Issues

Leadership is the process whereby one individual influences other group members toward the attainment of defined group or organizational goals. Leaders generally use noncoercive forms of influence and are influenced, in turn, by their followers. Not all managers function as leaders. Conversely, not all leaders are managers. Thus, the two terms should not be treated as synonyms.

Leader Traits and Leader Behaviors

Early efforts to identify key traits that set leaders apart from other people generally failed. However, recent evidence suggests that leaders do differ from followers in certain respects. They are higher in leadership motivation, drive, honesty, self-confidence, and several other traits. In addition, successful leaders appear to be high in *flexibility*—the ability to adapt their style to the followers' needs and to the requirements of specific situations. Conversely, certain traits, such as arrogance, can interfere with leaders' performance.

Leaders differ greatly in their style or approach to leadership. One key dimension involves the extent to which leaders are *directive* or *permissive* toward subordinates. Another involves the extent to which they are **participative** or **autocratic** in their decision making. Leaders also vary along two other key dimensions: concern with, and efforts to attain, successful task performance (**initiating structure**) and concern with maintaining favorable personal relations with subordinates (**consideration**). Organizational factors (e.g., technology, the presence and strength of unions) can strongly determine leaders' behavior.

Major Theories of Leadership

Major theories of leadership differ in many respects, but all the theories share a concern with the determinants of leader effectiveness. Fiedler's **contingency theory** suggests that both a leader's characteristics and situational factors are crucial. Task-oriented leaders are more effective than people-oriented leaders under conditions where the leader has either high or low control over the group in question. In contrast, people-oriented leaders are more effective under conditions where the leader has moderate control. Vroom and Yetton's **normative theory** focuses on decision making as a key determinant of leader effectiveness. According to normative theory, different situations call for different styles of decision making (e.g., autocratic, consultative, participative) by leaders. Recent evidence suggests that personal characteristics of leaders, too, are important in determining which of these styles is best. The **path-goal theory** of leadership suggests that leaders' behavior will be accepted by subordinates and will enhance their motivation only to the extent that it helps them progress toward valued goals and provides guidance or clarification not already present in work settings.

Transformational and Charismatic Leaders

Some leaders exert profound effects on the beliefs, perceptions, and actions of their followers; they are often termed **transformational** or **charismatic leaders.** Such leaders have a special relationship with their followers, in which they can call forth exceptionally high levels of performance, loyalty, and enthusiasm. An important factor in the impressive influence of transformational leaders over others involves their proposal of an emotion-provoking *vision*. Other actions by transformational leaders involve *framing*—defining the purpose of their movement or organization in highly meaningful terms—and the willingness to take risks and engage in unconventional actions to reach stated goals. Transformational leaders are expert at impression management and often have outstanding communication skills.

Additional Theoretical Perspectives

The **vertical dyad linkage (VDL)** theory calls attention to the fact that leaders often have different relationships with different subordinates. These relationships, in turn, may strongly affect subordinates' satisfaction, performance, and perceptions of the leader. The quality of young managers' relations with their supervisors has been found to affect the course of their careers.

Growing evidence suggests that under some conditions (e.g., when subordinates are highly skilled or committed), directives or guidance from a leader may be superfluous. Such conditions are termed **substitutes for leadership.** That leaders are unnecessary in at least some situations has often been overlooked because of our strong tendency to romanticize leadership—to perceive it as more important than it actually is. The **situational theory of leadership** suggests that as they mature, followers may require different styles of leadership from their managers. Inexperienced subordinates may require a high level of structuring by their leaders. Ones who are moderately mature may require a high level of social and emotional support (showing consideration). However, those who are fully mature may require low levels of both types of behavior on the part of their leaders.

KEY TERMS

autocratic (leadership style): A style of leadership in which the leader makes all decisions unilaterally.

charismatic leaders: Leaders who exert powerful effects on their followers and to whom special traits are attributed (e.g., possession of an idealized vision or goal, willingness to engage in unconventional behaviors to reach it).

consideration: Actions by a leader that demonstrate concern with the welfare of subordinates and establish positive relations with them. Leaders who focus primarily on this task are often described as demonstrating a person-oriented style.

contingency theory: A theory suggesting that leader effectiveness is determined both by characteristics of leaders and by the level of situational control they are able to exert over subordinates.

great person theory: The view that leaders possess special *traits* that set them apart from others, and that these traits are responsible for their assuming positions of power and authority.

initiating structure: Activities by a leader designed to enhance productivity or task performance. Leaders who focus primarily on these goals are described as demonstrating a task-oriented style.

leader: An individual within a group or an organization who wields the most influence over others.

leadership: The process whereby one individual influences other group members toward the attainment of defined group or organizational goals.

leadership motivation: The desire to influence others, especially toward the attainment of shared goals.

normative theory: A theory of leader effectiveness focusing primarily on strategies for choosing the most effective approach to making decisions.

participative (leadership style): A style of leadership in which the leader permits subordinates to take part in decision making, and also permits them a considerable degree of autonomy in completing routine work activities.

path-goal theory: A theory of leadership suggesting that subordinates will be motivated by a leader only to the extent they perceive this individual as helping them to attain valued goals.

situational leadership theory: A theory suggesting that the most effective style of leadership varies with the maturity or experience of subordinates.

substitutes for leadership: The view that high levels of skill among subordinates or certain features of technology and organizational structure sometimes serve as substitutes for leaders, rendering their guidance or influence superfluous.

transformational leaders: Leaders who exert profound influence over followers by proposing an emotion-generating *vision*, *framing* the activities of their organization in highly meaningful terms, and several other techniques.

vertical dyad linkage (VDL): A theory suggesting that leaders form different relations with various subordinates and that the nature of such dyadic exchanges can exert strong effects on subordinates' performance and satisfaction.

QUESTIONS FOR DISCUSSION

1. It has often been said that "leaders are born, not made." Do you agree? If so, why? If not, why?

2. Under what conditions are people-oriented leaders more effective than task-oriented leaders and vice versa?

3. Most people prefer to be involved in decisions concerning their jobs. Is such participative decision making always preferable to a more directive approach?

4. Some authors have suggested that female leaders should adopt a different style from male leaders—a style that emphasizes and benefits from their uniquely feminine traits. Do you agree?

5. Recent findings suggest that Asian and American CEOs differ in important respects. Do you think such culture-based differences can be overcome, so that leaders in one culture can adopt beneficial practices used by leaders from another culture?

6. Arrogance seems to be an important stumbling block to being an effective leader. Can people who are arrogant learn a different approach to dealing with others? If so, how?

7. In your experience, do most leaders have a small in-group? If so, what are the effects of this clique on other group members?

8. Consider all the people who have been president of the United States during your lifetime. Which of these (if any) would you describe as charismatic? Why?

9. What style of leadership would be best for a newly formed group that was just "learning the ropes" with respect to its tasks and functions?

NOTES

1. Motowidlo, S. (1992). Leadership and leadership processes. In M. D. Dunnette (Ed.), *Handbook of industrial/organizational psychology* (2nd ed.). Palo Alto, CA: Consulting Psychologists Press.

2. Bass, B. M. (1981). *Stogdill's handbook of leadership: A survey of theory and research.* New York: Free Press.

3. Yukl, G. A. (1989). *Leadership in organizations* (2nd ed.). New York: Academic Press.

4. Cialdini, R. B. (1988). *Influence* (2nd ed.). Glenview, IL: Scott, Foresman.

5. Geier, J. G. (1969). A trait approach to the study of leadership in small groups. *Journal of Communication, 17,* 316–323.

6. Stogdill, R. (1974). *Handbook of leadership.* New York: Free Press.

7. See Note 3.

8. See Note 6.

9. Kirkpatrick, S. A., & Locke, E. A. (1991). Leadership: Do traits matter? *Academy of Management Executive, 5*(2), 48–60.

10. Lord, R. G., DeVader, C. L., & Alliger, G. M. (1986). A meta-analysis of the relation between personality traits and leadership perceptions: An application of validity generalization procedures. *Journal of Applied Psychology, 61,* 402–410.

11. Zaccaro, S. J., Foti, R. J., & Kenny, D. A. (1991). Self-monitoring and trait-based variance in leadership: An investigation of leader flexibility across multiple group situations. *Journal of Applied Psychology, 76,* 308–315.

12. See Note 9, p. 58.

13. Moskal, B. S. (1991, June 3). Arrogance: The executive Achilles' heel. *Industry Week,* p. 19.

14. See Note 13.

15. See Note 13.

16. Muczyk, J. P., & Reimann, B. C. (1987). The case for directive leadership. *Academy of Management Review, 12,* 637–647.

17. See Note 16.

18. Likert, R. (1961). *New patterns in management.* New York: McGraw-Hill.

19. See Note 6.

20. Weissenberg, P., & Kavanagh, M. H. (1972). The independence of initiating structure and consideration: A review of the evidence. *Personnel Psychology, 25,* 119–130.

21. Vroom, V. H. (1976). Leadership. In M. D. Dunnette (Ed.), *Handbook of industrial/organization psychology.* Palo Alto, CA: Consulting Psychologists Press.

22. Blake, R. R., & Mouton, J. S. (1978). *The new managerial grid.* Houston: Gulf.

23. Blake, R. R., & Mouton, J. S. (1985). *The managerial grid III.* Houston: Gulf.

24. Tjosvold, D. (1984). Effects of leader warmth and directiveness on subordinate performance on a subsequent task. *Journal of Applied Psychology, 69,* 222–232.

25. Bureau of Labor Statistics. (1989, October). *Employment and Earnings* (Tables 1–22, 29). Washington, DC: U.S. Department of Labor.

26. Grant, J. (1988). Women as managers: What they can offer to organizations. *Organizational Dynamics,* Winter, 56–63.

27. Loden, M. (1985). *Feminine leadership or how to succeed in business without being one of the boys.* New York: Times Books.

28. Powell, G. N. (1990). One more time: Do female and male managers differ? *Academy of Management Executive, 4*(3), 68–75.

29. Eagly, A. H., & Johnson, B. T. (1990). Gender and leadership style: A meta-analysis. *Psychological Bulletin, 108,* 233–256.

30. See Note 28.

31. See Note 28, p. 74.

32. Lee, C. (1991). Followership: The essence of leadership. *Training, 28,* 27–35.

33. See Note 1.

34. See Note 32.

35. Leana, C. R., Locke, E. A., & Schweiger, D. M. (1990). Fact and fiction in analyzing research on participative decision making: Critique of Cotton, Vollrath, Froggatt, Lengnick-Hall, & Jennings. *Academy of Management Review, 15,* 137–146.

36. Kotter, J. (1982). *The general managers.* New York: Free Press.

37. Doktor, R. H. (1990). Asian and American CEOs: A comparative study. *Organizational Dynamics, 18*(3), 46–56.

38. See Note 32.

39. Fiedler, F. E. (1978). Contingency model and the leadership process. In L. Berkowitz (Ed.), *Advances in experimental social psychology* (Vol. 11). New York: Academic Press.

40. Vroom, V. H., & Yetton, P. W. (1973). *Leadership and decision making.* Pittsburgh: University of Pittsburgh Press.

41. House, R. J., & Baetz, M. L. (1978). Leadership: Some generalizations and new research directions. In B. M. Staw (Ed.), *Research in organizational behavior.* Greenwich, CT: JAI Press.

42. See Note 39.

43. Strube, M. J., & Garcia, J. E. (1981). A meta-analytic investigation of Fiedler's contingency model of leadership effectiveness. *Psychological Bulletin, 90,* 307–321.

44. Chemers, M. M., Hays, R. B., Rhodewelt, F., & Wysocki, J. (1985). A person-environment analysis of job stress: A contingency model explanation. *Journal of Personality and Social Psychology, 49,* 628–635.

45. Peters, L. H., Hartke, D. D., & Pohlman, J. T. (1985). Fiedler's contingency theory of leadership: An application of the meta-analytic procedures of Schmidt and Hunter. *Psychological Bulletin, 97,* 274–385.

46. Ashour, A. S. (1973). The contingency model of leadership effectiveness: An evaluation. *Organizational Behavior and Human Performance, 9*, 339–355.

47. See Note 40.

48. Vroom, V. H., & Jago, A. G. (1978). On the validity of the Vroom–Yetton model. *Journal of Applied Psychology, 63*, 151–162.

49. Field, R. H. (1982). A test of the Vroom-Yetton normative model of leadership. *Journal of Applied Psychology, 67*, 532–537.

50. Heilman, M. E., Hornstein, H. A., Cage, J. H., & Herschlag, J. K. (1984). Reactions to prescribed leader behavior as a function of role perspective: The case of the Vroom–Yetton model. *Journal of Applied Psychology, 69*, 50–60.

51. See Note 50.

52. Crouch, A., & Yetton, P. (1987). Manager behavior, leadership style, and subordinate performance: An empirical extension of the Vroom–Yetton model. *Journal of Applied Psychology, 69*, 50–60.

53. Field, R. H. G., & House, R. J. (1990). A test of the Vroom-Yetton model using manager and subordinate reports. *Journal of Applied Psychology, 75*, 362–366.

54. House, R. J., & Baetz, M. L. (1979). Leadership: Some generalizations and new research directions. In B. M. Staw (Ed.), *Research in organizational behavior*. Greenwich, CT: JAI Press.

55. Schriesheim, C. A., & DeNisi, A. S. (1981). Task dimensions as moderators of the effects of instrumental leadership: A two-sample replicated test of path-goal leadership theory. *Journal of Applied Psychology, 66*, 589–597.

56. Milbank, D. (1990, March 5). Managers are sent to "Charm Schools" to discover how to polish up their acts. *Wall Street Journal*, pp. A14, B3.

57. See Note 56.

58. Bass, B. M. (1985). Leadership and performance beyond expectations. New York: Free Press.

59. See Note 3.

60. House, R. J., Spangler, W. D., & Woycke, J. (1991). Personality and charisma in the U.S. presidency: A psychological theory of leader effectiveness. *Administrative Science Quarterly, 36*, 364–396.

61. See Note 58.

62. House, R. J. (1977). A 1976 theory of charismatic leadership. In J. G. Hunt & L. L. Larson (Eds.), *Leadership: The cutting edge* (pp. 189–207). Carbondale, IL: Southern Illinois University Press.

63. See Note 62.

64. Conger, J. A. (1991). Inspiring others: The language of leadership. *Academy of Management Executive, 5*, 31–45.

65. See Note 64.

66. See Note 64, p. 44.

67. See Note 60.

68. Winter, D. G. (1987). Leader appeal, leader performance, and the motives profile of leaders and followers: A study of American presidents and elections. *Journal of Personality and Social Psychology, 52*, 92–102.

69. Simonton, D. K. (1988). Presidential style: Personality, biography, and performance. *Journal of Personality and Social Psychology, 55*, 928–936.

70. Dansereau, G., Graen, G., & Haga, G. (1975). A vertical dyad linkage approach to leadership within formal organizations: A longitudinal investigation of the role making process. *Organizational Behavior and Human Performance, 13*, 45–78.

71. Nadler, D. A., & Tushman, M. L. (1990). Beyond the charismatic leader: Leadership and organizational change. *California Management Review, 32*(2), 77–97.

72. Graen, G. B., & Scandura, T. A. (1987). Vertical dyad linkages theory of leadership. In A. Kiesler, G. Reber, & R. Wunderer (Eds.), *Encyclopedia of Leadership* (pp. 378–390). Kernerstrasse, FRG: C. E. Paeschel Verlag.

73. Scandura, T. A., & Graen, G. B. (1984). Moderating effects of initial leader-member exchange status on the effects of a leadership intervention. *Journal of Applied Psychology, 69*, 428–436.

74. Lord, R. G., & Maher, K. (1989). Perceptions in leadership and their implications in organizations. In J. Carroll (Ed.), *Applied social psychology and organizational settings* (Vol. 4, pp. 129–154). Hillsdale, NJ: Erlbaum.

75. Henneman, R. L., Greenberg, D. B., & Anonyuo, C. (1989). Attributions and exchanges: The effects of interpersonal factors on the diagnosis of employee performance. *Academy of Management Journal, 32*, 466–476.

76. Mitchell, T. R., & Wood, R. E. (1980). Supervisors' responses to subordinate poor performance: A test of an attribution model. *Organizational Behavior and Human Performance, 25*, 123–138.

77. Kerr, S., & Jermier, J. M. (1978). Substitutes for leadership: Their meaning and measurement. *Organizational Behavior and Human Performance, 22*, 375–403.

78. Sheridan, J. E., Vredenburgh, D. J., & Abelson, M. A. (1984). Contextual model of leadership influence in hospital units. *Academy of Management Journal, 27*, 57–78.

79. Meindl, J. R., & Ehrlich, S. B. (1987). The romance of leadership and the evaluation of organizational performance. *Academy of Management Journal, 30*, 91–109.

80. Hersey, P., & Blanchard, K. (1982). *Management of organizational behavior* (4th ed.). Englewood Cliffs, NJ: Prentice-Hall.

81. Hambleton, R. K., & Gumpert, R. (1982). The validity of Hersey and Blanchard's theory of leader effectiveness. *Group and Organization Studies, 7*, 225–242.

82. Vecchio, R. P. (1987). Situational leadership theory: An examination of a prescriptive theory. *Journal of Applied Psychology, 72*, 444–451.

**Leadership at
Levi Strauss**

Meet Robert D. Haas, chairman and chief executive officer of Levi Strauss and Company, one of this nation's most effective leaders. Haas took over as CEO of Levi Strauss in 1984. Known for its rugged blue jeans, Levi Strauss enjoyed enormous success as it rode the wave of blue jean popularity fueled by post–World War II baby boomers. But by the early 1980s, the company found itself in serious trouble. During the 1970s, it got caught up in the prevailing hysteria to diversify. Levi Strauss acquired new businesses and developed new products that differed from its traditional expertise—making blue jeans.

In an interview, Haas indicates that although Levi Strauss employees went along with corporate efforts to diversify, their hearts were not really in it.[1] By the time Haas took over as CEO, sales were falling and profits were suffering.

To Haas, a former Peace Corps volunteer and the great-great-grandnephew of the company's founder, the problem was obvious. The company needed to identify the values that would guide it into the future. "A company's values—what it stands for, what its people believe in—are crucial to its competitive success," says Haas.[2] Levi Strauss management and employees used to think about the company in terms of "soft stuff" and "hard stuff." Soft stuff refers to how the company treats its employees. But more important was the hard stuff, the actual manufacturing, distributing, and selling of jeans. To Haas, the soft stuff and the hard stuff are so intertwined that they must be treated equally.

Haas believes that "values drive the business."[3] He relies on shared values to guide employee decision making. The pressures of business today no longer allow us to view the employer-employee relationship as one of simple give and take. Employees can no longer expect to think about work only as the process of carrying out the commands of bosses in exchange for the company taking care of them. Today's workers must expect to make decisions for themselves and do whatever is needed to keep the company operating at peak performance.

Haas says that managers, too, must change. They must decentralize decision making throughout the organization and give employees the responsibility, authority, accountability, and skills necessary to make good decisions and act quickly in response to a changing business environment. Their job is to ensure that employees share the values of the company. Says Haas, "Values provide a common language for aligning a company's leadership and its people."[4] Through values alignment, employees are able to make independent decisions that are consistent with the values of the company rather than relying on bosses to tell them what to do.

How does Haas articulate the values of Levi Strauss to its employees? First, he states the company's values and the leadership actions in the "Aspirations Statement."[5] The aspirations statement is conspicuously displayed throughout the company.

Haas relies heavily on manager training to promote understanding and demonstration of Levi Strauss's values. Managers are trained to perform the leadership behaviors specified by the aspirations statement during one-week courses called "leadership weeks." During leadership week, managers are asked to consider their own personal values and how their values compare with Levi Strauss values. Managers most often come to recognize that their personal values are consistent or at least compatible with Levi Strauss values. Haas believes that one's personal values are too established to be changed by any leader but that if people can realize that the company's values are aligned with their own personal values, they will be more committed to helping Levi Strauss achieve its goals.

The training during leadership week clarifies the company's values. By the time the week is over, managers understand what the company's values are and the consequences of failing to act in accordance with these values. All Levi Strauss managers are evaluated on their ability to lead according to the aspirations statement, referred to by Haas as "aspirational" leadership. One-third of a manager's annual raise is based on demonstrating aspirational leadership. Promotion is not possible for managers who fail to lead aspirationally. Some managers cannot honestly agree with the company's values, and they leave Levi Strauss.

"People have unerring detection systems for fakes, and they won't put up with them. They won't put values into practice if you're not."[6] Haas and his managers openly discuss their vulnerabilities and failings with employees. Levi Strauss values innovation, and Haas knows that employees will not innovate if they are afraid to take risks. By admitting his own mistakes and failures, Haas lets everyone know that it's okay to fail. What is important is taking the risks necessary to innovate and taking responsibility for one's own contributions to a problem.

Haas also works hard to solicit the comments and opinions of employees. In 1989, he implemented a three-day course on "valuing diversity." All of the company's 31,000 employees will eventually take this course. According to Haas, the more perspectives you can bring to problem solving, the better the solutions.

His beliefs about leadership go beyond the need to articulate and convey the values of the company. "If the people on the front line really are the keys to our success, then the manager's job is to help those people and the people that they serve."[7] Haas argues that the leader's job is to clear away any obstacles that get in the way of employee performance. He firmly believes that deep down, people want to work to make a real contribution to something.

Haas has found that employees are very idealistic about what they want for the company and for themselves. He encourages their idealism and the realization of their dreams. Levi Strauss's efforts to facilitate the realization of employee ideals has released an incredible amount of power and energy.

How do managers at Levi Strauss go about removing obstacles? First, managers do not control all aspects of their subordinates' work. They set parameters within which employees exercise their own discretion. Some people are more skilled than others, and for those who don't understand how to do something, the leader should provide some form of guidance. The leader must consider each employee as a unique individual with different abilities and then assist the employee in improving his or her skills so that the parameters can be broadened.

Above all else, Haas believes that a leader must be absolutely clear about what is expected of his or her subordinates. This means that leaders must have good interpersonal and communication skills. Leaders must avoid becoming defensive and respect the decision-making authority that employees have been given. In addition, "managers still have to make decisions, serve as counselors and coaches, be there when things get sticky, and help sort out all the tangles."[8]

Haas believes that effective leaders are also concerned about employee well-being. "If [employees] feel supported—not just financially but psychically—then they are going to be more responsive to the needs of customers and of the business."[9] Haas created a task force to examine how Levi Strauss can modify its policies to better support employee efforts to balance their personal needs with work. Haas serves on this committee but does not run it. Employees run the task force because Haas knows that it is the employees who best understand their own needs and goals.

Haas realizes that technology and leadership are highly intertwined. Levi Strauss's LeviLink electronic data interchange system collects and analyzes point-of-sale information from the cash registers of customer stores. Its purpose is to provide information about inventory levels, thereby speeding up the order-replenishment cycle between the company and its customer stores.

LeviLink has dramatically increased the level of employee involvement with customers. Levi Strauss sales and distribution employees now know more about a store's inventory than do the people working in the store. They interpret information for the store owner, and because the information system takes care of most of the product ordering and distribution paperwork, employees now have time to provide a wider range of marketing services to customers.

LeviLink provides a necessary ingredient for effectively empowering employees—the information that employees need to make the decisions delegated to them. Other information technology in use at Levi Strauss is its production scanning system. Levi Strauss's factories contain sewing machines equipped with computers. Every bundle of fabric is identified by a bar code. As a bundle moves through a factory, it is read by a scanner on the sewing machine. The information provided by the scanning system allows employees to identify and solve production problems at their own work stations. The production scanning system, LeviLink, and other technologies have, according to Haas, freed employees to do "what human beings do best—think, plan, interact, see trends, humanize the business to make it more successful."[10] Haas's use of information processing technology has removed numerous obstacles that previously cluttered employee paths to success.

How successful have Haas's leadership actions been? During the first five years under Haas's leadership, Levi Strauss sales increased 31 percent (to $3.6 billion) and profits soared $272 million, a 500 percent increase. But perhaps the best measure of Haas's leadership is the feeling that now permeates the company. Says Haas, "Suddenly this $4 billion company feels like an owner-operated company, which is the goal."[11]

Questions for Discussion

1. Is Robert Haas a leader or a manager? Haas uses the terms interchangeably to describe his management personnel. What does this tell you about Haas's philosophy of management?
2. Haas is considered by many to be a transformational leader. Why? How does Haas articulate and convey the guiding values of Levi Strauss to its employees?
3. Using the leader behavior approach to leadership, describe Haas's leadership behavior.
4. Describe Haas's leadership behavior in terms of the path-goal theory.
5. According to Vroom and Yetton's normative theory, which decision strategies does Haas use?
6. What substitutes for leadership does Haas use at Levi Strauss?
7. Describe Levi Strauss's "aspirational" leadership. How is this type of leadership similar to other approaches to leadership that you have studied?

Notes

1. Howard, R. (1990, September–October). Values make the company: An interview with Robert Haas. *Harvard Business Review*, pp. 133–144.
2. See Note 1, p. 134.
3. See Note 1, p. 134.
4. See Note 1, p. 134.
5. See Note 1, p. 135.
6. See Note 1, p. 139.
7. See Note 1, p. 134.
8. See Note 1, p. 136.
9. See Note 1, p. 138.
10. See Note 1, p. 137.
11. See Note 1, p. 142.

This is a group exercise, so enlist the aid of two or three friends. Then, work together as described below. Your task is to identify *three great leaders*. These leaders can be historical figures from out of the past, or they can be people alive now. You can select your *great leaders* from any sphere of human activity:

**In Search of
Great Leaders**

- Politics
- Military
- Sports
- Business
- Science/Medicine
- Religion

After your group has agreed on three leaders, do the following.

Procedure

1. Indicate why each leader can be considered great—what did each do, what did he or she accomplish? Note: *great* does not necessarily mean *good*.

   Leader 1:

   Leader 2:

   Leader 3:

2. Now, indicate whether you think these people would have been great leaders at any time in history, in any culture, and in the face of any set of circumstances. Defend your decision.

   Leader 1:

   Leader 2:

   Leader 3:

Points to Consider

1. Do the leaders you identified as being great have any traits or characteristics in common? The chances are good that they do, for as noted earlier in this chapter, all transformational or charismatic leaders do seem to share some key characteristics.
2. Assuming such traits or skills *are* crucial for effective leadership, do you think they can be trained? In other words, can almost any individual be taught, through appropriate procedures, to be a great leader?

■ 13 ■

COMMUNICATION IN ORGANIZATIONS

CHAPTER OUTLINE

Communication: Its Basic Nature
    Communication: A Working Definition and a
      Model
    Forms of Communication: Verbal and Nonverbal
Major Influences on Organizational
Communication
    Organizational Structure: Directing the Flow of
      Messages
    Communication Networks: Formal Channels of
      Communication in Groups
    Informal Communication Networks: A Small
      World
    Communication and the Work Environment:
      Technology and Office Design
Overcoming Communication Barriers: Enhancing
the Flow of Information

Becoming a Better Communicator: Individual
    Strategies
Improving Communication on the Job:
    Organizational Strategies

Special Sections

OB in Practice   Layoffs at Middlebury College:
How *Not* to Communicate Bad News

A Question of Ethics   Privacy Rights and
E-Mail: Should Employers Have Access to
Employees' Electronic Mailboxes?

Focus on Research   How to Communicate with
Employees about a Merger

LEARNING OBJECTIVES

After reading this chapter, you should be able to:
1. Define the process of communication and describe its major forms.
2. Identify and describe the most prevalent nonverbal communication cues operating in organizations.
3. Distinguish between messages that are best communicated in written and spoken forms.
4. Describe how the formal structure of an organization influences the nature of the communication that occurs within it.
5. Distinguish between centralized and decentral-

ized communication networks with respect to their relative superiority in performing different tasks.
6. Describe how informal patterns of communication operate within organizations.
7. Understand the impact of technology and of the physical layout of offices on communication between people within and between offices.
8. Identify and describe measures that can be taken by individuals and by organizations to improve communication effectiveness.

F ew American citizens are more proud than Maria Sanchez. Having grown up in a poor, rural Mexican village, she is now a department manager at Desert Power and Light, one of the fastest-growing utility companies in the United States. And based on the performance evaluation interview she is having with her boss, Dan Haskins, she is obviously doing quite well.

"You're clearly a fast-tracker, Maria," says Dan, "exactly the kind of employee we like around here. You have great technical skills and you're highly motivated. No one works harder for the company than you do."

"Thank you very much, Dan," replies Maria. "That means a great deal coming from you."

"There's only one small matter," Dan adds. "You have a communication problem. It's nothing serious, mind you, but you do have to work on it."

Dan's intercom buzzes, interrupting them. It's the receptionist, informing Dan that he must leave right away for an important meeting with the Utilities Commission.

Hearing this, Maria immediately stands up and gathers her things to leave. Dan extends his hand and shakes Maria's hand firmly as they walk toward the door. "As you heard," he says, "I've got to go now. Again, you're doing a terrific job, just work on that communication problem and you'll be fine. We'll talk about it more at your next evaluation session, six months from now."

As she walks back to her desk, Maria thinks about Dan's remarks. She is truly pleased that her hard work has been appreciated. Optimistic about her future with the company, now she wants to please him more than ever. "I'll show him," she thinks aloud. "I'll work on that communication problem."

Although Maria is proud of her Mexican heritage, she knows that she speaks with an accent, which sometimes makes her feel a bit self-conscious. As a result, she frequently refrains from making presentations with all the poise and confidence that her superior skills and knowledge merit.

Determined to turn things around, she goes on an all-out campaign to improve herself. She hires a private English tutor and takes classes in English composition and public speaking at a local community college—all at considerable personal expense. As a result of these efforts, it soon becomes clear to everyone at Desert Power and Light that Maria has become a poised and polished communicator. Now, instead of shyly hiding in the corner at meetings, she always sits up front and confidently speaks her mind.

As the time approaches for Maria's next performance evaluation interview with Dan, she is certain that it will go quite well. Indeed, when they meet, Dan is quick to detail all the leadership skills that Maria has demonstrated lately. "Maria," he says, "there's no doubt that you're one of the best managers we have here at Desert. You really know what you're doing, and you've emerged into a real take-charge person—the kind who could eventually become a vice president."

Maria blushes, but she is beaming inside. She knows she has worked hard, and the recognition feels good.

"There's only one thing," Dan adds, "and I believe we spoke about it before."

"What's that, sir?" Maria questions formally.

"Well, Maria, it's that communication thing again. You still have a problem in that area."

Hearing this, Maria becomes confused and exasperated. She explains about all the courses she has taken off the job, and all the things she has done on the job to demonstrate her new communication skills. She can't figure out what Dan wants and is noticeably upset.

"Whoa, calm down," Dan interjects. "I'm not complaining about how you speak or write. You're as good as they come. In fact, you were even a good speaker and writer before taking all your classes."

"Well, then, what is it?" she asks. "You said I had a communication problem."

"Yes, you see, by that I meant that you were not sending me copies of your correspondence for our files. For years, department heads around here have been routinely 'cc-ing' their supervisors on important letters, and I've not been getting yours. That's your communication problem, Maria."

Frustrated, yet relieved, Maria doesn't know whether to laugh or cry. Pleased that the true problem is only minor, she is distressed that she wasted too much time and money working on something that was just fine. Still, she feels that her efforts were worthwhile and that she is now a very good communicator.

"No problem," says Maria as she composes herself. "From now on, I'll see to it that you get copies of all the correspondence coming from my office."

The irony of this story, of course, is that it was not Maria, but Dan who had "the communication problem." By being so ambiguous about what he had in mind—in part because he didn't have time to explain it—Dan failed to communicate the message he meant to send. This caused Maria to take the wrong corrective actions, which might have proved a waste of time. However, if one thinks about Maria's communication skills relative to those of Dan, her efforts might not represent such a waste of time after all. Indeed, the indirect effect of Dan's ambiguous directive may have been to select his own replacement. We'll leave it to you to decide how this story plays out, but its moral is clear: accurate communication is a critical element of effective organizational functioning.

Communication is considered a key process underlying all aspects of organizational operations.[1] In fact, research has shown that employees' overall performance assessments tend to be highly related to their competence as communicators.[2] Contemporary scholars have variously referred to organizational communication as "the social glue . . . that continues to keep the organization tied together,"[3] and "the essence of organization."[4] Writing many years earlier, well-known management theorist and former New Jersey Bell Telephone president Chester Barnard said, "The structure, extensiveness and scope of the organization are almost entirely determined by communication techniques."[5] This strong statement makes sense if you consider that supervisors spend as much as 80 percent of their workdays engaging in some form of communication, such as speaking or listening to others, or writing to and reading material from others.[6] Clearly, the process of communication is a very basic one with which we must be concerned in the study of organizational behavior.

Given the importance of communication in organizations, we will examine this process very closely in this chapter. First, we will carefully define communication and describe a basic *model of communication*—a framework for describing its fundamental steps. We will also review some of the most basic forms the communication process takes in organizations. Second, we will examine several of the major *influences on communication*—aspects of the social and work environments that shape the nature and direction of the flow of information. Finally, we will turn to several *barriers to effective communication* and consider techniques for overcoming them.

COMMUNICATION: ITS BASIC NATURE

Before we can fully appreciate the process of organizational communication, we need to address some basic issues. To begin, we will formally define what we mean by communication and then elaborate on the process by which it occurs. Following this, we will describe the various forms organizational communication may take.

Communication: A Working Definition and a Model

What do the following situations have in common? Your boss issues a memo limiting all employees' coffee breaks to ten minutes. A junior executive prepares and submits a report about the financial status of a potential corporate takeover prospect. The dispatcher of a taxi company directs Cab 706 to pick up a fare at 74 Cherry Drive. A foreman smiles at one of his workers and gives him a pat on the back in exchange for a job well done. You probably realize that each of these incidents involves some form of communication. Although most of us already have a good idea of what communication entails, we could better understand communication in organizations by more closely examining the meaning of the term.

With this in mind, we may define **communication** as *the process by which a person, group, or organization (the sender) transmits some type of information (the message) to another person, group, or organization (the receiver)*. To clarify this definition, and to further elaborate on how the process works, we have summarized the communication process in the model shown in Figure 13–1 (see p. 490). Refer to this diagram as we describe the various components of the model.

The process begins when one party has an idea that it wishes to transmit to another (either party may be an individual, a group, or an entire organization). It is the sender's mission to transform the idea into a form that can be sent to and understood by the intended *receiver*. This is what happens in the process of **encoding**—translating the idea into a form that can be recognized by the receiver, such as written or spoken language. We encode information when we select the words we use to write a letter or speak to someone in person. This process is critical if we hope to adequately communicate our ideas. Yet, the difficulty we all sometimes have thinking about the best way to say something suggests that our capacity to encode messages is far from perfect. As we will see later in this chapter, limitations in people's abilities to accurately encode their ideas are a serious weakness in the communication process, but, fortunately, one that can be corrected.

After a message is encoded, it is ready to be transmitted over one or more *channels of communication* to reach the intended receiver. These may be understood as pathways along which encoded information is transmitted. Telephone lines, radio and television signals, fiber-optic cables, mail routes, and even the air waves that

Managers need good communication skills, both oral and written, to be effective on the job. Unfortunately, many managers are poor communicators. Robert Lefton, president of the Psychological Associates consulting firm, estimates that only 10 percent of corporate executives are effective communicators, talking candidly with employees and encouraging them to contribute ideas. Businesses have also been complaining that new M.B.A.s lack adequate communication skills and have to be trained on the job by their organizations. As a result, many business schools have added communication courses to their M.B.A. programs to train students in these important job skills. [Rice, F. (1991, June 3). Champions of communication. *Fortune*, pp. 111–120; Fowler, E. M. (1992, February 11). Careers: Special training for MBAs. *The New York Times*, p. D11(L).]

Test Bank questions 13.1–13.4, 13.46, 13.56, and 13.66 relate to material on this page.

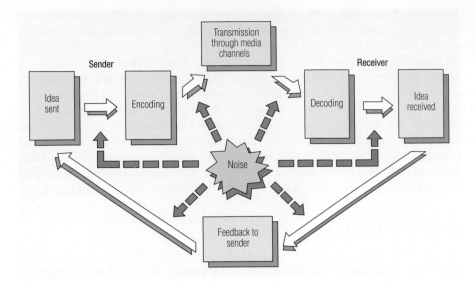

FIGURE 13-1   Communication: A Basic Model

In its most basic form, communication consists of the distinct steps shown here. First, a *sender* desires to make an idea known to a *receiver* (either party may be an individual, a group, or an organization). The idea must be *encoded*—converted into a form that can be transmitted (e.g., the written or spoken word). This message is then sent via one of several communication channels (e.g., telephone, and/or letter) to the receiver. This receiver must then *decode* the message—convert it back into an understandable idea. This idea may then be returned to the sender in the form of *feedback*. The model also recognizes that *noise,* factors distorting or limiting the flow of information, may enter into the process at any of several points.

carry the vibrations of our voices all represent potential channels of communication. Of course, the form of encoding largely determines the way information may be transmitted. Visual information—such as pictures and written words—may be mailed, delivered in person by a courier, shipped by an express delivery service, or, with increasing popularity, sent and received by fax machines and satellite dishes (see Figure 13–2). Oral information may be transmitted over the telephone, via radio and television waves, and of course the old-fashioned way—in person. (As we will see in the next section, the choice of a communication medium depends not only on the type of encoding used, but also on the nature of the message itself.) Whatever channel is used, the goal is to send the encoded message accurately to the desired receiver.

You will recall that the *receiver* is the desired target of a message, be it another person, group, organization, or even a computer. Once the message is received, the recipient must begin the process of **decoding**—converting the message back into ideas. This can involve many different subprocesses, such as comprehending spoken and written words, interpreting facial expressions, and the like. To the extent that the sender's message is accurately decoded by the receiver, the ideas understood will be the ones intended. Of course, our ability to accurately comprehend and interpret information received from others may be imperfect (e.g., restricted by unclear messages, or by the language skills of the receiver). Thus, as in the case of encoding, limitations in our ability to decode information represent another potential weakness in the communication process. Fortunately, as we will describe later in this chapter, the necessary skills may be improved.

FIGURE 13-2   Communication Media: Just Some of Many Forms

Fax machines and satellite dishes, once breakthrough communication technologies, are now commonly used to transmit and receive messages.

Finally, once a message has been decoded, the process can be reversed so that the receiver transmits a message back to the original sender. This is known as *feedback*—knowledge about the impact of messages on receivers. Receiving feedback allows senders to determine whether their messages have been understood and had the desired effects. At the same time, giving feedback can help convince receivers that the sender (e.g., a manager) really cares about what he or she has to say. Once received, feedback can trigger another idea from the sender, and another cycle of transferring information may begin. For this reason, we have characterized the process of communication summarized in Figure 13–1 as continuous.

Despite the apparent simplicity of the communication process, it rarely operates as flawlessly as we have described it here. As we will see, there are many potential barriers to effective communication. The name given to factors that distort the clarity of a message is **noise.** As we have shown in Figure 13–1, noise can occur at any point along the communication process. For example, messages that are poorly encoded (e.g., written in an unclear way) or poorly decoded (e.g., not comprehended), or channels of communication that are too full of static, may reduce communication's effectiveness. These factors, and others (e.g., time pressure, organizational politics), may contribute to the distortion of information transmitted from one party to another.

Organizational communication is really much more complex than we have described it here. In any organization, the process of encoding, transmitting, decoding, and sending feedback is likely to take place simultaneously among many people and groups at once. Furthermore, differences in communicators' authority levels, the purpose of the communication, management philosophy, limitations imposed by marketing considerations, and legal constraints are just a few of the many factors that make the process of communication so complicated. Organizational communication goes beyond simple words and messages alone, but also has to do with the meanings given those words and messages by the environments within which they occur.[7] In other words, it is important to consider the culture within which messages are communicated, because the culture may alter or qualify the meaning of the messages. For example, whereas diamond brokers in New York City are content to make multimillion-dollar deals on the basis of a handshake alone (because in that

Test Bank question 13.6 relates to material on this page.

culture an atmosphere of trust exists), the culture of most other businesses typically requires the use of more formal safeguards, such as written agreements.

Clearly, a great deal more is involved than just the simple transfer of information. As you continue reading this chapter, you will come to appreciate many of the factors that make the process of organizational communication so complex and so important.

Forms of Communication: Verbal and Nonverbal

As we have suggested, organizational communication can take several forms. It is obvious that we transfer information when we write to others and when we speak to them. Although sometimes less obvious, we also communicate *nonverbally*, through our gestures, our posture, the clothes we wear, the way we use time, the physical distances we keep from others, and so on.

Verbal Communication: Speaking with Words   Because you are reading this book, we know you are familiar with verbal communication—transmitting and receiving ideas using words. Verbal communication can be either *oral*, using spoken language in forms such as face-to-face talks, telephone conversations, tape recordings, and the like, or *written*, in forms such as memos, letters, order blanks, and electronic mail, to name just a few. Because both oral and written communications involve the use of words, they fall under the heading of verbal communications.

What types of verbal communication are most effective? Research has shown that reports written by hand and those composed at a word processor are relatively similar in most aspects of writing quality.[8] Where differences were found, they were inconsistent. Specifically, whereas handwritten reports contained more punctuation errors, they tended to be somewhat easier to read (using a standardized readability index). Thus, important differences as a function of the technology used in written communication have not been found. It has been established, however, that communication is most effective when it uses two different channels, such as oral messages and written ones. Specifically, supervisors believe that communication is most effective when oral messages are followed by written ones.[9] This combination is especially preferred under several conditions: when immediate action is required, an important policy change is being made, a praiseworthy employee is identified, and a company directive or order is announced. When the information to be communicated is of a general nature, or requires only future action, written forms are judged to be most effective.

Apparently, the oral message is useful in getting others' immediate attention, and the follow-up written portion helps make the message more permanent, something that can be referred to in the future. Oral messages also have the benefit of allowing for immediate two-way communication between parties, whereas written communiqués are frequently only one-way (or take too long for a response if they are two-way). Not surprisingly, researchers have found that two-way communications (e.g., face-to-face discussions, telephone conversations) are more commonly used in organizations than one-way communications (e.g., memos). For example, Klauss and Bass found that approximately 83 percent of the communications taking place among civilian employees of a U.S. Navy agency used two-way media.[10] In fact, 55 percent of all communications were individual face-to-face interactions. One-way, written communications tended to be reserved for more formal, official messages that needed to be referred to in the future at the receiver's convenience (e.g., official announcements about position openings). Apparently, both written and spoken communications have their place in organizational communication.

What factors determine when each of these forms of communication will be used? Recent research has shown that the choice of a communication medium greatly depends on a very important factor—the degree of clarity or ambiguity of the message being sent. Specifically, studying this factor, Daft, Lengel, and Trevino reasoned that oral media (e.g., telephone conversations, face-to-face meetings) are preferable to written media (e.g., notes, memos) when messages are ambiguous (requiring a great deal of assistance in interpreting them), whereas written media are preferable when messages are clear.[11] The researchers surveyed a sample of managers about the medium they preferred using to communicate messages that differed with respect to their clarity or ambiguity. (For example, "giving a subordinate a set of cost figures" was prejudged to be a very unambiguous type of message, whereas "getting an explanation about a complicated technical matter" was prejudged to be a very ambiguous type of message.) The results, summarized in Figure 13–3, show that the choice of medium was related to the clarity or ambiguity of the messages.

These data reveal two interesting trends. First, the more ambiguous the message, the more managers preferred using oral media (such as telephones or face-to-face contact). Second, the clearer the message, the more managers preferred using written media (such as letters or memos). Apparently, most managers were sensitive to the need to use communications media that allowed them to take advantage of the rich avenues for two-way oral communications when necessary, and to use the more efficient one-way, written communications when these were adequate.

Note, however, that whereas many managers selected media based on the pattern described here (those identified as being "media sensitive"), others did not. They made their media choices almost randomly (this group was identified as being "media insensitive"). Further analysis of the data revealed that these differences were related to the managers' job performance. Those who were media sensitive were expected to be more effective than those who were media insensitive. After all, effective

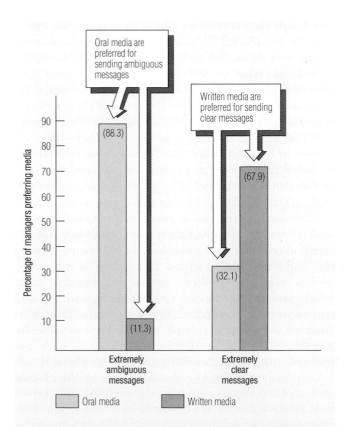

FIGURE 13–3

Oral or Written Communication? Matching the Medium to the Message

What type of communications medium do managers prefer using? The research findings reviewed here show that it depends on the degree of clarity or ambiguity of the message. Oral media (e.g., telephones or face-to-face contact) were preferred for ambiguous messages; written media (e.g., letters or memos) were preferred for clear messages. (*Source:* Based on data in Daft, Lengel, & Trevino, 1987; see Note 11.)

Test Bank questions 13.9–13.10, 13.47, and 13.58 relate to material on this page.

communication is an important part of managers' activities, and using the appropriate medium could enhance their effectiveness. Comparisons of the performance ratings of managers in the media-sensitive and media-insensitive groups supported this hypothesis. Specifically, whereas most of the media-sensitive managers (87 percent) received their company's highest performance ratings, only about half of the media-insensitive managers (47 percent) received equally high evaluations.

Apparently, the skill of selecting the appropriate communications medium is an important aspect of a manager's success. Unfortunately, it is difficult to say whether the managers' choices of communications media were directly responsible for their success, or whether their media sensitivity was part of an overall set of managerial skills that together led to their success. Still, these findings highlight the importance of making appropriate media choices in successful managerial communication.

It would be misleading to conclude this section with the idea that managerial communication occurs only at the verbal level. Although words are a very important part of communication, of course, they represent only one way of transmitting messages. Many messages in organizations are also communicated in the absence of words—that is, nonverbally.

Nonverbal Communication: Speaking without Words   As we have already noted in chapter 2, nonverbal cues represent an important source of information influencing our impressions of people. Others' smiles and eye contact tend to enhance our positive feelings about them. Here we will describe how other nonverbal cues may provide useful vehicles of communication. Simply put, **nonverbal communication** refers to the transmission of messages without the use of words. Some of the most prevalent nonverbal communication cues in organizations have to do with manners of dress and the uses of time and space.

Style of Dress.   If you have ever heard the expression "The clothes make the man," you are probably already aware of the importance of mode of dress as a communication vehicle. This is especially the case in organizations where, as self-styled "wardrobe engineer" John T. Malloy reminds us, what we wear communicates a great deal about our competence as employees.[12] Organizational researchers are becoming increasingly aware of the importance of style of dress as a communication vehicle. Consider, for example, a study by Forsythe, Drake, and Cox, who showed videotapes[13] of women dressed in one of four costumes to a group of personnel administrators. The costumes differed with respect to how masculine they were perceived to be by a panel of judges (the clothes ranged from a very masculine navy tailored business suit to a more feminine beige dress in a soft fabric). The personnel administrators were asked to view the applicants in their various costumes and rank how likely they would be to hire each one. The woman dressed in the most feminine costume was found the least likely to be hired. However, the most likely hired candidate was *not* the one wearing the most masculine costume, but something in between—a beige tailored suit with a blazer jacket and a rust blouse with a narrow bow at the neck.

Although these findings are interesting, it would be unwise to generalize them to other situations. In other words, women, please don't automatically rush out and buy this outfit, thinking it might be your key to success! As you might imagine, what we communicate by the clothing we wear is not a simple matter. We cannot make up for the absence of critical job skills simply by putting on the right clothes. People who are qualified for jobs, however, may communicate certain things about themselves by the way they dress. Clearly, one of the key messages sent by the clothes people wear is their understanding of the appropriate way of presenting themselves for the job. In general, the most positive images are communicated when someone is dressed appropriately for the occasion. An important reason for this appears to be

Four main types of nonverbal communication are often used in organizations. *Emblems* are common gestures used to stand for words, such as telling your boss that something is "okay" by holding up an open hand with the tips of the thumb and index finger touching each other. *Illustrators* accompany and complement spoken language, such as a professor holding up and pointing to a textbook and saying, "Here's your assignment!" *Regulators* help control the pace of speech, such as students nodding when they agree with a professor's lecture, or students looking out the window when they lose interest. *Affect displays* are body cues that indicate one's emotions, such as sticking out your tongue at your manager when you are upset with him or her. [Goldhaber, G. M. (1983). *Organizational communication.* Dubuque, IA: Wm. C. Brown.]

that people who are dressed just right for an occasion tend to feel better about themselves; they have higher levels of self-confidence. For example, in one study, student job candidates appeared for an interview wearing either their informal street clothes (e.g., T-shirts and jeans) or more formal garb (e.g., suits with shirts and ties). Those who wore the more formal clothing not only felt they made a more positive impression than those dressed less appropriately, but also tended to express this more positive self-image by requesting a starting annual salary that was, on average, $4,000 higher.[14] Apparently, then, clothing may be a powerful communication vehicle not only because of what it connotes about the wearer, but also because it changes the feelings and self-perceptions of the wearer.

Time: The Waiting Game. As we have noted, another important mechanism of nonverbal communication in organizations is the use of time. Indeed, the way we use time says a great deal about us. Have you ever waited for hours in the outer office of a doctor or dentist? Surely you have—after all, they have special "waiting rooms" just for this purpose! Why do you have to wait for such people? Mainly because they have special skills that put high demands on their services. Their time is organized in a manner that is most efficient for them—by keeping others lined up to see them.

Medical professionals are not the only ones who make people wait to see them. In fact, individuals in high-status positions often communicate the idea that their time is more valuable than others' (and therefore that they hold higher-status positions) by making others wait to see them. This is a very subtle, but important, form of nonverbal communication. Typically, the longer you have to wait to see someone, the higher the organizational status that person has attained. This has been shown in a study by Greenberg.[15] Participants in this investigation were applicants for a job as office manager at various companies who awaited interviews with people of higher status (vice presidents), lower status (assistant office managers), or equal status (another office manager). As summarized in Figure 13–4, the higher the status of the person job candidates waited to see, the longer they had to wait.

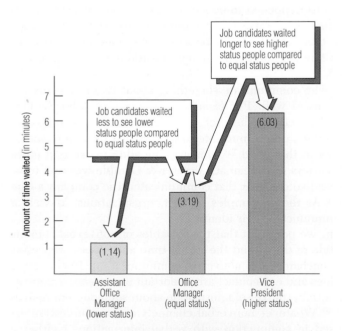

Person waiting to see for interview

FIGURE 13–4

Communicating Status through Time Delays: The Organizational Waiting Game

Research has shown that the higher another's status relative to oneself, the more one has to wait to see that person. These findings suggest that the use of time is a nonverbal mechanism for communicating one's organizational status. (*Source:* Based on data reported in Greenberg, 1989; see Note 15.)

Test Bank question 13.13 relates to material on this page.

The vice president interviewers communicated their higher status to the candidates by making them wait to see them. In contrast, assistant office manager interviewers communicated their lower status to candidates by being prompt—an act conveying deference and respect. Interviewers communicated their liking for prospective employees (whose application files they studied in advance) by not making them wait. Candidates who were subsequently hired had to wait less time to see their future bosses than those who were not hired. Apparently, interviewers wanted to communicate their liking for the most desirable candidates by treating them politely and not making them wait. If time is viewed as a resource, its use as a symbol of organizational status is not surprising. Important people can communicate their status nonverbally by making others wait for them. Hence, the use of time is an important mechanism of nonverbal communication in organizations.

People are concerned about the amount of personal space they maintain around their bodies, especially when space is limited, such as on a crowded elevator. The study of the use of space is called *proxemics*. According to E. T. Hall, in the United States there are four main zones of personal space: *intimate* (touching to about 18 inches); *personal* (18 inches to 4 feet); *social,* or "cocktail party," distance (4 to 12 feet); and *public* (12 to 15 feet or more). The norms of proxemics vary from culture to culture. For example, whereas Middle Easterners stand very close to others, Northern Europeans tend to position themselves more distantly. Amusingly, when an American and a Middle Eastern businessman have a conversation they can often be seen "dancing" around the room as the American backs up to increase the personal distance while the Middle Easterner moves forward to reduce the distance. [Goldhaber, G. M. (1983). *Organizational communication*. Dubuque, IA: Wm. C. Brown; Hall, E. T. (1959). *The hidden dimension*. New York: Doubleday.]

The Use of Space: What Does It Say about You? Like time, space is another important communication vehicle. Research has shown that one's organizational status is communicated by the amount of space at one's disposal. The more space one commands, the more powerful one is likely to be in an organization. For example, research has shown that higher-status life insurance underwriters have larger desks and larger offices than lower-status underwriter trainees.[16] Not only the amount of space communicates organizational status, but also the way that space is arranged. For example, among faculty members at a small college, senior professors were more likely to arrange their offices so as to separate themselves from visitors with their desks, whereas junior professors were less likely to impose such physical barriers. These various office arrangements systematically communicated different things about the occupants. Specifically, professors who did not distance themselves from their students by use of their desks were seen as more open and unbiased in their dealing with students than those who used their desks as a physical barrier.

The use of space appears to have symbolic value in communicating something about group interaction. Consider who usually sits at the head of a rectangular table. In most cases, it is the group leader. It is, in fact, traditional for leaders to do so. But at the same time, studies have shown that people emerging as the leaders of groups tend to be ones who just happened to be sitting at the table heads.[17] Apparently, where a person sits influences the available communication possibilities. Sitting at the head of a rectangular table enables a person to see everyone else and to be seen by them. That leaders tend to emerge from such positions is, therefore, not surprising (see Figure 13–5).

It is not only individuals who communicate something about themselves by the use of space, but organizations as well. For example, according to John Sculley, former president of PepsiCo (and current head of Apple Computer), his company's world headquarters were designed to communicate to visitors that they were seeing "the most important company in the world."[18] Similarly, by adding a second office tower to its company headquarters in Cincinnati, Procter & Gamble was said to be attempting to create a gatewaylike complex that communicated the company's connection to the community.[19] As these examples suggest, organizations, as well as individuals, use space to communicate their identities.

In concluding this section, we point out that the variables of nonverbal communication presented here—style of dress, and the use of time and space—represent only some of the important mechanisms of nonverbal communication. In chapter 2, we noted that facial expressions and eye contact are important cues to our emotional states. Indeed, they are also useful sources of information about someone's perceived suitability for employment.[20] Whatever nonverbal channels of communication are employed, they are also used in conjunction with verbal information. Neither is

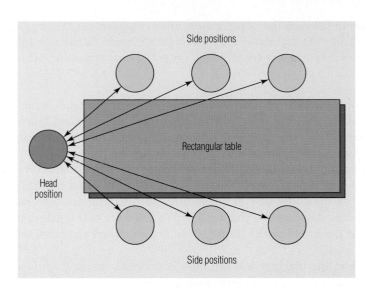

FIGURE 13–5

Head of the Table: A Good Location for Communication

In part because of the ease with which they can see others and be seen by them, people who sit at the heads of rectangular tables enjoy effective communication with others seated at the sides.

isolated; both work together as vehicles of communication in organizations. As you might imagine, verbal and nonverbal cues don't always provide consistent information. In such cases, which message form is given greater attention? Recent research suggests that people tend to rely on nonverbal, rather than verbal, cues when the two are incongruent, seemingly because they believe the nonverbal information is harder to disguise and therefore provides a better indication of one's true feelings.[21] In fact, people who believe they are particularly good decoders of messages on the job tend to pay especially careful attention to nonverbal cues. Obviously, nonverbal information is of prime importance in organizational communication.

MAJOR INFLUENCES ON ORGANIZATIONAL COMMUNICATION

It is a fact of life on the job that everyone engages in communication. Yet, whom we communicate with and how we do so vary considerably from person to person, from job to job, and from organization to organization. The communication process is influenced by many factors. For example, formal organizational rules require some people to communicate with others, although informal patterns of communication also tend to develop in organizations. The way we communicate is also affected by external factors such as the kinds of technology used on the job and the way offices are laid out. Because such factors can be important, we will now describe some of these key influences on organizational communication.

Organizational Structure: Directing the Flow of Messages

Although the basic process of communication as we have described it thus far is similar in many different social contexts, a unique feature of organizations has a profound impact on the communication process—namely, their structure. Organizations are often designed in ways that dictate who may and may not communicate with whom. Given this, we may ask: how is the communication process affected by the structure of an organization? To begin, we must first specify what is meant by **organizational structure.** We use this term to refer to the *formally prescribed pattern*

In Japan, cultural norms dictate the appropriate language used by businesspeople. From an early age, Japanese males are taught a rough, masculine way of expressing themselves, whereas Japanese females are taught a more polite, feminine form. This training is carried over into businesses. For example, a businessman would say, "It's cold, I say!" whereas a businesswoman would say, "It's cold, don't you think?" The use of male language is particularly troublesome for Japanese women in high-level roles. This is because they are traditionally trained to use female language but find themselves being taken less seriously than males when using female language in business settings. Some female Japanese executives are still trying to use female language because they don't believe that women have to use male language to be successful in Japan. [Rudolph, E. (1991, September 1). Women's talk. *The New York Times Magazine*, p. 8.]

of interrelationships existing between the various units of an organization. Although we will have a great deal more to say about organizational structure in chapter 15, here we describe the many important ways in which organizational structure influences communication.

Organizational Structure: Its Impact on Communication   An organization's structure may be described using a diagram referred to as an **organizational chart.** Such a diagram provides a graphic representation of an organization's structure. It may be likened to an X ray of an organization, a drawing that shows the planned, formal connections between its various units.[22] An organizational chart showing the structure of part of a fictitious organization is shown in Figure 13–6. (Keep in mind that this diagram represents only one possible way of structuring an organization. Several other possibilities are described in detail in chapter 15.) We will refer to this diagram to make several important points about the impact of an organization's structure on the flow of information.

Note the various boxes in the diagram and the lines connecting them. Each box represents an organizational unit—a person performing a specific job. The diagram shows the titles of the individuals performing the various jobs and the formally prescribed pattern of communication between them. These are relatively fixed and defined. Each individual is responsible for performing a certain job, playing a certain role. Should the people working in the organization leave their jobs, they must be replaced if their jobs are to be done. The key point is that the formal structure of an organization does not change just because the personnel changes. This is what keeps organizations stable and predictable. For example, the structure of the U.S. government does not change whenever a new president is elected. It remains the same even though new individuals may occupy the various positions.

The lines connecting the boxes in the organizational chart are lines of authority showing who must answer to whom. Each person is responsible to (or answers to) the person at the next higher level to which he or she is connected. At the same time, people are also responsible for (or give orders to) those who are immediately below them. The boxes and lines form a sort of blueprint of an organization showing not only what people have to do, but with whom they have to communicate for the organization to operate properly.

FIGURE 1 3 – 6

An Organizational Chart: A Map of an Organization's Formal Communication Networks

An *organizational chart* indicates the formally prescribed patterns of communication in an organization. Shown here is part of an organizational chart for one branch of a hypothetical manufacturing company.

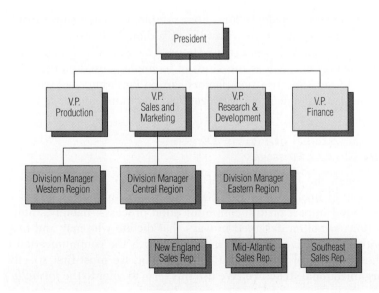

The organizational chart in Figure 13–6 makes it clear that people may be differentiated with respect to their levels in the organization's *hierarchy*. In other words, not all people are at the same level; some are higher up in terms of the formal organizational power they wield (e.g., the company president), and others are lower down (e.g., department managers). Such differences in one's level in an organizational hierarchy may be communicated in various ways. For example, people at higher levels tend to be called by their titles (e.g., "Mr. Chairman"), and are usually addressed in a formal manner. Such individuals may also communicate their higher positions by the way they dress (e.g., formal as opposed to informal attire) and by the size and location of their offices in the corporate complex. Indeed, differences in organizational level are communicated in many different ways.

That individuals are connected to each other by formal lines of communication can have important influences on organizational functioning. For example, it has been demonstrated that the more employees are integrated into an organization's formal structure, the better they adapt to using new technology.[23] If you consider that "being connected" to others promotes opportunities to learn, these findings should not be surprising. However, when formality is so great that individuals are denied opportunities to communicate their desires regarding the organization's operations, they tend to experience negative reactions such as stress, emotional exhaustion, and low levels of job satisfaction and commitment.[24] Such findings do not suggest that formal organizational structures are necessarily problematic—indeed, they are in many ways absolutely necessary for organizations to operate effectively.

Establishing formal communication channels, especially when companies are very large and have operations scattered all over the world, is critical. This is the case among *multinational corporations*—organizations that have operations in various countries. In some cases, these can be very extensive, such as in the case of N. V. Philips, an enormous multinational corporation headquartered in the Netherlands.[25] As shown in Figure 13–7 (see p. 500), this company's operations require intricate communication linkages between people in many different nations. Philips, and other large multinationals, such as U.S.-based Procter & Gamble, and Japan-based Matsushita Electric, face difficult communication challenges in view of the cultural and geographic barriers that must be confronted for them to survive.

Communicating Up, Down, and Across the Organizational Chart As you might imagine, the nature and form of communication vary greatly as a function of people's relative positions within an organization. Even a quick look at an organizational chart reveals that information may flow up (from lower to higher levels), down (from higher to lower levels), or horizontally (between people at the same level). However, as summarized in Figure 13–8 (see p. 501), different types of information typically travel in different directions within a hierarchy.

Imagine that you are a supervisor. What types of messages do you think would characterize communication between you and your subordinates? Typically, *downward communication* consists of instructions, directions, and orders—messages telling subordinates what they should be doing.[26] We would also expect to find feedback on past performance flowing in a downward direction (such as when managers tell subordinates how well they have been working). A vice president of sales, for example, might direct members of her sales force to promote a certain product among their customers, and she may then congratulate them for being successful in doing so.

Despite the fact that superiors mean to communicate certain information to their subordinates, the subordinates do not always accurately perceive their superiors' messages. This phenomenon was demonstrated in a recent questionnaire study by Schnake and his associates.[27] These researchers surveyed a large group of managers

FIGURE 13-7

Communication
Connections between
Subunits at N. V. Philips

As you might imagine,
the communication
linkages between
subunits of large
multinational
corporations, such as
N. V. Philips, can be
quite intricate. Circle
sizes are drawn in
proportion to the
relative number of
communications sent
and received. (*Source:*
From Ghoshal &
Bartlett, 1990; see Note
25. Reprinted by
permission of the
*Academy of
Management Review*
and the authors.)

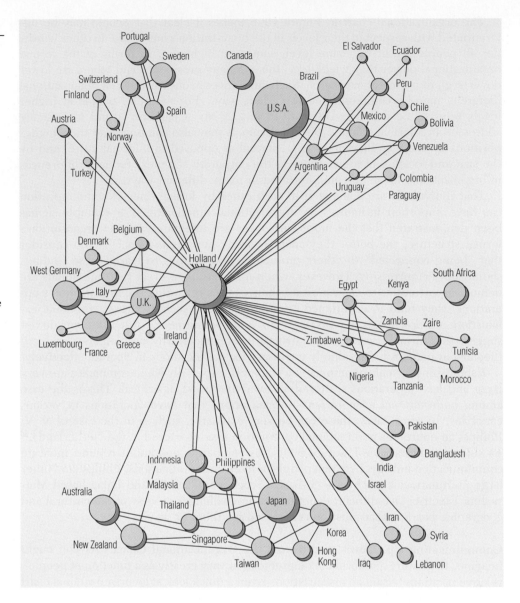

and their subordinates about the extent to which the managers communicated various
things to them (e.g., establish clear goals, clearly explain assignments). The study
revealed considerable disagreement between what the managers thought they communicated and what the subordinates thought their managers communicated. In all
cases, the managers perceived their own communications as more positive than their
subordinates believed them to be. What is interesting about these findings is that
the discrepancies were associated with negative outcomes such as low levels of job
satisfaction.

Downward communication flows from one level to the next lowest one, slowly
trickling down to the bottom. As a message passes through to the next lower level
on its way to the bottom, it often becomes less and less accurate (especially if the
information is spoken as opposed to written). Thus, it is not surprising to find that
the most effective downward communication techniques are ones directly aimed at
those who are most affected by the messages—namely, small group meetings and

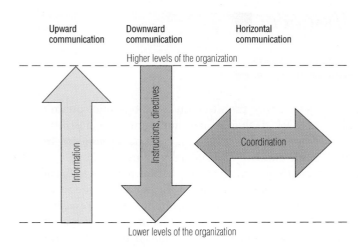

FIGURE 13-8

Upward, Downward, and Horizontal Communication: An Overview

The types of messages communicated within organizations tend to differ according to whether they are traveling upward (from lower to higher levels), downward (from higher to lower levels), or horizontally (across the same levels).

organizational publications targeting specific groups.[28] There are signs that such methods are being used—and successfully at that! For example, executives at Tandem Computers hold monthly teleconferences with their employees, and in-person discussions and a monthly newsletter are used to keep employees up-to-date on General Motors' activities in its Packard Electric plant in Mississippi. Such efforts at improving downward communication have been credited with improving productivity and reducing turnover in both companies.[29] (Despite such findings, downward communication is not always conducted in the most effective manner. Particularly problematic are those instances—and they are inevitable—in which superiors must communicate negative information, such as bad news regarding a layoff or a plant closing. As we will see in the **OB in Practice** feature on p. 502, communicating bad news inappropriately can have some devastating consequences.)

Upward communication flows from lower levels to higher levels within an organization, such as from a subordinate to her supervisor. Messages flowing in this direction tend to contain the information managers need to do their jobs, such as data required for decision making and the status of various projects. In short, upward communication is designed to keep managers aware of what is going on. Among the various types of information flowing upward are suggestions for improvement, status reports, reactions to work-related issues, new ideas, and so on.

Upward communication is not simply the reverse of downward communication. The difference in status between the communicating parties makes for some important distinctions. For example, it has been established that upward communication occurs much less frequently than downward communication. In fact, one classic study found that 70 percent of assembly line workers initiated communication with their supervisors less than once a month.[30] Among managers, a study revealed that less than 15 percent of their total communication was directed at their superiors.[31] Research has also shown that when people do communicate upward, their conversations tend to be shorter than discussions with their peers.[32]

Perhaps more important, upward communication often tends to suffer from serious inaccuracies. That subordinates frequently feel they must highlight their accomplishments and downplay their mistakes if they are to be looked on favorably is one factor.[33] Another factor that limits upward communication is the tendency of some individuals to fear that they will be rebuked by their supervisors if they speak to them, especially when they fear that their outspokenness will threaten their superiors and lessen their own chances for promotion.[34] Such dynamics commonly limit upward communication.

OB IN PRACTICE

**Layoffs at Middlebury College:
How *Not* to Communicate Bad News**

▶ Sometimes, organizational officials have to communicate bad news, such as layoffs and plant closings. Whether necessitated by a sluggish economy or stimulated by an interest in streamlining operations, such corporate decisions can have severe effects on employees. The trick is to communicate the bad news in such a manner that it minimizes the sting to the people who face unemployment. The effects of unemployment are negative enough; management's challenge is to avoid breaking the bad news in a way that adds insult to injury.

Unfortunately for the people dismissed from Vermont's Middlebury College in the spring of 1991, the layoffs were handled in a most insensitive manner.[35] In response to a budget crisis, seventeen secretaries and clerical workers, some of whom had as many as forty years' experience at the school, were abruptly told one morning that their jobs had been eliminated. They were then driven to a building at the edge of campus, where they met with members of the outplacement firm of Challenger, Gray, and Christmas, hired by the college to help the layoff victims adjust and find new jobs. They were not even permitted to finish their work or call their offices. An impersonal form letter from the president, Dr. Timothy Light, indicated that the college would continue their benefits, but only if they cooperated with the outplacement firm. The employees found the abrupt way their jobs were terminated shocking, as if they didn't really matter; and the complete lack of sensitivity shown for their feelings only made a difficult situation worse. After all, someone working at the same place for forty years should at least get a chance to say good-bye to her coworkers before leaving the job! Needless to say, the small community was shocked by the news. Shouldering the blame for the incident, President Light resigned several months later.

The college had followed a consultant's advice to structure the situation so that people couldn't go back to their offices and vent their hostility. Although this may be a reasonable concern in some industries (especially those in which disgruntled employees may be in a position to harm the company), people in this small college were used to confronting problems by expressing themselves in open discussions—a key reason for their vehement rejection of the strong-arm tactics. Experts disagree about the most appropriate way to handle layoffs. From the standpoint of James Challenger, president of the consulting firm used at Middlebury, the idea was to be as swift as possible and not allow people to return to their jobs, where they might spend time looking for new jobs or attempting to prove that the company made a mistake by laying them off. However, others disagree, such as William C. Norris, founder and former chief executive officer of Control Data Corporation. He contends that it is inexcusable to fire people abruptly and that employees will not be vindictive if dealt with openly and honestly.

Other experts agree that the college could have helped eliminate its budget problems by inviting employees to help find solutions. After all, people performing their jobs for many years might have excellent insight into where fat can be trimmed from budgets. They might be able to raise their productivity, reducing costs for the organization, thereby eliminating the need for layoffs. The point is that if a company doesn't give its employees information about the problems it is facing, it might not only miss out on finding potentially useful solutions, but also run the risk of alienating those who are adversely affected by the corporate actions. Should a layoff or pay cut be decided upon, it will surely hurt those who are affected, but it is more likely to be accepted as fair and reasonable when the basis for the action is thoroughly explained in a manner that shows sensitivity toward the injured parties.[36] This is one lesson Middlebury College learned the hard way.

Finally, we note the nature of *horizontal communication* within organizations. Messages that flow laterally (at the same organizational level) are characterized by efforts at coordination (attempts to work together). Consider, for example, how a vice president of marketing would have to coordinate her efforts to initiate an advertising campaign for a new product with information from the vice president of production about when the first products will be coming off the assembly line. Unlike vertical communication, in which the parties are at different status levels, horizontal communication involves people at the same level, and therefore tends to be easier and friendlier. Communication between peers also tends to be more casual and occurs more quickly because fewer social barriers exist between the parties. Note, however, that even horizontal communication can be problematic. For example, people in different departments may feel that they are competing against each other for valued organizational resources and may show resentment toward each other, thereby substituting an antagonistic, competitive orientation for the friendlier, cooperative one needed to get things done.[37]

Communication Networks: Formal Channels of Information in Groups

Imagine two different work groups in the Sales and Marketing Division of a large corporation. One consists of a team of creative writers, artists, and market researchers sitting around a table working together on developing the company's new advertising campaign. Another includes field representatives in various territories who report to regional sales managers throughout the country about consumers' preferences for various products. These people, in turn, analyze this information and report it to the vice president of sales and marketing. If you think about how these two groups differ, one key variable becomes obvious: the *pattern* of communication within them is not the same. Members of the creative team working on the advertising campaign can all communicate with each other at once, whereas people in the sales force speak only to those who are immediately above or below them. The patterns determining which organizational units (either people or groups) communicate to which other units are referred to as **communication networks.**

As you might imagine, there are many different possible communication networks within organizations. Do such arrangements matter? Do they make any difference in how well groups do their jobs and how satisfied group members feel? A considerable amount of research has shown that the nature of the communication linkages between group members can greatly influence group functioning.[38] So that we can appreciate these research findings, let's first consider some of the possible configurations of connections between people. Some of the most commonly studied possibilities are shown in Figure 13–9 (see p. 504). (These various diagrams depict communication networks that have five members, although they can have any number of members from three or more.) In each diagram, the circles represent individual people and the lines connecting them represent two-way lines of communication between them. (Some communication flows only in one direction, but for simplicity's sake only two-way, mutual communication flows will be used in our examples.)

As Figure 13–9 highlights, communication networks may differ with respect to a key feature: their degree of **centralization.** Briefly, this refers to the degree to which information must flow through a specific member of the network. As you can see in Figure 13–9, communication networks such as the *Y, Wheel,* and *Chain* are identified as **centralized networks.** For members within them to communicate with each other, they must go through a central person who is at the "crossroads" of the information

FIGURE 13-9

Communication Networks:
Some Basic Types

Some examples of five-person communication networks are shown here. Networks such as the *Circle* and *Comcon* give all members equal opportunities to communicate with each other, and are known as *decentralized networks*. In contrast, networks such as the *Y*, *Wheel*, and *Chain* contain members (marked by a filled-in circle) through whom messages must pass to reach others.

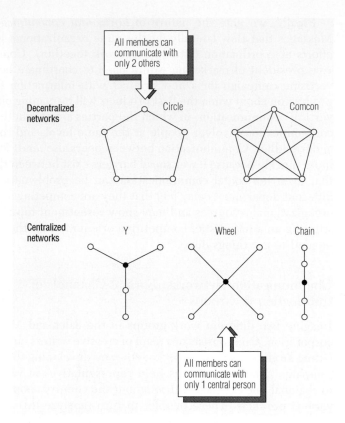

flow. In contrast, the *Circle* and *Comcon* are referred to as **decentralized networks** because information can freely flow between members without going through a central person. People in decentralized networks have equal access to information, whereas those in centralized networks are unequal because the individuals at the centers have access to more information than those at the periphery.

Research has shown that these differences in communication networks are responsible for determining how effectively groups will perform various jobs. Generally speaking, it has been found that when the tasks being performed are simple, centralized networks perform better, but when the tasks are complex, decentralized networks perform better.[39] Specifically, comparing these two types of network: *centralized networks are faster and more accurate on simple tasks, whereas decentralized networks are faster and more accurate on complex tasks.*

Why is this so? The answer has to do with the pressures put on the central member of a centralized network. The more information any one member of a group has to deal with, the greater the degree of **saturation** that person experiences. If you've ever tried working on several homework assignments at the same time, you probably already know how information saturation can cause performance to suffer. This is what happens when a centralized network performs a complex task. The central person becomes so overloaded with information that the group is slowed down and many errors are made. However, when the problem is simple, the central person can easily solve it alone after receiving all the information from the other members. Decentralized networks have no one central person, so information and work demands are more evenly distributed. As a result, on simple tasks the information needed to solve the problem may be spread out over all the group members, causing delays in coming to a solution. This same feature represents an advantage, however, when tasks are highly complex because it prevents any single member from becoming saturated and lowering the group's performance. (See our summary of these processes in Figure 13–10.) In short, centralization is a double-edged sword. When tasks are simple, centralization facilitates getting the job done. However, when tasks are complex, it may cause saturation, bringing performance to a halt.

Research also shows that centralized and decentralized networks differ in terms of their members' satisfaction. Would you be more satisfied as a member of a centralized or decentralized group? Most people enjoy the greater equality in decision making that occurs in decentralized networks. Such groups give everyone involved an equal status. In contrast, as a peripheral member of a centralized network, you would be less powerful than the central member and left out of the decision-making process. The central member controls more of the flow of information and is clearly more important, leading many peripheral members to feel that their contributions are not fully appreciated. Together, these factors combine to cause lower overall levels of satisfaction among members of centralized networks compared with those in decentralized networks.

In summary, formal communication networks clearly play an important role in organizations. However, formal communication networks may be only one of several factors responsible for organizational communication. One important consideration

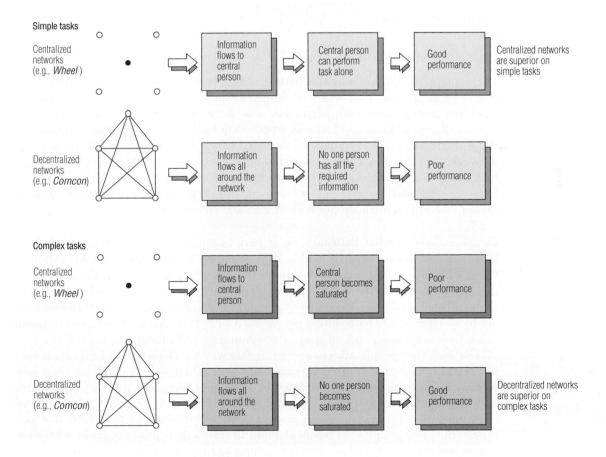

FIGURE 13–10   Comparing the Performance of Centralized and Decentralized Communication Networks: The Influence of Task Complexity

As shown here, centralized networks are superior on *simple* tasks (top), and decentralized networks are superior on *complex* tasks (bottom).

Test Bank questions 13.31–13.32 and 13.51 relate to material on this page.

is that although the lines of communication between people can greatly influence their job performance and satisfaction, the various advantages and limitations of different communication networks tend to disappear the longer the groups are in operation.[40] As group members gain more experience interacting with each other, they may learn to overcome the limitations imposed by their communication networks. (For example, they may learn to send messages to specific individuals who have proven themselves in the past to be particularly competent at solving certain kinds of problems.) In other words, although the differences between various communication networks may be quite significant, they may be only temporary, accounting for the behavior of newly formed groups more than the behavior of highly experienced groups.

Another important point is that any formal lines of communication operate in organizations in conjunction with widespread informal networks that also may help groups accomplish their goals. Even if formal channels impede the communication of information, informal connections between people—such as friendships, or contacts in other departments—may help the communication process. (Consider, for example, the widespread use of informal channels of communication by the character "Radar" O'Reilly on the old TV show "M*A*S*H." Using his contacts to trade his unit's hypodermic syringes for another unit's toilet paper represents the operation of informal as opposed to formal channels of communication.) As we will describe next, the informal connections between people are extremely important in organizational communications.

Informal Communication Networks: A Small World

For a moment, think about the people with whom you communicate during the course of an average day. Friends, family members, classmates, and colleagues at work are among those with whom you may have *informal communication*—information shared without any formally imposed obligations or restrictions. When you think about it carefully, you may be surprised to realize how widespread our informal networks can be. You know someone who knows someone else, who knows your best friend—and before long, your informal networks become very far-reaching. In fact, we often use the phrase "It's a small world" to describe our connections to others through an intricate network of informal connections.

Organizations' Hidden Pathways   It is easy to imagine how important the flow of informal information may be within organizations. People transmit information to those with whom they come into contact, thereby providing conduits through which messages can travel. We also tend to communicate most with those who are similar to ourselves on such key variables as age and time working on the job.[41] Because we are more comfortable with similar people than with dissimilar ones, we tend to spend more time with them and, of course, communicate with them more.

The idea that people are connected in this way has been used to explain a very important organizational phenomenon—turnover. Do people resign from their jobs in ways that are random and unrelated to each other? A recent study by Krackhardt and Porter suggests that they do not, but that turnover is related to the informal communication patterns between people.[42] These investigators theorized that voluntary turnover (employees freely electing to resign their jobs) occurs as a result of a *snowball effect*. A snowball does not accumulate snowflakes randomly, but collects those snowflakes that are in its path. Analogously, it was reasoned, patterns of voluntary turnover may not be independently distributed within a work group, but may be the result of people's influences on each other. Thus, predicting which people will resign from their jobs may be based, in large part, on knowledge of the communication patterns within groups. Someone who leaves her job for a better one in another organization may know someone who has already done so. Krackhardt and Porter found support for this snowball effect among teenagers working in fast-food restaurants. Specifically, turnover tended to be concentrated among groups of people who communicated informally with each other a great deal before they resigned. (For a suggestion regarding how this may operate, see Figure 13–11). This study provides an excellent example of the importance of informal patterns of communication in organizations.

Informal communication networks are characterized by the fact that they often are composed of individuals at different organizational levels. People can tell anyone in the network whatever informal information they wish. For example, one investigator found that jokes and funny stories tended to cross organizational boundaries, and were freely shared by those in both the managerial and nonmanagerial ranks of organizations.[43] On the other hand, it would be quite unlikely—and considered "out of line"—for a lower-level employee to communicate something about how to do the job to an upper-level employee. What flows within the pathways of informal communication is informal information, messages not necessarily related to individuals' work.

The Grapevine and the Rumor Mill   When anyone can tell something informal to anyone else, it results in a very rapid flow of information along the organizational **grapevine.** You are probably aware that the grapevine refers to the pathways along which unofficial, informal information travels. However, you may be unaware that the term is believed to have originated during the U.S. Civil War, when makeshift telegraph lines hastily strung up between trees hung loosely, resembling grapevines.[44] (The messages traveling along these lines were often garbled, thereby associating the grapevine with messages that are incomplete, distorted, or inaccurate.) In contrast to a formal organizational message, which might take several days to reach its desired audience, information traveling along the organizational grapevine tends to flow very rapidly, often within hours. This is not only because informal

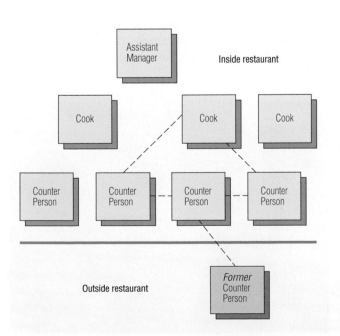

FIGURE 13–11

Informal Communication Networks: A Predictor of Turnover Patterns

The informal networks of communication between people (shown in dotted lines) provide channels through which messages about better job opportunities may be communicated. Patterns of voluntary turnover have been linked to the existence of such informal networks. (*Source:* Based on suggestions by Krackhardt & Porter, 1986; see Note 42.)

communication can cross formal organizational boundaries (e.g., you might be able to tell a good joke to almost anyone, not just your boss or subordinates with whom you are required to communicate), but also because informal information tends to be communicated orally. As we noted earlier, oral messages are communicated faster than written ones, but may become increasingly inaccurate as they flow from person to person in oral form. Because of the confusion grapevines may cause, some people have sought to eliminate them, but they are not necessarily bad. Informally socializing with our coworkers can help make work groups more cohesive (as you may recall from chapter 8), and may also provide excellent opportunities for desired human contact, keeping the work environment stimulating. Grapevines must be considered an inevitable fact of life in organizations.[45] Where there are people, there will be informal communication among them.

It is interesting to note that most of the information communicated along the grapevine is accurate. In fact, one study found that 82 percent of the information communicated along a particular company's organizational grapevine was accurate.[46] The problem with interpreting this figure is that the inaccurate portions of some messages may alter their overall meaning. If, for example, a story is going around that someone got passed by for promotion over a lower-ranking employee, it may cause quite a bit of dissension in the workplace. However, suppose everything is true except that the person turned down the promotion because it involved relocating. This important fact completely alters the situation. Only one fact needs to be inaccurate for the accuracy of communication to suffer.

This problem of inaccuracy is clearly responsible for giving the grapevine such a bad reputation. In extreme cases, information may be transmitted that is almost totally without any basis in fact and usually unverifiable. Such messages are known as **rumors.** Typically, rumors are based on speculation, an overactive imagination, and wishful thinking, rather than on facts. Rumors race like wildfire through organizations because the information they present is so interesting and ambiguous. The ambiguity leaves it open to embellishment as it passes orally from one person to the next (see Figure 13–12). Before you know it, almost everyone in the organization has heard the rumor, and its inaccurate message becomes taken as fact ("It must be true, everyone knows it"). Hence, even if there was, at one point, some truth to a rumor, the message quickly becomes untrue.

If you've ever been the victim of a rumor, you know how difficult it can be to negate and undo its effects. This is especially the case among organizations, which can also be the victims of rumors, such as commonly heard rumors about the pos-

Hey, did you hear that Equitable, the nation's third largest insurer, is going bankrupt? That rumor swept the financial world recently, but it's not true. Rumors like this one often occur when the incident is probable and partly based on real information. (In this case, the company was having minor difficulties.) But what should a company do when a rumor about it gets out of hand? Irv Schlenker of New York University recommends refuting the rumors quickly. Send a memo to your employees immediately, stating the facts of the case. If that doesn't work, call a meeting and tell your employees face-to-face. If the rumor has gone public, call a press conference and issue an official statement. Finally, take out an advertisement in the paper and let the world know that the rumor is false. [Light, L., & Landler, M. (1990, December 24). Killing a rumor before it kills a company. *Business Week*, p. 23.]

FIGURE 13–12

Hearing It through the Grapevine

Informal information flows very rapidly in organizations, in large part because the messages may be shared by many people at once.

sibility of corporate takeovers. Such rumors not only influence the value of the company's stock, but also threaten employees' feelings of job security. For example, a rumor about the use of worms in McDonald's hamburgers circulated in the Chicago area in the late 1970s. Even though the rumor was completely untrue, sales dropped as much as 30 percent in some restaurants.[47] McDonald's survived the rumor, but such a cut in business volume no doubt hurt.

What, then, can be done to counter the effects of rumors? Although this is a difficult question to answer, some research evidence suggests that directly refuting a rumor may *not* help counter its effects.[48] Directly refuting a rumor only serves to help spread it among those who have not already heard about it ("Oh, I didn't know people thought that") and strengthen it among those who have already heard it ("If it weren't true, they wouldn't be protesting so much"). Directing people's attention away from the rumor may help, focusing instead on other things they know about the target of the rumor. In research studying the McDonald's rumor, for example, it was found that reminding people about other things they thought about McDonald's (e.g., that it is a clean, family-oriented place) helped counter the negative effects of the rumor. Keep in mind that the rumored information that someone has about any target may be just part of the set of beliefs held. If you should ever become the victim of a rumor, remember: directing people's attention to other positive things they already believe about you may be a helpful way to counter the effects of the rumor. Although rumors may be impossible to stop, their effects can, with some effort, be effectively managed.

The Benefits of Informal Communication   To conclude by noting only the negative effects of informal communication networks would be misleading. It is also true that the informal flow of information from person to person can be beneficial. For example, research has shown that the more involved people are in their organizations' communication networks, the more powerful and influential they become on the job.[49] Informal connections apparently help people attain formal power (see chapter 11). It has also been shown that the informal connections between scientists become an important mechanism through which they share ideas, what has been referred to as an *invisible college*.[50] The transmittal of scientific knowledge is affected by the patterns of communication through which that knowledge is directed. Note that the communication here is strictly informal; it did not have to be shared, but it was, informally. Still, it was quite influential. Indeed, as we have shown, information that is communicated informally can have potent effects on organizational functioning.

Communication and the Work Environment: Technology and Office Design

Management theorists have long been aware of the importance of the work environment as a determinant of organizational communication. For example, in his book on office management written almost seventy years ago, William Henry Leffingwell noted that clerks could be more productive if they did not have to leave their desks to communicate with each other.[51] To avoid making clerks waste time by walking around, he recommended using devices such as pneumatic tubes, elevators, conveyor belts, and a variety of buzzers and bells to make communication more efficient for office workers. Such devices may seem primitive by today's modern technological standards (in which complex computer and telephone networks are commonly used to transmit messages), but the basic idea is the same: technology can enhance the flow of information and, hence, the quality of organizational functioning. (For a whimsical look at this process, see Figure 13–13 on p. 510.)

FIGURE 13–13

Modern Technology:
A Major Influence on
Communication

Although this example
may be a bit extreme,
modern advances in
technology have
changed many of
the ways in which
people communicate
with each other.
(*Source:* Reprinted by
permission of Cartoon
Features Syndicate,
Inc.)

*"No! I don't want any middlemen. Put me right
through to your computer."*

Computers, Electronic Mail, and Voice Messaging   It would be incorrect to assume
that modern technological advances have made the organizational communication
process any more pleasant for today's office workers than it was for those Leffingwell
studied in the 1920s. One of the key culprits seems to be the ever-present video
display terminals that have replaced the paper-cluttered desks of office workers in
the past. Clerical employees forced to do their work in the shadow of a green or
amber screen all day may miss human contact, especially when they are encased in
cubicles separated from others by tall partitions. In an attempt to escape such isolation, the employees in one office studied by Zuboff mischievously pried open the
seam of a metal partition that separated them from their coworkers.[52] People reported
feeling isolated and solitary, and longed for the kind of informal contact denied them
by the design of their surroundings.

In general, although the use of on-line technology can improve office productivity,
there is a hidden cost in using these methods. The problem, Zuboff notes, is that
such automation minimizes important contact between managers and their subordinates. Technology that takes away decision-making powers may preclude the need
for some management supervision. We are not saying that computers may make
supervisors obsolete, but that they may diminish subordinates' need to interact with
their supervisors during the course of their jobs. Thus, critical opportunities to help
identify and solve organizational problems may be lost (or at least temporarily mis-
placed) in the process. Machinery that makes interpersonal collaboration unnecessary
may add to feelings of social isolation. This idea applies to the shop floor, too, where
research has shown that the use of robots is recognized as a potential threat to
communication between supervisors and their subordinates.[53] Obviously, organizational scientists are just beginning to recognize the challenges to effective communication posed by the use of modern technology in the workplace.

One of the primary technological advances in organizational communication in
recent years has been the use of electronic mail, popularly referred to as *e-mail*, a
system whereby people use personal computer terminals to send and receive messages between each other (see Figure 13–14). As you might imagine, such systems
make communication within and between organizations easier than ever before. For
large multinational operations, they're vital. Los Angeles–based Hughes Aircraft,
for example, uses e-mail to connect more than 30,000 users in thirty-two different
locations worldwide.[54] The electronic transmission of messages represents a com-

Electronic communication
(through such networks as
Bitnet and Internet) is extremely fast and is changing the way researchers
around the world are solving problems. For exam-
ple, two U.S.
mathematicians were

munication revolution in that it allows for the very rapid transmission of information, and the simultaneous sharing of identical information by people regardless of how widely dispersed they may be. What may be lost in terms of depth and richness of communication is more than made up for by efficiency.[55]

E-mail systems have been used as alternatives to in-person meetings, permitting people to share information with many others on electronic bulletin boards. For example, a writer wishing to interview people who still use slide rules was able to contact a dozen such individuals in only two days by posting a message on an electronic bulletin board system.[56] As such systems proliferate, a problem has developed in that many different types of systems are in use, making communication between systems difficult if not impossible. Fortunately, a movement toward standardization has been noted, a step that can have profound implications for electronically interconnecting vast numbers of people. With such a development, it looks as if e-mail soon will be a reality for all organizations, large and small. (Along with the profound opportunities afforded by e-mail systems has come a serious ethical question regarding the right to privacy. For a closer look at this issue, see the **Question of Ethics** feature on p. 514.)

Although e-mail can be very quick and efficient, it lacks the capacity to send a personal message using one's own voice. However, another recent technology known as *voice messaging* allows for just that. A voice message system uses a computer to convert human speech into digital information saved on a hard disk for playback later by the receiver at any time from any touch-tone telephone. Because 76 percent of all business calls are nonimmediate in nature (i.e., they do not require instantaneous action), and 56 percent of all calls completed involve one-way communication (i.e., they either give or receive information, but not both), voice messaging may be very useful on many occasions.[57] Voice messaging allows people to avoid wasting time playing "telephone tag," and permits the highly efficient use of voice as an information tool because it precludes the need to translate messages into written characters or keystrokes. Voice messaging systems are so efficient, in fact, that they have been credited with saving an average of $2,000 per employee annually![58]

Recent research by Reinsch and Beswick has found that voice mail is generally well accepted.[59] These investigators had a variety of professional, technical, and administrative employees read a description of a situation describing a certain communication need, and asked them to express a preference for the channel they would use to initiate a message. Although the employees most frequently preferred face-

trying to solve a difficult large-number factoring problem. They let a few researchers know about the problem through electronic mail, and in turn, those researchers let other researchers know. In a short time, people at over 1,000 computers scattered around the world helped the two mathematicians solve different parts of the problem and sent answers back to them. With this help, the two mathematicians were able to put all of the pieces together and solve the problem. [Peterson, I. (1990, August 11). The electronic grapevine. *Science News, 138* 90–91.]

Although the telephone is an excellent device for business communication, about 75 percent of all business calls don't get through on the first try, resulting in the annoying phenomenon of "telephone tag," where the callers phone back and forth trying to reach each other. To combat this costly problem, about 85 percent of the nation's top 500 firms and 2 million smaller firms are using voice mail to answer calls for an employee who is not available. Despite the benefits of voice mail, these systems can sometimes be frustrating for users. For example, it is possible for users to get thrown into "voice mail jail," the state in which they repeatedly keep hearing a menu of items to select although no desirable alternative is offered and the option to break out to a live person is not given. [Porter, P. (1992, March 15). Voice mail sometimes gives callers the cold shoulder. *The Columbus Dispatch,* p. H1.]

FIGURE 13-14

E-Mail: Connecting People Worldwide

Electronic mail, or e-mail, systems are vital tools used to facilitate communication between individuals all over the world.

to-face communication, they preferred voice mail in a variety of circumstances. Specifically, people wish to use voice mail when

- The recipient is far away.
- The user is familiar with the technology.
- Messages are relatively brief.
- Messages are relatively simple.
- A positive response is anticipated.
- Documentation is not needed.
- The recipient works a different shift from the sender.

These findings suggest that we can expect voice mail to be accepted and widely used under limited circumstances (e.g., when a short, simple, noncontroversial, undocumented message needs to be sent to someone far away who works different hours). However, under other circumstances, alternative forms of communication may be preferred, such as face-to-face messages or communication using multiple channels. Thus, although voice messaging represents a very practical and efficient use of communication technology, its acceptance is likely to be limited to a restricted range of communication situations.

Office Design   In addition to the effects of high technology, another element of the work environment—a much more basic one, namely, the design of offices—may also have profound influences on communication. During the 1960s, offices designed without interior walls or partitions, using one large open space—referred to as the *open-plan office*—were very popular. The idea behind such designs was to encourage open communication between people by eliminating the walls that serve as barriers to communication in conventional, walled offices. The idea makes sense, especially if you consider that people tend to avoid communicating with others who are located more than twenty-five feet away from them.[60] However, open-plan offices have their problems, too. Notably, they have been found to be noisier, and to offer much less privacy, than traditional offices.[61]

FIGURE 13–15

Open versus Closed Offices: Which Are Preferred?

Research has shown that clerical employees were more satisfied working in partitioned offices than in open-plan offices. Partitioned offices were also recognized as providing greater possibilities for focusing on the task at hand, and for communicating in private. (*Source:* Based on data reported by Oldham, 1988; see Note 62.)

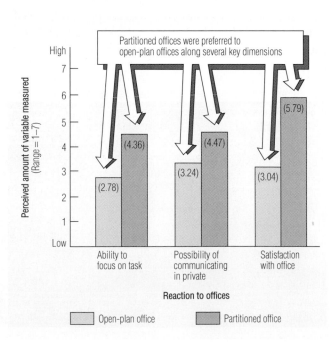

In a recent study, Oldham surveyed the reactions of insurance company claims adjusters at two different times—once while they were working in an open-plan office, and again after they moved to an office of the same size that had partitions (four to six feet high) separating them from each other.[62] As shown in Figure 13–15, the new offices with partitions brought about improvements in several areas. The employees studied believed they were better able to focus on the work at hand, and that they could more effectively communicate privately with others. They were also more satisfied with the office itself. Such research findings suggest that office design may have a complex effect on communication. Although open-plan offices may make it easier for clerical workers to interact with each other, the lack of privacy may actually make communication less effective than in traditional, closed-plan offices.

As we have noted here, the work environment can profoundly influence communication. Office machinery can make it easier than ever to communicate vast quantities of information to others. But such equipment may isolate employees, keeping them from the kinds of social interaction they seek and the formal interaction with their supervisors that may be most helpful to organizations. Research on the layout of open-plan offices leads to similarly complex conclusions. Although open-plan offices may make access to others easier, their characteristically high levels of background noise and their lack of privacy may actually make communication more difficult. In summary, there is no one best way to use machinery or to design an environment for effective communication. Clearly, tradeoffs are involved. Effective communication in today's high-tech world demands the use of impersonal machines, but using them creates an even greater need for the informal social contact that is so vital to effective organizational communication.

OVERCOMING COMMUNICATION BARRIERS: ENHANCING THE FLOW OF INFORMATION

Throughout this chapter, we have noted the central role of communication in organizational functioning. Given this, it is easy to understand how any efforts at improving the communication process in organizations may have highly desirable payoffs for organizations as well as for the individuals and groups working in them. Several steps can be taken to obtain the benefits of effective communication. In this final section, we will describe some of these techniques, including measures that can be taken by individuals, as well as tactics for improving communication that involve entire organizations.

Becoming a Better Communicator: Individual Strategies

Imagine that someone is talking to you, but you cannot understand what the speaker is saying. Now imagine reading a letter so clearly written that you know exactly what ideas the writer had in mind. If you've ever experienced any situations like these, you can appreciate the importance of communicating clearly and effectively. Bad communication is easy to recognize; you usually know it when someone isn't coming across to you. However, good communication isn't a skill we can take for granted, and it isn't easily acquired. Top executives often work long and hard at honing their communication skills. So, although we don't expect you to become an expert communicator just by taking the tips we describe here, we think you will find them a useful head start at understanding some of the necessary elements of effective interpersonal communication.

Keep Language Simple   Have you ever pulled your "previously owned motor vehicle" up to a gas pump and found yourself greeted by a "petroleum transfer engineer"

One of the largest barriers to international business is communicating with businesspeople who speak a different language. As a result, the translation business is booming, as the need for the translation of legal contracts, technical information, instruction manuals, and direct interpersonal communication is greater than ever. Including government and corporate business, the translation industry has grown to a whopping $10-billion-per-year industry

A QUESTION OF ETHICS

Privacy Rights and E-Mail: Should Employers Have Access to Employees' Electronic Mailboxes?

With the advent of advances in communication technology come new ethical challenges regarding their use. This is especially true in the case of electronic mail. Specifically, when e-mail messages are transmitted over company equipment, a critical question arises about the appropriate level of privacy that they should be accorded. Some assert that companies have the right to monitor messages communicated with their equipment, whereas others counter that doing so constitutes an invasion of employees' privacy.

Consider what happened to Alana Shoars, while she worked as an electronic mail administrator at Epson America.[63] She arrived at work one morning and found her supervisor printing out various employees' private e-mail messages. Ironically, when training employees how to use the system, she routinely explained that their mail was private. Apparently, this was untrue. When Shoars questioned this practice, she was fired on the grounds of insubordination (although company officials deny that her dismissal was related to her questions about the e-mail incident). Epson officials also have denied that the monitoring of e-mail is a corporate policy. Subsequently, Shoars filed a $1 million suit against the company on the grounds that she was wrongfully terminated, and has been working elsewhere in a similar capacity.

This incident highlights the basic issues involved. On the one hand, as Shoars contends, it's a basic matter of not invading privacy: "You don't read other people's mail, just as you don't listen to their phone conversations. Right is right and wrong is wrong."[64] Michael Simmons, the chief information officer at the Bank of Boston, believes otherwise. He contends that if the company owns the equipment, "it has a right to look and see if people are using it for purposes other than running the business."[65] Perhaps Simmons's views were tempered by experiences he had on a previous job. He discovered that one employee was using the company's computer system to run his own Amway business, and another was using it to handicap horse races (a task using 600 megabytes of memory!).

Some companies, such as Federal Express, American Airlines, and United Parcel Service, have e-mail systems that inform employees that their messages might be monitored. But some contend that simply informing employees that they *might* snoop does not give companies the right to actually do so; it's still wrong. Mitchell Kapor, founder of the Lotus Development Corporation, believes that companies should have clear policies about their examination of e-mail. Unfortunately, few corporations have codes of ethics that address the treatment of electronic messages. It has been argued that this might not be a problem because ordinary ethical values should apply. For example, according to Donn B. Parker, a senior management consultant at SRI International, no specific computer-related rules of conduct should be needed because "when people log onto a computer or network, they don't automatically turn off their ethical values."[66]

In recent years, laws have been enacted in the United States (e.g., the Federal Electronic Communications Privacy Act of 1986) that safeguard the privacy of electronic messages sent over public telephone lines. However, the law applies only to public networks, such as Compuserve and MCI Mail, and not to private facilities. Although such legislation is unlikely to be extended to private networks, experts believe that a more general ethical matter is at stake—namely, the ethical values of the organization at large. If organizations show disregard for the privacy of employees, they should not be surprised to find that employees are similarly tempted to test ethical boundaries.[67] To the extent that employees model the ethical standards communicated to them by company officials, the treatment of e-mail messages represents a prime avenue by which organizations can project their ethical values.

who filled your "fuel containment module"? Or perhaps you've gone to a "home improvement center" looking to purchase a "manually powered impact device." In either case, we wouldn't blame you if you went to another "operating entity" that had a better "customer interface capacity." Certainly, you've already encountered enough business double-talk without getting any more from us. Our point is that using such seemingly formal language may impose a serious barrier on communication.

Keep in mind that all organizations, fields, social groups, and professions have their **jargon**—their own specialized language. Your own college or university may have a "quad," or, as a student, you may have a "roomie" who wants to go "Greek," and is interested in "rushing." These terms are examples of a college student's jargon. No doubt, you've encountered a lot of language in this book that may at first sound strange to you. Our point is that the use of jargon is inevitable when people within the same field or social groups communicate with each other. Some degree of highly specialized language may help communication by providing an easy way for people in the same fields to share complex ideas. Jargon also allows professionals to identify unknown others as people in their field because they "speak the same language." For example, management professors would describe this book as dealing with the field of *OB*, a term that would have a very different meaning to medical doctors (for whom it refers to the field of obstetrics). Obviously, within professions jargon helps communication, but it can lead to confusion when used outside the groups within which it has meaning (refer to Table 13–1).

and is expected to continue growing rapidly. The largest translation companies charge anywhere from ten to fifty cents per word and even more for technical material. [Levy, C. J. (1991, October 20). The growing gelt in other's words. *The New York Times*, p. F5.]

TABLE 13–1   Can You Pass the Business Jargon Test?

The world of business is full of words and phrases that seem strange to the uninitiated. Using a field's specialized terms (known as *jargon*) may hinder communication with people who are outside the field. See how many of the business-related terms on the left you can correctly match with the meanings shown on the right. Compare your answers to the correct pairings shown below.

Term	Definition
1. Bean counter	a. A signal that a manager is close by
2. Unzip	
3. Turkey-shoot	b. Overly technical language, jargon
4. 13	
5. 30	c. A wastebasket
6. File 17	d. The lower echelons of an organization
7. Schmooz	
8. Where the rubber meets the road	e. A numerical clerk
	f. A wealthy rural businessman
9. Butter-and-egg man	g. Something that is easy to accomplish
10. Double Dutch	
	h. To converse informally
	i. The end of a story or message
	j. To find a solution to a problem in an organized fashion

The correct pairings are as follows: 1 = e, 2 = j, 3 = g, 4 = a, 5 = i, 6 = c, 7 = h, 8 = d, 9 = f, and 10 = b.

Source: Based on definitions appearing in Chapman, R. L. (1986). *New dictionary of American slang.* New York: Harper & Row.

Studying the use of jargon in one large organization, Kanter noted that a *COM-VOC*—itself a jargon term for "common vocabulary"—developed among its members.[68] For example, within some divisions there were "fast-trackers" who "shot from the hip" to go for "the big win." Unfortunately, people in other departments of the corporation who didn't understand this jargon often felt out of place, creating a barrier to clear communication. This happened not only between various departments of the large organization studied by Kanter, but also between various employees and their family members, who, as a result, often had great difficulty understanding what their spouses or parents did on the job. In fact, the wives of male executives identified over 100 unfamiliar work-related terms and phrases that they could not understand. Accordingly, we can safely say that jargon may be an effective communication device between people within one's social or professional group, but it should be avoided when attempting to communicate with outsiders. *You* might know what you mean, but using jargon others don't understand will not help you get your point across. And, of course, that is what communication is all about.

In addition to avoiding jargon, verbal communication between people should also tend to use language that is short, simple, and to the point. Hence, it is often wise to adopt the **K.I.S.S. principle** when communicating with others—that is, keep it short and simple.[69] People are better able to understand messages that do not overwhelm them with too much information at once than those that present more than they can absorb. A wise communicator is sensitive to this and knows how to monitor his or her audience for signs of overloading audience members' circuits with too much information. Again, although you may know what you are talking about, you may not be able to get your ideas across to others unless you package them in doses small and simple enough to be understood. When this is done effectively, even the most complex ideas can be clearly communicated.

Be an Active, Attentive Listener   Just as it is important to present your ideas in ways that make them understandable to others (i.e., sending messages), it is equally important to work at being a good listener (i.e., receiving messages). Although listening to others takes up a large percentage of the time spent communicating, it has been established that people tend to actually pay attention to and comprehend only a small percentage of the information directed at them in the course of doing their jobs.[70]

Most of us usually think of listening as a passive process of taking in information sent by others, but when done correctly the process of listening is much more active. For example, ask questions if you don't understand something, and nod or otherwise signal if you do understand. Such cues provide critical feedback to the communicator about the extent to which he or she is getting across to you. As a listener, you can do your share to help the communication process by letting the message-sender know if and how his or her messages are coming across to you. Asking questions and putting the speaker's ideas into your own words are helpful ways of staying alert and taking in all the information being presented.

It is also very useful to avoid distractions in the environment and concentrate on what the other person is saying. (As you may recall from chapter 2, attention is a critical part of the perception process.) When listening to others, also try to avoid immediately jumping to conclusions or evaluating their remarks. It is important to completely take in what is being said before you reach your own conclusions about it. Certainly, simply dismissing someone because you don't like what is being said is much too easy. Doing so, of course, poses a formidable barrier to effective communication. Being a good listener also involves making sure you are aware of others' main points. What is the speaker trying to say? Be sure you understand another's ideas before you formulate your reply. Too many of us interrupt speakers with our own ideas before we have fully heard theirs. If this sounds like something you do, rest assured that it is not only quite common, but also correctable. Although it requires some effort, incorporating these suggestions into your own listening habits cannot help but make you a better listener. Indeed, many organizations have sought to help their employees in this way. For example, the corporate giant Unisys has for some time (since it was known as the Sperry Corporation) systematically trained thousands of its employees in effective listening skills (using seminars and self-training cassettes). Clearly, Unisys is among those companies acknowledging the importance of good listening skills in promoting effective organizational communication.

The development of listening skills requires identifying the individual elements of listening, the separate skills that contribute to listening effectiveness. Brownell has proposed that listening effectiveness may be understood in terms of the behavioral indicators that individuals perceive as related to effective listening, skills clustered into six groups known as the **HURIER model.** The term *HURIER* is an acronym composed of the initials of the words reflecting the component skills of effective listening: hearing, understanding, remembering, interpreting, evaluating, and responding. For a summary of these individual skills, see Figure 13–16. Although it might seem easy to do the six things needed to be a good listener, we are not all as good as we think we are in this capacity, suggesting that listening might not be as easy as it seems.

Management consultant Nancy K. Austin would agree, and explains that when you invite people to talk to you about their problems on the job, you're implicitly making a promise to listen to them.[72] Of course, when you do, you may feel hostile

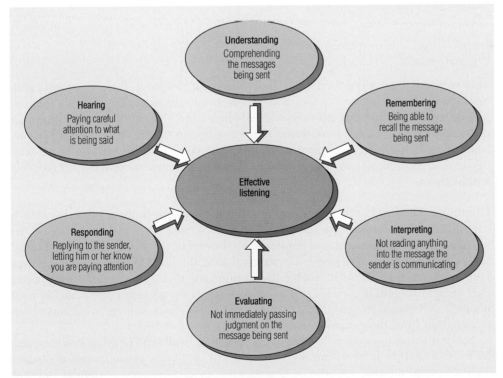

FIGURE 13–16

The HURIER Model: The Components of Effective Listening

What makes a listener effective? Research by Brownell has shown that the six skills identified here are recognized as contributing to effective listening. (*Source:* Based on suggestions by Brownell, 1985; see Note 71.)

and defensive toward the speaker, and become more interested in speaking up and setting the record straight if you don't like what you hear. This is the challenge of listening. Good listeners should resist this temptation and pay careful attention to the speaker. When they cannot do so, they should admit the problem and reschedule another opportunity to get together. Austin also advises people to "be an equal opportunity listener," that is, to pay attention not only to those whose high status commands our attention, but also to anyone at any level, and to make time to hear them all in a democratic fashion. The idea is not only that people at any job level might have something to say, but also that they may feel good about you as a manager for having shown consideration to them. Austin notes that by listening to an employee, you are saying, "You are smart and have important things to say; you are worth my time."[73] Such a message is critical to establishing the kind of open, two-way communication essential for top management.

Research has confirmed the importance of listening as a management skill. In fact, it has shown that the better a person is as a listener, the more likely he or she is to rapidly rise up the organizational hierarchy[74] and to perform well as a manager.[75] Apparently, good listening skills are an important aspect of one's ability to succeed as a manager (and to become a leader). Yet, people tend to be insensitive to how others perceive their listening skills. In a survey of employees in the hospitality industry, Brownell found that almost all the managers indicated that they felt their listening skills were either "good" or "very good," although most of their subordinates did not agree.[76] Such overconfidence in one's own listening ability can be a barrier to seeking training in listening skills inasmuch as people who believe they are already good listeners may have little motivation to seek training in that area. This is unfortunate, because Brownell also found that among those who were rated as better listeners by their subordinates was a significant number of managers who had earlier been trained in listening skills. This evidence suggests that this type of training may indeed pay off.

Improving Communication on the Job: Organizational Strategies

Thus far, we have described ways individuals can improve their communication abilities by being better senders and receivers of messages. In addition to these individual skills, there are also ways of enhancing the communication at the organizational level. Given the importance of information to the survival of organizations, communication must be as effective as possible. We will now consider some ways in which organizations can improve the quality of the communications that take place within them.

Obtaining Feedback   To operate most effectively, organizations must be able to communicate accurately with those who keep them running—their employees. Unfortunately, the vast majority of employees believe that the feedback between themselves and their organizations is not as good as it should be.[77] For various reasons, people are often unwilling or unable to communicate their ideas to top management. Part of the problem is the lack of available channels for upward communication and people's reluctance to use whatever ones exist. How, then, can organizations obtain information from their employees?

Several techniques exist for effectively soliciting feedback. *Employee surveys* can be used to gather information about employees' attitudes and opinions about key areas of organizational operations. Questionnaires administered at regular intervals may be useful for spotting changes in attitudes as they occur. Such surveys tend to be quite effective when their results are shared with employees, especially when the feedback is used as the basis for changing the way things are done.

A second means of facilitating upward communication in organizations is *suggestion systems*. Too often, employees' good ideas about how to improve organizational functioning fail to work their way up the organizational chart because the people with the ideas do not know how to reach the people who can implement them. Even worse, they may feel they will not be listened to even if they can reach the right person. *Suggestion boxes* are designed to help avoid these problems, to help provide a conduit for employees' ideas. Recent research has found that about 15 percent of employees use their companies' suggestion boxes, and that about 25 percent of the suggestions made are implemented.[78] Employees are usually rewarded for their successful suggestions, either with a flat monetary reward or some percentage of the money saved by implementing the suggestion. The oldest continuously operating suggestion system has been at the Eastman Kodak Company since 1898. At that time, a worker was awarded $2 for pointing out the advantages of washing the windows in the company's production department. Since then, almost 2 million suggestions have been made at Kodak, including one that yielded an award of $47,800 to the man who suggested mounting film boxes on cards for display racks at retail stores.[79]

A third method of providing important information is through *corporate hotlines*—telephone lines staffed by corporate personnel ready to answer employees' questions, listen to their comments, and the like.[80] A good example of this is the "Let's Talk" program that AT&T developed to answer its employees' questions at the time of the company's antitrust divestiture. By providing personnel with easy access to information, companies benefit in several ways. It not only shows employees that the company cares about them, but it also encourages them to address their concerns before the issues become more serious. In addition, by keeping track of the kinds of questions and concerns voiced, top management is given a good source of feedback about the things that are on employees' minds. Such information can be invaluable when attempting to improve organizational conditions.

A fourth set of techniques are *"brown bag" meetings* and *"skip level" meetings*. Both are methods designed to facilitate communication between people who don't usually get together because they're at different organizational levels.[81] The brown bag meetings are simply informal get-togethers over breakfast or lunch (brought in from home, hence the term "brown bag") at which people discuss what's going on in the company. The informal nature of the meetings is designed to encourage the open sharing of ideas (eating a sandwich out of a bag is an equalizer!). Skip level meetings do essentially the same thing. These are gatherings of employees with corporate superiors who are more than one level higher than they are in the organizational hierarchy. The idea is that new lines of communication can be established by bringing together people who are two or more levels apart, individuals who usually don't come into contact with each other. The new insight that both parties may derive from meeting with each other can be expected to facilitate the communication process within organizations.

Together, the four methods we have referred to here (see the summary in Table 13–2 on p. 520) can effectively break down the barriers that too frequently restrict the flow of information from lower-level personnel to upper-level managers. They represent ways of improving the upward flow of communication in organizations. Effective communication requires not only obtaining enough feedback, but also appropriately accessing it. In other words, it is important to control the amount of information being communicated at any one time so as to avoid being inundated.

TABLE 13-2   Obtaining Employee Feedback: Some Useful Techniques

The techniques summarized here are designed to improve organizational functioning by providing top management with information about the attitudes and ideas of the work force. They are used to promote the upward flow of information.

Technique	Description
Employee surveys	Questionnaires assessing workers' attitudes and opinions about key areas of organizational functioning, especially when results are shared with the work force
Suggestion systems	Formal mechanisms through which employees can submit ideas for improving things in organizations (often by putting a note in a *suggestion box*); good ideas are implemented and the people who submitted them are rewarded
Corporate hotlines	Telephone numbers employees may call to ask questions about important organizational matters; useful in addressing workers' concerns before they become too serious
Brown bag meetings	Sessions in which subordinates and superiors meet informally over breakfast or lunch to discuss organizational matters
Skip level meetings	Meetings between subordinates and superiors two or more levels above them in the organizational hierarchy

Gauging the Flow of Information   Imagine a busy manager surrounded by a tall stack of papers, with a telephone receiver in each ear and a crowd of people gathered around, waiting to talk to her. Obviously, the many demands put on this person can slow down the system and make its operation less effective. When any part of a communication network (be it an individual, a committee, or the like) becomes bogged down with more information than it can handle effectively, a condition of **overload** is said to exist. Consider, for example, the bottleneck in the flow of routine financial information that might result when the members of the Accounting Department of an organization are tied up preparing corporate tax returns. (Such an overloaded condition is analogous to the experience of saturation encountered by central members of a centralized communication network described earlier in this chapter.) Naturally, such a state poses a serious threat to effective organizational communication. Fortunately, however, several steps can be taken to manage information more effectively.

For one, organizations may employ *gatekeepers*, people whose jobs require them to control the flow of information to potentially overloaded units. For example, executive assistants are responsible for making sure that busy executives are not overloaded by the demands of other people or groups. Newspaper editors and television news directors may also be thought of as gatekeepers, since such individuals decide what news will and will not be shared with the public. It is an essential part of these individuals' jobs to avoid overloading others by gauging the flow of information to them.

Overload can also be avoided through *queuing*. This term refers to lining up incoming information so that it can be managed in an orderly fashion. The practices of "stacking" jets as they approach a busy airport and making customers take a number (i.e., defining their position in the line) at a busy deli counter are both designed to avoid the chaos that may otherwise result when too many demands are made on the system at once. For a summary of these techniques, see Figure 13–17.

When systems are overloaded, problems of *distortion* and *omission* are likely to result. That is, messages may be either changed or left out when they are passed on from one organizational unit to the next. If you've ever played the parlor game "telephone" (in which one person whispers a message to another, who passes it on to another, and so on until it reaches the last person), you have likely experienced— or contributed to—the ways messages get distorted and omitted. When you consider the important messages that are often communicated in organizations, these problems can be very serious. They also tend to be quite extreme. A dramatic demonstration of this was reported in a study tracing the flow of downward communication in more than 100 organizations. The researchers found that messages communicated downward over five levels lost approximately 80 percent of their original information by the time they reached their destination at the lowest level of the organizational hierarchy.[82] Obviously, something needs to be done.

One strategy that has proven effective in avoiding the problems of distortion and omission is *redundancy*. Making messages redundant involves transmitting them again, often in another form or via another channel. For example, in attempting to communicate an important message to her subordinates, a manager may tell them the message and then follow it up with a written memo. In fact, one study has found that managers frequently encourage this practice.[83] Another practice that can help avoid distortion and omission is *verification*. This refers to making sure messages have been received accurately. Pilots use verification when they repeat the messages given them by air traffic controllers. Doing so assures both parties that the messages the pilots heard were the actual messages the controllers sent. Given how busy pilots may be during takeoffs and landings and the interference inherent in radio transmissions, coupled with the importance of the messages themselves, the practice of verifying messages is a wise safety measure. The practice not only is used in airline communication systems, but may be used by individual communicators as well.

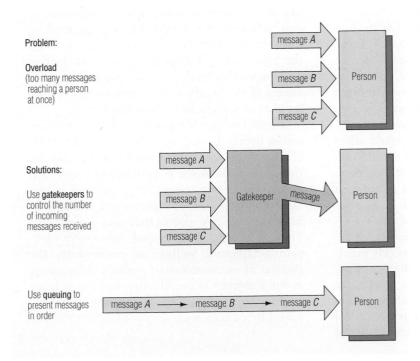

Problem:

Overload
(too many messages reaching a person at once)

Solutions:

Use **gatekeepers** to control the number of incoming messages received

Use **queuing** to present messages in order

FIGURE 13–17

Overload: A Problem That Can Be Solved

Overload, receiving too many messages at once, can seriously interfere with organizational functioning. It can be minimized by using *gatekeepers* and *queuing*.

Test Bank question 13.45 relates to material on this page.

Active listeners may wish to verify that they correctly understood a speaker, and do so by paraphrasing the speaker's remarks within a question, asking "If I heard you correctly, you were saying. . . ."

As we have noted here, for the communication process to operate as effectively as it can, a concerted effort is required of everyone involved in it. Those who send messages should make them clear and redundant, those who receive messages should listen actively and verify what they have heard, and the system within which communication occurs should provide gatekeepers and/or mechanisms for queuing that

 ## FOCUS ON RESEARCH

How to Communicate with Employees about a Merger

 Corporate mergers have become a reality of the business environment in the 1990s. With them has come another reality, often difficult for employees: facing uncertainty about the future. A lack of information about how one's job might change, or if it even will exist at all, can be a critical source of tension and stress.[84] Hence, managers would be wise to communicate information about mergers that may mitigate these negative effects. Exactly what should be done? How should companies go about providing information about a forthcoming merger to minimize the disruptive effects on employees?

A recent study by Schweiger and DeNisi provides critical insight into this question.[85] These investigators compared the reactions of people in two manufacturing plants whose operations were going to be affected by a friendly merger between their company and another. The employees in the experimental plant received a realistic preview of how the merger would affect them. They were given honest and detailed information about impending layoffs, transfers, promotions, demotions, as well as changes in pay, job responsibilities, and benefits. This information was presented in several forms—a bimonthly newsletter, a telephone hotline on which questions could be answered, and weekly meetings between managers and employees. Furthermore, the plant manager met with all employees to discuss decisions that affected them personally. In contrast, employees in the control plant were not given any formal information about

the merger, aside from a brief letter from the CEO.

What were the effects of the realistic preview communication on employees' reactions to the merger? As expected, employees expressed negative reactions to the merger immediately after it was announced. Among other things, they reported feeling higher amounts of uncertainty about the future (e.g., uncertainty about the possibility of relocating, being laid off, opportunities to advance). However, as shown in Figure 13–18, after the realistic merger information was communicated, the level of uncertainty experienced by employees of the control plant (who did not receive the information) continued to rise, whereas the uncertainty experienced by those in the experimental plant (who received the information) did *not* go up, but remained at an even level. Clearly, the information about the effects of the layoffs helped reduce employees' feelings of uncertainty about the future.

These findings demonstrate that communicating detailed, realistic information about the effects of a merger helped employees get through the process. Realistic communication can help employees better accept and cope with uncertain situations, thereby protecting themselves from any negative effects they may experience. Thus, although mergers may inherently instigate heightened feelings of uncertainty, the process of communicating realistic information about a merger is an effective tool for helping to minimize the degree of uncertainty experienced by employees.

guard against the possibility of overload. Together, these measures help ensure that communication occurs effectively, avoiding confusion and misunderstandings at all stages of the process. (Indeed, efforts to improve communication in organizations may require reducing employees' uncertainties about what is happening in the company, minimizing the chances that they misinterpret what they see or hear. These possibilities are especially likely during periods when two companies are merging. The **Focus on Research** section that starts on the preceding page describes a successful technique for reducing uncertainty under such conditions.)

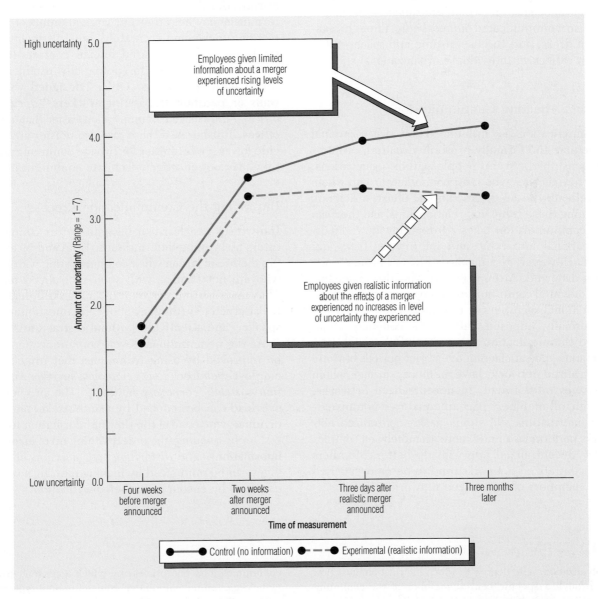

FIGURE 13–18   Effects of Realistic Merger Information on Experienced Uncertainty: An Experimental Demonstration

A recent experiment found that the levels of uncertainty that rise when a merger is announced tend to level off after realistic information about the merger is provided, whereas uncertainty levels tend to rise further when no such information is provided. (*Source:* Adapted from Schweiger & DeNisi, 1991; see Note 85.)

SUMMARY AND REVIEW

The Nature of Communication

The process of **communication** occurs when a sender of information *encodes* a message and transmits it over communication channels to a receiver, who *decodes* it and then sends feedback. Factors interfering with these processes are known as **noise.** Communication may be either verbal or nonverbal. Verbal messages may be either written (which are more enduring) or spoken (which are quicker). Messages are also communicated *nonverbally,* through manner of dress, and the use of time and space—all of which reflect an individual's organizational status.

Factors Affecting Communication

Communication is influenced by **organizational structure,** the formally prescribed pattern of interrelationships between people within organizations. Structure dictates who must communicate with whom (as reflected in an **organizational chart,** a diagram outlining these reporting relationships) and the form that communication takes. Orders flow down an organizational hierarchy, and information flows upward. However, the upward flow of information is often distorted. Attempts at coordination characterize horizontal communication, messages between organizational members at the same level.

Formally imposed patterns of communication, called **communication networks,** influence job performance and satisfaction over brief periods of time. **Centralized networks** have members through whom messages must travel. In **decentralized networks,** though, all members play an equal role in transmitting information. On simple tasks, centralized networks perform faster and more accurately; on complex tasks, decentralized networks do better. Members of decentralized networks tend to be more satisfied than members of centralized networks.

Information also flows along *informal communication networks.* These informal connections between people are responsible for spreading information very quickly because they transcend formal organizational boundaries. Informal pathways known as the **grapevine** are often responsible for the rapid transmission of partially inaccurate information.

Elements of the work environment also influence organizational communication. The use of computer terminals may help transmit large amounts of information quickly and accurately, but this technology tends to minimize desired human contact. It also reduces opportunities for potentially useful interaction with supervisors. Offices designed without walls or partitions separating workers—*open-plan offices*—may make communication easier than closed offices. But because these are also noisier and provide fewer opportunities for private communication, they may not effectively facilitate communication.

Improving the Communication Process

Individuals can learn to become better communicators by keeping their messages brief and by avoiding the use of **jargon** when communicating with those who are not familiar with such specialized terms. They may also improve their listening skills, learning to listen actively (thinking about and questioning the speaker) and attentively (without distraction).

At the organizational level, communication may be improved by using techniques that provide for employee feedback (e.g., *employee surveys, suggestion systems, corporate hotlines*). The problem of **overload** can be reduced by using gatekeepers (individuals who control the flow of information to others), or by *queuing* (the orderly lining up of incoming information). The *distortion and omission* of messages can be minimized by making messages *redundant* and by encouraging their *verification.*

KEY TERMS

centralization: The degree to which information must flow through a specific central member of the communication network.

centralized networks: Communication networks that have central members through which all information must pass to reach other members (e.g., the *Y,* the *Wheel,* and the *Chain*).

communication: The process by which a person, group, or organization (the sender) transmits some type of information (the message) to another person, group, or organization (the receiver).

communication networks: Preestablished patterns dictating who may communicate with whom. (See *centralized networks* and *decentralized networks.*)

decentralized networks: Communication networks in which all members play an equal role in the transmittal of information (e.g., the *Circle* and the *Comcon*).

decoding: The process by which a receiver of messages transforms them back into the sender's ideas.

encoding: The process by which an idea is transformed so that it can be transmitted to, and recognized by, a receiver (e.g., a written or spoken message).

grapevine: An organization's informal channels of communication, based mainly on friendship or acquaintance.

HURIER model: The conceptualization that describes effective listening as made up of six components: hearing, understanding, remembering, interpreting, evaluating, and responding.

jargon: The specialized language used by a particular group (e.g., people within a profession).

K.I.S.S. principle: A basic principle of communication advising that messages should be as short and simple as possible. (An abbreviation for keep it short and simple.)

noise: Factors capable of distorting the clarity of messages at any point during the communication process.

nonverbal communication: The transmission of messages without the use of words (e.g., by gestures, the use of space).

organizational chart: A diagram showing the formal structure of an organization, indicating who is to communicate with whom.

organizational structure: The formally prescribed pattern of interrelationships existing between the various units of an organization.

overload: The condition in which a unit of an organization becomes overburdened with too much incoming information.

rumors: Information with little basis in fact, often transmitted through informal channels. (See *grapevine*.)

saturation: The amount of information a single member of a communication network must handle.

QUESTIONS FOR DISCUSSION

1. Identify and describe the various elements of the model of communication effectiveness described in the text.

2. Describe how any three types of nonverbal cues influence communication within organizations.

3. Imagine that you are a manager attempting to explain the use of a certain new computer software package to a subordinate. Should this be accomplished using written communication, oral communication, or both? Explain.

4. What is an *organizational chart?* What does it reveal about the nature of communication within organizations?

5. Imagine that you are putting together groups of five employees to evaluate proposed methods for disposing of nuclear waste. What type of communication network would be most appropriate? Why?

6. Argue for or against the following statement: "Rumors pose a threat to the effective operation of organizations."

7. Suppose you were designing a new office. What con-

siderations of technology and physical design should enter into your plan if you are trying to make it as effective as possible for communication?

8. In Shakespeare's *Hamlet*, Polonius said, "Give every man thine ear, but few thy voice." Discuss the implications of this advice for being an effective listener. What other suggestions should be followed for enhancing the effectiveness of listening?

9. Identify any two problems of organizational communication, and measures that can be taken to overcome them.

10. Argue for or against the following statement: Employers have a right to access their employees' electronic mailboxes.

11. Suppose you are going to tell your company's employees about a forthcoming merger. What considerations will you take into account when doing so?

NOTES

1. Fulk, J., & Boyd, B. (1991). Emerging theories of communication in organizations. *Journal of Management, 17,* 407–446.

2. Scudder, J. N., & Guinan, P. J. (1989). Communication competencies as discriminators of superiors' ratings of employee performance. *Journal of Business Communication, 26,* 217–229.

3. Roberts, K. H. (1984). *Communicating in organizations* (p. 4). Chicago: Science Research Associates.

4. Weick, K. E. (1987). Theorizing about organizational communication. In F. M. Jablin, L. L. Putnam, K. H. Roberts, & L. W. Porter (Eds.), *Handbook of organizational communication* (pp. 97–122). Newbury Park, CA: Sage.

5. Barnard, C. I. (1938). *The functions of the executive.* Cambridge, MA: Harvard University Press.

6. Mintzberg, H. (1973). *The nature of managerial work.* New York: Harper & Row.

7. Reilly, B. J., & DiAngelo, J. A., Jr. (1990). Communication: A cultural system of meaning and value. *Human Relations, 43,* 129–140.

8. Pearce, C. G., & Barker, R. T. (1991). A comparison of business communication quality between computer written and handwritten samples. *Journal of Business Communication, 28,* 141–151.

9. Level, D. A. (1972). Communication effectiveness: Methods and situation. *Journal of Business Communication, 10,* 19–25.

10. Klauss, R., & Bass, B. M. (1982). *International communication in organizations.* New York: Academic Press.

11. Daft, R. L., Lengel, R. H., & Trevino, L. K. (1987). Message equivocality, media selection, and manager performance: Implications for information systems. *MIS Quarterly, 11,* 355–366.

12. Malloy, J. T. (1975). *Dress for success.* New York: Warner Books.

13. Forsythe, S., Drake, M. F., & Cox, C. E. (1985). Influence of applicant's dress on interviewer's selection decisions. *Journal of Applied Psychology, 70,* 374–378.

14. Solomon, M. R. (1986, April). Dress for effect. *Psychology Today,* pp. 20–28.

15. Greenberg, J. (1989). The organizational waiting game: Status as a status-asserting or status-neutralizing tactic. *Basic and Applied Social Psychology, 10,* 13–26.

16. Zweigenhaft, R. L. (1976). Personal space in the faculty office: Desk placement and student-faculty interaction. *Journal of Applied Psychology, 61,* 529–532.

17. Greenberg, J. (1976). The role of seating position in group interaction: A review, with applications for group trainers. *Group and Organization Studies, 1,* 310–327.

18. Scully, J. (1987). *Odyssey: Pepsi to Apple . . . a journey of adventure, ideas, and the future.* New York: Harper & Row.

19. Carstairs, E. (1986, February). No ivory tower for Procter & Gamble. *Corporate Design and Reality,* pp. 24–30.

20. Rasmussen, K. G., Jr. (1984). Nonverbal behavior, verbal behavior, résumé credentials, and selection interview outcomes. *Journal of Applied Psychology, 69,* 551–556.

21. See Note 8.

22. Argyris, C. (1974). *Behind the front page: Organizational self-renewal in a metropolitan newspaper.* San Francisco: Jossey-Bass.

23. Papa, M. J. (1990). Communication network patterns and employee performance with new technology. *Communication Research, 17,* 344–368.

24. Miller, K. I., Ellis, B. H., Zook, E. G., & Lyles, J. S. (1990). An integrated model of communication, stress, and burnout in the workplace. *Communication Research, 17,* 300–326.

25. Ghoshal, S., & Bartlett, C. A. (1990). The multinational corporation as an interorganizational network. *Academy of Management Review, 15,* 603–625.

26. Hawkins, B. L., & Preston, P. (1981). *Managerial communication.* Santa Monica, CA: Goodyear.

27. Schnake, M. E., Dumler, M. P., Cochran, D. S., & Barnett, T. R. (1990). Effects of differences in superior and subordinate perceptions of superiors' communication practices. *Journal of Business Communication, 27,* 37–50.

28. Szilagyi, A. (1981). *Management and performance.* Glenview, IL: Scott, Foresman.

29. Kiechell, W., III. (1986, January 6). No word from on high. *Fortune,* pp. 19, 26.

30. Walker, C. R., & Guest, R. H. (1952). *The man on the assembly line.* Cambridge, MA: Harvard University Press.

31. Luthans, F., & Larsen, J. K. (1986). How managers really communicate. *Human Relations, 39,* 161–178.

32. Kirmeyer, S. L., & Lin, T. (1987). Social support: Its relationship to observed communication with peers and superiors. *Academy of Management Journal, 30,* 138–151.

33. Read, W. (1962). Upward communication in industrial hierarchies. *Human Relations, 15,* 3–16.

34. Glauser, M. J. (1984). Upward information flow in organizations: Review and conceptual analysis. *Human Relations, 37,* 613–643.

35. Singer, A. (1991, November/December). Could Middlebury have found a "decent" middle way to conduct layoffs? *Ethikos, 5*(3), 1–4, 16.

36. Greenberg, J. (1992). The social side of fairness: Interpersonal and informational classes of organizational justice. In R. Cropanzano (Ed.), *Justice in the workplace: Approaching fairness in human resource management.* Hillsdale, NJ: Erlbaum.

37. Rogers, E. M., & Rogers, A. (1976). *Communication in organizations.* New York: Free Press.

38. Shaw, M. E. (1978). Communication networks fourteen years later. In L. Berkowitz (Ed.), *Group processes* (pp. 351–361). New York: Academic Press.

39. Forsyth, D. R. (1983). *An introduction to group dynamics.* Monterey, CA: Brooks/Cole.

40. Burgess, R. L. (1968). Communication networks: An experimental reevaluation. *Journal of Experimental Social Psychology, 4,* 324–327.

41. Zenger, T. R., & Lawrence, B. S. (1989). Organizational demography: The differential effects of age and tenure distributions on technical communication. *Academy of Management Journal, 32,* 353–376.

42. Krackhardt, D., & Porter, L. W. (1986). The snowball effect: Turnover embedded in communication networks. *Journal of Applied Psychology, 71,* 50–55.

43. Duncan, J. W. (1984). Perceived humor and social network patterns in a sample of task-oriented groups: A reexamination of prior research. *Human Relations, 37,* 895–907.

44. Flexner, S. B. (1982). *Listening to America.* New York: Simon and Schuster.

45. Baskin, O. W., & Aronoff, C. E. (1989). *Interpersonal communication in organizations.* Santa Monica, CA: Goodyear.

46. Walton, E. (1961). How efficient is the grapevine? *Personnel, 28,* 45–49.

47. Thibaut, A. M., Calder, B. J., & Sternthal, B. (1981).

Using information processing theory to design marketing strategies. *Journal of Marketing Research, 18,* 73–79.

48. See Note 47.

49. Brass, D. J. (1985). Men's and women's networks: A study of interaction patterns and influence in an organization. *Academy of Management Journal, 28,* 327–343.

50. West, C. K., & Hoerr, W. A. (1985). Communication and work patterns among productive scholars in psychoeducational research: The invisible college hypothesis. *Human Relations, 18,* 127–137.

51. Leffingwell, W. H. (1925). *Office management.* Chicago: A. W. Shaw.

52. Zuboff, S. (1988). *In the age of the smart machine.* New York: Basic Books.

53. Chao, G. T., & Kozlowski, S. W. J. (1986). Employee perceptions on the implementation of robotic manufacturing technology. *Journal of Applied Psychology, 71,* 70–76.

54. Medina, D. (1991, June 24). Management's e-mail message. *Information Week,* p. 60.

55. Ritchie, L. D. (1991). Another turn of the information revolution. *Communication Research, 18,* 412–427.

56. Begole, C. (1990, October). Five successful alternatives to in-person meetings. *Working Woman,* pp. 70–74.

57. Johnson, B. (1988, November/December). Streamlining corporate communications through voice imaging technology. *The Professional Communicator,* pp. 19–20.

58. See Note 57.

59. Reinsch, N. L., Jr., & Beswick, R. W. (1990). Voice mail versus conventional channels: A cost minimization analysis of individuals' preferences. *Academy of Management Journal, 33,* 801–816.

60. Allen, T. J. (1966). Performance information channels in the transfer of technology. *Industrial Management, 8,* 87–98.

61. Zalesny, M. D., & Farce, R. V. (1987). Traditional versus open offices: A comparison of sociotechnical, social relations, and symbolic meaning perspectives. *Academy of Management Journal, 30,* 240–259.

62. Oldham, G. R. (1988). Effects of changes in workspace partitions and spatial density on employee reactions: A quasi-experiment. *Journal of Applied Psychology, 73,* 253–258.

63. Rifkin, G. (1991, December 8). Do employees have a right to electronic privacy? *New York Times,* p. F8.

64. See Note 63.

65. See Note 63.

66. See Note 63.

67. Pettit, J. D., Jr., Vaught, B., & Pulley, K. J. (1990). The role of communication in organizations: Ethical considerations. *Journal of Business Communications, 27,* 233–249.

68. Kanter, R. M. (1977). *Men and women of the corporation.* New York: Basic Books.

69. Borman, E. (1982). *Interpersonal communication in the modern organization* (2nd ed.). Englewood Cliffs, NJ: Prentice-Hall.

70. Rowe, M. P., & Baker, M. (1984, May–June). Are you hearing enough employee concerns? *Harvard Business Review,* pp. 127–135.

71. Brownell, J. (1985). A model for listening instruction: Management applications. *ABCA Bulletin, 48*(3), 39–44.

72. Austin, N. K. (1991, March). Why listening's not as easy as it sounds. *Working Woman,* pp. 46–48.

73. See Note 72.

74. Sypher, B. D., Bostrom, R. N., & Seibert, J. H. (1989). Listening, communication abilities, and success at work. *Journal of Business Communication, 26,* 293–303.

75. Penley, L. E., Alexander, E. R., Jernigan, I. E., & Henwood, C. I. (1991). Communication abilities of managers: The relationship to performance. *Journal of Management, 17,* 57–76.

76. Brownell, J. (1990). Perceptions of effective listeners: A management study. *Journal of Business Communication, 27,* 401–415.

77. McCathrin, Z. (1990, Spring). The key to employee communication: Small group meetings. *The Professional Communicator,* pp. 6–7, 10.

78. Vernyi, B. (1987, April 26). Institute aims to boost quality of company suggestion boxes. *Toledo Blade,* p. B2.

79. Bergerson, A. W. (1977, May). Employee suggestion plan still going strong at Kodak. *Supervisory Management, 22,* 32–36.

80. Taft, W. F. (1985). Bulletin boards, exhibits, hotlines. In C. Reuss & D. Silvis (Eds.), *Inside organizational communication* (2nd ed.) (pp. 183–189). New York: Longman.

81. See Note 77.

82. Nichols, R. G. (1962, Winter). Listening is good business. *Management of Personnel Quarterly,* p. 4.

83. See Note 9.

84. Buono, A. F., & Bowditch, J. L. (1989). *The human side of mergers and acquisitions.* San Francisco: Jossey-Bass.

85. Schweiger, D. M., & DeNisi, A. S. (1991). Communication with employees following a merger: A longitudinal field experiment. *Academy of Management Journal, 34,* 110–135.

What do you do when more than half of your employees don't believe anything that management says? The Saginaw Division of General Motors met this problem head on by developing a multifaceted approach for improving communications.[1]

In 1982, Ron Actis, director of public affairs at General Motors' Saginaw Division, suspected that the communications system was inadequate. Actis conducted a survey of division employees to find out what they thought of the quality and quantity of communications. "We not only sensed . . . but found a lack of trust between management and labor, poor communications throughout the division, decision making limited to a handful, minimum employee involvement and unpredictable leadership."[2] Actis's suspicions were confirmed.

Actis knew that if the level of trust was to increase, he needed to devise a process for management and employees to start communicating with each other. An effective communications system would have to get "the right message to the right audience at the right time with the right medium . . . all the while with progress measured on a continuous basis."[3] A two-way dialogue had to be instituted; management would have to listen as well as talk to employees.

Actis developed the Synchronous Communication Process (SCP). The SCP consisted of educating top management about the advantages and requirements of an effective communications system, upgrading company publications, instituting a video magazine, creating a format for face-to-face meetings between management and employees, and establishing a means of appraising the effectiveness of the entire SCP.

The effectiveness of any change in an organization's communications methods depends largely on top management's support. Actis was especially interested in getting top managers to view internal communications as an important means of increasing organizational performance. He gave top managers numerous journal reports and magazine articles showing how effective communications can improve organizational productivity.

Actis knew that effective communications systems had to be designed correctly. He had to sell top managers on the idea of investing to build a good system. Actis provided managers with case illustrations of how other well-known companies had built their communications systems and promoted the idea of effective communications systems whenever he met with top managers.

Actis then set out to upgrade the company's publications. He changed the content of the *Daily Newsletter* from industry- and company wide news to 75 percent news about what was going on in the Saginaw Division. This one-page newsletter is distributed to the division's 20,000 employees each workday. Copies of the *Daily Newsletter* are available at various places throughout the plant. What did employees think of this change? They liked it. Employees at all levels of the division were reading the *Newsletter*.

Next, Actis started the *Steering Column,* a monthly tabloid mailed to the home of every employee. Saginaw employees were delighted with the tabloid. However, Actis's use of the *Steering Column* didn't stop with employees. He also put copies in the company's lobbies for visitors and sent the tabloid to retirees, area press, and local civic leaders. This four- to six-page tabloid extended the division's communications to the entire Saginaw community.

Actis realized the importance of targeting information to the appropriate audiences. He started a series of publications. To enable Saginaw's supervisors to communicate face-to-face with employees, Actis published the *Report to Supervisors*—a bimonthly, two-page newsletter filled with tips for improving communicating skills and advance information about key issues. For upper management, he published *Insight,* a summary of government and regulatory issues related to the auto industry. To improve relations between management and unions, *Joint Activities* was created. This publication includes features concerning quality, cost reduction, and competitiveness techniques. And for Saginaw's 7,000 suppliers, Actis created the *21st Century Supplier.* This publication includes features about the division's goals so that suppliers can better anticipate the division's future needs.

Actis then developed *Perspective,* a video magazine produced quarterly and shown to employees during work hours. *Perspective* is intended to communicate company information of a more confidential nature. Comprising a diverse mix of interviews with managers, customers, employees, suppliers, and union representatives, this video magazine achieved a high level of credibility.

The video format of *Perspective* encouraged employees and managers to engage in face-to-face discussions of company issues. Actis, however, wasn't about to rely on *Perspective* as the only means of assuring this two-way communication. He initiated a series of face-to-face meetings between employees and management. "The underlying premise behind such meetings was that upper management was out of touch with the work force and vice versa," he explains.[4] The face-to-face meetings were designed to be candid, nothing-barred, question-and-answer sessions.

The meetings soon turned into intense discussions of business issues. Stereotypes of employees interested only in pay and benefits all but vanished. Employees demonstrated that they were very concerned about what General Motors was trying to achieve and how they could become more involved in helping their division's productivity.

The response of both management and employees to the face-to-face meetings was so positive that seventeen different types of employee-management meetings are now scheduled every year. These meetings range in frequency from weekly to annual, depending on their purpose.

To provide the SCP with better focus, Actis assembled a Communications Review Group, a standing committee charged with critically reviewing all of the division's communications needs and activities. To better enable it to perform its review function, the Communications Review Group developed a communications mission statement that gives focus to communications strategies. In addition, the review group nominates story ideas for the division's publications and video magazine. The Communications Review Group also serves to institutionalize the communications system. The plant's general manager and executive staff regularly attend the meetings of the review group. Top managers at the Saginaw Division now consider communications as central to the division's effectiveness.

How is the effectiveness of the Saginaw Division's communications system assessed? With the help of the Communications Review Group, Actis uses a variety of measuring devices. At least once every two years, Actis conducts a divisionwide communications audit. All employees are asked to comment on the quality and quantity of communications as well as the degree to which they trust the communications. Prior to Actis's implementation of the SCP, fewer than 50 percent of employees believed anything management tried to communicate. Four years later, over 80 percent of employees not only believed what management had to say, but were pleased with the effectiveness of the SCP in getting important information to them. The trust between management and employees had grown dramatically.

Actis also uses an information tracking technique to find out how well information percolates throughout the division. Actis monitors information and messages that top managers send down the division's organizational hierarchy, and then interviews randomly selected employees from various levels of the division to determine how much of the original information actually reaches employees. Actis's first information tracking study—conducted prior to implementation of the SCP—showed that much of the original information sent down by managers was lost during its downward transmission to hourly employees. The SCP has substantially reduced the loss of downward-flowing information. Now, face-to-face meetings between employees and management are greater in number and more deliberate in focus. The division's various publications and magazines communicate important information more directly to employees who need the information. Use of the information tracking technique continues to help the division monitor the effectiveness of the SCP and make corrections where needed.

Other indicators of the success of the SCP are reflected financially by the bottom line. Annual decreases in operating costs ranging from 2.2 to 5.5 percent were achieved during the SCP's first seven years. Sales per employee doubled over the same time period. On-time delivery of parts also improved, reaching the ultimate level of zero parts past due in 1988! In addition, the savings generated by employee suggestions soared from an average of $864 per employee in 1981 to $5,748 per employee in 1987.

Actis admits that the SCP cannot take all the credit for productivity increases, but he is convinced that better communications are the driving force behind the improvements. The SCP developed by Actis for the Saginaw Division is now the communications model for all General Motors divisions.

Questions for Discussion

1. Describe the Saginaw Division's Synchronous Communication Process (SCP) in terms of the basic model of communications described in this text.
2. Which of the communication methods in the SCP involve verbal communications? Which methods involve nonverbal communications? Which of the methods involve both verbal and nonverbal communications?
3. Which of the SCP communication methods is most effective for communicating ambiguous messages? Clear messages? Explain your answers.
4. Which of the SCP communication methods is most useful for communicating up the organizational chart? Down and across the organizational chart?
5. How does the SCP work to get the right information to the right people?

Notes

1. McKeand, P. J. (1990, November). GM division builds a classic system to share internal information. *Public Relations Journal*, pp. 24–26, 41.
2. See Note 1, p. 24.
3. See Note 1, p. 24.
4. See Note 1, p. 25.

EXPERIENCING ORGANIZATIONAL BEHAVIOR

Becoming an Active Listener

What makes an effective communicator? Most people would probably say it's his or her ability to express ideas—to speak and write clearly. Of course these skills are important, but listening is, too. Being a good communicator requires listening carefully, picking up others' ideas. Although we might hear others, most of us tend to be very inefficient listeners. That is, we fail to pay attention to and understand most of what others are saying. When it comes to communication in organizations, this can be quite problematic. Recognizing this, many people in organizations are trained to become more *active listeners* (see pages 516–518).

Procedure

1. Review the following "dos and don'ts" of active listening.

Do	*Don't*
Show empathy; support the speaker.	Judge and draw conclusions.
Explain what you think was said.	Evaluate the ideas expressed.

2. As a class, consider how an active listener would respond to someone saying "I worked for hours on that stupid project, and the boss didn't like it. That'll be the last time I work so hard for him."

Listening actively, it would be correct to say "You seem disappointed that your boss didn't approve of your work." Such a response shows that you understand the speaker and encourages him or her to give more thought to the problem at hand. In contrast, it would be incorrect to say either "You should have started that project long ago" (too judgmental) or "At least you have a good job" (no empathy).

3. The instructor should now read each of the following statements out loud. Listen actively to each one and respond to it in a way that shows you've listened actively. Discuss several students' responses relative to the guidelines for active listening noted above.

a. I just found out my boss gave me only a 2 percent raise. If that's the kind of appreciation they show for hard work around here, they can get themselves another sucker!

b. Why did you take Barbara's side on that budget vote? I thought you agreed with me, but apparently not. Sometimes it's tough to tell your friends from your enemies.

c. It really sounds like a good offer. The pay is competitive, and I've always wanted to live in Crowdville.

d. I'm really tired of those staff meetings. All we ever do is gripe. If you ask me, they're just a waste of time.

e. Try as I might, I just can't get the hang of that new computer system. Yesterday, I messed with it for hours and got nowhere.

f. Being part of the Rafstone Products team is a dream come true. I just hope I can cut it around here with all those big shots.

g. Everybody's gone on vacation this week, but I have to hang around to get caught up on my work. At least that's what Mr. Nasty wanted. Sure wish I could be getting a tan like everyone else!

Points to Consider

1. Did it become easier for you to think of appropriate responses as you practiced more?
2. Had you not been attempting to listen actively, how would you have responded? More judgmentally?
3. What mistakes did your classmates make most commonly in responding to these statements?
4. Do you think you will be able to apply your active listening skills to your own interactions with others? Why or why not?
5. What personal benefits do you imagine will result for both speakers and listeners from using active listening techniques?
6. When do you think it would be most appropriate to use and to not use active listening skills in organizations?
7. How would you feel as the speaker if you heard the responses of your classmates?

■ 14 ■

DECISION MAKING IN ORGANIZATIONS

CHAPTER OUTLINE

Organizational Decision Making: Its Basic Nature
The Traditional, Analytical Model of Decision Making
An Intuitive Approach to Decision Making: Image Theory
Varieties of Organizational Decisions

Individual Decision Making in Organizations: An Imperfect Process
Two Approaches to Individual Decision Making: The Rational-Economic Model and the Administrative Model
Impediments to Optimal Individual Decisions

Group Decisions: Do Too Many Cooks Spoil the Broth?
Comparing Group and Individual Decisions: When Are Two (or More) Heads Better Than One?

Obstacles to Quality Group Decisions: Groupthink and Group Polarization
Improving the Effectiveness of Group Decisions: Some Techniques

Special Sections

OB in Practice Undoing Corporate Decisions: Toying Around at Fisher-Price and Taking the Fizzle Out of Coca-Cola

A Question of Ethics Ethical Decisions: The Result of "Bad Apples" in "Bad Barrels"

Focus on Research Training Pilots to Make Decisions about Avoiding Hazardous Weather

LEARNING OBJECTIVES

After reading this chapter, you should be able to:
1. Identify the steps in the traditional, analytic model of decision making.
2. Describe and give examples of the various types of organizational decisions (i.e., *programmed* versus *nonprogrammed*, and decisions made under high and low levels of risk).
3. Distinguish between the rational-economic model and the administrative model of decision making.
4. Describe the factors that dictate against high-quality individual decisions—both individual, cognitive biases and organizationally induced barriers.

5. Compare the advantages and disadvantages of using groups and individuals to make decisions in organizations.
6. Describe the conditions under which groups make better decisions than individuals, and the conditions under which individuals make better decisions than groups.
7. Identify the major obstacles to effective group decisions (*groupthink* and *group polarization*).
8. Describe techniques that can be used to improve the quality of group decisions (e.g., the *Delphi technique*, the *nominal group technique*, and *decision training*).

"Love that one," the deejay wails as the music fades, "the Playmates with 'Beep Beep' from back in '62."

The sound coming out of the studio monitor is unmistakably vintage rock 'n' roll. But just how long these "doo-wop ditties" will be booming from KZYN's transmitter is anybody's guess.

Diana Fordham has the volume on the receiver in her office turned all the way down, but the sound is ever-present in the suite of offices and studios that form this small-town radio station. As general manager, she is having her weekly meeting with her top staff members, Randy Harris, sales manager, and John Singh, program director.

"I'll be blunt," Di says. "The numbers are out, and they're not looking good." A hush falls over the room, confirming what everybody has been sensing. The station changed to an oldies format from country music only three months earlier, and there has been no sign that it has caught on.

"Just look," says Di, pointing to the fine print in the ratings book, "we have less than 5 percent of the market in the critical eighteen- to thirty-five-year-old age group—and no gain whatsoever during drive time."

"That's down from about 15 percent before the format change, isn't it?" Randy questions.

"I think so," John answers. "I don't think we were ever lower than 15 percent." Thinking a moment longer, he adds, "In fact, as I recall, it was our concern about the 15 percent that prompted the format change."

"That wasn't everything," Di interjects. "It was really the trend, down from a high of about 27 percent just two years ago."

"It all happened when Country Bob left us and took his Jamboree with him," John notes.

"Yeah," Randy agrees, "he was the core of our country air staff. We really panicked when he left and saw the numbers tumble."

"We all took it as a sign to change who we were, to alter our basic identity," Di explains, "and in retrospect, that might have been a mistake."

"I can't agree more," Randy says. "This is a farm community, and our listeners want to hear country music—with or without Country Bob! Selling the Supremes and the Beach Boys isn't easy down at Jones's Feed and Grain."

"I can imagine, Randy, and these ratings don't help either."

"That's for sure," Randy agrees. "They'd buy time *if* we had listeners, whether or not they really like the music—within limits, of course."

"So, it looks like a real no-win situation," Diana summarizes. "No listeners means no sponsors, and no sponsors means no money, which means no improvements."

"And maybe no jobs!" John chimes in.

Di is quick to assume the duties of her leadership role. "Gentlemen," she says, "it looks to me like our decision to switch to an oldies format was, probably, too hasty. Our faltering ratings as a country station shouldn't have signaled a need to change our format. All we may have really needed was a *better* country station, instead of a whole different musical format."

"We can't feel too bad," Randy says. "After all, we decided to go to an oldies format because we really believed it would make it. Remember, we had hoped that we'd pull in listeners from bigger cities nearby, yuppies who wanted to hear the music they grew up with."

"That trend is—and has been—hot all over the country," Di adds.

"The one thing we didn't plan on was that there'd be a much stronger FM station, OK95—right in the middle of the population center—that sounded better than we did," John explains. "And when you're riding to work in a nice car, you really want to have that radio station come in clearly, and not pull in static from a fringe reception area."

"So, what I'm hearing is that you think we might do best to return to what we really are deep inside—a country station for country people," Di observes.

"At least that way," Randy notes, "we can meet any competition on our home turf, so to speak."

"We would keep our sponsors loyal and get back our old listeners. I can just see the promotion now: 'We're back to country . . . and sounding better than ever!' "

"Well," Diana says, "it looks like the three of us are in agreement that KZYN should return to a country format, but that's a lot easier said than done. We still have to convince the board of directors at Paragon Broadcasting."

"Yeah," John remarks, "those eight guys in blue suits who now go around saying, 'rock 'n' roll is here to stay.' "

"Maybe they'll just have to learn a new tune," Di comments, "like 'Take Me Home, Country Roads.' "

———————————————■———————————————

Maybe you're not in charge of a radio station's operations and feeling the pressure of low ratings, but you can probably relate to the KZYN staff's dilemma. Anyone who has ever worked through a complex problem is probably aware of how difficult it is to take everything into account when deciding what to do. When you made a decision about which college or university to attend, you may have faced a broad array of considerations: curriculum, location, scholarship opportunities, tuition and living expenses, and so on. Because of these various factors, it may not have been an easy decision, with many critical options to carefully sort through and evaluate— all without knowing what is really best for you! That's often just how it is in the business world. As an example, the management of the radio station in our story has to decide what direction to take the station now that a previous decision (a format change) has failed. The people immediately closest to the problem seem to agree about what to do, but will they be able to convince those who are responsible for making a final decision? In the face of adversity, decision makers may attempt to analyze the facts carefully and make a good decision, but this is easier said than done. Ultimately, will the board of directors make the best decision for the station? Only time will tell. The only certainty is that the decision won't come easily. Some may wish to stay the course, whereas others may "cut their losses and run." From your own experiences, you probably know how difficult it can be for a group of people, no matter how well intentioned, to reach a decision. Thinking about the problems involved in making decisions in your own life may help you appreciate how complicated and important the process of **decision making** can be in organizations, where the stakes—for both the individual and the organization—may be greater.

This chapter will examine theories, research, and practical managerial techniques concerned with organizational decision making. We will explore the ways individuals make decisions, and then look at the decision-making processes of groups. Specifically, we will review the basic characteristics of individual decisions and group decisions. For each, we will identify factors that may adversely affect the quality of decisions and ways of combating them—that is, techniques for improving the quality of decisions. We will compare the quality of individual and group decisions on a variety of tasks and note the conditions under which individuals or groups are better suited for making decisions. But first, we will begin by taking a closer look at the general process of decision making and the varieties of decisions made in organizations.

ORGANIZATIONAL DECISION MAKING: ITS BASIC NATURE

It is safe to say that decision making is one of the most important—if not *the* most important—of all managerial activities.[1] Management theorists and researchers agree that decision making represents one of the most common and most crucial work roles of the executive. In fact, organizational scientist Herbert Simon, who won a Nobel prize for his work on decision making, has gone so far as to describe decision making as synonymous with managing (see Figure 14–1).[2]

Given the central importance of decision making in organizational life, we will begin our discussion by highlighting some of the basic steps in the decision-making process and noting the characteristics of organizational decisions. Specifically, two different approaches to decision making will be considered: the traditional orientation, which looks at decision making in terms of a continuous series of analytical steps, and a more contemporary approach, which looks at decision making as an automatic, intuitive process.

FIGURE 14–1

Decision Making: A Common Aspect of Managerial Jobs

As part of their jobs, managers are routinely required to make decisions. The process of decision making is one of the most basic duties of managerial work.

Even though making decisions is important, especially for managers in organizations, many people admit that they have trouble making even minor decisions. For example, in a survey of 1,000 Americans, people said that they have trouble making such kinds of decisions as buying life insurance (73 percent), making political choices (76 percent), choosing the best school for their children (72 percent), buying a new car (71 percent), selecting clothing to wear (63 percent), planning how to lose weight (61 percent), choosing a doctor (55 percent), and deciding on a vacation spot (52 percent). If people have trouble making even minor decisions, then good managerial decisions—which might cost the company thousands of dollars if incorrect—might be even harder to make. [Decisions, decisions. (1990, February 5). *U.S. News & World Report*, p. 74.]

The Traditional, Analytical Model of Decision Making

Traditionally, scientists have found it useful to conceptualize the process of decision making as a series of steps that groups or individuals take to solve problems.[3] A general model of the steps in the decision-making process can help us understand the complex nature of organizational decision making (see Figure 14–2).[4] As we present this model, remember that not all decisions fully conform to the neat, eight-step pattern described (e.g., steps may be skipped and/or combined).[5] However, for the purpose of pointing out the general way the decision making process operates, we think the model is quite effective.

The first step in decision making is *problem identification.* To decide how to solve a problem, one must first recognize and identify the problem. For example, an executive may identify as a problem the fact that the company cannot meet its payroll obligations. This step isn't always as easy as it sounds. In fact, research reviewed by Cowan has shown that people often distort, omit, ignore, and/or discount information around them that provides important cues regarding the existence of problems.[6] You may recall from our discussion of the social perception process (see chapter 2) that people do not always accurately perceive social situations. It is easy to imagine that someone may fail to recognize a problem if doing so makes him or her uncomfortable. Denying a problem may be the first impediment on the road to solving it!

After a problem is identified, the next step is to *define the objectives to be met in solving the problem.* It is important to conceive of problems in such a way that

FIGURE 14–2

The Decision-Making Process: The Traditional, Analytical Model

The process of decision making tends to follow the eight steps outlined here. Note how each step may be applied to a hypothetical organizational problem: having insufficient funds to meet payroll obligations. (*Source:* Based on information in Wedley & Field, 1984; see Note 4).

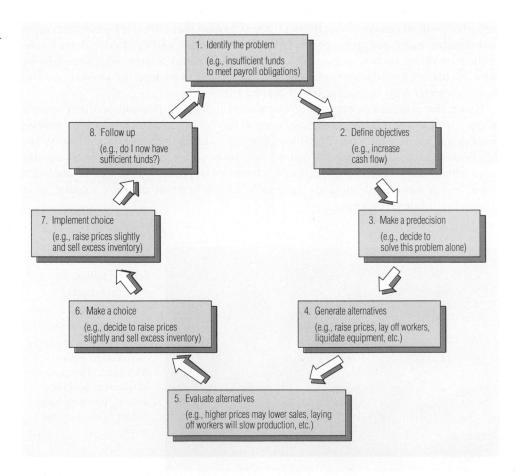

possible solutions can be identified. The problem identified in our example may be defined as not having enough money, or in business terms, "inadequate cash flow." By looking at the problem in this way, the objective is clear: increase available cash reserves. Any possible solution to the problem should be evaluated relative to this objective. A good solution is one that meets it.

The third step in the decision-making process is to *make a predecision*. **A predecision** is a decision about how to make a decision. By assessing the type of problem in question, the style of the decision maker, and other aspects of the situation, managers may opt to make a decision themselves, delegate the decision to another, or have a group make the decision. Decisions about how to make a decision should be based on research that tells us about the nature of the decisions made under different circumstances—many of which we will review later in this chapter. For many years, managers have been relying on their own intuition or, better yet, on empirically based information about organizational behavior (contained in books like this) for the guidance needed to make predecisions. Recently, however, computer programs have been developed summarizing much of this information in a form that gives practicing managers ready access to a wealth of social science information that may help them decide how to make decisions.[7] Note that such **decision support systems (DSS)**, as they are called, can only be as good as the social science information that goes into developing them. Research has shown that DSS techniques are effective in helping people make decisions about solving problems.[8] The use of decision-making technology leads to outcomes believed to be better than those made in the absence of such techniques. Moreover, computer-based DSS techniques have been found to be especially helpful in getting people to generate a higher number of alternative solutions.[9]

The fourth step in the process is *alternative generation*, the stage in which possible solutions to the problem are identified. In attempting to come up with solutions, people tend to rely on previously used approaches that might provide ready-made answers for them.[10] In our example, some possible ways of solving the revenue shortage problem would be to reduce the work force, sell unnecessary equipment and material, or increase sales.

Because all these possibilities may not be equally feasible, the fifth step calls for *evaluating alternative solutions*. Which solution is best? What would be the most effective way of raising the revenue needed to meet the payroll? The various alternatives need to be identified. Some may be more effective than others, and some may be more difficult to implement than others. For example, although increasing sales would help solve the problem, that is much easier said than done. It is a solution, but not an immediately practical one.

Next, in the sixth step, a *choice* is made. After several alternatives are evaluated, one that is considered acceptable is chosen. As we will describe shortly, different models of decision making offer different views of how thoroughly people consider alternatives and how optimal their chosen alternatives are. Choosing which course of action to take is the step that most often comes to mind when we think about the decision-making process.

The seventh step calls for *implementation of the chosen alternative*. That is, the chosen alternative is carried out. The eighth and final step is *follow-up*. Monitoring the effectiveness of the decisions they put into action is important to the success of organizations. Does the problem still exist? Have any new problems been caused by implementing the solution? In other words, it is important to seek feedback about the effectiveness of any attempted solution. For this reason, the decision-making process is presented as circular in Figure 14–2. If the solution works, the problem may be considered solved. If not, a new solution will have to be attempted.

Managers have had remarkable success in making decisions with the assistance of decision support systems (DSSs). Such systems have been used in a number of industries, such as oil drilling, where deciding where to drill an oil well is a complex and costly decision. The DSS assists the manager by providing information about geological, economic, and legal factors that could affect the decision. In the future, with the help of artificial intelligence, DSSs will be able not only to provide data but also to offer possible decisions and courses of action to the manager based on the data. [Williams, J., & Nelson, J. A. (1990, March 15). Striking oil in decision support. *Datamation*, pp. 83–86.]

Test Bank questions 14.3–14.5 and 14.56–14.57 relate to material on this page.

An Intuitive Approach to Decision Making: Image Theory

Another type of intuitive decision making is called "mixed scanning." It has been the subject of research by Amitai Etzioni at George Washington University. The oldest formal use of mixed scanning is in the field of medicine and concerns the way doctors make decisions. For example, physicians know what they want to achieve and what parts of the body need attention. Doctors do not commit all of their resources on the basis of one preliminary diagnosis, nor do they wait for every conceivable piece of evidence to emerge before starting treatment. Instead, doctors survey the general health of the patient, then zero in on his or her complaint. They initiate a preliminary treatment and then try something else if that fails. This type of intuitive "trial and error" is the same process often used by effective managers. [Etzioni, A. (1990, February). So much data, so little time. *Current*, pp. 10–14.]

If you think about it, you'll probably realize that some, but certainly not all, decisions are made following the logical steps of the traditional, analytical model of decision making. Consider Elizabeth Barrett Browning's poetic question "How do I love thee? Let me count the ways."[11] It's unlikely that one would ultimately make such a decision by carefully counting what one loves about another (although many such characteristics can be enumerated). Instead, a more intuitive-based decision making is likely, not only for matters of the heart, but for a variety of important organizational decisions as well.[12] The point is that selecting the best alternative by weighing all the options is not always a major concern when making a decision. People also consider how various decision alternatives fit with their personal standards as well as their personal goals and plans. The best decision for someone might not be the best for someone else. In other words, people may make decisions in a more automatic, intuitive fashion than is traditionally recognized. Representative of this approach is Beach and Mitchell's **image theory**.[13] This new approach to decision making is summarized in Figure 14–3.

Image theory deals primarily with decisions about adopting a certain course of action (e.g., should the company develop a new product line?) or changing a current course of action (e.g., should the company drop a present product line?). According to the theory, we make adoption decisions on the basis of a simple two-step process. The first step is the *compatibility test*, a comparison of the degree to which a particular course of action is consistent with various images—particularly individual principles, current goals, and plans for the future. If any lack of compatibility exists with respect to any of these considerations, a rejection decision is made. If the compatibility test

FIGURE 14–3

Image Theory: A Summary and Example

According to image theory, decisions are made in a relatively automatic, intuitive fashion following the two steps outlined here. (*Source:* Adapted from Mitchell & Beach, 1990; see Note 12.)

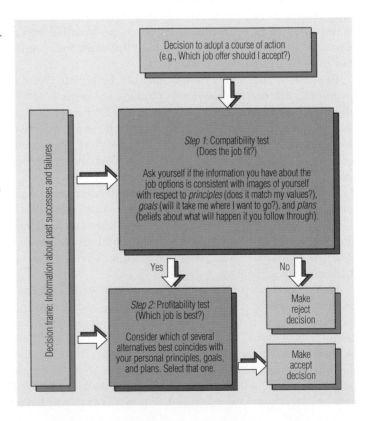

Test Bank questions 14.6, 14.10–14.11, 14.47, and 14.58 relate to material on this page.

is passed, then the *profitability test* is carried out. That is, people consider the extent to which using various alternatives best fits with their values, goals, and plans. The decision is then made to accept the best candidate. These tests are used within a certain *decision frame*—that is, with consideration of meaningful information about the decision context (such as past experiences). The basic idea is that we learn from the past and are guided by it when making decisions. The example shown in Figure 14–3 should help highlight this contemporary approach to decision making.

According to image theory, the decision-making process is very rapid and simple. The theory suggests that people do not ponder and reflect over decisions, but make them using a smooth, intuitive process with minimal cognitive processing. If you've ever found yourself saying that something "seemed like the right thing to do," or "something doesn't feel right," you're probably well aware of the kind of intuitive thinking that goes on in a great deal of decision making.

To summarize, we have described the traditional, analytical approach to decision making, and image theory—a newer, intuitive approach to decision making. Both approaches have received support, and neither one should be seen as a replacement for the other. Instead, several different processes may be involved in decision making. Not all decision making is carried out the same way: sometimes decision making might be analytical, and sometimes it might be more intuitive. Modern organizational behavior scholars recognize the value of both approaches. As you might imagine, both of the decision-making processes just outlined may be applied to making a variety of different decisions in organizations. To better appreciate the various types of decisions that are made, we will now consider some of the basic characteristics of organizational decisions.

Varieties of Organizational Decisions

Consider, for a moment, the variety of decisions likely to be made in organizations. Some decisions have far-reaching consequences (such as radio station KZYN management's decision to change its musical format in our opening story), and others are more mundane (such as the decision to reorder office supplies). People sometimes make decisions in situations in which the likely outcomes are well known (e.g., the decision to underwrite life insurance on the basis of actuarial data), whereas at other times the outcomes are much more uncertain (e.g., the decision to invade a hostile nation for purposes of freeing hostages). These examples are reflective of the two major characteristics of organizational decisions: how structured or unstructured is the situation, and how much certainty or risk is involved in the decision?

Programmed versus Nonprogrammed Decisions: How Well Structured Is the Decision Setting?   Think of a decision that is made repeatedly, according to a preestablished set of alternatives. For example, a word processing operator may decide to make a backup diskette of the day's work, or a manager of a fast-food restaurant may decide to place an order for hamburger buns as the supply starts to get low. Decisions such as these are known as **programmed decisions**—they are routine decisions, made by lower-level personnel, that rely on predetermined courses of action.

By contrast, we may identify **nonprogrammed decisions**—ones for which there are no ready-made solutions. The decision maker confronts a unique situation in which the solutions are novel. The research scientist attempting to find a cure for a rare disease faces a problem that is poorly structured. Unlike the order clerk whose course of action is clear when the supply of paper clips runs low, the scientist in this example must rely on creativity rather than preexisting answers to solve the problem

Test Bank questions 14.7–14.8, 14.48, 14.59, and 14.67 relate to material on this page.

TABLE 14-1   Programmed and Nonprogrammed Decisions: A Comparison

The two major types of organizational decisions—*programmed decisions* and *nonprogrammed decisions*—differ with respect to the types of task on which they are made, the degree to which solutions may be found in existing organizational policies, and the typical decision-making unit.

Variable	Type of Decision	
	Programmed Decisions	**Nonprogrammed Decisions**
Type of task	Simple, routine	Complex, creative
Reliance on organizational policies	Considerable guidance from past decisions	No guidance from past decisions
Typical decision maker	Lower-level workers (usually alone)	Upper-level supervisors (usually in groups)

at hand. Certain types of nonprogrammed decisions are known as *strategic decisions*.[14] These decisions are typically made by coalitions of high-level executives and have important long-term implications for the organization. Strategic decisions reflect a consistent pattern for directing the organization in some specified fashion—that is, according to an underlying organizational philosophy or mission. For example, an organization may make a strategic decision to grow at a specified yearly rate, or to be guided by a certain code of corporate ethics. Both of these decisions are likely to be considered "strategic" because they guide the future direction of the organization.

Table 14–1 summarizes the differences between programmed and nonprogrammed decisions with respect to three important questions. First, *what type of tasks* are involved? Programmed decisions are made on tasks that are common and routine, whereas nonprogrammed decisions are made on unique and novel tasks. Second, *how much reliance is there on organizational policies?* In making programmed decisions, the decision maker can count on guidance from statements of organizational policy and procedure. However, nonprogrammed decisions require the use of creative solutions that are implemented for the first time; past solutions may provide little guidance. Finally, *who makes the decisions?* Not surprisingly, nonprogrammed decisions typically are made by upper-level organizational personnel, whereas the more routine, well-structured decisions are usually relegated to lower-level personnel.[15]

Do male and female managers handle the risk involved in decision making in the same way? A common business misconception is that women are not as skilled as men at making the "big decisions" or those decisions that involve a great deal of risk or that have possible dire consequences. A study conducted by Paul Slovic found that at an early age, boys and girls take equal risks, but by their late teens, girls take fewer

Certain versus Uncertain Decisions: How Much Risk Is Involved?   Just think of how easy it would be to make decisions if we knew what the future held in store. Making the best investments in the stock market would simply be a matter of looking up the changes in tomorrow's newspaper. Of course, we never know exactly what the future holds, but we can be more certain at some times than others. Certainty about the factors on which decisions are made is highly desired in organizational decision making.

Degrees of certainty and uncertainty are expressed as statements of *risk*. All organizational decisions involve some degree of risk—ranging from complete certainty (no risk) to complete uncertainty, "a stab in the dark" (high risk). To make the best possible decisions in organizations, people seek to "manage" the risks they take—that is, to minimize the riskiness of a decision by gaining access to information relevant to the decision (see Figure 14–4).[16]

Test Bank questions 14.12–14.13 relate to material on this page.

"'Be careful!' All you can tell me is 'be careful'?"

FIGURE 14-4

Managing Risk: A Critical Organizational Task

Organizational decisions are made under conditions of varying degrees of risk. For those decisions to be successful, it is necessary to "manage" risk—that is, to gather information that can be used to maximize the possibility of obtaining the desired outcomes. (*Source:* Reprinted by permission of S. Harris.)

What makes an outcome risky or not is the *probability* of obtaining the desired outcome. Decision makers attempt to obtain information about the probabilities, or odds, of certain events occurring given that other events have occurred. For example, a financial analyst may report that a certain stock has risen 80 percent of the time that the prime rate has dropped, or a TV weather person may report that the precipitation probability is 50 percent (i.e., in the past it rained half the time certain meteorological conditions existed). These data may be considered reports of *objective* probabilities because they are based on concrete, verifiable data. Many decisions are also based on *subjective* probabilities—personal beliefs or hunches about what will happen (see Figure 14–5). For example, a gambler who bets on a horse because it has a name similar to one of his children's, or a person who suspects it's going to rain because he just washed his car, is basing these judgments on subjective probabilities.

risks than boys. Although women were found to be as skillful as men in making effective decisions, they tended to shy away from doing so. Slovic's conclusion was that society encourages women not to take risks, but to make decisions having more certain outcomes. [Dumas, L. (1991, June). Taking risks in business: Are women getting the hang of it? *Cosmopolitan*, pp. 229–231.]

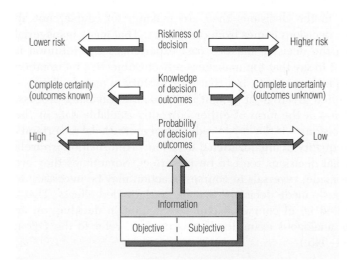

FIGURE 14-5

The Riskiness of a Decision: A Summary

Decisions differ with respect to their degree of riskiness, based on how certain (high probability) or uncertain (low probability) various outcomes may be. Information—both objective and subjective— is used as the basis for estimating the probability of a decision outcome.

Test Bank questions 14.14–14.15 and 14.60 relate to material on this page.

Obviously, uncertainty is an undesirable characteristic in decision-making situations. We may view much of what decision makers do in organizations as attempting to reduce uncertainty so they can make better decisions. How do organizations respond when faced with highly uncertain conditions, when they don't know what the future holds for them? Studies have shown that decision uncertainty can be reduced by establishing linkages with other organizations. The more an organization knows about what another organization will do, the greater certainty it will have in making decisions.[17] This is part of a general tendency for organizational decision makers to respond to uncertainty by reducing the unpredictability of other organizations in their business environments. Those outside organizations with which managers have the greatest contact are most likely to be the ones whose actions are copied.[18]

Research on this topic also has revealed that organizational uncertainty influences decisions regarding whether to make or buy components needed in the manufacturing process. When highly competitive conditions exist between organizations, a high degree of uncertainty regarding the availability of required technology leads organizations to buy the components they need rather than to make them.[19] Apparently, executives do not wish to bog their organizations down by investing in the technology for manufacturing needed components when an uncertain future and the prospect of high competition conspire to make organizational change likely. Under such conditions, organizations that simply buy the needed components can respond more quickly to change (for more on organizations' adaptations to technological changes, see chapter 16). Not surprisingly, the faster an organization has to change to operate effectively in the market, the more uncertainty it faces and the greater difficulty it confronts in making decisions. A good example of this is today's rapidly changing microcomputer business. Winners and losers in this market will be determined, in part, by how well they can predict what products will succeed. Clearly, organizations must be sensitive to conditions of uncertainty when making decisions; uncertain conditions qualify the nature of organizational decisions.

In general, what reduces uncertainty in decision-making situations? The answer is *information*. Knowledge about the past and the present can be used to help make projections about the future. A modern executive's access to data needed to make important decisions may be as close as the nearest computer terminal. Indeed, computer technology has greatly aided managers' ability to make decisions quickly, using the most accurate and thorough information available.[20] A variety of on-line information services are designed to provide organizational decision makers with the latest information relevant to the decisions they are making. Of course, not all information needed to make decisions comes from computers. That many managerial decisions are also based on the decision maker's past experiences and intuition is well established.[21] This is not to say that top managers rely on subjective information in making decisions (although they might), but that their history of past decisions—successes and failures—is often given great weight in the decision-making process. In other words, *information*—in the form of either currently available data or the collective wisdom of past decisions—is the key to reducing organizational uncertainty and thereby enhancing the quality of organizational decisions. (Information is rarely perfect, and so organizational decisions tend to be imperfect. Sometimes they are undone soon after they are made; reversals in courses of action may be necessary to correct the effects of previously made decisions that had unintended effects. That a certain course of action failed is, of course, useful information in deciding on an alternative action. For two analogous examples of this process, refer to the **OB in Practice** section on pp. 544–545.)

INDIVIDUAL DECISION MAKING IN ORGANIZATIONS: AN IMPERFECT PROCESS

Decision making is one of the most common processes in which we engage. We are always making decisions—whether they are simple ones, such as which television show to watch, or more complex ones with far-reaching consequences, such as whom a presidential candidate should select as a vice presidential running mate. Organizations represent a context within which decisions may be particularly important. Thus, an examination of some of the most basic characteristics of individual decision processes, and how organizational variables influence them, would be useful. This section will analyze the process of individual decision making in organizations and some of the major impediments to high-quality individual decisions.

Two Approaches to Individual Decision Making: The Rational-Economic Model and the Administrative Model

We all like to think that we are "rational" people who make the best possible decisions. What does it mean to make a *rational* decision? Organizational scientists view **rational decisions** as ones that maximize the attainment of goals, whether they are the goals of a person, a group, or an entire organization.[22] In this section, we will present two approaches to decision making that derive from different assumptions about the rationality of individual decision makers. For a summary of these approaches, see Table 14–2.

The Rational-Economic Model: In Search of the Ideal Decision What would be the most rational way for an individual to go about making a decision? Economists interested in predicting market conditions and prices have relied on a **rational-economic model** of decision making, which assumes that decisions are perfect and rational in every way. An economically rational decision maker will attempt to maximize his or her profits by systematically searching for the best possible solution to a problem. For this to occur, the decision maker must have complete and perfect information, and be able to process all this information in an accurate and unbiased fashion.[23]

In many respects, rational-economic decisions follow the same steps outlined in the traditional, analytical model of decision making (see Figure 14–2). However, what makes the rational-economic approach special is that it calls for the decision maker to recognize *all* alternative courses of action, and to accurately and completely evaluate each one. It views decision makers as attempting to make *optimal* decisions.

TABLE 14–2   The Administrative Model versus the Rational-Economic Model: A Summary Comparison

The *rational-economic model* and the *administrative model* of individual decision making are based on a variety of assumptions about how people make decisions.

Assumption	Rational-Economic Model	Administrative Model
Rationality of decision maker	Perfect rationality	Bounded rationality
Information available	Complete access	Limited access
Selection of alternatives	Optimal choice	Satisficing choice
Type of model	Normative	Descriptive

Of course, the rational-economic approach to decision making does not fully appreciate the fallibility of the human decision maker. Based on the assumption that people have access to complete and perfect information and use it to make perfect decisions, the model can be considered a *normative* (also called *prescriptive*) approach—one that describes how decision makers ideally ought to behave so as to make the best possible decisions. It does not describe how decision makers *actually* behave in most circumstances. This task is undertaken by the next major approach to individual decision making, the *administrative model*.

 OB IN PRACTICE

Undoing Corporate Decisions: Toying Around at Fisher-Price and Taking the Fizzle Out of Coca-Cola

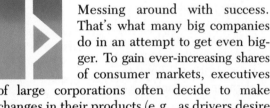 Messing around with success. That's what many big companies do in an attempt to get even bigger. To gain ever-increasing shares of consumer markets, executives of large corporations often decide to make changes in their products (e.g., as drivers desire either larger or smaller cars, auto company executives must be sensitive, and deliver as quickly as possible). Although change is necessary for growth to occur, not all organizational decisions are successful. In many cases, when feedback about failure is unmistakable, policymakers typically do not stay the course, but change again, often returning back to where things were originally. Let's now consider two good examples of such "undoing" of corporate decisions.

You probably know of Fisher-Price, the company specializing in simple, brightly colored toys for infants and toddlers. Until recently, it was owned by the giant food company Quaker Oats.[24] For many years, Fisher-Price sold basic preschool toys with timeless appeal, nothing trendy or flashy. It also enjoyed a huge proportion of market share. Then the company began to see other toy companies develop new, competitive lines (e.g., Mattel's Disney line, Hasbro's Playskool line). In response, in 1989 the company introduced the broadest and most sophisticated line in its history. It even planned a battery-powered $299 "Sport Car" that children could drive. Unfortunately, the company was plagued by both production problems (only a small percentage of the products planned hit the market on time) and image problems. After all, why would a more mature audience wish to buy a product from a company known for infant toys? By November 1989, retail orders were being canceled en masse. Understandably, the bottom line was bleak. Compared with the 17 percent annual growth Fisher-Price had enjoyed between 1984 and 1988, the company suffered a $100 million reversal in operating profits between 1988 and 1990.

What did the company do? Simple. It downsized and returned to its original product niche for the under-five set. Fisher-Price successfully competes in this market with Little Tikes and Playskool. So, rather than seeking to rebound by gaining a new territory, Fisher-Price retrenched and has decided to fight to keep its number one position on its own turf. Today, Fisher-Price is back where it started.

An analogous series of decisions was made by Coca-Cola (see Figure 14–6). Or should we say Coke Classic? On April 23, 1985, Coca-Cola's chief executive officer, Roberto Goizueta, announced that the company had decided to alter its extremely successful ninety-nine-year-old formula and to make an even better product.[25] This was not an overnight decision, but the result of four and a half years of consumer taste-testing on 200,000 people at a cost of $4 million. Coca-Cola bosses were confident that their new product would be a success.[26] Unfortunately, the public didn't see it that way, resulting in an immediate outcry. Consumers besieged the company with angry letters and phone calls. A black market for "old Coke" developed, and cases of the product were imported from foreign dis-

The Administrative Model: Exploring the Limits of Human Rationality   Not only are some people incapable of acting in a completely rational-economic manner, but in addition, the cost of such so-called rationality may be very high. In fact, research has shown that it may be more rational not to try to be so rational after all. For example, in one study, Fredrickson and Mitchell found that considering all possible solutions to problems might not be such an effective way of solving them.[27] They surveyed more than 100 executives in the forest products industry concerning how comprehensive and exhaustive their organizations were likely to be in making dif-

One way in which people are not very rational in their decision making is that they tend to calculate probabilities incorrectly and follow a supposed "law of averages" when making decisions. For example, many people believe that lightning never strikes in the same place

tributors to meet the demand. Such consumer reactions were completely inconsistent with the market research, and were totally unexpected by the company. Less than three months after the new formula was introduced, Coke announced that it would return to its original formula in a product called Coca-Cola Classic. To this day, Coke Classic continues to outsell the new formula.

The Fisher-Price and the Coca-Cola cases have an important element in common—they both made changes that met with failure, and then returned to their original way of operating.

Fisher-Price expanded into the sophisticated toy market, but dropped its plans about a year later. Coca-Cola introduced a new formula, but reintroduced the original formula less than three months later. Both cases clearly demonstrate the willingness of organizations faced with overwhelmingly negative evidence to return to earlier, more successful ways of operating. Business decisions may not be forever—especially those that have been previously unsuccessful. Clearly, information about the failure of previous decisions is an important stimulant to the making of new decisions.

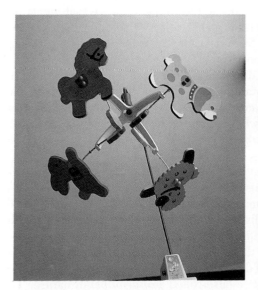

FIGURE 14-6   Fisher-Price and Coca-Cola: What Do They Have in Common?

In response to intense market competition, both Fisher-Price and Coca-Cola made unsuccessful decisions to change their product lines, but rapidly reversed them. In 1988, Fisher-Price, long known for its basic preschool toys, ventured into sophisticated toys. When these new products failed to catch on, the company reverted to its formerly successful line. Similarly, in 1985 Coca-Cola changed its formula, but met with massive consumer rejection. Less than three months later, the original product was returned to the shelves under the name "Coca-Cola Classic."

twice. Or in war, soldiers often shelter themselves in shell craters, believing that a second hit in that spot is unlikely. In reality, neither belief is true. Perhaps the best example of someone using the law of averages to make decisions is the story of a man who always carried a bomb with him whenever he traveled by plane. His reasoning was that two bombs on the same plane would be so improbable that it would never happen. Although these stories may be amusing, they should remind people that decisions based on the "law of averages" are often faulty. [Stewart, I. (1990, May 19). Risky business. *New Scientist,* pp. 1–4.]

ferent types of decisions. It was found that use of this seemingly rational strategy was not linked to organizational prosperity. In fact, the more comprehensive the executives reported their organizations' decision strategies were, the poorer their organizations performed financially. Particularly when organizations operate in very unstable environments (ones in which there is a great deal of change), the effort involved in making completely rational decisions can actually interfere with economic progress. In other words, the costs of attempting to make a seemingly rational economic decision may sometimes be so high that they cut into economic gains.

For example, consider how a personnel department might go about deciding on hiring a new receptionist. After several applicants are interviewed, the personnel director might select the best candidate seen so far and stop the selection process. Had the interviewer been following a rational-economic model, he or she would have had to interview all possible candidates before deciding on the *best* one. However, by ending the search after finding a candidate who was just *good enough,* the manager was using a much simpler approach. The decision strategy used by the personnel manager in this example typifies an approach to decision making known as the **administrative model.**[28] This conceptualization recognizes that decision makers may have a limited view of the problems confronting them. The number of solutions that can be recognized or implemented is limited by the capabilities of the decision maker and the available resources of the organization. Also, decision makers do not have perfect information about the consequences of their decisions, so they cannot tell which one is best.

How are decisions made according to the administrative model? Instead of considering all possible solutions, as suggested by the rational-economic model, the administrative model recognizes that decision makers consider solutions as they become available. Then they decide on the first alternative that meets their criteria for acceptability. Thus the decision maker selects a solution that may be just good enough, although not optimal. Such decisions are referred to as **satisficing decisions.** Of course, a satisficing decision is much easier for a decision maker to make than an optimal decision. In most decision-making situations, March and Simon note, satisficing decisions are acceptable and are more likely to be made than optimal ones.[29] They use the following analogy to compare the two types of decisions: *making an optimal decision is like searching a haystack for the sharpest needle, but making a satisficing decision is like searching a haystack for a needle just sharp enough with which to sew.*

As we have noted, it is often impractical for people to make completely optimal, rational decisions. The administrative model recognizes the **bounded rationality** under which most organizational decision makers must operate. The idea is that people lack the cognitive skills required to formulate and solve highly complex business problems in a completely objective, rational way.[30]

It should not be surprising that the administrative model does a better job than the rational-economic model of describing how decision makers actually behave. The approach is said to be *descriptive* (also called *proscriptive*) in nature. This interest in examining the actual, imperfect behavior of decision makers, rather than specifying the ideal, economically rational behaviors that decision makers ought to engage in, lies at the heart of the distinction between the administrative and rational-economic models (refer to the summary of these two approaches in Table 14–2). Our point is not that decision makers do not want to behave rationally, but that restrictions posed by the innate capabilities of the decision makers themselves and the social environments in which decisions are often made sometimes preclude "perfect" decisions. With this idea in mind, we will now explore some of the factors limiting optimal decisions.

Test Bank questions 14.20–14.23, 14.49, and 14.61 relate to material on this page.

Impediments to Optimal Individual Decisions

The picture of an imperfect decision maker operating in a complex world is supported by many studies that point to the seemingly confused and irrational decisions people make. The imperfections of decision makers take many forms, several of which we will review here.

Cognitive Biases in Decision Making: Framing and Heuristics   Probably the most obvious limitation on people's ability to make the best possible decisions is imposed by their restricted capacity to process information accurately and thoroughly (like a computer). For example, that people often focus on irrelevant information in making decisions has been established.[31] They also fail to use all the information made available to them.[32] Obviously, limitations in people's abilities to process complex information adversely influence their decisions. Beyond this general limitation in information-processing capacity, we may note the existence of several systematic biases in decision making.[33]

Framing   One well-established decision-making bias has to do with the tendency for people to make different decisions based on how the problem is presented to them—that is, the **framing** of a problem. Specifically, Kahneman and Tversky have noted that problems framed in a manner that emphasizes the positive gains to be received tend to encourage conservative decisions (i.e., decision makers are said to be *risk averse*), whereas problems framed in a manner that emphasizes the potential losses to be suffered lead to *risk-seeking* decisions.[34] Consider the following example:

> The government is preparing to combat a rare disease expected to take 600 lives. Two alternative programs to combat the disease have been proposed, each of which, scientists believe, will have certain consequences. *Program A* will save 200 people, if adopted. *Program B* has a one-third chance of saving all 600 people, but a two-thirds chance of saving no one. Which program do you prefer?

When Kahneman and Tversky presented such a problem to people, 72 percent expressed a preference for Program A, and 28 percent for Program B. In other words, they preferred the "sure thing" of saving 200 people over the one-third possibility of saving them all. However, a curious thing happened when the description of the programs was framed in negative terms. Specifically:

> *Program C* was described as allowing 400 people to die, if adopted. *Program D* was described as allowing a one-third probability that no one would die, and a two-thirds probability that all 600 would die. Now which program would you prefer?

Compare these four programs. Program C is just another way of stating the outcomes of Program A, and Program D is just another way of stating the outcomes of Program B. However, Programs C and D are framed in negative terms, which led to almost opposite preferences: 22 percent favored Program C and 78 percent favored Program D (for a summary, see Figure 14–7 on p. 548). In other words, people tended to avoid risk when the problem was framed in the "lives saved" version (i.e., in positive terms), but to seek risk when the problem was framed in the "lives lost" version (i.e., in negative terms). Findings such as these suggest that people are not completely rational decision makers, but are systematically biased by the aversiveness of the outcomes they confront as a result of their decisions.

Heuristics   Framing effects are not the only cognitive biases to which decision makers are subjected. It has also been established that people often attempt to simplify the complex decisions they face by using **heuristics**—simple rules of thumb

FIGURE 14-7

Framing Effects: An Empirical Demonstration

Research has found that differences in the *framing* of a problem have a profound effect on the decisions individuals make. As shown here, when a problem is framed in positive terms (e.g., lives saved by a medical decision), people prefer a certain outcome, a sure thing (i.e., they avoid risk). However, when the same problem is framed in negative terms (e.g., lives lost by a medical decision), people prefer a less certain outcome (i.e., they seek risk). (*Source:* Based on data reported by Kahneman & Tversky, 1984; see Note 34.)

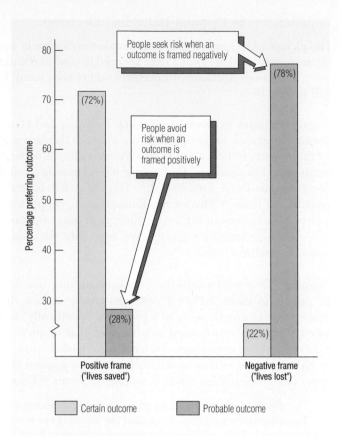

that guide them through a complex array of decision alternatives.[35] Although heuristics are potentially useful to decision makers, they represent potential impediments to decision making. Two very common types of heuristics may be identified.

1. The **availability heuristic** refers to the tendency for people to base their judgments on information that is readily available to them—even though it might not be accurate. Suppose, for example, that an executive needs to know the percentage of entering college freshmen who go on to graduate. There is not enough time to gather the appropriate statistics, so she bases her judgments on her own recollections of when she was a college student. If the percentage she recalls graduating, based on her own experiences, is higher or lower than the usual number, her estimate will be off accordingly. In other words, basing judgments solely on information that is conveniently available increases the possibility of making inaccurate decisions. Yet, the availability heuristic is often used when making decisions.[36]

2. The **representativeness heuristic** refers to the tendency to perceive others in stereotypical ways if they appear to be typical representatives of the category to which they belong. For example, suppose you believe that accountants are bright, mild-mannered individuals, whereas salespeople are less intelligent, but much more extroverted. Further, imagine that there are twice as many salespeople as accountants at a party. You meet someone at the party who is bright and mild-mannered. Although mathematically the odds are two-to-one that this person is a salesperson rather than an accountant, chances are you will guess that the individual is an accountant because he possesses the traits you associate with accountants. In other words, you believe

this person to be representative of accountants in general—so much so that you would knowingly go against the mathematical odds in making your judgment. Research has consistently found that people tend to make this type of error in judgment, thereby providing good support for the existence of the representativeness heuristic.[37]

Heuristics do not *always* deteriorate the quality of decisions made. In fact, they can be quite helpful. People often use rules of thumb to help simplify the complex decisions they face. For example, management scientists employ many useful heuristics to aid decisions regarding such matters as where to locate warehouses or how to compose an investment portfolio.[38] We also use heuristics in our everyday lives, such as when we play chess ("control the center of the board") or blackjack ("hit on 16, stick on 17"). However, the representativeness heuristic and the availability heuristic may be recognized as impediments to superior decisions because they discourage people from collecting and processing as much information as they should. Making judgments on the basis of only readily available information, or on stereotypical beliefs, although making things simple for the decision maker, does so at a potentially high cost—poor decisions. Thus, these systematic biases represent potentially serious impediments to individual decision making.

Escalation of Commitment   Because decisions are made all the time in organizations, some of these will inevitably be unsuccessful. What would you say is the *rational* thing to do when a poor decision has been made? Obviously, the ineffective action should be stopped or reversed. In other words, it would make sense to "cut your losses and run." (If you recall our **OB in Practice** section on pp. 544–545, this is what Fisher-Price and Coca-Cola did in response to some of their own ineffective actions.) However, it has been established that people don't always respond in this manner. Indeed, it is not unusual to find that ineffective decisions are sometimes followed up with still further ineffective decisions. Imagine, for example, that you have invested money in a company, but the company appears to be failing. Rather than lose your initial investment, you may invest still more money in the hope of salvaging your first investment. The more you invest, the more you may be tempted to save those earlier investments by making later investments. That is to say, people sometimes may be found "throwing good money after bad." This is known as the **escalation of commitment phenomenon**—the tendency for people to continue to support previously unsuccessful courses of action.[39]

Although this might not seem like a rational thing to do, this strategy is frequently followed. Consider, for example, how large banks and governments may invest money in foreign governments in the hope of turning them around even though such a result becomes increasingly unlikely. Similarly, the organizers of Expo 86 in British Columbia continued pouring money into the fair long after it became apparent that it would be a big money-losing proposition.[40] Why do people do this? If you think about it, you may realize that the failure to back your own previous courses of action in an organization would be taken as an admission of failure—a politically difficult act to face in an organization. In other words, people may be very concerned about "saving face"—looking good in the eyes of others. Staw and his associates have recognized that this tendency for *self-justification* is primarily responsible for people's inclination to protect their beliefs about themselves as rational, competent decision makers by convincing themselves and others that they made the right decision all along, and are willing to back it up.[41] Although there are other possible reasons for the escalation of commitment phenomenon, the research supports the self-justification explanation.[42,43] For a summary of the escalation of commitment phenomenon, see Figure 14–8 on p. 550.

Test Bank questions 14.28–14.29 and 14.51 relate to material on this page.

Escalation of Commitment:
Summary of the
Phenomenon

According to the
*escalation of
commitment
phenomenon,* people
who have repeatedly
made poor decisions
will continue to support
those failing courses of
action in order to justify
those decisions. Under
some conditions,
summarized here, the
effect will not occur.

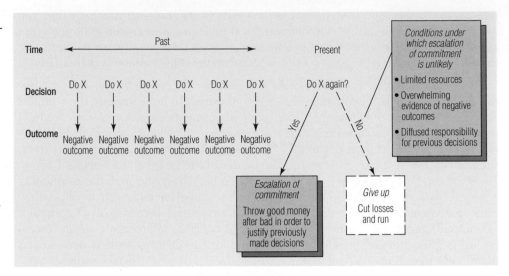

Recently, researchers have noted several conditions under which people will refrain from escalating their commitment to a failing course of action. Notably, in several studies, Garland and his associates have found that people will stop making failing investments under conditions in which the available funds for making further investments are limited, and the threat of failure is overwhelmingly obvious.[44] For example, they found that oil field geologists were unwilling to recommend the further drilling of holes in light of clear evidence that oil would not be found, even though they may have earlier recommended drilling.[45] It also has been found that people will refrain from escalating commitment when they can diffuse their responsibility for the earlier failing actions. That is, the more people felt they were just one of several people responsible for a failing course of action, the less likely they were to commit to further failing actions.[46] In other words, the less one is responsible for an earlier failure, the less one may be motivated to justify those earlier failures by making further investments in them. To conclude, the escalation of commitment phenomenon represents a type of irrational decision making that may occur, but only under certain circumstances.

Organizational Impediments to Decision Making   Thus far we have emphasized the human cognitive shortcomings and biases that limit effective decision making. However, we must not ignore several important organizational factors that also interfere with rational decisions. Indeed, the situations faced by many organizational decision makers cannot help but interfere with their capacity to make decisions.

One obvious factor is *time constraints.* Many important organizational decisions are made under severe time pressure. Under such circumstances, it is often impossible for more exhaustive decision-making processes to occur. This is particularly the case when organizations face crisis situations requiring immediate decisions. In crisis situations, decision makers have been found to limit their search for information that may help them make optimal decisions.[47]

The quality of many organizational decisions also may be limited by political *"face-saving" pressure.* In other words, decision makers may make decisions that help them save face at work, although the resulting decisions might not be in the best interest of their organizations. Imagine, for example, how an employee might distort the available information needed to make a decision if the correct decision would jeopardize his job. Unfortunately, such misuses of information to support desired decisions are common (recall our discussion of the problem of distorted communication in chapter 13). One study on this topic reported that a group of businessmen working on a group decision-making problem opted for an adequate—although less than optimal—decision rather than risk generating serious conflicts with their fellow group members.[48] In an actual case, a proponent of medical inoculation for the flu was reported as having decided to go ahead with the inoculation program on the basis of only a 2 percent chance of an epidemic.[49] Apparently, people may make the decisions they *want* to make even though these may not be the optimal ones for the organizations involved.

Besides the time constraints and political pressures that limit the quality of organizational decisions, note also the limitations imposed by moral and ethical constraints—what is known as *bounded discretion*.[50] According to this idea, decision makers limit their actions to those that fall within the bounds of current moral and ethical standards. So, although engaging in illegal activities such as stealing may optimize an organization's profits (at least in the short run), ethical considerations may discourage such actions. (As you must be aware, decision makers do not always act in an ethical manner. Sometimes unethical decisions are made because of the inherent tendency of some individuals to be unethical, and other times unethical decisions result from the tendency of the organization to encourage, or fail to discourage, unethical behavior. For a closer look at how these factors contribute to the ethicality of decision making in organizations, see the **Question of Ethics** section on pp. 552–553.)

GROUP DECISIONS: DO TOO MANY COOKS SPOIL THE BROTH?

Decision-making groups are a well-established fact of modern organizational life. Groups such as *committees, study teams, task forces,* or *review panels* are often charged with the responsibility for making important business decisions. They are so common, in fact, that it has been said that some administrators spend as much as 80 percent of their time in committee meetings.[51] Given this, it is important to consider the strengths and weaknesses of using groups to make organizational decisions. Refer to our summary of these factors in Figure 14–9.

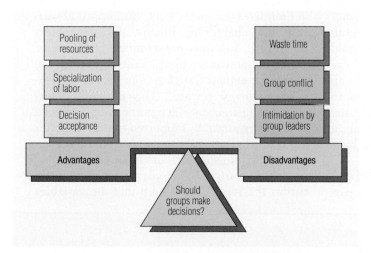

FIGURE 14–9

Group Decision Making: Advantages and Disadvantages

Should groups be used to make decisions? Both advantages and disadvantages are associated with using groups rather than individuals to make decisions.

A QUESTION OF ETHICS

Ethical Decisions: The Result of "Bad Apples" in "Bad Barrels"

 Newspapers are full of stories about unethical decisions in business: major brokerage firms manipulate accounts to fraudulently make money, oil companies pollute the environment to make profits, and religious organizations funnel charitable donations into the pockets of their leaders. Such accounts portray only too clearly the fact that many of the decisions made by people in organizations are unethical. What accounts for these unethical acts? Are they the result of "bad apples"—the practices of a few immoral individuals—or "bad barrels"—characteristics of the work environment that promote unethical activity? Recent research by Trevino and Youngblood suggests that the answer is *both*.[52]

The participants in their study were M.B.A. students who participated in an "in-basket" exercise—a task requiring them to play the role of a national sales manager for an electronics corporation. They were presented with various types of information (in the form of letters, memos, a company newsletter, and the like) on which they would have to rely as the basis for making several decisions. The two decisions of interest involved ethical issues. One decision concerned how they responded to a situation in which one of their sales representatives was paying kickbacks: did they stop the kickbacks (an ethical response) or permit them to continue (an unethical response)? Another decision concerned a production executive's action of changing the materials used in a particular product to cheaper but potentially problematic ones: would they inform customers of this change (an ethical response) or would they keep it a secret (an unethical response)? The participants were judged to have acted ethically if they made the ethical choice in both cases, and unethically if they made at least one of the two unethical decisions.

What factors influenced the likelihood of ethical or unethical behavior on the part of the par-

ticipants? Trevino and Youngblood considered several possibilities. These are summarized in a model appearing in Figure 14–10. As the figure reveals, the variables considered fell into both the "bad apples" and the "bad barrels" categories.

By providing appropriate in-basket material, the researchers manipulated information about how company management responded previously to incidents of other kinds of unethical behavior on the part of employees. In one case, participants were led to believe that previous unethical behaviors were disciplined (vicarious discipline condition), whereas in the other, they were led to believe that unethical behaviors were allowed to go on (vicarious reward condition). This represents a set of environmental conditions that either condone or discourage unethical action—that is, the "bad barrel" explanation.

The experimenters also examined the contributions of individual predispositions—that is, "bad apples." To do so, they measured several aspects of the participants' personalities and underlying beliefs. For example, measures of *cognitive moral development* were taken—a test tapping people's capacity to judge what is morally right. Higher scores reflect the use of basic moral principles (e.g., rights and justice), whereas lower scores reflect more selfish, less principled concerns. The experimenters also measured the participants' *locus of control*—a personality variable tapping the extent to which people believe they are responsible for the events in their lives (for more about this important variable, see chapter 6). Finally, the researchers measured *outcome expectancy*—participants' beliefs about management's most likely response to various actions (ranging from severe punishment to major reward). This measure determined the extent to which participants believed that the organization supported ethical behavior (by rewarding it) and discouraged unethical behavior (by punishing it), or the opposite.

Using a variety of complex correlational statistics, the researchers found that the variables

---

studied (as shown in Figure 14–10) all contributed somewhat to ethical decision-making behavior. However, some variables were not particularly strong. Notably, vicarious reward and vicarious punishment did not strongly influence ethical decision making directly, but they did so indirectly, by altering people's beliefs about outcome expectancies. The other variables were more strongly related to the making of ethical decisions, thereby supporting the model. Overall, the findings are consistent with the idea that the ethical or unethical decisions made by people are based on various personality characteristics (who they are, i.e., whether or not they are "bad apples") and the environment in which

they work—particularly, the extent to which they are expected to be punished for behaving unethically (i.e., whether or not they are put into "bad barrels"). Although the entire range of individual and environmental factors possibly affecting the ethicality of decision making was not tapped in this study, the results are quite revealing. They help make the point that ethical decisions result from inherently moral people operating in environments that encourage moral behavior. Therefore, our advice to the wise manager is simple: don't make an otherwise ethical person act unethically by tolerating (not punishing) unethical activity!

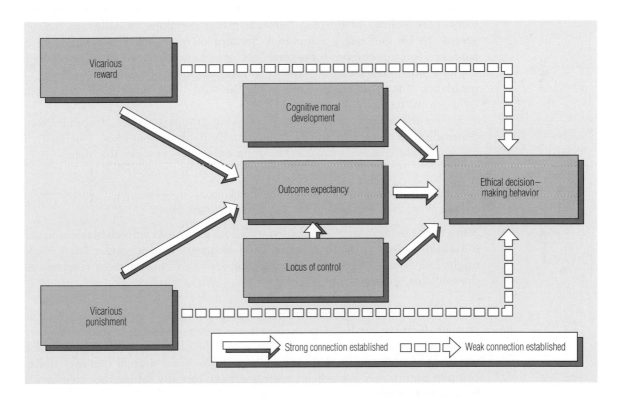

FIGURE 14–10   Ethical Decision Making: A Model

Trevino and Youngblood's model of ethical decision making posits that ethical decisions are influenced by both individual factors (cognitive moral development, locus of control, and outcome expectancy) and environmental factors (vicarious reward and punishment). The direct connections between environmental factors and ethical decisions were only weakly established. (*Source:* Adapted from Trevino & Youngblood, 1990; see Note 52.)

There is little doubt that much can be gained by using decision-making groups. Several potential advantages of this approach may be identified. First, bringing people together may increase the amount of knowledge and information available for making good decisions. In other words, there may be a *pooling of resources*. A related benefit is that in decision-making groups there can be a *specialization of labor*. With enough people around to share the work load, individuals can perform only those tasks at which they are best, thereby potentially improving the quality of the group's efforts. Another benefit is that group decisions are likely to enjoy *greater acceptance* than individual decisions. People involved in making decisions may be expected to understand those decisions better and be more committed to carrying them out than decisions made by someone else.[53]

Of course, there are also some problems associated with using decision-making groups. One obvious drawback is that groups are likely to *waste time*. The time spent socializing before getting down to business may be a drain on the group and be very costly to organizations. Another possible problem is that potential disagreement over important matters may breed ill will and *group conflict*. Although constructive disagreement can actually lead to better group outcomes, highly disruptive conflict may interfere with group decisions (see chapter 10). Indeed, with corporate power and personal pride at stake, it is not at all surprising to find that lack of agreement can cause bad feelings to develop between group members. Finally, we may expect groups to be ineffective sometimes because of members' *intimidation by group leaders*. A group composed of several "yes" men or women trying to please a dominant leader tends to discourage open and honest discussion of solutions. In view of these problems, it is no wonder we often hear the adage "A camel is a horse put together by a committee."

Given the several pros and cons of using groups to make decisions, we must conclude that neither groups nor individuals are always superior. Obviously, there are important trade-offs involved in using either one to make decisions.

Comparing Group and Individual Decisions: When Are Two (or More) Heads Better Than One?

Since there are advantages associated with both group and individual decision makers, a question arises as to *when* each should be used. That is, under what conditions might individuals or groups make superior decisions? Fortunately, research has addressed this important question.[54]

When Are Groups Superior to Individuals?   Imagine a situation in which an important decision has to be made about a complex problem—such as whether one company should acquire another. This is not the kind of problem about which any one individual working alone would be able to make a good decision. Its highly complex nature may overwhelm even an expert, thereby setting the stage for a group to do a better job.

Whether or not it actually will do better depends on several important considerations. For one, we must consider who is in the group. Successful groups tend to be composed of *heterogeneous group members with complementary skills*. So, for example, a group composed of lawyers, accountants, real estate agents, and other experts may make much better decisions on complex problems than one composed of specialists in only one field. Indeed, research has shown that the diversity of opinions offered by group members is one of the major advantages of using groups to make decisions.[55]

As you might imagine, it is not enough simply to have skills. For a group to be successful, its members must also be able to freely communicate their ideas to each other in an open, nonhostile manner (see chapter 13). Conditions under which one individual (or group) intimidates another from contributing his or her expertise can easily negate any potential gain associated with composing groups of heterogeneous experts (see chapter 8). After all, *having* expertise and being able to make a contribution by *using* that expertise are two different things. Indeed, research has shown that only when the contributions of the most qualified group members are given the greatest weight does the group derive any benefit from that member's presence.[56] Thus, for groups to be superior to individuals, they must be composed of a heterogeneous collection of experts with complementary skills who can freely and openly contribute to their group's product.

As an example of this, Michaelsen, Watson, and Black studied the performance of 222 groups of approximately six students who worked together extensively on class projects (team learning exercises) over the course of a semester.[57] Assignments to groups were made so as to create groups as broadly diversified as possible. The teams had to work together on answering exam questions about the material they studied. The questions were generally difficult, some requiring the ability to analyze and synthesize complex concepts. The researchers were interested in comparing the performance of the groups as a whole with that of individual members. Their findings are summarized in Figure 14–11.

As shown in Figure 14–11, the average score on the exams completed jointly by group members was not only higher than that of the average group member, but also higher than that of the best group member. In fact, of the 222 groups studied, 215 (97 percent) outperformed their best member, 4 groups tied their best member, and only 3 groups scored lower than their best member. Clearly, these findings support the idea that *on complex tasks, a benefit is derived from combining individuals into groups that goes beyond the contribution of what the best group member can do.* People can help each other solve complex problems not only by pooling

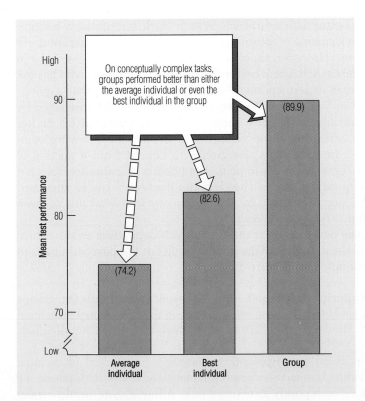

FIGURE 14–11

Group versus Individual Performance on a Complex Learning Task: Experimental Evidence

Research comparing the performance of groups and individuals on a complex learning task has shown that groups as a whole performed better than either the average individual or even the best individual member of the group. Such findings support the idea that the benefit of working in groups goes beyond the simple combination of individual skills. (*Source:* Based on data in Michaelsen, Watson, & Black, 1989; see Note 57.)

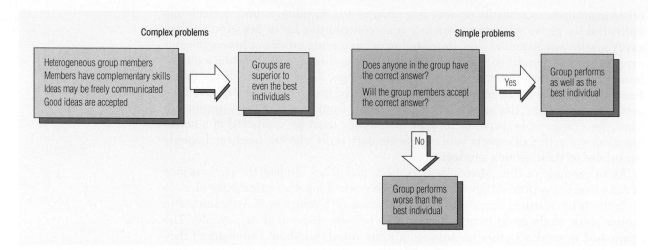

FIGURE 14–12   Group Decisions: When Are They Superior to Individual Decisions?

When performing complex problems, groups are superior to individuals if certain conditions prevail (i.e., group members have heterogeneous, complementary skills, they can freely share ideas, and good ideas are accepted). However, when performing simple problems, groups will perform only as well as the best individual in the group, and then only if that person has the correct answer and that response is accepted by the group.

their resources, but also by correcting each other's answers and assisting each other to come up with ideas. There is also likely to be the intangible *synergy* created when a group of people help each other and create a climate for success.

In contrast to complex decision tasks, imagine a situation in which a judgment is required on a simple problem with a readily verifiable answer. For example, imagine that you are asked to translate a phrase from a relatively obscure language into English. Groups might do better than individuals on such a task, but probably because the odds are increased that someone in the group knows the language and can perform the translation for the group. However, there is no reason to expect that even a large group will be able to perform such a task better than a single individual who has the required expertise. In fact, an expert working alone may do even better than a group. This is because an expert individual performing a simple task may be distracted by others and suffer from having to convince them of the correctness of his or her solution. For this reason, exceptional individuals tend to outperform entire committees on simple tasks.[58] In such cases, for groups to benefit from a pooling of resources, there must be some resources to pool. The pooling of ignorance does not help. In other words, the question "Are two heads better than one?" can be answered this way: *on simple tasks, two heads may be better than one if at least one of those heads has enough of what it takes to succeed.*

In summary, groups *may* perform better than individuals depending on the nature of the task performed and the expertise of the people involved. We have summarized some of these key considerations in Figure 14–12.

When Are Individuals Superior to Groups?   As we have described thus far, groups may be expected to perform better than the average or even the exceptional individual under certain conditions. However, there are also conditions under which individuals are superior to groups.

Most of the problems faced by organizations require a great deal of creative thinking. A company deciding how to use a newly developed adhesive in its consumer products is facing decisions on a poorly structured task. Although you would expect

Test Bank questions 14.36 and 14.52 relate to material on this page.

that the complexity of such creative problems would give groups a natural advantage, this is *not* the case. In fact, research has shown that on poorly structured, creative tasks, individuals perform better than groups.[59]

An approach to solving creative problems commonly used by groups is **brainstorming.** This technique was developed by advertising executive Alex Osborn of the Madison Avenue agency Batten, Barton, Durstine, and Osborn as a tool for coming up with creative, new ideas.[60] The members of brainstorming groups are encouraged to present their ideas in an uncritical way and to discuss freely and openly all ideas on the floor. Specifically, members of brainstorming groups are required to follow four main rules:

1. Avoid criticizing others' ideas.
2. Share even far-out suggestions.
3. Offer as many comments as possible.
4. Build on others' ideas to create your own.

Does brainstorming help improve the quality of creative decisions? To answer this question, Bouchard and his associates conducted a study in which they compared the effectiveness of individuals and brainstorming groups working on creative problems.[61] Specifically, participants were given thirty-five minutes to consider the consequences of situations such as "What if everybody went blind?" or "What if everybody grew an extra thumb on each hand?" Clearly, the novel nature of such problems requires a great deal of creativity. Comparisons were made of the number of solutions generated by groups of four or seven people and a like number of individuals working on the same problems alone. As shown in Figure 14–13, individuals were far more productive than groups.

In summary, groups perform worse than individuals when working on creative tasks. A great part of the problem—and it *is* a problem, given the prevalence of decision-making groups in organizations—is that some individuals feel inhibited by the presence of others even though one rule of brainstorming is that even far-out ideas may be shared. To the extent that people wish to avoid feeling foolish as a

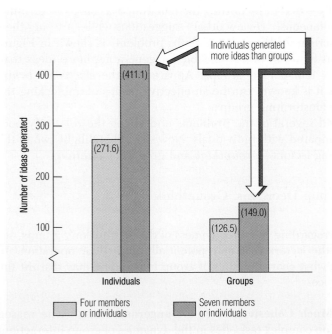

FIGURE 14–13

Brainstorming: Unsuccessful for Creative Problems

Research comparing the number of solutions to creative problems generated by brainstorming groups (of four or seven members) and a like number of individuals working alone has shown that individuals are more productive. (*Source:* Based on data in Bouchard, Barsaloux, & Drauden, 1974; see Note 61.)

FIGURE 14-14

Electronic Brainstorming: A Sample Display Screen

What would happen if everyone grew an extra thumb on each hand? By typing their responses into computer terminals, people can have access to other group members' ideas without interfering with them. A sample screen for the "extra thumb" problem is shown here. (*Source:* Adapted from Gallupe, Bastianutti, & Cooper, 1991; see Note 62.)

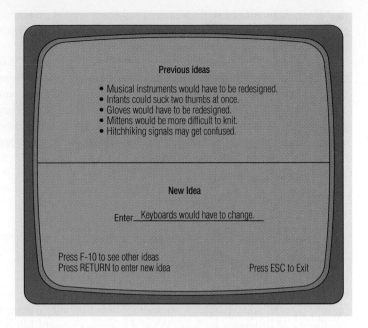

Previous ideas

- Musical instruments would have to be redesigned.
- Infants could suck two thumbs at once.
- Gloves would have to be redesigned.
- Mittens would be more difficult to knit.
- Hitchhiking signals may get confused.

New Idea

Enter Keyboards would have to change.

Press F-10 to see other ideas
Press RETURN to enter new idea   Press ESC to Exit

result of saying silly things, their creativity may be inhibited when in groups. Similarly, groups may inhibit creativity by slowing down the process of bringing ideas to fruition. Thus, although groups may be expected to help stimulate the creative process, any such benefits of groups are clearly more than offset when it comes to creative problems.

Fortunately, through the use of technology, a way has been found to combat the inefficiency of brainstorming groups. Part of the problem with the brainstorming process is that the production of ideas is blocked by others. In other words, people may be prevented from thinking of or expressing an idea because they are required to listen to someone else and, as a result, forget what they were about to say. To combat this possibility, Gallupe, Bastianutti, and Cooper had groups of people do brainstorming electronically—that is, by putting them in front of a computer terminal that allowed them to simultaneously review others' suggestions while entering their own.[62] A sample display screen for the "extra thumbs problem" is shown in Figure 14–14. This technique was found to be responsible for generating more ideas than standard brainstorming by four-person groups. Apparently, the *electronic brainstorming system (EBS)*, as it is known, can be an effective means of unblocking the presentation of ideas in brainstorming groups.

Thus far, we have noted several of the problems underlying the relatively poor performance of groups compared with individuals. Now we will highlight two of the most important contributing factors—*groupthink* and *group polarization*.

Obstacles to Quality Group Decisions: Groupthink and Group Polarization

Given the mixed findings regarding the effectiveness of decision-making groups, we should consider some of the factors that may potentially limit their operation. In other words, we may ask: what characteristics of group functioning may disrupt the group decision-making process?

Groupthink: When Too Much Cohesiveness Is a Dangerous Thing   One reason groups may fare so poorly on complex tasks lies in the dynamics of group interaction.

As we noted in chapter 8, when members of a group develop a very strong group spirit—or a high level of *cohesiveness*—they sometimes become so concerned about not disrupting the like-mindedness of the group that they may be reluctant to challenge the group's decisions. When this happens, group members tend to isolate themselves from outside information, and the process of critical thinking deteriorates. This phenomenon is referred to as **groupthink**.[63]

The concept of groupthink was proposed initially as an attempt to explain ineffective decisions made by U.S. government officials that led to fiascoes such as the Bay of Pigs invasion in Cuba and the Vietnam War.[64] Analyses of each of these cases have revealed that the president's advisers actually *discouraged* more effective decision making. A recent examination of the conditions under which the decision was made to launch the ill-fated space shuttle *Challenger* in January 1986 revealed that it too resulted from groupthink.[65] Post-hoc analyses of conversations between key personnel suggested that the team that made the decision to launch the shuttle under freezing conditions did so while insulating itself from the engineers who knew how the equipment should function. Given that NASA had such a successful history, the decision makers operated with a sense of invulnerability. They also worked so closely together and were under such intense pressure to launch the shuttle without further delay that they all collectively went along with the launch decision, creating the illusion of unanimous agreement. For a more precise description of groupthink (and a practical guide to recognizing its symptoms), see Table 14–3.

Groupthink doesn't occur only in governmental decision making, of course, but also in the private sector (although the failures may be less well publicized). For example, analyses of the business policies of large corporations such as Lockheed and Chrysler have suggested that it was the failure of top management teams to

Sometimes managers limit themselves to certain decisions by not considering all possibilities. For example, a manager in a conservative insurance company might ignore possibly risky decisions merely because the company is used to following conservative decisions. Thus, potentially beneficial decisions might be overlooked merely because they would not fit in with the usual "style" of the organization. By always making similar, routine decisions, managers could be limiting the possible advantages of new and different decisions and their outcomes. [Duchon, D., Ashmos, D., & Dunegan, K. J. (1991, Summer/Fall). Avoid decision making disaster by considering psychological bias. *Review of Business, 13,* 13–18.]

TABLE 14–3   Groupthink: Its Warning Signals

Sometimes in highly cohesive groups the members become more concerned about maintaining positive group spirit than about making the most realistic decisions—a phenomenon known as *groupthink*. The major symptoms of groupthink are identified and described here.

Symptom	Description
Illusion of *invulnerability*	Ignoring obvious danger signals, being overoptimistic, and taking extreme risks
Collective *rationalization*	Discrediting or ignoring warning signals that run contrary to group thinking
Unquestioned *morality*	Believing that the group's position is ethical and moral and that all others are inherently evil
Excessive negative *stereotyping*	Viewing the opposing side as being too negative to warrant serious consideration
Strong *conformity pressure*	Discouraging the expression of dissenting opinions under the threat of expulsion for disloyalty
Self-censorship of dissenting ideas	Withholding dissenting ideas and counterarguments, keeping them to oneself
Illusion of *unanimity*	Sharing the false belief that everyone in the group agrees with its judgments
Self-appointed *mindguards*	Protecting the group from negative, threatening information

Source: Adapted from Janis, 1982; see Note 63.

respond to changing market conditions that at one time led them to the brink of disaster.[66] The problem is that members of very cohesive groups may have considerable confidence in their group's decisions, making them unlikely to raise doubts about these actions (i.e., "the group seems to know what it's doing"). As a result, they may suspend their own critical thinking in favor of conforming to the group. When group members become fiercely loyal to each other, they may ignore potentially useful information from other sources that challenges the group's decisions. The result of this process is that the group's decisions may be completely uninformed, irrational, or even immoral.[67]

So as not to conclude on an entirely pessimistic note, we point out that several strategies can effectively combat groupthink. Here are a few proven techniques.

1. **Promote open inquiry.** Remember: groupthink arises in response to group members' reluctance to "rock the boat." Group leaders should encourage members to be skeptical of all solutions and to avoid reaching premature agreements. It sometimes helps to play the role of "devil's advocate," that is, to intentionally find fault with a proposed solution.[68] Research has shown that when this is done, groups make higher-quality decisions.[69] In fact, some corporate executives use exercises in which conflict is intentionally generated just so the negative aspects of a decision can be identified before it's too late.[70] This is not to say that leaders should be argumentative. Rather, raising a nonthreatening question to force both sides of an issue can be very helpful in improving the quality of decisions.

2. **Use subgroups.** Because the decisions made by any one group may be the result of groupthink, basing decisions on the recommendations of two groups is a useful check. If the two groups disagree, a discussion of their differences is likely to raise important issues. However, if the two groups agree, you can be relatively confident that their conclusions are not *both* the result of groupthink.

3. **Admit shortcomings.** When groupthink occurs, group members feel very confident that they are doing the right thing. Such feelings of perfection discourage people from considering opposing information. However, if group members acknowledge some of the flaws and limitations of their decisions, they may be more open to corrective influences. Keep in mind that no decision is perfect. Asking others to point out their misgivings about a group's decisions may help avoid the illusion of perfection that contributes to groupthink.

4. **Hold second-chance meetings.** Before implementing a decision, it is a good idea to hold a *second-chance meeting* during which group members are asked to express any doubts and propose any new ideas they may have. Alfred P. Sloan, former head of General Motors, is known to have postponed acting on important matters until any group disagreement was resolved.[71] As people get tired of working on problems, they may hastily reach agreement on a solution. Second-chance meetings can be useful devices for seeing if a solution still seems good even after "sleeping on it."

Given the extremely adverse effects groupthink can have on organizations, we encourage practicing managers to put these simple suggestions into action. The alternative—facing the consequences of groupthink—certainly suggests the need for serious consideration of this issue.

Group Polarization: The Extreme Nature of Group Decisions   Imagine that you are an investor considering diversifying your portfolio. Your present holdings yield a modest appreciation each year. Although the stocks you own are safe and very conservative, they are unlikely to produce any great gains. Now you have an opportunity to buy an interest in a new company that has a highly uncertain future. If the company succeeds, the payoff will be enormous. But you don't know how well it will do. Should you consider converting your safer investments into this much riskier, but potentially more lucrative, one?

What would the odds of the new company's success have to be before you would decide to "go for it" and make the investment? If you said that there would have to be a 90 percent chance of the company's succeeding before you would advocate making the investment, we could safely characterize your stance as conservative or cautious. However, if you were willing to make the investment when there was only a 10 percent chance of success, we would consider your stance quite risky. Now suppose we asked a group of investors (e.g., an investment club) to consider this same decision. The question we are interested in is: would the group make a riskier or a more conservative decision than an individual?

You might think that the give-and-take going on in a group's discussion sessions would cause the group to make more middle-of-the-road, neutral decisions—ones that shy away from risk. However, a considerable amount of research seriously challenges this popular belief. Systematic studies have shown that groups tended to make riskier decisions than individuals.[72] So, for example, if four individuals recommended that the riskier courses of action be taken if the odds of success were 40 percent, a group composed of these same individuals might recommend that the riskier course of action be taken if the odds of success were lower, say, 20 percent. Because of this shift in the direction of riskiness by groups compared with individuals, the phenomenon became known as the **risky shift.**

Scientists quickly became interested in the risky shift phenomenon. Their curiosity was sparked not only by the surprising nature of the effect, but also, no doubt, by the interesting implications that decision-making groups (such as juries, or business and governmental committees) might be biased toward making risky—perhaps even dangerous—decisions. As researchers continued to study the decisions made by groups, it became apparent that they were not only riskier—they were more extreme along several other dimensions as well. For example, studies have shown that liberal judges tend to hand down more liberal decisions when they convene in panels of three than when they decide cases alone.[73] Other studies have found that jury members who believe a defendant is innocent or guilty before deliberations tend to be even more certain of these convictions after joint discussions. Apparently, the risky shift is part of a more general tendency for group members to shift their individual views in a more extreme direction, a phenomenon known as **group polarization.**[74] The group polarization effect refers to the tendency for group members to shift their views about a given issue to ones that are more extreme in the same direction as the views they held initially. This effect is summarized in Figure 14–15. As

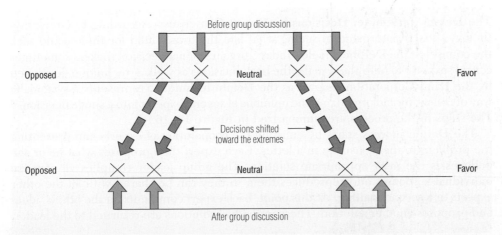

Before group discussion

Opposed   ✕   ✕   Neutral   ✕   ✕   Favor

← Decisions shifted →
toward the extremes

Opposed   ✕   ✕   Neutral   ✕   ✕   Favor

After group discussion

Test Bank questions 14.42 and 14.54 relate to material on this page.

FIGURE 14–15

The Group Polarization Effect: A Summary

The *group polarization effect* refers to the tendency for individuals initially in favor of or against a certain decision to become even more in favor of it or against it following group discussions.

you can see, someone who is initially in favor of a certain decision will be *more favorable* toward it following group discussion, and someone who is initially opposed to a certain decision will be *more opposed* to it following group discussion.

Apparently, the group interaction makes people more extremely disposed to their initially held beliefs. Why does this happen? In other words, what causes group polarization? One major explanation, the *social comparison* view, suggests that group members may want to make a positive impression on their fellow group members, and do so by strongly endorsing predominant cultural values. People wanting to impress their fellow group members (or at least to not embarrass themselves in front of them) will embrace the predominant cultural value—wanting to appear to do the right thing in front of others and therefore going to the extreme with respect to whatever perspective seems right. This explanation suggests that group polarization represents a serious bias in group decision-making processes.

Another possible explanation of the group polarization effect is that *persuasive information* is exchanged during the course of group deliberations. As deliberations progress, some group members may be exposed to arguments they had not previously considered. Since most of these arguments will favor the views initially held by the majority of the group members, there is a gradual shift toward extremity as more and more dissenters change their minds and "jump on the bandwagon." It is difficult to say which explanation of the group polarization effect is better since both are supported by research.[75]

Regardless of the precise basis for the group polarization effect, its existence has important implications for managers and organizations. Potentially, groups may make increasingly extreme decisions, and the results for both organizations and individuals can be disastrous. Because the group polarization effect, along with groupthink, is a potentially important negative influence on group decisions, it is clearly worthwhile to consider ways of overcoming such obstacles to effective group decision making.

Improving the Effectiveness of Group Decisions: Some Techniques

As we have made clear in this chapter, certain advantages can be gained from sometimes using individuals and sometimes using groups to make decisions. A decision-making technique that combines the best features of groups and individuals, while minimizing the disadvantages, would be ideal. Several techniques designed to realize the "best of both worlds" have been widely used in organizations. These include techniques that involve the structuring of group discussions in special ways, as well as improving the skills individuals may bring to the decision-making situation.

The Delphi Technique: Decisions by Expert Consensus According to Greek mythology, people interested in seeing what fate the future held for them could seek the counsel of the Delphic oracle. Today's organizational decision makers sometimes consult experts to help them make the best decisions as well. A technique developed by the Rand Corporation, known as the **Delphi technique,** represents a systematic way of collecting and organizing the opinions of several experts into a single decision.[76] The steps in the process are summarized in Figure 14–16.

The Delphi process starts by enlisting the cooperation of experts and presenting the problem to them, usually in a letter. Each expert then proposes what he or she believes is the most appropriate solution. The group leader compiles all of these individual responses and reproduces them so they can be shared with all the other experts in a second mailing. At this point, each expert comments on the others' ideas and proposes another solution. These individual solutions are returned to the leader,

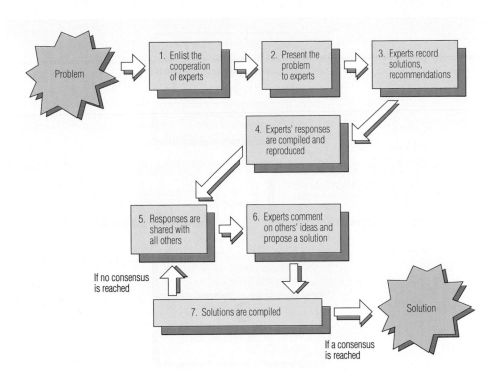

FIGURE 14–16

The Delphi Technique:
A Summary

The *Delphi technique* allows decisions to be made by several experts without encountering many of the disadvantages of face-to-face group interaction.

who compiles them and looks for a consensus of opinions. If a consensus is reached, the decision is made. If not, the process of sharing reactions with others is repeated until a consensus is eventually obtained.

The obvious advantage of using the Delphi technique to make decisions is that it allows the collection of expert judgments without the great costs and logistical difficulties of bringing many experts together for a face-to-face meeting. However, the technique is not without limitations. As you might imagine, the Delphi process can be very time-consuming. Sending out letters, waiting for everyone to respond, transcribing and disseminating the responses, and repeating the process until a consensus is reached can take quite a long time. Experts have estimated that the minimum time required to use the Delphi technique would be more than forty-four days. In one case, the process took five months to complete.[77] Obviously, the Delphi approach would not be appropriate for making decisions in crisis situations, or whenever else time is of the essence. However, the approach has been successfully employed to make decisions such as what items to put on a conference agenda and what the potential impact of implementing new land-use policies would be.[78]

The Nominal Group Technique: A Structured Group Meeting   When there are only a few hours available to make a decision, group discussion sessions can be held in which members interact with each other in an orderly, focused fashion aimed at solving problems. The **nominal group technique (NGT)** brings together a small number of individuals (usually about seven to ten) who systematically offer their individual solutions to a problem and share their personal reactions to others' solutions.[79] The technique is referred to as *nominal* because the individuals involved form a group *in name only*. The participants do not attempt to agree as a group on any solution, but rather vote on all the solutions proposed. For an outline of the steps in the process, see Figure 14–17 on p. 564.

FIGURE 14–17

The Nominal Group
Technique: A Summary

The *nominal group
technique* structures
face-to-face group
meetings in a way that
allows for the open
expression and
evaluation of ideas.

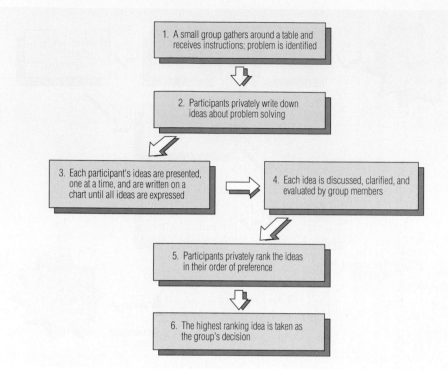

1. A small group gathers around a table and receives instructions; problem is identified

2. Participants privately write down ideas about problem solving

3. Each participant's ideas are presented, one at a time, and are written on a chart until all ideas are expressed

4. Each idea is discussed, clarified, and evaluated by group members

5. Participants privately rank the ideas in their order of preference

6. The highest ranking idea is taken as the group's decision

As shown in Figure 14–17, the nominal group process begins by gathering the group members together around a table and identifying the problem at hand. Then each member writes down his or her solutions. Next, one at a time, each member presents his or her solutions to the group and the leader writes these down on a chart. This process continues until all the ideas have been expressed. Following this, each solution is discussed, clarified, and evaluated by the group members. Each member is given a chance to voice his or her reactions to each idea. After all the ideas have been evaluated, the group members privately rank-order their preferred solutions. The idea that receives the highest rank is taken as the group's decision.

Although nominal groups traditionally meet in face-to-face settings, advances in modern technology enable nominal groups to meet even when its members are far away from each other. Specifically, a technique known as **automated decision conferencing** has been used, in which individuals in different locations participate in nominal group conferences by means of telephone lines or direct satellite transmissions.[80] The messages may be sent either via characters on a computer monitor or images viewed during a teleconference. Despite their high-tech look, automated decision conferences are really just nominal groups meeting in a manner that approximates face-to-face contact.

The NGT has several advantages and disadvantages.[81] We have already noted that this approach can be used to arrive at group decisions in only a few hours. The benefit of the technique is that it discourages any pressure to conform to the wishes of a high-status group member because *all* ideas are evaluated and the preferences are expressed in *private* balloting. The technique must be considered limited, however, in that it requires the use of a trained group leader. In addition, using NGT successfully requires that only one narrowly defined problem be considered at a time. So, for very complex problems, many NGT sessions would have to be run—and only *if* the problem under consideration can be broken down into smaller parts.

It is important to consider the relative effectiveness of nominal groups and Delphi groups over face-to-face interacting groups. In general, research has shown the superiority of these special approaches to decision making in many ways on a variety of decision problems.[82] For example, the effectiveness of both techniques has been demonstrated in a study by Van de Ven and Delbecq in which seven-member groups (nominal, Delphi, and interacting) worked on the task of defining the job of a dormitory counselor.[83] Nominal groups tended to be the most satisfied with their work and made the best-quality judgments. In addition, both nominal groups and Delphi groups were much more productive than interacting groups. As we noted earlier, however, there is a potential benefit to be derived from face-to-face interaction that cannot be realized in nominal and Delphi groups—that is, acceptance of the decision. Groups are likely to accept their decisions and be committed to them if members have been actively involved in making them. Thus the more detached and impersonal atmosphere of nominal and Delphi groups sometimes makes their members less likely to accept their groups' decisions. We may conclude, then, that there is no one best type of group used to make decisions. Which type is most appropriate depends on the trade-offs decision makers are willing to make in terms of speed, quality, and commitment.[84]

The nominal group technique and the Delphi technique represent two very useful and effective ways of improving group performance. The problem with using these techniques, however, is that they go outside the normal decision-making channels and call for certain procedures requiring the use of specialists to run group meetings. It may not always be feasible, of course, to conduct such meetings, suggesting a need for improving the quality of group decisions on a more regular basis. What else can be done to help improve the quality of group decisions? One promising answer appears to lie in the area of training individual decision makers to work more effectively in groups.

Training Individuals to Improve Group Performance. As we noted earlier in this chapter, how well groups solve problems depends in part on the composition of those groups. If at least one group member is capable of coming up with a solution, groups may benefit by that individual's expertise. Based on this reasoning, it follows that the more qualified individual group members are to solve problems, the better their groups as a whole will perform.

The researchers Bottger and Yetton found that individuals trained to avoid four common types of errors significantly reduced the number of mistakes made by their groups when attempting to solve a creative problem.[85] Specifically, participants in the study were asked to be aware of and to try to avoid four common problems.

1. **Hypervigilance.** This state involves frantically searching for quick solutions to problems, going from one idea to another out of a sense of desperation that one idea isn't working and that another needs to be considered before time runs out. A poor, "last chance" solution may be adopted to relieve anxiety. This problem may be avoided by keeping in mind that it is best to stick with one suggestion and work it out thoroughly, and reassuring the person solving the problem that his or her level of skill and education is adequate to perform the task at hand. In other words, a little reassurance may go a long way toward keeping individuals on the right track and avoiding the problem of hypervigilance.

2. **Unconflicted adherence.** Many decision makers make the mistake of sticking to the first idea that comes into their heads without more deeply evaluating the consequences. As a result, such people are unlikely to become aware of any problems associated with their ideas or to consider other possibilities. To avoid unconflicted adherence, decision makers are urged to (1) think about the difficulties associated

FOCUS ON RESEARCH

Training Pilots to Make Decisions about Avoiding Hazardous Weather

It's already 4:30 P.M., the time you were supposed to be landing in Los Angeles, but your flight hasn't even gotten off the ground. The cause of the delay: weather. Then, despite stormy conditions, your pilot begins taxiing down the runway in preparation for takeoff. As soon as the nose lifts off the ground, the pilot receives a "wind-shear alert." A microburst (a small area of very turbulent wind) is encountered, causing a sudden downdraft and a resulting loss of lift. At a "white knuckle time" like this, you hope—or pray—that your air crew can decide how to act appropriately! The question of what constitutes correct group decision making becomes a life and death matter. Unfortunately, such circumstances proved fatal for more than 400 people in fourteen separate air carrier accidents between 1975 and 1985, making wind shear the top cause of aircraft accidents in the United States.[86]

Our intention is not to frighten you with these statistics, but to illustrate the severity of the wind-shear problem and to highlight the importance of training pilots to make appropriate decisions under such hazardous conditions. Despite the development of technological tools to detect dangerous weather conditions and alert pilots to them (e.g., Doppler radar), the human factor—appropriately managing information—remains critical. For example, an analysis of a wind-shear accident in Denver on July 11, 1988, suggests that several pilots flew into an area reported to have microburst activity because the warnings they received did not enable them to determine whether the problem was a relatively common, very brief spurt of bad weather, or the rarer and more dangerous intense variety. Clearly, to the extent that pilots can accurately interpret the signals they receive, they are better able to take the correct, timely actions needed to guide their craft safely.

What can be done to help in such situations? In other words, what type of information should be presented to pilots, when, and in what form? This question was considered by Lee in an intensive investigation in which eighteen experienced commercial air crews (a captain and a first officer constituted a crew) were studied in an elaborate flight simulator.[87] Crews were familiarized with the training apparatus and were required to fly a simulated round trip between Salt Lake City and Denver. The flight conditions were made to closely match those of the July 1988 accident. Crews were assigned to one of three groups differing with respect to the nature of the weather-related information they received. In the *control group*, crews received only the standard weather briefings given by air traffic control transmissions. Two additional groups received one of two different types of display information. Both groups received a visual display of simulated ground-based Doppler radar automatically when the plane came within sixty nautical miles of Denver (supplementing the verbal information received by the control group). Microbursts were shown within three nautical miles of either end of the active runway. The two experimental groups differed with respect to the time at which the microburst/wind-shear alert was received. Specifically, warnings were issued within three nautical miles of the runway or twenty-five nautical miles of the runway. How did these differences in display mode (verbal only versus verbal plus visual display) and warning times (three versus twenty-five miles) influence air crews' decision-making behavior?

The results revealed some critical differences. First, an analysis was made of the topics of weather-related conversation that the pilot and first officer had between them. Although no significant differences emerged between the control group and the two experimental groups on unrelated weather matters (e.g., temperature, visibility), very important differences were found in discussions of critical wind-related matters. Specifically, whereas 17 percent of the discussion in the experimental groups dealt with wind shear, attention to the topic was virtually nonexistent in the control group. By contrast, control group members paid greater attention to surface winds, a less predictive measure of wind shear. Clearly, the use of visual information to supplement verbal warnings was effective in gaining the attention of cockpit crew members. This, of course, is a necessary preliminary step toward making the right decisions.

The investigators also analyzed the results with respect to decision time—that is, the average time that elapsed from the alert to the captain's decision about what approach to take in landing. The findings are summarized in Figure 14–18. Crews assigned to experimental groups (receiving both oral and visual information) made decisions more quickly than those assigned to the control group (receiving only oral information). No significant differences in decision time were found between the two experimental groups (differing in terms of the advance distances from the microbursts). These data reveal that the visual presentation of redundant data allowed airline cockpit crews to make critical decisions about avoiding microbursts much faster. In fact, a mean difference of approximately one minute (and 700–800 feet of additional altitude) was found—margins that may be critical to avoiding potentially dangerous conditions.

Although additional factors may be involved in potentially dangerous air travel situations, the present results strongly suggest the need to use redundant visual information to supplement oral information. Given that good information is the key to good decision making, such knowledge about the most effective ways to present critical information may be exceptionally useful. Although such redundant visual displays may be costly to introduce, one must consider these costs relative to the loss of life that might occur when the appropriate visual display technology is not put into place. Findings such as these strongly suggest that although human decision making is highly imperfect, the use of technology can greatly improve it.

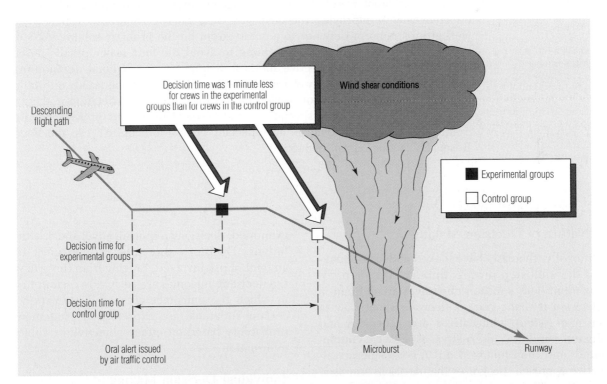

FIGURE 14–18   Decision Times Needed to Make Critical Air Safety Maneuvers: An Experimental Comparison of Two Methods

The time needed to make the critical decision to "go around" a microburst was significantly reduced when air crews received information about microburst activity both orally and visually (experimental groups) rather than when they received only oral information (control group). (*Source:* Adapted from Lee, 1991; see Note 87.)

with their ideas, (2) force themselves to consider different ideas, and (3) consider the special and unique characteristics of the problem they are facing and avoid carrying over assumptions from previous problems.

3. **Unconflicted change.** Sometimes people are too quick to change their minds and adopt the first new idea to come along. To avoid such unconflicted change, decision makers are encouraged to ask themselves about (1) the risks and problems of adopting that solution, (2) the good points of the first idea, and (3) the relative strengths and weaknesses of both ideas.

4. **Defensive avoidance.** Too often decision makers fail to solve problems effectively because they avoid working on the task at hand. To minimize this problem, they should do three things. First, they should attempt to *avoid procrastination.* Don't put off the problem indefinitely just because you cannot come up with a solution right away. Continue to budget some of your time on even the most frustrating problems. Second, *avoid disowning responsibility.* It is easy to minimize the importance of a problem by saying "It doesn't matter, so who cares?" Avoid giving up so soon. Finally, *don't ignore potentially corrective information.* It is tempting to put your nagging doubts about the quality of a solution to rest in order to be finished with it. Good decision makers would not do so. Rather, they use their doubts to test and potentially improve the quality of their ideas.

The encouraging aspect of Bottger and Yetton's findings is that merely having members of problem-solving groups consider these four potential pitfalls was an effective way of improving the quality of their groups' solutions. Apparently, how well groups perform depends to a great extent on the problem-solving skills of the individual group members. Attempting to avoid the four major pitfalls described here appears to be an effective method of improving individual decision-making skills—and hence the quality of group decisions. (Obviously, this is only one approach that can improve organizational decision making. Training in decision-making techniques can also be highly specialized with respect to various professions. For an example of decision training in an especially critical job context, see the **Focus on Research** section on pp. 566–567.)

> Probably one of the oldest decision-making strategies is not making a decision at all. For example, a manager may have an opportunity to buy a valuable warehouse, but might be given a two-week time limit in which to make an offer. One way the manager in this situation may make a decision is by merely letting the time lapse. In this way, not making a decision really is making a decision (here, not to buy the warehouse). This type of decision making can also be used to cover bad decisions. For example, if the manager were questioned about not buying the warehouse, he or she could just say that the offer lapsed before the company was able to pull enough resources together, thereby letting himself or herself off the hook for the bad decision. [Etzioni, A. (1990, February). So much data, so little time. *Current,* pp. 10–14.]

SUMMARY AND REVIEW

The Nature of Decision Making

Traditionally, theorists have looked at **decision making** as the multistep process through which a problem is identified, solution objectives are defined, a *predecision* is made (i.e., a decision about how to make a decision), alternatives are generated and evaluated, and an alternative is chosen, implemented, and then followed up. A contemporary alternative approach recognizes that decisions are made in an automatic, intuitive fashion. Specifically, **image theory** claims that people will adopt a course of action that best fits their individual principles, current goals, and plans for the future.

The decisions made in organizations can be characterized as **programmed,** routine decisions made according to preexisting guidelines, or **nonpro-** grammed, decisions requiring novel and creative solutions. Decisions also differ with respect to the amount of risk involved, ranging from those in which the decision outcomes are relatively *certain* to those in which the outcomes are highly *uncertain.* Uncertain situations are expressed as statements of probability based on either objective or subjective information.

Individual Decision Making

Two major approaches to individual decision making have been identified. The **rational-economic model** characterizes decision makers as thoroughly searching through perfect information to make an *optimal* decision. In contrast, the **administrative model** recognizes the inherent imperfections of decision makers and the social and organizational systems within which they operate. Limitations imposed by people's ability to process the information needed to make complex decisions (**bounded rationality**) restrict decision makers to making **satisficing decisions**—solutions that are not optimal, but good enough.

Impediments to optimal individual decisions include cognitive biases (such as **framing** and **heuristics**), the tendency for decision makers to escalate their commitment to failing courses of action, and various organizational factors (such as time constraints and political face-saving pressures).

Group Decision Making

Studies comparing the decisions made by groups and individuals reveal a complex pattern. Groups have proven superior to individual members when they are composed of a heterogeneous mix of experts who possess complementary skills. However, groups may not be any better than the best member of the group when performing a task that has a simple, verifiable answer. Compared with individuals, groups tend to make inferior decisions on creative problems.

Two major obstacles to good group decisions may be identified. One of these, **groupthink,** is the tendency for strong conformity pressures within groups to lead to the breakdown of critical thinking and to encourage premature acceptance of potentially questionable solutions. Another possible obstacle is known as **group polarization**—the tendency, following group discussions, for group members to shift their opinions to more extreme positions in the direction they initially favored. As a result, groups tend to make more extreme decisions than individuals.

The quality of group decisions can be enhanced by using the **nominal group technique**—a method of structuring group meetings so as to systematically elicit and evaluate all opinions—and the **Delphi technique**—a method in which experts are solicited through the mail for their proposed solutions to problems. The quality of group decisions has also been shown to improve following individual training in problem-solving skills.

KEY TERMS

administrative model: A model of decision making that recognizes the *bounded rationality* that limits the making of optimally rational-economic decisions.

automated decision conferencing: A technique in which decision-making groups are formed by connecting people in different locations via satellite transmissions or telephone lines.

availability heuristic: The tendency for people to base their judgments on information that is readily available to them although it may be potentially inaccurate, thereby adversely affecting decision quality.

bounded rationality: The major assumption of the administrative model—that organizational, social, and human limitations lead to the making of *satisficing* rather than optimal decisions.

brainstorming: A technique designed to foster group productivity by encouraging interacting group members to express their ideas in a noncritical fashion.

decision making: The process through which a problem is identified, solution objectives are defined, a *predecision* is made, alternatives are generated and evaluated, and an alternative is chosen, implemented, and followed up.

decision support systems (DSS): Computer programs in which information about organizational behavior is presented to decision makers in a manner that helps them structure their responses to decisions.

Delphi technique: A method of improving group decisions using the opinions of experts, which are solicited by mail and then compiled. The expert consensus of opinions is used to make a decision.

escalation of commitment phenomenon: The tendency for individuals to continue to support previously unsuccessful courses of action.

framing: The presentation of a problem to an individual, either in negative terms (leading to *risk seeking*) or positive terms (leading to *risk aversion*).

group polarization: The tendency for group members to shift to more extreme positions (in the direction they initially favored) following group interaction.

groupthink: The tendency for members of highly cohesive groups to so strongly conform to group pressures regarding a certain decision that they fail to think critically, rejecting the potentially correcting influences of outsiders.

heuristics: Simple decision rules (rules of thumb) used to make quick decisions about complex problems. (See *availability heuristic* and *representativeness heuristic*.)

image theory: A theory of decision making that recognizes that decisions are made in an automatic, intuitive fashion. According to the theory, people will adopt a course of action that best fits their individual principles, current goals, and plans for the future.

nominal group technique (NGT): A technique for improving group performance in which small groups of individuals systematically present and discuss their ideas before privately voting on their preferred solution. The most preferred solution is accepted as the group's decision.

nonprogrammed decisions: Decisions made about a highly novel problem for which there is no prespecified course of action.

predecision: A decision about what process to follow in making a decision.

programmed decisions: Highly routine decisions made according to preestablished organizational routines and procedures.

rational decisions: Decisions that maximize the chance of attaining an individual's, group's, or organization's goals.

rational-economic model: The model of decision making according to which decision makers consider all possible alternatives to problems before selecting the optimal solution.

representativeness heuristic: The tendency to perceive others in stereotypical ways if they appear to be typical representatives of the category to which they belong.

risky shift: The tendency for groups to make riskier decisions than individuals; a specific form of *group polarization.*

satisficing decisions: Decisions made by selecting the first minimally acceptable alternative as it becomes available.

QUESTIONS FOR DISCUSSION

1. Apply the eight-step model of decision making described in the text to any decision you recently made.

2. Distinguish between *programmed decisions* and *nonprogrammed decisions,* giving an example of each in an organization with which you are familiar.

3. Describe the various barriers to effective decision making recognized by the *rational-economic model.* Give an example of each.

4. Suppose you were hired as a consultant to improve the decision-making skills of an organization's personnel. Outline the things you would do, and justify these measures.

5. Imagine that you are a manager facing the problem of not attracting enough high-quality personnel to your organization. Would you attempt to solve this problem alone or by committee? Explain your reasoning.

6. *Groupthink* is a potentially serious impediment to group decision making. Describe this phenomenon, and review some things that can be done to avoid it.

7. Give an example of *group polarization* operating in any group in which you have been a member.

8. Suppose you find out that a certain important organizational decision has to be made by a group, but you suspect that a better decision might be made by an individual. How could you structure a group so as to derive its advantages while avoiding its disadvantages?

9. Describe how individuals can be trained to improve the quality of group decisions.

NOTES

1. Mintzberg, H. J. (1988). *Mintzberg on management: Inside our strange world of organizations.* New York: Free Press.

2. Simon, H. (1977). *The new science of management decisions* (2nd ed.). Englewood Cliffs, NJ: Prentice-Hall.

3. Harrison, E. F. (1987). *The managerial decision-making process* (3rd ed.). Boston: Houghton Mifflin.

4. Wedley, W. C., & Field, R. H. G. (1984). A predecision support system. *Academy of Management Review, 9,* 696–703.

5. Nutt, P. (1984). Types of organizational decision processes. *Administrative Science Quarterly, 29,* 414–450.

6. Cowan, D. A. (1986). Developing a process model of problem recognition. *Academy of Management Review, 11,* 763–776.

7. Dennis, T. L., & Dennis, L. B. (1988). *Microcomputer models for management decision making.* St. Paul, MN: West.

8. Fulk, J., & Boyd, B. (1991). Emerging theories of communication in organizations. *Journal of Management, 17,* 407–446.

9. Sainfort, F. C., Gustafson, D. H., Bosworth, K., & Hawkins, R. P. (1990). Decision support systems effectiveness: Conceptual framework and empirical evaluation. *Organizational Behavior and Human Decision Processes, 45,* 232–252.

10. Stevenson, M. K., Busemeyer, J. R., & Naylor, J. C. (1990). *Handbook of industrial and organizational psychology* (Vol. 1, pp. 283–374). Palo Alto, CA: Consulting Psychologists Press.

11. Browning, E. B. (1850/1950). *Sonnets from the Portuguese.* New York: Ratchford and Fulton.

12. Mitchell, T. R., & Beach, L. R. (1990). " . . . Do I love thee? Let me count . . ." Toward an understanding of intuitive and automatic decision making. *Organizational Behavior and Human Decision Processes, 47,* 1–20.

13. Beach, L. R., & Mitchell, T. R. (1990). Image theory: A behavioral theory of image making in organizations. In B. Staw and L. L. Cummings (Eds.), *Research in organizational behavior* (Vol. 12, pp. 1–41). Greenwich, CT: JAI Press.

14. Hill, C. W., & Jones, G. R. (1989). *Strategic management.* Boston: Houghton Mifflin.

15. See Note 3.

16. Amit, R., & Wernerfelt, B. (1990). Why do firms reduce business risk? *Academy of Management Journal, 33,* 520–533.

17. Provan, K. G. (1982). Interorganizational linkages and influence over decision making. *Academy of Management Journal, 25,* 443–451.

18. Galaskiewicz, J., & Wasserman, S. (1989). Mimetic processes within an interorganizational field: An empirical test. *Administrative Science Quarterly, 34,* 454–479.

19. Walker, G., & Weber, D. (1987). Supplier competition, uncertainty, and make-or-buy decisions. *Academy of Management Journal, 30,* 589–596.

20. Parsons, C. K. (1988). Computer technology: Implications for human resources management. In G. R. Ferris & K. M. Rowland (Eds.), *Research in personnel and human resources management* (Vol. 6, pp. 1–36). Greenwich, CT: JAI Press.

21. Simon, H. A. (1987). Making management decisions: The role of intuition and emotion. *Academy of Management Executive, 1,* 57–64.

22. Linstone, H. A. (1984). *Multiple perspectives for decision making.* New York: North-Holland.

23. Simon, H. A. (1979). Rational decision making in organizations. *American Economic Review, 69,* 493–513.

24. Saporito, B. (1990, October 8). How Quaker Oats got rolled. *Fortune,* pp. 129, 132, 134, 136, 138.

25. Greenwald, J. (1985, July 22). Coca-Cola's big fizzle. *Time,* pp. 48–52.

26. Gelb, B. D., & Gelb, G. M. (1986, Fall). New Coke's fizzle—Lessons for the rest of us. *Sloan Management Review,* pp. 71–76.

27. Fredrickson, J. W., & Mitchell, T. R. (1984). Strategic decision processes: Comprehensiveness and performance in an industry with an unstable environment. *Academy of Management Journal, 27,* 399–423.

28. March, J. G., & Simon, H. A. (1958). *Organizations.* New York: Wiley.

29. See Note 28.

30. Simon, H. A. (1957). *Models of man.* New York: Wiley.

31. Gaeth, G. J., & Shanteau, J. (1984). Reducing the influence of irrelevant information on experienced decision makers. *Organizational Behavior and Human Performance, 33,* 263–282.

32. Ginrich, G., & Soli, S. D. (1984). Subjective evaluation and allocation of resources in routine decision making. *Organizational Behavior and Human Performance, 33,* 187–203.

33. Abelson, R. P., & Levi, A. (1985). Decision-making and decision theory. In G. Lindzey & E. Aronson (Eds.), *Handbook of social psychology* (3rd ed.) (Vol. 1, pp. 231–309). Reading, MA: Addison-Wesley.

34. Kahneman, D., & Tversky, A. (1984). Choices, values, and frames. *American Psychologist, 39,* 341–350.

35. Nisbett, R. E., & Ross, L. (1980). *Human inference: Strategies and shortcomings of social judgment.* Englewood Cliffs, NJ: Prentice-Hall.

36. Dubé-Rioux, L., & Russo, J. R. (1988). An availability bias in professional judgment. *Journal of Behavioral Decision Making, 1,* 223–237.

37. Kahneman, D., & Tversky, A. (1973). On the psychology of prediction. *Psychological Review, 80,* 251–273.

38. Taylor, R. N. (1984). *Behavioral decision making.* Glenview, IL: Scott, Foresman.

39. Brockner, J. (1992). The escalation of commitment to a failing course of action: Toward theoretical progress. *Academy of Management Review, 17,* 39–61.

40. Ross, J., & Staw, B. M. (1986). Expo 86: An escalation prototype. *Administrative Science Quarterly, 31,* 274–297.

41. Staw, B. M. (1981). The escalation of commitment to a course of action. *Academy of Management Review, 6,* 577–587.

42. Whyte, G. (1986). Escalating commitment to a course of action: A reinterpretation. *Academy of Management Review, 11,* 311–321.

43. Bowen, M. G. (1987). The escalation phenomenon reconsidered: Decision dilemmas or decision errors? *Academy of Management Review, 12,* 52–66.

44. Garland, H., & Newport, S. (1991). Effects of absolute and relative sunk costs on the decision to persist with a course of action. *Organizational Behavior and Human Decision Processes, 48,* 55–69.

45. Garland, H., Sandefur, C. A., & Rogers, A. C. (1990). De-escalation of commitment in oil exploration: When sunk costs and negative feedback coincide. *Journal of Applied Psychology, 75,* 721–727.

46. Whyte, G. (1991). Diffusion of responsibility: Effects on the escalation tendency. *Journal of Applied Psychology, 76,* 408–415.

47. Tjosvold, D. (1984). Effects of crisis orientation on managers' approach to controversy in decision making. *Academy of Management Journal, 27,* 130–138.

48. Johnson, R. J. (1984). Conflict avoidance through acceptable decisions. *Human Relations, 27,* 71–82.

49. Neustadt, R. E., & Fineberg, H. (1978). *The swine flu affair: Decision making on a slippery disease.* Washington, DC: U.S. Department of Health, Education and Welfare.

50. Shull, F. A., Delbecq, A. L., & Cummings, L. L. (1970). *Organizational decision making.* New York: McGraw-Hill.

51. Delbecq, A. L., Van de Ven, A. H., & Gustafson, D. H. (1975). *Group techniques for program planning.* Glenview, IL: Scott, Foresman.

52. Trevino, L. K., & Youngblood, S. A. (1990). Bad ap-

ples in bad barrels: A causal analysis of ethical decision-making behavior. *Journal of Applied Psychology, 75,* 378–385.

53. Murninghan, J. K. (1981). Group decision making: What strategies should you use? *Management Review, 25,* 56–62.

54. Hill, G. W. (1982). Group versus individual performance: Are $N + 1$ heads better than one? *Psychological Bulletin, 91,* 517–539.

55. Wanous, J. P., & Youtz, M. A. (1986). Solution diversity and the quality of group decisions. *Academy of Management Journal, 29,* 149–159.

56. Yetton, P., & Bottger, P. (1983). The relationships among group size, member ability, social decision schemes, and performance. *Organizational Behavior and Human Performance, 32,* 145–149.

57. Michaelsen, L. K., Watson, W. E., & Black, R. H. (1989). A realistic test of individual versus group consensus decision making. *Journal of Applied Psychology, 74,* 834–839.

58. See Note 54.

59. See Note 54.

60. Osborn, A. F. (1957). *Applied imagination.* New York: Scribner's.

61. Bouchard, T. J., Jr., Barsaloux, J., & Drauden, G. (1974). Brainstorming procedure, group size, and sex as determinants of the problem-solving effectiveness of groups and individuals. *Journal of Applied Psychology, 59,* 135–138.

62. Gallupe, R. B., Bastianutti, L. M., & Cooper, W. H. (1991). Unblocking brainstorms. *Journal of Applied Psychology, 76,* 137–142.

63. Janis, I. L. (1982). *Groupthink: Psychological studies of policy decisions and fiascoes* (2nd ed.). Boston: Houghton Mifflin.

64. Whyte, G. (1989). Groupthink reconsidered. *Academy of Management Review, 14,* 40–56.

65. Morehead, G., Ference, R., & Neck, C. P. (1991). Group decision fiascoes continue: Space shuttle *Challenger* and a revised groupthink framework. *Human Relations, 44,* 539–550.

66. Janis, I. L. (1988). *Crucial decisions: Leadership in policy making and crisis management.* New York: Free Press.

67. Morehead, G., & Montanari, J. R. (1986). An empirical investigation of the groupthink phenomenon. *Human Relations, 39,* 399–410.

68. Schweiger, D. M., Sandberg, W. R., & Ragan, J. W. (1986). Group approaches for improving strategic decision making: A comparative analysis of dialectical inquiry, devil's advocacy, and consensus. *Academy of Management Journal, 29,* 51–71.

69. Schwenger, D. M., Sandberg, W. R., & Rechner, P. L. (1989). Experiential effects of dialectical inquiry, devil's advocacy, and consensus approaches to strategic decision making. *Academy of Management Journal, 32,* 745–772.

70. Cosier, R. A., & Schwenk, C. R. (1990). Agreement and thinking alike: Ingredients for poor decisions. *Academy of Management Executive, 4,* 69–74.

71. Sloan, A. P., Jr. (1964). *My years with General Motors.* New York: Doubleday.

72. Pruitt, D. G. (1971). Choice shifts in group discussion: An introductory review. *Journal of Personality and Social Psychology, 20,* 339–360.

73. Walker, T. G., & Main, E. C. (1973). Choice-shifts in political decision making: Federal judges and civil liberties cases. *Journal of Applied Social Psychology, 2,* 93–98.

74. Lamm, H., & Myers, D. G. (1978). Group-induced polarization of attitudes and behavior. In L. Berkowitz (Ed.), *Advances in experimental social psychology* (Vol. 11, pp. 145–195). New York: Academic Press.

75. See Note 74.

76. Dalkey, N. (1969). *The Delphi method: An experimental study of group decisions.* Santa Monica, CA: Rand Corporation.

77. Van de Ven, A. H., & Delbecq, A. L. (1971). Nominal versus interacting group processes for committee decision-making effectiveness. *Academy of Management Journal, 14,* 203–212.

78. See Note 77.

79. Gustafson, D. H., Shulka, R. K., Delbecq, A., & Walster, W. G. (1973). A comparative study of differences in subjective likelihood estimates made by individuals, interacting groups, Delphi groups, and nominal groups. *Organizational Behavior and Human Performance, 9,* 280–291.

80. See Note 38.

81. Ulshak, F. L., Nathanson, L., & Gillan, P. B. (1981). *Small group problem solving: An aid to organizational effectiveness.* Reading, MA: Addison-Wesley.

82. Willis, R. E. (1979). A simulation of multiple selection using nominal group procedures. *Management Science, 25,* 171–181.

83. Van de Ven, A. H., & Delbecq, A. L. (1974). The effectiveness of nominal, Delphi, and interacting group decision making processes. *Academy of Management Journal, 17,* 605–621.

84. Stumpf, S. A., Zand, D. E., & Freedman, R. D. (1979). Designing groups for judgmental decisions. *Academy of Management Review, 4,* 589–600.

85. Bottger, P. C., & Yetton, P. W. (1987). Improving group performance by training in individual problem solving. *Journal of Applied Psychology, 72,* 651–657.

86. Federal Aviation Administration. (1987, April). *Integrated FAA wind shear program plan.* Washington, DC: DOT/FAA/DI-87/1.

87. Lee, A. T. (1991). Aircrew decision-making behavior in hazardous weather avoidance. *Aviation, Space, and Environmental Medicine, 15,* 158–161.

CASE IN POINT

Xerox Corporation, a leading manufacturer of computers and photocopiers, is radically chang-ing the way its employees make decisions.[1] Xerox has a strong tradition of anchoring its decision making in terms of xerography. Now over fifty years old, xerography is a process very much like photography. An image of a document is projected by a light-lens onto a photoreceptor. Dry toner is then used to develop the image into a copy.[2] Decisions based on xerography have served Xerox well, but today's rapidly changing technological environment demands that Xerox broaden the way its employees think about technology if it is to remain competitive.

At Xerox, the driving force to change the way employees make decisions is the Xerox Palo Alto Research Center (PARC). PARC was created in 1970 to provide research and development in the areas of computer science and electronics.[3] PARC was staffed with "some of the best computer scientists in the world" and these scientists were given "virtually unlimited funding to pursue their ideas."[4] PARC performed basic laboratory research and then attempted to transfer its research for incorporation into Xerox products.

During its first ten years, PARC produced fundamental breakthroughs in computer and photocopying technology. PARC developed the point-and-click "mouse" editing feature used with many computer systems. Although PARC was a huge success in its research efforts, it was not effective in transferring its research knowledge to the rest of the company. According to John Brown, vice president and director of PARC, "Xerox gained a reputation for fumbling the future, and PARC for doing brilliant research but in isolation from the company's business."[5]

Something was wrong with the way Xerox employees thought about the connection between research and the company's products. Attempting to transfer even the greatest research ideas was doomed to fail if the people who were responsible for incorporating these ideas into real products couldn't get past their own decision-making biases. Xerox employees seemed to be blind to ideas that didn't fit their decision-making assumptions.

Brown decided to launch a systematic investigation to identify the obstacles that were undermining the decision-making processes of Xerox employees. He hired social science researchers (anthropologists, sociologists, psychologists, and linguists) to join PARC. His re-search unveiled several fundamental obstacles.

A major obstacle had to do with the way Xerox employees anchored decisions about technology. Traditionally, Xerox employees defined technology in terms of new computer and copier hardware and software. The technology that served as the basis for all photocopying decisions was xerography. Everyone at Xerox thought in terms of xerography. If a new idea was to be used by Xerox, it had to be similar in some way to xerographic technology. Essentially, Xerox decision makers began their thinking about technology with xerography, and then adjusted their decision making from that point forward. New technologies that were not anchored to the idea of xerography did not get used by Xerox decision makers.

Brown found that many scientists in PARC itself had far too limited a definition of tech-nology. Many PARC researchers framed research-and-development decisions only in terms of the physical sciences. With the introduction of social scientists into PARC (to study obstacles to effective decision making), Brown discovered that the way people interact with computer technology has important effects on their productivity.[6] Given the same computer equipment, employee productivity differed depending on how employees used the equipment. Speaking on the significance of this finding, Brown says "this means going beyond the typical view of technology as an artifact—hardware and software—to explore its potential for creating new and more effective ways of working, what we call studying technology in use."[7] The definition of technology at Xerox clearly had to be expanded to include the social science factors.

Brown's discovery of the importance of the social science side of Xerox technology led him to conclude not only that the role of research and development at Xerox was framed too narrowly, but also that the research process itself had to move out of the laboratory and into the workplace. PARC's social science research demonstrated the importance of *coproducing* research with the people who ultimately will be using it. This meant conducting research *in* the Xerox workplace, rather than exclusively in PARC laboratories. Xerox employees had to begin to think of themselves as integral parts of Xerox's research-and-development effort.

If Xerox employees could overcome their old decision-making biases, Brown believed, they would be better able to integrate new research into Xerox products. PARC started changing the way decisions are made at Xerox by updating its own decision-making practices. Like most research-and-development divisions of high-technology companies, PARC was staffed largely by researchers trained in the physical sciences, who viewed their job as the advancing of the physical sciences. Brown changed all of that when he broadened the definition of Xerox research to include not only advancements in computer science and electronics, but also advancements in understanding how people use technology in general. Brown championed a radically new focus for PARC, the study of how people interact with technology—how people go about doing work. The social scientists whom Brown hired are trained to study the interaction between people and their cultural and technological environments and quickly became important members of the redirected PARC.

Brown formally communicated Xerox's new definition of research and development through his "Letter to a Young Researcher." All PARC's researchers—not just the newly hired ones—were made familiar with this letter. Illustrative of the general content of this letter are Brown's comments regarding what types of decisions researchers at PARC should expect to be making. "If you come to work here, there will be no plotted path. The problems you work on will be ones you help to invent. When embarking on a project, you will have to be prepared to go in directions you couldn't have predicted at the outset. You will be challenged to take risks and to give up cherished methods and beliefs in order to find new approaches. You will encounter periods of deep uncertainty and frustration when it will seem that your efforts are leading nowhere. . . . Only by having deep intuitions, being able to trust them, and knowing how to run with them will you be able to keep your bearing and guide yourself through uncharted territory."[8]

But what is PARC doing to get Xerox employees throughout the rest of the company to radically change the way they make their decisions? Traditionally, Xerox employees thought about technology in general, and information processing technology in particular, "mainly as a way to make traditional copiers cheaper and better."[9] The challenge was to get people to frame their decisions about integrating information technology with Xerox products in new and different ways.

The "unfinished document" video was developed by Brown and his PARC scientists as a means of getting Xerox managers to envision Xerox and technology in new and different ways. The video shows PARC researchers discussing how digital technology could be used in copy machines and then—using mock-ups of what the new digital-based copiers would look like—acting out how the new copiers would affect the way people interact with the copiers. The video portrayed visually how a new technology could be used in a traditional Xerox product and, most important, how the use of a different technology affects the way people interact with such a new and different copier. The video was called the "unfinished document" because "the whole point of the exercise was to get the viewer to complete the video by suggesting their own ideas for how they might use the technology and what their new uses might mean for the business. In the process, they weren't just learning about a new technology, they were creating a new mental model of the business."[10]

Another way PARC researchers are trying to change the way Xerox employees make decisions is through "express teams," which are small groups made up of PARC researchers, Xerox engineers and marketers, and employees of Xerox corporate customers. These teams are assigned the task of speeding up the commercialization of Xerox research by sharing assumptions and perspectives about how new research and technology can be used to develop new Xerox products. Express teams create mutual understandings that form the basis for the groups' decision making.

PARC's social scientists even study the express teams to discover how team members go about developing shared understandings. The researchers have found that it takes a lot of time to develop the common language, sense of purpose, and definitions necessary to support decision making in the express teams. By videotaping the interactions of express-team members, PARC researchers are currently developing a decision support system (expert system) that can be used to facilitate the process of developing shared understandings in decision-making teams such as express teams.

Finally, PARC researchers are developing an "envisioning laboratory" to support decision making about how to integrate new research and technology into Xerox products. The envisioning laboratory is "a powerful computer environment where Xerox customers would have access to advanced programming tools for quickly modeling and envisioning the consequences of new systems."[11] Using the envisioning laboratory, Xerox employees, working with Xerox customers, could decide how to tailor new Xerox research and technology to fulfill customer needs. The envisioning laboratory would test the usefulness of new technological systems before such systems were even built.

The research-and-development process within PARC has changed dramatically. Social science research is now an integral part of PARC's mission. All employees are beginning to think about Xerox products not just in terms of hardware and software, but also in terms of how people can use these products to be more effective in their work. They also seem to be getting beyond anchoring decisions to xerography. The work of PARC to remove obstacles to effective decision making seems to be taking hold. In fact, Xerox's efforts to change the basic decision-making processes of its employees have resulted in nothing short of reinventing the entire corporation.[12]

Questions for Discussion

1. Xerox employees have traditionally based their decision making on the assumption that their business is derived from xerography technology. Which of the approaches described in the text provides the best description of the traditional decision-making practices used at Xerox: the traditional, analytical model, or image theory? Explain your choice.
2. How does the "unfinished document" exercise affect decision making?
3. Consider the impediments to optimal individual decision making described in the text. What impediments to optimal individual decision making do you find in this case? Are any of these impediments reduced by the decision-making strategies being offered by Xerox's PARC? How?
4. Xerox's PARC is working to provide the company's employees with new tools for decision making. Are these tools best used for programmed or nonprogrammed decisions? Explain your answer.

Notes

1. Brown, J. S. (1991, January–February). Research that reinvents the corporation. *Harvard Business Review, 69*(1), 102–111.
2. See Note 1.
3. See Note 1.
4. See Note 1, p. 103.
5. See Note 1, p. 102.
6. See Note 1.
7. See Note 1, p. 103.
8. See Note 1, p. 105.
9. See Note 1, p. 110.
10. See Note 1, p. 110.
11. See Note 1, p. 111.
12. See Note 1.

As noted in our discussion of decision framing (see p. 547), the level of risk that people are likely to take when making a decision will depend on how the decision is *framed*—that is, whether it is presented in a positive manner (in terms of gains) or in a negative manner (in terms of losses). When an outcome is framed in terms of a choice between losses, people tend to seek risk. However, when the same options are framed in terms of gains, people tend to avoid risk. You can demonstrate this phenomenon for yourself by considering the following situation.

Procedure

Read each of the following descriptions of hypothetical situations, and answer the questions that follow.

Situation 1: Imagine that you are an executive whose policies have recently resulted in a $1 million loss for your company. Now you're considering two new projects. One of them (Alpha) will provide a definite return of $500,000. The other (Beta) will provide a fifty-fifty chance of obtaining either a $1 million return or a zero return.

Question: Which project will you select: Alpha or Beta?

Situation 2: Imagine that you are considering one of two new projects to conduct in your company. The first project (Alpha) will provide a definite return of $500,000. The other project (Beta) will provide a fifty-fifty chance of obtaining a $1 million return, or a zero return.

Question: Which project will you select: Alpha or Beta?

Points to Consider

In Situation 1, your options follow a recent loss—a fact that causes you to frame the results of the two new options in a negative fashion (outcomes that have the effect of minimizing your losses). In other words, you can select between minimizing your loss by 50 percent (selecting Alpha) and having a fifty-fifty chance of undoing the loss completely (selecting Beta). Essentially, you are choosing between two losses. In such a case, most people would make a risky decision (select Beta). Did you?

However, the opposite would occur in Situation 2. Here, most people would select the sure thing (Alpha). The difference is that this situation is viewed from a positive perspective—that is, a "positive frame" (gains received). When selecting between the sure gain (Alpha) and the chancy but larger gain (Beta), people are unwilling to risk the "bird in the hand."

If you think about it, there is no rational reason for distinguishing between these two options, because they are mathematically identical. That people have strong preferences in such situations represents a bias in the way decision makers operate. Such framing effects may be responsible for many major decision failures (some of which were identified in the text; see Note 70). Sometimes, when decisions are framed between two losses, unusually high levels of risk are taken, resulting in failure. Some key failures in history may be seen as the result of taking high levels of risk when choosing between two apparent losses (whether or not they are recognized as such at the time). Here are a few:

- The Iran-contra affair during the Reagan administration (1980s)
- The 1986 decision to launch the space shuttle *Challenger*
- Coca-Cola's 1985 decision to change its formula
- The Iraqi invasion of Kuwait in 1990
- The Japanese attack on Pearl Harbor in 1941

Can you think of any others? For each case you identify, list the potential losses that might have been considered.

■ 15 ■

ORGANIZATIONAL STRUCTURE AND DESIGN

CHAPTER OUTLINE

Organizational Structure: The Basic Dimensions of Organizations

Organizational Charts: What Do They Reveal about Organizational Structure?

Approaches to Departmentalization: Various Ways of Structuring Organizations

Organizational Design: Coordinating the Structural Elements of Organizations

Classical and Neoclassical Approaches: The Quest for the One Best Design

The Contemporary Approach: Design Contingent on Environmental Conditions

Interorganizational Designs: Going Beyond the Single Organization

Technology: A Major Cause—and Consequence— of Design

Technology and Structure in Manufacturing Companies: The Woodward Studies

Work-Flow Integration: The Aston Studies
Technology and Interdependence

Special Sections

OB in Practice   Growing Pains Force CDP Publications to Restructure

An International/Multicultural Perspective   Structuring Organizations for Multinational Operations

A Question of Ethics   Who Takes the Rap for Unethical Corporate Behavior? Camouflaging Immorality within the Web of Organizational Structure

LEARNING OBJECTIVES

After reading this chapter, you should be able to:

1. Explain the basic characteristics of organizational structure revealed in an organization chart (*hierarchy of authority, division of labor, span of control, line versus staff,* and *decentralization*).
2. Describe different approaches to departmentalization—*functional organizations, product organizations,* and *matrix organizations.*
3. Distinguish between *classical* and *neoclassical* approaches to organizational design.
4. Explain how the contemporary approach to organizational design differs from the classical and neoclassical approaches.

5. Describe how an organization's design is influenced by the environment within which the organization operates.
6. Distinguish between *mechanistic organizations* and *organic organizations*, and describe the conditions under which each is most appropriate.
7. Characterize two forms of intraorganizational design—*joint ventures* and *conglomerates.*
8. Describe the relationship between organizational design and structure identified in the Woodward studies and in the Aston studies.
9. Explain the implications of *interdependence* on organizational structure.

After ten years in business, Harry Merkle has seen it all—good times, bad times, stagnant times. "The only thing you can count on," he tells his son and business partner, Vaughn, "is that things never stay the same." For Merkle and Sons Importing, this is certainly the case. At the end of a huge party celebrating Merkle's first decade in business, everyone's tie is loosened, and Harry is feeling nostalgic and waxing philosophical.

"I remember when we first got started," Harry reminisces, "it was just me and your mom, we did everything."

"Tell me about it," says Tess Merkle, Harry's wife of thirty-three years. "We placed the orders, unloaded trucks, swept the warehouse, fought with the customs agents—whatever it took to get ahead."

"How can I forget?" Harry acknowledges. "Back then, we grew so fast, things really got crazy. Tariffs got lifted, the dollar got strong, and imported goods were a bargain. We had all the business we could handle."

"That's when I graduated from college and went into the business," Vaughn recalled.

"It was crazy," Harry remembers. "We put Tess in charge of all the accounting, Vaughn here took care of the shipping and warehousing nightmares, and baby Scott—still over there dancing—handled most of the sales calls. The customers always liked him."

"I remember that," Vaughn says. "We each hired staff to help us, and before you knew it, we had what really looked like a company, not just a family."

Tess is nodding her head, and adds, "I even remember when we hired our first full-time lawyer, Sid Corey, I believe his name was, to check out all the contracts, deal with the customs regulations, and so on."

"I think his name was Sol Corey, Mom," Vaughn interrupts. "He was glad to help us almost full-time before he retired."

"You're both wrong, it was Sal Corey," Harry interjects, "but it doesn't matter. What really matters is that we realized we couldn't do everything by ourselves. We liked being a family business, but we couldn't pass up the opportunity to go big-time. And that meant yielding control to others, allowing non–family members to make decisions."

"I remember how that always scared you, Dad," Vaughn comments. "But you knew inside that having a *real* business meant not getting involved in everything firsthand."

"Yeah," Tess agrees, "Pop had to learn to be a boss, not a Superman!" Everyone laughs.

"Sure, it's funny," Harry says, "but I'm glad I learned how to do everything, because those days are over."

The mood suddenly grows somber. Harry continues: "I don't have to tell you, the last few years have been tough. The dollar's taken a dive. People want to 'buy American,' making foreign goods unpopular. Our rents have gone through the roof, not to mention our shipping costs. And then there's the outrageous insurance. . . ."

"We know, Dad, we know," Vaughn interrupts, not wanting his father to get all worked up, spoiling his good mood.

"That's business," Tess philosophizes. "You've got to take the good with the bad. I think we have been doing the best we can under the circumstances. We immediately eliminated some jobs. That's okay, 'cause we were getting too fat and lazy. Now we're a leaner and hungrier company. Our service is better, too. Someone sells an order, and now it's his responsibility to get it into the customer's hands. People can now really take responsibility for their work."

"I know what you mean," Vaughn remarks. "A few years ago, you just took the order and let someone else worry about everything else. People got lazy and lost sight of how things worked. They used to complain about getting the stuff in and warehousing it. Of course, it took forever. Slow was slow, but we were just so big, we couldn't operate any differently. Now the salespeople are right on top of everything."

"That's my wife, the big-time business tycoon," says Harry as he extends his arm and draws Tess closer to him. "We've had to change the way we operate in many ways over the years, but we survive. Why? Because we know that we have to change how we do the work around here, and we don't just continue with our old ways. As I said before, the only thing you can count on is that things won't stay the same—and that includes Merkle and Sons."

During its decade of business, Merkle and Sons has seen many changes in the world in which it operates and, as a result, in the way it conducts business. Over the years, the economy changed, governmental regulations were introduced, consumer preferences developed—all factors that influenced the growth and size of the company. When business boomed, the company grew as fast as it could—new positions were created, leading people to perform more specialized tasks and to take more responsibility for their actions. But when business slumped, cutbacks were made to keep the company afloat—fewer people were employed, requiring the remaining employees to perform many different tasks, leaving only a few top people to make decisions.

As this example illustrates, the environment within which organizations operate requires them to alter their basic designs to cope most effectively with the conditions they face. Our example makes clear that several different factors contribute to this notion of **organizational structure,** such as the level of specialization with which workers can afford to operate, and the degree to which employees are free to make decisions about their jobs. As you might imagine, factors such as these—and others— can be combined in various ways to intentionally create organizations that meet certain characteristics. This is the notion of **organizational design.** One key issue this chapter addresses is ways of designing organizations in the most effective manner. One of the major influences on the way organizations are designed is **technology,** the nature of the tools and machinery used to perform a job. (Just think, for example, how the personal computer has changed how you perform various tasks in the last few years!) This chapter is concerned with the basic structural characteristics of organizations, how they are combined into effective organizational designs, and the role of technology in this process.

Our coverage of this important topic represents a shift in emphasis that begins with this section of the book. Until now, we have been dealing with individual-level processes operating within people, what can be called a *micro* orientation to organizational behavior. We also have considered the dynamics of work groups, taking a *groups* orientation. Now, however, we will refocus our attention toward the organization as a whole—how it is structured and designed, and the factors that are responsible for its most effective form. This is referred to as a *macro* orientation to OB. Now that we have already examined organizations from a micro perspective, we think that you will appreciate the new insights created by the macro perspective, an approach that will be continued through the next chapter. For now, we will begin using the macro approach by looking at the issues we have identified above. First, we will identify the basic building blocks of organizations, which can be identified by the *organizational chart,* a useful pictorial way of depicting key features of organizational structure. Second, we will examine how these structural elements can be most effectively combined into productive organizational designs. Finally, we will discuss the role of technology as a cause—and a consequence—of organizational design. In so doing, we will be highlighting some basic facts regarding the role of the environment on organizational design.

ORGANIZATIONAL STRUCTURE: THE BASIC DIMENSIONS OF ORGANIZATIONS

Think about how a simple house is constructed. It is composed of a wooden frame positioned atop a concrete slab covered by a roof and siding materials. Within this basic structure are separate systems operating to provide electricity, water, and telephone services. Similarly, the structure of the human body is composed of a skeleton surrounded by various systems of organs, muscle, and tissue serving bodily functions such as respiration, digestion, and the like. Although you may not have thought about it much, we can also identify the structure of an organization. Consider, for example, the college or university you attend. It is probably composed of various groupings of people and departments working together to serve special functions. Individuals and groups are dedicated to tasks such as teaching, providing financial services, maintaining the physical facilities, and so on. Of course, within each group, even more distinctions can be found between the jobs people perform. For example, it's unlikely that the instructor for your organizational behavior course is also teaching seventeenth-century French literature! You can also distinguish between the various tasks and functions people perform in other organizations. In other words, an organization is not a haphazard collection of people, but a meaningful combination of groups and individuals working together purposefully to meet the goals of the organization.[1] The term **organizational structure** refers to the formal configuration between individuals and groups with respect to the allocation of tasks, responsibilities, and authority within organizations.[2]

Strictly speaking, one cannot see the structure of an organization; it is an abstract concept. However, the connections between various clusters of functions of which

Test Bank questions 15.1 and 15.46 relate to material on this page.

FIGURE 15–1

The Organizational Chart: A Valuable Guide to Organizational Structure

Organizational charts provide useful information about the interrelationships between various organizational units and the basic structural elements of organizations. (*Source:* Reprinted by permission of Nick Downes.)

"Clearly, someone's not holding up his end."

an organization is composed can be represented in the form of a diagram known as an **organizational chart.** In other words, an organizational chart can be considered a representation of an organization's internal structure. As you might imagine, organizational charts may be recognized as useful tools for avoiding confusion within organizations regarding how various tasks or functions are interrelated (see Figure 15–1). By carefully studying organizational charts, we can learn about some of the basic elements of organizational structure. With this in mind, we will now turn our attention to the five basic dimensions of organizational structure that can be revealed by organizational charts.

Organizational Charts: What Do They Reveal about Organizational Structure?

Organizational charts provide information about the various tasks performed within an organization and the formal lines of authority between them. For example, look at the chart depicting part of a hypothetical manufacturing organization shown in Figure 15–2 (see p. 582). Each box represents a specific job, and the lines connecting them reflect the formally prescribed lines of communication between the individuals performing those jobs (see chapter 13). To students of organizational behavior, however, such diagrams reveal a great deal more.

Hierarchy of Authority: Up and Down the Organizational Ladder   In particular, the organizational chart also provides information about who reports to whom—what is known as **hierarchy of authority.** The diagram reveals which particular lower-level employees are required to report to which particular individuals immediately above them in the organizational hierarchy. In our hypothetical example in Figure 15–2, the various regional salespeople (at the bottom of the hierarchy and the bottom of the diagram) report to their respective regional sales directors, who report to the vice president of sales, who reports to the president, who reports to the chief executive officer, who reports to the members of the board of directors. As we trace these reporting relationships, we work our way up the organization's hierarchy. In this case, the organization has six levels. Organizations may have many levels, in which case their structure is considered *tall*, or only a few, in which case their structure is considered *flat*.

FIGURE 15-2

Partial Organizational Chart of a Hypothetical Manufacturing Firm

An organizational chart, such as this one, identifies pictorially the various functions performed within an organization and the lines of authority between people performing those functions.

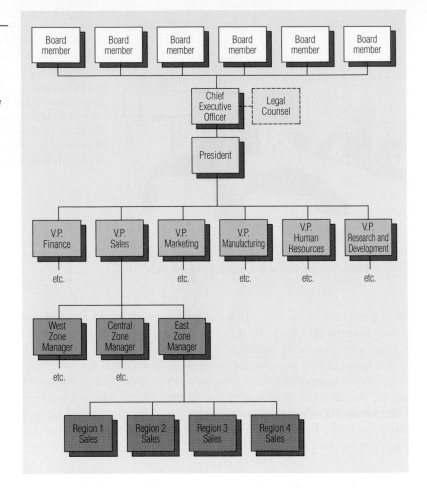

In recent years, a great deal has appeared in the news about organizations re-structuring their work forces by flattening them out. Although it is not uncommon for large companies to lay off people in low-level assembly line jobs (in fact, the "big three" automakers recently laid off a quarter of a million such employees), these days even middle managers and executives, long believed to be secure in their positions, find themselves unemployed as companies "downsize," "delayer," or "re-trench" by eliminating entire layers of organizational structure.[3] In fact, it has been estimated that during the 1980s, one-quarter of middle management jobs were elim-inated in American companies.[4] For example, in Motorola's Shaumburg, Illinois, portable-telephone plant, the number of organizational layers was recently reduced from seven to four.[5] Similar moves toward a flatter hierarchy also have been seen at IBM. In January 1986, John F. Akers, the president of IBM, announced a drastic change in the internal organizational structure of his company. Most notably, he changed the authority for making decisions, shifting it from just a few individuals in company headquarters to several general managers who were closer to the company's products and the people who made and sold them.[6] Five separate groups were created (personal computers, midrange systems, mainframes, communications, and chip technology), each of which had nearly complete authority to develop and market its products. Such changes do not come easily—in fact, in this case, more than 20,000 employees were affected by having to move to new jobs in new locations, changing jobs, or even having their jobs eliminated.

Test Bank question 15.5 relates to material on this page.

The underlying assumption of all these changes is that fewer layers reduce waste and enable people to make better decisions (by moving them closer to the problems at hand), thereby leading to greater profitability. Taking the American auto industry as an example, whereas Ford has seventeen layers of management between its CEO and its employees on the factory floor, and GM has as many as twenty-two, the more profitable Toyota has only seven![7] Although this is hardly conclusive evidence of the virtues of reducing the size of an organizational hierarchy, the differences are clearly remarkable. In general, most management experts claim that although hierarchy is necessary, too many layers of hierarchy can be hazardous to a company's bottom line.[8]

Division of Labor: Carving Up the Jobs Done   The organizational chart makes clear that the many tasks to be performed within an organization are divided into specialized jobs, a process known as the **division of labor.** The more that tasks are divided into separate jobs, the more those jobs are *specialized* and the narrower the range of activities that job incumbents are required to perform. In theory, the fewer tasks a person performs, the better he or she may be expected to perform them, freeing others to perform the tasks that they perform best. (We say "in theory" because if specialization is *too* great, people may lose their motivation to work at a high level and performance may suffer; see chapter 4.) Taken together, an entire organization is composed of people performing a collection of specialized jobs. This is probably the most obvious feature of an organization that can be observed from the organizational chart.

As you might imagine, the degree to which employees perform specialized jobs is likely to depend on the size of the organization. The larger the organization, the more the opportunities for specialization are likely to exist. For example, an individual working in a large advertising agency may get to specialize in a highly narrow field, such as writing jingles for radio and TV spots for automobiles. By contrast, someone working at a much smaller agency may be required to do all writing of print and broadcast ads in addition to helping out with the artwork and meeting with the clients. Obviously, the larger company might be expected to reap the benefits of efficiently using the talents of employees (a natural result of an extensive division of labor). As companies downsize, however, many managerial jobs become less specialized. For example, at General Electric, quite a few middle-management positions have been eliminated in recent years. As a consequence, the remaining managers must perform a wider variety of jobs, making their own jobs less specialized.[9] You can see this relationship in our summary in Figure 15–3.

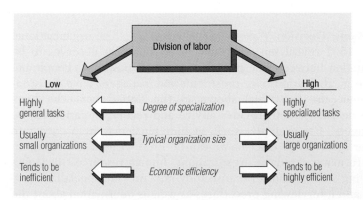

FIGURE 15–3

Division of Labor:
A Summary

In large organizations, the division of labor tends to be high, allowing people to perform highly specialized tasks in a highly efficient manner. The opposite is true in small organizations.

Test Bank questions 15.6–15.7 and 15.48 relate to material on this page.

A popular trend in organizational design has been to create flatter organizations by removing layers of middle managers and increasing the number of people who report to any one manager. These new designs are supposed to reduce cost and make the organization more adaptable and flexible to the demands of its customers. However, the reduction of middle managers has not been without costs in some cases. One employee of a newly "flattened" organization said that his department now looked like a wheel with spokes pointing toward the center. The employees were on the periphery and two managers were in the middle. Rather than increasing production, this design served only as a bottleneck, with all of the important information having to move through the two managers in the middle. Clearly, flat organizations are profitable for some organizations but not for others. [Cox, A. (1989, August 20). Even "flat" companies need leaders. *The New York Times*, p. F3(L).]

Span of Control: Breadth of Responsibility   Over how many individuals should a manager have responsibility? The earliest management theorists and practitioners alike (even the Roman legions) addressed this question.[10] When you look at an organizational chart, the number of people formally required to report to each individual manager is immediately clear. This number constitutes what is known as a manager's **span of control.** Those responsible for many individuals are said to have a *wide* span of control, whereas those responsible for fewer are said to have a *narrow* span of control. In our organizational chart (Figure 15–2), the CEO is responsible for only the actions of the president, giving this individual a narrower span of control than the president himself or herself, who has a span of control of five individuals. Sometimes, when organization leaders are concerned that they do not have enough control over lower-level employees, they restructure their organizations so that managers have responsibility over smaller numbers of subordinates. This is the case at Canada's largest bank, Royal Bank, where a team of top managers recently recommended that area managers reduce the number of branches under their control to between seven and twelve.[11]

When a manager's span of control is wide, the organization itself tends to have a flat hierarchy. In contrast, when a manager's span of control is narrow, the organization itself tends to have a tall hierarchy. This is demonstrated in Figure 15–4. The diagram at the top shows a tall organization—one in which the level of hierarchy is relatively high, but the span of control is relatively narrow. By contrast, the diagram at the bottom of Figure 15–4 shows a flat organization—one in which the level of hierarchy is relatively short, but the span of control is relatively wide. Note that both organizations depicted here have the same number of positions, but they are merely arranged differently.

The organizational chart may not reflect perfectly a manager's actual span of control. Other factors not immediately forthcoming from the chart itself may be involved. For example, managers may have additional responsibilities that do not appear on the chart—notably, assignments on various committees. Moreover, some subordinates (e.g., new people to the job) might require more attention than others. Also, the degree of supervisory control needed may increase (e.g., when jobs change), or decrease (e.g., when subordinates become more proficient). In fact, it is not readily possible to specify the "ideal" span of control that should be sought. Instead, consideration of what form of organization is best suited to various purposes makes better sense. Consider, for example, a military unit as compared to a research and development laboratory. Because supervisors in a military unit must have tighter control over subordinates and get them to respond quickly and precisely, a narrow span of control is likely to be effective (as a result, most military organizations are extremely tall). People working in a research and development lab, however, must have an open exchange of ideas and typically require little managerial guidance to be successful.

Line versus Staff Positions: Decision Makers versus Advisers   The organizational chart shown in Figure 15–2 reveals an additional distinction that deserves to be highlighted—the distinction between **line positions** and **staff positions.** People occupying line positions (e.g., the various vice presidents and managers) have decision-making power. However, the individual shown in the dotted box—the legal counsel—cannot make decisions, but provides advice and recommendations to be used by the line managers. For example, such an individual may help corporate officials decide whether a certain product name can be used without infringing on copyright restrictions. In many of today's organizations, human resources managers may be seen as occupying staff positions because they may provide specialized services regarding testing and interviewing procedures as well as information about the

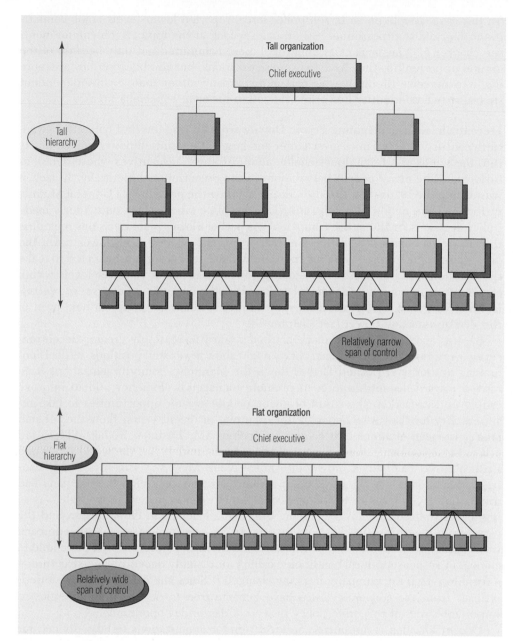

FIGURE 15–4

Tall versus Flat
Organizations:
A Comparison

In *tall organizations*, the hierarchy is tall (i.e., many layers from top to bottom) and managers have a narrow span of control (i.e., responsible for few subordinates). However, in *flat organizations*, the hierarchy is flat (i.e., few layers from top to bottom) and managers have a wide span of control (i.e., responsible for many subordinates). Both of the organizations depicted here have thirty-one members, although each is configured in a different form.

latest laws on personnel discrimination. However, the ultimate decisions on personnel selection might be made by more senior managers in specialized areas—that is, staff managers.

Differences between line and staff personnel are not unusual. Such differences may be conflict arousing, or even may be used to create intentional sources of conflict. For example, when Harold Green was the CEO of ITT, staff specialists in the areas of planning and strategy were regularly brought in from headquarters to challenge the decisions made by line managers in an attempt to "keep them on their toes."[12] Sociologists have long noted that staff managers tend to be younger, better educated, and more committed to their fields than the organizations employing them.[13] This tendency, no doubt, accounts for the recent finding by Kowlowsky that line personnel (in this case, people on an Israeli police force) reported lower levels of job commitment than did staff personnel.[14] (For a closer look at the topic of job commitment, see chapter 5). Line managers might feel more committed not only because of the greater opportunities they have to exercise decisions, but also because they are more likely to perceive themselves as part of a company rather than as an independent specialist (whose identity lies primarily within his or her specialty area).

Decentralization: Delegating Power Downward   During the first half of the twentieth century, as companies grew larger and larger, they shifted power and authority into the hands of a few upper-echelon administrators—executives whose decisions influenced the many people below them in the organizational hierarchy. In fact, it was during the 1920s that Alfred P. Sloan, Jr., then the president of General Motors, introduced the notion of a *central office,* the place where a few individuals made policy decisions for the entire company.[15] As part of Sloan's plan, decisions regarding the day-to-day operation of the company were pushed lower and lower down the organizational hierarchy, allowing those individuals who were most affected to make the decisions. This process of delegating power from higher to lower levels within organizations is known as **decentralization.** It is the opposite, of course, of *centralization,* the tendency for just a few powerful individuals or groups to hold most of the decision-making power (see chapter 14).

Recent years have seen a marked trend toward increasingly greater decentralization. As a result, organizational charts might show fewer staff positions, as decision-making authority is pushed farther down the hierarchy. Many organizations have moved toward decentralization to promote managerial efficiency and to improve employee satisfaction (the result of giving people greater opportunities to take responsibility for their own actions). For example, in recent years, thousands of staff jobs have been eliminated at companies such as 3M, Eastman Kodak, AT&T, and GE as these companies have decentralized.[16] In the mid-1980s, the world-renowned French resort company Club Mediterranée (Club Med) was run in a highly centralized fashion by its chief executive, Gilbert Trigano. Although the company had ninety holiday villages in twenty-six countries, Trigano's management style was so highly centralized that his overseeing the smallest details in club sites around the world from his Paris office was not unusual. As you might imagine, such an approach was impractical and could not continue. The individual resorts needed to be able to change in response to local conditions, calling for a highly decentralized structure—a form to which the company has now changed.[17] Since the company restructured, officials from the corporate office have become free to devote their energies to important issues of corporate policy instead of day-to-day operations.

Decentralization is *not always* an ideal step for organizations to take. In fact, for some types of jobs, it actually may be a serious hindrance to productivity. Consider production-oriented positions, like assembly line jobs. In a classic study, Lawrence and Lorsh found that decentralization improved the performance on some jobs—notably, the work of employees in a research lab—but interfered with the performance of people performing more routine, assembly line jobs.[18] These findings make sense once you consider that people working in research and development positions are likely to enjoy the autonomy to make decisions that decentralization allows, whereas people working on production jobs are likely to be less interested in taking responsibility for decisions and may enjoy *not* having to take such responsibility. As we have discussed in chapter 4, not everyone enjoys such responsibility. Thus the effects of decentralizing jobs on those who do not welcome the resulting gain in decision power are not likely to be positive. Negative effects of decentralization also may be expected under conditions in which only a centralized power has the knowl-

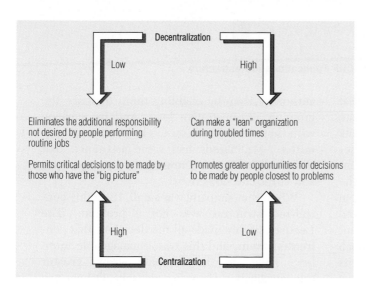

FIGURE 15–5

Decentralization: Benefits When Low and When High

Various benefits are associated with low decentralization (high centralization) and high decentralization (low centralization) within organizations.

edge to avoid a bad decision. At Delta Airlines, CEO Ronald W. Allen must personally approve every expenditure over $5,000 (except jet fuel).[19] By so doing, he can very carefully monitor the company's expenses and keep it afloat during difficult times. Despite the possible benefits likely to result from relieving Allen of these chores, he believes that it is necessary to tightly enforce the decisions made at times when the margin for error is small. To conclude, although the potential exists to derive considerable benefits from decentralization, the process should be avoided under certain conditions (see the summary in Figure 15–5).

The five elements described thus far—hierarchy of authority, division of labor, span of control, line versus staff positions, and decentralization—are some of the building blocks of organizational structure. In essence, they represent key dimensions along which organizations differ. (A key reason that organizations may need to be structured differently is that they experience growth and decline. Most of the contemporary examples we've discussed have focused on redesigning organizations to function effectively as they become smaller. Of course, organizations must change their structure when they experience growth as well. For an example of one company's reorganization in response to business success, see the **OB in Practice** section on p. 588.)

Approaches to Departmentalization: Various Ways of Structuring Organizations

Thus far, we have been talking about "the" organizational chart of an organization. Typically, such charts, like the one shown in Figure 15–2, divide the organization according to the various functions performed. However, as we will explain in this section, this is only one option. Organizations can be divided up not only by function, but also by product or market, and by a special blend of function and product or market known as the *matrix form*. We will now take a closer look at these various ways of breaking up organizations into coherent units—that is, the process of **departmentalization.**

Functional Organizations: Departmentalization by Task   Because it is the form organizations usually take when they are first created, and because it is how we

OB IN PRACTICE

Growing Pains Force CDP Publications to Restructure

The symptoms made it clear that something had to be done. In late 1986, people who wanted to talk to CDP Publications' cofounder Gerard G. Leeds had to start lining up outside his office by 8:00 A.M.[20] At the same time, answers to day-to-day questions from support departments, such as Accounting and Human Resources, were becoming very difficult to obtain. The company had experienced so much success that it was now being tripped up by its own corporate structure. CDP Publications is a family-owned business headquartered in Manhasset, New York, run by Gerard Leeds and his wife and cofounder, Lilo. The company publishes business newspapers and magazines that have all been very successful and grow rapidly each year. This growth, however, was causing the problems.

The Leedses' approach was to restructure the organization, which they did in two ways. First, they broke the company into two separate groups of more manageable size, essentially creating two companies within a company. A separate manager, called a "group publisher," was placed in charge of each, and was given total authority over that company. In addition, the Leedses added another tier to the organizational hierarchy by setting up a board, called the Publications Committee, that included the group publishers. As a result, instead of forcing people to line up outside his office, Gerard Leeds empowered other executives with decision-making authority, thereby enabling them to share the growing administrative load. And by working with these individuals on the Publications Committee, Mr. Leeds had some assurance that they'd all be working toward the same policies and corporate objectives.

When the company was small, its highly centralized structure was not a problem. The Leedses simply made all the decisions that confronted them, and this was a manageable number. Then, as the company grew, greater decentralization became necessary. Others had to make some of the decisions that the Leedses had formerly made because it had become impossible for them to sign off on everything. Giving up such control is usually difficult for entrepreneurs in family-owned businesses, but Gerard Leeds was wise to view it as necessary at CDP. In fact, this reorganization enabled the company to grow even more. In 1990, the company added several new publications to its roster (now up to fourteen), and sales climbed by 11 percent. Such figures are most impressive for this industry—especially during the difficult financial times in which the growth occurred. Obviously, although many factors are no doubt responsible for CDP's success (such as the Leedses' ability to produce publications that meet consumer demand), Gerard Leeds attributes a great deal of the company's growth to its new organizational structure. Under the old structure, a high degree of inefficiency would definitely have stunted the company's growth.

Although many organizations follow a functional design within a single operation, a functional organizational design is also possible across a number of individual organizations, such as across an entire chain of hotels. More than a decade ago, the Marriott Corporation was one of the first hotel chains to replace the separate reservation function of each

usually think of organizations, **functional organization** can be considered the most basic approach to departmentalization. Essentially, functional organizations departmentalize individuals according to the nature of the functions they perform, with people who perform similar functions assigned to the same department. For example, a manufacturing company might consist of separate departments devoted to basic functions such as production, sales, research and development, and accounting (see Figure 15–6).

Naturally, as organizations grow and become more complex, additional departments are added or deleted as the need arises. Consider, for example, what happened at Merkle and Sons Importing in our opening story. At first, just a few family members did everything. Then, as the business grew, groups of people were formed into

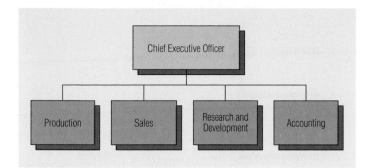

FIGURE 15–6

Functional Organization of a Typical Manufacturing Firm

Functional organizations are ones in which departments are formed on the basis of common functions performed. In the hypothetical manufacturing firm shown in this organizational chart, four typical functional departments are identified.

departments dealing with limited functions; some individuals took care of shipping, others worked at sales, and so on, resulting in a higher level of efficiency. Not only does this form of organizational structure take advantage of economies of scale (by allowing employees performing the same jobs to share facilities and not duplicate functions), but in addition it allows individuals to specialize, thereby performing only those tasks at which they are most expert. The result is a highly skilled work force, a direct benefit to the organization.

Partly offsetting these advantages, however, are several potential weaknesses. The most important of these stems from the fact that functional organizational structures encourage separate units to develop their own narrow perspectives, and to lose sight of overall organizational goals. For example, in a manufacturing company, an engineer might see the company's problems in terms of the reliability of its products, and lose sight of other key considerations, such as what the market really wants, overseas competition, and so on. Such narrow-mindedness is the inevitable result of functional specialization—the downside of people seeing the company's operations through a narrow lens. A related problem is that functional structures discourage innovation because they channel individual efforts toward narrow, functional areas and do not encourage coordination and cross-fertilization of ideas between areas. As a result, functional organizations are slow to respond to the challenges and opportunities they face from the environment (such as the need for new products and services). In summary, although functional organizations are certainly logical in nature and have proven useful in many contexts, they are by no means the perfect way to departmentalize people in organizations.

hotel with a computer reservation system for all of their hotels. Instead of following the old one-room, one-rate offering, the centralized reservation function allowed the hotel chain to take advantage of economies of scale, to allow for changing customer demographics, and to provide group rates. [Kaestle, P. (1990, July/August). A new rationale for organizational structure. *Planning Review,* pp. 20–27.]

Product Organizations: Departmentalization by Type of Output   Organizations—at least successful ones—do not stand still; they constantly change in size and scope. As they develop new products and seek new customers, they might find that a functional structure doesn't work as well as it once did. Manufacturing a wide range of products using a variety of different methods, for example, might put a strain on a manufacturing division of a functional organization. Similarly, keeping track of the varied tax requirements for different types of business (e.g., restaurants, farms, real estate, manufacturing) might pose quite a challenge for a single financial division of a company. In response to such strains, a **product organization** might be created. This type of departmentalization creates self-contained divisions, each of which is responsible for everything to do with a certain product or group of products. (For a look at the structure of a product organization, see Figure 15–7 on p. 590.)

When organizations are departmentalized by products, separate divisions are established, each of which is devoted to a certain product or group of products. Each unit contains all the resources needed to develop, manufacture, and sell its products. The organization is composed of separate divisions, operating separately, the heads

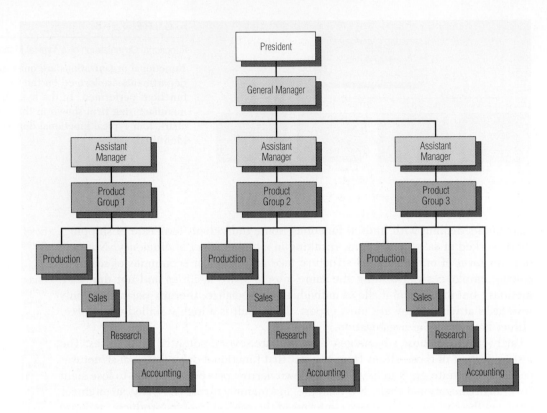

FIGURE 15-7   An Example of a Product Organization

In a *product organization,* separate units are established to handle different products or product lines. Each of these divisions contains all of the departments necessary for operating as an independent unit.

of which report to top management. Although some functions might be centralized within the parent company (e.g., human resource management or legal staff), on a day-to-day basis each division operates autonomously as a separate company—or, as accountants call them, "cost centers" of their own. Consider, for example, how separate divisions of General Motors are devoted to manufacturing cars, trucks, locomotives, refrigerators, auto parts, and the like. The managers of each division can devote their energies to one particular business. Organizations may be beneficial from a marketing perspective as well. Consider, for example, the example of Honda's 1987 introduction of its line of luxury cars, Acura.[21] By creating a separate division, manufactured in separate plants and sold by a separate network of dealers, the company made its higher-priced cars look special, and avoided making its less expensive cars look less appealing by putting them together with superior products on the same showroom floors. Given Honda's success with this configuration, it is not surprising that Toyota and Nissan followed suit when they introduced their own luxury lines, Lexus and Infiniti, in 1989.

This is not to say that product organizations do not have limitations. Indeed, they have several drawbacks. The most obvious of these is the loss of economies of scale stemming from the duplication of various departments within operating units. For example, if each unit carries out its own research and development functions, the need for costly equipment, facilities, and personnel may be multiplied. Another problem associated with product designs involves the organization's ability to attract and retain talented employees. Since each department within operating units is necessarily smaller than a single combined one would be, opportunities for advancement and career development may suffer. This, in turn, may pose a serious problem with respect to the long-term retention of talented employees. Finally, problems of coordination across product lines may arise. In fact, in extreme cases, actions taken by one operating division may have adverse effects on the outcomes of one or more others.

A clear example of such problems was provided by Hewlett-Packard, a major U.S. manufacturer of computers and a wide array of test and measurement equipment. During most of its history, Hewlett-Packard adopted a product design. It consisted of scores of small, largely autonomous divisions, each concerned with producing (and selling) certain products. As it grew in size and complexity, the company found itself in an increasingly untenable situation in which sales representatives from different divisions sometimes attempted to sell different lines of equipment, often to be used for the same basic purposes, to the same customers! To deal with such problems, top management at Hewlett-Packard decided to restructure the company into sectors based largely on the markets they served (business customers; scientific and manufacturing customers). In short, Hewlett-Packard switched from a fairly traditional product organization to an internal structure driven by market considerations.[22] Although it's too soon to determine whether the effects of this reorganization will be as positive as top management hopes, initial results, at least, are promising.

The Hewlett-Packard case points out a particular variation on the basic theme of market departmentalization. Self-contained operating units can also be established on the basis of specific geographic *regions* or territories, and even *customers* rather than different products. So, for example, a large retail chain might develop separate divisions for different regions of the country (e.g., Macy's–New York; and Macy's–California), or for different customer bases (e.g., Bloomingdales by Mail and Bloomingdales Retail). Similarly, a large record company (itself likely a division of a larger entertainment company) may establish independent divisions (each with its own labels) to sign, develop, produce, and promote recordings of interest to people in different markets (e.g., children, classical, Latin, pop). By departmentalizing in this fashion, like having separate companies within a large company (e.g., MCA or CBS), a company can give artists the attention they would expect from a smaller company, and the specialization and economies of scale they would expect from a large company. Regardless of the exact basis for departmentalizing—be it product, region, market, or customer group—the basic rationale remains the same: divide the organization's operations in a way that enhances efficiency.

Matrix Organizations: Departmentalization by Both Function and Product When the aerospace industry was first developing, the U.S. government demanded that a single manager in each company be assigned to each of its projects so that it was immediately clear who was responsible for the progress of each project. In response to this requirement, TRW established a "project leader" for each project, someone who shared authority with the leaders of the existing functional departments.[23] This temporary arrangement later evolved into what is called a **matrix organization,** the type of organization in which an employee is required to report to both a functional (or division) manager and the manager of a specific project (or product). In essence, they developed a complex type of organizational structure that combines both the function and product forms of departmentalization.[24] Recently, matrix organizational forms have been used in many organizations, such as Citibank and Liberty Mutual

Matrix organizations are supposed to enhance flexibility and communications, but their great complexity may bring great inefficiency. One profitable matrix organization decided to analyze

FIGURE 15–8

A Typical Example of a Matrix Organization

In a *matrix organization,* a product structure is superimposed on a basic functional structure. This results in a dual system of authority in which some managers report to two bosses—a project (product) manager and a functional (departmental) manager.

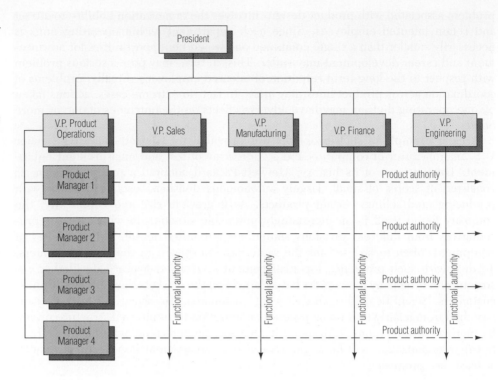

how long it took to get a proposal to a customer. They determined that a proposal required thirty-five people performing a total of seven days of value-added work to complete. With respect to time, they found that it took sixteen functional handoffs, twenty-five sign-offs, eleven transfers between locations, and ninety-one days to get the proposal out the door. This organization found out that the supposed advantages of a matrix organization, such as enhanced communication, came at great cost to efficiency. [Stalk G., Jr., & Hout, T. M. (1990, January/February). Redesign your organization for time-based management. *Planning Review,* pp. 4–9.]

Insurance.[25] To better understand matrix organizations, let's take a closer look at the organizational chart shown in Figure 15–8.

Employees in matrix organizations have two bosses (or, more technically, they are under *dual authority*). One line of authority, shown by the vertical axes on Figure 15–8, is *functional,* managed by vice presidents in charge of various functional areas; the other, shown by the horizontal axes, is *product* (or it may be a specific project or temporary business), managed by specific individuals in charge of certain products (or projects). In matrix designs, there are three major roles. First, there is the *top leader*—the individual who has authority over both lines (the one based on function and the one based on product or project). It is this individual's task to enhance coordination between functional and product managers and to maintain an appropriate balance of power between them. Second, there are the *matrix bosses*—people who head functional departments or specific projects. Since neither functional managers nor project managers nor matrix bosses have complete authority over subordinates, they must work together to assure that their efforts mesh rather than conflict. In addition, they must agree on issues such as promotions and raises for specific people working under their joint authority. Finally, there are *two-boss managers*—people who must report to both product and functional managers, and attempt to balance the demands of each.

Not all organizations using the matrix structure do so on a permanent basis. Several partial, or temporary, types of matrix design have been identified by Davis and Lawrence.[26] First, the *temporary overlay* is a form of matrix structure in which projects are crossed with functions on a special, short-term basis. This is in contrast to a *permanent overlay,* in which project teams are kept going after each project is completed. Finally, there are *mature matrix* organizations, those in which both the functional lines and the product lines are permanent, and equally strong within the organization. An example of such an organization is Dow Corning, where a matrix organization has been in effect for approximately twenty years.[27] At this company, each functional representative reports to the leaders of his or her own department, while also contributing to the design and operation of the particular product line for which he or she is responsible. Because people working in this fashion have two bosses, they must have sufficient freedom to attain their objectives. As you might imagine, a fair amount of coordination, flexibility, openness, and trust is essential for such a program to work, suggesting that not everyone adapts well to such a system.

Organizations are most likely to adopt matrix designs when they confront certain conditions. These include a complex and uncertain environment (one with frequent changes), and the need for economies of scale in the use of internal resources. Specifically, a matrix approach is often adopted by medium-size organizations with several product lines that do not possess sufficient resources to establish fully self-contained operating units. Under such conditions, a matrix design provides a useful compromise. Some companies that have adopted this structure, at least on a trial basis, are TRW Systems Group, Liberty Mutual Insurance, and Citibank.[28]

Key advantages offered by matrix designs have already been suggested by our discussion so far. First, they permit flexible use of an organization's human resources. Individuals within functional departments can be assigned to specific products or projects as the need arises and then return to their regular duties when this task is completed. Second, matrix designs offer medium-size organizations an efficient means of responding quickly to a changing, unstable environment. Third, such designs often enhance communication among managers; indeed, they literally force matrix bosses to discuss and agree on many matters. Disadvantages of such designs include the frustration and stress faced by two-boss managers in reporting to two different supervisors, the danger that one of the two authority systems (functional or product) will overwhelm the other, and the consistently high levels of cooperation required from the people involved for the organization to succeed. As we noted in chapter 10, this is sometimes far easier to imagine than to achieve! In situations where organizations must stretch their financial and human resources to meet challenges from the external environment or take advantage of new opportunities, however, matrix designs can often play a useful role. (All our examples of organizations we identified thus far have dealt with operations within a single country. However, as companies grow and seek new markets for their products and services, they often begin operating within foreign countries as well. For a look at the special design implications of such a move, refer to the **International/Multicultural Perspective** section on pp. 594–596.)

ORGANIZATIONAL DESIGN: COORDINATING THE STRUCTURAL ELEMENTS OF ORGANIZATIONS

We began the first major section of this chapter by likening the structure of an organization to the structure of a house. Now we are prepared to extend that analogy for purposes of introducing the concept of *organizational design*. Just as a house is designed in a particular fashion by combining its structural elements in various ways, so too can an organization be designed by combining its basic elements in certain ways. Accordingly, **organizational design** refers to the process of coordinating the structural elements of organizations in the most appropriate manner.

As you might imagine, this is no easy task. Although we might describe some options that sound neat and rational on the next few pages, in reality this is hardly ever the case. Even the most precisely designed organizations will face the need to change at one time or another, adjusting to the realities of technological changes, political pressures, accidents, and so on. Organizational designs might also be changed

AN INTERNATIONAL/MULTICULTURAL PERSPECTIVE

Structuring Organizations for Multinational Operations

After World War II, American industry turned its direction from the war effort to producing consumer goods. As companies prospered, they looked to offer their products and services to new markets. Because Japan and much of Europe were rebuilding after the war, foreign demand for American goods and services was considerable, and many American companies were more than happy to meet these needs by selling their wares abroad. Soon, many companies realized that it was most efficient not only to sell to various countries, but also to set up shop there on a permanent basis—that is, to invest in foreign property, equipment, and human capital. The term **multinational corporation (MNC)** is used to describe organizations that have significant operations spread throughout various nations, but that are headquartered in one nation.

Although many MNCs—such as General Motors, Mobil Oil, Firestone Tire and Rubber, and Massey-Ferguson—are American based, a good number are also based in Europe, such as British Petroleum and N. V. Philips (see chapter 13), and in Japan, such as Mitsubishi and Toyota. The involvement of these companies in various nations is not just a sideline, but an integral part of their business. In fact, in the case of many MNCs, over half of their total revenues come from foreign sources.[29]

As you might imagine, operating an organization in several different countries poses quite a challenge with respect to organizational structure. The ways organizations are structured for international operations depend on the degree to which the organization is involved in international activities. Three stages have been identified.[30] Initially, organizations begin their international activities simply, by exporting their products to foreign countries. During this *export* stage, the organization's basic structure remains unchanged. The only difference is that some individuals (or an outside trading company, in some cases) take on added responsibility for exporting a company's products.

As international activities increase, companies may develop separate international divisions—usually at the vice presidential level. This is known as the *international division* stage. A separate vice president of international affairs might exist (along with the vice presidents of other divisions, such as industrial products, consumer products, and the like). This individual would oversee responsibility for various operations in various countries. Separate international divisions have been established in giant companies such as IBM and Coca-Cola. With further growth, separate international divisions tend to become too large and cumbersome, calling for a more fully differentiated global approach to management—the *integrated structure* stage. At this point, organizations can be divided into departments as noted earlier—that is, either by function, by product, or by region.[31] These options are summarized in Figure 15–9.

In the case of a *functional* structure, a small group of executives can have control over operations, but the manufacturing, sales, and financial functions tend to lack coordination. Navistar (formerly International Harvester) is an example of a company organized with respect to separate internal divisions under each of its functional areas.[32]

Companies also may be organized according to *geographic region or territory*. This approach is particularly useful when the need to make comparisons between regions is important, and the company has a narrow range of similarly manufactured products. Oil companies tend to be organized in this manner, as is the large food-service company H. J. Heinz.[33]

Finally, products may be organized around a *product* internal structure. This approach works best when the company's product line is widely dispersed and different types of companies are held under different groupings in different nations. For example, Westinghouse has a power systems group (which runs a meter company in Argentina) and an industry and defense group (which runs an elevator company in Belgium and a construction products company in Italy).[34]

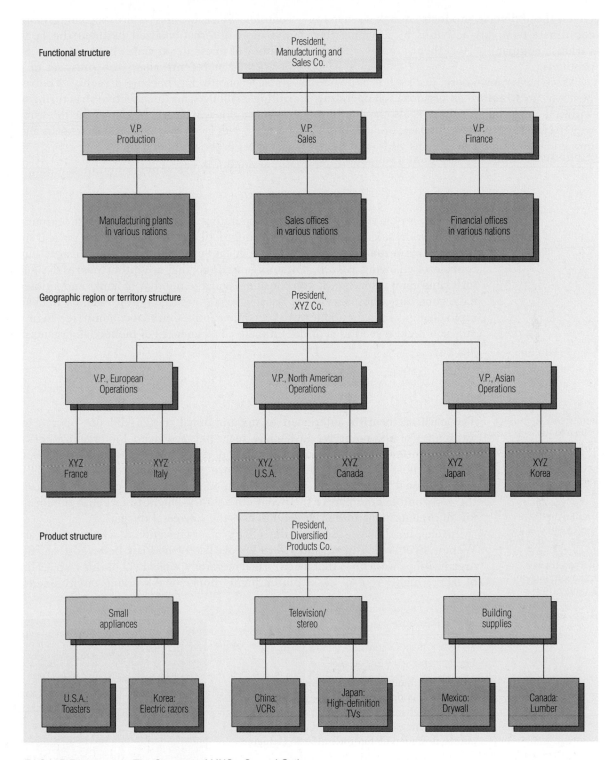

FIGURE 15–9   The Structure of MNCs: Several Options

Multinational corporations can be structured in many different ways. The international component can be treated like other bases for departmentalization—by function, by geographic region or territory, or by product.

(continued)

Given these diverse products, it makes sense to coordinate company activities by grouping the various companies together around related products.

As we have shown here, just as there is no one best way to structure an organization operating within a single nation, there is also no one best way to structure an MNC. In fact, because of the foreign involvement, the options grow even more complex. Since businesses are becoming more and more internationalized (witness the large number of foreign companies buying into U.S. businesses in recent years), the prospect of a global economy has become a reality. The resulting challenges for the effective structuring of organizations will clearly be one of the most important issues faced by organizational scholars and managers in the years to come.

purposely in an attempt to improve operating efficiency, such as the promise by some U.S. presidents to streamline the huge federal bureaucracy. Our point is simple: because organizations operate within a changing world, their own designs must be capable of changing as well. Those organizations that are either poorly designed or inflexible cannot survive. If you consider the large number of banks and airlines that have gone out of business in the last few years because of their inability to deal with rapid changes brought about by deregulation and a shifting economy (see Figure 15–10), you'll get a good idea of the ultimate consequences of ineffective organizational design.

Classical and Neoclassical Approaches: The Quest for the One Best Design

A contemporary approach to structure touted as being the best is known as *Just in Time* (JIT). JIT was invented by the Toyota Motor Company in the early 1950s. Using the JIT process, a company keeps no inventory of parts, but waits until orders are received. Then the supplier ships only what is immediately needed for production. Unfortunately, the JIT ap-

The earliest theorists interested in organizational design did not operate out of awareness of the point we just made regarding the need for organizations to be flexible. Instead, they approached the task of designing organizations as a search for "the one best way." Although today we are more attuned to the need to adapt organizational designs to various environmental and social conditions, theorists in the early and middle part of the twentieth century sought to establish the ideal form for all organizations under all conditions—the universal design.

In chapter 1, we described the efforts of organizational scholars such as Max Weber, Frederick Taylor, and Henri Fayol. These theorists believed that effective organizations were ones that had a formal hierarchy, a clear set of rules, specialization of labor, highly routine tasks, and a highly impersonal working environment. You

FIGURE 15–10

Failure to Adapt Quickly Enough to a Changing Environment: Some Examples

Given the changing world within which organizations operate, their own designs must be capable of changing to adapt. As evidenced here, organizations can fail when they are either poorly designed or too inflexible to change.

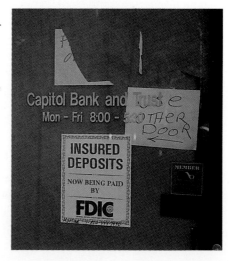

Test Bank questions 15.23, 15.52, and 15.72 relate to material on this page.

may recall that Weber referred to this form as a *bureaucracy*. This classical organizational theory has fallen into disfavor in large part because it is insensitive to human needs and is not suited to a changing environment. Unfortunately, the "ideal" form of an organization, according to Weber, did not take into account the realities of the world within which it operates. Apparently, what is ideal is not necessarily what is realistic.

In response to these conditions, and with inspiration from the Hawthorne studies (see chapter 1), the classical approach to the bureaucratic model gave way to more of a human relations orientation. Organizational scholars such as McGregor, Argyris, and Likert attempted to improve the classical model (which is why their approach is labeled *neoclassical*) by arguing that economic effectiveness is not the only goal of an industrial organization, but also employee satisfaction.

Douglas McGregor was an organizational theorist who objected to the rigid hierarchy imposed by Weber's bureaucratic form because it was based on negative assumptions about people—primarily that they lacked ambition and wouldn't work unless coerced (the *Theory X* approach).[35] In contrast, McGregor argued that people desire to achieve success by working and that they seek satisfaction by behaving responsibly (the *Theory Y* approach) (see also chapter 1). Another neoclassical theorist, Chris Argyris, expressed similar ideas.[36] Specifically, he argued that managerial domination of organizations blocks basic human needs to express oneself and to successfully accomplish tasks. Such dissatisfaction, he argues, would encourage turnover and lead to poor performance. Another neoclassical theorist, Rensis Likert, shared these perspectives, arguing that organizational performance is enhanced *not* by rigidly controlling people's actions, but by actively promoting their feelings of self-worth and their importance to the organization.[37] An effective organization, Likert proposed, was one in which individuals would have a great opportunity to participate in making organizational decisions—what he called a *System 4* organization. Doing this, he claimed, would enhance employees' personal sense of worth, motivating them to succeed. (Although this assumption appears a bit naive in view of the more complex approaches to motivation we examined in chapter 4, the same basic idea is inherent in even more sophisticated, contemporary approaches. Accordingly, rather than dismiss these approaches because of their simplicity, it makes more sense to applaud them for their insight and foresight.) Likert called the opposite type of organization *System 1*, the traditional form in which organizational power is distributed in the hands of a few top managers who tell lower-ranking people what to do. (*System 2* and *System 3* are intermediate forms between the *System 1* and *System 4* extremes.)

The organizational design implications of these neoclassical approaches are clear. In contrast to the classical approach, calling for organizations to be designed with a rigid, tall hierarchy, with a narrow span of control (allowing managers to maintain close supervision over their subordinates), the neoclassical approach argues for designing organizations with flat hierarchical structures (minimizing managerial control over subordinates) and a high degree of decentralization (encouraging employees to make their own decisions). Indeed, such design features may well serve the underlying neoclassical philosophy.

Like the classical approach, the neoclassical approach may also be faulted on the grounds that it is promoted as "the one best approach" to organizational design. Although the benefits of flat, decentralized designs may be many, to claim that this represents the universal, ideal form for all organizations would be naive. In response to this criticism, more contemporary approaches to organizational design have given up on finding the one best way to design organizations in favor of finding designs that are most appropriate to various circumstances and contexts within which organizations operate.

proach requires thousands of partially loaded trucks to make the daily deliveries, which pollutes the environment and causes traffic jams. For example, the JIT approach required supply trucks to visit a single 7-Eleven store in Tokyo seventy times a day to keep merchandise in stock! Because of the problems with JIT, the Japanese government is applauding organizations that are taking steps to reduce the number of trucks required. [Miller, K. L. (1991, June 17). "Just-in-time" is becoming just a pain. *Business Week*, p. 100H.]

The Contemporary Approach: Design Contingent on Environmental Conditions

The design of automobile plants is highly contingent upon environmental demands. As recently as fifteen years ago, automakers literally had to rip out their old assembly lines and replace them with new equipment for each new model produced. Today, with the use of computer software and robots, automobile assembly lines can be re-tooled in as little as two to three months instead of the traditional nine to twelve months, and at one-fifth the cost. Because most car companies sell only about 200,000 units of one particular model, the continued use and improvement of computer technology promises to vastly increase the speed at which assembly lines can be refitted for a new model. [Judge, P. C. (1991, August 25). Nissan's flexible, "thinking" line for auto body assembly. *The New York Times*, p. F11(L).]

The idea that *the best* design for an organization depends on the nature of the environment in which the organization is operating lies at the heart of the modern **contingency approach** to organizational design. We use the term "contingency" here in a manner similar to the way we used it in our discussion of leadership (chapter 12). But rather than considering the best approach to leadership for a given situation, we are considering the best way to design an organization given the environment within which the organization functions.

The External Environment: Its Connection to Organizational Design   If we assume that the most appropriate type of organizational design depends on the organization's external environment, it is critical to understand what is meant by the *external environment*. In general, the external environment is the sum of all the forces impinging on an organization with which it must deal effectively if it is to survive.[38] These forces include general work conditions, such as the economy, geography, and national resources, as well as the specific task environment within which the company operates—most notably, its competitors, customers, work force, and suppliers. Let's consider some examples. Banks operate within an environment that is highly influenced by the general economic environment (e.g., interest rates and government regulations) as well as a task environment sensitive to other banks' products (e.g., types of accounts) and services (e.g., service hours, access to account information by computers and/or telephone), the needs of the customer base (e.g., direct deposit for customers), the availability of trained personnel (e.g., individuals suitable for entry-level positions), as well as the existence of suppliers providing goods and services (e.g., automated teller equipment, surveillance equipment, computer workstations) necessary to deliver requisite services. Analogous examples can be found in other industries as well. For example, think about the environmental forces faced by the airlines, the computer industry, and automobile manufacturers (see Figure 15–11). It's easy to recognize the features of their environments that must be taken into account when considering how organizations in these industries could be designed.

Although many features of the environment may be taken into account when considering how an organization should be designed, a classic investigation by Burns and Stalker provides some useful guidance.[39] These two scientists interviewed people in twenty industrial organizations in the United Kingdom to determine the relationship between managerial activities and the external environment. In so doing,

FIGURE 15–11

Environmental Forces on Industry: One Example

Think about the many ways in which the changing environment influences the automobile industry. For example, as fuel prices increase, consumer demand for small, fuel-efficient cars increases and the demand for larger gas guzzlers goes down. Governmental regulations restricting foreign trade, requiring enhanced safety features, demanding increased fuel efficiency, and limiting levels of air pollution have had dramatic influences on the automobile industry.

they distinguished between organizations that operated in highly *stable*, unchanging environments, and those that operated in highly unstable, *turbulent* environments. For example, a rayon company in their sample operated in a highly stable environment: the environmental demands were predictable, people performed the same jobs in the same ways for a long time, and the organization had clearly defined lines of authority that helped get the job done. In contrast, a new electronics development company in their sample operated in a highly turbulent environment. Conditions changed on a daily basis, jobs were not well defined, and no clear organizational structure existed. Burns and Stalker noted that many of the organizations studied tended to be described in ways that were appropriate for their environments. For example, when the environment is stable, people can do the same tasks repeatedly, allowing them to perform highly specialized jobs. However, in turbulent environments, many different jobs may have to be performed, and such specialization should not be designed into the jobs. Clearly, a strong link exists between the stability of the work environment and the proper organizational form. It was Burns and Stalker's conclusion that two different approaches to management existed and that these are largely based on the degree of stability within the external environment. These two approaches are known as **mechanistic organizations** and **organic organizations.**

Mechanistic versus Organic Organizations: Designs for Stable versus Turbulent Conditions   If you've ever worked at a McDonald's, you probably know how highly standardized each step of the most basic processes must be.[40] Boxes of fries are to be stacked two inches from the wall in stacks one inch apart. Making those fries is another matter—one that requires nineteen distinct steps, each clearly laid out in a training film shown to new employees. The process is the same, whether it's done in Moscow, Idaho, or in Moscow, Russia. This is an example of a highly mechanistic task. Organizations can be highly mechanistic when conditions don't change. Although the fast-food industry has changed a great deal in recent years (with the introduction of new, healthier menu items, competitive pricing, and the like), the making of fries at McDonald's has not changed. The key to using mechanization is the lack of change. If the environment doesn't change, a highly mechanistic organizational form can be very efficient.

An environment is considered stable whenever there is little or no unexpected change in product, market demands, technology, and the like. Have you ever seen an old-fashioned–looking bottle of E. E. Dickinson's witch hazel (a topical astringent used to cleanse the skin in the area of a wound)? Since the company has been making the product following the same distillation process since 1866, it is certainly operating in a relatively stable manufacturing environment.[41] As we described earlier, stability affords the luxury of high employee specialization. Without change, people can easily specialize. When change is inevitable, specialization is impractical.

Mechanistic organizations can be characterized in several additional ways (for a summary, see Figure 15–12 on p. 600). Not only do mechanistic organizations allow for a high degree of specialization, but they also impose many rules. Authority is vested in a few people located at the top of a hierarchy who give direct orders to their subordinates. Mechanistic organizational designs tend to be most effective under conditions in which the external environment is stable and unchanging.

Now think about high-technology industries, such as those dedicated to computers, aerospace products, and biotechnology. Their environmental conditions are likely to be changing all the time. These industries are so prone to change that as soon as a new way of operating could be introduced into one of them, it would have to be altered. It isn't only technology, however, that makes an environment turbulent. Turbulence also can be high in industries in which adherence to rapidly changing

The extent to which an organization is mechanistic or organic may be reflected by the design of the building in which it is located. In the 1980s, corporations tried to make grand statements about themselves by constructing expensive monoliths of granite and marble. In the 1990s, the trend is toward constructing roomy, open, and less expensive buildings, often made of limestone and brick. Because researchers have found that employee communication falls off sharply if employees are separated by more than two floors, new office designs tend to be low-rise, with numerous break areas, concourses, and atriums where employees can meet and mingle casually (more organic designs). Importantly, these new designs are practical and much less costly too. [Alpert, M. (1991, November 18). Office buildings for the 1990s. *Fortune*, pp. 140–150.]

FIGURE 15–12

Mechanistic versus Organic Designs: Opposite Extremes
of Several Dimensions

Mechanistic and *organic* designs differ along several
key dimensions identified here. These represent
extremes; organizations can be relatively organic,
relatively mechanistic, or somewhere in between.

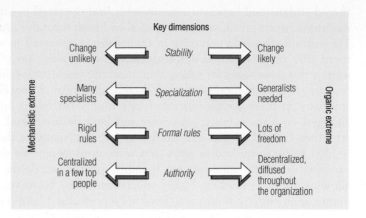

regulations is essential. For example, times were turbulent in the hospital industry
when new Medicaid legislation was passed, and times were turbulent in the nuclear
power industry when governmental regulations dictated the introduction of many
new standards that had to be followed. With the dominance of foreign automobiles
in the United States, the once-stable American auto industry has faced turbulent
times of late. Unfortunately, in this case, the design of the auto companies could not
rapidly accommodate the changes needed for more organic forms (since the American
auto industry was traditionally highly mechanistic).

The pure organic form of organization may be characterized in several different
ways (see Figure 15–12). The degree of job specialization possible is very low; instead,
a broad knowledge of many different jobs is required. Very little authority is exercised
from the top. Instead, self-control is expected, and an emphasis is placed on coordination between peers. As a result, decisions tend to be made in a highly democratic,
participative manner. Be aware that the mechanistic and organic types of organizational structure described here are ideal forms. The mechanistic-organic distinction
should be thought of as opposite poles along a continuum rather than as completely
distinct options for organization. Certainly, organizations can be relatively organic
or relatively mechanistic compared with others, but may not be located at either
extreme.

Finally, note that research supports the idea that organizational effectiveness is
related to the degree to which an organization's structure (mechanistic or organic)
is matched to its environment (stable or turbulent). In a classic study, Morse and
Lorsch evaluated four departments in a large company—two of which manufactured
containers (a relatively stable environment) and two of which dealt with communications research (a highly unstable environment).[42] One department in each pair was
evaluated as being more effective than the other. It was found that for the container
manufacturing departments, the more effective unit was the one structured in a
highly mechanistic form (roles and duties were clearly defined). In contrast, the
more effective communications research department was structured in a highly organic fashion (roles and duties were vague). Additionally, the other, less effective
departments were structured in the opposite manner (i.e., the less effective manufacturing department was organically structured, and the less effective research
department was mechanistically structured) (see Figure 15–13). Taken together, the
results made it clear that departments were most effective when their organizational
structures fit their environments. This notion of "Which design is best under which
conditions?" lies at the heart of the modern orientation—the contingency approach—
to organizational structure. Rather than specifying which structure is best, the contingency approach specifies when each type of organizational design is most effective.

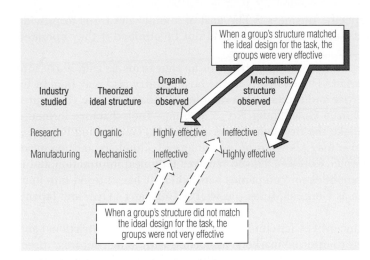

FIGURE 15-13

Design Effectiveness: Depends on Match between Ideal and Actual Design

In a classic study, Morse and Lorsch evaluated the performance of four departments in a large company. The most effective units were ones in which the way the group was structured (mechanistic or organic) matched the most appropriate form for the type of task performed (i.e., organic for research work, and mechanistic for manufacturing work). (*Source:* Based on suggestions by Morse & Lorsch, 1970; see Note 42.)

Free-Form Designs: The Ultimate in Flexibility   Not all organizations are designed in a specific, rigid fashion. Organizations that are not designed in a formal way are said to have **free-form designs.** Although employees of organizations using free-form designs have normal functional responsibilities, they spend most of their time on special teams and task forces that are created as the need arises.

As an example, consider Kyocera, the large Japanese diversified electronics firm. Under the guidance of company chairman Kazuo Inamori, Kyocera employees are arranged into relatively autonomous teams ranging in size from only two or three to several hundred, which Inamori calls "amoebas," reflecting their amorphous form.[43] These groups are created and dissolved as needed to perform various projects. Although amoebas require permission to make purchases, they are completely free to buy whatever they want from whomever they want to do their jobs appropriately. Part of the underlying idea is that by working on different problems or tasks at different times, people learn to appreciate how the entire organization operates. (The now-defunct People Express airline used to operate in this fashion as well.) Given that Kyocera performs a great deal of research and development work (mostly in the semiconductor and computer chip areas), it stands to benefit from the flexibility that free-form designs offer. The rapidly changing environment within which Kyocera operates is a key factor that makes such a flexible arrangement effective—a changing design for a changing environment. This notion is in keeping with the empirically established tendency for organizations to adapt more flexible ways of operating in response to highly complex work environments.[44]

Interorganizational Designs: Going Beyond the Single Organization

All the organizational designs we have examined thus far have concentrated on the arrangement of units *within* an organization—what may be termed *intraorganizational designs.* However, sometimes at least some parts of different organizations must operate jointly. To coordinate their efforts on such projects, organizations must create *interorganizational designs,* plans by which two or more organizations come together. Two such designs are commonly found in organizations: *joint ventures* and *conglomerates.*

Joint Ventures: Alliances for Mutual Benefit   A **joint venture** is a type of organizational design in which two or more separate companies legally combine forces to develop and operate a specific business.[45] The goal of a joint venture is to provide benefits to each individual organization that could not be attained if they operated separately.

Sometimes, companies form joint ventures with foreign firms to gain entry into that foreign country's market. The company in the host country also may benefit by the influx of foreign expertise and capital. For example, Florida's Orlando Helicopter Airway Company and China's Guangdung No. 3 Machine Tools Factory formed a joint venture in 1986 to make the first helicopters available in Guangdung Province, China.[46] Joint ventures also may allow for an exchange of technology and manufacturing services. For example, Korea's Daewoo receives technical information and is paid to manufacture automobiles for companies with which it has entered into joint venture agreements, such as General Motors, as well as Germany's Opel and Japan's Isuzu and Nissan.[47]

Besides the financial incentives (circumventing trade and tariff restrictions) and marketing benefits (access to internal markets) associated with joint ventures, direct managerial benefits also are associated with extending one company's organizational chart into another's. These benefits primarily come from improved technology and greater economies of scale (e.g., sharing functional operations across organizations). For these benefits to be derived, a high degree of coordination and fit must exist between the parties, each delivering on its promise to the other. Given the rapid move toward globalization of the economy, we may expect to see many companies seeking joint ventures in the future as a means for gaining or maintaining a competitive advantage.

Conglomerates: Diversified "Megacorporations"   When an organization diversifies by adding an entirely unrelated business or product to its organizational design, it may be said to have formed a **conglomerate**. Some of the world's largest conglomerates may be found in the Orient. For example, in Korea, companies such as Samsung and Hyundai produce home electronics, automobiles, textiles, and chemicals in large, unified conglomerates known as *chaebols*.[48] These are all separate companies overseen by the same parent company leadership. In Japan, the same type of arrangement is known as a *keiretsu*. A good example of a keiretsu is the Mitsubishi Group.[49] This enormous conglomerate consists of a bank (Mitsubishi Bank), a glass company (Asahi Glass), and many additional companies dealing in products as diverse as steel, mining, and cement (from Mitsubishi's various petroleum and heavy industries companies) (see Figure 15–14). These examples are not meant to suggest that conglomerates are unique to the Orient; many large U.S.-based corporations, such as IBM and Tenneco, are also conglomerates.

The term *keiretsu* is said to have its roots in Japan in the ancient relationships between feudal landlords and their samurai warriors who built the war machine of the first half of this century. *Keiretsu* are networks or families of

FIGURE 15–14

What Do These Items Have in Common?

The items shown here—and many, many more—are all made by the gigantic Mitsubishi Group *keiretsu* (Japanese for "conglomerate").

Companies form conglomerates for several reasons. First, as an independent business, the parent company can enjoy the benefits of diversification. Thus, as one industry languishes, another may excel, allowing for a stable economic outlook for the parent company. In addition, conglomerates may provide built-in markets and access to supplies, since companies typically support other organizations within the conglomerate. For example, General Motors cars and trucks are fitted with Delco radios, and Ford cars and trucks have engines with Autolite spark plugs, separate companies that are owned by their respective parent companies. In this manner, conglomerates can benefit by providing a network of organizations that are dependent on each other for products and services, thereby creating considerable advantages.

TECHNOLOGY: A MAJOR CAUSE—AND CONSEQUENCE—OF DESIGN

Organizations differ tremendously with respect to **technology**—the means by which they transform inputs into outputs. These can vary from the simplest of tools used by single individuals to huge machines and complex, automated equipment. Clearly, the technology employed by a given organization is closely linked to the work it performs and the major tasks it seeks to accomplish. But growing evidence indicates that this relationship, too, is something of a two-way street. Organizations not only choose the technology they will employ; they are also affected by such tools once they are selected. In short, just as the design of a specific building reflects the activities that take place within it, the structure of many organizations, too, tends to mirror the technologies they employ. In the discussion that follows, we will describe several major studies that point to this conclusion. As you will soon see, these investigations classify technology in contrasting ways and focus on a wide range of issues. Thus, their findings are often difficult to compare in a simple or direct manner. Generally, though, all point to the same basic conclusion: technology plays an important role in shaping both the design and performance of many organizations.

Technology and Structure in Manufacturing Companies: The Woodward Studies

Perhaps the best-known study on the effects of technology is one conducted in England during the 1960s by Woodward and her associates.[50] To determine the relationship between various structural characteristics (e.g., span of control, decentralization) and organizational performance (e.g., profitability, market share), these investigators gathered data about 100 manufacturing firms. In keeping with the classical view of management (described on pages 596–597), they initially expected that organizations classified as highly successful would share similar structural characteristics, and those classified as relatively unsuccessful would share other characteristics. Surprisingly, this was not the case. Instead, various aspects of organizational structure appeared to be just as common in successful and unsuccessful companies. Thus, there was little if any support for the accuracy of universal principles of management.

Instead, Woodward and her colleagues found that the organization's success depended on the degree to which it was structured in the most appropriate way given the technology used. Specifically, they compared organizations using each of three different types of technology in popular use at the time. In the first, labeled **small-batch production,** custom work was the norm. Capital equipment (machinery) was not highly mechanized, and the companies involved typically produced small batches of products to meet specific orders from customers. Employees were either skilled

corporations. They can be horizontal, spanning several industries and generally organized around a bank; or they can be vertical, composed of a major industrial corporation and its suppliers in a particular industry. Many U.S. companies are afraid of the unfair advantage seemingly caused by the "captive" suppliers in Japanese auto *keiretsu*. In reality, however, General Motors still makes more of its own parts than Toyota gets from captive suppliers. [Kinsley, M. (1991, July 1). Keiretsuphobia. *The New Republic*, p. 4.]

or unskilled, depending on the tasks they performed. Firms included in this category made items such as specialized construction equipment or custom-ordered electronic items. Other examples include dressmaking and printing.

Companies in the second category, known as **large-batch** or **mass production,** used basic assembly line procedures. These organizations typically engaged in long production runs of standardized parts or products. Their output then went into inventory from which orders were filled on a continuous basis. Employees were mainly unskilled or semiskilled, with a sprinkling of research and engineering personnel. The third category, known as **continuous-process production,** was the most technologically complex. Here, there was no start and no stop to production, which was automated and fully integrated. Employees were skilled workers or engineers. Among the organizations employing such advanced technology were oil refining and chemical companies.

When companies using these various types of technology were compared, important differences were noted. First, as expected, they demonstrated contrasting internal structures. For example, the span of control (of first-level supervisors) and centralization were higher in companies employing mass production than in ones using small-batch or continuous-process technologies. Similarly, chains of command were longest in organizations using continuous-process production, and shortest in those using small-batch methods. In short, the type of technology employed in production appeared to be an important variable in shaping organization structure. As Woodward herself put it, "Different technologies imposed different kinds of demands on individuals and organizations, and those demands had to be met through an appropriate structure."[51]

Perhaps even more important than these findings was the fact that the characteristics distinguishing highly successful from unsuccessful companies also varied with technology. At the low and high ends of the technology dimension described above, an *organic* management approach seemed best; companies showing this strategy were more successful than those demonstrating a *mechanistic* approach. In contrast, in the middle of the technology dimension (mass production), the opposite was true. Here, companies adopting a mechanistic approach tended to be more effective (see Figure 15–15). Another finding was that successful firms tended to have structures suited to their level of technology. Specifically, those with above-average performance showed structural characteristics similar to most other firms using the same type of production methods; in contrast, those with below-average records tended to depart from the median structure shown by companies in the same technology category. In summary, the results of Woodward's study indicated that important links exist between technology and performance.

Additional support for these conclusions was later obtained in several other studies. For example, in a project involving fifty-five U.S. firms, Zwerman found that organizations employing small-batch or continuous-process technology tended to adopt an organic management approach.[52] Those employing mass production generally showed a mechanistic approach. In general, research has shown that the more sophisticated technology is used, the greater are the opportunities for organizations to thrive when authority is decentralized (in essence, because the "smart" technology is making the decisions, eliminating the need for some people in the hierarchy).[53] Woodward's findings are valuable because they were among the first that recognized the value of the contemporary, contingency approach to organizational structure.

As you might imagine, we have learned a great deal about organizational design since Woodward's time—if for no other reason than technology has changed so very much. In addition to the three types of technology studied by Woodward, today some organizations produce highly customized, high-performance products in rela-

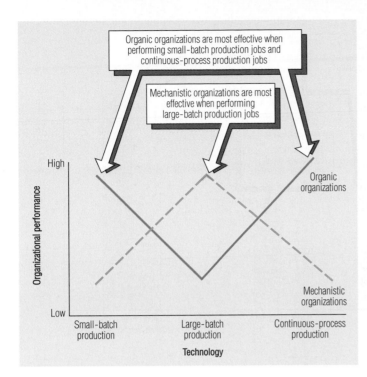

FIGURE 15–15

Relationship between Technology and Design: The Woodward Studies

In a classic study, Woodward found that organic organizations were most effective when performing small-batch production and continuous-batch production jobs, whereas mechanistic organizations were most effective when performing large-batch production jobs. (*Source:* Based on findings by Woodward, 1965; see Note 50.)

tively small runs. However, because these products are technologically advanced and complex, they are produced by highly automated, computer-controlled equipment. Moreover, the people involved in their manufacture must often possess a high level of professional or technical knowledge. In short, such companies share some characteristics with the traditional small-batch firms studied by Woodward, but share others with the technologically advanced continuous-process firms at the other end of her continuum. What type of internal structure do such *technical batch* organizations demonstrate? Evidence on this issue has been provided by Hull and Collins.[54]

These researchers examined the internal structure of 110 separate companies operating in the United States. On the basis of careful examination of their methods of production, Hull and Collins divided these organizations into four categories—traditional batch, technical batch, mass production, and process production. Then they compared the companies' internal structure along several key dimensions (e.g., supervisory span of control, occupational specialization, decentralization, formalization). As the examples in Figure 15–16 (see p. 606) show, the types differed in various ways. As predicted, organizations classified as traditional batch or technical batch in their methods of production showed contrasting structure in several respects. For example, the traditional batch companies possessed a larger supervisory span of control. In contrast, the technical batch companies showed a greater degree of occupational specialization and more decentralization. Further, and perhaps most important, the technical batch companies showed a much higher level of innovative activity (e.g., a higher percentage of employees involved in research and development activities).

In summary, expanding Woodward's original categories to reflect recent developments in methods of production yielded additional evidence for the powerful impact of technology on internal structure. Additional research along similar lines may help us to sharpen our knowledge of this important relationship still further.

Technology and Internal Structure: Some Recent Findings

Organizations employing technical batch technology differ in several respects from ones employing traditional batch technology. (*Source:* Based on data from Hull & Collins, 1987; see Note 54.)

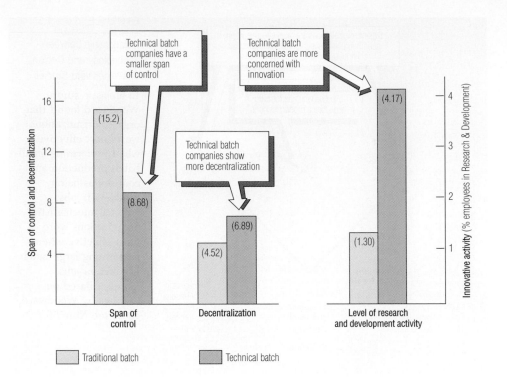

Work-Flow Integration: The Aston Studies

As the heading of the preceding section suggests, Woodward's project, and several subsequent investigations, focused primarily on the links between technology and structure in manufacturing companies. Thus, as thorough as this work was, it left a basic issue unresolved: would similar findings be observed in other types of companies as well? Evidence on this question was provided by another team of British researchers affiliated with the University of Aston.[55] After studying a wide range of both manufacturing and service organizations (e.g., savings banks, insurance companies, department stores), these researchers concluded that technology can be described in terms of three basic characteristics: *automation of equipment*—the extent to which work activities are performed by machines; *work-flow rigidity*—the extent to which the sequence of work activities is inflexible; and *specificity of evaluation*—the degree to which work activities can be assessed by specific, quantitative means. Since these three factors appeared to be highly associated, they were combined into a single scale labeled **work-flow integration.** The higher an organization's score on this scale, the more likely it was to employ automation, rigid task sequences, and quantitative measurement of its operations. The work-flow integration scores obtained by various companies are shown in Table 15–1. As you can see from this table, manufacturing firms generally score higher than those whose primary output is service.

When work-flow integration was related to structural characteristics in the organizations studied, no strong or general links were uncovered. Thus, at first glance, findings seemed contradictory to those reported by Woodward. Closer analysis of the data obtained, however, revealed that technological complexity *was* related to

TABLE 15-1   Work-Flow Integration in Different Organizations

Manufacturing firms generally score higher on work-flow integration than do service organizations (e.g., banks, stores).

Organization	Classification (Manufacturing or Service)	Work-Flow Integration Score
Vehicle manufacturer	Manufacturing	17
Metal-goods manufacturer	Manufacturing	14
Tire manufacturer	Manufacturing	12
Printer	Service	11
Local water department	Service	10
Insurance company	Service	7
Savings bank	Service	4
Department stores	Service	2
Chain of retail stores	Service	1

Source: Based on data from Hickson, Pugh, & Pheysey, 1969; see Note 55.

structural features in at least some ways. For example, as work-flow integration increased, so did specialization, standardization, and decentralization of authority. The magnitude of these findings was small, and they seemed to involve mainly those aspects of structure closely connected to actual work flow. Moreover, *size* exerted stronger effects on several aspects of structure than technology.

These findings, plus those obtained in later studies, point to two conclusions. First, although technology does indeed seem to affect the internal structure of organizations, it is only one of several influences. As a result, the so-called *technological imperative*—the view that technology always has a compelling influence on organizational structure—clearly overstates the case. Indeed, as noted by Singh, close examination of recent evidence for this view suggests that it is far from strong or consistent.[56] Second, technology probably exerts stronger effects on structure in small organizations, where such characteristics impinge directly on work flow, than in large ones, where structure is complex and often far removed from actual production. In any case, taken as a whole, the findings of the Aston studies can be interpreted as indicating that the impact of technology on organizational structure is not restricted to manufacturing concerns. Under certain conditions, it can be observed in other types of companies as well.

Technology and Interdependence

Another aspect of technology with important implications for organizational structure is **interdependence**. This refers to the extent to which individuals, departments, or units within a given organization depend on each other in accomplishing their tasks. Under conditions of low interdependence, each person, unit, or group can carry out its functions in the absence of assistance or input from others. Under high interdependence, in contrast, such coordination is essential. A framework proposed by Thompson helps clarify the various types of interdependence possible in organizations, and also the implications of this factor for effective structural design.[57]

What role does technology play in the competitiveness of U.S. companies in world markets? Norsworthy and Jang examined this question by comparing the technology used in U.S.-owned factories with that used by foreign-owned or affiliated plants in the United States. The researchers found that the foreign-controlled plants were far more up-to-date, using 30 percent more "high tech" machinery and computers in the production process. The differences were greatest in those industries in which the United States has been losing ground to foreign competitors, such as semiconductors and automobiles. [Templeton, F. (1992, February 10). Why U.S. companies are losing ground in their own backyard. *Business Week,* p. 124.]

The lowest level within this framework is known as **pooled interdependence.** Under such conditions, departments or units are part of an organization, but work does not flow between them. Rather, each carries out its tasks independently. One example of pooled interdependence is provided by the branch stores of a clothing retailer in many large shopping malls. Each contributes to the total earnings of the parent company, but there is little, if any, contact or coordination between them.

The next higher level suggested by Thompson is **sequential interdependence.** Here, the output of one department or subunit becomes the input for another. For example, the marketing department of a food company cannot proceed with promotional campaigns until it receives information about new products from the product development unit. Similarly, in a company that manufactures electronic toys, final assemblers cannot perform their jobs unless they receive a steady supply of component parts from other work units or outside suppliers. Note that in sequential interdependence, information, products, and components flow in one direction. Thus, units farther along the chain of production are dependent on ones that precede them, but the reverse is not true.

The highest level in Thompson's model is known as **reciprocal interdependence.** Here the output of each department or unit serves as the input for other departments or units in a reciprocal fashion. Thus, the output of Department A provides input for Department B, and the output of Department B serves as the input for Department A. An example of such reciprocal interdependence is provided by the operations of the marketing and production departments of many companies. Marketing, through appropriate surveys, may develop a profile of new products or product innovations attractive to potential customers. This serves as input for Production, which considers the feasibility of actually making such products and suggests modifications. The appeal of these modifications is then assessed by Marketing and the results obtained serve as the basis for further planning by Production. This process may be repeated until a plan for product innovations acceptable to both units is devised (see Figure 15–17).

These three forms of interdependence require varying levels of coordination between the units involved. The need for coordination is quite low under conditions of pooled interdependence, since each of the departments involved is relatively independent. Rules and standard operating procedures usually suffice. In contrast, sequential interdependence requires substantially greater coordination. Here, formal meetings and vertical communication are often needed. Finally, reciprocal interdependence calls for concerted efforts at coordination, including many meetings and a high level of horizontal communication.[58]

FIGURE 15–17

Reciprocal Interdependence: An Example

Under conditions of *reciprocal interdependence,* the output of two or more departments serves as the input for each other in a reciprocal fashion. (*Source:* Based on suggestions by Thompson, 1967; see Note 57.)

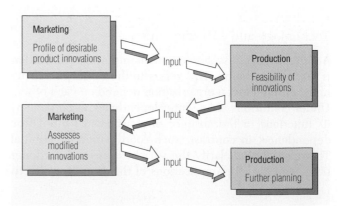

The level of interdependence existing between various units within an organization also has important implications for internal structure. Special attention should be directed in organizational design to departments or units that are reciprocally interdependent. These should be grouped together so that they can engage in continuous, mutual adjustment (e.g., they should be close to each other physically and should fall under the authority of the same person). Further, specific mechanisms for assuring a high degree of coordination between them (e.g., daily meetings, the creation of special liaison positions) should be developed. Although top priority in devising internal structure should be given to reciprocal interdependence, efforts to establish effective communication between units that are sequentially interdependent are important, too. These should have ready access to one another so that work flow between them can proceed in a smooth and orderly manner.

In summary, the kind of work activities performed within an organization, and the specific technologies it employs, often determine the level of interdependence between its various units. Such interdependence, in turn, should be taken into careful account when planning internal structure. (Because of the various interconnections between organizational elements, the exact organizational units responsible for specific policies and actions taken to carry them out are often difficult to identify. This is especially so in the case of policies that are of dubious ethical value. For a closer look at this phenomenon, see the **Question of Ethics** section on p. 610.)

SUMMARY AND REVIEW

Organizational Structure

The formal configuration between individuals and groups with respect to the allocation of tasks, responsibilities, and authority within organizations is known as **organizational structure,** an abstract concept that can be represented by an **organizational chart.** Such diagrams represent five different elemental building blocks of organizational structure: **hierarchy of authority** (a summary of reporting relationships), **division of labor** (the degree to which jobs are specialized), **span of control** (the number of individuals over which a manager has responsibility), **line** versus **staff positions** (jobs permitting direct decision-making power versus jobs in which advice is given), and **decentralization** (the degree to which decisions can be made by lower-ranking employees as opposed to a few higher-ranking individuals).

Within organizations, groups of people can be combined into departments in various ways. The most popular approach is the **functional organization,** organizations created by combining people in terms of the common functions they perform (e.g., sales, manufacturing). An alternative approach is to departmentalize people by virtue of the specific products for which they are responsible, known as the **product organization.** Another form of departmentalization combines both of these approaches into a single form known as the **matrix organization.** In

such organizations, people have at least two bosses; they are responsible to a superior in charge of the various functions and a superior in charge of the specific product. Employees also may have to answer to high-ranking people responsible for the entire organization, the *top leader.*

Organizational Design

The process of coordinating the structural elements of organizations in the most appropriate manner is known as **organizational design.** *Classical organizational theorists* (such as Weber and his notion of *bureaucracy*) believed that a universally best way to design organizations exists, an approach based on high efficiency. *Neoclassical organizational theorists* (such as McGregor, Argyris, and Likert) also believe that there is one best way to design organizations, although their approach emphasizes the need to pay attention to basic human needs to succeed and express oneself.

In contrast, the contemporary, **contingency approach** to organizational design is predicated on the belief that the most appropriate way to design organizations depends on the external environments within which they operate. Specifically, a key factor has to do with the degree to which the organization is subject to change: a stable environment is one in

A QUESTION OF ETHICS

Who Takes the Rap for Unethical Corporate Behavior? Camouflaging Immorality within the Web of Organizational Structure

History can provide valuable lessons. During the 1970s, U.S. president Richard Nixon was forced to resign from office in large part because the evidence was not convincing that he did not have any knowledge of—or actually authorize—the illegal acts associated with the Watergate break-in. A decade later, when some officials of President Ronald Reagan's administration were accused of selling arms to political factions in Nicaragua, they conscientiously distanced the president from their actions, keeping the nation's chief executive in the dark so that he could not be blamed for their questionable actions. Interestingly, when similar questions of unethical behavior by subordinates are raised about public and private institutions in Japan, the top leaders tend to resign in disgrace, shouldering the blame for their subordinates' conduct—whether or not they actually were directly responsible.

Although cultural differences are partly responsible for discrepancies in people's willingness to assume blame for wrongdoings that are not immediately under their own control, organizational structure cannot be overlooked as a factor. Given the complexity of most organizational designs—especially those for large bureaucratic organizations such as the federal government—it is usually difficult to identify who exactly is to blame for a particular unethical event. One individual may have committed the impropriety, but he or she may only be following the orders of an immediate superior, who is following the orders of a still-higher-ranking official, and so on. Who is *really* responsible? Philosophers would say that it is morally wrong to "pull the trigger," even if one is "only following orders" (a common plea made by people accused of committing the Nazi atrocities during World War II); to kill is morally wrong, for whatever reason. However, psychologists recognize the intense social pressures a subordinate is likely to feel when ordered by a superior to act unethically, especially when a superior explicitly shoulders the blame for their actions.

As a case in point, consider what happened at Hertz Car Rental's Boston office in the 1980s. The company was accused of overcharging rental customers by some $13 million by sending them phony and inflated bills for repair damage.[59] In response, the chairman of Hertz, Frank Olson, fired the head of the Boston office, Alan Blicker (who was five levels below Olson!), and eighteen others. He also redesigned the organization by shifting control over repair matters from the regional offices to the corporate office itself (increased centralization). Such actions ostensibly suggest that the company does not approve of these practices. Regardless, Mr. Blicker contended that he was made a scapegoat, and that management actually *approved* of these practices! By instituting a policy that lower-level employees have to follow, top-level employees may effectively make themselves immune from any questionable actions by lower-level employees that are taken in an attempt to implement the policy. Put differently, top officials may be able to camouflage themselves from unethical actions by hiding within the organizational chart.

Many business analysts argue that top management routinely should be held responsible for their subordinates' actions (as cultural norms already dictate in Japan). The idea is that until top officials are made responsible for the unethical practices of their subordinates, corporate cultures will continue endorsing—if only tacitly—unethical actions that yield short-term profit. In other words, top-down accountability may be the most effective way of inculcating a strong ethical culture within organizations. To the extent that officials can continue to hide behind the veil of a complex organizational chart, the prospect of further unethical episodes remains.

What is your opinion about this matter? Do you believe that top officials *are usually* held accountable for the unethical practices of lower-ranking employees? Can you think of any examples? Do you agree that more top-level managers *should be* held accountable?

Test Bank question 15.75 relates to material on this page.

which business conditions do not change, whereas a turbulent environment is one in which conditions change rapidly. Research has shown that when conditions are stable, a **mechanistic organization** is effective. A mechanistic organization is one in which people perform specialized jobs, many rigid rules are imposed, and authority is vested in a few top-ranking officials. When conditions are turbulent, an **organic organization** is effective. These are organizations in which jobs tend to be very general, there are few rules, and decisions can be made by lower-level employees. The mechanistic and organic forms are pure types, and organizations can be located in-between these two extremes.

Despite the existence of these popular types of organizational designs, some organizations are designed so that employees spend most of their time on special teams and task forces that are created as needed. These are known as **free-form designs.** Other organizational designs represent ways of combining more than one organization. Such *interorganizational designs* include the **joint venture** (organizations combining forces to operate a specific business)

and the **conglomerate** (large corporations that diversify by getting involved in unrelated businesses).

Technology as a Factor in Organizational Design

The **technology** employed by an organization often affects its internal structure. Companies employing **small-batch, large-batch (mass production),** and **continuous-process** technologies often differ with respect to their internal structure. In recent years, companies employing small-batch production coupled with a high-level technology have emerged. The internal characteristics of such companies are different from those of traditional small-batch organizations, which typically employ simpler means of production.

Organizations vary with respect to the level of **interdependence** between departments or other work units. The higher such interdependence, the greater the need for structural components that enhance coordination.

KEY TERMS

conglomerate: A form of organizational diversification in which an organization (usually a very large, multinational one) adds an entirely unrelated business or product to its organizational design.

contingency approach: The contemporary approach that recognizes that no one approach to organizational design is best, but that the best design is the one that best fits with the existing environmental conditions.

continuous-process production: A highly automated form of production that is continuous in nature and highly integrated in terms of component steps and processes.

decentralization: The extent to which authority and decision making are spread throughout all levels of an organization rather than being reserved for top management (*centralization*).

departmentalization: The process of breaking up organizations into coherent units.

division of labor: The process of dividing the many tasks performed within an organization into specialized jobs.

free-form designs: Organizations that are not designed in any formal way, but allow special teams to be created as needed.

functional organization: The type of departmentalization based on the activities or functions performed (e.g., sales, finance).

hierarchy of authority: A configuration of the reporting relationships within organizations; that is, who reports to whom.

interdependence: The extent to which the units or departments within an organization depend on each other to accomplish tasks.

joint venture: A type of organizational design in which two or more separate companies legally combine forces to develop and operate a specific business.

large-batch (mass) production: Technology based on long production runs of standardized parts or products.

line positions: Positions in organizations in which people can make decisions related to doing its basic work.

matrix organization: The type of departmentalization in which a product or project form is superimposed on a functional form.

mechanistic organization: An internal organizational structure in which people perform specialized jobs, many rigid rules are imposed, and authority is vested in a few top-ranking officials.

multinational corporation (MNC): Organizations that have significant operations spread throughout several nations, but that are headquartered in a single nation.

organic organization: An internal organizational structure in which jobs tend to be very general, there are few rules, and decisions can be made by lower-level employees.

organizational chart: A diagram representing the connections between the various departments within an organization; a graphic representation of organizational design.

organizational design: The process of coordinating the structural elements of an organization in the most appropriate manner.

organizational structure: The formal configuration between individuals and groups with respect to the allocation of tasks, responsibilities, and authorities within organizations.

pooled interdependence: A relatively low level of interdependence in which units within an organization operate in a largely independent manner.

product organization: The type of departmentalization based on the products (or product lines) produced.

reciprocal interdependence: A high level of interdependence in which the output of each unit within an organization serves as the input for others, and vice versa.

sequential interdependence: An intermediate level of interdependence in which the output of one unit serves as input for another.

small-batch production: A technology in which products are custom-produced in response to specific customer orders.

span of control: The number of subordinates in an organization who are supervised by managers.

staff positions: Positions in organizations in which people make recommendations to others, but are not themselves involved in making decisions concerning the organization's day-to-day operations.

technology: The knowledge, tools, and procedures used by an organization to perform its major work.

work-flow integration: A measure of technology that takes account of the degree of automation, work-flow rigidity, and specificity of evaluation within an organization.

QUESTIONS FOR DISCUSSION

1. How are the various elements of organizational design likely to be related to each other?

2. As organizations grow and become more complex, their designs are likely to change. Describe the various ways in which size may influence organizational design. How are these changes likely to influence individuals?

3. Describe the difficulties you believe will result from implementing a matrix organization.

4. In what ways may classical and neoclassical organizational designs be considered naive when it comes to describing the behavior of people in organizations?

5. Can you identify any examples of contemporary organizations that are relatively mechanistic or relatively organic? To what extent is each characterized by stable or turbulent environments as predicted by the contingency approach to organizational design?

6. What special organizational design considerations must be taken into account given the growing trend toward internationalization of industries?

7. Using an example of an organization you know, describe how its prevailing technology is related to its organizational design.

NOTES

1. Miller, D. (1987). The genesis of configuration. *Academy of Management Review, 12,* 686–701.

2. Galbraith, J. R. (1987). Organization design. In J. W. Lorsch (Ed.), *Handbook of organizational behavior* (pp. 343–357). Englewood Cliffs, NJ: Prentice-Hall.

3. Swoboda, F. (1990, May 28–June 3). For unions, maybe bitter was better. *Washington Post National Weekly Edition,* p. 20.

4. Weber, J. (1990, December 10). Farewell, fast track. *Business Week,* pp. 192–200.

5. Port, O. (1990, April 30). A smarter way to manufacture. *Business Week,* pp. 110–117.

6. Charles, R. (1988, February 15). Big changes at big blue. *Business Week,* pp. 92–98.

7. Treece, J. B. (1990, April 9). Will GM learn from its own role models? *Business Week,* pp. 62–64.

8. Lawler, E. E. (1988). Substitutes for hierarchy. *Organizational Dynamics,* 5–6, 15.

9. Speen, K. (1988, September 12). Caught in the middle. *Business Week,* pp. 80–88.

10. Urwick, L. F. (1956). The manager's span of control. *Harvard Business Review, 34*(3), 39–47.

11. Charan, R. (1991). How networks reshape organizations—for results. *Harvard Business Review, 69*(5), 104–115.

12. Green, H., & Moscow, A. (1984). *Managing.* New York: Doubleday.

13. Dalton, M. (1950). Conflicts between staff and line managerial officers. *American Sociological Review, 15,* 342–351.

14. Koslowsky, M. (1990). Staff/line distinctions in job and organizational commitment. *Journal of Occupational Psychology, 15,* 163–173.

15. Chandler, A. (1962). *Strategy and structure.* Cambridge, MA: MIT Press.

16. Mitchell, R. (1987, December 14). When Jack Welch

takes over: A guide for the newly acquired. *Business Week,* p. 93–97.

17. Mansford, J. (1984). Club Med management gives up some of its freewheeling style. *International Management, 39,* 27–29.

18. Lawrence, P., & Lorsch, J. (1967). *Organization and environment.* Boston: Harvard University.

19. Dumaine, B. (1990, November 5). How to manage in a recession. *Fortune,* pp. 72–75.

20. Richman, T. (1991, January). Reorganizing for growth. *Inc.,* pp. 110–111.

21. Toy, S. (1988, April 25). The Americanization of Honda. *Business Week,* pp. 90–96.

22. Uttal, B. (1985, June 29). Mettle test time for John Young. *Fortune,* pp. 242–244, 248.

23. Mee, J. F. (1964). Matrix organizations. *Business Horizons, 7*(2), 70–72.

24. Bartlett, C. A., & Ghoshal, S. (1990). Matrix management: Not a structure, a frame of mind. *Harvard Business Review, 68*(3), 138–145.

25. Wall, W. C., Jr. (1984). Integrated management in matrix organizations. *IEEE Transactions on Engineering Management, 20*(2), 30–36.

26. Davis, S. M., & Lawrence, P. R. (1977). *Matrix.* Reading, MA: Addison-Wesley.

27. Goggin, W. (1974). How the multidimensional structure works at Dow Corning. *Harvard Business Review, 56*(1), 33–52.

28. See Note 25.

29. Morgan, J. C. (1991). *Cracking the Japanese market.* New York: Free Press.

30. Perlmutter, H. V. (1969). The tortuous evolution of the multinational corporation. *Columbia Journal of World Business,* 9–18.

31. Robock, S. H., Simmonds, K., & Zwick, J. (1977). *International business and multinational enterprises.* Homewood, IL: Irwin.

32. Daniels, J. D., & Radebaugh, L. H. (1989). *International business* (5th ed.). Reading, MA: Addison-Wesley.

33. See Note 32.

34. See Note 32.

35. McGregor, D. (1960). *The human side of enterprise.* New York: McGraw-Hill.

36. Argyris, C. (1964). *Integrating the individual and the organization.* New York: Wiley.

37. Likert, R. (1961). *New patterns of management.* New York: McGraw-Hill.

38. Duncan, R. (1979, Winter). What is the right organization structure? *Organizational Dynamics,* pp. 59–69.

39. Burns, T., & Stalker, G. M. (1961). *The management of innovation.* London: Tavistock.

40. Deveney, K. (1986, October 13). Bag those fries, squirt that ketchup, fry that fish. *Business Week,* pp. 57–61.

41. Kerr, P. (1985, May 11). Witch hazel still made the old-fashioned way. *New York Times,* pp. 27–28.

42. Morse, J. J., & Lorsch, J. W. (1970). Beyond Theory Y. *Harvard Business Review, 48*(3), 61–68.

43. Bylinsky, G. (1990, January 1). The hottest high-tech company in Japan. *Fortune,* pp. 82–88.

44. Kukalis, S. (1989). The relationship among firm characteristics and design of strategic planning systems in large organizations. *Journal of Management, 15,* 565–579.

45. Hayden, C. L. (1986). *The handbook of strategic expertise.* New York: Free Press.

46. Fletcher, N. (1988, December 10). U.S., China form joint venture to manufacture helicopters. *Journal of Commerce,* p. 58.

47. Bransi, B. (1987, January 3). South Korea's carmakers count their blessings. *The Economist,* p. 45.

48. Steers, R., Shin, Y., & Ungson, G. (1989). *The chaebol: Korea's new industrial might.* New York: Harper & Row.

49. Dodwell Marketing Consultants. (1990). *Industrial groupings in Japan.* Tokyo: Author. [Cited in Steers, R. M. (1991). *Organizational behavior* (4th ed.). New York: Harper Collins.]

50. Woodward, J. (1965). *Industrial organization: Theory and practice.* London: Oxford University Press.

51. See Note 50, p. 58.

52. Zwerman, W. L. (1970). *New perspectives on organizational theory.* Westport, CT: Greenwood.

53. Huber, G. P. (1990). A theory of the effects of advanced information technologies on organizational design, intelligence, and decision making. *Academy of Management Review, 15,* 47–71.

54. Hull, F. M., & Collins, P. D. (1987). High-technology batch production systems: Woodward's missing type. *Academy of Management Journal, 30,* 786–797.

55. Hickson, D., Pugh, D., & Pheysey, D. (1969). Operations technology and organization structure: An empirical reappraisal. *Administrative Science Quarterly, 26,* 349–377.

56. Singh, J. V. (1986). Technology, size and organization structure: A reexamination of the Okayama study data. *Academy of Management Journal, 29,* 800–812.

57. Thompson, J. D. (1967). *Organizations in action.* New York: McGraw-Hill.

58. Daft, R. L. (1986). *Organizational theory and design* (2nd ed.). St. Paul, MN: West.

59. Alsway, W. (1988, February 15). Hertz is doing body work—on itself. *Business Week,* pp. 56–58.

CASE IN POINT

**Reorganizing
Apple Computer,
and Reorganizing
It Again . . . and
Again**

A CNN video is available
to accompany this case.
Additional information can
be found in the CNN
Video User's Guide.

Apple Computer, which began its existence in a garage, experienced tremendous early success. Within a few years of its founding, it sold more than $1 billion worth of personal computers.[1] The future looked bright, and Apple planned to take on "Big Blue" (IBM) with its new Macintosh line.

But the costs associated with this strategy were so great that by 1985, profits evaporated and the company had to cut more than 20 percent of its labor force. Friction developed between the young and charismatic Steven Jobs, Apple's founder and largest stockholder, and John Sculley, the high-powered executive whom Jobs had hired in 1983 to serve as Apple's chief executive officer.

John Sculley found himself in a difficult position. As chairman of the board, Steven Jobs had authority over him. But Jobs, as head of the Macintosh Division, reported to John Sculley. More important, the two men disagreed on how to solve the company's problems. Sculley, drawing on his long career as a top executive he achieved considerable success as president of PepsiCo),[2] wanted to change Apple's organizational structure to a functional design. Jobs wanted Apple to retain the informal, product division structure that it had used since its founding. Steven Jobs lost. With the board of directors' backing, Sculley forced Jobs to leave Apple.[3]

In 1985, Sculley implemented functional reorganization of Apple, hoping to gain control over its spiraling costs. Although the functional structure controlled operational costs and boosted profits, it also slowed Apple's ability to innovate. Since developing the Macintosh, Apple had lost its position as the computer industry's leading product innovator.

Sculley reorganized Apple again in 1988, this time opting for a decentralization of decision making throughout the company, reverting to a divisional design.[4] Three sales and marketing divisions were created, one to serve each of the United States, Pacific, and European markets, respectively, and a fourth division was created to carry out manufacturing operations and product development.

The results of this reorganization were mixed. The divisional approach worked well for the European and Pacific markets, but the U.S. division and the manufacturing and product development division failed, losing ground to IBM and IBM clone competitors. New product development slowed and manufacturing fell behind schedule. By the end of 1989, Apple's marketing divisions were at war with its manufacturing and product development division over product delays, and overall company sales were down 11 percent.[5]

Sculley responded by laying off 400 employees. The head of the U.S. division was fired, and the position of chief operating officer, abolished in 1988, was reestablished to oversee manufacturing operations, and staffed by the head of the successful European division, Michael Spindler. What used to be the manufacturing and product development division was reduced to product development only. By late 1989, Sculley had fired the head of the product development division and installed himself as its new head.

The product development division had always relied heavily on teams to develop new products. There was a team for each form of technology that went into a computer (e.g., disk drives, system software, and the like). Engineers reported to the team leader. To develop a new product, team leaders had to reach agreement on how all the technologies would fit together. This practice, which worked well during Apple's early years, resulted in considerable slowdowns in the larger, more mature Apple Computer. Sculley created new product teams, and engineers were assigned to product teams and reported directly to their respective product team managers.

Apple introduced three new Macintosh computers in late 1990—the Classic, the LC, and the IIsi. The distinguishing feature of these new products was their low price. The Classic was the most successful. The Classic was in such demand that Apple had a backlog of $525 million worth of orders after a month. By March 1991, Apple was selling 100,000 Classics per month and Apple's share of the U.S. computer market had doubled. Even in price sensitive foreign markets, Apple's new products were doing well. Revenues were up 19 percent and Apple had once again solidified its position as the largest personal computer company in the

United States—with 20 percent of the market (up from a low of 9 percent immediately prior to Apple's introduction of its new line of Macintosh computers).[6]

Things looked like they were turning around for Apple, except for one major problem. Apple's revenues and market share were up by the beginning of 1991, but its operating costs were so high that its profits were sharply lower. For the first time, Apple was not earning the large profit margins it traditionally made on its products—50 percent on average, compared with 40 percent by competitors such as IBM. Apple had become accustomed to earning the highest profit margins in the computer industry. But with their new Macintosh computers, Apple's profit margin fell to an average of 35 percent.

In addition, Apple was forced to run several of its manufacturing plants twenty-four hours a day to catch up with its backlog of orders, incurring substantial additional labor costs. Apple also had serious problems with its marketing and product distribution systems. They were very expensive! For example, Apple was accustomed to spending $750 to market each Macintosh it sold. That's about the same as the sticker price it charged for its new Classic computer.

Apple's move into producing low-profit-margin computer products marks an important strategic shift for the company. This change in strategy demanded that Apple's organization structure be designed to support its new business as a high-volume producer of low-profit computers, rather than a low-volume producer of high-profit computers. But Sculley also needed to evaluate Apple's business environment, and the rapidly changing technology of the computer products industry, when deciding on a new organizational structure.

The 1990s brought a devastating recession to the computer industry. Apple's customers were demanding lower-priced products, but they also wanted more new products, reflecting the latest in computer technology. Consumers were screaming for laptop and notebook computers, but until late 1991, Apple did not have a competitive laptop—its first laptop computer flopped because of its excessive weight and high cost. The company learned a lesson from this, and its first line of notebook computers (PowerBook Models 100, 140, and 170) were immediate hits with consumers.[7]

In 1991, more than 50 percent of Apple's revenues derived from international sales. Apple must adapt its products to numerous cultures and languages. Today, Apple develops computers for thirty-eight languages. In some countries, import regulations require Apple to make or buy various computer components within the buyer country.

Apple has had to adapt its organizational practices to satisfy the demands associated with selling in the international marketplace. For example, of the three manufacturing facilities that make the Classic computer, one facility is located in Singapore and another in Ireland. In each case, Apple had to modify its facilities to accommodate local norms, regulations, and laws.

Apple finally penetrated the Japanese computer market. But to do this, it had to establish "Apple Japan" and hire Japanese nationals to head the operation. To date, Apple has captured 5 percent of the Japanese computer market. Apple is also exploring the feasibility of expanding into Eastern European markets, and possibly the Commonwealth of Independent States (the former Soviet Union) and South Africa, depending on the political stability of these regions.

Apple has also lobbied to change the business environment in other countries. Apple lobbied hard to persuade Brazil and India to lift trade barriers that prevented certain Apple products from being sold. Apple also pushed for the recent free-trade agreement between Mexico and the United States, which resulted in its gaining 5 percent of the Mexican market in its first year.[8]

Apple has entered into joint venture agreements with other computer products companies, but these joint ventures have been disappointing. Work with Digital Equipment Corporation on a computer networking project resulted in nothing but numerous lawsuits. Apple's joint venture with Hewlett-Packard to develop imaging products fell apart after Apple filed a lawsuit against Hewlett-Packard over a disagreement. Hewlett-Packard and Apple eventually introduced new printers, but Hewlett-Packard beat Apple to the market with its popular DeskWriter printer. Apple's attempt to work with Microsoft to better support Apple's software language broke up too. Most recently, Apple has engaged forces with IBM to develop computer workstations. Apple's history casts serious doubt over the ultimate success of its IBM joint venture.

By the middle of 1991, Sculley had decided to reorganize again to make Apple more cost efficient. Ten percent of the work force (about 1,500 employees) were targeted for layoff. Sculley consolidated the U.S. division's five sales regions into three units. He closed regional headquarters in Chicago and San Jose, California, and moved several departments out of high-cost regions to lower-cost areas in the western United States. For the first time, the engineering and product development staff also were squeezed. Travel budgets and bonuses were slashed.

Sculley drastically changed the way Apple distributes its computers. Traditionally, Apple used a network of authorized dealers to sell its computers. Apple has now begun to sell its new line of products in low-cost, low-service superstores that operate and appear more like warehouses than computer stores.

Apple is in the process of trying "to produce technologically advanced products—on time—and to fill in the gaps in its current product line."[9] To achieve this aim, Sculley has created a dual hierarchy organization design. He made Michael Spindler president and chief operating officer responsible for manufacturing and Apple's three sales and marketing divisions—Apple USA, Apple Europe, and Apple Pacific. Spindler is also in charge of three newly formed Macintosh dedicated groups—Macintosh Hardware, Macintosh Software, and Enterprise Systems.

The second hierarchy, headed by Sculley, contains the Product Development Group—the Advanced Technology Group and two spin-off companies, Claris Corporation and General Magic. Apple spun off the two companies to allow them to pursue their entrepreneurial activities. Says one of Apple's general managers, "We want to isolate entrepreneurs. We don't expect revenue from them, but ideas. The other part of the organization has to deliver predictably, boringly good products. The mission of Sculley's Product Development Group is to define Apple's future."[10]

The philosophy behind the new dual hierarchy structure is that it is best to separate the normal operations of Apple from its creative activities. Within Spindler's operations, standard business operating procedures and strict policies and controls are being used to minimize costs. Spindler has also implemented regular monthly business forecasting and planning meetings that are new to Apple.

The reorganization is still being worked out. Sculley has become increasingly aware of the difficulties associated with running a company with a multiple personality. Designing for efficiency on the one hand, and innovating on the other, has created numerous problems and frustrations for Apple. Intended to be protected from the cost-cutting directives aimed at operations, his Product Development Group has nonetheless received cuts too.

Even Claris Corporation employees, who as members of the spin-offs were supposed to be protected from Apple's new efficiency mandates, accuse Sculley of frustrating their attempts to innovate and be entrepreneurial. It is believed that Sculley grew fearful that Claris's entrepreneurial success was becoming so great that Apple might lose control over the spin-off, so he tightened Apple's reins. The result is that seven of the original nine executives who formed Claris have left or are threatening to resign. Activity at Claris has slowed to a crawl.

Apple employees and investors are worried. Is Apple trying to do too much in its attempt to be a low-cost computer manufacturer *and* a leading innovator in the computer products industry?

Questions for Discussion

1. Describe Apple's business and technological environments using concepts discussed in the text. What type of organization design best fits Apple's environment—organic or mechanistic? Why?
2. Apple CEO John Sculley has reorganized the company several times. What organization designs has he used? Explain why he used each of these designs.
3. Why did Sculley go back to a divisional design in 1988? How did this design differ from Apple's pre-1985 organizational structure?
4. Following Apple's 1988 reorganization, the manufacturing and product development division failed to meet performance expectations. What about Apple's 1988 organization design might explain this failure?
5. Apple has entered into several joint ventures with other computer products companies—with very little success. Why do you think Apple continues to enter into these joint ventures?

6. Does Sculley's latest dual hierarchy organization design fit Apple's strategy, and business and technological environment? Explain. If you were CEO of Apple, how would you design the company? Explain your design choice.

Notes

1. Cassidy, T. (1991). Pinnacle: Interview with John Sculley of Apple Computer. *CNN/Allyn and Bacon Video.*
2. See Note 1.
3. See Note 1.
4. Schlender, B. R. (1990, October 22). Yet another strategy for Apple. *Fortune*, pp. 81–87.
5. See Note 4.
6. England, C. (1991, September). That vision thing. *MacWorld,* pp. 169–175.
7. Editors of MacUser (1992, March). The 7th annual editors choice awards. *MacUser*, p. 103.
8. See Note 6.
9. See Note 6, p. 172.
10. See Note 6, p. 175.

EXPERIENCING ORGANIZATIONAL BEHAVIOR

As we have described mechanistic and organic organizations, each is likely to be most effective under different sets of conditions. Several well-known studies cited in the chapter support this idea. Extending this work, it is an intriguing possibility that the effectiveness of each form is related to how the employees feel about that type of organization. After all, the conditions one can expect to experience in mechanistic and organic organizations are likely to be quite different—and people might not be equally comfortable with those conditions. This quiz is designed to be a self-assessment tool that helps you learn about your own preferences for each type of organization and, in so doing, learn about the various organizational forms themselves.

Mechanistic versus Organic Organizations: Which Do You Prefer?

Procedure

Each of the following questions deals with your preferences for various conditions that may exist where you work. Answer each one by checking the one alternative that best describes your feelings.

1. When I have a job-related decision to make, I usually prefer to
   _____ a. make the decision myself
   _____ b. have my boss make it for me

2. I usually find myself more interested in performing
   _____ a. a highly narrow, specialized task
   _____ b. many different types of tasks

3. I prefer to work in places in which working conditions
   _____ a. change a great deal
   _____ b. generally remain the same

4. When a lot of rules are imposed on me, I generally feel
_____ a. very comfortable
_____ b. very uncomfortable
5. I believe that governmental regulation of industry is
_____ a. usually best for all
_____ b. rarely good for anyone

Score your responses in the following manner. Each time you respond as follows, give yourself a point toward preferring *mechanistic organizations:* 1 = b; 2 = a; 3 = b; 4 = a; 5 = a. Subtract this number from 5 to get your score on preference for *organic organizations.* Whichever score is larger indicates your preference for that type of organization. The bigger the difference between the two scores (the extremes are 5 for one type and 0 for another), the stronger is your preference.

Points to Consider

1. How did you score? In other words, which type of organization does this quiz indicate you prefer?
2. Think back at organizations in which you've worked. Can you identify some that were mechanistic and others that were organic in design? (Although your information may not be perfect, base your judgment on the descriptions appearing in the text as closely as you can.)
3. How did your own preferences fit in with the nature of the organizations? Generally, was there a match (i.e., you preferred the type of organizations within which you usually worked) or mismatch (i.e., you did not prefer the type of organizations within which you usually worked)?
4. Although it might be difficult to answer this question in an unbiased way, please give it careful thought: How were your work performance and attitudes related to any matches or mismatches? In other words, did you perform better and enjoy the job more when you worked in the type of organization you preferred? Or did this not really make any difference?
5. Consider some of the factors that might account for your responses to question 4 above. Given that we *could* carefully assess your job performance and attitudes (although these are not being carefully measured here), why would you expect them to be related or not related to a match between the type of organization that exists and the type of organization that is preferred?
6. What could be done to improve this questionnaire? What other items might be added, or how could the items be rewritten to better measure one's preference for each type of organizational design?

■ 16 ■

ORGANIZATIONAL CHANGE AND DEVELOPMENT

CHAPTER OUTLINE

LEARNING OBJECTIVES

After reading this chapter, you should be able to:
1. Identify the major forces responsible for organizational change.
2. Describe the primary targets of organizational change efforts.
3. Identify the conditions under which organizational change is likely to occur.
4. Explain the major factors making people resistant to organizational change—and some ways of overcoming them.
5. Describe the major techniques of organizational development.
6. Evaluate the effectiveness of organizational development efforts.
7. Debate the idea that organizational development is inherently unethical.
8. Explain the potential cultural barriers to effective organizational development.

L ate Friday afternoons are special at Coronado Industries. Most of the executives gather informally in the break room at about 4:00 P.M. to enjoy the day's last cups of coffee from the firm's eighty-cup urn (often having to tip it forward to get the last few cups) and chat about whatever they have in mind. This Friday, as the company's ninth birthday approaches, people feel like reminiscing.

"It's amazing," remarks Rusty Burlson, Coronado's founder and chief executive officer, "we've only been in business for eight years, and we hardly do anything like we did when we first opened."

Ed Grimley, the manager of the accounting department at Coronado, nods, adding, "I know what you mean, Rusty. In my department alone we changed from keeping financial records mostly by hand when we first opened, to now entering data completely on computers."

"Tell me about it," comments Susan Mulhouse, the office manager. "I don't think I'd even know how to use a typewriter anymore. We still have a few old models gathering dust in our storage closet; we moved them there when we first changed over to word processors."

"You keep them for emergency backups?" Ed questions.

"Originally, yes," Susan replies. "We never quite trusted the computers at first, but now that we've gotten used to them, we don't know what to do anymore with the typewriters. Anyone want to take them off our hands? I'll give you a good price."

Ed chuckles, pointing to a room on the other side of the building. "It's not just typewriters, but lots of very expensive manufacturing equipment over there in the shop—stuff that all had to be retrofitted with computer interfaces to work fast enough, and accurately enough, for us to stay competitive."

"Listening to you folks," interjects Matt Solomon, the corporate attorney for Coronado, "you'd think it's only computers that have made things change around here, but that's just part of it."

"C'mon, Matt, you use computers, too," Susan points out.

"Sure, I do," Matt replies, adding, "and they've made my life—or my secretary's life—a lot easier and more efficient. My point is that it's not *only* computers that have changed the way we operate around here. Much of my job has changed from reviewing contracts with suppliers and customers to filling out forms for the federal government."

"We've got plenty of forms to fill out in accounting, too," Susan adds.

"Yeah, mostly tax forms, I'm afraid," says Rusty as he shakes his head with displeasure.

"Just think about it," Matt says, returning the conversation to his earlier point. "A lot of what we do is based on governmental regulations. Those goggles and hard hats worn on the shop floor, they're all required by OSHA."

"Oh, what?" Ed asks, only half joking.

"OSHA, the Occupational Safety and Health Administration," Matt answers. "That's not all. For example, we now have to make sure that we dispose of our waste products the right way. The EPA monitors us to make sure we don't pollute the air and streams by emitting dangerous—or at least polluting—substances into the environment."

"Our company was never really much of an environmental threat," Rusty comments, "but there *are* a lot of things we now have to do differently with our waste. It's not all so obnoxious, though. In fact, some of what we used to think of as waste is now recyclable; we actually make money on our scrap metal."

"See, there's even been a change in what constitutes garbage!" Matt chuckles.

"And don't forget that new law, the Americans with Disabilities Act," says Susan. "In the old days, I remember public service announcements encouraged us to 'hire the handicapped.' Now we have to make it possible for them to work in our facility. Maybe you've seen all those new ramps and wide toilet stalls with railings they're installing in our part of the building? That's all part of it."

"That's gotta cost a fortune," Ed observes.

"It's costing us a lot in construction fees, sure," Rusty acknowledges, "but it's something we really *should* be doing—for everyone's good. After all, remember when you were in a wheelchair for a week or so last year, Matt, because of your skiing accident? It would have really been a problem if you couldn't come to work just because the facilities didn't allow you to get around."

"Maybe yes, maybe no," Matt answers jokingly, and everyone laughs.

"Well, there's no 'maybe' about it," Rusty summarizes, "just about everything's changed. Whether it's for better or for worse, only time will tell. But there's no 'maybe' about one thing, and that's change itself!"

"Well, one thing hasn't changed, Rusty," Ed notes. "After eight years, we *still* continue to gab away our Friday afternoons."

This conversation at Coronado Industries focuses on a key concern in organizations, sources of change responsible for the way work is performed. You can be sure that if we revealed even more of what was said, we'd become aware of additional factors that have changed life at Coronado (and other companies as well) in the last eight years. Specifically, what else besides the two factors identified in the story—advances in computer technology and the imposition of governmental regulations—might be responsible for change? In answering this question, we must consider forces acting on the organization, such as the changing demands of the marketplace (e.g., do people want to buy small cars or large ones?), the availability of human resources (e.g., is there a skilled labor force nearby?) and other natural resources (e.g., is there an ample supply of water and coal to manufacture steel?), and shifting political and social movements (e.g., pressure to be an "equal opportunity" employer). We should also take into account changes intentionally brought about by the organization itself,

FIGURE 16–1   Signs of the Times: Signals of Organizational Change

Signs such as these provide a good indication of changing environmental conditions that influence organizational functioning. Organizational growth places demands on the pool of available human resources (left), sometimes compensating for increased supply generated by organizational decline elsewhere (right).

self-improvement measures, so to speak—actions designed to avoid problems such as high absenteeism and turnover, and low morale (job dissatisfaction). These various considerations underscore some of the major factors that we will examine in this chapter on **organizational change.**

As you might imagine, it is not difficult for business executives to chronicle the varying environmental forces acting on their organizations that have produced change. In fact, signs of the impact of change in organizations can be found everywhere (see Figure 16–1). People do have difficulty, however, accepting that they may have to alter their work methods to adapt to change. After all, if you're used to doing things a certain way at work, a sudden change can be very unsettling. Fortunately, social scientists have developed various methods, known collectively as **organizational development** techniques, that are designed to implement needed organizational change in a manner that both is acceptable to employees and enhances the effectiveness of the organizations involved.[1] We will examine these techniques and their effectiveness in this chapter. Before doing so, however, we will take a closer look at the organizational change process by chronicling different forces for change acting on organizations. Then we will explore some major issues involved in the organizational change process, such as *what* is changed, *when* change will occur, and *why* people are resistant to change.

ORGANIZATIONAL CHANGE: SOME DETERMINING FACTORS

As you look around you today, the sight of portable computers is hardly uncommon. Indeed, that they can be easily transported from home to car to airplane to office is a major reason for their popularity. Given this, it is difficult to understand why the developers of the first portable computers, Osborne Computer, found itself $45 million in debt and was forced to declare bankruptcy just two years after its first portable computer was introduced in January 1981. This is especially surprising because the company enjoyed sales of nearly $100 million in the two years of its existence.[2]

How does a company go from boom to bust so quickly? Although there were undoubtedly many reasons for Osborne's failure, one key factor was its inability to manage the rapid growth and complex changes brought about by the introduction of giants such as IBM into the field. As the market for computer products changed, along with the technology needed to make them, other companies, such as the much larger IBM and the highly aggressive upstart Apple Computer, were better suited to making the changes necessary to create and meet the growing demand for home computers.

As you might imagine, Osborne is hardly alone in its inability to adapt to change. Companies such as Xerox, Texas Instruments, American Motors, and Eastman Kodak, to name just a few, have encountered difficulties at various times in their histories trying to meet rapidly changing technological and marketing conditions. No organization is immune. Even General Motors, one of the world's largest companies, lost an unprecedented $4.45 billion in 1991, resulting in the planned reduction of over 16,000 jobs and a dozen plant closings in the early 1990s.[3] Sometimes, as in the case of Osborne Computer, the inability to respond to changing conditions leads to organizational decline and eventual dissolution. Indeed, as shown in Figure 16–2, the survival rate of U.S corporations tends to be rather low, with 62 percent failing within their first five years of operation.[4]

Obviously, everchanging conditions present a formidable challenge to organizations, which must learn to be flexible and adapt to them. However, not all organizational changes are the result of unplanned, externally imposed factors. Some organizational changes are planned, and quite intentional. The large variety of determinants of organizational change—forces dictating change—can be organized into four major categories. These categories are created by combining two key distinctions: (1) whether the organizational change is *planned* or *unplanned* by the organization, and (2) whether it derives from factors *internal* or *external* to the organization. The

Organizational change is a fact of working life. In the past ten years, over 35,000 corporate mergers and acquisitions were completed in the United States. These organizational changes resulted in reconstructions, reconfigurings, and the displacement of millions of employees. In fact, the entire face of business has been rapidly changing. By 1990, 22 of the top 100 companies listed by *Fortune* magazine in 1979 no longer existed. This rapid pace of organizational change is not a fad but is expected to continue into the next century. [Berger, L., Gouillart, F. J., King, W. C., Useem, M., & Georges, J. A. (1991, Fall). The age of alignment. *Directors & Boards*, pp. 13–18.]

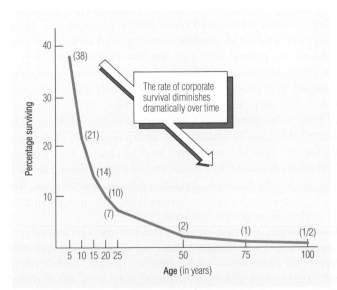

FIGURE 16–2

Survival Rates of American Corporations: The Grim Picture

As these data reveal, only 38 percent of organizations survive their first five years in business—and even fewer make it longer than that. The failure to successfully make needed changes is undoubtedly one key reason behind these statistics. (*Source:* Based on data reported by Nystrom & Starbuck, 1984; see Note 4.)

TABLE 16–1   Categories of Organizational Change: A Taxonomy and Some Examples

Organizational changes may be either planned or unplanned, and based on either internal or external causes. Some examples of changes within each of the four categories are listed here.

	Planned Change	Unplanned Change
Internal Change	Changes in products or services Changes in administrative systems	Changing employee demographics Performance gaps
External Change	Introduction of new technologies Advances in information processing and communication	Government regulations External competition

taxonomy that results from combining these two dimensions—as shown in Table 16–1—provides a useful way of summarizing the major determinants of organizational change.

Planned Internal Change

A great deal of organizational change comes from the conscious decision to alter the way an organization does business or the very nature of the business itself. For example, when one company takes over another, it must plan how it will change its operations and management to accommodate the new acquisition. Two examples of planned organizational change can be identified—changes in products or services, and changes in administrative systems.

Changes in Products or Services   Imagine that you and a friend begin a small janitorial business. The two of you divide the duties, each doing some cleaning, buying supplies, and performing some administrative work. Before long, the business grows and you expand, adding new employees, and really begin "cleaning up." Many of your commercial clients express interest in window cleaning, and so you and your partner think it over and decide to expand into the window-cleaning business as well. This decision to take on a new direction to the business, to add a new, specialized service, will require a fair amount of organizational change. Not only will new equipment and supplies be needed, but also new personnel will have to be hired and trained, new insurance will have to be purchased, and new accounts will have to be secured. In short, the planned decision to change the company's line of services necessitates organizational change. This is exactly the kind of change that Federal Express encountered in 1989 when it sought to expand its package delivery service, formerly limited exclusively to North America, to international markets, or that Citicorp, a longtime leader in consumer banking, encountered when it attempted to become an international leader in corporate banking.[5,6]

As you are undoubtedly well aware, the rash of new products and services offered to consumers each year is staggering. Unfortunately, many of these are unsuccessful; only about one out of every eight ever becomes profitable. In fact, both Federal Express and Citicorp have experienced difficult financial battles in their recent attempts to expand their service markets beyond their traditional boundaries. In

British Petroleum Exploration (BPX), the arm of British Petroleum that finds and develops oil and gas reserves, recently underwent a massive planned internal transformation. Although BPX is a successful company that employs some 10,000 people, a 1989 survey showed that most of the employees felt stifled by paperwork and were unable to get things done in the company's existing structure. In 1990 a new CEO implemented a plan to create a culture of personal responsibility to replace its rigid hierarchy. He wanted to establish a global culture that transcended national boundaries, to create a company where people and ideas could move freely. One of the major changes made was to implement dual career paths: one for would-be managers and another for individual contributors. [Moravec, M., & Tucker, R. (1991, October). Transforming organizations for good. *HRMagazine*, pp. 74–76.]

general, what accounts for these difficulties, and what can be done to improve the odds?

Some valuable insight into this question is provided by the **horizontal linkage model**.[7] In brief, this model specifies that the success of a new product is based on the success of the *marketing* and *research* departments in interacting with their external environments and with each other. The marketing and research areas are singled out because these are typically the ones most concerned with effecting change. Moreover, experts in these fields are expected to keep close tabs on the environment external to the organization. Specifically, employees involved in research are expected to make themselves aware of new technological developments and advances in areas relevant to the organization as soon as they occur. Analogously, people involved in marketing are expected to be able to monitor changes in consumers' preferences and the product introductions by competitors. In short, both departments are expected to serve important *boundary-spanning* roles—that is, to connect the organization to its external environment.

However, it is not sufficient that these two units only gather information; they must also establish *horizontal linkages* between themselves. In other words, they must coordinate their efforts, sharing the information they receive and giving each other advice. The absence of such communication not only can cause a great deal of confusion within the organization (see chapter 13), but is also greatly responsible for the failure of many organizations to successfully change as desired. Organizations whose critical marketing and research subunits function effectively not only with the outside world, but with each other as well, tend to be ones whose products are best accepted. By carefully paying attention to the advice of the horizontal linkage model (summarized in Figure 16–3), organizations can increase the odds that they will be effectively—and profitably—able to change the products and services they offer.

Changes in Administrative Systems   Although an organization may be forced to change its policies, reward structure, goals, and management style in response to outside competition, governmental regulation, and economic changes (as we will note later), it is also quite common for changes in administrative systems to be strategically planned in advance. Such changes may stem from a desire to improve efficiency, to change the company's image, or to gain a political power advantage within the organization (see chapter 11).[8] As an example of this, let's consider a recent decision to structurally reorganize at PepsiCo.[9] Until recently, PepsiCo had a separate

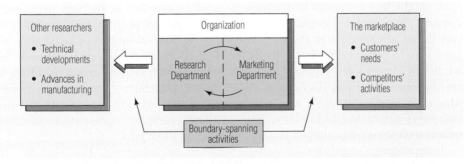

FIGURE 16–3   The Horizontal Linkage Model: A Summary

According to the *horizontal linkage model*, new products and services will be successful if they result from the boundary-spanning activities of an organization's marketing and research staffs, and from the coordinated interaction between these two units. (*Source:* Based on suggestions by Daft, 1986; see Note 7.)

Test Bank questions 16.3, 16.48, and 16.57 relate to material on this page.

international food service division, which included the operation of sixty-two foreign locations of the company's Pizza Hut and Taco Bell restaurants. Because of the great profit potential of these foreign restaurants, PepsiCo officials decided to reorganize, putting these restaurants directly under the control of the same executives responsible for the successful national operations of Pizza Hut (Steve Reinemund) and Taco Bell (John Martin). This type of departmentalization allows the foreign operations to be managed under the same careful guidance as the national operations (see chapter 15).

Typically, the pressure to bring about changes in the administration of organizations (e.g., to coordinate activities, set goals and priorities) comes from upper management—that is, from the top down. In contrast, pressure to change the central work of the organization (i.e., the production of goods and services) comes from the technical side of the organization, from the bottom upward.[10] This is the idea behind the **dual-core model** of organizations. Many organizations, especially medium-size ones, may be characterized by potential conflicts between the administrative and the technical cores—each faction wishing to change the organization according to its own vested interests.

Which side usually wins? Research suggests that the answer depends on the design of the organization in question (refer to chapter 15). Organizations that are highly *mechanistic* as opposed to *organic* in their approach (i.e., they are highly formal and centralized) tend to be successful in introducing administrative changes.[11] The high degree of control wielded by the administrative core tends to facilitate the introduction of administrative change. Obviously, factors such as the need to make administrative changes in order to support the technical changes required for organizational success make the issue more complex. Regardless, changes in the administrative systems of organizations clearly represent a good example of planned internal change.

Planned External Change

In addition to planning changes in the ways organizations are run, it is often possible to plan which change variables originating outside the organization will be incorporated into it. Introductions of new technology and advances in information processing and communication fall into this category. Both of these advances typically originate outside the organization and are introduced into it in some planned fashion.

Introduction of New Technologies: From Slide Rules to Computers   There can be little doubt that advances in technology produce changes in the way organizations operate. Scientists and engineers, for example, can probably tell you how their work was drastically altered in the mid-1970s, when their ubiquitous plastic slide rules gave way to powerful pocket calculators. Things changed again only a decade later, when calculators were supplanted by powerful desktop microcomputers, which have revolutionized the way documents are prepared, transmitted, and filed in an office. Manufacturing plants have also seen a great deal of growth recently in the use of computer-automated technology. Each of these examples represents an instance in which technology has altered the way people do their jobs.

Technological changes take various forms in organizations. For example, technological advances are commonly applied in the cockpits of airplanes, where computer-based devices are routinely used to guide, assist, or take over many functions performed by pilots. This is in keeping with a prediction by John Naisbitt, in his best-selling book, *Megatrends*, that high-tech devices would become friendlier and easier to use.[12] Anyone who has used computer software packages to make complex mathematical calculations during the last several years will surely recognize how

Boeing, the airplane manufacturer, is trying to incorporate a new technology called *concurrent engineering (CE)* into its operations. The technology has been used by other industries and by one of Boeing's competitors, Airbus. CE is a technique in which engineers work side by side with designers rather than separately. Boeing hopes that using the new CE technology will save as much as 20 percent of the estimated $4 to $5 billion it plans to spend to develop its new wide-body 777 airplane. If successful, the use of CE will enable the 777 to be designed without paper blueprints—a completely computer-based, "paperless" design will be used. The design project is massive, involving 7,000 people in 238 design teams linked together through 2,033 com-

much easier modern programs are to use than older programming languages (e.g., FORTRAN). As computer-based technology is applied to more and more life activities, new products emerge, such as books on compact disc (that add pictures and sound to words) and portable wireless cash registers (hand-held devices that allow clerks to enter credit card transactions wherever customers and bar-coded merchandise are located).[13] Only time will tell, of course, which devices will catch on, making life easier, and which will end up in the technological graveyard. Regardless of the eventual fate of high-tech devices, organizations must stay abreast of such changes if they are to remain competitive in today's world.

In keeping with this ease-of-use theme, note that technological advances applied to the shop floor have been responsible for the introduction of complex microelectronic, computer-based devices—*robots*. The use of robots has clearly taken hold in manufacturing industries, especially in the performance of monotonous or dangerous jobs. Such devices are commonly used in automobile manufacturing (see Figure 16–4). Automated assembly plants are so important to automobile manufacturing that in the 1991 fiscal year, Toyota increased capital spending by 39 percent, to nearly $4.2 billion.[14] Toyota already uses robots to perform routine tasks such as applying adhesive to windshields and dropping spare tires into trunks. However, currently only 5 percent of Toyota's assembly line tasks are automated—but because of labor shortages (over two jobs are available for each worker in the areas near Toyota factories), the automation rate is likely to increase in the future. In fact, in European Fiat and Volkswagen plants, where labor shortages have long existed, some assembly plants are as much as 30 percent automated.

Automated production is being used more often in other types of industries as well. For example, the use of robots has reportedly helped General Electric to produce 20 percent more dishwashers in 20 percent less floor space in its Louisville, Kentucky, plant. Robots have also helped the Walgreen's drugstore chain increase the rate of packing shipments from its distribution center to its stores by over 800 percent.[15] Naturally, because robots are so efficient, they pose a challenge to workers who fear being replaced by them. (As we will describe later in this chapter, such a fear represents one especially potent source of workers' resistance to organizational change.) Obviously, the introduction of new technology poses an important challenge to today's businesses. The primary challenge is to use machines to spare human beings from dangerous and undesirable working conditions, freeing people to use their creativity and talents in ways that machines cannot, thereby improving the quality of working life.

puter workstations. If the 777 project is successful, Boeing plans to integrate the CE technology companywide. [Jones Yang, D. (1991, October 28). Boeing knocks down the wall between the dreamers and the doers. *Business Week,* pp. 120–121.]

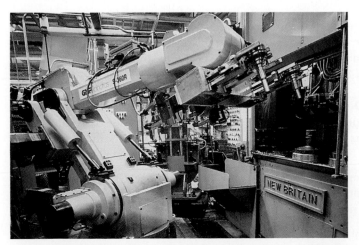

FIGURE 16–4

Robots: An Important Source of Technological Change

Robots are now used for many of the monotonous or dangerous jobs that used to be performed by people on automobile assembly lines. Such a change not only relieves people from undesirable jobs, but also dramatically improves the quality of manufacturing—hence, organizational functioning.

Test Bank questions 16.7–16.8 relate to material on this page.

Advances in Information Processing and Communication   Although we now easily take for granted everyday events such as television transmissions and long-distance telephone calls, these things were merely exotic dreams not too long ago. If you've ever seen an old western film in which the Pony Express rider struggled through uncharted territories to deliver messages to people in distant western cities, you are well aware of the difficulties that people faced—and in the not too distant past—to communicate over long distances. Of course, with today's sophisticated satellite transmission systems, fiber-optic cables crisscrossing the planet, fax machines, portable telephones, teleconferencing facilities (see chapter 13) and the like, it is easier than ever for businesses to communicate with each other and with their clients. The key point is that as such communication systems improve, opportunities for organizational growth and improvement immediately follow.[16] One key to organizational success is to selectively incorporate advances in communication technology that allow organizations to share vast amounts of information faster and more widely than ever before.

One company that has been using high-tech communication techniques very effectively is U.S. Healthcare, one of the largest private practice–based health maintenance organizations (HMOs) in the United States.[17] With the aim of improving the quality of health-care services, the company relies on technological assistance in its new, futuristic office facility in Blue Bell, Pennsylvania. Company executives were careful to focus on their objectives when selecting technology, letting the technology be a means to an end, rather than making the expensive mistake of using it as an end in itself. Among other things, the company installed large electronic bulletin boards, cleverly called "Vital Signs," on which progress toward various performance goals was monitored (which, as you may recall from chapter 4, can greatly enhance motivation). For two-way communication, the company installed an electronic mail system (see chapter 13), but found that low-tech face-to-face meetings, informal brown bag sessions, were preferred. Still, sophisticated technology is used at U.S. Healthcare to automate tasks such as delivering the mail (for which a robot is now used) and accessing customers' files (for which a sophisticated automated answering machine hooked up to a computer is used to allow agents to focus their attention on customers' concerns). The idea is that the more that mundane tasks can be automated, the more people can be used to provide valuable human contact. Given that improving customer service was one of the company's goals, U.S. Healthcare's use of advanced communication technology to help achieve this goal does indeed make the technology a useful means to a desired end.

Unplanned Internal Change

Not all forces for change are the result of strategic planning. Indeed, organizations must often be responsive to changes that are unplanned—especially those derived from factors internal to the organization. Two such forces are changes in the demographic composition of the work force, and performance gaps.

Changing Employee Demographics   It is easy to see how, even within your own lifetime, the composition of the work force has changed. Consider these illustrative statistics and projections for the American work force as the twentieth century draws to a close.

■ **The percentage of women in the American work force is greater than ever before.** In 1976, women accounted for 40.5 percent of the adult work force, a figure that had increased to 45 percent by 1988 and is projected to rise to 47.3 percent by 2000.[18]

Test Bank question 16.9 relates to material on this page.

- **The American work force is getting older.** People aged thirty-five to fifty-four constituted 38 percent of the work force in 1985, but they will be 51 percent of the work force by the year 2000.[19]
- **The American work force is becoming more culturally diverse.** In 1980, 10 percent of the work force was composed of blacks, and 6 percent was composed of Hispanics. By the year 2000, blacks are expected to represent 12 percent of the work force, Hispanics will account for 10 percent, and Asians, 4 percent.[20]

These statistics represent only some of the major demographic changes that have occurred, and that will be occurring, in the American labor force. To people concerned with the long-term operation of organizations, these are not simply curious sociological trends, but sets of shifting conditions that will force organizations to change. Questions regarding how many people will be working, what skills they will bring to their jobs, and what new influences they will bring to the workplace are of key interest to human resource management professionals. In the words of Frank Doyle, corporate vice president for external and industrial relations at General Electric, the impending changes in work force demographics "will turn the professional human-resources world upside down."[21] Indeed, some companies such as American Express have already responded to these changes by educating their supervisors on how to manage a changing, increasingly diversified work force.[22]

Let's consider some of the implications of these demographic forces with which today's organizations must wrestle. In the 1980s, baby boomers (people born in the decade immediately following World War II) became more of an economic force than ever—their high income and educational levels forced organizations to make a wide variety of comfort and convenience items available (e.g., luxury cars; convenience foods, and microwave ovens in which to cook them).[23] With more female employees of childbearing age in the work force than ever before, organizations have had to make child-care facilities available and to allow many employees to work on a part-time basis or to "share" jobs. As workers grow older, they put an increasing burden on pension systems. If they live longer lives, and work farther into their lives, the drain on health insurance may become severe. Even if higher levels of affluence allow people to retire earlier than ever before, the lack of experienced personnel may pose a formidable organizational problem.[24] In the 1990s, these trends have begun to change somewhat in response to the harsh economic realities faced. The affluent baby-boom generation of the 1980s has given way to the more modest "baby-bust" generation of the 1990s. Today, fewer young people graduate from college and become as affluent as quickly as they did just a few years ago (see Figure 16–5 on page 630). As you might imagine, this too represents an important shift in worker expectations, a key change of which organizations must be aware.

Scientists are just beginning to understand how the everchanging composition of the work force is influencing the operation of organizations.[25] Although the exact nature of the changes forced by shifting demographics is complex and not yet fully understood, one thing is certain—changes in the composition of the work force demand corresponding changes in organizations.

Performance Gaps   If you've ever heard the phrase "If it's not broken, don't fix it," you already have a good feel for one of the most potent sources of unplanned internal changes in organizations—performance gaps. A product line that isn't moving, a vanishing profit margin, a level of sales that isn't up to corporate expectations—these are examples of gaps between real and expected levels of organizational performance. Few things force change more than sudden and unexpected information about poor organizational performance. Organizations often stay with a winning course of action, and they often change in response to failure; in other words, they follow a *win-stay/*

FIGURE 16–5   Shifting from the Baby-Boom Generation to the Baby-Bust Generation: Harsh Lessons

The levels of affluence to which people aspire often must be adjusted in response to changing economic realities. As employee demographics shift over time, organizations must accommodate new demands of the work force. (*Source:* © King Features Syndicate, Inc.)

lose-change rule. Indeed, several research projects have shown that a performance gap is one of the key factors providing an impetus for organizational innovation.[26] Those organizations that are best prepared to mobilize change in response to unexpected downturns may well be the ones that succeed.

One company that has not changed fast enough is Digital Equipment Corporation, a key player in the rapidly changing world of computers.[27] Although Digital's VAX family of computers was successful in the late 1980s, the company was rapidly losing sales to a new type of desktop computer—the workstation, especially Sun Microsystems' powerful and popular SPARC systems. Instead of rushing to market competitive workstations, Digital stood still, losing billions of dollars in sales. Recent figures reveal that the company lost over $40 million and had stock valued at only about half of IBM's (although as recently as 1987, both companies' stocks traded at about $165). This is surely a "performance gap"! To turn things around, former company CEO Ken Olsen invested over $1 billion on a new computer chip design called *Alpha*, an extremely fast, "open" design that can be built on in the future and that is compatible with most of today's operating systems. Olsen's hope was to regain leadership in the computer marketplace by making all the competitors play catch-up. On the strength of the *Alpha* line, Olsen put into practice a lesson he had already learned the hard way: "If anyone is going to make your product obsolete, it had better be you."[28]

Unplanned External Change

One of the greatest challenges faced by an organization is its ability to respond to changes from the outside world over which it has little or no control. As the environment changes, organizations must follow suit. Research has shown that organizations that can best adapt to changing conditions tend to survive.[29] Two of the most important unplanned external factors are governmental regulation and economic competition.

Government Regulation   One of the most commonly witnessed unplanned organizational changes results from government regulations. In the late 1980s, restaurant owners in the United States had to completely change the way they report the income of waiters and waitresses to the federal government for purposes of collecting income taxes. Similarly, any change in the minimum wage law greatly influences organizations, forcing them to revise the amount they pay their lowest-paid employees. In recent years the U.S. federal government has been involved in both imposing and eliminating regulations in industries such as commercial airlines (e.g., mandating inspection schedules, but no longer controlling fares) and banks (e.g., restricting the amount of time checks can be held before clearing, but no longer regulating interest rates). No doubt, such activities have greatly influenced the way business is conducted in these industries.

An excellent example of how government activities drive organizational change is provided by the 1984 divestiture of AT&T. A settlement of antitrust proceedings dramatically rearranged the activities of almost 1 million employees of the Bell System—a company with $103 billion in assets. Among other things, the agreement led to the creation of seven new independent companies. At Southwestern Bell, CEO Zane Barnes remarked that the divestiture forced them to "rethink the functions of some 90,000 employees," a process that was likened to "taking apart and reassembling a jumbo jet while in flight."[30] Not surprisingly, the company relied on its expertise in satellite and communications technology to provide information about the change process to its employees in fifty-seven locations.

Government regulations are often imposed on organizations following some crisis of public health or safety. Such was the case when the Nuclear Regulatory Commission (NRC) imposed safety standards on nuclear power plants following the 1979 accident at Three Mile Island. Among other things, the NRC imposed a set of guidelines for improving the safety of all nuclear power plants. A study by Marcus compared the safety records of power plants that responded to the NRC's guidelines either exactly as established (i.e., they were *rule-bound*), or by customizing the regulations to their individual circumstances (i.e., they were *autonomous*).[31] As shown in Figure 16–6, the autonomous power plants operated significantly more safely than

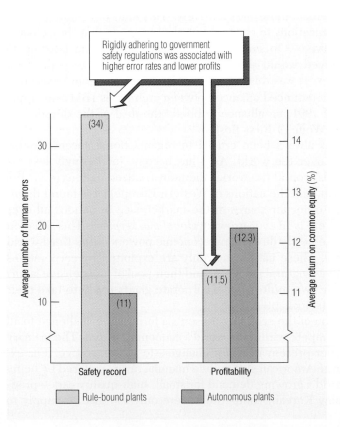

FIGURE 16–6

Rigid Adherence to Government Regulations: Some Unsettling Effects in Nuclear Power Plants

Research comparing several nuclear power plants found those that adapted government safety guidelines to their own operations (i.e., *auto-nomous* plants) operated more safely and at a higher profit margin than those that adhered rigidly to the guidelines (i.e., *rule-bound* plants). (*Source:* Based on data reported by Marcus, 1988; see Note 31.)

the rule-bound ones (they had one-third as many human-caused errors), and more profitably, too.

As Marcus explains, a good safety record encouraged the use of discretion in following the NRC's rules, whereas a poor safety record encouraged the NRC to require stricter adherence to its policies. Unfortunately, because plants that were allowed to customize the rules performed more safely than those that did not, insisting on close adherence to the rules may have only kept the dangerous power plants performing dangerously. These self-defeating actions are clearly responsible for the mixed effectiveness of government regulation in this case. Regardless, this research provides a clear example of the organizational changes created by government regulation in one important industry.

Sometimes, government intervention can stretch across several different industries at once. An example is the *Americans with Disabilities Act*—legislation passed by Congress in July 1990 and phased in during 1992. This law guarantees accessibility and employment rights to the 43 million Americans with physical and mental impairments.[32] Although some critics of the law argue that it places an unfair disadvantage on small businesses (whose owners must now endure the expense of retrofitting their existing facilities to make them more accessible to disabled people), proponents argue that it is the only effective way to make people "temporarily without" disabilities more sensitive to those with them. Although only time will tell how effective this legislation will be in actually combating prejudice toward the handicapped, one thing is certain: legislation protecting the rights of disabled people represents a serious force effecting change within all organizations.

Economic Competition   It happens every day: someone builds a better mousetrap—or at least a cheaper one, or one that's marketed more effectively. As a result, companies must often fight to maintain their share of the market, advertise more effectively, and produce products more inexpensively. This kind of economic competition not only forces organizations to change, but also demands that they change effectively if they are to survive. On some occasions, competition can become so fierce that the parties involved would actually be more effective if they dropped their swords and joined forces. It was this "if you can't beat 'em, join 'em" reasoning that was responsible for the announced alliance between arch rivals IBM and Apple Computer in the summer of 1991, an alliance dubbed "the deal of the decade" by financial analyst Charles R. Wolfe of First Boston.[33]

Although competition has always been crucial to organizational success, today competition comes from all over the world. As it has become increasingly less expensive to transport materials around the world, the industrialized nations (e.g., the United States, Canada, Japan, and the nations of Western Europe) have found themselves competing with each other for shares of the marketplace in nations all over the world. In other words, there is an ever-growing *global marketplace*. This situation is made more complex by the newly developing economic powers of the third world (e.g., Mexico, South Korea). These nations not only are exploited by corporations from other nations for their vast natural resources and their pool of inexpensive labor, but are also developing their own multinational corporate giants ready to take their place in the world's market (see chapter 15).[34]

This extensive globalization of the economy presents a formidable challenge to all organizations who wish to compete within the world's economic system. The primary challenge is to meet the ever-present need for change—to be innovative. For example, consider how the large American automobile manufacturers suffered by being unprepared to meet the world's growing demand for small, high-quality cars—products their Japanese (and now Korean) competitors were only too glad to supply to

One company that has recently undergone a massive restructuring is Caterpillar International (Cat), the manufacturer of construction and mining equipment. A reason for the change is increasing economic competition from Japanese firms such as Komatsu, Kubota, Hitachi, and Kawasaki. The reorganization of Cat moved the firm from an archaic functional structure to a modern, product orientation. The new organization revolves around thirteen profit centers spread around the world, each divided into specific products, and four service divisions. Cat also streamlined its work force, cutting 1,000 jobs. With changes in plants called PWAF ("Plant with a Future"), Cat hopes to return to its once dominant position in the construction equipment market. [Benson, T., E. (1991, May 20). Caterpillar wakes up. *Industry Week,* pp. 33–37.]

an eager marketplace. One thing is certain: as the stakes get higher and the number of players increases, the world marketplace becomes an arena where only the most adaptive organizations can survive.

THE PROCESS OF ORGANIZATIONAL CHANGE: SOME BASIC ISSUES

Clearly, organizations change in many ways and for many reasons. However, as you might imagine, the process of changing organizations is not haphazard; rather, it proceeds according to some well-established, orderly pattern. It is well known, for example, what the targets of organizational change efforts may be. Under which conditions organizational change is likely to occur, and when people will be most likely to resist making such changes, are also known. We will address these basic issues in this section.

Targets of Organizational Change: What Is Changed?

Imagine that you are an engineer responsible for overseeing the operation of a large office building. The property manager has noted a dramatic increase in the use of heat in the building, causing operating costs to skyrocket. In other words, a need for change exists—specifically, a reduction in the building's heat usage is deemed necessary. You cannot get the power company to lower its rates, so you realize you must bring about changes in the use of heat. How do you do this? Working with the manager, you consider some ways to achieve this goal. One possibility calls for rearranging job responsibilities so that only maintenance personnel are permitted to adjust thermostats. Another possibility is to put timers on all thermostats so that the building temperature is automatically lowered during periods of nonuse. Finally, you consider the idea of putting stickers next to the thermostats, requesting that occupants refrain from turning the heat up beyond 68 degrees. Although there are clearly other possibilities, these three options represent excellent examples of the three potential targets of organizational change we will consider here—changes in *structure*, *technology*, and *people* (see Figure 16–7).

People, structure, and technology have recently been targets of change in a number of well-known organizations. Over the past fourteen years, Conrail has cut its work force by 61 percent and has gained market share in the process. Eastman Kodak eliminated 24,000 jobs between 1983 and 1986, a reduction of 17.5 percent of its work force. The downsizing allowed the company to reorganize its structure, giving managers much more direct responsibility. Apple Computer consolidated its operating division, closed plants, and laid off one-fifth of its employees after the failure of the Lisa computer. Overall, the companies that survived the 1980s the best were those that stayed lean by modifying their use of people, structure, and technology. [Shuger, S. (1990, June). How to cut bureaucracy in half. *The Washington Monthly*, pp. 38–51.]

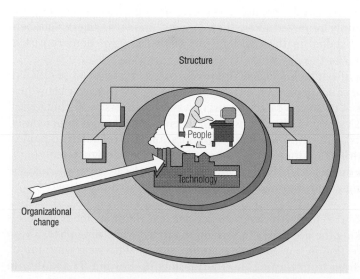

FIGURE 16–7

Organizational Change Targets: Structure, Technology, People

To effect change in organizations, one can rely on altering organizational structure, technology, and/or people. Changes in any one of these areas may necessitate changes in the others.

Test Bank questions 16.14, 16.49, 16.58, and 16.67 relate to material on this page.

Changes in Organizational Structure   In chapter 15 we described in detail the key characteristics of organizational structure. Here we note that altering the structure of an organization may be a reasonable way of responding to a need for change. In the above example, a structural solution to the heat regulation problem came in the form of reassigning job responsibilities. Indeed, modifying rules, responsibilities, and procedures may be an effective way to manage change. Changing the control of heat from a highly decentralized design (whereby anyone can adjust the thermostats) to a centralized design (whereby only maintenance personnel may do so) may be one way of implementing organizational change in response to a problem. This particular structural solution called for changing the power structure (i.e., who was in charge of a particular task).

Different types of structural changes may take other forms.[35] For example, changes can be made in an organization's span of control, altering the number of employees for which supervisors are responsible. Structural changes may also take the form of revising the basis for creating departments—such as from product-based departments to functional departments (see chapter 15). Other structural changes may be quite simple, such as clarifying someone's job description or the written policies and procedures followed.

Structural changes are not uncommon in organizations. Consider, for example, some changes reported in recent years at the huge consumer products company Procter & Gamble.[36] In response to growing competition, the company was forced to make a number of changes that streamlined its highly bureaucratic organizational structure. For example, the decision-making process used to be so centralized that many decisions that could have been made at lower levels were being made by top corporate personnel (such as the color of the cap on the can of decaffeinated instant Folgers coffee). Now decentralized business teams have been instituted and are permitted to make all the necessary decisions about developing, manufacturing, and marketing products. These represent good examples of structural changes made in organizations.

Changes in Technology   In the example used to open this section, we noted that one possible solution to the heat conservation problem would be to use thermostats that automatically reduce the building's temperature while it is not in use. This is an example of a technological approach to the need to conserve heat in the building. Placement of regulating devices on the thermostats that would thwart attempts to raise the temperature would also be possible. The thermostats also could be encased in a locked box, or simply removed altogether. A new, modern, energy-efficient furnace could also be installed in the building. All of these suggestions represent technological approaches to the need for change.

The underlying idea is that technological improvements can lead to more efficient work. Indeed, if you've ever prepared a term paper on a typewriter, you know how much more efficient it is to do the same job using a word processor. Technological changes may involve a variety of alterations, such as changing the equipment used to do jobs (e.g., robots), substituting microprocessors for less reliable mechanical components (e.g., on airline equipment), or simply using better-designed tools (e.g., chairs that conform to one's body). Each of these changes, large or small, may be used effectively to bring about improvements in organizational functioning.

Changes in People   You've probably seen stickers next to light switches in hotels and office buildings asking the occupants to turn off the lights when not in use. These are similar to the suggestion in our opening example to affix signs near thermostats asking occupants to refrain from turning the thermostats up beyond 68 degrees (in

Test Bank questions 16.15–16.16 relate to material on this page.

the winter). Such efforts represent attempts to respond to the needed organizational change by altering the way people behave. The basic assumption is that the effectiveness of organizations is greatly dependent on the behavior of the people working within them. To the extent that employees are motivated to meet organizational goals (see chapter 4), and are rewarded for working efficiently (see chapter 3), organizations will be able to change as necessary.

As you might imagine, the process of changing people is not easy—indeed, it lies at the core of most of the topics discussed in this book. However, theorists have identified three basic steps that summarize what's involved in the process of changing people.[37,38] The first step is known as *unfreezing*. This refers to the process of recognizing that the current state of affairs is undesirable and in need of change. Realizing that change is needed may be the result of some serious organizational crisis (e.g., a serious profit loss, a strike, or a major lawsuit), or simply becoming aware that current conditions are unacceptable (e.g., antiquated equipment, inadequately trained employees). After unfreezing, *changing* may occur. This step occurs when some planned attempt is made to create a more desirable state for the organization and its members. Change attempts may be quite ambitious (e.g., an organizationwide restructuring) or only minor (e.g., a change in a training program). (A thorough discussion of such planned change techniques will be presented in the next major part of this chapter.) Finally, *refreezing* occurs when the changes made are incorporated into the employees' thinking and the organization's operations (e.g., mechanisms for rewarding behaviors that maintain the changes are put in place). Hence, the new attitudes and behaviors become a new, enduring aspect of the organizational system. For a summary of these three steps in the individual change process, please see Figure 16–8. Despite the simplicity of this model, it does a good job of identifying some of the factors that make people willing to change their behavior—thereby potentially improving organizational effectiveness.

We close this section with the reminder that organizational change efforts may be directed at the organizational structure, the technology used, or the people involved. As you might imagine, however, changes made with respect to one of these targets may very well necessitate changes with respect to another. As a simple example, imagine how a change in the machinery used to perform a job requires changes in the skills needed by the employees who operate it. In fact, almost any change, be it in organizational structure or technology, may be expected to have

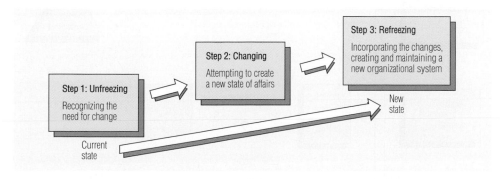

FIGURE 16–8   Changing People: Some Basic Steps

Many planned organizational change efforts are directed at changing people. In general, the process of changing people involves the steps outlined here. (*Sources*. Based on ideas suggested by Lewin, 1951; see Note 37; and Schein, 1968; see Note 38.)

Test Bank questions 16.17–16.19 and 16.59 relate to material on this page.

profound effects on the way people do their jobs. For this reason, it is important to pay careful attention to the kinds of factors that may make people more or less willing to accept organizational changes.

Readiness for Change: When Will Organizational Change Occur?

As you might imagine, there are times when organizations are likely to change, and times during which change is less likely. Even if the need for change is high and resistance to change is low (two important factors), organizational change does not automatically occur. Other factors are involved, and we have summarized some of the key variables in Figure 16–9.

As Figure 16–9 summarizes, change is likely to occur when the people involved believe that the benefits associated with making a change outweigh the costs involved. The factors contributing to the benefits of making a change are: (1) the amount of dissatisfaction with current conditions, (2) the availability of a desirable alternative, and (3) the existence of a plan for achieving that alternative. Theorists have claimed that these three factors combine multiplicatively to determine the benefits of making a change.[39] Thus, if any one of these factors is very low (or zero), the benefits of making a change, and the likelihood of change itself, are very low (or zero). If you think about it, this will begin to make sense to you. After all, people are unlikely to initiate change if they are not at all dissatisfied, or if they don't have any desirable alternative in mind (or any way of attaining that alternative, if they do have one in mind). Of course, for change to occur, the expected benefits must outweigh the likely costs involved (e.g., disruption, uncertainties). Professionals in the field of organizational development pay careful attention to these factors before they attempt to initiate any formal, ambitious organizational change programs. Only when the readiness for change is high will organizational change efforts be successful. (Having established that there are certain conditions under which change is likely, an interesting follow-up question comes to mind: are some individuals more predisposed to accept and foster organizational change than others? In other words, are there pre-

In organizations, especially mature organizations, great pressure not to accept change exists. Sometimes when the status quo is very strong, the only way change can occur is through a "champion of change." A champion of change is someone who believes so strongly in the change that he or she is willing to take whatever risk is necessary to see it through, including going to the highest authority if the situation requires it. William Sims was such a champion of change. As a mere Navy lieutenant, he put his career on the line by going straight to President Theodore Roosevelt in order to get the reluctant Navy to

---

FIGURE 16–9

Organizational Change: When Will It Occur?

Whether or not an organizational change will be made depends on members' beliefs regarding the relative benefits and costs of making the change. The benefits are reflected by three considerations reviewed here. (*Source:* Based on suggestions by Beer, 1980; see Note 39.)

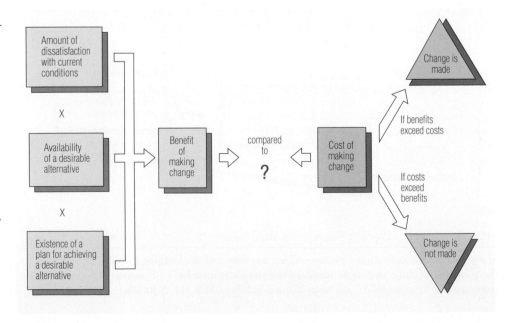

Test Bank questions 16.20–16.22 and 16.50 relate to material on this page.

dictable differences in people's willingness to change? Might people from one demographic group be more inclined to accept change than those from other demographic groups? For an examination of recent research relevant to these questions, see the **Focus on Research** section on pp. 638–640.)

Resistance to Change: Will Organizational Change Be Accepted?

Although people may be unhappy with the current state of affairs confronting them in organizations, they may be afraid that any changes will be potentially disruptive and will only make things worse. Indeed, fear of new conditions is quite real; it creates unwillingness to accept change. Organizational scientists have recognized that **resistance to change** comes from both individual and organizational variables.

Individual Barriers to Change Researchers have noted several key factors that are known to make people resistant to change in organizations.[40]

1. **Economic insecurity.** Because any changes on the job have the potential to threaten one's livelihood—by either loss of job or reduced pay—some degree of resistance to change is inevitable unless job security can be assured.

2. **Fear of the unknown.** It is well accepted that employees derive a sense of security from doing things the same way, knowing who their coworkers will be, and whom they're supposed to answer to from day to day. Disrupting these well-established, comfortable patterns creates unfamiliar conditions, a state of affairs that is often rejected.

3. **Threats to social relationships.** As people continue to work within organizations, they form strong social bonds with their coworkers. Many organizational changes (e.g., the reassignment of job responsibilities) threaten the integrity of friendship groups that provide an important source of social rewards for many employees.

4. **Habit.** Jobs that are well learned and become habitual are easy to perform. The prospect of changing the way jobs are done challenges workers to relearn their jobs and to develop new job skills. Doing this is clearly more difficult than continuing to perform the job as it was originally learned.

5. **Failure to recognize need for change.** Unless employees can recognize and fully appreciate the need for changes in organizations, any vested interests they may have in keeping things the same may overpower their willingness to accept change.

Organizational Barriers to Change As we noted earlier, resistance to organizational change arises not only from individual forces, but also from several factors associated with the organization itself.[41]

1. **Structural inertia.** Organizations are designed to promote stability. To the extent that employees are carefully selected and trained to perform certain jobs, and rewarded for performing them, the forces acting on individuals to perform in certain ways are very powerfully determined—that is, jobs have **structural inertia**.[42] In other words, because jobs are designed to have stability, it is often difficult to overcome the resistance created by the many forces that create the stability.

2. **Work group inertia.** Inertia to continue performing jobs in a specified way comes not only from the jobs themselves but also from the social groups within which many employees work. Because of the development of strong social norms within work groups (see chapter 8), potent pressures exist to perform jobs in certain ways and at certain accepted rates. Introducing change causes disruption in these established normative expectations, which imposes formidable barriers to change.

adopt a new technology called continuous-aim-firing (CAF) guns. [Gautschi, T. F. (1989, January 2). Champions of change can move mountains. *Design News*, pp. 172–173.]

Any type of organizational change can be very hard on employees. In some cases, people's responses to change resemble the four stages of the bereavement process: denial, resistance, anger, and depression. Some employees worry that their jobs may be phased out or that they'll have to take on more work that they won't be able to handle. Some employees think of changing an organizational routine or procedure as being like losing an old friend. It's no wonder that employees express their feelings of loss through absenteeism, lowered production, and decreased morale. [First, S. E. (1990, April). All systems go: How to manage technological change. *Working Woman*, pp. 47–54.]

FOCUS ON RESEARCH

When Does Strategic Change Occur? A Comparative Study of Executive Team Demographics

 Imagine that you are part of a team of top executives deciding what course your firm will take in the future. Should it diversify its line of products, expanding into new areas? Or should it take the opposite approach, narrowing its focus on a smaller line of products? Perhaps no change should be made at all in product diversification, leaving things as they are. Such carefully planned decisions about changing the basic nature of organizations, decisions made with the organization's long-term goals in mind, are known as *strategic decisions*—a type of decision made almost exclusively by teams of top executives. Given how important such decisions are to organizational functioning, it would be interesting to see if strategic decisions to change an organization in one way or another can be predicted in advance. That is, could it be determined which organizations' top teams will make strategic change decisions and which ones will not? A fascinating recent study by Wiersema and Bantel addresses this issue.[43]

These investigators reasoned that it might, in fact, be possible to predict the making of strategic change decisions by knowing about certain key demographic factors, that is, personal characteristics of the top team members. If you assume that certain types of people might be more predisposed to making changes than other types, it follows that demographic variables may be good predictors of when strategic change will occur. This was Wiersema and Bantel's underlying general hypothesis.

They tested this notion in an investigation focusing on the top management teams within eighty-seven different *Fortune* 500 companies (i.e., those top executives who were most responsible for determining the directions taken by their organizations). For each company, a measure was made of its level of diversification—that is, the degree to which it has a varied product line. (This measure was based on a sophisticated mathematical formula that took into account the proportion of total sales accounted for by the company's various product lines.) Relying on huge databases of corporate facts and figures, these measures were computed reflecting two time periods: once for 1980, and again for 1983. By comparing these figures, the investigators determined how much change took place with respect to diversification. Specifically, they determined which companies made decisions to change a great deal (such as by adding or dropping several product lines) and which made no decisions to change. Such comparisons were made as a function of several key demographic variables in which the investigators were interested. These included the average *age* of the team members during the study period; *organizational tenure* (how long team members had worked for this organization); *team tenure* (how long team members had worked together); *education level;* within-team *heterogeneity of education* (how varied the educational backgrounds of team members were); and degree of *academic training in the sciences* (the extent to which team members were trained in scientific fields). Again, the researchers measured these variables using records of top team members appearing on large corporate databases.

Did these variables predict the amount of change that occurred in the teams' organizations? In all cases, the answer was "yes"! Specifically, more change occurred in organizations whose top team members were younger, better educated, worked less time in their teams and in their organizations, were more diverse in educational specialization, and had more academic training in the sciences compared with those who were opposite along these dimensions (see Figure 16–10). Intuitively, these findings make a great deal of sense. After all, younger people— those who have spent less time in their teams and their organizations—are not likely to have as much invested in keeping things the same, maintaining the status quo, as those who are older and more experienced. Similarly, more educated people, and those working in educationally diverse teams, may be more sensitive to the benefits of change than those with narrower educational perspectives. Finally, because those trained in science are expected to be aware of the need for progress, invention, and improvement, they would likely be predisposed to change. Not only do these findings make good intuitive sense, but they are also impressive because they were obtained in a large sample of different types of industries, organizations that were of different sizes, ones that were structured differently, had different performance records, and had different size management teams. By statistically controlling for these factors (i.e., holding constant any effects they may have had), researchers could be assured that the pattern of demographic differences we just described was valid, and not the result of any of these other factors (i.e., organizational size, structure, and performance) entering into the situation. (This is important insofar as any of these factors themselves might have influenced the results.)

Taken together, these findings are important for at least two reasons. First, they highlight how profoundly the directions a firm can take may be influenced by the decisions of only a few top individuals. Second, the findings make clear that *who* is at the helm of the company is likely to dictate the extent to which change may be predicted. In this sample, for example, the top executives who managed the American Can Company and the Allied Corporation were younger (average of 51.5 years) and more educated (average of 16.5 years) than their counterparts in the Westinghouse Electric Corporation and the Phillips Petroleum Company (average of 60 years of age and 15.8 years of

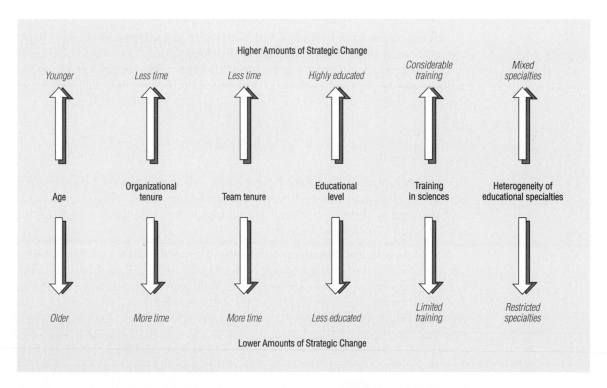

FIGURE 16-10   Which Executives Promote Strategic Change? Research Evidence

Recent research in a sample of *Fortune* 500 organizations has shown that strategic change is most likely to occur in organizations whose executive teams match a certain demographic profile, summarized here. (*Source:* Based on data reported by Wiersema & Bantel, 1992; see Note 43.)

(*continued*)

education). Based on only these measures, which companies do you think experienced more change? Consistent with the overall findings, American Can and Allied had more strategic change than Westinghouse and Phillips.

Such predictions cannot be perfect, of course, and not all people within the same demographic groups are necessarily identical in all ways.

Moreover, many different variables can be responsible for the way strategic decisions are made, not only those factors predictable from demographic variables. Still, the present findings support the interesting idea that strategic decisions regarding organizational change may be predicted from knowledge of a few key demographic characteristics.

3. **Threats to existing balance of power.** If changes are made with respect to who's in charge and how things are done, a shift in the balance of power between individuals and organizational subunits is likely to occur (see chapter 11). Those units that now control the resources, have the expertise, and wield the power may fear losing their advantageous positions as a result of any organizational change.

4. **Previously unsuccessful change efforts.** Anyone who has lived through a past disaster may be understandably reluctant to endure another attempt at the same thing. Similarly, groups or entire organizations that have been unsuccessful in introducing change in the past may be understandably reluctant to accept further attempts at introducing change into the system.

Having summarized some of the barriers to organizational change, we should consider some of the ways to overcome resistance. After all, unless these barriers to change can be effectively overcome, any attempts to systematically change organizations may be doomed to failure. With this in mind, we will now outline some of the major methods used to overcome resistance to organizational change.

Overcoming Resistance to Organizational Change: Some Guidelines

Because organizational change is inevitable, managers should be sensitive to the barriers to change so that such resistance can be overcome. This, of course, is easier said than done. However, several useful approaches have been suggested, and the key ones are summarized here.[44,45]

1. **Shape political dynamics.** In chapter 11, we described the important role of organizational politics in achieving desired goals. Political variables are crucial to getting organizational changes accepted. Politically, resistance to change can be overcome by winning the support of the most powerful and influential individuals. Doing so builds a critical internal mass of support for change. Demonstrating clearly that key organizational leaders support the change is an effective way of getting others to go along with it—either because they share the leader's vision or because they fear the leader's retaliation. Either way, political support for change will facilitate acceptance of change.

2. **Educate the work force.** Sometimes, people are reluctant to change because they fear what the future has in store for them. Fears about economic security, for example, may be easily put to rest by a few reassuring words from organizational powerholders. As part of educating employees about what organizational changes may mean for them, top management must show a considerable amount of emotional sensitivity. Doing so makes it possible for the people affected by the change to

become instrumental in making it work. This philosophy of educating employees, providing them with information that helped them better understand organizational goals, has been cited as one of the elements responsible for successfully implementing the large-scale organizational changes at Honeywell that were needed to make it competitive with IBM.[46]

A straightforward example of this principle in practice may be seen in the way New Jersey–based Sandoz Pharmaceuticals introduced laptop computers to its 1,000 salespeople.[47] In 1988, the company wanted a more immediate and efficient way of collecting information about sales calls than the written reports that had been filed weekly, but management was concerned that the salespeople might balk at having to learn the new technology. So, in addition to making the system very easy to use, Brad Fackler, the company's manager for field planning, also pointed out to the salespeople the many good features of the new system that "were in it for them." In this case, it was easy. The new system required the salespeople to enter a few remarks into their computers immediately after each visit to a doctor's office. Transmitting this information back to the company helped the company learn immediately how the physicians felt. It also helped the salespeople themselves by precluding the need to spend weekends handwriting reports of their weekly activities. In essence, the new technology allowed the reports to write themselves, thereby freeing the salespeople from the drudgery of the paperwork they faced in the old system. By selling workers on these benefits, the company effectively persuaded employees to embrace the new technology.

3. **Involve employees in the change efforts.** It is well established that people who participate in making a decision tend to be more committed to the outcomes of the decision than are those who are not involved.[48] Accordingly, employees who are involved in responding to unplanned change, or who are made part of the team charged with planning a needed organizational change, may be expected to have very little resistance to change. Organizational changes that are "sprung" on the work force with little or no warning might be expected to encounter resistance simply as a knee-jerk reaction until employees have a chance to assess how the change affects them. In contrast, employees who are involved in the change process are better positioned to understand the need for change, and are therefore less likely to resist it. It is precisely these kinds of efforts at participative management that are credited with the successful changes in Southwestern Bell in the aftermath of the breakup of AT&T.[49]

4. **Reward constructive behaviors.** One rather obvious, and quite successful, mechanism for facilitating organizational change is rewarding people for behaving in the desired fashion (recall our discussion of organizational rewards in chapter 3). Changing organizational operations may necessitate a change in the kinds of behaviors that need to be rewarded by the organization. This is especially critical when an organization is in the transition period of introducing the change. For example, employees who are required to learn to use new equipment should be praised for their successful efforts. Feedback on how well they are doing not only provides a great deal of useful assurance to uncertain employees, but also goes a long way toward shaping the desired behavior (see chapter 3).

Although these four suggestions may be easier to state than to implement, any effort to follow them will be well rewarded. Given the many forces that make employees resistant to change, managers should keep these guidelines in mind. If organizational change is to be beneficial, all employees must work toward accepting the change rather than using it as a rallying point around which organizational conflict may focus.

ORGANIZATIONAL DEVELOPMENT: THE IMPLEMENTATION OF PLANNED ORGANIZATIONAL CHANGE

Now that we have shed some light on the basic issues surrounding organizational change, we are ready to look at planned ways of implementing it—collectively known as techniques of **organizational development (OD).** More formally, we may define organizational development as *a set of social science techniques designed to plan and implement change in work settings for purposes of enhancing the personal development of individuals and improving the effectiveness of organizational functioning.*[50] By planning organizationwide changes involving people, OD seeks to enhance organizational performance by improving the quality of the work environment and the attitudes and well-being of employees.

Over the years, a vast array of strategies for implementing planned organizational change (referred to as *OD interventions*) have been used by specialists attempting to improve organizational functioning (referred to as *OD practitioners*).[51] All too often, some such techniques are merely managerial fads and fashions that do not stand the test of time.[52] Fortunately, however, several well-established OD techniques have been developed over the years. We will begin this section by summarizing several major OD techniques. Following this, we will conclude by assessing their overall effectiveness, addressing the important question: do they work?

Organizational Development Interventions: Major Techniques

As organizational development (OD) is gaining maturity as a profession, researchers have become increasingly interested in learning what specific actions are taken by successful OD practitioners. A survey of organizations that used OD practitioners considered what specific OD-practitioner behaviors were believed to be the most important. Twenty-eight percent of the respondents said "implementation of the OD action," 21 percent said "managing group processes and building teams," 21 percent said "formal and informal strategies for collecting data about the organization and

All the major methods of organizational development attempt to produce some kind of change in individual employees, work groups, and/or entire organizations. This is the goal of the six well-known OD techniques we will review—*survey feedback, sensitivity training, team building, grid training, quality of work life programs,* and *management by objectives.*

Survey Feedback: Inducing Change by Sharing Information For effective organizational change to occur, employees must understand the organization's current strengths and weaknesses. That's the underlying rationale behind the **survey feedback** method.

This technique follows three simple steps (summarized in Figure 16–11).[53] First (usually with the help of an outside consultant retained by top management), data are collected that provide information about matters of general concern to the employees, such as organizational climate, leadership style, degree of satisfaction, and similar themes. This may take the form of intensive interviews or structured questionnaires (either standardized, or developed specifically for the organization studied), or both. Because it is important that this information be as accurate as possible, employees providing feedback are assured that their responses will be kept confidential.

FIGURE 16-11

Survey Feedback: An Overview

The *survey feedback* technique of organizational development follows the three stages outlined here.

Data collection
Employees complete surveys to provide information about problems in their organization

Feedback
Feelings about the organization are summarized and shared with all employees

Develop action plans
Through group discussions, specific plans for overcoming problems are identified and developed

Test Bank questions 16.28–16.31, 16.53, 16.62, and 16.69 relate to material on this page.

The second step calls for reporting the information obtained to the employees during small group meetings. Typically, this consists of summarizing the average scores on the various work-related attitudes measured in the survey. Profiles are created of feelings about the organization, its leadership, the work done, and related topics. Discussions also focus on why the scores are as they are, and what problems are revealed by the feedback. The third and final step involves analyzing problems dealing with communication, decision making, and other organizational processes in order to make plans for dealing with them. Such discussions are usually most effective when they are carefully documented and a specific plan of implementation is made (with someone put in charge of carrying it out).

Survey feedback is a widely used organizational development technique.[54] This is not surprising in view of the advantages it offers. It is efficient, allowing a great deal of information to be collected relatively quickly. Also, it is very flexible and can be tailored to the needs of different organizations facing a variety of problems. However, the technique can be no better than the quality of the questionnaire used— it must measure the things that really matter to the employees. Of course, to derive the maximum benefit from survey feedback, it must have the support of top management. Specifically, the plans developed by the small discussion groups must be capable of implementation with the full approval of the organization. When these conditions are met, survey feedback can be a very effective OD technique.

Sensitivity Training: Developing Personal Insight The method by which small, face-to-face group interaction experiences are used to give people insight into themselves (e.g., who they are, the way others respond to them) is known as **sensitivity training.** Developed in the 1940s, sensitivity training groups (also referred to as *encounter groups, laboratory groups,* or *T-groups*) were among the first organizational development techniques used in organizations (such as Standard Oil and Union Carbide).[55]

The rationale behind sensitivity training is that people are usually not completely open and honest with each other, a condition that thwarts insights into oneself and others. However, when people are placed in special situations within which open, honest communication is allowed and encouraged, personal insights may be gained. To do this, small groups (usually of about eight to fifteen) are created and meet away from the pressures of the job site for several days. An expert trainer (referred to as the *facilitator*) guides the group at all times, helping assure that the proper atmosphere is maintained.

The sessions themselves are completely open with respect to what is discussed. Often, to get the ball rolling, the facilitator will frustrate the group members by not getting involved at all and appearing to be passively goofing off. As members sit around and engage in meaningless chit-chat, they begin to feel angry at the change agent for wasting their time. Once these expressions of anger begin to emerge, the change agent has created the important first step needed to make the session work— he or she has given the group a chance to focus on a current event. At this point, the discussion may be guided into how each of the group members expresses his or her anger toward the others. They are encouraged to continue discussing these themes openly and honestly, and not to hide their true feelings as they would often do on the job. The rule is to openly and honestly share your feelings about others. So, for example, if you think someone is goofing off and relying too much on you, this is the time to say so. Participants are encouraged to respond by giving each other *immediate feedback* to what was said. By doing this, it is reasoned, people will come to learn more about how they interrelate with others, and will become more skilled at interpersonal relations. These are among the major goals of sensitivity groups.

its problems," 14 percent said "negotiating a contract and relationship between the OD practitioner and the organization," 8 percent said "interpersonal skills," and 8 percent said "maintaining the client relationship and following up on the OD intervention." [Eubanks, J. L., Marshall, J. B., & O'Driscoll, M. P. (1990, November). A competency model for OD practitioners. *Training & Development Journal,* pp. 85–90.]

It probably comes as no surprise to you that the effectiveness of sensitivity training is difficult to assess. After all, measuring insight into one's own personality is clearly elusive. Even if interpersonal skills seem to be improved, people will not always be able to successfully transfer their newly learned skills when they leave the artificial training atmosphere and return to their jobs.[56] As a result, sensitivity training tends *not* to be used extensively by itself for OD purposes. Rather, as we will see, it is often used in conjunction with, or as part of, other OD techniques.

Team Building: Creating Effective Work Groups   The technique of **team building** developed in an attempt to apply the techniques and rationale of sensitivity training to work groups. The approach attempts to get members of a work group to diagnose how they work together, and to plan how this may be improved.[57] Given the importance of group efforts in effective organizational functioning, attempts to improve the effectiveness of work groups are likely to have profound effects on organizations. If one assumes that work groups are the basic building blocks of organizations, it follows that organizational change should emphasize changing groups instead of individuals.[58]

Team building begins when members of a group admit that they have a problem and gather data to provide insight about it. The problems that are identified may come from sensitivity training sessions, or more objective sources, such as production figures or attitude surveys. These data are then shared, in a *diagnostic session*, to develop a consensus regarding the group's current strengths and weaknesses. From this, a list of desired changes is created, along with some plans for implementing these changes. In other words, an *action plan* is developed—some task-oriented approach to solving the group's problems as diagnosed. Following this step, the plan is carried out, and its progress is evaluated to determine whether the originally identified problems remain. If the problems are solved, the process is completed and the team may stop meeting. If not, the process should be restarted. (See Figure 16–12 for a summary of these steps.)

Work teams have been used effectively to combat a variety of important organizational problems.[59] For these efforts to be successful, however, all group members must participate in the gathering and evaluating of information as well as in the planning and implementing of action plans. Input from group members is also especially crucial in evaluating the effectiveness of the team building program.[60] Keep in mind that because the team building approach is highly task-oriented, interpersonal problems between group members may be disruptive and need to be neutralized by an outside party. With interpersonal strain out of the way, the stage is set for groups to learn to effectively solve their own problems. However, this does not happen overnight. To be most effective, team building should not be approached as a one-time exercise undertaken during a few days away from the job. Rather, it should be thought of as an ongoing process that takes several months (or even years) to develop. Given the great impact effective groups can have on organizational functioning, efforts to build effective work teams seem quite worthwhile.

An example of a successful team building program can be seen at the France-based multinational corporation Groupe Bull.[61] Instead of using team building exercises among top leaders (who presumably have already bought into the company's philosophies), lower-level executives and managers from companies on several different continents are brought together for several two- to three-week sessions in which they try to solve problems of mutual interest. In one meeting, for example, group participants formulated a worldwide strategy for advertising and consolidated worldwide engineering designs. According to Dr. David L. Dotlich, executive vice president of the Massachusetts-based Bull subsidiary, Bull HN Information Systems,

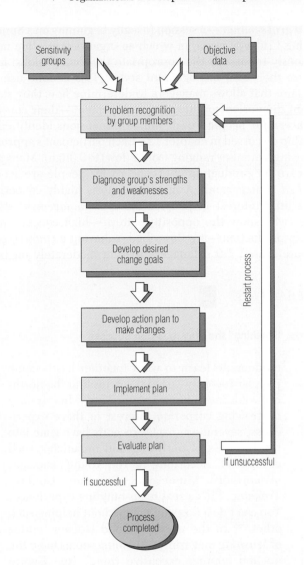

FIGURE 16-12

Team Building: An Overview

Team building, a popular technique of organizational development, follows the steps outlined here.

it is very difficult to develop new relationships and tap new resources and new sources of information during group meetings, but they do it because it is an effective way of getting everyone to understand the global nature of the company's activities. In his own words, "Only those global teams that really have trust and interdependence, are able to see the world as a global business, can make decisions in the company's best interest."[62] (Some other techniques used in team building exercises for attaining high levels of interpersonal trust are not exactly what you might expect. For some interesting examples, see the **OB in Practice** section on pp. 646–647.)

Grid Training: Improving Managerial Effectiveness   Improving the total organization on a long-term basis is the goal of **grid training.** This approach, developed by Blake and Mouton, seeks to promote organizational excellence by fostering concern for both production and people.[69] Working on the premise that most organizational problems stem from poor communication and inadequate planning, Blake and Mouton propose a multistep process for improving organizations by attempting to cultivate these skills.

The initial step consists of a *grid seminar*—a session (usually beginning on a Sunday night and ending the following Friday at noon) in which an organization's line managers (who have been previously trained in the appropriate theory and skills) help organization members analyze their own management styles. This is done using a specially designed questionnaire that allows managers to determine how they stand with respect to two important dimensions of effective management—their *concern for production* and their *concern for people* (recall similar dimensions identified in several approaches to leadership discussed in chapter 12). Each participant's approach on each dimension is scored using a number ranging from 1 (low) to 9 (high). Managers who score low on both concern for production and concern for people are scored *1,1*—evidence of *impoverished management*. A manager who is highly concerned about production but shows little interest in people, the *task management* style, scores *9,1*. In contrast, ones who show the opposite pattern—high concern with people but little concern with production—are described as having a *country club* style of management; they are scored *1,9*. Managers scoring moderately on both

  OB IN PRACTICE

Developing Teamwork in the Wilderness: "Mushing" the Way to Group Success

Getting members of a work group to understand how they work together as a unit, the goal of team building, is certainly challenging. Such a challenging goal calls for challenging measures. Indeed, as part of many team building exercises, group members are put into highly challenging real-life situations that are metaphors for how they have to pull together to meet difficult challenges on the job. The idea is that by facing these difficult off-the-job challenges successfully, they will develop the skills needed for working together effectively on the job. An example is the case of Groupe Bull. The executives in this company did not develop all their team skills by sitting around a conference table and talking. Far from it—they took an adventurous white water rafting trip in the swirling waters of the river Spey in the mountains of Scotland.[63] Learning to work together on navigating the treacherous river while staying afloat, it is assumed, will help team members recognize how they interact with each other while navigating the rough waters of the highly competitive world of international business.

White water rafting is not the only metaphor that has been called on in recent times to help develop work teams. Another challenging activity that takes business executives to the great outdoors to learn to work together has become popular recently—sled dog trips into the northern wilderness, known as *mushing*.[64] In response to growing corporate interest in these experiences, several companies recently have gone into the business of outfitting and organizing such excursions. According to Ted Young, manager of northern Minnesota's Boundary Country Trekking, "It's a real team-building experience. You can't do a dog sled trip without helping each other."[65] In the words of Todd Hoener, editor of *Mushing* magazine, "Mushing seems to be the up and coming executive thing" (see Figure 16–13).[66]

The analogies between mushing and managing people back on the job are interesting. One of the first steps in preparing an expedition into the wild calls for harnessing the five to seven dogs to each sled. In completing this process, which takes about an hour, executives can see how the dogs react differently based on whom each one is paired with. Working with the dogs, one quickly learns that each dog is an individual, and can be a bit ornery; the trick is to put them together so they can perform effectively. The parallel to composing effective work groups on the job is one to which managers can easily relate. The analogy to different corporate types can also be seen in the different dogs' personalities.

dimensions, the 5,5 pattern, are said to follow a *middle-of-the-road management style*. Finally, there are individuals who are highly concerned with both production and people, those scoring 9,9. This is the most desirable pattern, and it represents what is known as *team management*. These various patterns are represented in a diagram like that shown in Figure 16–14 (see p. 648), known as the *managerial grid.*®

After a manager's position along the grid is determined, training begins to improve concern over production (planning skills) and concern over people (communication skills) in order to reach the ideal, *9,9* state. This training consists of organizationwide team training aimed at helping work group members interact more effectively with each other. Then this training is expanded to help reduce conflict between groups that must work with each other. Additional phases of training include efforts to identify the extent to which the organization is meeting its strategic goals and then comparing this performance to an ideal. Next, plans are made to meet these goals, and these plans are implemented in the organization. Finally, progress toward the goals is continuously assessed, and problem areas are identified.

There's Wyoming, the leader who never seems to have any fun. If the team stops and the other dogs start playing, he just stands there, his brown eyes focused on the trail ahead. On the other hand, there are the leaders Gillis and Sag, sisters who keep up team morale by such antics as jumping in the sled when no one is looking. . . . Smoky is the leader of the group . . . he's respected because he works his buns off. What Smoky says, others do.[67]

Probably the ultimate lesson to be learned from the mushing experience was articulated by Walter Kissling, the chief operating officer of the Minneapolis-based chemical maker H. B. Fuller Company: Five rather small dogs [35 to 55 pounds] can be very powerful. If you can get a team pulling in one direction, you can get enormous power out of them. If you can do that in management, think of what the results are."[68] As fascinating as these techniques are, their effectiveness will depend ultimately on the extent to which participants actually come away from the experience with the type of insight desired—and translate these insights into meaningful work-related activities. Thus, these fascinating wilderness experiences must be integrated into a highly work focused team building plan (as summarized in Figure 16–12) rather than left as one-time, stand-alone experiences.

FIGURE 16–13

"Mushing": A Technique for Developing Effective Teamwork

As a means of creating a spirit of cooperation and a sense of trust in one another, members of work teams sometimes participate in challenging physical activities, such as sled dog racing—known as *mushing*—shown here. The underlying idea is that the challenges confronted in the wild are useful metaphors for appreciating the challenges faced on the job, thereby helping to develop cooperative relations between coworkers.

FIGURE 16-14

The Managerial Grid®: Key
Dimensions of Management

A manager's standing
along two key
dimensions—concern
for production, and
concern for people—can
be illustrated by means
of a diagram such as this
one, known as the
managerial grid.® Blake
and Mouton, the
developers of the
popular organizational
development technique
grid training, suggest
that organizational
effectiveness results
when managers are
trained to score high
on both dimensions.
(*Source:* Based on
suggestions by Blake &
Mouton, 1969; see Note
69.)

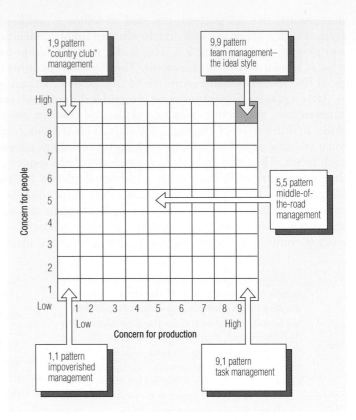

As you can tell, full implementation of grid training involves many changes, making it difficult to tell which aspects of the program may be responsible for improved organizational functioning. Some skeptics would argue that because grid training is prepackaged and designed to be used in all organizations, it may not meet the special development needs of any particular organization. Specifically, it always assumes that being concerned about both people and production is the best management style. However, as we described in chapter 12, there are many situations in which effective leadership requires much more of one of these skills than the other. Regardless, the technique has been identified as a successful mechanism for implementing planned organizational change in several studies.[70] Because the grid approach trains managers to train their coworkers, it has been widely used—allowing several hundred thousand people to reap its benefits.

Quality of Work Life Programs: Humanizing the Workplace   When you think of work, do you think of drudgery? Although many people believe these two terms go together naturally, it has become increasingly popular in recent years to systematically improve the quality of life on many jobs. As more and more people demand satisfying and personally fulfilling places to work (a movement that became popular in the 1970s), organizational development practitioners have attempted to systematically create work situations that enhance employees' motivation, satisfaction, and commitment—factors that may contribute to high levels of organizational performance. Such efforts are known collectively as **quality of work life** (**QWL**) programs. Specifically, such programs are ways of increasing organizational output and improving quality by involving employees in the decisions that affect them on their jobs. Typically, such programs support highly democratic treatment of employees at all levels and encourage their participation in decision making. Although many approaches to

Test Bank question 16.41 relates to material on this page.

improving the quality of work life exist, they all share the common goal of humanizing the workplace.[71]

One popular approach to improving the quality of work life involves *work restructuring*—the process of changing the way jobs are done to make them more interesting to workers.[72] If this sounds familiar to you, it might be because we already discussed several such approaches to redesigning jobs—including *job enlargement, job enrichment,* and the *job characteristics model*—in our discussion of motivation in chapter 4. In the present context, note that such techniques represent effective ways of improving the quality of work life for employees.

Another approach to improving the quality of work life, and an increasingly popular one in recent years, has been imported from Japan—**quality circles (QCs).** These are small groups of volunteers (usually around ten) who meet regularly (usually weekly) to identify and solve problems related to (1) the quality of the work they perform, and (2) the conditions under which people do their jobs.[73] An organization may have several QCs operating at once, each dealing with a particular work area about which it has the most expertise. To help them work effectively, the members of the circle usually receive some form of training in problem solving. Large companies such as Westinghouse, Hewlett-Packard, and Eastman Kodak, to name only a few, have included QCs as part of their QWL efforts.[74] Groups have dealt with issues such as how to reduce vandalism, how to create safer and more comfortable working environments, and how to improve product quality. Research has shown that although quality circles are very effective at bringing about short-term improvements in quality of work life (i.e., those lasting up to eighteen months), they are less effective at creating more permanent changes.[75] Thus, they may be recognized as useful temporary strategies for enhancing organizational effectiveness.

As you might imagine, a variety of benefits (even if short-term ones) might result from QWL programs—both work restructuring and QCs. These fall into three major categories.[76] The most direct benefit is usually increased job satisfaction and organizational commitment among the work force. A second benefit is increased productivity. In fact, a recent study comparing the performance of employees who participated in a QC program with a control group (an equivalent group that had not participated in such a program) revealed that in the year following the group involvement, those who had participated received higher job performance ratings and were more likely to get promoted than those who had not participated in the QC program.[77] To the extent that the company benefits from having such highly valued employees, QC programs clearly help improve company performance. Related to these first two benefits is a third—namely, increased organizational effectiveness (e.g., profitability, goal attainment). Many companies, including industrial giants such as Ford, General Electric, and AT&T, have active QWL programs and are reportedly quite pleased with their results.[78]

Achieving these benefits is not automatic, however. Two major potential pitfalls must be avoided for QWL programs to be successfully implemented. First, both management and labor must cooperate in designing the program. Should any one side believe that the program is really just a method of gaining an advantage over the other, it is doomed to fail. Second, the plans agreed to by all concerned parties must be fully implemented. It is too easy for action plans developed in QWL groups to be forgotten amid the hectic pace of daily activities. It is the responsibility of employees at all levels—from the highest-ranking manager to the lowest-level laborer—to follow through on their part of the plan.

Management by Objectives: Clarifying Organizational Goals You may recall that in chapter 4 we detailed the positive motivational benefits of setting specific goals. As you might imagine, not only individuals but also entire organizations stand to benefit from setting specific goals. For example, an organization may strive to "raise production" and "improve the quality" of its manufactured goods. These goals, noble and well intentioned though they may be, may not be as useful to an organization as more specific ones, such as "increase production of widgets by 15 percent" or "lower the failure rate of widgets by 25 percent." After all, as the old saying goes, "It's usually easier to get somewhere if you know where you're going." Peter Drucker, consulting for General Electric during the early 1950s, was well aware of this idea, and is credited with promoting the benefits of specifying clear organizational goals—a technique known as **management by objectives (MBO)**.[79]

The MBO process, summarized in Figure 16–15, consists of three basic steps. First, goals are selected that employees will try to attain to best serve the needs of the organization. The goals should be selected by managers and their subordinates together. The goals must be set mutually, not imposed on subordinates by their managers. Further, these goals should be directly measurable and have some time frame attached to them. Goals that cannot be measured, or that have no time limits (e.g., "make the company better"), are useless. As part of this first step, it is crucial that managers and their subordinates work together to plan ways of attaining the goals they have selected—what is known as an *action plan*.

After goals are set and action plans have been developed to attain them, the second step calls for *implementation*—carrying out the plan and regularly assessing its progress. Is the plan working? Are the goals being approximated? Are there any problems being encountered in attempting to meet the goals? Such questions need to be considered while implementing an action plan. If the plan is failing, a mid-course correction may be in order—changing the plan, the way it's carried out, or even the goal itself.

After monitoring progress toward the goal, the third step may be instituted: *evaluation*—that is, assessing goal attainment. Were the organization's goals reached? If so, what new goals should be set to improve things still further? If not, what new plans can be initiated to help meet the goals? Because the ultimate assessment of the extent to which goals are met helps determine the selection of new goals, the MBO process is shown in Figure 16–15 as a continuous one.

As described here, MBO represents a potentially effective source of planning and implementing strategic change for organizations. Individual efforts designed to meet

FIGURE 16–15

Management by Objectives: Developing Organizations through Goal Setting

The organizational development technique of *management by objectives* requires managers and their subordinates to work together on setting and trying to achieve important organizational goals. The steps in the process are outlined here.

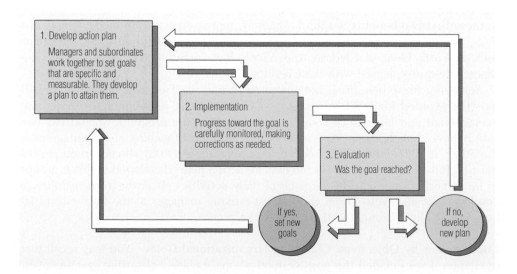

Test Bank questions 16.43, 16.65, and 16.71 relate to material on this page.

**NORTHWEST AIRLINES—ATLANTA
1989 CONTINUOUS IMPROVEMENT**
The Year of the Customer . . . External and Internal

1989 Strategic Objectives for the Atlanta Base

1. A 50 percent reduction in number of on-the-job injuries.
2. JT8D engine turn time of 43 work days.
3. DC-9 check average turn time of 10 days—nonpaint; 14 days—with paint.
4. Component shops turn 90 percent of the rotable—repairable in 14 days.
5. Metal finishing turn 98 percent of the units in 20 days.
6. 98 percent of M & E personnel receive 40 hours of training.
7. 95 percent on-time Atlanta launch departures.

FIGURE 16–16   Signs of MBO at Northwest Airlines

As part of an MBO program at Northwest Airlines, this document (only part of which is shown here) was prepared to remind employees of some of the key objectives sought for Atlanta-based employees in 1989. (*Source:* Based on material in Midas & Devine, 1991; see Note 81. Reprinted with permission from *National Productivity Review, 10* (3), Summer 1991. Copyright 1991 by Executive Enterprises, Inc., 22 West 21st Street, New York, NY 10010-6904. All Rights Reserved.)

organizational goals get the individual employee and the organization itself working together toward common ends. Hence, systemwide change results. Of course, for MBO to work, everyone involved in the process has to buy into it. Because the program typically entails a great amount of participation by lower-level employees, top managers must be willing to accept and support the cooperation and involvement of all employees. Making MBO work also requires a great deal of time—anywhere from three to five years.[80] Hence, MBO may be inappropriate in organizations that do not have the time to commit to making it work. Despite these considerations, MBO has become one of the most widely used techniques for affecting organizational change in recent years. It not only is used on an ad hoc basis by many organizations, but also constitutes an ingrained element of the organizational culture in some companies, such as Hewlett-Packard and IBM. An MBO program was used effectively by Northwest Airlines in 1989 to help improve various areas of performance in its Atlanta-based crew.[81] Figure 16-16 shows part of a Northwest Airlines internal document listing the key objectives sought. The program was reportedly effective in meeting these and other vital goals, thereby helping to improve Northwest's overall safety and performance record. Given the success MBO has experienced (not only as an organizational development technique, but also as a motivational tool and an aid to effective performance appraisals), its widespread use today is not surprising.[82]

The Effectiveness of Organizational Development: Does It Really Work?

Thus far, we have described some of the major techniques used by OD practitioners to improve organizational functioning. As is probably clear, carrying out these techniques requires a considerable amount of time, money, and effort. Accordingly, it is appropriate to ask if the investment involved in implementing OD interventions is worth it. In other words, does OD really work? Given the increasing popularity of OD in a wide variety of organizations, the question is more important than ever.[83]

Research has revealed that the answer to the question is a qualified "yes." In other words, although many studies have revealed beneficial effects associated with OD programs, the findings are far from unanimous. Consider, for example, research on quality circles. Although many researchers have found that quality circles help reduce organizational costs and improve employees' attitudes, other studies reported no such beneficial effects.[84] Mixed results have also been obtained in many studies assessing the effectiveness of sensitivity training programs. For example, whereas such programs often lead to temporary differences in the way people interact with others, the results tend to be short-lived on the job, and are not related to permanent changes in the way people behave.[85] Thus, whereas OD may have many positive effects, not all desired outcomes may be realized.

A recent review by Porras, Robertson, and Goldman compared the results of forty-nine OD studies published between 1975 and 1986.[86] Among the different types of OD interventions studied were those we have described: *grid training, MBO, QWL, survey feedback, sensitivity groups,* and *team building.* The investigators categorized the research with respect to whether they found the effects of the interventions to be beneficial, negative, or nonexistent. The outcomes studied were both individual (e.g., job satisfaction) and organizational (e.g., profit, productivity) in nature. The results, summarized in Figure 16–17, reveal some interesting findings.

A sizable percentage of the studies found effects of the various interventions beneficial. However, these beneficial results were not as impressive for individual outcomes (where the vast majority of the studies demonstrated no effects of any of the interventions) as they were for organizational outcomes (where many studies found positive effects). Clearly, the benefits of OD techniques are more firmly established with respect to improving organizational functioning than with respect to improving individuals' job attitudes. Nevertheless, a recent review of the evidence

FIGURE 16–17

Organizational Development: Evidence of Its Effectiveness

In reviewing forty-nine studies of organizational development techniques published between 1975 and 1986, Porras, Robertson, and Goldman found that organizational outcomes (e.g., pro-ductivity) benefited more often than individual outcomes (e.g., job satisfaction). (*Source:* Based on data reported by Porras, Robertson, & Goldman, 1992; see Note 50.)

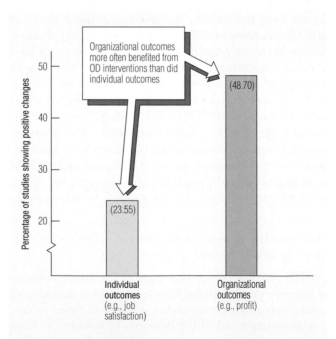

reveals that team building is the most effective technique for changing work attitudes (closely followed by sensitivity training).[87]

We hasten to add that any conclusions about where the effectiveness of OD lies or what techniques are most effective should be qualified in several important ways. First, research has shown that OD interventions tend to be more effective among blue-collar employees than among white-collar employees.[88] Second, it has been found that the beneficial effects of OD can be enhanced by using several techniques instead of just one. Specifically, studies in which four or more OD programs were used together yielded positive findings more frequently than those in which fewer techniques were used.[89] Thus, it appears that the effectiveness of OD efforts can be enhanced by relying not on any one single technique, but rather on a combination of several.[90]

Despite the importance of attempting to evaluate the effectiveness of OD interventions, a great many of them go unevaluated. Although there are undoubtedly many reasons for this, one key factor is the difficulty of assessing change. Because many factors can cause people to behave differently in organizations, and because such behaviors may be difficult to measure, many OD practitioners avoid the problem of measuring change altogether. In a related vein, political pressures to justify OD programs may discourage some OD professionals from honestly and accurately assessing their effectiveness. After all, in doing so, one runs the risk of scientifically demonstrating one's wasted time and money (a similar point was made in chapter 3 regarding the assessment of organizational training programs).

In cases where OD has been studied, however, the research is more often than not conducted in a manner that leaves its conclusions seriously open to question.[91] In particular, it is often very difficult to isolate exactly which aspects of an organizational intervention were responsible for the changes noted. Also, because OD practices are a novelty to most employees, they may have a tendency to produce temporary improvements (recall our discussion of the Hawthorne effect in chapter 1).[92] In other words, serious questions may be raised about the true effectiveness of organizational development efforts as revealed in existing research.

We may conclude that organizational development is an approach that shows considerable promise in its ability to benefit organizations and the individuals working within them. With further refinements in assessing the value of OD programs, a great many benefits may be derived—benefits for the OD practitioner who seeks to improve organizations, for the organizational scientist who seeks to understand organizational behavior, and ultimately, of course, for the people who make up the organizations themselves.

Controversial Aspects of Organizational Development

If you think about the great variety of (sometimes unusual) methods used in organizational development interventions, coupled with the complicated mosaic pattern of their success, you shouldn't be surprised that these techniques sometimes generate controversy.[93] Although scientists and practitioners alike may take issue with just about any aspect of OD, two key focal issues have emerged lately—first, whether OD should focus on process or take a more results-oriented approach, and second, whether OD is inherently unethical.

Focus on Process or Results?   For the most part, the OD techniques we've described (as well as a variety of other different management tools) have focused on *how* to get things done (e.g., using certain exercises ranging from simple group discussions to elaborate treks in the wilderness) more than on exactly *what* should be accomplished. Certainly, some general goals are often stated, but the emphasis is generally on using the techniques assuming that they will sometime yield benefits. Although OD *is* by definition results-oriented, there can be no doubt that practitioners have become preoccupied by the processes themselves. Indeed, as we noted earlier, OD activities frequently become management fads; as one company uses a technique, others quickly jump on the bandwagon, for fear of not remaining competitive. Management scholars Mitroff and Mohrman expressed this situation clearly by noting that "U.S. business easily fall prey to every new management fad promising a painless solution, especially when it was presented in a neat, bright package. But all simple formulas are eventually bound to fail."[94]

In agreement with this pessimistic observation are management consultants Robert H. Schaffer and Harvey A. Thomson, who have recently countered the process orientation of organizational development by arguing that successful change programs should begin with results, and not with an assortment of activities.[95] They call existing OD programs "corporate rain dances" in that they *may* yield positive results, but not necessarily as a result of the programs themselves. Schaffer and Thomson's prescription calls for using results-driven programs—those that lead to specific, measurable improvements in a short period of time. (This idea may sound familiar, because it follows from the basic tenet of goal setting described in chapter 4—namely, to set *specific* goals. Unfortunately, when applied to management by objectives programs, the goals set are sometimes far too general to be as useful as possible.) A problem noted about OD techniques is that they too often define effort in a general, long-term fashion (e.g., "We're going to be considered to have the best-quality production in the industry") instead of as measurable, short-term goals for improvement (e.g., "By two months from today, we will settle 95 percent of all claims within one week").

As an example of their approach in action, Schaffer and Thomson describe an automotive parts plant plagued by problems of poor quality. The plant superintendent asked the manager of one assembly line to work with the employees and the plant engineers to reduce their most prevalent defect by 30 percent within two months. This goal was met on time, and the effort soon was extended to other assembly lines, where the effects were equally positive. In essence, "the results-driven path strikes out specific targets and matches resources, tools, and action plans to the requirements of reaching those targets. As a consequence, managers know what they are trying to achieve and when it should be done, and how it can be evaluated."[96]

Clearly, Schaffer and Thomson's approach makes good sense. (Indeed, it is founded on one of the best established principles of organizational behavior described in this text!) Their approach, however, does not necessarily render OD techniques obsolete, in large part because these tools are not necessarily designed to have an immediate impact on organizational functioning. In fact, by definition, a *development* tool is meant to have the long-term benefit of developing managerial talent for the long run (as opposed to *training* people to solve immediate problems). If you think of OD as a long-term investment in improving the insight and managerial skills of supervisory personnel, it's difficult to accept Schaffer and Thomson's approach as a substitute for OD. Instead, it appears that *both* long-term (process-oriented) and more immediate (results-oriented) techniques may have their place in the toolbox of today's organizational practitioner. Imagine a physician encouraging patients to lead a healthy lifestyle marked by good nutrition and exercise; to condemn this advice simply because it does not also provide relief from an immediate ailment would be misleading. In organizations, too, long-term, healthy development, *as well as* seeking solutions to immediate problems, is important.

Is Organizational Development Inherently Unethical?   By its very nature, OD applies powerful social science techniques in an attempt to change individual attitudes and behaviors. From the perspective of a manager attempting to accomplish various goals, such tools are immediately recognized as very useful. However, if you think about it from the perspective of the individual being affected, several ethical questions immediately come to mind.

For example, it has been argued that OD techniques impose the values of the organization on the individual without taking the individual's own attitudes into account.[97] This is a very one-sided approach, reflecting the imposition of the more powerful organization on the less powerful individual. A related issue is that this process does not provide any free choice on the part of the employees.[98] As a result, it may be seen as *coercive and manipulative*. When faced with a "do it, or else" situation, employees tend to have little free choice, and are forced to allow themselves to be manipulated, a degrading and humiliating prospect. Another issue is that the unequal power relationship between the organization and its employees makes it possible for the true intent of OD techniques to be misrepresented. As an example, imagine that an MBO technique is presented to employees as a means of allowing greater organizational participation, whereas in reality it is used as a means for holding individuals responsible for their poor performance and punishing them as a result. Although such a thing might not happen, the potential for abuse of this type *might* exist, and the potential to misuse the technique—even if not originally intended— might later prove to be too great a temptation.

Despite these considerations, many professionals do not agree that OD is inherently unethical. To claim that OD is unethical, it has been countered, is to say that the practice of management is itself unethical. After all, the very act of going to work for an organization requires one to submit to the organization's values and the overall values of the society at large.[99] One cannot help but face life situations in which others' values are imposed. This is not to say that organizations have the right to impose patently unethical values on people for the purpose of making a profit (e.g., stealing from customers). Indeed, because they have the potential to abuse their power (such as in the MBO example above), organizations have a special obligation to refrain from doing so. Although abuses of organizational power are all too common (see chapter 11), OD itself is not necessarily the culprit. Indeed, like any other tool (even a gun!), OD is not inherently good or evil. Instead, *whether the tool is used for good or evil will depend on the individual using it*. With this in mind, the ethical use of OD interventions will require that they be supervised by professionals in an organization that places a high value on ethics. To the extent that top management officials embrace ethical values and behave ethically themselves, norms for behaving ethically are likely to develop in organizations. When an organization has a strong ethical culture, it is unlikely that OD practitioners would even think of misusing their power to harm individuals. The need to develop such a culture has been recognized as a way for organizations to take not only moral leadership in their communities, but financial leadership as well.

After considering both sides of this issue, you will probably wish to draw your own conclusions about this matter. The only thing we can be sure about here is that the debate is not settled, and it is likely to remain a key question for years to come. One reason the issue might not be put to rest anytime soon is that executives are becoming increasingly concerned about the importance of ethics in their organizations. Given corporations' ongoing concerns about being competitive, it is also likely that techniques of organizational development will remain popular in the years to come. (At least, this is likely to be the case in the United States. Given the proliferation of multinational corporations, the question of whether this social technology

AN INTERNATIONAL/MULTICULTURAL PERSPECTIVE

Cultural Barriers to Effective OD Interventions: The Importance of Matching OD Values to National Culture Values

Warren Bennis, an expert in organizational development, recounts an incident in which a large Swiss company terminated an OD program after the company president found the program's egalitarian values inconsistent with the values of his Swiss Army training—that authority is based on one's position in an organizational hierarchy.[100] Steele tells a similar story of his failed experiences at attempting to introduce OD to Great Britain.[101] Apparently, there was a clash between the expectations of openness underlying the OD techniques and British norms encouraging the avoidance of "unsuitable" topics. These examples suggest that the underlying assumptions behind many OD interventions may clash with cultural values operating in organizations. Thus, OD practitioners apparently require a great deal of knowledge about the culture of the nations in which their techniques are to be used before they can expect beneficial results.

What elements of social culture are most likely to account for cross-national differences in organizational functioning? Based on a questionnaire administered to 116,000 employees of a large multinational corporation (IBM) working in forty countries, Hofstede identified four critical elements of culture.[102]

1. **Power distance.** The degree to which the unequal distribution of power within organizations is accepted by members of society
2. **Uncertainty avoidance.** How much members of a society are threatened by uncertain and ambiguous situations
3. **Individualism-collectivism.** The tendency to take care of oneself and one's family versus

the tendency to work together for the collective good of everyone
4. **Masculinity-femininity.** The extent to which highly assertive values predominate (e.g., acquiring money and goods at the expense of others) versus showing sensitivity and concern for others' welfare

In recent years, organizational scientists have disclosed some very interesting and important findings regarding these cultural dimensions. For example, Kedia and Bhagat reviewed literature revealing that nations were most likely to accept new technologies when certain cultural elements prevailed.[103] Specifically, among other things, they note that technology is more likely to be accepted and successfully implemented by nations that have an individualistic orientation (e.g., Germany), than those with a collective one (e.g., Venezuela). The point is that cultural values operating within nations are expected to influence the likelihood that new technology will be adopted. If a culture's prevailing norms and values are threatened by a new technology, it is unlikely to be accepted (e.g., a machine that makes workers' jobs more equal might not be accepted in a culture like India's, where high degrees of power distance are culturally embraced). In fact, in the case of developing nations, cultural factors may be even more important than the strategic value of the technology itself when it comes to the willingness to import new technology.

Given that Hofstede's four key cultural dimensions are critical to the successful adoption of new technologies, they may likewise be an important part of any planned organizational change efforts. With this in mind, Jaeger argued

can be effectively imported to other nations is extremely important. As shown in the **International/Multicultural Perspective** section that begins on the preceding page, American OD practitioners may be in for some serious surprises—and disappointments—when they try to practice their work in different nations.)

that the values underlying most OD techniques may be described as low on power distance, uncertainty avoidance, and masculinity, and moderate on individualism.[104] He reasoned that countries whose national values come closest to this pattern (e.g., the Scandinavian nations) may be the most successful in using OD techniques, whereas those that are highly different (e.g., most Latin American nations) may be most unsuccessful (see summary in Figure 16–18).

However, because not all OD techniques are alike, Jaeger analyzed specific intervention techniques with respect to their underlying cultural values. For example, management by objectives, a very popular OD technique in the United States, may have caught on because it promotes the American values of willingness to take risks and working aggressively at attaining high performance. However, because MBO also encourages superiors and subordinates to negotiate freely with each other, the technique has been generally unsuccessful in France, where high power distance between superiors and subordinates is culturally accepted.[105] Following similar reasoning, one may expect OD techniques

such as survey feedback to be unsuccessful in the Southeast Asian nation of Brunei, where the prevailing cultural value is such that problems are unlikely to be confronted openly.[106] These and other examples illustrate an important point: *the effectiveness of OD techniques will depend, in part, on the extent to which the values of the technique match the underlying values of the national culture in which it is employed.*

Given this, we may conclude that OD practitioners must fully appreciate the cultural norms of the nations where they are operating. Failure to do so not only may make OD interventions unsuccessful, but in addition may even have dangerous negative consequences. Therefore, as part of planning an OD intervention, OD practitioners are strongly advised to carefully match the techniques they use to the values of the host culture. The most rigidly held values of a culture should never be challenged by the OD techniques. Remember: these techniques are designed to improve the functioning of the organization *within its culture.* Any techniques that clash with prevailing cultural norms should be avoided.

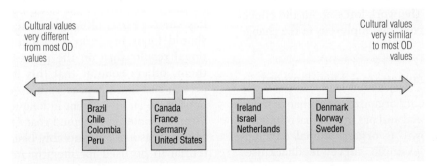

FIGURE 16–18 Organizational Development: Its Fit with Cultural Values

Organizational development (OD) techniques are more successful when the underlying values of the technique match the cultural values of the nation in which it is used. General OD values conform more to the cultural values of some nations, shown on the right (where OD is more likely to be accepted), and less to others, shown on the left (where OD is less likely to be accepted). (*Source:* Based on suggestions by Jaeger, 1986; see Note 104.)

SUMMARY AND REVIEW

Forces behind Organizational Change

Changes in organizations may be either planned or unplanned, and they may be based internal or external to the organization. Planned internal changes may include changes in products or services and changes in administrative systems. Planned external changes include the introduction of new technologies and advances in information processing and communication. Unplanned internal changes include shifts in the demographic characteristics of the work force and responses to performance gaps. Unplanned external change may result from governmental regulation as well as from economic competition.

The Process of Organizational Change

Organizations may change with respect to their organizational structure (responsibilities and procedures used), the technology used on the job, and the people who perform the work. Change is likely to occur whenever the benefits associated with making a change (i.e., dissatisfaction with current conditions, the availability of desirable alternatives, and the existence of a plan for achieving that alternative) outweigh the costs involved. In general, people are resistant to change because of individual factors (e.g., economic insecurity, fear of the unknown) and organizational factors (e.g., the stability of work groups, threats to the existing balance of power). However, resistance to change can be overcome in several ways, including educating the work force about the effects of the changes and involving employees in the change process.

Techniques of Organizational Development

Techniques for planning organizational change in order to enhance personal and organizational outcomes are collectively known as **organizational development** practices. For example, **survey feedback** uses questionnaires and/or interviews as the basis for identifying organizational problems, which are then addressed in planning sessions. **Sensitivity training** is a technique in which group discussions are used to enhance interpersonal awareness and reduce interpersonal friction. **Team building** involves using work groups to diagnose and develop specific plans for solving problems with respect to their functioning as a work unit. **Grid training** focuses on efforts to improve managers' concern for people and their concern for production by training them in communication skills and planning skills. **Quality of work life** programs attempt to humanize the workplace by involving employees in the decisions affecting them (e.g., through **quality circle** meetings) and by restructuring the jobs themselves. Finally, **management by objectives** focuses on attempts by managers and their subordinates to work together at setting important organizational goals and developing a plan to help meet them. The rationale underlying all six of these techniques is that they may enhance organizational functioning by involving employees in identifying and solving organizational problems.

The effectiveness of most organizational development programs is not systematically assessed in practice, and the few studies that do attempt to measure the success of such programs are not carefully conducted. However, those studies that have systematically evaluated organizational development programs generally find them to be successful in improving organizational functioning and, to a lesser degree, individual satisfaction.

Controversial Aspects of OD

Finally, OD has proven to be controversial in two key areas. First, although some believe that OD should focus more on attaining specific organizational results than on the processes used to attain them, others counter that this is a short-term approach and that the processes used in OD interventions make an investment in long-term improvement. Second, some have argued that OD is unethical for several reasons, most notably because it has the potential to be used for illegitimate purposes. However, others counter that OD is just a tool and that it is people who are at fault for using it inappropriately.

KEY TERMS

dual-core model: The theory recognizing that changes in the administration of organizations come from upper management (i.e., from the top down), whereas changes in the work performed come from the technical specialists within organizations (i.e., from the bottom up).

grid training: The OD technique designed to strengthen

managers' communication skills (their concern for people) and their planning skills (their concern for production).

horizontal linkage model: The theory specifying the importance of the marketing and research functions of organizations in the introduction of new products and services.

management by objectives (MBO): The technique by which managers and their subordinates work together to set, and then meet, organizational goals.

organizational change: Alterations in the operations of organizations that are either planned or unplanned, and are a result of either internal or external influences.

organizational development (OD): A set of social science techniques designed to plan change in organizational work settings, for purposes of enhancing the personal development of individuals and improving the effectiveness of organizational functioning.

quality circles (QCs): An approach to improving the quality of work life, in which small groups of volunteers meet regularly to identify and solve problems related to the work they perform and the conditions under which they work.

quality of work life (QWL): An OD technique designed to improve organizational functioning by humanizing the workplace, making it more democratic, and involving employees in decision making.

resistance to change: The tendency for employees to be unwilling to go along with organizational changes, either because of individual fears of the unknown, or organizational impediments (such as *structural inertia*).

sensitivity training: An OD technique that seeks to enhance employees' understanding of their own behavior and its impact on others. Such changes, it is believed, will reduce the interpersonal conflicts that interfere with organizational effectiveness.

structural inertia: The organizational forces acting on employees, encouraging them to perform their jobs in certain ways (e.g., training, reward systems), thereby making them resistant to change.

survey feedback: An OD technique in which questionnaires and interviews are used to collect information about issues of concern to an organization. This information is shared with employees and is used as the basis for planning organizational change.

team building: An OD technique in which employees discuss problems related to their work group's performance. On the basis of these discussions, specific problems are identified and plans for solving them are devised and implemented.

QUESTIONS FOR DISCUSSION

1. Some changes in organizations are unplanned, whereas others are the result of deliberate, planned actions. Give examples of each of these varieties of change and explain their implications for organizational functioning.

2. Suppose you are having difficulty managing a small group of subordinates who work in an office 1,000 miles away from your home base. What kinds of changes in *structure, technology,* and *people* can be implemented to more closely supervise these distant employees?

3. Under what conditions will people be most willing to make changes in organizations? Explain your answer and give an example.

4. Suppose that you are a top executive of a large organization about to undertake an ambitious restructuring involving massive changes in job responsibilities for most employees. Explain why people might be resistant to such changes and what steps could be taken to overcome this resistance.

5. Imagine that you are supervising ten employees who are not getting along. Their constant fighting is interfering with their job performance. Identify any two different *organizational development* techniques that might be employed to address this problem. Explain why they may help. Describe the steps taken to implement these techniques.

6. Overall, how effective is organizational development in improving organizational functioning? With respect to what factors does it work or not work?

7. Argue for or against the following statement: "Organizational development techniques are universally effective and may be effectively applied in any culture."

8. Argue for or against each of the following statements: (1) "Organizational development techniques focus too much on the process used at the expense of the results desired." (2) "Organizational development is inherently unethical and should not be used."

NOTES

1. Woodman, R. W. (1989). Organizational change and development: New arenas for inquiry and action. *Journal of Management, 15,* 205–228.

2. Barczak, G., Smith, C., & Wilemon, D. (1987, Autumn). Managing large-scale organizational change. *Organizational Dynamics,* 23–35.

3. Ingrassia, P., & White, J. B. (1992, February 25). GM posts record '91 loss of $4.45 billion, sends tough messages to UAW on closings. *Wall Street Journal*, pp. A3, A5.

4. Nystrom, P. C., & Starbuck, W. H. (1984, Spring). To avoid organizational crises, unlearn. *Organizational Dynamics*, 44–60.

5. Calonius, E. (1990, December 3). Federal Express's battle overseas. *Fortune*, pp. 137–140.

6. Tichy, N., & Charan, R. (1990, November–December). Citicorp faces the world: An interview with John Reed. *Harvard Business Review*, pp. 135–144.

7. Daft, R. L. (1986). *Organization theory and design* (2nd ed.). St. Paul, MN: West.

8. Cobb, A. T., & Marguiles, N. (1981). Organizational development: A political perspective. *Academy of Management Review*, 6, 49–59.

9. McCarty, M. (1990, October 30). PepsiCo to consolidate its restaurants, combining U.S. and foreign operations. *Wall Street Journal*, p. A4.

10. Daft, R. L. (1982). Bureaucratic versus nonbureaucratic structure and the process of innovation and change. In S. B. Bachrach (Ed.), *Research in the sociology of organizations* (Vol. 1, pp. 56–88). Greenwich, CT: JAI Press.

11. Gaertner, G. H., Gaertner, K. N., & Akinnusi, D. M. (1984). Environment, strategy, and implementation of administrative change: The case of civil service reform. *Academy of Management Journal*, 27, 525–543.

12. Naisbitt, J. (1982). *Megatrends*. New York: Warner.

13. Carroll, P. B. (1992, February 25). Technology. *Wall Street Journal*, p. B1.

14. Taylor, A. (1990, November 19). Why Toyota keeps getting better and better and better. *Fortune*, pp. 66–79.

15. Foulkes, F. K., & Hirsch, J. L. (1984). People make robots work. *Harvard Business Review*, 62 (1), pp. 94–102.

16. Keen, P. G. W. (1988). *Competing in time: Using telecommunications for competitive advantage* (rev. ed.). Cambridge, MA: Ballinger.

17. Begole, C. (1991, May). How to get the productivity edge. *Working Woman*, pp. 47–60.

18. Miller, W. A. (1991, May 6). A new perspective for tomorrow's workforce. *Industry Week*, pp. 7–8, 17.

19. Johnson, W. R., & Packer, A. H. (1987). *Workforce 2000*. Indianapolis: Hudson Institute.

20. Kiplinger, A. A., & Kiplinger, K. A. (1989). *America in the global '90s*. Washington, DC: Kiplinger Books.

21. See Note 18.

22. See Note 18.

23. Colvin, G. (1984, October 15). What baby boomers will buy next. *Fortune*, pp. 28–34.

24. Dennis, H. (1988). *Fourteen steps in managing an aging work force*. Lexington, MA: Lexington Books.

25. Loden, M., & Rosener, J. B. (1991). *Workforce America! Managing employee diversity as a vital resource*. Homewood, IL: Business One Irwin.

26. Wheelen, T. L., & Hunger, J. D. (1989). *Strategic management and business policy* (3rd ed.). Reading, MA: Addison-Wesley.

27. Sherman, S. P. (1991, January 14). Digital's daring comeback. *Fortune*, pp. 100–103.

28. See Note 26.

29. Singh, J. V., House, R. J., & Tucker, D. J. (1986). Organizational change and mortality. *Administrative Science Quarterly*, 31, 587–611.

30. Barnes, Z. E. (1987). Change in the Bell System. *Academy of Management Executive*, 1, 43–46. (Quote from p. 43.)

31. Marcus, A. A. (1988). Implementing externally induced innovations: A comparison of rule-bound and autonomous approaches. *Academy of Management Journal*, 31, 235–256.

32. Noble, B. P. (1992, January 26). As seen from a wheelchair. *New York Times*, p. F25.

33. Powell, B., & Stone, J. (1991, July 15). "The deal of the decade." *Newsweek*, p. 40.

34. Kilmann, R. H., & Covin, T. J. (1987). *Corporate transformation: Revitalizing organizations for a competitive world*. San Francisco: Jossey-Bass.

35. Glueck, W. F. (1979). *Personnel: A diagnostic approach*. Dallas: Business Publications.

36. Solomon, J. B., & Bussey, J. (1985, May 20). Cultural change: Pressed by its rivals, Procter & Gamble is altering its ways. *Wall Street Journal*, p. 1.

37. Lewin, K. (1951). *Field theory in social science*. New York: Harper & Row.

38. Schein, E. H. (1968). Organizational socialization and the profession of management. *Industrial Management Review*, 9, 1–16.

39. Beer, M. (1980). *Organizational change and development: A systems view*. Glenview, IL: Scott, Foresman.

40. Nadler, D. A. (1987). The effective management of organizational change. In J. W. Lorsch (Ed.), *Handbook of organizational behavior* (pp. 358–369). Englewood Cliffs, NJ: Prentice-Hall.

41. Katz, D., & Kahn, R. L. (1978). *The social psychology of organizations* (2nd ed.). New York: Wiley.

42. Hannan, M. T., & Freeman, J. (1984). Structural inertia and organizational change. *American Sociological Review*, 49, 149–164.

43. Wiersema, M. F., & Bantel, K. A. (1992). Top management team demography and corporate strategic change. *Academy of Management Journal*, 35, 91–121.

44. Kotter, J. P., & Schlesinger, L. A. (1979, March–April). Choosing strategies for change. *Harvard Business Review*, pp. 106–114.

45. See Note 40.

46. Reiner, J. J. (1987). Turnaround of information systems at Honeywell. *Academy of Management Executive*, 1, 47–50.

47. Farber, S. (1989, September). When employees ask: "What's in it for me?" *Business Month*, p. 79.

48. Cotton, J. L., Vollrath, D. A., Froggatt, K. L., Lengnick-Hall, M. L., & Jennings, K. R. (1988). Employee participation: Diverse forms and different outcomes. *Academy of Management Review*, 13, 8–22.

49. See Note 30.

50. Porras, J. I., Robertson, P. J., & Goldman, L. (1992). Organization development: Theory, practice, and research. In M. D. Dunnette (Ed.), *Handbook of industrial/organizational psychology* (2nd ed.). Palo Alto, CA: Consulting Psychologists Press.

51. Huse, E. F., & Cummings, T. G. (1985). *Organization development and change* (3rd ed.). St. Paul, MN: West.

52. Abrahamson, E. (1991). Managerial fads and fashions: The diffusion and rejection of innovations. *Academy of Management Review, 16,* 586–612.

53. See Note 51.

54. Franklin, J. L. (1978, May–June). Improving the effectiveness of survey feedback. *Personnel,* pp. 11–17.

55. Golombiewski, R. T. (1972). *Reviewing organizations: A laboratory approach to planned change.* Itasca, IL: Peacock.

56. Campbell, J. P., & Dunnette, M. D. (1968). Effectiveness of T-group experiences in managerial training and development. *Psychological Bulletin, 70,* 73–104.

57. See Note 39.

58. Sherwood, J. J. (1972). An introduction to organization development. In J. W. Pfeiffer & J. E. Jones (Eds.), *The 1972 handbook for group facilitators* (pp. 122–168). La Jolla, CA: Univ. Assoc.

59. Beckhard, R. (1972, Summer). Optimizing team-building efforts. *Journal of Contemporary Business,* pp. 23–32.

60. Vicars, W. M., & Hartke, D. D. (1984). Evaluating OD evaluations: A status report. *Group and Organization Studies, 9,* 177–188.

61. McClenahen, J. S. (1990, October 15). Not fun in the sun. *Industry Week,* pp. 22–24.

62. See Note 61, pp. 22–23.

63. See Note 61.

64. Fisher, L. (1992, January 12). The latest word on teamwork? "Mush." *New York Times,* p. B16.

65. See Note 64.

66. See Note 64.

67. See Note 64.

68. See Note 64.

69. Blake, R. R., & Mouton, J. S. (1969). *Building a dynamic corporation through grid organizational development.* Reading, MA: Addison-Wesley.

70. Porras, J. I., & Berg, P. O. (1978). The impact of organization development. *Academy of Management Review, 3,* 249–266.

71. Burke, W. W. (1982). *Organization development: Principles and practices.* Boston: Little, Brown.

72. Hackman, J. R., & Oldham, G. R. (1980). *Work redesign.* Reading, MA: Addison-Wesley.

73. Munchus, G. (1983). Employer-employee based quality circles in Japan: Human resource implications for American firms. *Academy of Management Review, 8,* 255–261.

74. Meyer, G. W., & Scott, R. G. (1985, Spring). Quality circles: Panacea or Pandora's box? *Organizational Dynamics,* 34–50.

75. Griffin, R. W. (1988). Consequences of quality circles in an industrial setting: A longitudinal assessment. *Academy of Management Journal, 31,* 338–358.

76. Suttle, J. L. (1977). Improving life at work—problems and prospects. In J. R. Hackman & J. L. Suttle (Eds.), *Improving life at work: Behavioral science approaches to organizational change* (pp. 1–29). Santa Monica, CA: Goodyear.

77. Buch, K., & Spangler, R. (1990). The effects of quality circles on performance and promotions. *Human Relations, 43,* 573–582.

78. Jick, T. D., & Ashkenas, R. N. (1985). Involving employees in productivity and QWL improvements: What OD can learn from the manager's perspective. In D. D. Warrick (Ed.), *Contemporary organization development: Current thinking and applications* (pp. 218–230). Glenview, IL: Scott, Foresman.

79. Drucker, P. (1954). *The practice of management.* New York: Harper & Row.

80. Kondrasuk, J. N., Flager, K., Morrow, D., & Thompson, R. (1984). The effect of management by objectives on organization results. *Group and Organization Studies, 9,* 531–539.

81. Midas, M. T., Jr., & Devine, T. E. (1991, Summer). A look at continuous improvement at Northwest Airlines. *National Productivity Review, 10,* 379–394.

82. Kondrasuk, J. N. (1981). Studies in MBO effectiveness. *Academy of Management Review, 6,* 419–430.

83. French, W. L., Bell, C. H., Jr., & Zawacki, R. A. (1989). *Organization development: Theory, practice, & research* (3rd ed.). Homewood, IL: BPI/Irwin.

84. Steel, R. P., & Shane, G. S. (1986). Evaluation research on quality circles: Technical and analytical implications. *Human Relations, 39,* 449–468.

85. See Note 56.

86. See Note 50.

87. Neuman, G. A., Edwards, J. E., & Raju, N. S. (1989). Organizational development interventions: A meta-analysis of their effects on satisfaction and other attitudes. *Personnel Psychology, 42,* 461–483.

88. Nicholas, J. M. (1982). The comparative impact of organization development interventions on hard criteria measures. *Academy of Management Review, 7,* 531–542.

89. See Note 70.

90. See Note 87.

91. Nicholas, J. M., & Katz, M. (1985). Research methods and reporting practices in organization development: A review and some guidelines. *Academy of Management Review, 10,* 737–749.

92. White, S. E., & Mitchell, T. R. (1976). Organization development: A review of research content and research design. *Academy of Management Review, 1,* 57–73.

93. Beer, M., & Walton, A. E. (1987). Organizational change and development. In M. Rosenzweig & L. W. Porter, (Eds.), *Annual review of psychology.* Palo Alto, CA: Annual Reviews.

94. Mitroff, I., & Mohrman, S. (1987). The slack is gone: How the United States lost its competitive edge in the

world economy. *Academy of Management Executive, 1,* 65–70.

95. Schaffer, R. H., & Thomson, H. H. (1992, January–February). Successful change processes begin with results. *Harvard Business Review,* pp. 80–91.

96. See Note 95, p. 82.

97. Greiner, L., & Schein, V. (1988). *Power and organization development: Mobilizing power to implement change.* Reading, MA: Addison-Wesley.

98. Cobb, A. T. (1986). Political diagnosis: Applications in organizational development. *Academy of Management Review, 11,* 482–496.

99. White, L. P., & Wotten, K. C. (1983). Ethical dilemmas in various stages of organizational development. *Academy of Management Review, 8,* 690–697.

100. Bennis, W. (1977). Bureaucracy and social change: An anatomy of a training failure. In P. H. Mirvis & D. N. Berg (Eds.), *Failures in organizational development and change: Cases and essays for learning* (pp. 191–215). New York: Wiley.

101. Steele, F. (1977). Is culture hostile to organization development? The UK example. In P. H. Mirvis & D. N. Berg (Eds.), *Failures in organization development and change: Cases and essays for learning* (pp. 23–31). New York: Wiley.

102. Hofstede, G. (1980). *Culture's consequences.* Beverly Hills, CA: Sage.

103. Kedia, B. L., & Bhagat, R. S. (1988). Cultural constraints on transfer of technology across nations: Implications for research in international and comparative management. *Academy of Management Review, 13,* 559–571.

104. Jaeger, A. M. (1986). Organizational development and national culture: Where's the fit? *Academy of Management Review, 11,* 178–190.

105. Trepo, G. (1973, Autumn). Management style *a la française. European Business, 39,* 71–79.

106. Blunt, P. (1988). Cultural consequences for organization change in a southeast Asian state: Brunei. *Academy of Management Executive, 2,* 235–240.

CASE IN POINT

Transforming the Bell Atlantic Corporation

A CNN video is available to accompany this case. Additional information can be found in the CNN Video User's Guide.

How do you transform a rigid bureaucracy into an innovative and entrepreneurial organization? Bell Atlantic Corporation has done just that, under the leadership of its chief executive officer and change master, Raymond Smith. In an interview, Smith describes how he changed Bell Atlantic from bureaucracy to entrepreneur.[1]

Bell Atlantic is one of the seven "Baby Bells" born out of the 1984 breakup of AT&T's Bell System. Bell Atlantic is chartered to provide local telephone services to six mid-Atlantic states plus the District of Columbia. Bell Atlantic has expanded to become the most innovative and profitable of all the Baby Bells—bringing a wide array of new products to the market, starting new ventures with other companies throughout the world, and solidifying its strong position in the information technology industry.

What caused Bell Atlantic to change? The telecommunications industry itself is rapidly changing. The explosion of information technologies has blurred any distinction that may have once existed between the telecommunications and information technology industries. Bell Atlantic must keep up with the latest changes in information technology if it is to remain competitive.

Bell Atlantic now has competitors. In the pre-1984 days, Bell enjoyed a monopoly on telephone services. Things changed dramatically when the court ordered the breakup of the Bell System. Competition in telecommunications and information technologies is now fierce.

Bell Atlantic remains regulated, too, thereby limiting what Bell Atlantic can earn from local telephone services. If Bell Atlantic wanted to earn anything more than minimal return on investment, it had to develop additional products and services that would be competitive in the global marketplace.

Bell Atlantic really had no choice but to change—and CEO Raymond Smith knew it. Having worked his way up through various key management positions at the company, Smith was keenly aware of the forces demanding change. On becoming president and chief operating officer in 1988, and CEO in 1989, Smith set out to drastically change Bell Atlantic.

Smith describes traditional Bell Atlantic managers as "maintenance managers, not business managers."[2] They avoided risks, focusing instead on maintaining the status quo. They were highly parochial. They didn't understand or care about anything beyond their own departments. And Smith knew why. Bell Atlantic's old organizational structure rewarded bureaucratic behavior. It encouraged a mind-set that all but precluded any possibility of companywide innovation. Protection of turf, not cooperation, was standard operating procedure at Bell Atlantic.

Prior to Smith's taking over as CEO, attempts were made to change Bell Atlantic. Bell Atlantic's 1,400 managers participated in a series of concept design retreats. Smith, one of the coleaders of the retreats, started the concept design process by writing a statement of what he believed should be the underlying values of Bell Atlantic. Small groups of managers then worked to edit the document—offering changes, clarifying the wording, and generally thinking about what should really be important to the company. The concept design seminars produced a statement of Bell Atlantic's values based on the five values of "integrity, respect and trust, excellence, individual fulfillment, and profitable growth."[3]

Smith realized that the values statement was not enough of a beacon to get Bell Atlantic employees to change, to become entrepreneurial. The values statement was too general. According to Smith, "We needed to move from a general statement of values to concrete behavior and work practices, or what we called the *conventions* of day-to-day business life."[4]

When Smith was promoted to CEO, he initiated a ten-year plan for transforming the company into an innovative, entrepreneurial firm. One of his first acts was to bring the company's top fifty managers together to think about their obligations to Bell Atlantic (beyond those to their own divisions). Smith prepared a list of the twelve obligations of leadership that he believed were necessary to support the company's new values. He then challenged his top managers to internalize these obligations so that they could serve as role models for all employees.

Smith coined the slogan "the Bell Atlantic Way," which he describes as "an organized, participative method of working together that allows us to get the most out of our own efforts and maximize our contribution to team goals."[5] The Bell Atlantic Way now serves as the unifying philosophy that the company's employees use to guide day-to-day business life.

The company's 20,000 managers and supervisors were introduced to the Bell Atlantic Way by a series of specially designed forums. The company's top fifty managers were the first to participate in these educational forums. These top managers then served as executives-in-residence for the manager and supervisor forums that followed. After completing the forums, all participants were expected to talk about the Bell Atlantic Way with their employees.

Smith's strategy for communicating the change in values did not end with educating employees about the Bell Atlantic Way. He believed that the nature of the intended changes had to be made even more specific and concrete. Smith and his executive team wrote down what they believed to be the basic business problem facing Bell Atlantic. They then identified the problems that needed to be solved by each division and department in the company.

To communicate the basic business problem—and the questions and subproblems associated with it—Smith brought together the company's top 400 key communicators and managers, who were educated as to the overall strategy of the company and its basic business problem. They then studied the questions and subproblems. Their job was to go back to their work sites and communicate the work to be done to their employees and coworkers.

This communication method was quite successful. With the group of 400 talking about Bell Atlantic's strategy and business problems, it wasn't long before the company's thousands of employees understood their tasks. They also came to understand how their actions, the actions of their departments, and the actions of everyone else in the company needed to fit together to help solve the company's basic business problem.

Experiential exercises were used to illustrate the need for employees to work as a team. One game the company uses to impress on employees the need to cooperate is called "breaking the squares." Participants gather into small teams. Each team is provided with puzzle pieces that can be arranged to form squares, and is assigned the task of making six squares. Group members must cooperate as a team to successfully generate six squares. There are fifty-seven ways to form five squares, but only one way to form six squares. Typically, individual team members begin by working independently to make a complete square. Individual members wait for everyone else to finish their squares; the attitude is that they are done. However, team members eventually realize that for the team to make six squares, everyone needs to break their own squares and start over again—that is, collectively rearrange their pieces to make six squares. They learn that they must cooperate and work as a team, not as individuals, if they are to succeed.

Smith made major changes to the company's employee reward structure. Employees are now compensated based on team and corporate results in addition to their individual performance. Customer service is of paramount importance to Bell Atlantic. Regular telephone surveys are used to measure customer opinions of Bell Atlantic service. A specified minimal level of customer satisfaction is required to trigger a team performance reward. Moreover, compensation reflecting corporate performance is differentiated by short-term and long-term performance. Representing a substantial portion of managers' pay, this change in reward structure focuses attention on the long term. Even individual performance rewards emphasize the teamwork values of the company. One of the major criteria in assessing individual performance is contribution to overall team goals.

Clearly, the development and use of teams is central to the Bell Atlantic Way philosophy, making it an important part of Smith's change strategy. Bell Atlantic instituted the Champion Program, which "provides seed money, guidance, and training to potential entrepreneurs who propose new products and services. People at any level can make proposals. If projects are accepted, their proposers can run them. And they can invest a portion of their wages in the project, in exchange for the prospect of a piece of the action when their product has been marketed."[6]

The Champion Program has been very successful. During the program's first year, thirty-six champion projects were begun. Thirty-nine additional projects were started in 1989, and by 1990 several products had already been introduced into the marketplace and thirty-three new products were nearing the commercial stage of development. One example of the program's success is Jack Coppley's *Thinx*, a computer program that integrates data with graphics so that users can visually manipulate data in all sorts of ways to better understand it. Coppley put together a twenty-member team to develop the idea, and the rest is history. *Thinx* quickly became a huge success following its introduction in 1990. Initially created to stimulate innovative and entrepreneurial behavior among employees and thus facilitate organizational change, the Champion Program not only has fulfilled its mission, but has also become a substantial revenue generator.

The final change strategy is that of employee participation in decision making. Practicing the Bell Atlantic Way, all layoff decisions are made at the local level. Top management indicates the degree of downsizing needed, but it is up to each division and department to decide where and how layoffs should be made. Allowing for employee participation in making these painful decisions has resulted in staff reductions that make sense for each division and has increased acceptance by Bell Atlantic employees.

In three years, Bell Atlantic employees shed their bureaucratic ways to become team-oriented and desirous of increased responsibility and accountability. Top management took about a year to internalize the new values in the Bell Atlantic Way. But once the change process took hold, things sped up. According to Smith, "Now changes have started to accelerate. We're seeing as much change every three months as we used to see in three years."[7] Corporate earnings are up, and a wide range of new products are being marketed. Bell Atlantic employees are more satisfied, too. Even the downsizing seems to have had a positive effect on morale. Employees claim that many cynical bureaucrats who used to undermine the company's atmosphere have left the company. Less bureaucracy has resulted in a much more positive workplace.

Perhaps Smith describes the success of Bell Atlantic's change strategies best with this statement: "I really know we're doing well when I walk into a room of people and they are discussing a project with tremendous excitement, a project that is going to move our corporation ahead significantly, and I've never heard of it. That is a wonderful feeling."[8]

Questions for Discussion

1. What were the internal and external sources of pressure for change at Bell Atlantic?
2. What individual barriers to change existed at Bell Atlantic?
3. What organizational barriers to change existed at Bell Atlantic?
4. Describe Bell Atlantic's change strategies. What methods for overcoming resistance to change did Bell Atlantic use?

Notes

1. Kanter, R. M. (1991). Championing change: An interview with Bell Atlantic's CEO Raymond Smith. *Harvard Business Review, 69*(1), 119–130.
2. See Note 1, p. 120.
3. See Note 1, p. 121.
4. See Note 1, p. 121.
5. See Note 1, p. 122.
6. See Note 1, p. 127.
7. See Note 1, p. 123.
8. See Note 1, p. 130.

EXPERIENCING ORGANIZATIONAL BEHAVIOR

If there's any one constant in the world, it's that things change, and the same truism applies to organizations. As technology advances, the composition of the work force shifts, and new markets evolve, people must confront the reality of organizational change. Such changes are often quite threatening to people, and pose serious challenges to managers attempting to implement the changes needed for organizations to survive. This exercise will help you appreciate the resistance to change that many supervisors encounter and to consider some ways to overcome it.

Facing Up to Organizational Change

Procedure

Listed below are two situations involving organizational change. For each one, list (a) some of the impediments that are likely to arise on the part of employees, and (b) things that managers can do to overcome this resistance.

Situation 1: A secretarial staff very familiar with using typewriters must now face using a word processing system.

Impediments to Change	Ways to Overcome Impediments
1.	1.
2.	2.
3.	3.

Situation 2: An older, well-liked supervisor is retiring and will be replaced by a younger person hired from outside the company.

Impediments to Change	Ways to Overcome Impediments
1.	1.
2.	2.
3.	3.

Points to Consider

1. For each of the different situations described, were the impediments to change similar or different?
2. For each of the different situations described, were the ways of overcoming these impediments similar or different?
3. In what ways do you think the nature of the organizational change situation may dictate the types of change barriers likely to be encountered and the ease with which these may be overcome?

Name Index

Subject Index

(Continued from inside front cover)

1965

Dimensions of negotiation and conflict resolution
R. Walton and *Robert B. McKersie* described two key underlying dimensions of conflict resolution: concern with one's own outcomes, known as *distribution;* and concern with others' outcomes, known as *integration* (see chapter 10).

R. Walton   Robert B. McKersie

1966

Open systems approach
Daniel Katz and *Robert L. Kahn* advanced the open systems approach to studying organizational processes (see chapter 1).

Daniel Katz   Robert L. Kahn

1968

Goal setting
Edwin Locke and his associates developed the very effective motivational technique of goal setting (see chapter 4).

Edwin Locke

1978

Resource dependency view
Jeffrey Pfeffer and *Gerald Salancik* advocated the idea that power rests with those who control valued resources (see chapter 11).

Jeffrey Pfeffer   Gerald Salancik

1982

Development of the concept of burnout
Christina Maslach proposed a theoretical model that linked burnout to prolonged exposure to high levels of work-related stress (see chapter 7).

Christina Maslach

Note: These events were selected on the basis of suggestions in the following sources:

Lawrence, P.R. (1987). Historical development of organizational behavior. In J.W. Lorsch (Ed.), *Handbook of organizational behavior*, (pp. 1–9). Englewood Cliffs, NJ: Prentice-Hall.

Pugh, D.S., Hickson, D.J., & Hinings, C.R. (1985). *Writers on organizations*. Newbury Park, CA: Sage.